Kelley Blue Book

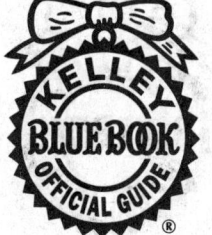

80th Anniversary Edition

USED CAR GUIDE
Consumer Edition
1991– 2005 Models

Vol. 14	January—2006—June	No. 1

LES KELLEY - *Founder*
PAUL C. JOHNSON - - - - - - - - - - - - - - - - - - *Publisher*
PATRICIA A. DEBACKER - - - - - - - - - - *Editor-in-Chief*
LESA SPEROU - - - - - - - - - - - - - - - - - - *Senior Editor*

Kelley Blue Book Used Car Guide, Consumer Edition is published two times per year in January and July for $9.95 per issue by Kelley Blue Book Co., P.O. Box 19691, Irvine, CA 92623. POSTMASTER: Send address changes to Kelley Blue Book Auto Market Report, P.O. Box 19691, Irvine, CA 92623.

This publication is distributed to the book trade by Publishers Group West, 1700 4th Street, Berkeley, CA 94710.

Published at:

P.O. Box 19691, Irvine, California 92623

We assume no responsibility for errors or omissions.

Official Guidebooks Since 1926

ORDER YOUR BLUE BOOK NOW!

Kelley Blue Book
P.O. Box 19691
Irvine, California 92623

Please accept our order for _____ copies of the Kelley Blue Book Used Car Guide Consumer Edition, at $9.95 per copy, including shipping.

NAME _____

ADDRESS _____

CITY _____

STATE _____ ZIP _____

PHONE (_____)_____

VISA or MASTER CARD # _____

EXP. DATE _____ SIGNATURE _____

Visa ☐   MasterCard ☐   Check Enclosed ☐

California residents please add sales tax. Shipping outside U.S. extra.

THE HISTORY OF KELLEY BLUE BOOK

In 1918, a young man named Les Kelley parked three Model T Fords in an open lot, put $450 in the till and started the Kelley Kar Company. It was to become the largest dealership in the world and along the way, spawn a need for placing values on used and even new cars, known as Blue Book values. Here is the story of how it all happened.

Les Kelley, the son of a preacher from Arkansas, made his way to California in 1914 at the age of 17. Les had no money and no job but he owned an old car. It was in fine shape because he had a knack for mechanics and had overhauled it himself. All of his friends admired his car and frequently tried to buy it. After much persuasion he finally did sell it to one of them. With the money he received from this deal Les bought another old Ford. After giving this car a thorough overhauling, he traded it off, taking in two used cars and a little money on the deal. He reconditioned these cars and sold them. With the money he bought other used automobiles and found himself making enough money to pay his way through college.

Like many young men at the end of the war, Les Kelley sought to establish himself in the business world. In 1918 he leased part of a lot from another car dealer in Los Angeles and started the Kelley Kar Company with three cars for sale. His brother, Buster, joined Les as a lot boy at age 13 changing tires and washing cars.

In the early 1920s, to help acquire new inventory, Les Kelley distributed to other dealers and to banks a list of automobiles he wished to buy and the prices he was willing to pay for them. The automotive community began to trust his judgment so much as an accurate reflection of current values they started to request the list for their own use. It didn't take long for Les Kelley to realize that he could provide an ongoing service to dealers and bankers alike.

In 1926, Les Kelley decided to expand the list of automobile values he had been producing since 1918 and published the first Blue Book of Motor Car Values. He showed factory list price and cash value on thousands of vehicles, from Cadillacs to Duesenbergs, from Pierce-Arrows to Hupmobiles. A 1926 Packard sedan limousine with balloon tires might fetch as much as $3,825. But a 1921 Nash touring car, even with a clock, was only worth $50. Les named the publication Blue Book after the Social Register because it meant that you would find valuable information inside. And Les Kelley was to make Kelley Blue Book synonymous with the authoritative source for car values. To this day, across the country, people ask the question, "What's the Blue Book value of my car?" At the dealership Les was selling "Selected Blue Seal Automobiles," so he carried the blue and gold ribbon medallion onto the cover of the Blue Book, where it remains today.

Both the dealership and the publication continued to flourish. Buster Kelley eventually worked his way up to General Manager of the dealership and Publisher of the Blue Book. Kelley Kar Company

THE HISTORY OF KELLEY BLUE BOOK

had moved to the corner of Figueroa Street and Pico in Los Angeles and took up nearly an entire block. The repair/body shop at another location on Pico employed more than a hundred people. For many years the dealership operated solely as a used car operation, which was to become the largest in the world. In those days new car dealerships didn't sell used cars, so the Kelleys bought vehicles that new car dealers were taking in trade, as well as directly from the public.

The 1930s and '40s were a different world from the car business today. Often, as a part of the sale, Buster had to spend Saturday or Sunday teaching the buyers how to drive! The Kelleys opened their own insurance company and auto club and sold the whole package with the automobile.

World War II brought with it a shortage of cars. Used car prices got so high the government decided to put a ceiling on prices and used the Blue Book as the ceiling for both wholesale and retail values. Subscribing to the book became a must for dealers. At the dealership the Kelleys continued to innovate. They bought cars in the East and shipped as many as 1,000 a month to Los Angeles in freight cars. A person about to be drafted could sell his car to Kelley Kar Company and then continue to drive it right up until he left for the war. When the war was over, Kelley offered the "G.I Credit Plan," which included no money down and up to five years to pay.

Les Kelley bought a small Ford franchise during the war and afterward the Kelley Kar Company operated as both a used and new car dealership. Full-page newspaper ads invited crowds into the Kelley showroom. And Buster became perhaps the nation's first dealer to use a new medium-television!

Commercials showed Buster walking around the showroom pointing out specials that offered a guarantee: return the car within 30 days and you could trade it for any other car at the same or higher price. More success followed. By the 1950s they had become the largest Ford dealer in addition to being the largest used car dealership in the world.

By the late 1950s Les Kelley, then in his sixties, decided to sell the dealerships rather than move them again. By 1962 the Kelleys were completely out of the car business and devoting full time to the Blue Book, with Buster as Publisher and Buster's son Bob as Assistant Publisher. The company moved to Long Beach and later to Orange County. Les continued to be active in the business until his death in 1990, at age 93.

For the next 30 years the Blue Book was to thrive as a "trade" publication, sold to businesses involved in the automotive industry such as car dealers, financial institutions and insurance companies.

THE HISTORY OF KELLEY BLUE BOOK

These customers used the bimonthly book to determine everything from loan values to suggested retail prices. Kelley Blue Book continued to innovate, becoming the first publication to show the effect of high or low mileage on a car's value.

As a natural evolution, the compnay began publishing other value guides for the industry. A New Car Price Manual was added in 1966 and the company became the industry's leading provider of pricing services. Next, Kelley Blue Book developed RV guides that place values on everything from travel trailers to campers to Motor Homes to Van Conversions. A separate Manufactured Housing Guide came out of the RV lineup and a separate Motorcycle Guide was published with values for ATVs, Snowmobiles, and Personal Watercraft.

As the quality of cars improved, people began to drive them longer. The average age of a vehicle on the road today has been estimated to be about nine years. The Blue Book covered seven years, so it made sense to produce a sister publication, the Older Car Guide, that provided values another 14 years back. Then came the Early Model Guide, which today provides values all the way back to 1946!

The Kelley family tradition reached a third generation when Bob's son, Mike, joined the company in 1978. Mike's background in computer science made him a natural to usher in the computer age for vehicle values. In essence, ever since Les Kelley's first newsletter, the company has really been in the information business. The delivery method of that information keeps evolving, from a letter to books to PC-based software to the Internet! Mike Kelley became General Manager in 1981 and helped develop systems for dealers to get trade-in values online. That led to PC software for new and used car pricing.

As late as the 1990s car dealers still promoted used cars on the lot with hand-made signs and window paint touting "low mileage!" or "fully loaded!" It was time for Kelley Blue Book to innovate again. They created desktop software for dealers to use to print the Blue Book window sticker listing the mileage, equipment, etc, on the used car, along with its Blue Book Suggested Retail Value compared to the dealer's asking price. Once again the result was increased customer confidence. Since 1992, every year several million used cars are sold displaying the Blue Book label.

In 1993 Kelley Blue Book made its initial venture into the consumer marketplace by publishing a Consumer Edition of the Blue Book. It quickly became the nation's number-one-selling automotive book, often making the USA Today best-seller list. It features 15 years of used car values on more than 10,000 models of cars, trucks and vans and is available in bookstores, auto supply stores and other locations.

THE HISTORY OF KELLEY BLUE BOOK

As the 90s continued, something called the World Wide Web was introducing regular people to a medium called the Internet. It was innovation time again and Kelley Blue Book saw a further opportunity to facilitate transactions between consumers and retailers. The company created a Web site, kbb.com, running on a single PC and offering first, new car prices in 1995 and then its famous used car values in 1996. Early in 1996, 20,000 people a month found their way to the site, largely by word-of-mouth. That number has grown a bit since then and now exceeds seven million visitors a month coming to kbb.com and millions more viewing Blue Book information on numerous portals and other automotive sites, including those of auto manufacturers and car dealers.

In 2000, Bob and Mike Kelley retired from the company but the entrepreneurial spirit lives on with today's company leaders. Even though Kelley Blue Book exited the insurance, auto club and warranty businesses decades ago, the company leaders were always interested in new ways to help connect consumers and the auto industry. While the Kelley Blue Book brand has remained focused on providing the trusted information needed in the buying and selling of vehicles, the breadth of what information is necessary has grown considerably. At one time, new car buyers used just MSRP as a reference point and later, the invoice price. But studies showed that there was a desire to know actual transaction prices for new cars. Kelley Blue Book went to work gathering and analyzing transactions from thousands of dealers across the United States and in 2002, introduced kbb.com visitors to the Blue Book value for new cars - what other consumers are really paying for them.

In the 10 years since kbb.com was launched the Internet has become not only an integral part of everyday life, but has also fueled the biggest growth in Kelley Blue Book's history. A recent independent survey of car-shoppers nationwide rated kbb.com "Best Overall Customer Experience" and tops in 11 other categories, including "Most Reliable," "Most Trustworthy" and "Most Dependable."

Today we offer you the best of both worlds - access to Blue Book values online and this book to take with you anywhere you go.

2006 is our 80th anniversary and we are pleased to be given the opportunity to, yet again, play a part of your vehicle buying and selling experience by providing you with the information that America has relied on since 1926.

INTRODUCTION

Since 1926, Kelley Blue Book has provided the automotive industry with used vehicle values. Today we are the trusted resource relied upon by both the automotive industry and consumers. This **Consumer Edition** has been prepared to provide values and information relevant to the different types of consumer transactions.

What is a guidebook?

A guidebook such as this one is just that, a guide. To produce the most timely, accurate and trusted used vehicle values, Kelley Blue Book's pricing analysts constantly collect and review new and used vehicle transaction data, as well as information on each vehicle's current supply and demand. They then meticulously determine and report used car values based on real market information.

This guidebook represents the educated opinion of Kelley Blue Book's staff and each value is determined after carefully studying information we deem complete and reliable. We assume no responsibility for errors or omissions.

Is this book the same as the Kelley Blue Book trade publication?

This book contains the trusted values you have come to expect from Kelley Blue Book. The values in the Consumer Guide represent transactions relevant to consumers including Trade-In, Private Party and used Retail Values.

What is the difference between Trade-In, Private Party and Retail Values?

Kelley Blue Book provides several different values representing different types of transactions.

Trade-In Value is what consumers can expect to receive from a dealer for a Trade-In vehicle assuming an accurate appraisal of condition. This value will likely be less than the Private Party Value because the dealer incurs the cost of safety inspections, reconditioning and other costs of doing business.

Kelley Blue Book factors the following into our Trade-In values:

Safety Inspections — The dealer will incur the cost of inspecting and repairing the vehicle to ensure that it meets government requirements for safety and smog emissions.

Reconditioning — Before reselling a vehicle a dealer can spend hundreds or even thousands of dollars performing repairs, routine maintenance and cosmetic detailing and touch up.

The dealer also hopes to make a fair profit for his efforts.

INTRODUCTION

Private Party Value is what a buyer can expect to pay when buying a used car from a private party. The Private Party Value assumes the vehicle is sold "As Is" and carries no warranty (other than the continuing factory warranty). The final sale price will vary depending on the vehicle's actual condition and local maket conditions. This value may also be used to derive Fair Market Value for insurance and vehicle donation purposes.

Suggested Retail Value is representative of dealers' asking prices and is the starting point for negotiation between a consumer and a dealer. This Suggested Retail Value assumes that the vehicle has been fully reconditioned and has a clean Title History. This value also takes into account the dealers' profit, costs for advertising, sales commissions and other costs of doing business. The final sale price will likely be less depending on the vehicle's actual condition, popularity, type of warranty offered and local market conditions.

How does Condition affect the value of the vehicle and what is the difference between "Fair," "Good," and "Excellent" ratings? There is never a single correct value for a used vehicle. The value of a vehicle depends on several factors, most importantly condition and overall appearance. Supply and demand for a particular vehicle, local market conditions and the economy also play a role in determining a car's value.

Kelley Blue Book provides additional vales for used vehicles in each of the following conditions:

"Excellent" condition means that the vehicle looks new, is in excellent mechanical condition and needs no reconditioning. This vehicle has never had any body or paint work and is free of rust. The vehicle has a clean Title History and will pass a smog and safety inspection. The engine compartment is clean, with no fluid leaks and is free of visible defects. The vehicle also has complete and verifiable service and maintenance records. Less than 5% of all used vehicles fall into this category.

"Good" condition means that the vehicle is free of any major defects. This vehicle has a clean Title History, the paint, body and interior have only minor (if any) blemishes and there are no major mechanical problems. There should be little or no rust on this vehicle. The tires match and have substantial tread wear left. A "good" vehicle will need some reconditioning or routine servicing to be sold at retail. Most consumer owned vehicles fall into this catagory.

"Fair" condition means that the vehicle has some mechanical or cosmetic defects and needs servicing but is still in reasonable running condition. This vehicle has a clean Title History, the paint, body and/or interior need work performed by a professional. The tires may need to be replaced. There may be some repairable rust damage.

HOW TO USE THE BLUE BOOK

FINDING A VEHICLE

There are two sections in this book, the Automobile or Car section up front and the Truck & Van Section in the back. The Truck & Van section is marked by black tabs on each page. Within each section, the makes are listed alphabetically and models are listed by size within each make. Model years are listed oldest to newest.

EQUIPMENT ADJUSTMENTS

To get the most accurate value, you will need to add or deduct from the base value depending on the equipment. "Adds" and "Deducts" appear underneath individual vehicles and in separate Equipment Schedules. A value in parentheses represents a "Deduct." More generic equipment adjustments appear in the Equipment Schedules. Schedules for cars are at the front of the book. Equipment schedules for trucks and vans are at the back of the book.

You should always add or subtract for each item that is listed separately, even if it is part of a package that you have already added for or if it was considered original standard equipment. If an equipment item is listed both underneath the vehicle listing and in the Equipment Schedule, use the value underneath the vehicle listing because it is specific to that vehicle.

MILEAGE

Mileage must also be taken into consideration to derive the most accurate valuation of a used vehicle. On page 13 we have listed an "acceptable" range of mileage for each model year. The range does not represent the average mileage driven for the model year but the point of resistence where value can be affected. As a vehicle gets older, condition is more important than mileage. Vehicles with more miles may sometimes be worth more than lower mileage vehicles if its condition is better. It is important to note that the values we list are intended for vehicles within the acceptable mileage range.

HOW TO USE THE BLUE BOOK

ABBREVIATIONS USED IN THIS BOOK

VIN — Vehicle Identification Number. The VIN may vary depending on model, engine, transmission and option packages.

W.B. — Wheelbase. This is the distance from the center of the front wheel to the center of the rear wheel.

CID/L — Engine size displacement in cubic inches or liters.

List — This is the original suggested suggested retail price of the vehicle when it was sold new, including destination charges and equipment as indicated on the equipment schedule.

Trucks — Trucks listed in this guide have a smooth exterior with the rear wheel wells inside the bed. Value adjustments for models with the rear wheel wells on the outside of the bed can be found on the Truck Equipment Schedules under the Stepside listing.

Premium Sound — This refers to an upgraded sound system (Bose, JBL, Infinity, etc.) not simply a CD changer, equalizer or an aftermarket receiver.

VEHICLE IDENTIFICATION NUMBERS (VINs)

If you are not sure of the year or model of a vehicle, you can often determine them from the Vehicle Identification Number or VIN. Using VINs can get a bit technical. If you already know the year and the model of the vehicle you can skip this information.

Under 1995 Lincoln, you will see the heading "1995 LINCOLN - 1LN(LM81W)-S-#." What this means is that all 1995 Lincolns have a VIN starting with 1LN and have an S in the 10th position. The fourth through eighth positions determine the specific Linoln model and are marked by parentheses. The hyphens indicate positions which can be ignored and the # symbol represents the individual vehicle's serial number.

Please note that we do not have room in this guidebook to list all the VIN information. There are some VINs that you cannot decode using the information provided. Also there are some VINs that indicate two or more possible models. In these cases you must determine the particular model by inspecting the vehicle.

TIPS ON BUYING A USED CAR

DEALER vs PRIVATE PARTY

There are advantages and disadvantages to buying a car from a dealer vs a Private Party. With a dealer, you may get a warranty and some dealerships offer certification programs for late model vehicles that will extend the original factory warranty. While buying from a dealership provides security, buying from a Private Party can save you money. When buying from a private party, ask for all repair and maintenance records and contact information of the previous owner in case you have questions later.

TRADING-IN YOUR VEHICLE

If you are trading your vehicle to a dealer, be sure to check the Trade-In Value and the Private Party Value of your vehicle. You may find it to your benefit to sell the vehicle yourself.

CHECKING OUT A USED VEHICLE

If you are contacting a private party, be sure to ask why they are selling the vehicle. Ask them to describe the condition of the vehicle and how it was used (daily, as a second car, kids car). Ask if they have all of the repair and maintenance records for the vehicle. Ask if you can take the car to a mechanic for an inspection. This is extremely important as private party sales are "As Is" and once you have bought the vehicle, it's yours. If your state requires a smog certificate, insist that the vehicle pass a smog test before buying the car. Smog checks are the current owner's responsibility. Also be certain the vehicle's registration is current and paid to date. It can be costly to reinstate an expired registration. Registration fees vary from state to state, be sure to consult your state's Department of Motor Vehicles.

— Write down the VIN. For a fee, services such as CARFAX can provide you with the vehicle's history (www.kbb.com/carfax).

— Stand away from the vehicle and look at its body panels. Do they all match in color? Do they line up?

— Check the tires for wear. Uneven tire wear, balding on the sides or in the middle, could indicate the need for an alignment or a costly repair to the vehicle's suspension.

— Open the trunk, hood and doors. Look for paint specks or over spray, a sign that all or part of the vehicle has been repainted. If the vehicle has been repainted it is often a sign of some previous damage.

— Check the radiator fluid. If it is very dark or has oil droplets in it, there is a good chance the vehicle has a cracked head gasket meaning that coolant and oil are mixing together.

— Look at the condition of the rubber on each foot pedal and the leather on the steering wheel. Do they show heavy wear? Heavy wear in a low mileage vehicle may indicate that the vehicle has seen more mileage then the odometer indicates.

TIPS ON BUYING A USED CAR

— Spend as much time as you can inside the vehicle. Feel the seat, and we mean really feel it. Take a good long time to sit, because really, the seat is one of the most important parts of the vehicle.

— What about the steering wheel? Is it too high up or too close to the dash? When adjusted comfortably, does it cut off any or all the gauges? Look at the layout of the radio and heater controls. Can they be easily adjusted without taking your eyes off the road? Look over your shoulders, are there any blind spots that you cannot compensate for by using your mirrors? Climb into the seats, front and back. Is there enough legroom and headroom? Do the headrests come up far enough? Do they touch your head or are they raked back at an angle away from you? Does the seatbelt have an adjustable anchor or does it cut into your neck? Check to see how far the rear windows roll down. Some models have windows that only go down a few inches or are sealed in place and don't roll down at all. Take your time to explore all these areas.

— Then take it for a drive. How does it sound? A prolonged tapping could be the valves needing adjustment or a bad hydraulic lifter. Pump the brake pedal a few times and then press hard with your foot. If it slowly sinks all the way to the floor, there is either a leak in the line or the master cylinder/brake booster is dying. Shift into gear. If the vehicle is an automatic, the transmission should engage immediately and shifts should be crisp and quick. With your foot firmly on the brake, shift from drive to reverse; clunks or grinding noises could indicate a worn or broken engine/transmission mount, bad U-joints or differential wear.

— As you drive along, does the steering wheel shake or vibrate? It shouldn't. Vibration in the steering wheel can mean anything from an unbalanced wheel to a loose steering rack. Cars with ABS (anti-lock brakes) will have a slight pulsating action in the brake pedal when the brakes are applied with some force. Cars without ABS should not have a pulsating brake pedal.

— We also recommend that you contact your local Department of Motor Vehicles. Ask them what forms are required to transfer the vehicle title as well as any other required information. For example, some states require a smog certificate while others require the bill of sale from the current owner.

— Lastly, whatever you do, get it in WRITING. This means if you settle with a private party, write up a contract stating what you are paying for the vehicle and under what terms it is to be delivered. Likewise with a dealer, any work they promise to do or options they intend to add, get it in writing before you close the deal.

MILEAGE RANGES

ACCEPTABLE MILEAGE RANGES

The following are acceptable mileage ranges for each model year. They do **not** represent the average miles driven. Rather, they represent an accepted mileage range as demonstrated by market research. If a vehicle's mileage is outside of the accepted range, dollar adjustments may be necessary. Mileage higher than shown on the guidelines below can expect to encounter resistance from a buyer.

YEAR	ACCEPTABLE MILEAGE RANGE
1991 – 1992	99,000 – 104,000
1993	95,000 – 100,000
1994	92,000 – 97,000
1995	89,000 – 94,000
1996	86,000 – 91,000
1997	83,000 – 88,000
1998	80,000 – 85,000
1999	77,000 – 82,000
2000	71,000 – 76,000
2001	65,000 – 70,000
2002	55,000 – 60,000
2003	43,000 – 48,000
2005	29,000 – 34,000
2004	13,000 – 18,000

PRIVATE PARTY & RETAIL EQUIPMENT VALUE CONVERSION

Use the chart below to convert Trade-In Equipment Values to Private Party and Retail Values. Simply find your total Trade-In Equipment Value under the Trade-In (TI) column then follow across to the Private Party and Retail (PP/R) column. This new figure will be your Private Party or Retail Equipment Value.

TI	PP/R	TI	PP/R	TI	PP/R	TI	PP/R	TI	PP/R
25	35	225	300	425	565	625	835	825	1100
50	65	250	335	450	600	650	865	850	1135
75	100	275	365	475	635	675	900	875	1165
100	135	300	400	500	665	700	935	900	1200
125	165	325	435	525	700	725	965	925	1235
150	200	350	465	550	735	750	1000	950	1265
175	235	375	500	575	765	775	1035	975	1300
200	265	400	535	600	800	800	1065	1000	1335

1991–1992 FACTORY EQUIP. TRADE-IN VALUES

Equipment	1	2	3	4	5	6
Automatic Trans	—	—	100	—	*	150
Power Steering	*	*	*	*	*	50
Air Conditioning	*	*	*	*	*	50
GROUP TOTAL	*	*	100	*	*	250
Cassette	*	*	*	50	25	25
Power Windows	*	*	*	25	0	0
Power Door Locks	*	*	25	25	0	0
Tilt Wheel	*	*	25	25	25	0
Cruise Control	*	*	25	25	25	0
BOTH GROUPS	*	*	175	150	75	275
CD (Single Disc)	50	50	50	50	50	25
CD (Multi Disc)	100	100	100	100	100	75
Leather	*	100	100	50	25	25
Sun Roof (Flip-up)	*	—	50	50	25	25
Sun Roof (Sliding)	*	50	50	50	50	25
Moon Roof (Sldng)	*	75	75	75	50	25
T-Bar Roof	—	—	200	200	—	100
Alloy Wheels	*	*	25	25	25	25
Premium Wheels	75	75	50	50	50	25
Third Seat (Wagon)	100	50	50	50	50	50
DEDUCT FOR:						
Manual Trans	—	(200)	*	(175)	(150)	*
w/o Power Steering	—	—	—	(50)	(50)	(50)
w/o Air Cond	(125)	(125)	(75)	(75)	(50)	(50)
w/o AM/FM Stereo	(25)	(25)	(25)	(25)	0	0
w/o Power Windows	—	(25)	—	(25)	—	—
w/o Pwr Door Locks	—	(25)	—	(25)	—	—

* — EQUIPMENT INCLUDED IN BASE PRICE

1993 FACTORY EQUIPMENT TRADE-IN VALUES

Equipment	1	2	3	4	5	6
Automatic Trans	—	—	—	—	*	175
Power Steering	*	*	*	*	*	*
Air Conditioning	*	*	*	*	*	*
Power Windows	*	*	*	*	0	0
Power Door Locks	*	*	*	*	0	0
Tilt Wheel	*	*	*	*	25	0
Cruise Control	*	*	*	*	25	0
Cassette	*	*	*	*	25	25
GROUP TOTAL	*	*	*	*	75	200
Power Seat	*	*	25	25	0	—
Dual Power Seats	*	*	25	25	25	—
ABS (4 Wheel)	*	*	50	50	25	0
CD (Single Disc)	50	50	50	50	50	25
CD (Multi Disc)	100	100	100	100	100	75
Premium Sound	25	25	25	25	25	25
Leather	*	*	100	50	25	25
Sun Roof (Flip-up)	—	—	50	50	25	25
Sun Roof (Sliding)	*	50	50	50	50	25
Moon Roof (Sldng)	*	100	75	75	50	25
T-Bar Roof	—	—	225	225	—	100
Alloy Wheels	*	*	25	25	25	25
Premium Wheels	100	100	50	50	50	25
Roof Rack (Wagon)	25	25	25	25	0	0
Third Seat (Wagon)	125	50	50	50	50	50
DEDUCT FOR:						
Manual Trans	—	—	—	—	(200)	*
w/o Power Steering	—	—	—	(50)	(50)	(50)
w/o Air Cond	(150)	(150)	(100)	(100)	(50)	(50)
w/o AM/FM Stereo	(25)	(25)	(25)	(25)	0	0
w/o Power Windows	—	(25)	—	(25)	—	—
w/o Pwr Door Locks	—	(25)	—	(25)	—	—
w/o Tilt Wheel	—	(50)	—	(50)	—	—
w/o Cruise Control	—	(25)	—	(25)	—	—
w/o Leather	(100)	(100)	—	—	—	—
w/o Sun/Moon Roof	(225)	—	—	—	—	—

* — EQUIPMENT INCLUDED IN BASE PRICE

SEE PAGE 13 FOR PVT PARTY & RETAIL EQUIPMENT

1994 FACTORY EQUIPMENT TRADE-IN VALUES

Equipment	1	2	3	4	5	6
Automatic Trans	—	—	—	—	*	200
Power Steering	*	*	*	*	*	*
Air Conditioning	*	*	*	*	*	*
Power Windows	*	*	*	*	0	0
Power Door Locks	*	*	*	*	0	0
Tilt Wheel	*	*	*	*	25	0
Cruise Control	*	*	*	*	25	0
Cassette	*	*	*	*	25	25
GROUP TOTAL	*	*	*	*	75	225
Power Seat	*	*	25	25	0	—
Dual Power Seats	*	*	25	25	25	—
ABS (4 Wheel)	*	*	50	50	25	0
CD (Single Disc)	50	50	50	50	50	25
CD (Multi Disc)	125	125	125	125	100	75
Premium Sound	25	25	25	25	25	25
Leather	*	*	100	50	25	25
Sun Roof (Flip-up)	—	—	50	50	25	25
Sun Roof (Sliding)	*	50	50	50	50	25
Moon Roof (Sldng)	*	125	75	75	50	25
T-Bar Roof	—	—	250	250	—	100
Alloy Wheels	*	*	25	25	25	25
Premium Wheels	125	125	75	75	50	25
Roof Rack (Wagon)	25	25	25	25	0	0
Third Seat (Wagon)	175	75	75	75	50	50
DEDUCT FOR:						
Manual Trans	—	—	—	—	(250)	*
w/o Power Steering	—	—	—	(50)	(50)	(50)
w/o Air Cond	(175)	(175)	(125)	(125)	(50)	(50)
w/o AM/FM Stereo	(25)	(25)	(25)	(25)	0	0
w/o Power Windows	—	(25)	—	(25)	—	—
w/o Pwr Door Locks	—	(25)	—	(25)	—	—
w/o Tilt Wheel	—	(50)	—	(50)	—	—
w/o Cruise Control	—	(25)	—	(25)	—	—
w/o Leather	(100)	(100)	—	—	—	—
w/o Sun/Moon Roof	(275)	—	—	—	—	—

* — EQUIPMENT INCLUDED IN BASE PRICE

1995 FACTORY EQUIPMENT TRADE-IN VALUES

Equipment	1	2	3	4	5	6
Automatic Trans	—	—	—	—	*	225
Power Steering	*	*	*	*	*	*
Air Conditioning	*	*	*	*	*	*
Power Windows	*	*	*	*	25	0
Power Door Locks	*	*	*	*	0	0
Tilt Wheel	*	*	*	*	25	0
Cruise Control	*	*	*	*	25	0
Cassette	*	*	*	*	25	25
GROUP TOTAL	*	*	*	*	100	250
Power Seat	*	*	25	25	0	0
Dual Power Seats	*	*	25	25	25	0
ABS (4 Wheel)	*	*	50	50	25	0
CD (Single Disc)	50	50	50	50	50	25
CD (Multi Disc)	150	150	150	150	100	75
Premium Sound	25	25	25	25	25	25
Leather	*	*	100	75	25	25
Sun Roof (Flip-up)	—	—	50	50	25	25
Sun Roof (Sliding)	*	50	50	50	50	25
Moon Roof (Sldng)	*	150	100	100	75	50
T-Bar Roof	—	—	275	275	—	100
Rear Spoiler	25	25	25	25	25	25
Alloy Wheels	*	*	25	25	25	25
Premium Wheels	150	150	100	100	50	25
Roof Rack (Wagon)	25	25	25	25	0	0
Third Seat (Wagon)	225	100	100	100	50	50
DEDUCT FOR:						
Manual Trans	—	—	—	—	(300)	*
w/o Power Steering	—	—	—	(50)	(50)	(50)
w/o Air Cond	(200)	(200)	(150)	(150)	(50)	(50)
w/o AM/FM Stereo	(25)	(25)	(25)	(25)	0	0
w/o Power Windows	—	(50)	—	(50)	—	—
w/o Pwr Door Locks	—	(25)	—	(25)	—	—
w/o Tilt Wheel	—	(50)	—	(50)	—	—
w/o Cruise Control	—	(25)	—	(25)	—	—
w/o Leather	(100)	(100)	—	—	—	—
w/o Sun/Moon Roof	(300)	—	—	—	—	—

* — EQUIPMENT INCLUDED IN BASE PRICE

1996 FACTORY EQUIPMENT TRADE-IN VALUES

Equipment	1	2	3	4	5	6
Automatic Trans	—	—	—	—	*	250
Power Steering	*	*	*	*	*	*
Air Conditioning	*	*	*	*	*	*
Power Windows	*	*	*	*	50	0
Power Door Locks	*	*	*	*	0	0
Tilt Wheel	*	*	*	*	25	0
Cruise Control	*	*	*	*	25	0
Cassette	*	*	*	*	25	25
GROUP TOTAL	*	*	*	*	125	275
Power Seat	*	*	25	25	0	0
Dual Power Seats	*	*	25	25	25	0
ABS (4 Wheel)	*	*	50	50	25	0
CD (Single Disc)	75	75	75	75	50	25
CD (Multi Disc)	175	175	175	175	125	100
Premium Sound	50	50	25	25	25	25
Navigation System	125	—	—	—	—	—
Leather	*	*	125	100	25	25
Sun Roof (Flip-up)	—	—	50	50	25	25
Sun Roof (Sliding)	*	75	50	50	25	25
Moon Roof (Sldng)	*	175	125	125	100	75
T-Bar Roof	—	—	300	300	—	—
Rear Spoiler	25	25	25	25	25	25
Alloy Wheels	*	*	25	25	25	25
Premium Wheels	175	175	125	125	75	25
Roof Rack (Wagon)	25	25	25	25	0	0
Third Seat (Wagon)	275	125	125	125	75	75
DEDUCT FOR:						
Manual Trans	—	—	—	—	(350)	*
w/o Power Steering	—	—	—	(75)	(50)	(50)
w/o Air Cond	(225)	(225)	(175)	(175)	(75)	(75)
w/o AM/FM Stereo	(25)	(25)	(25)	(25)	0	0
w/o Power Windows	—	(75)	—	(75)	—	—
w/o Pwr Door Locks	—	(25)	—	(25)	—	—
w/o Tilt Wheel	—	(50)	—	(50)	—	—
w/o Cruise Control	—	(25)	—	(25)	—	—
w/o Leather	(125)	(125)	—	—	—	—
w/o Sun/Moon Roof	(325)	—	—	—	—	—

* — EQUIPMENT INCLUDED IN BASE PRICE

1997 FACTORY EQUIPMENT TRADE-IN VALUES

Equipment	1	2	3	4	5	6
Automatic Trans	—	—	—	—	*	275
Power Steering	*	*	*	*	*	*
Air Conditioning	*	*	*	*	*	*
Power Windows	*	*	*	*	75	25
Power Door Locks	*	*	*	*	0	0
Tilt Wheel	*	*	*	*	50	0
Cruise Control	*	*	*	*	25	0
Cassette	*	*	*	*	25	25
GROUP TOTAL	*	*	*	*	175	325
Power Seat	*	*	25	25	0	0
Dual Power Seats	*	*	25	25	25	0
ABS (4 Wheel)	*	*	50	50	25	0
CD (Single Disc)	100	100	100	100	50	50
CD (Multi Disc)	200	200	200	200	150	125
Premium Sound	75	75	25	25	25	25
Navigation System	125	—	—	—	—	—
Leather	*	*	150	125	25	25
Sun Roof (Flip-up)	—	—	50	50	25	25
Sun Roof (Sliding)	*	100	75	75	50	25
Moon Roof (Sldng)	*	200	150	150	125	100
T-Bar Roof	—	—	—	325	—	—
Imitation Conv Top	—	50	—	25	—	—
Rear Spoiler	25	25	25	25	25	25
Alloy Wheels	*	*	50	50	25	25
Premium Wheels	225	225	150	150	100	50
Roof Rack (Wagon)	25	25	25	25	0	0
Third Seat (Wagon)	325	150	150	150	100	100
DEDUCT FOR:						
Manual Trans	—	—	—	—	(375)	*
w/o Power Steering	—	—	—	(100)	(50)	(50)
w/o Air Cond	(250)	(250)	(200)	(200)	(100)	(100)
w/o AM/FM Stereo	(25)	(25)	(25)	(25)	0	0
w/o Power Windows	—	(100)	—	(100)	—	—
w/o Pwr Door Locks	—	(25)	—	(25)	—	—
w/o Tilt Wheel	—	(75)	—	(75)	—	—
w/o Cruise Control	—	(25)	—	(25)	—	—
w/o Leather	(150)	(150)	—	—	—	—
w/o Sun/Moon Roof	(350)	—	—	—	—	—

* — EQUIPMENT INCLUDED IN BASE PRICE

1998 FACTORY EQUIPMENT TRADE-IN VALUES

Equipment	1	2	3	4	5	6
Automatic Trans	—	—	—	—	*	300
Power Steering	*	*	*	*	*	*
Air Conditioning	*	*	*	*	*	*
Power Windows	*	*	*	*	100	50
Power Door Locks	*	*	*	*	25	0
Tilt Wheel	*	*	*	*	75	25
Cruise Control	*	*	*	*	25	0
Cassette	*	*	*	*	50	25
GROUP TOTAL	*	*	*	*	275	400
Power Seat	*	*	25	25	0	0
Dual Power Seats	*	*	50	50	25	0
ABS (4 Wheel)	*	*	75	75	25	25
CD (Single Disc)	125	125	125	125	75	75
CD (Multi Disc)	225	225	225	225	175	150
Premium Sound	100	100	50	50	50	50
Navigation System	125	—	—	—	—	—
Leather	*	*	175	150	25	25
Sun Roof (Flip-up)	—	—	50	50	25	25
Sun Roof (Sliding)	*	125	100	100	75	50
Moon Roof (Sldng)	*	225	175	175	150	125
Imitation Conv Top	—	75	—	25	—	—
Rear Spoiler	25	25	25	25	25	25
Alloy Wheels	*	*	75	75	50	25
Premium Wheels	275	275	175	175	125	75
Roof Rack (Wagon)	25	25	25	25	0	0
Third Seat (Wagon)	375	175	175	175	125	125
DEDUCT FOR:						
Manual Trans	—	—	—	—	(400)	*
w/o Power Steering	—	—	—	(125)	(75)	(75)
w/o Air Cond	(275)	(275)	(225)	(225)	(125)	(125)
w/o AM/FM Stereo	(25)	(25)	(25)	(25)	0	0
w/o Power Windows	—	(125)	—	(125)	—	—
w/o Pwr Door Locks	—	(25)	—	(25)	—	—
w/o Tilt Wheel	—	(100)	—	(100)	—	—
w/o Cruise Control	—	(25)	—	(25)	—	—
w/o Leather	(175)	(175)	—	—	—	—
w/o Sun/Moon Roof	(375)	—	—	—	—	—

* — EQUIPMENT INCLUDED IN BASE PRICE

1999 FACTORY EQUIPMENT TRADE-IN VALUES

Equipment	1	2	3	4	5	6
Automatic Trans	—	—	—	—	*	300
Power Steering	*	*	*	*	*	*
Air Conditioning	*	*	*	*	*	*
Power Windows	*	*	*	*	125	75
Power Door Locks	*	*	*	*	50	25
Tilt Wheel	*	*	*	*	100	50
Cruise Control	*	*	*	*	50	25
Cassette	*	*	*	*	75	50
GROUP TOTAL	*	*	*	*	400	525
Power Seat	*	*	50	50	25	25
Dual Power Seats	*	*	75	75	50	25
ABS (4 Wheel)	*	*	100	100	50	50
CD (Single Disc)	150	150	150	150	100	100
CD (Multi Disc)	250	250	250	250	200	175
Premium Sound	125	125	75	75	75	75
Integrated Phone	175	175	150	150	—	—
Navigation System	300	—	—	—	—	—
Leather	*	*	200	175	50	25
Sun Roof (Flip-up)	—	—	50	50	25	25
Sun Roof (Sliding)	*	150	125	125	100	75
Moon Roof (Slдng)	*	250	200	200	175	150
Imitation Conv Top	—	100	—	50	—	—
Rear Spoiler	25	25	25	25	25	25
Parking Sensors	200	—	—	—	—	—
Alloy Wheels	*	*	100	100	75	50
Premium Wheels	300	300	200	200	150	100
Roof Rack (Wagon)	25	25	25	25	0	0
Third Seat (Wagon)	400	200	200	200	150	150
DEDUCT FOR:						
Manual Trans	—	—	—	—	(425)	*
w/o Power Steering	—	—	—	(150)	(100)	(100)
w/o Air Cond	(325)	(325)	(250)	(250)	(150)	(150)
w/o AM/FM Stereo	(50)	(50)	(50)	(50)	(25)	(25)
w/o Power Windows	—	(150)	—	(150)	—	—
w/o Pwr Door Locks	—	(50)	—	(50)	—	—
w/o Tilt Wheel	—	(125)	—	(125)	—	—
w/o Cruise Control	—	(25)	—	(25)	—	—
w/o Leather	(200)	(200)	—	—	—	—
w/o Sun/Moon Roof	(425)	—	—	—	—	—

* — EQUIPMENT INCLUDED IN BASE PRICE

SEE PAGE 13 FOR PVT PARTY & RETAIL EQUIPMENT 21

2000 FACTORY EQUIPMENT TRADE-IN VALUES

Equipment	1	2	3	4	5	6
Automatic Trans	—	—	—	—	*	350
Power Steering	*	*	*	*	*	*
Air Conditioning	*	*	*	*	*	*
Power Windows	*	*	*	*	125	75
Power Door Locks	*	*	*	*	50	25
Tilt Wheel	*	*	*	*	100	50
Cruise Control	*	*	*	*	50	25
Cassette	*	*	*	*	75	50
GROUP TOTAL	*	*	*	*	400	575
Power Seat	*	*	50	50	25	25
Dual Power Seats	*	*	100	100	50	25
ABS (4 Wheel)	*	*	100	100	50	50
CD (Single Disc)	150	150	150	150	100	100
CD (Multi Disc)	275	275	275	275	225	200
Premium Sound	150	150	100	100	75	75
Integrated Phone	200	200	150	150	—	—
Navigation System	325	325	325	—	—	—
Leather	*	*	250	200	75	50
Sun Roof (Flip-up)	—	—	75	75	25	25
Sun Roof (Sliding)	*	200	150	150	125	100
Moon Roof (Sldng)	*	325	250	250	200	175
Imitation Conv Top	—	125	—	75	—	—
Rear Spoiler	50	50	50	50	50	50
Sensing Cruise Ctrl	375	—	—	—	—	—
Parking Sensors	225	150	—	—	—	—
Alloy Wheels	*	*	100	100	75	50
Premium Wheels	325	325	225	225	150	100
Roof Rack (Wagon)	50	50	50	50	25	25
Third Seat (Wagon)	425	225	225	225	175	175
DEDUCT FOR:						
Manual Trans	—	—	—	—	(450)	*
w/o Power Steering	—	—	—	(175)	(125)	(100)
w/o Air Cond	(400)	(400)	(300)	(300)	(200)	(200)
w/o AM/FM Stereo	(50)	(50)	(50)	(50)	(25)	(25)
w/o Power Windows	—	(175)	—	(175)	—	—
w/o Pwr Door Locks	—	(50)	—	(50)	—	—
w/o Tilt Wheel	—	(150)	—	(150)	—	—
w/o Cruise Control	—	(50)	—	(50)	—	—
w/o Leather	(250)	(250)	—	—	—	—
w/o Sun/Moon Roof	(500)	—	—	—	—	—

* — EQUIPMENT INCLUDED IN BASE PRICE

2001 FACTORY EQUIPMENT TRADE-IN VALUES

Equipment	1	2	3	4	5	6
Automatic Trans	—	—	—	—	*	400
Power Steering	*	*	*	*	*	*
Air Conditioning	*	*	*	*	*	*
Power Windows	*	*	*	*	150	75
Power Door Locks	*	*	*	*	50	25
Tilt Wheel	*	*	*	*	100	50
Cruise Control	*	*	*	*	50	25
Cassette	*	*	*	*	75	50
GROUP TOTAL	*	*	*	*	425	625
Power Seat	*	*	50	50	25	25
Dual Power Seats	*	*	125	125	50	25
ABS (4 Wheel)	*	*	100	100	50	50
CD (Single Disc)	175	175	175	175	125	100
CD (Multi Disc)	300	300	300	300	250	225
Premium Sound	175	175	125	125	75	75
Integrated Phone	225	225	175	175	—	—
Navigation System	350	350	350	—	—	—
Leather	*	*	300	225	100	75
Sun Roof (Flip-up)	—	—	100	100	25	25
Sun Roof (Sliding)	*	250	200	200	150	125
Moon Roof (Sldng)	*	400	300	300	250	200
Imitation Conv Top	—	150	—	100	—	—
Rear Spoiler	75	75	75	75	75	75
Sensing Cruise Ctrl	400	—	—	—	—	—
Parking Sensors	250	175	—	—	—	—
Alloy Wheels	*	*	100	100	75	50
Premium Wheels	350	350	250	250	175	100
Roof Rack (Wagon)	75	75	75	75	50	50
Third Seat (Wagon)	450	250	250	250	200	200
DEDUCT FOR:						
Manual Trans	—	—	—	—	(475)	*
w/o Power Steering	—	—	—	(200)	(150)	(100)
w/o Air Cond	(475)	(475)	(350)	(350)	(250)	(250)
w/o AM/FM Stereo	(75)	(75)	(75)	(75)	(25)	(25)
w/o Power Windows	—	(200)	—	(200)	—	—
w/o Pwr Door Locks	—	(75)	—	(75)	—	—
w/o Tilt Wheel	—	(175)	—	(175)	—	—
w/o Cruise Control	—	(75)	—	(75)	—	—
w/o Leather	(300)	(300)	—	—	—	—
w/o Sun/Moon Roof	(550)	—	—	—	—	—

* — EQUIPMENT INCLUDED IN BASE PRICE

SEE PAGE 13 FOR PVT PARTY & RETAIL EQUIPMENT

2002 FACTORY EQUIPMENT TRADE-IN VALUES

Equipment	1	2	3	4	5	6
Automatic Trans	—	—	—	—	*	450
Power Steering	*	*	*	*	*	*
Air Conditioning	*	*	*	*	*	*
Power Windows	*	*	*	*	175	75
Power Door Locks	*	*	*	*	50	25
Tilt Wheel	*	*	*	*	100	50
Cruise Control	*	*	*	*	50	25
Cassette	*	*	*	*	75	50
GROUP TOTAL	*	*	*	*	450	675
Power Seat	*	*	50	50	25	25
Dual Power Seats	*	*	150	150	50	25
ABS (4 Wheel)	*	*	100	100	50	50
CD (Single Disc)	200	200	200	200	150	100
CD (Multi Disc)	325	325	325	325	275	250
Premium Sound	200	200	150	150	100	75
Integrated Phone	250	250	200	200	—	—
Navigation System	400	400	400	400	—	—
Leather	*	*	350	250	125	100
Sun Roof (Flip-up)	—	—	125	125	50	50
Sun Roof (Sliding)	*	300	250	250	175	150
Moon Roof (Sldng)	*	475	350	350	300	250
Imitation Conv Top	—	200	—	125	—	—
Rear Spoiler	100	100	100	100	100	100
Sensing Cruise Ctrl	425	—	—	—	—	—
Parking Sensors	275	200	100	—	—	—
Alloy Wheels	*	*	100	100	75	50
Premium Wheels	400	400	275	275	200	100
Roof Rack (Wagon)	100	100	100	100	50	50
Third Seat (Wagon)	475	275	275	275	225	225
DEDUCT FOR:						
Manual Trans	—	—	—	—	(500)	*
w/o Power Steering	—	—	—	(225)	(175)	(100)
w/o Air Cond	(550)	(550)	(425)	(425)	(300)	(300)
w/o AM/FM Stereo	(100)	(100)	(100)	(100)	(50)	(25)
w/o Power Windows	—	(225)	—	(225)	—	—
w/o Pwr Door Locks	—	(100)	—	(100)	—	—
w/o Tilt Wheel	—	(200)	—	(200)	—	—
w/o Cruise Control	—	(100)	—	(100)	—	—
w/o Leather	(350)	(350)	—	—	—	—
w/o Sun/Moon Roof	(600)	—	—	—	—	—

* — EQUIPMENT INCLUDED IN BASE PRICE

2003 FACTORY EQUIPMENT TRADE-IN VALUES

Equipment	1	2	3	4	5	6
Automatic Trans	—	—	—	—	*	475
Power Steering	*	*	*	*	*	*
Air Conditioning	*	*	*	*	*	*
Power Windows	*	*	*	*	200	100
Power Door Locks	*	*	*	*	75	25
Tilt Wheel	*	*	*	*	100	75
Cruise Control	*	*	*	*	75	25
Cassette	*	*	*	*	100	75
GROUP TOTAL	*	*	*	*	550	775
Power Seat	*	*	75	75	25	25
Dual Power Seats	*	*	175	175	75	25
ABS (4 Wheel)	*	*	125	125	75	50
CD (Single Disc)	225	225	225	225	175	125
CD (Multi Disc)	350	350	350	350	300	275
Premium Sound	225	225	175	175	125	75
Integrated Phone	275	275	225	225	—	—
Video/DVD	500	500	500	500	500	500
Navigation System	450	450	450	450	—	—
Leather	*	*	400	300	150	125
Sun Roof (Flip-up)	—	—	150	150	75	75
Sun Roof (Sliding)	*	350	300	300	200	175
Moon Roof (Sldng)	*	550	425	425	350	300
Imitation Conv Top	—	250	—	150	—	—
Rear Spoiler	100	100	100	100	100	100
Sensing Cruise Ctrl	450	—	—	—	—	—
Parking Sensors	300	225	125	—	—	—
Alloy Wheels	*	*	125	125	100	75
Premium Wheels	450	450	300	300	225	125
Roof Rack (Wagon)	100	100	100	100	50	50
Third Seat (Wagon)	500	300	300	300	250	250
DEDUCT FOR:						
Manual Trans	—	—	—	—	(525)	*
w/o Power Steering	—	—	—	(250)	(200)	(125)
w/o Air Cond	(625)	(625)	(500)	(500)	(350)	(350)
w/o AM/FM Stereo	(125)	(125)	(125)	(125)	(75)	(25)
w/o Power Windows	—	(250)	—	(250)	—	—
w/o Pwr Door Locks	—	(125)	—	(125)	—	—
w/o Tilt Wheel	—	(250)	—	(225)	—	—
w/o Cruise Control	—	(125)	—	(125)	—	—
w/o Leather	(400)	(400)	—	—	—	—
w/o Sun/Moon Roof	(650)	—	—	—	—	—

* — EQUIPMENT INCLUDED IN BASE PRICE

SEE PAGE 13 FOR PVT PARTY & RETAIL EQUIPMENT

2004 FACTORY EQUIPMENT TRADE-IN VALUES

Equipment	1	2	3	4	5	6
Automatic Trans	—	—	—	—	*	500
Power Steering	*	*	*	*	*	*
Air Conditioning	*	*	*	*	*	*
Power Windows	*	*	*	*	225	125
Power Door Locks	*	*	*	*	100	50
Tilt Wheel	*	*	*	*	125	100
Cruise Control	*	*	*	*	100	50
Cassette	*	*	*	*	125	100
GROUP TOTAL	*	*	*	*	675	925
Power Seat	*	*	100	100	50	25
Dual Power Seats	*	*	200	200	100	50
ABS (4 Wheel)	*	*	150	150	100	50
CD (Single Disc)	250	250	250	250	200	150
CD (Multi Disc)	400	400	400	400	325	300
Premium Sound	250	250	200	200	150	100
Integrated Phone	300	300	250	250	—	—
Video/DVD	500	500	500	500	500	500
Navigation System	500	500	500	500	500	—
Leather	*	*	475	350	200	150
Sun Roof (Flip-up)	—	—	200	200	100	100
Sun Roof (Sliding)	*	425	350	350	250	200
Moon Roof (Sldng)	*	625	500	500	400	350
Imitation Conv Top	—	300	—	200	—	—
Rear Spoiler	100	100	100	100	100	100
Sensing Cruise Ctrl	475	—	—	—	—	—
Parking Sensors	325	250	150	—	—	—
Alloy Wheels	*	*	150	150	125	100
Premium Wheels	500	500	350	350	250	150
Roof Rack (Wagon)	100	100	100	100	50	50
Third Seat (Wagon)	525	350	350	350	275	275
DEDUCT FOR:						
Manual Trans	—	—	—	—	(550)	*
w/o Power Steering	—	—	—	(275)	(225)	(150)
w/o Air Cond	(700)	(700)	(575)	(575)	(400)	(400)
w/o AM/FM Stereo	(150)	(150)	(150)	(150)	(100)	(50)
w/o Power Windows	—	(275)	—	(275)	—	—
w/o Pwr Door Locks	—	(150)	—	(150)	—	—
w/o Tilt Wheel	—	(300)	—	(250)	—	—
w/o Cruise Control	—	(150)	—	(150)	—	—
w/o Leather	(475)	(475)	—	—	—	—
w/o Sun/Moon Roof	(700)	—	—	—	—	—

* — EQUIPMENT INCLUDED IN BASE PRICE

2005 FACTORY EQUIPMENT TRADE-IN VALUES

Equipment	1	2	3	4	5	6
Automatic Trans	—	—	—	—	*	525
Power Steering	*	*	*	*	*	*
Air Conditioning	*	*	*	*	*	*
Power Windows	*	*	*	*	250	150
Power Door Locks	*	*	*	*	125	75
Tilt Wheel	*	*	*	*	150	125
Cruise Control	*	*	*	*	125	75
Cassette	*	*	*	*	150	125
GROUP TOTAL	*	*	*	*	800	1075
Power Seat	*	*	125	125	75	25
Dual Power Seats	*	*	225	225	125	75
ABS (4 Wheel)	*	*	175	175	125	75
CD (Single Disc)	275	275	275	275	225	175
CD (Multi Disc)	450	450	450	450	350	325
Premium Sound	275	275	225	225	175	125
Integrated Phone	350	350	275	275	—	—
Video/DVD	500	500	500	500	500	500
Navigation System	550	550	550	550	—	—
Leather	*	*	550	400	250	175
Sun Roof (Flip-up)	—	—	250	250	125	125
Sun Roof (Sliding)	*	500	400	400	300	250
Moon Roof (Sldng)	*	700	575	575	450	400
Imitation Conv Top	—	350	—	250	—	—
Rear Spoiler	100	100	100	100	100	100
Sensing Cruise Ctrl	500	500	—	—	—	—
Parking Sensors	350	275	175	—	—	—
Alloy Wheels	*	*	175	175	150	125
Premium Wheels	550	550	400	400	275	175
Roof Rack (Wagon)	100	100	100	100	50	50
Third Seat (Wagon)	550	400	400	400	300	300
DEDUCT FOR:						
Manual Trans	—	—	—	—	(575)	*
w/o Power Steering	—	—	—	(300)	(250)	(175)
w/o Air Cond	(775)	(775)	(650)	(650)	(450)	(450)
w/o AM/FM Stereo	(175)	(175)	(175)	(175)	(125)	(75)
w/o Power Windows	—	(300)	—	(300)	—	—
w/o Pwr Door Locks	—	(175)	—	(175)	—	—
w/o Tilt Wheel	—	(350)	—	(275)	—	—
w/o Cruise Control	—	(175)	—	(175)	—	—
w/o Leather	(550)	(550)	—	—	—	—
w/o Sun/Moon Roof	(750)	—	—	—	—	—

* — EQUIPMENT INCLUDED IN BASE PRICE

SEE PAGE 13 FOR PVT PARTY & RETAIL EQUIPMENT

Body	Type	VIN	List	Trade-In Fair	Good	Pvt-Party Good	Retail Excellent

Automobile Section

ACURA

1991 ACURA — JH4(DB164)–M–#

INTEGRA—4-Cyl.—Equipment Schedule 3
W.B. 100.4", 102.4" (4D); 1.8 Liter.

RS Sedan 4D	DB164	13870	800	1150	2275	3900
RS Hatchback 2D	DA944	12970	825	1175	2325	3975
LS Sedan 4D	DB165	15565	900	1275	2475	4175
LS Hatchback 2D	DA945	14845	900	1275	2475	4175
LS Special H'Back 2D	DA939	14985	925	1300	2525	4200
GS Sedan 4D	DB166	17470	1000	1425	2675	4400
GS Hatchback 2D	DA946	16945	1000	1425	2675	4400
Manual Trans (Sedan)	3,5		(175)	(175)	(235)	(235)

LEGEND—V6—Equipment Schedule 1
W.B. 111.4", 114.6" (4D); 3.2 Liter.

Sedan 4D	KA763	27910	2475	3075	4525	6575
L Sedan 4D	KA765	29910	2925	3600	5150	7300
L Coupe 2D	KA825	32010	3000	3650	5250	7450
LS Sedan 4D	KA767	34510	3075	3725	5325	7575
LS Coupe 2D	KA827	36610	3150	3800	5400	7675
Manual Trans (Sedan)	1,5		(200)	(200)	(265)	(265)

NSX—V6—Equipment Schedule 2
W.B. 99.6"; 3.0 Liter.

Sport Coupe 2D	NA126	64600	13375	15125	19100	24600

1992 ACURA — JH4(DB164)–N–#

INTEGRA—4-Cyl.—Equipment Schedule 3
W.B. 100.4", 102.4" (4D); 1.7 Liter, 1.8 Liter.

RS Sedan 4D	DB164	14335	925	1300	2550	4325
RS Hatchback 2D	DA944	13410	950	1325	2625	4400
LS Sedan 4D	DB165	16065	1050	1450	2800	4600
LS Hatchback 2D	DA945	15315	1050	1450	2800	4600
GS Sedan 4D	DB166	18025	1175	1625	3000	4875
GS Hatchback 2D	DA946	17485	1175	1625	3000	4875
GS-R Hatchback 2D	DB238	18255	1225	1725	3100	5000
Manual Trans (Sedan)	3,5		(100)	(100)	(135)	(135)

VIGOR—5-Cyl.—Equipment Schedule 1
W.B. 110.4"; 2.5 Liter.

LS Sedan 4D	CC264	24340	1975	2525	3950	5925
GS Sedan 4D	CC265	26325	2175	2775	4225	6250
w/o Leather			0	0	0	0
Manual Trans			(200)	(200)	(265)	(265)

LEGEND—V6—Equipment Schedule 1
W.B. 111.4", 114.6" (4D); 3.2 Liter.

Sedan 4D	KA763	28595	2825	3450	5025	7200
L Sedan 4D	KA765	30975	3325	4025	5700	8025
L Coupe 2D	KA825	32425	3400	4100	5800	8150
LS Sedan 4D	KA767	35475	3500	4200	5925	8325
LS Coupe 2D	KA827	36825	3575	4275	6025	8425
Manual Trans (Sedan)	1,5		(200)	(200)	(265)	(265)

NSX—V6—Equipment Schedule 2
W.B. 99.6"; 3.0 Liter.

Sport Coupe 2D	NA126	67600	15075	16975	21400	27500
Manual Trans			0	0	0	0

1993 ACURA — JH4(DA944)–P–#

INTEGRA—4-Cyl.—Equipment Schedule 3
W.B. 100.4", 102.4" (4D); 1.7 Liter, 1.8 Liter.

RS Sedan 2D	DA944	14045	1125	1575	2950	4875
RS Sedan 4D	DB164	14970	1075	1500	2875	4775
LS Sedan 2D	DA945	15950	1250	1750	3200	5175
LS Sedan 4D	DB165	16700	1250	1750	3175	5125
LS Special Sedan 2D	DA948	17450	1250	1750	3200	5175
GS Sedan 2D	DA946	18120	1450	1950	3425	5425
GS Sedan 4D	DB166	18680	1450	1950	3425	5425
GS-R Sedan 2D	DB238	18625	1550	2050	3575	5600

1993 ACURA

Body Type	VIN	List	Trade-In Fair	Trade-In Good	Pvt-Party Good	Retail Excellent
Manual Trans (Sedan) 3,5			**(125)**	**(125)**	**(165)**	**(165)**
VIGOR—5-Cyl.—Equipment Schedule 1						
W.B. 110.4"; 2.5 Liter.						
LS Sedan 4D	CC264	25380	**2350**	**2925**	**4450**	**6575**
GS Sedan 4D	CC266	27865	**2600**	**3225**	**4775**	**6950**
w/o Leather 4			**0**	**0**	**0**	**0**
Manual Trans 5			**(250)**	**(250)**	**(335)**	**(335)**
LEGEND—V6—Equipment Schedule 1						
W.B. 111.4", 114.6" (4D); 3.2 Liter.						
Sedan 4D	KA763	30365	**3250**	**3925**	**5600**	**7925**
L Sedan 4D	KA766	33865	**3850**	**4600**	**6375**	**8875**
L Coupe 2D	KA826	35915	**4000**	**4750**	**6575**	**9125**
LS Sedan 4D	KA767	36865	**4050**	**4825**	**6675**	**9225**
LS Coupe 2D	KA827	39315	**4225**	**5000**	**6850**	**9425**
Manual Trans (Sedan) 1,5			**(250)**	**(250)**	**(335)**	**(335)**
NSX—V6—Equipment Schedule 2						
W.B. 99.6"; 3.0 Liter.						
Sport Coupe 2D	NA126	73250	**16625**	**18725**	**23300**	**29700**

1994 ACURA — JH4(DB764)-R-#

Body Type	VIN	List	Trade-In Fair	Trade-In Good	Pvt-Party Good	Retail Excellent
INTEGRA—4-Cyl.—Equipment Schedule 3						
W.B. 101.2", 103.1" (4D); 1.8 Liter.						
RS Sedan 4D	DB764	16695	**1425**	**1925**	**3250**	**5075**
RS Sport Coupe 2D	DC444	15935	**1525**	**2025**	**3375**	**5225**
LS Sedan 4D	DB765	18565	**1700**	**2225**	**3600**	**5475**
LS Sport Coupe 2D	DC445	18565	**1725**	**2250**	**3625**	**5525**
GS-R Sedan 4D	DB858	20345	**2025**	**2575**	**4000**	**5975**
GS-R Sport Coupe 2D	DC238	20015	**2050**	**2625**	**4050**	**6050**
Manual Trans (Sedan) 3,5			**(150)**	**(150)**	**(200)**	**(200)**
VIGOR—5-Cyl.—Equipment Schedule 1						
W.B. 110.4"; 2.5 Liter.						
LS Sedan 4D	CC264	27485	**2800**	**3425**	**5025**	**7250**
GS Sedan 4D	CC266	29485	**3075**	**3725**	**5400**	**7700**
w/o Leather 4			**0**	**0**	**0**	**0**
Manual Trans 5			**(300)**	**(300)**	**(400)**	**(400)**
LEGEND—V6—Equipment Schedule 1						
W.B. 111.4", 114.6" (4D); 3.2 Liter.						
L Sedan 4D	KA766	36485	**4450**	**5250**	**7100**	**9750**
L Coupe 2D	KA826	38085	**4650**	**5500**	**7425**	**10150**
LS Sedan 4D	KA767	38985	**4675**	**5525**	**7450**	**10150**
LS Coupe 2D	KA827	41885	**4925**	**5775**	**7725**	**10500**
GS Sedan 4D	KA768	41085	**4925**	**5775**	**7725**	**10500**
Manual Trans (Sedan) 1,5			**(300)**	**(300)**	**(400)**	**(400)**
NSX—V6—Equipment Schedule 2						
W.B. 99.6"; 3.0 Liter.						
Sport Coupe 2D	NA126	77200	**18275**	**20575**	**25300**	**32000**

1995 ACURA — JH4(DB764)-S-#

Body Type	VIN	List	Trade-In Fair	Trade-In Good	Pvt-Party Good	Retail Excellent
INTEGRA—4-Cyl.—Equipment Schedule 3						
W.B. 101.2", 103.1" (4D); 1.8 Liter.						
RS Sedan 4D	DB764	17390	**1825**	**2350**	**3750**	**5675**
RS Sport Coupe 2D	DC444	16630	**1925**	**2450**	**3850**	**5800**
LS Sedan 4D	DB765	20110	**2125**	**2700**	**4100**	**6075**
LS Sport Coupe 2D	DC445	19310	**2150**	**2750**	**4175**	**6175**
Special Ed Sedan 4D	DB766	21610	**2125**	**2725**	**4125**	**6100**
Special Ed Coupe 2D	DC446	21060	**2250**	**2825**	**4275**	**6275**
GS-R Sedan 4D	DB858	21100	**2475**	**3075**	**4550**	**6650**
GS-R Sport Coupe 2D	DC238	20770	**2550**	**3150**	**4625**	**6725**
Manual Trans (Sedan) 3,5			**(175)**	**(175)**	**(235)**	**(235)**
TL—5-Cyl.—Equipment Schedule 1						
W.B. 111.8"; 2.5 Liter.						
2.5 Sedan 4D	UA265	30370	**3650**	**4375**	**6125**	**8600**
LEGEND—V6—Equipment Schedule 1						
W.B. 111.4", 114.6" (4D); 3.2 Liter.						
L Sedan 4D	KA766	38220	**5050**	**5925**	**7875**	**10650**
L Coupe 2D	KA826	39820	**5350**	**6250**	**8300**	**11150**
SE Sedan 4D	KA769	39320	**5175**	**6050**	**8050**	**10850**
LS Sedan 4D	KA767	40120	**5325**	**6225**	**8275**	**11150**
LS Coupe 2D	KA827	43620	**5650**	**6575**	**8650**	**11600**
GS Sedan 4D	KA768	42420	**5575**	**6500**	**8575**	**11500**
Manual Trans (Sedan) 1,5			**(350)**	**(350)**	**(465)**	**(465)**
NSX-T—V6—Equipment Schedule 2						
W.B. 99.6"; 3.0 Liter.						

1995 ACURA

Body	Type	VIN	List	Trade-In Fair	Trade-In Good	Pvt-Party Good	Retail Excellent
T-Targa 2D		NA128	85225	22225	24825	30100	37600

1996 ACURA — JH4(DB764)-T-#

INTEGRA—4-Cyl.—Equipment Schedule 3
W.B. 101.2", 103.1" (4D); 1.8 Liter.

RS Sedan 4D		DB764	18080	2275	2825	4300	6325
RS Sport Coupe 2D		DC444	17320	2350	2925	4425	6450
LS Sedan 4D		DB765	20870	2575	3200	4675	6775
LS Sport Coupe 2D		DC445	20070	2650	3275	4775	6875
Special Ed Sedan 4D		DB766	22370	2600	3225	4700	6800
Special Ed Coupe 2D		DC446	21820	2725	3325	4850	6950
GS-R Sedan 4D		DB858	21820	2975	3650	5200	7375
GS-R Sport Coupe 2D		DC238	21520	3050	3725	5275	7500
Manual Trans (Sedan)		3,5		(200)	(200)	(265)	(265)

TL—5-Cyl.—Equipment Schedule 1
W.B. 111.8"; 2.5 Liter.

2.5 Sedan 4D		UA265	30370	4175	4950	6850	9450

TL—V6—Equipment Schedule 1
W.B. 111.8"; 3.2 Liter.

3.2 Sedan 4D		UA365	35920	4850	5700	7675	10500

RL—V6—Equipment Schedule 1
W.B. 114.6"; 3.5 Liter.

3.5 Sedan 4D		KA964	41435	5425	6350	8250	10950
Traction Control		5,6		200	200	265	265

NSX—V6—Equipment Schedule 2
W.B. 99.6"; 3.0 Liter.

Sport Coupe 2D		NA126	83725	21825	24550	29700	37100
T-Targa 2D		NA128	87725	24150	26975	32500	40400

1997 ACURA — JH4(DC444)-V-#

INTEGRA—4-Cyl.—Equipment Schedule 3
W.B. 101.2", 103.1" (4D); 1.8 Liter.

RS Sport Coupe 2D		DC444	17335	2850	3500	5050	7200
LS Sedan 4D		DB765	20885	3100	3750	5325	7550
LS Sport Coupe 2D		DC445	20085	3175	3850	5425	7675
GS Sedan 4D		DB766	22385	3400	4100	5700	7975
GS Sport Coupe 2D		DC446	21835	3475	4175	5800	8075
GS-R Sedan 4D		DB858	21835	3525	4225	5875	8175
GS-R Sport Coupe 2D		DC238	21535	3625	4350	6000	8325
Type R Sport Cpe 2D		DC238	23535	****	****	****	12350
Manual Trans (Sedan)		3,5		(200)	(200)	(265)	(265)

CL—4-Cyl.—Equipment Schedule 1
W.B. 106.9"; 2.2 Liter.

2.2 Coupe 2D		YA125	24395	3900	4650	6550	9175
Manual Trans				(400)	(400)	(535)	(535)

CL—V6—Equipment Schedule 1
W.B. 106.9"; 3.0 Liter.

3.0 Coupe 2D		YA225	26895	4450	5250	7200	9950

TL—5-Cyl.—Equipment Schedule 1
W.B. 111.8"; 2.5 Liter.

2.5 Sedan 4D		UA265	30935	4775	5600	7600	10400

TL—V6—Equipment Schedule 1
W.B. 111.8"; 3.2 Liter.

3.2 Sedan 4D		UA365	33385	5525	6450	8525	11500
Traction Control				225	225	300	300

RL—V6—Equipment Schedule 1
W.B. 114.6"; 3.5 Liter.

3.5 Sedan 4D		KA964	41435	6300	7325	9325	12200
Traction Control				225	225	300	300

NSX—V6—Equipment Schedule 2
W.B. 99.6"; 3.0 Liter, 3.2 Liter.

Sport Coupe 2D		NA123	84725	23850	26675	32000	39800
T-Targa 2D		NA126	88725	26275	29400	35000	43200

1998 ACURA — JH4(DC444)-W-#

INTEGRA—4-Cyl.—Equipment Schedule 3
W.B. 101.2", 103.1" (4D); 1.8 Liter.

RS Sport Coupe 2D		DC444	17435	3400	4100	5750	8050
LS Sedan 4D		DB765	21235	3650	4400	6075	8450
LS Sport Coupe 2D		DC445	20435	3750	4475	6175	8550
GS Sedan 4D		DB766	22635	3975	4725	6475	8900
GS Sport Coupe 2D		DC446	22085	4050	4825	6575	9025

1998 ACURA

Body	Type	VIN	List	Trade-In Fair	Trade-In Good	Pvt-Party Good	Retail Excellent
GS-R Sedan 4D		DB858	22035	4100	4875	6625	9075
GS-R Sport Coupe 2D		DC238	21735	4225	5025	6775	9250
Type R Sport Cpe 2D		DC231	23500	****	****	****	13600
Manual Trans (Sedan)		3,5	....	(200)	(200)	(265)	(265)

CL—4-Cyl.—Equipment Schedule 1
W.B. 106.9"; 2.3 Liter.

Body	Type	VIN	List	Fair	Good	Good	Excellent
2.3 Coupe 2D		YA325	24595	4500	5325	7375	10200
Manual Trans		1	....	(425)	(425)	(565)	(565)

CL—V6—Equipment Schedule 1
W.B. 106.9"; 3.0 Liter.

Body	Type	VIN	List	Fair	Good	Good	Excellent
3.0 Coupe 2D		YA225	27095	5100	6000	8075	11000

TL—5-Cyl.—Equipment Schedule 1
W.B. 111.8"; 2.5 Liter.

Body	Type	VIN	List	Fair	Good	Good	Excellent
2.5 Sedan 4D		UA265	31135	5450	6375	8500	11450

TL—V6—Equipment Schedule 1
W.B. 111.8"; 3.2 Liter.

Body	Type	VIN	List	Fair	Good	Good	Excellent
3.2 Sedan 4D		UA364	33585	6250	7250	9475	12600
Traction Control			....	275	275	365	365

RL—V6—Equipment Schedule 1
W.B. 114.6"; 3.5 Liter.

Body	Type	VIN	List	Fair	Good	Good	Excellent
3.5 Sedan 4D		KA964	41635	7250	8350	10500	13600
Traction Control			....	275	275	365	365

NSX—V6—Equipment Schedule 2
W.B. 99.6"; 3.0 Liter, 3.2 Liter.

Body	Type	VIN	List	Fair	Good	Good	Excellent
Sport Coupe 2D		NA123	84725	26000	29100	34600	42800
T-Targa 2D		NA126	88725	28625	32000	37800	46400

1999 ACURA — (JH4or19U)(DB765)–X–#

INTEGRA—4-Cyl.—Equipment Schedule 3
W.B. 101.2", 103.1" (4D); 1.8 Liter.

Body	Type	VIN	List	Fair	Good	Good	Excellent
LS Sedan 4D		DB765	21255	4300	5100	6850	9300
LS Sport Coupe 2D		DC445	20455	4400	5200	6950	9450
GS Sedan 4D		DB766	22655	4625	5450	7225	9750
GS Sport Coupe 2D		DC446	22105	4725	5575	7350	9900
GS-R Sedan 4D		DB858	22855	4775	5600	7425	10000
GS-R Sport Coupe 2D		DC238	22555	4900	5750	7575	10150
Manual Trans (Sedan)		3,5	....	(200)	(200)	(265)	(265)

CL—4-Cyl.—Equipment Schedule 3
W.B. 106.9"; 2.3 Liter.

Body	Type	VIN	List	Fair	Good	Good	Excellent
2.3 Coupe 2D		YA325	24355	5250	6125	8225	11150
Manual Trans			....	(450)	(450)	(600)	(600)

CL—V6—Equipment Schedule 1
W.B. 106.9"; 3.0 Liter.

Body	Type	VIN	List	Fair	Good	Good	Excellent
3.0 Coupe 2D		YA225	26605	5900	6875	9000	12050

TL—V6—Equipment Schedule 1
W.B. 108.1"; 3.2 Liter.

Body	Type	VIN	List	Fair	Good	Good	Excellent
3.2 Sedan 4D		UA564	28405	7450	8550	10600	13650

RL—V6—Equipment Schedule 1
W.B. 114.6"; 3.5 Liter.

Body	Type	VIN	List	Fair	Good	Good	Excellent
3.5 Sedan 4D		KA964	42355	8325	9525	11650	14800

NSX—V6—Equipment Schedule 2
W.B. 99.6"; 3.0 Liter, 3.2 Liter.

Body	Type	VIN	List	Fair	Good	Good	Excellent
Sport Coupe 2D		NA123	84745	28625	32000	37400	45700
T-Targa 2D		NA126	88745	31425	35025	40700	49400

2000 ACURA — (JH4or19U)(DB765)–Y–#

INTEGRA—4-Cyl.—Equipment Schedule 3
W.B. 101.2", 103.1" (4D); 1.8 Liter.

Body	Type	VIN	List	Fair	Good	Good	Excellent
LS Sedan 4D		DB765	21355	4950	5825	7675	10350
LS Sport Coupe 2D		DC445	20555	5100	5975	7800	10500
GS Sedan 4D		DB766	22755	5275	6175	8075	10750
GS Sport Coupe 2D		DC446	22205	5400	6325	8225	10900
GS-R Sedan 4D		DB859	22955	5500	6425	8325	11050
GS-R Sport Coupe 2D		DC239	22655	5650	6575	8500	11250
Type R Sport Cpe 2D		DC231	24805	****	****	****	16400
Manual Trans (Sedan)		3,5	....	(225)	(225)	(300)	(300)

TL—V6—Equipment Schedule 1
W.B. 108.1"; 3.2 Liter.

Body	Type	VIN	List	Fair	Good	Good	Excellent
3.2 Sedan 4D		UA566	28855	8825	10100	12250	15450

RL—V6—Equipment Schedule 1
W.B. 114.6"; 3.5 Liter.

Body	Type	VIN	List	Fair	Good	Good	Excellent
3.5 Sedan 4D		KA965	42455	10050	11400	13950	17700

2000 ACURA

Body	Type	VIN	List	Trade-In Fair	Trade-In Good	Pvt-Party Good	Retail Excellent
NSX—V6—Equipment Schedule 2							
W.B. 99.6"; 3.0 Liter, 3.2 Liter.							
Sport Coupe 2D		NA123	84745	32600	36375	42200	51000
T-Targa 2D		NA126	88745	35800	39375	46000	55300

2001 ACURA — JH4or19U(DB765)-1-#

Body	Type	VIN	List	Fair	Good	Good	Excellent
INTEGRA—4-Cyl.—Equipment Schedule 3							
W.B. 101.2", 103.1" (4D); 1.8 Liter.							
LS Sedan 4D		DB765	21480	5700	6650	8650	11500
LS Sport Coupe 2D		DC445	20680	5850	6825	8825	11700
GS Sedan 4D		DB766	22880	6050	7000	9050	11950
GS Sport Coupe 2D		DC446	22330	6175	7175	9225	12150
GS-R Sedan 4D		DB859	23080	6300	7325	9325	12250
GS-R Sport Coupe 2D		DC239	22780	6475	7500	9550	12500
Type R Coupe 2D		DC231	24930	****	****	****	18250
Manual Trans (Sedan)		3,5		(250)	(250)	(335)	(335)
CL—V6—Equipment Schedule 1							
W.B. 106.9"; 3.2 Liter.							
3.2 Coupe 2D		YA424	28460	9200	10475	12750	16100
3.2 Type Coupe 2D		YA426	30810	10375	11825	14150	17700
TL—V6—Equipment Schedule 1							
W.B. 108.1"; 3.2 Liter.							
3.2 Sedan 4D		UA566	29030	10275	11700	13950	17400
RL—V6—Equipment Schedule 1							
W.B. 114.6"; 3.5 Liter.							
3.5 Sedan 4D		KA965	42630	11975	13575	16350	20500
NSX—V6—Equipment Schedule 2							
W.B. 99.6"; 3.0 Liter, 3.2 Liter.							
Sport Coupe 2D		NA123	84845	36950	41225	47300	56800
T-Targa 2D		NA126	88845	40450	45000	51500	61400

2002 ACURA — JH4or19U(DC548)-2-#

Body	Type	VIN	List	Fair	Good	Good	Excellent
RSX—4-Cyl.—Equipment Schedule 3							
W.B. 101.2"; 2.0 Liter.							
Sport Coupe 2D		DC548	21330	8550	9800	11850	14900
Type S Sport Cpe 2D		DC530	23650	9700	11050	13150	16300
CL—V6—Equipment Schedule 1							
W.B. 106.9"; 3.2 Liter.							
3.2 Coupe 2D		YA424	28510	10675	12125	14500	18100
3.2 Type S Coupe 2D		YA426	30860	11975	13575	16050	19800
TL—V6—Equipment Schedule 1							
W.B. 108.1"; 3.2 Liter.							
3.2 Sedan 4D		UA566	29360	11925	13525	15950	19700
3.2 Type S Sedan 4D		UA568	31710	12850	14550	17000	20900
RL—V6—Equipment Schedule 1							
W.B. 114.6"; 3.5 Liter.							
3.5 Sedan 4D		KA965	43630	14150	15950	18850	23300
NSX-T—V6—Equipment Schedule 2							
W.B. 99.6"; 3.0 Liter, 3.2 Liter.							
Targa 2D		NA126	89745	42200	46950	53300	63100

2003 ACURA — JH4or19U(DC548)-3-#

Body	Type	VIN	List	Fair	Good	Good	Excellent
RSX—4-Cyl.—Equipment Schedule 3							
W.B. 101.2"; 2.0 Liter.							
Sport Coupe 2D		DC548	21375	9800	11200	13350	16650
Type S Sport Cpe 2D		DC530	23770	11050	12550	14800	18250
CL—V6—Equipment Schedule 1							
W.B. 106.9"; 3.2 Liter.							
3.2 Coupe 2D		YA424	28700	12225	13875	16400	20300
3.2 Type S Coupe 2D		YA426	31050	13725	15525	18100	22100
TL—V6—Equipment Schedule 1							
W.B. 108.1"; 3.2 Liter.							
3.2 Sedan 4D		UA566	29480	13725	15525	18100	22000
3.2 Type S Sedan 4D		UA568	31830	14800	16675	19250	23300
RL—V6—Equipment Schedule 1							
W.B. 114.6"; 3.5 Liter.							
3.5 Sedan 4D		KA965	43650	16450	18525	21600	26300
NSX-T—V6—Equipment Schedule 2							
W.B. 99.6"; 3.0 Liter, 3.2 Liter.							
Targa 2D		NA126	89765	46950	52275	58900	69400

Body	Type	VIN	List	Trade-In Fair	Good	Pvt-Party Good	Retail Excellent

2004 ACURA — (JH4or19U)(DC548)-4-#

RSX—4-Cyl.—Equipment Schedule 3
W.B. 101.2"; 2.0 Liter.

| Sport Coupe 2D | | DC548 | 21470 | **11200** | **12700** | **14900** | **18300** |
| Type S Sport Cpe 2D | | DC530 | 23865 | **12600** | **14250** | **16550** | **20100** |

TL—V6—Equipment Schedule 1
W.B. 107.9"; 3.2 Liter.

| 3.2 Sedan 4D | | UA566 | 33195 | **19975** | **22400** | **25100** | **29600** |

TSX—4-Cyl.—Equipment Schedule 3
W.B. 105.1"; 2.4 Liter.

| Sedan 4D | | CL958 | 26990 | **15325** | **17275** | **19600** | **23300** |

RL—V6—Equipment Schedule 1
W.B. 114.6"; 3.5 Liter.

| 3.5 Sedan 4D | | KA965 | 46100 | **19000** | **21350** | **24600** | **29700** |

NSX-T—V6—Equipment Schedule 2
W.B. 99.6"; 3.0 Liter, 3.2 Liter.

| Targa 2D | | NA126 | 89765 | **52675** | **58500** | **65500** | **76700** |

2005 ACURA — (JH4or19U)(DC548)-5-#

RSX—4-Cyl.—Equipment Schedule 3
W.B. 101.2"; 2.0 Liter.

| Sport Coupe 2D | | DC548 | 21745 | **12375** | **14025** | **16200** | **19700** |
| Type S Sport Cpe 2D | | DC530 | 24240 | **13975** | **15775** | **18050** | **21700** |

TL—V6—Equipment Schedule 1
W.B. 107.9"; 3.2 Liter.

| 3.2 Sedan 4D | | UA662 | 33670 | **22600** | **25325** | **28100** | **33000** |

TSX—4-Cyl.—Equipment Schedule 3
W.B. 105.1"; 2.4 Liter.

| Sedan 4D | | CL958 | 27760 | **16875** | **18975** | **21300** | **25200** |

RL SH-AWD—V6—Equipment Schedule 1
W.B. 110.2"; 3.5 Liter.

| 3.5 Sedan 4D | | KB165 | 49670 | **30175** | **33650** | **36900** | **42500** |

NSX-T—V6—Equipment Schedule 2
W.B. 99.6"; 3.0 Liter, 3.2 Liter.

| Targa 2D | | NA126 | 89765 | | | | |

ALFA ROMEO

1991 ALFA ROMEO — ZAR(BB32G)-M-#

SPIDER—4-Cyl.—Equipment Schedule 6
W.B. 88.6"; 2.0 Liter.

Convertible 2D		BB32G	22320	**2975**	**3650**	**5425**	**7875**
Veloce Convertible 2D		BB32N	23325	**3250**	**3925**	**5775**	**8325**
Hard Top/Soft Top				**100**	**100**	**135**	**135**

164—V6—Equipment Schedule 3
W.B. 104.7"; 3.0 Liter.

Sedan 4D		EA33A	25525	**675**	**975**	**1950**	**3400**
L Sedan 4D		EA33L	28525	**775**	**1125**	**2250**	**3900**
S Sedan 4D		EA33E	29875	**1100**	**1550**	**2825**	**4600**

1992 ALFA ROMEO — ZAR(BB32G)-N-#

SPIDER—4-Cyl.—Equipment Schedule 6
W.B. 88.6"; 2.0 Liter.

Convertible 2D		BB32G	22654	**3425**	**4125**	**6050**	**8650**
Veloce Convertible 2D		BB32N	24704	**3725**	**4450**	**6450**	**9175**
Hard Top/Soft Top				**100**	**100**	**135**	**135**

164—V6—Equipment Schedule 3
W.B. 104.7"; 3.0 Liter.

| L Sedan 4D | | EA33L | 29885 | **925** | **1300** | **2550** | **4325** |
| S Sedan 4D | | EA33E | 35385 | **1350** | **1850** | **3225** | **5150** |

1993 ALFA ROMEO — ZAR(BB32G)-P-#

SPIDER—4-Cyl.—Equipment Schedule 6
W.B. 88.6"; 2.0 Liter.

Convertible 2D		BB32G	23174	**3900**	**4650**	**6725**	**9525**
Veloce Convertible 2D		BB32N	25265	**4275**	**5075**	**7175**	**10100**
Hard Top/Soft Top				**100**	**100**	**135**	**135**

164—V6—Equipment Schedule 3
W.B. 104.7"; 3.0 Liter.

1993 ALFA ROMEO

Body	Type	VIN	List	Trade-In Fair	Trade-In Good	Pvt-Party Good	Retail Excellent
L Sedan 4D		EA33L	30635	1075	1525	2900	4775
S Sedan 4D		EA33E	35385	1675	2175	3675	5725

1994 ALFA ROMEO — ZAR(BB32G)-R-#

SPIDER—4-Cyl.—Equipment Schedule 6
W.B. 88.6"; 2.0 Liter.

Body	Type	VIN	List	Fair	Good	Good	Excellent
Convertible 2D		BB32G	24095	4450	5250	7475	10500
Veloce Ce Conv 2D		BB32N	28015	4850	5700	7950	11050
Hard Top/Soft Top				100	100	135	135

164—V6—Equipment Schedule 3
W.B. 104.7"; 3.0 Liter.

LS Sedan 4D		ED33E	35315	2025	2575	4200	6425
Q Sedan 4D		ED33R	38115	2225	2825	4450	6750

1995 ALFA ROMEO — ZAR(ED33E)-S-#

164—V6—Equipment Schedule 3
W.B. 104.7"; 3.0 Liter.

LS Sedan 4D		ED33E	36600	2425	3025	5300	8275
Q Sedan 4D		ED33R	39400	3950	4700	6725	9475

AUDI

1991 AUDI — WAU(EC58A)-M-#

AUDI—5-Cyl.—Equipment Schedule 3
W.B. 99.9" (80 & 90 Sed), 100.3" (80 & 90 Quattro), 105.6" (100), 105.9" (100 Quattro); 2.3 Liter.

80 Sedan 4D		EC58A	21400	725	1050	2025	3475
80 Quattro Sedan 4D		FC58A	25165	875	1225	2425	4100
90 Sedan 4D		GC58A	26045	875	1225	2400	4075
90 Quattro 20V Sed 4D		HE58A	28935	1275	1775	3075	4900
100 Sedan 4D		BC544	28505	775	1125	2250	3900
100 Quattro Sedan 4D		CC544	30865	1125	1575	2900	4725
Manual Trans				(100)	(100)	(135)	(135)

QUATTRO—5-Cyl.—Equipment Schedule 1
W.B. 100.4"; 2.3 Liter.

Coupe 2D		GE58B	31345	3075	3725	5425	7775

200—5-Cyl. Turbo—Equipment Schedule 1
W.B. 105.6", 106.1" (Quattro); 2.2 Liter.

Sedan 4D		FD544	34935	1050	1450	2750	4475
Quattro Sedan 4D		GD544	42755	1750	2275	3725	5750
Quattro Wagon 4D		HD544	42755	1900	2425	3925	5975

QUATTRO—V8—Equipment Schedule 1
W.B. 106.4"; 3.6 Liter.

Sedan 4D		KE544	50555	3025	3700	5450	7875
Manual Trans				(200)	(200)	(265)	(265)

1992 AUDI — WAU(ED58A)-N-#

80—5-Cyl.—Equipment Schedule 3
W.B. 100.2", 99.9" (Quattro); 2.3 Liter.

Sedan 4D		ED58A	23055	825	1175	2375	4100
Quattro Sedan 4D		FD58A	26655	1000	1425	2725	4525
Manual Trans				(100)	(100)	(135)	(135)

100—V6—Equipment Schedule 3
W.B. 105.8", 106.0" (Quattro); 2.8 Liter.

Sedan 4D		AK54A	28105	1075	1525	2850	4700
S Sedan 4D		BK54A	30305	1225	1675	3050	4950
CS Sedan 4D		DK54A	33305	1550	2050	3550	5525
CS Quattro Sedan 4D		EK54A	36805	1925	2450	4000	6075
CS Quattro Wagon 4D		FK54A	41205	2500	3100	4725	6975
Manual Trans				(100)	(100)	(135)	(135)

S4—5-Cyl. Turbo—Equipment Schedule 1
W.B. 106.0"; 2.2 Liter.

Quattro Sedan 4D		HP54A	44155	3800	4550	6450	9075

QUATTRO—V8—Equipment Schedule 1
W.B. 106.4"; 4.2 Liter.

Sedan 4D		BW84C	53505	4800	5650	7675	10500

1993 AUDI — WAU(BK58C)-P-#

90—V6—Equipment Schedule 3
W.B. 102.8", 102.2" (Quattro); 2.8 Liter.

1993 AUDI

Body	Type	VIN	List	Trade-In Fair	Trade-In Good	Pvt-Party Good	Retail Excellent
S Sedan 4D		BK58C	26295	1225	1675	3075	5000
CS Sedan 4D		DK58C	29145	1400	1900	3350	5300
CS Quattro Sedan 4D		EK58C	32695	2300	2875	4500	6725
Manual Trans				**(125)**	**(125)**	**(165)**	**(165)**
100—V6—Equipment Schedule 3 W.B. 105.8", 106.0" (Quattro); 2.8 Liter.							
Sedan 4D		AK84A	30845	1375	1875	3325	5275
S Sedan 4D		BK84A	33695	1575	2075	3600	5625
CS Sedan 4D		DK84A	38195	2000	2550	4125	6275
CS Quattro Sedan 4D		EK848	41395	2475	3075	4750	7025
CS Quattro Wagon 4D		FK84A	44695	3150	3800	5575	8025
Manual Trans				**(125)**	**(125)**	**(165)**	**(165)**
S4—5-Cyl. Turbo—Equipment Schedule 1 W.B. 106.0"; 2.2 Liter.							
Quattro Sedan 4D		HR84A	47295	4775	5600	7675	10550
QUATTRO—V8—Equipment Schedule 1 W.B. 106.4"; 4.2 Liter.							
Sedan 4D		BW84C	58945	5500	6425	8575	11600

1994 AUDI — WAU(BK88C)-R-#

Body	Type	VIN	List	Trade-In Fair	Trade-In Good	Pvt-Party Good	Retail Excellent
90—V6—Equipment Schedule 3 W.B. 102.8", 102.2" (Quattro); 2.8 Liter.							
S Sedan 4D		BK88C	28265	1525	2025	3575	5675
CS Sedan 4D		DK88C	31215	1750	2275	3850	6000
CS Quattro Sedan 4D		EK88C	34865	2800	3425	5200	7600
Manual Trans				**(150)**	**(150)**	**(200)**	**(200)**
100—V6—Equipment Schedule 3 W.B. 105.8", 106.0" (Quattro); 2.8 Liter.							
S Sedan 4D		BK84A	35565	2000	2550	4200	6425
S Wagon 4D		CK84A	38515	2575	3175	4925	7300
CS Sedan 4D		DK84A	41015	2450	3050	4775	7125
CS Quattro Sedan 4D		EK84A	43465	3075	3725	5575	8100
CS Quattro Wagon 4D		FK84A	47465	3825	4575	6525	9200
Manual Trans				**(150)**	**(150)**	**(200)**	**(200)**
CABRIOLET—V6—Equipment Schedule 1 W.B. 100.6"; 2.8 Liter.							
Convertible 2D		BL88G	39395	3550	4250	6125	8700
S4—5-Cyl. Turbo—Equipment Schedule 1 W.B. 106.0"; 2.2 Liter.							
Quattro Sedan 4D		HR84A	51615	5775	6725	8975	12150
QUATTRO—V8—Equipment Schedule 1 W.B. 106.4"; 4.2 Liter.							
Sedan 4D		BW84C	59145	6225	7225	9525	12750

1995 AUDI — WAU(BK88C)-S-#

Body	Type	VIN	List	Trade-In Fair	Trade-In Good	Pvt-Party Good	Retail Excellent
90—V6—Equipment Schedule 3 W.B. 102.8", 102.2" (Quattro); 2.8 Liter.							
Sedan 4D		BK88C	26115	1900	2425	4150	6425
Sport Sedan 4D		DK88C	26515	2125	2725	4450	6800
Quattro AWD		C,E		1300	1300	1735	1735
Manual Trans				**(175)**	**(175)**	**(235)**	**(235)**
A6—V6—Equipment Schedule 3 W.B. 105.8", 106.0" (Quattro); 2.8 Liter.							
Sedan 4D		FA84A	31045	2725	3350	5200	7675
Wagon 4D		HA84A	33615	3350	4050	6000	8625
Quattro AWD		G,J		1300	1300	1735	1735
Manual Trans				**(175)**	**(175)**	**(235)**	**(235)**
CABRIOLET—V6—Equipment Schedule 1 W.B. 100.6"; 2.8 Liter.							
Convertible 2D		BL88G	36345	4150	4925	6950	9750
S6—5-Cyl. Turbo—Equipment Schedule 1 W.B. 106.0"; 2.2 Liter.							
Quattro Sedan 4D		KA84A	45715	7075	8175	10650	14150
Quattro Wagon 4D		LA84A	48385	7925	9125	11700	15350

1996 AUDI — WAU(DA88D)-T-#

Body	Type	VIN	List	Trade-In Fair	Trade-In Good	Pvt-Party Good	Retail Excellent
A4—V6—Equipment Schedule 3 W.B. 103.0". 2.8 Liter.							
Sedan 4D		DA88D	26975	3625	4325	6050	8475
Quattro AWD		E		1325	1325	1765	1765
Manual Trans				**(200)**	**(200)**	**(265)**	**(265)**

1996 AUDI

Body Type	VIN	List	Trade-In Fair	Good	Pvt-Party Good	Retail Excellent
A6—V6—Equipment Schedule 3						
W.B. 105.8"; 2.8 Liter.						
Sedan 4D	FA84A	32775	3300	3975	6000	8700
Wagon 4D	HA84A	34475	3975	4725	6850	9700
Quattro AWD	G,J		1325	1325	1765	1765
CABRIOLET—V6—Equipment Schedule 3						
W.B. 100.6"; 2.8 Liter.						
Convertible 2D	AA88G	37275	4825	5675	7875	10900

1997 AUDI — WAU(DA88A)-V-#

Body Type	VIN	List	Trade-In Fair	Good	Pvt-Party Good	Retail Excellent
A4—V6—Equipment Schedule 3						
W.B. 103.0"; 2.8 Liter.						
Sedan 4D	DA88A	28905	4375	5150	7000	9600
Quattro AWD	C,E		1350	1350	1800	1800
Manual Trans			(200)	(200)	(265)	(265)
4-Cyl. 1.8L Turbo	B		(925)	(925)	(1235)	(1235)
A6—V6—Equipment Schedule 3						
W.B. 105.8"; 2.8 Liter.						
Sedan 4D	FA84A	33100	3950	4700	6875	9850
Wagon 4D	HA84A	34900	4700	5550	7825	10950
Quattro AWD	G,J		1350	1350	1800	1800
A8—V8—Equipment Schedule 1						
W.B. 113.0"; 3.7 Liter, 4.2 Liter.						
Sedan 4D	AF84D	57400	7350	8475	11950	16600
Quattro AWD Sed 4D	AG84D	65000	9350	10675	14400	19500
CABRIOLET—V6—Equipment Schedule 1						
W.B. 100.6"; 2.8 Liter.						
Convertible 2D	AA88G	38800	5625	6550	8950	12200

1998 AUDI — WAU(DD68D)-W-#

Body Type	VIN	List	Trade-In Fair	Good	Pvt-Party Good	Retail Excellent
A4—V6—Equipment Schedule 3						
W.B. 103.0"; 2.8 Liter.						
Sedan 4D	DD68D	29965	5250	6100	8125	10950
Avant Wagon 4D	FD68D	30965	5625	6550	8600	11500
Quattro AWD	G,C,E		1375	1375	1835	1835
Manual Trans			(200)	(200)	(265)	(265)
4-Cyl. 1.8L Turbo	B		(975)	(975)	(1300)	(1300)
A6—V6—Equipment Schedule 3						
W.B. 105.8", 108.7" (Sed); 2.8 Liter.						
Sedan 4D	AA74B	34250	5250	6125	8575	11950
Wagon 4D	JA84A	38050	6050	7000	9550	13050
Quattro AWD	B,J		1375	1375	1835	1835
A8—V8—Equipment Schedule 1						
W.B. 113.0"; 3.7 Liter, 4.2 Liter.						
Sedan 4D	AF74D	57900	8600	9850	13700	18750
Quattro AWD Sed 4D	BG74D	65500	10775	12275	16300	21800
CABRIOLET—V6—Equipment Schedule 1						
W.B. 100.6"; 2.8 Liter.						
Convertible 2D	AA88G	38800	6575	7600	10250	13800

1999 AUDI — WAU(DD38D)-X-#

Body Type	VIN	List	Trade-In Fair	Good	Pvt-Party Good	Retail Excellent
A4—V6—Equipment Schedule 3						
W.B. 103.0"; 2.8 Liter.						
Sedan 4D	DD38D	28890	6300	7300	9350	12300
Quattro AWD	C,E		1400	1400	1865	1865
Manual Trans			(200)	(200)	(265)	(265)
4-Cyl. 1.8L Turbo	B		(1025)	(1025)	(1365)	(1365)
A4 AVANT QUATTRO AWD—V6—Equipment Schedule 3						
W.B. 102.6"; 2.8 Liter.						
Wagon 4D	GD38D	31540	7275	8375	10500	13700
Manual Trans			(200)	(200)	(265)	(265)
4-Cyl. 1.8L Turbo	B		(1025)	(1025)	(1365)	(1365)
A6—V6—Equipment Schedule 3						
W.B. 108.7"; 2.8 Liter.						
Sedan 4D	AA24B	34250	6300	7325	9850	13400
Quattro AWD	B		1400	1400	1865	1865
A6 AVANT QUATTRO AWD—V6—Equipment Schedule 3						
W.B. 108.6"; 2.8 Liter.						
Wagon 4D	DA24B	37100	7350	8450	11100	14800
A8—V8—Equipment Schedule 1						
W.B. 113.0"; 3.7 Liter, 4.2 Liter.						
Sedan 4D	AF34D	57900	10050	11400	15350	20700

Body Type	VIN	List	Trade-In Fair	Trade-In Good	Pvt-Party Good	Retail Excellent
Quattro AWD Sed 4D	BG34D	65500	12425	14075	18250	24000

2000 AUDI — (WAUorTRU)(AH28D)–Y–#

A4—V6—Equipment Schedule 3
W.B. 103.0"; 2.8 Liter.

Body Type	VIN	List	Fair	Good	Good	Excellent
Sedan 4D	AH28D	30390	7625	8750	11000	14300
Quattro AWD	D		1450	1450	1935	1935
Manual Trans			(225)	(225)	(300)	(300)
4-Cyl. 1.8L Turbo	C		(1175)	(1175)	(1565)	(1565)

A4 AVANT QUATTRO AWD—V6—Equipment Schedule 3
W.B. 102.6"; 2.8 Liter.

Wagon 4D	KH28D	33140	8725	10000	12350	15800
Manual Trans			(225)	(225)	(300)	(300)
4-Cyl. 1.8L Turbo	C		(1175)	(1175)	(1565)	(1565)

S4 QUATTRO AWD—V6 Turbo—Equipment Schedule 3
W.B. 102.6"; 2.7 Liter.

2.7T Sedan 4D	DD68D	39625	11500	13050	16050	20500

A6—V6—Equipment Schedule 3
W.B. 108.7"; 2.8 Liter.

Sedan 4D	BH24B	34475	7750	8900	11700	15500
Quattro AWD	G,J		1450	1450	1935	1935

A6 AVANT QUATTRO AWD—V6—Equipment Schedule 3
W.B. 108.6"; 2.8 Liter.

Wagon 4D	LH24B	37425	8950	10225	13050	17050

A6 QUATTRO AWD—V6 Turbo—Equipment Schedule 3
W.B. 108.7"; 2.7 Liter.

2.7T Sedan 4D	ED24B	39075	10225	11650	14600	18800

A6 QUATTRO AWD—V8—Equipment Schedule 3
W.B. 108.6"; 4.2 Liter.

4.2 Sedan 4D	ZL54B	49425	14200	16000	19300	24200

A8 QUATTRO AWD—V8—Equipment Schedule 1
W.B. 113.4", 118.5" (L); 4.2 Liter.

Sedan 4D	FL54D	62525	14500	16350	20900	27100
L Sedan 4D	FL54D	66775	18875	23600	30200	

TT—4-Cyl. Turbo—Equipment Schedule 2
W.B. 95.4", 95.6"; 1.8 Liter

Coupe 2D	TC28N	31025	8500	9700	11800	14900
Quattro AWD	U		1450	1450	1935	1935

2001 AUDI — (WAUorTRU)(AH68D)–1–#

A4—V6—Equipment Schedule 3
W.B. 103.0"; 2.8 Liter.

Sedan 4D	AH68D	30890	9150	10425	12950	16600
Quattro AWD	C,E		1475	1475	1965	1965
4-Cyl. 1.8L Turbo	C		(1325)	(1325)	(1765)	(1765)

A4 AVANT QUATTRO AWD—V6—Equipment Schedule 3
W.B. 102.6"; 2.8 Liter.

Wagon 4D	KH68D	33640	10425	11875	14450	18300
Manual Trans			(250)	(250)	(335)	(335)
4-Cyl. 1.8L Turbo	C		(1325)	(1325)	(1765)	(1765)

S4 QUATTRO AWD—V6 Turbo—Equipment Schedule 3
W.B. 102.6"; 2.7 Liter.

2.7T Sedan 4D	RD58D	39450	13475	15225	18550	23300
2.7T Avant Wagon 4D	XD68D	41050	14550	16450	19800	24600

A6—V6—Equipment Schedule 3
W.B. 108.7"; 2.8 Liter.

Sedan 4D	BH54B	34950	9425	10775	13750	17900
Quattro AWD	G,J		1475	1475	1965	1965

A6 AVANT QUATTRO AWD—V6—Equipment Schedule 3
W.B. 108.6"; 2.8 Liter.

Wagon 4D	LH54B	37900	10775	12275	15350	19700

A6 QUATTRO AWD—V6 Turbo—Equipment Schedule 3
W.B. 108.7"; 2.7 Liter.

2.7T Sedan 4D	ED54B	40050	12175	13825	17000	21500
Sport Pkg			400	400	535	535

ALLROAD QUATTRO AWD—V6 Turbo—Equipment Sch 1
W.B. 108.5"; 2.7 Liter.

2.7T Wagon 4D	YP54B	43450	15675	17650	21000	26100

A6 QUATTRO AWD—V8—Equipment Schedule 3
W.B. 108.6"; 4.2 Liter.

4.2 Sedan 4D	ZL54B	49950	16675	18775	22300	27500
Sport Pkg			400	400	535	535

2001 AUDI

Body	Type	VIN	List	Trade-In Fair	Trade-In Good	Pvt-Party Good	Retail Excellent
A8 QUATTRO AWD—V8—Equipment Schedule 1							
W.B. 113.4", 118.5" (L); 4.2 Liter.							
Sedan 4D		FL54D	62750	16925	19050	24000	30700
L Sedan 4D		ML54D	68450	19500	21925	27000	34100
S8 QUATTRO AWD—V8—Equipment Schedule 1							
W.B. 113.4"; 4.2 Liter.							
Sedan 4D		GU54D	73050	23775	26575	32000	39800
TT—4-Cyl. Turbo—Equipment Schedule 2							
W.B. 95.4"; 1.8 Liter.							
Coupe 2D		SC58N	31750	9800	11200	13500	16900
Roadster 2D		TT58N	33750	11100	12600	15000	18600
Power Folding Roof				400	400	535	535
Quattro AWD				1475	1475	1965	1965
TT QUATTRO AWD—4-Cyl. HO Turbo—Equipment Schedule 2							
W.B. 95.4"; 1.8 Liter.							
Coupe 2D		WT58N	36650	12125	13725	16150	19900
Roadster 2D		UT58N	39450	13425	15175	17700	21600

2002 AUDI — (WAUorTRU)(JT58E)-2-#

Body	Type	VIN	List	Trade-In Fair	Trade-In Good	Pvt-Party Good	Retail Excellent
A4—V6—Equipment Schedule 3							
W.B. 104.3"; 3.0 Liter.							
Sedan 4D		JT58E	31965	12375	14025	16250	19800
Sport Pkg				300	300	400	400
Quattro AWD		L		1500	1500	2000	2000
5-Spd Manual Trans				(275)	(275)	(365)	(365)
4-Cyl. 1.8L Turbo		C		(1475)	(1475)	(1965)	(1965)
A4 AVANT QUATTRO AWD—V6—Equipment Schedule 3							
W.B. 104.3"; 3.0 Liter.							
Wagon 4D		VT58E	34715	13775	15575	17900	21600
Sport Pkg				300	300	400	400
5-Spd Manual Trans				(275)	(275)	(365)	(365)
4-Cyl. 1.8L Turbo		C		(1475)	(1475)	(1965)	(1965)
S4 QUATTRO AWD—V6 Turbo—Equipment Schedule 3							
W.B. 102.6"; 2.7 Liter.							
2.7T Sedan 4D		RD68D	39475	15775	17750	21200	26500
2.7T Avant Wagon 4D		XD68D	41075	16925	19050	22700	28500
A6—V6—Equipment Schedule 3							
W.B. 108.7"; 3.0 Liter.							
Sedan 4D		JT54B	35975	11350	12900	16100	20700
Quattro AWD		L		1500	1500	2000	2000
A6 AVANT QUATTRO AWD—V6—Equipment Schedule 3							
W.B. 108.6"; 3.0 Liter.							
Wagon 4D		VT54B	38925	12800	14500	17800	22600
A6 QUATTRO AWD—V6 Turbo—Equipment Schedule 3							
W.B. 108.7"; 2.7 Liter.							
2.7T Sedan 4D		LD54B	40325	14400	16250	19700	24600
Sport Pkg				425	425	565	565
ALLROAD QUATTRO AWD—V6 Turbo—Equipment Sch 1							
W.B. 108.5"; 2.7 Liter.							
2.7T Wagon 4D		YD54B	43325	18150	20375	24100	29500
A6 QUATTRO AWD—V8—Equipment Schedule 3							
W.B. 108.6"; 4.2 Liter.							
4.2 Sedan 4D		ML54B	50225	19350	21725	25500	31100
Sport Pkg				425	425	565	565
S6 AVANT QUATTRO AWD—V8—Equipment Schedule 1							
W.B. 108.6"; 4.2 Liter.							
Wagon 4D		XU54B	61375	23575	26375	30400	36500
A8 QUATTRO AWD—V8—Equipment Schedule 1							
W.B. 113.4", 118.5" (L); 4.2 Liter.							
Sedan 4D		FL44D	62775	19700	22125	27500	35000
L Sedan 4D		ML44D	67775	22600	25325	30800	38800
S8 QUATTRO AWD—V8—Equipment Schedule 1							
W.B. 113.4"; 4.2 Liter.							
Sedan 4D		GU44D	74775	27250	30450	36400	44900
TT—4-Cyl. Turbo—Equipment Schedule 2							
W.B. 95.4"; 1.8 Liter.							
Coupe 2D		SC28N	31775	11550	13100	15650	19500
Roadster 2D		TC28N	33775	12950	14650	17250	21200
Power Folding Roof				400	400	535	535
TT QUATTRO AWD—4-Cyl. Turbo—Equipment Schedule 2							
W.B. 95.4"; 1.8 Liter.							
180 Coupe 2D		WX28N	33595	12750	14450	17050	21000

2002 AUDI

Body	Type	VIN	List	Trade-In Fair	Trade-In Good	Pvt-Party Good	Retail Excellent
TT QUATTRO AWD—4-Cyl. HO Turbo—Equipment Schedule 2							
W.B. 95.6"; 1.8 Liter.							
225 Coupe 2D		WT28N	36675	14075	15900	18600	22800
225 Roadster 2D		UT28N	39475	15525	17500	20300	24600
225 ALMS Comm Cpe		WT28N	40245	16350	18425	21200	25700

2003 AUDI — (WAU,WUA,WA1orTRU)(JT58E)–3–#

Body	Type	VIN	List	Trade-In Fair	Trade-In Good	Pvt-Party Good	Retail Excellent
A4—V6—Equipment Schedule 3							
W.B. 104.3", 104.5" (Cabriolet); 3.0 Liter.							
Sedan 4D		JT58E	32250	14550	16400	18900	22900
Cabriolet 2D		AT28H	42160	21825	24450	27300	32100
Sport Pkg				325	325	435	435
Quattro AWD		L		1525	1525	2035	2035
5-Spd Manual Trans				(300)	(300)	(400)	(400)
4-Cyl. 1.8L Turbo		C		(1625)	(1625)	(2165)	(2165)
A4 AVANT QUATTRO AWD—V6—Equipment Schedule 3							
W.B. 104.3"; 3.0 Liter.							
Wagon 4D		VT58E	35000	16100	18150	20800	24900
Sport Pkg				325	325	435	435
5-Spd Manual Trans				(300)	(300)	(400)	(400)
4-Cyl. 1.8L Turbo		C		(1625)	(1625)	(2165)	(2165)
A6—V6—Equipment Schedule 3							
W.B. 108.7"; 3.0 Liter.							
Sedan 4D		JT54B	36360	13575	15325	18850	24000
Quattro AWD		L		1525	1525	2035	2035
A6 AVANT QUATTRO AWD—V6—Equipment Schedule 3							
W.B. 108.7"; 3.0 Liter.							
Wagon 4D		VT54B	39310	15175	17125	20800	26000
A6 QUATTRO AWD—V6 Turbo—Equipment Schedule 3							
W.B. 108.7"; 2.7 Liter.							
2.7T Wagon 4D		LD54B	41510	16925	19050	22800	28200
ALLROAD QUATTRO AWD—V6 Turbo—Equipment Schedule 1							
W.B. 108.5"; 2.7 Liter.							
2.7T Wagon 4D		YD54B	45110	20850	23375	27400	33300
A6 QUATTRO AWD—V8—Equipment Schedule 3							
W.B. 108.6"; 4.2 Liter.							
4.2 Sedan 4D		ML54B	48460	22400	25025	29100	35200
Sport Pkg				450	450	600	600
S6 AVANT QUATTRO AWD—V8—Equipment Schedule 1							
W.B. 108.6"; 4.2 Liter.							
Wagon 4D		XU54B	61060	26875	30075	34200	40900
RS6 QUATTRO AWD—V8 Bi Turbo—Equipment Schedule 1							
W.B. 108.8"; 4.2 Liter.							
Sedan 4D		PV54B	84660	45200	50350	57600	68800
A8 QUATTRO AWD—V8—Equipment Schedule 1							
W.B. 113.4", 118.5" (L); 4.2 Liter.							
Sedan 4D		FL44D	68260	23075	25800	31600	39900
L Sedan 4D		ML44D	67860	26200	29300	35300	43900
S8 QUATTRO AWD—V8—Equipment Schedule 1							
W.B. 113.4"; 4.2 Liter.							
Sedan 4D		GU44D	74460	31325	34925	41200	50400
TT—4-Cyl. Turbo—Equipment Schedule 3							
W.B. 95.4"; 1.8 Liter.							
Coupe 2D		SC28N	33145	13775	15575	18450	22800
Roadster 2D		TC28N	35145	15375	17325	20300	24800
Power Folding Roof				400	400	535	535
TT QUATTRO AWD—4-Cyl. HO Turbo—Equipment Schedule 1							
W.B. 95.4"; 1.8 Liter.							
Coupe 2D		WT28N	36845	16625	18725	21700	26400
Roadster 2D		UT28N	39645	18200	20475	23600	28400

2004 AUDI — (WAU,WA1orTRU)(JT58E)–4–#

Body	Type	VIN	List	Trade-In Fair	Trade-In Good	Pvt-Party Good	Retail Excellent
A4—V6—Equipment Schedule 3							
W.B. 104.3", 104.5" (Cabriolet); 3.0 Liter.							
Sedan 4D		JT58E	31840	17225	19350	21100	26500
Cabriolet 2D		AT48H	42490	25125	28125	31200	36600
Sport Pkg				350	350	465	465
Ultra Sport Pkg				1000	1000	1335	1335
Quattro AWD		L		1550	1550	2065	2065
5-Spd Manual Trans				(300)	(300)	(400)	(400)
4-Cyl. 1.8L Turbo		C		(1775)	(1775)	(2365)	(2365)
A4 AVANT QUATTRO AWD—V6—Equipment Schedule 3							
W.B. 104.3"; 3.0 Liter.							

Body	Type	VIN	List	Trade-In Fair	Trade-In Good	Pvt-Party Good	Retail Excellent
Wagon 4D		VT58E	35480	18875	21150	24100	28600
Sport Pkg				350	350	465	465
Ultra Sport Pkg				1000	1000	1335	1335
4-Cyl. 1.8L Turbo		C		(1775)	(1775)	(2365)	(2365)

S4 QUATTRO AWD—V8—Equipment Schedule 1
W.B. 104.3"; 4.2 Liter.

Body	Type	VIN	List	Fair	Good	Good	Excellent
Sedan 4D		PL58E	47490	25600	28625	32900	39400
Cabriolet 2D		RL48H	55720	31425	35125	39500	46600

S4 AVANT QUATTRO AWD—V8—Equipment Schedule 1
W.B. 104.3"; 4.2 Liter.

Body	Type	VIN	List	Fair	Good	Good	Excellent
Wagon 4D		XL68E	48490	27150	30275	34500	41100

A6—V6—Equipment Schedule 3
W.B. 108.7"; 3.0 Liter.

Body	Type	VIN	List	Fair	Good	Good	Excellent
Sedan 4D		JT54B	36640	16300	18325	22100	27600
Quattro AWD		L		1550	1550	2065	2065

A6 AVANT QUATTRO AWD—V6—Equipment Schedule 3
W.B. 108.6"; 3.0 Liter.

Body	Type	VIN	List	Fair	Good	Good	Excellent
Wagon 4D		VT54B	40840	18050	20275	24200	29900

A6 QUATTRO AWD—V6 Turbo—Equipment Schedule 3
W.B. 108.7"; 2.7 Liter.

Body	Type	VIN	List	Fair	Good	Good	Excellent
2.7T Sedan 4D		LD54B	42840	19975	22400	26400	32300
2.7T S-Line Sedan 4D		CD64B	43870	20275	22800	26800	32700

ALLROAD QUATTRO AWD—V6 Turbo—Equipment Schedule 1
W.B. 108.5"; 2.7 Liter.

Body	Type	VIN	List	Fair	Good	Good	Excellent
2.7T Wagon 4D		YD54B	40640	23575	26375	29500	34600

ALLROAD QUATTRO AWD—V8—Equipment Schedule 1
W.B. 108.5"; 4.2 Liter.

Body	Type	VIN	List	Fair	Good	Good	Excellent
4.2 Wagon 4D		YL64B	47640	26100	29200	33500	40100

A6 QUATTRO AWD—V8—Equipment Schedule 3
W.B. 108.6"; 4.2 Liter.

Body	Type	VIN	List	Fair	Good	Good	Excellent
4.2 Sedan 4D		ML54B	49690	25900	28900	33200	39800
Sport Pkg				475	475	635	635

A8 QUATTRO AWD—V8—Equipment Schedule 1
W.B. 121.1"; 4.2 Liter.

Body	Type	VIN	List	Fair	Good	Good	Excellent
L Sedan 4D		ML44E	69190	37625	41900	46900	55200

TT—4-Cyl. Turbo—Equipment Schedule 2
W.B. 95.4"; 1.8 Liter.

Body	Type	VIN	List	Fair	Good	Good	Excellent
Coupe 2D		SC28N	33940	16875	18975	22300	27400
Roadster 2D		TC28N	35940	18525	20850	24300	29500
Power Folding Roof				400	400	535	535

TT QUATTRO AWD—4-Cyl. HO Turbo—Equipment Schedule 2
W.B. 95.6"; 1.8 Liter.

Body	Type	VIN	List	Fair	Good	Good	Excellent
Coupe 2D		WT28N	37390	19975	22400	25900	31200
Roadster 2D		UT28N	40190	21725	24350	27800	33500

TT QUATTRO AWD—V6—Equipment Schedule 2
W.B. 95.6"; 3.2 Liter.

Body	Type	VIN	List	Fair	Good	Good	Excellent
Coupe 2D		WF28N	40590	21250	23775	27300	32800
Roadster 2D		UF28N	43590	22700	25425	29000	34700

A4—V6—Equipment Schedule 3
W.B. 104.3", 104.5" (Cabriolet); 3.0 Liter.

Body	Type	VIN	List	Fair	Good	Good	Excellent
Sedan 4D		JT58E	32670	19975	22400	25400	30300
Cabriolet 2D		AT48H	43020	28525	31925	35200	40800
Sport Pkg				375	375	500	500
Ultra Sport Pkg				1000	1000	1335	1335
S-Line Pkg				500	500	665	665
Quattro AWD		L		1575	1575	2100	2100
5-Spd Manual Trans				(300)	(300)	(400)	(400)
4-Cyl. 1.8L Turbo		C		(1900)	(1900)	(2535)	(2535)

A4 AVANT QUATTRO AWD—V6—Equipment Schedule 3
W.B. 104.3"; 3.0 Liter.

Body	Type	VIN	List	Fair	Good	Good	Excellent
Wagon 4D		VT58E	36510	21825	24450	27500	32600
Sport Pkg				375	375	500	500
Ultra Sport Pkg				1000	1000	1335	1335
4-Cyl. 1.8L Turbo		C		(1900)	(1900)	(2535)	(2535)

A4 (2005.5)—4-Cyl. Turbo—Equipment Schedule 3
W.B. 104.3"; 2.0 Liter.

Body	Type	VIN	List	Fair	Good	Good	Excellent
2.0T Sedan 4D		AF78E	29270				
Sport Pkg							
Quattro AWD							

A4 AVANT QUATTRO (2005.5)—4-Cyl. Turbo—Equipment Sch 3
W.B. 104.3"; 2.0 Liter.

Body	Type	VIN	List	Trade-In Fair	Trade-In Good	Pvt-Party Good	Retail Excellent
2.0T Wagon 4D		KF78E	32370				
Sport Pkg							

A4 QUATTRO (2005.5)—V6—Equipment Schedule 3
W.B. 104.3"; 3.2 Liter.

Body	Type	VIN	List	Fair	Good	Good	Excellent
3.2 Sedan 4D		DG78E	36120				
Sport Pkg							

A4 AVANT QUATTRO (2005.5)—V6—Equipment Schedule 3
W.B. 104.3"; 3.2 Liter.

| 3.2 Wagon 4D | | KG78E | 37120 | | | | |
| Sport Pkg | | | | | | | |

S4 QUATTRO AWD—V8—Equipment Schedule 1
W.B. 104.3", 104.5" (Cabriolet); 4.2 Liter.

| Sedan 4D | | PL58E | 47770 | 29000 | 32400 | 36900 | 43800 |
| Cabriolet 2D | | RL48H | 55870 | 35400 | 39475 | 44000 | 51600 |

S4 AVANT QUATTRO AWD—V8—Equipment Schedule 1
W.B. 104.3"; 4.2 Liter.

| Wagon 4D | | XL58E | 48770 | | | | |

S4 QUATTRO AWD (2005.5)—V8—Equipment Schedule 1
W.B. 104.3"; 4.2 Liter.

| Sedan 4D | | GL68E | 49320 | | | | |

S4 AVANT QUATTRO AWD (2005.5)—V8— Equipment Sch 1
W.B. 104.3"; 4.2 Liter.

| Wagon 4D | | KF68E | 50320 | | | | |

A6 QUATTRO AWD—V6—Equipment Schedule 3
W.B. 108.7"; 3.2 Liter.

| Sedan 4D | | DG54F | 41620 | | | | |
| Sport Pkg | | | | | | | |

A6 QUATTRO AWD—V8—Equipment Schedule 3
W.B. 108.6"; 4.2 Liter.

4.2 Sedan 4D		DL54F	51220				
Sport Pkg							
S-Line Pkg		E					

ALLROAD QUATTRO AWD—V6 Turbo—Equipment Schedule 1
W.B. 108.5"; 2.7 Liter.

| 2.7T Wagon 4D | | YD54B | 44570 | 26875 | 30075 | 33300 | 38800 |

ALLROAD QUATTRO AWD—V8—Equipment Schedule 1
W.B. 108.5"; 4.2 Liter.

| 4.2 Wagon 4D | | YL54B | 47970 | 29575 | 33075 | 37500 | 44500 |

A8 QUATTRO AWD—V8—Equipment Schedule 1
W.B. 115.9", 121.0" (L); 4.2 Liter.

| Sedan 4D | | LL44E | 67310 | 39375 | 43850 | 49300 | 58100 |
| L Sedan 4D | | ML44E | 70620 | 43250 | 48100 | 53600 | 62800 |

A8 QUATTRO AWD—W12—Equipment Schedule 1
W.B. 121.0"; 6.0 Liter.

| L Sedan 4D | | MR44E | 118120 | | | | |

TT—4-Cyl. Turbo—Equipment Schedule 2
W.B. 95.4"; 1.8 Liter.

Coupe 2D		SC68N	34220	19600	22025	26100	32200
Roadster 2D		SG228	36220	21425	24050	28200	34400
Power Folding Roof				400	400	535	535

TT QUATTRO AWD—4-Cyl. HO Turbo—Equipment Schedule 2
W.B. 95.6"; 1.8 Liter.

| Coupe 2D | | WT28N | 37620 | 23000 | 25700 | 29900 | 36300 |
| Roadster 2D | | UT28N | 40420 | 24825 | 27750 | 32000 | 38500 |

TT QUATTRO AWD—V6—Equipment Schedule 2
W.B. 95.6"; 3.2 Liter.

| Coupe 2D | | WF68N | 40870 | 24350 | 27250 | 31500 | 38000 |
| Roadster 2D | | UF68N | 43870 | 26000 | 29000 | 33300 | 40000 |

BMW

1991 BMW — WB(AorS)(AJ931)-M-#

3 SERIES—4-Cyl.—Equipment Schedule 1
W.B. 101.0" (M3), 101.2"; 1.8 Liter, 2.3 Liter.

318i Sedan 4D		AJ931	20275	775	1125	2450	4300
318is Sedan 2D		AF931	21875	825	1175	2500	4375
318i Convertible 2D		BA731	28875	1125	1575	3100	5125
M3 Sedan 2D		AK031	36275	5450	6375	9050	12650

3 SERIES—6-Cyl.—Equipment Schedule 1
W.B. 101.2"; 2.5 Liter.

| 325i Sedan 2D | | AA231 | 26700 | 1125 | 1575 | 3025 | 5025 |
| 325i Sedan 4D | | AD231 | 27500 | 1225 | 1675 | 3200 | 5250 |

1991 BMW

Body Type	VIN	List	Trade-In Fair	Good	Pvt-Party Good	Retail Excellent
325iX 4WD Sedan 2D	AB031	32200	1900	2425	4125	6375
325iX 4WD Sedan 4D	AE031	33000	1950	2475	4200	6525
325i Convertible 2D	BB231	35650	2025	2575	4300	6625
5 SERIES—6-Cyl.—Equipment Schedule 1						
W.B. 108.7"; 2.5 Liter, 3.5 Liter.						
525i Sedan 4D	HC231	35600	2575	3175	4950	7350
535i Sedan 4D	HD231	43625	3225	3900	5800	8400
M5 Sedan 4D	HD931	58450	5625	6550	8900	12150
Traction Control			100	100	135	135
Manual Trans (Ex M5)			(350)	(350)	(465)	(465)
7 SERIES—6-Cyl.—Equipment Schedule 1						
W.B. 111.5", 116.0" (iL); 3.5 Liter.						
735i Sedan 4D	GB431	51925	2850	3500	5300	7775
735iL Sedan 4D	GC431	56025	3225	3900	5800	8400
Traction Control			100	100	135	135
7 SERIES—V12—Equipment Schedule 1						
W.B. 116.0"; 5.0 Liter.						
750iL Sedan 4D	GC831	75875	3500	4200	6125	8775
8 SERIES—V12—Equipment Schedule 1						
W.B. 105.7"; 5.0 Liter.						
850i Sedan 2D	EG231	75100	9075	10375	13350	17450
Traction Control			100	100	135	135

1992 BMW — WB(AorS)(CA531)–N–#

Body Type	VIN	List	Trade-In Fair	Good	Pvt-Party Good	Retail Excellent
3 SERIES—4-Cyl.—Equipment Schedule 1						
W.B. 101.2" (Conv), 106.3"; 1.8 Liter.						
318i Sedan 4D	CA531	23275	1200	1650	3275	5400
318is Coupe 2D	BE531	23975	1250	1750	3375	5525
318i Convertible 2D	BA731	29245	1925	2450	4200	6550
w/o Leather			0	0	0	0
3 SERIES—6-Cyl.—Equipment Schedule 1						
W.B. 101.2" (Conv), 106.3"; 2.5 Liter.						
325i Sedan 4D	CB431	30265	2025	2600	4375	6750
325is Coupe 2D	BF431	30275	2025	2575	4350	6700
325i Convertible 2D	BB231	37495	3275	3950	5950	8625
Manual Trans (Sedan)			(300)	(300)	(400)	(400)
5 SERIES—6-Cyl.—Equipment Schedule 1						
W.B. 108.7"; 2.5 Liter, 3.5 Liter.						
525i Sedan 4D	HD631	37975	2975	3650	5575	8225
525i Touring Wagon 4D	HJ231	40175	2875	3550	5475	8100
535i Sedan 4D	HD231	45725	3750	4475	6575	9425
M5 Sedan 4D	HD931	58600	6475	7500	10100	13700
Traction Control			100	100	135	135
Manual Trans (Ex M5)			(375)	(375)	(500)	(500)
7 SERIES—6-Cyl.—Equipment Schedule 1						
W.B. 111.5", 116.0" (iL); 3.5 Liter.						
735i Sedan 4D	GB431	54665	3325	4025	6025	8725
735iL Sedan 4D	GC431	58625	3750	4500	6600	9425
Traction Control			100	100	135	135
7 SERIES—V12—Equipment Schedule 1						
W.B. 116.0"; 5.0 Liter.						
750iL Sedan 4D	GC831	79875	4050	4825	6950	9850
8 SERIES—V12—Equipment Schedule 1						
W.B. 105.7"; 5.0 Liter.						
850i Coupe 2D	EG231	81500	10375	11825	15150	19800

1993 BMW — WB(AorS)(CA531)–P–#

Body Type	VIN	List	Trade-In Fair	Good	Pvt-Party Good	Retail Excellent
3 SERIES—4-Cyl.—Equipment Schedule 1						
W.B. 106.3"; 1.8 Liter.						
318i Sedan 4D	CA531	25420	1375	1900	3650	5950
318is Coupe 2D	BE531	26520	1450	1950	3700	6050
w/o Leather			0	0	0	0
Manual Trans (Sedan)			(325)	(325)	(435)	(435)
3 SERIES—6-Cyl.—Equipment Schedule 1						
W.B. 101.2" (Conv), 106.3"; 2.5 Liter.						
325i Sedan 4D	CB431	32055	2375	2950	4875	7450
325is Coupe 2D	BF431	32205	2325	2900	4825	7375
325iC Convertible 2D	BB131	36725	3725	4450	6600	9500
Manual Trans (Sedan)			(325)	(325)	(435)	(435)
5 SERIES—6-Cyl.—Equipment Schedule 1						
W.B. 108.7"; 2.5 Liter, 3.4 Liter, 3.6 Liter.						
525i Sedan 4D	HD231	38355	3475	4200	6275	9125
525i Touring Wagon 4D	HJ631	41505	3400	4100	6175	9000

Body	Type	VIN	List	Trade-In Fair	Trade-In Good	Pvt-Party Good	Retail Excellent
535i Sedan 4D		HD231	45755	4375	5175	7425	10500
M5 Sedan 4D		HD931	63300	7500	8625	11450	15350
Traction Control				125	125	165	165
Manual Trans (Ex M5)				(425)	(425)	(565)	(565)

7 SERIES—V8—Equipment Schedule 1
W.B. 111.5", 116.0" (iL); 4.0 Liter.

Body	Type	VIN	List	Fair	Good	Good	Excellent
740i Sedan 4D		GD432	55705	4225	5025	7250	10300
740iL Sedan 4D		GD832	59705	4550	5375	7725	10900
Traction Control				125	125	165	165

7 SERIES—V12—Equipment Schedule 1
W.B. 116.0"; 5.0 Liter.

750iL Sedan 4D		GC832	84305	5075	5950	8300	11550

8 SERIES—V12—Equipment Schedule 1
W.B. 105.7"; 5.0 Liter.

850Ci Coupe 2D		EG232	86400	12025	13625	17200	22200

3 SERIES—4-Cyl.—Equipment Schedule 1
W.B. 106.3"; 1.8 Liter.

318i Sedan 4D		CA632	26720	3275	3950	5425	7575
318is Coupe 2D		BE632	27845	3300	3975	5450	7600
318i Convertible 2D		BK632	31945	4450	5250	6900	9300
w/o Leather				0	0	0	0
Hard Top (Conv)				375	375	500	500
Rollover Pkg (Conv)				225	225	300	300
Manual Trans (Sedan)				(350)	(350)	(465)	(465)

3 SERIES—6-Cyl.—Equipment Schedule 1
W.B. 106.3"; 2.5 Liter.

325i Sedan 4D		CB432	33350	4375	5150	6825	9200
325is Coupe 2D		BF432	33550	4325	5125	6775	9150
325i Convertible 2D		BJ632	40150	6300	7325	9300	12150
Hard Top (Conv)				375	375	500	500
Rollover Pkg (Conv)				225	225	300	300
Traction Control				150	150	200	200
Manual Trans (Sedan)				(350)	(350)	(465)	(465)

5 SERIES—6-Cyl.—Equipment Schedule 1
W.B. 108.7"; 2.5 Liter.

525i Sedan 4D		HD632	39775	4325	5125	7425	10550
525i Touring Wagon 4D		HJ632	41050	4200	4975	7250	10350
Traction Control				150	150	200	200
w/o Premium Pkg				(450)	(450)	(600)	(600)
Manual Trans				(475)	(475)	(635)	(635)

5 SERIES—V8—Equipment Schedule 1
W.B. 108.7"; 3.0 Liter, 4.0 Liter.

530i Sedan 4D		HE232	43050	5225	6075	8525	11900
530i Touring Wagon 4D		HK232	46250	4950	5800	8225	11500
540i Sedan 4D		HE632	48950	6000	6950	9550	13100
Traction Control (Sedan)				150	150	200	200

7 SERIES—V8—Equipment Schedule 1
W.B. 111.5", 116.0" (iL); 4.0 Liter.

740i Sedan 4D		GD432	57400	4875	5725	8125	11400
740iL Sedan 4D		GD832	61400	5225	6075	8650	12150
Traction Control				150	150	200	200

7 SERIES—V12—Equipment Schedule 1
W.B. 116.0"; 5.0 Liter.

750iL Sedan 4D		GC832	87400	5825	6775	9300	12800

8 SERIES—V8—Equipment Schedule 1
W.B. 105.7"; 4.0 Liter.

840Ci Coupe 2D		EF632	69850	12025	13625	17150	22100

8 SERIES—V12—Equipment Schedule 1
W.B. 105.7"; 5.0 Liter, 5.6 Liter.

850Ci Coupe 2D		EG232	88500	13725	15525	19350	24700
850CSi Coupe 2D		EG932	101500	18375	20650	25100	31600

3 SERIES—4-Cyl.—Equipment Schedule 1
W.B. 106.3"; 1.8 Liter.

318ti H'Back Coupe 2D		CG632	25295	2400	2975	4400	6350
318i Sedan 4D		CA632	27645	3825	4575	6175	8500
318is Coupe 2D		BE632	29690	3825	4575	6175	8500
318i Convertible 2D		BK632	33965	5100	6000	7775	10400
w/o Leather				0	0	0	0
Sport Pkg				250	250	335	335

1995 BMW

Body	Type	VIN	List	Trade-In Fair	Good	Pvt-Party Good	Retail Excellent
	Hard Top (Conv)			400	400	535	535
	Rollover Pkg (Conv)			250	250	335	335
	Manual Trans (Sedan)			(375)	(375)	(500)	(500)
3 SERIES—6-Cyl.—Equipment Schedule 1							
W.B. 106.3"; 2.5 Liter.							
325i	Sedan 4D	CB432	34120	5025	5900	7675	10250
325is	Coupe 2D	BF432	34220	4975	5850	7625	10200
325i	Convertible 2D	BJ632	40970	7175	8300	10400	13450
	Sport Pkg			250	250	335	335
	Hard Top (Conv)			400	400	535	535
	Rollover Pkg (Conv)			250	250	335	335
	Traction Control			175	175	235	235
	Manual Trans (Sedan)			(375)	(375)	(500)	(500)
M3—6-Cyl.—Equipment Schedule 1							
W.B. 106.7"; 3.0 Liter.							
	Sedan 2D	BF932	38845	7350	8450	10550	13700
5 SERIES—6-Cyl.—Equipment Schedule 1							
W.B. 108.7"; 2.5 Liter.							
525i	Sedan 4D	HD632	40195	4950	5800	8275	11650
525i	Touring Wagon 4D	HJ632	42795	4775	5600	8075	11400
	Traction Control			175	175	235	235
	w/o Premium Pkg			(550)	(550)	(735)	(735)
	Manual Trans			(525)	(525)	(700)	(700)
5 SERIES—V8—Equipment Schedule 1							
W.B. 108.7"; 3.0 Liter, 4.0 Liter.							
530i	Sedan 4D	HE232	44320	5900	6875	9500	13100
530i	Touring Wagon 4D	HK232	47520	5675	6600	9225	12750
540i	Sedan 4D	HE632	48420	6825	7875	10650	14450
	Traction Control			175	175	235	235
7 SERIES—V8—Equipment Schedule 1							
W.B. 115.4", 120.9" (iL); 4.0 Liter.							
740i	Sedan 4D	GF632	59370	6450	7475	10200	13900
740iL	Sedan 4D	GJ632	61470	6800	7850	10750	14700
	Traction Control			175	175	235	235
7 SERIES—V12—Equipment Schedule 1							
W.B. 120.9"; 5.4 Liter.							
750iL	Sedan 4D	GK232	89770	8550	9800	12850	17050
8 SERIES—V8—Equipment Schedule 1							
W.B. 105.7"; 4.0 Liter.							
840Ci	Coupe 2D	EF632	71670	13575	15325	19100	24400
8 SERIES—V12—Equipment Schedule 1							
W.B. 105.7"; 5.4 Liter, 5.6 Liter.							
850Ci	Coupe 2D	EG432	90150	14850	16775	20800	26400
850CSi	Coupe 2D	EG932	104650	20650	23075	27900	34900

1996 BMW — WBA(CG732)-T-#

Body	Type	VIN	List	Trade-In Fair	Good	Pvt-Party Good	Retail Excellent
3 SERIES—4-Cyl.—Equipment Schedule 1							
W.B. 106.3"; 1.9 Liter.							
318ti	H'Back Coupe 2D	CG732	26180	2875	3550	5100	7250
318i	Sedan 4D	CD732	30120	4475	5275	7025	9525
318is	Coupe 2D	BE732	30995	4450	5250	7000	9500
318i	Convertible 2D	BH732	35745	5850	6825	8750	11550
	w/o Leather			0	0	0	0
	Sport Pkg			275	275	365	365
	Hard Top (Conv)			425	425	565	565
	Rollover Pkg (Conv)			275	275	365	365
	Traction Control			200	200	265	265
	Manual Trans (Sedan)			(400)	(400)	(535)	(535)
3 SERIES—6-Cyl.—Equipment Schedule 1							
W.B. 106.3"; 2.8 Liter.							
328i	Sedan 4D	CD132	36410	5775	6725	8625	11400
328is	Coupe 2D	BG132	36500	5725	6675	8575	11350
328i	Convertible 2D	BK832	42875	8150	9325	11600	14900
	Sport Pkg			275	275	365	365
	Hard Top (Conv)			425	425	565	565
	Rollover Pkg (Conv)			275	275	365	365
	Traction Control			200	200	265	265
	Manual Trans (Sedan)			(400)	(400)	(535)	(535)
M3—6-Cyl.—Equipment Schedule 1							
W.B. 106.7"; 3.2 Liter.							
	Coupe 2D	BG932	41205	8325	9525	11800	15150
Z3—4-Cyl.—Equipment Schedule 1							
W.B. 96.3"; 1.9 Liter.							

Body	Type	VIN	List	Trade-In Fair	Good	Pvt-Party Good	Retail Excellent
Roadster 2D		CH732	31445	4825	5675	7475	10050
Hard Top		-------	425	425	565	565
Traction Control		-------	200	200	265	265
7 SERIES—V8—Equipment Schedule 1							
W.B. 120.9"; 4.4 Liter.							
740iL Sedan 4D		GJ832	63060	7675	8800	11950	16200
7 SERIES—V12—Equipment Schedule 1							
W.B. 120.9"; 5.4 Liter.							
750iL Sedan 4D		GK232	92630	9650	11000	14250	18750
8 SERIES—V8—Equipment Schedule 1							
W.B. 105.7"; 4.4 Liter.							
840Ci Coupe 2D		EF832	76670	15225	17175	21100	26900
8 SERIES—V12—Equipment Schedule 1							
W.B. 105.7"; 5.4 Liter.							
850Ci Coupe 2D		EG432	95460	16775	18875	23100	29100

1997 BMW — WBA(CG732)-V-#

Body	Type	VIN	List	Trade-In Fair	Good	Pvt-Party Good	Retail Excellent
3 SERIES—4-Cyl.—Equipment Schedule 1							
W.B. 106.3"; 1.9 Liter.							
318ti H'Back Coupe 2D		CG732	26535	3500	4200	5900	8275
318i Sedan 4D		CC932	30745	5250	6100	8025	10700
318is Coupe 2D		BE732	31645	5200	6075	7975	10650
318i Convertible 2D		BH732	36145	6725	7750	9850	12850
w/o Leather		-------	0	0	0	0
Sport Pkg		-------	300	300	400	400
Hard Top (Conv)		-------	450	450	600	600
Rollover Pkg (Conv)		-------	300	300	400	400
Manual Trans		-------	(425)	(425)	(565)	(565)
3 SERIES—6-Cyl.—Equipment Schedule 1							
W.B. 106.3"; 2.8 Liter.							
328i Sedan 4D		CD332	36845	6625	7675	9750	12750
328is Coupe 2D		BG132	36935	6600	7625	9675	12650
328i Convertible 2D		BK832	42935	9250	10525	12950	16450
Sport Pkg		-------	300	300	400	400
Hard Top (Conv)		-------	450	450	600	600
Rollover Pkg (Conv)		-------	300	300	400	400
Manual Trans (Sedan)		-------	(425)	(425)	(565)	(565)
M3—6-Cyl.—Equipment Schedule 1							
W.B. 106.3"; 3.2 Liter.							
Sedan 4D		CD932	45400	9900	11300	13750	17400
Coupe 2D		BG932	44200	9400	10725	13150	16750
Z3—4-Cyl.—Equipment Schedule 1							
W.B. 96.3"; 1.9 Liter.							
Roadster 2D		CH732	31695	5600	6525	8475	11250
Hard Top		-------	450	450	600	600
Z3—6-Cyl.—Equipment Schedule 1							
W.B. 96.3"; 2.8 Liter.							
Roadster 2D		CJ332	37445	6950	8025	10150	13200
Hard Top		-------	450	450	600	600
5 SERIES—6-Cyl.—Equipment Schedule 1							
W.B. 111.4"; 2.8 Liter.							
528i Sedan 4D		DD532	43895	7775	8925	12100	16400
w/o Premium Pkg		-------	(700)	(700)	(935)	(935)
Manual Trans		-------	(625)	(625)	(835)	(835)
5 SERIES—V8—Equipment Schedule 1							
W.B. 111.4"; 4.4 Liter.							
540i Sedan 4D		DE632	50470	10325	11725	15200	20000
7 SERIES—V8—Equipment Schedule 1							
W.B. 115.4", 120.9"; 4.4 Liter.							
740i Sedan 4D		GF832	61420	8325	9525	12650	17000
740iL Sedan 4D		GJ832	65370	8650	9900	13250	17850
7 SERIES—V12—Equipment Schedule 1							
W.B. 120.9"; 5.4 Liter.							
750iL Sedan 4D		GK232	93370	10875	12325	15750	20600
8 SERIES—V8—Equipment Schedule 1							
W.B. 105.7"; 4.4 Liter.							
840Ci Coupe 2D		EF832	77970	16925	19050	23300	29300
8 SERIES—V12—Equipment Schedule 1							
W.B. 105.7"; 5.4 Liter.							
850Ci Coupe 2D		EG432	96800	18775	21050	25600	32000

Body	Type	VIN	List	Trade-In Fair	Good	Pvt-Party Good	Retail Excellent

1998 BMW — WBA(CG832)-W-#

3 SERIES—4-Cyl.—Equipment Schedule 1
W.B. 106.3"; 1.9 Liter.

Body	Type	VIN	List	Fair	Good	Good	Excellent
318ti Coupe 2D		CG832	26685	4225	5000	6875	9475
318i Sedan 4D		CC032	31045	6075	7050	9150	12150
w/o Leather				0	0	0	0
Sport Pkg				325	325	435	435
Manual Trans (Sedan)				(425)	(425)	(565)	(565)

3 SERIES—6-Cyl.—Equipment Schedule 1
W.B. 106.3"; 2.5 Liter, 2.8 Liter.

Body	Type	VIN	List	Fair	Good	Good	Excellent
323is Coupe 2D		BF832	32370	6250	7250	9325	12300
323i Convertible 2D		BJ832	38995	9025	10325	12700	16250
328i Sedan 4D		CD432	36770	7600	8725	10950	14200
328is Coupe 2D		BG232	36870	7550	8675	10900	14150
328i Convertible 2D		BK832	44495	10375	11825	14400	18150
Sport Pkg				325	325	435	435
Hard Top (Conv)				475	475	635	635
Rollover Pkg (Conv)				325	325	435	435
Manual Trans (Sedan)				(425)	(425)	(565)	(565)

M3—6-Cyl.—Equipment Schedule 1
W.B. 106.7"; 3.2 Liter.

Body	Type	VIN	List	Fair	Good	Good	Excellent
Sedan 4D		CD032	43840	11200	12700	15350	19300
Coupe 2D		BG932	42640	10625	12075	14650	18450
Convertible 2D		BK033	46470	12025	13625	16400	20500
Hard Top (Conv)				475	475	635	635

Z3—4-Cyl.—Equipment Schedule 1
W.B. 96.3"; 1.9 Liter.

Body	Type	VIN	List	Fair	Good	Good	Excellent
Roadster 2D		CH732	32120	6475	7500	9625	12650
Hard Top				475	475	635	635

Z3—6-Cyl.—Equipment Schedule 1
W.B. 96.3"; 2.8 Liter, 3.2 Liter.

Body	Type	VIN	List	Fair	Good	Good	Excellent
Roadster 2D		CJ332	37445	7925	9125	11350	14650
M. Roadster 2D		CK932	42770	9800	11200	13700	17300
Hard Top				475	475	635	635

5 SERIES—6-Cyl.—Equipment Schedule 1
W.B. 111.4"; 2.8 Liter.

Body	Type	VIN	List	Fair	Good	Good	Excellent
528i Sedan 4D		DD632	43895	8850	10125	13500	18100
w/o Premium Pkg				(775)	(775)	(1035)	(1035)
Sport Pkg				575	575	765	765
Manual Trans		5		(675)	(675)	(900)	(900)

5 SERIES—V8—Equipment Schedule 1
W.B. 111.4"; 4.4 Liter.

Body	Type	VIN	List	Fair	Good	Good	Excellent
540i Sedan 4D		DE632	51070	11650	13200	16900	22000
Sport Pkg				575	575	765	765

7 SERIES—V8—Equipment Schedule 1
W.B. 115.4", 120.9" (iL); 4.4 Liter.

Body	Type	VIN	List	Fair	Good	Good	Excellent
740i Sedan 4D		GF832	62070	9400	10725	14100	18700
740iL Sedan 4D		GJ832	66070	9750	11100	14700	19600

7 SERIES—V12—Equipment Schedule 1
W.B. 120.9"; 5.4 Liter.

Body	Type	VIN	List	Fair	Good	Good	Excellent
750iL Sedan 4D		GK232	92670	12175	13775	17450	22600

1999 BMW — (4UorWB)(SorA)(CG833)-X-#

3 SERIES—4-Cyl.—Equipment Schedule 1
W.B. 106.3"; 1.9 Liter.

Body	Type	VIN	List	Fair	Good	Good	Excellent
318ti Coupe 2D		CG833	26270	6675	7700	9525	12200
w/o Leather				0	0	0	0

3 SERIES—6-Cyl.—Equipment Schedule 1
W.B. 106.3", 107.3" (Sedan); 2.5 Liter, 2.8 Liter.

Body	Type	VIN	List	Fair	Good	Good	Excellent
323i Sedan 4D		AM332	30670	9800	11150	13250	16450
323is Coupe 2D		BF833	32645	8900	10175	12200	15300
323i Convertible 2D		BJ833	37695	11925	13525	15850	19400
328i Sedan 4D		AM633	37670	11450	13000	15250	18700
328is Coupe 2D		BG233	37145	10325	11725	13900	17200
328i Convertible 2D		BK833	43045	13375	15125	17600	21400
Sport Pkg				350	350	465	465
Hard Top (Conv)				500	500	665	665
Rollover Pkg (Conv)				350	350	465	465
Manual Trans (ex 2D)				(425)	(425)	(565)	(565)

M3—6-Cyl.—Equipment Schedule 1
W.B. 106.3", 106.7" (Coupe); 3.2 Liter.

Body	Type	VIN	List	Fair	Good	Good	Excellent
Coupe 2D		BG933	41695	13625	15375	17850	21700

1999 BMW

Body	Type	VIN	List	Trade-In Fair	Trade-In Good	Pvt-Party Good	Retail Excellent
Convertible 2D		BK033	48145	**15175**	**17125**	**19800**	**23900**
Hard Top (Conv)				**500**	**500**	**665**	**665**

Z3—6-Cyl.—Equipment Schedule 1
W.B. 96.3", 96.8" (M); 2.5 Liter, 2.8 Liter, 3.2 Liter.

Body	Type	VIN	List	Fair	Good	Good	Excellent
Coupe 2D		CK533	38045	**10375**	**11775**	**13950**	**17250**
2.3 Roadster 2D		CH933	33120	**8675**	**9950**	**11950**	**15000**
2.8 Roadster 2D		CH333	37745	**10725**	**12225**	**14400**	**17750**
M Coupe 2D		CM933	42670	**12175**	**13775**	**16100**	**19700**
M Roadster 2D		CK933	43270	**12750**	**14450**	**16850**	**20600**
Hard Top (Roadster)				**500**	**500**	**665**	**665**

5 SERIES—6-Cyl.—Equipment Schedule 1
W.B. 111.4"; 2.8 Liter.

Body	Type	VIN	List	Fair	Good	Good	Excellent
528i Sedan 4D		DM633	42945	**10100**	**11500**	**14900**	**19600**
528iT Wagon 4D		DP633	44745	**9425**	**10775**	**14100**	**18650**
w/o Premium Pkg				**(800)**	**(800)**	**(1065)**	**(1065)**
Sport Pkg				**625**	**625**	**835**	**835**
Manual Trans				**(725)**	**(725)**	**(965)**	**(965)**

5 SERIES—V8—Equipment Schedule 1
W.B. 111.4"; 4.4 Liter.

Body	Type	VIN	List	Fair	Good	Good	Excellent
540i Sedan 4D		DN633	51670	**13150**	**14900**	**18600**	**23800**
540iT Wagon 4D		DR633	54050	**12425**	**14075**	**17650**	**22700**
Sport Pkg				**625**	**625**	**835**	**835**

7 SERIES—V8—Equipment Schedule 1
W.B. 115.4", 120.9" (iL); 4.4 Liter.

Body	Type	VIN	List	Fair	Good	Good	Excellent
740i Sedan 4D		GG833	62970	**10875**	**12325**	**16250**	**20800**
740iL Sedan 4D		GH833	66970	**11250**	**12750**	**16550**	**21700**
Sport Pkg				**625**	**625**	**835**	**835**

7 SERIES—V12—Equipment Schedule 1
W.B. 120.9"; 5.4 Liter.

Body	Type	VIN	List	Fair	Good	Good	Excellent
750iL Sedan 4D		GJ033	92670	**13825**	**15625**	**19400**	**24800**

2000 BMW — (4UorWB)(SorA)(AM334)-Y-#

3 SERIES—6-Cyl.—Equipment Schedule 1
W.B. 107.3"; 2.5 Liter, 2.8 Liter.

Body	Type	VIN	List	Fair	Good	Good	Excellent
323i Sedan 4D		AM334	32680	**11200**	**12700**	**15300**	**18400**
323i Wagon 4D		AR334	32985	**11100**	**12600**	**14850**	**18300**
323Ci Coupe 2D		BM334	34280	**11875**	**13425**	**15700**	**19250**
323Ci Convertible 2D		BR334	38285	**15375**	**17325**	**19900**	**24000**
328i Sedan 4D		AM534	37670	**13150**	**14900**	**17250**	**21000**
328Ci Coupe 2D		BM534	38335	**13575**	**15325**	**17750**	**21500**
Hard Top (Conv)				**525**	**525**	**700**	**700**
Premium Pkg				**350**	**350**	**465**	**465**
Sport Pkg				**400**	**400**	**535**	**535**
Sport Premium Pkg				**500**	**500**	**665**	**665**
Manual Trans (ex 2D)				**(475)**	**(475)**	**(635)**	**(635)**

Z3—6-Cyl.—Equipment Schedule 1
W.B. 96.3"; 2.5 Liter, 2.8 Liter.

Body	Type	VIN	List	Fair	Good	Good	Excellent
Coupe 2D		CK534	38395	**11875**	**13475**	**15750**	**19300**
2.3 Roadster 2D		CH933	34470	**10000**	**11350**	**13500**	**16750**
2.8 Roadster 2D		CH334	38445	**12325**	**13975**	**16300**	**19900**
Hard Top (Roadster)				**525**	**525**	**700**	**700**

M—6-Cyl.—Equipment Schedule 1
W.B. 96.8"; 3.2 Liter.

Body	Type	VIN	List	Fair	Good	Good	Excellent
Coupe 2D		CM934	42670	**13975**	**15775**	**18200**	**22000**
Roadster 2D		CK934	43270	**14650**	**16550**	**19050**	**23000**
Hard Top (Roadster)				**525**	**525**	**700**	**700**

Z8—V8—Equipment Schedule 1
W.B. 98.9"; 5.0 Liter.

Body	Type	VIN	List	Fair	Good	Good	Excellent
Roadster 2D		EJ134	130670	********	********	********	**75900**

5 SERIES—6-Cyl.—Equipment Schedule 1
W.B. 111.4"; 2.8 Liter.

Body	Type	VIN	List	Fair	Good	Good	Excellent
528i Sedan 4D		DM634	44595	**11725**	**13300**	**16950**	**22000**
528iT Wagon 4D		DP634	46545	**10950**	**12425**	**16050**	**21000**
w/o Premium Pkg				**(850)**	**(850)**	**(1135)**	**(1135)**
Sport Pkg				**725**	**725**	**965**	**965**
Manual Trans				**(800)**	**(800)**	**(1065)**	**(1065)**

5 SERIES—V8—Equipment Schedule 1
W.B. 111.4"; 4.4 Liter.

Body	Type	VIN	List	Fair	Good	Good	Excellent
540i Sedan 4D		DN634	52970	**15325**	**17275**	**21100**	**27000**
540iT Wagon 4D		DR634	55350	**14400**	**16250**	**20100**	**25600**
Sport Pkg				**725**	**725**	**965**	**965**

M5—V8—Equipment Schedule 1
W.B. 111.4"; 5.0 Liter.

Body Type	VIN	List	Trade-In Fair	Good	Pvt-Party Good	Retail Excellent
Sedan 4D	DE934	72070	24825	27850	32600	39700
7 SERIES—V8—Equipment Schedule 1						
W.B. 115.4", 120.9" (iL); 4.4 Liter.						
740i Sedan 4D	GG834	64670	15950	17950	22700	27400
740iL Sedan 4D	GH834	66970	16550	18625	22700	28600
Sport Pkg			725	725	965	965
7 SERIES—V12—Equipment Schedule 1						
W.B. 120.9"; 5.4 Liter.						
750iL Sedan 4D	GJ034	95270	19500	21825	26000	32100

2001 BMW — WBAorWBS(AV334)-1-#

Body Type	VIN	List	Trade-In Fair	Good	Pvt-Party Good	Retail Excellent
3 SERIES—6-Cyl.—Equipment Schedule 1						
W.B. 107.3"; 2.5 Liter, 3.0 Liter.						
325i Sedan 4D	AV334	30060	12800	14500	16900	20600
325xi AWD Sedan 4D	AV334	31810	13475	15225	17650	21400
325Ci Coupe 2D	BN334	32060	13525	15275	17700	21400
325Cic Convertible 2D	BS334	38010	17550	19700	22400	26800
325iT Wagon 4D	AW334	32470	12750	14400	16800	20500
325xiT AWD Wagon 4D	AW334	34220	13100	14850	17200	21000
330i Sedan 4D	AV534	39280	14975	16875	19400	23400
330xi AWD Sedan 4D	AV534	41030	15625	17600	20200	24300
330Ci Coupe 2D	BN534	39935	15525	17500	20100	24200
330Cic Convertible 2D	BS534	44245	19100	21425	24300	28800
Hard Top (Conv)			550	550	735	735
Premium Pkg			400	400	535	535
Sport Pkg			450	450	600	600
Manual Trans (ex 2D)			(500)	(500)	(665)	(665)
M3—6-Cyl.—Equipment Schedule 1						
W.B. 107.5"; 3.2 Liter.						
Coupe 2D	BL934	46045	22225	24825	27900	32900
Convertible 2D	BR934	54045	25700	28700	32000	37500
Hard Top (Conv)			550	550	735	735
Z3—6-Cyl.—Equipment Schedule 1						
W.B. 96.3"; 2.5 Liter, 3.0 Liter.						
2.5i Roadster 2D	CN334	34295	11500	13050	15300	18750
3.0i Coupe 2D	CK734	39845	13625	15375	17800	21600
3.0i Roadster 2D	CN534	39745	14075	15900	18350	22200
Hard Top (Roadster)			550	550	735	735
M—6-Cyl.—Equipment Schedule 1						
W.B. 96.8"; 3.2 Liter.						
Coupe 2D	CN934	45635	15900	17900	20500	24600
Roadster 2D	CL934	46635	16675	18775	21400	25700
Hard Top (Roadster)			550	550	735	735
Z8—V8—Equipment Schedule 1						
W.B. 98.6"; 5.0 Liter.						
Roadster 2D	EJ134	130745	****	****	****	84000
5 SERIES—6-Cyl.—Equipment Schedule 1						
W.B. 111.4"; 2.5 Liter, 3.0 Liter.						
525i Sedan 4D	DT334	40195	14975	16875	20700	26000
525iT Wagon 4D	DS334	41995	14125	15950	19600	24800
530i Sedan 4D	DT534	44345	16775	18875	22700	28300
w/o Premium Pkg			(875)	(875)	(1165)	(1165)
Sport Pkg			825	825	1100	1100
Manual Trans			(875)	(875)	(1165)	(1165)
5 SERIES—V8—Equipment Schedule 1						
W.B. 111.4"; 4.4 Liter.						
540i Sedan 4D	DN634	51670	19100	21425	25500	31500
540iT Wagon 4D	DR634	54050	18050	20275	24200	30000
Sport Pkg			825	825	1100	1100
M5—V8—Equipment Schedule 1						
W.B. 111.4"; 5.0 Liter.						
Sedan 4D	DE934	69970	29775	33275	38000	45500
7 SERIES—V8—Equipment Schedule 1						
W.B. 115.4", 120.9" (iL); 4.4 Liter.						
740i Sedan 4D	GG834	63470	18275	20575	24600	30700
740iL Sedan 4D	GH834	67470	19100	21425	25800	32200
Sport Pkg			825	825	1100	1100
7 SERIES—V12—Equipment Schedule 1						
W.B. 120.9"; 5.4 Liter.						
750iL Sedan 4D	GJ034	92670	22300	24925	29400	35900
Sport Pkg			275	275	365	365

2002 BMW

Body	Type	VIN	List	Trade-In Fair	Trade-In Good	Pvt-Party Good	Retail Excellent

2002 BMW — WBA,WBS,4USor5UM(ET374)-2-#

3 SERIES—6-Cyl.—Equipment Schedule 1
W.B. 107.3"; 2.5 Liter, 3.0 Liter.

Body	Type	VIN	List	Fair	Good	Good	Excellent
325i Sedan 4D		ET374	32465	14550	16450	19000	23000
325xi AWD Sedan 4D		EU334	34215	15375	17325	19900	24000
325Ci Coupe 2D		BN334	34465	15425	17375	20000	24100
325Cic Convertible 2D		BS334	39470	19800	22225	25100	29900
325iT Wagon 4D		EN334	34465	14500	16350	18900	22900
325xiT AWD Wagon 4D		EP334	36615	14900	16825	19400	23500
330i Sedan 4D		EV334	38410	17025	19150	21800	26200
330xi AWD Sedan 4D		EW534	40160	17700	19875	22700	27200
330Ci Coupe 2D		BN534	39410	17700	19875	22600	27100
330Cic Convertible 2D		BS534	46820	21625	24250	27200	32100
Hard Top (Conv)		......		575	575	765	765
Premium Pkg		......		450	450	600	600
Sport Pkg		......		500	500	665	665
Manual Trans (ex 2D)		......		(525)	(525)	(700)	(700)

M3—6-Cyl.—Equipment Schedule 1
W.B. 107.5"; 3.2 Liter.

Body	Type	VIN	List	Fair	Good	Good	Excellent
Coupe 2D		BL934	49745	25800	28800	32100	37500
Convertible 2D		BR934	55545	29000	32300	35800	41700

Z3—6-Cyl.—Equipment Schedule 1
W.B. 96.3"; 2.5 Liter, 3.0 Liter.

Body	Type	VIN	List	Fair	Good	Good	Excellent
2.5i Roadster 2D		CN334	34370	13100	14850	17300	21100
3.0i Coupe 2D		CK734	39920	15475	17450	20100	24300
3.0i Roadster 2D		CN534	39820	16000	18000	20700	24800
Hard Top (Roadster)		......		575	575	765	765

M—6-Cyl.—Equipment Schedule 1
W.B. 96.8"; 3.2 Liter.

Body	Type	VIN	List	Fair	Good	Good	Excellent
Coupe 2D		CN934	45635	18050	20275	23100	27500
Roadster 2D		CL934	46635	18875	21150	24100	28600
Hard Top (Roadster)		......		575	575	765	765

Z8—V8—Equipment Schedule 1
W.B. 98.6"; 5.0 Liter.

Body	Type	VIN	List	Fair	Good	Good	Excellent
Roadster 2D		EJ134	132745	****	****	****	92200

5 SERIES—6-Cyl.—Equipment Schedule 1
W.B. 111.4"; 2.5 Liter, 3.0 Liter.

Body	Type	VIN	List	Fair	Good	Good	Excellent
525i Sedan 4D		DT434	41070	17125	19250	23300	29200
525iT Wagon 4D		DS334	42870	16100	18150	22100	27800
530i Sedan 4D		DT634	44670	19100	21425	25700	31800
w/o Premium Pkg		......		(900)	(900)	(1200)	(1200)
Sport Pkg		......		925	925	1235	1235
Manual Trans		......		(950)	(950)	(1265)	(1265)

5 SERIES—V8—Equipment Schedule 1
W.B. 111.4"; 4.4 Liter.

Body	Type	VIN	List	Fair	Good	Good	Excellent
540i Sedan 4D		DN634	53145	21825	24450	28700	35200
540iT Wagon 4D		DR634	55545	20575	23000	27400	33700
Sport Pkg		......		925	925	1235	1235

M5—V8—Equipment Schedule 1
W.B. 111.4"; 5.0 Liter.

Body	Type	VIN	List	Fair	Good	Good	Excellent
Sedan 4D		DE934	72645	33475	37350	42400	50300

7 SERIES—V8—Equipment Schedule 1
W.B. 117.7", 123.2" (Li); 4.4 Liter.

Body	Type	VIN	List	Fair	Good	Good	Excellent
745i Sedan 4D		GL634	68495	33950	37825	42500	50000
745Li Sedan 4D		GN634	72495	35025	39100	43900	51800

2003 BMW — WBA,WBSor4US(EV334)-3-#

3 SERIES—6-Cyl.—Equipment Schedule 1
W.B. 107.3"; 2.5 Liter, 3.0 Liter.

Body	Type	VIN	List	Fair	Good	Good	Excellent
325i Sedan 4D		EV334	32270	16625	18725	21400	25800
325xi AWD Sedan 4D		EU334	34020	17450	19600	22400	26900
325Ci Coupe 2D		BN334	34070	17550	19700	22500	27000
325Cic Convertible 2D		BS334	40120	22400	25025	28000	33100
325iT Wagon 4D		EN334	33820	16550	18625	21300	25700
325xiT AWD Wagon 4D		EP334	35570	17025	19150	21900	26300
330i Sedan 4D		EV534	39070	19300	21625	24500	29200
330xi AWD Sedan 4D		EW534	40820	20075	22500	25400	30200
330Ci Coupe 2D		BN534	40070	20075	22600	25500	30300
330Cic Convertible 2D		BS534	44870	24250	27150	30300	35500
Hard Top (Conv)		......		600	600	800	800
Premium Pkg		......		500	500	665	665
Sport Pkg		......		325	325	435	435

2003 BMW

Body	Type	VIN	List	Trade-In Fair	Trade-In Good	Pvt-Party Good	Retail Excellent
	Performance Pkg			500	500	665	665
	5-Spd Manual (ex 2D)			(550)	(550)	(735)	(735)

M3—6-Cyl.—Equipment Schedule 1
W.B. 107.5"; 3.2 Liter.

Body	Type	VIN	List	Fair	Good	Good	Excellent
	Coupe 2D	BL934	49345	29575	32975	36400	42200
	Convertible 2D	BR934	55195	32600	36275	39900	46100
	Hard Top (Conv)			600	600	800	800

Z4—6-Cyl.—Equipment Schedule 1
W.B. 98.2"; 2.5 Liter, 3.0 Liter.

	2.5i Roadster 2D	BT334	37690	18875	21150	24100	28600
	3.0i Roadster 2D	BT534	43215	21525	24150	27200	32000
	Sport Pkg			325	325	435	435
	Premium Pkg			500	500	665	665

Z8—V8—Equipment Schedule 1
W.B. 98.6"; 4.8 Liter, 5.0 Liter.

	Roadster 2D	EJ134	134295	****	****	****	100200
	Alpina Roadster 2D	EJ134	139295				

5 SERIES—6-Cyl.—Equipment Schedule 1
W.B. 111.4"; 2.5 Liter, 3.0 Liter.

	525i Sedan 4D	DT334	41770	19500	21925	26200	32500
	525iT Wagon 4D	DS334	43470	18425	20750	24900	31000
	530i Sedan 4D	DT534	45370	21725	24350	28700	35200
	w/o Premium Pkg			(925)	(925)	(1235)	(1235)
	Sport Pkg			1000	1000	1335	1335
	Manual Trans			(675)	(675)	(900)	(900)

5 SERIES—V8—Equipment Schedule 1
W.B. 111.4"; 4.4 Liter.

	540i Sedan 4D	DN634	52495	24725	27650	32200	39100
	540iT Wagon 4D	DR634	56085	23275	26100	30600	37200
	Sport Pkg			1000	1000	1335	1335

M5—V8—Equipment Schedule 1
W.B. 111.4"; 5.0 Liter.

	Sedan 4D	DE934	73195	37550	41800	47000	55400

7 SERIES—V8—Equipment Schedule 1
W.B. 117.7", 123.2" (Li); 4.4 Liter.

	745i Sedan 4D	GL634	70895	38125	42475	47200	55100
	745Li Sedan 4D	GN634	73195	39375	43850	48900	57100

7 SERIES—V12—Equipment Schedule 1
W.B. 123.2"; 6.0 Liter.

	760Li Sedan 4D	GN834	118195	62950	69850	75900	86600

2004 BMW — WBA,WBSor4US(EV334)-4-#

3 SERIES—6-Cyl.—Equipment Schedule 1
W.B. 107.3"; 2.5 Liter, 3.0 Liter.

	325i Sedan 4D	EV334	33265	19200	21525	24400	29100
	325xi AWD Sedan 4D	EU334	35015	20075	22600	25500	30300
	325Ci Coupe 2D	BD334	34570	20175	22700	25600	30400
	325Cic Convertible 2D	BW334	40720	25425	28425	31700	37100
	325iT Wagon 4D	EN334	34815	19100	21425	24300	29000
	325xiT AWD Wagon 4D	EP334	36565	19600	22025	24900	29700
	330i Sedan 4D	EV534	39270	22125	24725	27800	32800
	330xi AWD Sedan 4D	EW534	41020	23000	25700	28800	33900
	330Ci Coupe 2D	BD534	40770	23075	25800	28900	34000
	330Cic Convertible 2D	BW534	44570	27550	30750	34000	39700
	Hard Top (Conv)			625	625	835	835
	Premium Pkg			550	550	735	735
	Sport Pkg			350	350	465	465
	Performance Pkg			500	500	665	665
	5-Spd Manual (ex 2D)			(575)	(575)	(765)	(765)

M3—6-Cyl.—Equipment Schedule 1
W.B. 107.5"; 3.2 Liter.

	Coupe 2D	BL934	51340	33750	37625	41200	47500
	Convertible 2D	BR934	56595	36575	40750	44400	50900
	Hard Top (Conv)			625	625	835	835

Z4—6-Cyl.—Equipment Schedule 1
W.B. 98.2"; 2.5 Liter, 3.0 Liter.

	2.5i Roadster 2D	BT334	37790	21625	24250	27300	32300
	3.0i Roadster 2D	BT534	43315	24550	27450	30700	35900
	Sport Pkg			350	350	465	465
	Premium Pkg			550	550	735	735

5 SERIES—6-Cyl.—Equipment Schedule 1
W.B. 113.7"; 2.5 Liter, 3.0 Liter.

	525i Sedan 4D	NA535	43670	25800	28800	32900	39200

2004 BMW

Body	Type	VIN	List	Trade-In Fair	Good	Pvt-Party Good	Retail Excellent
530i Sedan 4D		NA735	48670	28125	31425	35500	42100
w/o Premium Pkg				(950)	(950)	(1265)	(1265)
Sport Pkg				1075	1075	1435	1435
Manual Trans				(700)	(700)	(935)	(935)

5 SERIES—V8—Equipment Schedule 1
W.B. 113.7"; 4.4 Liter.

Body	Type	VIN	List	Fair	Good	Good	Excellent
545i Sedan 4D		NB335	54995	33375	37250	41500	48600
Sport Pkg				1075	1075	1435	1435

6 SERIES—V8—Equipment Schedule 1
W.B. 109.4"; 4.4 Liter.

Body	Type	VIN	List	Fair	Good	Good	Excellent
645Ci Coupe 2D		EH734	69995	47625	52950	57800	66400
645Cic Convertible 2D		EK734	76995	52100	57900	63000	72000
Sport Pkg				1075	1075	1435	1435

7 SERIES—V8—Equipment Schedule 1
W.B. 117.7", 123.2" (Li); 4.4 Liter.

Body	Type	VIN	List	Fair	Good	Good	Excellent
745i Sedan 4D		GL634	69195	42675	47525	52500	60800
745Li Sedan 4D		GN634	73195	44225	49175	54400	63100
Sport Pkg				1075	1075	1435	1435

7 SERIES—V12—Equipment Schedule 1
W.B. 117.7", 123.2" (Li); 6.0 Liter.

Body	Type	VIN	List	Fair	Good	Good	Excellent
760i Sedan 4D		GL834	111795	68100	75575	81500	92500
760Li Sedan 4D		GN834	117795	69750	77400	83400	94700

2005 BMW — WBA,WBSor4US(EV334)-5-#

3 SERIES—6-Cyl.—Equipment Schedule 1
W.B. 107.3"; 2.5 Liter, 3.0 Liter.

Body	Type	VIN	List	Fair	Good	Good	Excellent
325i Sedan 4D		EV334	33715	22500	25225	28600	34000
325xi AWD Sedan 4D		EU334	35465	23575	26375	29800	35200
325Ci Coupe 2D		BD334	36115	23675	26475	29800	35300
325Cic Convertible 2D		BW334	42425	29300	32700	36300	42300
325iT Wagon 4D		EN334	35615	22500	25125	28500	33900
325xiT AWD Wagon 4D		EP334	37365	23075	25800	29200	34600
330i Sedan 4D		EV534	39120	25700	28700	32200	37900
330xi AWD Sedan 4D		EW534	40870	26575	29675	33200	38900
330Ci Coupe 2D		BD534	40720	26675	29875	33400	39100
330Cic Convertible 2D		BW534	46470	31525	35200	38900	45100
Hard Top (Conv)				650	650	865	865
Premium Pkg				575	575	765	765
Sport Pkg				375	375	500	500
Performance Pkg				500	500	665	665
5-Spd Manual (ex 2D)				(600)	(600)	(800)	(800)

M3—6-Cyl.—Equipment Schedule 1
W.B. 107.5"; 3.2 Liter.

Body	Type	VIN	List	Fair	Good	Good	Excellent
Coupe 2D		BL934	51140				
Convertible 2D		BR934	56495				
Hard Top (Conv)							
Club Sport Pkg							

Z4—6-Cyl.—Equipment Schedule 1
W.B. 98.2"; 2.5 Liter, 3.0 Liter.

Body	Type	VIN	List	Fair	Good	Good	Excellent
2.5i Roadster 2D		BT335	38415	25125	28125	31500	37200
3.0i Roadster 2D		BT535	44265	28325	31625	35100	41000
Sport Pkg				375	375	500	500
Premium Pkg				575	575	765	765

5 SERIES—6-Cyl.—Equipment Schedule 1
W.B. 113.7"; 2.5 Liter, 3.0 Liter.

Body	Type	VIN	List	Fair	Good	Good	Excellent
525i Sedan 4D		NA535	44720	29675	33175	37500	44500
530i Sedan 4D		NA735	48820	32200	35900	40400	47600
w/o Premium Pkg				(975)	(975)	(1300)	(1300)
Sport Pkg				1150	1150	1535	1535
Manual Trans				(725)	(725)	(965)	(965)

5 SERIES—V8—Equipment Schedule 1
W.B. 113.7"; 4.4 Liter.

Body	Type	VIN	List	Fair	Good	Good	Excellent
545i Sedan 4D		NB335	56495	37925	42300	46900	54700
Sport Pkg				1150	1150	1535	1535

6 SERIES—V8—Equipment Schedule 1
W.B. 109.4"; 4.4 Liter.

Body	Type	VIN	List	Fair	Good	Good	Excellent
645Ci Coupe 2D		EH734	70595				
645Cic Convertible 2D		EK734	78895				
Sport Pkg							

7 SERIES—V8—Equipment Schedule 1
W.B. 117.7", 123.2" (Li); 4.4 Liter.

Body	Type	VIN	List	Fair	Good	Good	Excellent
745i Sedan 4D		GL635	70595				
745Li Sedan 4D		GN635	74595				

Body	Type	VIN	List	Trade-In Fair	Good	Pvt-Party Good	Retail Excellent

Sport Pkg ....
7 SERIES—V12—Equipment Schedule 1
W.B. 117.7", 123.2" (Li); 6.0 Liter.
760i Sedan 4D GL835 111895
760Li Sedan 4D GN835 119295

BUICK

1991 BUICK — 1G4(NV54U)–M–#

SKYLARK—4-Cyl.—Equipment Schedule 5
W.B. 103.4"; 2.5 Liter.

Sedan 4D	NV54U	12036	400	550	1025	1775
Coupe 2D	NV14U	12136	400	550	1025	1775
Custom Sedan 4D	NC54U	13653	400	550	1025	1775
Custom Coupe 2D	NJ14U	13653	400	550	1025	1775
Luxury Sedan 4D	ND54U	15335	400	600	1100	1875
Gran Sport Coupe 2D	NM14U	15135	450	650	1175	2000
Gran Touring Pkg			50	50	65	65
4-Cyl. 2.3L Quad 4	D		100	100	135	135
V6 3.3 Liter	N		125	125	165	165

CENTURY—V6—Equipment Schedule 4
W.B. 104.8"; 3.3 Liter.

Special Sedan 4D	AG54N	15798	475	675	1175	2000
Custom Sedan 4D	AH54N	16805	475	675	1175	2000
Custom Coupe 2D	AH14N	16800	475	675	1175	2000
Custom Wagon 4D	AH84N	18865	525	750	1250	2100
Limited Sedan 4D	AL54N	17786	600	850	1425	2375
Limited Wagon 4D	AL84N	19656	525	750	1250	2100
4-Cyl. 2.5 Liter	R		(150)	(150)	(200)	(200)

REGAL—V6—Equipment Schedule 4
W.B. 107.5"; 3.1 Liter.

Custom Sedan 4D	WB54T	17295	700	1025	1775	3000
Custom Coupe 2D	WB14T	17075	600	850	1550	2675
Limited Sedan 4D	WD54T	18501	675	950	1700	2875
Limited Coupe 2D	WD14T	18116	600	875	1600	2775
Gran Touring Pkg			50	50	65	65
Gran Sport Pkg			75	75	100	100
V6 3.8 Liter	L		150	150	200	200

LeSABRE—V6—Equipment Schedule 4
W.B. 110.8"; 3.8 Liter.

Coupe 2D	HP14C	19019	550	775	1300	2200
Custom Sedan 4D	HP54C	19024	675	950	1550	2550
Limited Sedan 4D	HR54C	20481	675	950	1550	2550
Limited Coupe 2D	HR14C	20276	575	825	1350	2275
Gran Touring Pkg			50	50	65	65

PARK AVENUE—V6—Equipment Schedule 4
W.B. 110.8"; 3.8 Liter.

Sedan 4D	CW53L	25594	900	1275	2075	3350
Ultra Sedan 4D	CU53L	28000	1150	1600	2675	4175
Gran Touring Pkg			50	50	65	65
V6 3.8L Supercharged	1		150	150	200	200

ROADMASTER—V8—Equipment Schedule 2
W.B. 115.9"; 5.0 Liter.
| Estate Wagon 4D | BR83E | 24642 | 1850 | 2375 | 3550 | 5225 |

RIVIERA—V6—Equipment Schedule 2
W.B. 108.0"; 3.8 Liter.
| Coupe 2D | EZ13L | 26250 | 825 | 1175 | 2125 | 3625 |
| Gran Touring Pkg | | | 50 | 50 | 65 | 65 |

REATTA—V6—Equipment Schedule 2
W.B. 98.5"; 3.8 Liter.
| Coupe 2D | EC14C | 29880 | 1375 | 1875 | 3150 | 4925 |
| Convertible 2D | EC34C | 36545 | 2600 | 3225 | 4725 | 6875 |

1992 BUICK — 1G4(NJ543)–N–#

SKYLARK—4-Cyl.—Equipment Schedule 5
W.B. 103.4"; 2.3 Liter.

Sedan 4D	NJ543	15180	450	650	1225	2075
Coupe 2D	NJ143	15180	450	650	1225	2075
V6 3.3 Liter	N		125	125	165	165

SKYLARK—V6—Equipment Schedule 5
W.B. 103.4"; 3.3 Liter.

1992 BUICK

Body Type	VIN	List	Trade-In Fair	Good	Pvt-Party Good	Retail Excellent
Gran Sport Sedan 4D	NM54N	17175	575	825	1425	2450
Gran Sport Coupe 2D	NM14N	17175	575	825	1425	2450
CENTURY—V6—Equipment Schedule 4						
W.B. 104.9"; 3.3 Liter.						
Special Sedan 4D	AG54N	16337	550	775	1325	2250
Custom Sedan 4D	AH54N	16897	550	775	1325	2250
Custom Coupe 2D	AH14N	16627	550	775	1325	2250
Custom Wagon 4D	AH84N	17375	600	850	1425	2375
Limited Sedan 4D	AL54N	17894	675	975	1600	2675
Limited Wagon 4D	AL84N	18969	600	875	1450	2425
4-Cyl. 2.5 Liter	R		(150)	(150)	(200)	(200)
REGAL—V6—Equipment Schedule 4						
W.B. 107.5"; 3.1 Liter.						
Custom Sedan 4D	WB54T	18370	800	1150	2025	3400
Custom Coupe 2D	WB14T	18050	675	950	1750	3000
Limited Sedan 4D	WD54T	19700	750	1075	1950	3275
Limited Coupe 2D	WD14T	19315	700	1000	1825	3100
Gran Sport Sedan 4D	WF54L	21098	875	1225	2200	3650
Gran Sport Coupe 2D	WF14L	20333	775	1125	2075	3350
Gran Touring Pkg			50	50	65	65
V6 3.8 Liter	L		150	150	200	200
LeSABRE—V6—Equipment Schedule 4						
W.B. 110.8"; 3.8 Liter.						
Custom Sedan 4D	HP53L	19615	625	900	1550	2600
Limited Sedan 4D	HR53L	21695	975	1375	2275	3625
Gran Touring Pkg			50	50	65	65
PARK AVENUE—V6—Equipment Schedule 4						
W.B. 110.8"; 3.8 Liter.						
Sedan 4D	CW53L	26569	1075	1500	2550	4050
Gran Touring Pkg			50	50	65	65
PARK AVENUE—V6 Supercharged—Equipment Schedule 4						
W.B. 110.8"; 3.8 Liter.						
Ultra Sedan 4D	CU531	29380	1425	1925	3050	4675
Gran Touring Pkg			50	50	65	65
ROADMASTER—V8—Equipment Schedule 2						
W.B. 115.9"; 5.7 Liter.						
Sedan 4D	BN537	24255	1225	1700	2800	4325
Limited Sedan 4D	BT537	25835	1375	1900	3000	4575
Estate Wagon 4D	BR837	25110	2250	2825	4100	5925
RIVIERA—V6—Equipment Schedule 2						
W.B. 108.0"; 3.8 Liter.						
Coupe 2D	EZ13L	27080	975	1350	2600	4325
Gran Touring Pkg			50	50	65	65

1993 BUICK — 1G4(NV543)-P-#

Body Type	VIN	List	Trade-In Fair	Good	Pvt-Party Good	Retail Excellent
SKYLARK—4-Cyl.—Equipment Schedule 5						
W.B. 103.4"; 2.3 Liter.						
Custom Sedan 4D	NV543	14260	550	775	1375	2375
Custom Coupe 2D	NV143	14260	525	750	1350	2325
Limited Sedan 4D	NJ543	15180	550	800	1425	2425
Limited Coupe 2D	NJ143	15180	550	775	1375	2375
V6 3.3 Liter	N		150	150	200	200
SKYLARK—V6—Equipment Schedule 5						
W.B. 103.4"; 3.3 Liter.						
Gran Sport Sedan 4D	NM54N	17065	700	1000	1675	2800
Gran Sport Coupe 2D	NM14N	17065	700	1000	1675	2800
CENTURY—V6—Equipment Schedule 4						
W.B. 104.9"; 3.3 Liter.						
Special Sedan 4D	AG54N	16627	625	900	1525	2550
Special Wagon 4D	AG84N	17681	650	925	1550	2600
Custom Sedan 4D	AH55N	18955	625	900	1525	2550
Custom Coupe 2D	AH15N	17958	625	900	1500	2500
Custom Wagon 4D	AH85N	20597	700	1000	1625	2725
Limited Sedan 4D	AL55N	19468	825	1175	1925	3100
4-Cyl. 2.2 Liter	4		(175)	(175)	(235)	(235)
REGAL—V6—Equipment Schedule 4						
W.B. 107.5"; 3.1 Liter.						
Custom Sedan 4D	WB54T	18195	900	1250	2375	4000
Custom Coupe 2D	WB14T	17875	775	1100	2025	3400
Limited Sedan 4D	WD54T	20045	900	1250	2350	3900
Limited Coupe 2D	WD14T	19780	800	1150	2050	3475
Gran Sport Sedan 4D	WF54L	21103	1025	1450	2575	4200
Gran Sport Coupe 2D	WF14L	20823	925	1300	2400	3975

Body Type	VIN	List	Trade-In Fair	Trade-In Good	Pvt-Party Good	Retail Excellent
Gran Touring Pkg			75	75	100	100
V6 3.8 Liter	L		175	175	235	235
LeSABRE—V6—Equipment Schedule 4						
W.B. 110.8"; 3.8 Liter.						
90th Anniv Sedan 4D	HP53L	19554	775	1100	1825	3000
Custom Sedan 4D	HP53L	21651	775	1100	1825	3000
Limited Sedan 4D	HR53L	23886	1200	1650	2725	4250
Gran Touring Pkg			75	75	100	100
PARK AVENUE—V6—Equipment Schedule 4						
W.B. 110.8"; 3.8 Liter.						
Sedan 4D	CW53L	26640	1400	1900	3025	4625
Gran Touring Pkg			75	75	100	100
PARK AVENUE—V6 Supercharged—Equipment Schedule 4						
W.B. 110.8"; 3.8 Liter.						
Ultra Sedan 4D	CU531	29995	1875	2400	3625	5325
Gran Touring Pkg			75	75	100	100
ROADMASTER—V8—Equipment Schedule 2						
W.B. 115.9"; 5.7 Liter.						
Sedan 4D	BN537	25895	1575	2075	3250	4875
Limited Sedan 4D	BT537	26235	1750	2275	3450	5125
Estate Wagon 4D	BR837	27895	2725	3350	4700	6625
RIVIERA—V6—Equipment Schedule 2						
W.B. 108.0"; 3.8 Liter.						
Coupe 2D	EZ13L	28125	1200	1650	3025	4900
Gran Touring Pkg			75	75	100	100

1994 BUICK — 1G4(NV553)-R-#

Body Type	VIN	List	Trade-In Fair	Trade-In Good	Pvt-Party Good	Retail Excellent
SKYLARK—4-Cyl.—Equipment Schedule 5						
W.B. 103.4"; 2.3 Liter.						
Custom Sedan 4D	NV553	14914	650	925	1625	2775
Custom Coupe 2D	NV153	14914	625	900	1600	2725
Limited Sedan 4D	NJ553	16684	675	950	1650	2800
V6 3.1 Liter	M		175	175	235	235
SKYLARK—V6—Equipment Schedule 5						
W.B. 103.4"; 3.1 Liter.						
Gran Sport Sedan 4D	NM55M	18784	825	1175	1975	3225
Gran Sport Coupe 2D	NM15M	18784	825	1175	1975	3225
CENTURY—V6—Equipment Schedule 4						
W.B. 104.9"; 3.1 Liter.						
Special Sedan 4D	AG55M	17325	725	1050	1775	2925
Special Wagon 4D	AG85M	18175	750	1075	1825	3000
Custom Sedan 4D	AH55M	19686	725	1050	1775	2925
4-Cyl. 2.2 Liter	4		(200)	(200)	(265)	(265)
REGAL—V6—Equipment Schedule 4						
W.B. 107.5"; 3.1 Liter.						
Custom Sedan 4D	WB55M	19672	1000	1400	2675	4425
Custom Coupe 2D	WB15M	19372	900	1250	2375	4000
Limited Sedan 4D	WD55L	21242	1050	1450	2650	4325
Gran Sport Sedan 4D	WF55L	21724	1200	1650	2875	4575
Gran Sport Coupe 2D	WF15L	21442	1075	1500	2700	4375
Gran Touring Pkg			100	100	135	135
V6 3.8 Liter	L		200	200	265	265
LeSABRE—V6—Equipment Schedule 4						
W.B. 110.8"; 3.8 Liter.						
Custom Sedan 4D	HP52L	22541	925	1300	2150	3475
Limited Sedan 4D	HR52L	24995	1500	2000	3125	4725
Gran Touring Pkg			100	100	135	135
PARK AVENUE—V6—Equipment Schedule 4						
W.B. 110.8"; 3.8 Liter.						
Sedan 4D	CW52L	27624	1825	2350	3575	5250
Gran Touring Pkg			100	100	135	135
PARK AVENUE—V6 Supercharged—Equipment Schedule 4						
W.B. 110.8"; 3.8 Liter.						
Ultra Sedan 4D	CU521	32324	2325	2900	4200	6050
Gran Touring Pkg			100	100	135	135
ROADMASTER—V8—Equipment Schedule 2						
W.B. 115.9"; 5.7 Liter.						
Sedan 4D	BN52P	27224	1975	2525	3725	5475
Limited Sedan 4D	BT52P	27734	2125	2725	3950	5725
Estate Wagon 4D	BR82P	29078	3250	3925	5350	7400

1995 BUICK

Body	Type	VIN	List	Trade-In Fair	Trade-In Good	Pvt-Party Good	Retail Excellent
1995 BUICK — (1or2)G4(NV55D)–S–#							
SKYLARK—4-Cyl.—Equipment Schedule 5							
W.B. 103.4"; 2.3 Liter.							
Custom Sedan 4D		NV55D	16070	775	1100	1925	3175
Custom Coupe 2D		NV15D	16070	750	1075	1875	3125
Gran Sport Pkg				100	100	135	135
V6 3.1 Liter		M		200	200	265	265
CENTURY—V6—Equipment Schedule 4							
W.B. 104.9"; 3.1 Liter.							
Special Sedan 4D		AG55M	19171	850	1200	2025	3350
Special Wagon 4D		AG85M	19989	900	1250	2125	3475
Custom Sedan 4D		AH55M	18865	850	1200	2025	3350
4-Cyl. 2.2 Liter		4		(225)	(225)	(300)	(300)
REGAL—V6—Equipment Schedule 4							
W.B. 107.5"; 3.1 Liter.							
Custom Sedan 4D		WB52M	20650	1125	1575	2925	4775
Custom Coupe 2D		WB12M	20333	1025	1450	2650	4350
Limited Sedan 4D		WD52L	22243	1225	1675	2925	4650
Gran Sport Sedan 4D		WF52L	22878	1400	1900	3200	4975
Gran Sport Coupe 2D		WF12L	19995	1225	1725	2975	4725
Gran Touring Pkg				100	100	135	135
V6 3.8 Liter		L		200	200	265	265
LeSABRE—V6—Equipment Schedule 4							
W.B. 110.8"; 3.8 Liter.							
Custom Sedan 4D		HP52L	23481	1075	1525	2625	4175
Limited Sedan 4D		HR52L	26050	1825	2350	3575	5300
Gran Touring Pkg				100	100	135	135
PARK AVENUE—V6—Equipment Schedule 4							
W.B. 110.8"; 3.8 Liter.							
Sedan 4D		CW52K	28879	2250	2825	4125	5975
Gran Touring Pkg				100	100	135	135
PARK AVENUE—V6 Supercharged—Equipment Schedule 4							
W.B. 110.8"; 3.8 Liter.							
Ultra Sedan 4D		CU521	33719	2800	3425	4800	6800
Gran Touring Pkg				100	100	135	135
ROADMASTER—V8—Equipment Schedule 2							
W.B. 115.9"; 5.7 Liter.							
Sedan 4D		BN52P	28425	2400	2975	4325	6175
Limited Sedan 4D		BT52P	29930	2575	3175	4500	6425
Estate Wagon 4D		BR82P	30365	3775	4525	6075	8250
RIVIERA—V6—Equipment Schedule 2							
W.B. 113.8"; 3.8 Liter.							
Coupe 2D		GD12K	28857	1775	2300	3225	4625
V6 3.8L Supercharged		1		250	250	335	335
1996 BUICK — (1,2or3)G4(NJ52T)–T–#							
SKYLARK—4-Cyl.—Equipment Schedule 5							
W.B. 103.4"; 2.4 Liter.							
Custom Sedan 4D		NJ52T	15995	900	1275	2350	3900
Custom Coupe 2D		NJ12T	15995	900	1250	2225	3675
Gran Sport Pkg				100	100	135	135
V6 3.1 Liter		M		225	225	300	300
CENTURY—V6—Equipment Schedule 4							
W.B. 104.9"; 3.1 Liter.							
Sedan 4D		AG55M	18235	1000	1400	2475	4025
Wagon 4D		AG85M	19040	1050	1450	2575	4125
4-Cyl. 2.2 Liter		4		(250)	(250)	(335)	(335)
REGAL—V6—Equipment Schedule 4							
W.B. 107.5"; 3.1 Liter.							
Custom Sedan 4D		WB52M	20280	1300	1800	3250	5225
Custom Coupe 2D		WB12M	19985	1200	1650	2950	4750
Limited Sedan 4D		WD52K	21735	1425	1925	3250	5100
Gran Sport Sedan 4D		WF52K	22340	1675	2175	3550	5425
Gran Sport Coupe 2D		WF12K	21495	1475	1975	3325	5175
Gran Touring Pkg				100	100	135	135
V6 3.8 Liter		K		200	200	265	265
LeSABRE—V6—Equipment Schedule 4							
W.B. 110.8"; 3.8 Liter.							
Custom Sedan 4D		HP52K	22345	1375	1875	3025	4675
Limited Sedan 4D		HR52K	25975	2200	2800	4075	5925
Gran Touring Pkg				100	100	135	135

EQUIPMENT & MILEAGE PAGE 13 TO 27

1996 BUICK

Body	Type	VIN	List	Trade-In Fair	Trade-In Good	Pvt-Party Good	Retail Excellent
PARK AVENUE—V6—Equipment Schedule 4							
W.B. 110.8"; 3.8 Liter.							
Sedan 4D		CW52K	28845	2750	3375	4750	6725
Gran Touring Pkg				100	100	135	135
PARK AVENUE—V6 Supercharged—Equipment Schedule 4							
W.B. 110.8"; 3.8 Liter.							
Ultra Sedan 4D		CU521	33460	3325	4025	5475	7575
Gran Touring Pkg				100	100	135	135
ROADMASTER—V8—Equipment Schedule 4							
W.B. 115.9"; 5.7 Liter.							
Sedan 4D		BN52P	28590	2875	3550	4925	6875
Limited Sedan 4D		BT52P	30125	3050	3725	5125	7125
Estate Wagon 4D		BR82P	30230	4400	5200	6775	9075
RIVIERA—V6—Equipment Schedule 2							
W.B. 113.8"; 3.8 Liter.							
Coupe 2D		GD12K	30715	2275	2850	3950	5550
V6 3.8L Supercharged		1		275	275	365	365

1997 BUICK — (1,2or3)G4(NJ52T)-V-#

Body	Type	VIN	List	Trade-In Fair	Trade-In Good	Pvt-Party Good	Retail Excellent
SKYLARK—4-Cyl.—Equipment Schedule 5							
W.B. 103.4"; 2.4 Liter.							
Custom Sedan 4D		NJ52T	16495	1050	1475	2675	4325
Custom Coupe 2D		NJ12T	16495	1050	1450	2650	4300
Gran Sport Pkg				100	100	135	135
V6 3.1 Liter		M		250	250	335	335
CENTURY—V6—Equipment Schedule 4							
W.B. 109.0"; 3.1 Liter.							
Custom Sedan 4D		WS52M	18590	1375	1900	3225	5100
Limited Sedan 4D		WY52M	19965	1850	2375	3800	5750
REGAL—V6—Equipment Schedule 4							
W.B. 109.0"; 3.8 Liter.							
LS Sedan 4D		WB52K	21095	1950	2475	3875	5850
Gran Touring Pkg				100	100	135	135
REGAL—V6 Supercharged—Equipment Schedule 4							
W.B. 109.0"; 3.8 Liter.							
GS Sedan 4D		WF521	23495	3025	3700	5100	7100
LeSABRE—V6—Equipment Schedule 4							
W.B. 110.8"; 3.8 Liter.							
Custom Sedan 4D		HP52K	23040	1750	2275	3550	5300
Limited Sedan 4D		HR52K	26170	2675	3275	4675	6650
Gran Touring Pkg				100	100	135	135
PARK AVENUE—V6—Equipment Schedule 4							
W.B. 113.8"; 3.8 Liter.							
Sedan 4D		CW52K	30660	3425	4125	5575	7675
Gran Touring Pkg				100	100	135	135
PARK AVENUE—V6 Supercharged—Equipment Schedule 4							
W.B. 113.8"; 3.8 Liter.							
Ultra Sedan 4D		CU521	35660	4050	4800	6350	8600
Gran Touring Pkg				100	100	135	135
RIVIERA—V6—Equipment Schedule 2							
W.B. 113.8"; 3.8 Liter.							
Coupe 2D		GD22K	31375	2925	3600	4850	6725
V6 3.8L Supercharged		1		300	300	400	400

1998 BUICK — (1,2or3)G4(NJ52M)-W-#

Body	Type	VIN	List	Trade-In Fair	Trade-In Good	Pvt-Party Good	Retail Excellent
SKYLARK—V6—Equipment Schedule 5							
W.B. 103.4"; 3.1 Liter.							
Custom Sedan 4D		NJ52M	16755	1250	1750	3025	4800
CENTURY—V6—Equipment Schedule 4							
W.B. 109.0"; 3.1 Liter.							
Custom Sedan 4D		WS52M	19185	1700	2225	3650	5650
Limited Sedan 4D		WY52M	20545	2200	2800	4275	6350
REGAL—V6—Equipment Schedule 4							
W.B. 109.0"; 3.8 Liter.							
LS Sedan 4D		WB52K	21495	2300	2875	4400	6450
Gran Touring Pkg				100	100	135	135
REGAL—V6 Supercharged—Equipment Schedule 4							
W.B. 109.0"; 3.8 Liter.							
GS Sedan 4D		WF521	24240	3475	4200	5650	7725
LeSABRE—V6—Equipment Schedule 4							
W.B. 110.8"; 3.8 Liter.							
Custom Sedan 4D		HP52K	23265	2200	2800	4150	6075
Limited Sedan 4D		HR52K	26395	3200	3875	5375	7500

1998 BUICK

Body Type	VIN	List	Trade-In Fair	Trade-In Good	Pvt-Party Good	Retail Excellent
Gran Touring Pkg			100	100	135	135
PARK AVENUE—V6—Equipment Schedule 4						
W.B. 113.8"; 3.8 Liter.						
Sedan 4D	CW52K	31340	4000	4750	6325	8575
Gran Touring Pkg			100	100	135	135
PARK AVENUE—V6 Supercharged—Equipment Schedule 4						
W.B. 113.8"; 3.8 Liter.						
Ultra Sedan 4D	CU521	36215	4650	5500	7150	9525
Gran Touring Pkg			100	100	135	135
RIVIERA—V6 Supercharged—Equipment Schedule 2						
W.B. 113.8"; 3.8 Liter.						
Coupe 2D	GD221	33165	3775	4525	6050	8200

1999 BUICK — (1,2or3)G4(WS52M)-X-#

Body Type	VIN	List	Trade-In Fair	Trade-In Good	Pvt-Party Good	Retail Excellent
CENTURY—V6—Equipment Schedule 4						
W.B. 109.0"; 3.1 Liter.						
Custom Sedan 4D	WS52M	19755	2100	2675	4200	6300
Limited	Y		675	675	900	900
REGAL—V6—Equipment Schedule 4						
W.B. 109.0"; 3.8 Liter.						
LS Sedan 4D	WB52K	22255	2775	3400	4950	7125
Gran Touring Pkg			100	100	135	135
REGAL—V6 Supercharged—Equipment Schedule 4						
W.B. 109.0"; 3.8 Liter.						
GS Sedan 4D	WF521	24955	4025	4775	6275	8475
LeSABRE—V6—Equipment Schedule 4						
W.B. 110.8"; 3.8 Liter.						
Custom Sedan 4D	HP52K	23535	2800	3425	4850	6875
Limited Sedan 4D	HR52K	26605	3900	4650	6175	8425
Gran Touring Pkg			100	100	135	135
PARK AVENUE—V6—Equipment Schedule 4						
W.B. 113.8"; 3.8 Liter.						
Sedan 4D	CW52K	31800	4675	5525	7125	9475
Gran Touring Pkg			100	100	135	135
PARK AVENUE—V6 Supercharged—Equipment Schedule 4						
W.B. 113.8"; 3.8 Liter.						
Ultra Sedan 4D	CU521	36695	5400	6325	8000	10500
Gran Touring Pkg			100	100	135	135
RIVIERA—V6 Supercharged—Equipment Schedule 2						
W.B. 113.8"; 3.8 Liter.						
Coupe 2D	GD221	35830	4800	5625	7300	9700

2000 BUICK — (1,2or3)G4(WS52J)-Y-#

Body Type	VIN	List	Trade-In Fair	Trade-In Good	Pvt-Party Good	Retail Excellent
CENTURY—V6—Equipment Schedule 4						
W.B. 109.0"; 3.1 Liter.						
Custom Sedan 4D	WS52J	20592	2700	3300	4950	7225
Century 2000 Pkg			275	275	365	365
Limited	Y		775	775	1035	1035
REGAL—V6—Equipment Schedule 4						
W.B. 109.0"; 3.8 Liter.						
LS Sedan 4D	WB52K	22780	3325	4025	5725	8075
Gran Touring Pkg			125	125	165	165
REGAL—V6 Supercharged—Equipment Schedule 4						
W.B. 109.0"; 3.8 Liter.						
GS Sedan 4D	WF521	25625	4775	5600	7225	9550
LeSABRE—V6—Equipment Schedule 4						
W.B. 112.2"; 3.8 Liter.						
Custom Sedan 4D	HP54K	24115	3700	4450	5875	7925
Limited Sedan 4D	HR54K	27310	5000	5875	7400	9675
Gran Touring Pkg			125	125	165	165
PARK AVENUE—V6—Equipment Schedule 4						
W.B. 113.8"; 3.8 Liter.						
Sedan 4D	CW52K	32395	5675	6600	8325	10850
Gran Touring Pkg			125	125	165	165
PARK AVENUE—V6 Supercharged—Equipment Schedule 4						
W.B. 113.8"; 3.8 Liter.						
Ultra Sedan 4D	CU521	37470	6550	7575	9350	12050
Gran Touring Pkg			125	125	165	165

2001 BUICK — (1or2)G4(WS52J)-2-#

CENTURY—V6—Equipment Schedule 4
W.B. 109.0"; 3.1 Liter.

2001 BUICK

Body	Type	VIN	List	Trade-In Fair	Good	Pvt-Party Good	Retail Excellent
Custom Sedan 4D	WS52J	20870	**3400**	**4100**	**5900**	**8375**
Limited	Y		**875**	**875**	**1165**	**1165**

REGAL—V6—Equipment Schedule 4
W.B. 109.0"; 3.1 Liter.

LS Sedan 4D	WB52K	23445	**4450**	**5250**	**7025**	**9525**
Abboud Pkg			**150**	**150**	**200**	**200**
Gran Touring Pkg			**150**	**150**	**200**	**200**

REGAL—V6 Supercharged—Equipment Schedule 4
W.B. 109.0"; 3.8 Liter.

| GS Sedan 4D | WF521 | 26695 | **6075** | **7050** | **8700** | **11150** |
| Abboud Pkg | | | **150** | **150** | **200** | **200** |

LeSABRE—V6—Equipment Schedule 4
W.B. 112.2"; 3.8 Liter.

Custom Sedan 4D	HP54K	24762	**4625**	**5450**	**6975**	**9250**
Limited Sedan 4D	HR54K	29451	**6075**	**7050**	**8700**	**11150**
Gran Touring Pkg			**150**	**150**	**200**	**200**

PARK AVENUE—V6—Equipment Schedule 4
W.B. 113.8"; 3.8 Liter.

| Sedan 4D | CW52K | 33700 | **6875** | **7900** | **9750** | **12500** |
| Gran Touring Pkg | | | **150** | **150** | **200** | **200** |

PARK AVENUE—V6 Supercharged—Equipment Schedule 4
W.B. 113.8"; 3.8 Liter.

| Ultra Sedan 4D | CU521 | 38210 | **7900** | **9075** | **11000** | **13850** |
| Gran Touring Pkg | | | **150** | **150** | **200** | **200** |

2002 BUICK — (1or2)G4(WS52J)-2-#

CENTURY—V6—Equipment Schedule 4
W.B. 109.0"; 3.1 Liter.

| Custom Sedan 4D | WS52J | 21325 | **4275** | **5075** | **7000** | **9700** |
| Limited | Y | | **975** | **975** | **1300** | **1300** |

REGAL—V6—Equipment Schedule 4
W.B. 109.0"; 3.8 Liter.

LS Sedan 4D	WB52K	23840	**5350**	**6250**	**8175**	**10900**
Abboud Pkg			**175**	**175**	**235**	**235**
Gran Touring Pkg			**175**	**175**	**235**	**235**

REGAL—V6 Supercharged—Equipment Schedule 4
W.B. 109.0"; 3.8 Liter.

| GS Sedan 4D | WF521 | 27895 | **7175** | **8275** | **10050** | **12750** |
| Abboud Pkg | | | **175** | **175** | **235** | **235** |

LeSABRE—V6—Equipment Schedule 4
W.B. 112.2"; 3.8 Liter.

| Custom Sedan 4D | HP54K | 24975 | **5800** | **6750** | **8400** | **10850** |
| Limited Sedan 4D | HR54K | 30675 | **7425** | **8525** | **10300** | **12950** |

PARK AVENUE—V6—Equipment Schedule 4
W.B. 113.8"; 3.8 Liter.

| Sedan 4D | CW52K | 34165 | **8275** | **9475** | **11450** | **14400** |
| Gran Touring Pkg | | | **175** | **175** | **235** | **235** |

PARK AVENUE—V6 Supercharged—Equipment Schedule 4
W.B. 113.8"; 3.8 Liter.

| Ultra Sedan 4D | CU521 | 38675 | **9425** | **10775** | **12800** | **15950** |
| Gran Touring Pkg | | | **175** | **175** | **235** | **235** |

2003 BUICK — (1or2)G4(WS52J)-3-#

CENTURY—V6—Equipment Schedule 4
W.B. 109.0"; 3.1 Liter.

| Sedan 4D | WS52J | 21685 | **5325** | **6225** | **8350** | **11300** |
| Limited | Y | | **1075** | **1075** | **1435** | **1435** |

REGAL—V6—Equipment Schedule 4
W.B. 109.0"; 3.8 Liter.

LS Sedan 4D	WB52K	24230	**6450**	**7475**	**9650**	**12750**
Abboud Pkg			**200**	**200**	**265**	**265**
Gran Touring Pkg			**200**	**200**	**265**	**265**

REGAL—V6 Supercharged—Equipment Schedule 4
W.B. 109.0"; 3.8 Liter.

| GS Sedan 4D | WF521 | 28175 | **8450** | **9675** | **11650** | **14650** |
| Abboud Pkg | | | **200** | **200** | **265** | **265** |

LeSABRE—V6—Equipment Schedule 4
W.B. 112.2"; 3.8 Liter.

Custom Sedan 4D	HP52K	25730	**7225**	**8350**	**10150**	**12850**
Limited Sedan 4D	HR54K	31360	**9075**	**10375**	**12250**	**15200**
Celebration Edition			**500**	**500**	**665**	**665**

PARK AVENUE—V6—Equipment Schedule 4
W.B. 113.8"; 3.8 Liter.

2003 BUICK

Body	Type	VIN	List	Trade-In Fair	Good	Pvt-Party Good	Retail Excellent
Sedan 4D		CW54K	34615	9950	11350	13500	16750
Gran Touring Pkg				200	200	265	265

PARK AVENUE—V6 Supercharged—Equipment Schedule 4
W.B. 113.8"; 3.8 Liter.

| Ultra Sedan 4D | | CU541 | 39915 | 11300 | 12800 | 15050 | 18450 |

2004 BUICK — (1or2)G4(WS52J)-4-#

CENTURY—V6—Equipment Schedule 4
W.B. 109.0"; 3.1 Liter.

| Sedan 4D | | WS52J | 22415 | 6650 | 7675 | 9900 | 13000 |
| Limited | | | | 1175 | 1175 | 1565 | 1565 |

REGAL—V6—Equipment Schedule 4
W.B. 109.0"; 3.8 Liter.

LS Sedan 4D		WB52K	24895	7900	9075	11400	14750
Abboud Pkg				200	200	265	265
Gran Touring Pkg				225	225	300	300

REGAL—V6 Supercharged—Equipment Schedule 4
W.B. 109.0"; 3.8 Liter.

| GS Sedan 4D | | WF521 | 28345 | 10100 | 11450 | 13650 | 16900 |
| Abboud Pkg | | | | 200 | 200 | 265 | 265 |

LeSABRE—V6—Equipment Schedule 4
W.B. 112.2"; 3.8 Liter.

Custom Sedan 4D		HP54K	26470	9125	10425	12300	15250
Limited Sedan 4D		HR54K	32245	11100	12600	14600	17750
Celebration Edition				500	500	665	665

PARK AVENUE—V6—Equipment Schedule 4
W.B. 113.8"; 3.8 Liter.

| Sedan 4D | | CW52K | 35545 | 12075 | 13675 | 15950 | 19500 |
| Gran Touring Pkg | | | | 225 | 225 | 300 | 300 |

PARK AVENUE—V6 Supercharged—Equipment Schedule 4
W.B. 113.8"; 3.8 Liter.

| Ultra Sedan 4D | | CU521 | 40720 | 13525 | 15275 | 17650 | 21300 |

2005 BUICK — (1or2)G4(WS52J)-5-#

CENTURY—V6—Equipment Schedule 4
W.B. 109.0"; 3.1 Liter.

Sedan 4D		WS52J	22950	8450	9675	12050	15450
Special Edition				400	400	535	535
Limited				1275	1275	1700	1700

LACROSSE—V6—Equipment Schedule 4
W.B. 110.5"; 3.6 Liter, 3.8 Liter.

CX Sedan 4D		WC532	23495	12275	13925	16200	19800
CXL Sedan 4D		WD532	25995	13475	15225	17600	21300
CXS Sedan 4D		WE537	27995	14650	16550	18900	22700

LeSABRE—V6—Equipment Schedule 4
W.B. 112.2"; 3.8 Liter.

Custom Sedan 4D		HP52K	27270	11350	12900	15000	18250
Limited Sedan 4D		HR54K	32930	13575	15325	17500	21000
Celebration Edition				500	500	665	665

PARK AVENUE—V6—Equipment Schedule 4
W.B. 113.8"; 3.8 Liter.

| Sedan 4D | | CW54K | 36350 | 14550 | 16450 | 18900 | 22800 |

PARK AVENUE—V6 Supercharged—Equipment Schedule 4
W.B. 113.8"; 3.8 Liter.

| Special Ed Ultra 4D | | CU541 | 41525 | 16150 | 18200 | 20700 | 24700 |

CADILLAC

1991 CADILLAC — 1G6(EL13B)-M-#

ELDORADO—V8—Equipment Schedule 2
W.B. 108.0"; 4.9 Liter.

Coupe 2D		EL13B	32380	1050	1450	2675	4375
Biarritz Coupe 2D		EL13B	35005	1125	1575	2850	4600
Touring Coupe 2D		EL13B	33875	1100	1550	2800	4500

SEVILLE—V8—Equipment Schedule 2
W.B. 108.0"; 4.9 Liter.

| Sedan 4D | | KS53B | 34975 | 1150 | 1600 | 2850 | 4600 |
| STS Touring Sedan 4D | | KY53B | 37715 | 1425 | 1925 | 3250 | 5100 |

DeVILLE—V8—Equipment Schedule 2
W.B. 110.8", 113.8" (Sed); 4.9 Liter.

| Sedan 4D | | CD53B | 31925 | 925 | 1300 | 2550 | 4300 |

1991 CADILLAC

Body Type	VIN	List	Trade-In Fair	Trade-In Good	Pvt-Party Good	Retail Excellent
Coupe 2D	CD13B	31675	825	1175	2375	4075
Touring Sedan 4D	CD53B	34375	1125	1575	2875	4700
FLEETWOOD—V8—Equipment Schedule 2						
W.B. 110.8", 113.8" (Sed); 4.9 Liter.						
Sedan 4D	CB53B	36095	975	1375	2650	4400
Coupe 2D	CB13B	35845	975	1375	2650	4400
FLEETWOOD SIXTY SPECIAL—V8—Equipment Schedule 2						
W.B. 113.8"; 4.9 Liter.						
Sedan 4D	CG53B	38925	950	1325	2600	4375
BROUGHAM—V8—Equipment Schedule 2						
W.B. 121.5"; 5.7 Liter.						
Sedan 4D	DW547	31375	925	1300	2525	4225
V8 5.0 Liter	E		(200)	(200)	(265)	(265)
ALLANTE—V8—Equipment Schedule 2						
W.B. 99.4"; 4.5 Liter.						
Convertible Coupe 2D	VS338	55250	4650	5500	7400	10100
Hard Top	R		1100	1100	1465	1465

1992 CADILLAC — 1G6(EL13B)–N–#

Body Type	VIN	List	Trade-In Fair	Trade-In Good	Pvt-Party Good	Retail Excellent
ELDORADO—V8—Equipment Schedule 2						
W.B. 108.0"; 4.9 Liter.						
Coupe 2D	EL13B	33720	1850	2375	3600	5300
Touring Coupe 2D	EL13B	35570	1975	2525	3750	5525
SEVILLE—V8—Equipment Schedule 2						
W.B. 111.0"; 4.9 Liter.						
Sedan 4D	KS53B	36225	1425	1925	3325	5250
STS Touring Sedan 4D	KY53B	38575	1725	2250	3700	5725
DeVILLE—V8—Equipment Schedule 2						
W.B. 110.8", 113.8 (Sed); 4.9 Liter.						
Sedan 4D	CD53B	32910	1100	1550	2925	4800
Coupe 2D	CD13B	32910	975	1375	2725	4525
Touring Sedan 4D	CT53B	35790	1375	1875	3300	5250
FLEETWOOD—V8—Equipment Schedule 2						
W.B. 110.8", 113.8 (Sed); 4.9 Liter.						
Sedan 4D	CB53B	37530	1175	1625	3025	4925
Coupe 2D	CB13B	37530	1175	1625	3025	4925
FLEETWOOD SIXTY SPECIAL—V8—Equipment Schedule 2						
W.B. 113.8"; 4.9 Liter.						
Sedan 4D	CG53B	40460	1125	1575	2950	4875
BROUGHAM—V8—Equipment Schedule 2						
W.B. 121.5"; 5.7 Liter.						
Sedan 4D	DW547	32910	1075	1525	2875	4725
d'Elegance			100	100	135	135
V8 5.0 Liter	E		(200)	(200)	(265)	(265)
ALLANTE—V8—Equipment Schedule 2						
W.B. 99.4"; 4.5 Liter.						
Convertible Coupe 2D	VS338	58470	5600	6525	8725	11800
Hard Top	R		1150	1150	1535	1535

1993 CADILLAC — 1G6(EL12B)–P–#

Body Type	VIN	List	Trade-In Fair	Trade-In Good	Pvt-Party Good	Retail Excellent
ELDORADO—V8—Equipment Schedule 2						
W.B. 108.0"; 4.6 Liter, 4.9 Liter.						
Coupe 2D	EL12B	35240	2275	2825	4125	5975
Sport Coupe 2D	EL12Y	38240	2600	3225	4550	6500
Touring Coupe 2D	EL129	39590	2675	3275	4650	6600
SEVILLE—V8—Equipment Schedule 2						
W.B. 111.0"; 4.6 Liter, 4.9 Liter.						
Sedan 4D	KS52B	38240	2575	3200	4425	6175
STS Touring Sedan 4D	KY529	42590	3325	4025	5375	7350
DeVILLE—V8—Equipment Schedule 2						
W.B. 110.8", 113.8" (Sed); 4.9 Liter.						
Sedan 4D	CD53B	34160	1400	1900	3425	5475
Coupe 2D	CD13B	35085	1225	1725	3200	5225
Touring Sedan 4D	CT53B	36910	1750	2275	3850	6025
FLEETWOOD—V8—Equipment Schedule 2						
W.B. 121.5"; 5.7 Liter.						
Sedan 4D	DW527	35160	2575	3175	4875	7225
Brougham Pkg			250	250	335	335
SIXTY SPECIAL—V8—Equipment Schedule 2						
W.B. 113.8"; 4.9 Liter.						
Sedan 4D	CB53B	38400	1550	2050	3625	5725
ALLANTE—V8—Equipment Schedule 2						
W.B. 99.4"; 4.6 Liter.						

1993 CADILLAC

Body Type	VIN	List	Trade-In Fair	Good	Pvt-Party Good	Retail Excellent
Convertible Coupe 2D	VS339	61675	9850	11250	14100	18200
Hard Top			1325	1325	1765	1765

1994 CADILLAC — 1G6(EL12Y)-R-#

ELDORADO—V8—Equipment Schedule 2
W.B. 108.0"; 4.6 Liter.

Coupe 2D	EL12Y	38565	2725	3350	4750	6775
Touring Coupe 2D	ET129	41215	3200	3875	5375	7525

SEVILLE—V8—Equipment Schedule 2
W.B. 111.0"; 4.6 Liter.

SLS Sedan 4D	KS52Y	42265	3000	3650	4975	6875
STS Touring Sedan 4D	KY529	45515	3850	4600	6075	8175

DeVILLE—V8—Equipment Schedule 2
W.B. 113.8"; 4.6 Liter, 4.9 Liter.

Sedan 4D	KD52B	34400	1825	2350	3825	5875
Concours Sedan 4D	KF52Y	37215	2525	3125	4700	6900

FLEETWOOD—V8—Equipment Schedule 2
W.B. 121.5"; 5.7 Liter.

Sedan 4D	DW52P	35185	3075	3725	5600	8150
Brougham Pkg			275	275	365	365

1995 CADILLAC — 1G6(EL12Y)-S-#

ELDORADO—V8—Equipment Schedule 2
W.B. 108.0"; 4.6 Liter.

Coupe 2D	EL12Y	39505	3300	3975	5525	7725
Touring Coupe 2D	ET129	42170	3850	4600	6225	8550

SEVILLE—V8—Equipment Schedule 2
W.B. 111.0"; 4.6 Liter.

SLS Sedan 4D	KS52Y	43220	3525	4225	5675	7750
STS Touring Sedan 4D	KY529	46570	4475	5275	6875	9175

DeVILLE—V8—Equipment Schedule 2
W.B. 113.8"; 4.6 Liter, 4.9 Liter.

Sedan 4D	KD52B	36320	2375	2950	4500	6675
Concours Sedan 4D	KF52Y	40035	3150	3800	5475	7800

FLEETWOOD—V8—Equipment Schedule 2
W.B. 121.5"; 5.7 Liter.

Sedan 4D	DW52P	37015	3675	4425	6450	9225
Brougham Pkg			300	300	400	400

1996 CADILLAC — 1G6(EL12Y)-T-#

ELDORADO—V8—Equipment Schedule 2
W.B. 108.0"; 4.6 Liter.

Coupe 2D	EL12Y	41020	3925	4675	6425	8850
Touring Coupe 2D	ET129	43635	4575	5400	7225	9800

SEVILLE—V8—Equipment Schedule 2
W.B. 111.0"; 4.6 Liter.

SLS Sedan 4D	KS52Y	44420	4150	4925	6525	8800
STS Touring Sedan 4D	KY529	48135	5225	6075	7825	10350

DeVILLE—V8—Equipment Schedule 2
W.B. 113.8"; 4.6 Liter.

Sedan 4D	KD52Y	37420	2975	3650	5325	7675
Concours Sedan 4D	KF529	41135	3800	4550	6350	8875

FLEETWOOD—V8—Equipment Schedule 2
W.B. 121.5"; 5.7 Liter.

Sedan 4D	DW52P	38420	4375	5175	7400	10450
Brougham Pkg			325	325	435	435

1997 CADILLAC — (Wor1)(GorO)6(VR52R)-V-#

CATERA—V6—Equipment Schedule 2
W.B. 107.4"; 3.0 Liter.

Sedan 4D	VR52R	33635	2075	2650	3975	5850

ELDORADO—V8—Equipment Schedule 2
W.B. 108.0"; 4.6 Liter.

Coupe 2D	EL12Y	39883	4700	5550	7500	10250
Touring Coupe 2D	ET129	42060	5425	6350	8425	11300

SEVILLE—V8—Equipment Schedule 2
W.B. 111.0"; 4.6 Liter.

SLS Sedan 4D	KS52Y	41883	4900	5750	7575	10150
STS Touring Sedan 4D	KY529	45660	6075	7025	8975	11800

DeVILLE—V8—Equipment Schedule 2
W.B. 113.8"; 4.6 Liter.

Sedan 4D	KD54Y	38445	3700	4450	6300	8875

1997 CADILLAC

Body	Type	VIN	List	Trade-In Fair	Trade-In Good	Pvt-Party Good	Retail Excellent
d'Elegance Sedan 4D		KE54Y	40660	4175	4950	6875	9500
Concours Sedan 4D		KF549	42660	4600	5425	7400	10150

1998 CADILLAC — (Wor1)(Gor0)6(VR52R)-W-#

CATERA—V6—Equipment Schedule 2
W.B. 107.4"; 3.0 Liter.

Body	Type	VIN	List	Fair	Good	Good	Excellent
Sedan 4D		VR52R	34250	2600	3225	4750	6900

ELDORADO—V8—Equipment Schedule 2
W.B. 108.0"; 4.6 Liter.

| Coupe 2D | | EL12Y | 39945 | 5675 | 6600 | 8800 | 11900 |
| Touring Coupe 2D | | ET129 | 43360 | 6450 | 7475 | 9800 | 13050 |

SEVILLE—V8—Equipment Schedule 2
W.B. 112.2"; 4.6 Liter.

| SLS Sedan 4D | | KS52Y | 43160 | 4975 | 5850 | 7800 | 10550 |
| STS Touring Sedan 4D | | KY529 | 47660 | 6250 | 7250 | 9350 | 12350 |

DeVILLE—V8—Equipment Schedule 2
W.B. 113.8"; 4.6 Liter.

Sedan 4D		KD54Y	39145	4600	5400	7500	10350
d'Elegance Sedan 4D		KE54Y	41960	5100	5975	8075	11000
Concours Sedan 4D		KF549	42960	5550	6500	8650	11700

1999 CADILLAC — (Wor1)(Gor0)6(VR52R)-X-#

CATERA—V6—Equipment Schedule 2
W.B. 107.5"; 3.0 Liter.

| Sedan 4D | | VR52R | 34820 | 3325 | 4000 | 5800 | 8275 |
| Sport | | | | 300 | 300 | 400 | 400 |

ELDORADO—V8—Equipment Schedule 2
W.B. 108.0"; 4.6 Liter.

| Coupe 2D | | EL12Y | 40690 | 6850 | 7875 | 10300 | 13650 |
| Touring Coupe 2D | | ET129 | 44165 | 7675 | 8825 | 11300 | 14800 |

SEVILLE—V8—Equipment Schedule 2
W.B. 112.2"; 4.6 Liter.

| SLS Sedan 4D | | KS52Y | 44025 | 6150 | 7150 | 9000 | 11700 |
| STS Touring Sedan 4D | | KY529 | 48520 | 7500 | 8625 | 10650 | 13650 |

DeVILLE—V8—Equipment Schedule 2
W.B. 113.8"; 4.6 Liter.

Sedan 4D		KD54Y	40085	5700	6625	8725	11700
d'Elegance Sedan 4D		KE54Y	43400	6150	7150	9300	12350
Concours Sedan 4D		KF549	43900	6675	7700	9900	13050

2000 CADILLAC — (Wor1)(Gor0)6(VR52R)-Y-#

CATERA—V6—Equipment Schedule 2
W.B. 107.5"; 3.0 Liter.

| Sedan 4D | | VR52R | 31500 | 3725 | 4450 | 6425 | 9150 |
| Sport | | | | 300 | 300 | 400 | 400 |

ELDORADO—V8—Equipment Schedule 2
W.B. 108.0"; 4.6 Liter.

| ESC Coupe 2D | | EL12Y | 39790 | 8025 | 9225 | 11700 | 15250 |
| ETC Coupe 2D | | ET129 | 43365 | 9025 | 10325 | 12900 | 16600 |

SEVILLE—V8—Equipment Schedule 2
W.B. 112.2"; 4.6 Liter.

| SLS Sedan 4D | | KS52Y | 44550 | 7350 | 8475 | 10500 | 13400 |
| STS Touring Sedan 4D | | KY529 | 49150 | 8725 | 10000 | 12200 | 15500 |

DeVILLE—V8—Equipment Schedule 2
W.B. 115.3"; 4.6 Liter.

Sedan 4D		KD54Y	40955	7175	8275	10400	13450
DHS Sedan 4D		KE54Y	45370	9700	11050	13400	16900
DTS Sedan 4D		KF549	45370	10325	11725	14100	17650

2001 CADILLAC — (Wor1)(Gor0)6(VR52R)-1-#

CATERA—V6—Equipment Schedule 2
W.B. 107.4"; 3.0 Liter.

| Sedan 4D | | VR52R | 31945 | 5075 | 5950 | 8300 | 11500 |
| Sport | | | | 300 | 300 | 400 | 400 |

ELDORADO—V8—Equipment Schedule 2
W.B. 108.0"; 4.6 Liter.

| ESC Coupe 2D | | EL12Y | 40756 | 10000 | 11350 | 14250 | 18350 |
| ETC Coupe 2D | | ET129 | 44331 | 11150 | 12650 | 15600 | 19900 |

SEVILLE—V8—Equipment Schedule 2
W.B. 112.2"; 4.6 Liter.

| SLS Sedan 4D | | KS52Y | 42655 | 8950 | 10225 | 12400 | 15650 |
| STS Touring Sedan 4D | | KY529 | 48765 | 10325 | 11725 | 14300 | 18050 |

2001 CADILLAC

Body Type	VIN	List	Trade-In Fair	Good	Pvt-Party Good	Retail Excellent
DeVILLE—V8—Equipment Schedule 2						
W.B. 115.3"; 4.6 Liter.						
Sedan 4D	KD54Y	42000	8850	10125	12550	16100
DHS Sedan 4D	KE54Y	46987	11775	13350	16000	20000
DTS Sedan 4D	KF549	46987	12475	14125	16800	20900

2002 CADILLAC — 1G6(EL12Y)-2-#

Body Type	VIN	List	Trade-In Fair	Good	Pvt-Party Good	Retail Excellent
ELDORADO—V8—Equipment Schedule 2						
W.B. 108.0"; 4.6 Liter.						
ESC Coupe 2D	EL12Y	42610	12425	14075	17350	22100
ETC Coupe 2D	ET129	45745	13675	15475	18850	23800
ECS Coupe 2D	ET129	48405	13975	15775	19150	24100
SEVILLE—V8—Equipment Schedule 2						
W.B. 112.2"; 4.6 Liter.						
SLS Sedan 4D	KS52Y	44269	11000	12475	15000	18750
STS Touring Sedan 4D	KY529	49825	12325	13975	16950	21200
DeVILLE—V8—Equipment Schedule 2						
W.B. 115.3"; 4.6 Liter.						
Sedan 4D	KD54Y	43070	10925	12375	15250	19300
DHS Sedan 4D	KE54Y	48000	14200	16000	19050	23600
DTS Sedan 4D	KF549	48000	14900	16825	19900	24500

2003 CADILLAC — 1G6(DM57N)-3-#

Body Type	VIN	List	Trade-In Fair	Good	Pvt-Party Good	Retail Excellent
CTS—V6—Equipment Schedule 2						
W.B. 113.4"; 3.2 Liter.						
Sedan 4D	DM57N	29990	14600	16500	19600	24300
Luxury Sport Pkg			650	650	865	865
SEVILLE—V8—Equipment Schedule 2						
W.B. 112.2"; 4.6 Liter.						
SLS Sedan 4D	KS54Y	45200	13625	15375	18400	22800
STS Touring Sedan 4D	KY529	51175	14975	16875	20400	25500
DeVILLE—V8—Equipment Schedule 2						
W.B. 115.3"; 4.6 Liter.						
Sedan 4D	KD54Y	43995	13300	15025	18300	23000
DHS Sedan 4D	KE54Y	48825	16925	19050	22400	27500
DTS Sedan 4D	KF549	48825	17700	19875	23400	28600

2004 CADILLAC — 1G6(DM57N)-4-#

Body Type	VIN	List	Trade-In Fair	Good	Pvt-Party Good	Retail Excellent
CTS—V6—Equipment Schedule 2						
W.B. 113.4"; 3.2 Liter.						
Sedan 4D	DM57N	33155	16350	18425	21300	25800
Luxury Sport Pkg			700	700	935	935
V6 3.6 Liter	7		600	600	800	800
CTS-V—V8—Equipment Schedule 2						
W.B. 113.4"; 5.7 Liter.						
Sedan 4D	DN57S	49995	30175	33650	36400	41400
SEVILLE—V8—Equipment Schedule 2						
W.B. 112.2"; 4.6 Liter.						
SLS Sedan 4D	KS52Y	47955	17025	19150	22800	28100
DeVILLE—V8—Equipment Schedule 2						
W.B. 115.3"; 4.6 Liter.						
Sedan 4D	KD54Y	45445	16100	18150	21800	27300
DHS Sedan 4D	KE54Y	50595	20075	22600	26500	32300
DTS Sedan 4D	KF549	50595	21050	23575	27500	33400
XLR—V8—Equipment Schedule 1						
W.B. 105.7"; 4.6 Liter.						
Hardtop Conv 2D	YV34A	76200	45100	50150	55000	63500

2005 CADILLAC — 1G6(DM56T)-5-#

Body Type	VIN	List	Trade-In Fair	Good	Pvt-Party Good	Retail Excellent
CTS—V6—Equipment Schedule 2						
W.B. 113.4"; 2.8 Liter.						
Sedan 4D	DM56T	33745	18775	21050	24300	29400
Luxury Pkg			750	750	1000	1000
V6 3.6 Liter	7		600	600	800	800
CTS-V—V8—Equipment Schedule 2						
W.B. 113.4"; 5.7 Liter.						
Sedan 4D	DN56S	49995	33750	37625	40400	45800
STS—V6—Equipment Schedule 2						
W.B. 116.6"; 3.6 Liter.						
Sedan 4D	DW677	40995	24450	27350	31300	37400
STS—V8—Equipment Schedule 2						
W.B. 116.6"; 4.6 Liter.						

Body	Type	VIN	List	Trade-In Fair	Good	Pvt-Party Good	Retail Excellent
Sedan 4D		DC67A	47495	29200	32600	36800	43400
AWD				3000	3000	4000	4000

DEVILLE—V8—Equipment Schedule 2
W.B. 115.3"; 4.6 Liter.

Sedan 4D		KD54Y	46490	19600	22025	26300	32600
DHS Sedan 4D		KE54Y	52045	24050	26875	31300	38000
DTS Sedan 4D		KF549	52045	24925	27925	32300	39100

XLR—V8—Equipment Schedule 1
W.B. 105.7"; 4.6 Liter.

Hardtop Conv 2D		YV34A	76650				

CHEVROLET

1991 CHEVROLET — 1G1(JC54G)-M-#

CAVALIER—4-Cyl.—Equipment Schedule 5
W.B. 101.3"; 2.2 Liter.

VL Sedan 4D		JC54G	10252	250	350	700	1300
VL Coupe 2D		JC14G	9977	250	350	700	1300
VL Wagon 4D		JC84G	10742	275	400	800	1425
RS Sedan 4D		JC54G	10915	275	400	800	1425
RS Coupe 2D		JC14G	10715	275	400	800	1425
RS Wagon 4D		JC84G	11455	275	400	800	1425
V6 3.1 Liter		T		100	100	135	135

CAVALIER—V6—Equipment Schedule 5
W.B. 101.3"; 3.1 Liter.

RS Convertible 2D		JF34T	16929	750	1050	1700	2800
Z24 Coupe 2D		JF14T	13700	500	725	1225	2100

CORSICA—4-Cyl.—Equipment Schedule 5
W.B. 103.4"; 2.2 Liter.

LT Notchback Sed 4D		LT54G	11845	350	475	900	1600
LT Hatchback Sed 4D		LT64G	12520	350	475	900	1600
V6 3.1 Liter		T		125	125	165	165

BERETTA—4-Cyl.—Equipment Schedule 5
W.B. 103.4"; 2.2 Liter.

Coupe 2D		LV14G	12140	400	575	1050	1825
V6 3.1 Liter		T		125	125	165	165

BERETTA—4-Cyl. Quad—Equipment Schedule 5
W.B. 103.4"; 2.3 Liter.

GTZ Coupe 2D		LZ14A	15545	600	850	1425	2425
Manual Trans				0	0	0	0
V6 3.1 Liter		T		125	125	165	165

BERETTA—V6—Equipment Schedule 5
W.B. 103.4"; 3.1 Liter.

GT Coupe 2D		LW14T	14145	525	750	1300	2200

LUMINA—V6—Equipment Schedule 4
W.B. 107.5"; 3.1 Liter, 3.4 Liter.

Sedan 4D		WL54T	15200	450	650	1275	2250
Coupe 2D		WL14T	15095	425	625	1225	2150
Euro Sedan 4D		WN54T	16060	550	800	1475	2600
Euro Coupe 2D		WN14T	16055	550	800	1475	2600
Z34 Coupe 2D		WP14X	18455	725	1050	1825	3050
Manual Trans				(50)	(50)	(65)	(65)
4-Cyl. 2.5 Liter		R		(250)	(250)	(335)	(335)

CAMARO—V6—Equipment Schedule 4
W.B. 101.0"; 3.1 Liter.

RS Coupe 2D		FP23T	14496	850	1200	1950	3125
RS Convertible 2D		FP33T	20134	1375	1875	2925	4475
Manual Trans				(150)	(150)	(200)	(200)
V8 5.0 Liter		E		200	200	265	265

CAMARO—V8—Equipment Schedule 4
W.B. 101.0"; 5.0 Liter.

Z28 Coupe 2D		FP23T	18276	1125	1575	2600	4075
Z28 Convertible 2D		FP33F	23504	1975	2500	3675	5400
Manual Trans				(100)	(100)	(135)	(135)
V8 5.7 Liter TPI		8		250	250	335	335

CAPRICE—V8—Equipment Schedule 4
W.B. 115.9"; 5.0 Liter.

Sedan 4D		BL53E	18040	550	800	1375	2325
Classic Sedan 4D		BN53E	19938	700	1025	1675	2775
Wagon 4D		BL83E	19590	1075	1525	2525	3975
LTZ Pkg				50	50	65	65

Body	Type	VIN	List	Trade-In Fair	Good	Pvt-Party Good	Retail Excellent
CORVETTE—V8—Equipment Schedule 2							
W.B. 96.2"; 5.7 Liter.							
Hatchback Coupe 2D		YY248	33990	4825	5675	7975	11100
Convertible 2D		YY348	40305	5700	6625	9100	12450
ZR1 H'Back Coupe 2D		YZ238	64668	14200	16000	20100	25700
Glass Roof Panel				250	250	335	335
Dual Roof Panels				300	300	400	400
Handling Pkg				50	50	65	65
Hard Top				200	200	265	265
6-Spd Manual Trans				0	0	0	0

1992 CHEVROLET — 1G1(JC544)-N-#

Body	Type	VIN	List	Trade-In Fair	Good	Pvt-Party Good	Retail Excellent
CAVALIER—4-Cyl.—Equipment Schedule 5							
W.B. 101.3"; 2.2 Liter.							
VL Sedan 4D		JC544	11046	275	375	800	1475
VL Coupe 2D		JC144	10946	275	375	800	1475
VL Wagon 4D		JC844	11651	325	450	925	1650
RS Sedan 4D		JC544	12419	325	450	925	1650
RS Coupe 2D		JC144	11714	325	450	925	1650
RS Wagon 4D		JC844	12419	325	450	925	1650
RS Convertible 2D		JC344	17720	750	1050	1775	2925
V6 3.1 Liter		T		125	125	165	165
CAVALIER—V6—Equipment Schedule 5							
W.B. 101.3"; 3.1 Liter.							
Z24 Coupe 2D		JF14T	14710	575	825	1425	2450
Z24 Convertible 2D		JF34T	20020	850	1225	2025	3275
CORSICA—4-Cyl.—Equipment Schedule 5							
W.B. 103.4"; 2.2 Liter.							
LT Sedan 4D		LT534	12834	400	525	1050	1825
V6 3.1 Liter		T		125	125	165	165
BERETTA—4-Cyl.—Equipment Schedule 5							
W.B. 103.4"; 2.2 Liter.							
Coupe 2D		LV134	12834	450	650	1225	2075
GT Coupe 2D		LW134	14410	550	775	1350	2325
V6 3.1 Liter		T		125	125	165	165
BERETTA—4-Cyl. Quad 4—Equipment Schedule 5							
W.B. 103.4"; 2.3 Liter.							
GTZ Coupe 2D		LZ13A	16620	675	975	1650	2775
Manual Trans				0	0	0	0
V6 3.1 Liter		T		125	125	165	165
LUMINA—V6—Equipment Schedule 4							
W.B. 107.5"; 3.1 Liter.							
Sedan 4D		WL54T	15850	525	750	1450	2550
Coupe 2D		WL14T	15745	500	725	1375	2450
Euro Sedan 4D		WN54T	16860	650	925	1700	2925
Euro Coupe 2D		WN14T	16755	650	925	1700	2925
Z34 Coupe 2D		WP14X	19580	850	1200	2100	3475
Manual Trans				(50)	(50)	(65)	(65)
4-Cyl. 2.5 Liter		R		(275)	(275)	(365)	(365)
V6 3.4 Liter		X		150	150	200	200
CAMARO—V6—Equipment Schedule 4							
W.B. 101.0"; 3.1 Liter.							
RS Coupe 2D		FP23T	14132	975	1375	2250	3575
RS Convertible 2D		FP33T	19960	1675	2175	3325	4950
Manual Trans				(175)	(175)	(235)	(235)
V8 5.0 Liter		E		225	225	300	300
CAMARO—V8—Equipment Schedule 4							
W.B. 101.0"; 5.0 Liter.							
Z28 Coupe 2D		FP23F	18112	1350	1850	2925	4475
Z28 Convertible 2D		FP33F	23405	2325	2900	4200	6025
Manual Trans				(100)	(100)	(135)	(135)
V8 5.7 Liter TPI		8		250	250	335	335
CAPRICE—V8—Equipment Schedule 4							
W.B. 115.9"; 5.0 Liter.							
Sedan 4D		BL53E	19018	650	925	1575	2675
Classic Sedan 4D		BN53E	21746	825	1175	1975	3175
Wagon 4D		BL83E	20433	1300	1800	2875	4450
LTZ Pkg				50	50	65	65
V6 4.3 Liter		Z		(100)	(100)	(135)	(135)
V8 5.7 Liter		7		100	100	135	135
CORVETTE—V8—Equipment Schedule 2							
W.B. 96.2"; 5.7 Liter.							
Hatchback Coupe 2D		YY23P	35270	5350	6250	8700	12100

Body Type	VIN	List	Trade-In Fair	Trade-In Good	Pvt-Party Good	Retail Excellent
Convertible 2D	YY33P	41780	6300	7300	9950	13550
ZR1 H'Back Coupe 2D	YZ23J	72378	15625	17600	21900	27900
Glass Roof Panel			250	250	335	335
Dual Roof Panels			300	300	400	400
Hard Top			225	225	300	300
Suspension Pkg			50	50	65	65
6-Spd Manual Trans			0	0	0	0

1993 CHEVROLET — 1G1(JC544)-P-#

CAVALIER—4-Cyl.—Equipment Schedule 5
W.B. 101.3"; 2.2 Liter.

Body Type	VIN	List	Trade-In Fair	Trade-In Good	Pvt-Party Good	Retail Excellent
VL Sedan 4D	JC544	10667	325	425	900	1650
VL Coupe 2D	JC144	10567	325	425	900	1650
VL Wagon 4D	JC844	11287	375	500	1025	1825
RS Sedan 4D	JC544	11335	400	525	1050	1875
RS Coupe 2D	JC144	11235	400	525	1050	1875
RS Wagon 4D	JC844	12005	400	550	1100	1925
RS Convertible 2D	JC344	17110	850	1225	2025	3300
V6 3.1 Liter	T		150	150	200	200

CAVALIER—V6—Equipment Schedule 5
W.B. 101.3"; 3.1 Liter.

Body Type	VIN	List	Trade-In Fair	Trade-In Good	Pvt-Party Good	Retail Excellent
Z24 Coupe 2D	JF14T	14215	700	1000	1700	2825
Z24 Convertible 2D	JF34T	20020	1025	1450	2475	3950

CORSICA—4-Cyl.—Equipment Schedule 5
W.B. 103.4"; 2.2 Liter.

Body Type	VIN	List	Trade-In Fair	Trade-In Good	Pvt-Party Good	Retail Excellent
LT Sedan 4D	LT534	13230	425	625	1175	2025
V6 3.1 Liter	T		150	150	200	200

BERETTA—4-Cyl.—Equipment Schedule 5
W.B. 103.4"; 2.2 Liter.

Body Type	VIN	List	Trade-In Fair	Trade-In Good	Pvt-Party Good	Retail Excellent
Coupe 2D	LV134	13230	525	750	1325	2275
GT Coupe 2D	LW134	14830	625	900	1525	2600
V6 3.1 Liter	T		150	150	200	200

BERETTA—4-Cyl. Quad 4—Equipment Schedule 5
W.B. 103.4"; 2.2 Liter.

Body Type	VIN	List	Trade-In Fair	Trade-In Good	Pvt-Party Good	Retail Excellent
GTZ Coupe 2D	LZ13A	17025	775	1125	1900	3100
Manual Trans			0	0	0	0
V6 3.1 Liter	T		150	150	200	200

LUMINA—V6—Equipment Schedule 5
W.B. 107.5"; 3.1 Liter.

Body Type	VIN	List	Trade-In Fair	Trade-In Good	Pvt-Party Good	Retail Excellent
Sedan 4D	WL54T	15550	550	775	1500	2675
Coupe 2D	WL14T	15735	500	725	1425	2550
Euro Sedan 4D	WN54T	17040	700	1000	1825	3125
Euro Coupe 2D	WN14T	16810	700	1000	1825	3125
Z34 Coupe 2D	WP14X	19370	900	1275	2350	3900
Manual Trans			(75)	(75)	(100)	(100)
4-Cyl. 2.2 Liter	4		(325)	(325)	(435)	(435)
V6 3.4 Liter	X		175	175	235	235

CAMARO—V6—Equipment Schedule 4
W.B. 101.1"; 3.4 Liter.

Body Type	VIN	List	Trade-In Fair	Trade-In Good	Pvt-Party Good	Retail Excellent
Coupe 2D	FP22S	16385	1500	2000	3025	4525
Manual Trans			(225)	(225)	(300)	(300)

CAMARO—V8—Equipment Schedule 4
W.B. 101.1"; 5.7 Liter.

Body Type	VIN	List	Trade-In Fair	Trade-In Good	Pvt-Party Good	Retail Excellent
Z28 Coupe 2D	FP22P	20125	2050	2625	3750	5400

CAPRICE CLASSIC—V8—Equipment Schedule 4
W.B. 115.9"; 5.0 Liter.

Body Type	VIN	List	Trade-In Fair	Trade-In Good	Pvt-Party Good	Retail Excellent
Sedan 4D	BL53E	19223	800	1150	1925	3125
LS Sedan 4D	BN53E	20950	1000	1425	2425	3900
Wagon 4D	BL83E	21318	1675	2175	3350	5000
LTZ Pkg			75	75	100	100
V8 5.7 Liter	7		125	125	165	165

CORVETTE—V8—Equipment Schedule 2
W.B. 96.2"; 5.7 Liter.

Body Type	VIN	List	Trade-In Fair	Trade-In Good	Pvt-Party Good	Retail Excellent
Coupe 2D	YY23P	36230	6000	6950	9525	13050
Convertible 2D	YY33P	42830	7075	8175	10900	14750
ZR1 Coupe 2D	YZ2JP	66828	17600	19800	24300	30700
Anniversary Edition			625	625	835	835
Glass Roof Panel			250	250	335	335
Dual Roof Panels			300	300	400	400
Hard Top (Convertible)			275	275	365	365
Suspension Pkg			75	75	100	100
6-Spd Manual Trans			25	25	35	35

Body	Type	VIN	List	Trade-In Fair	Good	Pvt-Party Good	Retail Excellent

1994 CHEVROLET — 1G1(JC544)-R-#

CAVALIER—4-Cyl.—Equipment Schedule 5
W.B. 101.3"; 2.2 Liter.

Body	Type	VIN	List	Fair	Good	Good	Excellent
VL Sedan 4D		JC544	11082	375	500	1075	1925
VL Coupe 2D		JC144	10932	375	500	1075	1925
Wagon 4D		JC844	12375	475	675	1275	2250
RS Sedan 4D		JC544	11790	450	625	1225	2150
RS Coupe 2D		JC144	11685	450	625	1225	2150
RS Convertible 2D		JC344	17470	1000	1400	2450	3950
V6 3.1 Liter		T		175	175	235	235

CAVALIER—V6—Equipment Schedule 5
W.B. 101.3"; 3.1 Liter.

Z24 Coupe 2D		JF14T	14965	825	1175	2025	3300
Z24 Convertible 2D		JF34T	20965	1225	1700	2825	4375

CORSICA—4-Cyl.—Equipment Schedule 5
W.B. 103.4"; 2.2 Liter.

LT Sedan 4D		LD554	13630	500	725	1325	2325
V6 3.1 Liter		M		175	175	235	235

BERETTA—4-Cyl.—Equipment Schedule 5
W.B. 103.4"; 2.2 Liter.

Coupe 2D		LV154	13455	600	875	1525	2625
V6 3.1 Liter		M		175	175	235	235

BERETTA—4-Cyl. Quad 4—Equipment Schedule 5
W.B. 103.4"; 2.3 Liter.

Z26 Coupe 2D		LW15A	15795	900	1275	2175	3525
Manual Trans				0	0	0	0
V6 3.1 Liter		M		175	175	235	235

LUMINA—V6—Equipment Schedule 4
W.B. 107.5"; 3.1 Liter.

Sedan 4D		WL54T	16645	575	825	1625	2875
Euro Sedan 4D		WN54T	17815	750	1075	2025	3450
Euro Coupe 2D		WN14T	17625	750	1075	2025	3450
Z34 Coupe 2D		WP14X	19835	975	1375	2525	4150
V6 3.4 Liter		X		200	200	265	265

CAMARO—V6—Equipment Schedule 4
W.B. 101.1"; 3.4 Liter.

Coupe 2D		FP22S	16250	1825	2350	3450	5050
Convertible 2D		FP32S	22021	2725	3350	4600	6425
Manual Trans				(275)	(275)	(365)	(365)

CAMARO—V8—Equipment Schedule 4
W.B. 101.1"; 5.7 Liter.

Z28 Coupe 2D		FP22P	19900	2475	3075	4300	6075
Z28 Convertible 2D		FP32P	25351	3675	4425	5825	7875

CAPRICE CLASSIC—V8—Equipment Schedule 4
W.B. 115.9"; 4.3 Liter.

Sedan 4D		BL52W	20698	975	1375	2300	3675
LS Sedan 4D		BN52W	22010	1225	1725	2825	4375
Wagon 4D		BL82P	22703	2050	2625	3850	5600
V8 5.7 Liter		P		150	150	200	200

IMPALA SS—V8—Equipment Schedule 2
W.B. 115.9"; 5.7 Liter.

Sedan 4D		BN52P	23355	4850	5700	7375	9800

CORVETTE—V8—Equipment Schedule 2
W.B. 96.2"; 5.7 Liter.

Coupe 2D		YY22P	37345	6725	7750	10500	14200
Convertible 2D		YY32P	44120	7925	9125	12050	16050
ZR1 Coupe 2D		YZ22J	67993	19600	22025	26800	33700
Glass Roof Panel				250	250	335	335
Dual Roof Panels				300	300	400	400
Hard Top (Convertible)				325	325	435	435
Suspension Pkg				100	100	135	135
6-Spd Manual Trans				50	50	65	65

1995 CHEVROLET — (1or2)G1(JC524)-S-#

CAVALIER—4-Cyl.—Equipment Schedule 5
W.B. 104.1"; 2.2 Liter, 2.3 Liter.

Sedan 4D		JC524	12030	525	750	1400	2450
Coupe 2D		JC124	11825	525	750	1400	2450
LS Sedan 4D		JF524	12950	700	1025	1775	3000
LS Convertible 2D		JF324	17695	1475	1975	3125	4775
Z24 Coupe 2D		JF12D	14295	800	1150	2000	3300

1995 CHEVROLET

Body Type	VIN	List	Trade-In Fair	Trade-In Good	Pvt-Party Good	Retail Excellent
CORSICA—4-Cyl.—Equipment Schedule 5						
W.B. 103.4"; 2.2 Liter.						
Sedan 4D	LD554	14385	**600**	**850**	**1550**	**2675**
V6 3.1 Liter	M		**200**	**200**	**265**	**265**
BERETTA—4-Cyl.—Equipment Schedule 5						
W.B. 103.4"; 2.2 Liter.						
Coupe 2D	LV154	14045	**700**	**1025**	**1775**	**3000**
V6 3.1 Liter	M		**200**	**200**	**265**	**265**
BERETTA—V6—Equipment Schedule 5						
W.B. 103.4"; 3.1 Liter.						
Z26 Coupe 2D	LW15M	16790	**1050**	**1450**	**2550**	**4100**
LUMINA—V6—Equipment Schedule 4						
W.B. 107.5"; 3.1 Liter.						
Sedan 4D	WL52M	16837	**825**	**1175**	**1875**	**3000**
LS Sedan 4D	WN52M	17712	**975**	**1375**	**2200**	**3475**
V6 3.4 Liter	X		**225**	**225**	**300**	**300**
MONTE CARLO—V6—Equipment Schedule 4						
W.B. 107.5"; 3.1 Liter, 3.4 Liter.						
LS Coupe 2D	WW12M	17512	**925**	**1300**	**2100**	**3350**
Z34 Coupe 2D	WX12X	19495	**1150**	**1600**	**2625**	**4100**
CAMARO—V6—Equipment Schedule 4						
W.B. 101.1"; 3.4 Liter.						
Coupe 2D	FP22S	17536	**2150**	**2750**	**3900**	**5600**
Convertible 2D	FP32S	22781	**3175**	**3825**	**5175**	**7075**
Manual Trans			**(325)**	**(325)**	**(435)**	**(435)**
V6 3.8 Liter	K		**175**	**175**	**235**	**235**
CAMARO—V8—Equipment Schedule 4						
W.B. 101.1"; 5.7 Liter.						
Z28 Coupe 2D	FP22P	21236	**2925**	**3600**	**4875**	**6775**
Z28 Convertible 2D	FP32P	26388	**4250**	**5050**	**6525**	**8675**
CAPRICE CLASSIC—V8—Equipment Schedule 4						
W.B. 115.9"; 4.3 Liter.						
Sedan 4D	BL52W	21798	**1200**	**1650**	**2800**	**4400**
Wagon 4D	BL82P	24373	**2475**	**3075**	**4425**	**6300**
V8 5.7 Liter	P		**175**	**175**	**235**	**235**
IMPALA SS—V8—Equipment Schedule 2						
W.B. 115.9"; 5.7 Liter.						
Sedan 4D	BL52P	24385	**5550**	**6500**	**8275**	**10850**
CORVETTE—V8—Equipment Schedule 2						
W.B. 96.2"; 5.7 Liter.						
Coupe 2D	YY22P	37955	**7500**	**8625**	**11450**	**15350**
Convertible 2D	YY32P	44835	**8850**	**10125**	**13150**	**17350**
ZR1 Coupe 2D	YZ22J	68603	**21825**	**24450**	**29300**	**36500**
Glass Roof Panel			**250**	**250**	**335**	**335**
Dual Roof Panels			**300**	**300**	**400**	**400**
Hard Top (Convertible)			**375**	**375**	**500**	**500**
Suspension Pkg			**125**	**125**	**165**	**165**
6-Spd Manual Trans			**75**	**75**	**100**	**100**

1996 CHEVROLET — (1,2or4)G1(JC524)-T-#

Body Type	VIN	List	Trade-In Fair	Trade-In Good	Pvt-Party Good	Retail Excellent
CAVALIER—4-Cyl.—Equipment Schedule 5						
W.B. 104.1"; 2.2 Liter, 2.4 Liter.						
Sedan 4D	JC524	12872	**625**	**900**	**1675**	**2925**
Coupe 2D	JC124	12672	**625**	**900**	**1675**	**2925**
LS Sedan 4D	JF524	13395	**825**	**1175**	**2100**	**3525**
LS Convertible 2D	JF324	17995	**1750**	**2275**	**3525**	**5275**
Z24 Coupe 2D	JF12T	15490	**925**	**1300**	**2425**	**4000**
CORSICA—4-Cyl.—Equipment Schedule 5						
W.B. 103.4"; 2.2 Liter.						
Sedan 4D	LD554	14885	**700**	**1000**	**1825**	**3125**
V6 3.1 Liter	M		**225**	**225**	**300**	**300**
BERETTA—4-Cyl.—Equipment Schedule 5						
W.B. 103.4"; 2.2 Liter.						
Coupe 2D	LV154	14545	**825**	**1175**	**2100**	**3525**
V6 3.1 Liter	M		**225**	**225**	**300**	**300**
BERETTA—V6—Equipment Schedule 5						
W.B. 103.4"; 3.1 Liter.						
Z26 Coupe 2D	LW15M	17190	**1225**	**1675**	**2850**	**4500**
LUMINA—V6—Equipment Schedule 4						
W.B. 107.5"; 3.1 Liter.						
Sedan 4D	WL52M	17863	**1000**	**1425**	**2275**	**3575**
LS Sedan 4D	WN52M	18812	**1225**	**1675**	**2700**	**4150**
V6 3.4 Liter	X		**250**	**250**	**335**	**335**

1996 CHEVROLET

Body	Type	VIN	List	Trade-In Fair	Good	Pvt-Party Good	Retail Excellent
MONTE CARLO—V6—Equipment Schedule 4							
W.B. 107.5"; 3.1 Liter, 3.4 Liter.							
LS Coupe 2D		WW12M	18012	1150	1600	2625	4050
Z34 Coupe 2D		WX12X	19995	1450	1950	3000	4525
CAMARO—V6—Equipment Schedule 4							
W.B. 101.1"; 3.8 Liter.							
Coupe 2D		FP22K	18411	2575	3175	4450	6250
Convertible 2D		FP32K	23796	3650	4375	5775	7825
RS Coupe 2D		FP22K	20911	3050	3725	5075	7000
RS Convertible 2D		FP32K	25246	4125	4900	6375	8525
Manual Trans				(375)	(375)	(500)	(500)
CAMARO—V8—Equipment Schedule 4							
W.B. 101.1"; 5.7 Liter.							
Z28 Coupe 2D		FP22P	21951	3450	4150	5525	7550
Z28 Convertible 2D		FP32P	27016	4850	5700	7275	9600
SS Pkg				1250	1250	1665	1665
CAPRICE CLASSIC—V8—Equipment Schedule 4							
W.B. 115.9"; 4.3 Liter.							
Sedan 4D		BL52W	21495	1525	2025	3225	4925
Wagon 4D		BL82P	22995	2975	3650	5025	7000
V8 5.7 Liter		P		200	200	265	265
IMPALA SS—V8—Equipment Schedule 2							
W.B. 115.9"; 5.7 Liter.							
Sedan 4D		BL52W	24995	6350	7375	9225	11950
CORVETTE—V8—Equipment Schedule 2							
W.B. 96.2"; 5.7 Liter.							
Coupe 2D		YY22P	38400	8375	9575	12550	16700
Convertible 2D		YY32P	46235	9850	11250	14400	18800
Collector Edition				675	675	900	900
Grand Sport				1875	1875	2500	2500
Glass Roof Panel				250	250	335	335
Dual Roof Panels				300	300	400	400
Hard Top (Convertible)				425	425	565	565
Suspension Pkg				150	150	200	200
6-Spd Manual Trans				100	100	135	135
V8 5.7 Liter LT4		5		925	925	1235	1235

1997 CHEVROLET — (1,2or4)G1(JC524)-V-#

Body	Type	VIN	List	Trade-In Fair	Good	Pvt-Party Good	Retail Excellent
CAVALIER—4-Cyl.—Equipment Schedule 5							
W.B. 104.1"; 2.2 Liter, 2.4 Liter.							
Sedan 4D		JC524	13357	750	1075	2025	3475
Coupe 2D		JC124	13157	750	1075	2025	3475
RS Coupe 2D		JC124	14070	925	1300	2425	4050
LS Sedan 4D		JF524	13880	975	1375	2550	4175
LS Convertible 2D		JF324	18265	2050	2625	3950	5825
Z24 Coupe 2D		JF12T	15760	1100	1550	2775	4450
MALIBU—V6—Equipment Schedule 5							
W.B. 107.0"; 3.1 Liter.							
Sedan 4D		ND52M	16390	1050	1475	2500	3975
LS Sedan 4D		NE52M	18715	1275	1775	2825	4350
4-Cyl. 2.4 Liter		T		(200)	(200)	(265)	(265)
LUMINA—V6—Equipment Schedule 4							
W.B. 107.5"; 3.1 Liter.							
Sedan 4D		WL52M	18485	1250	1750	2800	4300
LS Sedan 4D		WL52M	19695	1525	2025	3075	4625
LTZ Sedan 4D		WN52M	20200	1550	2050	3150	4700
V6 3.4 Liter		X		275	275	365	365
MONTE CARLO—V6—Equipment Schedule 4							
W.B. 107.5"; 3.1 Liter, 3.4 Liter.							
LS Coupe 2D		WW12M	18220	1475	1975	3050	4575
Z34 Coupe 2D		WX12X	20495	1825	2350	3475	5100
CAMARO—V6—Equipment Schedule 4							
W.B. 101.1"; 3.8 Liter.							
Coupe 2D		FP22K	18786	3000	3675	5025	6975
Convertible 2D		FP32K	24341	4175	4950	6450	8625
RS Coupe 2D		FP22K	20541	3600	4300	5725	7800
RS Convertible 2D		FP32K	25741	4700	5550	7100	9375
Manual Trans				(400)	(400)	(535)	(535)
CAMARO—V8—Equipment Schedule 4							
W.B. 101.1"; 5.7 Liter.							
Z28 Coupe 2D		FP22P	22721	4000	4750	6225	8400
Z28 Convertible 2D		FP32P	28091	5525	6450	8100	10550
SS Pkg				1350	1350	1800	1800

1997 CHEVROLET

Body	Type	VIN	List	Trade-In Fair	Good	Pvt-Party Good	Retail Excellent
CORVETTE—V8—Equipment Schedule 2							
W.B. 104.5"; 5.7 Liter.							
Coupe 2D		YY22G	38365	10225	11650	15050	19700
Glass Roof Panel				250	250	335	335
Dual Roof Panels				300	300	400	400
Suspension Pkg				175	175	235	235
6-Spd Manual Trans				125	125	165	165

1998 CHEVROLET–(1,2or4)(C,GorY)1(MR226)–W–

Body	Type	VIN	List	Trade-In Fair	Good	Pvt-Party Good	Retail Excellent
METRO—3-Cyl.—Equipment Schedule 6							
W.B. 93.1"; 1.0 Liter.							
Coupe 2D		MR226	10110	575	825	1750	3175
METRO—4-Cyl.—Equipment Schedule 6							
W.B. 93.1"; 1.3 Liter.							
LSi Sedan 4D		MR522	11800	1000	1400	2650	4375
LSi Coupe 2D		MR222	10910	750	1075	2125	3675
PRIZM—4-Cyl.—Equipment Schedule 6							
W.B. 97.0"; 1.8 Liter.							
Sedan 4D		SK528	15248	1650	2150	3550	5450
LSi Sedan 4D		SK528	16208	1825	2350	3750	5700
CAVALIER—4-Cyl.—Equipment Schedule 5							
W.B. 104.1"; 2.2 Liter, 2.4 Liter.							
Sedan 4D		JC524	13705	925	1300	2500	4200
Coupe 2D		JC124	13505	925	1300	2500	4200
RS Coupe 2D		JC124	14945	1100	1550	2800	4525
LS Sedan 4D		JF524	14750	1175	1625	2900	4650
LS Convertible 2D		JF324		2100	2675	4050	6000
Z24 Coupe 2D		JF12T	16990	1350	1850	3125	4925
Z24 Convertible 2D		JF32T	20690	2400	2975	4400	6375
MALIBU—V6—Equipment Schedule 5							
W.B. 107.0"; 3.1 Liter.							
Sedan 4D		ND52M	16690	1325	1825	2900	4475
LS Sedan 4D		NE52M	18995	1625	2125	3275	4900
4-Cyl. 2.4 Liter		T		(200)	(200)	(265)	(265)
LUMINA—V6—Equipment Schedule 4							
W.B. 107.5"; 3.1 Liter.							
Sedan 4D		WL52M	18785	1650	2150	3275	4850
LS Sedan 4D		WL52M	20020	1900	2425	3575	5225
LTZ Sedan 4D		WN52M	20520	1975	2500	3650	5275
V6 3.8 Liter		K		300	300	400	400
MONTE CARLO—V6—Equipment Schedule 4							
W.B. 107.5"; 3.1 Liter, 3.8 Liter.							
LS Coupe 2D		WW12M	18570	1850	2375	3525	5150
Z34 Coupe 2D		WX12K	20845	2225	2825	3975	5700
CAMARO—V6—Equipment Schedule 4							
W.B. 101.1"; 3.8 Liter.							
Coupe 2D		FP22K	19196	3575	4275	5725	7800
Convertible 2D		FP32K	24771	4775	5600	7200	9500
T-Bar Roof				375	375	500	500
Manual Trans				(425)	(425)	(565)	(565)
CAMARO—V8—Equipment Schedule 4							
W.B. 101.1"; 5.7 Liter.							
Z28 Coupe 2D		FP22G	22571	4650	5475	7025	9325
Z28 Convertible 2D		FP32G	27975	6275	7275	9000	11600
T-Bar Roof				375	375	500	500
SS Pkg				1450	1450	1935	1935
CORVETTE—V8—Equipment Schedule 2							
W.B. 104.5"; 5.7 Liter.							
Coupe 2D		YY22G	38365	11300	12850	16350	21200
Convertible 2D		YY32G	45295	13725	15525	19300	24600
Glass Roof Panel				250	250	335	335
Dual Roof Panels				300	300	400	400
Suspension Pkg				200	200	265	265
6-Spd Manual Trans				150	150	200	200

1999 CHEVROLET — (1,2or3)(C,GorY)1(MR226)–X–

Body	Type	VIN	List	Trade-In Fair	Good	Pvt-Party Good	Retail Excellent
METRO—3-Cyl.—Equipment Schedule 6							
W.B. 93.1"; 1.0 Liter.							
Coupe 2D		MR226	10488	750	1050	2100	3650
METRO—4-Cyl.—Equipment Schedule 6							
W.B. 93.1"; 1.3 Liter.							
LSi Sedan 4D		MR522	12187	1225	1700	2975	4725
LSi Coupe 2D		MR222	11285	925	1300	2500	4200

1999 CHEVROLET

Body	Type	VIN	List	Trade-In Fair	Trade-In Good	Pvt-Party Good	Retail Excellent
PRIZM—4-Cyl.—Equipment Schedule 6 W.B. 97.1"; 1.8 Liter.							
Sedan 4D		SK528	13828	**1975**	**2500**	**3975**	**6000**
LSi Sedan 4D		SK528	15269	**2125**	**2700**	**4175**	**6200**
CAVALIER—4-Cyl.—Equipment Schedule 5 W.B. 104.1"; 2.2 Liter, 2.4 Liter.							
Sedan 4D		JC524	13876	**1150**	**1600**	**2925**	**4725**
Coupe 2D		JC124	13776	**1150**	**1600**	**2925**	**4725**
RS Coupe 2D		JC124	15216	**1375**	**1900**	**3225**	**5075**
LS Sedan 4D		JF524	14921	**1525**	**2025**	**3375**	**5250**
Z24 Coupe 2D		JF12T	17261	**1700**	**2225**	**3625**	**5500**
Z24 Convertible 2D		JF32T	20861	**2825**	**3475**	**4950**	**7025**
MALIBU—V6—Equipment Schedule 5 W.B. 107.5"; 3.1 Liter.							
Sedan 4D		ND52M,J	17080	**1700**	**2225**	**3400**	**5075**
LS Sedan 4D		NE52M,J	19445	**2025**	**2575**	**3775**	**5500**
4-Cyl. 2.4 Liter		T		**(200)**	**(200)**	**(265)**	**(265)**
LUMINA—V6—Equipment Schedule 4 W.B. 107.5"; 3.1 Liter, 3.8 Liter.							
Sedan 4D		WL52M	18982	**2050**	**2625**	**3775**	**5475**
LS Sedan 4D		WL52M	20480	**2300**	**2875**	**4100**	**5825**
LTZ Sedan 4D		WN52K	20920	**2425**	**3000**	**4225**	**5975**
MONTE CARLO—V6—Equipment Schedule 4 W.B. 107.5"; 3.1 Liter, 3.8 Liter.							
LS Coupe 2D		WW12M	19070	**2275**	**2825**	**4025**	**5750**
Z34 Coupe 2D		WX12K	21095	**2725**	**3325**	**4550**	**6350**
CAMARO—V6—Equipment Schedule 4 W.B. 101.1"; 3.8 Liter.							
Coupe 2D		FP22K	19221	**4200**	**4975**	**6550**	**8825**
Convertible 2D		FP32K	24796	**5475**	**6400**	**8100**	**10550**
T-Bar Roof				**425**	**425**	**565**	**565**
Manual Trans				**(450)**	**(450)**	**(600)**	**(600)**
CAMARO—V8—Equipment Schedule 4 W.B. 101.1"; 5.7 Liter.							
Z28 Coupe 2D		FP22G	22996	**5400**	**6300**	**8000**	**10500**
Z28 Convertible 2D		FP32G	28385	**7150**	**8250**	**10100**	**12850**
T-Bar Roof				**425**	**425**	**565**	**565**
SS Pkg				**1550**	**1550**	**2065**	**2065**
CORVETTE—V8—Equipment Schedule 2 W.B. 104.5"; 5.7 Liter.							
Hard Top 2D		YY12G	39082	**10950**	**12425**	**15900**	**20800**
Coupe 2D		YY22G	39476	**12475**	**14125**	**17700**	**22800**
Convertible 2D		YY32G	45884	**15075**	**16975**	**20900**	**26300**
Glass Roof Panel				**250**	**250**	**335**	**335**
Dual Roof Panels				**300**	**300**	**400**	**400**
Suspension Pkg				**200**	**200**	**265**	**265**
6-Spd Manual Trans				**150**	**150**	**200**	**200**

2000 CHEVROLET — (1,2or3)(C,GorY)1(MR226)-Y-

Body	Type	VIN	List	Trade-In Fair	Trade-In Good	Pvt-Party Good	Retail Excellent
METRO—3-Cyl.—Equipment Schedule 6 W.B. 93.1"; 1.0 Liter.							
Coupe 2D		MR226	10680	**850**	**1225**	**2475**	**4250**
METRO—4-Cyl.—Equipment Schedule 6 W.B. 93.1"; 1.3 Liter.							
LSi Sedan 4D		MR522	12395	**1500**	**2000**	**3375**	**5250**
LSi Coupe 2D		MR222	11530	**1075**	**1500**	**2825**	**4625**
PRIZM—4-Cyl.—Equipment Schedule 6 W.B. 97.1"; 1.8 Liter.							
Sedan 4D		SK528	14246	**2375**	**2950**	**4500**	**6650**
LSi Sedan 4D		SK528	16272	**2575**	**3200**	**4750**	**6925**
CAVALIER—4-Cyl.—Equipment Schedule 5 W.B. 104.1"; 2.2 Liter, 2.4 Liter.							
Sedan 4D		JC524	14275	**1850**	**2375**	**3675**	**5525**
Coupe 2D		JC124	14175	**1825**	**2350**	**3650**	**5475**
LS Sedan 4D		JF524	15220	**2275**	**2850**	**4225**	**6100**
Z24 Coupe 2D		JF12T	17560	**2500**	**3100**	**4450**	**6400**
Z24 Convertible 2D		JF32T	21025	**3775**	**4525**	**6000**	**8125**
MALIBU—V6—Equipment Schedule 5 W.B. 107.0"; 3.1 Liter.							
Sedan 4D		ND52J	16995	**2225**	**2825**	**4050**	**5850**
LS Sedan 4D		NE52J	19625	**2575**	**3200**	**4450**	**6300**
LUMINA—V6—Equipment Schedule 4 W.B. 107.5"; 3.1 Liter.							

Body	Type	VIN	List	Trade-In Fair	Good	Pvt-Party Good	Retail Excellent
Sedan 4D		WL52J	19350	**2475**	**3075**	**4350**	**6125**

IMPALA—V6—Equipment Schedule 4
W.B. 110.5"; 3.4 Liter, 3.8 Liter.

Body	Type	VIN	List	Fair	Good	Good	Excellent
Sedan 4D		WF52E	19787	**3725**	**4450**	**6025**	**8250**
LS Sedan 4D		WH52K	22925	**4475**	**5275**	**6900**	**9275**

MONTE CARLO—V6—Equipment Schedule 4
W.B. 110.5"; 3.4 Liter, 3.8 Liter.

LS Coupe 2D		WW12E	20090	**4075**	**4850**	**6225**	**8300**
SS Coupe 2D		WX12K	22295	**5575**	**6500**	**8025**	**10350**

CAMARO—V6—Equipment Schedule 4
W.B. 101.1"; 3.8 Liter.

Coupe 2D		FP22K	19360	**5050**	**5925**	**7600**	**10050**
Convertible 2D		FP32K	25490	**6525**	**7550**	**9350**	**12050**
T-Bar Roof				**500**	**500**	**665**	**665**
Manual Trans				**(500)**	**(500)**	**(665)**	**(665)**

CAMARO—V8—Equipment Schedule 4
W.B. 101.1"; 5.7 Liter.

Z28 Coupe 2D		FP22G	23515	**6550**	**7575**	**9350**	**12050**
Z28 Convertible 2D		FP32G	28900	**8500**	**9700**	**11700**	**14700**
T-Bar Roof				**500**	**500**	**665**	**665**
SS Pkg				**1775**	**1775**	**2365**	**2365**

CORVETTE—V8—Equipment Schedule 2
W.B. 104.5"; 5.7 Liter.

Hard Top 2D		YY12G	39205	**14125**	**15950**	**19200**	**24000**
Coupe 2D		YY22G	40085	**15800**	**17800**	**21200**	**26300**
Convertible 2D		YY32G	46510	**18775**	**21050**	**24700**	**30300**
Glass Roof Panel				**275**	**275**	**365**	**365**
Dual Roof Panels				**350**	**350**	**465**	**465**
Suspension Pkg				**250**	**250**	**335**	**335**
6-Spd Manual Trans				**175**	**175**	**235**	**235**

2001 CHEVROLET — (1or2)(C,GorY)(MR522)-1-#

METRO—4-Cyl.—Equipment Schedule 6
W.B. 93.1"; 1.3 Liter.

LSi Sedan 4D		MR522	12915	**1925**	**2450**	**3950**	**6000**

PRIZM—4-Cyl.—Equipment Schedule 6
W.B. 97.0"; 1.8 Liter.

Sedan 4D		SK528	14460	**2850**	**3500**	**5125**	**7400**
LSi Sedan 4D		SK528	16525	**3100**	**3750**	**5425**	**7725**

CAVALIER—4-Cyl.—Equipment Schedule 5
W.B. 104.1"; 2.2 Liter, 2.4 Liter.

Sedan 4D		JC524	14480	**2300**	**2875**	**4300**	**6275**
Coupe 2D		JC124	14250	**2250**	**2825**	**4225**	**6175**
LS Sedan 4D		JF524	15375	**2825**	**3450**	**4900**	**6925**
Z24 Coupe 2D		JF12T	17665	**3025**	**3700**	**5175**	**7225**

MALIBU—V6—Equipment Schedule 5
W.B. 107.0"; 3.1 Liter.

Sedan 4D		ND52J	17595	**2850**	**3525**	**4850**	**6800**
LS Sedan 4D		NE52J	19875	**3275**	**3950**	**5325**	**7325**

LUMINA—V6—Equipment Schedule 4
W.B. 107.5"; 3.1 Liter.

Sedan 4D		WL52J	19490	**3025**	**3700**	**5075**	**7025**

IMPALA—V6—Equipment Schedule 4
W.B. 110.5"; 3.4 Liter, 3.8 Liter.

Sedan 4D		WF52E	20271	**4475**	**5275**	**7000**	**9475**
LS Sedan 4D		WH52K	23825	**5325**	**6225**	**8025**	**10600**

MONTE CARLO—V6—Equipment Schedule 4
W.B. 110.5"; 3.4 Liter, 3.8 Liter.

LS Coupe 2D		WW12E	20410	**4850**	**5700**	**7200**	**9425**
SS Coupe 2D		WX15K	23000	**6525**	**7550**	**9175**	**11650**

CAMARO—V6—Equipment Schedule 4
W.B. 101.1"; 3.8 Liter.

Coupe 2D		FP22K	19635	**6000**	**6950**	**8750**	**11400**
Convertible 2D		FP32K	25760	**7675**	**8800**	**10750**	**13650**
T-Bar Roof				**575**	**575**	**765**	**765**
RS				**250**	**250**	**335**	**335**
Manual Trans				**(525)**	**(525)**	**(700)**	**(700)**

CAMARO—V8—Equipment Schedule 4
W.B. 101.1"; 5.7 Liter.

Z28 Coupe 2D		FP22G	23935	**7775**	**8950**	**10850**	**13750**
Z28 Convertible 2D		FP32G	29325	**9950**	**11350**	**13400**	**16600**
T-Bar Roof				**575**	**575**	**765**	**765**
SS Pkg				**2000**	**2000**	**2665**	**2665**

Body	Type	VIN	List	Trade-In Fair	Trade-In Good	Pvt-Party Good	Retail Excellent
CORVETTE—V8—Equipment Schedule 2							
W.B. 104.5"; 5.7 Liter.							
Coupe 2D		YY22G	40475	17600	19800	23300	28500
Z06 Hard Top 2D		YY12G	47500	20075	22500	26100	31700
Convertible 2D		YY32G	47000	20950	23475	27200	32900
Glass Roof Panel		-------		300	300	400	400
Dual Roof Panels		-------		400	400	535	535
Suspension Pkg		-------		275	275	365	365
6-Spd Manual Trans		-------		200	200	265	265

2002 CHEVROLET — (1or2)(GorY)1(SK528)-2-#

Body	Type	VIN	List	Trade-In Fair	Trade-In Good	Pvt-Party Good	Retail Excellent
PRIZM—4-Cyl.—Equipment Schedule 6							
W.B. 97.0"; 1.8 Liter.							
Sedan 4D		SK528	14815	3425	4125	5875	8325
LSi Sedan 4D		SK528	16880	3700	4450	6200	8675
CAVALIER—4-Cyl.—Equipment Schedule 5							
W.B. 104.1"; 2.2 Liter, 2.4 Liter.							
Sedan 4D		JC524	15280	2875	3550	5075	7225
Coupe 2D		JC124	15180	2825	3450	4975	7125
LS Sedan 4D		JF524	16330	3450	4150	5700	7925
LS Coupe 2D		JS124	16230	3300	3975	5525	7725
LS Sport Sedan 4D		JF52F	17700	3625	4350	5925	8175
LS Sport Coupe 2D		JS12F	17600	3500	4200	5800	8025
Z24 Sedan 4D		JH52T	17900	3825	4575	6150	8450
Z24 Coupe 2D		JF12T	17800	3700	4450	6050	8300
MALIBU—V6—Equipment Schedule 5							
W.B. 107.0"; 3.1 Liter.							
Sedan 4D		ND52J	18120	3675	4425	5875	7950
LS Sedan 4D		NE52J	20325	4100	4875	6350	8500
IMPALA—V6—Equipment Schedule 5							
W.B. 110.5"; 3.4 Liter, 3.8 Liter.							
Sedan 4D		WF52E	20820	5375	6275	8200	10900
LS Sedan 4D		WH52K	24270	6300	7325	9300	12150
MONTE CARLO—V6—Equipment Schedule 4							
W.B. 110.5"; 3.4 Liter, 3.8 Liter.							
LS Coupe 2D		WW12E	20920	5775	6725	8375	10800
SS Coupe 2D		WX12K	23470	7650	8775	10500	13250
CAMARO—V6—Equipment Schedule 4							
W.B. 101.1"; 3.8 Liter.							
Coupe 2D		FP22K	20640	7150	8250	10150	12950
Convertible 2D		FP32K	26650	9025	10325	12300	15350
T-Bar Roof		-------		650	650	865	865
RS		-------		275	275	365	365
Manual Trans		-------		(550)	(550)	(735)	(735)
CAMARO—V8—Equipment Schedule 4							
W.B. 101.1"; 5.7 Liter.							
Z28 Coupe 2D		FP22G	24770	9250	10525	12550	15650
Z28 Convertible 2D		FP32G	30165	11600	13150	15300	18650
35th Annv Coupe 2D		FP22G	27270	10325	11725	13800	17050
35th Annv Conv 2D		FP32G	32665	12525	14150	16450	20000
T-Bar Roof		-------		650	650	865	865
SS Pkg		-------		2225	2225	2965	2965
CORVETTE—V8—Equipment Schedule 2							
W.B. 104.5"; 5.7 Liter.							
Coupe 2D		YY22G	41650	19500	21925	25500	30900
Z06 Hard Top 2D		YY12G	50350	22225	24825	28600	34300
Convertible 2D		YY32G	48175	23275	26100	29900	35800
Glass Roof Panel		-------		325	325	435	435
Dual Roof Panels		-------		450	450	600	600
Suspension Pkg		-------		300	300	400	400
6-Spd Manual Trans		-------		225	225	300	300

2003 CHEVROLET — (1or2)G1(JC52F)-3-#

Body	Type	VIN	List	Trade-In Fair	Trade-In Good	Pvt-Party Good	Retail Excellent
CAVALIER—4-Cyl.—Equipment Schedule 5							
W.B. 104.1"; 2.2 Liter.							
Sedan 4D		JC52F	15520	3650	4400	6075	8475
Coupe 2D		JC12F	15370	3575	4275	5975	8350
LS Sedan 4D		JF52F	16920	4250	5050	6775	9225
LS Coupe 2D		JF12F	16770	4100	4875	6600	9025
LS Sport Sedan 4D		JH52T	18120	4450	5250	7000	9475
LS Sport Coupe 2D		JH12F	17970	4350	5125	6875	9325
MALIBU—V6—Equipment Schedule 5							
W.B. 107.0"; 3.1 Liter.							

2003 CHEVROLET

Body · Type	VIN	List	Trade-In Fair	Trade-In Good	Pvt-Party Good	Retail Excellent
Sedan 4D	ND52J	18290	4650	5500	7075	9400
LS Sedan 4D	NE52J	20575	5100	6000	7600	9950
IMPALA—V6—Equipment Schedule 4						
W.B. 110.5"; 3.4 Liter, 3.8 Liter.						
Sedan 4D	WF52E	21350	6450	7475	9600	12650
LS Sedan 4D	WH52K	24460	7500	8600	10800	13950
MONTE CARLO—V6—Equipment Schedule 4						
W.B. 110.5"; 3.4 Liter, 3.8 Liter.						
LS Coupe 2D	WW12E	21350	6875	7950	9800	12550
SS Coupe 2D	WX12K	23665	8950	10225	12150	15150
CORVETTE—V8—Equipment Schedule 2						
W.B. 104.5"; 5.7 Liter.						
Coupe 2D	YY22G	43895	21625	24250	27900	33700
Z06 Hard Top 2D	YY12S	51155	24550	27450	31300	37300
Convertible 2D	YY32G	50370	25700	28700	32600	38800
50th Anniversary			3000	3000	4000	4000
Glass Roof Panel			350	350	465	465
Dual Roof Panels			500	500	665	665
Suspension Pkg			325	325	435	435
6-Spd Manual Trans			250	250	335	335

2004 CHEVROLET — (1,2orK)(GorL)1(TD526)-4-#

Body · Type	VIN	List	Trade-In Fair	Trade-In Good	Pvt-Party Good	Retail Excellent
AVEO—4-Cyl.—Equipment Schedule 6						
W.B. 97.6"; 1.6 Liter.						
SVM Sedan 4D	TD526	9995	3275	3950	5575	7875
SVM Hatchback 4D	TD626	9995	3275	3950	5575	7875
Sedan 4D	TD526	11690	3850	4600	6250	8625
Hatchback 4D	TD626	11690	3850	4600	6250	8625
LS Sedan 4D	TJ526	12585	4225	5025	6725	9125
LS Hatchback 4D	TJ626	12585	4225	5025	6725	9125
CAVALIER—4-Cyl.—Equipment Schedule 5						
W.B. 104.1"; 2.2 Liter.						
Sedan 4D	JC52F	15995	4650	5500	7275	9800
Coupe 2D	JC12F	15810	4525	5350	7125	9650
LS Sedan 4D	JF52F	17230	5275	6175	8000	10600
LS Coupe 2D	JF12F	17030	5150	6050	7825	10450
LS Sport Sedan 2D	JH52F	18635	5525	6450	8275	10900
LS Sport Coupe 2D	JH12F	18435	5375	6275	8100	10700
CLASSIC—4-Cyl.—Equipment Schedule 5						
W.B. 107.0" 2.2 Liter.						
Sedan 4D	ND52F	19380	5250	6150	8025	10700
MALIBU—V6—Equipment Schedule 5						
W.B. 106.3", 112.3" (MAXX); 3.5 Liter.						
Sedan 4D	ZS52F	18995	7350	8475	10500	13400
MAXX Hatchback 4D	ZS638	21725	7725	8875	10900	13850
LS Sedan 4D	ZT528	20995	7800	8975	10950	13950
LS MAXX H'Back 4D	ZT638	22225	7925	9125	11150	14150
LT Sedan 4D	ZU528	23495	8025	9225	11250	14250
LT MAXX H'Back 4D	ZU668	24725	8200	9375	11400	14450
4-Cyl. 2.2 Liter	F		(500)	(500)	(665)	(665)
IMPALA—V6—Equipment Schedule 4						
W.B. 110.5"; 3.4 Liter, 3.8 Liter.						
Sedan 4D	WF52E	22150	7800	8975	11200	14450
LS Sedan 4D	WH52K	25000	8950	10225	12500	15900
IMPALA—V6 Supercharged—Equipment Schedule 4						
W.B. 110.5"; 3.8 Liter.						
SS Sedan 4D	WP521	27995	12525	14150	16700	20500
MONTE CARLO—V6—Equipment Schedule 4						
W.B. 110.5"; 3.4 Liter, 3.8 Liter.						
LS Coupe 2D	WW12E	22075	8375	9575	11500	14450
SS Coupe 2D	WX12K	24225	10625	12075	14150	17350
MONTE CARLO—V6 Supercharged—Equipment Schedule 4						
W.B. 110.5"; 3.8 Liter.						
SS Coupe 2D	WZ121	27795	11650	13200	15350	18650
CORVETTE—V8—Equipment Schedule 2						
W.B. 104.5"; 5.7 Liter.						
Coupe 2D	YY22G	44535	23775	26575	30400	36200
Z06 Hard Top 2D	YY12S	52385	26975	30175	34000	40200
Convertible 2D	YY32G	51535	28225	31525	35400	41700
Commemorative Ed			600	600	800	800
Glass Roof Panel			375	375	500	500
Dual Roof Panels			550	550	735	735
Handling Pkg			350	350	465	465

2004 CHEVROLET

Body	Type	VIN	List	Trade-In Fair	Good	Pvt-Party Good	Retail Excellent
6-Spd Manual Trans				275	275	365	365

2005 CHEVROLET—(1,2orK)(GorL)1(TD526)-5-#

AVEO—4-Cyl.—Equipment Schedule 6
W.B. 97.6"; 1.6 Liter.

Body Type	VIN	List	Fair	Good	Pvt Good	Excellent
SVM Sedan 4D	TD526	9995	4100	4875	6575	9000
SVM Hatchback 4D	TD626	9995	4100	4875	6575	9000
LS Sedan 4D	TD526	11840	5125	6025	7775	10350
LS Hatchback 4D	TD626	11840	5125	6025	7775	10350
LT Sedan 4D	TG526	13110	5350	6250	8050	10600
LT Hatchback 4D	TG626	13335	5425	6350	8125	10700

COBALT—4-Cyl.—Equipment Schedule 5
W.B. 103.3"; 2.2 Liter.

Sedan 4D	AJ52F	15040	6475	7500	9700	12800
Coupe 2D	AJ12F	15240	6200	7325	9475	12550
LS Sedan 4D	AL52F	17335	7150	8250	10500	13700
LS Coupe 2D	AL12F	17335	7000	8075	10300	13500
LT Sedan 4D	AM52F	18760	7450	8550	10800	14000

COBALT—4-Cyl. Supercharged—Equipment Schedule 5
W.B. 103.3"; 2.0 Liter.

SS Coupe 2D	AP12P	21995				
Manual Trans						

CAVALIER—4-Cyl.—Equipment Schedule 5
W.B. 104.1"; 2.2 Liter.

Sedan 4D	JC52F	16025	5925	6875	8775	11550
Coupe 2D	JC12F	15825	5775	6725	8600	11350
LS Sedan 4D	JF52F	17705	6600	7625	9575	12400
LS Coupe 2D	JF12F	17505	6450	7450	9375	12200
LS Sport Sedan 4D	JH52F	19125	6850	7875	9850	12700
LS Sport Coupe 2D	JH12F	18925	6675	7700	9650	12500

CLASSIC—4-Cyl.—Equipment Schedule 5
W.B. 107.0"; 2.2 Liter.

Sedan 4D	ND52F	20130	6875	7925	10000	12950

MALIBU—V6—Equipment Schedule 5
W.B. 106.3", 112.3" (MAXX); 3.5 Liter.

Sedan 4D	ZS528	19710	9150	10425	12650	15900
MAXX Hatchback 4D	ZS628	21475	9575	10925	13150	16450
LS Sedan 4D	ZT528	21775	9650	11000	13200	16550
LS MAXX H'Back 4D	ZT628	21975	9800	11150	13400	16750
LT Sedan 4D	ZU548	24570	9850	11250	13500	16850
LT MAXX H'Back 4D	ZU648	25120	10050	11400	13650	17000
4-Cyl. 2.2 Liter	F		(500)	(500)	(665)	(665)

IMPALA—V6—Equipment Schedule 4
W.B. 110.5"; 3.4 Liter, 3.8 Liter.

Sedan 4D	WF52E	23130	9650	11000	13500	17050
LS Sedan 4D	WH52K	25990	10875	12325	14900	18650

IMPALA—V6 Supercharged—Equipment Schedule 4
W.B. 110.5"; 3.8 Liter.

SS Sedan 4D	WP521	29085	14900	16825	19500	23800

MONTE CARLO—V6—Equipment Schedule 4
W.B. 110.5"; 3.4 Liter, 3.8 Liter.

LS Coupe 2D	WW12E	23060	10100	11500	13750	17150
LT Coupe 2D	WX12E	25220	12525	14150	16600	20300

MONTE CARLO—V6 Supercharged—Equipment Schedule 4
W.B. 110.5"; 3.8 Liter.

SS Coupe 2D	WZ121	28885	13675	15425	17900	21700

CORVETTE—V8—Equipment Schedule 2
W.B. 105.8"; 6.0 Liter.

Coupe 2D	YY22U	44245				
Convertible 2D	YY34U	52245				
Glass Roof Panel						
Dual Roof Panels						
Suspension Pkg						
6-Spd Manual Trans						

CHRYSLER

1991 CHRYSLER — (1C3orZC2)–(J41K)–M–#

LeBARON—4-Cyl.—Equipment Schedule 4
W.B. 100.3"; 2.5 Liter.

Highline Coupe 2D	J41K	15389	450	625	1125	1925

1991 CHRYSLER

Body	Type	VIN	List	Trade-In Fair	Trade-In Good	Pvt-Party Good	Retail Excellent
Highline Conv 2D		J45K	18021	625	900	1475	2450
Manual Trans				**(175)**	**(175)**	**(235)**	**(235)**
4-Cyl. 2.5 Liter Turbo		J	......	0	0	0	0
V6 3.0 Liter		3	......	200	200	265	265

LeBARON—V6—Equipment Schedule 4
W.B. 100.3", 103.3" (Sed); 3.0 Liter.

Sedan 4D		A563	16915	725	1050	1650	2725
Premium LX Coupe 2D		J513	16580	475	700	1225	2075
Premium LX Conv 2D		J553	20235	850	1225	1975	3125
GTC Coupe 2D		J413	16655	575	825	1375	2325
GTC Convertible 2D		J453	19160	750	1075	1750	2825
Manual Trans				**(100)**	**(100)**	**(135)**	**(135)**
4-Cyl. 2.5 Liter		K	......	**(150)**	**(150)**	**(200)**	**(200)**
4-Cyl. 2.5 Liter		J	......	0	0	0	0

NEW YORKER—V6—Equipment Schedule 4
W.B. 104.3"; 3.3 Liter.

| Salon Sedan 4D | | C66R | 18990 | 675 | 975 | 1575 | 2625 |

FIFTH AVE—V6—Equipment Schedule 4
W.B. 109.3"; 3.3 Liter, 3.8 Liter.

| Sedan 4D | | Y66R | 23405 | 1000 | 1425 | 2275 | 3575 |

IMPERIAL—V6—Equipment Schedule 2
W.B. 109.3"; 3.3 Liter, 3.8 Liter.

| Sedan 4D | | Y56L | 27515 | 1225 | 1725 | 2750 | 4225 |

TC—V6—Equipment Schedule 2
W.B. 93.0"; 3.0 Liter.

| Convertible 2D | | S120 | 37570 | 2550 | 3150 | 4725 | 6925 |

1992 CHRYSLER — (1or3)C3–(A46K)–N–#

LeBARON—4-Cyl.—Equipment Schedule 4
W.B. 100.5", 103.5" (Sed); 2.5 Liter.

Sedan 4D		A46K	15253	650	925	1525	2550
Landau Sedan 4D		A56K	16195	675	975	1575	2625
Coupe 2D		U41K	14787	525	750	1275	2150
Convertible 2D		U45K	18631	725	1050	1700	2800
Manual Trans				**(175)**	**(175)**	**(235)**	**(235)**
4-Cyl. 2.5 Liter Turbo		J	......	0	0	0	0
V6 3.0 Liter		3	......	200	200	265	265

LeBARON—V6—Equipment Schedule 4
W.B. 100.5", 103.5" (Sed); 3.0 Liter.

LX Sedan 4D		A763	16624	850	1200	1950	3100
LX Coupe 2D		U513	16894	575	825	1400	2375
LX Convertible 2D		U553	20930	1000	1425	2300	3625
GTC Coupe 2D		U413	17356	675	950	1575	2625
GTC Convertible 2D		U453	20177	875	1225	2025	3225
4-Cyl. 2.5 Liter Turbo		J	......	0	0	0	0

NEW YORKER—V6—Equipment Schedule 4
W.B. 104.5"; 3.3 Liter.

| Salon Sedan 4D | | C66R | 20134 | 800 | 1150 | 1850 | 3000 |

FIFTH AVE—V6—Equipment Schedule 4
W.B. 109.5"; 3.3 Liter, 3.8 Liter.

| Sedan 4D | | V66R | 23906 | 1200 | 1650 | 2700 | 4175 |

IMPERIAL—V6—Equipment Schedule 2
W.B. 109.6"; 3.8 Liter.

| Sedan 4D | | V56L | 29063 | 1525 | 2025 | 3125 | 4700 |

1993 CHRYSLER — (1or3)C3–(U41K)–P–#

LeBARON—4-Cyl.—Equipment Schedule 4
W.B. 100.6", 103.5" (Sed); 2.5 Liter.

Coupe 2D		U41K	15594	600	850	1425	2425
Convertible 2D		U45K	19569	825	1175	1950	3125
LE Sedan 4D		A36K	15774	750	1050	1725	2825
Manual Trans				**(225)**	**(225)**	**(300)**	**(300)**
V6 3.0 Liter		3	......	225	225	300	300

LeBARON—V6—Equipment Schedule 4
W.B. 100.6", 103.5" (Sed); 3.0 Liter.

Landau Sedan 4D		A563	17689	900	1250	2025	3275
LX Coupe 2D		U513	17351	675	975	1600	2675
LX Convertible 2D		U553	21675	1125	1575	2625	4100
GTC Coupe 2D		U413	18040	775	1100	1800	2950
GTC Convertible 2D		U453	21015	975	1375	2250	3575

CONCORDE—V6—Equipment Schedule 4
W.B. 113.0"; 3.3 Liter.

| Sedan 4D | | L56T | 19718 | 1100 | 1550 | 2600 | 4075 |

Body	Type	VIN	List	Trade-In Fair	Good	Pvt-Party Good	Retail Excellent
V6 3.5 Liter		F		125	125	165	165

NEW YORKER—V6—Equipment Schedule 4
W.B. 104.5"; 3.3 Liter.

| Salon Sedan 4D | | C66R | 20000 | 925 | 1300 | 2150 | 3450 |

FIFTH AVE—V6—Equipment Schedule 4
W.B. 109.6"; 3.3 Liter, 3.8 Liter.

| Sedan 4D | | V66R | 22723 | 1450 | 1950 | 3050 | 4600 |

IMPERIAL—V6—Equipment Schedule 2
W.B. 109.6"; 3.8 Liter.

| Sedan 4D | | V56L | 29991 | 1825 | 2350 | 3525 | 5200 |

1994 CHRYSLER — (1or3)C3-(A363)-R-#

LeBARON—V6—Equipment Schedule 4
W.B. 100.6", 103.5" (Sed); 3.0 Liter.

LE Sedan 4D		A363	17226	925	1300	2150	3475
Landau Sedan 4D		A563	18438	1000	1400	2325	3675
GTC/LX Convertible 2D		U453	18239	1075	1525	2600	4100
4-Cyl. 2.5 Liter		K		(200)	(200)	(265)	(265)

CONCORDE—V6—Equipment Schedule 4
W.B. 113.0"; 3.3 Liter.

| Sedan 4D | | L56T | 21017 | 1275 | 1775 | 2875 | 4450 |
| V6 3.5 Liter | | F | | 200 | 200 | 265 | 265 |

NEW YORKER—V6—Equipment Schedule 4
W.B. 113.0"; 3.5 Liter.

| Sedan 4D | | D46F | 26126 | 1325 | 1825 | 2900 | 4450 |

LHS—V6—Equipment Schedule 2
W.B. 113.0"; 3.5 Liter.

| Sedan 4D | | D56F | 30868 | 1750 | 2275 | 3450 | 5125 |

1995 CHRYSLER — (1,2or4)C3-(U42Y)-S-#

SEBRING—4-Cyl.—Equipment Schedule 4
W.B. 103.7"; 2.0 Liter.

LX Coupe 2D		U42Y	17636	1275	1775	3025	4775
Manual Trans				(325)	(325)	(435)	(435)
V6 2.5 Liter		H,N		275	275	365	365

SEBRING—V6—Equipment Schedule 4
W.B. 103.7"; 2.5 Liter.

| LXi Coupe 2D | | U52H,N | 20548 | 1700 | 2225 | 3575 | 5425 |

CIRRUS—V6—Equipment Schedule 4
W.B. 108.0"; 2.5 Liter.

LX Sedan 4D		J56H,N	17970	1225	1700	2825	4375
LXi				100	100	135	135
4-Cyl. 2.4 Liter		X		(250)	(250)	(335)	(335)

LeBARON—V6—Equipment Schedule 4
W.B. 100.6"; 3.0 Liter.

| GTC/LX Convertible 2D | | U453 | 18709 | 1225 | 1725 | 2825 | 4425 |

CONCORDE—V6—Equipment Schedule 4
W.B. 113.0"; 3.3 Liter.

| Sedan 4D | | D56T | 21085 | 1525 | 2025 | 3225 | 4875 |
| V6 3.5 Liter | | F | | 225 | 225 | 300 | 300 |

NEW YORKER—V6—Equipment Schedule 2
W.B. 113.0"; 3.5 Liter.

| Sedan 4D | | C46F | 26191 | 1625 | 2125 | 3325 | 5000 |

LHS—V6—Equipment Schedule 2
W.B. 113.0"; 3.5 Liter.

| Sedan 4D | | C56F | 30190 | 2075 | 2650 | 3900 | 5700 |

1996 CHRYSLER — (1,2or4)C3-(U42Y)-T-#

SEBRING—4-Cyl.—Equipment Schedule 4
W.B. 103.7", 106.0" (Conv); 2.0 Liter, 2.4 Liter.

LX Coupe 2D		U42Y	18418	1525	2025	3400	5300
JX Convertible 2D		L45X	19995	2450	3050	4550	6675
Manual Trans				(375)	(375)	(500)	(500)
V6 2.5 Liter		H,N		325	325	435	435

SEBRING—V6—Equipment Schedule 4
W.B. 103.7", 106.0" (Conv); 2.5 Liter.

| LXi Coupe 2D | | U52N | 20685 | 1975 | 2525 | 3975 | 6000 |
| JXi Convertible 2D | | L55H | 25210 | 2825 | 3475 | 5050 | 7225 |

CIRRUS—V6—Equipment Schedule 4
W.B. 108.0"; 2.5 Liter.

| LX Sedan 4D | | J56H | 18895 | 1475 | 1975 | 3150 | 4800 |
| LXi | | | | 100 | 100 | 135 | 135 |

Body Type	VIN	List	Trade-In Fair	Good	Pvt-Party Good	Retail Excellent
4-Cyl. 2.4 Liter	X		(275)	(275)	(365)	(365)
CONCORDE—V6—Equipment Schedule 4						
W.B. 113.0"; 3.3 Liter.						
LX Sedan 4D	D56T	19995	1825	2350	3625	5350
LXi			100	100	135	135
V6 3.5 Liter	F		250	250	335	335
NEW YORKER—V6—Equipment Schedule 2						
W.B. 113.0"; 3.5 Liter.						
Sedan 4D	C46F	27895	2000	2550	3800	5575
LHS—V6—Equipment Schedule 2						
W.B. 113.0"; 3.5 Liter.						
Sedan 4D	C56F	30850	2500	3100	4450	6325

1997 CHRYSLER — (1,2,3or4)C3–(U42Y)–V–#

Body Type	VIN	List	Trade-In Fair	Good	Pvt-Party Good	Retail Excellent
SEBRING—4-Cyl.—Equipment Schedule 4						
W.B. 103.7", 106.0" (Conv); 2.0 Liter, 2.4 Liter.						
LX Coupe 2D	U42Y	18541	1800	2325	3800	5850
JX Convertible 2D	L45X	21560	2825	3450	5075	7300
JXi Convertible 2D	L55X	25195	2850	3525	5150	7400
Manual Trans			(400)	(400)	(535)	(535)
V6 2.5 Liter	H,N		350	350	465	465
SEBRING—V6—Equipment Schedule 4						
W.B. 103.7"; 2.5 Liter.						
LXi Coupe 2D	U52N	21555	2275	2850	4450	6575
CIRRUS—V6—Equipment Schedule 4						
W.B. 108.0"; 2.5 Liter.						
LX Sedan 4D	J56H	19265	1800	2325	3550	5275
LXi			100	100	135	135
4-Cyl. 2.4 Liter	X		(300)	(300)	(400)	(400)
CONCORDE—V6—Equipment Schedule 4						
W.B. 113.0"; 3.5 Liter.						
LX Sedan 4D	D56F	20985	2175	2775	4025	5850
LXi			100	100	135	135
LHS—V6—Equipment Schedule 2						
W.B. 113.0"; 3.5 Liter.						
Sedan 4D	C56F	30850	2975	3650	5050	7075

1998 CHRYSLER — (1,2,3or4)C3–(U49Y)–W–#

Body Type	VIN	List	Trade-In Fair	Good	Pvt-Party Good	Retail Excellent
SEBRING—4-Cyl.—Equipment Schedule 4						
W.B. 103.7", 106.0" (Conv); 2.0 Liter, 2.4 Liter.						
LX Coupe 2D	U49Y	18850	2100	2675	4275	6450
JX Convertible 2D	L45X	21985	3200	3875	5600	8000
JXi Convertible 2D	L55X	25575	3300	3975	5725	8125
Limited			300	300	400	400
Manual Trans			(425)	(425)	(565)	(565)
V6 2.5 Liter	H,N		375	375	500	500
SEBRING—V6—Equipment Schedule 4						
W.B. 103.7"; 2.5 Liter.						
LXi Coupe 2D	U59N	21310	2650	3275	4925	7225
CIRRUS—V6—Equipment Schedule 4						
W.B. 108.0"; 2.5 Liter.						
LXi Sedan 4D	J56H	19995	2300	2875	4225	6100
CONCORDE—V6—Equipment Schedule 4						
W.B. 113.0"; 2.7 Liter.						
LX Sedan 4D	D46R	21855	2500	3100	4475	6450
LXi			100	100	135	135
V6 3.2 Liter			250	250	335	335

1999 CHRYSLER — (1,2,3or4)C3–(U42Y)–X–#

Body Type	VIN	List	Trade-In Fair	Good	Pvt-Party Good	Retail Excellent
SEBRING—4-Cyl.—Equipment Schedule 4						
W.B. 103.7"; 2.0 Liter.						
LX Coupe 2D	U42Y	19390	2475	3075	4775	7100
Manual Trans			(450)	(450)	(600)	(600)
V6 2.5 Liter	N		250	250	335	335
SEBRING—V6—Equipment Schedule 4						
W.B. 103.7", 106.0" (Conv); 2.5 Liter.						
LXi Coupe 2D	U52N	21860	3075	3725	5500	7925
JX Convertible 2D	L45H	24505	3900	4650	6475	9025
JXi Convertible 2D	L55H	26820	4300	5100	6950	9575
Limited			300	300	400	400
CIRRUS—V6—Equipment Schedule 4						
W.B. 108.0"; 2.5 Liter.						

Body	Type	VIN	List	Trade-In Fair	Good	Pvt-Party Good	Retail Excellent
LXi Sedan 4D		J56H	19995	2750	3375	4775	6800

CONCORDE—V6—Equipment Schedule 4
W.B. 113.0"; 2.7 Liter.

LX Sedan 4D		D46R	22115	2975	3650	5100	7150
LXi				100	100	135	135
V6 3.2 Liter		J		250	250	335	335

300M—V6—Equipment Schedule 2
W.B. 113.0"; 3.5 Liter.

Sedan 4D		E66G	29445	4975	5850	7575	10050

LHS—V6—Equipment Schedule 2
W.B. 113.0"; 3.5 Liter.

Sedan 4D		C56G	29445	3925	4675	6300	8625

2000 CHRYSLER — (1,2,3or4)C3-(U42N)-Y-#

SEBRING—V6—Equipment Schedule 4
W.B. 103.7", 106.0" (Conv); 2.5 Liter.

LX Coupe 2D		U42N	19635	3250	3925	5800	8375
LXi Coupe 2D		U52N	22015	3725	4450	6375	9000
JX Convertible 2D		L45H	24790	4625	5450	7425	10200
JXi Convertible 2D		L55H	27105	5075	5950	7950	10750
Limited				325	325	435	435

CIRRUS—4-Cyl.—Equipment Schedule 4
W.B. 108.0"; 2.0 Liter, 2.4 Liter.

LX Sedan 4D		J46B	17675	2600	3225	4550	6450
Manual Trans				(450)	(450)	(600)	(600)

CIRRUS—V6—Equipment Schedule 4
W.B. 108.0"; 2.5 Liter.

LXi Sedan 4D		J56H	20480	3425	4125	5625	7750

CONCORDE—V6—Equipment Schedule 4
W.B. 113.0"; 2.7 Liter, 3.2 Liter.

LX Sedan 4D		D46R	22550	3675	4425	6000	8225
LXi Sedan 4D		D36J	26480	4225	5000	6600	8900

300M—V6—Equipment Schedule 2
W.B. 113.0"; 3.5 Liter.

Sedan 4D		E66G	29690	5975	6925	8750	11450

LHS—V6—Equipment Schedule 2
W.B. 113.0"; 3.5 Liter.

Sedan 4D		C56G	28695	4750	5575	7325	9800

2001 CHRYSLER — 1C(4or8)-(Y4BB)-1-#

PT CRUISER—4-Cyl.—Equipment Schedule 4
W.B. 103.0"; 2.4 Liter.

Sport Wagon 4D		Y4BB	18325	4300	5100	6700	9000
Limited Sport Wag 4D		Y4BB	20685	5025	5900	7550	9950
Touring				250	250	335	335

SEBRING—4-Cyl.—Equipment Schedule 4
W.B. 103.7", 108.0" (Sed); 2.4 Liter.

LX Sedan 4D		L46G	18520	3275	3950	5375	7450
LX Coupe 2D		G42G	20495	3550	4250	6250	8975
V6 2.7/3.0 Liter		R,H		550	550	735	735

SEBRING—V6—Equipment Schedule 4
W.B. 103.7", 106.0" (Conv), 108.0" (Sed); 2.7 Liter, 3.0 Liter.

LXi Sedan 4D		L66R	21405	4225	5000	6625	8950
LXi Coupe 2D		G62H	22885	4475	5275	7350	10200
LX Convertible 2D		L55U	24945	5450	6375	8500	11500
LXi Convertible 2D		L65U	27405	5950	6900	9075	12150
Limited Convertible 2D		L65U	29490	6500	7525	9750	12900

CONCORDE—V6—Equipment Schedule 4
W.B. 113.0"; 2.7 Liter, 3.2 Liter.

LX Sedan 4D		D46R	22995	4500	5325	7025	9450
LXi Sedan 4D		D36J	27240	5150	6050	7750	10300

300M—V6—Equipment Schedule 2
W.B. 113.0"; 3.5 Liter.

Sedan 4D		E66G	30170	7125	8225	10200	13050

LHS—V6—Equipment Schedule 2
W.B. 113.0"; 3.5 Liter.

Sedan 4D		C56G	29210	5750	6700	8550	11250

PROWLER—V6—Equipment Schedule 1
W.B. 113.3"; 3.5 Liter.

Roadster 2D		W65G	45400	19875	22300	26800	33300

Body	Type	VIN	List	Trade-In Fair	Good	Pvt-Party Good	Retail Excellent

2002 CHRYSLER–(1,2,3or4)C(3,4or8)–(Y48B)–2–#

PT CRUISER–4-Cyl.—Equipment Schedule 4
W.B. 103.0"; 2.4 Liter.

Sport Wagon 4D	Y48B	18395	**4950**	**5825**	**7600**	**10150**
Touring Sport Wag 4D	Y58B	19540	**5450**	**6375**	**8200**	**10800**
Limited Sport Wag 4D	Y68B	21655	**5775**	**6725**	**8525**	**11200**
Dream Cruiser Wag 4D	Y68B	23395	**6375**	**7400**	**9250**	**12000**
Woodie Edition		......	**275**	**275**	**365**	**365**

SEBRING–4-Cyl.—Equipment Schedule 4
W.B. 103.7", 106.0" (Conv), 108.0" (Sed); 2.4 Liter.

LX Sedan 4D	L46X	18535	**4100**	**4875**	**6425**	**8650**
LX Coupe 2D	G42G	20615	**4250**	**5050**	**7200**	**10200**
LX Convertible 2D	L55G	23905	**6425**	**7425**	**9750**	**13000**
V6 2.7/3.0 Liter	R,H	......	**600**	**600**	**800**	**800**

SEBRING–V6—Equipment Schedule 4
W.B. 103.7", 106.0" (Conv), 108.0" (Sed); 2.7 Liter, 3.0 Liter.

LXi Sedan 4D	L56R	20875	**5150**	**6050**	**7750**	**10300**
LXi Coupe 2D	G52H	23130	**5350**	**6250**	**8500**	**11600**
LXi Convertible 2D	L55H	26755	**6925**	**8000**	**10450**	**13700**
GTC Convertible 2D	L75R	25875	**6375**	**7400**	**9700**	**12950**
Limited Convertible 2D	L65K	29390	**7550**	**8675**	**11050**	**14500**

CONCORDE–V6—Equipment Schedule 4
W.B. 113.0"; 2.7 Liter, 3.5 Liter.

LX Sedan 4D	D46R	22995	**5525**	**6450**	**8275**	**10900**
LXi Sedan 4D	D36M	25600	**6250**	**7250**	**9125**	**11850**
Limited Sedan 4D	D56G	28495	**6675**	**7700**	**9600**	**12350**

300M–V6—Equipment Schedule 2
W.B. 113.0"; 3.5 Liter.

Sedan 4D	E66G	28995	**8525**	**9750**	**11900**	**15050**
Special Sedan 4D	E76K	32595	**8825**	**10100**	**12200**	**15350**

PROWLER–V6—Equipment Schedule 1
W.B. 113.0"; 3.5 Liter.

Roadster 2D	W65G	45400	**22125**	**24725**	**29300**	**36000**

2003 CHRYSLER–(1,2,3or4)C(3,4or8)–(Y48B)–3–

PT CRUISER–4-Cyl.—Equipment Schedule 4
W.B. 103.0"; 2.4 Liter.

Sport Wagon 4D	Y48B	18815	**5800**	**6750**	**8675**	**11500**
Touring Sport Wag 4D	Y58B	19940	**6325**	**7350**	**9300**	**12150**
Limited Sport Wag 4D	Y68B	22180	**6700**	**7725**	**9750**	**12650**
Woodie Edition		......	**300**	**300**	**400**	**400**

PT CRUISER–4-Cyl. HO Turbo—Equipment Schedule 4
W.B. 103.0"; 2.4 Liter.

GT Sport Wagon 4D	Y78C	23170	**8725**	**10000**	**11950**	**14850**
Dream Cruiser		......	**600**	**600**	**800**	**800**

SEBRING–4-Cyl.—Equipment Schedule 4
W.B. 103.7", 106.0" (Conv), 108.0" (Sed); 2.4 Liter.

LX Sedan 4D	L46X	19930	**5125**	**6025**	**7675**	**10150**
LX Coupe 2D	G42G	21560	**5150**	**6050**	**8375**	**11600**
LX Convertible 2D	L45X	24560	**7550**	**8675**	**11150**	**14650**
V6 2.7/3.0 Liter	U,R	......	**650**	**650**	**865**	**865**

SEBRING–V6—Equipment Schedule 4
W.B. 103.7", 106.0" (Conv), 108.0" (Sed); 2.7 Liter, 3.0 Liter.

LXi Sedan 4D	L56R	21295	**6275**	**7275**	**9150**	**11900**
LXi Coupe 2D	G52H	23835	**6425**	**7425**	**9850**	**13250**
GTC Convertible 2D	L75R	26160	**7500**	**8600**	**11100**	**14600**
LXi Convertible 2D	L55T	27410	**8150**	**9325**	**11850**	**15400**
Limited Convertible 2D	L65K	30045	**8775**	**10050**	**12600**	**16250**

CONCORDE–V6—Equipment Schedule 4
W.B. 113.0"; 2.7 Liter, 3.5 Liter.

LX Sedan 4D	D46R	23510	**6700**	**7725**	**9700**	**12600**
LXi Sedan 4D	D36M	26240	**7525**	**8650**	**10650**	**13700**
Limited Sedan 4D	D56G	29135	**7925**	**9125**	**11150**	**14150**

300M–V6—Equipment Schedule 2
W.B. 113.0"; 3.5 Liter.

Sedan 4D	E66G	29245	**10175**	**11600**	**13850**	**17300**
Special Sedan 4D	E76K	32895	**10525**	**11975**	**14250**	**17750**

2004 CHRYSLER–(1,2,3or4)C(3,4or8)–(Y48B)–4–#

PT CRUISER–4-Cyl.—Equipment Schedule 4
W.B. 103.0"; 2.4 Liter.

Body	Type	VIN	List	Trade-In Fair	Trade-In Good	Pvt-Party Good	Retail Excellent
Sport Wagon 4D		Y48B	19515	6825	7875	9850	12700
Touring Sport Wag 4D		Y58B	20585	7400	8500	10500	13450
Limited Sport Wag 4D		Y68B	22825	7775	8950	10950	13950
4-Cyl. 2.4L Turbo		8	------	900	900	1200	1200

PT CRUISER—4-Cyl. HO Turbo—Equipment Schedule 4
W.B. 103.0"; 2.4 Liter.

Body	Type	VIN	List	Fair	Good	Good	Excellent
GT Sport Wagon 4D		Y78G	26245	10050	11400	13350	16300

SEBRING—4-Cyl.—Equipment Schedule 4
W.B. 103.7", 106.0" (Conv), 108.0" (Sed); 2.4 Liter.

Sedan 4D		Y46X	19360	6175	7175	8875	11400
Coupe 2D		G42G	22305	6275	7275	9750	13200
Convertible 2D		L45J	25570	8550	9800	12400	16100
LX Sedan 4D		L46X	19500	6400	7425	9125	11700
LX Convertible 2D		L45X	25215	8900	10175	12800	16550
V6 2.7 Liter		T	------	700	700	935	935

SEBRING—V6—Equipment Schedule 4
W.B. 103.7", 106.0" (Conv), 108.0" (Sed); 2.7 Liter, 3.0 Liter.

LXi Sedan 4D		L56R	21840	7675	8800	10750	13700
LXi Convertible 2D		L55T	28140	9575	10925	13600	17400
GTC Convertible 2D		L75R	27045	8825	10100	12700	16450
Touring Sedan 4D		L55T	21200	7400	8500	10800	14050
Touring Convertible 2D		L55T	28370	9800	11150	13800	17650
Limited Sedan 4D		L66R	23490	8275	9475	11800	15200
Limited Coupe 2D		G52H	24580	8500	9700	12300	16000
Limited Convertible 2D		L65R	31180	10225	11650	14350	18250

CONCORDE—V6—Equipment Schedule 4
W.B. 113.0"; 2.7 Liter, 3.5 Liter.

LX Sedan 4D		D46R	24130	8150	9325	11400	14400
LXi Sedan 4D		D36M	26860	9075	10375	12450	15650
Limited Sedan 4D		D56G	29755	9475	10825	12950	16200

300M—V6—Equipment Schedule 2
W.B. 113.0"; 3.5 Liter.

| Sedan 4D | | E66G | 29865 | 12325 | 13975 | 16350 | 20000 |
| Special Sedan 4D | | E76K | 33295 | 12700 | 14350 | 16800 | 20500 |

CROSSFIRE—V6—Equipment Schedule 1
W.B. 94.5"; 3.2 Liter.

| Coupe 2D | | N69L | 35570 | 14900 | 16825 | 19800 | 24300 |

2005 CHRYSLER — (1,2,3or4)C(4or8)-(Y48B)-5

PT CRUISER—4-Cyl.—Equipment Schedule 4
W.B. 103.0"; 2.4 Liter.

Sport Wagon 4D		Y48B	15820	8075	9275	11200	14150
Convertible 2D		Y45X	20820	9900	11300	13350	16550
Touring Sport Wag 4D		Y58B	17070	8675	9950	11950	15000
Touring Convertible 2D		Y55X	24490	10275	11700	13750	17000
Limited Sport Wag 4D		Y68B	18730	9125	10425	12400	15500
4-Cyl. 2.4L Turbo		E	------	950	950	1265	1265

PT CRUISER—4-Cyl. HO Turbo—Equipment Schedule 4
W.B. 103.0"; 2.4 Liter.

| GT Sport Wagon 4D | | Y78S | 23935 | 11550 | 13100 | 15050 | 18150 |
| GT Convertible 2D | | Y75S | 28860 | 13100 | 14850 | 16900 | 20200 |

SEBRING—4-Cyl.—Equipment Schedule 4
W.B. 103.7", 106.0" (Conv), 108.0" (Sed); 2.4 Liter.

Sedan 4D		L46X	19975	7925	9125	10950	13750
Coupe 2D		G42G	22770	7650	8800	11500	15250
Convertible 2D		L45X	26035	10125	11550	14400	18550
V6 2.7 Liter		R	------	750	750	1000	1000

SEBRING—V6—Equipment Schedule 4
W.B. 103.7", 106.0" (Conv), 108.0" (Sed); 2.7 Liter, 3.0 Liter.

GTC Convertible 2D		L75R	27510	10375	11825	14700	18800
Touring Sedan 4D		L56R	20695	9250	10525	13050	16650
Touring Convertible 2D		L55T	28835	11450	13000	15900	20200
Limited Sedan 4D		L66R	23985	10175	11600	14100	17850
Limited Coupe 2D		G52H	25045	10050	11400	14250	18350
Limited Convertible 2D		L65R	31645	11145	13925	16550	20900
TSi Sedan 4D		L56R	24455	11600	13200	15400	18900

300—V6—Equipment Schedule 2
W.B. 120.0"; 2.7 Liter, 3.5 Liter.

Sedan 4D		A43R	24695	16625	18725	20600	24000
Touring Sedan 4D		A53G	27720	18975	21250	23300	27000
Touring AWD Sedan 4D		K53G	29995	19800	22225	24300	28000
Signature Series			------	500	500	665	665
Limited			------	1000	1000	1335	1335

Body	Type	VIN	List	Trade-In Fair	Trade-In Good	Pvt-Party Good	Retail Excellent
300C—V8 HEMI—Equipment Schedule 2							
W.B. 120.0"; 5.7 Liter, 6.1 Liter.							
Sedan 4D		A63H	33495	24450	27350	29600	33800
AWD Sedan 4D		K63H	34820	25325	28325	30600	34800
SRT-8 Sedan 4D		A73W	39995				
CROSSFIRE—V6—Equipment Schedule 1							
W.B. 94.5"; 3.2 Liter.							
Coupe 2D		N69L	29920	15175	17125	20300	24900
Roadster 2D		N65L	34960	17550	19700	22900	27700
Limited Coupe 2D		N69L	35695	17375	19500	22700	27500
Limited Roadster 2D		N65L	39995	19700	22125	25300	30500
CROSSFIRE—V6 Supercharged—Equipment Schedule 1							
W.B. 94.5"; 3.2 Liter.							
SRT-6 Coupe 2D		N79N	45695	22900	25600	28900	34300
SRT-6 Roadster 2D		N75N	49995	25225	28225	31600	37200

DAEWOO

1999 DAEWOO — KLA(TA226)-X-#

Body	Type	VIN	List	Trade-In Fair	Trade-In Good	Pvt-Party Good	Retail Excellent
LANOS—4-Cyl.—Equipment Schedule 6							
W.B. 99.0"; 1.6 Liter.							
S Hatchback 2D		TA226	9699	750	1050	1825	3050
S Sedan 4D		TA526	10399	825	1175	2025	3300
SE Hatchback 2D		TB226	11300	900	1250	2125	3475
SE Sedan 4D		TB526	11600	925	1300	2200	3575
SX Hatchback 2D		TC226	11669	900	1275	2175	3525
SX Sedan 4D		TC526	11969	925	1300	2225	3625
NUBIRA—4-Cyl.—Equipment Schedule 5							
W.B. 101.0"; 2.0 Liter.							
SX Sedan 4D		JA52Z	13300	900	1275	2250	3675
SX Hatchback 4D		JA62Z	13300	875	1225	2175	3625
SX Wagon 4D		JA82Z	13900	925	1300	2375	3925
CDX Sedan 4D		JB52Z	14610	1025	1450	2550	4100
CDX Hatchback 4D		JB62Z	14610	1000	1400	2500	4050
CDX Wagon 4D		JB82Z	15210	1050	1475	2600	4175
LEGANZA—4-Cyl.—Equipment Schedule 5							
W.B. 105.1"; 2.2 Liter.							
SE Sedan 4D		VB692	15590	900	1250	2500	4275
SX Sedan 4D		VA692	16910	1150	1600	2925	4750
CDX Sedan 4D		VA692	18910	1425	1925	3300	5175

2000 DAEWOO — KLA(TA226)-Y-#

Body	Type	VIN	List	Trade-In Fair	Trade-In Good	Pvt-Party Good	Retail Excellent
LANOS—4-Cyl.—Equipment Schedule 6							
W.B. 99.2"; 1.6 Liter.							
S Hatchback 2D		TA226	9699	850	1200	2150	3575
S Sedan 4D		TA526	10479	950	1325	2425	4000
SE Hatchback 2D		TB226	11230	1025	1450	2550	4125
SX Sedan 4D		TC526	12049	1075	1525	2650	4250
NUBIRA—4-Cyl.—Equipment Schedule 5							
W.B. 101.2"; 2.0 Liter.							
SE Sedan 4D		JC52Z	12885	1100	1550	2700	4325
CDX Sedan 4D		JB52Z	14755	1275	1775	2950	4600
CDX Wagon 4D		JB82Z	15355	1325	1825	3000	4650
LEGANZA—4-Cyl.—Equipment Schedule 5							
W.B. 105.1"; 2.2 Liter.							
SE Sedan 4D		VB692	14865	1050	1475	2850	4750
SX Sedan 4D		VA692	17065	1425	1925	3375	5300
CDX Sedan 4D		VA692	19060	1775	2300	3750	5750

2001 DAEWOO — KLA(TA226)-1-#

Body	Type	VIN	List	Trade-In Fair	Trade-In Good	Pvt-Party Good	Retail Excellent
LANOS—4-Cyl.—Equipment Schedule 6							
W.B. 99.2"; 1.6 Liter.							
S Hatchback 2D		TA226	10329	1000	1425	2600	4275
S Sedan 4D		TA526	11229	1125	1575	2800	4475
Sport Hatchback 2D		TB226	13429	1225	1725	2950	4650
NUBIRA—4-Cyl.—Equipment Schedule 5							
W.B. 101.2"; 2.0 Liter.							
SE Sedan 4D		JC52Z	13329	1400	1900	3150	4875
CDX Sedan 4D		JB52Z	15429	1650	2150	3425	5175
CDX Wagon 4D		JB82Z	16029	1700	2225	3500	5250

Body Type	VIN	List	Trade-In Fair	Good	Pvt-Party Good	Retail Excellent
LEGANZA—4-Cyl.—Equipment Schedule 5						
W.B. 105.1"; 2.2 Liter.						
SE Sedan 4D	VB692	15429	1325	1825	3325	5375
SX Sedan 4D	VA692	17929	1800	2325	3875	6000
CDX Sedan 4D	VA692	19429	2175	2775	4350	6525

2002 DAEWOO — KLA(TA226)-2-#

Body Type	VIN	List	Trade-In Fair	Good	Pvt-Party Good	Retail Excellent
LANOS—4-Cyl.—Equipment Schedule 6						
W.B. 99.2"; 1.6 Liter.						
S Hatchback 2D	TA226	10644	1250	1750	3050	4875
S Sedan 4D	TA526	11544	1450	1950	3275	5125
Sport Hatchback 2D	TB226	13494	1600	2100	3450	5300
NUBIRA—4-Cyl.—Equipment Schedule 5						
W.B. 101.2"; 2.0 Liter.						
SE Sedan 4D	JC52Z	13844	1825	2350	3675	5550
CDX Wagon 4D	JB82Z	15294	2150	2750	4100	6000
LEGANZA—4-Cyl.—Equipment Schedule 5						
W.B. 105.1"; 2.2 Liter.						
SE Sedan 4D	VB692	16094	1800	2325	3975	6225
CDX Sedan 4D	VA692	19094	2725	3350	5100	7450
DAEWOO — No Longer Produced						

DAIHATSU

1991 DAIHATSU — JD1(EG112)-M-#

Body Type	VIN	List	Trade-In Fair	Good	Pvt-Party Good	Retail Excellent
CHARADE—4-Cyl.—Equipment Schedule 6						
W.B. 92.1"; 1.3 Liter.						
SE Sedan 4D	EG112	9768	450	650	1225	2075
SE Hatchback 2D	FG112	8968	350	475	950	1700
SX Hatchback 2D	EG122	10719	475	700	1250	2150
3-Cyl. 1.0 Liter	0		(100)	(100)	(135)	(135)

1992 DAIHATSU — JD1(EG112)-N-#

Body Type	VIN	List	Trade-In Fair	Good	Pvt-Party Good	Retail Excellent
CHARADE—4-Cyl.—Equipment Schedule 6						
W.B. 92.1"; 1.3 Liter.						
SE Sedan 4D	EG112	9074	500	725	1300	2275
SE Hatchback 2D	FG112	7774	375	500	1025	1825
SX Hatchback 2D	EG122	10274	525	750	1375	2375
3-Cyl. 1.0 Liter	0		(100)	(100)	(135)	(135)

DODGE

1991 DODGE — (1orJ)B(3or4)-(U14A)-M-#

Body Type	VIN	List	Trade-In Fair	Good	Pvt-Party Good	Retail Excellent
COLT—4-Cyl.—Equipment Schedule 6						
W.B. 93.9"; 1.5 Liter.						
Hatchback 2D	U14A	8247	400	525	1050	1825
GL Hatchback 2D	U24A	9143	400	525	1050	1825
COLT VISTA—4-Cyl.—Equipment Schedule 6						
W.B. 103.3", 103.5" (AWD); 2.0 Liter.						
Wagon 4D	G39V	13695	625	900	1500	2550
AWD Wagon 4D	H49V	14462	625	900	1550	2625
SHADOW—4-Cyl.—Equipment Schedule 5						
W.B. 97.0"; 2.2 Liter, 2.5 Liter.						
America H'Back 2D	P24D	9786	325	425	850	1525
America H'Back 4D	P28D	10086	350	475	900	1600
Highline H'Back 2D	P44D	10702	350	475	900	1600
Highline H'Back 4D	P48D	11002	350	475	900	1600
Highline Conv 2D	P45K	14758	500	725	1225	2100
ES Hatchback 2D	P64K	12178	400	550	1025	1775
ES Hatchback 4D	P68K	12478	400	550	1025	1775
ES Convertible 2D	P65K	15871	500	725	1225	2100
4-Cyl. 2.5 Liter Turbo	J		50	50	65	65
DAYTONA—4-Cyl.—Equipment Schedule 4						
W.B. 97.0"; 2.5 Liter.						
Hatchback 2D	G24K	12428	625	900	1525	2550
ES Hatchback 2D	G44K	14011	675	950	1575	2625
4-Cyl. 2.5 Liter Turbo	J		0	0	0	0
V6 3.0 Liter	3		200	200	265	265

1991 DODGE

Body	Type	VIN	List	Trade-In Fair	Trade-In Good	Pvt-Party Good	Retail Excellent
DAYTONA—4-Cyl. Turbo—Equipment Schedule 4							
W.B. 97.0"; 2.5 Liter.							
Shelby H'Back 2D		G74J	15752	750	1075	1800	2925
DAYTONA—V6—Equipment Schedule 4							
W.B. 97.0"; 3.0 Liter.							
IROC H'Back 2D		G743	15687	800	1150	1875	3050
4-Cyl. 2.5 Liter Turbo		J		0	0	0	0
SPIRIT—4-Cyl.—Equipment Schedule 5							
W.B. 103.3"; 2.5 Liter.							
Sedan 4D		A46K	12852	375	500	925	1600
LE Sedan 4D		A56K	14211	400	550	1000	1700
4-Cyl. 2.5 Liter Turbo		J		0	0	0	0
V6 3.0 Liter				150	200	200	200
SPIRIT—4-Cyl. Turbo—Equipment Schedule 5							
W.B. 103.3"; 2.2 Liter, 2.5 Liter.							
ES Sedan 4D		A76J	17341	450	650	1150	1950
R/T Sedan 4D		A66A	18285	725	1050	1650	2725
Manual Trans (R/T)				0	0	0	0
V6 3.0 Liter (ES)		3		200	200	265	265
DYNASTY—V6—Equipment Schedule 4							
W.B. 104.3"; 3.0 Liter, 3.3 Liter.							
Sedan 4D		C46U	16741	525	750	1275	2150
LE Sedan 4D		C56U	17341	600	875	1425	2375
4-Cyl. 2.5 Liter		K		(150)	(150)	(200)	(200)
MONACO—V6—Equipment Schedule 4							
W.B. 106.0"; 3.0 Liter.							
LE Sedan 4D		B56U	16461	250	350	1000	2000
ES Sedan 4D		B66U	18060	325	425	1150	2200
STEALTH—V6—Equipment Schedule 4							
W.B. 97.2"; 3.0 Liter.							
Coupe 2D		D44S	18484	900	1250	2625	4500
ES Coupe 2D		D54B	20121	1025	1450	2850	4800
R/T Coupe 2D		D64B	24483	1375	1875	3375	5425
Auto Trans				100	100	135	135
STEALTH—V6 Turbo—Equipment Schedule 4							
W.B. 97.2"; 3.0 Liter.							
R/T AWD Coupe 2D		E74C	30438	2375	2950	4650	6975

1992 DODGE — (1,3orJ)B3–(U14A)–N–#

Body	Type	VIN	List	Trade-In Fair	Trade-In Good	Pvt-Party Good	Retail Excellent
COLT—4-Cyl.—Equipment Schedule 6							
W.B. 93.9"; 1.5 Liter.							
Hatchback 2D		U14A	8640	400	600	1175	2025
GL Hatchback 2D		U24A	9304	400	600	1175	2025
SHADOW—4-Cyl.—Equipment Schedule 5							
W.B. 97.0"; 2.2 Liter, 2.5 Liter.							
America Hatchback 2D		P24D	10210	350	475	975	1700
America Hatchback 4D		P28D	10610	400	525	1025	1775
Highline Hatchback 2D		P44D	11188	400	525	1025	1775
Highline Hatchback 4D		P48D	11588	400	525	1025	1775
Highline Convertible 2D		P45K	15399	550	800	1400	2375
ES Hatchback 2D		P64K	12854	425	625	1125	1950
ES Hatchback 4D		P68K	13176	450	625	1175	2000
ES Convertible 2D		P65K	16627	550	800	1400	2375
4-Cyl. 2.5 Liter Turbo		J		50	50	65	65
V6 3.0 Liter		3		100	100	135	135
DAYTONA—4-Cyl.—Equipment Schedule 4							
W.B. 97.2"; 2.5 Liter.							
Hatchback 2D		W24K	12918	750	1050	1750	2875
ES Hatchback 2D		W44K	13959	775	1100	1800	2950
V6 3.0 Liter		3		200	200	265	265
DAYTONA—V6—Equipment Schedule 4							
W.B. 97.2"; 3.0 Liter.							
IROC Hatchback 2D		W743	15254	925	1300	2175	3475
4-Cyl. 2.5 Liter Turbo		J		0	0	0	0
DAYTONA—4-Cyl. Turbo—Equipment Schedule 4							
W.B. 97.2"; 2.2 Liter.							
IROC R/T Hatchback 2D		W64A	20093	1200	1650	2725	4225
Manual Trans				0	0	0	0
SPIRIT—4-Cyl.—Equipment Schedule 5							
W.B. 103.5"; 2.5 Liter.							
Sedan 4D		A46K	13343	400	600	1075	1825
LE Sedan 4D		A56K	14846	450	625	1125	1925
4-Cyl. 2.5 Liter Turbo		J		0	0	0	0

Body	Type	VIN	List	Trade-In Fair	Trade-In Good	Pvt-Party Good	Retail Excellent
	V6 3.0 Liter	3	......	175	175	235	235
SPIRIT—4-Cyl. Turbo—Equipment Schedule 5							
W.B. 103.5"; 2.2 Liter, 2.5 Liter.							
	ES Sedan 4D	A76J	16314	525	750	1300	2200
	R/T Sedan 4D	A66A	19159	850	1200	1950	3100
	Manual Trans (R/T)			0	0	0	0
	V6 3.0 Liter	3	......	200	200	265	265
DYNASTY—V6—Equipment Schedule 4							
W.B. 104.5"; 3.0 Liter, 3.3 Liter.							
	Sedan 4D	C463	17006	625	900	1475	2450
	LE Sedan 4D	C563	17658	700	1025	1650	2725
	4-Cyl. 2.5 Liter	K		(150)	(150)	(200)	(200)
MONACO—V6—Equipment Schedule 4							
W.B. 106.0"; 3.0 Liter.							
	LE Sedan 4D	B56U	16673	250	350	1100	2200
	ES Sedan 4D	B66U	18883	325	425	1225	2450
STEALTH—V6—Equipment Schedule 4							
W.B. 97.2"; 3.0 Liter.							
	Coupe 2D	D44S	19525	1050	1450	2925	4950
	ES Coupe 2D	D54B	21428	1225	1675	3225	5300
	R/T Coupe 2D	D64B	25868	1650	2150	3775	5975
	Auto Trans			100	100	135	135
STEALTH—V6 Turbo—Equipment Schedule 2							
W.B. 97.2"; 3.0 Liter.							
	R/T AWD Coupe 2D	E74C	32096	2800	3425	5250	7775
	Manual Trans			0	0	0	0
VIPER—V10—Equipment Schedule 2							
W.B. 96.2"; 8.0 Liter.							
	RT/10 Roadster 2D	R65E	50700	15275	17225	21700	27900
	Manual Trans			0	0	0	0

1993 DODGE — (1,3orJ)B3—(A11A)—P—#

Body	Type	VIN	List	Trade-In Fair	Trade-In Good	Pvt-Party Good	Retail Excellent
COLT—4-Cyl.—Equipment Schedule 6							
W.B. 96.1", 98.4" (4D); 1.5 Liter, 1.8 Liter.							
	Sedan 2D	A11A	9260	525	750	1375	2425
	Sedan 4D	A26A	10902	625	900	1625	2775
	GL Sedan 2D	A21A	10376	575	825	1500	2600
	GL Sedan 4D	A46C	12260	675	975	1725	2925
SHADOW—4-Cyl.—Equipment Schedule 5							
W.B. 97.2"; 2.2 Liter, 2.5 Liter.							
	Hatchback Sedan 4D	P28D	11023	400	575	1100	1950
	Hatchback 2D	P24D	10623	400	525	1050	1875
	Highline Convertible 2D	P25K	15970	625	900	1575	2675
	ES Hatchback Sedan 4D	P68K	12146	500	725	1300	2250
	ES Hatchback 2D	P64K	11746	475	700	1275	2200
	ES Convertible 2D	P65K	16109	625	900	1575	2675
	V6 3.0 Liter	3		125	125	165	165
DAYTONA—4-Cyl.—Equipment Schedule 4							
W.B. 97.2"; 2.5 Liter.							
	Hatchback 2D	W24K	13500	900	1275	2100	3400
	ES Hatchback 2D	W44K	14556	950	1325	2200	3525
	V6 3.0 Liter	3		225	225	300	300
DAYTONA—V6—Equipment Schedule 4							
W.B. 97.2"; 3.0 Liter.							
	IROC Hatchback 2D	W743	15980	1175	1625	2700	4225
DAYTONA—4-Cyl. Turbo—Equipment Schedule 4							
W.B. 97.2"; 2.2 Liter.							
	IROC R/T Hatchback 2D	W64A	21436	1525	2025	3150	4750
SPIRIT—4-Cyl.—Equipment Schedule 5							
W.B. 103.5"; 2.5 Liter.							
	Highline Sedan 4D	A46K	13455	450	650	1175	2000
	ES Sedan 4D	A56K	15827	600	875	1450	2425
	4-Cyl. Flexible Fuel	V		0	0	0	0
	V6 3.0 Liter	3		225	225	300	300
INTREPID—V6—Equipment Schedule 4							
W.B. 113.0"; 3.3 Liter.							
	Sedan 4D	D46T	18005	900	1250	2125	3450
	ES Sedan 4D	D56T	19520	1075	1500	2575	4075
	V6 3.5 Liter	F		175	175	235	235
DYNASTY—V6—Equipment Schedule 4							
W.B. 104.5"; 3.0 Liter, 3.3 Liter.							
	Sedan 4D	C463	17535	725	1050	1700	2800
	LE Sedan 4D	C563	18228	825	1175	1925	3100

Body	Type	VIN	List	Trade-In Fair	Good	Pvt-Party Good	Retail Excellent
	4-Cyl. 2.5 Liter	K	......	**(175)**	**(175)**	**(235)**	**(235)**
STELLTH—V6—Equipment Schedule 4							
W.B. 97.2"; 3.0 Liter.							
Coupe 2D		M44H	20863	**1225**	**1700**	**3325**	**5475**
ES Coupe 2D		M54J	22974	**1475**	**1975**	**3650**	**5875**
R/T Coupe 2D		M64J	27766	**1975**	**2525**	**4275**	**6625**
Auto Trans				**125**	**125**	**165**	**165**
STEALTH—V6 Turbo—Equipment Schedule 2							
W.B. 97.2"; 3.0 Liter.							
R/T AWD Coupe 2D		N74K	34350	**3325**	**4000**	**5975**	**8650**
VIPER—V10—Equipment Schedule 2							
W.B. 96.2"; 8.0 Liter.							
RT/10 Roadster 2D		R65E	53300	**16050**	**18050**	**22600**	**29000**

1994 DODGE — (1,3orJ)B3–(A11A)–R–#

Body	Type	VIN	List	Trade-In Fair	Good	Pvt-Party Good	Retail Excellent
COLT—4-Cyl.—Equipment Schedule 5							
W.B. 96.1", 98.4" (4D); 1.5 Liter, 1.8 Liter.							
Sedan 2D		A11A	10779	**600**	**875**	**1575**	**2725**
Sedan 4D		A36C	13248	**750**	**1050**	**1850**	**3100**
ES Sedan 2D		A21A	11876	**675**	**950**	**1700**	**2875**
ES Sedan 4D		A46C	13824	**800**	**1150**	**1975**	**3275**
SHADOW—4-Cyl.—Equipment Schedule 5							
W.B. 97.2"; 2.2 Liter, 2.5 Liter.							
Hatchback Sedan 4D		P28D	11452	**450**	**650**	**1250**	**2200**
Hatchback 2D		P24D	11052	**425**	**625**	**1200**	**2100**
ES H'Back Sedan 4D		P68K	12614	**600**	**850**	**1500**	**2600**
ES Hatchback 2D		P64K	12214	**575**	**825**	**1475**	**2550**
V6 3.0 Liter		3		**150**	**150**	**200**	**200**
SPIRIT—4-Cyl.—Equipment Schedule 5							
W.B. 103.5"; 2.5 Liter.							
Sedan 4D		A46K	14154	**500**	**725**	**1300**	**2250**
4-Cyl. Flexible Fuel		V		**0**	**0**	**0**	**0**
V6 3.0 Liter		3		**275**	**275**	**365**	**365**
INTREPID—V6—Equipment Schedule 4							
W.B. 113.0"; 3.3 Liter.							
Sedan 4D		D46T	19106	**1000**	**1425**	**2525**	**4075**
ES Sedan 4D		D56T	21423	**1225**	**1725**	**2850**	**4450**
V6 3.5 Liter		F		**200**	**200**	**265**	**265**
STEALTH—V6—Equipment Schedule 4							
W.B. 97.2"; 3.0 Liter.							
Coupe 2D		M44H	23659	**1500**	**2000**	**3725**	**6075**
R/T Coupe 2D		M64J	26404	**1800**	**2325**	**4125**	**6525**
Auto Trans				**150**	**150**	**200**	**200**
STEALTH—V6 Turbo—Equipment Schedule 2							
W.B. 97.2"; 3.0 Liter.							
R/T AWD Coupe 2D		N74K	38785	**3850**	**4600**	**6725**	**9600**
VIPER—V10—Equipment Schedule 2							
W.B. 96.2"; 8.0 Liter.							
RT/10 Roadster 2D		R65E	58500	**16775**	**18875**	**23600**	**30100**

1995 DODGE — (1,4orJ)B3–(S27C)–S–#

Body	Type	VIN	List	Trade-In Fair	Good	Pvt-Party Good	Retail Excellent
NEON—4-Cyl.—Equipment Schedule 6							
W.B. 104.0"; 2.0 Liter.							
Sedan 4D		S27C	12195	**500**	**725**	**1275**	**2200**
Highline Sedan 4D		S47C	12443	**600**	**875**	**1475**	**2500**
Highline Coupe 2D		S41C	12443	**575**	**825**	**1425**	**2425**
Sport Sedan 4D		S67C	14393	**750**	**1050**	**1750**	**2875**
Sport Coupe 2D		S61C	14693	**850**	**1200**	**1975**	**3175**
Competition Pkg				**50**	**50**	**65**	**65**
AVENGER—4-Cyl.—Equipment Schedule 4							
W.B. 103.7"; 2.0 Liter.							
Coupe 2D		U42Y	16309	**1125**	**1575**	**2825**	**4525**
Manual Trans				**(325)**	**(325)**	**(435)**	**(435)**
AVENGER—V6—Equipment Schedule 4							
W.B. 103.7"; 2.5 Liter.							
ES Coupe 2D		U52H,N	18260	**1525**	**2025**	**3350**	**5150**
SPIRIT—4-Cyl.—Equipment Schedule 5							
W.B. 103.5"; 2.5 Liter.							
Sedan 4D		A46K	14828	**575**	**825**	**1475**	**2550**
V6 3.0 Liter		3		**300**	**300**	**400**	**400**
STRATUS—4-Cyl.—Equipment Schedule 5							
W.B. 108.0"; 2.0 Liter, 2.4 Liter.							
Sedan 4D		J46C	15230	**750**	**1050**	**1800**	**3000**

1995 DODGE

Body	Type	VIN	List	Trade-In Fair	Trade-In Good	Pvt-Party Good	Retail Excellent
STRATUS—V6—Equipment Schedule 4							
W.B. 108.0"; 2.5 Liter.							
ES Sedan 4D		J56H,N	17800	**1100**	**1550**	**2725**	**4375**
Manual Trans				(325)	(325)	(435)	(435)
4-Cyl. 2.0L/2.4 Liter		C,X		(250)	(250)	(335)	(335)
INTREPID—V6—Equipment Schedule 4							
W.B. 113.0"; 3.3 Liter.							
Sedan 4D		D46T	19232	**1175**	**1625**	**2825**	**4450**
ES Sedan 4D		D56T	21379	**1500**	**2000**	**3200**	**4875**
V6 3.3L Flexible Fuel		U		0	0	0	0
V6 3.5 Liter		F		225	225	300	300
STEALTH—V6—Equipment Schedule 4							
W.B. 97.2"; 3.0 Liter.							
Hatchback 2D		M84H	24572	**1825**	**2350**	**4275**	**6775**
R/T Hatchback 2D		M44J	27756	**2150**	**2750**	**4675**	**7250**
Auto Trans				175	175	235	235
STEALTH—V6 Turbo—Equipment Schedule 2							
W.B. 97.2"; 3.0 Liter.							
R/T AWD H'Back 2D		N74K	39178	**4450**	**5250**	**7550**	**10600**
VIPER—V10—Equipment Schedule 2							
W.B. 96.2"; 8.0 Liter.							
RT/10 Roadster 2D		R65E	60500	**17700**	**19875**	**24600**	**31200**

1996 DODGE — (1,4orJ)B3–(S27C)–T–#

Body	Type	VIN	List	Trade-In Fair	Trade-In Good	Pvt-Party Good	Retail Excellent
NEON—4-Cyl.—Equipment Schedule 6							
W.B. 104.0"; 2.0 Liter.							
Sedan 4D		S27C	11730	**600**	**875**	**1525**	**2625**
Coupe 2D		S22C	11230	**575**	**825**	**1475**	**2550**
Highline Sedan 4D		S47C	12735	**700**	**1025**	**1750**	**2925**
Highline Coupe 2D		S42C	12535	**675**	**975**	**1675**	**2825**
Sport Sedan 4D		S67C	14165	**850**	**1225**	**2050**	**3350**
Sport Coupe 2D		S62C	13965	**975**	**1350**	**2275**	**3650**
AVENGER—4-Cyl.—Equipment Schedule 4							
W.B. 103.7"; 2.0 Liter.							
Coupe 2D		U41B	17008	**1325**	**1825**	**3175**	**5050**
Manual Trans				(375)	(375)	(500)	(500)
AVENGER—V6—Equipment Schedule 4							
W.B. 103.7"; 2.5 Liter.							
ES Coupe 2D		U51H,N	19190	**1800**	**2325**	**3725**	**5700**
Manual Trans				(375)	(375)	(500)	(500)
4-Cyl. 2.0 Liter		B		(225)	(225)	(300)	(300)
STRATUS—4-Cyl.—Equipment Schedule 5							
W.B. 108.0"; 2.0 Liter, 2.4 Liter.							
Sedan 4D		J46C	15820	**875**	**1225**	**2150**	**3525**
STRATUS—V6—Equipment Schedule 4							
W.B. 108.0"; 2.5 Liter.							
ES Sedan 4D		J56H,N	18720	**1300**	**1800**	**3050**	**4800**
Manual Trans				(375)	(375)	(500)	(500)
4-Cyl. 2.0L/2.4 Liter		C,X		(275)	(275)	(365)	(365)
INTREPID—V6—Equipment Schedule 4							
W.B. 113.0"; 3.3 Liter.							
Sedan 4D		D46T	18995	**1400**	**1900**	**3150**	**4900**
ES Sedan 4D		D56F	22810	**1775**	**2300**	**3575**	**5350**
V6 3.5 Liter		F		250	250	335	335
STEALTH—V6—Equipment Schedule 4							
W.B. 97.2"; 3.0 Liter.							
Hatchback 2D		M84J	25651	**2200**	**2800**	**4825**	**7525**
R/T Hatchback 2D		M54J	29207	**2575**	**3175**	**5250**	**8025**
Auto Trans				200	200	265	265
STEALTH—V6 Turbo—Equipment Schedule 2							
W.B. 97.2"; 3.0 Liter.							
R/T AWD H'Back 2D		N74K	35355	**5100**	**6000**	**8425**	**11750**
VIPER—V10—Equipment Schedule 2							
W.B. 96.2"; 8.0 Liter.							
RT/10 Roadster 2D		R65E	63100	**18625**	**20950**	**25700**	**32500**
GTS Coupe 2D		R69E	66700	**20650**	**23075**	**28200**	**35500**

1997 DODGE — (1or4)B3–(S27C)–V–#

Body	Type	VIN	List	Trade-In Fair	Trade-In Good	Pvt-Party Good	Retail Excellent
NEON—4-Cyl.—Equipment Schedule 6							
W.B. 104.0"; 2.0 Liter.							
Sedan 4D		S27C	12430	**750**	**1075**	**1875**	**3125**
Coupe 2D		S22C	12230	**725**	**1050**	**1825**	**3050**
Highline Sedan 4D		S47C	13170	**850**	**1225**	**2100**	**3450**

1997 DODGE

Body	Type	VIN	List	Trade-In Fair	Trade-In Good	Pvt-Party Good	Retail Excellent
Highline Coupe 2D		S42C	12970	**825**	**1175**	**2025**	**3350**
AVENGER—V6—Equipment Schedule 4							
W.B. 103.7"; 2.5 Liter.							
Coupe 2D		U42N	18857	**1925**	**2450**	**3950**	**6025**
ES Coupe 2D		U52N	19971	**2075**	**2650**	**4175**	**6250**
Manual Trans		Y		**(400)**	**(400)**	**(535)**	**(535)**
4-Cyl. 2.0 Liter				**(250)**	**(250)**	**(335)**	**(335)**
STRATUS—4-Cyl.—Equipment Schedule 5							
W.B. 108.0"; 2.0 Liter, 2.4 Liter.							
Sedan 4D		J46C	16545	**1050**	**1475**	**2600**	**4175**
STRATUS—V6—Equipment Schedule 4							
W.B. 108.0"; 2.5 Liter.							
ES Sedan 4D		J56H	19390	**1600**	**2100**	**3450**	**5275**
Manual Trans				**(400)**	**(400)**	**(535)**	**(535)**
4-Cyl. 2.0L/2.4 Liter		C		**(300)**	**(300)**	**(400)**	**(400)**
INTREPID—V6—Equipment Schedule 4							
W.B. 113.0"; 3.3 Liter.							
Sedan 4D		D46T	19955	**1725**	**2250**	**3550**	**5325**
ES Sedan 4D		D56F	23460	**2100**	**2675**	**4000**	**5875**
V6 3.5 Liter		F		**250**	**250**	**335**	**335**
VIPER—V10—Equipment Schedule 2							
W.B. 96.2"; 8.0 Liter.							
GTS Coupe 2D		R69E	69300	**21825**	**24450**	**29600**	**37100**

1998 DODGE — (1,2or4)B3–(S47C)–W–#

Body	Type	VIN	List	Trade-In Fair	Trade-In Good	Pvt-Party Good	Retail Excellent
NEON—4-Cyl.—Equipment Schedule 6							
W.B. 104.0"; 2.0 Liter.							
Highline Sedan 4D		S47C	12855	**1050**	**1475**	**2575**	**4150**
Highline Coupe 2D		S42C	12655	**1025**	**1450**	**2525**	**4075**
Competition Sedan 4D		S27C	14660	**1450**	**1950**	**3100**	**4750**
Competition Coupe 2D		S22Y	14480	**1400**	**1900**	**3050**	**4675**
R/T or Sport Pkg				**50**	**50**	**65**	**65**
AVENGER—V6—Equipment Schedule 4							
W.B. 103.7"; 2.5 Liter.							
Coupe 2D		U42N	18685	**2225**	**2825**	**4425**	**6625**
ES Coupe 2D		U52N	20525	**2425**	**3000**	**4650**	**6875**
Manual Trans				**(425)**	**(425)**	**(565)**	**(565)**
4-Cyl. 2.0 Liter		Y		**(275)**	**(275)**	**(365)**	**(365)**
STRATUS—4-Cyl.—Equipment Schedule 5							
W.B. 108.0"; 2.0 Liter, 2.4 Liter.							
Sedan 4D		J46C	16425	**1300**	**1800**	**3000**	**4675**
STRATUS—V6—Equipment Schedule 4							
W.B. 108.0"; 2.5 Liter.							
ES Sedan 4D		J56H	19000	**1950**	**2475**	**3900**	**5875**
4-Cyl. 2.4 Liter		X		**(325)**	**(325)**	**(435)**	**(435)**
INTREPID—V6—Equipment Schedule 4							
W.B. 113.0"; 2.7 Liter, 3.2 Liter.							
Sedan 4D		D46M	20235	**2000**	**2550**	**3950**	**5925**
ES Sedan 4D		D56J	23015	**2400**	**2975**	**4450**	**6475**
VIPER—V10—Equipment Schedule 2							
W.B. 96.2"; 8.0 Liter.							
RT/10 Roadster 2D		R65E	64700	**20650**	**23175**	**28200**	**35300**
GTS Coupe 2D		R69E	67900	**23075**	**25800**	**31000**	**38600**

1999 DODGE — (1,2or4)B3–(S47C)–X–#

Body	Type	VIN	List	Trade-In Fair	Trade-In Good	Pvt-Party Good	Retail Excellent
NEON—4-Cyl.—Equipment Schedule 6							
W.B. 104.0"; 2.0 Liter.							
Highline Sedan 4D		S47C	13320	**1350**	**1850**	**3000**	**4675**
Highline Coupe 2D		S42C	13120	**1300**	**1800**	**2975**	**4625**
Competition Sedan 4D		S27C	14985	**1825**	**2350**	**3600**	**5325**
Competition Coupe 2D		S22Y	14805	**1800**	**2325**	**3550**	**5250**
R/T or Sport Pkg				**50**	**50**	**65**	**65**
AVENGER—V6—Equipment Schedule 4							
W.B. 103.7"; 2.5 Liter.							
Coupe 2D		U42N	19665	**2600**	**3225**	**4925**	**7275**
ES Coupe 2D		U52N	20975	**2825**	**3475**	**5225**	**7600**
Manual Trans				**(450)**	**(450)**	**(600)**	**(600)**
4-Cyl. 2.0 Liter		Y		**(300)**	**(300)**	**(400)**	**(400)**
STRATUS—4-Cyl.—Equipment Schedule 5							
W.B. 108.0"; 2.0 Liter, 2.4 Liter.							
Sedan 4D		J46C	16865	**1650**	**2150**	**3450**	**5250**
STRATUS—V6—Equipment Schedule 4							
W.B. 108.0"; 2.5 Liter.							

1999 DODGE

Body	Type	VIN	List	Trade-In Fair	Good	Pvt-Party Good	Retail Excellent
ES Sedan 4D		J56H	19495	2350	2925	4450	6550
INTREPID—V6—Equipment Schedule 4							
W.B. 113.0"; 2.7 Liter, 3.2 Liter.							
Sedan 4D		D46R	20495	2425	3000	4475	6575
ES Sedan 4D		D56J	23340	2850	3500	5025	7175
VIPER—V10—Equipment Schedule 2							
W.B. 96.2"; 8.0 Liter.							
RT/10 Roadster 2D		R65E	66425	22125	24725	29900	37200
GTS Coupe 2D		R69E	68925	24725	27650	32900	40600
Competition Group				2050	2050	2735	2735

2000 DODGE — (1,2or4)B3–(S46C)–Y–#

NEON—4-Cyl.—Equipment Schedule 4							
W.B. 105.0"; 2.0 Liter.							
Highline Sedan 4D		S46C	13890	1500	2000	3325	5150
ES Sedan 4D		S56C	14680	2025	2575	3925	5850
AVENGER—V6—Equipment Schedule 4							
W.B. 103.7"; 2.5 Liter.							
Coupe 2D		U42N	18840	3100	3750	5625	8175
ES Coupe 2D		U52N	21130	3375	4075	5950	8525
STRATUS—4-Cyl.—Equipment Schedule 5							
W.B. 108.0"; 2.0 Liter, 2.4 Liter.							
SE Sedan 4D		J46C	17525	2125	2700	4075	6050
STRATUS—V6—Equipment Schedule 4							
W.B. 108.0"; 2.5 Liter.							
ES Sedan 4D		J56H	20655	2975	3650	5250	7525
INTREPID—V6—Equipment Schedule 4							
W.B. 113.0"; 2.7 Liter, 3.2 Liter, 3.5 Liter.							
Sedan 4D		D46R	20950	3025	3700	5300	7575
ES Sedan 4D		D56J	23550	3550	4250	5925	8250
R/T Sedan 4D		D76V	24995	4950	5825	7525	10000
VIPER—V10—Equipment Schedule 2							
W.B. 96.2"; 8.0 Liter.							
RT/10 Roadster 2D		R65E	70925	24925	27925	33200	40800
GTS Coupe 2D		R69E	73425	27850	31125	36600	44700
Competition Group				2350	2350	3135	3135

2001 DODGE — (1,2or4)B3–(S46C)–1–#

NEON—4-Cyl.—Equipment Schedule 6							
W.B. 105.0"; 2.0 Liter.							
Highline Sedan 4D		S46C	14275	1950	2475	3900	5875
ES Sedan 4D		S56C	15095	2525	3125	4575	6625
Competition Sedan 4D		S66C	15155	2575	3175	4625	6700
R/T Sedan 4D		S66F	16845	2925	3600	5075	7175
STRATUS—4-Cyl.—Equipment Schedule 4							
W.B. 103.7", 108.0" (Sed); 2.4 Liter.							
SE Sedan 4D		J46X	18425	2725	3350	4875	6975
SE Coupe 2D		G42X	19230	3550	4250	6250	8975
Manual Trans				(525)	(525)	(700)	(700)
V6 2.7/3.0 Liter		U,H		550	550	735	735
STRATUS—V6—Equipment Schedule 4							
W.B. 103.7", 108.0" (Sed); 2.7 Liter, 3.0 Liter.							
ES Sedan 4D		J56U	21010	3725	4450	6200	8650
R/T Coupe 2D		G52H	22115	4800	5625	7700	10600
INTREPID—V6—Equipment Schedule 4							
W.B. 113.0"; 2.7 Liter, 3.2 Liter, 3.5 Liter.							
SE Sedan 4D		D46R	21395	3775	4525	6275	8750
ES Sedan 4D		D56J	23090	4375	5150	6925	9475
R/T Sedan 4D		D66V	25460	5950	6900	8725	11400
VIPER—V10—Equipment Schedule 2							
W.B. 96.2"; 8.0 Liter.							
RT/10 Roadster 2D		R65E	67950	27850	31125	36600	44600
GTS Coupe 2D		R69E	70450	31225	34825	40400	49000
Competition Group				2650	2650	3530	3530

2002 DODGE — (1,2or4)B3–(S26C)–2–#

NEON—4-Cyl.—Equipment Schedule 6							
W.B. 105.0"; 2.0 Liter.							
S Sedan 4D		S26C	10570	2375	2950	4475	6575
Sedan 4D		S26C	13805	2525	3125	4650	6775
SXT Sedan 4D		S66C	14130	2875	3550	5100	7250
ACR Sedan 4D		S66F	14795	2850	3525	5075	7225

Body	Type	VIN	List	Trade-In Fair	Trade-In Good	Pvt-Party Good	Retail Excellent
SE Sedan 4D		S46C	15330	2875	3550	5100	7250
ES Sedan 4D		S56C	15860	3175	3825	5400	7625
R/T Sedan 4D		S76F	16680	3625	4350	5950	8200
STRATUS—4-Cyl.—Equipment Schedule 4							
W.B. 103.7", 108.0" (Sed); 2.4 Liter.							
SE Sedan 4D		L46X	18290	3500	4200	5850	8150
SE Coupe 2D		G42X	19340	4250	5050	7200	10200
SXT Sedan 4D		L66X	19345	3825	4575	6225	8575
SXT Coupe 2D		G42G	19695	4625	5450	7675	10650
Manual Trans				(550)	(550)	(735)	(735)
V6 2.7/3.0 Liter		R,H		600	600	800	800
STRATUS—V6—Equipment Schedule 4							
W.B. 103.7", 108.0" (Sed); 2.7 Liter, 3.0 Liter.							
ES Sedan 4D		J56R	21255	5175	5450	7350	10050
R/T Sedan 4D		L76R	22150	5550	6500	8450	11200
R/T Coupe 2D		G52H	22360	5650	6575	8825	12000
INTREPID—V6—Equipment Schedule 4							
W.B. 113.0"; 2.7 Liter, 3.5 Liter.							
SE Sedan 4D		D46R	21230	4700	5550	7450	10150
ES Sedan 4D		D56J	23155	5325	6225	8175	10900
SXT Sedan 4D		D66G	24170	6000	6950	8750	11400
R/T Sedan 4D		D66V	27240	7075	8175	10150	13000
VIPER—V10—Equipment Schedule 2							
W.B. 96.2"; 8.0 Liter.							
RT/10 Roadster 2D		R65E	75500	30950	34525	40100	48500
GTS Coupe 2D		R69E	76000	34625	38600	44400	53300
Competition Group				2950	2950	3930	3930

2003 DODGE — (1,2or4)B3–(S46C)–3–#

Body	Type	VIN	List	Trade-In Fair	Trade-In Good	Pvt-Party Good	Retail Excellent
NEON—4-Cyl.—Equipment Schedule 6							
W.B. 105.0"; 2.0 Liter.							
SE Sedan 4D		S46C	14100	3650	4400	6075	8425
SXT Sedan 4D		S66C	14295	3650	4400	6075	8425
R/T Sedan 4D		S76F	17250	4450	5250	6975	9425
NEON—4-Cyl. Turbo—Equipment Schedule 6							
W.B. 105.0"; 2.4 Liter.							
SRT-4 Sedan 4D		S66S	19965	8850	10125	12100	15050
STRATUS—4-Cyl.—Equipment Schedule 4							
W.B. 103.7", 108.0" (Sed); 2.4 Liter.							
SE Sedan 4D		L46X	18470	4450	5250	7050	9575
SE Coupe 2D		G42G	20680	5150	6050	8375	11600
SXT Sedan 4D		L46X	18340	4800	5650	7475	10050
SXT Coupe 2D		G42GX	20680	5550	6500	8850	12150
Manual Trans				(575)	(575)	(765)	(765)
V6 2.7/3.0 Liter		R,H		650	650	865	865
STRATUS—V6—Equipment Schedule 4							
W.B. 103.7", 108.0" (Sed); 2.7 Liter, 3.0 Liter.							
ES Sedan 4D		J56U	21980	5700	6650	8700	11650
R/T Sedan 4D		L76R	22340	6725	7750	9850	12900
R/T Coupe 2D		G52H	23175	6675	7700	10150	13550
INTREPID—V6—Equipment Schedule 4							
W.B. 113.0"; 2.7 Liter, 3.5 Liter.							
SE Sedan 4D		D46R	21720	5800	6750	8825	11800
ES Sedan 4D		D56J	25515	6475	7400	9625	12650
SXT Sedan 4D		D66G	24335	7175	8300	10250	13150
VIPER—V10—Equipment Schedule 2							
W.B. 98.8"; 8.3 Liter.							
SRT-10 Roadster 2D		R65Z	83795	46650	51900	57800	67600

2004 DODGE — (1,2or4)B3–(S46C)–4–#

Body	Type	VIN	List	Trade-In Fair	Trade-In Good	Pvt-Party Good	Retail Excellent
NEON—4-Cyl.—Equipment Schedule 6							
W.B. 105.0"; 2.0 Liter.							
SE Sedan 4D		S46C	14745	4625	5450	7100	9500
SXT Sedan 4D		S66C	15115	4625	5450	7100	9500
R/T Sedan 4D		S76F	17895	5475	6400	8100	10600
NEON—4-Cyl. HO Turbo—Equipment Schedule 6							
W.B. 105.0"; 2.4 Liter.							
SRT-4 Sedan 4D		S66S	20995	10175	11600	13600	16650
STRATUS—4-Cyl.—Equipment Schedule 4							
W.B. 103.7", 108.0" (Sed); 2.4 Liter.							
SXT Sedan 4D		L66X	19155	6075	7025	8900	11600
SXT Coupe 2D		G42G	20535	6750	7775	10300	13750
SE Sedan 4D		L46X	20315	5700	6625	8475	11100

2004 DODGE

Body	Type	VIN	List	Trade-In Fair	Trade-In Good	Pvt-Party Good	Retail Excellent
Manual Trans				(600)	(600)	(800)	(800)
V6 2.7 Liter		T		700	700	935	935

STRATUS—V6—Equipment Schedule 4
W.B. 103.7", 108.0" (Sed); 2.7 Liter, 3.0 Liter.

Body	Type	VIN	List	Fair	Good	Good	Excellent
ES Sedan 4D		J56R	22600	7050	8150	10300	13400
R/T Sedan 4D		L76R	23135	8150	9325	11550	14750
R/T Coupe 2D		G52H	23030	7925	9125	11700	15350

INTREPID—V6—Equipment Schedule 4
W.B. 113.0"; 2.7 Liter, 3.5 Liter.

Body	Type	VIN	List	Fair	Good	Good	Excellent
SE Sedan 4D		D46R	22270	7150	8250	10450	13550
ES Sedan 4D		D56J	26065	7900	9075	11250	14450
SXT Sedan 4D		D66G	24485	8675	9950	11950	15000

VIPER—V10—Equipment Schedule 2
W.B. 98.8"; 8.3 Liter.

Body	Type	VIN	List	Fair	Good	Good	Excellent
SRT/10 Roadster 2D		R65Z	84795	51025	56750	62800	72800

2005 DODGE — (1,2or4)B3–(S26C)–5–#

NEON—4-Cyl.—Equipment Schedule 6
W.B. 105.0"; 2.0 Liter.

Body	Type	VIN	List	Fair	Good	Good	Excellent
SE Sedan 4D		S26C	15160	5800	6750	8400	10850
SXT Sedan 4D		S56C	15530	5825	6775	8450	10900
Special Edition				100	100	135	135

NEON—4-Cyl. HO Turbo—Equipment Schedule 6
W.B. 105.0"; 2.4 Liter.

Body	Type	VIN	List	Fair	Good	Good	Excellent
SRT-4 Sedan 4D		S66S	21195	11775	13350	15400	18650

STRATUS—4-Cyl.—Equipment Schedule 4
W.B. 103.7", 108.0" (Sed); 2.4 Liter.

Body	Type	VIN	List	Fair	Good	Good	Excellent
SXT Sedan 4D		L46J	19770	7775	8950	10950	13900
SXT Coupe 2D		G42G	21825	8150	9325	12100	15900
Special Edition				200	200	265	265
Manual Trans				(625)	(625)	(835)	(835)
V6 2.7 Liter		R		750	750	1000	1000

STRATUS—V6—Equipment Schedule 4
W.B. 103.7", 108.0" (Sed); 2.7 Liter, 3.0 Liter.

Body	Type	VIN	List	Fair	Good	Good	Excellent
R/T Sedan 4D		L76T	22250	10175	11600	13750	17000
R/T Coupe 2D		G52H	24320	9425	10775	13600	17600

MAGNUM—V6—Equipment Schedule 4
W.B. 120.0"; 2.7 Liter, 3.5 Liter.

Body	Type	VIN	List	Fair	Good	Good	Excellent
SE Sport Wagon 4D		V48T	22495	13100	14850	17250	21000
SXT Sport Wagon 4D		V48T	26145	13475	15225	17700	21500
SXT AWD Sport Wagon		Z48V	28525	14075	15900	18350	22200
Special Edition Pkg				200	200	265	265

MAGNUM—V8 HEMI—Equipment Schedule 4
W.B. 120.0"; 5.7 Liter.

Body	Type	VIN	List	Fair	Good	Good	Excellent
RT Sport Wagon 4D		V582	29995	18375	20650	23300	27500
RT AWD Sport Wagon		Z582	31995	19100	21425	24100	28400

VIPER—V10—Equipment Schedule 2
W.B. 98.8"; 8.3 Liter.

Body	Type	VIN	List	Fair	Good	Good	Excellent
SRT-10 Roadster 2D		R65H	85395				

EAGLE

1991 EAGLE — (1,4orJ)E3C(U36A)–M–#

SUMMIT—4-Cyl.—Equipment Schedule 6
W.B. 93.9", 96.7" (Sed); 1.5 Liter.

Body	Type	VIN	List	Fair	Good	Good	Excellent
Sedan 4D		U36A	10454	500	725	1275	2200
Hatchback Coupe 2D		U14A	8506	400	550	1075	1875
ES Sedan 4D		U56A	11212	525	750	1300	2250
ES Hatchback Coupe 2D		U24A	9402	450	625	1175	2025

TALON—4-Cyl.—Equipment Schedule 4
W.B. 97.2"; 2.0 Liter.

Body	Type	VIN	List	Fair	Good	Good	Excellent
Coupe 2D		S44R	14906	375	500	1250	2375
Auto Trans				100	100	135	135

TALON—4-Cyl. Turbo—Equipment Schedule 4
W.B. 97.2"; 2.0 Liter.

Body	Type	VIN	List	Fair	Good	Good	Excellent
TSi Coupe 2D		S54U	16525	525	750	1600	2925
TSi AWD Coupe 2D		T64U	18429	700	1000	1950	3400
Manual Trans				0	0	0	0

PREMIER—V6—Equipment Schedule 4
W.B. 106.0"; 3.0 Liter.

Body	Type	VIN	List	Fair	Good	Good	Excellent
LX Sedan 4D		B56U	16249	250	350	1000	2000

EQUIPMENT & MILEAGE PAGE 13 TO 27

1991 EAGLE

Body	Type	VIN	List	Trade-In Fair	Trade-In Good	Pvt-Party Good	Retail Excellent
ES Sedan 4D		B66U	18061	325	425	1150	2200
ES Ltd Sedan 4D		B66U	19975	350	475	1200	2275

1992 EAGLE — (1,4orJ)E3C(U36A)-N-#

SUMMIT—4-Cyl.—Equipment Schedule 6
W.B. 93.9", 96.7" (Sed), 99.2" (Wag); 1.5 Liter, 1.8 Liter, 2.4 Liter.

Body	Type	VIN	List	Fair	Good	Good	Excellent
Sedan 4D		U36A	10661	550	775	1400	2425
Hatchback 2D		U14A	8640	425	625	1175	2025
ES Sedan 4D		U56A	11419	550	800	1425	2450
ES Hatchback 2D		U24A	10057	475	700	1275	2200
DL Wagon 3D		V20D	12806	975	1350	2250	3625
LX Wagon 3D		V50D	13262	1000	1400	2425	3900
AWD Wagon 3D		W40D	14878	1200	1650	2750	4300
TALON—4-Cyl.—Equipment Schedule 4 W.B. 97.2"; 2.0 Liter.							
Coupe 2D		S44R	15854	450	625	1500	2825
Auto Trans				100	100	135	135
TALON—4-Cyl. Turbo—Equipment Schedule 4 W.B. 97.2"; 2.0 Liter.							
TSi Coupe 2D		S54U	17375	625	900	1900	3400
TSi AWD Coupe 2D		T64U	19382	825	1175	2375	4075
Manual Trans				0	0	0	0
PREMIER—V6—Equipment Schedule 4 W.B. 106.0"; 3.0 Liter.							
LX Sedan 4D		B56U	17016	250	350	1100	2200
ES Sedan 4D		B66U	18743	325	425	1225	2425
ES Ltd Sedan 4D		B66U	20712	350	475	1300	2550

1993 EAGLE — (1,4orJ)E3-(A36B)-P-#

SUMMIT—4-Cyl.—Equipment Schedule 6
W.B. 96.1", 98.4" (Sed), 99.2" (Wag); 1.5 Liter, 1.8 Liter, 2.4 Liter.

Body	Type	VIN	List	Fair	Good	Good	Excellent
DL Sedan 4D		A36B	10902	700	1000	1725	2875
DL Coupe 2D		A11B	9260	550	775	1425	2450
ES Sedan 4D		A46B	12260	700	1025	1775	2950
ES Coupe 2D		A21B	9888	600	875	1525	2625
DL Wagon 3D		B20B	12926	1100	1550	2625	4175
LX Wagon 3D		B50B	14060	1175	1625	2750	4325
AWD Wagon 3D		C40B	15010	1400	1900	3050	4675
VISION—V6—Equipment Schedule 4 W.B. 113.0"; 3.3 Liter, 3.5 Liter.							
ESi Sedan 4D		D56T	18725	875	1225	2025	3275
TSi Sedan 4D		D66F	21935	950	1325	2200	3525
TALON—4-Cyl.—Equipment Schedule 4 W.B. 97.2"; 1.8 Liter, 2.0 Liter.							
DL Coupe 2D		F34B	13910	475	675	1650	3100
ES Coupe 2D		F44E	16243	525	750	1775	3300
Auto Trans				125	125	165	165
TALON—4-Cyl. Turbo—Equipment Schedule 4 W.B. 97.2"; 2.0 Liter.							
TSi Coupe 2D		F54F	17749	725	1050	2250	4000
TSi AWD Coupe 2D		G64F	20034	950	1325	2650	4450
Auto Trans				125	125	165	165

1994 EAGLE — (1,4orJ)E3-(A11A)-R-#

SUMMIT—4-Cyl.—Equipment Schedule 6
W.B. 96.1", 98.4" (Sed), 99.2" (Wag); 1.5 Liter, 1.8 Liter, 2.4 Liter.

Body	Type	VIN	List	Fair	Good	Good	Excellent
DL Coupe 2D		A11A	10779	625	900	1600	2775
LX Sedan 4D		A36C	13248	775	1125	1950	3225
ES Sedan 4D		A46C	13824	825	1175	2000	3300
ES Coupe 2D		A21A	11876	675	975	1725	2925
ESi Sedan 4D		A46C	14607	925	1300	2225	3650
ESi Coupe 2D		A31C	12924	750	1075	1875	3125
DL Wagon 3D		B30C	14565	1275	1775	2900	4525
LX Wagon 3D		B50G	16233	1400	1900	3075	4725
AWD Wagon 3D		C40G	16685	1675	2175	3400	5125
VISION—V6—Equipment Schedule 4 W.B. 113.0"; 3.3 Liter, 3.5 Liter.							
ESi Sedan 4D		D56T	20272	975	1375	2300	3675
TSi Sedan 4D		D66F	23737	1125	1575	2650	4200
TALON—4-Cyl.—Equipment Schedule 4 W.B. 97.2"; 1.8 Liter, 2.0 Liter.							
DL Coupe 2D		F34B	14080	550	775	1950	3625

1994 EAGLE

Body	Type	VIN	List	Trade-In Fair	Good	Pvt-Party Good	Retail Excellent
ES Coupe 2D		F44E	16438	650	925	2225	4075
Auto Trans				150	150	200	200

TALON—4-Cyl. Turbo—Equipment Schedule 4
W.B. 97.2"; 2.0 Liter.

TSi Coupe 2D		F54F	18479	850	1200	2575	4450
TSi AWD Coupe 2D		G64F	20270	1100	1550	3000	5000
Auto Trans				150	150	200	200

1995 EAGLE — (1,4orJ)E3–(A11A)–S–#

SUMMIT—4-Cyl.—Equipment Schedule 6
W.B. 96.1", 98.4" (Sed), 99.2" (Wag); 1.5 Liter, 1.8 Liter, 2.4 Liter.

DL Coupe 2D		A11A	11878	725	1050	1850	3100
LX Sedan 4D		A36C	13553	900	1275	2200	3625
ESi Sedan 4D		A46C	15497	1050	1475	2575	4150
ESi Sedan 4D		A31C	13257	875	1225	2150	3525
DL Wagon 3D		B30C	15799	1525	2025	3225	4900
LX Wagon 3D		B50G	17305	1700	2225	3450	5200
AWD Wagon 3D		C50G	18461	1975	2500	3750	5550

VISION—V6—Equipment Schedule 4
W.B. 113.0"; 3.3 Liter.

ESi Sedan 4D		D56T	20232	1125	1575	2675	4225
TSi Sedan 4D		D66F	23406	1350	1850	2975	4600
V6 3.5 Liter		F		225	225	300	300

TALON—4-Cyl.—Equipment Schedule 4
W.B. 98.8"; 2.0 Liter.

| ESi Coupe 2D | | K44Y | 16927 | 1225 | 1700 | 3125 | 5075 |
| Auto Trans | | | | 175 | 175 | 235 | 235 |

TALON—4-Cyl. Turbo—Equipment Schedule 4
W.B. 98.8"; 2.0 Liter.

TSi Coupe 2D		K54F	19270	1700	2225	3725	5800
TSi AWD Coupe 2D		L54F	20758	2100	2675	4225	6350
Auto Trans				175	175	235	235

1996 EAGLE — (J,2or4)E3–(A31A)–T–#

SUMMIT—4-Cyl.—Equipment Schedule 6
W.B. 96.1", 98.4" (Sed), 99.2" (Wag); 1.5 Liter, 1.8 Liter, 2.4 Liter.

DL Coupe 2D		A31A	12271	825	1175	2100	3525
LX Sedan 4D		A56C	14474	1025	1450	2575	4150
ESi Sedan 4D		A46C	16411	1225	1675	2850	4500
ESi Sedan 4D		A41A	13759	1000	1400	2525	4100
DL Wagon 3D		B30C	16347	1800	2325	3575	5325
LX Wagon 3D		B50G	17873	2000	2550	3850	5675
AWD Wagon 3D		C60G	19009	2250	2825	4150	6025

VISION—V6—Equipment Schedule 4
W.B. 113.0"; 3.5 Liter.

ESi Sedan 4D		D56T	19795	1325	1825	2975	4625
TSi Sedan 4D		D66F	24385	1650	2150	3375	5100
V6 3.5 Liter		F		250	250	335	335

TALON—4-Cyl.—Equipment Schedule 4
W.B. 98.8"; 2.0 Liter.

Hatchback 2D		K24Y	15954	1450	1950	3450	5475
ESi Hatchback 2D		K44Y	17563	1525	2025	3575	5625
Auto Trans				200	200	265	265

TALON—4-Cyl. Turbo—Equipment Schedule 4
W.B. 98.8"; 2.0 Liter.

TSi Hatchback 2D		K54F	20140	2075	2650	4250	6450
TSi AWD H'Back 2D		L54F	21695	2525	3125	4775	7050
Auto Trans				200	200	265	265

1997 EAGLE — (2or4)E3–(D56F)–V–#

VISION—V6—Equipment Schedule 4
W.B. 113.0"; 3.5 Liter.

| ESi Sedan 4D | | D56F | 20855 | 1625 | 2125 | 3350 | 5050 |
| TSi Sedan 4D | | D66F | 25035 | 2000 | 2550 | 3800 | 5600 |

TALON—4-Cyl.—Equipment Schedule 4
W.B. 98.8"; 2.0 Liter.

Hatchback 2D		K24Y	16701	1800	2325	3950	6125
ESi Hatchback 2D		K44Y	17587	1925	2450	4125	6350
Auto Trans				200	200	265	265

TALON—4-Cyl. Turbo—Equipment Schedule 4
W.B. 98.8"; 2.0 Liter.

| TSi Hatchback 2D | | K54F | 20164 | 2500 | 3100 | 4850 | 7200 |

1997 EAGLE

Body Type	VIN	List	Trade-In Fair	Good	Pvt-Party Good	Retail Excellent
TSi AWD H'Back 2D	L54F	21666	2975	3650	5400	7850
Auto Trans			200	265	200	265

1998 EAGLE — 4E3-(K24Y)-W-#

TALON—4-Cyl.—Equipment Schedule 4
W.B. 98.8"; 2.0 Liter.
Hatchback 2D	K24Y	16400	2200	2800	4550	6950
ESi Hatchback 2D	K44Y	18550	2375	2950	4775	7200
Auto Trans			200	265	200	265

TALON—4-Cyl. Turbo—Equipment Schedule 4
W.B. 98.8"; 2.0 Liter.
TSi Hatchback 2D	K54F	21000	3000	3650	5525	8100
TSi AWD H'Back 2D	L54F	22110	3525	4225	6150	8800
Auto Trans			200	265	200	265

FORD

1991 FORD — (1FA,KNJor1ZV)-(T05H)-M-#

FESTIVA—4-Cyl.—Equipment Schedule 6
W.B. 90.2"; 1.3 Liter.
L Hatchback 2D	T05H	7150	250	350	825	1575
GL Hatchback 2D	T06H	8844	275	400	900	1650

ESCORT—4-Cyl.—Equipment Schedule 6
W.B. 98.4"; 1.9 Liter.
Pony Hatchback 2D	P10J	8586	400	575	975	1650
LX Hatchback 2D	P11J	10011	400	575	1000	1700
LX Hatchback 4D	P14J	11024	400	600	1050	1750
LX Wagon 4D	P15J	11435	475	675	1125	1875
GT Hatchback 2D	P128	12593	450	625	1100	1825

TEMPO—4-Cyl.—Equipment Schedule 5
W.B. 99.9"; 2.3 Liter.
L Sedan 2D	P30X	10141	200	300	625	1200
L Sedan 4D	P35X	10284	200	300	650	1225
GL Sedan 2D	P31X	11376	325	425	850	1525
GL Sedan 4D	P36X	11526	325	425	850	1525
GLS Sedan 2D	P33S	12193	325	425	850	1525
GLS Sedan 4D	P38S	12341	325	450	900	1575
LX Sedan 4D	P37X	12498	325	450	900	1575
AWD Sedan 4D	P39S	12662	400	550	1050	1825

MUSTANG—4-Cyl.—Equipment Schedule 4
W.B. 100.5"; 2.3 Liter.
LX Sedan 2D	P40M	12321	675	950	1575	2600
LX Hatchback 2D	P41M	12827	675	950	1575	2600
LX Convertible 2D	P44M	18271	925	1300	2125	3400
Manual Trans			(150)	(150)	(200)	(200)

MUSTANG—V8—Equipment Schedule 4
W.B. 100.5"; 5.0 Liter.
LX 5.0L Sedan 2D	P40E	15609	1100	1550	2550	3975
LX 5.0L H'Back 2D	P41E	16394	1125	1575	2600	4050
LX 5.0L Conv 2D	P44E	21016	1475	1975	3050	4625
Manual Trans			(100)	(100)	(135)	(135)

MUSTANG—V8—Equipment Schedule 4
W.B. 100.5"; 5.0 Liter.
GT Hatchback 2D	P42E	17373	1175	1625	2650	4125
GT Convertible 2D	P45E	21638	1625	2125	3250	4825

PROBE—4-Cyl.—Equipment Schedule 5
W.B. 99.0"; 2.2 Liter.
GL Hatchback 2D	T20C	13680	300	400	1125	2150

PROBE—V6—Equipment Schedule 5
W.B. 99.0"; 3.0 Liter.
LX Hatchback 2D	T21U	15281	400	600	1350	2550

PROBE—4-Cyl. Turbo—Equipment Schedule 5
W.B. 99.0"; 2.2 Liter.
GT Hatchback 2D	T22L	17016	400	600	1350	2550
Manual Trans			0	0	0	0

TAURUS—V6—Equipment Schedule 4
W.B. 106.0"; 3.0 Liter.
L Sedan 4D	P50U	16075	425	625	1100	1875
L Wagon 4D	P55U	16986	575	825	1375	2325
GL Sedan 4D	P52U	16595	475	675	1175	2000
GL Wagon 4D	P57U	17482	600	875	1450	2425

Body Type	VIN	List	Trade-In Fair	Trade-In Good	Pvt-Party Good	Retail Excellent
LX Sedan 4D	P53U	18218	**525**	**750**	**1300**	**2200**
LX Wagon 4D	P584	19808	**700**	**1000**	**1625**	**2675**
SHO Sedan 4D	P54Y	22551	**700**	**1000**	**1625**	**2675**
4-Cyl. 2.5 Liter	N		**(150)**	**(150)**	**(200)**	**(200)**
V6 3.8 Liter	4		**100**	**100**	**135**	**135**
THUNDERBIRD—V6—Equipment Schedule 4 W.B. 113.0"; 3.8 Liter.						
Coupe 2D	P604	16548	**475**	**675**	**1300**	**2325**
LX Coupe 2D	P624	18219	**575**	**825**	**1500**	**2625**
V8 5.0 Liter	T		**250**	**250**	**335**	**335**
THUNDERBIRD—V6 Supercharged—Equipment Schedule 4 W.B. 113.0"; 3.8 Liter.						
Super Coupe 2D	P64R	22079	**850**	**1200**	**2075**	**3450**
CROWN VICTORIA—V8—Equipment Schedule 4 W.B. 114.3"; 5.0 Liter, 5.8 Liter.						
S Sedan 4D	P72F	18776	**500**	**725**	**1225**	**2100**
Sedan 4D	P73F	19403	**550**	**775**	**1325**	**2250**
Wagon 4D	P76F	19274	**500**	**725**	**1225**	**2100**
LX Sedan 4D	P74F	20039	**675**	**975**	**1575**	**2625**
LX Wagon 4D	P77F	20024	**550**	**800**	**1350**	**2275**
Country Squire Wag 4D	P78F	19256	**1050**	**1475**	**2375**	**3675**
Country Sq LX Wag 4D	P79F	20276	**1050**	**1475**	**2375**	**3675**

1992 FORD — (1FA,KNJor1ZV)-(T05H)-N-#

Body Type	VIN	List	Trade-In Fair	Trade-In Good	Pvt-Party Good	Retail Excellent
FESTIVA—4-Cyl.—Equipment Schedule 6 W.B. 90.2"; 1.3 Liter.						
L Hatchback 2D	T05H	7548	**275**	**400**	**925**	**1750**
GL Hatchback 2D	T06H	9138	**325**	**425**	**975**	**1825**
ESCORT—4-Cyl.—Equipment Schedule 6 W.B. 98.4"; 1.8 Liter, 1.9 Liter.						
Pony Hatchback 2D	P10J	9883	**450**	**650**	**1125**	**1875**
LX Sedan 4D	P13J	11177	**475**	**675**	**1175**	**1950**
LX Hatchback 2D	P11J	10437	**450**	**650**	**1150**	**1925**
LX Hatchback 4D	P14J	10865	**475**	**675**	**1175**	**1950**
LX Wagon 4D	P15J	11449	**525**	**750**	**1250**	**2100**
GT Hatchback 2D	P128	12800	**500**	**725**	**1225**	**2025**
LX-E Sedan 4D	P168	12862	**500**	**725**	**1225**	**2025**
TEMPO—4-Cyl.—Equipment Schedule 5 W.B. 99.9"; 2.3 Liter.						
GL Sedan 2D	P31X	11808	**350**	**475**	**975**	**1700**
GL Sedan 4D	P36X	11958	**350**	**475**	**975**	**1700**
LX Sedan 4D	P37X	12936	**375**	**500**	**1000**	**1750**
V6 3.0 Liter	U		**125**	**125**	**165**	**165**
TEMPO—V6—Equipment Schedule 5 W.B. 99.9"; 3.0 Liter.						
GLS Sedan 2D	P33U	13656	**400**	**600**	**1125**	**1950**
GLS Sedan 4D	P38U	13804	**450**	**625**	**1175**	**2025**
MUSTANG—4-Cyl.—Equipment Schedule 4 W.B. 100.5"; 2.3 Liter.						
LX Sedan 2D	P40M	12343	**775**	**1100**	**1800**	**2925**
LX Hatchback 2D	P41M	12849	**775**	**1100**	**1800**	**2925**
LX Convertible 2D	P44M	18873	**1075**	**1525**	**2550**	**4000**
Manual Trans			**(175)**	**(175)**	**(235)**	**(235)**
MUSTANG—V8—Equipment Schedule 4 W.B. 100.5"; 5.0 Liter.						
LX 5.0L Sedan 2D	P40E	15825	**1300**	**1800**	**2850**	**4400**
LX 5.0L H'Back 2D	P41E	16610	**1375**	**1875**	**2925**	**4475**
LX 5.0L Conv 2D	P44E	21496	**1775**	**2300**	**3475**	**5150**
Manual Trans			**(100)**	**(100)**	**(135)**	**(135)**
MUSTANG—V8—Equipment Schedule 4 W.B. 100.5"; 5.0 Liter.						
GT Hatchback 2D	P42E	17645	**1400**	**1900**	**3000**	**4575**
GT Convertible 2D	P45E	21997	**1950**	**2475**	**3675**	**5400**
PROBE—4-Cyl.—Equipment Schedule 5 W.B. 99.0"; 2.2 Liter.						
GL Hatchback 2D	T20C	14140	**400**	**525**	**1400**	**2725**
PROBE—V6—Equipment Schedule 5 W.B. 99.0"; 3.0 Liter.						
LX Hatchback 2D	T21U	15140	**525**	**750**	**1700**	**3175**
PROBE—4-Cyl. Turbo—Equipment Schedule 5 W.B. 99.0"; 2.2 Liter.						
GT Hatchback 2D	T22L	16740	**525**	**750**	**1700**	**3175**
Manual Trans			**0**	**0**	**0**	**0**

Body	Type	VIN	List	Trade-In Fair	Trade-In Good	Pvt-Party Good	Retail Excellent
TAURUS—V6—Equipment Schedule 4							
W.B. 106.0"; 3.0 Liter.							
L Sedan 4D		P50U	17164	500	725	1225	2100
L Wagon 4D		P55U	18197	675	975	1600	2675
GL Sedan 4D		P52U	17619	550	800	1350	2275
GL Wagon 4D		P57U	18629	700	1025	1675	2775
LX Sedan 4D		P53U	18660	625	900	1500	2500
LX Wagon 4D		P584	20349	825	1175	1900	3050
SHO Sedan 4D		P54Y	24262	825	1175	1900	3050
V6 3.8 Liter		4		100	100	135	135
THUNDERBIRD—V6—Equipment Schedule 4							
W.B. 113.0"; 3.8 Liter.							
Coupe 2D		P604	17676	550	775	1475	2625
LX Coupe 2D		P624	18278	675	950	1725	2950
V8 5.0 Liter		T		250	250	335	335
THUNDERBIRD—V6 Supercharged—Equipment Schedule 4							
W.B. 113.0"; 3.8 Liter.							
Super Coupe 2D		P64R	23052	975	1375	2475	4050
THUNDERBIRD—V8—Equipment Schedule 4							
W.B. 113.0"; 5.0 Liter.							
Sport Coupe 2D		P60T	19787	750	1050	1925	3225
CROWN VICTORIA—V8—Equipment Schedule 4							
W.B. 114.4"; 4.6 Liter.							
Sedan 4D		P73W	21051	750	1075	1800	2950
LX Sedan 4D		P74W	22259	925	1300	2200	3525
Touring Sedan 4D		P75W	24842	975	1375	2275	3650

1993 FORD — (1FA,KNJor1ZV)–(T05H)–P–#

Body	Type	VIN	List	Trade-In Fair	Trade-In Good	Pvt-Party Good	Retail Excellent
FESTIVA—4-Cyl.—Equipment Schedule 6							
W.B. 90.2"; 1.3 Liter.							
L Hatchback 2D		T05H	7548	325	450	1025	1925
GL Hatchback 2D		T06H	9027	375	500	1125	2025
ESCORT—4-Cyl.—Equipment Schedule 6							
W.B. 98.4"; 1.8 Liter, 1.9 Liter.							
Hatchback 2D		P10J	9883	475	700	1200	2000
LX Sedan 4D		P13J	11423	525	750	1275	2150
LX Hatchback 2D		P11J	10746	500	725	1225	2075
LX Hatchback 4D		P14J	11179	525	750	1275	2150
LX Wagon 4D		P15J	11749	600	875	1425	2375
GT Hatchback 2D		P128	12800	575	825	1350	2275
LX-E Sedan 4D		P168	12862	575	825	1350	2275
TEMPO—4-Cyl.—Equipment Schedule 5							
W.B. 99.9"; 2.3 Liter.							
GL Sedan 2D		P31X	11599	400	525	1050	1825
GL Sedan 4D		P36X	11949	400	550	1075	1875
LX Sedan 4D		P37X	13605	400	600	1125	1950
V6 3.0 Liter		U		150	150	200	200
MUSTANG—4-Cyl.—Equipment Schedule 4							
W.B. 100.5"; 2.3 Liter.							
LX Sedan 2D		P40M	12847	875	1225	2025	3300
LX Hatchback 2D		P41M	13352	900	1250	2075	3350
LX Convertible 2D		P44M	19706	1350	1850	2925	4500
Manual Trans				(225)	(225)	(300)	(300)
MUSTANG—V8—Equipment Schedule 4							
W.B. 100.5"; 5.0 Liter.							
LX 5.0L Sedan 2D		P40E	16345	1600	2100	3250	4875
LX 5.0L H'Back 2D		P41E	17129	1675	2200	3350	5000
LX 5.0L Conv 2D		P44E	22145	2200	2800	4050	5850
Manual Trans				(125)	(125)	(165)	(165)
MUSTANG—V8—Equipment Schedule 4							
W.B. 100.5"; 5.0 Liter.							
GT Hatchback 2D		P42E	18165	1775	2300	3475	5175
GT Convertible 2D		P45E	22662	2375	2950	4250	6075
Cobra Hatchback 2D		P42D	19935	2575	3200	4500	6400
PROBE—4-Cyl.—Equipment Schedule 5							
W.B. 102.9"; 2.0 Liter.							
Hatchback 2D		T20A	15119	325	425	1275	2550
SE Pkg				75	75	100	100
PROBE—V6—Equipment Schedule 5							
W.B. 102.9"; 2.5 Liter.							
GT Hatchback 2D		T22B	17687	600	850	1900	3450
TAURUS—V6—Equipment Schedule 4							
W.B. 106.0"; 3.0 Liter, 3.2 Liter.							

1993 FORD

Body Type	VIN	List	Trade-In Fair	Trade-In Good	Pvt-Party Good	Retail Excellent
GL Sedan 4D	P52U	17675	600	850	1425	2425
GL Wagon 4D	P57U	18840	800	1150	1875	3050
LX Sedan 4D	P53U	19291	750	1050	1725	2825
LX Wagon 4D	P584	21181	950	1325	2175	3475
SHO Sedan 4D	P54Y	25960	1125	1575	2600	4075
Manual Trans			(225)	(225)	(300)	(300)
V6 3.0L Flexible Fuel	1		0	0	0	0
V6 3.8 Liter	4		125	125	165	165
THUNDERBIRD—V6—Equipment Schedule 4						
W.B. 113.0"; 3.8 Liter.						
LX Coupe 2D	P624	15833	625	900	1675	2925
V8 5.0 Liter	T		275	275	365	365
THUNDERBIRD—V6 Supercharged—Equipment Schedule 4						
W.B. 113.0"; 3.8 Liter.						
Super Coupe 2D	P64R	23120	1150	1600	2800	4450
CROWN VICTORIA—V8—Equipment Schedule 4						
W.B. 114.4"; 4.6 Liter.						
Sedan 4D	P73W	21247	775	1125	2000	3350
LX Sedan 4D	P74W	23180	1000	1400	2525	4100

1994 FORD — (1FA,KNJor1ZV)–(T05H)–R–#

Body Type	VIN	List	Trade-In Fair	Trade-In Good	Pvt-Party Good	Retail Excellent
ASPIRE—4-Cyl.—Equipment Schedule 6						
W.B. 90.7", 93.9" (5D); 1.3 Liter.						
Hatchback 2D	T05H	9660	275	375	875	1650
Hatchback 4D	T06H	10525	400	550	1175	2075
SE Hatchback 2D	T07H	10315	400	550	1150	2025
ESCORT—4-Cyl.—Equipment Schedule 6						
W.B. 98.4"; 1.8 Liter, 1.9 Liter.						
Hatchback 2D	P10J	10510	525	750	1300	2200
LX Sedan 4D	P13J	11885	600	875	1450	2450
LX Hatchback 2D	P11J	11225	550	800	1375	2325
LX Hatchback 4D	P14J	11660	600	875	1450	2450
LX Wagon 4D	P15J	12215	700	1000	1625	2725
GT Hatchback 2D	P128	12675	675	950	1575	2625
TEMPO—4-Cyl.—Equipment Schedule 5						
W.B. 99.9"; 2.3 Liter.						
GL Sedan 2D	P31X	12065	400	600	1175	2025
GL Sedan 4D	P36X	12065	450	625	1225	2100
LX Sedan 4D	P37X	13350	475	700	1275	2250
V6 3.0 Liter	U		175	175	235	235
MUSTANG—V6—Equipment Schedule 4						
W.B. 101.3"; 3.8 Liter.						
Coupe 2D	P404	16455	1225	1725	2825	4425
Convertible 2D	P444	22840	1925	2450	3725	5525
Manual Trans			(275)	(275)	(365)	(365)
MUSTANG—V8—Equipment Schedule 4						
W.B. 101.3"; 5.0 Liter.						
GT Coupe 2D	P42T	19950	2200	2800	4050	5850
GT Convertible 2D	P45T	24640	3050	3725	5125	7125
Cobra Coupe 2D	P42D	22425	3875	4625	6125	8350
Cobra Convertible 2D	P45D	26845	4675	5525	7175	9575
PROBE—4-Cyl.—Equipment Schedule 5						
W.B. 102.8"; 2.0 Liter.						
Hatchback 2D	T20A	15975	400	600	1575	3050
SE Pkg			100	100	135	135
PROBE—V6—Equipment Schedule 5						
W.B. 102.8"; 2.5 Liter.						
GT Hatchback 2D	T22B	19105	750	1075	2350	4150
GT Plus Pkg			100	100	135	135
TAURUS—V6—Equipment Schedule 4						
W.B. 106.0"; 3.0 Liter, 3.2 Liter.						
GL Sedan 4D	P52U	18280	675	975	1650	2800
GL Wagon 4D	P57U	19340	925	1300	2175	3525
LX Sedan 4D	P53U	19825	850	1200	2025	3275
LX Wagon 4D	P584	21630	1075	1525	2600	4100
SHO Sedan 4D	P54Y	25240	1300	1800	2875	4450
Manual Trans			(275)	(275)	(365)	(365)
V6 3.0L Flexible Fuel	1		0	0	0	0
V6 3.8 Liter	4		150	150	200	200
THUNDERBIRD—V6—Equipment Schedule 4						
W.B. 113.0"; 3.8 Liter.						
LX Coupe 2D	P624	17325	725	1050	1950	3350
V8 4.6 Liter	W		300	300	400	400

1994 FORD

Body Type	VIN	List	Trade-In Fair	Good	Pvt-Party Good	Retail Excellent
THUNDERBIRD—V6 Supercharged—Equipment Schedule 4						
W.B. 113.0"; 3.8 Liter.						
Super Coupe 2D	P64R	23525	1375	1900	3150	4900
CROWN VICTORIA—V8—Equipment Schedule 4						
W.B. 114.4"; 4.6 Liter.						
Sedan 4D	P73W	19345	850	1200	2325	3975
LX Sedan 4D	P74W	20995	1075	1525	2775	4475

1995 FORD — (K,1,2,3or4)(FA,NJorZV)–(T05H)–S–#

Body Type	VIN	List	Trade-In Fair	Good	Pvt-Party Good	Retail Excellent
ASPIRE—4-Cyl.—Equipment Schedule 6						
W.B. 90.7", 93.9" (5D); 1.3 Liter.						
Hatchback 2D	T05H	9860	325	425	1000	1875
Hatchback 4D	T06H	10425	450	650	1325	2375
SE Hatchback 2D	T07H	10535	450	625	1275	2275
ESCORT—4-Cyl.—Equipment Schedule 6						
W.B. 98.4"; 1.8 Liter, 1.9 Liter.						
Hatchback 2D	P10J	11115	600	875	1450	2450
LX Sedan 4D	P13J	12390	700	1025	1675	2800
LX Hatchback 2D	P11J	11785	650	925	1550	2625
LX Hatchback 4D	P14J	12220	700	1025	1675	2800
LX Wagon 4D	P15J	12775	825	1175	1925	3100
GT Hatchback 2D	P128	13530	775	1125	1850	3000
CONTOUR—4-Cyl.—Equipment Schedule 5						
W.B. 106.5"; 2.0 Liter.						
GL Sedan 4D	P653	15470	475	675	1300	2325
LX Sedan 4D	P663	16655	525	750	1425	2500
V6 2.5 Liter	L		175	175	235	235
CONTOUR—V6—Equipment Schedule 5						
W.B. 106.5"; 2.5 Liter.						
SE Sedan 4D	P67L	18355	750	1050	1875	3125
MUSTANG—V6—Equipment Schedule 4						
W.B. 101.3"; 3.8 Liter.						
Coupe 2D	P404	17550	1550	2050	3250	4900
Convertible 2D	P444	23610	2225	2825	4150	6075
Hard Top (Conv)			500	500	665	665
Manual Trans			(325)	(325)	(435)	(435)
MUSTANG—V8—Equipment Schedule 4						
W.B. 101.3"; 5.0 Liter.						
GTS Coupe 2D	P42T	19080	2025	2575	3825	5600
GT Coupe 2D	P42T	20710	2650	3275	4600	6525
GT Convertible 2D	P45T	25400	3550	4250	5725	7850
Cobra Coupe 2D	P42D	23060	4450	5250	6850	9150
Cobra Convertible 2D	P45D	27365	5325	6225	7950	10500
Hard Top (Conv)			500	500	665	665
PROBE—4-Cyl.—Equipment Schedule 5						
W.B. 102.8"; 2.0 Liter.						
Hatchback 2D	T20A	15890	550	800	2000	3675
SE Pkg			100	100	135	135
PROBE—V6—Equipment Schedule 5						
W.B. 102.8"; 2.5 Liter.						
GT Hatchback 2D	T22B	19485	950	1325	2775	4700
TAURUS—V6—Equipment Schedule 4						
W.B. 106.0"; 3.0 Liter, 3.2 Liter.						
GL Sedan 4D	P52U	18295	800	1150	1975	3225
GL Wagon 4D	P57U	19390	1075	1500	2600	4125
SE Sedan 4D	P52U	19165	825	1175	2025	3300
LX Sedan 4D	P53U	20290	975	1375	2400	3900
LX Wagon 4D	P584	22090	1275	1775	2875	4475
SHO Sedan 4D	P54Y	26465	1550	2050	3225	4875
Manual Trans			(325)	(325)	(435)	(435)
V6 3.0L Flexible Fuel	1		0	0	0	0
V6 3.8 Liter	4		175	175	235	235
THUNDERBIRD—V6—Equipment Schedule 4						
W.B. 113.0"; 3.8 Liter.						
LX Coupe 2D	P624	17895	825	1175	2300	3925
V8 4.6 Liter	W		300	300	400	400
THUNDERBIRD—V6 Supercharged—Equipment Schedule 4						
W.B. 113.0"; 3.8 Liter.						
Super Coupe 2D	P64R	24195	1650	2150	3500	5325
CROWN VICTORIA—V8—Equipment Schedule 4						
W.B. 114.4"; 4.6 Liter.						
Sedan 4D	P73W	21315	925	1300	2600	4425
LX Sedan 4D	P74W	23365	1225	1675	3075	5000

1996 FORD

Body Type	VIN	List	Trade-In Fair	Trade-In Good	Pvt-Party Good	Retail Excellent

1996 FORD — (K,1,2or3)(NJ,FAorZV)-(T05H)-T-#

ASPIRE—4-Cyl.—Equipment Schedule 6
W.B. 90.7", 93.9" (5D); 1.3 Liter.
| Hatchback 2D | T05H | 10225 | 375 | 500 | 1150 | 2100 |
| Hatchback 4D | T06H | 11090 | 550 | 775 | 1500 | 2675 |

ESCORT—4-Cyl.—Equipment Schedule 6
W.B. 98.4"; 1.8 Liter, 1.9 Liter.
Hatchback 2D	P10J	11615	700	1000	1700	2825
LX Sedan 4D	P13J	12890	825	1175	2000	3275
LX Hatchback 2D	P11J	12335	750	1075	1850	3050
LX Hatchback 4D	P14J	12720	825	1175	2000	3275
LX Wagon 4D	P15J	13275	950	1325	2250	3625
GT Hatchback 2D	P128	14040	925	1300	2175	3525

CONTOUR—4-Cyl.—Equipment Schedule 5
W.B. 106.5"; 2.0 Liter.
GL Sedan 4D	P653	15980	575	825	1575	2775
LX Sedan 4D	P663	16995	650	925	1725	2950
V6 2.5 Liter	L		200	200	265	265

CONTOUR—V6—Equipment Schedule 5
W.B. 106.5"; 2.5 Liter.
| SE Sedan 4D | P67L | 18865 | 875 | 1225 | 2200 | 3650 |

MUSTANG—V6—Equipment Schedule 4
W.B. 101.3"; 3.8 Liter.
Coupe 2D	P404	18485	1925	2450	3725	5525
Convertible 2D	P444	23935	2575	3200	4625	6675
Manual Trans			(375)	(375)	(500)	(500)

MUSTANG—V8—Equipment Schedule 4
W.B. 101.3"; 4.6 Liter.
GT Coupe 2D	P42X	21740	3125	3775	5225	7275
GT Convertible 2D	P45X	26430	4050	4825	6400	8650
Cobra Coupe 2D	P47V	26645	5050	5925	7600	10050
Cobra Convertible 2D	P46V	29415	6025	6975	8825	11500

PROBE—4-Cyl.—Equipment Schedule 6
W.B. 102.8"; 2.0 Liter.
| SE Hatchback 2D | T20A | 16240 | 750 | 1050 | 2475 | 4450 |

PROBE—V6—Equipment Schedule 6
W.B. 102.8"; 2.5 Liter.
| GT Hatchback 2D | T22B | 19545 | 1175 | 1625 | 3200 | 5300 |

TAURUS—V6—Equipment Schedule 4
W.B. 108.5"; 3.0 Liter.
G Sedan 4D	P51U	18545	900	1250	2025	3225
GL Sedan 4D	P52U	19390	1000	1425	2300	3625
GL Wagon 4D	P57U	20470	1375	1875	2900	4450
LX Sedan 4D	P53S	21680	1225	1700	2750	4225
LX Wagon 4D	P58S	22700	1625	2125	3225	4800
V6 3.0L Flexible Fuel	1,2		0	0	0	0

TAURUS—V8—Equipment Schedule 4
W.B. 108.5"; 3.4 Liter.
| SHO Sedan 4D | P54N | 27805 | 2725 | 3350 | 4600 | 6400 |

THUNDERBIRD—V6—Equipment Schedule 4
W.B. 113.0"; 3.8 Liter.
| LX Coupe 2D | P624 | 17995 | 975 | 1375 | 2625 | 4375 |
| V8 4.6 Liter | W | | 300 | 300 | 400 | 400 |

CROWN VICTORIA—V8—Equipment Schedule 4
W.B. 114.4"; 4.6 Liter.
| Sedan 4D | P73W | 21780 | 1075 | 1500 | 2950 | 4925 |
| LX Sedan 4D | P74W | 23895 | 1450 | 1950 | 3500 | 5550 |

1997 FORD — (K,1,2or3)(NJ,FAorZV)-(T05H)-V-#

ASPIRE—4-Cyl.—Equipment Schedule 6
W.B. 90.7", 93.9" (5D); 1.3 Liter.
| Hatchback 2D | T05H | 10655 | 425 | 625 | 1350 | 2500 |
| Hatchback 4D | T06H | 11285 | 625 | 900 | 1775 | 3100 |

ESCORT—4-Cyl.—Equipment Schedule 6
W.B. 98.4"; 2.0 Liter.
Sedan 4D	P10P	12225	975	1350	2150	3400
LX Sedan 4D	P13P	12975	1075	1500	2375	3675
LX Wagon 4D	P15P	13630	1225	1675	2675	4125

CONTOUR—4-Cyl.—Equipment Schedule 5
W.B. 106.5"; 2.0 Liter.
| Sedan 4D | P653 | 16015 | 600 | 875 | 1675 | 2925 |
| GL Sedan 4D | P653 | 16945 | 725 | 1050 | 1925 | 3275 |

1997 FORD

Body Type	VIN	List	Trade-In Fair	Trade-In Good	Pvt-Party Good	Retail Excellent
LX Sedan 4D	P663	17480	825	1175	2100	3525
V6 2.5 Liter	L		200	200	265	265
CONTOUR—V6—Equipment Schedule 5						
W.B. 106.5"; 2.5 Liter.						
SE Sedan 4D	P67L	19350	1050	1475	2650	4275
MUSTANG—V6—Equipment Schedule 4						
W.B. 101.3"; 3.8 Liter.						
Coupe 2D	P404	18810	2325	2900	4300	6200
Convertible 2D	P444	23710	3000	3650	5200	7375
Manual Trans			(400)	(400)	(535)	(535)
MUSTANG—V8—Equipment Schedule 4						
W.B. 101.3"; 4.6 Liter.						
GT Coupe 2D	P42X	20790	3650	4375	5900	8075
GT Convertible 2D	P45X	27010	4650	5475	7125	9500
Cobra Coupe 2D	P47V	27195	5700	6650	8425	11000
Cobra Convertible 2D	P46V	29995	6775	7825	9700	12500
PROBE—4-Cyl.—Equipment Schedule 5						
W.B. 102.8"; 2.0 Liter.						
Hatchback 2D	T20A	16235	950	1325	2950	5125
PROBE—V6—Equipment Schedule 5						
W.B. 102.8"; 2.5 Liter.						
GT Hatchback 2D	T22B	18735	1500	2000	3700	6025
GTS Pkg			100	100	135	135
TAURUS—V6—Equipment Schedule 4						
W.B. 108.5"; 3.0 Liter.						
G Sedan 4D	P51U	19005	1075	1500	2475	3900
GL Sedan 4D	P52U	19785	1225	1725	2775	4250
GL Wagon 4D	P57U	20995	1700	2225	3300	4875
LX Sedan 4D	P53S	22880	1525	2025	3100	4625
LX Wagon 4D	P58S	23985	1975	2500	3650	5250
V6 3.0L Flexible Fuel	1,2		0	0	0	0
TAURUS—V8—Equipment Schedule 4						
W.B. 108.5"; 3.4 Liter.						
SHO Sedan 4D	P54N	28220	3175	3850	5150	7000
THUNDERBIRD—V6—Equipment Schedule 4						
W.B. 113.0"; 3.8 Liter.						
LX Coupe 2D	P624	18395	1175	1625	3000	4875
V8 4.6 Liter	W		300	300	400	400
CROWN VICTORIA—V8—Equipment Schedule 4						
W.B. 114.4"; 4.6 Liter.						
Sedan 4D	P73W	21425	1300	1800	3400	5550
LX Sedan 4D	P74W	23440	1775	2300	3950	6200

1998 FORD — (1,2or3)FA–(P10P)–W–#

Body Type	VIN	List	Trade-In Fair	Trade-In Good	Pvt-Party Good	Retail Excellent
ESCORT—4-Cyl.—Equipment Schedule 6						
W.B. 98.4"; 2.0 Liter.						
LX Sedan 4D	P10P	12490	1225	1675	2675	4125
SE Sedan 4D	P13P	12995	1375	1875	2850	4350
SE Wagon 4D	P15P	14195	1525	2025	3075	4575
ZX2 Coupe 2D	P113	14325	1675	2200	3250	4775
CONTOUR—4-Cyl.—Equipment Schedule 5						
W.B. 106.5"; 2.0 Liter.						
Sedan 4D	P653	15980	775	1125	2125	3625
GL Sedan 4D	P653	17305	900	1275	2425	4050
LX Sedan 4D	P653	17760	1000	1400	2575	4225
SE Sedan 4D	P663	19475	1075	1500	2700	4375
V6 2.5 Liter	L		200	200	265	265
CONTOUR—V6—Equipment Schedule 5						
W.B. 106.5"; 2.5 Liter.						
SVT Sedan 4D	P68G	22900	2500	3100	4475	6425
Manual Trans			0	0	0	0
MUSTANG—V6—Equipment Schedule 4						
W.B. 101.3"; 3.8 Liter.						
Coupe 2D	P404	17805	2825	3475	4925	6950
Convertible 2D	P444	22305	3500	4200	5850	8150
Manual Trans			(425)	(425)	(565)	(565)
MUSTANG—V8—Equipment Schedule 4						
W.B. 101.3"; 4.6 Liter.						
GT Coupe 2D	P42X	21605	4250	5050	6650	8950
GT Convertible 2D	P45X	25665	5300	6200	7950	10500
Cobra Coupe 2D	P47V	26155	6450	7475	9300	12050
Cobra Convertible 2D	P46V	28955	7625	8750	10700	13700

1998 FORD

Body	Type	VIN	List	Trade-In Fair	Trade-In Good	Pvt-Party Good	Retail Excellent
TAURUS—V6—Equipment Schedule 4							
W.B. 108.5"; 3.0 Liter.							
LX Sedan 4D		P52U	19255	**1575**	**2075**	**3175**	**4750**
SE Sedan 4D		P52U	19995	**1900**	**2425**	**3575**	**5200**
SE Wagon 4D		P57U	21655	**2325**	**2900**	**4100**	**5825**
V6 3.0 Liter 24V		S	....	**200**	**200**	**265**	**265**
V6 3.0L Flexible Fuel		1,2	....	**0**	**0**	**0**	**0**
TAURUS—V8—Equipment Schedule 4							
W.B. 108.5"; 3.4 Liter.							
SHO Sedan 4D		P54N	29470	**3675**	**4425**	**5750**	**7700**
CROWN VICTORIA—V8—Equipment Schedule 4							
W.B. 114.7"; 4.6 Liter.							
Sedan 4D		P73W	21725	**1675**	**2175**	**3950**	**6325**
LX Sedan 4D		P74W	23740	**2125**	**2725**	**4525**	**6975**

1999 FORD — (1,2or3)FA-(P10P)-X-#

Body	Type	VIN	List	Trade-In Fair	Trade-In Good	Pvt-Party Good	Retail Excellent
ESCORT—4-Cyl.—Equipment Schedule 6							
W.B. 98.4"; 2.0 Liter.							
LX Sedan 4D		P10P	12665	**1575**	**2075**	**3175**	**4650**
SE Sedan 4D		P13P	13350	**1750**	**2275**	**3325**	**4875**
SE Wagon 4D		P15P	14550	**1950**	**2475**	**3575**	**5150**
ZX2 Coupe 2D		P113	13705	**2075**	**2650**	**3725**	**5325**
S/R Pkg			....	**200**	**200**	**265**	**265**
CONTOUR—4-Cyl.—Equipment Schedule 5							
W.B. 106.5"; 2.0 Liter.							
LX Sedan 4D		P653	15810	**1025**	**1450**	**2700**	**4425**
SE Sedan 4D		P663	17305	**1150**	**1600**	**2875**	**4650**
V6 2.5 Liter		L	....	**200**	**200**	**265**	**265**
CONTOUR—V6—Equipment Schedule 5							
W.B. 106.5"; 2.5 Liter.							
SVT Sedan 4D		P68G	23200	**2975**	**3650**	**5100**	**7150**
Manual Trans			....	**0**	**0**	**0**	**0**
MUSTANG—V6—Equipment Schedule 5							
W.B. 101.3"; 3.8 Liter.							
Coupe 2D		P404	18360	**3375**	**4075**	**5425**	**7400**
Convertible 2D		P444	22960	**4075**	**4850**	**6400**	**8650**
Manual Trans			....	**(450)**	**(450)**	**(600)**	**(600)**
MUSTANG—V8—Equipment Schedule 4							
W.B. 101.3"; 4.6 Liter.							
GT Coupe 2D		P42X	22760	**4950**	**5800**	**7300**	**9525**
GT Convertible 2D		P45X	26760	**6075**	**7050**	**8675**	**11100**
Cobra Coupe 2D		P47V	27995	**7350**	**8450**	**10200**	**12800**
Cobra Convertible 2D		P46V	31995	**8550**	**9800**	**11650**	**14500**
TAURUS—V6—Equipment Schedule 4							
W.B. 108.5"; 3.0 Liter.							
LX Sedan 4D		P52U	18670	**1925**	**2450**	**3650**	**5350**
SE Sedan 4D		P53U	18995	**2275**	**2825**	**4075**	**5850**
SE Wagon 4D		P58U	19995	**2725**	**3350**	**4625**	**6475**
V6 3.0 Liter 24V		S	....	**200**	**200**	**265**	**265**
V6 3.0L Flexible Fuel		2	....	**0**	**0**	**0**	**0**
TAURUS—V8—Equipment Schedule 4							
W.B. 108.5"; 3.4 Liter.							
SHO Sedan 4D		P54N	29550	**4225**	**5025**	**6425**	**8500**
CROWN VICTORIA—V8—Equipment Schedule 4							
W.B. 114.7"; 4.6 Liter.							
Sedan 4D		P73W	22510	**2125**	**2700**	**4600**	**7150**
LX Sedan 4D		P74W	24530	**2650**	**3275**	**5225**	**7850**

2000 FORD — (1,2or3)FA-(P33P)-Y-#

Body	Type	VIN	List	Trade-In Fair	Trade-In Good	Pvt-Party Good	Retail Excellent
FOCUS—4-Cyl.—Equipment Schedule 6							
W.B. 103.0"; 2.0 Liter.							
LX Sedan 4D		P33P	13335	**2175**	**2775**	**4050**	**5900**
SE Sedan 4D		P34P	13980	**2525**	**3125**	**4450**	**6350**
SE Wagon 4D		P36P	15795	**2775**	**3400**	**4750**	**6675**
Sony Special Edition			....	**75**	**75**	**100**	**100**
4-Cyl. 2.0 Liter 16V		3	....	**125**	**125**	**165**	**165**
FOCUS—4-Cyl. 16V—Equipment Schedule 6							
W.B. 103.0"; 2.0 Liter.							
ZX3 Hatchback 2D		P313	13075	**2775**	**3400**	**4750**	**6675**
ZTS Sedan 4D		P383	15580	**2825**	**3450**	**4800**	**6750**
Kona Limited Edition			....	**75**	**75**	**100**	**100**
ESCORT—4-Cyl.—Equipment Schedule 6							
W.B. 98.4"; 2.0 Liter.							

Body	Type	VIN	List	Trade-In Fair	Good	Pvt-Party Good	Retail Excellent
Sedan 4D		P13P	12440	2125	2700	3775	5400
ZX2 Coupe 2D		P113	12970	2500	3100	4250	5925
S/R Pkg				250	250	335	335
CONTOUR—V6—Equipment Schedule 5							
W.B. 106.5"; 2.5 Liter.							
SE Sedan 4D		P66L	17265	1400	1900	3300	5225
SE Sport Sedan 4D		P66L	18195	2250	2825	4300	6350
SVT Sedan 4D		P68G	23250	3700	4450	6050	8300
Manual Trans (SVT)				0	0	0	0
4-Cyl. 2.0 Liter		Z,3		(250)	(250)	(335)	(335)
MUSTANG—V6—Equipment Schedule 4							
W.B. 101.3"; 3.8 Liter.							
Coupe 2D		P404	18410	3900	4650	6150	8375
Convertible 2D		P444	23260	4800	5625	7375	9850
Manual Trans				(500)	(500)	(665)	(665)
MUSTANG—V8—Equipment Schedule 4							
W.B. 101.3"; 4.6 Liter.							
GT Coupe 2D		P42X	22905	5775	6725	8400	10850
GT Convertible 2D		P45X	27160	7075	8175	9950	12650
TAURUS—V6—Equipment Schedule 4							
W.B. 108.5"; 3.0 Liter.							
LX Sedan 4D		P52U	18995	2200	2800	4175	6125
SE Sedan 4D		P53U	19295	2625	3250	4675	6725
SE Wagon 4D		P58U	20450	3150	3800	5275	7400
SES Sedan 4D		P55U	20290	2725	3325	4775	6825
SES Wagon 4D		P55U	20870	3150	3800	5275	7400
SEL Sedan 4D		P56U	21565	2850	3500	4950	7000
V6 3.0 Liter 24V		S		250	250	335	335
V6 3.0L Flexible Fuel		2		0	0	0	0
CROWN VICTORIA—V8—Equipment Schedule 4							
W.B. 114.7"; 4.6 Liter.							
Sedan 4D		P73W	22610	2725	3325	5425	8225
LX Sedan 4D		P74W	24725	3325	4000	6125	9025

2001 FORD — (1,2or3)FA–(P33P)–1–#

Body	Type	VIN	List	Trade-In Fair	Good	Pvt-Party Good	Retail Excellent
FOCUS—4-Cyl.—Equipment Schedule 6							
W.B. 103.0"; 2.0 Liter.							
LX Sedan 4D		P33P	13645	2725	3325	4725	6700
SE Sedan 4D		P34P	14505	3075	3725	5175	7175
SE Wagon 4D		P363	16700	3375	4075	5500	7575
Street Edition				150	150	200	200
4-Cyl. 2.0 Liter 16V		3		150	150	200	200
FOCUS—4-Cyl. 16V—Equipment Schedule 6							
W.B. 103.0"; 2.0 Liter.							
ZX3 Hatchback 2D		P313	13385	3375	4075	5500	7575
ZTS Sedan 4D		P383	15725	3425	4125	5550	7625
Street Edition				150	150	200	200
S2 Feature Car				150	150	200	200
ZTW				275	275	365	365
Traction Control				275	275	365	365
ESCORT—4-Cyl.—Equipment Schedule 6							
W.B. 98.4"; 2.0 Liter.							
Sedan 4D		P13P	14230	2600	3225	4400	6100
ZX2—4-Cyl.—Equipment Schedule 6							
W.B. 98.4"; 2.0 Liter.							
Coupe 2D		P113	13310	3000	3650	4850	6625
MUSTANG—V6—Equipment Schedule 4							
W.B. 101.3"; 3.8 Liter.							
Coupe 2D		P404	18195	4525	5350	7050	9475
Convertible 2D		P444	23610	5600	6525	8475	11250
Manual Trans				(525)	(525)	(700)	(700)
MUSTANG—V8—Equipment Schedule 4							
W.B. 101.3"; 4.6 Liter.							
GT Coupe 2D		P42X	23830	6725	7750	9625	12350
GT Convertible 2D		P45X	28085	8225	9425	11400	14350
Bullitt Coupe 2D		P42X	26830	7825	9000	10900	13800
Cobra Coupe 2D		P47V	29205	10000	11350	13450	16650
Cobra Convertible 2D		P46V	33205	11500	13050	15250	18650
TAURUS—V6—Equipment Schedule 4							
W.B. 108.5"; 3.0 Liter.							
LX Sedan 4D		P52U	19455	2650	3275	4900	7125
SE Sedan 4D		P53U	19635	3125	3775	5450	7750
SE Wagon 4D		P58U	20790	3700	4450	6125	8525

Body Type	VIN	List	Trade-In Fair	Trade-In Good	Pvt-Party Good	Retail Excellent
SES Sedan 4D	P55U	20650	3200	3875	5550	7850
SES Wagon 4D	P55S	21225	3700	4450	6125	8525
SEL Sedan 4D	P56U	22135	3375	4075	5750	8100
V6 3.0 Liter 24V	S		275	275	365	365
V6 3.0L Flexible Fuel	2		0	0	0	0

CROWN VICTORIA—V8—Equipment Schedule 4
W.B. 114.7"; 4.6 Liter.

Body Type	VIN	List	Trade-In Fair	Trade-In Good	Pvt-Party Good	Retail Excellent
Sedan 4D	P73W	22620	3500	4200	6500	9550
LX Sedan 4D	P74W	24735	4200	4975	7325	10500

2002 FORD — (1,2or3)FA-(P33P)-2-#

FOCUS—4-Cyl.—Equipment Schedule 6
W.B. 103.0"; 2.0 Liter.

Body Type	VIN	List	Trade-In Fair	Trade-In Good	Pvt-Party Good	Retail Excellent
LX Sedan 4D	P33P	13220	3375	4075	5550	7675
SE Sedan 4D	P34P	14810	3775	4525	6050	8200
SE Wagon 4D	P36P	17015	4125	4900	6425	8625
4-Cyl. 2.0 Liter 16V	3		150	150	200	200

FOCUS—4-Cyl. 16V—Equipment Schedule 6
W.B. 103.0"; 2.0 Liter.

Body Type	VIN	List	Trade-In Fair	Trade-In Good	Pvt-Party Good	Retail Excellent
ZX3 Hatchback 2D	P313	13700	4125	4900	6425	8625
ZTS Sedan 4D	P383	15730	4175	4950	6475	8675
ZX5 Hatchback 4D	P373	16105	4550	5375	6925	9225
SVT Hatchback 2D	P395	17995	5350	6250	7625	9700
ZTW Wagon 4D	P383	18195	4550	5375	6925	9225

ESCORT—4-Cyl.—Equipment Schedule 6
W.B. 98.4"; 2.0 Liter.

Body Type	VIN	List	Trade-In Fair	Trade-In Good	Pvt-Party Good	Retail Excellent
Sedan 4D	P13P	14450	3225	3900	5150	6975

ZX2—4-Cyl.—Equipment Schedule 6
W.B. 98.4"; 2.0 Liter.

Body Type	VIN	List	Trade-In Fair	Trade-In Good	Pvt-Party Good	Retail Excellent
Coupe 2D	P113	13655	3650	4375	5625	7525

MUSTANG—V6—Equipment Schedule 4
W.B. 101.3"; 3.8 Liter.

Body Type	VIN	List	Trade-In Fair	Trade-In Good	Pvt-Party Good	Retail Excellent
Coupe 2D	P404	18635	5375	6275	8175	10850
Convertible 2D	P444	23955	6600	7650	9800	12850
Manual Trans			(550)	(550)	(735)	(735)

MUSTANG—V8—Equipment Schedule 4
W.B. 101.3"; 4.6 Liter.

Body Type	VIN	List	Trade-In Fair	Trade-In Good	Pvt-Party Good	Retail Excellent
GT Coupe 2D	P42X	24175	7825	9000	11050	14050
GT Convertible 2D	P45X	28430	9525	10875	13000	16250

TAURUS—V6—Equipment Schedule 4
W.B. 108.5"; 3.0 Liter.

Body Type	VIN	List	Trade-In Fair	Trade-In Good	Pvt-Party Good	Retail Excellent
LX Sedan 4D	P52U	19445	3250	3925	5775	8325
SE Sedan 4D	P53U	20070	3775	4525	6400	9025
SE Wagon 4D	P58U	22005	4450	5250	7150	9850
SES Sedan 4D	P55U	21085	3875	4625	6500	9125
SEL Sedan 4D	P56S	22995	4300	5100	7000	9675
SEL Wagon 4D	P59S	23265	4600	5425	7375	10100
V6 3.0 Liter 24V	S		300	300	400	400
V6 3.0L Flexible Fuel	2		0	0	0	0

CROWN VICTORIA—V8—Equipment Schedule 4
W.B. 114.7"; 4.6 Liter.

Body Type	VIN	List	Trade-In Fair	Trade-In Good	Pvt-Party Good	Retail Excellent
Sedan 4D	P73W	23435	4500	5325	7800	11150
LX Sedan 4D	P74W	27025	5275	6175	8725	12150

THUNDERBIRD—V8—Equipment Schedule 2
W.B. 107.2"; 3.9 Liter.

Body Type	VIN	List	Trade-In Fair	Trade-In Good	Pvt-Party Good	Retail Excellent
Soft Top Conv 2D	P60A	35495	13100	14800	17250	21100
Hard Top			800	800	1065	1065

2003 FORD — (1,2or3)FA-(P33P)-3-#

FOCUS—4-Cyl.—Equipment Schedule 6
W.B. 103.0"; 2.0 Liter, 2.3 Liter.

Body Type	VIN	List	Trade-In Fair	Trade-In Good	Pvt-Party Good	Retail Excellent
LX Sedan 4D	P33P	13505	4225	5000	6575	8850
SE Sedan 4D	P34P	15175	4650	5500	7100	9425
SE Wagon 4D	P36P	17525	5025	5900	7525	9900
4-Cyl. 2.3 Liter 16V	Z		150	150	200	200

FOCUS—4-Cyl. 16V—Equipment Schedule 6
W.B. 103.0"; 2.0 Liter, 2.3 Liter.

Body Type	VIN	List	Trade-In Fair	Trade-In Good	Pvt-Party Good	Retail Excellent
ZX3 Hatchback 2D	P313	13990	5025	5900	7525	9900
ZX5 Hatchback 4D	P373	15900	5500	6425	8050	10450
ZTS Sedan 4D	P383	16095	5100	5975	7575	9950
ZTW Wagon 4D	P363	17870	5550	6500	8125	10550
ZX3 SVT Hatchback 2D	P395	19100	6400	7425	8825	11050
ZX5 SVT Hatchback 4D	P375	19600	7475	8575	10050	12400

Body	Type	VIN	List	Trade-In Fair	Good	Pvt-Party Good	Retail Excellent
ZX2—4-Cyl.—Equipment Schedule 6							
W.B. 98.4"; 2.0 Liter.							
Coupe 2D		P113	14250	**4450**	**5250**	**6600**	**8625**
MUSTANG—V6—Equipment Schedule 4							
W.B. 101.3"; 3.8 Liter.							
Coupe 2D		P404	18915	**6425**	**7425**	**9525**	**12550**
Convertible 2D		P444	24585	**7800**	**8975**	**11350**	**14800**
Manual Trans				**(575)**	**(575)**	**(765)**	**(765)**
MUSTANG—V8—Equipment Schedule 4							
W.B. 101.3"; 4.6 Liter.							
GT Coupe 2D		P42X	24785	**9200**	**10475**	**12700**	**16050**
GT Convertible 2D		P45X	29060	**11050**	**12550**	**14900**	**18450**
Mach 1 Coupe 2D		P42R	29810	**11650**	**13200**	**15550**	**19150**
MUSTANG—V8 Supercharged—Equipment Schedule 4							
W.B. 101.3"; 4.6 Liter.							
Cobra Coupe 2D		P48Y	33750	**16450**	**18525**	**21100**	**25300**
Cobra Convertible 2D		P49Y	37995	**18275**	**20575**	**23300**	**27600**
10th Anniversary Edition				**300**	**300**	**400**	**400**
TAURUS—V6—Equipment Schedule 4							
W.B. 108.5"; 3.0 Liter.							
LX Sedan 4D		P52U	20230	**4050**	**4800**	**6900**	**9800**
SE Sedan 4D		P53U	20345	**4650**	**5475**	**7600**	**10500**
SE Wagon 4D		P58U	21995	**5325**	**6225**	**8425**	**11450**
SES Sedan 4D		P55U	21670	**4725**	**5575**	**7700**	**10650**
SEL Sedan 4D		P56S	23570	**5200**	**6075**	**8250**	**11250**
SEL Wagon 4D		P59U	23820	**5375**	**6275**	**8475**	**11500**
V6 3.0 Liter 24V		S		**325**	**325**	**435**	**435**
V6 3.0L Flexible Fuel		2		**0**	**0**	**0**	**0**
CROWN VICTORIA—V8—Equipment Schedule 4							
W.B. 114.7"; 4.6 Liter.							
Sedan 4D		P73W	24510	**5850**	**6800**	**9525**	**13250**
LX Sedan 4D		P74W	27780	**6675**	**7700**	**10500**	**14300**
THUNDERBIRD—V8—Equipment Schedule 2							
W.B. 107.2"; 3.9 Liter.							
Soft Top Conv 2D		P60A	36895	**15025**	**16925**	**19700**	**23900**
007 Hard Top Conv 2D		P62A	43995				
Hard Top				**875**	**875**	**1165**	**1165**

2004 FORD — (1,2or3)FA–(P333)–4–#

Body	Type	VIN	List	Trade-In Fair	Good	Pvt-Party Good	Retail Excellent
FOCUS—4-Cyl.—Equipment Schedule 6							
W.B. 103.0"; 2.0 Liter.							
LX Sedan 4D		P333	14640	**5250**	**6100**	**7675**	**10000**
SE Wagon 4D		P363	17675	**6100**	**7075**	**8675**	**11100**
4-Cyl. 2.0/2.3L 16V		P,Z		**150**	**150**	**200**	**200**
FOCUS—4-Cyl. 16V—Equipment Schedule 6							
W.B. 103.0"; 2.0 Liter, 2.3 Liter.							
ZX3 Hatchback 2D		P313	14180	**6100**	**7075**	**8675**	**11100**
ZX5 Hatchback 4D		P373	15580	**6625**	**7675**	**9300**	**11750**
SE Sedan 4D		P34Z	15460	**5725**	**6675**	**8250**	**10600**
ZTS Sedan 4D		P38Z	16080	**6175**	**7175**	**8775**	**11200**
ZTW Wagon 4D		P35Z	18290	**6750**	**7800**	**9425**	**11950**
SVT Hatchback 2D		P395	19375	**7650**	**8775**	**10150**	**12400**
SVT Hatchback 4D		P375	19630	**8775**	**10050**	**11500**	**13850**
MUSTANG—V6—Equipment Schedule 4							
W.B. 101.3"; 3.8 Liter.							
Coupe 2D		P404	19160	**7775**	**8925**	**11100**	**14250**
Convertible 2D		P444	24895	**9350**	**10675**	**13200**	**16900**
Manual Trans				**(600)**	**(600)**	**(800)**	**(800)**
MUSTANG—V8—Equipment Schedule 4							
W.B. 101.3"; 4.6 Liter.							
GT Coupe 2D		P42X	24685	**10825**	**12275**	**14650**	**18250**
GT Convertible 2D		P45X	29025	**12900**	**14600**	**17100**	**21000**
Mach 1 Coupe 2D		P42R	30260	**13525**	**15275**	**17800**	**21700**
MUSTANG—V8 Supercharged—Equipment Schedule 4							
W.B. 101.3"; 4.6 Liter.							
Cobra Coupe 2D		P48Y	35200	**18875**	**21150**	**24000**	**28400**
Cobra Convertible 2D		P49Y	39575	**20850**	**23375**	**26300**	**31000**
TAURUS—V6—Equipment Schedule 4							
W.B. 108.5"; 3.0 Liter.							
LX Sedan 4D		P52U	20720	**5100**	**6000**	**8250**	**11350**
SE Sedan 4D		P53U	20855	**5775**	**6725**	**9000**	**12150**
SE Wagon 4D		P58S	22290	**6500**	**7525**	**9850**	**13150**
SES Sedan 4D		P55S	22040	**5850**	**6825**	**9100**	**12250**

0106

Body	Type	VIN	List	Trade-In Fair	Trade-In Good	Pvt-Party Good	Retail Excellent
SEL Sedan 4D		P56S	23965	6350	7375	9675	12950
SEL Wagon 4D		P59U	24115	6550	7575	9900	13200
V6 3.0 Liter 24V		S		350	350	465	465
V6 3.0L Flexible Fuel		2		0	0	0	0

CROWN VICTORIA—V8—Equipment Schedule 4
W.B. 114.7"; 4.6 Liter.

Sedan 4D		P73W	24345	7600	8725	11650	15650
LX Sedan 4D		P74W	27370	8500	9700	12700	16850

THUNDERBIRD—V8—Equipment Schedule 2
W.B. 107.2"; 3.9 Liter.

Soft Top Conv 2D		P60A	37530	17375	19500	22400	27000
Pacific Coast Conv 2D		P63A	43995				
Hard Top				950	950	1265	1265

2005 FORD — (1,2or3)(FAorZV)–(P31N)–5

FOCUS—4-Cyl.—Equipment Schedule 6
W.B. 102.9"; 2.0 Liter, 2.3 Liter.

ZX3 S Hatchback 2D		P31N	14545	7175	8300	10050	12650
ZX3 SE Hatchback 2D		P31N	15135	7175	8300	10050	12650
ZX3 SES Hatchback 2D		P31N	16235	7375	8500	10250	12900
ZX4 S Sedan 4D		P34N	15145	6800	7850	9550	12150
ZX4 SE Sedan 4D		P34N	15735	6800	7850	9550	12150
ZX4 SES Sedan 4D		P34N	16835	7000	8075	9800	12400
ZX4 ST Sedan 4D		P38Z	18335	7600	8725	10500	13150
ZX5 S Hatchback 4D		P35N	15845	7750	8900	10650	13400
ZX5 SE Hatchback 4D		P37N	16435	7750	8900	10650	13400
ZX5 SES Hatchback 4D		P37N	17535	7775	8950	10700	13450
ZXW SE Wagon 4D		P35N	17435	7175	8300	10050	12650
ZXW SES Wagon 4D		P33N	18535	7375	8500	10250	12900

MUSTANG—V6—Equipment Schedule 4
W.B. 107.1"; 4.0 Liter.

Coupe 2D		T80N	20405	12700	14350	16550	20000
Convertible 2D		T84N	24495				
Manual Trans				(625)	(625)	(835)	(835)

MUSTANG—V8—Equipment Schedule 4
W.B. 107.1"; 4.6 Liter.

GT Coupe 2D		T82H	25990				
GT Convertible 2D		T85H	29995				

TAURUS—V6—Equipment Schedule 4
W.B. 108.5"; 3.0 Liter.

SE Sedan 4D		P53U	21145	7350	8450	11000	14600
SE Wagon 4D		P58U	23015	8150	9325	11950	15600
SEL Sedan 4D		P56U	23055	7975	9175	11800	15450
SEL Wagon 4D		P59U	24005	8200	9375	12000	15650
V6 3.0 Liter 24V		S		375	375	500	500
V6 3.0L Flexible Fuel		2		0	0	0	0

FIVE HUNDRED—V6—Equipment Schedule 4
W.B. 112.9"; 3.0 Liter.

SE Sedan 4D		P231	22795	11925	13525	15850	19400
SE AWD Sedan 4D		P261	24495	12375	14025	16300	19900
SEL Sedan 4D		P241	24795	12475	14125	16450	20100
SEL AWD Sedan 4D		P271	26495	12800	14500	16900	20600
Limited Sedan 4D		P251	26795	12900	14600	17000	20700
Limited AWD Sedan 4D		P281	28495	13675	15475	17850	21600

CROWN VICTORIA—V8—Equipment Schedule 4
W.B. 114.7"; 4.6 Liter.

Sedan 4D		P73W	24810	9750	11100	14250	18650
LX Sedan 4D		P74W	27945	10675	12175	15350	19900

THUNDERBIRD—V8—Equipment Schedule 2
W.B. 107.2"; 3.9 Liter.

Soft Top Conv 2D		P60A	38065	19975	22400	25500	30600
50th Anniv Conv 2D		P69A	44430				
Hard Top				1025	1025	1365	1365

GT—V8—Equipment Schedule 2
W.B. 106.7"; 5.4 Liter.

Coupe 2D		P90S	143345				

0106

Body	Type	VIN	List	Trade-In Fair	Good	Pvt-Party Good	Retail Excellent

GEO

1991 GEO — (1Y,JGorJ8)1(MS246)-M-#

METRO—3-Cyl.—Equipment Schedule 6
W.B. 89.2", 93.1" (4D); 1.0 Liter.

Body	Type	VIN	List	Fair	Good	Good	Excellent
XFi Hatchback 2D	MS246	7361	175	225	650	1300	
Hatchback 2D	MR246	8031	150	225	625	1250	
Hatchback 4D	MR646	8231	175	225	650	1300	
LSi Hatchback 2D	MR246	9031	200	275	725	1400	
LSi Hatchback 4D	MR646	9231	225	325	775	1475	
LSi Convertible 2D	MR336	10966	300	400	925	1700	

STORM—4-Cyl.—Equipment Schedule 6
W.B. 96.5"; 1.6 Liter.

2+2 Coupe 2D	RF236	11685	250	350	1025	2025	
Hatchback Coupe 2D	RF436	11720	275	400	1075	2100	
GSi 2+2 Coupe 2D	RT235	13410	375	500	1250	2375	

PRIZM—4-Cyl.—Equipment Schedule 6
W.B. 95.7"; 1.6 Liter.

Notchback Sedan 4D	SK546	11555	400	600	1275	2375	
Hatchback Sedan 4D	SK646	11992	400	600	1275	2375	
GSi N'Back Sedan 4D	SL545	13599	475	675	1400	2550	
GSi Hatchback 4D	SL645	13949	500	725	1450	2625	
LSi Pkg			100	100	135	135	

1992 GEO — (1Y,JGorJ8)1(MS246)-N-#

METRO—3-Cyl.—Equipment Schedule 6
W.B. 89.2", 93.1" (4D); 1.0 Liter.

XFi Hatchback 2D	MS246	7585	175	250	700	1400	
Hatchback 2D	MR246	8305	175	225	675	1350	
Hatchback 4D	MR646	8705	175	250	700	1400	
LSi Hatchback 2D	MR246	9505	200	300	750	1475	
LSi Hatchback 4D	MR646	9905	250	350	825	1575	
LSi Convertible 2D	MR336	11275	325	425	975	1775	

STORM—4-Cyl.—Equipment Schedule 6
W.B. 96.5"; 1.6 Liter, 1.8 Liter.

2+2 Coupe 2D	RF236	12560	325	425	1275	2375	
Hatchback Coupe 2D	RF436	13330	350	475	1250	2450	
GSi 2+2 Coupe 2D	RT238	14530	400	600	1450	2775	

PRIZM—4-Cyl.—Equipment Schedule 6
W.B. 95.7"; 1.6 Liter.

Sedan 4D	SK546	11995	475	675	1425	2600	
GSi Sedan 4D	SL545	14135	525	750	1550	2775	
LSi Pkg			100	100	135	135	

1993 GEO — (1Y,JGorJ8)1(MS246)-P-#

METRO—3-Cyl.—Equipment Schedule 6
W.B. 89.2", 93.1" (4D); 1.0 Liter.

XFi Hatchback 2D	MS246	7296	200	275	750	1475	
Hatchback 2D	MR246	8016	175	250	725	1425	
Hatchback 4D	MR646	8505	200	275	750	1475	
LSi Hatchback 2D	MR246	9505	250	350	825	1600	
LSi Hatchback 4D	MR646	9905	275	400	925	1750	
LSi Convertible 2D	MR336	10749	350	475	1075	1950	

STORM—4-Cyl.—Equipment Schedule 6
W.B. 96.5"; 1.6 Liter, 1.8 Liter.

2+2 Coupe 2D	RF236	12620	400	525	1425	2800	
GSi 2+2 Coupe 2D	RT238	14585	500	725	1725	3225	

PRIZM—4-Cyl.—Equipment Schedule 6
W.B. 97.1"; 1.6 Liter, 1.8 Liter.

Sedan 4D	SK536	11662	550	775	1575	2825	
LSi Sedan 4D	SK536	12482	650	925	1800	3125	

1994 GEO — (1Y,JGorJ8)1(MS246)-R-#

METRO—3-Cyl.—Equipment Schedule 6
W.B. 89.2", 93.1" (5D); 1.0 Liter.

XFi Hatchback 2D	MS246	7791	200	300	825	1650	
Hatchback 2D	MR246	8511	200	275	800	1600	
Hatchback 4D	MR646	9011	200	300	825	1650	

PRIZM—4-Cyl.—Equipment Schedule 6
W.B. 97.1"; 1.6 Liter, 1.8 Liter.

Body Type	VIN	List	Trade-In Fair	Good	Pvt-Party Good	Retail Excellent
Sedan 4D	SK536	12480	625	900	1800	3175
LSi Sedan 4D	SK536	13410	750	1050	2025	3525

1995 GEO — (JG,2Cor1Y)1(MR226)–S–#

METRO—3-Cyl.—Equipment Schedule 6
W.B. 93.1"; 1.0 Liter.

Hatchback 2D	MR226	9481	225	325	850	1650
LSi Hatchback 2D	MR226	9781	325	425	1025	1925
4-Cyl. 1.3 Liter	9		100	100	135	135

METRO—4-Cyl.—Equipment Schedule 6
W.B. 93.1"; 1.3 Liter.

Sedan 4D	MR529	10741	450	625	1300	2375
LSi Sedan 4D	MR529	11141	475	675	1350	2450

PRIZM—4-Cyl.—Equipment Schedule 6
W.B. 97.1"; 1.6 Liter, 1.8 Liter.

Sedan 4D	SK526	13435	725	1050	2075	3650
LSi Sedan 4D	SK526	14260	850	1200	2400	4100

1996 GEO — (1Yor2C)1(MR226)–T–#

METRO—3-Cyl.—Equipment Schedule 6
W.B. 93.1"; 1.0 Liter.

Coupe 2D	MR226	9988	275	375	975	1875
LSi Coupe 2D	MR226	10271	375	500	1175	2150
4-Cyl. 1.3 Liter	9		100	100	135	135

METRO—4-Cyl.—Equipment Schedule 6
W.B. 93.1"; 1.3 Liter.

Sedan 4D	MR529	11026	525	750	1525	2725
LSi Sedan 4D	MR529	11426	575	825	1600	2825

PRIZM—4-Cyl.—Equipment Schedule 6
W.B. 97.1"; 1.6 Liter, 1.8 Liter.

Sedan 4D	SK526	14300	850	1200	2450	4225
LSi Sedan 4D	SK526	15010	975	1350	2650	4450

1997 GEO — (1Yor2C)1(MR226)–V–#

METRO—3-Cyl.—Equipment Schedule 6
W.B. 93.1"; 1.0 Liter.

Coupe 2D	MR226	10185	350	475	1200	2250

METRO—4-Cyl.—Equipment Schedule 6
W.B. 93.1"; 1.3 Liter.

LSi Sedan 4D	MR529	11546	700	1000	1925	3350
LSi Coupe 2D	MR229	10606	500	725	1525	2775

PRIZM—4-Cyl.—Equipment Schedule 6
W.B. 97.1"; 1.6 Liter, 1.8 Liter.

Sedan 4D	SK526	14375	975	1375	2750	4625
LSi Sedan 4D	SK526	15020	1100	1550	2950	4875

HONDA

1991 HONDA — (1HGorJHM)(ED836)–M–#

CIVIC—4-Cyl.—Equipment Schedule 6
W.B. 98.4", 90.6" (CRX); 1.5 Liter, 1.6 Liter.

CRX HF H'Back 2D	ED836	9405	700	1000	1975	3450
CRX Hatchback 2D	ED835	9670	750	1050	2050	3575
CRX Si Hatchback 2D	ED836	11390	900	1250	2425	4100
Hatchback 2D	ED634	7155	600	875	1775	3175
Wagon 4D	EE275	10585	725	1050	2025	3525
DX Sedan 4D	ED354	9750	775	1100	2125	3650
DX Hatchback 2D	ED635	9005	600	850	1750	3125
Si Hatchback 2D	ED736	10555	825	1175	2300	3950
LX Sedan 4D	ED355	10760	775	1125	2150	3675
EX Sedan 4D	ED456	11455	825	1175	2350	4050
4WD Wagon 4D	EE476	12670	825	1175	2300	3950

ACCORD—4-Cyl.—Equipment Schedule 3
W.B. 107.1"; 2.2 Liter.

DX Sedan 4D	CB764	13555	925	1300	2500	4175
DX Coupe 2D	CB724	13355	950	1325	2525	4225
LX Sedan 4D	CB765	16105	1075	1500	2750	4475
LX Coupe 2D	CB725	15905	1150	1600	2875	4625
LX Wagon 4D	CB985	18325	1100	1550	2825	4550
EX Sedan 4D	CB766	17805	1100	1550	2825	4550
EX Coupe 2D	CB726	17605	1200	1650	2925	4700

Body	Type	VIN	List	Trade-In Fair	Good	Pvt-Party Good	Retail Excellent
EX Wagon 4D		CB986	20075	1350	1850	3150	4975
SE Sedan 4D		CB768	19805	1125	1575	2850	4600
Manual Trans				(175)	(175)	(235)	(235)

PRELUDE—4-Cyl.—Equipment Schedule 3
W.B. 101.0"; 2.0 Liter.

Body	Type	VIN	List	Fair	Good	Good	Excellent
2.0 Si Coupe 2D		BA412	15955	900	1275	2450	4100
Si Coupe 2D		BA413	18175	975	1350	2550	4225
Si 4WS Coupe 2D		BA414	19460	975	1350	2550	4225
Si ALB Coupe 2D		BA415	19710	975	1350	2550	4225
Auto Trans				100	100	135	135

1992 HONDA — (1HGorJHM)(EH234)–N–#

CIVIC—4-Cyl.—Equipment Schedule 6
W.B. 101.3", 103.2" (Sed); 1.5 Liter, 1.6 Liter.

Body	Type	VIN	List	Fair	Good	Good	Excellent
CX Hatchback 2D		EH234	8190	625	900	1850	3300
DX Sedan 4D		EG854	10845	975	1350	2625	4375
DX Hatchback 2D		EH235	9940	775	1125	2300	3975
VX Hatchback 2D		EH236	10640	900	1275	2500	4225
Si Hatchback 2D		EH338	11990	1025	1450	2725	4500
LX Sedan 4D		EG855	11675	975	1375	2650	4425
EX Sedan 4D		EH959	13865	1075	1500	2825	4600

ACCORD—4-Cyl.—Equipment Schedule 6
W.B. 107.1"; 2.2 Liter.

Body	Type	VIN	List	Fair	Good	Good	Excellent
DX Sedan 4D		CB764	14265	1050	1475	2800	4600
DX Coupe 2D		CB724	14065	1075	1525	2850	4675
LX Sedan 4D		CB765	16865	1250	1750	3125	5025
LX Coupe 2D		CB725	16665	1350	1850	3250	5200
LX Wagon 4D		CB985	18490	1300	1800	3175	5100
EX Sedan 4D		CB767	19285	1300	1800	3175	5100
EX Coupe 2D		CB727	19085	1400	1900	3325	5250
EX Wagon 4D		CB987	20940	1600	2100	3575	5525
Manual Trans				(175)	(175)	(235)	(235)

PRELUDE—4-Cyl.—Equipment Schedule 3
W.B. 100.4"; 2.2 Liter, 2.3 Liter.

Body	Type	VIN	List	Fair	Good	Good	Excellent
S Coupe 2D		BA814	16540	1575	2075	3525	5450
Si Coupe 2D		BB215	19540	1750	2275	3725	5750
Si 4WS Coupe 2D		BB216	21860	1750	2275	3725	5750
Auto Trans				100	100	135	135

1993 HONDA — (1HGorJHM)(EH235)–P–#

CIVIC—4-Cyl.—Equipment Schedule 6
W.B. 101.3", 103.2" (2D, 4D); 1.5 Liter, 1.6 Liter.

Body	Type	VIN	List	Fair	Good	Good	Excellent
CX Hatchback 2D		EH235	8730	675	975	2050	3650
DX Sedan 4D		EG854	11385	1075	1525	2875	4725
DX Coupe 2D		EJ114	10980	950	1325	2650	4450
DX Hatchback 2D		EH236	10430	875	1225	2500	4300
VX Hatchback 2D		EH237	11130	1025	1450	2775	4600
Si Hatchback 2D		EH338	12530	1200	1650	3050	4950
LX Sedan 4D		EG855	12215	1125	1575	2925	4825
EX Sedan 4D		EH959	14365	1250	1750	3150	5075
EX Coupe 2D		EJ115	12730	1225	1725	3125	5050

CIVIC del SOL—4-Cyl.—Equipment Schedule 6
W.B. 93.3"; 1.5 Liter, 1.6 Liter.

Body	Type	VIN	List	Fair	Good	Good	Excellent
S Coupe 2D		EG114	13530	1275	1775	3025	4775
Si Coupe 2D		EH616	15330	1525	2025	3325	5125

ACCORD—4-Cyl.—Equipment Schedule 6
W.B. 107.1"; 2.2 Liter.

Body	Type	VIN	List	Fair	Good	Good	Excellent
DX Sedan 4D		CB764	15030	1225	1700	3125	5075
DX Coupe 2D		CB724	14830	1250	1750	3175	5125
LX Sedan 4D		CB765	17630	1575	2075	3600	5625
LX Coupe 2D		CB725	17430	1625	2125	3675	5800
LX Wagon 4D		CB985	19055	1625	2125	3650	5700
10th Annv Sedan 4D		CB769	18780	1550	2050	3575	5600
EX Sedan 4D		CB767	20050	1650	2150	3675	5750
EX Coupe 2D		CB727	19850	1725	2250	3800	5925
EX Wagon 4D		CB987	21505	1950	2475	4025	6150
SE Sedan 4D		CB768	22050	1675	2200	3725	5800
SE Coupe 2D		CB728	21850	1625	2125	3650	5700
Manual Trans				(225)	(225)	(300)	(300)

PRELUDE—4-Cyl.—Equipment Schedule 3
W.B. 100.4"; 2.2 Liter, 2.3 Liter.

Body	Type	VIN	List	Fair	Good	Good	Excellent
S Coupe 2D		BA814	17330	1900	2425	3975	6075
Si Coupe 2D		BB215	20330	2100	2675	4250	6400

1993 HONDA

Body Type	VIN	List	Trade-In Fair	Good	Pvt-Party Good	Retail Excellent
Si 4WS Coupe 2D	BB216	22650	2100	2675	4250	6400
VTEC Coupe 2D	BB117	23020	2425	3000	4650	6875
Auto Trans			125	125	165	165

1994 HONDA — (1HGorJHM)(EH235)–R–#

CIVIC—4-Cyl.—Equipment Schedule 6
W.B. 101.3", 103.2" (2D, 4D); 1.5 Liter, 1.6 Liter.

Body Type	VIN	List	Trade-In Fair	Good	Pvt-Party Good	Retail Excellent
CX Hatchback 2D	EH235	9750	750	1075	2350	4150
DX Sedan 4D	EG854	12100	1225	1725	3175	5150
DX Coupe 2D	EJ212	11570	1075	1500	2900	4825
DX Hatchback 2D	EH236	11150	975	1375	2775	4650
VX Hatchback 2D	EH237	11850	1150	1600	3050	5000
Si Hatchback 2D	EH338	13520	1375	1900	3375	5250
LX Sedan 4D	EG855	13300	1300	1800	3250	5250
EX Sedan 4D	EH959	16090	1525	2025	3550	5575
EX Coupe 4D	EJ112	13950	1475	1975	3475	5500

del SOL—4-Cyl.—Equipment Schedule 6
W.B. 93.3"; 1.5 Liter, 1.6 Liter.

Body Type	VIN	List	Trade-In Fair	Good	Pvt-Party Good	Retail Excellent
S Coupe 2D	EG114	14450	1525	2025	3400	5250
Si Coupe 2D	EH616	16450	1800	2325	3675	5600
VTEC Coupe 2D	EG217	17850	1950	2475	3875	5850

ACCORD—4-Cyl.—Equipment Schedule 3
W.B. 106.9"; 2.2 Liter.

Body Type	VIN	List	Trade-In Fair	Good	Pvt-Party Good	Retail Excellent
DX Sedan 4D	CD562	15430	1375	1875	3300	5250
DX Coupe 2D	CD722	15230	1375	1900	3325	5250
LX Sedan 4D	CD563	18330	1800	2325	3800	5875
LX Coupe 2D	CD723	18180	1825	2350	3925	6075
LX Wagon 4D	CE182	19280	1850	2375	3900	6075
EX Sedan 4D	CD565	20850	1900	2425	3975	6075
EX Coupe 4D	CD725	20650	1975	2500	4100	6250
EX Wagon 4D	CE189	21850	2175	2775	4325	6450
Manual Trans			(275)	(275)	(365)	(365)

PRELUDE—4-Cyl.—Equipment Schedule 3
W.B. 100.4"; 2.2 Liter, 2.3 Liter.

Body Type	VIN	List	Trade-In Fair	Good	Pvt-Party Good	Retail Excellent
S Coupe 2D	BA814	18450	2250	2825	4475	6750
Si Coupe 2D	BB215	21750	2500	3100	4800	7125
4WS Coupe 2D	BB216	24510	2500	3100	4800	7125
VTEC Coupe 2D	BB117	24850	2850	3500	5250	7675
Auto Trans			150	150	200	200

1995 HONDA — (1HGorJHM)(EH235)–S–#

CIVIC—4-Cyl.—Equipment Schedule 6
W.B. 101.3", 103.2" (2D, 4D); 1.5 Liter, 1.6 Liter.

Body Type	VIN	List	Trade-In Fair	Good	Pvt-Party Good	Retail Excellent
CX Hatchback 2D	EH235	10130	875	1225	2625	4525
DX Sedan 4D	EG854	12360	1500	2000	3550	5625
DX Coupe 2D	EJ212	11970	1250	1750	3275	5300
DX Hatchback 2D	EH236	11480	1125	1575	3075	5100
VX Hatchback 2D	EH237	12180	1375	1875	3400	5450
Si Hatchback 2D	EH338	13920	1675	2175	3750	5925
LX Sedan 4D	EG855	13700	1550	2050	3625	5725
EX Sedan 4D	EH959	16580	1825	2350	3975	6150
EX Coupe 2D	EJ112	14410	1775	2300	3900	6075

del SOL—4-Cyl.—Equipment Schedule 6
W.B. 93.3"; 1.5 Liter, 1.6 Liter.

Body Type	VIN	List	Trade-In Fair	Good	Pvt-Party Good	Retail Excellent
S Coupe 2D	EG114	15160	1825	2350	3750	5725
Si Coupe 2D	EH616	17330	2075	2650	4100	6100
VTEC Coupe 2D	EG217	19580	2275	2825	4350	6425

ACCORD—4-Cyl.—Equipment Schedule 3
W.B. 106.9"; 2.2 Liter.

Body Type	VIN	List	Trade-In Fair	Good	Pvt-Party Good	Retail Excellent
DX Sedan 4D	CD562	15930	1675	2200	3725	5825
LX Sedan 4D	CD563	18880	2150	2750	4350	6550
LX Coupe 2D	CD723	18680	2150	2750	4450	6775
LX Wagon 4D	CE182	19840	2250	2825	4450	6675
EX Sedan 4D	CD565	21440	2300	2875	4550	6850
EX Coupe 2D	CD725	21240	2325	2900	4650	7000
EX Wagon 4D	CE189	22470	2600	3225	4875	7175
Manual Trans			(325)	(325)	(435)	(435)
V6 2.7 Liter			325	325	435	435

PRELUDE—4-Cyl.—Equipment Schedule 3
W.B. 100.4"; 2.2 Liter, 2.3 Liter.

Body Type	VIN	List	Trade-In Fair	Good	Pvt-Party Good	Retail Excellent
S Coupe 2D	BA814	19930	2650	3275	5075	7500
Si Coupe 2D	BB215	22580	2925	3600	5425	7925
SE Coupe 2D	BB217	23780	2925	3600	5425	7925

Body Type	VIN	List	Trade-In Fair	Good	Pvt-Party Good	Retail Excellent
VTEC Coupe 2D	BB117	25730	**3325**	**4025**	**5925**	**8500**
Auto Trans			**175**	**175**	**235**	**235**

1996 HONDA — (1HG,2HGorJHM)(EJ632)-T-#

CIVIC—4-Cyl.—Equipment Schedule 6
W.B. 103.2"; 1.6 Liter.

CX Hatchback 2D	EJ632	10360	**1800**	**2325**	**3575**	**5300**
DX Sedan 4D	EJ652	12630	**2575**	**3175**	**4525**	**6450**
DX Coupe 2D	EJ612	12280	**2325**	**2900**	**4250**	**6100**
DX Hatchback 2D	EJ634	11630	**2150**	**2750**	**4025**	**5875**
HX Coupe 2D	EJ650	13480	**2600**	**3225**	**4550**	**6500**
LX Sedan 4D	EJ712	13980	**2650**	**3275**	**4625**	**6575**
EX Sedan 4D	EJ854	16660	**2975**	**3650**	**5050**	**7050**
EX Coupe 2D	EJ814	15330	**2875**	**3550**	**4950**	**6950**

del SOL—4-Cyl.—Equipment Schedule 6
W.B. 93.3"; 1.6 Liter.

S Coupe 2D	EH614	15475	**2100**	**2675**	**4150**	**6200**
Si Coupe 2D	EH616	17695	**2400**	**2975**	**4500**	**6625**
VTEC Coupe 2D	EG217	19995	**2600**	**3225**	**4775**	**6950**

ACCORD—4-Cyl.—Equipment Schedule 3
W.B. 106.9"; 2.2 Liter.

DX Sedan 4D	CD562	16280	**2025**	**2600**	**4250**	**6500**
Anniversary Ed Sed 4D	CD568	17390	**2250**	**2825**	**4500**	**6800**
LX Sedan 4D	CD563	19270	**2575**	**3200**	**4925**	**7300**
LX Coupe 2D	CD723	19070	**2575**	**3175**	**5050**	**7550**
LX Wagon 4D	CE182	20170	**2675**	**3275**	**5050**	**7425**
EX Sedan 4D	CD565	21780	**2775**	**3425**	**5225**	**7675**
EX Coupe 2D	CD725	21580	**2750**	**3375**	**5250**	**7825**
EX Wagon 4D	CE189	22810	**3050**	**3725**	**5525**	**8000**
Manual Trans	1,5,7		**(375)**	**(375)**	**(500)**	**(500)**
V6 2.7 Liter			**375**	**375**	**500**	**500**

PRELUDE—4-Cyl.—Equipment Schedule 3
W.B. 100.4"; 2.2 Liter, 2.3 Liter.

S Coupe 2D	BA814	20340	**3075**	**3725**	**5700**	**8325**
Si Coupe 2D	BB215	23035	**3425**	**4125**	**6100**	**8825**
VTEC Coupe 2D	BB117	26260	**3850**	**4600**	**6650**	**9450**
Auto Trans			**200**	**200**	**265**	**265**

1997 HONDA — (1HG,2HGorJHM)(EJ632)-V-#

CIVIC—4-Cyl.—Equipment Schedule 6
W.B. 103.2"; 1.6 Liter.

CX Hatchback 2D	EJ632	10945	**2200**	**2800**	**4075**	**5900**
DX Sedan 4D	EJ652	13030	**3000**	**3675**	**5075**	**7075**
DX Coupe 2D	EJ612	12675	**2800**	**3425**	**4775**	**6750**
DX Hatchback 2D	EJ634	12195	**2600**	**3225**	**4550**	**6500**
HX Coupe 2D	EJ712	13795	**3075**	**3725**	**5150**	**7150**
LX Sedan 4D	EJ657	15045	**3125**	**3775**	**5225**	**7225**
EX Sedan 4D	EJ854	16875	**3500**	**4200**	**5675**	**7775**
EX Coupe 2D	EJ814	15645	**3425**	**4125**	**5575**	**7675**

del SOL—4-Cyl.—Equipment Schedule 6
W.B. 93.3"; 1.6 Liter.

S Coupe 2D	EH614	15475	**2425**	**3000**	**4575**	**6750**
Si Coupe 2D	EH616	17695	**2725**	**3325**	**4925**	**7150**
VTEC Coupe 2D	EG217	19995	**2950**	**3625**	**5250**	**7550**

ACCORD—4-Cyl.—Equipment Schedule 3
W.B. 106.9"; 2.2 Liter.

DX Sedan 4D	CD562	16295	**2450**	**3050**	**4850**	**7275**
LX Sedan 4D	CD563	19385	**3050**	**3725**	**5600**	**8175**
LX Coupe 2D	CD723	19185	**3000**	**3675**	**5675**	**8400**
LX Wagon 4D	CE182	20285	**3150**	**3800**	**5700**	**8275**
Special Edition 4D	CD560	20795	**3050**	**3725**	**5600**	**8175**
Special Edition 2D	CD720	20595	**3000**	**3675**	**5675**	**8400**
EX Sedan 4D	CD565	21895	**3275**	**3950**	**5950**	**8625**
EX Coupe 2D	CD725	21695	**3225**	**3900**	**5975**	**8750**
EX Wagon 4D	CE189	22925	**3575**	**4275**	**6200**	**8875**
Manual Trans	1,5,7		**(400)**	**(400)**	**(535)**	**(535)**
V6 2.7 Liter			**425**	**425**	**565**	**565**

PRELUDE—4-Cyl.—Equipment Schedule 3
W.B. 101.8"; 2.2 Liter.

Coupe 2D	BB614	23595	**4525**	**5350**	**7400**	**10250**
Type SH Coupe 2D	BB615	26095	**5000**	**5875**	**7950**	**10850**
Auto Trans			**200**	**200**	**265**	**265**

Body	Type	VIN	List	Trade-In Fair	Trade-In Good	Pvt-Party Good	Retail Excellent

1998 HONDA — (1HG,2HGorJHM)(EJ632)-W-#

CIVIC—4-Cyl.—Equipment Schedule 6
W.B. 103.2"; 1.6 Liter.

CX Hatchback 2D	EJ632	11045	2675	3275	4650	6600
DX Sedan 4D	EJ652	13130	3525	4225	5700	7800
DX Coupe 2D	EJ612	12975	3300	3975	5425	7500
DX Hatchback 2D	EJ634	12495	3075	3725	5175	7200
HX Coupe 2D	EJ712	13795	3625	4325	5800	7925
LX Sedan 4D	EJ657	15145	3650	4375	5850	7975
EX Sedan 4D	EJ854	16875	4050	4825	6350	8575
EX Coupe 2D	EJ814	15645	3975	4725	6250	8475

ACCORD—4-Cyl.—Equipment Schedule 3
W.B. 105.1", 106.9" (Sed); 2.3 Liter.

DX Sedan 4D	CF864	16295	3650	4400	5875	8000
LX Sedan 4D	CG564	19485	4350	5125	6700	8950
LX Coupe 2D	CG324	19485	4275	5075	6775	9200
EX Sedan 4D	CG565	21995	4550	5375	7075	9500
EX Coupe 2D	CG325	21995	4500	5300	7075	9600
Manual Trans	1,3,5,7	....	(425)	(425)	(565)	(565)
4-Cyl. 2.3L ULEV			0	0	0	0
V6 3.0 Liter VTEC			475	475	635	635

PRELUDE—4-Cyl.—Equipment Schedule 3
W.B. 101.8"; 2.2 Liter.

Coupe 2D	BB614	23695	5225	6075	8275	11300
Type SH Coupe 2D	BB615	26195	5700	6625	8850	12000
Auto Trans			200	200	265	265

1999 HONDA — (1HG,2HGorJHM)(EJ632)-X-#

CIVIC—4-Cyl.—Equipment Schedule 6
W.B. 103.2"; 1.6 Liter.

CX Hatchback 2D	EJ632	11065	3175	3825	5250	7275
DX Sedan 4D	EJ652	13200	4075	4850	6325	8500
DX Coupe 2D	EJ612	12995	3850	4600	6075	8200
DX Hatchback 2D	EJ634	12515	3650	4375	5825	7925
VP Sedan 4D	EJ661	15045	4325	5125	6625	8825
HX Coupe 2D	EJ712	13815	4175	4950	6450	8625
LX Sedan 4D	EJ657	15245	4250	5050	6550	8750
EX Sedan 4D	EJ854	17145	4675	5525	7050	9325
EX Coupe 2D	EJ814	15865	4600	5425	6975	9250
Si Coupe 2D	EM115	17860	6050	7000	8675	11150

ACCORD—4-Cyl.—Equipment Schedule 3
W.B. 105.1", 106.9" (Sed); 2.3 Liter.

DX Sedan 4D	CF864	16415	4325	5125	6600	8775
LX Sedan 4D	CG564	19605	5075	5950	7500	9800
LX Coupe 2D	CG324	19605	4975	5850	7575	10050
EX Sedan 4D	CG565	22115	5325	6225	7950	10500
EX Coupe 2D	CG325	22115	5250	6125	7925	10500
Manual Trans	1,3,5	....	(450)	(450)	(600)	(600)
4-Cyl. 2.3L ULEV			0	0	0	0
V6 3.0 Liter VTEC			525	525	700	700

PRELUDE—4-Cyl.—Equipment Schedule 3
W.B. 101.8"; 2.2 Liter.

Coupe 2D	BB614	23865	6000	6950	9250	12400
Type SH Coupe 2D	BB615	26365	6500	7525	9850	13150
Auto Trans			200	200	265	265

2000 HONDA — (1HG,2HGorJHM)(ZE137)-Y-#

INSIGHT—3-Cyl. Hybrid—Equipment Schedule 3
W.B. 94.5"; 1.0 Liter.

Hatchback 2D	ZE137	20495	5950	6900	8575	11100

CIVIC—4-Cyl.—Equipment Schedule 6
W.B. 103.2"; 1.6 Liter.

CX Hatchback 2D	EJ632	11165	3550	4250	5800	8000
DX Sedan 4D	EJ652	13300	4550	5375	7000	9350
DX Coupe 2D	EJ612	13095	4375	5150	6775	9100
DX Hatchback 2D	EJ634	12615	4100	4875	6475	8750
VP Sedan 4D	EJ661	15145	4875	5725	7400	9800
HX Coupe 2D	EJ712	13915	4675	5525	7150	9525
LX Sedan 4D	EJ657	15345	4850	5700	7350	9750
EX Sedan 4D	EJ854	17245	5350	6250	7950	10450
EX Coupe 2D	EJ814	15965	5250	6100	7800	10300

Body Type	VIN	List	Trade-In Fair	Trade-In Good	Pvt-Party Good	Retail Excellent
Si Coupe 2D	EM115	17960	6875	7900	9700	12350

ACCORD—4-Cyl.—Equipment Schedule 3
W.B. 105.1", 106.9" (Sed); 2.3 Liter.

Body Type	VIN	List	Fair	Good	Good	Excellent
DX Sedan 4D	CF864	16565	4800	5650	7275	9625
LX Sedan 4D	CG564	19755	5875	6850	8525	11050
LX Coupe 2D	CG324	19755	5750	6700	8550	11250
SE Sedan 4D	CG567	20905	6150	7150	8875	11450
EX Sedan 4D	CG565	22265	6150	7150	9050	11800
EX Coupe 2D	CG325	22265	6075	7050	9025	11850
Manual Trans			(500)	(500)	(665)	(665)
4-Cyl. 2.3L ULEV			0	0	0	0
V6 3.0 Liter VTEC			600	600	800	800

PRELUDE—4-Cyl.—Equipment Schedule 3
W.B. 101.8"; 2.2 Liter.

Body Type	VIN	List	Fair	Good	Good	Excellent
Coupe 2D	BB614	23915	6925	8000	10500	13900
Type SH Coupe 2D	BB615	26415	7550	8675	11200	14750
Auto Trans			225	225	300	300

S2000—4-Cyl.—Equipment Schedule 3
W.B. 94.5"; 2.0 Liter.

Body Type	VIN	List	Fair	Good	Good	Excellent
Convertible 2D	AP114	32415	11000	12525	14750	18150
Hard Top			675	675	900	900

2001 HONDA — (1HGorJHM)(ZE135)-1-#

INSIGHT—3-Cyl. Hybrid—Equipment Schedule 3
W.B. 94.5"; 1.0 Liter.

Body Type	VIN	List	Fair	Good	Good	Excellent
Hatchback 2D	ZE135	20620	6775	7825	9625	12300

CIVIC—4-Cyl.—Equipment Schedule 6
W.B. 103.1"; 1.7 Liter.

Body Type	VIN	List	Fair	Good	Good	Excellent
DX Sedan 4D	ES151	13400	5475	6400	7775	9950
DX Coupe 2D	EM212	13200	5275	6175	7575	9675
HX Coupe 2D	EM217	14000	5650	6575	7975	10150
LX Sedan 4D	ES155	15450	5900	6875	8275	10500
LX Coupe 2D	EM215	15250	5800	6750	8150	10350
EX Sedan 4D	ES257	17350	6450	7475	8925	11200
EX Coupe 2D	EM219	16850	6300	7300	8750	11000
GX Sedan 4D	EN264	20670				

ACCORD—4-Cyl.—Equipment Schedule 3
W.B. 105.1", 106.9" (Sed); 2.3 Liter.

Body Type	VIN	List	Fair	Good	Good	Excellent
DX Sedan 4D	CF864	16640	5400	6300	8075	10650
VP Sedan 4D	CF866	17640	5600	6525	8325	10900
LX Sedan 4D	CG564	20030	6750	7800	9650	12400
LX Coupe 2D	CG324	20030	6600	7650	9700	12650
EX Sedan 4D	CG565	22640	7075	8175	10250	13300
EX Coupe 2D	CG325	22640	6975	8050	10250	13350
Manual Trans	1,5		(525)	(525)	(700)	(700)
4-Cyl. 2.3L ULEV/SULEV			0	0	0	0
V6 3.0 Liter VTEC			675	675	900	900

PRELUDE—4-Cyl.—Equipment Schedule 3
W.B. 101.8"; 2.2 Liter.

Body Type	VIN	List	Fair	Good	Good	Excellent
Coupe 2D	BB614	24040	8025	9225	11850	15500
Type SH Coupe 2D	BB615	26540	8725	10000	12650	16500
Auto Trans			250	250	335	335

S2000—4-Cyl.—Equipment Schedule 2
W.B. 94.5"; 2.0 Liter.

Body Type	VIN	List	Fair	Good	Good	Excellent
Convertible 2D	AP114	32740	12325	13975	16250	19800
Hard Top			700	700	935	935

2002 HONDA — (1HG,SHHorJHM)(ZE135)-2-#

INSIGHT—3-Cyl. Hybrid—Equipment Schedule 3
W.B. 94.5"; 1.0 Liter.

Body Type	VIN	List	Fair	Good	Good	Excellent
Hatchback 2D	ZE135	21720	7675	8825	10750	13650

CIVIC—4-Cyl.—Equipment Schedule 6
W.B. 101.2", 103.1" (Sed & Cpe); 1.7 Liter, 2.0 Liter.

Body Type	VIN	List	Fair	Good	Good	Excellent
DX Sedan 4D	ES151	13450	6225	7225	8650	10900
DX Coupe 2D	EM212	13250	6075	7025	8500	10700
HX Coupe 2D	EM217	14050	6425	7425	8875	11150
LX Sedan 4D	ES155	15550	6775	7825	9300	11650
LX Coupe 2D	EM215	15350	6650	7675	9175	11500
EX Sedan 4D	ES257	17450	7400	8500	10050	12450
EX Coupe 2D	EM219	16950	7175	8300	9800	12150
Si Hatchback 2D	EP335	19440	6950	8025	9900	12700

ACCORD—4-Cyl.—Equipment Schedule 3
W.B. 105.1", 106.9" (Sed); 2.3 Liter.

2002 HONDA

Body Type	VIN	List	Trade-In Fair	Good	Pvt-Party Good	Retail Excellent
DX Sedan 4D	CF864	16740	6100	7075	9025	11850
VP Sedan 4D	CF866	17740	6350	7375	9325	12150
LX Sedan 4D	CG564	20130	7750	8900	10950	13950
LX Coupe 2D	CG324	20130	7600	8725	10950	14200
SE Sedan 4D	CG567	21290	8100	9300	11350	14400
SE Coupe 2D	CG320	21290	8325	9525	11650	14750
EX Sedan 4D	CG566	22740	8150	9325	11600	14900
EX Coupe 2D	CG325	22740	8025	9225	11600	15000
Manual Trans	1,5		(550)	(550)	(735)	(735)
4-Cyl. 2.3L ULEV/SULEV			0	0	0	0
V6 3.0 Liter VTEC			750	750	1000	1000
S2000—4-Cyl.—Equipment Schedule 2						
W.B. 94.5"; 2.0 Liter.						
Convertible 2D	AP114	32840	13775	15575	17950	21700
Hard Top			725	725	965	965

2003 HONDA — (1HG,SHHorJHM)(ZE135)-3-#

INSIGHT—3-Cyl. Hybrid—Equipment Schedule 3
W.B. 94.5"; 1.0 Liter.

Hatchback 2D	ZE135	21740	8725	10000	12000	15050

CIVIC—4-Cyl.—Equipment Schedule 6
W.B. 101.2", 103.1" (Sed & Cpe), 103.2" (Hybrid); 1.3 Liter, 1.7 Liter, 2.0 Liter.

DX Sedan 4D	ES151	13470	7075	8175	9700	12150
DX Coupe 2D	EM212	13270	6925	8000	9550	11950
HX Coupe 2D	EM217	14170	7300	8400	9900	12400
LX Sedan 4D	ES155	15670	7750	8900	10500	13000
LX Coupe 2D	EM215	15470	7625	8750	10350	12800
EX Sedan 4D	ES257	17520	8450	9675	11300	13850
EX Coupe 2D	EM219	17270	8200	9375	11000	13550
Si Hatchback 2D	EP335	19460	7925	9125	11100	14050
Hybrid Sedan 4D	ES956	19990	11550	13100	14800	17600

ACCORD—4-Cyl.—Equipment Schedule 6
W.B. 105.1", 107.9" (Sed); 2.4 Liter.

DX Sedan 4D	CM551	17060	7900	9075	10900	13750
LX Sedan 4D	CM564	20460	10000	11350	13250	16150
LX Coupe 2D	CM712	20560	10000	11350	13300	16350
EX Sedan 4D	CM556	22860	10675	12125	14050	17100
EX Coupe 2D	CM716	22960	10275	11700	13850	17200
5-Spd Manual Trans	1,5		(575)	(575)	(765)	(765)
6-Spd Manual Trans			0	0	0	0
V6 3.0 Liter VTEC			825	825	1100	1100

S2000—4-Cyl.—Equipment Schedule 2
W.B. 94.5"; 2.0 Liter.

Convertible 2D	AP114	33060	15425	17375	19900	24000
Hard Top			750	750	1000	1000

2004 HONDA — (1HG,SHHorJHM)(ZE135)-4-#

INSIGHT—3-Cyl. Hybrid—Equipment Schedule 3
W.B. 94.5"; 1.0 Liter.

Hatchback 2D	ZE135	21870	9900	11300	13300	16450

CIVIC—4-Cyl.—Equipment Schedule 6
W.B. 101.2", 103.1" (Sed & Cpe); 1.3 Liter, 1.7 Liter, 2.0 Liter.

DX Sedan 4D	ES151	13500	8100	9300	10750	13200
Value Sedan 4D	ES163	14900	8500	9700	11200	13700
Value Coupe 2D	EM221	13900	7975	9175	10650	13050
HX Coupe 2D	EM217	14200	8325	9525	11050	13500
LX Sedan 4D	ES155	15850	8900	10175	11700	14200
LX Coupe 2D	EM215	15650	8725	10000	11550	14000
EX Sedan 4D	ES257	17750	9600	10950	12500	15150
EX Coupe 2D	EM219	17350	9350	10675	12200	14800
Si Hatchback 2D	EP335	19560	9025	10325	12300	15350
Hybrid Sedan 4D	ES956	20140	12950	14650	16300	19150
GX Sedan 4D	EN264	21250				

ACCORD—4-Cyl.—Equipment Schedule 3
W.B. 105.1", 107.9" (Sed); 2.4 Liter.

DX Sedan 4D	CM551	17190	9025	10325	12150	15100
LX Sedan 4D	CM553	20590	11450	13000	14850	17850
LX Coupe 2D	CM712	20690	11400	12950	14950	18100
EX Sedan 4D	CM556	22990	12175	13775	15700	18900
EX Coupe 2D	CM716	23090	11775	13350	15550	19000
5-Spd Manual Trans	1,5		(600)	(600)	(800)	(800)
6-Spd Manual Trans			0	0	0	0
V6 3.0 Liter VTEC			900	900	1200	1200

Body	Type	VIN	List	Trade-In Fair	Trade-In Good	Pvt-Party Good	Retail Excellent

S2000—4-Cyl.—Equipment Schedule 2
W.B. 94.5"; 2.2 Liter.

| Convertible 2D | AP214 | 33290 | **17275** | **19400** | **22200** | **26700** |
| Hard Top | | | 775 | 775 | 1035 | 1035 |

2005 HONDA — (1HG,SHHorJHM)(ZE137)-5-#

INSIGHT—3-Cyl. Hybrid—Equipment Schedule 3
W.B. 94.5"; 1.0 Liter.

| Hatchback 3D | ZE137 | 22045 | **10675** | **12125** | **14150** | **17300** |

CIVIC—4-Cyl.—Equipment Schedule 6
W.B. 101.2", 103.1" (Sed & Cpe); 1.3 Liter, 1.7 Liter, 2.0 Liter.

DX Sedan 4D	ES151	13675	**8675**	**9950**	**11250**	**13550**
Value Sedan 4D	ES163	15075	9175	10425	11800	14100
Value Coupe 2D	EM221	14075	8600	9850	11200	13450
HX Coupe 2D	EM217	14375	8950	10225	11600	13850
LX Sedan 4D	ES155	16025	9600	10950	12300	14700
LX Coupe 2D	EM215	15825	9425	10775	12150	14500
LX Special Ed Sed 4D	ES155	16775	9800	11150	12550	14950
LX Special Ed Cpe 2D	EM215	16575	9600	10950	12300	14700
EX Sedan 4D	ES257	17925	10375	11775	13200	15650
EX Coupe 2D	EM219	17525	10100	11500	12950	15350
EX Special Ed Sed 4D	ES257	18375	10625	12075	13500	16000
EX Special Ed Cpe 2D	EM219	17975	10425	11875	13300	15750
Si Hatchback 2D	EP335	19735	9750	11100	12950	15900
Hybrid Sedan 4D	ES956	20315	13975	15775	17200	20000

ACCORD—4-Cyl.—Equipment Schedule 6
W.B. 105.1", 107.9" (Sed); 2.4 Liter.

DX Sedan 4D	CM561	17510	**10050**	**11400**	**13200**	**16050**
LX Sedan 4D	CM564	20990	12750	14400	16200	19250
LX Coupe 2D	CM723	21090	12700	14350	16300	19500
LX Special Ed Cpe 2D	CM723	25065	13150	14900	16850	20100
EX Sedan 4D	CM567	23415	13475	15225	17150	20400
EX Coupe 2D	CM726	23515	13100	14800	17000	20500
5-Spd Manual Trans			(625)	(625)	(835)	(835)
5-Spd Manual Trans			0	0	0	0
V6 3.0 Liter VTEC			950	950	1265	1265

ACCORD—V6 Hybrid—Equipment Schedule 3
W.B. 107.9"; 3.0 Liter.

| Sedan 4D | CN364 | 30655 | **20750** | **23275** | **25600** | **29800** |

S2000—4-Cyl.—Equipment Schedule 2
W.B. 94.5"; 2.2 Liter.

| Convertible 2D | AP214 | 33465 | **18725** | **21050** | **23700** | **28000** |

HYUNDAI

1991 HYUNDAI — (KMHor2HM)(VF12J)-M-#

EXCEL—4-Cyl.—Equipment Schedule 6
W.B. 93.8"; 1.5 Liter.

Sedan 4D	VF12J	9100	**225**	**325**	**775**	**1475**
Hatchback 2D	VD12J	7965	175	250	700	1350
GL Sedan 4D	VF22J	9755	275	375	850	1600
GL SE Sedan 4D	VF22J	8875	275	375	850	1600
GS Hatchback 2D	VD32J	8785	250	350	800	1525
GS SE Hatchback 2D	VD32J	7745	250	350	800	1525
GLS Sedan 4D	VF32J	10110	300	400	925	1700

SCOUPE—4-Cyl.—Equipment Schedule 6
W.B. 93.8"; 1.5 Liter.

Coupe 2D	VE12J	10030	250	350	800	1525
SE Coupe 2D	VE22J	10095	300	400	925	1700
LS Coupe 2D	VE32J	10815	400	525	1100	1950

SONATA—4-Cyl.—Equipment Schedule 5
W.B. 104.3"; 2.4 Liter.

Sedan 4D	BF12S	12540	325	425	850	1525
SE Sedan 4D	BF22S	12320	325	425	850	1525
GLS Sedan 4D	BF32S	15090	375	500	975	1700
GLS SE Sedan 4D	BF32T	15320	375	500	975	1700
V6 3.0 Liter	T		100	100	135	135

1992 HYUNDAI — (KMHor2HM)(VF12J)-N-#

EXCEL—4-Cyl.—Equipment Schedule 6
W.B. 93.8"; 1.5 Liter.

Body	Type	VIN	List	Trade-In Fair	Good	Pvt-Party Good	Retail Excellent
Sedan 4D		VF12J	9490	225	325	800	1525
Hatchback 2D		VD12J	8390	175	250	700	1400
GS Hatchback 2D		VD32J	9034	250	350	825	1575
GL Sedan 4D		VF22J	9934	275	375	900	1700
SCOUPE—4-Cyl.—Equipment Schedule 6							
W.B. 93.8"; 1.5 Liter.							
Coupe 2D		VE22J	10569	275	375	875	1650
LS Coupe 2D		VE32J	11174	400	575	1175	2075
ELANTRA—4-Cyl.—Equipment Schedule 5							
W.B. 98.4"; 1.6 Liter.							
Sedan 4D		JF22R	11155	300	400	950	1750
GLS Sedan 4D		JF32R	12051	400	525	1100	2000
SONATA—4-Cyl.—Equipment Schedule 5							
W.B. 104.3"; 2.0 Liter.							
Sedan 4D		BF22S	13130	325	425	950	1750
GLS Sedan 4D		BF32S	15125	375	500	1075	1925
V6 3.0 Liter		T		150	150	200	200

1993 HYUNDAI — (KMHor2HM)(VF12J)-P-#

Body	Type	VIN	List	Trade-In Fair	Good	Pvt-Party Good	Retail Excellent
EXCEL—4-Cyl.—Equipment Schedule 6							
W.B. 93.8"; 1.5 Liter.							
Sedan 4D		VF12J	9534	225	325	825	1575
Hatchback 2D		VD12J	8634	175	225	700	1400
GS Hatchback 2D		VD32J	9174	250	350	825	1600
GL Sedan 4D		VF22J	10074	275	400	925	1750
SCOUPE—4-Cyl.—Equipment Schedule 6							
W.B. 93.8"; 1.5 Liter.							
Coupe 2D		VE22N	10879	400	550	1175	2100
LS Coupe 2D		VE32N	11414	550	775	1475	2600
SCOUPE—4-Cyl. Turbo—Equipment Schedule 6							
W.B. 93.8"; 1.5 Liter.							
Coupe 2D		VE32N	12669	675	975	1750	3000
ELANTRA—4-Cyl.—Equipment Schedule 5							
W.B. 98.4"; 1.6 Liter, 1.8 Liter.							
Sedan 4D		JF22R	11749	325	450	1025	1875
GLS Sedan 4D		JF32M	12214	400	600	1225	2150
SONATA—4-Cyl.—Equipment Schedule 5							
W.B. 104.3"; 2.0 Liter.							
Sedan 4D		BF22F	13554	350	475	1050	1950
GLS Sedan 4D		BF32F	14954	400	575	1200	2150
V6 3.0 Liter		T		225	225	300	300

1994 HYUNDAI — (KMHor2HM)(VD12J)-R-#

Body	Type	VIN	List	Trade-In Fair	Good	Pvt-Party Good	Retail Excellent
EXCEL—4-Cyl.—Equipment Schedule 6							
W.B. 93.8"; 1.5 Liter.							
Hatchback 2D		VD12J	9140	200	275	800	1575
GL Sedan 4D		VF22J	9659	325	450	1050	1950
GS Hatchback 2D		VD32J	9659	275	400	950	1825
SCOUPE—4-Cyl.—Equipment Schedule 6							
W.B. 93.8"; 1.5 Liter.							
Coupe 2D		VE22N	11409	425	625	1275	2325
LS Coupe 2D		VE32N	11889	600	875	1625	2825
SCOUPE—4-Cyl. Turbo—Equipment Schedule 6							
W.B. 93.8"; 1.5 Liter.							
Coupe 2D		VE32N	13189	750	1075	1975	3300
ELANTRA—4-Cyl.—Equipment Schedule 5							
W.B. 98.4"; 1.6 Liter, 1.8 Liter.							
Sedan 4D		JF22R	12674	350	475	1125	2075
GLS Sedan 4D		JF32M	13392	450	650	1350	2425
SONATA—4-Cyl.—Equipment Schedule 5							
W.B. 104.3"; 2.0 Liter.							
Sedan 4D		BF22F	13984	400	550	1225	2200
GLS Sedan 4D		BF32F	15884	475	675	1350	2450
V6 3.0 Liter		T		275	275	365	365

1995 HYUNDAI — KMH(VD14N)-S-#

Body	Type	VIN	List	Trade-In Fair	Good	Pvt-Party Good	Retail Excellent
ACCENT—4-Cyl.—Equipment Schedule 6							
W.B. 94.5"; 1.5 Liter.							
L Hatchback 2D		VD14N	9674	400	525	1075	1925
Hatchback 2D		VD14N	10310	475	700	1275	2250
Sedan 4D		VF14N	10834	575	825	1450	2500

1995 HYUNDAI

Body Type	VIN	List	Trade-In Fair	Good	Pvt-Party Good	Retail Excellent
SCOUPE—4-Cyl.—Equipment Schedule 6						
W.B. 93.8"; 1.5 Liter.						
Coupe 2D	VE12N	11905	475	700	1450	2625
LS Coupe 2D	VE32N	12735	675	975	1850	3175
SCOUPE—4-Cyl. Turbo—Equipment Schedule 6						
W.B. 93.8"; 1.5 Liter.						
Coupe 2D	VE32N	14045	850	1200	2200	3675
ELANTRA—4-Cyl.—Equipment Schedule 5						
W.B. 98.4"; 1.6 Liter, 1.8 Liter.						
Sedan 4D	JF13M	13149	400	575	1275	2375
SE Sedan 4D	JF23M	13848	450	650	1400	2550
GLS Sedan 4D	JF33M	14032	525	750	1550	2775
SONATA—4-Cyl.—Equipment Schedule 5						
W.B. 106.3"; 2.0 Liter.						
Sedan 4D	CF14F	14614	450	650	1300	2325
GL Sedan 4D	CF24F	15334	475	700	1350	2425
V6 3.0 Liter	T		325	325	435	435
SONATA—V6—Equipment Schedule 5						
W.B. 106.3"; 3.0 Liter.						
GLS Sedan 4D	CF34T	17804	775	1125	2050	3475

1996 HYUNDAI — KMH(VD14N)-T-#

Body Type	VIN	List	Trade-In Fair	Good	Pvt-Party Good	Retail Excellent
ACCENT—4-Cyl.—Equipment Schedule 6						
W.B. 94.5"; 1.5 Liter.						
L Hatchback 2D	VD14N	8690	450	650	1250	2200
Hatchback 2D	VD14N	10770	600	850	1500	2600
Sedan 4D	VF14N	11270	700	1000	1725	2875
GT Hatchback 2D	VD34N	11679	700	1000	1850	3175
ELANTRA—4-Cyl.—Equipment Schedule 5						
W.B. 100.4"; 1.8 Liter.						
Sedan 4D	JF24M	13434	700	1025	1975	3400
Wagon 4D	JW24M	14334	975	1350	2525	4175
GLS Sedan 4D	JF34M	14679	850	1225	2350	3975
GLS Wagon 4D	JW34M	15329	1100	1550	2775	4475
SONATA—4-Cyl.—Equipment Schedule 5						
W.B. 106.3"; 2.0 Liter.						
Sedan 4D	CF14F	15204	600	875	1675	2950
GL Sedan 4D	CF24F	16104	625	900	1750	3050
V6 3.0 Liter	T		375	375	500	500
SONATA—V6—Equipment Schedule 5						
W.B. 106.3"; 3.0 Liter.						
GLS Sedan 4D	CF34T	18404	975	1350	2575	4275

1997 HYUNDAI — KMH(VD14N)-V-#

Body Type	VIN	List	Trade-In Fair	Good	Pvt-Party Good	Retail Excellent
ACCENT—4-Cyl.—Equipment Schedule 6						
W.B. 94.5"; 1.5 Liter.						
L Hatchback 2D	VD14N	9014	550	800	1500	2625
GS Hatchback 2D	VD34N	11419	700	1025	1800	3050
GL Sedan 4D	VF24N	11819	825	1175	2025	3330
GT Hatchback 2D	VD34N	12139	825	1175	2175	3675
ELANTRA—4-Cyl.—Equipment Schedule 5						
W.B. 100.4"; 1.8 Liter.						
Sedan 4D	JF24M	13659	825	1175	2325	4025
Wagon 4D	JW24M	14559	1075	1525	2800	4550
GLS Sedan 4D	JF34M	14879	975	1375	2625	4350
GLS Wagon 4D	JW34M	15529	1250	1750	3050	4875
TIBURON—4-Cyl.—Equipment Schedule 5						
W.B. 97.4"; 1.8 Liter, 2.0 Liter.						
Coupe 2D	JG24M	15609	925	1300	2675	4550
FX Coupe 2D	JG34F	17539	1125	1575	3025	4975
SONATA—4-Cyl.—Equipment Schedule 5						
W.B. 106.3"; 2.0 Liter.						
Sedan 4D	CF24F	15964	500	725	2075	4000
GL Sedan 4D	CF24F	16764	525	750	2125	4050
V6 3.0 Liter	T		425	425	565	565
SONATA—V6—Equipment Schedule 5						
W.B. 106.3"; 3.0 Liter.						
GLS Sedan 4D	CF34T	18964	900	1250	2825	4975

1998 HYUNDAI — KMH(VD14N)-W-#

ACCENT—4-Cyl.—Equipment Schedule 6
W.B. 94.5"; 1.5 Liter.

1998 HYUNDAI

Body Type	VIN	List	Trade-In Fair	Good	Pvt-Party Good	Retail Excellent
L Hatchback 2D	VD14N	9534	700	1025	1850	3125
GS Hatchback 2D	VD34N	11328	875	1225	2175	3625
GL Sedan 4D	VF24N	11728	975	1375	2475	4025
GSi Hatchback 2D	VD34N	12573	975	1375	2600	4300
ELANTRA—4-Cyl.—Equipment Schedule 5						
W.B. 100.4"; 1.8 Liter.						
Sedan 4D	JF24M	13728	975	1350	2650	4450
Wagon 4D	JW24M	14628	1275	1775	3125	4975
GLS Sedan 4D	JF34M	15023	1150	1600	2925	4775
GLS Wagon 4D	JW34M	15673	1525	2025	3400	5300
TIBURON—4-Cyl.—Equipment Schedule 5						
W.B. 97.4"; 2.0 Liter.						
Coupe 2D	JG24F	16217	1225	1725	3250	5275
FX Coupe 2D	JG34F	17717	1550	2050	3625	5725
SE Pkg			100	100	135	135
SONATA—4-Cyl.—Equipment Schedule 5						
W.B. 106.3"; 2.0 Liter.						
Sedan 4D	CF24F	15984	700	1025	2550	4625
GL Sedan 4D	CF24F	16784	750	1050	2600	4675
V6 3.0 Liter	T		475	475	635	635
SONATA—V6—Equipment Schedule 5						
W.B. 106.3"; 3.0 Liter.						
GLS Sedan 4D	CF34T	18984	1125	1575	3350	5650

1999 HYUNDAI — KMH(VD14N)-X-#

Body Type	VIN	List	Trade-In Fair	Good	Pvt-Party Good	Retail Excellent
ACCENT—4-Cyl.—Equipment Schedule 6						
W.B. 94.5"; 1.5 Liter.						
L Hatchback 2D	VD14N	9434	875	1225	2200	3650
GS Hatchback 2D	VD34N	12129	1050	1475	2600	4200
GL Sedan 4D	VF24N	12129	1200	1650	2800	4425
Sport Pkg			150	150	200	200
ELANTRA—4-Cyl.—Equipment Schedule 5						
W.B. 100.4"; 2.0 Liter.						
GL Sedan 4D	JF24F	12734	2025	2600	3650	5200
GL Wagon 4D	JW24F	13634	2475	3075	4175	5800
GLS Sedan 4D	JF34F	13934	2300	2875	3975	5550
GLS Wagon 4D	JW34F	14434	2725	3350	4450	6125
TIBURON—4-Cyl.—Equipment Schedule 5						
W.B. 97.4"; 2.0 Liter.						
Coupe 2D	JG24F	16229	1700	2225	3825	6025
FX Coupe 2D	JG34F	17729	2050	2625	4275	6500
SONATA—4-Cyl.—Equipment Schedule 5						
W.B. 106.3"; 2.4 Liter.						
Sedan 4D	WF24S	16234	2600	3225	4525	6400
V6 2.5 Liter	V		525	525	700	700
SONATA—V6—Equipment Schedule 5						
W.B. 106.3"; 3.0 Liter.						
GLS Sedan 4D	WF34V	18234	3200	3875	5325	7400

2000 HYUNDAI — KMH(CF35G)-Y-#

Body Type	VIN	List	Trade-In Fair	Good	Pvt-Party Good	Retail Excellent
ACCENT—4-Cyl.—Equipment Schedule 6						
W.B. 96.1"; 1.5 Liter.						
L Hatchback 2D	CF35G	9434	1700	2225	3325	4925
GS Hatchback 2D	CG35G	10784	2000	2550	3675	5300
GL Sedan 4D	CG58G	10884	2225	2825	3950	5625
ELANTRA—4-Cyl.—Equipment Schedule 5						
W.B. 100.4"; 2.0 Liter.						
GLS Sedan 4D	JF34F	12984	2825	3475	4600	6275
GLS Wagon 4D	JW34F	13684	3250	3925	5100	6850
TIBURON—4-Cyl.—Equipment Schedule 5						
W.B. 97.4"; 2.0 Liter.						
Coupe 2D	JG24F	15184	2625	3250	5100	7600
SONATA—4-Cyl.—Equipment Schedule 5						
W.B. 106.3"; 2.4 Liter.						
Sedan 4D	WF14S	15934	3150	3800	5175	7100
V6 2.5 Liter	V		600	600	800	800
SONATA—V6—Equipment Schedule 5						
W.B. 106.3"; 2.5 Liter.						
GLS Sedan 4D	WF34V	17934	3825	4575	6075	8225

2001 HYUNDAI

Body	Type	VIN	List	Trade-In Fair	Good	Pvt-Party Good	Retail Excellent
2001 HYUNDAI — KMH(CF35G)-1-#							
ACCENT—4-Cyl.—Equipment Schedule 6							
W.B. 96.1"; 1.5 Liter, 1.6 Liter.							
L Hatchback 2D		CF35G	10184	**2225**	**2825**	**3925**	**5575**
GS Hatchback 2D		CH35C	10584	**2575**	**3175**	**4325**	**6025**
GL Sedan 4D		CG45C	11084	**2850**	**3500**	**4650**	**6400**
ELANTRA—4-Cyl.—Equipment Schedule 5							
W.B. 102.7"; 2.0 Liter.							
GLS Sedan 4D		JF35D	13734	**3400**	**4100**	**5300**	**7125**
GT Hatchback 4D		JF35D	15234	**3850**	**4600**	**5850**	**7725**
TIBURON—4-Cyl.—Equipment Schedule 5							
W.B. 97.4"; 2.0 Liter.							
Coupe 2D		JG25D	15734	**3175**	**3825**	**5850**	**8550**
SONATA—4-Cyl.—Equipment Schedule 5							
W.B. 106.3"; 2.4 Liter.							
Sedan 4D		WF15S	15934	**3750**	**4500**	**5925**	**7950**
V6 2.5 Liter		V		**675**	**675**	**900**	**900**
SONATA—V6—Equipment Schedule 5							
W.B. 106.3"; 2.5 Liter.							
GLS Sedan 4D		WF35V	17934	**4525**	**5350**	**6900**	**9200**
XG300—V6—Equipment Schedule 3							
W.B. 108.3"; 3.0 Liter.							
Sedan 4D		FU45D	23934	**4175**	**4950**	**7100**	**10050**
L Sedan 4D		FU45D	25434	**4400**	**5200**	**7375**	**10350**
2002 HYUNDAI — KMH(CF35G)-2-#							
ACCENT—4-Cyl.—Equipment Schedule 6							
W.B. 96.1"; 1.5 Liter, 1.6 Liter.							
L Hatchback 2D		CF35G	10244	**2825**	**3475**	**4650**	**6400**
GS Hatchback 2D		CH35C	10744	**3200**	**3875**	**5100**	**6875**
GL Sedan 4D		CG45C	11144	**3550**	**4250**	**5475**	**7325**
ELANTRA—4-Cyl.—Equipment Schedule 5							
W.B. 102.7"; 2.0 Liter.							
GLS Sedan 4D		DN45D	13794	**4050**	**4800**	**6125**	**8100**
GT Hatchback 4D		DN55D	15294	**4500**	**5325**	**6700**	**8725**
SONATA—4-Cyl.—Equipment Schedule 5							
W.B. 106.3"; 2.4 Liter.							
Sedan 4D		WF15S	16494	**4500**	**5300**	**6800**	**8975**
V6 2.7 Liter		H		**600**	**600**	**800**	**800**
SONATA—V6—Equipment Schedule 5							
W.B. 106.3"; 2.7 Liter.							
GLS Sedan 4D		WF35H	17994	**5375**	**6275**	**7900**	**10350**
LX Sedan 4D		WF35H	19319	**5650**	**6575**	**8300**	**10800**
XG350—V6—Equipment Schedule 3							
W.B. 108.3"; 3.5 Liter.							
Sedan 4D		FU45E	24494	**7175**	**8275**	**9750**	**12100**
L Sedan 4D		FU45E	26094	**7425**	**8525**	**10050**	**12400**
2003 HYUNDAI — KMH(CF35C)-3-#							
ACCENT—4-Cyl.—Equipment Schedule 6							
W.B. 96.1"; 1.6 Liter.							
Hatchback 2D		CF35C	10745	**3525**	**4225**	**5475**	**7350**
GL Hatchback 2D		CG35C	11144	**3925**	**4675**	**5975**	**7875**
GL Sedan 4D		CG45C	11544	**4325**	**5125**	**6400**	**8375**
ELANTRA—4-Cyl.—Equipment Schedule 5							
W.B. 102.7"; 2.0 Liter.							
GLS Sedan 4D		DN45D	13794	**4775**	**5600**	**7050**	**9200**
GT Sedan 4D		DN55D	15444	**4675**	**5525**	**7250**	**9750**
GT Hatchback 4D		DN55D	15444	**5275**	**6175**	**7650**	**9850**
TIBURON—4-Cyl.—Equipment Schedule 5							
W.B. 99.6"; 2.0 Liter.							
Coupe 2D		HM65D	16494	**6875**	**7900**	**9800**	**12550**
5-Spd Manual Trans				**(525)**	**(525)**	**(700)**	**(700)**
TIBURON—V6—Equipment Schedule 3							
W.B. 99.6"; 2.7 Liter.							
GT Coupe 2D		HN65F	19244	**7575**	**8700**	**10550**	**13450**
5-Spd Manual Trans				**(525)**	**(525)**	**(700)**	**(700)**
6-Spd Manual Trans				**0**	**0**	**0**	**0**
SONATA—4-Cyl.—Equipment Schedule 5							
W.B. 106.3"; 2.4 Liter.							
Sedan 4D		WF15S	16494	**5350**	**6250**	**7825**	**10200**

2003 HYUNDAI

Body Type	VIN	List	Trade-In Fair	Trade-In Good	Pvt-Party Good	Retail Excellent
V6 2.7 Liter	H		650	650	865	865
SONATA—V6—Equipment Schedule 5						
W.B. 106.3"; 2.7 Liter.						
GLS Sedan 4D	WF35H	18094	6325	7350	9100	11700
LX Sedan 4D	WF35H	19319	6625	7675	9475	12150
XG350—V6—Equipment Schedule 3						
W.B. 108.3"; 3.5 Liter.						
Sedan 4D	FU45E	24494	8400	9625	11200	13750
L Sedan 4D	FU45E	26094	8675	9950	11550	14100

2004 HYUNDAI — KMH(CF35C)-4-#

Body Type	VIN	List	Trade-In Fair	Trade-In Good	Pvt-Party Good	Retail Excellent
ACCENT—4-Cyl.—Equipment Schedule 6						
W.B. 96.1"; 1.6 Liter.						
Hatchback 2D	CF35C	11289	4325	5125	6325	8200
GL Hatchback 2D	CG35C	11439	4775	5600	6875	8775
GL Sedan 4D	CG45C	11839	5200	6075	7350	9300
GT Hatchback 2D	CG45C	11939	5075	5950	7425	9625
ELANTRA—4-Cyl.—Equipment Schedule 5						
W.B. 102.7"; 2.0 Liter.						
GLS Sedan 4D	DN46D	14639	5600	6525	7975	10200
GT Sedan 4D	DN55D	16189	5525	6450	8225	10800
GT Hatchback 4D	DN55D	16189	6150	7150	8625	10900
TIBURON—4-Cyl.—Equipment Schedule 3						
W.B. 99.6"; 2.0 Liter						
Coupe 2D	HM65D	18439	8075	9275	11200	14100
5-Spd Manual Trans			(550)	(550)	(735)	(735)
TIBURON—V6—Equipment Schedule 3						
W.B. 99.6"; 2.7 Liter.						
GT Coupe 2D	HN65F	19639	8825	10100	12100	15150
GT Special Ed Cpe 2D	HN65F	20987	9475	10825	12850	15950
5-Spd Manual Trans			(550)	(550)	(735)	(735)
6-Spd Manual Trans			0	0	0	0
SONATA—4-Cyl.—Equipment Schedule 5						
W.B. 106.3"; 2.4 Liter.						
Sedan 4D	WF15S	17339	6350	7375	8950	11350
V6 2.7 Liter	H		700	700	935	935
SONATA—V6—Equipment Schedule 5						
W.B. 106.3"; 2.7 Liter.						
GLS Sedan 4D	WF35H	19339	7450	8550	10350	13050
LX Sedan 4D	WF35H	20339	7750	8900	10750	13600
XG350—V6—Equipment Schedule 3						
W.B. 108.3"; 3.5 Liter.						
Sedan 4D	FU45E	24589	9800	11200	12850	15550
L Sedan 4D	FU45E	26189	10100	11500	13200	15950

2005 HYUNDAI — KMH(CG35C)-5-#

Body Type	VIN	List	Trade-In Fair	Trade-In Good	Pvt-Party Good	Retail Excellent
ACCENT—4-Cyl.—Equipment Schedule 6						
W.B. 96.1"; 1.6 Liter.						
GLS Hatchback 2D	CG35C	11339	5800	6750	7975	9950
GLS Sedan 4D	CG45C	11839	6250	7250	8500	10500
GT Hatchback 2D	CG35C	11939	6100	7075	8575	10850
ELANTRA—4-Cyl.—Equipment Schedule 5						
W.B. 102.7"; 2.0 Liter.						
GLS Sedan 4D	DN46D	14644	6625	7675	9175	11500
GLS Hatchback 4D	DN56D	14944	6850	7875	9400	11800
GT Sedan 4D	DN46D	16194	6525	7550	9400	12150
GT Hatchback 4D	DN56D	16194	7200	8325	9850	12250
TIBURON—4-Cyl.—Equipment Schedule 3						
W.B. 99.6"; 2.0 Liter.						
GS Coupe 2D	HM65D	17494	8200	9375	11750	15200
5-Spd Manual Trans			(575)	(575)	(765)	(765)
TIBURON—V6—Equipment Schedule 3						
W.B. 99.6"; 2.7 Liter.						
GT Coupe 2D	HN65F	19494	9075	10375	12800	16350
SE Coupe 2D	HN65F	20594	9800	11150	13650	17250
5-Spd Manual Trans			(575)	(575)	(765)	(765)
6-Spd Manual Trans			0	0	0	0
SONATA—4-Cyl.—Equipment Schedule 5						
W.B. 106.3"; 2.4 Liter.						
GL Sedan 4D	WF25S	17394	7150	8250	9750	12150
V6 2.7 Liter	H		750	750	1000	1000
SONATA—V6—Equipment Schedule 5						
W.B. 106.3"; 2.7 Liter.						

2005 HYUNDAI

Body	Type	VIN	List	Trade-In Fair	Good	Pvt-Party Good	Retail Excellent
GLS Sedan 4D		WF35H	19394	8375	9575	11300	13950
LX Sedan 4D		WF35H	20394	8650	9900	11750	14600
XG350—V6—Equipment Schedule 3							
W.B. 108.3"; 3.5 Liter.							
Sedan 4D		FU45E	24994	11100	12600	14350	17250
L Sedan 4D		FU45E	26594	11450	13000	14750	17700

INFINITI

1991 INFINITI — JN(KorX)(CP01P)–M–#

G20—4-Cyl.—Equipment Schedule 1
W.B. 104.0"; 2.0 Liter.

Sedan 4D		CP01P	18650	1350	1850	2825	4300
Manual Trans				(200)	(200)	(265)	(265)

M30—V6—Equipment Schedule 1
W.B. 103.0"; 3.0 Liter.

Coupe 2D		HF14C	24885	975	1375	2525	4125
Convertible 2D		HF16C	31385	1875	2400	3750	5650

Q45—V8—Equipment Schedule 1
W.B. 113.2"; 4.5 Liter.

Sedan 4D		NG01G	40385	850	1225	2575	4450
Active Suspension				200	200	265	265
Touring Pkg				100	100	135	135
Traction Control				100	100	135	135

1992 INFINITI — JN(KorX)(CP01P)–N–#

G20—4-Cyl.—Equipment Schedule 1
W.B. 100.4"; 2.0 Liter.

Sedan 4D		CP01P	19585	1550	2050	3100	4625
Manual Trans				(200)	(200)	(265)	(265)

M30—V6—Equipment Schedule 1
W.B. 103.0"; 3.0 Liter.

Coupe 2D		HF14C	25385	1100	1550	2775	4475
Convertible 2D		HF16C	33385	2150	2750	4175	6175

Q45—V8—Equipment Schedule 1
W.B. 113.2"; 4.5 Liter.

Sedan 4D		NG01C	42385	975	1350	2850	4875
Active Suspension				250	250	335	335
Touring Pkg				125	125	165	165
Traction Control				100	100	135	135

1993 INFINITI — JNK(CP01P)–P–#

G20—4-Cyl.—Equipment Schedule 1
W.B. 100.4"; 2.0 Liter.

Sedan 4D		CP01P	22750	1700	2225	3400	5075
Manual Trans				(250)	(250)	(335)	(335)

J30—V6—Equipment Schedule 1
W.B. 108.7"; 3.0 Liter.

Sedan 4D		AY21D	34485	2450	3050	4400	6300
Touring Pkg				175	175	235	235

Q45—V8—Equipment Schedule 1
W.B. 113.2"; 4.5 Liter.

Sedan 4D		NG01C	45850	975	1350	2925	5075
Active Suspension				325	325	435	435
Touring Pkg				175	175	235	235
Traction Control				125	125	165	165

1994 INFINITI — JNK(CP01D)–R–#

G20—4-Cyl.—Equipment Schedule 1
W.B. 100.4"; 2.0 Liter.

Sedan 4D		CP01D	25625	1925	2450	3725	5525
Touring				150	150	200	200
Manual Trans				(300)	(300)	(400)	(400)

J30—V6—Equipment Schedule 1
W.B. 108.7"; 3.0 Liter.

Sedan 4D		AY21D	37400	2800	3425	4875	6900
Touring				225	225	300	300

Q45—V8—Equipment Schedule 1
W.B. 113.2"; 4.5 Liter.

Sedan 4D		NG01D	50900	1350	1850	3550	5800
Active Suspension				400	400	535	535

1994 INFINITI

Body	Type	VIN	List	Trade-In Fair	Good	Pvt-Party Good	Retail Excellent
Touring				225	225	300	300
Traction Control				150	150	200	200

1995 INFINITI — JNK(CP01D)-S-#

G20—4-Cyl.—Equipment Schedule 1
W.B. 100.4"; 2.0 Liter.

Sedan 4D		CP01D	26625	2125	2725	4125	6075
Touring				175	175	235	235
Manual Trans				(350)	(350)	(465)	(465)

J30—V6—Equipment Schedule 1
W.B. 108.7"; 3.0 Liter.

Sedan 4D		AY21D	39000	3150	3800	5375	7625
Touring				275	275	365	365

Q45—V8—Equipment Schedule 1
W.B. 113.4"; 4.5 Liter.

Sedan 4D		NG01D	52850	1700	2225	4100	6550
Active Suspension				475	475	635	635
Touring				275	275	365	365
Traction Control				175	175	235	235

1996 INFINITI — JNK(CP01D)-T-#

G20—4-Cyl.—Equipment Schedule 1
W.B. 100.4"; 2.0 Liter.

Sedan 4D		CP01D	27630	2425	3025	4575	6750
Touring				200	200	265	265
Manual Trans				(400)	(400)	(535)	(535)

I30—V6—Equipment Schedule 1
W.B. 106.3"; 3.0 Liter.

Sedan 4D		CA21D	32000	3325	4025	5600	7825
Touring				325	325	435	435
Manual Trans				(400)	(400)	(535)	(535)

J30—V6—Equipment Schedule 1
W.B. 108.7"; 3.0 Liter.

Sedan 4D		AY21D	40400	3575	4275	6000	8400
Touring				325	325	435	435

Q45—V8—Equipment Schedule 1
W.B. 113.4"; 4.5 Liter.

Sedan 4D		NG01D	54000	2150	2750	4800	7525
Touring				325	325	435	435
Traction Control				200	200	265	265

1997 INFINITI — JNK(CA21D)-V-#

I30—V6—Equipment Schedule 1
W.B. 106.3"; 3.0 Liter.

Sedan 4D		CA21D	30395	3800	4550	6225	8600
Touring				350	350	465	465
Manual Trans				(450)	(450)	(600)	(600)

J30—V6—Equipment Schedule 1
W.B. 108.7"; 3.0 Liter.

Sedan 4D		AY21D	36245	4050	4800	6650	9250
Touring				350	350	465	465

Q45—V8—Equipment Schedule 1
W.B. 111.4"; 4.1 Liter.

Sedan 4D		BY31D	48395	4950	5800	8550	12200
Touring				350	350	465	465

1998 INFINITI — JNK(CA21D)-W-#

I30—V6—Equipment Schedule 1
W.B. 106.3"; 3.0 Liter.

Sedan 4D		CA21D	30695	4775	5600	7475	10100
Touring				375	375	500	500
Manual Trans				(475)	(475)	(635)	(635)

Q45—V8—Equipment Schedule 1
W.B. 111.4"; 4.1 Liter.

Sedan 4D		BY31D	48395	6000	6950	10000	14000
Touring				375	375	500	500

1999 INFINITI — JNK(CP11A)-X-#

G20—4-Cyl.—Equipment Schedule 1
W.B. 102.4"; 2.0 Liter.

Sedan 4D		CP11A	23820	5250	6125	7550	9675

1999 INFINITI

Body	Type	VIN	List	Trade-In Fair	Trade-In Good	Pvt-Party Good	Retail Excellent
Touring				200	200	265	265
Manual Trans				(500)	(500)	(665)	(665)
I30—V6—Equipment Schedule 1							
W.B. 106.3"; 3.0 Liter.							
Sedan 4D		CA21A	30725	5500	6425	8325	11050
Limited Sedan 4D		CA21A	31625	5550	6475	8375	11100
Touring				425	425	565	565
Manual Trans				(500)	(500)	(665)	(665)
Q45—V8—Equipment Schedule 1							
W.B. 111.4"; 4.1 Liter.							
Sedan 4D		BY31A	48725	7225	8350	11400	15550
Touring				425	425	565	565

2000 INFINITI — JNK(CP11A)-Y-#

Body	Type	VIN	List	Trade-In Fair	Trade-In Good	Pvt-Party Good	Retail Excellent
G20—4-Cyl.—Equipment Schedule 1							
W.B. 102.4"; 2.0 Liter.							
Sedan 4D		CP11A	24220	6200	7200	8675	10950
Touring				250	250	335	335
Manual Trans				(550)	(550)	(735)	(735)
I30—V6—Equipment Schedule 1							
W.B. 108.3"; 3.0 Liter.							
Sedan 4D		CA21A	29990	7800	8975	10850	13750
Touring				500	500	665	665
Q45—V8—Equipment Schedule 1							
W.B. 111.4"; 4.1 Liter.							
Sedan 4D		BY31A	49420	8500	9700	13000	17450
Touring				500	500	665	665
Anniversary Edition				350	350	465	465

2001 INFINITI — JNK(CP11A)-1-#

Body	Type	VIN	List	Trade-In Fair	Trade-In Good	Pvt-Party Good	Retail Excellent
G20—4-Cyl.—Equipment Schedule 1							
W.B. 102.4"; 2.0 Liter.							
Sedan 4D		CP11A	24220	7300	8400	10000	12400
Touring				275	275	365	365
Manual Trans				(600)	(600)	(800)	(800)
I30—V6—Equipment Schedule 1							
W.B. 108.3"; 3.0 Liter.							
Sedan 4D		CA31A	29990	9200	10475	12500	15600
Touring				550	550	735	735
Q45—V8—Equipment Schedule 1							
W.B. 111.4"; 4.1 Liter.							
Sedan 4D		BY31A	49420	10050	11400	15050	20000
Touring				550	550	735	735

2002 INFINITI — JNK(CP11A)-2-#

Body	Type	VIN	List	Trade-In Fair	Trade-In Good	Pvt-Party Good	Retail Excellent
G20—4-Cyl.—Equipment Schedule 1							
W.B. 102.4"; 2.0 Liter.							
Sedan 4D		CP11A	24340	8600	9850	11550	14150
Sport Pkg				300	300	400	400
Manual Trans				(650)	(650)	(865)	(865)
I35—V6—Equipment Schedule 1							
W.B. 108.3"; 3.5 Liter.							
Sedan 4D		DA31A	29295	9800	11150	13250	16400
Sport Pkg				600	600	800	800
Q45—V8—Equipment Schedule 1							
W.B. 113.0"; 4.5 Liter.							
Sedan 4D		BF01A	51045	17550	19700	24400	31100
Sport Pkg				600	600	800	800
Premium Pkg				1475	1475	1965	1965

2003 INFINITI — JNK(CV51E)-3-#

Body	Type	VIN	List	Trade-In Fair	Trade-In Good	Pvt-Party Good	Retail Excellent
G35—V6—Equipment Schedule 1							
W.B. 112.2"; 3.5 Liter.							
Sedan 4D		CV51E	29495	15850	17850	20300	24300
Coupe 2D		CV54E	32945	18975	21250	23900	28200
I35—V6—Equipment Schedule 1							
W.B. 108.3"; 3.5 Liter.							
Sedan 4D		DA31A	30995	13875	15675	17800	21300
Sport Pkg				650	650	865	865
M45—V8—Equipment Schedule 1							
W.B. 110.2"; 4.5 Liter.							
Sedan 4D		AY41E	43845	19975	22400	26500	32500

2003 INFINITI

Body	Type	VIN	List	Trade-In Fair	Good	Pvt-Party Good	Retail Excellent
Q45—V8—Equipment Schedule 1							
W.B. 113.0"; 4.5 Liter.							
Sedan 4D		BF01A	52545	**20750**	**23275**	**28500**	**35900**
Premium Sedan 4D		BF01A	62145	**24250**	**27075**	**32500**	**40300**

2004 INFINITI — JNK(CV51E)-4-#

Body	Type	VIN	List	Trade-In Fair	Good	Pvt-Party Good	Retail Excellent
G35—V6—Equipment Schedule 1							
W.B. 112.2"; 3.5 Liter.							
Sedan 4D		CV51E	31690	**18150**	**20375**	**22800**	**26900**
AWD Sedan 4D		CV51E	33490	**19600**	**22025**	**24500**	**28800**
Coupe 2D		CV54E	33140	**21425**	**24050**	**26700**	**31100**
I35—V6—Equipment Schedule 1							
W.B. 108.3"; 3.5 Liter.							
Sedan 4D		DA31A	31190	**15950**	**17950**	**20200**	**24000**
M45—V8—Equipment Schedule 1							
W.B. 110.2"; 4.5 Liter.							
Sedan 4D		AY41E	44840	**22400**	**25025**	**29300**	**35700**
Q45—V8—Equipment Schedule 1							
W.B. 113.0"; 4.5 Liter.							
Sedan 4D		BF01A	52990	**24725**	**27650**	**33500**	**41900**
Premium Sedan 4D		BF01A	62190	**28425**	**31825**	**37800**	**46600**
Journey Pkg				**1775**	**1775**	**2365**	**2365**

2005 INFINITI — JNK(CV51E)-5-#

Body	Type	VIN	List	Trade-In Fair	Good	Pvt-Party Good	Retail Excellent
G35—V6—Equipment Schedule 1							
W.B. 112.2"; 3.5 Liter.							
Sedan 4D		CV51E	32460	**20650**	**23075**	**25700**	**30200**
AWD Sedan 4D		CV51E	34260	**22225**	**24825**	**27500**	**32200**
Coupe 2D		CV54E	34160	**24250**	**27075**	**29900**	**34600**
Q45—V8—Equipment Schedule 1							
W.B. 113.0"; 4.5 Liter.							
Sedan 4D		BF01A	56810	**29400**	**32775**	**39400**	**48800**
Premium Pkg				**1900**	**1900**	**2535**	**2535**

ISUZU

1991 ISUZU — JABRT(536)-M-#

Body	Type	VIN	List	Trade-In Fair	Good	Pvt-Party Good	Retail Excellent
STYLUS—4-Cyl.—Equipment Schedule 6							
W.B. 96.5"; 1.6 Liter.							
S Sedan 4D		536	10728	**350**	**475**	**950**	**1700**
XS Sedan 4D		535	12348	**450**	**625**	**1175**	**2025**
IMPULSE—4-Cyl.—Equipment Schedule 6							
W.B. 96.5"; 1.6 Liter.							
XS Coupe 2D		235	13363	**250**	**350**	**1025**	**2025**
XS Hatchback 2D		435	13668	**350**	**475**	**1200**	**2275**
IMPULSE AWD—4-Cyl. Turbo—Equipment Schedule 6							
W.B. 96.5"; 1.6 Liter.							
RS Coupe 2D		234	16073	**375**	**500**	**1250**	**2375**

1992 ISUZU — JABRT(536)-N-#

Body	Type	VIN	List	Trade-In Fair	Good	Pvt-Party Good	Retail Excellent
STYLUS—4-Cyl.—Equipment Schedule 6							
W.B. 96.5"; 1.6 Liter, 1.8 Liter.							
S Sedan 4D		536	10798	**400**	**525**	**1050**	**1875**
RS Sedan 4D		538	11838	**450**	**650**	**1225**	**2100**
IMPULSE—4-Cyl.—Equipment Schedule 6							
W.B. 96.5"; 1.8 Liter.							
XS Coupe 2D		238	13588	**325**	**425**	**1225**	**2375**
XS Hatchback 2D		438	14188	**400**	**550**	**1375**	**2625**
IMPULSE AWD—4-Cyl. Turbo—Equipment Schedule 6							
W.B. 96.5"; 1.6 Liter.							
RS Coupe 2D		234	16018	**400**	**600**	**1450**	**2775**

1993 ISUZU — JABRT(536)-P-#

Body	Type	VIN	List	Trade-In Fair	Good	Pvt-Party Good	Retail Excellent
STYLUS—4-Cyl.—Equipment Schedule 6							
W.B. 96.5"; 1.6 Liter.							
S Sedan 4D		536	11168	**400**	**600**	**1175**	**2075**

Body	Type	VIN	List	Trade-In Fair	Good	Pvt-Party Good	Retail Excellent

JAGUAR

1991 JAGUAR — SAJ(FY17)4-M-#

XJ6—6-Cyl.—Equipment Schedule 1
W.B. 113.0"; 4.0 Liter.

Sedan 4D		FY17	40425	**1375**	**1900**	**3450**	**5550**
Sovereign Sedan 4D		HY17	45425	**1775**	**2300**	**3950**	**6150**
Vanden Plas Sedan 4D		KY17	50425	**1900**	**2425**	**4125**	**6375**

XJS—V12—Equipment Schedule 2
W.B. 102.0"; 5.3 Liter.

Coupe 2D		NW58	53580	**2425**	**3000**	**4650**	**6925**
Convertible 2D		NW48	64180	**4575**	**5400**	**7475**	**10350**

1992 JAGUAR — SAJ(FY17)4-N-#

XJ6—6-Cyl.—Equipment Schedule 1
W.B. 113.0"; 4.0 Liter.

Sedan 4D		FY17	45080	**1750**	**2275**	**4025**	**6350**
Sovereign Sedan 4D		HY17	50080	**2175**	**2775**	**4575**	**7050**
Vanden Plas Sedan 4D		KY17	55080	**2325**	**2900**	**4800**	**7300**
Majestic Sedan 4D		MY17	60080	**2625**	**3250**	**5175**	**7725**

XJS—V12—Equipment Schedule 2
W.B. 102.0"; 5.3 Liter.

Coupe 2D		NW58	61080	**2925**	**3600**	**5425**	**7925**
Convertible 2D		NW48	68080	**5500**	**6425**	**8725**	**11950**

1993 JAGUAR — SAJ(HW174)-P-#

XJ6—6-Cyl.—Equipment Schedule 1
W.B. 113.0"; 4.0 Liter.

Sedan 4D		HW174	51830	**2575**	**3200**	**5225**	**7925**
Vanden Plas Sedan 4D		KW174	57330	**2825**	**3450**	**5525**	**8325**

XJS—6-Cyl.—Equipment Schedule 2
W.B. 102.0"; 4.0 Liter.

Coupe 2D		NW574	50330	**3400**	**4100**	**6100**	**8850**
Convertible 2D		NW474	57330	**5325**	**6225**	**8550**	**11800**
Manual Trans				**(250)**	**(250)**	**(335)**	**(335)**

XJ—V12—Equipment Schedule 1
W.B. 102.0", 113.0" (XJ12); 6.0 Liter.

XJ12 Sedan 4D		MW134	72330	**2700**	**3300**	**5375**	**8125**
XJR-S Coupe 2D		SW534	73600	**5100**	**5975**	**8275**	**11450**
XJR-S Convertible 2D		SW434	80700	**6125**	**7100**	**9600**	**13050**

1994 JAGUAR — SAJ(HX174)-R-#

XJ6—6-Cyl.—Equipment Schedule 1
W.B. 113.0"; 4.0 Liter.

Sedan 4D		HX174	52330	**3075**	**3725**	**6000**	**8975**
Vanden Plas Sedan 4D		KX174	59980	**3400**	**4100**	**6400**	**9475**

XJS—6-Cyl.—Equipment Schedule 2
W.B. 102.0"; 4.0 Liter.

Coupe 2D		NX574	52530	**4150**	**4925**	**7150**	**10200**
2+2 Convertible 2D		NX474	60530	**6300**	**7300**	**9850**	**13400**
Manual Trans				**(300)**	**(300)**	**(400)**	**(400)**

XJS—V12—Equipment Schedule 2
W.B. 102.0"; 6.0 Liter.

Coupe 2D		NX534	70530	**5725**	**6675**	**9175**	**12550**
2+2 Convertible 2D		NX234	80530	**7175**	**8300**	**11000**	**14750**

XJ12—V12—Equipment Schedule 1
W.B. 113.0"; 6.0 Liter.

Sedan 4D		MX134	72330	**3275**	**3950**	**6225**	**9300**

1995 JAGUAR — SAJ(HX174)-S-#

XJ6—6-Cyl.—Equipment Schedule 1
W.B. 113.0"; 4.0 Liter.

Sedan 4D		HX174	54030	**3625**	**4325**	**6475**	**9375**
Vanden Plas Sedan 4D		KX174	62780	**4525**	**5350**	**7650**	**10750**
Traction Control				**175**	**175**	**235**	**235**

XJR—6-Cyl. Supercharged—Equipment Schedule 1
W.B. 113.0"; 4.0 Liter.

Sedan 4D		PX114	65580	**5575**	**6500**	**8975**	**12350**

1995 JAGUAR

Body	Type	VIN	List	Trade-In Fair	Trade-In Good	Pvt-Party Good	Retail Excellent
XJS—6-Cyl.—Equipment Schedule 2							
W.B. 102.0"; 4.0 Liter.							
Coupe 2D		NX574	53980	**5000**	**5875**	**8375**	**11750**
2+2 Convertible 2D		NX274	62130	**7350**	**8475**	**11350**	**15300**
XJS—V12—Equipment Schedule 2							
W.B. 102.0"; 6.0 Liter.							
Coupe 2D		NX534	72930	**6750**	**7775**	**10500**	**14300**
2+2 Convertible 2D		NX234	83130	**8325**	**9525**	**12500**	**16650**
XJ12—V12—Equipment Schedule 1							
W.B. 113.0"; 6.0 Liter.							
Sedan 4D		MX134	77830	**3875**	**4625**	**6825**	**9800**

1996 JAGUAR — SAJ(HX174)-T-#

Body	Type	VIN	List	Trade-In Fair	Trade-In Good	Pvt-Party Good	Retail Excellent
XJ6—6-Cyl.—Equipment Schedule 1							
W.B. 113.0", 117.9" (Vanden Plas); 4.0 Liter.							
Sedan 4D		HX174	56900	**4450**	**5250**	**7675**	**10950**
Vanden Plas Sedan 4D		KX674	65000	**6400**	**7425**	**10100**	**13750**
Traction Control				**200**	**200**	**265**	**265**
XJR—6-Cyl. Supercharged—Equipment Schedule 1							
W.B. 113.0"; 4.0 Liter.							
Sedan 4D		PX114	66850	**6875**	**7900**	**10650**	**14500**
XJS—6-Cyl.—Equipment Schedule 2							
W.B. 102.0"; 4.0 Liter.							
2+2 Convertible 2D		NX274	62150	**8600**	**9850**	**12950**	**17250**
XJ12—V12—Equipment Schedule 1							
W.B. 117.9"; 6.0 Liter.							
Sedan 4D		MX634	79950	**7125**	**8225**	**11000**	**14850**

1997 JAGUAR — SAJ(HX124)-V-#

Body	Type	VIN	List	Trade-In Fair	Trade-In Good	Pvt-Party Good	Retail Excellent
XJ6—6-Cyl.—Equipment Schedule 1							
W.B. 113.0", 117.9" (L & Vanden Plas); 4.0 Liter.							
Sedan 4D		HX124	54980	**5650**	**6575**	**9325**	**13050**
L Sedan 4D		HX624	59980	**5950**	**6900**	**9675**	**13450**
Vanden Plas Sedan 4D		KX624	64380	**7600**	**8725**	**11750**	**15850**
Traction Control				**225**	**225**	**300**	**300**
XJR—6-Cyl. Supercharged—Equipment Schedule 1							
W.B. 113.0"; 4.0 Liter.							
Sedan 4D		PX114	67980	**8325**	**9525**	**12600**	**16850**
XK8—V8—Equipment Schedule 2							
W.B. 101.9", 109.9" (Conv); 4.0 Liter.							
Coupe 2D		GX574	65480	**10425**	**11875**	**14950**	**19300**
Convertible 2D		GX274	70480	**11500**	**13050**	**16200**	**20800**
Traction Control				**225**	**225**	**300**	**300**

1998 JAGUAR — SAJ(HX124)-W-#

Body	Type	VIN	List	Trade-In Fair	Trade-In Good	Pvt-Party Good	Retail Excellent
XJ8—V8—Equipment Schedule 1							
W.B. 113.0", 117.9" (L & Vanden Plas); 4.0 Liter.							
Sedan 4D		HX124	55330	**7075**	**8175**	**10900**	**14750**
L Sedan 4D		HX624	60330	**7775**	**8950**	**11800**	**15750**
Vanden Plas Sedan 4D		KX624	64380	**9075**	**10375**	**13350**	**17500**
Traction Control				**275**	**275**	**365**	**365**
XJR—V8 Supercharged—Equipment Schedule 1							
W.B. 113.0"; 4.0 Liter.							
Sedan 4D		PX184	67980	**11725**	**13300**	**16600**	**21200**
XK8—V8—Equipment Schedule 2							
W.B. 101.9"; 4.0 Liter.							
Coupe 2D		GX524	65480	**12175**	**13825**	**17150**	**21900**
Convertible 2D		GX224	70480	**13350**	**15025**	**18550**	**23500**
Traction Control				**275**	**275**	**365**	**365**

1999 JAGUAR — SAJ(HX104)-X-#

Body	Type	VIN	List	Trade-In Fair	Trade-In Good	Pvt-Party Good	Retail Excellent
XJ8—V8—Equipment Schedule 1							
W.B. 113.0", 117.9" (L & Vanden Plas); 4.0 Liter.							
Sedan 4D		HX104	55780	**7775**	**8950**	**11900**	**15900**
L Sedan 4D		HX604	60830	**8550**	**9800**	**12800**	**17000**
Vanden Plas Sedan 4D		KX604	64880	**9950**	**11350**	**14450**	**18850**
Traction Control				**300**	**300**	**400**	**400**
XJR—V8 Supercharged—Equipment Schedule 1							
W.B. 113.0"; 4.0 Liter.							
Sedan 4D		PX184	69030	**12900**	**14600**	**17950**	**22800**
XK8—V8—Equipment Schedule 2							
W.B. 101.9"; 4.0 Liter.							

1999 JAGUAR

Body	Type	VIN	List	Trade-In Fair	Trade-In Good	Pvt-Party Good	Retail Excellent
Coupe 2D		GX504	66330	14250	16100	19400	24300
Convertible 2D		GX204	71330	15475	17450	20900	25800
Traction Control				300	300	400	400

2000 JAGUAR — SAJ(DorJ)(A01C)-Y-#

S-TYPE—V6—Equipment Schedule 1
W.B. 114.5"; 3.0 Liter.

Body	Type	VIN	List	Trade-In Fair	Trade-In Good	Pvt-Party Good	Retail Excellent
Sedan 4D		A01C	44980	9850	11250	13700	17250
Sport Pkg				175	175	235	235

S-TYPE—V8—Equipment Schedule 1
W.B. 114.5"; 4.0 Liter.

| Sedan 4D | | A01D | 48580 | 11300 | 12850 | 15350 | 19200 |
| Sport Pkg | | | | 175 | 175 | 235 | 235 |

XJ8—V8—Equipment Schedule 1
W.B. 113.0", 117.9" (L & Vanden Plas); 4.0 Liter.

Sedan 4D		A14C	56245	10175	11600	14950	19600
L Sedan 4D		A23C	61295	11100	12600	16000	20800
Vanden Plas Sedan 4D		A24C	65345	12750	14450	18000	23000

XJR—V8 Supercharged—Equipment Schedule 1
W.B. 113.0"; 4.0 Liter.

| Sedan 4D | | A15B | 69145 | 16300 | 18325 | 21900 | 27300 |

XJ8—V8 Supercharged—Equipment Schedule 1
W.B. 113.0"; 4.0 Liter.

| Vanden Plas Sedan 4D | | A14B | 81245 | 20850 | 23375 | 27500 | 33900 |

XK8—V8—Equipment Schedule 2
W.B. 101.9"; 4.0 Liter.

| Coupe 2D | | A41C | 66795 | 17125 | 19250 | 22900 | 28300 |
| Convertible 2D | | A42C | 71795 | 18425 | 20750 | 24400 | 30100 |

XKR—V8 Supercharged—Equipment Schedule 2
W.B. 101.9"; 4.0 Liter.

| Coupe 2D | | A41B | 77395 | 21150 | 23675 | 27600 | 33700 |
| Convertible 2D | | A42B | 82395 | 23275 | 26100 | 30300 | 36600 |

2001 JAGUAR — SAJD(A01C)-1-#

S-TYPE—V6—Equipment Schedule 1
W.B. 114.5"; 3.0 Liter.

| Sedan 4D | | A01C | 46250 | 11600 | 13200 | 15900 | 20000 |
| Sport Pkg | | | | 200 | 200 | 265 | 265 |

S-TYPE—V8—Equipment Schedule 1
W.B. 114.5"; 4.0 Liter.

| Sedan 4D | | A01D | 49950 | 13300 | 15025 | 17900 | 22200 |
| Sport Pkg | | | | 200 | 200 | 265 | 265 |

XJ8—V8—Equipment Schedule 1
W.B. 113.0", 117.9" (L & Vanden Plas); 4.0 Liter.

Sedan 4D		A14C	56950	12900	14600	18400	23700
L Sedan 4D		A23C	62950	13925	15725	19600	25000
Vanden Plas Sedan 4D		A24C	68250	15900	17900	21900	27600

XJR—V8 Supercharged—Equipment Schedule 1
W.B. 113.0"; 4.0 Liter.

| Sedan 4D | | A15B | 69930 | 19975 | 22400 | 26400 | 32300 |

XJ8—V8 Supercharged—Equipment Schedule 1
W.B. 117.9"; 4.0 Liter.

| Vanden Plas Sedan 4D | | A25B | 83950 | 24825 | 27850 | 32500 | 39600 |

XK8—V8—Equipment Schedule 2
W.B. 101.9"; 4.0 Liter.

| Coupe 2D | | A41C | 69750 | 20275 | 22800 | 26800 | 32900 |
| Convertible 2D | | A42C | 74750 | 21825 | 24450 | 28600 | 34900 |

XKR—V8 Supercharged—Equipment Schedule 2
W.B. 101.9"; 4.0 Liter.

Coupe 2D		A41B	80750	24825	27750	32100	38900
Convertible 2D		A42B	85750	27250	30350	35000	42100
Silverstone Coupe 2D		A41B	97500	****	****	****	54300
Silverstone Conv 2D		A42B	97500	****	****	****	57700

2002 JAGUAR — SAJ-(A51D)-2-#

X-TYPE AWD—V6—Equipment Schedule 2
W.B. 106.7"; 2.5 Liter, 3.0 Liter.

2.5L Sedan 4D		A51D	34370	9300	10625	13000	16450
2.5L Sport Sedan 4D		A53D	36370	9950	11350	13700	17200
3.0L Sedan 4D		A51C	39095	11450	13000	15400	19150
3.0L Sport Sedan 4D		A53C	41095	12075	13675	16200	20000
Manual Trans				(750)	(750)	(1000)	(1000)

2002 JAGUAR

Body	Type	VIN	List	Trade-In Fair	Good	Pvt-Party Good	Retail Excellent
S-TYPE—V6—Equipment Schedule 1 W.B. 114.5"; 3.0 Liter.							
Sedan 4D		A01C	46320	**13875**	**15675**	**18800**	**23500**
Sport				**1000**	**1000**	**1335**	**1335**
Manual Trans				**(750)**	**(750)**	**(1000)**	**(1000)**
S-TYPE—V8—Equipment Schedule 1 W.B. 114.5"; 4.0 Liter.							
Sedan 4D		A01D	49975	**15725**	**17700**	**21000**	**25800**
Sport				**1000**	**1000**	**1335**	**1335**
XJ8—V8—Equipment Schedule 1 W.B. 113.0"; 4.0 Liter.							
Sedan 4D		A14C	56975	**16050**	**18100**	**22400**	**28400**
XJ SPORT—V8—Equipment Schedule 1 W.B. 113.0"; 4.0 Liter.							
Sedan 4D		A14C	59975	**16200**	**18225**	**22500**	**28600**
VANDEN PLAS—V8—Equipment Schedule 1 W.B. 117.9"; 4.0 Liter.							
Sedan 4D		A24C	68975	**19500**	**21825**	**26400**	**32900**
XJR—V8 Supercharged—Equipment Schedule 1 W.B. 113.0"; 4.0 Liter.							
Sedan 4D		A15B	72475	**24050**	**26875**	**31200**	**37700**
100 Sedan 4D		A15B		**26000**	**29100**	**34000**	**41300**
XJ SUPER—V8 Supercharged—Equipment Schedule 1 W.B. 117.9"; 4.0 Liter.							
Sedan 4D		A25B	79975	**29400**	**32775**	**37900**	**45700**
XK8—V8—Equipment Schedule 1 W.B. 101.9"; 4.0 Liter.							
Coupe 2D		A41C	69975	**23850**	**26675**	**31200**	**38000**
Convertible 2D		A42C	74975	**25500**	**28525**	**33200**	**40350**
XKR—V8 Supercharged—Equipment Schedule 2 W.B. 101.9"; 4.0 Liter.							
Coupe 2D		A41B	82975	**28900**	**32200**	**37100**	**44500**
Convertible 2D		A42B	87975	**31525**	**35200**	**40200**	**48000**
100 Coupe 2D		A41B	84000	********	********	********	**61300**
100 Convertible 2D		A42B	86975	********	********	********	**65000**

2003 JAGUAR — SAJ–(A51D)–3–#

Body	Type	VIN	List	Trade-In Fair	Good	Pvt-Party Good	Retail Excellent
X-TYPE AWD—V6—Equipment Schedule 2 W.B. 106.7"; 2.5L, 3.0 Liter.							
2.5L Sedan 4D		A51D	29950	**11250**	**12750**	**15500**	**19600**
3.0L Sedan 4D		A51C	36950	**13575**	**15325**	**18200**	**22500**
Sport Pkg				**1300**	**1300**	**1735**	**1735**
Manual Trans				**(825)**	**(825)**	**(1100)**	**(1100)**
S-TYPE—V6—Equipment Schedule 1 W.B. 114.5"; 3.0 Liter.							
Sedan 4D		A01T	44975	**16350**	**18425**	**21900**	**27200**
Sport				**1000**	**1000**	**1335**	**1335**
Manual Trans				**(825)**	**(825)**	**(1100)**	**(1100)**
S-TYPE—V8—Equipment Schedule 1 W.B. 114.5"; 4.2 Liter.							
Sedan 4D		A01U	49975	**18375**	**20650**	**24300**	**29700**
Sport				**1000**	**1000**	**1335**	**1335**
S-TYPE R—V8 Supercharged—Equipment Schedule 1 W.B. 114.5"; 4.2 Liter.							
Sedan 4D		A03V	62400	**25425**	**28425**	**32300**	**38600**
XJ8—V8—Equipment Schedule 1 W.B. 113.0"; 4.0 Liter.							
Sedan 4D		A14C	56975	**19500**	**21825**	**26600**	**33400**
XJ SPORT—V8—Equipment Schedule 1 W.B. 113.0"; 4.0 Liter.							
Sedan 4D		A12C	59975	**19600**	**22025**	**26800**	**33700**
VANDEN PLAS—V8—Equipment Schedule 1 W.B. 117.9"; 4.0 Liter.							
Sedan 4D		A24C	68975	**23275**	**26100**	**31000**	**38300**
XJR—V8 Supercharged—Equipment Schedule 1 W.B. 113.0"; 4.0 Liter.							
Sedan 4D		A15B	72475	**28425**	**31725**	**36400**	**43600**
XJ SUPER—V8 Supercharged—Equipment Schedule 1 W.B. 117.9"; 4.0 Liter.							
Sedan 4D		A25B	79975	**34150**	**38025**	**43600**	**52100**
XK8—V8—Equipment Schedule 2 W.B. 101.9"; 4.2 Liter.							
Coupe 2D		A41U	69975	**27750**	**30950**	**35800**	**43300**

Body	Type	VIN	List	Trade-In Fair	Good	Pvt-Party Good	Retail Excellent
Convertible 2D		A42U	74975	29575	32975	37900	45600
XKR—V8 Supercharged—Equipment Schedule 2							
W.B. 101.9"; 4.2 Liter.							
Coupe 2D		A41V	81975	33175	37050	42200	50300
Convertible 2D		A42V	86975	36175	40250	45600	54000
Handling Pkg				2000	2000	2665	2665

2004 JAGUAR — SAJ-(A51D)-4-#

X-TYPE AWD—V6—Equipment Schedule 2
W.B. 106.7"; 2.5 Liter, 3.0 Liter.

Body	Type	VIN	List	Fair	Good	Good	Excellent
2.5L Sedan 4D		A51D	30520	13925	15725	18900	23700
3.0L Sedan 4D		A51C	33995	16450	18525	21900	27000
Sport Pkg				1400	1400	1865	1865
Manual Trans				(900)	(900)	(1200)	(1200)
S-TYPE—V6—Equipment Schedule 2							
W.B. 114.5"; 3.0 Liter.							
Sedan 4D		A01T	44995	19600	22025	26000	31900
Sport				1000	1000	1335	1335
Manual Trans				(900)	(900)	(1200)	(1200)
S-TYPE—V8—Equipment Schedule 1							
W.B. 114.5"; 4.2 Liter.							
Sedan 4D		A01U	49995	21825	24450	28500	34600
Sport				1000	1000	1335	1335
S-TYPE R—V8 Supercharged—Equipment Schedule 1							
W.B. 114.5"; 4.2 Liter.							
Sedan 4D		A03V	63120	29400	32775	37200	44100
XJ8—V8—Equipment Schedule 1							
W.B. 119.4"; 4.2 Liter.							
Sedan 4D		A71C	59995	25800	28800	33600	40700
VANDEN PLAS—V8—Equipment Schedule 1							
W.B. 119.4"; 4.2 Liter.							
Sedan 4D		A74C	68995	30075	33550	38400	46100
XJR—V8 Supercharged—Equipment Schedule 1							
W.B. 119.4"; 4.2 Liter.							
Sedan 4D		A73B	74995	35700	39775	44100	51500
XK8—V8—Equipment Schedule 2							
W.B. 101.9"; 4.2 Liter.							
Coupe 2D		A41C	69995	32300	35975	41400	49700
Convertible 2D		A42C	74995	34350	38225	43700	52200
XKR—V8 Supercharged—Equipment Schedule 2							
W.B. 101.9"; 4.2 Liter.							
Coupe 2D		A41B	82995	38325	42675	48300	57200
Convertible 2D		A42B	87995	41525	46175	51900	61200
Handling Pkg				2000	2000	2665	2665

2005 JAGUAR — SAJD(A51D)-5-#

X-TYPE AWD—V6—Equipment Schedule 2
W.B. 106.7"; 2.5 Liter, 3.0 Liter.

Body	Type	VIN	List	Fair	Good	Good	Excellent
2.5L Sedan 4D		A51D	32245	17275	19400	23400	29200
3.0L Sedan 4D		A51C	34995	20075	22500	26600	32600
3.0L Wagon 4D		A54C	36995	20850	23375	27500	33600
Sport Pkg				1500	1500	2000	2000
VDP Edition				500	500	665	665
Manual Trans				(950)	(950)	(1265)	(1265)
S-TYPE—V6—Equipment Schedule 1							
W.B. 114.5"; 3.0 Liter.							
Sedan 4D		A01T	45995	23575	26375	30900	37800
Sport				1000	1000	1335	1335
S-TYPE—V8—Equipment Schedule 1							
W.B. 114.5"; 4.2 Liter.							
Sedan 4D		A01U	51995	25900	28900	33600	40600
VDP Edition				500	500	665	665
Sport				1000	1000	1335	1335
S-TYPE R—V8 Supercharged—Equipment Schedule 1							
W.B. 114.5"; 4.2 Liter.							
Sedan 4D		A03V	58995	34150	38025	43000	50800
XJ8—V8—Equipment Schedule 1							
W.B. 119.4"; 4.2 Liter.							
Sedan 4D		A71C	61495	30350	33950	39200	47300
L Sedan 4D		A79C	63495	32000	35700	41000	49300
VANDEN PLAS—V8—Equipment Schedule 1							
W.B. 124.4"; 4.2 Liter.							
Sedan 4D		A82C	70995				

2005 JAGUAR

Body	Type	VIN	List	Trade-In Fair	Good	Pvt-Party Good	Retail Excellent
XJR—V8 Supercharged—Equipment Schedule 1 W.B. 119.4"; 4.2 Liter.							
Sedan 4D		A73B	75995				
XJ SUPER—V8 Supercharged—Equipment Schedule 1 W.B. 124.4"; 4.2 Liter.							
Sedan 4D		A86B	89995				
XK8—V8—Equipment Schedule 2 W.B. 101.9"; 4.2 Liter.							
Coupe 2D		A41C	70495				
Convertible 2D		A42C	75495				
XKR—V8 Supercharged—Equipment Schedule 2 W.B. 101.9"; 4.2 Liter.							
Coupe 2D		A41B	82995				
Convertible 2D		A42B	87995				
Handling Pkg							

KIA

1994 KIA — KNA(FA121)–R–#

SEPHIA—4-Cyl.—Equipment Schedule 6
W.B. 98.4"; 1.6 Liter.

Body	Type	VIN	List	Fair	Good	Good	Excellent
RS Sedan 4D		FA121	10130	250	350	850	1600
LS Sedan 4D		FA121	10674	325	450	1000	1825
GS Sedan 4D		FA121	11420	400	575	1175	2075

1995 KIA — KNA(FA121)–S–#

SEPHIA—4-Cyl.—Equipment Schedule 6
W.B. 98.4"; 1.6 Liter, 1.8 Liter.

RS Sedan 4D		FA121	10140	300	400	1000	1875
LS Sedan 4D		FA121	10730	400	525	1175	2100
GS Sedan 4D		FA121	11630	450	650	1325	2375

1996 KIA — KNA(FA125)–T–#

SEPHIA—4-Cyl.—Equipment Schedule 6
W.B. 98.4"; 1.6 Liter, 1.8 Liter.

RS Sedan 4D		FA125	11040	350	475	1150	2150
LS Sedan 4D		FA125	11980	425	625	1325	2425
GS Sedan 4D		FA125	12880	525	750	1525	2725

1997 KIA — KNA(FA125)–V–#

SEPHIA—4-Cyl.—Equipment Schedule 6
W.B. 98.4"; 1.6 Liter, 1.8 Liter.

RS Sedan 4D		FA125	11350	400	600	1375	2600
LS Sedan 4D		FA125	12190	500	725	1550	2825
GS Sedan 4D		FA125	13250	625	900	1800	3175

1998 KIA — KNA(FB121)–W–#

SEPHIA—4-Cyl.—Equipment Schedule 6
W.B. 100.8"; 1.8 Liter.

| Sedan 4D | | FB121 | 11605 | 825 | 1175 | 2175 | 3675 |
| LS Sedan 4D | | FB121 | 12345 | 900 | 1275 | 2425 | 4050 |

1999 KIA — KNA(FB121)–X–#

SEPHIA—4-Cyl.—Equipment Schedule 6
W.B. 100.8"; 1.8 Liter.

| Sedan 4D | | FB121 | 11605 | 1000 | 1400 | 2575 | 4250 |
| LS Sedan 4D | | FB121 | 12345 | 1075 | 1525 | 2750 | 4425 |

2000 KIA — KNA(FA121)–Y–#

SEPHIA—4-Cyl.—Equipment Schedule 6
W.B. 100.8"; 1.8 Liter.

| Sedan 4D | | FA121 | 11605 | 1225 | 1675 | 2975 | 4775 |
| LS Sedan 4D | | FA121 | 12345 | 1350 | 1850 | 3150 | 4975 |

SPECTRA—4-Cyl.—Equipment Schedule 6
W.B. 100.8"; 1.8 Liter.

| GS Sedan 4D | | FB161 | 11245 | 2125 | 2725 | 3850 | 5525 |
| GSX Sedan 4D | | FB161 | 13445 | 2400 | 2975 | 4175 | 5875 |

2001 KIA

Body Type	VIN	List	Trade-In Fair	Good	Pvt-Party Good	Retail Excellent

2001 KIA — KNA(DC123)-1-#

RIO—4-Cyl.—Equipment Schedule 6
W.B. 94.9"; 1.5 Liter.

| Sedan 4D | DC123 | 10175 | 2650 | 3275 | 4250 | 5750 |

SEPHIA—4-Cyl.—Equipment Schedule 6
W.B. 100.8"; 1.8 Liter.

| Sedan 4D | FB121 | 11945 | 1800 | 2325 | 3750 | 5750 |
| LS Sedan 4D | FB121 | 12645 | 1975 | 2500 | 3950 | 5975 |

SPECTRA—4-Cyl.—Equipment Schedule 6
W.B. 100.8"; 1.8 Liter.

| GS Hatchback 4D | FB161 | 12345 | 2725 | 3325 | 4525 | 6275 |
| GSX Hatchback 4D | FB161 | 13645 | 3000 | 3650 | 4875 | 6675 |

OPTIMA—4-Cyl.—Equipment Schedule 5
W.B. 106.3"; 2.4 Liter.

LX Sedan 4D	GD126	16599	2350	2925	4725	7125
SE Sedan 4D	GD126	18899	3075	3725	5575	8100
V6 2.5 Liter			675	675	900	900

2002 KIA — KNA(DC123)-2-#

RIO—4-Cyl.—Equipment Schedule 6
W.B. 94.9"; 1.5 Liter.

| Sedan 4D | DC123 | 10660 | 3175 | 3850 | 4925 | 6550 |
| Cinco Wagon 4D | DC163 | 11630 | 3450 | 4150 | 5225 | 6875 |

SPECTRA—4-Cyl.—Equipment Schedule 6
W.B. 100.8"; 1.8 Liter.

Sedan 4D	FB121	12450	3200	3875	5125	6925
GS Hatchback 4D	FB161	12850	3350	4050	5275	7125
LS Sedan 4D	FB121	13090	3500	4200	5450	7325
GSX Hatchback 4D	FB161	14090	3675	4425	5675	7575

OPTIMA—4-Cyl.—Equipment Schedule 5
W.B. 106.3"; 2.4 Liter.

LX Sedan 4D	GD126	16244	2850	3525	5450	8075
SE Sedan 4D	GD126	17894	3675	4425	6400	9125
V6 2.7 Liter	8		750	750	1000	1000

2003 KIA — KNA(DC125)-3-#

RIO—4-Cyl.—Equipment Schedule 6
W.B. 94.9"; 1.6 Liter.

| Sedan 4D | DC125 | 10495 | 3825 | 4575 | 5750 | 7525 |
| Cinco Wagon 4D | DC165 | 11995 | 4100 | 4875 | 6050 | 7850 |

SPECTRA—4-Cyl.—Equipment Schedule 5
W.B. 100.8"; 1.8 Liter.

Sedan 4D	FB121	12715	3925	4675	5975	7900
GS Hatchback 4D	FB161	13140	4100	4875	6175	8125
LS Sedan 4D	FB121	13320	4275	5075	6375	8350
GSX Hatchback 4D	FB161	14360	4450	5250	6600	8575

OPTIMA—4-Cyl.—Equipment Schedule 5
W.B. 106.3"; 2.4 Liter.

LX Sedan 4D	GD126	16915	3525	4225	6325	9200
SE Sedan 4D	GD126	18590	4425	5225	7375	10350
V6 2.7 Liter			825	825	1100	1100

2004 KIA — KNA(DC125)-4-#

RIO—4-Cyl.—Equipment Schedule 6
W.B. 94.9"; 1.6 Liter.

| Sedan 4D | DC125 | 11030 | 4575 | 5400 | 6550 | 8375 |
| Cinco Wagon 4D | DC165 | 12655 | 4875 | 5725 | 6900 | 8750 |

SPECTRA—4-Cyl.—Equipment Schedule 6
W.B. 100.8"; 1.8 Liter, 2.0 Liter.

Sedan 4D	FB121	13320	4800	5625	6875	8800
GS Hatchback 4D	FB161	13580	4950	5825	7075	9025
LS Sedan 4D	FB121	13590	5125	6025	7250	9225
LX Sedan 4D	FB121	14120	5200	6075	7350	9300
EX Sedan 4D	FB121	14290	5250	6125	7400	9375
GSX Hatchback 4D	FB161	14630	5325	6225	7500	9475

OPTIMA—4-Cyl.—Equipment Schedule 5
W.B. 106.3"; 2.4 Liter.

LX Sedan 4D	GD126	16960	4325	5125	7300	10300
EX Sedan 4D	GD126	18635	5275	6175	8425	11500
V6 2.7 Liter	8		900	900	1200	1200

Body	Type	VIN	List	Trade-In Fair	Good	Pvt-Party Good	Retail Excellent
AMANTI—V6—Equipment Schedule 3 W.B. 110.2"; 3.5 Liter.							
Sedan 4D		LD124	25535	**8550**	**9800**	**13150**	**17650**

2005 KIA — KNA(DC125)-5-#

Body	Type	VIN	List	Trade-In Fair	Good	Pvt-Party Good	Retail Excellent
RIO—4-Cyl.—Equipment Schedule 6 W.B. 94.9"; 1.6 Liter.							
Sedan 4D		DC125	11080	**5525**	**6450**	**7625**	**9500**
Cinco Wagon 4D		DC165	12705	**5850**	**6800**	**7975**	**9900**
SPECTRA—4-Cyl.—Equipment Schedule 6 W.B. 102.8"; 2.0 Liter.							
LX Sedan 4D		FB121	14120	**6225**	**7225**	**8500**	**10500**
EX Sedan 4D		FB121	14290	**6300**	**7300**	**8550**	**10600**
SX Sedan 4D		FB121	15535	**6775**	**7825**	**9125**	**11200**
SPECTRA 5—4-Cyl.—Equipment Schedule 6 W.B. 102.8"; 2.0 Liter.							
Hatchback 4D		FE161	15535	**6775**	**7825**	**9125**	**11200**
OPTIMA—4-Cyl.—Equipment Schedule 5 W.B. 106.3"; 2.4 Liter.							
LX Sedan 4D		GD126	17740	**4900**	**5750**	**7900**	**10900**
EX Sedan 4D		GD126	19190	**5950**	**6900**	**9150**	**12250**
V6 2.7 Liter		8		**950**	**950**	**1265**	**1265**
AMANTI—V6—Equipment Schedule 3 W.B. 110.2"; 3.5 Liter.							
Sedan 4D		LD124	25840	**9850**	**11250**	**14850**	**19800**

LEXUS

1991 LEXUS — JT8(VV22T)-M-#

Body	Type	VIN	List	Trade-In Fair	Good	Pvt-Party Good	Retail Excellent
ES 250—V6—Equipment Schedule 1 W.B. 102.4"; 2.5 Liter.							
Sedan 4D		VV22T	24500	**1225**	**1725**	**2925**	**4625**
Manual Trans				**(200)**	**(200)**	**(265)**	**(265)**
LS 400—V8—Equipment Schedule 1 W.B. 110.8"; 4.0 Liter.							
Sedan 4D		UF11E	41650	**2850**	**3525**	**5650**	**8500**
Traction Control				**100**	**100**	**135**	**135**

1992 LEXUS — JT8(VK13T)-N-#

Body	Type	VIN	List	Trade-In Fair	Good	Pvt-Party Good	Retail Excellent
ES 300—V6—Equipment Schedule 1 W.B. 103.1"; 3.0 Liter.							
Sedan 4D		VK13T	28650	**2850**	**3525**	**4875**	**6850**
Manual Trans				**(200)**	**(200)**	**(265)**	**(265)**
SC 300—6-Cyl.—Equipment Schedule 1 W.B. 105.9"; 3.0 Liter.							
Sport Coupe 2D		JZ31C	35000	**3650**	**4400**	**6425**	**9225**
Traction Control				**100**	**100**	**135**	**135**
SC 400—V8—Equipment Schedule 1 W.B. 105.9"; 4.0 Liter.							
Sport Coupe 2D		UZ30C	39100	**4300**	**5100**	**7225**	**10200**
Traction Control				**100**	**100**	**135**	**135**
LS 400—V8—Equipment Schedule 1 W.B. 110.8"; 4.0 Liter.							
Sedan 4D		UF11E	43600	**3300**	**3975**	**6325**	**9425**
Traction Control				**100**	**100**	**135**	**135**

1993 LEXUS — JT8(VK13T)-P-#

Body	Type	VIN	List	Trade-In Fair	Good	Pvt-Party Good	Retail Excellent
ES 300—V6—Equipment Schedule 1 W.B. 103.1"; 3.0 Liter.							
Sedan 4D		VK13T	31030	**3350**	**4050**	**5550**	**7675**
Manual Trans				**(250)**	**(250)**	**(335)**	**(335)**
GS 300—6-Cyl.—Equipment Schedule 1 W.B. 109.4"; 3.0 Liter.							
Sedan 4D		JS47E	40130	**4575**	**5400**	**7325**	**10050**
Traction Control				**125**	**125**	**165**	**165**
SC 300—6-Cyl.—Equipment Schedule 1 W.B. 105.9"; 3.0 Liter.							
Sport Coupe 2D		JZ31C	38730	**4200**	**4975**	**7150**	**10150**
Traction Control				**125**	**125**	**165**	**165**
SC 400—V8—Equipment Schedule 1 W.B. 105.9"; 4.0 Liter.							

1993 LEXUS

Body	Type	VIN	List	Trade-In Fair	Good	Pvt-Party Good	Retail Excellent
Sport Coupe 2D		UZ30C	42730	4925	5775	8075	11250
Traction Control				125	125	165	165
LS 400—V8—Equipment Schedule 1							
W.B. 110.8"; 4.0 Liter.							
Sedan 4D		UF11E	48030	3750	4500	7025	10400
Traction Control				125	125	165	165

1994 LEXUS — JT8(GK13T)-R-#

Body	Type	VIN	List	Trade-In Fair	Good	Pvt-Party Good	Retail Excellent
ES 300—V6—Equipment Schedule 1							
W.B. 103.1"; 3.0 Liter.							
Sedan 4D		GK13T	31070	3875	4625	6250	8575
GS 300—6-Cyl.—Equipment Schedule 1							
W.B. 109.4"; 3.0 Liter.							
Sedan 4D		JS47E	40370	5550	6500	8550	11500
Traction Control				150	150	200	200
SC 300—6-Cyl.—Equipment Schedule 1							
W.B. 105.9"; 3.0 Liter.							
Sport Coupe 2D		JZ31C	39370	4800	5625	8025	11250
Traction Control				150	150	200	200
SC 400—V8—Equipment Schedule 1							
W.B. 105.9"; 4.0 Liter.							
Sport Coupe 2D		UZ30C	45570	5600	6525	9050	12450
Traction Control				150	150	200	200
LS 400—V8—Equipment Schedule 1							
W.B. 110.8"; 4.0 Liter.							
Sedan 4D		UF11E	50370	4325	5125	7850	11500
Traction Control				150	150	200	200

1995 LEXUS — JT8(GK13T)-S-#

Body	Type	VIN	List	Trade-In Fair	Good	Pvt-Party Good	Retail Excellent
ES 300—V6—Equipment Schedule 1							
W.B. 103.1"; 3.0 Liter.							
Sedan 4D		GK13T	34180	4425	5225	6975	9500
GS 300—6-Cyl.—Equipment Schedule 1							
W.B. 109.4"; 3.0 Liter.							
Sedan 4D		JS47E	45380	6575	7600	9850	13000
Traction Control				175	175	235	235
SC 300—6-Cyl.—Equipment Schedule 1							
W.B. 105.9"; 3.0 Liter.							
Sport Coupe 2D		JZ31C	44980	5525	6450	9025	12500
Traction Control				175	175	235	235
SC 400—V8—Equipment Schedule 1							
W.B. 105.9"; 4.0 Liter.							
Sport Coupe 2D		UZ30C	49780	6425	7425	10150	13850
Traction Control				175	175	235	235
LS 400—V8—Equipment Schedule 1							
W.B. 112.2"; 4.0 Liter.							
Sedan 4D		UF22E	52680	5250	6150	9225	13250
Traction Control				175	175	235	235

1996 LEXUS — JT8(BF12G)-T-#

Body	Type	VIN	List	Trade-In Fair	Good	Pvt-Party Good	Retail Excellent
ES 300—V6—Equipment Schedule 1							
W.B. 103.1"; 3.0 Liter.							
Sedan 4D		BF12G	34895	5025	5900	7800	10500
GS 300—6-Cyl.—Equipment Schedule 1							
W.B. 109.4"; 3.0 Liter.							
Sedan 4D		BD42S	48445	7650	8775	11150	14550
Traction Control				200	200	265	265
SC 300—6-Cyl.—Equipment Schedule 1							
W.B. 105.9"; 3.0 Liter.							
Sport Coupe 2D		CD32Z	47695	6350	7375	10200	13950
Traction Control				200	200	265	265
SC 400—V8—Equipment Schedule 1							
W.B. 105.9"; 4.0 Liter.							
Sport Coupe 2D		CH32Y	53845	7350	8450	11350	15350
Traction Control				200	200	265	265
LS 400—V8—Equipment Schedule 1							
W.B. 112.2"; 4.0 Liter.							
Sedan 4D		BH33F	54445	6075	7050	10400	14800
Traction Control				200	200	265	265

1997 LEXUS

Body	Type	VIN	List	Trade-In Fair	Good	Pvt-Party Good	Retail Excellent

1997 LEXUS — JT8(BF22G)-V-#

ES 300—V6—Equipment Schedule 1
W.B. 105.1"; 3.0 Liter.

Sedan 4D		BF22G	33045	**6250**	**7250**	**9300**	**12200**

GS 300—6-Cyl.—Equipment Schedule 1
W.B. 109.4"; 3.0 Liter.

| Sedan 4D | | BD42S | 48595 | **8775** | **10050** | **12550** | **16200** |
| Traction Control | | | | **225** | **225** | **300** | **300** |

SC 300—6-Cyl.—Equipment Schedule 1
W.B. 105.9"; 3.0 Liter.

| Sport Coupe 2D | | CD32Z | 43445 | **7350** | **8450** | **11500** | **15650** |
| Traction Control | | | | **225** | **225** | **300** | **300** |

SC 400—V8—Equipment Schedule 1
W.B. 105.9"; 4.0 Liter.

| Sport Coupe 2D | | CH32Y | 52295 | **8400** | **9625** | **12800** | **17150** |
| Traction Control | | | | **225** | **225** | **300** | **300** |

LS 400—V8—Equipment Schedule 1
W.B. 112.2"; 4.0 Liter.

| Sedan 4D | | BH28F | 54495 | **8225** | **9425** | **12950** | **17700** |
| Traction Control | | | | **225** | **225** | **300** | **300** |

1998 LEXUS — JT8(BF28G)-W-#

ES 300—V6—Equipment Schedule 1
W.B. 105.1"; 3.0 Liter.

Sedan 4D		BF28G	33935	**7400**	**8500**	**10700**	**13850**

GS 300—6-Cyl.—Equipment Schedule 1
W.B. 110.2"; 3.0 Liter.

| Sedan 4D | | BD68S | 40025 | **10000** | **11350** | **14000** | **17900** |

GS 400—V8—Equipment Schedule 1
W.B. 110.2"; 4.0 Liter.

| Sedan 4D | | BH68X | 46315 | **11875** | **13475** | **16350** | **20600** |

SC 300—6-Cyl.—Equipment Schedule 1
W.B. 105.9"; 3.0 Liter.

| Sport Coupe 2D | | CD32Z | 44565 | **8500** | **9700** | **13050** | **17600** |
| Traction Control | | | | **275** | **275** | **365** | **365** |

SC 400—V8—Equipment Schedule 1
W.B. 105.9"; 4.0 Liter.

| Sport Coupe 2D | | CH32Y | 54315 | **9600** | **10950** | **14450** | **19200** |
| Traction Control | | | | **275** | **275** | **365** | **365** |

LS 400—V8—Equipment Schedule 1
W.B. 112.2"; 4.0 Liter.

| Sedan 4D | | BH28F | 54515 | **9525** | **10875** | **14700** | **19900** |

1999 LEXUS — JT8(BF28G)-X-#

ES 300—V6—Equipment Schedule 1
W.B. 110.2"; 3.0 Liter.

| Sedan 4D | | BF28G | 34235 | **8600** | **9850** | **12100** | **15350** |
| Coach Edition | | | | **200** | **200** | **265** | **265** |

GS 300—6-Cyl.—Equipment Schedule 1
W.B. 110.2"; 3.0 Liter.

| Sedan 4D | | BD68S | 40580 | **11350** | **12900** | **15550** | **19500** |

GS 400—V8—Equipment Schedule 1
W.B. 110.2"; 4.0 Liter.

| Sedan 4D | | BH68X | 47020 | **13425** | **15175** | **18100** | **22400** |

SC 300—6-Cyl.—Equipment Schedule 1
W.B. 105.9"; 3.0 Liter.

| Sport Coupe 2D | | CD32Z | 46640 | **9800** | **11150** | **14600** | **19350** |
| Traction Control | | | | **300** | **300** | **400** | **400** |

SC 400—V8—Equipment Schedule 1
W.B. 105.9"; 4.0 Liter.

| Sport Coupe 2D | | CH32Y | 56830 | **11000** | **12525** | **16100** | **21000** |
| Traction Control | | | | **300** | **300** | **400** | **400** |

LS 400—V8—Equipment Schedule 1
W.B. 112.2"; 4.0 Liter.

| Sedan 4D | | BH28F | 55220 | **11050** | **12550** | **16500** | **21800** |

2000 LEXUS — JT8(BF28G)-Y-#

ES 300—V6—Equipment Schedule 1
W.B. 105.1"; 3.0 Liter.

| Sedan 4D | | BF28G | 34785 | **9950** | **11350** | **13750** | **17250** |
| Platinum Series | | | | **250** | **250** | **335** | **335** |

2000 LEXUS

Body	Type	VIN	List	Trade-In Fair	Good	Pvt-Party Good	Retail Excellent
GS 300—6-Cyl.—Equipment Schedule 1 W.B. 110.2"; 3.0 Liter.							
Sedan 4D		BD68S	40880	**13300**	**15025**	**17800**	**22000**
Platinum Series				250	250	335	335
GS 400—V8—Equipment Schedule 1 W.B. 110.2"; 4.0 Liter.							
Sedan 4D		BH68X	47520	**15775**	**17800**	**20800**	**25400**
Platinum Series				250	250	335	335
SC 300—6-Cyl.—Equipment Schedule 1 W.B. 105.9"; 3.0 Liter.							
Sport Coupe 2D		CD32Z	47140	**11250**	**12750**	**16500**	**21600**
Traction Control				325	325	435	435
SC 400—V8—Equipment Schedule 1 W.B. 105.9"; 4.0 Liter.							
Sport Coupe 2D		CH32Y	57530	**12800**	**14500**	**18400**	**23800**
Traction Control				325	325	435	435
LS 400—V8—Equipment Schedule 1 W.B. 112.2"; 4.0 Liter.							
Sedan 4D		BH28F	55420	**12900**	**14600**	**18750**	**24500**
Platinum Series				250	250	335	335

2001 LEXUS — JT(8orH)(BF28G)-1-#

Body	Type	VIN	List	Trade-In Fair	Good	Pvt-Party Good	Retail Excellent
ES 300—V6—Equipment Schedule 1 W.B. 105.1"; 3.0 Liter.							
Sedan 4D		BF28G	34935	**11400**	**12950**	**15500**	**19350**
Coach Edition				250	250	335	335
IS 300—6-Cyl.—Equipment Schedule 1 W.B. 105.1"; 3.0 Liter.							
Sedan 4D		BD182	34055	**11875**	**13475**	**15700**	**19200**
GS 300—6-Cyl.—Equipment Schedule 1 W.B. 110.2"; 3.0 Liter.							
Sedan 4D		BD68S	41780	**15275**	**17225**	**20100**	**24500**
GS 430—V8—Equipment Schedule 1 W.B. 110.2"; 4.3 Liter.							
Sedan 4D		BN68X	50580	**18200**	**20475**	**23600**	**28400**
LS 430—V8—Equipment Schedule 1 W.B. 115.2"; 4.3 Liter.							
Sedan 4D		BN30F	54550	**21725**	**24350**	**28900**	**35600**
Ultra Luxury Pkg				2725	2725	3630	3630

2002 LEXUS — JT(8orH)(BF30G)-2-#

Body	Type	VIN	List	Trade-In Fair	Good	Pvt-Party Good	Retail Excellent
ES 300—V6—Equipment Schedule 1 W.B. 105.1"; 3.0 Liter.							
Sedan 4D		BF30G	33640	**14800**	**16675**	**19100**	**23000**
IS 300—6-Cyl.—Equipment Schedule 1 W.B. 105.1"; 3.0 Liter.							
Sedan 4D		BD192	33655	**13675**	**15425**	**17800**	**21500**
Sport Cross H'Back 4D		ED192	35195	**13825**	**15625**	**18000**	**21700**
Manual Trans				(500)	(500)	(665)	(665)
GS 300—6-Cyl.—Equipment Schedule 1 W.B. 110.2"; 3.0 Liter.							
Sedan 4D		BD69S	41840	**17450**	**19600**	**22600**	**27400**
SportDesign				750	750	1000	1000
GS 430—V8—Equipment Schedule 1 W.B. 110.2"; 4.3 Liter.							
Sedan 4D		BL69S	48980	**20750**	**23275**	**26600**	**31700**
LS 430—V8—Equipment Schedule 1 W.B. 115.2"; 4.3 Liter.							
Sedan 4D		BN30F	56080	**24550**	**27450**	**32400**	**39700**
Ultra Luxury Pkg				2800	2800	3730	3730
SC 430—V8—Equipment Schedule 1 W.B. 103.1"; 4.3 Liter.							
Convertible 2D		FN48Y	59030	**27075**	**30275**	**34600**	**41500**

2003 LEXUS — JT(8orH)(BF30G)-3-#

Body	Type	VIN	List	Trade-In Fair	Good	Pvt-Party Good	Retail Excellent
ES 300—V6—Equipment Schedule 1 W.B. 107.1"; 3.0 Liter.							
Sedan 4D		BF30G	33780	**16775**	**18875**	**21400**	**25500**
IS 300—6-Cyl.—Equipment Schedule 1 W.B. 105.1"; 3.0 Liter.							
Sedan 4D		BD192	32485	**15625**	**17600**	**20000**	**24000**
Sport Cross H'Back 4D		ED192	32525	**15775**	**17800**	**20200**	**24200**

2003 LEXUS

Body	Type	VIN	List	Trade-In Fair	Good	Pvt-Party Good	Retail Excellent
	SportDesign			800	800	1065	1065
	Manual Trans			(500)	(500)	(665)	(665)
GS 300—6-Cyl.—Equipment Schedule 1							
W.B. 110.2"; 3.0 Liter.							
Sedan 4D		BD69S	40960	19800	22225	25300	30400
	SportDesign			1350	1350	1800	1800
GS 430—V8—Equipment Schedule 1							
W.B. 110.2"; 4.3 Liter.							
Sedan 4D		BL69S	48400	23575	26375	29700	35100
LS 430—V8—Equipment Schedule 1							
W.B. 115.2"; 4.3 Liter.							
Sedan 4D		BN30F	56600	27925	31225	36500	44400
	Ultra Luxury Pkg			2875	2875	3830	3830
SC 430—V8—Equipment Schedule 1							
W.B. 103.1"; 4.3 Liter.							
Convertible 2D		FN48Y	62600	30950	34525	39300	46800

2004 LEXUS — JT(8orH)(BA30G)-4-#

Body	Type	VIN	List	Trade-In Fair	Good	Pvt-Party Good	Retail Excellent
ES 330—V6—Equipment Schedule 1							
W.B. 107.1"; 3.3 Liter.							
Sedan 4D		BA30G	32350	19100	21425	24100	28300
IS 300—6-Cyl.—Equipment Schedule 1							
W.B. 105.1"; 3.0 Liter.							
Sedan 4D		BD192	32815	17800	19975	22500	26700
Sport Cross H'Back 4D		ED192	32855	17950	20175	22700	26900
	Manual Trans			(500)	(500)	(665)	(665)
GS 300—6-Cyl.—Equipment Schedule 1							
W.B. 110.2"; 3.0 Liter.							
Sedan 4D		BD68S	41010	22400	25025	28300	33600
GS 430—V8—Equipment Schedule 1							
W.B. 110.2"; 4.3 Liter.							
Sedan 4D		BL69S	48450	26475	29575	33000	38700
LS 430—V8—Equipment Schedule 1							
W.B. 115.2"; 4.3 Liter.							
Sedan 4D		BN30F	55750	32100	35800	41700	50500
	Ultra Luxury Pkg			2950	2950	3930	3930
SC 430—V8—Equipment Schedule 1							
W.B. 103.1"; 4.3 Liter.							
Convertible 2D		FN48Y	63200	35700	39775	45000	53400

2005 LEXUS — JT(8orH)(BA30G)-5-#

Body	Type	VIN	List	Trade-In Fair	Good	Pvt-Party Good	Retail Excellent
ES 330—V6—Equipment Schedule 1							
W.B. 107.1"; 3.3 Liter.							
Sedan 4D		BA30G	32600	21625	24250	27000	31600
IS 300—6-Cyl.—Equipment Schedule 1							
W.B. 105.1"; 3.0 Liter.							
Sedan 4D		BD192	34315	20275	22800	25400	29900
Sport Cross H'Back 4D		ED192	34355	20475	22900	25600	30100
	Manual Trans			(500)	(500)	(665)	(665)
GS 300—6-Cyl.—Equipment Schedule 1							
W.B. 110.2"; 3.0 Liter.							
Sedan 4D		BD69S	41160	25325	28325	31600	37200
GS 430—V8—Equipment Schedule 1							
W.B. 110.2"; 4.3 Liter.							
Sedan 4D		BL69S	48600	29775	33275	36800	42700
LS 430—V8—Equipment Schedule 1							
W.B. 115.2"; 4.3 Liter.							
Sedan 4D		BN36F	56300				
	Ultra Luxury Pkg						
SC 430—V8—Equipment Schedule 1							
W.B. 103.1"; 4.3 Liter.							
Convertible 2D		FN48Y	63800				

LINCOLN

1991 LINCOLN — 1LN(LM81W)-M-#

Body	Type	VIN	List	Trade-In Fair	Good	Pvt-Party Good	Retail Excellent
TOWN CAR—V8—Equipment Schedule 2							
W.B. 117.4"; 4.6 Liter.							
Executive Sedan 4D		LM81W	31908	875	1225	2425	4125
Signature Sedan 4D		LM82W	33566	925	1300	2550	4300
Cartier Dsgnr Sed 4D		LM83W	35084	975	1350	2625	4375

1991 LINCOLN

Body Type	VIN	List	Trade-In Fair	Good	Pvt-Party Good	Retail Excellent
MARK VII—V8—Equipment Schedule 2						
W.B. 108.5"; 5.0 Liter.						
Bill Blass Sedan 2D	CM92E	30942	725	1050	2000	3450
LSC Sedan 2D	CM93E	30818	725	1050	2025	3475
Special Edition Pkg			50	50	65	65
CONTINENTAL—V6—Equipment Schedule 2						
W.B. 109.0"; 3.8 Liter.						
Executive Sedan 4D	LM974	32175	650	925	1900	3350
Signature Sedan 4D	LM984	32700	700	1000	2000	3475

1992 LINCOLN — 1LN(LM81W)–N–#

Body Type	VIN	List	Trade-In Fair	Good	Pvt-Party Good	Retail Excellent
TOWN CAR—V8—Equipment Schedule 2						
W.B. 117.4"; 4.6 Liter.						
Executive Sedan 4D	LM81W	33585	1025	1450	2775	4600
Signature Sedan 4D	LM82W	35968	1100	1550	2925	4800
Cartier Dsgnr Sed 4D	LM83W	36930	1125	1575	2975	4875
MARK VII—V8—Equipment Schedule 2						
W.B. 108.5"; 5.0 Liter.						
Bill Blass Designer 2D	CM92E	32746	850	1225	2450	4175
LSC Sedan 2D	CM93E	32622	850	1225	2450	4200
Special Edition Pkg			50	50	65	65
CONTINENTAL—V6—Equipment Schedule 2						
W.B. 109.0"; 3.8 Liter.						
Executive Sedan 4D	LM974	34237	775	1100	2300	4050
Signature Sedan 4D	LM984	34843	825	1175	2425	4175

1993 LINCOLN — 1LN(LM81W)–P–#

Body Type	VIN	List	Trade-In Fair	Good	Pvt-Party Good	Retail Excellent
TOWN CAR—V8—Equipment Schedule 2						
W.B. 117.4"; 4.6 Liter.						
Executive Sedan 4D	LM81W	35350	1225	1700	3175	5175
Signature Sedan 4D	LM82W	36654	1375	1900	3400	5425
Cartier Dsgnr Sed 4D	LM83W	38171	1450	1950	3475	5525
CONTINENTAL—V6—Equipment Schedule 2						
W.B. 109.0"; 3.8 Liter.						
Executive Sedan 4D	LM974	33918	900	1250	2600	4450
Signature Sedan 4D	LM984	35909	950	1325	2725	4600
MARK VIII—V8—Equipment Schedule 2						
W.B. 113.0"; 4.6 Liter.						
Coupe 2D	LM91V	37230	1075	1525	2775	4500

1994 LINCOLN — 1LN(LM81W)–R–#

Body Type	VIN	List	Trade-In Fair	Good	Pvt-Party Good	Retail Excellent
TOWN CAR—V8—Equipment Schedule 2						
W.B. 117.4"; 4.6 Liter.						
Executive Sedan 4D	LM81W	35930	1525	2025	3650	5825
Signature Sedan 4D	LM82W	37230	1775	2300	3950	6175
Cartier Dsgnr Sed 4D	LM83W	38725	1825	2350	4025	6275
CONTINENTAL—V6—Equipment Schedule 2						
W.B. 109.0"; 3.8 Liter.						
Executive Sedan 4D	LM974	34375	1050	1475	2975	5025
Signature Sedan 4D	LM984	36225	1125	1575	3100	5150
MARK VIII—V8—Equipment Schedule 2						
W.B. 113.0"; 4.6 Liter.						
Coupe 2D	LM91V	38675	1225	1725	3025	4825

1995 LINCOLN — 1LN(LM81W)–S–#

Body Type	VIN	List	Trade-In Fair	Good	Pvt-Party Good	Retail Excellent
TOWN CAR—V8—Equipment Schedule 2						
W.B. 117.4"; 4.6 Liter.						
Executive Sedan 4D	LM81W	37595	2075	2650	4225	6350
Signature Sedan 4D	LM82W	39695	2375	2950	4575	6825
Cartier Sedan 4D	LM83W	41825	2425	3025	4650	6900
Spinnaker Edition			75	75	100	100
CONTINENTAL—V8—Equipment Schedule 2						
W.B. 109.0"; 4.6 Liter.						
Sedan 4D	LM97V	41375	1475	1975	3450	5425
MARK VIII—V8—Equipment Schedule 2						
W.B. 113.0"; 4.6 Liter.						
Coupe 2D	LM91V	39425	1525	2025	3425	5325
LSC			175	175	235	235

1996 LINCOLN

Body	Type	VIN	List	Trade-In Fair	Good	Pvt-Party Good	Retail Excellent
1996 LINCOLN — 1LN(LM81W)–T–#							
TOWN CAR—V8—Equipment Schedule 2							
W.B. 117.4"; 4.6 Liter.							
Executive Sedan 4D		LM81W	38120	2475	3075	4800	7150
Signature Sedan 4D		LM82W	40170	2825	3475	5250	7675
Cartier Sedan 4D		LM83W	42600	2875	3550	5325	7775
CONTINENTAL—V8—Equipment Schedule 2							
W.B. 109.0"; 4.6 Liter.							
Sedan 4D		LM97V	42440	1975	2525	4150	6325
MARK VIII—V8—Equipment Schedule 2							
W.B. 113.0"; 4.6 Liter.							
Coupe 2D		LM91V	40290	1950	2475	3975	6025
LSC				200	200	265	265
1997 LINCOLN — 1LN(LM81W)–V–#							
TOWN CAR—V8—Equipment Schedule 2							
W.B. 117.4"; 4.6 Liter.							
Executive Sedan 4D		LM81W	38720	3000	3650	5575	8175
Signature Sedan 4D		LM82W	41080	3425	4125	6075	8775
Cartier Sedan 4D		LM83W	43870	3475	4200	6150	8875
CONTINENTAL—V8—Equipment Schedule 2							
W.B. 109.0"; 4.6 Liter.							
Sedan 4D		LM97V	37850	2600	3225	5025	7475
MARK VIII—V8—Equipment Schedule 2							
W.B. 113.0"; 4.6 Liter.							
Coupe 2D		LM91V	36950	2450	3050	4725	7000
LSC				200	200	265	265
1998 LINCOLN — 1LN(LM81W)–W–#							
TOWN CAR—V8—Equipment Schedule 2							
W.B. 117.7"; 4.6 Liter.							
Executive Sedan 4D		LM81W	38330	4450	5250	6675	8775
Signature Sedan 4D		LM82W	40150	4925	5775	7250	9450
Cartier Sedan 4D		LM83W	42500	5000	5875	7350	9550
CONTINENTAL—V8—Equipment Schedule 2							
W.B. 109.0"; 4.6 Liter.							
Sedan 4D		LM97V	38500	3350	4050	6050	8725
MARK VIII—V8—Equipment Schedule 2							
W.B. 113.0"; 4.6 Liter.							
Coupe 2D		LM91V	37500	3175	3825	5725	8325
LSC				200	200	265	265
1999 LINCOLN — 1LN(LM81W)–X–#							
TOWN CAR—V8—Equipment Schedule 2							
W.B. 117.7"; 4.6 Liter.							
Executive Sedan 4D		LM81W	38995	5575	6500	7975	10250
Signature Sedan 4D		LM82W	40995	6100	7075	8600	10900
Cartier Sedan 4D		LM83W	43495	6225	7225	8750	11100
CONTINENTAL—V8—Equipment Schedule 2							
W.B. 109.0"; 4.6 Liter.							
Sedan 4D		LM97V	38995	4375	5150	7300	10250
2000 LINCOLN — 1LN(HM81W)–Y–#							
TOWN CAR—V8—Equipment Schedule 2							
W.B. 117.7", 123.7" (L Pkg); 4.6 Liter.							
Executive Sedan 4D		HM81W	39300	6850	7875	9550	12100
Signature Sedan 4D		HM82W	41300	7500	8600	10350	12950
Cartier Sedan 4D		HM83W	43800	7800	8975	10700	13400
L Pkg				1725	1725	2300	2300
Touring Pkg				125	125	165	165
CONTINENTAL—V8—Equipment Schedule 2							
W.B. 117.7"; 4.6 Liter.							
Sedan 4D		HM97V	39550	5800	6750	8750	11650
LS—V6—Equipment Schedule 2							
W.B. 114.5"; 3.0 Liter.							
Sedan 4D		HM86S	31450	6000	6950	9000	11900
Sport Pkg				125	125	165	165
Manual Trans				(550)	(550)	(735)	(735)
LS—V8—Equipment Schedule 2							
W.B. 114.5"; 3.9 Liter.							

2000 LINCOLN

Body	Type	VIN	List	Trade-In Fair	Trade-In Good	Pvt-Party Good	Retail Excellent
Sedan 4D		HM87A	35225	7700	8850	11000	14150
Sport Pkg				125	125	165	165

2001 LINCOLN — 1LN(HM81W)-1-#

TOWN CAR—V8—Equipment Schedule 2
W.B. 117.7", 123.7" (L); 4.6 Liter.

Executive Sedan 4D		HM81W	39865	8400	9625	11550	14450
Executive L Sed 4D		HM84W	44225	10675	12175	14200	17450
Signature Sedan 4D		HM82W	42035	9150	10425	12400	15400
Signature Touring 4D		HM82W	42745	9275	10575	12550	15600
Cartier Sedan 4D		HM83W	44420	9750	11100	13100	16200
Cartier L Sedan 4D		HM85W	49230	12600	14250	16500	20000

CONTINENTAL—V8—Equipment Schedule 2
W.B. 109.0"; 4.6 Liter.

Sedan 4D		HM97V	40100	7400	8500	10850	14200

LS—V6—Equipment Schedule 2
W.B. 114.5"; 3.0 Liter.

Sedan 4D		HM86S	32250	7500	8600	10950	14350
Sport Pkg				150	150	200	200
Manual Trans				(600)	(600)	(800)	(800)

LS—V8—Equipment Schedule 2
W.B. 114.5"; 3.9 Liter.

Sedan 4D		HM87A	36280	9400	10725	13250	16900
Sport Pkg				150	150	200	200

2002 LINCOLN — 1LN(HM81W)-2-#

TOWN CAR—V8—Equipment Schedule 2
W.B. 117.7", 123.7" (L); 4.6 Liter.

Executive Sedan 4D		HM81W	40540	10375	11775	14050	17450
Executive L Sed 4D		HM84W	44600	12900	14600	17000	20800
Signature Sedan 4D		HM82W	42710	11250	12750	15050	18600
Signature Touring 4D		HM82W	43420	11350	12900	15250	18750
Cartier Sedan 4D		HM83W	45095	12025	13625	15950	19600
Cartier L Sedan 4D		HM85W	49605	15025	16925	19500	23600

CONTINENTAL—V8—Equipment Schedule 2
W.B. 109.0"; 4.6 Liter.

Sedan 4D		HM97V	38555	9400	10725	13500	17400

LS—V6—Equipment Schedule 2
W.B. 114.5"; 3.0 Liter.

Sedan 4D		HM86S	33455	9425	10775	13600	17550
LSE				1500	1500	2000	2000
Manual Trans				(650)	(650)	(865)	(865)

LS—V8—Equipment Schedule 2
W.B. 114.5"; 3.9 Liter.

Sedan 4D		HM87A	37630	11600	13150	16050	20300
LSE				1500	1500	2000	2000

2003 LINCOLN — 1LN(HM81W)-3-#

TOWN CAR—V8—Equipment Schedule 2
W.B. 117.7", 123.7" (L); 4.6 Liter.

Executive Sedan 4D		HM81W	41140	12600	14250	16900	20900
Executive L Sed 4D		HM84W	45115	15425	17375	20200	24400
Signature Sedan 4D		HM82W	43600	13575	15325	18050	22100
Cartier Sedan 4D		HM83W	46110	14600	16500	19250	23500
Cartier L Sedan 4D		HM85W	51570	17800	19975	22900	27500
Limited Edition				500	500	665	665

LS—V6—Equipment Schedule 2
W.B. 114.5"; 3.0 Liter.

Sedan 4D		HM86S	34495	12025	13625	17000	21700

LS—V8—Equipment Schedule 2
W.B. 114.5"; 3.9 Liter.

Sedan 4D		HM87A	40695	14350	16200	19700	24700

2004 LINCOLN — 1LN(HM81W)-4-#

TOWN CAR—V8—Equipment Schedule 2
W.B. 117.7", 123.7" (L); 4.6 Liter.

Executive Sedan 4D		HM81W	42810	15375	17325	20400	25000
Executive L Sedan 4D		HM84W	45790	18425	20750	24000	28900
Signature Sedan 4D		HM81W	41815	16450	18525	21600	26400
Ultimate Sedan 4D		HM83W	44925	17700	19875	23100	27900
Ultimate L Sedan 4D		HM85W	50470	20950	23475	26800	32000

Body	Type	VIN	List	Trade-In Fair	Trade-In Good	Pvt-Party Good	Retail Excellent

LS—V6—Equipment Schedule 2
W.B. 114.5"; 3.0 Liter.

| Sedan 4D | | HM86S | 32495 | **13475** | **15225** | **18600** | **23500** |

LS—V8—Equipment Schedule 2
W.B. 114.5"; 3.9 Liter.

| Sedan 4D | | HM87A | 40095 | **16050** | **18050** | **21500** | **26800** |
| LSE | | | | **1500** | **1500** | **2000** | **2000** |

TOWN CAR—V8—Equipment Schedule 2
W.B. 117.7", 123.7" (L); 4.6 Liter.

Signature Sedan 4D		M81W	42470	**19875**	**22300**	**26000**	**31500**
Signature Ltd Sed		M83W	21350	**23950**	**27600**	**33400**
Signature L Sedan		M85W	50915	**24825**	**27750**	**31500**	**37500**
Executive L Sedan		M84W	46445	**22025**	**24725**	**28400**	**34200**
Limited Edition				**300**	**300**	**400**	**400**

LS—V6—Equipment Schedule 2
W.B. 114.5"; 3.0 Liter.

| Sedan 4D | | M86S | 32965 | **15950** | **17950** | **21700** | **27200** |

LS—V8—Equipment Schedule 2
W.B. 114.5"; 3.9 Liter.

| Sedan 4D | | M87A | 40515 | **18725** | **21050** | **24800** | **30600** |
| LSE | | | | **1500** | **1500** | **2000** | **2000** |

MAZDA

323—4-Cyl.—Equipment Schedule 6
W.B. 96.5"; 1.6 Liter.

| Hatchback 2D | | BG232 | 8243 | **475** | **700** | **1250** | **2150** |
| SE Hatchback 2D | | BG234 | 9693 | **550** | **775** | **1350** | **2325** |

PROTEGE—4-Cyl.—Equipment Schedule 6
W.B. 98.4"; 1.8 Liter.

DX Sedan 4D		BG224	11063	**475**	**700**	**1425**	**2600**
LX Sedan 4D		BG226	12393	**550**	**775**	**1550**	**2775**
4WD Sedan 4D		BG228	12783	**625**	**900**	**1700**	**2950**

626—4-Cyl.—Equipment Schedule 4
W.B. 101.4"; 2.2 Liter.

DX Sedan 4D		GD222	14448	**575**	**825**	**1700**	**3050**
LX Sedan 4D		GD222	15938	**625**	**900**	**1825**	**3225**
LX Touring Sedan 4D		GD242	16338	**675**	**950**	**1900**	**3300**
LE Sedan 4D		GD222	17269	**750**	**1050**	**2025**	**3525**
Manual Trans				**(175)**	**(175)**	**(235)**	**(235)**

626—4-Cyl. Turbo—Equipment Schedule 4
W.B. 101.4"; 2.2 Liter.

| GT Touring Sedan 4D | | GD244 | 17938 | **700** | **1025** | **2000** | **3450** |

MX-6—4-Cyl.—Equipment Schedule 4
W.B. 99.0"; 2.2 Liter.

DX Coupe 2D		GD312	14384	**575**	**825**	**1700**	**3050**
LX Coupe 2D		GD312	15938	**575**	**825**	**1700**	**3050**
LE Coupe 2D		GD312	16549	**575**	**825**	**1700**	**3050**
Manual Trans				**(175)**	**(175)**	**(235)**	**(235)**

MX-6—4-Cyl. Turbo—Equipment Schedule 4
W.B. 99.0"; 2.2 Liter.

| GT Coupe 2D | | GD314 | 18258 | **575** | **825** | **1700** | **3050** |

MX-5 MIATA—4-Cyl.—Equipment Schedule 6
W.B. 89.2"; 1.6 Liter.

MX-5 Convertible 2D		NA351	14499	**825**	**1175**	**2275**	**3900**
MX-5 Spcl Ed Conv 2D		NA351	19548	**1150**	**1600**	**2875**	**4625**
Auto Trans				**0**	**0**	**0**	**0**
Hard Top				**300**	**300**	**400**	**400**

RX-7—Rotary—Equipment Schedule 4
W.B. 95.7"; 1.3 Liter.

| Coupe 2D | | FC331 | 20799 | **900** | **1250** | **2700** | **4675** |
| Convertible 2D | | FC352 | 29199 | **1950** | **2475** | **4175** | **6475** |

RX-7—Rotary Turbo—Equipment Schedule 4
W.B. 95.7"; 1.3 Liter.

| Coupe 2D | | FC332 | 28149 | **1075** | **1525** | **3050** | **5100** |

929—Equipment Schedule 4
W.B. 106.7"; 3.0 Liter.

| Sedan 4D | | HC222 | 23799 | **600** | **850** | **2100** | **3900** |

1991 MAZDA

Body	Type	VIN	List	Trade-In Fair	Good	Pvt-Party Good	Retail Excellent
S Sedan 4D		HC224	25299	650	925	2225	4050

1992 MAZDA — (JM1or1YV)(BG232)-N-#

323—4-Cyl.—Equipment Schedule 6
W.B. 96.5"; 1.6 Liter.

Hatchback 2D		BG232	8439	550	775	1400	2425
SE Hatchback 2D		BG232	10189	600	875	1525	2625

MX-3—4-Cyl.—Equipment Schedule 6
W.B. 96.3"; 1.6 Liter.

Hatchback 2D		EC431	12630	900	1275	2150	3475

MX-3—V6—Equipment Schedule 6
W.B. 96.3"; 1.8 Liter.

GS Hatchback 2D		EC432	15430	1175	1625	2725	4275

PROTEGE'—4-Cyl.—Equipment Schedule 6
W.B. 98.4"; 1.8 Liter.

DX Sedan 4D		BG224	11769	550	800	1600	2825
LX Sedan 4D		BG226	12889	625	900	1725	3000

626—4-Cyl.—Equipment Schedule 4
W.B. 101.4"; 2.2 Liter.

DX Sedan 4D		GD22B	15685	650	925	1950	3475
LX Sedan 4D		GD22B	16585	700	1025	2075	3650
Manual Trans				(175)	(175)	(235)	(235)

MX-6—4-Cyl.—Equipment Schedule 4
W.B. 99.0"; 2.2 Liter.

DX Coupe 2D		GD31B	15475	650	925	1950	3475
LX Coupe 2D		GD31B	16575	650	925	1950	3475
Manual Trans				(175)	(175)	(235)	(235)

MX-6—4-Cyl. Turbo—Equipment Schedule 4
W.B. 99.0"; 2.2 Liter.

GT Coupe 2D		GD31D	18895	675	950	2025	3575

MX-5 MIATA—4-Cyl.—Equipment Schedule 6
W.B. 89.2"; 1.6 Liter.

MX-5 Convertible 2D		NA351	15150	975	1350	2625	4375
Auto Trans				(25)	(25)	(35)	(35)
Hard Top				325	325	435	435

929—V6—Equipment Schedule 4
W.B. 112.2"; 3.0 Liter.

Sedan 4D		HD461	28150	1125	1575	3100	5150

1993 MAZDA — (JM1or1YV)(BG232)-P-#

323—4-Cyl.—Equipment Schedule 6
W.B. 96.5"; 1.6 Liter.

Hatchback 2D		BG232	9219	625	900	1575	2725
SE Hatchback 2D		BG232	10889	700	1025	1775	2950

MX-3—4-Cyl.—Equipment Schedule 6
W.B. 96.3"; 1.6 Liter.

Hatchback 2D		EC431	13055	1000	1425	2475	4000

MX-3—V6—Equipment Schedule 6
W.B. 96.3"; 1.8 Liter.

GS Hatchback 2D		EC432	15825	1400	1900	3050	4675
Spcl Edition H'Back 2D		EC432	17660	1400	1900	3050	4675

PROTEGE'—4-Cyl.—Equipment Schedule 6
W.B. 98.4"; 1.8 Liter.

DX Sedan 4D		BG224	12374	625	900	1775	3125
LX Sedan 4D		BG226	13539	700	1000	1925	3350

626—4-Cyl.—Equipment Schedule 4
W.B. 102.8"; 2.0 Liter.

DX Sedan 4D		GE22A	17495	650	925	1950	3475
LX Sedan 4D		GE22A	17590	700	1025	2075	3650
Manual Trans				(225)	(225)	(300)	(300)

626—V6—Equipment Schedule 4
W.B. 102.8"; 2.5 Liter.

ES Sedan 4D		GE22B	19875	975	1375	2675	4450
Manual Trans				(225)	(225)	(300)	(300)

MX-6—4-Cyl.—Equipment Schedule 4
W.B. 102.8"; 2.0 Liter.

Coupe 2D		GE31A	18300	675	950	2000	3525
Manual Trans				(225)	(225)	(300)	(300)

MX-6—V6—Equipment Schedule 4
W.B. 102.8"; 2.5 Liter.

LS Coupe 2D		GE31B	20575	775	1100	2275	4000
Manual Trans				(225)	(225)	(300)	(300)

Body	Type	VIN	List	Trade-In Fair	Good	Pvt-Party Good	Retail Excellent
MX-5 MIATA—4-Cyl.—Equipment Schedule 6							
W.B. 89.2"; 1.6 Liter.							
MX-5 Convertible 2D		NA351	15650	1125	1575	2925	4825
MX-5 Ltd Ed Conv 2D		NA351	22350	1675	2200	3675	5725
Auto Trans				(75)	(75)	(100)	(100)
Hard Top				350	350	465	465
RX-7—Rotary Turbo—Equipment Schedule 3							
W.B. 95.5"; 1.3 Liter.							
Coupe 2D		FD331	32850	5400	6300	8950	12500
Auto Trans				(75)	(75)	(100)	(100)
929—V6—Equipment Schedule 4							
W.B. 112.2"; 3.0 Liter.							
Sedan 4D		HD461	29550	1300	1800	3425	5600

1994 MAZDA — (JM1or1YV)(BG232)–R–#

Body	Type	VIN	List	Trade-In Fair	Good	Pvt-Party Good	Retail Excellent
323—4-Cyl.—Equipment Schedule 6							
W.B. 96.5"; 1.6 Liter.							
Hatchback 2D		BG232	10220	700	1025	1800	3050
MX-3—4-Cyl.—Equipment Schedule 6							
W.B. 96.3"; 1.6 Liter.							
Hatchback 2D		EC435	14840	1125	1575	2725	4325
MX-3—V6—Equipment Schedule 6							
W.B. 96.3"; 1.8 Liter.							
GS Hatchback 2D		EC436	17340	1675	2200	3425	5150
PROTEGE'—4-Cyl.—Equipment Schedule 6							
W.B. 98.4"; 1.8 Liter.							
Sedan 4D		BG224	10570	525	750	1650	3000
DX Sedan 4D		BG224	13070	700	1000	2025	3525
LX Sedan 4D		BG226	14770	775	1125	2275	3950
626—4-Cyl.—Equipment Schedule 4							
W.B. 102.8"; 2.0 Liter.							
DX Sedan 4D		GE22C	15450	675	975	2075	3675
LX Sedan 4D		GE22C	17735	725	1050	2250	3975
Manual Trans				(275)	(275)	(365)	(365)
V6 2.5 Liter		D		225	225	300	300
626—V6—Equipment Schedule 4							
W.B. 102.8"; 2.5 Liter.							
ES Sedan 4D		GE22D	22740	1150	1600	2975	4875
Manual Trans				(275)	(275)	(365)	(365)
MX-6—4-Cyl.—Equipment Schedule 4							
W.B. 102.8"; 2.0 Liter.							
Coupe 2D		GE31C	19540	800	1150	2375	4125
Manual Trans				(275)	(275)	(365)	(365)
MX-6—V6—Equipment Schedule 4							
W.B. 102.8"; 2.5 Liter.							
LS Coupe 2D		GE31D	22690	1000	1400	2725	4550
Manual Trans				(275)	(275)	(365)	(365)
MX-5 MIATA—4-Cyl.—Equipment Schedule 6							
W.B. 89.2"; 1.8 Liter.							
MX-5 Convertible 2D		NA353	17045	1200	1650	3075	5025
MX-5 M-Ed Conv 2D		NA353	21645	1825	2350	3875	5975
Auto Trans				0	0	0	0
Hard Top				375	375	500	500
RX-7—Rotary Turbo—Equipment Schedule 3							
W.B. 95.5"; 1.3 Liter.							
Coupe 2D		FD333	36395	6450	7475	10400	14250
Auto Trans				(125)	(125)	(165)	(165)
929—V6—Equipment Schedule 4							
W.B. 112.2"; 3.0 Liter.							
Sedan 4D		HD461	31895	1550	2050	3825	6150

1995 MAZDA — (JM1or1YV)(EC435)–S–#

Body	Type	VIN	List	Trade-In Fair	Good	Pvt-Party Good	Retail Excellent
MX-3—4-Cyl.—Equipment Schedule 6							
W.B. 96.3"; 1.6 Liter.							
Hatchback 2D		EC435	15780	1325	1825	2975	4600
PROTEGE'—4-Cyl.—Equipment Schedule 6							
W.B. 98.4"; 1.5 Liter, 1.8 Liter.							
DX Sedan 4D		BA141	14010	700	1000	1975	3450
LX Sedan 4D		BA141	14980	800	1150	2275	3900
ES Sedan 4D		BA142	16585	975	1350	2575	4275
626—4-Cyl.—Equipment Schedule 4							
W.B. 102.8"; 2.0 Liter.							
DX Sedan 4D		GE22C	17630	825	1175	2475	4300

Body	Type	VIN	List	Trade-In Fair	Good	Pvt-Party Good	Retail Excellent
LX Sedan 4D		GE22C	18635	875	1225	2575	4425
Manual Trans				(325)	(325)	(435)	(435)
V6 2.5 Liter		D		275	275	365	365
626—V6—Equipment Schedule 4							
W.B. 102.8"; 2.5 Liter.							
ES Sedan 4D		GE22D	23935	1400	1900	3375	5375
Manual Trans				(325)	(325)	(435)	(435)
MX-6—4-Cyl.—Equipment Schedule 4							
W.B. 102.8"; 2.0 Liter.							
Coupe 2D		GE31C	20713	975	1350	2725	4600
Manual Trans				(325)	(325)	(435)	(435)
MX-6—V6—Equipment Schedule 4							
W.B. 102.8"; 2.5 Liter.							
LS Coupe 2D		GE31D	22888	1275	1775	3225	5225
Manual Trans				(325)	(325)	(435)	(435)
MX-5 MIATA—4-Cyl.—Equipment Schedule 6							
W.B. 89.2"; 1.8 Liter.							
MX-5 Convertible 2D		NA353	17940	1475	1975	3525	5600
MX-5 M-Ed Conv 2D		NA353	23970	2125	2725	4375	6600
Auto Trans				0	0	0	0
Hard Top				400	400	535	535
RX-7—Rotary Turbo—Equipment Schedule 3							
W.B. 95.5"; 1.3 Liter.							
Coupe 2D		FD333	37950	7600	8725	11800	16000
Auto Trans				(150)	(150)	(200)	(200)
MILLENIA—V6—Equipment Schedule 2							
W.B. 108.3"; 2.5 Liter.							
Sedan 4D		TA221	29335	1100	1550	3250	5475
MILLENIA—V6 Supercharged—Equipment Schedule 2							
W.B. 108.3"; 2.3 Liter.							
S Sedan 4D		TA222	32435	2150	2750	4575	7075
929—V6—Equipment Schedule 4							
W.B. 112.2"; 3.0 Liter.							
Sedan 4D		HD461	36235	1875	2400	4300	6800

1996 MAZDA — JM1(BB141)-T-#

Body	Type	VIN	List	Trade-In Fair	Good	Pvt-Party Good	Retail Excellent
PROTEGE—4-Cyl.—Equipment Schedule 6							
W.B. 102.6"; 1.5 Liter, 1.8 Liter.							
DX Sedan 4D		BB141	13720	825	1175	2350	4050
LX Sedan 4D		BB141	14590	950	1325	2575	4300
ES Sedan 4D		BB142	15145	1125	1575	2875	4675
626—4-Cyl.—Equipment Schedule 4							
W.B. 102.8"; 2.0 Liter.							
DX Sedan 4D		GE22C	17960	975	1375	2825	4800
LX Sedan 4D		GE22C	18945	1050	1475	2950	4950
Manual Trans				(375)	(375)	(500)	(500)
V6 2.5 Liter		D		325	325	435	435
626—V6—Equipment Schedule 4							
W.B. 102.8"; 2.5 Liter.							
ES Sedan 4D		GE22D	24045	1725	2250	3825	6000
Manual Trans				(375)	(375)	(500)	(500)
MX-6—V6—Equipment Schedule 4							
W.B. 102.8"; 2.0 Liter.							
Coupe 2D		GE31C	21745	1175	1625	3125	5175
Manual Trans				(375)	(375)	(500)	(500)
MX-6—V6—Equipment Schedule 4							
W.B. 102.8"; 2.5 Liter.							
LS Coupe 2D		GE31D	24100	1675	2200	3775	5950
M-Edition Coupe 2D		GE31D	27600	1975	2500	4150	6350
Manual Trans				(375)	(375)	(500)	(500)
MX-5 MIATA—4-Cyl.—Equipment Schedule 6							
W.B. 89.2"; 1.8 Liter.							
MX-5 Convertible 2D		NA353	18900	1825	2350	4050	6325
MX-5 M-Ed Conv 2D		NA353	25210	2525	3125	4925	7375
Auto Trans				0	0	0	0
Hard Top				425	425	565	565
MILLENIA—V6—Equipment Schedule 2							
W.B. 108.3"; 2.5 Liter.							
Sedan 4D		TA221	28445	1275	1775	3600	6000
L Sedan 4D		TA221	31845	1375	1875	3675	6100
MILLENIA—V6 Supercharged—Equipment Schedule 2							
W.B. 108.3"; 2.3 Liter.							
S Sedan 4D		TA222	34845	2575	3175	5175	7825

1997 MAZDA

Body	Type	VIN	List	Trade-In Fair	Trade-In Good	Pvt-Party Good	Retail Excellent
1997 MAZDA — JM1(BC141)-V-#							
PROTEGE'—4-Cyl.—Equipment Schedule 6							
W.B. 102.6"; 1.5 Liter, 1.8 Liter.							
DX Sedan 4D		BC141	14170	975	1375	2700	4475
LX Sedan 4D		BC141	15140	1125	1575	2900	4750
ES Sedan 4D		BC142	15745	1375	1875	3250	5150
626—4-Cyl.—Equipment Schedule 4							
W.B. 102.8"; 2.0 Liter.							
DX Sedan 4D		GE22C	18160	1225	1675	3300	5425
LX Sedan 4D		GE22C	19145	1325	1825	3450	5600
Manual Trans				(400)	(400)	(535)	(535)
V6 2.5 Liter		D		350	350	465	465
626—V6—Equipment Schedule 4							
W.B. 102.8"; 2.5 Liter.							
ES Sedan 4D		GE22D	24245	2100	2675	4400	6725
Manual Trans				(400)	(400)	(535)	(535)
MX-6—4-Cyl.—Equipment Schedule 4							
W.B. 102.8"; 2.0 Liter.							
Coupe 2D		GE31C	22345	1500	2000	3650	5850
Manual Trans				(400)	(400)	(535)	(535)
MX-6—V6—Equipment Schedule 4							
W.B. 102.8"; 2.5 Liter.							
LS Coupe 2D		GE31D	25200	2125	2700	4425	6750
Manual Trans				(400)	(400)	(535)	(535)
MX-5 MIATA—4-Cyl.—Equipment Schedule 6							
W.B. 89.2"; 1.8 Liter.							
MX-5 Convertible 2D		NA353	20775	2175	2775	4625	7125
MX-5 STO-Ed Conv 2D		NA353	22970	2725	3350	5300	7925
MX-5 M-Ed Conv 2D		NA353	24935	2925	3600	5550	8225
Auto Trans				0	0	0	0
Hard Top				450	450	600	600
MILLENIA—V6—Equipment Schedule 2							
W.B. 108.3"; 2.5 Liter.							
Sedan 4D		TA221	29445	1675	2175	4200	6850
L Sedan 4D		TA221	33445	1750	2275	4300	6950
MILLENIA—V6 Supercharged—Equipment Schedule 2							
W.B. 108.3"; 2.3 Liter.							
S Sedan 4D		TA222	37045	3000	3675	5875	8775
1998 MAZDA — JM1(BB141)-W-#							
PROTEGE'—4-Cyl.—Equipment Schedule 6							
W.B. 102.6"; 1.5 Liter, 1.8 Liter.							
DX Sedan 4D		BB141	14170	1200	1650	3050	4975
LX Sedan 4D		BB141	15140	1375	1900	3325	5250
ES Sedan 4D		BB142	15745	1675	2175	3650	5650
626—4-Cyl.—Equipment Schedule 4							
W.B. 105.1"; 2.0 Liter.							
DX Sedan 4D		GE22C	18690	1675	2175	3850	6100
LX Sedan 4D		GE22C	19395	1825	2350	4025	6300
Manual Trans				(425)	(425)	(565)	(565)
V6 2.5 Liter		D		375	375	500	500
626—V6—Equipment Schedule 4							
W.B. 105.1"; 2.5 Liter.							
ES Sedan 4D		GE22D	25495	2625	3250	5050	7475
Manual Trans				(425)	(425)	(565)	(565)
MILLENIA—V6—Equipment Schedule 2							
W.B. 108.3"; 2.5 Liter.							
Sedan 4D		TA221	33445	2250	2825	5050	7950
MILLENIA—V6 Supercharged—Equipment Schedule 2							
W.B. 108.3"; 2.3 Liter.							
S Sedan 4D		TA222	37045	3625	4325	6700	9850
1999 MAZDA — (Jor1)(M1orYV)(BJ222)-X-#							
PROTEGE'—4-Cyl.—Equipment Schedule 6							
W.B. 102.8"; 1.6 Liter, 1.8 Liter.							
DX Sedan 4D		BJ222	13995	2200	2800	4175	6125
LX Sedan 4D		BJ222	14725	2425	3000	4425	6400
ES Sedan 4D		BJ221	15375	2725	3350	4800	6850
626—4-Cyl.—Equipment Schedule 4							
W.B. 105.1"; 2.0 Liter.							
LX Sedan 4D		GF22C	19165	2275	2850	4650	7050

1999 MAZDA

Body	Type	VIN	List	Trade-In Fair	Good	Pvt-Party Good	Retail Excellent
ES Sedan 4D		GF22C	20245	2800	3425	5250	7750
Manual Trans				(450)	(450)	(600)	(600)
V6 2.5 Liter		D		425	425	565	565

MX-5 MIATA—4-Cyl.—Equipment Schedule 6
W.B. 89.2"; 1.8 Liter.

Convertible 2D		NB353	21420	4350	5125	7200	10050
10th Anniversary Conv		NB353	27325	6475	7500	9800	13000
Auto Trans				0	0	0	0
Hard Top				500	500	665	665

MILLENIA—V6—Equipment Schedule 2
W.B. 108.3"; 2.5 Liter.

| Sedan 4D | | TA221 | 28995 | 4500 | 5325 | 7175 | 9800 |

MILLENIA—V6 Supercharged—Equipment Schedule 2
W.B. 108.3"; 2.3 Liter.

| S Sedan 4D | | TA222 | 31495 | 6000 | 6950 | 8925 | 11800 |

2000 MAZDA — (Jor1)(M1orYV)(BJ222)-Y-#

PROTEGE'—4-Cyl.—Equipment Schedule 6
W.B. 102.8"; 1.6 Liter, 1.8 Liter.

DX Sedan 4D		BJ222	13995	2650	3275	4725	6825
LX Sedan 4D		BJ222	14840	2875	3550	5050	7150
ES Sedan 4D		BJ221	15490	3250	3925	5450	7650

626—4-Cyl.—Equipment Schedule 4
W.B. 105.1"; 2.0 Liter.

LX Sedan 4D		GF22C	19695	2725	3325	5250	7800
ES Sedan 4D		GF22C	21095	3300	3975	5925	8575
Manual Trans				(500)	(500)	(665)	(665)
V6 2.5 Liter		D		500	500	665	665

MX-5 MIATA—4-Cyl.—Equipment Schedule 6
W.B. 89.2"; 1.8 Liter.

Convertible 2D		NB353	22595	5075	5950	8175	11250
LS Convertible 2D		NB353	25345	5825	6775	9050	12200
Special Ed Conv 2D		NB353	25505	6050	7000	9325	12550
Auto Trans				0	0	0	0
Hard Top				525	525	700	700

MILLENIA—V6—Equipment Schedule 2
W.B. 108.3"; 2.5 Liter.

| Sedan 4D | | TA221 | 25445 | 5100 | 6000 | 7950 | 10700 |

MILLENIA—V6 Supercharged—Equipment Schedule 2
W.B. 108.3"; 2.3 Liter.

| S Sedan 4D | | TA222 | 30445 | 6800 | 7850 | 9950 | 13000 |
| Millennium Edition | | | | 175 | 175 | 235 | 235 |

2001 MAZDA — (Jor1)(M1orYV)(BJ222)-1-#

PROTEGE'—4-Cyl.—Equipment Schedule 6
W.B. 102.8"; 1.6 Liter, 2.0 Liter.

DX Sedan 4D		BJ222	14095	3150	3800	5375	7600
LX Sedan 4D		BJ222	14895	3450	4150	5725	7975
ES Sedan 4D		BJ225	16015	3825	4575	6200	8500
MP3 Sedan 4D		BJ227	18500	5400	6300	8050	10550

626—4-Cyl.—Equipment Schedule 4
W.B. 105.1"; 2.0 Liter.

LX Sedan 4D		GF22C	20015	3200	3875	5950	8700
ES Sedan 4D		GF22C	21415	3875	4625	6725	9575
Manual Trans				(525)	(525)	(700)	(700)
V6 2.5 Liter		D		550	550	735	735

MX-5 MIATA—4-Cyl.—Equipment Schedule 6
W.B. 89.2"; 1.8 Liter.

Convertible 2D		NB353	21660	5850	6800	9050	12200
LS Convertible 2D		NB353	24410	6650	7675	10050	13350
SE Convertible 2D		NB353	26195	6925	8000	10400	13750
Auto Trans				0	0	0	0
Hard Top				550	550	735	735

MILLENIA—V6—Equipment Schedule 2
W.B. 108.3"; 2.5 Liter.

| Sedan 4D | | TA221 | 28505 | 5825 | 6775 | 8900 | 11950 |

MILLENIA—V6 Supercharged—Equipment Schedule 2
W.B. 108.3"; 2.3 Liter.

| S Sedan 4D | | TA222 | 31505 | 7725 | 8875 | 11150 | 14450 |

2002 MAZDA

Body Type	VIN	List	Trade-In Fair	Good	Pvt-Party Good	Retail Excellent

2002 MAZDA — (Jor1)(M1orYV)(BJ222)-2-#

PROTEGE—4-Cyl.—Equipment Schedule 6
W.B. 102.8"; 2.0 Liter.

DX Sedan 4D	BJ222	14530	3725	4450	6125	8500
LX Sedan 4D	BJ222	15335	4050	4825	6525	8925
ES Sedan 4D	BJ221	16060	4500	5300	7025	9500

PROTEGE'5—4-Cyl.—Equipment Schedule 6
W.B. 102.8"; 2.0 Liter.

Hatchback 4D	BJ245	16815	5650	6575	8475	11150

626—4-Cyl.—Equipment Schedule 6
W.B. 105.1"; 2.0 Liter.

LX Sedan 4D	GF22C	20015	3825	4575	6800	9800
ES Sedan 4D	GF22C	22915	4575	5400	7675	10750
Manual Trans			(550)	(550)	(735)	(735)
V6 2.5 Liter	D		600	600	800	800

MX-5 MIATA—4-Cyl.—Equipment Schedule 6
W.B. 89.2"; 1.8 Liter.

Convertible 2D	NB353	21660	6875	7925	10400	13750
LS Convertible 2D	NB353	24410	7750	8900	11400	14900
SE Convertible 2D	NB353	26275	8100	9300	11800	15350
Auto Trans			0	0	0	0
Hard Top			575	575	765	765

MILLENIA—V6—Equipment Schedule 2
W.B. 108.3"; 2.5 Liter.

Sedan 4D	TA221	28505	6750	7775	10100	13400

MILLENIA—V6 Supercharged—Equipment Schedule 2
W.B. 108.3"; 2.3 Liter.

S Sedan 4D	TA222	31505	8900	10175	12600	16200

2003 MAZDA — (Jor1)(M1orYV)(BJ225)-3-#

PROTEGE—4-Cyl.—Equipment Schedule 6
W.B. 102.8"; 2.0 Liter.

DX Sedan 4D	BJ225	14690	4375	5175	6950	9500
LX Sedan 4D	BJ225	15575	4725	5575	7375	9950
ES Sedan 4D	BJ225	16300	5225	6075	7925	10550

PROTEGE'5—4-Cyl.—Equipment Schedule 6
W.B. 102.8"; 2.0 Liter.

Hatchback 4D	BJ245	17055	6475	7500	9475	12350

PROTEGE—4-Cyl. Turbo—Equipment Schedule 6
W.B. 102.8"; 2.0 Liter.

Mazdaspeed Sedan 4D	BJ227	20500	****	****	****	17400

6—4-Cyl.—Equipment Schedule 4
W.B. 105.3"; 2.3 Liter.

i Sedan 4D	FP80C	19900	8100	9300	11550	14850
Sport Pkg			300	300	400	400
Manual Trans			(575)	(575)	(765)	(765)

6—V6—Equipment Schedule 4
W.B. 105.3"; 3.0 Liter.

s Sedan 4D	FP80D	22520	9850	11250	12950	15750
Sport Pkg			300	300	400	400
Manual Trans			(575)	(575)	(765)	(765)

MX-5 MIATA—4-Cyl.—Equipment Schedule 6
W.B. 89.2"; 1.8 Liter.

Club Sport Conv 2D	NB353	20000				
Convertible 2D	NB353	22125	8075	9275	11850	15500
Shinsen Conv 2D	NB353	23625				
LS Convertible 2D	NB353	24905	8975	10275	12900	16700
SE Convertible 2D	NB353	26550	8950	10225	13300	17600
Auto Trans			0	0	0	0
Hard Top			600	600	800	800

2004 MAZDA — (Jor1)(M1orYV)(BK12F)-4-#

MAZDA3—4-Cyl.—Equipment Schedule 6
W.B. 103.9"; 2.0 Liter, 2.3 Liter.

i Sedan 4D	BK12F	14200	9600	10950	12100	14150
s Sedan 4D	BK123	16925	10425	11875	13450	16100
s Hatchback 4D	BK143	17415	10825	12275	13900	16600

MAZDA6—4-Cyl.—Equipment Schedule 4
W.B. 105.3"; 2.3 Liter.

i Sedan 4D	FP80C	20120	9275	10575	12950	16400
i Hatchback 4D	FP84C	22165	10375	11825	14000	17350

2004 MAZDA

Body	Type	VIN	List	Trade-In Fair	Trade-In Good	Pvt-Party Good	Retail Excellent
	Sport Pkg		....	300	300	400	400
	Manual Trans		....	(600)	(600)	(800)	(800)
MAZDA6—V6—Equipment Schedule 4							
W.B. 105.3"; 3.0 Liter.							
s	Sedan 4D	FP80D	22765	11200	12700	14500	17450
s	Hatchback 4D	FP84D	24315	11600	13150	15150	18400
s	Wagon 4D	FP82D	23645	9800	11150	13950	18000
	Sport Pkg		....	300	300	400	400
	Manual Trans		....	(600)	(600)	(800)	(800)
MX-5 MIATA—4-Cyl.—Equipment Schedule 6							
W.B. 89.2"; 1.8 Liter.							
	Convertible 2D	NB353	22388	9425	10775	13500	17350
LS	Convertible 2D	NB353	25193	10375	11825	14600	18600
	Auto Trans		....	0	0	0	0
	Hard Top		....	625	625	835	835
MX-5 MIATA—4-Cyl. Turbo—Equipment Schedule 6							
W.B. 89.2"; 1.8 Liter.							
	Mazdaspeed Conv	NB354	26020	11600	13150	15950	20100
RX-8—Rotary—Equipment Schedule 3							
W.B. 106.4"; 1.3 Liter.							
	Coupe 4D	FE173	25700	14025	15850	18600	22800
	Sport Pkg		....	500	500	665	665
	Touring Pkg		....	700	700	935	935
	Grand Touring Pkg		....	1000	1000	1335	1335

2005 MAZDA — (Jor1)(M1orYV)-(K12F)-5-#

Body	Type	VIN	List	Trade-In Fair	Trade-In Good	Pvt-Party Good	Retail Excellent
MAZDA3—4-Cyl.—Equipment Schedule 6							
W.B. 103.9"; 2.0 Liter, 2.3 Liter.							
i	Sedan 4D	K12F	15075	10925	12375	13500	15600
s	Sedan 4D	K123	17160	11775	13350	15000	17750
s	Hatchback 4D	K143	17650	12175	13825	15450	18300
sp	Sedan 4D	K323	19245	13150	14900	16100	18550
sp	Hatchback 4D	K343	19245	13575	15325	16600	19050
MAZDA6—4-Cyl.—Equipment Schedule 4							
W.B. 105.3"; 2.3 Liter.							
i	Sedan 4D	P80C	20590	10275	11700	14100	17700
i	Sport Sedan 4D	P80C	23090	11050	12550	15050	18700
i	Sport Hatchback 4D	P84C	23620	12225	13875	15950	19250
i	Grand Touring Sed	P80C	24940	11500	13050	15750	19800
	Manual Trans		....	(625)	(625)	(835)	(835)
MAZDA6—V6—Equipment Schedule 4							
W.B. 105.3"; 3.0 Liter.							
s	Sedan 4D	P80D	24990	12325	13975	15750	18800
s	Hatchback 4D	P84D	25690	12750	14400	16500	19900
s	Base Sport Wag 4D	P82D	24590	10825	12275	15250	19500
s	Sport Wagon 4D	P82D	25720	12025	13625	16150	20000
s	Grand Touring Sed	P80D	26870	12225	13875	16400	20300
s	Grand Touring Wag	P82D	27540	12650	14300	16900	20800
	Manual Trans		....	(625)	(625)	(835)	(835)
MX-5 MIATA—4-Cyl.—Equipment Schedule 6							
W.B. 89.2"; 1.8 Liter.							
	Convertible 2D	B353	22643	10475	11925	14700	18650
LS	Convertible 2D	B353	25448	11500	13050	15850	20000
MX-5 MIATA—4-Cyl. Turbo—Equipment Schedule 6							
W.B. 89.2"; 1.8 Liter.							
	Mazdaspeed Conv 2D	B354	26325	12750	14450	17350	21600
RX-8—Rotary—Equipment Schedule 3							
W.B. 106.4"; 1.3 Liter.							
	Coupe 4D	E173	26120	15175	17125	19900	24100
	Shinka Special Ed 4D	E173	32220	14750	16625	21700	28600
	Sport Pkg		....	500	500	665	665
	Touring Pkg		....	700	700	935	935
	Grand Touring Pkg		....	1000	1000	1335	1335

MERCEDES-BENZ

1991 MERCEDES-BENZ — WDB(DA28D)-M-#

Body	Type	VIN	List	Trade-In Fair	Trade-In Good	Pvt-Party Good	Retail Excellent
MERCEDES—4-Cyl.—Equipment Schedule 1							
W.B. 104.9"; 2.3 Liter.							
	190E 2.3 Sedan 4D	DA28D	31260	1175	1625	3150	5225
	Leather		....	100	100	135	135

Body Type	VIN	List	Trade-In Fair	Trade-In Good	Pvt-Party Good	Retail Excellent
Manual Trans			(200)	(200)	(265)	(265)

MERCEDES—6-Cyl.—Equipment Schedule 1
W.B. 104.9", 110.2" (300E, 300TE); 2.6 Liter, 3.0 Liter.

Body Type	VIN	List	Fair	Good	Good	Excellent
190E 2.6 Sedan 4D	DA29D	34050	1550	2050	3400	5250
300E 2.6 Sedan 4D	EA28D	41350	2025	2575	4000	5975
300TE Wagon 4D	EA90D	52000	3200	3875	5550	7875
300TE 4-M 4WD Wag 4D	ED90D	59370	3925	4675	6475	9000
Leather			100	100	135	135
Slip Control			100	100	135	135
Manual Trans			(200)	(200)	(265)	(265)

MERCEDES—6-Cyl.—Equipment Schedule 1
W.B. 99.0", 106.9" (CE), 110.2" (E), 115.6" (SEL), 121.1" (SEL); 3.0L.

Body Type	VIN	List	Fair	Good	Good	Excellent
300E 3.0 Sedan 4D	EA30D	47550	2450	3050	4550	6675
300E 4-M 4WD Sed 4D	ED30D	55000	3500	4200	5925	8300
300CE Coupe 2D	EA51D	57700	3000	3675	5300	7600
300SE Sedan 4D	CA24D	54250	3150	3800	5450	7750
300SEL Sedan 4D	CA25D	58150	3325	4000	5675	8000
300SL Roadster 2D	FA61E	79350	7825	9000	12200	16600
Slip Control			100	100	135	135
Manual Trans			(200)	(200)	(265)	(265)

MERCEDES—6-Cyl. Turbo Diesel—Equipment Schedule 1
W.B. 110.2"; 2.5 Liter.

Body Type	VIN	List	Fair	Good	Good	Excellent
300D Sedan 4D	EB28D	41350	2700	3300	5175	7675
Leather			100	100	135	135

MERCEDES—6-Cyl. Turbo Diesel—Equipment Schedule 1
W.B. 115.6", 121.1" (SDL); 3.5 Liter.

Body Type	VIN	List	Fair	Good	Good	Excellent
350SD Sedan 4D	CB34D	54250	4250	5050	7150	10050
350SDL Sedan 4D	CB35D	58150	4650	5475	7675	10650

MERCEDES—V8—Equipment Schedule 1
W.B. 99.0", 112.2" (SEC), 121.1" (SEL); 4.2L, 5.0L, 5.6L.

Body Type	VIN	List	Fair	Good	Good	Excellent
420SEL Sedan 4D	CA35E	64800	3375	4075	6250	9200
560SEL Sedan 4D	CA39E	76750	3750	4475	6800	9900
560SEC Coupe 2D	CA45E	84550	4550	5375	7925	11350
500SL Roadster 2D	FA66E	90700	8450	9675	13050	17650
Slip Control			100	100	135	135

MERCEDES—4-Cyl.—Equipment Schedule 1
W.B. 104.9"; 2.3 Liter.

Body Type	VIN	List	Fair	Good	Good	Excellent
190E 2.3 Sedan 4D	DA28D	30200	1425	1925	3600	5825
Leather			100	100	135	135
Manual Trans			(200)	(200)	(265)	(265)

MERCEDES—5-Cyl. Turbo Diesel—Equipment Schedule 1
W.B. 110.2"; 2.5 Liter.

Body Type	VIN	List	Fair	Good	Good	Excellent
300D Sedan 4D	EB28D	43300	2975	3650	5625	8325
Leather			100	100	135	135

MERCEDES—6-Cyl.—Equipment Schedule 1
W.B. 104.9", 110.2" (300E, 300TE); 2.6 Liter, 3.0 Liter.

Body Type	VIN	List	Fair	Good	Good	Excellent
190E 2.6 Sedan 4D	DA29D	35250	1875	2400	3850	5850
300E 2.6 Sedan 4D	EA26D	43300	2425	3000	4550	6700
300TE Wagon 4D	EA90D	55250	3775	4525	6350	8875
300TE 4-M 4WD Wag 4D	ED90D	61450	4625	5450	7400	10150
Leather			100	100	135	135
Slip Control			100	100	135	135
Manual Trans			(200)	(200)	(265)	(265)

MERCEDES—6-Cyl.—Equipment Schedule 1
W.B. 99.0", 106.9" (CE), 110.2" (E), 119.7" (SE); 3.0 Liter.

Body Type	VIN	List	Fair	Good	Good	Excellent
300E 3.0 Sedan 4D	EA30D	49850	2900	3575	5225	7500
300E 4-M 4WD Sed 4D	ED30D	58450	4125	4900	6775	9350
300CE Coupe 2D	EA51D	60750	3575	4275	6075	8550
300SE Sedan 4D	GA32D	71850	6850	7875	10250	13550
300SL Roadster 2D	FA61E	84850	8975	10275	13800	18600
Slip Control			100	100	135	135
Manual Trans			(200)	(200)	(265)	(265)

MERCEDES—6-Cyl. Turbo Diesel—Equipment Schedule 1
W.B. 119.7"; 3.5 Liter.

Body Type	VIN	List	Fair	Good	Good	Excellent
300SD Sedan 4D	GB34E	69750	6575	7600	10250	13850

MERCEDES—V8—Equipment Schedule 1
W.B. 110.2", 112.2" (E), 119.7" (SE), 123.6" (SEL); 4.2L, 5.0L.

Body Type	VIN	List	Fair	Good	Good	Excellent
400E Sedan 4D	EA34E	56150	3150	3800	5750	8400
400SE Sedan 4D	GA42D	78250	6000	6950	9400	12800
500E Sedan 4D	EA36E	82150	8375	9575	12450	16500
500SEL Sedan 4D	GA51E	96850	6900	7975	10550	14200

1992 MERCEDES-BENZ

Body	Type	VIN	List	Trade-In Fair	Good	Pvt-Party Good	Retail Excellent
500SL Roadster 2D	FA66E	99950	**9650**	**11000**	**14800**	**19900**
Slip Control (400)			100	100	135	135

MERCEDES—V12—Equipment Schedule 1
W.B. 123.6"; 6.0 Liter.

| 600SEL Sedan 4D | GA57E | 132650 | **5925** | **6875** | **9475** | **13050** |

1993 MERCEDES-BENZ — WDB(DA28D)-P-#

MERCEDES—4-Cyl.—Equipment Schedule 1
W.B. 104.9"; 2.3 Liter.

190E 2.3 Sedan 4D	DA28D	33930	**1575**	**2075**	**3875**	**6250**
Leather			100	100	135	135
Manual Trans			(250)	(250)	(335)	(335)

MERCEDES—5-Cyl. Turbo Diesel—Equipment Schedule 1
W.B. 110.2"; 2.5 Liter.

| 300D Sedan 4D | EB28E | 46115 | **3625** | **4325** | **6500** | **9400** |
| Leather | | | 100 | 100 | 135 | 135 |

MERCEDES—6-Cyl.—Equipment Schedule 1
W.B. 104.9", 110.2" (300E, 300TE); 2.6L, 2.8L, 3.0L, 3.2L.

190E 2.6 Sedan 4D	DA29D	36865	**2175**	**2775**	**4325**	**6450**
300E 2.8 Sedan 4D	EA28E	46115	**2850**	**3500**	**5175**	**7475**
300TE Wagon 4D	EA92E	56365	**4500**	**5300**	**7300**	**10050**
300TE 4-M 4WD Wag 4D	ED90D	63100	**5400**	**6325**	**8450**	**11400**
Leather			100	100	135	135
Slip Control			125	125	165	165
Manual Trans			(250)	(250)	(335)	(335)

MERCEDES—6-Cyl.—Equipment Schedule 1
W.B. 99.0", 106.9" (CE), 110.2" (SE), 119.7" (SE); 3.0 Liter, 3.2 Liter.

300E 3.2 Sedan 4D	EA32E	50300	**3450**	**4150**	**5925**	**8375**
300E 4-M 4WD Sed 4D	ED30D	59100	**4700**	**5550**	**7550**	**10350**
300CE Coupe 2D	EA52E	61400	**4425**	**5225**	**7200**	**9950**
300CE Cabriolet 2D	EA66E	76900	**11000**	**12525**	**15600**	**20000**
300SE Sedan 4D	GA32E	72000	**7600**	**8725**	**11200**	**14700**
300SL Roadster 2D	FA61E	85800	**8950**	**10225**	**13850**	**18800**
Slip Control			125	125	165	165
Manual Trans			(250)	(250)	(335)	(335)

MERCEDES—6-Cyl. Turbo Diesel—Equipment Schedule 1
W.B. 119.7"; 3.5 Liter.

| 300SD Sedan 4D | GB34E | 70300 | **7675** | **8825** | **11700** | **15650** |

MERCEDES—V8—Equipment Schedule 1
W.B. 99.0", 110.2" (E), 115.9" (SEC), 123.6" (SEL); 4.2L, 5.0L.

400E Sedan 4D	EA34E	56800	**3750**	**4475**	**6575**	**9425**
400SEL Sedan 4D	GA43E	81200	**7000**	**8075**	**10750**	**14450**
500E Sedan 4D	EA58E	81700	**9700**	**11050**	**14150**	**18500**
500SEL Sedan 4D	GA51E	97800	**7850**	**9025**	**11800**	**15650**
500SEC Coupe 2D	GA70E	102300	**11250**	**12750**	**16100**	**20900**
500SL Roadster 2D	FA67E	100200	**10375**	**11775**	**15750**	**21100**
Slip Control (400)			125	125	165	165

MERCEDES—V12—Equipment Schedule 1
W.B. 99.0", 115.9" (SEC), 123.6 (SEL); 6.0 Liter.

600SEL Sedan 4D	GA57E	133100	**6750**	**7775**	**10600**	**15650**
600SEC Coupe 2D	GA76E	136100	**8550**	**9800**	**12800**	**16950**
600SL Roadster 2D	FA76E	122900	**10625**	**12075**	**16050**	**21400**

1994 MERCEDES-BENZ — WDB(HA22E)-R-#

C-CLASS—4-Cyl.—Equipment Schedule 1
W.B. 105.9"; 2.2 Liter.

| C220 Sedan 4D | HA22E | 31085 | **3075** | **3725** | **5800** | **8550** |

C-CLASS—6-Cyl.—Equipment Schedule 1
W.B. 105.9"; 2.8 Liter.

| C280 Sedan 4D | HA28E | 37105 | **2900** | **3575** | **5700** | **8550** |
| Slip Control | | | 150 | 150 | 200 | 200 |

E-CLASS—6-Cyl.—Equipment Schedule 1
W.B. 106.9", 110.2" (4D); 3.2 Liter.

E320 Sedan 4D	EA32E	42975	**3575**	**4275**	**6525**	**9525**
E320 Coupe 2D	EA52E	62075	**5100**	**6000**	**8500**	**11900**
E320 Cabriolet 2D	EA66E	77775	**12275**	**13925**	**17500**	**22600**
E320 Wagon 4D	EA92E	46675	**5200**	**6075**	**8575**	**12000**
Slip Control			150	150	200	200
Sport Pkg			275	275	365	365

E-CLASS—V8—Equipment Schedule 1
W.B. 110.2"; 4.2 Liter.

| E420 Sedan 4D | EA34E | 51475 | **4925** | **5775** | **7925** | **10900** |
| Slip Control | | | 150 | 150 | 200 | 200 |

Body	Type	VIN	List	Trade-In Fair	Good	Pvt-Party Good	Retail Excellent
S-CLASS—6-Cyl.—Equipment Schedule 1							
W.B. 119.7"; 3.2 Liter.							
S320 Sedan 4D		GA32E	71075	**6600**	**7650**	**10400**	**14150**
Slip Control				**150**	**150**	**200**	**200**
S-CLASS—6-Cyl. Turbo Diesel—Equipment Schedule 1							
W.B. 119.7"; 3.5 Liter.							
S350D Sedan 4D		GB34E	71075	**8900**	**10175**	**13250**	**17500**
S-CLASS—V8—Equipment Schedule 1							
W.B. 115.9", 123.6" (S420, S500 4D); 4.2 Liter, 5.0 Liter.							
S420 Sedan 4D		GA43E	81675	**8150**	**9325**	**12050**	**15750**
S500 Sedan 4D		GA51E	97875	**8900**	**10175**	**13200**	**17350**
S500 Coupe 2D		GA70E	102375	**12700**	**14350**	**17950**	**23000**
Slip Control				**150**	**150**	**200**	**200**
S-CLASS—V12—Equipment Schedule 1							
W.B. 115.9", 123.6" (4D); 6.0 Liter.							
S600 Sedan 4D		GA57E	134455	**7675**	**8825**	**11900**	**16500**
S600 Coupe 2D		GA76E	136775	**9850**	**11250**	**14400**	**18850**
SL-CLASS—6-Cyl.—Equipment Schedule 1							
W.B. 99.0"; 3.2 Liter.							
SL320 Roadster 2D		FA63E	85675	**8975**	**10275**	**14000**	**19100**
Slip Control				**150**	**150**	**200**	**200**
SL-CLASS—V8—Equipment Schedule 1							
W.B. 99.0"; 5.0 Liter.							
SL500 Roadster 2D		FA67E	101275	**11150**	**12650**	**16850**	**22500**
SL-CLASS—V12—Equipment Schedule 1							
W.B. 99.0"; 6.0 Liter.							
SL600 Roadster 2D		FA76E	123575	**11300**	**12850**	**17000**	**22700**

1995 MERCEDES-BENZ — WDB(HA22E)-S-#

Body	Type	VIN	List	Trade-In Fair	Good	Pvt-Party Good	Retail Excellent
C-CLASS—4-Cyl.—Equipment Schedule 1							
W.B. 105.9"; 2.2 Liter.							
C220 Sedan 4D		HA22E	32000	**3500**	**4200**	**6400**	**9325**
Traction Control				**175**	**175**	**235**	**235**
C-CLASS—6-Cyl.—Equipment Schedule 1							
W.B. 105.9"; 2.8 Liter, 3.6 Liter.							
C280 Sedan 4D		HA28E	38400	**3475**	**4200**	**6500**	**9600**
C36 Sedan 4D		HM36E	50500	**6575**	**7600**	**10400**	**14150**
Slip Control				**175**	**175**	**235**	**235**
E-CLASS—6-Cyl.—Equipment Schedule 1							
W.B. 106.9", 110.2" (4D); 3.2 Liter.							
E320 Sedan 4D		EA32E	43975	**4225**	**5000**	**7425**	**10650**
E320 Coupe 2D		EA52E	63475	**6100**	**7075**	**9800**	**13550**
E320 Cabriolet 2D		EA66E	79475	**13975**	**15800**	**19700**	**25200**
E320 Wagon 4D		EA92E	49600	**6000**	**6950**	**9675**	**13350**
Slip Control				**175**	**175**	**235**	**235**
Sport Pkg				**300**	**300**	**400**	**400**
E-CLASS—6-Cyl. Diesel—Equipment Schedule 1							
W.B. 110.2"; 3.0 Liter.							
E300D Sedan 4D		EB31E	43100	**5100**	**6000**	**8550**	**12050**
E-CLASS—V8—Equipment Schedule 1							
W.B. 110.2"; 4.2 Liter.							
E420 Sedan 4D		EA34E	52975	**4450**	**5250**	**7875**	**11350**
Slip Control				**175**	**175**	**235**	**235**
S-CLASS—6-Cyl.—Equipment Schedule 1							
W.B. 119.7", 123.6" (LWB); 3.2 Liter.							
S320 SWB Sedan 4D		GA32E	63175	**7350**	**8450**	**11350**	**15350**
S320 LWB Sedan 4D		GA33E	66375	**7575**	**8700**	**11650**	**15650**
Slip Control				**175**	**175**	**235**	**235**
S-CLASS—6-Cyl. Turbo Diesel—Equipment Schedule 1							
W.B. 119.7"; 3.5 Liter.							
S350D Sedan 4D		GB34E	66375	**10125**	**11550**	**14900**	**19500**
S-CLASS—V8—Equipment Schedule 1							
W.B. 115.9", 123.6" (4D); 4.2 Liter, 5.0 Liter.							
S420 Sedan 4D		GA43E	76075	**7825**	**9000**	**12100**	**16300**
S500 Sedan 4D		GA51E	89675	**8725**	**10000**	**13450**	**18100**
S500 Coupe 2D		GA70E	94075	**12900**	**14600**	**18600**	**24300**
S-CLASS—V12—Equipment Schedule 1							
W.B. 115.9", 123.6" (4D); 6.0 Liter.							
S600 Sedan 4D		GA57E	133775	**8850**	**10125**	**13450**	**17950**
S600 Coupe 2D		GA76E	136775	**11300**	**12850**	**16300**	**21100**
SL-CLASS—6-Cyl.—Equipment Schedule 1							
W.B. 99.0"; 3.2 Liter.							
SL320 Roadster 2D		FA63E	78775	**10000**	**11350**	**14950**	**19800**

1995 MERCEDES-BENZ

Body	Type	VIN	List	Trade-In Fair	Trade-In Good	Pvt-Party Good	Retail Excellent
Slip Control				175	175	235	235
SL-CLASS—V8—Equipment Schedule 1							
W.B. 99.0"; 5.0 Liter.							
SL500 Roadster 2D		FA67E	91675	12325	13975	17850	23300
SL-CLASS—V12—Equipment Schedule 1							
W.B. 99.0"; 6.0 Liter.							
SL600 Roadster 2D		FA76E	123175	12950	14650	18650	24300

1996 MERCEDES-BENZ — WDB(HA22E)-T-#

Body	Type	VIN	List	Trade-In Fair	Trade-In Good	Pvt-Party Good	Retail Excellent
C-CLASS—4-Cyl.—Equipment Schedule 1							
W.B. 105.9"; 2.2 Liter.							
C220 Sedan 4D		HA22E	33055	4000	4750	7125	10300
Traction Control				200	200	265	265
C-CLASS—6-Cyl.—Equipment Schedule 1							
W.B. 105.9"; 2.8 Liter, 3.6 Liter.							
C280 Sedan 4D		HA28E	37815	4450	5250	7275	10100
C36 Sedan 4D		HM36E	51595	7175	8275	10850	14500
Slip Control				200	200	265	265
Sport Pkg				325	325	435	435
E-CLASS—6-Cyl.—Equipment Schedule 1							
W.B. 111.5"; 3.2 Liter.							
E320 Sedan 4D		JF55F	45165	6500	7525	10050	13500
Slip Control				200	200	265	265
E-CLASS—6-Cyl. Diesel—Equipment Schedule 1							
W.B. 111.5"; 3.0 Liter.							
E300D Sedan 4D		JF20F	42465	7125	8225	11150	15200
S-CLASS—6-Cyl.—Equipment Schedule 1							
W.B. 119.2", 123.6" (LWB); 3.2 Liter.							
S320 SWB Sedan 4D		GA32E	63295	7975	9175	11850	15600
S320 LWB Sedan 4D		GA33E	66495	8225	9425	12150	15950
Slip Control				200	200	265	265
S-CLASS—V8—Equipment Schedule 1							
W.B. 115.9", 123.6" (4D); 4.2 Liter, 5.0 Liter.							
S420 Sedan 4D		GA43E	74495	9075	10375	13650	18150
S500 Sedan 4D		GA51E	88095	10100	11450	15150	20200
S500 Coupe 2D		GA70E	92495	14650	16550	20800	26800
S-CLASS—V12—Equipment Schedule 1							
W.B. 115.9", 123.6" (4D); 6.0 Liter.							
S600 Sedan 4D		GA57E	130895	10225	11650	15250	20200
S600 Coupe 2D		GA76E	133895	13000	14700	18450	23700
SL-CLASS—6-Cyl.—Equipment Schedule 1							
W.B. 99.0"; 3.2 Liter.							
SL320 Roadster 2D		FA63F	78895	10575	12025	15700	20800
Slip Control				200	200	265	265
Sport Pkg				1350	1350	1800	1800
SL-CLASS—V8—Equipment Schedule 1							
W.B. 99.0"; 5.0 Liter.							
SL500 Roadster 2D		FA67F	90495	13475	15225	19350	25000
Sport Pkg				1350	1350	1800	1800
SL-CLASS—V12—Equipment Schedule 1							
W.B. 99.0"; 6.0 Liter.							
SL600 Roadster 2D		FA76F	122595	14150	15950	20200	26100
Sport Pkg				1350	1350	1800	1800

1997 MERCEDES-BENZ — WDB(HA23E)-V-#

Body	Type	VIN	List	Trade-In Fair	Trade-In Good	Pvt-Party Good	Retail Excellent
C-CLASS—4-Cyl.—Equipment Schedule 1							
W.B. 105.9"; 2.3 Liter.							
C230 Sedan 4D		HA23E	33235	4125	4900	7375	10650
Traction Control				225	225	300	300
C-CLASS—6-Cyl.—Equipment Schedule 1							
W.B. 105.9"; 2.8 Liter, 3.6 Liter.							
C280 Sedan 4D		HA28E	37985	5100	5975	8175	11250
C36 Sedan 4D		HM36E	52520	8375	9575	12400	16400
Slip Control				225	225	300	300
Sport Pkg				350	350	465	465
E-CLASS—6-Cyl.—Equipment Schedule 1							
W.B. 111.5"; 3.2 Liter.							
E320 Sedan 4D		JF55F	46485	7650	8775	11500	15350
Slip Control				225	225	300	300
E-CLASS—6-Cyl. Diesel—Equipment Schedule 1							
W.B. 111.5"; 3.0 Liter.							
E300D Sedan 4D		JF20F	42475	8200	9375	12550	16900

1997 MERCEDES-BENZ

Body	Type	VIN	List	Trade-In Fair	Good	Pvt-Party Good	Retail Excellent
E-CLASS—V8—Equipment Schedule 1							
W.B. 111.5"; 4.2 Liter.							
E420 Sedan 4D	JF72F	51585	8725	10000	13350	17900
Sport Pkg			625	625	835	835
S-CLASS—6-Cyl.—Equipment Schedule 1							
W.B. 119.7"; 123.6" (LWB); 3.2 Liter.							
S320 SWB Sedan 4D	GA32G	63895	9200	10475	13450	17550
S320 LWB Sedan 4D	GA33G	67195	9425	10775	13750	17900
Slip Control			225	225	300	300
S-CLASS—V8—Equipment Schedule 1							
W.B. 115.9", 123.6" (4D); 4.2 Liter, 5.0 Liter.							
S420 Sedan 4D	GA43G	75795	10525	11975	15450	20400
S500 Sedan 4D	GA51G	89795	11650	13200	17150	22600
S500 Coupe 2D	GA70G	93795	16625	18725	23300	29700
S-CLASS—V12—Equipment Schedule 1							
W.B. 115.9", 123.6" (4D); 6.0 Liter.							
S600 Sedan 4D	GA57G	133895	11825	13375	17350	22800
S600 Coupe 2D	GA76G	136495	14850	16775	20900	26700
SL-CLASS—6-Cyl.—Equipment Schedule 1							
W.B. 99.0"; 3.2 Liter.							
SL320 Roadster 2D	FA63F	80195	11400	12950	16750	22000
Slip Control			225	225	300	300
Sport Pkg			1350	1350	1800	1800
SL-CLASS—V8—Equipment Schedule 1							
W.B. 99.0"; 5.0 Liter.							
SL500 Roadster 2D	FA67F	91795	14900	16825	21000	27100
Sport Pkg			625	625	835	835
SL-CLASS—V12—Equipment Schedule 1							
W.B. 99.0"; 6.0 Liter.							
SL600 Roadster 2D	FA76F	125895	15675	17650	22000	28100
Sport Pkg			1475	1475	1965	1965

1998 MERCEDES-BENZ — WDB(KK47F)-W-#

Body	Type	VIN	List	Trade-In Fair	Good	Pvt-Party Good	Retail Excellent
SLK-CLASS—4-Cyl. Supercharged—Equipment Schedule 1							
W.B. 94.5"; 2.3 Liter.							
SLK230 Roadster 2D	KK47F	40295	8325	9525	12600	16900
C-CLASS—4-Cyl.—Equipment Schedule 1							
W.B. 105.9" 2.3 Liter.							
C230 Sedan 4D	HA23G	33235	5025	5900	8600	12200
Slip Control			275	275	365	365
C-CLASS—V6—Equipment Schedule 1							
W.B. 105.9"; 2.8 Liter.							
C280 Sedan 4D	HA29G	37985	5875	6850	9250	12550
Sport Pkg			375	375	500	500
C-CLASS—V8—Equipment Schedule 1							
W.B. 105.9"; 4.3 Liter.							
C43 Sedan 4D	HA33G	53345	10050	11400	15150	20200
CLK-CLASS—V6—Equipment Schedule 1							
W.B. 105.9"; 3.2 Liter.							
CLK320 Coupe 2D	LJ65G	41555	9025	10325	13100	17000
E-CLASS—V6—Equipment Schedule 1							
W.B. 111.5"; 3.2 Liter.							
E320 Sedan 4D	JF65F	47205	8900	10175	13150	17250
E320 4Matic Sedan 4D	JF82F	49955	9750	11100	14150	18500
E320 Wagon 4D	JH65F	49900	9700	11050	14100	18450
E320 4Matic Wagon 4D	JH82F	52650	10475	11925	15100	19500
E-CLASS—6-Cyl. Turbo Diesel—Equipment Schedule 1							
W.B. 111.5"; 3.0 Liter.							
E300TD Sedan 4D	JF25F	45200	10925	12375	15950	21000
E-CLASS—V8—Equipment Schedule 1							
W.B. 111.5"; 4.3 Liter.							
E430 Sedan 4D	JF70F	52305	10825	12275	15850	20900
Sport Pkg			625	625	835	835
CL-CLASS—V8—Equipment Schedule 1							
W.B. 115.9"; 5.0 Liter.							
CL500 Coupe 2D	GA70G	92495	18875	21150	26000	32900
CL-CLASS—V12—Equipment Schedule 1							
W.B. 115.9"; 6.0 Liter.							
CL600 Coupe 2D	GA76G	135895	17025	19150	23700	30000
S-CLASS—6-Cyl.—Equipment Schedule 1							
W.B. 119.7", 123.6" (LWB); 3.2 Liter.							
S320 SWB Sedan 4D	GA32G	64595	10575	12025	15150	19600
S320 LWB Sedan 4D	GA33G	67895	10825	12275	15400	19900

Body	Type	VIN	List	Trade-In Fair	Good	Pvt-Party Good	Retail Excellent
S-CLASS—V8—Equipment Schedule 1							
W.B. 123.6"; 4.2 Liter, 5.0 Liter.							
S420 Sedan 4D		GA43G	75795	**12325**	**13975**	**17700**	**23000**
S500 Sedan 4D		GA51G	89795	**13625**	**15375**	**19500**	**25300**
S-CLASS—V12—Equipment Schedule 1							
W.B. 123.6"; 6.0 Liter.							
S600 Sedan 4D		GA57G	135845	**13675**	**15475**	**19800**	**25800**
SL-CLASS—V8—Equipment Schedule 1							
W.B. 99.0"; 5.0 Liter.							
SL500 Roadster 2D		FA67F	81495	**16625**	**18725**	**23300**	**29700**
Sport Pkg			....	**1600**	**1600**	**2135**	**2135**
SL-CLASS—V12—Equipment Schedule 1							
W.B. 99.0"; 6.0 Liter.							
SL600 Roadster 2D		FA76F	127695	**17450**	**19600**	**24300**	**30700**
Sport Pkg			....	**1600**	**1600**	**2135**	**2135**

1999 MERCEDES-BENZ — WDB(KK47F)-X-#

Body	Type	VIN	List	Trade-In Fair	Good	Pvt-Party Good	Retail Excellent
SLK-CLASS—4-Cyl. Supercharged—Equipment Schedule 1							
W.B. 94.5"; 2.3 Liter.							
SLK230 Roadster 2D		KK47F	41495	**11825**	**13375**	**15600**	**19100**
Sport Pkg			....	**650**	**650**	**865**	**865**
Manual Trans			....	**(500)**	**(500)**	**(665)**	**(665)**
C-CLASS—4-Cyl. Supercharged—Equipment Schedule 1							
W.B. 105.9"; 2.3 Liter.							
C230 Sedan 4D		HA24G	34795	**8225**	**9425**	**11350**	**14250**
Sport Pkg			....	**425**	**425**	**565**	**565**
C-CLASS—V6—Equipment Schedule 1							
W.B. 105.9"; 2.8 Liter.							
C280 Sedan 4D		HA29G	38630	**6850**	**7875**	**10400**	**13800**
Sport Pkg			....	**425**	**425**	**565**	**565**
C-CLASS—V8—Equipment Schedule 1							
W.B. 105.9"; 4.3 Liter.							
C43 Sedan 4D		HA33G	53595	**11875**	**13475**	**17300**	**22600**
CLK-CLASS—V6—Equipment Schedule 1							
W.B. 105.9"; 3.2 Liter.							
CLK320 Coupe 2D		LJ65G	42485	**10475**	**11925**	**14800**	**18850**
CLK320 Cabriolet 2D		LK65G	47795	**14500**	**16350**	**19500**	**24300**
CLK-CLASS—V8—Equipment Schedule 1							
W.B. 105.9"; 4.3 Liter.							
CLK430 Coupe 2D		LJ70G	49785	**12525**	**14150**	**17600**	**22500**
E-CLASS—V6—Equipment Schedule 1							
W.B. 111.5"; 3.2 Liter.							
E320 Sedan 4D		JF65R	47905	**10375**	**11775**	**14800**	**19100**
E320 AWD Sedan 4D		JF82F	50695	**11300**	**12800**	**15900**	**20400**
E320 Wagon 4D		JH65F	48905	**11250**	**12750**	**15900**	**20400**
E320 AWD Wagon 4D		JH82F	51695	**12075**	**13675**	**16900**	**21400**
E-CLASS—6-Cyl. Turbo Diesel—Equipment Schedule 1							
W.B. 111.5"; 3.0 Liter.							
E300TD Sedan 4D		JF25F	45430	**12375**	**14025**	**17600**	**22800**
E-CLASS—V8—Equipment Schedule 1							
W.B. 111.5"; 4.3 Liter, 5.5 Liter.							
E430 Sedan 4D		JF70F	53005	**12275**	**13925**	**17600**	**22800**
E55 Sedan 4D		JF744	69695	**17800**	**19975**	**24400**	**30700**
Sport Pkg (E430)			....	**650**	**650**	**865**	**865**
CL-CLASS—V8—Equipment Schedule 1							
W.B. 115.9"; 5.0 Liter.							
CL500 Coupe 2D		GA70G	93795	**21425**	**24050**	**28900**	**35900**
CL-CLASS—V12—Equipment Schedule 1							
W.B. 115.9"; 6.0 Liter.							
CL600 Coupe 2D		GA76G	140495	**19500**	**21825**	**26500**	**33200**
S-CLASS—6-Cyl.—Equipment Schedule 1							
W.B. 119.7", 123.6" (LWB); 3.2 Liter.							
S320 SWB Sedan 4D		GA32G	65345	**12175**	**13775**	**16950**	**21500**
S320 LWB Sedan 4D		GA33G	68595	**12475**	**14125**	**17350**	**22000**
S-CLASS—V8—Equipment Schedule 1							
W.B. 123.6"; 4.2 Liter, 5.0 Liter.							
S420 Sedan 4D		GA43G	75795	**14250**	**16050**	**20000**	**25500**
S500 Sedan 4D		GA51G	89795	**15775**	**17750**	**22000**	**28000**
Grand Edition (S500)			....	**200**	**200**	**265**	**265**
S-CLASS—V12—Equipment Schedule 1							
W.B. 123.6"; 6.0 Liter.							
S600 Sedan 4D		GA57G	137845	**15850**	**17850**	**22400**	**28700**

1999 MERCEDES-BENZ

Body	Type	VIN	List	Trade-In Fair	Trade-In Good	Pvt-Party Good	Retail Excellent
SL-CLASS—V8—Equipment Schedule 1							
W.B. 99.0"; 5.0 Liter.							
SL500 Roadster 2D	FA68F	82695	**18725**	**21050**	**25600**	**32300**
Sport Pkg			**1650**	**1650**	**2200**	**2200**
SL-CLASS—V12—Equipment Schedule 1							
W.B. 99.0"; 6.0 Liter.							
SL600 Roadster 2D	FA76F	130095	**19700**	**22125**	**26900**	**33700**
Sport Pkg			**1650**	**1650**	**2200**	**2200**

2000 MERCEDES-BENZ — WDB(KK47F)-Y-#

Body	Type	VIN	List	Trade-In Fair	Trade-In Good	Pvt-Party Good	Retail Excellent
SLK-CLASS—4-Cyl. Supercharged—Equipment Schedule 1							
W.B. 94.5"; 2.3 Liter.							
SLK230 Roadster 2D	KK47F	42495	**13675**	**15475**	**17800**	**21500**
Sport Pkg			**725**	**725**	**965**	**965**
designo Edition			**350**	**350**	**465**	**465**
Manual Trans			**(500)**	**(500)**	**(665)**	**(665)**
C-CLASS—4-Cyl. Supercharged—Equipment Schedule 1							
W.B. 105.9"; 2.3 Liter.							
C230 Sedan 4D	HA24G	34820	**9650**	**11000**	**13000**	**16100**
Sport Pkg			**500**	**500**	**665**	**665**
C-CLASS—V6—Equipment Schedule 1							
W.B. 105.9"; 2.8 Liter.							
C280 Sedan 4D	HA29G	39020	**7900**	**9075**	**11900**	**15750**
Sport Pkg			**500**	**500**	**665**	**665**
C-CLASS—V8—Equipment Schedule 1							
W.B. 105.9"; 4.3 Liter.							
C43 Sedan 4D	HA33G	53595	**14550**	**16400**	**20000**	**25100**
CLK-CLASS—V6—Equipment Schedule 1							
W.B. 105.9"; 3.2 Liter.							
CLK320 Coupe 2D	LJ65G	43505	**12225**	**13875**	**17000**	**21500**
CLK320 Cabriolet 2D	LK65G	48695	**16775**	**18875**	**22400**	**27700**
designo Edition			**350**	**350**	**465**	**465**
CLK-CLASS—V8—Equipment Schedule 1							
W.B. 105.9"; 4.3 Liter.							
CLK430 Coupe 2D	LJ70G	51005	**15225**	**17175**	**20300**	**25000**
CLK430 Cabriolet 2D	LK70G	56195	**19200**	**21525**	**25000**	**30300**
designo Edition			**350**	**350**	**465**	**465**
E-CLASS—V6—Equipment Schedule 1							
W.B. 111.5"; 3.2 Liter.							
E320 Sedan 4D	JF65G	48825	**12075**	**13675**	**17050**	**21900**
E320 AWD Sedan 4D	JF82G	51625	**13100**	**14850**	**18300**	**23300**
E320 Wagon 4D	JH65F	49675	**13100**	**14800**	**18300**	**23300**
E320 AWD Wagon 4D	JH82F	52475	**14025**	**15850**	**19350**	**24400**
designo Edition			**350**	**350**	**465**	**465**
E-CLASS—V8—Equipment Schedule 1							
W.B. 111.5"; 4.3 Liter, 5.5 Liter.							
E430 Sedan 4D	JF70G	54175	**14550**	**16400**	**19900**	**24900**
E430 AWD Sedan 4D	JF83G	56975	**15175**	**17075**	**20500**	**25500**
E55 Sedan 4D	JF74G	71395	**21350**	**23950**	**28100**	**34300**
Sport Pkg (E430)			**725**	**725**	**965**	**965**
designo Edition			**350**	**350**	**465**	**465**
CL-CLASS—V8—Equipment Schedule 1							
W.B. 113.6"; 5.0 Liter.							
CL500 Coupe 2D	PJ75J	87145	**32000**	**35800**	**40800**	**48700**
S-CLASS—V8—Equipment Schedule 1							
W.B. 121.5"; 4.3 Liter, 5.0 Liter.							
S430 Sedan 4D	NG70J	70295	**20750**	**23275**	**27500**	**33700**
S500 Sedan 4D	NG75J	79445	**23675**	**26575**	**31100**	**38100**
Sport Pkg			**1700**	**1700**	**2265**	**2265**
designo Edition			**875**	**875**	**1165**	**1165**
SL-CLASS—V8—Equipment Schedule 1							
W.B. 99.0"; 5.0 Liter.							
SL500 Roadster 2D	FA68F	84195	**21350**	**23950**	**29000**	**36200**
Sport Pkg			**1700**	**1700**	**2265**	**2265**
designo Edition			**875**	**875**	**1165**	**1165**
SL-CLASS—V12—Equipment Schedule 1							
W.B. 99.0"; 6.0 Liter.							
SL600 Roadster 2D	FA76F	132145	**23275**	**26100**	**31200**	**38800**
Sport Pkg			**1700**	**1700**	**2265**	**2265**
designo Edition			**875**	**875**	**1165**	**1165**

Body	Type	VIN	List	Trade-In Fair	Good	Pvt-Party Good	Retail Excellent

2001 MERCEDES-BENZ — WDB(KK49F)-1-#

SLK-CLASS—4-Cyl. Supercharged—Equipment Schedule 1
W.B. 94.5"; 2.3 Liter.

Body	Type	VIN	List	Fair	Good	Good	Excellent
SLK230 Roadster 2D	KK49F	40495	15775	17750	20200	24200
Sport Pkg			800	800	1065	1065
designo Edition			475	475	635	635
Manual Trans			(500)	(500)	(665)	(665)

SLK-CLASS—V6—Equipment Schedule 1
W.B. 94.5"; 3.2 Liter.

SLK320 Roadster 2D	KK65F	45495	16450	18525	21900	27100
Sport Pkg			800	800	1065	1065
designo Edition			475	475	635	635
Manual Trans			(500)	(500)	(665)	(665)

C-CLASS—V6—Equipment Schedule 1
W.B. 106.9"; 2.6 Liter, 3.2 Liter.

C240 Sedan 4D	RF61G	34610	10050	11400	14400	18600
C320 Sedan 4D	RF64G	40310	12750	14400	17600	22200
Sport Pkg			550	550	735	735
Manual Trans			(500)	(500)	(665)	(665)

CLK-CLASS—V6—Equipment Schedule 1
W.B. 105.9"; 3.2 Liter.

CLK320 Coupe 2D	LJ65G	42595	16775	18875	22100	27000
CLK320 Cabriolet 2D	LK65G	49545	21825	24550	28000	33700
designo Edition			475	475	635	635

CLK-CLASS—V8—Equipment Schedule 1
W.B. 105.9"; 4.3 Liter, 5.5 Liter.

CLK430 Coupe 2D	LJ70G	50295	18050	20275	23800	29000
CLK430 Cabriolet 2D	LK70G	57145	22500	25125	28900	34800
CLK55 Coupe 2D	LJ74G	68045	23075	25800	30300	37000
designo Edition			900	900	1200	1200

E-CLASS—V6—Equipment Schedule 1
W.B. 111.5"; 3.2 Liter.

E320 Sedan 4D	JF65F	48495	16625	18725	22200	27400
E320 AWD Sedan 4D	JF82F	51345	17800	19975	23500	28800
E320 Wagon 4D	JH65F	49295	17800	19975	23500	28800
E320 AWD Wagon 4D	JH82F	52145	18775	21050	24700	30200
Sport Pkg			800	800	1065	1065
designo Edition			475	475	635	635

E-CLASS—V8—Equipment Schedule 1
W.B. 111.5"; 4.3 Liter, 5.5 Liter.

E430 Sedan 4D	JF70F	53845	16875	18975	22300	28500
E430 AWD Sedan 4D	JF83G	56695	17450	19600	23300	29100
E55 Sedan 4D	JF744	70945	25025	28025	32500	39300
Sport Pkg			800	800	1065	1065
designo Edition			475	475	635	635

CL-CLASS—V8—Equipment Schedule 1
W.B. 113.6"; 5.0 Liter, 5.5 Liter.

CL500 Coupe 2D	PJ75J	89145	36950	41225	46500	55000
CL55 Coupe 2D	PJ73J	100145	42875	47725	53500	62900
Sport Pkg			1750	1750	2335	2335
designo Edition			900	900	1200	1200

CL-CLASS—V12—Equipment Schedule 1
W.B. 113.6"; 5.8 Liter.

CL600 Coupe 2D	PJ78J	119145	44325	49275	55900	66300
Sport Pkg			1750	1750	2335	2335
designo Edition			900	900	1200	1200

S-CLASS—V8—Equipment Schedule 1
W.B. 121.5"; 4.3 Liter, 5.0 Liter, 5.5 Liter.

S430 Sedan 4D	NG70J	71445	24350	27250	31700	38500
S500 Sedan 4D	NG75J	80595	27650	30850	35900	43500
S55 Sedan 4D	NG73J	98645	39775	44325	49400	57700
Sport Pkg			1750	1750	2335	2335
designo Edition			900	900	1200	1200

S-CLASS—V12—Equipment Schedule 1
W.B. 121.5"; 6.0 Liter.

S600 Sedan 4D	NG78J	115985	35800	39875	46100	55500
Sport Pkg			1750	1750	2335	2335
designo Edition			900	900	1200	1200

SL-CLASS—V8—Equipment Schedule 1
W.B. 99.0"; 5.0 Liter.

SL500 Roadster 2D	FA68F	84445	24450	27350	32500	40600
Sport Pkg			1750	1750	2335	2335

2001 MERCEDES-BENZ

Body	Type	VIN	List	Trade-In Fair	Good	Pvt-Party Good	Retail Excellent
	designo Edition			900	900	1200	1200
SL-CLASS—V12—Equipment Schedule 1							
W.B. 99.0"; 6.0 Liter.							
SL600 Roadster 2D		FA76F	129595	27250	30450	36100	44300
	designo Edition			900	900	1200	1200

2002 MERCEDES-BENZ — WDB(KK49F)-2-#

Body	Type	VIN	List	Trade-In Fair	Good	Pvt-Party Good	Retail Excellent
SLK-CLASS—4-Cyl. Supercharged—Equipment Schedule 1							
W.B. 94.5"; 2.3 Liter.							
SLK230 Roadster 2D		KK49F	41345	18150	20375	23000	27300
	Sport Pkg			875	875	1165	1165
	designo Edition			600	600	800	800
	Manual Trans			(500)	(500)	(665)	(665)
SLK-CLASS—V6—Equipment Schedule 1							
W.B. 94.5"; 3.2 Liter.							
SLK320 Roadster 2D		KK65F	46745	18975	21250	24900	30500
	Sport Pkg			875	875	1165	1165
	designo Edition			600	600	800	800
	Manual Trans			(500)	(500)	(665)	(665)
SLK-CLASS—V6 Supercharged—Equipment Schedule 1							
W.B. 94.5"; 3.2 Liter.							
SLK32 Roadster 2D		KK66F	55545	22300	24925	28800	34800
	designo Edition			600	600	800	800
C-CLASS—4-Cyl. Supercharged—Equipment Schedule 1							
W.B. 106.9"; 2.3 Liter.							
C230 Sport Coupe 2D		RN47J	29490	10625	12075	14200	17500
	Manual Trans			(500)	(500)	(665)	(665)
C-CLASS—V6—Equipment Schedule 1							
W.B. 106.9"; 2.6 Liter, 3.2 Liter.							
C240 Sedan 4D		RF61J	33680	11825	13375	16650	21200
C320 Sedan 4D		RF64J	38780	14850	16725	20100	25100
C320 Wagon 4D		RH64J	40280	15475	17450	20900	25900
	Sport Pkg			600	600	800	800
	Manual Trans			(500)	(500)	(665)	(665)
C-CLASS—V6 Supercharged—Equipment Schedule 1							
W.B. 106.9"; 3.2 Liter.							
C32 Sedan 4D		RF65J	50545	20650	23075	26600	32000
CLK-CLASS—V6—Equipment Schedule 1							
W.B. 105.9"; 3.2 Liter.							
CLK320 Coupe 2D		LJ65G	44565	19300	21625	25000	30300
CLK320 Cabriolet 2D		LK65G	50245	24925	27925	31600	37600
	Sport Pkg			875	875	1165	1165
	designo Edition			600	600	800	800
CLK-CLASS—V8—Equipment Schedule 1							
W.B. 105.9"; 4.3 Liter, 5.5 Liter.							
CLK430 Coupe 2D		LJ70G	52265	21350	23950	27700	33700
CLK430 Cabriolet 2D		LK70G	57945	26275	29400	33500	40000
CLK55 Coupe 2D		LJ74G	69095	26975	30175	35000	42500
CLK55 Cabriolet 2D		LK74G	79645	30275	33850	39000	46900
	designo Edition			925	925	1235	1235
E-CLASS—V6—Equipment Schedule 1							
W.B. 111.5"; 3.2 Liter.							
E320 Sedan 4D		JF65J	50280	19100	21425	25100	30700
E320 AWD Sedan 4D		JF82J	53130	20375	22900	26600	32300
E320 Wagon 4D		JH65J	51080	20475	22900	26700	32400
E320 AWD Wagon 4D		JH82J	53130	21525	24150	27900	33900
	Sport Pkg			875	875	1165	1165
	designo Edition			600	600	800	800
E-CLASS—V8—Equipment Schedule 1							
W.B. 111.5"; 4.3 Liter, 5.5 Liter.							
E430 Sedan 4D		JF70J	55680	19700	22125	26500	32900
E430 AWD Sedan 4D		JF83J	58530	20275	22800	27100	33400
E55 Sedan 4D		JF74J	71995	29200	32600	37400	45000
	Sport Pkg (E430)			875	875	1165	1165
	designo Edition			925	925	1235	1235
CL-CLASS—V8—Equipment Schedule 1							
W.B. 113.6"; 5.0 Liter, 5.5 Liter.							
CL500 Coupe 2D		PJ75J	92395	42400	47150	52900	62200
CL55 Coupe 2D		PJ73J	105145	48975	54425	60600	70700
	Sport Pkg			1800	1800	2400	2400
	designo Edition			925	925	1235	1235
CL-CLASS—V12—Equipment Schedule 1							
W.B. 113.6"; 5.8 Liter.							

Body Type	VIN	List	Trade-In Fair	Good	Pvt-Party Good	Retail Excellent
CL600 Coupe 2D	PJ78J	120895	50450	56075	63100	74200
Sport Pkg			1800	1800	2400	2400
designo Edition			925	925	1235	1235

S-CLASS—V8—Equipment Schedule 1
W.B. 121.5"; 4.3 Liter, 5.0 Liter, 5.5 Liter.

Body Type	VIN	List	Fair	Good	Good	Excellent
S430 Sedan 4D	NG70J	72495	28425	31825	36700	44100
S500 Sedan 4D	NG75J	81845	32000	35700	41100	49500
S55 Sedan 4D	NG73J	101145	45600	50625	56000	65000
Sport Pkg			1800	1800	2400	2400
designo Edition			925	925	1235	1235

S-CLASS—V12—Equipment Schedule 1
W.B. 121.5"; 6.0 Liter.

Body Type	VIN	List	Fair	Good	Good	Excellent
S600 Sedan 4D	NG78J	117545	40925	45600	52200	62400
Sport Pkg			1800	1800	2400	2400
designo Edition			925	925	1235	1235

SL-CLASS—V8—Equipment Schedule 1
W.B. 99.0"; 5.0 Liter.

Body Type	VIN	List	Fair	Good	Good	Excellent
SL500 Roadster 2D	FA68F	85445	27925	31225	37100	45600
Sport Pkg			1800	1800	2400	2400
Silver Arrow Edition			2100	2100	2800	2800

SL-CLASS—V12—Equipment Schedule 1
W.B. 99.0"; 6.0 Liter.

Body Type	VIN	List	Fair	Good	Good	Excellent
SL600 Roadster 2D	FA76F	132195	31825	35500	41500	50600
Silver Arrow Edition			2100	2100	2800	2800

2003 MERCEDES-BENZ — WDB(KK49F)-3-#

SLK-CLASS—4-Cyl. Supercharged—Equipment Schedule 1
W.B. 94.5"; 2.3 Liter.

Body Type	VIN	List	Fair	Good	Good	Excellent
SLK230 Roadster 2D	KK49F	40265	20650	23175	26000	30600
Sport Pkg			950	950	1265	1265
Manual Trans			(500)	(500)	(665)	(665)

SLK-CLASS—V6—Equipment Schedule 1
W.B. 94.5"; 3.2 Liter.

Body Type	VIN	List	Fair	Good	Good	Excellent
SLK320 Roadster 2D	KK65F	45715	22600	25325	28500	33700
Sport Pkg			950	950	1265	1265
designo Edition			725	725	965	965
Manual Trans			(500)	(500)	(665)	(665)

SLK-CLASS—V6 Supercharged—Equipment Schedule 1
W.B. 94.5"; 3.2 Liter.

Body Type	VIN	List	Fair	Good	Good	Excellent
SLK32 Roadster 2D	KK66F	56115	26275	29400	32700	38300
designo Edition			725	725	965	965

C-CLASS—4-Cyl. Supercharged—Equipment Schedule 1
W.B. 106.9"; 1.8 Liter.

Body Type	VIN	List	Fair	Good	Good	Excellent
C230 Sport Sedan 4D	RF40J	30310	13050	14750	17050	20800
C230 Sport Coupe 2D	RN40J	28270	12225	13875	16200	19800
Manual Trans			(500)	(500)	(665)	(665)

C-CLASS—V6—Equipment Schedule 1
W.B. 106.9"; 2.6 Liter, 3.2 Liter.

Body Type	VIN	List	Fair	Good	Good	Excellent
C240 Sedan 4D	RF61J	32165	14800	16675	19400	23700
C240 4Matic Sedan 4D	RF81J	33965	15475	17400	20200	24400
C240 Wagon 4D	RH61J	33544	15475	17400	20200	24400
C240 4Matic Wagon 4D	RH81J	35344	16450	18525	21300	25800
C320 Sedan 4D	RF64J	38790	18050	20275	23200	27700
C320 4Matic Sedan 4D	RF84J	40590	18775	21050	24100	28700
C320 Coupe 2D	RN64J	30620	13725	15525	18200	22300
C320 Wagon 4D	RH64J	38840	18775	21050	24100	28700
C320 4Matic Wagon 4D	RH84J	40640	19500	21825	24800	29600
Sport Pkg			950	950	1265	1265
Manual Trans			(500)	(500)	(665)	(665)

C-CLASS—V6 Supercharged—Equipment Schedule 1
W.B. 106.9"; 3.2 Liter.

Body Type	VIN	List	Fair	Good	Good	Excellent
C32 Sedan 4D	RF65J	52065	24350	27250	30200	35200

CLK-CLASS—V6—Equipment Schedule 1
W.B. 105.9", 106.9" (Coupe); 3.2 Liter.

Body Type	VIN	List	Fair	Good	Good	Excellent
CLK320 Coupe 2D	TJ65J	44565	23075	25800	28600	33400
CLK320 Cabriolet 2D	LK65G	50615	29200	32600	35800	41300
Sport Pkg			950	950	1265	1265
designo Edition			725	725	965	965

CLK-CLASS—V8—Equipment Schedule 1
W.B. 105.9", 106.9" (Coupe); 4.3 Liter, 5.0 Liter, 5.5 Liter.

Body Type	VIN	List	Fair	Good	Good	Excellent
CLK430 Cabriolet 2D	LK70G	58315	30750	34250	38800	46100
CLK500 Coupe 2D	TJ75J	52865	28425	32700	39300	
CLK55 Coupe 2D	TJ76H	69470	31425	35125	40400	48700

2003 MERCEDES-BENZ

Body	Type	VIN	List	Trade-In Fair	Good	Pvt-Party Good	Retail Excellent
	designo Edition			950	950	1265	1265
E-CLASS—V6—Equipment Schedule 1							
W.B. 111.5"; 3.2 Liter.							
	E320 Sedan 4D	UF65J	49165	24150	26975	30000	35000
	E320 Wagon 4D	JH65J	55415	24250	27075	30300	35600
	E320 4Matic Wagon 4D	JH82J	55415	25425	28425	31700	37200
	Sport Pkg			950	950	1265	1265
E-CLASS—V8—Equipment Schedule 1							
W.B. 112.4"; 5.0 Liter.							
	E500 Sedan 4D	UF70J	57065	28425	31825	35900	42600
	Sport Pkg			950	950	1265	1265
E-CLASS—V8 Supercharged—Equipment Schedule 1							
W.B. 112.4"; 5.5 Liter.							
	E55 Sedan 4D	UF72J	76720	44050	48975	55100	64800
CL-CLASS—V8—Equipment Schedule 1							
W.B. 113.6"; 5.0 Liter.							
	CL500 Coupe 2D	PJ75J	93315	48500	53925	59900	69900
	Sport Pkg			1850	1850	2465	2465
	designo Edition			950	950	1265	1265
CL-CLASS—V8 Supercharged—Equipment Schedule 1							
W.B. 113.6"; 5.5 Liter.							
	CL55 Coupe 2D	PJ74J	115265	55675	61800	68300	79200
	designo Edition			950	950	1265	1265
CL-CLASS—V12—Equipment Schedule 1							
W.B. 113.6"; 5.5 Liter.							
	CL600 Coupe 2D	PJ76J	127265	57125	63450	70900	82900
	Sport Pkg			1850	1850	2465	2465
	designo Edition			950	950	1265	1265
S-CLASS—V8—Equipment Schedule 1							
W.B. 121.5"; 4.3 Liter, 5.0 Liter.							
	S430 Sedan 4D	NG70J	73265	33175	36950	42300	50500
	S430 4Matic Sedan 4D	NG83J	76165	34050	37925	43500	52000
	S500 Sedan 4D	NG75J	82665	37050	41325	47100	56300
	S500 4Matic Sedan 4D	NG84J	85565	38900	43250	49100	58200
	Sport Pkg			1850	1850	2465	2465
	designo Edition			950	950	1265	1265
S-CLASS—V8 Supercharged—Equipment Schedule 1							
W.B. 100.8"; 5.5 Liter.							
	S55 Sedan 4D	NG74J	107165	51900	57725	63300	73000
	designo Edition			950	950	1265	1265
S-CLASS—V12—Equipment Schedule 1							
W.B. 121.5"; 5.8 Liter.							
	S600 Sedan 4D	NG76J	121205	46850	52100	59100	70100
	Sport Pkg			1850	1850	2465	2465
	designo Edition			950	950	1265	1265
SL-CLASS—V8—Equipment Schedule 1							
W.B. 100.8"; 5.0 Liter.							
	SL500 Roadster 2D	SK75F	87655	50450	56075	63100	74400
	Sport Pkg			1850	1850	2465	2465
	designo Edition			950	950	1265	1265
SL-CLASS—V8 Supercharged—Equipment Schedule 1							
W.B. 100.8"; 5.5 Liter.							
	SL55 Roadster 2D	SK74F	114915	63450	70425	78100	90900
	designo Edition			950	950	1265	1265

2004 MERCEDES BENZ — WDB(KK49F)-4-#

Body	Type	VIN	List	Trade-In Fair	Good	Pvt-Party Good	Retail Excellent
SLK-CLASS—4-Cyl. Supercharged—Equipment Schedule 1							
W.B. 94.5"; 2.3 Liter.							
	SLK230 Roadster 2D	KK49F	40320	24050	26875	29900	34900
	Sport Pkg			1000	1000	1335	1335
	designo Edition			825	825	1100	1100
	Manual Trans			(500)	(500)	(665)	(665)
SLK-CLASS—V6—Equipment Schedule 1							
W.B. 94.5"; 3.2 Liter.							
	SLK320 Roadster 2D	KK65F	47330	26000	29000	32500	38200
	Sport Pkg			1000	1000	1335	1335
	designo Edition			825	825	1100	1100
	Manual Trans			(500)	(500)	(665)	(665)
SLK-CLASS—V6 Supercharged—Equipment Schedule 1							
W.B. 94.5"; 3.2 Liter.							
	SLK32 Roadster 2D	KK66F	56170	30075	33550	37200	43400
	designo Edition			825	825	1100	1100

Body	Type	VIN	List	Trade-In Fair	Good	Pvt-Party Good	Retail Excellent
C-CLASS—4-Cyl. Supercharged—Equipment Schedule 1							
W.B. 106.9"; 1.8 Liter.							
C230 Sport Sedan 4D	RF40J	33180	15675	17650	20300	24300
C230 Sport Coupe 2D	RN47J	30090	14500	16350	18850	22800
Manual Trans			(500)	(500)	(665)	(665)
C-CLASS—V6—Equipment Schedule 1							
W.B. 106.9"; 2.6 Liter, 3.2 Liter.							
C240 Sedan 4D	RF61J	33920	17550	19700	22800	27500
C240 4Matic Sedan 4D	RF81J	35120	18200	20475	23600	28400
C240 Wagon 4D	RH61J	35290	18625	20950	24100	28900
C240 4Matic Wagon 4D	RH81J	36490	19300	21625	24800	29800
C320 Sedan 4D	RF64J	39270	21050	23575	26900	32000
C320 4Matic Sedan 4D	RF84J	40470	21825	24550	27800	33100
C320 Coupe 2D	RN64J	29610	16350	18425	21400	26100
C320 Wagon 4D	RH64J	40640	21825	24550	27800	33100
C320 4Matic Wagon 4D	RH84J	41840	22600	25325	28600	34000
Sport Pkg			1000	1000	1335	1335
Manual Trans			(500)	(500)	(665)	(665)
C-CLASS—V6 Supercharged—Equipment Schedule 1							
W.B. 106.9"; 3.2 Liter.							
C32 Sedan 4D	RF65J	53120	27925	31225	34400	40000
CLK-CLASS—V6—Equipment Schedule 1							
W.B. 106.9"; 3.2 Liter.							
CLK320 Coupe 2D	TJ65J	46480	26475	29575	32700	38100
CLK320 Cabriolet 2D	LK65G	52120	33175	37050	40400	46600
designo Edition			825	825	1100	1100
CLK-CLASS—V8—Equipment Schedule 1							
W.B. 106.9"; 5.0 Liter, 5.5 Liter.							
CLK500 Coupe 2D	TJ75J	54520	30450	33950	38800	46400
CLK500 Cabriolet 2D	TK75G	61570	36675	40825	46800	56000
CLK55 Coupe 2D	TJ76H	70620	37150	41325	47300	56600
CLK55 Cabriolet 2D	LJ74G	80220	41125	45775	51900	61600
designo Edition			975	975	1300	1300
E-CLASS—V6—Equipment Schedule 1							
W.B. 112.4"; 3.2 Liter.							
E320 Sedan 4D	UF65J	49410	27650	30850	34100	39800
E320 Wagon 4D	JH65J	51910	27850	31050	34600	40500
Sport/Appearance Pkg			1000	1000	1335	1335
designo Edition			825	825	1100	1100
E-CLASS—V8—Equipment Schedule 1							
W.B. 112.4"; 5.0 Liter.							
E500 Sedan 4D	UF70J	58510	33750	37625	42300	49900
E500 4Matic Wagon 4D	UH83J	63210	37050	41325	44600	50900
Sport/Appearance Pkg			1000	1000	1335	1335
designo Edition			975	975	1300	1300
E-CLASS—V8 Supercharged—Equipment Schedule 1							
W.B. 112.4"; 5.5 Liter.							
E55 Sedan 4D	UF76J	80070	50825	56450	63100	73700
designo Edition			975	975	1300	1300
CL-CLASS—V8—Equipment Schedule 1							
W.B. 113.6"; 5.0 Liter.							
CL500 Coupe 2D	PJ75J	94520	55575	61700	68300	79200
Sport Pkg			1900	1900	2535	2535
designo Edition			975	975	1300	1300
CL-CLASS—V8 Supercharged—Equipment Schedule 1							
W.B. 113.6"; 5.5 Liter.							
CL55 Coupe 2D	PJ74J	119520	63525	70525	77300	89100
designo Edition			975	975	1300	1300
CL-CLASS—V12 Twin Turbo—Equipment Schedule 1							
W.B. 113.6"; 5.5 Liter.							
CL600 Coupe 2D	PJ76J	129320	70325	78075	84700	96700
Sport Pkg			1900	1900	2535	2535
designo Edition			975	975	1300	1300
S-CLASS—V8—Equipment Schedule 1							
W.B. 121.5"; 4.3 Liter, 5.0 Liter.							
S430 Sedan 4D	NG70J	74320	39000	43350	49300	58500
S430 4Matic Sedan 4D	NG83J	78220	39875	44425	50500	60000
S500 Sedan 4D	NG75J	83770	43175	48025	54400	64600
S500 4Matic Sedan 4D	NG84J	86970	45200	50350	56600	66700
Sport Pkg			1900	1900	2535	2535
designo Edition			975	975	1300	1300
S-CLASS—V8 Supercharged—Equipment Schedule 1							
W.B. 121.5"; 5.5 Liter.							

2004 MERCEDES-BENZ

Body	Type	VIN	List	Trade-In Fair	Good	Pvt-Party Good	Retail Excellent
S55 Sedan 4D		NG74J	111870	59375	65950	72000	82500
designo Edition				975	975	1300	1300

S-CLASS—V12 Twin Turbo—Equipment Schedule 1
W.B. 121.5"; 5.5 Liter.

Body	Type	VIN	List	Trade-In Fair	Good	Pvt-Party Good	Retail Excellent
S600 Sedan 4D		NG76J	124260	65275	72450	79700	92200
Sport Pkg				1900	1900	2535	2535
designo Edition				975	975	1300	1300

SL-CLASS—V8—Equipment Schedule 1
W.B. 100.8"; 5.0 Liter.

Body	Type	VIN	List	Trade-In Fair	Good	Pvt-Party Good	Retail Excellent
SL500 Roadster 2D		SK75F	89800	55875	61975	69500	81500
Sport Pkg				1900	1900	2535	2535
designo Edition				975	975	1300	1300

SL-CLASS—V8 Supercharged—Equipment Schedule 1
W.B. 100.8"; 5.5 Liter.

Body	Type	VIN	List	Trade-In Fair	Good	Pvt-Party Good	Retail Excellent
SL55 Roadster 2D		SK74F	121450	71875	79725	87800	101600
designo Edition				975	975	1300	1300

SL-CLASS—V12 Bi-Turbo—Equipment Schedule 1
W.B. 100.8"; 5.5 Liter.

Body	Type	VIN	List	Trade-In Fair	Good	Pvt-Party Good	Retail Excellent
SL600 Roadster 2D		SK76F	128550	68575	76150	84100	97500
Sport Pkg				1900	1900	2535	2535
designo Edition				975	975	1300	1300

2005 MERCEDES-BENZ — WDBorWDD(WK56F)-5

SLK-CLASS—V6—Equipment Schedule 1
W.B. 95.7"; 3.5 Liter.

Body	Type	VIN	List	Trade-In Fair	Good	Pvt-Party Good	Retail Excellent
SLK350 Roadster 2D		WK56F	47610	31425	35025	38900	45500
Sport Pkg				1050	1050	1400	1400
designo Edition				925	925	1235	1235
Manual Trans				(500)	(500)	(665)	(665)

SLK-CLASS—V8—Equipment Schedule 1
W.B. 95.7"; 5.5 Liter.

Body	Type	VIN	List	Trade-In Fair	Good	Pvt-Party Good	Retail Excellent
SLK55 Roadster 2D		WK73F	61220				
designo Edition							

C-CLASS—4-Cyl. Supercharged—Equipment Schedule 1
W.B. 106.9"; 1.8 Liter.

Body	Type	VIN	List	Trade-In Fair	Good	Pvt-Party Good	Retail Excellent
C230 Sport Sedan 4D		RF40J	34650	19500	21925	25100	30100
C230 Sport Coupe 2D		RN40J	30850	18050	20275	23400	28200
Manual Trans				(500)	(500)	(665)	(665)

C-CLASS—V6—Equipment Schedule 1
W.B. 106.9"; 2.6 Liter, 3.2 Liter.

Body	Type	VIN	List	Trade-In Fair	Good	Pvt-Party Good	Retail Excellent
C240 Sedan 4D		RF61J	36660	21525	24150	27700	33400
C240 4Matic Sedan 4D		RF81J	37860	22400	25025	28700	34400
C240 Wagon 4D		RH61J	38030	22700	25425	29100	34800
C240 4Matic Wagon 4D		RH81J	39230	23575	26375	30100	35900
C320 Sedan 4D		RF64J	41960	25425	28425	32100	38100
C320 4Matic Sedan 4D		RF84J	43160	26275	29400	33200	39200
C320 Coupe 2D		RN64J	33250	20275	22800	26300	31800
Sport Pkg				1050	1050	1400	1400
Manual Trans				(500)	(500)	(665)	(665)

C-CLASS—V8 Supercharged—Equipment Schedule 1
W.B. 106.9"; 5.5 Liter.

Body	Type	VIN	List	Trade-In Fair	Good	Pvt-Party Good	Retail Excellent
C55 Sedan 4D		RF76J	54620				

CLK-CLASS—V6—Equipment Schedule 1
W.B. 106.9"; 3.2 Liter.

Body	Type	VIN	List	Trade-In Fair	Good	Pvt-Party Good	Retail Excellent
CLK320 Coupe 2D		TJ65G	47410	31225	34825	38300	44400
CLK320 Cabriolet 2D		TK65G	53420				
designo Edition				925	925	1235	1235

CLK-CLASS—V8—Equipment Schedule 1
W.B. 106.9"; 5.0 Liter, 5.5 Liter.

Body	Type	VIN	List	Trade-In Fair	Good	Pvt-Party Good	Retail Excellent
CLK500 Coupe 2D		TJ75G	55910				
CLK500 Cabriolet 2D		TK75G	61920				
CLK55 Coupe 2D		TJ76G	71620				
CLK55 Cabriolet 2D		TK76G	82870				
designo Edition							

E-CLASS—6-Cyl. Turbo Diesel—Equipment Schedule 1
W.B. 112.4"; 3.2 Liter.

Body	Type	VIN	List	Trade-In Fair	Good	Pvt-Party Good	Retail Excellent
E320 CDI Sedan 4D		UF26J	52855	34150	38025	42100	48900

E-CLASS—V6—Equipment Schedule 1
W.B. 112.4"; 3.2 Liter.

Body	Type	VIN	List	Trade-In Fair	Good	Pvt-Party Good	Retail Excellent
E320 Sedan 4D		UF65J	52280	32500	36175	39900	46300
E320 4Matic Sedan 4D		UF82J	54770	32600	36375	40400	47000
E320 Wagon 4D		UH65J	54400	32700	36475	40400	47100
E320 4Matic Wagon 4D		UH82J	56900	34050	37925	42000	48800

Body	Type	VIN	List	Trade-In Fair	Good	Pvt-Party Good	Retail Excellent
	Sport/Appearance Pkg			1050	1050	1400	1400
	designo Edition			925	925	1235	1235
E-CLASS—V8—Equipment Schedule 1							
W.B. 112.4"; 5.0 Liter.							
E500 Sedan 4D		UF70J	60480				
E500 4Matic Sedan 4D		UF83J	61420				
E500 4Matic Wagon 4D		UH83J	63950				
	Sport/Appearance Pkg						
	designo Edition						
E-CLASS—V8 Supercharged—Equipment Schedule 1							
W.B. 112.4"; 5.5 Liter.							
E55 Sedan 4D		UF76J	81920				
E55 Wagon 4D		UF86J	83220				
	designo Edition						
CL-CLASS—V8—Equipment Schedule 1							
W.B. 113.6"; 5.0 Liter.							
CL500 Coupe 2D		PJ75J	94620				
	Sport Pkg						
	designo Edition						
CL-CLASS—V8 Supercharged—Equipment Schedule 1							
W.B. 113.6"; 5.5 Liter.							
CL55 Coupe 2D		PJ74J	119620				
	designo Edition						
CL-CLASS—V12 Twin Turbo—Equipment Schedule 1							
W.B. 113.6"; 5.5 Liter, 6.0 Liter.							
CL600 Coupe 2D		PJ76J	128620				
CL65 Coupe 2D		PJ79J	178220				
	Sport Pkg						
	designo Edition						
S-CLASS—V8—Equipment Schedule 1							
W.B. 121.5"; 4.3 Liter, 5.0 Liter.							
S430 Sedan 4D		NG70J	76020				
S430 4Matic Sedan 4D		NG83J	76020				
S500 Sedan 4D		NG75J	84620				
S500 4Matic Sedan 4D		NG84J	84620				
	Sport Pkg						
	designo Edition						
S-CLASS—V8 Supercharged—Equipment Schedule 1							
W.B. 121.5"; 5.5 Liter.							
S55 Sedan 4D		NG74J	112620				
	designo Edition						
S-CLASS—V12 Twin Turbo—Equipment Schedule 1							
W.B. 121.5"; 5.5 Liter.							
S600 Sedan 4D		NG76J	125470				
	Sport Pkg						
	designo Edition						
SL-CLASS—V8—Equipment Schedule 1							
W.B. 100.8"; 5.0 Liter.							
SL500 Roadster 2D		SK75F	91920				
	Sport Pkg						
	designo Edition						
SL-CLASS—V8 Supercharged—Equipment Schedule 1							
W.B. 100.8"; 5.5 Liter.							
SL55 Roadster 2D		SK74F	120120				
	designo Edition						
SL-CLASS—V12 Twin Turbo—Equipment Schedule 1							
W.B. 100.8"; 5.5 Liter, 6.0 Liter.							
SL600 Roadster 2D		SK76F	125620				
SL65 Roadster 2D		SK79F	182720				
	Sport Pkg						
	designo Edition						

MERCURY

1991 MERCURY — (1,3or6)M(E,AorP)(PM10J)-M-#

TRACER—4-Cyl.—Equipment Schedule 6
W.B. 98.4"; 1.8 Liter, 1.9 Liter.

Body	Type	VIN	List	Fair	Good	Good	Excellent
Notchback 4D		PM10J	10730	400	575	1025	1750
Wagon 4D		PM15J	11516	450	650	1150	1925
LTS Notchback 4D		PM148	12745	475	675	1175	2000

CAPRI—4-Cyl.—Equipment Schedule 6
W.B. 94.7"; 1.6 Liter.

1991 MERCURY

Body	Type	VIN	List	Trade-In Fair	Good	Pvt-Party Good	Retail Excellent
Convertible 2D		PT01Z	14172	**400**	**600**	**1350**	**2550**
Hard Top				**300**	**300**	**400**	**400**
CAPRI—4-Cyl. Turbo—Equipment Schedule 6							
W.B. 94.7"; 1.6 Liter.							
XR2 Convertible 2D		PT036	16285	**525**	**750**	**1600**	**2875**
Hard Top				**300**	**300**	**400**	**400**
TOPAZ—4-Cyl.—Equipment Schedule 5							
W.B. 99.9"; 2.3 Liter.							
GS Sedan 2D		PM31X	11900	**250**	**350**	**750**	**1350**
GS Sedan 4D		PM36X	12057	**275**	**375**	**775**	**1400**
LS Sedan 4D		PM37X	13436	**300**	**400**	**825**	**1475**
XR5 Sedan 2D		PM33S	12899	**275**	**375**	**775**	**1400**
LTS Sedan 4D		PM38S	13644	**350**	**475**	**950**	**1650**
Four Wheel Drive Pkg				**250**	**250**	**335**	**335**
SABLE—V6—Equipment Schedule 4							
W.B. 106.0"; 3.0 Liter.							
GS Sedan 4D		CM50U	16748	**475**	**675**	**1175**	**2000**
GS Wagon 4D		CM55U	17643	**625**	**900**	**1500**	**2500**
LS Sedan 4D		CM53U	17225	**550**	**800**	**1350**	**2250**
LS Wagon 4D		CM58U	18195	**700**	**1000**	**1625**	**2675**
V6 3.8 Liter		4		**100**	**100**	**135**	**135**
COUGAR—V6—Equipment Schedule 4							
W.B. 113.0"; 3.8 Liter.							
LS Coupe 2D		PM604	16890	**575**	**825**	**1500**	**2625**
V8 5.0 Liter		T		**250**	**250**	**335**	**335**
COUGAR—V8—Equipment Schedule 4							
W.B. 113.0"; 5.0 Liter.							
XR-7 Coupe 2D		PM62T	22166	**975**	**1375**	**2450**	**3975**
GRAND MARQUIS—V8—Equipment Schedule 4							
W.B. 114.3"; 5.0 Liter.							
GS Sedan 4D		CM74F	19917	**450**	**650**	**1175**	**2000**
GS Colony Park Wag 4D		CM78F	20109	**475**	**675**	**1200**	**2025**
LS Sedan 4D		CM75F	20417	**550**	**775**	**1350**	**2275**
LS Colony Park Wag 4D		CM79F	20681	**525**	**750**	**1275**	**2150**

1992 MERCURY — (1,3or6)M(E,AorP)(PM10J)–N–#

Body	Type	VIN	List	Trade-In Fair	Good	Pvt-Party Good	Retail Excellent
TRACER—4-Cyl.—Equipment Schedule 5							
W.B. 98.4"; 1.8 Liter, 1.9 Liter.							
Notchback 4D		PM10J	11168	**450**	**650**	**1150**	**1925**
Wagon 4D		PM15J	11928	**525**	**750**	**1225**	**2075**
LTS Notchback 4D		PM148	13157	**550**	**775**	**1300**	**2200**
CAPRI—4-Cyl.—Equipment Schedule 6							
W.B. 94.7"; 1.6 Liter.							
Convertible 2D		CT01Z	15644	**475**	**700**	**1575**	**2925**
Hard Top				**325**	**325**	**435**	**435**
CAPRI—4-Cyl. Turbo—Equipment Schedule 6							
W.B. 94.7"; 1.6 Liter.							
XR2 Convertible 2D		CT036	17625	**600**	**875**	**1825**	**3275**
Hard Top				**325**	**325**	**435**	**435**
TOPAZ—4-Cyl.—Equipment Schedule 5							
W.B. 99.9"; 2.3 Liter.							
GS Sedan 2D		PM31X	12332	**300**	**400**	**850**	**1525**
GS Sedan 4D		PM36X	12498	**325**	**425**	**875**	**1575**
LS Sedan 4D		PM37X	13878	**350**	**475**	**925**	**1650**
V6 3.0 Liter		U		**125**	**125**	**165**	**165**
TOPAZ—V6—Equipment Schedule 5							
W.B. 99.9"; 3.0 Liter.							
XR5 Sedan 2D		PM33U	14456	**425**	**625**	**1150**	**2000**
LTS Sedan 4D		PM38U	15248	**450**	**650**	**1225**	**2075**
SABLE—V6—Equipment Schedule 4							
W.B. 106.0"; 3.0 Liter.							
GS Sedan 4D		CM50U	17917	**550**	**800**	**1350**	**2275**
GS Wagon 4D		CM55U	18895	**750**	**1050**	**1725**	**2825**
LS Sedan 4D		CM53U	18510	**650**	**925**	**1550**	**2600**
LS Wagon 4D		CM58U	19537	**825**	**1175**	**1900**	**3050**
V6 3.8 Liter		4		**100**	**100**	**135**	**135**
COUGAR—V6—Equipment Schedule 4							
W.B. 113.0"; 3.8 Liter.							
LS Coupe 2D		PM604	17790	**675**	**950**	**1725**	**2950**
V8 5.0 Liter		T		**250**	**250**	**335**	**335**
COUGAR—V8—Equipment Schedule 4							
W.B. 113.0"; 5.0 Liter.							
XR-7 Coupe 2D		PM62T	23384	**1125**	**1575**	**2750**	**4375**

Body	Type	VIN	List	Trade-In Fair	Trade-In Good	Pvt-Party Good	Retail Excellent

GRAND MARQUIS—V8—Equipment Schedule 4
W.B. 114.4"; 4.6 Liter.

GS Sedan 4D		CM74W	21450	775	1100	1825	3000
LS Sedan 4D		CM75W	21878	925	1300	2150	3475

1993 MERCURY — (1,3or6)M(E,AorP)(PM10J)–P–#

TRACER—4-Cyl.—Equipment Schedule 6
W.B. 98.4"; 1.8 Liter, 1.9 Liter.

Sedan 4D		PM10J	11289	500	725	1225	2075
Wagon 4D		PM15J	12116	575	825	1350	2275
LTS Notchback 4D		PM148	12398	625	900	1475	2450

CAPRI—4-Cyl.—Equipment Schedule 6
W.B. 94.7"; 1.6 Liter.

Convertible 2D		CT01Z	15874	500	725	1700	3175
Hard Top				350	350	465	465

CAPRI—4-Cyl. Turbo—Equipment Schedule 6
W.B. 94.7"; 1.6 Liter.

XR2 Convertible 2D		CT036	17625	625	900	2000	3575
Hard Top				350	350	465	465

TOPAZ—4-Cyl.—Equipment Schedule 6
W.B. 99.9"; 2.3 Liter.

GS Sedan 2D		PM31X	12141	325	450	925	1650
GS Sedan 4D		PM36X	12181	375	500	1000	1775
V6 3.0 Liter		U		150	150	200	200

SABLE—V6—Equipment Schedule 4
W.B. 106.0"; 3.0 Liter.

GS Sedan 4D		LM50U	18909	675	950	1575	2625
GS Wagon 4D		LM55U	20019	850	1225	2000	3225
LS Sedan 4D		LM53U	20379	775	1100	1800	2950
LS Wagon 4D		LM58U	21406	975	1375	2250	3575
V6 3.8 Liter		4		125	125	165	165

COUGAR—V8—Equipment Schedule 4
W.B. 113.0"; 5.0 Liter.

XR-7 Coupe 2D		PM62T	17833	800	1150	2050	3450
V6 3.8 Liter		4		(100)	(100)	(135)	(135)

GRAND MARQUIS—V8—Equipment Schedule 4
W.B. 114.4"; 4.6 Liter.

GS Sedan 4D		LM74W	23420	825	1175	2075	3475
LS Sedan 4D		LM75W	24184	1000	1425	2550	4125

1994 MERCURY — (1,3or6)M(E,AorP)(PM10J)–R–#

TRACER—4-Cyl.—Equipment Schedule 6
W.B. 98.4"; 1.8 Liter, 1.9 Liter.

Sedan 4D		PM10J	11350	575	825	1400	2375
Wagon 4D		PM15J	11620	675	950	1575	2625
LTS Notchback 4D		PM148	13660	725	1050	1725	2825

CAPRI—4-Cyl.—Equipment Schedule 6
W.B. 94.7"; 1.6 Liter.

Convertible 2D		CT01Z	13565	550	775	1925	3575

CAPRI—4-Cyl. Turbo—Equipment Schedule 6
W.B. 94.7"; 1.6 Liter.

XR2 Convertible 2D		CT036	15275	700	1000	2275	4100

TOPAZ—4-Cyl.—Equipment Schedule 5
W.B. 99.9"; 2.3 Liter.

GS Sedan 2D		PM31X	12585	375	500	1050	1875
GS Sedan 4D		PM36X	12625	425	625	1200	2075
V6 3.0 Liter		U		175	175	235	235

SABLE—V6—Equipment Schedule 4
W.B. 106.0"; 3.0 Liter.

GS Sedan 4D		LM50U	19230	775	1100	1850	3050
GS Wagon 4D		LM55U	20390	975	1375	2300	3675
LS Sedan 4D		LM53U	21625	900	1250	2125	3450
LS Wagon 4D		LM58U	22735	1150	1600	2700	4225
LTS Pkg				100	100	135	135
V6 3.8 Liter				150	150	200	200

COUGAR—V8—Equipment Schedule 4
W.B. 113.0"; 4.6 Liter.

XR-7 Coupe 2D		LM62W	18360	975	1375	2525	4150
V6 3.8 Liter		4		(125)	(125)	(165)	(165)

GRAND MARQUIS—V8—Equipment Schedule 4
W.B. 114.4"; 4.6 Liter.

GS Sedan 4D		LM74W	21130	925	1300	2475	4125
LS Sedan 4D		LM75W	23130	1125	1575	2825	4575

Body	Type	VIN	List	Trade-In Fair	Good	Pvt-Party Good	Retail Excellent

1995 MERCURY — (1ME,2MEor3MA)(SM10J)-S-#

TRACER—4-Cyl.—Equipment Schedule 6
W.B. 98.4"; 1.8 Liter, 1.9 Liter.

Sedan 4D		SM10J	12040	675	975	1625	2725
Wagon 4D		SM15J	12310	775	1125	1850	3000
LTS Notchback 4D		SM148	14445	850	1225	2025	3275

MYSTIQUE—4-Cyl.—Equipment Schedule 5
W.B. 106.5"; 2.0 Liter.

GS Sedan 4D		LM653	16060	400	600	1225	2150
LS Sedan 4D		LM663	17920	550	775	1450	2550
Young America Edition				175	175	235	235
V6 2.5 Liter		L		175	175	235	235

SABLE—V6—Equipment Schedule 4
W.B. 106.0"; 3.0 Liter.

GS Sedan 4D		LM50U	19710	900	1275	2175	3525
GS Wagon 4D		LM55U	20860	1125	1575	2700	4250
LS Sedan 4D		LM53U	21450	1050	1450	2525	4050
LS Wagon 4D		LM58U	22550	1400	1900	3025	4650
LTS Pkg				100	100	135	135
V6 3.8 Liter		4		175	175	235	235

COUGAR—V8—Equipment Schedule 4
W.B. 113.0"; 4.6 Liter.

XR-7 Coupe 2D		LM62W	18960	1125	1575	2800	4500
V6 3.8 Liter		4		(150)	(150)	(200)	(200)

GRAND MARQUIS—V8—Equipment Schedule 4
W.B. 114.4"; 4.6 Liter.

GS Sedan 4D		LM74W	22130	1025	1450	2800	4625
LS Sedan 4D		LM75W	24335	1300	1800	3200	5125

1996 MERCURY — (1,2or3)M(EorA)-(M10J)-T-#

TRACER—4-Cyl.—Equipment Schedule 6
W.B. 98.4"; 1.8 Liter, 1.9 Liter.

Sedan 4D		M10J	12540	800	1150	1950	3175
Wagon 4D		M15J	12810	925	1300	2175	3525
LTS Notchback 4D		M148	14945	1000	1425	2475	3975

MYSTIQUE—4-Cyl.—Equipment Schedule 5
W.B. 106.5"; 2.0 Liter.

GS Sedan 4D		M653	16570	525	750	1450	2600
LS Sedan 4D		M663	19280	675	950	1750	3000
V6 2.5 Liter		L		200	200	265	265

SABLE—V6—Equipment Schedule 4
W.B. 108.5"; 3.0 Liter.

G Sedan 4D		M51U	18910	1000	1425	2300	3625
GS Sedan 4D		M50U	19755	1125	1575	2600	4050
GS Wagon 4D		M55U	20775	1450	1950	3025	4550
LS Sedan 4D		M53S	21995	1325	1825	2850	4400
LS Wagon 4D		M58S	23055	1825	2350	3475	5075

COUGAR—V8—Equipment Schedule 4
W.B. 113.0"; 4.6 Liter.

XR-7 Coupe 2D		M62W	18445	1325	1825	3125	4950
V6 3.8 Liter		4		(150)	(150)	(200)	(200)

GRAND MARQUIS—V8—Equipment Schedule 4
W.B. 114.4"; 4.6 Liter.

GS Sedan 4D		M74W	22595	1225	1675	3175	5200
LS Sedan 4D		M75W	24785	1550	2050	3625	5700

1997 MERCURY — (1,2or3)ME-(M10P)-V-#

TRACER—4-Cyl.—Equipment Schedule 6
W.B. 98.4"; 2.0 Liter.

GS Sedan 4D		M10P	12355	825	1175	1950	3125
LS Sedan 4D		M13P	13200	975	1350	2200	3525
LS Wagon 4D		M15P	13855	1200	1650	2700	4175

MYSTIQUE—4-Cyl.—Equipment Schedule 5
W.B. 106.5"; 2.0 Liter.

Sedan 4D		M653	16105	550	800	1575	2800
GS Sedan 4D		M653	17605	675	950	1800	3100
LS Sedan 4D		M663	19920	825	1175	2100	3525
V6 2.5 Liter		L		200	200	265	265

SABLE—V6—Equipment Schedule 4
W.B. 108.5"; 3.0 Liter.

GS Sedan 4D		M50U	20295	1400	1900	2950	4450

Body	Type	VIN	List	Trade-In Fair	Trade-In Good	Pvt-Party Good	Retail Excellent
GS Wagon 4D		M55U	20295	1800	2325	3425	5025
LS Sedan 4D		M53S	23350	1675	2175	3275	4825
LS Wagon 4D		M58S	23350	2200	2800	3925	5600

COUGAR—V8—Equipment Schedule 4
W.B. 113.0"; 4.6 Liter.

XR-7 Sedan 2D		M62W	19685	1600	2100	3550	5500
V6 3.8 Liter		4		(150)	(150)	(200)	(200)

GRAND MARQUIS—V8—Equipment Schedule 4
W.B. 114.4"; 4.6 Liter.

GS Sedan 4D		M74W	23140	1500	2000	3650	5875
LS Sedan 4D		M75W	25330	1875	2400	4125	6400

1998 MERCURY — (1,2or3)ME–(M10P)–W–#

TRACER—4-Cyl.—Equipment Schedule 6
W.B. 98.4"; 2.0 Liter.

GS Sedan 4D		M10P	12565	1050	1450	2475	3925
LS Sedan 4D		M13P	13125	1200	1650	2700	4200
LS Wagon 4D		M15P	14620	1500	2000	3075	4625

MYSTIQUE—4-Cyl.—Equipment Schedule 5
W.B. 106.5"; 2.0 Liter.

Sedan 4D		M653	16105	750	1050	2025	3475
GS Sedan 4D		M653	18230	850	1200	2325	3925

MYSTIQUE—V6—Equipment Schedule 5
W.B. 106.5"; 2.5 Liter

LS Sedan 4D		M66L	19295	1100	1550	2775	4450

SABLE—V6—Equipment Schedule 4
W.B. 108.5"; 3.0 Liter.

GS Sedan 4D		M50U	19995	1750	2275	3375	4975
LS Sedan 4D		M53U	20995	2025	2575	3700	5350
LS Wagon 4D		M58U	22835	2650	3275	4475	6250
V6 3.0 Liter 24V		S		200	200	265	265

GRAND MARQUIS—V8—Equipment Schedule 4
W.B. 114.7"; 4.6 Liter.

GS Sedan 4D		M74W	22495	1875	2400	4250	6675
LS Sedan 4D		M75W	24395	2275	2825	4725	7225

1999 MERCURY — (1,2or3)(MEorZW)–(M10P)–X–#

TRACER—4-Cyl.—Equipment Schedule 6
W.B. 98.4"; 2.0 Liter.

GS Sedan 4D		M10P	12740	1325	1825	2900	4475
LS Sedan 4D		M13P	13485	1525	2025	3125	4725
LS Wagon 4D		M15P	14690	1875	2400	3575	5225

MYSTIQUE—4-Cyl.—Equipment Schedule 5
W.B. 106.5"; 2.0 Liter.

GS Sedan 4D		M653	17740	1075	1525	2800	4525

MYSTIQUE—V6—Equipment Schedule 5
W.B. 106.5"; 2.5 Liter.

LS Sedan 4D		M66L	19095	1450	1950	3250	5075

SABLE—V6—Equipment Schedule 4
W.B. 108.5"; 3.0 Liter.

GS Sedan 4D		M50U	18995	2100	2675	3875	5625
LS Sedan 4D		M53U	20095	2400	2975	4225	6025
LS Wagon 4D		M58U	21195	3050	3725	5025	6925
V6 3.0 Liter 24V		S		200	200	265	265

COUGAR—V6—Equipment Schedule 4
W.B. 106.4"; 2.5 Liter.

Coupe 2D		T61L	18630	2625	3250	5050	7500
Manual Trans				(250)	(250)	(335)	(335)
4-Cyl. 2.0 Liter		3		(400)	(400)	(535)	(535)

GRAND MARQUIS—V8—Equipment Schedule 4
W.B. 114.7"; 4.6 Liter.

GS Sedan 4D		M74W	22825	2375	2950	4925	7525
LS Sedan 4D		M75W	24725	2825	3450	5425	8125

2000 MERCURY — (1,2or3)(MEorZW)–(M653)–Y–#

MYSTIQUE—4-Cyl.—Equipment Schedule 5
W.B. 106.5"; 2.0 Liter.

GS Sedan 4D		M653	17495	1500	2000	3400	5325

MYSTIQUE—V6—Equipment Schedule 5
W.B. 106.5"; 2.5 Liter.

LS Sedan 4D		M66L	18795	1975	2525	3975	6000

2000 MERCURY

Body	Type	VIN	List	Trade-In Fair	Trade-In Good	Pvt-Party Good	Retail Excellent
SABLE—V6—Equipment Schedule 4							
W.B. 108.5"; 3.0 Liter.							
GS Sedan 4D		M50U	19395	2475	3075	4500	6500
GS Wagon 4D		M58U	21195	3000	3675	5150	7225
LS Sedan 4D		M53U	20495	2775	3400	4850	6900
V6 3.0 Liter 24V		S		250	250	335	335
SABLE—V6 24V—Equipment Schedule 4							
W.B. 108.5"; 3.0 Liter.							
LS Premium Sedan 4D		M55S	21795	3225	3900	5400	7525
LS Premium Wagon 4D		M59S	22895	3775	4525	6075	8275
COUGAR—V6—Equipment Schedule 4							
W.B. 106.4"; 2.5 Liter.							
Coupe 2D		T61L	18880	3100	3750	5725	8400
Manual Trans				(275)	(275)	(365)	(365)
4-Cyl. 2.0 Liter		3		(450)	(450)	(600)	(600)
GRAND MARQUIS—V8—Equipment Schedule 4							
W.B. 114.7"; 4.6 Liter.							
GS Sedan 4D		M74W	23020	3000	3650	5800	8650
LS Sedan 4D		M75W	24920	3500	4200	6400	9325

2001 MERCURY — (1or2)(MEorZW)–(M50U)–1–#

Body	Type	VIN	List	Trade-In Fair	Trade-In Good	Pvt-Party Good	Retail Excellent
SABLE—V6—Equipment Schedule 4							
W.B. 108.5"; 3.0 Liter.							
GS Sedan 4D		M50U	19785	3000	3650	5300	7600
GS Wagon 4D		M58U	21585	3625	4350	6050	8425
LS Sedan 4D		M53U	20885	3275	3950	5625	7950
V6 3.0 Liter 24V		S		275	275	365	365
V6 3.0L Flex Fuel		2		0	0	0	0
SABLE—V6 24V—Equipment Schedule 4							
W.B. 108.5"; 3.0 Liter.							
LS Premium Sedan 4D		M55S	22285	3775	4525	6225	8625
LS Premium Wagon 4D		M59S	23285	4475	5275	7050	9550
COUGAR—V6—Equipment Schedule 4							
W.B. 106.4"; 2.5 Liter.							
Coupe 2D		T61L	18545	4425	5225	7250	10050
C2 Coupe 2D		T61L	20660	4975	5850	7900	10750
Zn Coupe 2D		T61L	21645	5200	6075	8150	11050
Manual Trans				(300)	(300)	(400)	(400)
4-Cyl. 2.0 Liter		3		(475)	(475)	(635)	(635)
GRAND MARQUIS—V8—Equipment Schedule 4							
W.B. 114.7"; 4.6 Liter.							
GS Sedan 4D		M74W	23460	3825	4575	6900	10050
LS Sedan 4D		M75W	24580	4400	5200	7575	10750

2002 MERCURY — (1or2)(MEorZW)–(M50U)–2–#

Body	Type	VIN	List	Trade-In Fair	Trade-In Good	Pvt-Party Good	Retail Excellent
SABLE—V6—Equipment Schedule 4							
W.B. 108.5"; 3.0 Liter.							
GS Sedan 4D		M50U	20255	3675	4425	6275	8875
GS Wagon 4D		M58U	21665	4400	5200	7100	9800
SABLE—V6 24V—Equipment Schedule 4							
W.B. 108.5"; 3.0 Liter.							
LS Premium Sedan 4D		M55S	22680	4500	5325	7250	9950
LS Premium Wagon 4D		M59S	23845	5325	6225	8225	11000
COUGAR—V6—Equipment Schedule 4							
W.B. 106.4"; 2.5 Liter.							
Coupe 2D		M61L	18490	5225	6075	8275	11300
Sport Coupe 2D		M62L	18990	5700	6650	8875	12000
C2 Coupe 2D		M62L	19505	5850	6800	9025	12150
Xr Coupe 2D		M62L	19940	6075	7025	9275	12400
Manual Trans				(325)	(325)	(435)	(435)
4-Cyl. 2.0 Liter		3		(500)	(500)	(665)	(665)
35th Anniversary Ed				200	200	265	265
GRAND MARQUIS—V8—Equipment Schedule 4							
W.B. 114.7"; 4.6 Liter.							
GS Sedan 4D		M74W	24325	4900	5750	8300	11750
LS Sedan 4D		M75W	27800	5525	6450	9025	12500
LSE Sedan 4D		M75W	29305	6125	7100	9750	13350

2003 MERCURY — (1or2)ME–(M50U)–3–#

Body	Type	VIN	List	Trade-In Fair	Trade-In Good	Pvt-Party Good	Retail Excellent
SABLE—V6—Equipment Schedule 4							
W.B. 108.5"; 3.0 Liter.							
GS Sedan 4D		M50U	20770	4550	5375	7500	10450

EQUIPMENT & MILEAGE PAGE 13 TO 27

Body	Type	VIN	List	Trade-In Fair	Good	Pvt-Party Good	Retail Excellent
GS Wagon 4D		M58U	22180	**5350**	**6250**	**8425**	**11450**
V6 3.0L Flex Fuel				**0**	**0**	**0**	**0**
SABLE—V6 24V—Equipment Schedule 4							
W.B. 108.5"; 3.0 Liter.							
LS Premium Sedan 4D		M55S	23145	**5425**	**6350**	**8500**	**11550**
LS Premium Wagon 4D		M59S	24310	**6375**	**7400**	**9600**	**12750**
GRAND MARQUIS—V8—Equipment Schedule 4							
W.B. 114.7"; 4.6 Liter.							
GS Sedan 4D		M74W	24875	**6275**	**7275**	**10050**	**13800**
LS Sedan 4D		M75W	28605	**6950**	**8025**	**10850**	**14700**
LSE Sedan 4D		M75W	30110	**7650**	**8775**	**11650**	**15550**
Limited Edition				**500**	**500**	**665**	**665**
MARAUDER—V8—Equipment Schedule 2							
W.B. 114.7"; 4.6 Liter.							
Sedan 4D		M75V	34495	**11550**	**13100**	**15350**	**18750**

Body	Type	VIN	List	Trade-In Fair	Good	Pvt-Party Good	Retail Excellent
SABLE—V6—Equipment Schedule 4							
W.B. 108.5"; 3.0 Liter.							
GS Sedan 4D		M50U	21595	**5700**	**6650**	**8950**	**12150**
GS Wagon 4D		M58U	22595	**6600**	**7625**	**9950**	**13250**
V6 3.0L Flex Fuel				**0**	**0**	**0**	**0**
SABLE—V6 24V—Equipment Schedule 4							
W.B. 108.5"; 3.0 Liter.							
LS Premium Sedan 4D		M55S	23895	**6625**	**7675**	**10000**	**13300**
LS Premium Wagon 4D		M59S	24795	**7675**	**8825**	**11250**	**14650**
GRAND MARQUIS—V8—Equipment Schedule 4							
W.B. 114.7"; 4.6 Liter.							
GS Sedan 4D		M74W	24695	**8100**	**9300**	**12200**	**16300**
LS Sedan 4D		M75W	29595	**8850**	**10125**	**13100**	**17200**
Limited Edition				**500**	**500**	**665**	**665**
MARAUDER—V8—Equipment Schedule 2							
W.B. 114.7"; 4.6 Liter.							
Sedan 4D		M79V	34495	**13775**	**15575**	**17900**	**21600**

Body	Type	VIN	List	Trade-In Fair	Good	Pvt-Party Good	Retail Excellent
SABLE—V6—Equipment Schedule 4							
W.B. 108.5"; 3.0 Liter.							
GS Sedan 4D		M50U	21525	**7325**	**8425**	**11000**	**14600**
V6 3.0L Flex Fuel		2		**0**	**0**	**0**	**0**
SABLE—V6 24V—Equipment Schedule 4							
W.B. 108.5"; 3.0 Liter.							
LS Sedan 4D		M55S	24490	**8275**	**9475**	**12150**	**15850**
LS Wagon 4D		M59S	25800	**9425**	**10775**	**13500**	**17350**
MONTEGO—V6—Equipment Schedule 4							
W.B. 112.9"; 3.0 Liter.							
Luxury Sedan 4D		M401	24995	**12475**	**14125**	**16450**	**20100**
Luxury AWD Sedan 4D		M411	26695	**12800**	**14500**	**16900**	**20600**
Premier Sedan 4D		M421	27195	**12900**	**14600**	**17000**	**20700**
Premier AWD Sedan 4D		M431	28895	**13675**	**15475**	**17850**	**21600**
GRAND MARQUIS—V8—Equipment Schedule 4							
W.B. 114.7"; 4.6 Liter.							
GS Sedan 4D		M74W	25095	**10275**	**11700**	**14900**	**19400**
LS Sedan 4D		M75W	30150	**11050**	**12550**	**15850**	**20500**
LSE Sedan 4D		M75W	30620	**11250**	**12750**	**16000**	**20700**

MINI

Body	Type	VIN	List	Trade-In Fair	Good	Pvt-Party Good	Retail Excellent
COOPER—4-Cyl.—Equipment Schedule 3							
W.B. 97.1"; 1.6 Liter.							
Hatchback 2D		RC334	16850	**10225**	**11650**	**13400**	**16250**
Sport Pkg				**500**	**500**	**665**	**665**
COOPER S—4-Cyl. Supercharged—Equipment Schedule 3							
W.B. 97.1"; 1.6 Liter.							
Hatchback 2D		RE334	19850	**12125**	**13725**	**15600**	**18650**
Sport Pkg				**500**	**500**	**665**	**665**

COOPER—4-Cyl.—Equipment Schedule 3
W.B. 97.1"; 1.6 Liter.

2003 MINI

Body	Type	VIN	List	Trade-In Fair	Good	Pvt-Party Good	Retail Excellent
Hatchback 2D		RC334	18575	**11700**	**13250**	**15150**	**18200**
Sport Pkg				**550**	**550**	**735**	**735**
COOPER S—4-Cyl. Supercharged—Equipment Schedule 3							
W.B. 97.1"; 1.6 Liter.							
Hatchback 2D		RE334	20325	**13725**	**15525**	**17450**	**20800**
Sport Pkg				**550**	**550**	**735**	**735**

2004 MINI — WMW(RC334)-4-#

COOPER—4-Cyl.—Equipment Schedule 3
W.B. 97.1"; 1.6 Liter.

Body	Type	VIN	List	Trade-In Fair	Good	Pvt-Party Good	Retail Excellent
Hatchback 2D		RC334	18299	**13300**	**15025**	**16900**	**20000**
Sport Pkg				**600**	**600**	**800**	**800**
COOPER S—4-Cyl. Supercharged—Equipment Schedule 3							
W.B. 97.1"; 1.6 Liter.							
Hatchback 2D		RE334	19999	**15475**	**17450**	**19400**	**22800**
Sport Pkg				**600**	**600**	**800**	**800**

2005 MINI — WMW(RC334)-5-#

COOPER—4-Cyl.—Equipment Schedule 3
W.B. 97.1"; 1.6 Liter.

Body	Type	VIN	List	Trade-In Fair	Good	Pvt-Party Good	Retail Excellent
Hatchback 2D		RC334	18299	**14500**	**16350**	**18150**	**21200**
Convertible 2D		RF334	22800	**17600**	**19800**	**22300**	**26400**
Sport Pkg				**650**	**650**	**865**	**865**
COOPER S—4-Cyl. Supercharged—Equipment Schedule 3							
W.B. 97.1"; 1.6 Liter.							
Hatchback 2D		RE334	20449	**16875**	**18975**	**21000**	**24300**
Convertible 2D		RH334	24950	**20750**	**23275**	**25400**	**29300**
Sport Pkg				**650**	**650**	**865**	**865**

MITSUBISHI

1991 MITSUBISHI — (JA3,4A3orKPH)(VD12J)-M-#

PRECIS—4-Cyl.—Equipment Schedule 6
W.B. 93.8"; 1.5 Liter.

Body	Type	VIN	List	Trade-In Fair	Good	Pvt-Party Good	Retail Excellent
Hatchback 2D		VD12J	7107	**175**	**250**	**700**	**1350**
RS Hatchback 2D		VD22J	8761	**250**	**350**	**800**	**1525**
MIRAGE—4-Cyl.—Equipment Schedule 6							
W.B. 93.9", 96.7" (Sed); 1.5 Liter, 1.6 Liter.							
VL Hatchback 2D		CU14X	8508	**275**	**375**	**975**	**1875**
Sedan 4D		CU26X	10190	**325**	**450**	**1100**	**2025**
Hatchback 2D		CU24X	9303	**325**	**450**	**1100**	**2025**
Special Ed H'Back 2D		CU24X	8652	**350**	**475**	**1125**	**2075**
LS Sedan 4D		CU36X	10977	**400**	**550**	**1225**	**2250**
GS DOHC Sedan 4D		CU56Y	12115	**325**	**450**	**1100**	**2025**
ECLIPSE—4-Cyl.—Equipment Schedule 4							
W.B. 97.2"; 1.8 Liter, 2.0 Liter.							
Coupe 2D		CS34T	12655	**375**	**500**	**1250**	**2375**
GS Coupe 2D		CS44T	13697	**400**	**600**	**1350**	**2550**
GS 16V DOHC Cpe 2D		CS44R	14597	**475**	**700**	**1500**	**2775**
Auto Trans				**100**	**100**	**135**	**135**
ECLIPSE—4-Cyl. Turbo—Equipment Schedule 4							
W.B. 97.2"; 2.0 Liter.							
GS DOHC Coupe 2D		CS54U	16697	**600**	**875**	**1750**	**3100**
GSX Coupe 2D		CT64U	18357	**900**	**1275**	**2450**	**4100**
Manual Trans				**0**	**0**	**0**	**0**
GALANT—4-Cyl.—Equipment Schedule 4							
W.B. 102.4"; 2.0 Liter.							
Sedan 4D		CR46V	14098	**450**	**650**	**1475**	**2725**
LS Sedan 4D		CR56V	15124	**575**	**825**	**1700**	**3050**
GS Sport Sedan 4D		CR56R	16144	**750**	**1050**	**2025**	**3525**
GSR Sport Sedan 4D		CR56R	17714	**775**	**1125**	**2150**	**3675**
GSX Sport Sedan 4D		CX56R	18104	**775**	**1125**	**2150**	**3675**
Manual Trans				**(175)**	**(175)**	**(235)**	**(235)**
GALANT—4-Cyl. Turbo—Equipment Schedule 4							
W.B. 102.4"; 2.0 Liter.							
VR-4 Sport Sedan 4D		CX56U	22145	**950**	**1325**	**2525**	**422?**
3000GT—V6—Equipment Schedule 4							
W.B. 97.2"; 3.0 Liter.							
Coupe 2D		XD54B	21161	**1300**	**1800**	**3525**	**5?**
SL Coupe 2D		XD64B	25092	**1700**	**2225**	**4025**	**?**
Auto Trans				**100**	**100**	**135**	**?**

0106   **EQUIPMENT & MILEAGE PAGE 13 TO 27**   ,

1991 MITSUBISHI

Body	Type	VIN	List	Trade-In Fair	Trade-In Good	Pvt-Party Good	Retail Excellent
3000GT—V6 Turbo—Equipment Schedule 2							
W.B. 97.2"; 3.0 Liter.							
VR-4 Coupe 2D		XE74C	32265	**3600**	**4300**	**6425**	**9300**
Manual Trans				**0**	**0**	**0**	**0**

1992 MITSUBISHI — (JA3,4A3orKPH)(VD11J)–N–#

Body	Type	VIN	List	Trade-In Fair	Trade-In Good	Pvt-Party Good	Retail Excellent
PRECIS—4-Cyl.—Equipment Schedule 6							
W.B. 93.8"; 1.5 Liter.							
Hatchback 2D		VD11J	8436	**175**	**250**	**700**	**1400**
MIRAGE—4-Cyl.—Equipment Schedule 6							
W.B. 93.9", 96.7" (Sed); 1.5 Liter, 1.6 Liter.							
VL Hatchback 2D		CU14A	8823	**325**	**425**	**1125**	**2150**
Special Ed H'Back 2D		CU14A	8927	**325**	**425**	**1125**	**2150**
Sedan 4D		CU26A	10605	**375**	**500**	**1225**	**2325**
Hatchback 2D		CU24A	9638	**375**	**500**	**1250**	**2375**
LS Sedan 4D		CU36A	11120	**450**	**650**	**1450**	**2675**
GS DOHC Sedan 4D		CU56Y	12530	**400**	**525**	**1275**	**2425**
EXPO—4-Cyl.—Equipment Schedule 6							
W.B. 99.2" (LRV), 107.1"; 1.8 Liter, 2.4 Liter.							
LRV Wagon 3D		CV20D	12639	**1000**	**1400**	**2325**	**3675**
LRV Sport Wagon 3D		CV40D	13459	**1050**	**1475**	**2550**	**4050**
LRV Sport AWD Wag 3D		CW40D	15359	**1200**	**1650**	**2750**	**4300**
Wagon 4D		CY29W	14692	**1225**	**1700**	**2825**	**4375**
SP Wagon 4D		CY59W	15652	**1375**	**1900**	**3000**	**4600**
SP AWD Wagon 4D		CZ59W	16982	**1625**	**2125**	**3300**	**4950**
ECLIPSE—4-Cyl.—Equipment Schedule 4							
W.B. 97.2"; 1.8 Liter, 2.0 Liter.							
Coupe 2D		CS34T	12894	**425**	**625**	**1450**	**2775**
GS Coupe 2D		CS44T	14396	**500**	**725**	**1625**	**3000**
GS 16V DOHC Cpe 2D		CS44R	15336	**600**	**850**	**1825**	**3275**
Auto Trans				**100**	**100**	**135**	**135**
ECLIPSE—4-Cyl. Turbo—Equipment Schedule 4							
W.B. 97.2"; 2.0 Liter.							
GS DOHC Coupe 2D		CS54U	17477	**700**	**1025**	**2050**	**3625**
GSX Coupe 2D		CT64U	19217	**1050**	**1450**	**2750**	**4500**
Manual Trans				**0**	**0**	**0**	**0**
GALANT—4-Cyl.—Equipment Schedule 4							
W.B. 102.4"; 2.0 Liter.							
Sedan 4D		CR46V	15487	**525**	**750**	**1675**	**3100**
LS Sedan 4D		CR56V	15979	**625**	**900**	**1950**	**3475**
GS Sport Sedan 4D		CR56R	17109	**825**	**1175**	**2400**	**4125**
GSR Sport Sedan 4D		CR56R	17859	**900**	**1250**	**2500**	**4275**
GSX Sport Sedan 4D		CX56R	18899	**900**	**1250**	**2500**	**4275**
Manual Trans (Ex GSR)				**(175)**	**(175)**	**(235)**	**(235)**
GALANT—4-Cyl. Turbo—Equipment Schedule 4							
W.B. 102.4"; 2.0 Liter.							
VR-4 Sport Sedan 4D		CX56U	22868	**1075**	**1500**	**2825**	**4625**
Manual Trans				**0**	**0**	**0**	**0**
3000GT—V6—Equipment Schedule 4							
W.B. 97.2"; 3.0 Liter.							
Coupe 2D		XD54B	21826	**1625**	**2125**	**4025**	**6500**
SL Coupe 2D		XD64B	26577	**2075**	**2650**	**4625**	**7250**
Auto Trans				**100**	**100**	**135**	**135**
3000GT—V6 Turbo—Equipment Schedule 4							
W.B. 97.2"; 3.0 Liter.							
VR-4 Coupe 2D		XE74C	34288	**4075**	**4850**	**7175**	**10350**
Manual Trans				**0**	**0**	**0**	**0**
DIAMANTE—V6—Equipment Schedule 4							
W.B. 107.1"; 3.0 Liter.							
Sedan 4D		XC47S	21375	**600**	**850**	**2150**	**4000**
LS Sedan 4D		XC57B	26007	**900**	**1275**	**2725**	**4700**
Euro-Handling Pkg				**275**	**275**	**365**	**365**

1993 MITSUBISHI — (JA3,4A3orKPH)(VD12J)–P–#

Body	Type	VIN	List	Trade-In Fair	Trade-In Good	Pvt-Party Good	Retail Excellent
PRECIS—4-Cyl.—Equipment Schedule 6							
W.B. 93.8"; 1.5 Liter.							
Hatchback 2D		VD12J	8360	**175**	**225**	**700**	**1400**
MIRAGE—4-Cyl.—Equipment Schedule 6							
W.B. 96.1", 98.4" (Sed); 1.5 Liter, 1.8 Liter.							
S Sedan 4D		CA26A	11208	**500**	**725**	**1525**	**2775**
S Coupe 2D		CA11A	8822	**400**	**525**	**1250**	**2375**
S Sedan 4D		CA36C	11986	**450**	**650**	**1450**	**2675**
S Coupe 2D		CA21A	10708	**400**	**600**	**1325**	**2500**

Body	Type	VIN	List	Trade-In Fair	Trade-In Good	Pvt-Party Good	Retail Excellent
LS Sedan 4D		CA46C	13252	475	700	1500	2775
LS Coupe 2D		CA31A	11472	450	625	1400	2625

EXPO—4-Cyl.—Equipment Schedule 4
W.B. 99.2" (LRV), 107.1"; 1.8 Liter, 2.4 Liter.

Body Type	VIN	List	Fair	Good	Good	Excellent
LRV Wagon 3D	CB20C	12988	1150	1600	2700	4250
LRV Sport Wagon 3D	CB40G	15494	1225	1725	2825	4450
LRV AWD Wagon 3D	CC20G	14728	1450	1950	3100	4750
Wagon 4D	CD49G	15213	1500	2000	3175	4825
AWD Wagon 4D	CE49G	16533	1900	2425	3650	5400
SP Wagon 4D	CD59G	17211	1675	2200	3400	5100
SP AWD Wagon 4D	CE59G	18561	1950	2475	3700	5475

ECLIPSE—4-Cyl.—Equipment Schedule 4
W.B. 97.2"; 1.8 Liter, 2.0 Liter.

Body Type	VIN	List	Fair	Good	Good	Excellent
Coupe 2D	CF34B	13399	475	700	1675	3125
GS Coupe 2D	CF44B	15350	600	875	1950	3525
GS 16V DOHC Cpe 2D	CF44E	16280	700	1025	2225	3975
Auto Trans			125	125	165	165

ECLIPSE—4-Cyl. Turbo—Equipment Schedule 4
W.B. 97.2"; 2.0 Liter.

Body Type	VIN	List	Fair	Good	Good	Excellent
GS DOHC Coupe 2D	CF54F	18442	850	1200	2475	4250
GSX AWD Coupe 2D	CG64F	21162	1225	1675	3075	4975
Auto Trans			125	125	165	165

GALANT—4-Cyl.—Equipment Schedule 4
W.B. 102.4"; 2.0 Liter.

Body Type	VIN	List	Fair	Good	Good	Excellent
S Sedan 4D	CH46D	16024	600	875	1975	3575
ES Sedan 4D	CH56D	16704	750	1075	2325	4100
LS Sport Sedan 4D	CH56D	17734	975	1350	2700	4550
Manual Trans			(225)	(225)	(300)	(300)

3000GT—V6—Equipment Schedule 4
W.B. 97.2"; 3.0 Liter.

Body Type	VIN	List	Fair	Good	Good	Excellent
Coupe 2D	BM54J	24102	2125	2700	4700	7350
SL Coupe 2D	BM64J	29152	2700	3300	5400	8225
Auto Trans			125	125	165	165

3000GT—V6 Turbo—Equipment Schedule 2
W.B. 97.2"; 3.0 Liter.

Body Type	VIN	List	Fair	Good	Good	Excellent
VR-4 Coupe 2D	BN74K	37693	4950	5800	8275	11650

DIAMANTE—V6—Equipment Schedule 4
W.B. 107.1"; 107.2" (Wag); 3.0 Liter.

Body Type	VIN	List	Fair	Good	Good	Excellent
ES Luxury Sedan 4D	BP47H	22842	675	975	2375	4350
LS Luxury Sedan 4D	BP57J	30293	1050	1450	3025	5125
Wagon 4D	XC49S	22869	550	800	2175	4100
Euro-Handling Pkg			300	300	400	400

1994 MITSUBISHI — (JA3,4A3orKPH)(VD12J)–R–#

PRECIS—4-Cyl.—Equipment Schedule 6
W.B. 93.8"; 1.5 Liter.

Body Type	VIN	List	Fair	Good	Good	Excellent
Hatchback 2D	VD12J		200	275	800	1575

MIRAGE—4-Cyl.—Equipment Schedule 6
W.B. 96.1", 98.4" (Sed); 1.5 Liter, 1.8 Liter.

Body Type	VIN	List	Fair	Good	Good	Excellent
S Sedan 4D	EA26A	12928	550	800	1700	3100
S Coupe 2D	EA11A	10548	400	575	1375	2625
ES Sedan 4D	EA36C	13488	525	750	1675	3050
ES Coupe 2D	EA21A	11918	450	650	1500	2800
LS Sedan 4D	EA46C	15754	600	850	1800	3225
LS Coupe 2D	EA31C	13104	525	750	1625	3000

EXPO—4-Cyl.—Equipment Schedule 6
W.B. 99.2" (LRV), 107.1"; 1.8 Liter, 2.4 Liter.

Body Type	VIN	List	Fair	Good	Good	Excellent
LRV Wagon 3D	EB30C	14627	1375	1875	3000	4650
LRV Sport Wagon 3D	EB40G	17244	1500	2000	3200	4875
Wagon 4D	ED59G	17429	1800	2325	3550	5275
AWD Wagon 4D	EE59G	18869	2175	2775	4050	5875

ECLIPSE—4-Cyl.—Equipment Schedule 4
W.B. 97.2"; 1.8 Liter, 2.0 Liter.

Body Type	VIN	List	Fair	Good	Good	Excellent
Coupe 2D	CF34B	13686	575	825	2000	3675
GS Coupe 2D	CF44B	16037	750	1050	2375	4250
GS 16V DOHC Cpe 2D	CF44E	16711	850	1225	2600	4475
Auto Trans			150	150	200	200

ECLIPSE—4-Cyl. Turbo—Equipment Schedule 4
W.B. 97.2"; 2.0 Liter.

Body Type	VIN	List	Fair	Good	Good	Excellent
GS DOHC Coupe 2D	CF54F	18949	1000	1400	2825	4775
GSX AWD Coupe 2D	CG64F	21689	1450	1950	3475	5525
Auto Trans			150	150	200	200

1994 MITSUBISHI

Body	Type	VIN	List	Trade-In Fair	Trade-In Good	Pvt-Party Good	Retail Excellent
GALANT—4-Cyl.—Equipment Schedule 4							
W.B. 103.7"; 2.4 Liter.							
S Sedan 4D	AJ46G	16204	550	800	2100	3950
ES Sedan 4D	AJ56G	17195	725	1050	2375	4275
LS Sport Sedan 4D	AJ56G	18635	975	1350	2825	4800
GS DOHC Sedan 4D	AJ56L	21697	1000	1400	2875	4875
Manual Trans			(275)	(275)	(365)	(365)
3000GT—V6—Equipment Schedule 4							
W.B. 97.2"; 3.0 Liter.							
Coupe 2D	AM54J	27745	2675	3275	5400	8250
SL Coupe 2D	AM64J	32120	3325	4000	6250	9250
Auto Trans			150	150	200	200
3000GT—V6 Turbo—Equipment Schedule 2							
W.B. 97.2"; 3.0 Liter.							
VR-4 Coupe 2D	BN74K	41370	5850	6800	9400	13000
DIAMANTE—V6—Equipment Schedule 4							
W.B. 107.1", 107.2" (Wag); 3.0 Liter.							
ES Luxury Sedan 4D	AP47H	25995	800	1150	2700	4800
LS Luxury Sedan 4D	AP57J	32970	1225	1700	3425	5675
Wagon 4D	AC49S	26320	675	950	2450	4525
Traction Control			125	125	165	165

1995 MITSUBISHI — (J,4or6)(A3orMM)A(A26A)–S–

Body	Type	VIN	List	Trade-In Fair	Trade-In Good	Pvt-Party Good	Retail Excellent
MIRAGE—4-Cyl.—Equipment Schedule 6							
W.B. 96.1", 98.4" (Sed); 1.5 Liter, 1.8 Liter.							
S Sedan 4D	A26A	13707	650	925	1975	3525
S Coupe 2D	A11A	11563	475	675	1600	3000
ES Sedan 4D	A36C	14627	625	900	1975	3525
ES Coupe 2D	A21A	13367	525	750	1725	3175
LS Coupe 2D	A31C	14696	625	900	1925	3475
EXPO—4-Cyl.—Equipment Schedule 6							
W.B. 107.1"; 2.4 Liter.							
Wagon 4D	D59G	17894	2100	2675	3925	5750
AWD Wagon 4D	E59G	19364	2525	3125	4450	6350
ECLIPSE—4-Cyl.—Equipment Schedule 4							
W.B. 98.8"; 2.0 Liter.							
RS Coupe 2D	K34Y	15891	1275	1775	3200	5150
GS Coupe 2D	K44Y	18544	1750	2275	3775	5850
Auto Trans			175	175	235	235
ECLIPSE—4-Cyl. Turbo—Equipment Schedule 4							
W.B. 98.8"; 2.0 Liter.							
GS-T Coupe 2D	K54F	20419	1975	2500	4050	6150
GSX Coupe 2D	L54F	23349	2525	3125	4725	6950
Auto Trans			175	175	235	235
GALANT—4-Cyl.—Equipment Schedule 4							
W.B. 103.7"; 2.4 Liter.							
S Sedan 4D	J46G	17017	700	1000	2425	4425
ES Sedan 4D	J56G	19089	875	1225	2750	4775
LS Sedan 4D	J56G	20689	1075	1525	3100	5250
Manual Trans			(325)	(325)	(435)	(435)
3000GT—V6—Equipment Schedule 4							
W.B. 97.2"; 3.0 Liter.							
Coupe 2D	M84Y	28920	3250	3925	6200	9250
SL Coupe 2D	M54J	34220	3975	4725	7125	10350
SL Spyder Conv 2D	V65J	57969	8600	9850	12950	17200
Auto Trans			175	175	235	235
3000GT—V6 Turbo—Equipment Schedule 2							
W.B. 97.2"; 3.0 Liter.							
VR-4 Coupe 2D	N74K	43520	6750	7800	10550	14400
VR-4 Spyder Conv 2D	W75K	64919	10725	12225	15550	20300
DIAMANTE—V6—Equipment Schedule 4							
W.B. 107.1", 107.2" (Wag); 3.0 Liter.							
ES Luxury Sedan 4D	P47H	28370	975	1350	3050	5325
LS Luxury Sedan 4D	P57J	35720	1525	2025	3850	6275
Wagon 4D	P49H	28720	825	1175	2800	5025
Traction Control			150	150	200	200

1996 MITSUBISHI — (Jor4)A3A(A26A)–T–#

Body	Type	VIN	List	Trade-In Fair	Trade-In Good	Pvt-Party Good	Retail Excellent
MIRAGE—4-Cyl.—Equipment Schedule 6							
W.B. 96.1", 98.4" (Sed); 1.5 Liter, 1.8 Liter.							
S Sedan 4D	A26A	14834	775	1100	2350	4125
S Coupe 2D	A11A	12422	575	825	1900	3475
LS Coupe 2D	A31C	14924	750	1075	2325	4125

Body	Type	VIN	List	Trade-In Fair	Good	Pvt-Party Good	Retail Excellent

ECLIPSE—4-Cyl.—Equipment Schedule 4
W.B. 98.8"; 2.0 Liter, 2.4 Liter.

Body	Type	VIN	List	Fair	Good	Good	Excellent
Coupe 2D		K34Y	15135	1300	1800	3300	5300
RS Coupe 2D		K34Y	16281	1625	2125	3650	5750
GS Coupe 2D		K44Y	19310	2125	2725	4325	6525
GS Spyder Conv 2+2		X35G	21227	2825	3475	5175	7525
Auto Trans				200	200	265	265

ECLIPSE—4-Cyl. Turbo—Equipment Schedule 4
W.B. 98.8"; 2.0 Liter.

GS-T Coupe 2D		K54F	21360	2375	2950	4600	6875
GS-T Spyder Conv 2+2		X55F	25410	3525	4225	6050	8525
GSX Coupe 2D		L54F	24330	2975	3650	5325	7700
Auto Trans				200	200	265	265

GALANT—4-Cyl.—Equipment Schedule 4
W.B. 103.7"; 2.4 Liter.

S Sedan 4D		J46G	18535	850	1225	2825	4975
ES Sedan 4D		J56G	20210	1050	1475	3150	5350
LS Sedan 4D		J56G	23280	1325	1825	3550	5850
Manual Trans				(375)	(375)	(500)	(500)

3000GT—V6—Equipment Schedule 4
W.B. 97.2"; 3.0 Liter.

Coupe 2D		M84J	31110	3875	4625	7050	10300
SL Coupe 2D		M54J	36250	4675	5525	8075	11500
SL Spyder Conv 2D		V65J	58600	9850	11250	14500	19000
Auto Trans				200	200	265	265

3000GT—V6 Turbo—Equipment Schedule 4
W.B. 97.2"; 3.0 Liter.

VR-4 Coupe 2D		N74K	46878	7700	8850	11800	15850
VR-4 Spyder Conv 2D		W75K	65740	12075	13675	17200	22200

DIAMANTE—V6—Equipment Schedule 4
W.B. 107.1"; 3.0 Liter.

ES Luxury Sedan 4D		P47H	27540	1200	1650	3550	5900

1997 MITSUBISHI—(J,4or6)(A3orMM)A(Y26A)-V-#

MIRAGE—4-Cyl.—Equipment Schedule 6
W.B. 95.1", 98.4" (Sed); 1.5 Liter, 1.8 Liter.

DE Sedan 4D		Y26A	13390	1200	1650	2800	4425
DE Coupe 2D		Y11A	11962	975	1350	2450	4000
LS Sedan 4D		Y36C	14907	1225	1675	2825	4450
LS Coupe 2D		Y31C	14547	1200	1650	2825	4450

ECLIPSE—4-Cyl.—Equipment Schedule 4
W.B. 98.8"; 2.0 Liter, 2.4 Liter.

Coupe 2D		K24Y	15821	1675	2175	3800	6000
RS Coupe 2D		K34Y	18219	2000	2550	4200	6450
GS Coupe 2D		K44Y	20623	2575	3200	4925	7300
GS Spyder Conv 2D		X35G	22411	3325	4000	5825	8350
Auto Trans				200	200	265	265

ECLIPSE—4-Cyl. Turbo—Equipment Schedule 4
W.B. 98.8"; 2.0 Liter.

GS-T Coupe 2D		K54F	22440	2825	3475	5250	7675
GS-T Spyder Conv 2D		X55F	26800	4050	4825	6775	9425
GSX Coupe 2D		L54F	24490	3475	4200	6025	8550
Auto Trans				200	200	265	265

GALANT—4-Cyl.—Equipment Schedule 4
W.B. 103.7"; 2.4 Liter.

DE Sedan 4D		J46G	17964	975	1350	2925	5050
ES Sedan 4D		J56G	18535	1200	1650	3275	5450
LS Sedan 4D		J56G	24400	1525	2025	3700	5975
Manual Trans				(400)	(400)	(535)	(535)

3000GT—V6—Equipment Schedule 4
W.B. 97.2"; 3.0 Liter.

Coupe 2D		M44H	28400	4550	5375	7975	11450
SL Coupe 2D		M84J	34460	5450	6375	9100	12750
Auto Trans				200	200	265	265

3000GT—V6 Turbo—Equipment Schedule 2
W.B. 97.2"; 3.0 Liter.

VR-4 Coupe 2D		N74K	45060	8725	10000	13100	17400

DIAMANTE—V6—Equipment Schedule 4
W.B. 107.1"; 3.5 Liter.

ES Luxury Sedan 4D		P37P	26370	2250	2825	4150	6050
LS Luxury Sedan 4D		P47P	30460	3000	3650	5075	7125

1998 MITSUBISHI

Body	Type	VIN	List	Trade-In Fair	Good	Pvt-Party Good	Retail Excellent

1998 MITSUBISHI–(J,4or6)(A3orMM)A(Y26A)–W–#

MIRAGE—4-Cyl.—Equipment Schedule 6
W.B. 95.1", 98.4" (Sed); 1.5 Liter, 1.8 Liter.

DE Sedan 4D	Y26A	13660	1475	1975	3150	4825
DE Coupe 2D	Y11A	12130	1200	1650	2825	4450
LS Sedan 4D	Y36C	15320	1525	2025	3250	4950
LS Coupe 2D	Y31C	14750	1525	2025	3225	4925

ECLIPSE—4-Cyl.—Equipment Schedule 4
W.B. 98.8"; 2.0 Liter, 2.4 Liter.

RS Coupe 2D	K24Y	17775	2450	3050	4875	7325
GS Coupe 2D	K44Y	20171	3100	3750	5675	8250
GS Spyder Conv 2D	X35G	22311	3875	4625	6600	9300
Auto Trans			200	200	265	265

ECLIPSE—4-Cyl. Turbo—Equipment Schedule 4
W.B. 98.8"; 2.0 Liter.

GS-T Coupe 2D	K54F	22380	3375	4075	6000	8600
GS-T Spyder Conv 2D	X55F	27080	4675	5525	7600	10500
GSX Coupe 2D	L54F	25740	4050	4800	6800	9525
Auto Trans			200	200	265	265

GALANT—4-Cyl.—Equipment Schedule 4
W.B. 103.7"; 2.4 Liter.

DE Sedan 4D	J46G	18222	1250	1750	3500	5825
ES Sedan 4D	J56G	18870	1575	2075	3875	6250
LS Sedan 4D	J56G	25730	1950	2475	4325	6775
Manual Trans			(425)	(425)	(565)	(565)

3000GT—V6—Equipment Schedule 4
W.B. 97.2"; 3.0 Liter.

Coupe 2D	M44H	28240	5325	6225	8975	12650
SL Coupe 2D	M84J	35660	6300	7325	10200	14100
Auto Trans			200	200	265	265

3000GT—V6 Turbo—Equipment Schedule 2
W.B. 97.2"; 3.0 Liter.

VR-4 Coupe 2D	N74K	46700	9850	11250	14500	19000

DIAMANTE—V6—Equipment Schedule 4
W.B. 107.1"; 3.5 Liter.

ES Luxury Sedan 4D	P37P	28120	2875	3550	4950	6950
LS Luxury Sedan 4D	P47P	33520	3675	4425	5925	8100

1999 MITSUBISHI — (J,4or6)(A3orMM)A(Y26A)–X–

MIRAGE—4-Cyl.—Equipment Schedule 6
W.B. 95.1", 98.4" (Sed); 1.5 Liter, 1.8 Liter.

DE Sedan 4D	Y26A	14405	1775	2300	3575	5325
DE Coupe 2D	Y11A	12455	1475	1975	3200	4925
LS Sedan 4D	Y36C	15432	1900	2425	3700	5500
LS Coupe 2D	Y31C	15025	1850	2375	3650	5450

ECLIPSE—4-Cyl.—Equipment Schedule 4
W.B. 98.8"; 2.0 Liter, 2.4 Liter.

RS Coupe 2D	K34Y	18474	2925	3600	5500	8100
GS Coupe 2D	K44Y	20214	3650	4375	6350	9075
GS Spyder Conv 2D	X35G	22836	4475	5275	7350	10200
Auto Trans			200	200	265	265

ECLIPSE—4-Cyl. Turbo—Equipment Schedule 4
W.B. 98.8"; 2.0 Liter.

GS-T Coupe 2D	K54F	23645	3925	4675	6700	9450
GS-T Spyder Conv 2D	X55F	27395	5375	6275	8425	11400
GSX Coupe 2D	L54F	26985	4650	5475	7550	10450
Auto Trans			200	200	265	265

GALANT—4-Cyl.—Equipment Schedule 4
W.B. 103.7"; 2.4 Liter.

DE Sedan 4D	A36G	17425	2550	3150	4700	6350
ES Sedan 4D	A46G	18425	2850	3525	4875	6825
V6 3.0 Liter	L		525	525	700	700

GALANT—V6—Equipment Schedule 4
W.B. 103.7"; 3.0 Liter.

LS Sedan 4D	A56L	24685	4450	5250	6775	8975
GTZ Sedan 4D	A46L	24785	4325	5125	6800	9200

3000GT—V6—Equipment Schedule 4
W.B. 97.2"; 3.0 Liter.

Coupe 2D	M44H	25920	5400	6300	9075	12800
SL Coupe 2D	M84J	33870	7275	8375	11350	15350
Auto Trans			200	200	265	265

Body	Type	VIN	List	Trade-In Fair	Trade-In Good	Pvt-Party Good	Retail Excellent

3000GT—V6 Turbo—Equipment Schedule 2
W.B. 97.2"; 3.0 Liter.

	Type	VIN	List	Fair	Good	Good	Excellent
VR-4 Coupe 2D		N74K	45070	11100	12600	15900	20600

DIAMANTE—V6—Equipment Schedule 4
W.B. 107.1"; 3.5 Liter.

	Type	VIN	List	Fair	Good	Good	Excellent
Luxury Sedan 4D		P37P	27669	3600	4300	5800	7925
Traction Control				250	250	335	335

2000 MITSUBISHI — (J,4or6)(A3orMM)A(Y26A)-Y-

MIRAGE—4-Cyl.—Equipment Schedule 6
W.B. 95.1", 98.4" (Sed); 1.5 Liter, 1.8 Liter.

	Type	VIN	List	Fair	Good	Good	Excellent
DE Sedan 4D		Y26A	14412	2125	2700	4025	5900
DE Coupe 2D		Y11A	13062	1775	2300	3600	5400
LS Sedan 4D		Y36C	17372	2250	2825	4175	6075
LS Coupe 2D		Y31C	15032	2200	2800	4125	6025

ECLIPSE—4-Cyl.—Equipment Schedule 4
W.B. 100.8"; 2.4 Liter.

	Type	VIN	List	Fair	Good	Good	Excellent
RS Coupe 2D		C34G	18932	3875	4625	5950	7900
GS Coupe 2D		C44G	20482	4675	5525	6900	9000
Auto Trans				225	225	300	300

ECLIPSE—V6—Equipment Schedule 4
W.B. 100.8"; 3.0 Liter.

	Type	VIN	List	Fair	Good	Good	Excellent
GT Coupe 2D		C84L	21622	5300	6200	7775	10150
Traction Control				275	275	365	365
Auto Trans				225	225	300	300

GALANT—4-Cyl.—Equipment Schedule 4
W.B. 103.7"; 2.4 Liter.

	Type	VIN	List	Fair	Good	Good	Excellent
DE Sedan 4D		A36G	17792	3000	3650	5025	7000
ES Sedan 4D		A46G	18692	3375	4075	5475	7525
V6 3.0 Liter		L		600	600	800	800

GALANT—V6—Equipment Schedule 4
W.B. 103.7"; 3.0 Liter.

	Type	VIN	List	Fair	Good	Good	Excellent
LS Sedan 4D		A56L	24092	5200	6075	7650	9950
GTZ Sedan 4D		A46L	24192	5025	5900	7650	10200

DIAMANTE—V6—Equipment Schedule 4
W.B. 107.1"; 3.5 Liter.

	Type	VIN	List	Fair	Good	Good	Excellent
ES Sedan 4D		P57P	25467	4175	4950	6475	8675
LS Sedan 4D		P67P	28367	5150	6050	7650	10000

2001 MITSUBISHI-(J,4or6)(A3orMM)A(Y11A)-1-#

MIRAGE—4-Cyl.—Equipment Schedule 6
W.B. 95.1", 98.4" (Sed); 1.5 Liter, 1.8 Liter.

	Type	VIN	List	Fair	Good	Good	Excellent
DE Coupe 2D		Y11A	13277	2125	2700	4075	6000
ES Sedan 4D		Y26C	14147	2550	3150	4550	6550
LS Sedan 4D		Y36C	14997	2675	3275	4700	6725
LS Coupe 2D		Y31C	15237	2625	3250	4650	6675

ECLIPSE—4-Cyl.—Equipment Schedule 4
W.B. 100.8"; 2.4 Liter.

	Type	VIN	List	Fair	Good	Good	Excellent
RS Coupe 2D		C31G	18507	4525	5350	6775	8875
GS Coupe 2D		C41G	19317	5450	6375	7850	10100
GS Spyder Conv 2D		E35G	23927	6250	7250	8975	11550
Auto Trans				250	250	335	335

ECLIPSE—V6—Equipment Schedule 4
W.B. 100.8"; 3.0 Liter.

	Type	VIN	List	Fair	Good	Good	Excellent
GT Coupe 2D		C81H	21467	6125	7100	8800	11300
GT Spyder Conv 2D		E55H	25927	7725	8875	10650	13450
Auto Trans				250	250	335	335
Traction Control				300	300	400	400

GALANT—4-Cyl.—Equipment Schedule 4
W.B. 103.7"; 2.4 Liter.

	Type	VIN	List	Fair	Good	Good	Excellent
DE Sedan 4D		A36G	18077	3550	4250	5725	7825
ES Sedan 4D		A46G	18927	3950	4700	6200	8400
V6 3.0 Liter		H		675	675	900	900

GALANT—V6—Equipment Schedule 4
W.B. 103.7"; 3.0 Liter.

	Type	VIN	List	Fair	Good	Good	Excellent
LS Sedan 4D		A56H	24427	6000	6950	8625	11100
GTZ Sedan 4D		A46H	24527	5825	6775	8625	11350

DIAMANTE—V6—Equipment Schedule 4
W.B. 107.1"; 3.5 Liter.

	Type	VIN	List	Fair	Good	Good	Excellent
ES Sedan 4D		P57P	25907	4875	5725	7350	9700
LS Sedan 4D		P67P	26907	6000	6950	8625	11150

Body	Type	VIN	List	Trade-In Fair	Trade-In Good	Pvt-Party Good	Retail Excellent

2002 MITSUBISHI–(J,4or6)(A3orMM)A(Y11A)–2–#

MIRAGE—4-Cyl.—Equipment Schedule 6
W.B. 95.1"; 1.5 Liter, 1.8 Liter.

Body	Type	VIN	List	Fair	Good	Good	Excellent
DE Coupe 2D		Y11A	13362	2575	3175	4650	6725
LS Coupe 2D		Y31C	15332	3125	3775	5300	7450

LANCER—4-Cyl.—Equipment Schedule 6
W.B. 102.4"; 2.0 Liter.

ES Sedan 4D		J26E	15242	4375	5150	6525	8550
LS Sedan 4D		J36E	16442	4600	5425	6825	8875
OZ Rally Sedan 4D		J86E	16832	5275	6175	7575	9675

ECLIPSE—4-Cyl.—Equipment Schedule 4
W.B. 100.8"; 2.4 Liter.

RS Coupe 2D		C31G	18642	5325	6225	7775	10100
GS Coupe 2D		C41G	19512	6350	7375	8975	11400
GS Spyder Conv 2D		E35G	24172	7225	8350	10200	12950
Auto Trans				275	275	365	365

ECLIPSE—V6—Equipment Schedule 4
W.B. 100.8"; 3.0 Liter.

GT Coupe 2D		C81G	21702	7050	8150	10000	12700
GT Spyder Conv 2D		E55H	26152	8900	10175	12100	15050
Auto Trans				275	275	365	365
Traction Control				325	325	435	435

GALANT—4-Cyl.—Equipment Schedule 4
W.B. 103.7"; 2.4 Liter.

DE Sedan 4D		A36G	18262	4225	5000	6575	8850
ES Sedan 4D		A46G	19072	4650	5500	7100	9450
LS Sedan 4D		A46G	21672	5300	6200	7850	10300
V6 3.0 Liter		L		750	750	1000	1000

GALANT—V6—Equipment Schedule 4
W.B. 103.7"; 3.0 Liter.

| GTZ Sedan 4D | | A46H | 24712 | 6750 | 7775 | 9800 | 12700 |

DIAMANTE—V6—Equipment Schedule 4
W.B. 107.1"; 3.5 Liter.

ES Sedan 4D		P57P	26247	5775	6725	8500	11050
VR-X Sedan 4D		P67P	27557	6400	7425	9200	11850
LS Sedan 4D		P67P	29007	7000	8075	9900	12650

2003 MITSUBISHI — (J,4or6)(A3orMM)A(J26E)–3–#

LANCER—4-Cyl.—Equipment Schedule 6
W.B. 102.4"; 2.0 Liter.

ES Sedan 4D		J26E	14587	5175	6050	7450	9550
LS Sedan 4D		J36E	16617	5425	6350	7750	9900
OZ Rally Sedan 4D		J86E	16317	6175	7175	8575	10750

LANCER AWD—4-Cyl. Turbo—Equipment Schedule 4
W.B. 103.1"; 2.0 Liter.

| Evolution Sedan 4D | | H86F | 29582 | 15675 | 17650 | 20800 | 25500 |

ECLIPSE—4-Cyl.—Equipment Schedule 4
W.B. 100.8"; 2.4 Liter.

RS Coupe 2D		C34G	18717	6275	7275	8975	11500
GS Coupe 2D		C44G	19617	7400	8500	10300	12950
GS Spyder Conv 2D		E45G	24397	8375	9575	11600	14600
Auto Trans				300	300	400	400

ECLIPSE—V6—Equipment Schedule 4
W.B. 100.8"; 3.0 Liter.

GT Coupe 2D		C84H	21807	8150	9325	11350	14300
GT Spyder Conv 2D		E85H	26477	10175	11600	13700	16850
GTS Coupe 2D		C74H	24777	9550	10925	13200	16600
GTS Spyder Conv 2D		E75H	28847	10775	12275	14450	17850
Auto Trans				300	300	400	400
Traction Control				350	350	465	465

GALANT—4-Cyl.—Equipment Schedule 4
W.B. 103.7"; 2.4 Liter.

DE Sedan 4D		A36G	18347	5000	5875	7600	10100
ES Sedan 4D		A46G	19157	5500	6425	8175	10700
LS Sedan 4D		A46G	21757	6200	7200	8975	11600
V6 3.0 Liter		H		825	825	1100	1100

GALANT—V6—Equipment Schedule 4
W.B. 103.7"; 3.0 Liter.

| GTZ Sedan 4D | | A46H | 25047 | 7775 | 8925 | 11100 | 14250 |

DIAMANTE—V6—Equipment Schedule 4
W.B. 107.1"; 3.5 Liter.

| ES Sedan 4D | | P57P | 26557 | 6875 | 7925 | 9850 | 12700 |

2003 MITSUBISHI

Body	Type	VIN	List	Trade-In Fair	Trade-In Good	Pvt-Party Good	Retail Excellent
VR-X Sedan 4D		P87P	27677	7575	8700	10650	13600
LS Sedan 4D		P67P	29027	8225	9425	11450	14450

2004 MITSUBISHI — (J,4or6)(A3orMM)A(J26E)-4-#

LANCER—4-Cyl.—Equipment Schedule 6
W.B. 102.4"; 2.0 Liter, 2.4 Liter.

Body	Type	VIN	List	Fair	Good	Good	Excellent
ES Sedan 4D		J26E	14172	6100	7075	8375	10450
LS Sedan 4D		J36E	16572	6400	7425	8700	10800
LS Wagon 4D		D29F	17172	6700	7725	9075	11200
OZ Rally Sedan 4D		J86E	16372	7200	8325	9600	11750
Ralliart Sedan 4D		J66F	18572	8325	9525	10900	13250
Ralliart Wagon 4D		D69F	19772	9025	10325	11800	14200

LANCER AWD—4-Cyl. Turbo—Equipment Schedule 6
W.B. 102.4"; 2.0 Liter.

Body	Type	VIN	List	Fair	Good	Good	Excellent
Evolution RS Sedan 4D		H36D	27374	16000	18000	21100	25800
Evolution Sedan 4D		H86D	30574	17450	19600	22800	27700

ECLIPSE—4-Cyl.—Equipment Schedule 4
W.B. 100.8"; 2.4 Liter.

Body	Type	VIN	List	Fair	Good	Good	Excellent
RS Coupe 2D		C34G	18892	7375	8500	10300	13000
GS Coupe 2D		C44G	19892	8600	9850	11750	14600
GS Spyder Conv 2D		E45G	24892	9650	11000	13150	16350
Auto Trans				300	300	400	400

ECLIPSE—V6—Equipment Schedule 4
W.B. 100.8"; 3.0 Liter.

Body	Type	VIN	List	Fair	Good	Good	Excellent
GT Coupe 2D		C84H	22092	9350	10675	12750	15950
GT Spyder Conv 2D		E85H	26992	11600	13200	15350	18800
GTS Coupe 2D		C74H	25092	11000	12475	14900	18550
GTS Spyder Conv 2D		E75H	29372	12275	13925	16250	19900
Auto Trans				300	300	400	400

GALANT—4-Cyl.—Equipment Schedule 4
W.B. 108.3"; 2.4 Liter.

Body	Type	VIN	List	Fair	Good	Good	Excellent
DE Sedan 4D		A36G	18592	8400	9625	11500	14350
ES Sedan 4D		A46G	19592	8950	10225	12150	15050
V6 3.8 Liter		S		900	900	1200	1200

GALANT—V6—Equipment Schedule 4
W.B. 108.3"; 3.8 Liter.

Body	Type	VIN	List	Fair	Good	Good	Excellent
LS Sedan 4D		A46H	21592	11300	12850	14900	18100
GTS Sedan 4D		A46H	26292	11450	13000	15350	18900

DIAMANTE—Equipment Schedule 4
W.B. 107.1"; 3.5 Liter.

Body	Type	VIN	List	Fair	Good	Good	Excellent
ES Sedan 4D		P57P	25594	8200	9375	11400	14450
VR-X Sedan 4D		P87P	27414	8950	10225	12300	15400
LS Sedan 4D		P67P	28214	9700	11050	13200	16400

2005 MITSUBISHI — (J,4or6)(A3orMM)A(J26E)-5-#

LANCER—4-Cyl.—Equipment Schedule 6
W.B. 102.4"; 2.0 Liter, 2.4 Liter.

Body	Type	VIN	List	Fair	Good	Good	Excellent
ES Sedan 4D		J26E	14574	7225	8350	9600	11700
OZ Rally Sedan 4D		J86E	16974	8450	9675	10950	13150
Ralliart Sedan 4D		J66F	18774	9600	10950	12350	14800

LANCER AWD—4-Cyl. Turbo—Equipment Schedule 6
W.B. 102.4"; 2.0 Liter.

Body	Type	VIN	List	Fair	Good	Good	Excellent
Evolution RS Sedan 4D		H36D	28774	17275	19400	22600	27500
Evolution VIII Sedan		H76D	31074	18875	21150	24400	29500
Evolution MR Ed Sed		H86D	35574	20475	22900	26200	31400

ECLIPSE—4-Cyl.—Equipment Schedule 4
W.B. 100.8"; 2.4 Liter.

Body	Type	VIN	List	Fair	Good	Good	Excellent
GS Coupe 2D		C44G	20044	9525	10875	12700	15900
GS Spyder Conv 2D		E45G	25494	10675	12125	14200	17500
Auto Trans				300	300	400	400

ECLIPSE—V6—Equipment Schedule 4
W.B. 100.8"; 3.0 Liter.

Body	Type	VIN	List	Fair	Good	Good	Excellent
GT Coupe 2D		C84H	23494	10325	11725	13800	17050
GT Spyder Conv 2D		E55H	27694	12750	14450	16750	20300
GTS Coupe 2D		C74H	25244	12075	13675	16200	20000
GTS Spyder Conv 2D		E75H	30094	13475	15225	17650	21400
Auto Trans				300	300	400	400

GALANT—4-Cyl.—Equipment Schedule 4
W.B. 108.3"; 2.4 Liter.

Body	Type	VIN	List	Fair	Good	Good	Excellent
DE Sedan 4D		B26F	19294	9300	10625	12500	15450
ES Sedan 4D		B46F	20194	9900	11300	13200	16200

GALANT—V6—Equipment Schedule 4
W.B. 108.3"; 3.8 Liter.

Body	Type	VIN	List	Trade-In Fair	Trade-In Good	Pvt-Party Good	Retail Excellent
LS Sedan 4D		B46S	22894	12475	14125	16250	19600
GTS Sedan 4D		B76S	26894	12600	14250	16750	20500

NISSAN

1991 NISSAN — (1N4orJN1)(EB32A)–M–#

SENTRA—4-Cyl.—Equipment Schedule 6
W.B. 95.7"; 1.6 Liter, 2.0 Liter.

Body	Type	VIN	List	Fair	Good	Good	Excellent
E Sedan 2D		EB32A	9099	275	400	1100	2150
E Sedan 4D		EB31B	10000	275	400	1100	2150
XE Sedan 2D		EB32A	10370	350	475	1225	2375
XE Sedan 4D		EB31B	10035	350	475	1225	2375
SE Sedan 2D		EB32A	10855	350	475	1225	2325
SE-R Sedan 2D		GB32A	11245	525	750	1625	2950
GXE Sedan 4D		EB31B	12325	450	650	1475	2725

STANZA—4-Cyl.—Equipment Schedule 5
W.B. 100.4"; 2.4 Liter.

| XE Sedan 4D | | FU21P | 13900 | 450 | 650 | 1475 | 2725 |
| GXE Sedan 4D | | FU21P | 16300 | 525 | 750 | 1600 | 2925 |

NX—4-Cyl.—Equipment Schedule 6
W.B. 95.7"; 1.6 Liter, 2.0 Liter.

| 1600 Hatchback Cpe 2D | | EB34C | 12240 | 775 | 1100 | 1825 | 3000 |
| 2000 Hatchback Cpe 2D | | GB34C | 14120 | 925 | 1300 | 2150 | 3450 |

240SX—4-Cyl.—Equipment Schedule 5
W.B. 97.4"; 2.4 Liter.

Coupe 2D		MS34P	15539	750	1050	2025	3525
Fastback 2D		MS36P	15789	750	1075	2075	3575
SE Coupe 2D		MS34P	17579	750	1075	2075	3575
SE Fastback 2D		MS36P	17764	775	1100	2100	3625
LE Fastback 2D		MS36P	18664	750	1075	2075	3575

MAXIMA—V6—Equipment Schedule 4
W.B. 104.3"; 3.0 Liter.

GXE Sedan 4D		HJ01P	18974	700	1025	2325	4175
SE Sedan 4D		HJ01P	20994	700	1025	2325	4175
Manual Trans				(175)	(175)	(235)	(235)

300ZX—V6—Equipment Schedule 3
W.B. 96.5", 101.2" (2+2); 3.0 Liter.

| Coupe 2D | | RZ24A | 30175 | 2275 | 2850 | 4775 | 7350 |
| 2+2 Coupe 2D | | RZ26A | 31375 | 2475 | 3075 | 5025 | 7650 |

300ZX—V6 Turbo—Equipment Schedule 3
W.B. 96.5"; 3.0 Liter.

| Coupe 2D | | CZ24A | 34575 | 3125 | 3775 | 5875 | 8650 |

1992 NISSAN — (1N4orJN1)(EB32A)–N–#

SENTRA—4-Cyl.—Equipment Schedule 6
W.B. 95.7"; 1.6 Liter, 2.0 Liter.

E Sedan 2D		EB32A	9645	350	475	1275	2500
E Sedan 4D		EB31B	10700	350	475	1275	2500
XE Sedan 2D		EB32A	11175	400	600	1425	2725
XE Sedan 4D		EB31B	11860	400	600	1425	2725
SE Sedan 2D		EB32A	12155	400	575	1400	2675
SE-R Sedan 2D		GB32A	13445	625	900	1900	3400
GXE Sedan 4D		EB31B	13250	550	775	1700	3100

STANZA—4-Cyl.—Equipment Schedule 5
W.B. 100.4"; 2.4 Liter.

XE Sedan 4D		FU21P	14000	525	750	1675	3100
GXE Sedan 4D		FU21P	17370	600	850	1850	3350
SE Sedan 4D		FU21P	17825	675	950	2025	3575

NX—4-Cyl.—Equipment Schedule 6
W.B. 95.7"; 1.6 Liter, 2.0 Liter.

| 1600 H'Back Cpe 2D | | EB34C | 12900 | 875 | 1225 | 2050 | 3350 |
| 2000 H'Back Cpe 2D | | GB34C | 14630 | 1025 | 1450 | 2475 | 3975 |

240SX—4-Cyl.—Equipment Schedule 5
W.B. 97.4"; 2.4 Liter.

Coupe 2D		MS34P	16495	875	1225	2450	4175
Fastback 2D		MS36P	16765	900	1250	2475	4200
SE Coupe 2D		MS34P	18665	900	1250	2475	4200
SE Fastback 2D		MS36P	18865	900	1275	2500	4225
SE Convertible 2D		MS36A	22295	1400	1900	3300	5200
LE Fastback 2D		MS36P	19025	900	1250	2475	4200

Body	Type	VIN	List	Trade-In Fair	Trade-In Good	Pvt-Party Good	Retail Excellent
MAXIMA—V6—Equipment Schedule 4							
W.B. 104.3"; 3.0 Liter.							
GXE Sedan 4D		HJ01P	19995	825	1175	2575	4500
SE Sedan 4D		EJ01P	22050	850	1200	2625	4575
Manual Trans				(175)	(175)	(235)	(235)
300ZX—V6—Equipment Schedule 3							
W.B. 96.5", 101.2" (2+2); 3.0 Liter.							
Coupe 2D		RZ24H	31490	2725	3325	5400	8150
2+2 Coupe 2D		RZ26H	32740	2900	3575	5675	8500
300ZX—V6 Turbo—Equipment Schedule 3							
W.B. 96.5"; 3.0 Liter.							
Coupe 2D		CZ24H	36190	3650	4375	6625	9625

1993 NISSAN — (1N4orJN1)(EB32A)-P-#

Body	Type	VIN	List	Trade-In Fair	Trade-In Good	Pvt-Party Good	Retail Excellent
SENTRA—4-Cyl.—Equipment Schedule 6							
W.B. 95.7"; 1.6 Liter, 2.0 Liter.							
E Sedan 2D		EB32A	10310	375	500	1400	2775
E Sedan 4D		EB31P	11760	400	525	1425	2800
XE Sedan 2D		EB32A	11850	450	625	1575	3000
XE Sedan 4D		EB31P	12540	450	625	1575	3000
SE Sedan 2D		EB32A	12845	425	625	1550	2950
SE-R Sedan 2D		GB32A	14400	675	975	2175	3900
GXE Sedan 4D		EB31C	14495	575	825	1875	3400
NX—4-Cyl.—Equipment Schedule 6							
W.B. 95.7"; 1.6 Liter, 2.0 Liter.							
1600 Coupe 2D		EB34C	13285	1000	1400	2450	3950
2000 Coupe 2D		GB36C	15920	1200	1650	2775	4350
240SX—4-Cyl.—Equipment Schedule 5							
W.B. 97.4"; 2.4 Liter.							
Coupe 2D		MS34P	16785	1000	1425	2775	4600
Fastback 2D		MS36P	17500	1050	1450	2825	4650
SE Coupe 2D		MS34P	19245	1050	1450	2825	4650
SE Fastback 2D		MS36P	19705	1050	1475	2825	4675
SE Convertible 2D		MS36A	23545	1725	2250	3750	5800
ALTIMA—4-Cyl.—Equipment Schedule 6							
W.B. 103.1"; 2.4 Liter.							
XE Sedan 4D		BU31F	16229	525	750	1850	3450
GXE Sedan 4D		BU31F	16199	550	800	1875	3475
SE Sedan 4D		BU31F	17699	650	925	2175	3975
GLE Sedan 4D		BU31F	18699	875	1225	2575	4450
Manual Trans				(225)	(225)	(300)	(300)
MAXIMA—V6—Equipment Schedule 4							
W.B. 104.3"; 3.0 Liter.							
GXE Sedan 4D		HJ01F	23525	950	1325	2850	4900
SE Sedan 4D		EJ01F	23310	1000	1425	2975	5075
Manual Trans				(225)	(225)	(300)	(300)
300ZX—V6—Equipment Schedule 3							
W.B. 96.5", 101.2" (2+2); 3.0 Liter.							
Coupe 2D		RZ24H	30445	3200	3875	6100	9100
2+2 Coupe 2D		RZ26H	33875	3475	4175	6450	9500
Convertible 2D		RZ27H	36920	4225	5025	7425	10650
300ZX—V6 Turbo—Equipment Schedule 3							
W.B. 96.5"; 3.0 Liter.							
Coupe 2D		CZ24H	37440	4300	5100	7525	10750

1994 NISSAN — (1N4orJN1)(EB32A)-R-#

Body	Type	VIN	List	Trade-In Fair	Trade-In Good	Pvt-Party Good	Retail Excellent
SENTRA—4-Cyl.—Equipment Schedule 6							
W.B. 95.7"; 1.6 Liter, 2.0 Liter.							
E Sedan 2D		EB32A	11924	400	575	1575	3100
E Sedan 4D		EB31P	12474	425	625	1650	3175
XE Sedan 2D		EB32A	12479	475	700	1775	3350
XE Sedan 4D		EB31P	12679	500	725	1800	3400
Limited Ed Sedan 2D		EB32A	13029	575	825	1975	3625
Limited Ed Sedan 4D		EB31P	13249	600	875	2100	3900
SE Sedan 2D		EB32A	13974	475	700	1775	3350
SE-R Sedan 2D		GB32A	15174	750	1075	2375	4200
GXE Sedan 4D		EB31C	15049	625	900	2150	3950
240SX—4-Cyl.—Equipment Schedule 5							
W.B. 97.4"; 2.4 Liter.							
SE Convertible 2D		MS36A	25344	2075	2650	4250	6450
ALTIMA—4-Cyl.—Equipment Schedule 6							
W.B. 103.1"; 2.4 Liter.							
XE Sedan 4D		BU31F	16904	625	900	2200	4075

1994 NISSAN

Body	Type	VIN	List	Trade-In Fair	Good	Pvt-Party Good	Retail Excellent
GXE Sedan 4D		BU31F	17264	**675**	**975**	**2250**	**4100**
SE Sedan 4D		BU31F	19384	**775**	**1100**	**2475**	**4425**
GLE Sedan 4D		BU31F	19559	**1000**	**1425**	**2875**	**4900**
Manual Trans				**(275)**	**(275)**	**(365)**	**(365)**
MAXIMA—V6—Equipment Schedule 4							
W.B. 104.3"; 3.0 Liter.							
GXE Sedan 4D		HJ01F	22579	**1125**	**1575**	**3250**	**5450**
SE Sedan 4D		EJ01F	24614	**1225**	**1700**	**3425**	**5675**
Manual Trans				**(275)**	**(275)**	**(365)**	**(365)**
300ZX—V6—Equipment Schedule 3							
W.B. 96.5", 101.2" (2+2); 3.0 Liter.							
Coupe 2D		RZ24D	34079	**3750**	**4475**	**6875**	**10100**
2+2 Coupe 2D		RZ26D	36869	**4050**	**4800**	**7275**	**10550**
Convertible 2D		RZ27D	41259	**4900**	**5750**	**8350**	**11850**
300ZX—V6 Turbo—Equipment Schedule 3							
W.B. 96.5"; 3.0 Liter.							
Coupe 2D		CZ24D	40479	**4975**	**5850**	**8450**	**11950**

1995 NISSAN — (1N4orJN1)(AB41D)-S-#

Body	Type	VIN	List	Trade-In Fair	Good	Pvt-Party Good	Retail Excellent
SENTRA—4-Cyl.—Equipment Schedule 6							
W.B. 99.8"; 1.6 Liter.							
Sedan 4D		AB41D	11389	**900**	**1275**	**2500**	**4225**
XE Sedan 4D		AB41D	13139	**1000**	**1400**	**2650**	**4400**
GXE Sedan 4D		AB41D	13839	**1075**	**1500**	**2775**	**4525**
GLE Sedan 4D		AB41D	14839	**1300**	**1800**	**3125**	**4975**
200SX—4-Cyl.—Equipment Schedule 6							
W.B. 99.8"; 1.6 Liter, 2.0 Liter.							
Coupe 2D		AB42D	13874	**1000**	**1425**	**2675**	**4425**
SE Coupe 2D		AB42D	14674	**1075**	**1525**	**2825**	**4575**
SE-R Coupe 2D		BB42D	15674	**1275**	**1775**	**3100**	**4950**
240SX—4-Cyl.—Equipment Schedule 5							
W.B. 99.4"; 2.4 Liter.							
Coupe 2D		AS44D	19758	**1975**	**2500**	**4200**	**6450**
SE Coupe 2D		AS44D	22439	**2375**	**2950**	**4700**	**7075**
ALTIMA—4-Cyl.—Equipment Schedule 4							
W.B. 103.1"; 2.4 Liter.							
XE Sedan 4D		BU31D	17848	**750**	**1050**	**2525**	**4525**
GXE Sedan 4D		BU31D	18218	**825**	**1175**	**2625**	**4575**
SE Sedan 4D		BU31D	20089	**925**	**1300**	**2825**	**4950**
GLE Sedan 4D		BU31D	20279	**1200**	**1650**	**3275**	**5450**
Manual Trans				**(325)**	**(325)**	**(435)**	**(435)**
MAXIMA—V6—Equipment Schedule 4							
W.B. 106.3"; 3.0 Liter.							
GXE Sedan 4D		CA21D	21989	**1900**	**2425**	**4000**	**6150**
SE Sedan 4D		CA21D	22989	**2050**	**2625**	**4225**	**6425**
GLE Sedan 4D		CA21D	25209	**2600**	**3225**	**4900**	**7200**
Manual Trans				**(325)**	**(325)**	**(435)**	**(435)**
300ZX—V6—Equipment Schedule 3							
W.B. 96.5", 101.2" (2+2); 3.0 Liter.							
Coupe 2D		RZ24D	35399	**4375**	**5150**	**7725**	**11150**
2+2 Coupe 2D		RZ26D	38189	**4675**	**5525**	**8150**	**11650**
Convertible 2D		RZ27D	42579	**5625**	**6550**	**9300**	**13050**
300ZX—V6 Turbo—Equipment Schedule 3							
W.B. 96.5"; 3.0 Liter.							
Coupe 2D		CZ24D	41799	**5700**	**6650**	**9425**	**13200**

1996 NISSAN — (1N4or3N1)(AB41D)-T-#

Body	Type	VIN	List	Trade-In Fair	Good	Pvt-Party Good	Retail Excellent
SENTRA—4-Cyl.—Equipment Schedule 6							
W.B. 99.8"; 1.6 Liter.							
Sedan 4D		AB41D	11904	**1100**	**1550**	**2825**	**4625**
XE Sedan 4D		AB41D	13934	**1225**	**1675**	**2975**	**4800**
GXE Sedan 4D		AB41D	14864	**1325**	**1825**	**3150**	**4975**
GLE Sedan 4D		AB41D	15634	**1625**	**2125**	**3525**	**5425**
200SX—4-Cyl.—Equipment Schedule 6							
W.B. 99.8"; 1.6 Liter, 2.0 Liter.							
Coupe 2D		AB42D	14303	**1225**	**1700**	**3000**	**4825**
SE Coupe 2D		AB42D	15274	**1350**	**1850**	**3175**	**5025**
SE-R Coupe 2D		BB42D	16474	**1600**	**2100**	**3500**	**5400**
240SX—4-Cyl.—Equipment Schedule 5							
W.B. 99.4"; 2.4 Liter.							
Coupe 2D		AS44D	20563	**2325**	**2900**	**4750**	**7225**
SE Coupe 2D		AS44D	23454	**2825**	**3450**	**5350**	**7925**

Body	Type	VIN	List	Trade-In Fair	Trade-In Good	Pvt-Party Good	Retail Excellent
ALTIMA—4-Cyl.—Equipment Schedule 4							
W.B. 103.1"; 2.4 Liter.							
XE Sedan 4D		BU31D	18783	**900**	**1250**	**2875**	**5100**
GXE Sedan 4D		BU31D	19533	**1000**	**1425**	**3000**	**5150**
SE Sedan 4D		BU31D	20534	**1100**	**1550**	**3275**	**5550**
GLE Sedan 4D		BU31D	21404	**1450**	**1950**	**3725**	**6075**
Manual Trans		------		**(375)**	**(375)**	**(500)**	**(500)**
MAXIMA—V6—Equipment Schedule 4							
W.B. 106.3"; 3.0 Liter.							
GXE Sedan 4D		CA21D	23084	**2325**	**2900**	**4575**	**6850**
SE Sedan 4D		CA21D	24084	**2550**	**3150**	**4850**	**7150**
GLE Sedan 4D		CA21D	26684	**3100**	**3750**	**5525**	**7950**
Manual Trans		------		**(375)**	**(375)**	**(500)**	**(500)**
300ZX—V6—Equipment Schedule 3							
W.B. 96.5", 101.2" (2+2); 3.0 Liter.							
Coupe 2D		RZ24D	37844	**5000**	**5875**	**8625**	**12300**
2+2 Coupe 2D		RZ26D	40594	**5350**	**6250**	**9050**	**12800**
Convertible 2D		RZ27D	45084	**6400**	**7425**	**10400**	**14350**
300ZX Turbo—V6—Equipment Schedule 3							
W.B. 96.5"; 3.0 Liter.							
Coupe 2D		CZ24D	44384	**6475**	**7500**	**10500**	**14500**

Body	Type	VIN	List	Trade-In Fair	Trade-In Good	Pvt-Party Good	Retail Excellent
SENTRA—4-Cyl.—Equipment Schedule 6							
W.B. 99.8"; 1.6 Liter.							
Sedan 4D		AB41D	11919	**1400**	**1900**	**3275**	**5175**
XE Sedan 4D		AB41D	14069	**1525**	**2025**	**3425**	**5325**
GXE Sedan 4D		AB41D	15219	**1675**	**2200**	**3625**	**5550**
GLE Sedan 4D		AB41D	16069	**2000**	**2550**	**4000**	**6025**
200SX—4-Cyl.—Equipment Schedule 6							
W.B. 99.8"; 1.6 Liter, 2.0 Liter.							
Coupe 2D		AB42D	14418	**1550**	**2050**	**3475**	**5375**
SE Coupe 2D		AB42D	15769	**1675**	**2200**	**3625**	**5550**
SE-R Coupe 2D		BB42D	17169	**1975**	**2525**	**3975**	**5975**
240SX—4-Cyl.—Equipment Schedule 5							
W.B. 99.4"; 2.4 Liter.							
Coupe 2D		AS44D	20628	**2750**	**3375**	**5375**	**8075**
SE Coupe 2D		AS44D	23269	**3300**	**3975**	**6075**	**8875**
LE Coupe 2D		AS44D	25719	**3325**	**4000**	**6075**	**8900**
ALTIMA—4-Cyl.—Equipment Schedule 4							
W.B. 103.1"; 2.4 Liter.							
XE Sedan 4D		BU31D	18798	**1075**	**1525**	**3350**	**5750**
GXE Sedan 4D		BU31D	19548	**1225**	**1725**	**3475**	**5800**
SE Sedan 4D		BU31D	20549	**1375**	**1900**	**3775**	**6250**
GLE Sedan 4D		BU31D	21419	**1775**	**2300**	**4250**	**6800**
Manual Trans		------		**(400)**	**(400)**	**(535)**	**(535)**
MAXIMA—V6—Equipment Schedule 4							
W.B. 106.3"; 3.0 Liter.							
GXE Sedan 4D		CA21D	23669	**2825**	**3475**	**5250**	**7675**
SE Sedan 4D		CA21D	24719	**3075**	**3725**	**5575**	**8075**
GLE Sedan 4D		CA21D	27319	**3650**	**4400**	**6275**	**8900**
Manual Trans		------		**(400)**	**(400)**	**(535)**	**(535)**

Body	Type	VIN	List	Trade-In Fair	Trade-In Good	Pvt-Party Good	Retail Excellent
SENTRA—4-Cyl.—Equipment Schedule 6							
W.B. 99.8"; 1.6 Liter, 2.0 Liter.							
Sedan 4D		AB41D	11989	**1800**	**2325**	**3775**	**5800**
XE Sedan 4D		AB41D	14189	**1925**	**2450**	**3925**	**5975**
GXE Sedan 4D		AB41D	15389	**2075**	**2650**	**4125**	**6175**
GLE Sedan 4D		AB41D	16239	**2425**	**3000**	**4525**	**6675**
SE Sedan 4D		AB41D	17239	**2575**	**3200**	**4750**	**6900**
200SX—4-Cyl.—Equipment Schedule 6							
W.B. 99.8"; 1.6 Liter, 2.0 Liter.							
Coupe 2D		AB42D	14638	**1950**	**2475**	**3950**	**6000**
SE Coupe 2D		AB42D	15889	**2050**	**2625**	**4100**	**6150**
SE-R Coupe 2D		BB42D	17239	**2375**	**2950**	**4475**	**6600**
240SX—4-Cyl.—Equipment Schedule 5							
W.B. 99.4"; 2.4 Liter.							
Coupe 2D		AS44D	20648	**3250**	**3925**	**6100**	**9050**
SE Coupe 2D		AS44D	23289	**3825**	**4575**	**6850**	**9900**
LE Coupe 2D		AS44D	25739	**3875**	**4625**	**6875**	**9950**
ALTIMA—4-Cyl.—Equipment Schedule 4							
W.B. 103.1"; 2.4 Liter.							

1998 NISSAN

Body	Type	VIN	List	Trade-In Fair	Trade-In Good	Pvt-Party Good	Retail Excellent
XE Sedan 4D		DL01D	18179	**1925**	**2450**	**4350**	**6875**
GXE Sedan 4D		DL01D	18480	**2125**	**2700**	**4475**	**6875**
SE Sedan 4D		DL01D	19780	**2275**	**2850**	**4800**	**7400**
GLE Sedan 4D		DL01D	20380	**2675**	**3275**	**5250**	**7925**
Manual Trans				**(425)**	**(425)**	**(565)**	**(565)**
MAXIMA—V6—Equipment Schedule 4							
W.B. 106.3"; 3.0 Liter.							
GXE Sedan 4D		CA21D	23739	**3475**	**4175**	**6075**	**8700**
SE Sedan 4D		CA21D	24989	**3750**	**4475**	**6450**	**9150**
GLE Sedan 4D		CA21D	27389	**4350**	**5125**	**7150**	**9950**
Manual Trans				**(425)**	**(425)**	**(565)**	**(565)**

1999 NISSAN — (1N4,JN1or3N1)(AB41D)-X-#

SENTRA—4-Cyl.—Equipment Schedule 6
W.B. 99.8"; 1.6 Liter, 2.0 Liter.

Body	Type	VIN	List	Fair	Good	Good	Excellent
XE Sedan 4D		AB41D	13319	**2325**	**2900**	**4375**	**6400**
GXE Sedan 4D		AB41D	14719	**2500**	**3100**	**4575**	**6650**
SE Sedan 4D		BB41D	15719	**3025**	**3700**	**5225**	**7375**
ALTIMA—4-Cyl.—Equipment Schedule 4							
W.B. 103.1"; 2.4 Liter.							
XE Sedan 4D		DL01D	18209	**2400**	**2975**	**4950**	**7550**
GXE Sedan 4D		DL01D	18510	**2625**	**3250**	**5100**	**7600**
SE Sedan 4D		DL01D	19810	**2825**	**3475**	**5450**	**8150**
GLE Sedan 4D		DL01D	20510	**3200**	**3875**	**5925**	**8650**
Manual Trans				**(450)**	**(450)**	**(600)**	**(600)**
MAXIMA—V6—Equipment Schedule 4							
W.B. 106.3"; 3.0 Liter.							
GXE Sedan 4D		CA21D	23769	**4125**	**4900**	**6875**	**9600**
SE Sedan 4D		CA21D	25019	**4475**	**5275**	**7300**	**10100**
GLE Sedan 4D		CA21D	27419	**5075**	**5950**	**7975**	**10850**
Manual Trans				**(450)**	**(450)**	**(600)**	**(600)**

2000 NISSAN — (1N4,JN1or3N1)(CB51D)-Y-#

SENTRA—4-Cyl.—Equipment Schedule 6
W.B. 99.8"; 1.8 Liter, 2.0 Liter.

Body	Type	VIN	List	Fair	Good	Good	Excellent
XE Sedan 4D		CB51D	12169	**2675**	**3275**	**4850**	**7025**
GXE Sedan 4D		CB51D	14019	**2825**	**3475**	**5075**	**7275**
CA Sedan 4D		DB51D	15319	**3175**	**3825**	**5450**	**7700**
SE Sedan 4D		BB51D	15419	**3425**	**4125**	**5750**	**8050**
ALTIMA—4-Cyl.—Equipment Schedule 4							
W.B. 103.1"; 2.4 Liter.							
XE Sedan 4D		DL01D	18459	**2875**	**3550**	**5875**	**8925**
GXE Sedan 4D		DL01D	18659	**3175**	**3825**	**6050**	**8975**
SE Sedan 4D		DL01D	19960	**3400**	**4100**	**6450**	**9575**
GLE Sedan 4D		DL01D	20910	**3825**	**4575**	**6975**	**10200**
Manual Trans				**(500)**	**(500)**	**(665)**	**(665)**
MAXIMA—V6—Equipment Schedule 4							
W.B. 108.3"; 3.0 Liter.							
GXE Sedan 4D		CA31A	23269	**5700**	**6625**	**8625**	**11500**
SE Sedan 4D		CA31A	24669	**6150**	**7150**	**9200**	**12150**
GLE Sedan 4D		CA31A	26769	**6775**	**7825**	**9950**	**12950**
Manual Trans				**(500)**	**(500)**	**(665)**	**(665)**

2001 NISSAN — (1N4,JN1or3N1)(CB51D)-1-#

SENTRA—4-Cyl.—Equipment Schedule 6
W.B. 99.8"; 1.8 Liter, 2.0 Liter.

Body	Type	VIN	List	Fair	Good	Good	Excellent
XE Sedan 4D		CB51D	13368	**3725**	**4450**	**5900**	**8000**
GXE Sedan 4D		CB51D	14019	**3900**	**4650**	**6100**	**8225**
CA Sedan 4D		DB51D	15319	**4300**	**5100**	**6575**	**8750**
SE Sedan 4D		BB51D	15419	**4500**	**5300**	**6825**	**9025**
ALTIMA—4-Cyl.—Equipment Schedule 4							
W.B. 103.1"; 2.4 Liter.							
XE Sedan 4D		DL01D	18459	**3425**	**4125**	**6625**	**9950**
GXE Sedan 4D		DL01D	18659	**3725**	**4450**	**6850**	**10000**
SE Sedan 4D		DL01D	19960	**3975**	**4725**	**7300**	**10650**
GLE Sedan 4D		DL01D	20190	**4475**	**5275**	**7875**	**11350**
LE				**150**	**150**	**200**	**200**
Manual Trans				**(525)**	**(525)**	**(700)**	**(700)**
MAXIMA—V6—Equipment Schedule 4							
W.B. 108.3"; 3.0 Liter.							
GXE Sedan 4D		CA31D	23469	**6500**	**7525**	**9750**	**12850**
SE Sedan 4D		CA31D	24869	**7100**	**8200**	**10450**	**13650**

Body Type	VIN	List	Trade-In Fair	Good	Pvt-Party Good	Retail Excellent
SE 20th Anniv Sed 4D	CA31A	28169	7900	9075	11350	14650
GLE Sedan 4D	CA31D	26969	7725	8875	11150	14450
Manual Trans			(525)	(525)	(700)	(700)

2002 NISSAN — (1N4,JN1or3N1)(CB51D)-2-#

SENTRA—4-Cyl.—Equipment Schedule 6
W.B. 99.8"; 1.8 Liter, 2.5 Liter.

XE Sedan 4D	CB51D	13588	4375	5175	6700	8900
GXE Sedan 4D	CB51D	14289	4525	5350	6875	9125
CA Sedan 4D	DB51D	15439	5000	5875	7425	9700
SE-R Sedan 4D	AB51A	16539	5425	6350	7775	10000
SE-R Spec V Sedan 4D	AB51A	17539	6400	7425	8900	11200

ALTIMA—4-Cyl.—Equipment Schedule 4
W.B. 110.2"; 2.5 Liter.

2.5 Sedan 4D	AL11D	17869	7675	8825	10600	13350
2.5 S Sedan 4D	AL11D	19389	8400	9625	11250	13850
2.5 SL Sedan 4D	AL11D	23239	8650	9900	11750	14600
Manual Trans			(550)	(550)	(735)	(735)

ALTIMA—V6—Equipment Schedule 4
W.B. 110.2"; 3.5 Liter.

3.5 SE Sedan 4D	BL11D	23689	9250	10525	12400	15350
Manual Trans			(550)	(550)	(735)	(735)

MAXIMA—V6—Equipment Schedule 4
W.B. 108.3"; 3.5 Liter.

GXE Sedan 4D	CA31D	25239	7500	8625	11000	14400
SE Sedan 4D	CA31D	25989	8225	9425	11850	15350
GLE Sedan 4D	CA31D	27639	8850	10125	12600	16150

2003 NISSAN — (1N4,JN1or3N1)(CB51D)-3-#

SENTRA—4-Cyl.—Equipment Schedule 6
W.B. 99.8"; 1.8 Liter, 2.5 Liter.

XE Sedan 4D	CB51D	13888	5125	6025	7625	10000
GXE Sedan 4D	CB51D	14639	5275	6175	7800	10200
Limited Sedan 4D	AB51D	17139	5825	6775	8425	10850
SE-R Sedan 4D	AB51D	16739	6300	7325	8825	11150
SE-R Spec V Sed 4D	AB51D	17739	7375	8500	10050	12450

ALTIMA—4-Cyl.—Equipment Schedule 4
W.B. 110.2"; 2.5 Liter.

2.5 Sedan 4D	AL11D	17689	8825	10100	12000	14950
2.5 S Sedan 4D	AL11D	19539	9575	10925	12650	15450
2.5 SL Sedan 4D	AL11D	23539	9850	11250	13200	16250
Manual Trans			(575)	(575)	(765)	(765)

ALTIMA—V6—Equipment Schedule 4
W.B. 110.2"; 3.5 Liter.

3.5 SE Sedan 4D	BL11D	23689	10475	11925	13900	17050
Manual Trans			(575)	(575)	(765)	(765)

MAXIMA—V6—Equipment Schedule 4
W.B. 108.3"; 3.5 Liter.

GXE Sedan 4D	DA31D	25439	8725	10000	12550	16250
SE Sedan 4D	DA31D	26189	9575	10925	13550	17300
GLE Sedan 4D	DA31D	28089	10175	11600	14250	18150

350Z—V6—Equipment Schedule 3
W.B. 104.3"; 3.5 Liter.

Coupe 2D	AZ34D	26809	12025	13625	16850	21400
Enthusiast Coupe 2D	AZ34D	29759	12375	14025	17550	22600
Performance Cpe 2D	AZ34D	30969	12950	14650	18350	23600
Touring Coupe 2D	AZ34D	32129	13375	15125	18950	24300
Track Coupe 2D	AZ34D	34619	14400	16250	20200	25800

2004 NISSAN — (1N4,JN1or3N1)(CB51D)-4-#

SENTRA—4-Cyl.—Equipment Schedule 6
W.B. 99.8"; 1.8 Liter, 2.5 Liter.

Sedan 4D	CB51D	12740	6050	7000	8575	10950
1.8 S Sedan 4D	CB51D	14740	6200	7200	8775	11150
2.5 S Sedan 4D	AB51D	17360	6550	7575	9175	11600
SE-R Sedan 4D	AB51D	17640	7350	8475	9900	12200
SE-R Spec V Sed 4D	AB51D	17840	8525	9750	11250	13700

ALTIMA—4-Cyl.—Equipment Schedule 4
W.B. 110.2"; 2.5 Liter.

2.5 Sedan 4D	AL11D	17890	10100	11450	13400	16400
2.5 S Sedan 4D	AL11D	19740	10925	12375	14100	17000
2.5 SL Sedan 4D	AL11D	23740	11200	12700	14650	17800

Body	Type	VIN	List	Trade-In Fair	Good	Pvt-Party Good	Retail Excellent
Manual Trans		......		**(600)**	**(600)**	**(800)**	**(800)**

ALTIMA—V6—Equipment Schedule 4
W.B. 110.2"; 3.5 Liter.

Body	Type	VIN	List	Fair	Good	Good	Excellent
3.5 SE Sedan 4D		BL11D	23790	**11875**	**13475**	**15500**	**18700**
Manual Trans		......		**(600)**	**(600)**	**(800)**	**(800)**

MAXIMA—V6—Equipment Schedule 4
W.B. 111.2"; 3.5 Liter.

Body	Type	VIN	List	Fair	Good	Good	Excellent
SE Sedan 4D		BA41E	27490	**14125**	**15950**	**18400**	**22200**
SL Sedan 4D		BA41E	29440	**15125**	**17025**	**19500**	**23500**

350Z—V6—Equipment Schedule 3
W.B. 104.3"; 3.5 Liter.

Body	Type	VIN	List	Fair	Good	Good	Excellent
Coupe 2D		AZ34D	26910	**13725**	**15525**	**18850**	**23800**
Enthusiast Coupe 2D		AZ34D	29860	**14125**	**15950**	**19700**	**25000**
Enthusiast Roadster		AZ36A	35360	**20575**	**23000**	**25200**	**29200**
Performance Cpe 2D		AZ34D	31070	**14800**	**16675**	**20600**	**26100**
Track Coupe 2D		AZ34D	34720	**16350**	**18425**	**22600**	**28500**
Touring Coupe 2D		AZ34D	33820	**15275**	**17225**	**21200**	**26900**
Touring Roadster 2D		AZ36A	37730	**21725**	**24350**	**26600**	**30700**

SENTRA—4-Cyl.—Equipment Schedule 6
W.B. 99.8"; 1.8 Liter, 2.5 Liter.

Body	Type	VIN	List	Fair	Good	Good	Excellent
Sedan 4D		CB51D	14310	**6575**	**7600**	**9000**	**11200**
S Sedan 4D		CB51D	15060	**6750**	**7775**	**9200**	**11450**
SE-R Sedan 4D		AB51D	17960	**8025**	**9225**	**10500**	**12650**
SE-R Spec V Sed 4D		AB51D	18160	**9250**	**10525**	**11900**	**14200**

ALTIMA—4-Cyl.—Equipment Schedule 4
W.B. 110.2"; 2.5 Liter.

Body	Type	VIN	List	Fair	Good	Good	Excellent
2.5 Sedan 4D		AL11D	17760	**11150**	**12650**	**14550**	**17550**
2.5 S Sedan 4D		AL11D	20110	**12025**	**13625**	**15300**	**18150**
SL		......		**900**	**900**	**1200**	**1200**
5-Spd Manual Trans		......		**(625)**	**(625)**	**(835)**	**(835)**

ALTIMA—V6—Equipment Schedule 4
W.B. 110.2"; 3.5 Liter.

Body	Type	VIN	List	Fair	Good	Good	Excellent
3.5 SE Sedan 4D		BL11D	24310	**13975**	**15800**	**17450**	**20400**
3.5 SL Sedan 4D		BL11D	27460	**14900**	**16825**	**18500**	**21400**
3.5 SE-R Sedan 4D		BL11D	29760	**16550**	**18625**	**20400**	**23600**
5-Spd Manual Trans		......		**(625)**	**(625)**	**(835)**	**(835)**

MAXIMA—V6—Equipment Schedule 4
W.B. 111.2"; 3.5 Liter.

Body	Type	VIN	List	Fair	Good	Good	Excellent
SE Sedan 4D		BA41E	27660	**15850**	**17850**	**20500**	**24500**
SL Sedan 4D		BA41E	29910	**16925**	**19050**	**21700**	**25900**

350Z—V6—Equipment Schedule 3
W.B. 104.3"; 3.5 Liter.

Body	Type	VIN	List	Fair	Good	Good	Excellent
Coupe 2D		AZ34D	27060	**14900**	**16825**	**20300**	**25300**
Enthusiast Coupe 2D		AZ34D	30010	**15275**	**17225**	**21100**	**26700**
Enthusiast Roadster		AZ36A	34710	**22300**	**24925**	**27200**	**31100**
Performance Cpe 2D		AZ34D	31210	**16000**	**18000**	**22000**	**27800**
Touring Coupe 2D		AZ34D	32360	**16550**	**18625**	**22800**	**28700**
Touring Roadster 2D		AZ36A	38110	**23575**	**26375**	**28500**	**32700**
Track Coupe 2D		AZ34D	34860	**17700**	**19875**	**24200**	**30300**
35th Anniv Coupe 2D		AZ34D	37660				
Grand Touring Rdstr		AZ36D	39780				

OLDSMOBILE

CALAIS—4-Cyl.—Equipment Schedule 5
W.B. 103.4"; 2.5 Liter.

Body	Type	VIN	List	Fair	Good	Good	Excellent
Sedan 4D		NL54U	12793	**400**	**550**	**1025**	**1775**
Coupe 2D		NL14U	12753	**400**	**550**	**1025**	**1775**
S Sedan 4D		NF54U	13310	**450**	**625**	**1150**	**1950**
S Coupe 2D		NF14U	13210	**450**	**625**	**1150**	**1950**
Quad 442 Sport Pkg		......		**50**	**50**	**65**	**65**
4-Cyl. 2.3L Quad 4		A,D		**100**	**100**	**135**	**135**

CALAIS—4-Cyl. Quad 4—Equipment Schedule 5
W.B. 103.4"; 2.3 Liter.

Body	Type	VIN	List	Fair	Good	Good	Excellent
SL Sedan 4D		NT54D	15650	**450**	**625**	**1150**	**1950**
SL Coupe 2D		NT14D	15550	**450**	**625**	**1150**	**1950**
International Sed 4D		NK54A	16500	**475**	**700**	**1225**	**2075**
International Cpe 2D		NK14A	16750	**475**	**700**	**1225**	**2075**

1991 OLDSMOBILE

Body	Type	VIN	List	Trade-In Fair	Trade-In Good	Pvt-Party Good	Retail Excellent
V6 3.3 Liter		N		125	125	165	165
CIERA—V6—Equipment Schedule 4							
W.B. 104.9"; 3.3 Liter.							
Sedan 4D		AL54N	15605	475	675	1175	2000
S Sedan 4D		AJ54N	15945	475	675	1200	2025
S Coupe 2D		AJ14N	16345	475	675	1175	2000
S Cruiser Wagon 4D		AJ84N	16935	525	750	1300	2200
SL Sedan 4D		AM54N	17165	550	775	1300	2200
SL Cruiser Wagon 4D		AM84N	17955	550	775	1325	2250
4-Cyl. 2.5 Liter		R		(150)	(150)	(200)	(200)
CUTLASS SUPREME—V6—Equipment Schedule 4							
W.B. 107.5"; 3.1 Liter, 3.4 Liter.							
Sedan 4D		WH54T	16812	600	875	1575	2725
Coupe 2D		WH14T	16607	575	825	1500	2625
Convertible Cpe 2D		WT34T	22047	1125	1575	2700	4275
SL Sedan 4D		WS54T	18407	625	900	1625	2800
SL Coupe 2D		WS14T	18232	600	850	1550	2675
International Sed 4D		WR54T	20685	725	1050	1825	3050
International Cpe 2D		WR14T	20510	675	975	1750	2950
Manual Trans				(50)	(50)	(65)	(65)
4-Cyl. 2.3L Quad 4		D		(200)	(200)	(265)	(265)
V6 3.4 Liter		X		150	150	200	200
EIGHTY EIGHT—V6—Equipment Schedule 4							
W.B. 110.8"; 3.8 Liter.							
Royale Sedan 4D		HN54C	18969	525	750	1225	2075
Royale Coupe 2D		HN14C	18764	550	775	1300	2200
Royale Brhm Sedan 4D		HY54C	20596	625	900	1475	2450
Royale Brhm Coupe 2D		HY14C	20381	575	825	1350	2275
CUSTOM CRUISER—V8—Equipment Schedule 4							
W.B. 115.9"; 5.0 Liter.							
Wagon 4D		BP83E	23668	1225	1675	2725	4225
NINETY EIGHT—V6—Equipment Schedule 4							
W.B. 110.8"; 3.8 Liter.							
Regency Elite Sedan 4D		CW53L	25129	750	1050	1725	2825
Touring Sedan 4D		CV53L	29175	925	1300	2150	3450
TORONADO—V6—Equipment Schedule 2							
W.B. 108.0"; 3.8 Liter.							
Coupe 2D		EZ13L	25579	800	1150	2100	3575
Trofeo Coupe 2D		EV13L	27075	850	1200	2200	3675

1992 OLDSMOBILE — (1or3)G3(NL543)–N–#

Body	Type	VIN	List	Trade-In Fair	Trade-In Good	Pvt-Party Good	Retail Excellent
ACHIEVA—4-Cyl.—Equipment Schedule 5							
W.B. 103.4"; 2.3 Liter.							
S Sedan 4D		NL543	14675	375	500	1000	1775
S Coupe 2D		NL143	14575	375	500	1000	1775
SL Sedan 4D		NF54D	15900	400	600	1125	1950
SL Coupe 2D		NF14D	15800	400	550	1075	1875
SCX Coupe 2D		NL14A	16495	450	650	1225	2075
SC Pkg				50	50	65	65
V6 3.3 Liter		N		125	125	165	165
CIERA—V6—Equipment Schedule 4							
W.B. 104.9"; 3.3 Liter.							
S Sedan 4D		AL54N	15855	525	750	1275	2150
S Cruiser Wagon 4D		AJ84N	16900	600	850	1425	2375
SL Sedan 4D		AM54N	18230	625	900	1450	2425
SL Cruiser Wagon 4D		AM84N	18730	625	900	1475	2450
4-Cyl. 2.5 Liter		R		(150)	(150)	(200)	(200)
CUTLASS SUPREME—V6—Equipment Schedule 4							
W.B. 107.5"; 3.1 Liter.							
S Sedan 4D		WH54T	17425	700	1000	1800	3050
S Coupe 2D		WH14T	17220	675	950	1725	2950
Convertible Cpe 2D		WT34T	23205	1325	1825	3000	4675
International Sed 4D		WR54T	22740	825	1175	2075	3475
International Cpe 2D		WR14T	22575	775	1125	2000	3350
SL Pkg				50	50	65	65
Manual Trans				(50)	(50)	(65)	(65)
V6 3.4 Liter		X		150	150	200	200
EIGHTY EIGHT—V6—Equipment Schedule 4							
W.B. 110.8"; 3.8 Liter.							
Royale Sedan 4D		HN53L	20502	475	700	1225	2100
Royale LdS Sedan 4D		HY53L	21950	500	725	1275	2200
CUSTOM CRUISER—V8—Equipment Schedule 4							
W.B. 115.9"; 5.0 Liter.							

1992 OLDSMOBILE

Body	Type	VIN	List	Trade-In Fair	Trade-In Good	Pvt-Party Good	Retail Excellent
Wagon 4D		BP83E	23983	**1475**	**1975**	**3100**	**4725**
V8 5.7 Liter		7		**100**	**100**	**135**	**135**

NINETY EIGHT—V6—Equipment Schedule 4
W.B. 110.7"; 3.8 Liter.

Body	Type	VIN	List	Fair	Good	Good	Excellent
Regency Sedan 4D		CX53L	25943	**875**	**1225**	**2025**	**3275**
Reg Elite Sed 4D		CW53L	26795	**875**	**1225**	**2025**	**3300**
Touring Sedan 4D		CV53L	29595	**1100**	**1550**	**2600**	**4100**
V6 3.8L Supercharged		1		**175**	**175**	**235**	**235**

TORONADO—V6—Equipment Schedule 2
W.B. 108.0"; 3.8 Liter.

Body	Type	VIN	List	Fair	Good	Good	Excellent
Coupe 2D		EZ13L	26539	**950**	**1325**	**2550**	**4275**
Trofeo Coupe 2D		EV13L	27895	**1000**	**1425**	**2675**	**4400**

1993 OLDSMOBILE — (1or3)G3(NL543)-P-#

ACHIEVA—4-Cyl.—Equipment Schedule 5
W.B. 103.4"; 2.3 Liter.

Body	Type	VIN	List	Fair	Good	Good	Excellent
S Sedan 4D		NL543	15009	**450**	**625**	**1200**	**2075**
S Coupe 2D		NL143	14909	**425**	**625**	**1175**	**2025**
SL Sedan 4D		NF54D	16254	**525**	**750**	**1325**	**2275**
SL Coupe 2D		NF14D	16154	**475**	**700**	**1275**	**2200**
SC Pkg				**75**	**75**	**100**	**100**
SCX Pkg				**175**	**175**	**235**	**235**
V6 3.3 Liter		N		**150**	**150**	**200**	**200**

CIERA—V6—Equipment Schedule 4
W.B. 104.9"; 3.3 Liter.

Body	Type	VIN	List	Fair	Good	Good	Excellent
S Sedan 4D		AG54N	16234	**600**	**850**	**1425**	**2375**
SL Sedan 4D		AM55N	18964	**675**	**950**	**1575**	**2600**
4-Cyl. 2.2 Liter		4		**(175)**	**(175)**	**(235)**	**(235)**

CUTLASS SUPREME—V6—Equipment Schedule 4
W.B. 107.5"; 3.1 Liter.

Body	Type	VIN	List	Fair	Good	Good	Excellent
S Sedan 4D		WH54T	17175	**825**	**1175**	**2075**	**3475**
S Coupe 2D		WH14T	17010	**775**	**1100**	**2000**	**3350**
Convertible Cpe 2D		WT34T	23574	**1625**	**2125**	**3400**	**5175**
International Sed 4D		WR54T	23744	**975**	**1375**	**2500**	**4100**
International Cpe 2D		WR14T	23579	**925**	**1300**	**2400**	**3975**
SL Pkg				**75**	**75**	**100**	**100**
V6 3.4 Liter		X		**175**	**175**	**235**	**235**

CUTLASS CRUISER—V6—Equipment Schedule 4
W.B. 104.9"; 3.3 Liter.

Body	Type	VIN	List	Fair	Good	Good	Excellent
S Wagon 4D		AJ84N	16934	**650**	**925**	**1525**	**2550**
SL Wagon 4D		AM85N	19464	**675**	**975**	**1575**	**2625**
4-Cyl. 2.2 Liter		4		**(175)**	**(175)**	**(235)**	**(235)**

EIGHTY EIGHT—V6—Equipment Schedule 4
W.B. 110.8"; 3.8 Liter.

Body	Type	VIN	List	Fair	Good	Good	Excellent
Royale Sedan 4D		HN53L	21251	**575**	**825**	**1425**	**2425**
Royale LS Sedan 4D		HY53L	22504	**600**	**875**	**1500**	**2550**
LSS Pkg				**75**	**75**	**100**	**100**

NINETY EIGHT—V6—Equipment Schedule 4
W.B. 110.8"; 3.8 Liter.

Body	Type	VIN	List	Fair	Good	Good	Excellent
Regency Sedan 4D		CX53L	25839	**1075**	**1525**	**2550**	**4025**
Reg Elite Sed 4D		CW53L	27599	**1125**	**1575**	**2625**	**4125**
Touring Sedan 4D		CV53L	30299	**1525**	**2025**	**3200**	**4825**
V6 3.8L Supercharged		1		**225**	**225**	**300**	**300**

1994 OLDSMOBILE — (1or3)G3(NL553)-R-#

ACHIEVA—4-Cyl.—Equipment Schedule 5
W.B. 103.4"; 2.3 Liter.

Body	Type	VIN	List	Fair	Good	Good	Excellent
S Sedan 4D		NL553	16045	**550**	**775**	**1425**	**2450**
S Coupe 2D		NL153	15945	**525**	**750**	**1350**	**2375**
SL Sedan 4D		NF55A	18715	**625**	**900**	**1600**	**2725**
SC Coupe 2D		NF15A	18715	**600**	**875**	**1525**	**2625**
V6 3.1 Liter		M		**175**	**175**	**235**	**235**

CIERA—V6—Equipment Schedule 4
W.B. 104.9"; 3.1 Liter.

Body	Type	VIN	List	Fair	Good	Good	Excellent
S Sedan 4D		AG55M	17725	**625**	**900**	**1550**	**2625**
4-Cyl. 2.2 Liter		4		**(200)**	**(200)**	**(265)**	**(265)**

CUTLASS SUPREME—V6—Equipment Schedule 4
W.B. 107.5"; 3.1 Liter.

Body	Type	VIN	List	Fair	Good	Good	Excellent
S Sedan 4D		WH55M	18827	**925**	**1300**	**2450**	**4075**
S Coupe 2D		WH15M	18662	**875**	**1225**	**2350**	**3950**
Convertible Cpe 2D		WT35M	25800	**1925**	**2450**	**3800**	**5675**
V6 3.4 Liter		X		**200**	**200**	**265**	**265**

1994 OLDSMOBILE

Body	Type	VIN	List	Trade-In Fair	Good	Pvt-Party Good	Retail Excellent
CUTLASS CRUISER—V6—Equipment Schedule 4							
W.B. 104.9"; 3.1 Liter.							
S Wagon 4D		AJ85M	18757	700	1000	1675	2800
EIGHTY EIGHT—V6—Equipment Schedule 4							
W.B. 110.8"; 3.8 Liter.							
Royale Sedan 4D		HN52L	22480	700	1000	1675	2800
Royale LS Sedan 4D		HY52L	23450	750	1050	1800	2950
LSS Pkg				100	100	135	135
NINETY EIGHT—V6—Equipment Schedule 4							
W.B. 110.8"; 3.8 Liter.							
Regency Sedan 4D		CX52L	26695	1375	1900	2975	4550
Reg Elite Sed 4D		CW53L	28600	1475	1975	3100	4700
V6 3.8L Supercharged		1		275	275	365	365

1995 OLDSMOBILE — (1or2)G3(NL55D)–S–#

Body	Type	VIN	List	Trade-In Fair	Good	Pvt-Party Good	Retail Excellent
ACHIEVA—4-Cyl.—Equipment Schedule 5							
W.B. 103.4"; 2.3 Liter.							
S Sedan 4D		NL55D	14750	650	925	1650	2825
S Coupe 2D		NL15D	14750	625	900	1600	2775
V6 3.1 Liter		M		200	200	265	265
CIERA—V6—Equipment Schedule 4							
W.B. 104.9"; 3.1 Liter.							
SL Sedan 4D		AJ55M	16595	775	1125	1900	3125
SL Wagon 4D		AJ85M	17595	800	1150	1950	3175
4-Cyl. 2.2 Liter		4		(225)	(225)	(300)	(300)
CUTLASS SUPREME—V6—Equipment Schedule 4							
W.B. 107.5"; 3.1 Liter.							
S Sedan 4D		WH52M	18995	1075	1500	2725	4425
S Coupe 2D		WH12M	18995	1000	1400	2600	4275
Convertible 2D		WT32M	26531	2200	2800	4200	6150
V6 3.4 Liter		X		225	225	300	300
EIGHTY EIGHT—V6—Equipment Schedule 4							
W.B. 110.8"; 3.8 Liter.							
Royale Sedan 4D		HN52K	20995	825	1175	2025	3350
Royale LS Sedan 4D		HY52K	23295	900	1250	2175	3575
LSS Pkg				100	100	135	135
V6 3.8L Supercharged		1		300	300	400	400
NINETY EIGHT—V6—Equipment Schedule 4							
W.B. 110.7"; 3.8 Liter.							
Reg Elite Sed 4D		CX52K	26695	1875	2400	3650	5375
V6 3.8L Supercharged		1		300	300	400	400
AURORA—V8—Equipment Schedule 2							
W.B. 113.8"; 4.0 Liter.							
Sedan 4D		GR52C	31995	1825	2350	3425	4975

1996 OLDSMOBILE — (1or2)G3(NL52T)–T–#

Body	Type	VIN	List	Trade-In Fair	Good	Pvt-Party Good	Retail Excellent
ACHIEVA—4-Cyl.—Equipment Schedule 5							
W.B. 103.4"; 2.4 Liter.							
SL Sedan 4D		NL52T	15790	775	1100	2000	3350
SC Coupe 2D		NL12T	15790	750	1050	1950	3275
V6 3.1 Liter		M		225	225	300	300
CIERA—V6—Equipment Schedule 4							
W.B. 104.9"; 3.1 Liter.							
SL Sedan 4D		AJ55M	15305	900	1250	2175	3575
SL Wagon 4D		AJ85M	17995	900	1275	2200	3625
4-Cyl. 2.2 Liter		4		(250)	(250)	(335)	(335)
CUTLASS SUPREME—V6—Equipment Schedule 4							
W.B. 107.5"; 3.1 Liter.							
SL Sedan 4D		WH52M	17995	1250	1750	3050	4875
SL Coupe 2D		WH12M	17995	1150	1600	2900	4675
V6 3.4 Liter		X		250	250	335	335
EIGHTY EIGHT—V6—Equipment Schedule 4							
W.B. 110.8"; 3.8 Liter.							
Sedan 4D		HN52K	21370	1025	1450	2550	4100
LS Sedan 4D		HN52K	23400	1100	1550	2675	4275
LSS Sedan 4D		HY52K	26600	1825	2350	3600	5325
V6 3.8L Supercharged		1		325	325	435	435
NINETY EIGHT—V6—Equipment Schedule 4							
W.B. 110.7"; 3.8 Liter.							
Reg Elite Sed 4D		CX52K	28800	2325	2900	4225	6075
AURORA—V8—Equipment Schedule 2							
W.B. 113.8"; 4.0 Liter.							
Sedan 4D		GR62C	35000	2050	2625	3800	5525

EQUIPMENT & MILEAGE PAGE 13 TO 27

1997 OLDSMOBILE

Body	Type	VIN	List	Trade-In Fair	Good	Pvt-Party Good	Retail Excellent

1997 OLDSMOBILE — (1or2)G3(NL52T)-V-#

ACHIEVA—4-Cyl.—Equipment Schedule 5
W.B. 103.4"; 2.4 Liter.

SL Sedan 4D	NL52T	15750	925	1300	2425	4050
SC Coupe 2D	NL12T	15950	900	1250	2375	4000
V6 3.1 Liter	M		250	250	335	335

CUTLASS—V6—Equipment Schedule 4
W.B. 107.0"; 3.1 Liter.

| Sedan 4D | WH52T | 18170 | 1275 | 1775 | 2925 | 4575 |
| GLS Sedan 4D | WH52M | 19225 | 1625 | 2125 | 3350 | 5050 |

CUTLASS SUPREME—V6—Equipment Schedule 4
W.B. 107.5"; 3.1 Liter.

| SL Sedan 4D | WH52M | 19500 | 1525 | 2025 | 3450 | 5375 |
| SL Coupe 2D | WH12M | 19500 | 1375 | 1900 | 3275 | 5200 |

EIGHTY EIGHT—V6—Equipment Schedule 4
W.B. 110.8"; 3.8 Liter.

| Sedan 4D | HN52K | 23100 | 1300 | 1800 | 3000 | 4675 |
| LS Sedan 4D | HN52K | 24400 | 1425 | 1925 | 3150 | 4875 |

LSS—V6—Equipment Schedule 4
W.B. 110.8"; 3.8 Liter.

| Sedan 4D | HY52K | 28300 | 2225 | 2825 | 4125 | 6025 |
| V6 3.8L Supercharged | 1 | | 350 | 350 | 465 | 465 |

REGENCY—V6—Equipment Schedule 4
W.B. 110.8"; 3.8 Liter.

| Sedan 4D | HC52K | 28600 | 2425 | 3025 | 4400 | 6300 |

AURORA—V8—Equipment Schedule 2
W.B. 113.8"; 4.0 Liter.

| Sedan 4D | GR62C | 36400 | 2425 | 3000 | 4400 | 6350 |

1998 OLDSMOBILE — (1or2)G3(NL52T)-W-#

ACHIEVA—4-Cyl.—Equipment Schedule 5
W.B. 103.4"; 2.4 Liter.

| SL Sedan 4D | NL52T | 18340 | 1225 | 1675 | 2950 | 4700 |
| V6 3.1 Liter | M | | 250 | 250 | 335 | 335 |

CUTLASS—V6—Equipment Schedule 4
W.B. 107.0"; 3.1 Liter.

| GL Sedan 4D | NB52M | 18950 | 1600 | 2100 | 3375 | 5125 |
| GLS Sedan 4D | NG52M | 19950 | 1975 | 2500 | 3775 | 5600 |

INTRIGUE—V6—Equipment Schedule 4
W.B. 109.0"; 3.8 Liter.

Sedan 4D	WH52K	21250	1800	2325	3675	5575
GL Sedan 4D	WS52K	22650	2025	2600	4000	5975
GLS Sedan 4D	WX52K	24660	2450	3050	4500	6525

EIGHTY EIGHT—V6—Equipment Schedule 4
W.B. 110.8"; 3.8 Liter.

| Sedan 4D | HN52K | 23400 | 1725 | 2250 | 3575 | 5400 |
| LS Sedan 4D | HN52K | 24800 | 1875 | 2400 | 3725 | 5600 |

LSS—V6—Equipment Schedule 4
W.B. 110.8"; 3.8 Liter.

| Sedan 4D | HY52K | 28700 | 2725 | 3350 | 4775 | 6825 |
| V6 3.8L Supercharged | 1 | | 375 | 375 | 500 | 500 |

REGENCY—V6—Equipment Schedule 4
W.B. 110.8"; 3.8 Liter.

| Sedan 4D | HC52K | 29000 | 2925 | 3600 | 5050 | 7100 |

AURORA—V8—Equipment Schedule 2
W.B. 113.8"; 4.0 Liter.

| Sedan 4D | GR62C | 36625 | 2950 | 3625 | 5250 | 7500 |

1999 OLDSMOBILE — (1or2)G3(NK52T)-X-#

ALERO—4-Cyl.—Equipment Schedule 4
W.B. 107.0"; 2.4 Liter.

GX Sedan 2D	NK52T	16850	1575	2075	3450	5325
GX Coupe 2D	NK12T	16850	1500	2000	3350	5225
GL Sedan 4D	NL52T	18745	1950	2475	3875	5825
GL Coupe 2D	NL12T	19180	1825	2350	3750	5675
V6 3.4 Liter	E		200	200	265	265

ALERO—V6—Equipment Schedule 4
W.B. 107.0"; 3.4 Liter.

| GLS Sedan 4D | NF52E | 21400 | 2650 | 3275 | 4725 | 6800 |
| GLS Coupe 2D | NF12E | 21400 | 2525 | 3125 | 4575 | 6625 |

1999 OLDSMOBILE

Body	Type	VIN	List	Trade-In Fair	Trade-In Good	Pvt-Party Good	Retail Excellent
CUTLASS—V6—Equipment Schedule 4							
W.B. 107.0"; 3.1 Liter.							
GL Sedan 4D		NB52M	19325	**2000**	**2550**	**3875**	**5750**
GLS Sedan 4D		NG52M	20250	**2400**	**2975**	**4375**	**6300**
INTRIGUE—V6—Equipment Schedule 4							
W.B. 109.0"; 3.5 Liter, 3.8 Liter.							
GX Sedan 4D		WH52K	21735	**2200**	**2800**	**4250**	**6275**
GL Sedan 4D		WS52K	23135	**2500**	**3100**	**4575**	**6675**
GLS Sedan 4D		WX52H	25505	**2975**	**3650**	**5175**	**7325**
EIGHTY EIGHT—V6—Equipment Schedule 4							
W.B. 110.8"; 3.8 Liter.							
Sedan 4D		HN52K	24170	**2275**	**2825**	**4250**	**6175**
LS Sedan 4D		HN52K	25720	**2425**	**3025**	**4450**	**6400**
LSS—V6—Equipment Schedule 4							
W.B. 110.8"; 3.8 Liter.							
Sedan 4D		HY52K	29720	**3375**	**4075**	**5550**	**7675**
V6 3.8L Supercharged		1		**425**	**425**	**565**	**565**
AURORA—V8—Equipment Schedule 2							
W.B. 113.8"; 4.0 Liter.							
Sedan 4D		GR62C	36899	**3700**	**4450**	**6075**	**8450**
2000 OLDSMOBILE — (1or2)G3(NK52T)-Y-#							
ALERO—4-Cyl.—Equipment Schedule 5							
W.B. 107.0"; 2.4 Liter.							
GX Sedan 4D		NK52T	16995	**1950**	**2475**	**3950**	**6000**
GX Coupe 2D		NK12T	16995	**1825**	**2350**	**3825**	**5850**
GL Sedan 4D		NL52T	18185	**2350**	**2925**	**4450**	**6550**
GL Coupe 2D		NL12T	18185	**2225**	**2825**	**4300**	**6375**
V6 3.4 Liter		E		**225**	**225**	**300**	**300**
ALERO—V6—Equipment Schedule 4							
W.B. 107.0"; 3.4 Liter.							
GLS Sedan 4D		NF52E	21900	**3175**	**3825**	**5400**	**7650**
GLS Coupe 2D		NF12E	21900	**3000**	**3675**	**5250**	**7450**
INTRIGUE—V6—Equipment Schedule 4							
W.B. 109.0"; 3.5 Liter.							
GX Sedan 4D		WH52H	22650	**2850**	**3525**	**5100**	**7300**
GL Sedan 4D		WS52H	24280	**3200**	**3875**	**5475**	**7725**
GLS Sedan 4D		WX52H	26280	**3750**	**4500**	**6150**	**8500**
Sterling Edition				**75**	**75**	**100**	**100**
2001 OLDSMOBILE — 1G3(NK52T)-1-#							
ALERO—4-Cyl.—Equipment Schedule 5							
W.B. 107.0"; 2.4 Liter.							
GX Sedan 4D		NK52T	17785	**2400**	**2975**	**4575**	**6775**
GX Coupe 2D		NK12T	17785	**2275**	**2825**	**4450**	**6600**
GL Sedan 4D		NL52T	19195	**2850**	**3500**	**5125**	**7375**
GL Coupe 2D		NL12T	19195	**2725**	**3350**	**4975**	**7200**
V6 3.4 Liter		E		**250**	**250**	**335**	**335**
ALERO—V6—Equipment Schedule 4							
W.B. 107.0"; 3.4 Liter.							
GLS Sedan 4D		NF52E	22540	**3750**	**4500**	**6200**	**8575**
GLS Coupe 2D		NF12E	22765	**3625**	**4350**	**6050**	**8400**
INTRIGUE—V6—Equipment Schedule 4							
W.B. 109.0"; 3.5 Liter.							
GX Sedan 4D		WH52H	22995	**3650**	**4400**	**6100**	**8500**
GL Sedan 4D		WS52H	24750	**4050**	**4800**	**6550**	**9000**
GLS Sedan 4D		WX52H	27115	**4650**	**5500**	**7300**	**9850**
AURORA—V6—Equipment Schedule 2							
W.B. 112.2"; 3.5 Liter.							
Sedan 4D		GR64H	31579	**5875**	**6850**	**8925**	**11900**
AURORA—V8—Equipment Schedule 2							
W.B. 112.2"; 4.0 Liter.							
Sedan 4D		GS64C	35314	**6975**	**8050**	**10250**	**13350**
2002 OLDSMOBILE — 1G3(NK52T)-2-#							
ALERO—4-Cyl.—Equipment Schedule 5							
W.B. 107.0"; 2.2 Liter.							
GX Sedan 4D		NK52T	18055	**2975**	**3650**	**5375**	**7775**
GX Coupe 2D		NK12T	18055	**2825**	**3475**	**5225**	**7600**
GL Sedan 4D		NL52T	20040	**3475**	**4200**	**5975**	**8425**
GL Coupe 2D		NL12T	20265	**3350**	**4050**	**5825**	**8275**
V6 3.4 Liter		E		**275**	**275**	**365**	**365**

Body	Type	VIN	List	Trade-In Fair	Good	Pvt-Party Good	Retail Excellent

ALERO—V6—Equipment Schedule 4
W.B. 107.0"; 3.4 Liter.

GLS Sedan 4D		NF52E	22675	**4500**	**5300**	**7150**	**9750**
GLS Coupe 2D		NF12E	22900	**4350**	**5125**	**6950**	**9525**

INTRIGUE—V6—Equipment Schedule 4
W.B. 109.0"; 3.5 Liter.

GX Sedan 4D		WH52H	23427	**4625**	**5450**	**7300**	**9900**
GL Sedan 4D		WS52H	25012	**5050**	**5925**	**7775**	**10450**
GLS Sedan 4D		WX52H	28502	**5725**	**6675**	**8575**	**11350**

AURORA—V6—Equipment Schedule 2
W.B. 112.2"; 3.5 Liter.

Sedan 4D		GR64H	31665	**7300**	**8400**	**10900**	**14400**

AURORA—V8—Equipment Schedule 2
W.B. 112.2"; 4.0 Liter.

Sedan 4D		GS64C	35660	**8525**	**9750**	**12300**	**16000**

2003 OLDSMOBILE — 1G3(NK52F)-3-#

ALERO—4-Cyl.—Equipment Schedule 5
W.B. 107.0"; 2.2 Liter.

GX Sedan 4D		NK52F	18335	**3750**	**4475**	**6400**	**9025**
GX Coupe 2D		NK12F	18335	**3600**	**4300**	**6200**	**8825**
GL Sedan 4D		NL52F	20175	**4300**	**5100**	**7000**	**9700**
GL Coupe 2D		NL12F	20175	**4175**	**4950**	**6875**	**9550**
V6 3.4 Liter		E		**300**	**300**	**400**	**400**

ALERO—V6—Equipment Schedule 4
W.B. 107.0"; 3.4 Liter.

GLS Sedan 4D		NF52E	22755	**5400**	**6325**	**8325**	**11150**
GLS Coupe 2D		NF12E	23005	**5250**	**6100**	**8100**	**10900**

AURORA—V8—Equipment Schedule 2
W.B. 112.2"; 4.0 Liter.

Sedan 4D		GS64C	34775	**10675**	**12175**	**15250**	**19600**

2004 OLDSMOBILE — 1G3(NK52F)-4-#

ALERO—4-Cyl.—Equipment Schedule 5
W.B. 107.0"; 2.2 Liter.

GX Sedan 4D		NK52F	18825	**4750**	**5575**	**7600**	**10400**
GX Coupe 2D		NK12F	18825	**4575**	**5400**	**7400**	**10200**
GL Sedan 4D		NL52F	20775	**5325**	**6225**	**8275**	**11150**
GL Coupe 2D		NL12F	20775	**5225**	**6075**	**8125**	**10950**
V6 3.4 Liter		E		**300**	**300**	**400**	**400**

ALERO—V6—Equipment Schedule 4
W.B. 107.0"; 3.4 Liter.

GLS Sedan 4D		NF52E	23425	**6575**	**7600**	**9700**	**12700**
GLS Coupe 2D		NF12E	23675	**6350**	**7375**	**9450**	**12450**

2005 OLDSMOBILE — No Longer Produced

PEUGEOT

1991 PEUGEOT — VF3(DA131)-M-#

PEUGEOT—4-Cyl.—Equipment Schedule 3
W.B. 105.1", 114.2" (505); 1.9 Liter, 2.2 Liter.

405 DL Sedan 4D		DA131	16350	**50**	**75**	**700**	**1600**
405 DL Sportswagon 4D		DA231	17040	**125**	**175**	**825**	**1775**
405 S Sedan 4D		DA132	18750	**175**	**225**	**925**	**1950**
405 S Sportswagon 4D		DA232	19545	**225**	**325**	**1050**	**2100**
405 Mi 16 Sedan 4D		DB133	22100	**325**	**450**	**1225**	**2425**
505 DL Wagon 4D		BF221	19640	**250**	**350**	**1075**	**2150**
505 SW8 Wagon 4D		BF327	21450	**475**	**675**	**1550**	**2875**
Auto Trans				**100**	**100**	**135**	**135**

PEUGEOT—4-Cyl. Turbo—Equipment Schedule 3
W.B. 114.2"; 2.2 Liter.

505 SW8 Wagon 4D		BE328	26500	**675**	**975**	**2000**	**3525**
Auto Trans				**100**	**100**	**135**	**135**

Body	Type	VIN	List	Trade-In Fair	Trade-In Good	Pvt-Party Good	Retail Excellent

PLYMOUTH

1991 PLYMOUTH — (1P3,JP3orJP4)(CU14A)–M–#

COLT—4-Cyl.—Equipment Schedule 6
W.B. 93.9"; 1.5 Liter.

Body	Type	VIN	List	Fair	Good	Good	Excellent
Hatchback 2D		CU14A	8247	400	525	1050	1825
GL Hatchback 2D		CU24A	9559	400	525	1050	1825

COLT VISTA—4-Cyl.—Equipment Schedule 6
W.B. 103.3", 103.5" (4WD); 2.0 Liter.

| Wagon 4D | | CG39V | 13695 | 625 | 900 | 1500 | 2550 |
| 4WD Wagon 4D | | EH31V | 14662 | 625 | 900 | 1550 | 2625 |

SUNDANCE—4-Cyl.—Equipment Schedule 5
W.B. 97.0"; 2.2 Liter, 2.5 Liter.

America Sedan 4D		XP28D	10086	350	475	900	1600
America Coupe 2D		XP24D	9786	325	425	850	1525
Highline Sedan 4D		XP48D	11002	350	475	900	1600
Highline Coupe 2D		XP44D	10702	350	475	900	1600
RS Sedan 4D		XP68K	12228	400	550	1025	1775
RS Coupe 2D		XP64K	11902	400	550	1025	1775
4-Cyl. 2.5 Liter Turbo		J		50	50	65	65

LASER—4-Cyl.—Equipment Schedule 4
W.B. 97.2"; 1.8 Liter, 2.0 Liter.

Liftback Coupe 2D		CS34T	12958	325	450	1175	2250
RS Liftback Coupe 2D		CS44R	14966	400	550	1300	2450
Auto Trans				100	100	135	135

LASER—4-Cyl. Turbo—Equipment Schedule 4
W.B. 97.2"; 2.0 Liter.

| RS Liftback Coupe 2D | | CS44U | 16150 | 450 | 625 | 1400 | 2625 |
| Auto Trans | | | | 100 | 100 | 135 | 135 |

ACCLAIM—4-Cyl.—Equipment Schedule 5
W.B. 103.3"; 2.5 Liter.

Sedan 4D		XA46K	12752	375	500	925	1600
LE Sedan 4D		XA56K	14166	400	550	1000	1700
V6 3.0 Liter		3		150	150	200	200

ACCLAIM—V6—Equipment Schedule 5
W.B. 103.3"; 3.0 Liter.

| LX Sedan 4D | | XA763 | 15666 | 575 | 825 | 1350 | 2275 |

1992 PLYMOUTH — (1,3,4orJ)P3(CU14A)–N–#

COLT—4-Cyl.—Equipment Schedule 6
W.B. 93.9"; 1.5 Liter.

| Hatchback 2D | | CU14A | 8640 | 400 | 600 | 1175 | 2025 |
| GL Hatchback 2D | | CU24A | 9304 | 400 | 600 | 1175 | 2025 |

COLT VISTA—4-Cyl.—Equipment Schedule 6
W.B. 99.2"; 1.8 Liter, 2.4 Liter.

Wagon 3D		CV20D	12426	1025	1450	2475	3950
SE Wagon 3D		CV50D	13262	1075	1525	2600	4100
AWD Wagon 3D		CW40D	14381	1225	1725	2825	4400

SUNDANCE—4-Cyl.—Equipment Schedule 5
W.B. 97.0"; 2.2 Liter, 2.5 Liter.

America Sedan 4D		XP28D	10610	400	525	1025	1775
America H'Back 2D		XP24D	10210	350	475	975	1700
Highline Sedan 4D		XP48D	11588	400	525	1025	1775
Highline H'Back 2D		XP44D	11188	400	525	1025	1775

SUNDANCE—V6—Equipment Schedule 5
W.B. 97.0"; 3.0 Liter.

Duster Hatchback 2D		XP643	11924	450	650	1200	2025
Duster Sedan 4D		XP683	12324	475	700	1250	2150
4-Cyl. 2.5 Liter		K		(125)	(125)	(165)	(165)

LASER—4-Cyl.—Equipment Schedule 4
W.B. 97.2"; 1.8 Liter, 2.0 Liter.

Hatchback 2D		CS34T	13398	400	550	1375	2625
RS Hatchback 2D		CS44R	15631	450	650	1525	2875
Auto Trans				100	100	135	135

LASER—4-Cyl. Turbo—Equipment Schedule 4
W.B. 97.2"; 2.0 Liter.

RS Hatchback 2D		CS44U	17110	525	750	1650	3050
RS AWD Hatchback 2D		CT44U	19152	825	1175	2375	4075
Auto Trans				100	100	135	135

Body	Type	VIN	List	Trade-In Fair	Good	Pvt-Party Good	Retail Excellent

ACCLAIM—4-Cyl.—Equipment Schedule 5
W.B. 103.5"; 2.5 Liter.

| Sedan 4D | XA46K | 13343 | 400 | 600 | 1075 | 1825 |
| V6 3.0 Liter | 3 | | 175 | 175 | 235 | 235 |

1993 PLYMOUTH — (1,3,4orJ)P3-(A11A)-P-#

COLT—4-Cyl.—Equipment Schedule 6
W.B. 96.1", 98.4" (4D); 1.5 Liter, 1.8 Liter.

Sedan 2D	A11A	9260	525	750	1375	2425
Sedan 4D	A26A	10902	625	900	1625	2775
GL Sedan 2D	A21A	9888	575	825	1500	2600
GL Sedan 4D	A46C	12260	675	975	1725	2925

COLT VISTA—4-Cyl.—Equipment Schedule 6
W.B. 99.2"; 1.8 Liter, 2.4 Liter.

Wagon 3D	B20C	12926	1200	1650	2775	4325
SE Wagon 3D	B50G	14060	1275	1775	2900	4500
AWD Wagon 3D	C40C	15010	1500	2000	3175	4825

SUNDANCE—4-Cyl.—Equipment Schedule 5
W.B. 97.2"; 2.2 Liter, 2.5 Liter.

| Hatchback 2D | P24D | 10623 | 400 | 525 | 1050 | 1875 |
| Sedan 4D | P28D | 11023 | 400 | 575 | 1100 | 1950 |

SUNDANCE—V6—Equipment Schedule 5
W.B. 97.2"; 3.0 Liter.

Duster Hatchback 2D	P643	12440	525	750	1325	2275
Duster Sedan 4D	P683	12840	550	800	1425	2425
4-Cyl. 2.5 Liter	K		(150)	(150)	(200)	(200)

LASER—4-Cyl.—Equipment Schedule 4
W.B. 97.2"; 1.8 Liter, 2.0 Liter.

Hatchback 2D	F34B	13876	450	650	1625	3100
RS Hatchback 2D	F44E	16273	550	775	1850	3400
Auto Trans			125	125	165	165

LASER—4-Cyl. Turbo—Equipment Schedule 4
W.B. 97.2"; 2.0 Liter.

RS Hatchback 2D	F44F	17680	600	875	1975	3575
RS AWD H'Back 2D	G44F	19784	950	1325	2675	4500
Auto Trans			125	125	165	165

ACCLAIM—4-Cyl.—Equipment Schedule 5
W.B. 103.5"; 2.5 Liter.

Sedan 4D	A46K	13455	450	650	1175	2000
V6 3.0 Liter	3		225	225	300	300
4-Cyl. 2.5L Flexible Fuel	V		0	0	0	0

1994 PLYMOUTH — (1,3,4orJ)P3-(A11A)-R-#

COLT—4-Cyl.—Equipment Schedule 6
W.B. 96.1", 98.4" (4D); 1.5 Liter, 1.8 Liter.

Sedan 2D	A11A	10779	600	875	1575	2725
Sedan 4D	A36C	13428	750	1050	1850	3100
GL Sedan 2D	A21A	11400	675	950	1700	2875
GL Sedan 4D	A46C	13824	800	1150	1975	3275

COLT VISTA—4-Cyl.—Equipment Schedule 6
W.B. 99.2"; 1.8 Liter, 2.4 Liter.

Wagon 3D	B30C	14565	1400	1900	3050	4700
SE Wagon 3D	B50G	16233	1525	2025	3225	4925
AWD Wagon 3D	C40G	16777	1775	2300	3525	5250

SUNDANCE—4-Cyl.—Equipment Schedule 5
W.B. 97.2"; 2.2 Liter, 2.5 Liter.

| Hatchback 2D | P24D | 11052 | 425 | 625 | 1200 | 2100 |
| Sedan 4D | P28D | 11452 | 450 | 650 | 1250 | 2200 |

SUNDANCE—V6—Equipment Schedule 5
W.B. 97.2"; 3.0 Liter.

Duster Hatchback 2D	P643	13008	600	875	1525	2625
Duster Sedan 4D	P683	13408	650	925	1625	2775
4-Cyl. 2.5 Liter	K		(175)	(175)	(235)	(235)

LASER—4-Cyl.—Equipment Schedule 4
W.B. 97.2"; 1.8 Liter, 2.0 Liter.

Hatchback 2D	F34B	14042	575	825	2000	3675
RS Hatchback 2D	F44E	16353	675	975	2275	4125
Auto Trans			150	150	200	200

LASER—4-Cyl. Turbo—Equipment Schedule 4
W.B. 97.2"; 2.0 Liter.

RS Hatchback 2D	F44F	17887	750	1050	2375	4250
RS AWD H'Back 2D	G44F	20015	1125	1575	3025	5025
Auto Trans			150	150	200	200

1994 PLYMOUTH

Body	Type	VIN	List	Trade-In Fair	Good	Pvt-Party Good	Retail Excellent
ACCLAIM—4-Cyl.—Equipment Schedule 5							
W.B. 103.5"; 2.5 Liter.							
Sedan 4D		A46K	14154	**500**	**725**	**1300**	**2250**
V6 3.0 Liter		3		**275**	**275**	**365**	**365**
4-Cyl. 2.5L Flexible Fuel		V		**0**	**0**	**0**	**0**

1995 PLYMOUTH — (1,3,4orJ)P3–(S27C)–S–#

Body	Type	VIN	List	Trade-In Fair	Good	Pvt-Party Good	Retail Excellent
NEON—4-Cyl.—Equipment Schedule 6							
W.B. 104.0"; 2.0 Liter.							
Sedan 4D		S27C	12195	**500**	**725**	**1275**	**2200**
Highline Sedan 4D		S47C	12443	**600**	**875**	**1475**	**2500**
Highline Sedan 2D		S41C	12443	**575**	**825**	**1425**	**2425**
Sport Sedan 4D		S67C	14393	**750**	**1050**	**1750**	**2875**
Sport Coupe 2D		S61C	14693	**850**	**1200**	**1975**	**3175**
ACCLAIM—4-Cyl.—Equipment Schedule 5							
W.B. 103.5"; 2.5 Liter.							
Sedan 4D		A46K	14828	**575**	**825**	**1475**	**2550**
V6 3.0 Liter		3		**300**	**300**	**400**	**400**

1996 PLYMOUTH — (1or3)P3–(S27C)–T–#

Body	Type	VIN	List	Trade-In Fair	Good	Pvt-Party Good	Retail Excellent
NEON—4-Cyl.—Equipment Schedule 6							
W.B. 104.0"; 2.0 Liter.							
Sedan 4D		S27C	11730	**600**	**875**	**1525**	**2625**
Coupe 2D		S22C	11230	**575**	**825**	**1475**	**2550**
Highline Sedan 4D		S47C	12735	**700**	**1025**	**1750**	**2925**
Highline Coupe 2D		S42C	12535	**675**	**975**	**1675**	**2825**
Sport Sedan 4D		S67C	14165	**850**	**1225**	**2050**	**3350**
Sport Coupe 2D		S62C	13965	**975**	**1350**	**2275**	**3650**
BREEZE—4-Cyl.—Equipment Schedule 5							
W.B. 108.0"; 2.0 Liter.							
Sedan 4D		J46C	15645	**600**	**875**	**1600**	**2775**

1997 PLYMOUTH — (1or3)P3–(S27C)–V–#

Body	Type	VIN	List	Trade-In Fair	Good	Pvt-Party Good	Retail Excellent
NEON—4-Cyl.—Equipment Schedule 6							
W.B. 104.0"; 2.0 Liter.							
Sedan 4D		S27C	12430	**750**	**1075**	**1875**	**3125**
Coupe 2D		S22C	12230	**725**	**1050**	**1825**	**3050**
Highline Sedan 4D		S47C	13170	**850**	**1225**	**2100**	**3450**
Highline Coupe 2D		S42C	12970	**825**	**1175**	**2025**	**3350**
BREEZE—4-Cyl.—Equipment Schedule 5							
W.B. 108.0"; 2.0 Liter.							
Sedan 4D		J46C	16380	**775**	**1100**	**1975**	**3300**
PROWLER—V6—Equipment Schedule 1							
W.B. 113.0"; 3.5 Liter.							
Roadster 2D		W65F	39000	**13250**	**14975**	**18850**	**24300**

1998 PLYMOUTH — (1or3)P3–(S47C)–W–#

Body	Type	VIN	List	Trade-In Fair	Good	Pvt-Party Good	Retail Excellent
NEON—4-Cyl.—Equipment Schedule 6							
W.B. 104.0"; 2.0 Liter.							
Highline Sedan 4D		S47C	12855	**1050**	**1475**	**2575**	**4150**
Highline Coupe 2D		S42C	12655	**1025**	**1450**	**2525**	**4075**
Competition Sedan 4D		S27C	14660	**1450**	**1950**	**3100**	**4750**
Competition Coupe 2D		S22C	14480	**1400**	**1900**	**3050**	**4675**
Expresso or Style				**50**	**50**	**65**	**65**
BREEZE—4-Cyl.—Equipment Schedule 5							
W.B. 108.0"; 2.0 Liter, 2.4 Liter.							
Sedan 4D		J46C	16260	**975**	**1350**	**2500**	**4125**
Expresso				**50**	**50**	**65**	**65**

1999 PLYMOUTH — (1or3)P3(EorH)(S47C)–X–#

Body	Type	VIN	List	Trade-In Fair	Good	Pvt-Party Good	Retail Excellent
NEON—4-Cyl.—Equipment Schedule 6							
W.B. 104.0"; 2.0 Liter.							
Highline Sedan 4D		S47C	13320	**1350**	**1850**	**3000**	**4675**
Highline Coupe 2D		S42C	13120	**1300**	**1800**	**2975**	**4625**
Competition Sedan 4D		S27C	14985	**1825**	**2350**	**3600**	**5325**
Competition Coupe 2D		S22C	14805	**1800**	**2325**	**3550**	**5250**
Expresso or Style				**50**	**50**	**65**	**65**
BREEZE—4-Cyl.—Equipment Schedule 5							
W.B. 108.0"; 2.0 Liter, 2.4 Liter.							
Sedan 4D		J46C	16700	**1225**	**1700**	**2950**	**4700**
Expresso				**50**	**50**	**65**	**65**

Body	Type	VIN	List	Trade-In Fair	Good	Pvt-Party Good	Retail Excellent
PROWLER—V6—Equipment Schedule 1							
W.B. 113.3"; 3.5 Liter.							
Roadster 2D		W65G	40000	15850	17850	22000	27900

2000 PLYMOUTH — (1or3)P3(EorH)(S46C)-Y-#

Body	Type	VIN	List	Fair	Good	Good	Excellent
NEON—4-Cyl.—Equipment Schedule 6							
W.B. 105.0"; 2.0 Liter.							
Highline Sedan 4D		S46C	13890	1500	2000	3325	5150
LX Sedan 4D		S46C	14680	2025	2575	3925	5850
BREEZE—4-Cyl.—Equipment Schedule 5							
W.B. 108.0"; 2.0 Liter, 2.4 Liter.							
Sedan 4D		J46C	17525	1650	2150	3525	5375
PROWLER—V6—Equipment Schedule 1							
W.B. 113.3"; 3.5 Liter.							
Roadster 2D		W65G	43500	17800	19975	24300	30600

2001 PLYMOUTH — 1P3(EorH)(S46C)-1-#

Body	Type	VIN	List	Fair	Good	Good	Excellent
NEON—4-Cyl.—Equipment Schedule 6							
W.B. 105.0"; 2.0 Liter.							
Highline Sedan 4D		S46C	14275	1950	2475	3900	5875
LX Sedan 4D		S46C	15095	2525	3125	4575	6625

PONTIAC

1991 PONTIAC — (1GorKL)2(TX246)-M-#

Body	Type	VIN	List	Fair	Good	Good	Excellent
LeMANS—4-Cyl.—Equipment Schedule 6							
W.B. 99.2"; 1.6 Liter.							
VL Aerocoupe 2D		TX246	8206	225	325	775	1475
LE Aerocoupe 2D		TN246	9523	350	475	1000	1825
LE Sedan 4D		TN546	9973	400	525	1100	1950
SUNBIRD—4-Cyl.—Equipment Schedule 5							
W.B. 101.2"; 2.0 Liter.							
Sedan 4D		JC54K	10424	400	525	1000	1750
Coupe 2D		JC14K	10324	400	525	1000	1750
LE Sedan 4D		JB54K	11184	400	550	1025	1775
LE Coupe 2D		JB14K	11084	400	550	1025	1775
LE Convertible 2D		JB34K	16054	725	1050	1675	2775
SE Coupe 2D		JD14K	12334	400	575	1050	1825
V6 3.1 Liter		T		100	100	135	135
SUNBIRD—V6—Equipment Schedule 5							
W.B. 101.2"; 3.1 Liter.							
GT Coupe 2D		JU14T	14084	525	750	1300	2200
GRAND AM—4-Cyl.—Equipment Schedule 5							
W.B. 103.4"; 2.5 Liter.							
Sedan 4D		NG54U	12089	425	625	1125	1925
Coupe 2D		NG14U	11889	425	625	1125	1925
LE Sedan 4D		NE54U	13039	500	725	1225	2075
LE Coupe 2D		NE14U	12839	500	725	1225	2075
4-Cyl. 2.3L Quad 4		A,D		100	100	135	135
GRAND AM—4-Cyl.—Quad 4—Equipment Schedule 5							
W.B. 103.4"; 2.3 Liter.							
SE Sedan 4D		NW54A	17539	625	900	1475	2450
SE Coupe 2D		NW14A	17339	600	850	1425	2375
Manual Trans				0	0	0	0
FIREBIRD—V6—Equipment Schedule 4							
W.B. 101.0"; 3.1 Liter.							
Hatchback 2D		FS23T	14624	900	1275	2050	3300
Convertible 2D		FS33T	21033	1475	1975	3050	4625
Manual Trans				(150)	(150)	(200)	(200)
V8 5.0 Liter		E		200	200	265	265
FIREBIRD—V8—Equipment Schedule 4							
W.B. 101.0"; 5.0 Liter.							
Formula H'Back 2D		FS23F	17174	1050	1475	2500	3950
Trans Am H'Back 2D		FW23F	19174	1200	1650	2700	4200
Trans Am Conv 2D		FW33F	25054	2050	2625	3825	5550
Manual Trans				(100)	(100)	(135)	(135)
V8 5.7 Liter TPI		8		250	250	335	335
FIREBIRD—V8—Equipment Schedule 4							
W.B. 101.0"; 5.7 Liter.							
GTA Hatchback 2D		FW238	24999	1375	1900	2975	4550
Manual Trans				(100)	(100)	(135)	(135)

1991 PONTIAC

Body	Type	VIN	List	Trade-In Fair	Trade-In Good	Pvt-Party Good	Retail Excellent
V8 5.0 Liter TPI		F		(50)	(50)	(65)	(65)

6000—V6—Equipment Schedule 4
W.B. 104.9"; 3.1 Liter.

Body	Type	VIN	List	Fair	Good	Good	Excellent
LE Sedan 4D		AF54T	15628	475	675	1200	2025
LE Wagon 4D		AF84T	18314	475	675	1200	2025
SE Sedan 4D		AJ54T	18879	575	825	1375	2325
4-Cyl. 2.5 Liter		R		(150)	(150)	(200)	(200)

GRAND PRIX—V6—Equipment Schedule 4
W.B. 107.5"; 3.1 Liter.

LE Sedan 4D		WH54T	15869	400	600	1225	2150
SE Sedan 4D		WJ54T	16992	525	750	1400	2450
SE Coupe 2D		WJ14T	16379	475	700	1350	2375
GT Coupe 2D		WP14T	19639	625	900	1650	2825
STE Sedan 4D		WT54T	20479	675	950	1725	2925
GTP Pkg				100	100	135	135
Manual Trans				(50)	(50)	(65)	(65)
4-Cyl. 2.3L Quad 4		D		(200)	(200)	(265)	(265)
V6 3.4 Liter		X		150	150	200	200

BONNEVILLE—V6—Equipment Schedule 4
W.B. 110.8"; 3.8 Liter.

LE Sedan 4D		HX54C	18548	400	575	1050	1825
SE Sedan 4D		HZ54C	20999	600	850	1425	2375
SSE Sedan 4D		HY54C	25799	775	1125	1800	2925

1992 PONTIAC — (1G,JGorKL)2(TX246)–N–#

LeMANS—4-Cyl.—Equipment Schedule 6
W.B. 99.2"; 1.6 Liter.

VL Aerocoupe 2D		TX246	8702	225	325	800	1525
SE Aerocoupe 2D		TN246	10025	350	475	1050	1925
SE Sedan 4D		TN546	10740	400	550	1175	2075

SUNBIRD—4-Cyl.—Equipment Schedule 5
W.B. 101.3"; 2.0 Liter.

LE Sedan 4D		JC54H	11435	400	600	1125	1950
LE Coupe 2D		JC14H	11335	400	600	1125	1950
SE Sedan 4D		JB54H	12195	425	625	1150	2000
SE Coupe 2D		JB14H	12095	425	625	1150	2000
SE Convertible 2D		JB34H	17060	825	1175	1925	3125
V6 3.1 Liter		T		125	125	165	165

SUNBIRD—V6—Equipment Schedule 5
W.B. 101.3"; 3.1 Liter.

GT Coupe 2D		JD14T	14535	600	850	1475	2500

GRAND AM—4-Cyl.—Equipment Schedule 5
W.B. 103.4"; 2.3 Liter.

SE Sedan 4D		NE543	13859	575	825	1425	2450
SE Coupe 2D		NE143	13759	575	825	1425	2450
GT Sedan 4D		NW54A	15659	675	950	1625	2725
GT Coupe 2D		NW14A	15559	675	950	1625	2725
Manual Trans				0	0	0	0
V6 3.3 Liter		N		125	125	165	165

FIREBIRD—V6—Equipment Schedule 4
W.B. 101.0"; 3.1 Liter.

Hatchback 2D		FS23T	15070	1050	1475	2500	3950
Convertible 2D		FS33T	21940	1800	2325	3475	5150
Manual Trans				(175)	(175)	(235)	(235)
V8 5.0 Liter		H		225	225	300	300

FIREBIRD—V8—Equipment Schedule 4
W.B. 101.0"; 5.0 Liter.

Formula H'Back 2D		FS23E	17940	1250	1750	2825	4375
Trans Am H'Back 2D		FW23F	19840	1450	1950	3050	4625
Trans Am Conv 2D		FW33F	25610	2475	3075	4375	6225
Manual Trans				(100)	(100)	(135)	(135)
V8 5.7 Liter TPI		8		250	250	335	335

FIREBIRD—V8—Equipment Schedule 4
W.B. 101.0"; 5.7 Liter.

GTA Hatchback 2D		FW238	26370	1700	2225	3400	5050
Manual Trans				(100)	(100)	(135)	(135)
V8 5.0 Liter TPI		F		(50)	(50)	(65)	(65)

GRAND PRIX—V6—Equipment Schedule 4
W.B. 107.5"; 3.1 Liter.

LE Sedan 4D		WH54T	16575	475	675	1350	2425
SE Sedan 4D		WJ54T	17875	600	850	1575	2775
SE Coupe 2D		WJ14T	16753	550	800	1525	2675
GT Coupe 2D		WP14T	20845	725	1050	1875	3175

1992 PONTIAC

Body	Type	VIN	List	Trade-In Fair	Good	Pvt-Party Good	Retail Excellent
STE Sedan 4D		WT54T	22140	750	1075	1950	3275
GTP Pkg				50	50	65	65
Manual Trans				(50)	(50)	(65)	(65)
V6 3.4 Liter		X		150	150	200	200
BONNEVILLE—V6—Equipment Schedule 4							
W.B. 110.8"; 3.8 Liter.							
SE Sedan 4D		HX53L	19677	600	850	1450	2450
SSE Sedan 4D		HZ53L	24554	775	1125	1875	3050
V6 3.8L Supercharged		1		175	175	235	235
BONNEVILLE—V6 Supercharged—Equipment Schedule 4							
W.B. 110.8"; 3.8 Liter.							
SSEi Sedan 4D		HY521	28600	1375	1900	2975	4525

1993 PONTIAC — (1G,JGorKL)2(TX246)–P–#

Body	Type	VIN	List	Trade-In Fair	Good	Pvt-Party Good	Retail Excellent
LeMANS—4-Cyl.—Equipment Schedule 6							
W.B. 99.2"; 1.6 Liter.							
VL Aerocoupe 2D		TX246	8806	225	325	825	1575
SE Aerocoupe 2D		TN246	10329	375	500	1100	2000
SE Sedan 4D		TN546	11129	400	600	1225	2150
SUNBIRD—4-Cyl.—Equipment Schedule 5							
W.B. 101.3"; 2.0 Liter.							
LE Sedan 4D		JC54H	11097	500	725	1300	2250
LE Coupe 2D		JC14H	11097	500	725	1300	2250
SE Sedan 4D		JB54H	12095	525	750	1350	2325
SE Coupe 2D		JB14H	12095	525	750	1350	2325
SE Convertible 2D		JB34H	17118	950	1325	2225	3575
V6 3.1 Liter		T		150	150	200	200
SUNBIRD—V6—Equipment Schedule 5							
W.B. 101.3"; 3.1 Liter.							
GT Coupe 2D		JD14T	14535	700	1025	1725	2875
GRAND AM—4-Cyl.—Equipment Schedule 5							
W.B. 103.4"; 2.3 Liter.							
SE Sedan 4D		NE543	14484	675	975	1650	2800
SE Coupe 2D		NE143	14384	675	975	1650	2800
GT Sedan 4D		NW54A	15884	775	1125	1900	3100
GT Coupe 2D		NW14A	15784	750	1075	1825	3000
Manual Trans				0	0	0	0
V6 3.3 Liter		N		150	150	200	200
FIREBIRD—V6—Equipment Schedule 4							
W.B. 101.2"; 3.4 Liter.							
Hatchback 2D		FS22S	16710	1500	2000	3025	4525
Manual Trans				(225)	(225)	(300)	(300)
FIREBIRD—V8—Equipment Schedule 4							
W.B. 101.2"; 5.7 Liter.							
Formula H'Back 2D		FV22P	19815	2050	2625	3750	5400
Trans Am H'Back 2D		FV22P	22480	2350	2925	4150	5875
GRAND PRIX—V6—Equipment Schedule 4							
W.B. 107.5"; 3.1 Liter.							
LE Sedan 4D		WH54T	16245	550	800	1550	2775
SE Sedan 4D		WJ54T	17545	700	1000	1825	3125
SE Coupe 2D		WJ14T	16680	650	925	1750	3000
GT Coupe 2D		WP14T	20845	850	1225	2175	3650
STE Sedan 4D		WT54T	22140	925	1300	2400	3975
GTP Pkg				75	75	100	100
Manual Trans				(75)	(75)	(100)	(100)
V6 3.4 Liter		X		175	175	235	235
BONNEVILLE—V6—Equipment Schedule 4							
W.B. 110.8"; 3.8 Liter.							
SE Sedan 4D		HX53L	20522	700	1025	1700	2825
SSE Sedan 4D		HZ53L	25399	975	1375	2275	3650
V6 3.8L Supercharged		1		225	225	300	300
BONNEVILLE—V6 Supercharged—Equipment Schedule 4							
W.B. 110.8"; 3.8 Liter.							
SSEi Sedan 4D		HY521	29999	1700	2225	3400	5050

1994 PONTIAC — (1G,JGorKL)2(JB54H)–R–#

Body	Type	VIN	List	Trade-In Fair	Good	Pvt-Party Good	Retail Excellent
SUNBIRD—4-Cyl.—Equipment Schedule 5							
W.B. 101.3"; 2.0 Liter.							
LE Sedan 4D		JB54H	11519	600	850	1500	2600
LE Coupe 2D		JB14H	11519	600	850	1500	2600
LE Convertible 2D		JB34H	17279	1075	1500	2575	4100
V6 3.1 Liter		T		175	175	235	235

1994 PONTIAC

Body	Type	VIN	List	Trade-In Fair	Good	Pvt-Party Good	Retail Excellent
SUNBIRD—V6—Equipment Schedule 5							
W.B. 101.3"; 3.1 Liter.							
SE Coupe 2D	JL14T	14179	675	975	1700	2875
GRAND AM—4-Cyl.—Equipment Schedule 5							
W.B. 103.4"; 2.3 Liter.							
SE Sedan 4D	NE553	14484	800	1150	1975	3225
SE Coupe 2D	NE153	14384	800	1150	1975	3225
GT Sedan 4D	NW55A	16354	925	1300	2200	3575
GT Coupe 2D	NW15A	16254	875	1225	2100	3450
Manual Trans			0	0	0	0
V6 3.1 Liter	M		175	175	235	235
FIREBIRD—V6—Equipment Schedule 4							
W.B. 101.1"; 3.4 Liter.							
Hatchback 2D	FS22S	16735	1825	2350	3450	5050
Convertible 2D	FS32S	22444	2800	3425	4675	6525
Manual Trans			(275)	(275)	(365)	(365)
FIREBIRD—V8—Equipment Schedule 4							
W.B. 101.1"; 5.7 Liter.							
Formula H'Back 2D	FV22P	19615	2475	3075	4300	6075
Formula Convertible 2D	FV32P	25544	3725	4450	5875	7925
Trans Am H'Back 2D	FV22P	21005	2825	3475	4750	6625
Trans Am GT H'Back 2D	FV22P	22505	3125	3775	5100	7000
Trans Am GT Conv 2D	FV32P	27744	4375	5150	6650	8850
GRAND PRIX—V6—Equipment Schedule 4							
W.B. 107.5"; 3.1 Liter.							
SE Sedan 4D	WJ52M	17094	825	1175	2125	3625
SE Coupe 2D	WJ16M	17295	750	1075	2025	3450
GT/GTP Pkg			100	100	135	135
V6 3.4 Liter	X		200	200	265	265
BONNEVILLE—V6—Equipment Schedule 4							
W.B. 110.8"; 3.8 Liter.							
SE Sedan 4D	HX52L	21627	850	1225	2025	3300
SSE Sedan 4D	HZ52L	26459	1225	1700	2800	4350
SLE Pkg			125	125	165	165
BONNEVILLE—V6 Supercharged—Equipment Schedule 4							
W.B. 110.8"; 3.8 Liter.							
SSEi Sedan 4D	HZ521	29141	1900	2425	3650	5325

1995 PONTIAC — (1G,JGorKL)2(JB524)-S-#

Body	Type	VIN	List	Trade-In Fair	Good	Pvt-Party Good	Retail Excellent
SUNFIRE—4-Cyl.—Equipment Schedule 5							
W.B. 104.1"; 2.2 Liter, 2.3 Liter.							
SE Sedan 4D	JB524	12989	675	975	1725	2925
SE Coupe 2D	JB124	12839	650	925	1650	2825
SE Convertible 2D	JB324	18034	1525	2025	3225	4875
GT Coupe 2D	JD12D	14824	875	1225	2125	3475
GRAND AM—4-Cyl.—Equipment Schedule 5							
W.B. 103.4"; 2.3 Liter.							
SE Sedan 4D	NE55D	15084	925	1300	2275	3675
SE Coupe 2D	NE15D	14984	925	1300	2275	3675
GT Sedan 4D	NW55D	16204	1050	1475	2575	4125
GT Coupe 2D	NW15D	16104	1000	1425	2500	4025
Manual Trans			0	0	0	0
V6 3.1 Liter	M		200	200	265	265
FIREBIRD—V6—Equipment Schedule 4							
W.B. 101.1"; 3.4 Liter.							
Hatchback 2D	FS22S	17764	2150	2750	3900	5600
Convertible 2D	FS32S	23214	3250	3925	5250	7200
Manual Trans			(325)	(325)	(435)	(435)
V6 3.8 Liter	K		175	175	235	235
FIREBIRD—V8—Equipment Schedule 4							
W.B. 101.1"; 5.7 Liter.							
Formula H'Back 2D	FV22P	21450	2925	3600	4875	6775
Formula Convertible 2D	FV32P	26404	4300	5100	6575	8750
Trans Am H'Back 2D	FV22P	22344	3350	4050	5400	7400
Trans Am Conv 2D	FV32P	28414	4950	5825	7400	9700
GRAND PRIX—V6—Equipment Schedule 4							
W.B. 107.5"; 3.1 Liter.							
SE Sedan 4D	WJ52M	17589	925	1300	2400	4150
SE Coupe 2D	WJ16M	17919	875	1225	2375	4025
GT/GTP Pkg			100	100	135	135
V6 3.4 Liter	X		225	225	300	300
BONNEVILLE—V6—Equipment Schedule 4							
W.B. 110.8"; 3.8 Liter.							

1995 PONTIAC

Body Type	VIN	List	Trade-In Fair	Good	Pvt-Party Good	Retail Excellent
SE Sedan 4D	HX52K	21584	1025	1450	2525	4050
SSE Sedan 4D	HZ52K	26389	1550	2050	3250	4950
SLE Pkg			150	150	200	200
V6 3.8L Supercharged (SE)	1		300	300	400	400
BONNEVILLE—V6 Supercharged—Equipment Schedule 4						
W.B. 110.8"; 3.8 Liter.						
SSEi Sedan 4D	HZ521	27556	**2275**	**2825**	**4125**	**5975**

1996 PONTIAC — (1,2,3or4)G2(JB524)–T–#

SUNFIRE—4-Cyl.—Equipment Schedule 5
W.B. 104.1"; 2.2 Liter, 2.4 Liter.

Body Type	VIN	List	Fair	Good	Good	Excellent
SE Sedan 4D	JB524	13514	800	1150	2050	3450
SE Coupe 2D	JB124	13344	775	1100	2000	3350
SE Convertible 2D	JB324	18229	1850	2375	3650	5425
GT Coupe 2D	JD12T	15299	1000	1425	2550	4125
GRAND AM—4-Cyl.—Equipment Schedule 5						
W.B. 103.4"; 2.4 Liter.						
SE Sedan 4D	NE52T	15624	1075	1525	2675	4300
SE Coupe 2D	NE12T	15624	1075	1525	2675	4300
GT Sedan 4D	NW52T	16794	1225	1700	2875	4525
GT Coupe 2D	NW12T	16794	1175	1625	2800	4450
Manual Trans			0	0	0	0
V6 3.1 Liter	M		225	225	300	300
FIREBIRD—V6—Equipment Schedule 4						
W.B. 101.1"; 3.8 Liter.						
Coupe 2D	FS22K	19408	2575	3175	4450	6250
Convertible 2D	FS32K	23739	3750	4475	5925	8000
Manual Trans			(375)	(375)	(500)	(500)
FIREBIRD—V8—Equipment Schedule 4						
W.B. 101.1"; 5.7 Liter.						
Formula Coupe 2D	FV22P	22363	3450	4150	5525	7550
Formula Conv 2D	FV32P	26579	4900	5750	7325	9650
Trans Am Coupe 2D	FV22P	26579	3900	4650	6125	8275
Trans Am Conv 2D	FV32P	28659	5600	6525	8200	10650
Ram Air Handling Pkg			850	850	1135	1135
GRAND PRIX—V6—Equipment Schedule 4						
W.B. 107.5"; 3.1 Liter.						
SE Sedan 4D	WJ52M	18049	1075	1525	2800	4550
SE Coupe 2D	WJ12M	18899	1025	1450	2700	4450
GT/GTP Pkg			100	100	135	135
V6 3.4 Liter	X		250	250	335	335
BONNEVILLE—V6—Equipment Schedule 4						
W.B. 110.8"; 3.8 Liter.						
SE Sedan 4D	HX52K	22374	1275	1775	2925	4550
SSE Sedan 4D	HZ52K	27149	1975	2525	3775	5575
SLE Pkg			150	150	200	200
V6 3.8L Supercharged (SE)	1		325	325	435	435
BONNEVILLE—V6 Supercharged—Equipment Schedule 4						
W.B. 110.8"; 3.8 Liter.						
SSEi Sedan 4D	HZ521	28491	**2725**	**3350**	**4700**	**6650**

1997 PONTIAC — (1,2,3or4)G2(JB524)–V–#

SUNFIRE—4-Cyl.—Equipment Schedule 5
W.B. 104.1"; 2.2 Liter, 2.4 Liter.

Body Type	VIN	List	Fair	Good	Good	Excellent
SE Sedan 4D	JB524	14079	950	1325	2500	4125
SE Coupe 2D	JB124	13939	925	1300	2425	4050
SE Convertible 2D	JB324	19399	2200	2800	4125	6025
GT Coupe 2D	JD12T	15859	1200	1650	2850	4550
GRAND AM—4-Cyl.—Equipment Schedule 5						
W.B. 103.4"; 2.4 Liter.						
SE Sedan 4D	NE52T	15969	1300	1800	3025	4750
SE Coupe 2D	NE12T	15969	1300	1800	3025	4750
GT Sedan 4D	NW52T	17209	1475	1975	3225	5000
GT Coupe 2D	NW12T	17209	1400	1900	3150	4900
Manual Trans			0	0	0	0
V6 3.1 Liter	M		250	250	335	335
FIREBIRD—V6—Equipment Schedule 4						
W.B. 101.1"; 3.8 Liter.						
Coupe 2D	FS22K	19209	3000	3675	5025	6975
Convertible 2D	FS32K	24374	4300	5100	6600	8800
Manual Trans			(400)	(400)	(535)	(535)
FIREBIRD—V8—Equipment Schedule 4						
W.B. 101.1"; 5.7 Liter.						

1997 PONTIAC

Body	Type	VIN	List	Trade-In Fair	Trade-In Good	Pvt-Party Good	Retail Excellent
Formula Coupe 2D		FV22P	21179	4000	4750	6225	8400
Formula Coupe 2D		FV32P	26979	5550	6500	8150	10600
Trans Am Coupe 2D		FV22P	23339	4525	5350	6900	9200
Trans Am Conv 2D		FV32P	28899	6300	7325	9075	11700
Ram Air Handling Pkg				925	925	1235	1235
GRAND PRIX—V6—Equipment Schedule 4							
W.B. 110.5"; 3.8 Liter.							
SE Sedan 4D		WJ52K	19249	1800	2325	3425	5000
GT Sedan 4D		WP52K	20359	2300	2875	4050	5750
GT Coupe 2D		WP12K	20029	2175	2775	3900	5575
GTP Pkg				100	100	135	135
V6 3.1 Liter		M		(250)	(250)	(335)	(335)
V6 3.8L Supercharged		1		350	350	465	465
BONNEVILLE—V6—Equipment Schedule 4							
W.B. 110.8"; 3.8 Liter.							
SE Sedan 4D		HX52K	22914	1675	2175	3450	5200
SSE Sedan 4D		HZ52K	27769	2425	3025	4400	6300
SLE				150	150	200	200
V6 3.8L Superchrgd (SE)		1		350	350	465	465
BONNEVILLE—V6 Supercharged—Equipment Schedule 4							
W.B. 110.8"; 3.8 Liter.							
SSEi Sedan 4D		HZ521	29111	3225	3900	5350	7425

1998 PONTIAC — (1,2,3or4)G2(JB524)-W-#

Body	Type	VIN	List	Trade-In Fair	Trade-In Good	Pvt-Party Good	Retail Excellent
SUNFIRE—4-Cyl.—Equipment Schedule 5							
W.B. 104.1"; 2.2 Liter, 2.4 Liter.							
SE Sedan 4D		JB524	14425	1125	1575	2850	4600
SE Coupe 2D		JB124	14425	1100	1550	2800	4525
SE Convertible 2D		JB324	19995	2600	3225	4650	6675
GT Coupe 2D		JD12T	16805	1425	1925	3225	5050
GRAND AM—4-Cyl.—Equipment Schedule 5							
W.B. 103.4"; 2.4 Liter.							
SE Sedan 4D		NE52T	16359	1600	2100	3450	5275
SE Coupe 2D		NE12T	16209	1600	2100	3450	5275
GT Sedan 4D		NW52T	17809	1775	2300	3650	5525
GT Coupe 2D		NW12T	17659	1700	2225	3575	5425
Manual Trans				0	0	0	0
V6 3.1 Liter		M		250	250	335	335
FIREBIRD—V6—Equipment Schedule 4							
W.B. 101.1"; 3.8 Liter.							
Coupe 2D		FS22P	20380	3575	4275	5725	7800
Convertible 2D		FS32P	25545	4925	5775	7375	9700
T-Bar Roof				375	375	500	500
Manual Trans				(425)	(425)	(565)	(565)
FIREBIRD—V8—Equipment Schedule 4							
W.B. 101.1"; 5.7 Liter.							
Formula Coupe 2D		FV22P	23290	4650	5475	7025	9325
Trans Am Coupe 2D		FV22P	26400	5250	6125	7775	10200
Trans Am Conv 2D		FV32P	30140	7075	8175	10000	12750
T-Bar Roof				375	375	500	500
Ram Air Handling Pkg				975	975	1300	1300
GRAND PRIX—V6—Equipment Schedule 4							
W.B. 110.5"; 3.8 Liter.							
SE Sedan 4D		WJ52K	19885	2200	2800	3925	5575
GT Sedan 4D		WP52K	21215	2800	3425	4625	6425
GT Coupe 2D		WP12K	20965	2650	3275	4450	6175
GTP Pkg				100	100	135	135
V6 3.1 Liter		M		(250)	(250)	(335)	(335)
V6 3.8L Supercharged		1		375	375	500	500
BONNEVILLE—V6—Equipment Schedule 4							
W.B. 110.8"; 3.8 Liter.							
SE Sedan 4D		HX52K	23215	2125	2700	4050	5975
SSE Sedan 4D		HZ52K	29895	2975	3650	5100	7175
SLE Pkg				150	150	200	200
BONNEVILLE—V6 Supercharged—Equipment Schedule 4							
W.B. 110.8"; 3.8 Liter.							
SSEi Sedan 4D		HZ521	31165	3800	4550	6075	8325

1999 PONTIAC — (1,2,3or4)G2(JB524)-X-#

Body	Type	VIN	List	Trade-In Fair	Trade-In Good	Pvt-Party Good	Retail Excellent
SUNFIRE—4-Cyl.—Equipment Schedule 5							
W.B. 104.1"; 2.2 Liter, 2.4 Liter.							
SE Sedan 4D		JB524	14685	1425	1925	3275	5150
SE Coupe 2D		JB124	14685	1375	1900	3225	5075

1999 PONTIAC

Body	Type	VIN	List	Trade-In Fair	Good	Pvt-Party Good	Retail Excellent
	GT Coupe 2D	JD12T	17065	**1775**	**2300**	**3650**	**5575**
	GT Convertible 2D	JB32T	21655	**3100**	**3750**	**5250**	**7400**

GRAND AM—4-Cyl.—Equipment Schedule 5
W.B. 106.7"; 2.4 Liter.

	SE Sedan 4D	NE52T	16995	**2200**	**2800**	**4125**	**6025**
	SE Coupe 2D	NE12T	16595	**2200**	**2800**	**4125**	**6025**
	V6 3.4 Liter	E		**250**	**250**	**335**	**335**

GRAND AM—V6—Equipment Schedule 5
W.B. 107.0"; 3.4 Liter.

| | GT Sedan 4D | NW52E | 19995 | **3025** | **3700** | **5000** | **6875** |
| | GT Coupe 2D | NW12E | 19595 | **2775** | **3400** | **4800** | **6800** |

FIREBIRD—V6—Equipment Schedule 5
W.B. 101.1"; 3.8 Liter.

	Coupe 2D	FS22K	20540	**4200**	**4975**	**6550**	**8825**
	Convertible 2D	FS32K	26465	**5650**	**6575**	**8300**	**10800**
	T-Bar Roof			**425**	**425**	**565**	**565**
	Manual Trans			**(450)**	**(450)**	**(600)**	**(600)**

FIREBIRD—V8—Equipment Schedule 5
W.B. 101.1"; 5.7 Liter.

	Formula Coupe 2D	FV22G	23930	**5400**	**6300**	**8000**	**10500**
	Trans Am Coupe 2D	FV22G	27040	**6100**	**7075**	**8850**	**11450**
	Trans Am Conv 2D	FV32G	31110	**8025**	**9225**	**11150**	**14050**
	T-Bar Roof			**425**	**425**	**565**	**565**
	Ram Air Handling Pkg			**1025**	**1025**	**1365**	**1365**

GRAND PRIX—V6—Equipment Schedule 4
W.B. 110.5"; 3.8 Liter.

	SE Sedan 4D	WJ52K	20210	**2700**	**3300**	**4475**	**6225**
	GT Sedan 4D	WP52K	21705	**3325**	**4025**	**5275**	**7125**
	GT Coupe 2D	WP12K	21555	**3175**	**3825**	**5075**	**6875**
	V6 3.1 Liter	M		**(250)**	**(250)**	**(335)**	**(335)**

GRAND PRIX—V6 Supercharged—Equipment Schedule 4
W.B. 110.5"; 3.8 Liter.

| | GTP Sedan 4D | WR521 | 24470 | **4425** | **5225** | **6575** | **8600** |
| | GTP Coupe 2D | WR121 | 24320 | **4225** | **5025** | **6350** | **8350** |

BONNEVILLE—V6—Equipment Schedule 4
W.B. 110.8"; 3.8 Liter.

	SE Sedan 4D	HX52K	23715	**2700**	**3300**	**4750**	**6775**
	SSE Sedan 4D	HZ52K	30715	**3650**	**4400**	**5925**	**8100**
	SLE Pkg			**150**	**150**	**200**	**200**

BONNEVILLE—V6 Supercharged—Equipment Schedule 4
W.B. 110.8"; 3.8 Liter.

| | SSEi Sedan 4D | HZ521 | 31665 | **4550** | **5375** | **6975** | **9300** |

2000 PONTIAC — (1,2,3or4)G2(JB524)-Y-#

SUNFIRE—4-Cyl.—Equipment Schedule 5
W.B. 104.1"; 2.2 Liter, 2.4 Liter.

	SE Sedan 4D	JB524	15120	**2175**	**2775**	**4025**	**5850**
	SE Coupe 2D	JB124	15020	**2125**	**2700**	**3950**	**5750**
	GT Coupe 2D	JD12T	17530	**2600**	**3225**	**4525**	**6400**
	GT Convertible 2D	JD32T	22120	**4075**	**4850**	**6275**	**8400**

GRAND AM—4-Cyl.—Equipment Schedule 5
W.B. 107.0"; 2.4 Liter.

	SE Sedan 4D	NE52T	17540	**2650**	**3275**	**4725**	**6775**
	SE Coupe 2D	NE12T	17240	**2625**	**3250**	**4700**	**6750**
	V6 3.4 Liter	E		**300**	**300**	**400**	**400**

GRAND AM—V6—Equipment Schedule 5
W.B. 107.0"; 3.4 Liter.

| | GT Sedan 4D | NW52E | 20385 | **3625** | **4350** | **5725** | **7750** |
| | GT Coupe 2D | NW12E | 20085 | **3325** | **4025** | **5525** | **7675** |

FIREBIRD—V6—Equipment Schedule 4
W.B. 101.1"; 3.8 Liter.

	Coupe 2D	FS22K	20535	**5050**	**5925**	**7600**	**10050**
	Convertible 2D	FS32K	26460	**6750**	**7775**	**9600**	**12300**
	T-Bar Roof			**500**	**500**	**665**	**665**
	Manual Trans			**(500)**	**(500)**	**(665)**	**(665)**

FIREBIRD—V8—Equipment Schedule 4
W.B. 101.1"; 5.7 Liter.

	Formula Coupe 2D	FV22G	24055	**6550**	**7575**	**9350**	**12050**
	Trans Am Coupe 2D	FV22G	27165	**7425**	**8525**	**10450**	**13250**
	Trans Am Conv 2D	FV32G	31235	**9475**	**10825**	**12850**	**16000**
	T-Bar Roof			**500**	**500**	**665**	**665**
	Ram Air Handling Pkg			**1175**	**1175**	**1565**	**1565**

Body Type	VIN	List	Trade-In Fair	Trade-In Good	Pvt-Party Good	Retail Excellent
GRAND PRIX—V6—Equipment Schedule 4						
W.B. 110.5"; 3.8 Liter.						
SE Sedan 4D	WJ52J	20610	3275	3950	5225	7075
GT Sedan 4D	WP52K	22105	4025	4775	6100	8075
GT Coupe 2D	WP12K	21955	3825	4575	5900	7825
V6 3.1 Liter	J		(250)	(250)	(335)	(335)
GRAND PRIX—V6 Supercharged—Equipment Schedule 4						
W.B. 110.5"; 3.8 Liter.						
GTP Sedan 4D	WR521	24870	5275	6175	7625	9800
GTP Coupe 2D	WR121	24720	5050	5925	7325	9450
BONNEVILLE—V6—Equipment Schedule 4						
W.B. 112.2"; 3.8 Liter.						
SE Sedan 4D	HX52K	24295	3550	4250	6025	8500
SLE Sedan 4D	HY52K	27995	4350	5125	6950	9550
SSEi Sedan 4D	HZ52K	32250	5950	6900	8750	11450
V6 3.8L Supercharged	1		500	500	665	665

2001 PONTIAC — (1,2or3)G(2or7)(JB524)-1-#

Body Type	VIN	List	Trade-In Fair	Trade-In Good	Pvt-Party Good	Retail Excellent
SUNFIRE—4-Cyl.—Equipment Schedule 5						
W.B. 104.1"; 2.2 Liter, 2.4 Liter.						
SE Sedan 4D	JB524	15650	2700	3300	4700	6675
SE Coupe 2D	JB124	15395	2600	3225	4575	6550
GT Coupe 2D	JD12T	17625	3175	3850	5275	7325
GRAND AM—4-Cyl.—Equipment Schedule 5						
W.B. 107.0"; 2.4 Liter.						
SE Sedan 4D	NE52T	17800	3175	3850	5400	7625
SE Coupe 2D	NE12T	17500	3150	3800	5375	7575
V6 3.4 Liter	E		325	325	435	435
GRAND AM—V6—Equipment Schedule 5						
W.B. 107.0"; 3.4 Liter.						
GT Sedan 4D	NW52E	21110	4325	5125	6600	8775
GT Coupe 2D	NW12E	20810	4000	4750	6375	8700
FIREBIRD—V6—Equipment Schedule 4						
W.B. 101.1"; 3.8 Liter.						
Coupe 2D	FS22K	20810	6000	6950	8750	11400
Convertible 2D	FS32K	26735	7925	9125	11050	13950
T-Bar Roof			575	575	765	765
Manual Trans			(525)	(525)	(700)	(700)
75th Anniversary			475	475	635	635
FIREBIRD—V8—Equipment Schedule 4						
W.B. 101.1"; 5.7 Liter.						
Formula Coupe 2D	FV22G	24480	7775	8950	10850	13750
Trans Am Coupe 2D	FV22G	27590	8825	10100	12100	15100
Trans Am Conv 2D	FV32G	31660	11050	12550	14750	18100
T-Bar Roof			575	575	765	765
Ram Air Handling Pkg			1325	1325	1765	1765
75th Anniversary			475	475	635	635
NHRA Pkg			250	250	335	335
GRAND PRIX—V6—Equipment Schedule 4						
W.B. 110.5"; 3.1 Liter, 3.8 Liter.						
SE Sedan 4D	WJ52J	21135	3950	4700	6075	8125
GT Sedan 4D	WP52K	22615	4800	5650	7075	9250
GT Coupe 2D	WP12K	22465	4575	5400	6850	8950
Special Edition			150	150	200	200
GRAND PRIX—V6 Supercharged—Equipment Schedule 4						
W.B. 110.5"; 3.8 Liter.						
GTP Sedan 4D	WR521	26135	6275	7275	8800	11150
GTP Coupe 2D	WR121	25935	5950	6900	8425	10750
Special Edition			150	150	200	200
BONNEVILLE—V6—Equipment Schedule 4						
W.B. 112.2"; 3.8 Liter.						
SE Sedan 4D	HX52K	25730	4375	5175	7075	9750
SLE Sedan 4D	HY52K	28700	5250	6150	8150	10950
BONNEVILLE—V6 Supercharged—Equipment Schedule 4						
W.B. 112.2"; 3.8 Liter.						
SSEi Sedan 4D	HZ521	33070	7300	8400	10350	13200

2002 PONTIAC — (1or2)G2(JB524)-2-#

Body Type	VIN	List	Trade-In Fair	Trade-In Good	Pvt-Party Good	Retail Excellent
SUNFIRE—4-Cyl.—Equipment Schedule 5						
W.B. 104.1"; 2.2 Liter, 2.4 Liter.						
SE Sedan 4D	JB524	16545	3325	4000	5400	7675
SE Coupe 2D	JB124	16045	3225	3900	5400	7575
GT Coupe 2D	JD12T	18205	3875	4625	6150	8400

2002 PONTIAC

Body Type	VIN	List	Trade-In Fair	Good	Pvt-Party Good	Retail Excellent
GRAND AM—4-Cyl.—Equipment Schedule 5						
W.B. 107.0"; 2.2 Liter.						
SE Sedan 4D	NE52T	18360	3850	4600	6275	8675
SE Coupe 2D	NE12T	18210	3775	4525	6225	8600
V6 3.4 Liter	E		350	350	465	465
GRAND AM—V6—Equipment Schedule 5						
W.B. 107.0"; 3.4 Liter.						
GT Sedan 4D	NW52E	21425	5125	6025	7625	10000
GT Coupe 2D	NW12E	21275	4800	5625	7400	9900
FIREBIRD—V6—Equipment Schedule 4						
W.B. 101.1"; 3.8 Liter.						
Coupe 2D	FS22K	21105	7150	8250	10150	12950
Convertible 2D	FS32K	27205	9275	10575	12600	15700
T-Bar Roof			650	650	865	865
GT Pkg			275	275	365	365
Manual Trans			(550)	(550)	(735)	(735)
FIREBIRD—V8—Equipment Schedule 4						
W.B. 101.1"; 5.7 Liter.						
Formula Coupe 2D	FV22G	26235	9250	10525	12550	15650
Trans Am Coupe 2D	FV22G	28265	10375	11825	13900	17150
Trans Am Conv 2D	FV32G	32335	12800	14500	16750	20300
Collector Ed Cpe 2D	FV22G	31265	11600	13200	15350	18750
Collector Ed Conv 2D	FV32G	35335	13875	15675	17950	21600
T-Bar Roof			650	650	865	865
NHRA Pkg			275	275	365	365
Ram Air Handling Pkg			1475	1475	1965	1965
GRAND PRIX—V6—Equipment Schedule 4						
W.B. 110.5"; 3.1 Liter, 3.8 Liter.						
SE Sedan 4D	WJ52J	21575	4800	5650	7175	9425
GT Sedan 4D	WP52K	23695	5750	6700	8275	10600
GT Coupe 2D	WP12K	23545	5500	6425	7975	10350
40th Anniversary Edition			100	100	135	135
GRAND PRIX—V6 Supercharged—Equipment Schedule 4						
W.B. 110.5"; 3.8 Liter.						
GTP Sedan 4D	WR521	26415	7425	8525	10250	12800
GTP Coupe 2D	WR121	26235	7000	8075	9750	12250
40th Anniversary Edition			100	100	135	135
BONNEVILLE—V6—Equipment Schedule 4						
W.B. 112.2"; 3.8 Liter.						
SE Sedan 4D	HX52K	26355	5425	6350	8425	11350
SLE Sedan 4D	HY52K	29545	6450	7450	9600	12650
BONNEVILLE—V6 Supercharged—Equipment Schedule 4						
W.B. 112.2"; 3.8 Liter.						
SSEi Sedan 4D	HZ521	33605	8900	10175	12150	15150

2003 PONTIAC — (1or5)G2orY2(JB12F)-3-#

Body Type	VIN	List	Trade-In Fair	Good	Pvt-Party Good	Retail Excellent
SUNFIRE—4-Cyl.—Equipment Schedule 5						
W.B. 104.1"; 2.2 Liter.						
Coupe 2D	JB12F	15435	4050	4800	6475	8825
VIBE—4-Cyl.—Equipment Schedule 6						
W.B. 102.4"; 1.8 Liter.						
Sport Wagon 4D	SL628	16900	6500	7525	9175	11650
GT Sport Wagon 4D	SN62L	19900	6825	7875	9500	12050
AWD Sport Wagon 4D	SM628	20100	7125	8225	9900	12400
GRAND AM—4-Cyl.—Equipment Schedule 5						
W.B. 107.0"; 2.2 Liter.						
SE Sedan 4D	NE52T	18465	4700	5550	7375	10000
V6 3.4 Liter	E		375	375	500	500
GRAND AM—V6—Equipment Schedule 5						
W.B. 107.0"; 3.4 Liter.						
GT Sedan 4D	NW52E	21640	6125	7100	8850	11450
GT Coupe 2D	NW12E	21640	5750	6700	8600	11350
GRAND PRIX—V6—Equipment Schedule 4						
W.B. 110.5"; 3.1 Liter, 3.8 Liter.						
SE Sedan 4D	WK52J	22140	5875	6850	8525	11050
GT Sedan 4D	WP52K	23990	6875	7950	9700	12350
Wide Track Sport Pkg			400	400	535	535
GRAND PRIX—V6 Supercharged—Equipment Schedule 4						
W.B. 110.5"; 3.8 Liter.						
GTP Sedan 4D	WR521	26800	8775	10050	11950	14800
BONNEVILLE—V6—Equipment Schedule 4						
W.B. 112.2"; 3.8 Liter.						
SE Sedan 4D	HX52K	26665	6800	7850	10150	13350

0106

2003 PONTIAC

Body	Type	VIN	List	Trade-In Fair	Good	Pvt-Party Good	Retail Excellent
SLE Sedan 4D		HY52K	29855	**7900**	**9075**	**11400**	**14800**
BONNEVILLE—V6 Supercharged—Equipment Schedule 4							
W.B. 112.2"; 3.8 Liter.							
SSEi Sedan 4D		HZ541	34085	**10775**	**12275**	**14250**	**17450**

2004 PONTIAC — (1,2,5or6)G2orY2(JB12F)-4-#

Body	Type	VIN	List	Trade-In Fair	Good	Pvt-Party Good	Retail Excellent
SUNFIRE—4-Cyl.—Equipment Schedule 5							
W.B. 104.1"; 2.2 Liter.							
Coupe 2D		JB12F	16695	**5100**	**5975**	**7675**	**10200**
VIBE—4-Cyl.—Equipment Schedule 6							
W.B. 102.4" 1.8 Liter.							
Sport Wagon 4D		SL628	17045	**7775**	**8925**	**10550**	**13100**
GT Sport Wagon		SN62L	19995	**8100**	**9300**	**10950**	**13550**
AWD Sport Wagon 4D		SM628	20345	**8500**	**9700**	**11350**	**13950**
GRAND AM—4-Cyl.—Equipment Schedule 5							
W.B. 107.0"; 2.2 Liter.							
SE Sedan 4D		NE52F	18545	**5800**	**6750**	**8675**	**11450**
V6 3.4 Liter		E		**400**	**400**	**535**	**535**
GRAND AM—V6—Equipment Schedule 5							
W.B. 107.0"; 3.4 Liter.							
GT Sedan 4D		NW52E	22450	**7350**	**8475**	**10300**	**13050**
GT Coupe 2D		NW12E	22450	**6925**	**8000**	**10050**	**12950**
GRAND PRIX—V6—Equipment Schedule 4							
W.B. 110.5"; 3.8 Liter.							
GT Sedan 4D		WP522	22395	**8400**	**9625**	**11500**	**14400**
GRAND PRIX—V6 Supercharged—Equipment Schedule 4							
W.B. 110.5"; 3.8 Liter.							
GTP Sedan 4D		WR524	26495	**10475**	**11925**	**13900**	**17050**
BONNEVILLE—V6—Equipment Schedule 4							
W.B. 112.2"; 3.8 Liter.							
SE Sedan 4D		HX52K	27570	**8600**	**9850**	**12200**	**15700**
SLE Sedan 4D		HY52K	30420	**9800**	**11200**	**13650**	**17200**
BONNEVILLE—V8—Equipment Schedule 4							
W.B. 112.2"; 4.6 Liter.							
GXP Sedan 4D		HZ54Y	35995	**10825**	**12275**	**15150**	**19250**
GTO—V8—Equipment Schedule 2							
W.B. 109.8"; 5.7 Liter.							
Coupe 2D		VX13G	33495	**14650**	**16550**	**19500**	**24000**

2005 PONTIAC — (1,2,3,5or6)G2orY2(JB12F)-5

Body	Type	VIN	List	Trade-In Fair	Good	Pvt-Party Good	Retail Excellent
SUNFIRE—4-Cyl.—Equipment Schedule 5							
W.B. 104.1"; 2.2 Liter.							
Coupe 2D		JB12F	15650	**6375**	**7400**	**9250**	**12000**
VIBE—4-Cyl.—Equipment Schedule 6							
W.B. 102.4" 1.8 Liter.							
Sport Wagon 4D		SL628	18735	**9275**	**10575**	**12200**	**14850**
GT Sport Wagon 4D		SN62L	20535	**9650**	**11000**	**12650**	**15350**
AWD Sport Wagon 4D		SM628	20885	**10050**	**11400**	**13100**	**15850**
GRAND AM—4-Cyl.—Equipment Schedule 5							
W.B. 107.0"; 2.2 Liter.							
SE Sedan 4D		NE52F	20580	**7125**	**8225**	**10300**	**13350**
V6 3.4 Liter		E		**425**	**425**	**565**	**565**
GRAND AM—V6—Equipment Schedule 5							
W.B. 107.0"; 3.4 Liter.							
GT Coupe 2D		NW12E	22990	**8400**	**9625**	**11800**	**15000**
GRAND PRIX—V6—Equipment Schedule 4							
W.B. 110.5"; 3.8 Liter.							
Sedan 4D		WP522	23560	**9750**	**11100**	**13250**	**16500**
GT Sedan 4D		WS522	25460	**10125**	**11550**	**13750**	**17000**
GRAND PRIX—V6 Supercharged—Equipment Schedule 4							
W.B. 110.5"; 3.8 Liter.							
GTP Sedan 4D		WR524	27220	**12475**	**14125**	**16450**	**20100**
GRAND PRIX—V8—Equipment Schedule 4							
W.B. 110.5"; 5.3 Liter.							
GXP Sedan 4D		WC52C	29995				
G6—V6—Equipment Schedule 4							
W.B. 112.3"; 3.5 Liter.							
Sedan 4D		ZG528	21700	**11300**	**12800**	**15350**	**19050**
GT Sedan 4D		ZH528	23925	**12075**	**13675**	**16250**	**20100**
BONNEVILLE—V6—Equipment Schedule 4							
W.B. 112.2"; 3.8 Liter.							
SE Sedan 4D		HX52K	28650	**10775**	**12275**	**14850**	**18700**
SLE Sedan 4D		HY52K	31085	**12075**	**13675**	**16400**	**20500**

Body	Type	VIN	List	Trade-In Fair	Good	Pvt-Party Good	Retail Excellent

BONNEVILLE—V8—Equipment Schedule 4
W.B. 112.2"; 4.6 Liter.

| GXP Sedan 4D | | HZ54Y | 36120 | **13150** | **14900** | **17950** | **22500** |

GTO—V8—Equipment Schedule 2
W.B. 109.8"; 5.7 Liter.

| Coupe 2D | | VX12U | 34295 | **18725** | **21050** | **24300** | **29400** |

PORSCHE

1991 PORSCHE — WPO(AB294)–M–#

944—4-Cyl.—Equipment Schedule 1
W.B. 94.5"; 3.0 Liter.

| S2 Coupe 2D | | AB294 | 47290 | **4000** | **4750** | **6150** | **8200** |
| S2 Cabriolet 2D | | CB294 | 54290 | **7050** | **8150** | **9850** | **12400** |

911 CARRERA 2—6-Cyl.—Equipment Schedule 1
W.B. 89.5"; 3.6 Liter.

Coupe 2D		AB296	64850	**11500**	**13050**	**17050**	**22600**
Targa 2D		BB296	66350	**11300**	**12800**	**16850**	**22300**
Cabriolet 2D		CB296	73450	**14550**	**16450**	**21000**	**27400**
Full Leather				100	100	135	135
Tiptronic Auto Trans				300	300	400	400

911 CARRERA 4—6-Cyl.—Equipment Schedule 1
W.B. 89.5"; 3.6 Liter.

AWD Coupe 2D		AB296	73550	**12650**	**14300**	**18550**	**24300**
AWD Targa 2D		BB296	75050	**12425**	**14075**	**18300**	**24100**
AWD Cabriolet 2D		CB296	82150	**14150**	**15950**	**20600**	**26800**
Full Leather				100	100	135	135

911 TURBO—6-Cyl. Turbo—Equipment Schedule 1
W.B. 89.4"; 3.3 Liter.

| Coupe 2D | | AA296 | 97800 | **18525** | **20850** | **26200** | **33700** |

928—V8—Equipment Schedule 1
W.B. 98.4"; 5.0 Liter.

| S4 Coupe 2D | | AA292 | 79050 | **9600** | **10950** | **14150** | **18650** |
| GT Coupe 2D | | AA292 | 79500 | **9600** | **10950** | **14150** | **18650** |

1992 PORSCHE — WPO(AA296)–N–#

968—4-Cyl.—Equipment Schedule 1
W.B. 94.5"; 3.0 Liter.

Coupe 2D		AA296	48350	**6025**	**6975**	**9350**	**12650**
Cabriolet 2D		CA296	56850	**8825**	**10100**	**12950**	**17000**
Tiptronic Auto Trans				325	325	435	435

911 CARRERA 2—6-Cyl.—Equipment Schedule 1
W.B. 89.4"; 3.6 Liter.

America Roadster 2D		CB296	91750	********	********	********	**39500**
Coupe 2D		AB296	67750	**12475**	**14125**	**18400**	**24300**
Targa 2D		BB296	69350	**12175**	**13825**	**18050**	**23900**
Cabriolet 2D		CB296	76750	**15775**	**17800**	**22700**	**29400**
Full Leather				100	100	135	135
Tiptronic Auto Trans				325	325	435	435

911 CARRERA 4—6-Cyl.—Equipment Schedule 1
W.B. 89.4"; 3.6 Liter.

AWD Coupe 2D		AB296	77780	**13675**	**15475**	**20000**	**26100**
AWD Targa 2D		BB296	79380	**13325**	**15100**	**19600**	**25700**
AWD Cabriolet 2D		CB296	86780	**15325**	**17275**	**22100**	**28700**
Full Leather				100	100	135	135

911 TURBO—6-Cyl. Turbo—Equipment Schedule 1
W.B. 89.4"; 3.3 Liter.

| Coupe 2D | | AA296 | 101675 | **20075** | **22500** | **28100** | **36100** |

1993 PORSCHE — WPO(AA296)–P–#

968—4-Cyl.—Equipment Schedule 1
W.B. 94.5"; 3.0 Liter.

Coupe 2D		AA296	47157	**6875**	**7925**	**10500**	**14000**
Cabriolet 2D		CA296	58800	**10100**	**11450**	**14550**	**18850**
Tiptronic Auto Trans				375	375	500	500

911 CARRERA 2—6-Cyl.—Equipment Schedule 1
W.B. 89.4"; 3.6 Liter.

RS America Coupe 2D		AB296	62742	**13100**	**14800**	**19200**	**25300**
America Roadster 2D		CB296	94301	********	********	********	**41300**
Coupe 2D		AB296	69941	**13725**	**15525**	**20100**	**26400**
Targa 2D		BB296	71551	**13475**	**15225**	**19800**	**26000**

Body Type	VIN	List	Trade-In Fair	Trade-In Good	Pvt-Party Good	Retail Excellent
Cabriolet 2D	CB296	79141	**16925**	**19050**	**24200**	**31100**
Full Leather			100	100	135	135
Tiptronic Auto Trans			375	375	500	500
911 CARRERA 4 AWD—6-Cyl.—Equipment Schedule 1						
W.B. 89.4"; 3.6 Liter.						
Coupe 2D	AB296	80151	**14900**	**16825**	**21500**	**28100**
Targa 2D	BB296	81761	**14650**	**16550**	**21200**	**27700**
Cabriolet 2D	CB296	89351	**17025**	**19150**	**24300**	**31300**
Full Leather			100	100	135	135
928 GTS—V8—Equipment Schedule 1						
W.B. 98.4"; 5.4 Liter.						
Coupe 2D	AA292	85085	**14900**	**16825**	**21800**	**28700**

1994 PORSCHE — WPO(AA296)-R-#

Body Type	VIN	List	Trade-In Fair	Trade-In Good	Pvt-Party Good	Retail Excellent
968—4-Cyl.—Equipment Schedule 1						
W.B. 94.5"; 3.0 Liter.						
Coupe 2D	AA296	43887	**7775**	**8925**	**11600**	**15350**
Cabriolet 2D	CA296	55530	**11350**	**12900**	**16150**	**20800**
Tiptronic Auto Trans			425	425	565	565
911 CARRERA 2—6-Cyl.—Equipment Schedule 1						
W.B. 89.4"; 3.6 Liter.						
RS America Coupe 2D	AB296	55525	**14250**	**16050**	**20800**	**27300**
Coupe 2D	AB296	65715	**15175**	**17075**	**21900**	**28600**
Cabriolet 2D	CB296	74915	**18200**	**20475**	**25700**	**33000**
Carrera 2 Speedster	CB296	70916	********	********	********	**41900**
Full Leather			100	100	135	135
Tiptronic Auto Trans			425	425	565	565
911 CARRERA 4 AWD—6-Cyl.—Equipment Schedule 1						
W.B. 89.4"; 3.6 Liter.						
Coupe 2D	AB296	81551	**16625**	**18725**	**23800**	**30800**
Full Leather			100	100	135	135
911 TURBO 3.6—6-Cyl. Turbo—Equipment Schedule 1						
W.B. 89.4"; 3.6 Liter.						
Coupe 2D	AC296	101825	**25225**	**28225**	**34500**	**43600**
928 GTS—V8—Equipment Schedule 1						
W.B. 98.4"; 5.4 Liter.						
Coupe 2D	AA292	85085	**16550**	**18625**	**23900**	**31100**

1995 PORSCHE — WPO(AA296)-S-#

Body Type	VIN	List	Trade-In Fair	Trade-In Good	Pvt-Party Good	Retail Excellent
968—4-Cyl.—Equipment Schedule 1						
W.B. 94.5"; 3.0 Liter.						
Coupe 2D	AA296	43887	**8725**	**10000**	**12800**	**16800**
Cabriolet 2D	CA296	55530	**12700**	**14350**	**17750**	**22600**
Tiptronic Auto Trans			475	475	635	635
911 CARRERA—6-Cyl.—Equipment Schedule 1						
W.B. 89.4"; 3.6 Liter.						
Coupe 2D	AA299	63055	**15575**	**17550**	**22700**	**29700**
Cabriolet 2D	CA299	71355	**18425**	**20750**	**26300**	**34000**
Full Leather			100	100	135	135
Hard Top (Cabriolet)			400	400	535	535
Aero Kit			1550	1550	2065	2065
Tiptronic Auto Trans			475	475	635	635
911 CARRERA 4 AWD—6-Cyl.—Equipment Schedule 1						
W.B. 89.4"; 3.6 Liter.						
Coupe 2D	AA299	70055	**16675**	**18775**	**24100**	**31200**
Cabriolet 2D	CA299	78355	**19600**	**22025**	**27600**	**35500**
Full Leather			100	100	135	135
Hard Top (Cabriolet)			400	400	535	535
Aero Kit			1550	1550	2065	2065
928 GTS—V8—Equipment Schedule 1						
W.B. 98.4"; 5.4 Liter.						
Coupe 2D	AA292	85085	**18275**	**20575**	**26100**	**33700**

1996 PORSCHE — WPO(AA299)-T-#

Body Type	VIN	List	Trade-In Fair	Trade-In Good	Pvt-Party Good	Retail Excellent
911 CARRERA—6-Cyl.—Equipment Schedule 1						
W.B. 89.5"; 3.6 Liter.						
Coupe 2D	AA299	67043	**17125**	**19250**	**24500**	**31900**
Targa 2D	DA299	74043	**18975**	**21250**	**26900**	**34800**
Cabriolet 2D	CA299	76293	**19875**	**22300**	**27900**	**35800**
Full Leather			125	125	165	165
Hard Top (Cabriolet)			425	425	565	565
Aero Kit			1625	1625	2165	2165

1996 PORSCHE

Body	Type	VIN	List	Trade-In Fair	Good	Pvt-Party Good	Retail Excellent
Tiptronic Auto Trans				525	525	700	700

911 CARRERA 4 AWD—6-Cyl.—Equipment Schedule 1
W.B. 89.5"; 3.6 Liter.

Body	Type	VIN	List	Trade-In Fair	Good	Pvt-Party Good	Retail Excellent
Coupe 2D		AA299	73393	18200	20475	25800	33300
4S Coupe 2D		AA299	76289	19975	22400	27900	35800
Cabriolet 2D		CA299	82643	21525	24150	30000	38100
Full Leather				125	125	165	165
Hard Top (Cabriolet)				425	425	565	565
Aero Kit				1625	1625	2165	2165

911 TURBO—6-Cyl. Turbo—Equipment Schedule 1
W.B. 89.5"; 3.6 Liter.

Body	Type	VIN	List	Trade-In Fair	Good	Pvt-Party Good	Retail Excellent
Coupe 2D		AC299	115050	37250	41425	49400	60900

1997 PORSCHE — WPO(CA298)-V-#

BOXSTER—6-Cyl.—Equipment Schedule 1
W.B. 95.1"; 2.5 Liter.

Body	Type	VIN	List	Trade-In Fair	Good	Pvt-Party Good	Retail Excellent
Cabriolet 2D		CA298	43086	10375	11775	14950	19400
Full Leather				150	150	200	200
Hard Top				450	450	600	600
Aero Kit				1700	1700	2265	2265
Sport Touring Pkg				1425	1425	1900	1900
Tiptronic Auto Trans				550	550	735	735

911 CARRERA—6-Cyl.—Equipment Schedule 1
W.B. 89.5"; 3.6 Liter.

Body	Type	VIN	List	Trade-In Fair	Good	Pvt-Party Good	Retail Excellent
Coupe 2D		AA299	67063	18375	20650	26100	33700
S Coupe 2D		AA299	67063	18875	21150	26800	34500
Targa 2D		DA299	74063	20850	23375	29300	37400
Cabriolet 2D		CA299	76313	21525	24150	30000	38200
Full Leather				150	150	200	200
Hard Top (Cabriolet)				450	450	600	600
Aero Kit				1700	1700	2265	2265
Tiptronic Auto Trans				550	550	735	735

911 CARRERA 4 AWD—6-Cyl.—Equipment Schedule 1
W.B. 89.5"; 3.6 Liter.

Body	Type	VIN	List	Trade-In Fair	Good	Pvt-Party Good	Retail Excellent
4S Coupe 2D		AA299	76313	21825	24550	30400	38600
Cabriolet 2D		CA299	81663	23675	26475	32500	41100
Full Leather				150	150	200	200
Hard Top (Cabriolet)				450	450	600	600
Aero Kit				1700	1700	2265	2265

911 TURBO—6-Cyl. Turbo—Equipment Schedule 1
W.B. 89.5"; 3.6 Liter.

Body	Type	VIN	List	Trade-In Fair	Good	Pvt-Party Good	Retail Excellent
Coupe 2D		AC299	105765	40750	45300	53500	65700
S Coupe 2D		AC299	153365	****	****	****	82500

1998 PORSCHE — WPO(CA298)-W-#

BOXSTER—6-Cyl.—Equipment Schedule 1
W.B. 95.2"; 2.5 Liter.

Body	Type	VIN	List	Trade-In Fair	Good	Pvt-Party Good	Retail Excellent
Cabriolet 2D		CA298	44316	11350	12900	16250	21000
Full Leather				175	175	235	235
Hard Top				475	475	635	635
Aero Kit				1775	1775	2365	2365
Sport Touring Pkg				1475	1475	1965	1965
Tiptronic Auto Trans				575	575	765	765

911 CARRERA—6-Cyl.—Equipment Schedule 1
W.B. 89.4"; 3.6 Liter.

Body	Type	VIN	List	Trade-In Fair	Good	Pvt-Party Good	Retail Excellent
S Coupe 2D		AA299	67461	19100	21425	27100	34900
Targa 2D		DA299	74461	21250	23850	29800	38000
Cabriolet 2D		CA299	76711	21625	24250	30200	38400
Full Leather				175	175	235	235
Hard Top (Cabriolet)				475	475	635	635
Aero Kit				1775	1775	2365	2365
Tiptronic Auto Trans				575	575	765	765

911 CARRERA 4 AWD—6-Cyl.—Equipment Schedule 1
W.B. 89.4"; 3.6 Liter.

Body	Type	VIN	List	Trade-In Fair	Good	Pvt-Party Good	Retail Excellent
4S Coupe 2D		AA299	76711	22300	24925	30800	39100
Cabriolet 2D		CA299	82061	24250	27150	33300	42000
Full Leather				175	175	235	235
Hard Top (Cabriolet)				475	475	635	635
Aero Kit				1775	1775	2365	2365

Body	Type	VIN	List	Trade-In Fair	Trade-In Good	Pvt-Party Good	Retail Excellent

1999 PORSCHE — WPO(CA298)-X-#

BOXSTER—6-Cyl.—Equipment Schedule 1
W.B. 95.2"; 2.5 Liter.

Type	VIN	List	Fair	Good	Good	Excellent
Cabriolet 2D	CA298	44316	**13875**	**15675**	**18600**	**23000**
Full Leather			200	200	265	265
Hard Top			500	500	665	665
Aero Kit			1825	1825	2435	2435
Sport Design Pkg			525	525	700	700
Sport Touring Pkg			1525	1525	2035	2035
Tiptronic Auto Trans			625	625	835	835

911 CARRERA—6-Cyl.—Equipment Schedule 1
W.B. 92.6"; 3.4 Liter.

Type	VIN	List	Fair	Good	Good	Excellent
Coupe 2D	AA299	70815	**22225**	**24825**	**30000**	**37300**
Cabriolet 2D	CA299	80245	**24725**	**27650**	**33000**	**40700**
Full Leather			200	200	265	265
Hard Top (Cabriolet)			500	500	665	665
Aero Kit			1825	1825	2435	2435
Tiptronic Auto Trans			625	625	835	835

911 CARRERA 4 AWD—6-Cyl.—Equipment Schedule 1
W.B. 92.6"; 3.4 Liter.

Type	VIN	List	Fair	Good	Good	Excellent
Coupe 2D	AA299	75980	**25600**	**28625**	**34000**	**42000**
Cabriolet 2D	CA299	85420	**27850**	**31050**	**36700**	**45000**
Full Leather			200	200	265	265
Hard Top (Cabriolet)			500	500	665	665
Aero Kit			1825	1825	2435	2435
Tiptronic Auto Trans			625	625	835	835

2000 PORSCHE — WPO(CA298)-Y-#

BOXSTER—6-Cyl.—Equipment Schedule 1
W.B. 95.2"; 2.7 Liter, 3.2 Liter.

Type	VIN	List	Fair	Good	Good	Excellent
Cabriolet 2D	CA298	44745	**14550**	**16450**	**19500**	**24100**
S Cabriolet 2D	CB298	53245	**18425**	**20750**	**24200**	**29300**
Full Leather			250	250	335	335
Hard Top			550	550	735	735
Aero Kit			1950	1950	2600	2600
Sport Design Pkg			600	600	800	800
Sport Touring Pkg			1600	1600	2135	2135
Tiptronic Auto Trans			725	725	965	965

911 CARRERA—6-Cyl.—Equipment Schedule 1
W.B. 92.6"; 3.4 Liter.

Type	VIN	List	Fair	Good	Good	Excellent
Coupe 2D	AA299	71375	**25325**	**28325**	**33700**	**41500**
Cabriolet 2D	CA299	80755	**28225**	**31525**	**37200**	**45400**
Full Leather			250	250	335	335
Hard Top (Cabriolet)			550	550	735	735
Aero Kit			1950	1950	2600	2600
Tiptronic Auto Trans			725	725	965	965

911 CARRERA 4 AWD—6-Cyl.—Equipment Schedule 1
W.B. 92.6"; 3.4 Liter.

Type	VIN	List	Fair	Good	Good	Excellent
Coupe 2D	AA299	76805	**29200**	**32600**	**38300**	**46800**
Cabriolet 2D	CA299	86185	**31625**	**35300**	**41100**	**50000**
Full Leather			250	250	335	335
Hard Top (Cabriolet)			550	550	735	735
Aero Kit			1950	1950	2600	2600
Millennium Pkg			4350	4350	5800	5800
Tiptronic Auto Trans			725	725	965	965

2001 PORSCHE — WPO(CA298)-1-#

BOXSTER—6-Cyl.—Equipment Schedule 1
W.B. 95.2"; 2.7 Liter, 3.2 Liter.

Type	VIN	List	Fair	Good	Good	Excellent
Cabriolet 2D	CA298	42865	**15575**	**17550**	**20900**	**25700**
S Cabriolet 2D	CB298	50965	**19975**	**22400**	**26000**	**31500**
Full Leather			300	300	400	400
Hard Top			575	575	765	765
Aero Kit			2075	2075	2765	2765
Sport Design Pkg			675	675	900	900
Sport Touring Pkg			1675	1675	2235	2235
Tiptronic Auto Trans			825	825	1100	1100

911 CARRERA—6-Cyl.—Equipment Schedule 1
W.B. 92.6"; 3.4 Liter.

Type	VIN	List	Fair	Good	Good	Excellent
Coupe 2D	AA299	70275	**28525**	**31925**	**37500**	**46000**
Cabriolet 2D	CA299	79775	**31925**	**35600**	**41500**	**50400**

Body	Type	VIN	List	Trade-In Fair	Trade-In Good	Pvt-Party Good	Retail Excellent
Full Leather				300	300	400	400
Hard Top (Cabriolet)				575	575	765	765
Aero Kit				2075	2075	2765	2765
Tiptronic Auto Trans				825	825	1100	1100

911 CARRERA 4 AWD—6-Cyl.—Equipment Schedule 1
W.B. 92.6"; 3.4 Liter.

Body	Type	VIN	List	Fair	Good	Good	Excellent
Coupe 2D		AA299	75320	32975	36775	42800	51900
Cabriolet 2D		CA299	84820	35600	39675	46000	55400
Full Leather				300	300	400	400
Hard Top (Cabriolet)				575	575	765	765
Aero Kit				2075	2075	2765	2765
Tiptronic Auto Trans				825	825	1100	1100

911 TURBO AWD—6-Cyl. Turbo—Equipment Schedule 1
W.B. 92.6"; 3.6 Liter.

Body	Type	VIN	List	Fair	Good	Good	Excellent
Coupe 2D		AB299	111765	51700	57525	64900	76600
Full Leather				300	300	400	400
Aero Kit				2075	2075	2765	2765
Tiptronic Auto Trans				825	825	1100	1100

2002 PORSCHE — WPO(CA298)-2-#

BOXSTER—6-Cyl.—Equipment Schedule 1
W.B. 95.2"; 2.7 Liter, 3.2 Liter.

Body	Type	VIN	List	Fair	Good	Good	Excellent
Cabriolet 2D		CA298	43365	16875	18975	22500	27700
S Cabriolet 2D		CB298	52365	21725	24350	28100	34000
Full Leather				350	350	465	465
Hard Top				600	600	800	800
Aero Kit				2200	2200	2935	2935
Sport Design Pkg				750	750	1000	1000
Sport Touring Pkg				1750	1750	2335	2335
Tiptronic Auto Trans				900	900	1200	1200

911 CARRERA—6-Cyl.—Equipment Schedule 1
W.B. 92.6"; 3.6 Liter.

Body	Type	VIN	List	Fair	Good	Good	Excellent
Coupe 2D		AA299	73450	32200	35900	41900	50900
Targa 2D		AA299	75965	35800	39875	46100	55600
Cabriolet 2D		CA299	83150	35975	40050	46300	55800
Full Leather				350	350	465	465
Hard Top (Cabriolet)				600	600	800	800
Aero Kit				2200	2200	2935	2935
Tiptronic Auto Trans				900	900	1200	1200

911 CARRERA 4 AWD—6-Cyl.—Equipment Schedule 1
W.B. 92.6"; 3.6 Liter.

Body	Type	VIN	List	Fair	Good	Good	Excellent
4S Coupe 2D		AA299	80965	37050	41325	47600	57200
Cabriolet 2D		CA299	88750	40450	44725	51200	61200
Full Leather				350	350	465	465
Hard Top (Cabriolet)				600	600	800	800
Aero Kit				2200	2200	2935	2935
Tiptronic Auto Trans				900	900	1200	1200

911 TURBO AWD—6-Cyl. Turbo—Equipment Schedule 1
W.B. 92.6"; 3.6 Liter.

Body	Type	VIN	List	Fair	Good	Good	Excellent
Coupe 2D		AB299	115765	57900	64300	71900	84200
Full Leather				350	350	465	465
Aero Kit				2200	2200	2935	2935
Tiptronic Auto Trans				900	900	1200	1200

911 TURBO—6-Cyl. Turbo—Equipment Schedule 1
W.B. 92.6"; 3.6 Liter.

Body	Type	VIN	List	Fair	Good	Good	Excellent
GT2 Coupe 2D		AB299	180665	****	****	****	129500

2003 PORSCHE — WPO(CA298)-3-#

BOXSTER—6-Cyl.—Equipment Schedule 1
W.B. 95.2"; 2.7 Liter, 3.2 Liter.

Body	Type	VIN	List	Fair	Good	Good	Excellent
Cabriolet 2D		CA298	45485	18625	20950	24800	30600
S Cabriolet 2D		CB298	54485	23950	26775	30900	37300
Full Leather				400	400	535	535
Hard Top				625	625	835	835
Aero Kit				2325	2325	3100	3100
Sport Design Pkg				825	825	1100	1100
Tiptronic Auto Trans				975	975	1300	1300

911 CARRERA—6-Cyl.—Equipment Schedule 1
W.B. 92.6"; 3.6 Liter.

Body	Type	VIN	List	Fair	Good	Good	Excellent
Coupe 2D		AA299	72435	36275	40450	46800	56300
Targa 2D		BA299	79835	40250	44825	51200	61200
Cabriolet 2D		CA299	82235	40450	45000	51500	61600
Full Leather				400	400	535	535

2003 PORSCHE

Body	Type	VIN	List	Trade-In Fair	Good	Pvt-Party Good	Retail Excellent
Hard Top (Cabriolet)				625	625	835	835
Aero Kit				2325	2325	3100	3100
Tiptronic Auto Trans				975	975	1300	1300

911 CARRERA 4 AWD—6-Cyl.—Equipment Schedule 1
W.B. 92.6"; 3.6 Liter.

Body	Type	VIN	List	Trade-In Fair	Good	Pvt-Party Good	Retail Excellent
4S Coupe 2D		AA299	82565	41625	46375	52900	63100
Cabriolet 2D		CA299	87835	45000	50050	56700	67300
Full Leather				400	400	535	535
Hard Top (Cabriolet)				625	625	835	835
Aero Kit				2325	2325	3100	3100
Tiptronic Auto Trans				975	975	1300	1300

911 TURBO AWD—6-Cyl. Turbo—Equipment Schedule 1
W.B. 92.6"; 3.6 Liter.

Body	Type	VIN	List	Trade-In Fair	Good	Pvt-Party Good	Retail Excellent
Coupe 2D		AB299	118265	64500	71575	79300	92200
Full Leather				400	400	535	535
Aero Kit				2325	2325	3100	3100
Tiptronic Auto Trans				975	975	1300	1300

911 TURBO—6-Cyl. Turbo—Equipment Schedule 1
W.B. 92.6"; 3.6 Liter.

Body	Type	VIN	List	Trade-In Fair	Good	Pvt-Party Good	Retail Excellent
GT2 Coupe 2D		AB299	183765				

2004 PORSCHE — WPO(CA298)-4-#

BOXSTER—6-Cyl.—Equipment Schedule 1
W.B. 95.1"; 2.7 Liter, 3.2 Liter.

Body	Type	VIN	List	Trade-In Fair	Good	Pvt-Party Good	Retail Excellent
Cabriolet 2D		CA298	45485	21050	23575	27800	34200
S Cabriolet 2D		CB298	54485	26875	30075	34500	41500
Full Leather				475	475	635	635
Hard Top				650	650	865	865
Aero Kit				2425	2425	3235	3235
Sport Design Pkg				900	900	1200	1200
Special Edition				2000	2000	2665	2665
Tiptronic Auto Trans				1050	1050	1400	1400

911 CARRERA—6-Cyl.—Equipment Schedule 1
W.B. 92.5", 92.6" (Targa); 3.6 Liter.

Body	Type	VIN	List	Trade-In Fair	Good	Pvt-Party Good	Retail Excellent
Coupe 2D		AA299	72435	41025	45675	52400	62600
Targa 2D		BA299	79835	45300	50450	57100	67800
Cabriolet 2D		CA299	82235	45600	50625	57500	68200
40th Anniversary Ed				5000	5000	6665	6665
Full Leather				475	475	635	635
Hard Top (Cabriolet)				650	650	865	865
Aero Kit				2425	2425	3235	3235
Tiptronic Auto Trans				1050	1050	1400	1400

911 CARRERA 4 AWD—6-Cyl.—Equipment Schedule 1
W.B. 92.5"; 3.6 Liter.

Body	Type	VIN	List	Trade-In Fair	Good	Pvt-Party Good	Retail Excellent
Cabriolet 2D		CA299	86285	50450	56075	63100	74300
4S Coupe 2D		AA299	84165	46850	52175	59000	69800
4S Cabriolet 2D		CA299	93965	53925	59850	67000	78600
Full Leather				475	475	635	635
Hard Top (Cabriolet)				650	650	865	865
Aero Kit				2425	2425	3235	3235
Tiptronic Auto Trans				1050	1050	1400	1400

911 TURBO AWD—6-Cyl. Turbo—Equipment Schedule 1
W.B. 92.5"; 3.6 Liter.

Body	Type	VIN	List	Trade-In Fair	Good	Pvt-Party Good	Retail Excellent
Coupe 2D		AB299	120465	71875	79725	87600	101000
Cabriolet 2D		CB299	130265	75375	83625	91600	105400
Full Leather				475	475	635	635
Aero Kit				2425	2425	3235	3235
Tiptronic Auto Trans				1050	1050	1400	1400

911 TURBO—6-Cyl. Turbo—Equipment Schedule 1
W.B. 92.7"; 3.6 Liter.

Body	Type	VIN	List	Trade-In Fair	Good	Pvt-Party Good	Retail Excellent
GT2 Coupe 2D		AB299	193765				

911—6-Cyl.—Equipment Schedule 1
W.B. 92.7"; 3.6 Liter.

Body	Type	VIN	List	Trade-In Fair	Good	Pvt-Party Good	Retail Excellent
GT3 Coupe 2D		AC299	101965	62850	69750	77200	89700

CARRERA GT—V10—Equipment Schedule 1
W.B. 107.5"; 5.7 Liter.

Body	Type	VIN	List	Trade-In Fair	Good	Pvt-Party Good	Retail Excellent
Roadster 2D		CA298	446165				

2005 PORSCHE — WPO(CA298)-5-#

BOXSTER—6-Cyl.—Equipment Schedule 1
W.B. 95.1"; 2.7 Liter, 3.2 Liter.

Body	Type	VIN	List	Trade-In Fair	Good	Pvt-Party Good	Retail Excellent
Cabriolet 2D		CA298	44595	26100	29200	34500	42300
S Cabriolet 2D		CB298	53895	32500	36175	41700	50100

Body	Type	VIN	List	Trade-In Fair	Trade-In Good	Pvt-Party Good	Retail Excellent
Full Leather			....	550	550	735	735
Hard Top			....	675	675	900	900
Aero Kit			....	2525	2525	3365	3365
Sport Pkg			....	950	950	1265	1265
Tiptronic Auto Trans			....	1125	1125	1500	1500

911 CARRERA—6-Cyl.—Equipment Schedule 1
W.B. 92.5", 92.6" (Targa); 3.6 Liter, 3.8 Liter.

Coupe 2D	AA299	73165					
Targa 2D	BA299	79865					
Cabriolet 2D	CA299	82965					
S Coupe 2D	AB299	79895					
S Cabriolet 2D	CB299	89695					
Full Leather		....					
Hard Top (Cabriolet)		....					
Aero Kit		....					
Tiptronic Auto Trans		....					

911 CARRERA 4 AWD—6-Cyl.—Equipment Schedule 1
W.B. 92.5"; 3.6 Liter.

4S Coupe 2D	AA299	84195					
4S Cabriolet 2D	CA299	93995					
Full Leather		....					
Hard Top (Cabriolet)		....					
Aero Kit		....					
Tiptronic Auto Trans		....					

911 TURBO AWD—6-Cyl. Turbo—Equipment Schedule 1
W.B. 92.5"; 3.6 Liter.

Cabriolet 2D	CB299	130295					
S Coupe 2D	AB299	133495					
S Cabriolet 2D	CB299	143295					
Full Leather		....					
Aero Kit		....					
Tiptronic Auto Trans		....					

911 TURBO—6-Cyl. Turbo—Equipment Schedule 1
W.B. 92.7"; 3.6 Liter.

GT2 Coupe 2D	AB299	193795					

911—6-Cyl.—Equipment Schedule 1
W.B. 92.7"; 3.6 Liter.

GT3 Coupe 2D	AC299	101995					

CARRERA GT—V10—Equipment Schedule 1
W.B. 107.5"; 5.7 Liter.

Roadster 2D	CA298	448400					

SAAB

1991 SAAB — YS3(AK45E)–M–#

900—4-Cyl.—Equipment Schedule 3
W.B. 99.1"; 2.1 Liter.

Sedan 4D	AK45E	19812		300	400	1150	2200
Hatchback 2D	AK35E	19292		300	400	1150	2200
S Sedan 4D	AK45E	23992		500	725	1550	2825
S Hatchback 2D	AK35E	23442		500	725	1550	2825
S Convertible 2D	AK75E	29292		1275	1775	3075	4900

900—4-Cyl. Turbo—Equipment Schedule 3
W.B. 99.1"; 2.0 Liter.

Hatchback 2D	AL35L	27292		775	1100	2125	3650
Convertible 2D	AL75L	34292		2025	2600	4075	6100
SE Convertible 2D	AL75L	35792		2100	2675	4150	6200
Spcl Performance Group		....		300	300	400	400

9000—4-Cyl.—Equipment Schedule 2
W.B. 105.2"; 2.3 Liter.

Hatchback 4D	CK58B	24077		850	1200	2375	4050
S Hatchback 4D	CK58B	28177		850	1225	2400	4075
CD Sedan 4D	CK48B	29412		925	1300	2550	4275
Manual Trans		....		(200)	(200)	(265)	(265)

9000—4-Cyl. Turbo—Equipment Schedule 2
W.B. 105.2"; 2.3 Liter.

Hatchback 4D	CL58M	34177		1225	1700	3000	4825
CD Sedan 4D	CL48M	34412		1325	1825	3175	5025
Manual Trans		....		(200)	(200)	(265)	(265)

1992 SAAB

Body Type	VIN	List	Trade-In Fair	Good	Pvt-Party Good	Retail Excellent
1992 SAAB — YS3(AK45E)-N-#						
900—4-Cyl.—Equipment Schedule 3						
W.B. 99.1"; 2.1 Liter.						
Sedan 4D	AK45E	20435	350	475	1275	2500
Hatchback 2D	AK35E	19835	350	475	1275	2500
S Sedan 4D	AK45E	24435	600	850	1825	3275
S Hatchback 2D	AK35E	23835	600	850	1825	3275
S Convertible 2D	AK75E	31035	1600	2100	3550	5500
900—4-Cyl. Turbo—Equipment Schedule 3						
W.B. 99.1"; 2.0 Liter.						
Hatchback 2D	AL35L	29085	900	1275	2525	4275
Convertible 2D	AL75L	35785	2475	3075	4675	6875
9000—4-Cyl.—Equipment Schedule 2						
W.B. 105.2"; 2.3 Liter.						
Hatchback 4D	CK58B	26175	975	1375	2700	4475
S Hatchback 4D	CK58B	29425	1000	1425	2725	4525
CD Sedan 4D	CK48B	30635	1100	1550	2875	4725
Manual Trans			(200)	(200)	(265)	(265)
9000—4-Cyl. Turbo—Equipment Schedule 2						
W.B. 105.2"; 2.3 Liter.						
Hatchback 4D	CL58M	37375	1525	2025	3475	5425
CD Sedan 4D	CL48M	37135	1625	2125	3625	5625
CD Griffin Ed Sedan 4D	CL48M	42635	1825	2350	3850	5925
Manual Trans			(200)	(200)	(265)	(265)
1993 SAAB — YS3(AK45E)-P-#						
900—4-Cyl.—Equipment Schedule 3						
W.B. 99.1"; 2.1 Liter.						
S Sedan 4D	AK45E	21400	575	825	1875	3400
S Hatchback 2D	AK35E	20785	575	825	1875	3400
S Convertible 2D	AK75E	32600	1850	2375	3900	5975
900—4-Cyl. Turbo—Equipment Schedule 3						
W.B. 99.1"; 2.0 Liter.						
Hatchback 2D	AL35L	30995	975	1375	2725	4525
Convertible 2D	AL75L	37500	2875	3550	5250	7600
9000—4-Cyl.—Equipment Schedule 2						
W.B. 105.2"; 2.3 Liter.						
CS Hatchback 4D	CK68B	28570	1375	1875	3325	5300
CD Sedan 4D	CK48B	27670	1225	1725	3150	5125
CSE Hatchback 4D	CK58B	32420	1625	2125	3650	5725
CDE Sedan 4D	CK48B	32190	1650	2150	3675	5750
Manual Trans			(250)	(250)	(335)	(335)
4-Cyl. 2.3 Liter Turbo	M		875	875	1165	1165
9000—4-Cyl. Turbo—Equipment Schedule 2						
W.B. 105.2"; 2.3 Liter.						
Aero Hatchback 4D	CL68M	38695	2150	2750	4375	6575
Manual Trans			(125)	(125)	(165)	(165)
1994 SAAB — YS3(DM35B)-R-#						
900—4-Cyl.—Equipment Schedule 3						
W.B. 99.1" (Conv), 102.4"; 2.1 Liter, 2.3 Liter.						
S Coupe 2D	DM35B	22750	400	575	1600	3125
S Hatchback 4D	DM55B	21450	375	500	1500	3000
S Convertible 2D	AK75E	33735	2150	2750	4400	6625
V6 2.5 Liter	V		275	275	365	365
900—V6—Equipment Schedule 3						
W.B. 102.4"; 2.5 Liter.						
SE Hatchback 4D	DM55V	27450	1000	1400	2825	4725
Auto Trans			150	150	200	200
900—4-Cyl. Turbo—Equipment Schedule 3						
W.B. 99.1"; 2.0 Liter.						
SE Coupe 2D	DN35L	27740	1000	1400	2825	4725
Convertible 2D	AL75L	38875	3375	4075	5925	8475
Commem Ed Conv 2D	AL75T	40875	3500	4200	6075	8625
9000—4-Cyl.—Equipment Schedule 2						
W.B. 105.2"; 2.3 Liter.						
CS Hatchback 4D	CM68B	30670	1375	1900	3425	5475
CD Sedan 4D	CM48B	32775	1250	1750	3250	5275
CSE Hatchback 4D	CM68B	34450	1675	2200	3775	5950
CDE Sedan 4D	CM48B	34090	1675	2200	3775	5925
Manual Trans			(300)	(300)	(400)	(400)

1994 SAAB

Body Type	VIN	List	Trade-In Fair	Good	Pvt-Party Good	Retail Excellent
4-Cyl. 2.3 Liter Turbo .... M			1000	1000	1335	1335
9000—4-Cyl. Turbo—Equipment Schedule 2						
W.B. 105.2"; 2.3 Liter.						
Aero Hatchback 4D CN68M	39150		2450	3050	4775	7125
Manual Trans			(150)	(150)	(200)	(200)
Traction Control			150	150	200	200

1995 SAAB — YS3(DD35B)–S–#

Body Type	VIN	List	Trade-In Fair	Good	Pvt-Party Good	Retail Excellent
900—4-Cyl.—Equipment Schedule 3						
W.B. 102.4"; 2.3 Liter.						
S Coupe 2D DD35B	24545		600	850	2200	4100
S Hatchback 4D DD55B	24225		525	750	2050	3925
S Convertible 2D DD75B	33465		2125	2700	4400	6700
Auto Trans			175	175	235	235
900—V6—Equipment Schedule 3						
W.B. 102.4"; 2.3 Liter.						
SE Hatchback 4D DF55V	29150		1250	1750	3325	5425
Auto Trans			175	175	235	235
900—4-Cyl. Turbo—Equipment Schedule 3						
W.B. 102.4"; 2.3 Liter.						
SE Coupe 2D DF35N	29460		1250	1750	3325	5425
SE Convertible 2D DF78N	39990		3125	3775	5650	8175
Auto Trans			175	175	235	235
V6 2.5 Liter V			300	300	400	400
9000—4-Cyl. Light Pressure Turbo—Equipment Schedule 2						
W.B. 105.2"; 2.3 Liter.						
CS Hatchback 4D CD68U	32695		1775	2300	3975	6225
Manual Trans			(350)	(350)	(465)	(465)
9000—4-Cyl. Turbo—Equipment Schedule 2						
W.B. 105.2"; 2.3 Liter.						
Aero Hatchback 4D CH68M,R	41770		3025	3700	5600	8175
Manual Trans			(175)	(175)	(235)	(235)
9000—V6—Equipment Schedule 2						
W.B. 105.2"; 3.0 Liter.						
CSE Hatchback 4D.............. CF68W	39120		2275	2825	4600	7000
CDE Sedan 4D..................... CF48W	39465		2175	2775	4500	6875
Manual Trans			(350)	(350)	(465)	(465)
4-Cyl. 2.3 Liter Turbo .... M			0	0	0	0

1996 SAAB — YS3(DD35B)–T–#

Body Type	VIN	List	Trade-In Fair	Good	Pvt-Party Good	Retail Excellent
900—4-Cyl.—Equipment Schedule 3						
W.B. 102.4"; 2.3 Liter.						
S Coupe 2D DD35B	24490		850	1225	2775	4875
S Hatchback 4D DD55B	25190		750	1075	2600	4650
S Convertible 2D DD75B	34490		2650	3275	5125	7650
Auto Trans			200	200	265	265
900—4-Cyl. Turbo—Equipment Schedule 3						
W.B. 102.4"; 2.0 Liter.						
SE Coupe 2D DF35N	29490		1700	2225	3950	6250
SE Hatchback 4D DF55N	30190		1675	2175	3900	6200
SE Convertible 2D DF75N	40490		3825	4575	6600	9350
Auto Trans			200	200	265	265
V6 2.5 Liter V			325	325	435	435
9000—4-Cyl. Light Pressure Turbo—Equipment Schedule 2						
W.B. 105.2"; 2.3 Liter.						
CS Hatchback 4D CD68U	32695		2250	2825	4675	7150
Manual Trans 5			(400)	(400)	(535)	(535)
9000—4-Cyl. Turbo—Equipment Schedule 2						
W.B. 105.2"; 2.3 Liter.						
Aero Hatchback 4D CH58M,R	42735		3725	4450	6550	9350
Manual Trans 5			(200)	(200)	(265)	(265)
9000—V6—Equipment Schedule 2						
W.B. 105.2"; 3.0 Liter.						
CSE Hatchback 4D.............. CF68W	40690		2800	3425	5350	7950
Manual Trans			(400)	(400)	(535)	(535)
4-Cyl. 2.3 Liter Turbo .... M			0	0	0	0

1997 SAAB — YS3(DD35B)–V–#

Body Type	VIN	List	Trade-In Fair	Good	Pvt-Party Good	Retail Excellent
900—4-Cyl.—Equipment Schedule 3						
W.B. 102.4"; 2.3 Liter.						
S Coupe 2D DD35B	25520		1225	1725	3475	5800
S Hatchback 4D DD55B	26520		1100	1550	3275	5550

1997 SAAB

Body Type	VIN	List	Trade-In Fair	Good	Pvt-Party Good	Retail Excellent
S Convertible 2D	DD75B	35520	**3300**	**3975**	**6000**	**8725**
Auto Trans			**200**	**200**	**265**	**265**
900—4-Cyl. Turbo—Equipment Schedule 3						
W.B. 102.4"; 2.0 Liter.						
SE Coupe 2D	DF35N	30520	**2275**	**2825**	**4725**	**7250**
SE Hatchback 4D	DF55N	31520	**2200**	**2800**	**4650**	**7150**
SE Convertible 2D	DF75N	41520	**4650**	**5475**	**7675**	**10650**
Auto Trans			**200**	**200**	**265**	**265**
V6 2.5 Liter	V		**350**	**350**	**465**	**465**
9000—4-Cyl. Light Pressure Turbo—Equipment Schedule 2						
W.B. 105.2"; 2.3 Liter.						
CS Hatchback 4D	CD68U	35360	**2825**	**3475**	**5500**	**8225**
Manual Trans			**(450)**	**(450)**	**(600)**	**(600)**
9000—4-Cyl. Turbo—Equipment Schedule 3						
W.B. 105.2"; 2.3 Liter.						
Aero Hatchback 4D	CH68M	43065	**4500**	**5325**	**7600**	**10650**
Manual Trans			**(200)**	**(200)**	**(265)**	**(265)**
9000—V6—Equipment Schedule 2						
W.B. 105.2"; 3.0 Liter.						
CSE Hatchback 4D	CF68W	41020	**3425**	**4125**	**6225**	**9075**
Manual Trans	5		**(450)**	**(450)**	**(600)**	**(600)**
4-Cyl. 2.3 Liter Turbo	U		**0**	**0**	**0**	**0**

1998 SAAB — YS3(DD55B)-W-#

Body Type	VIN	List	Trade-In Fair	Good	Pvt-Party Good	Retail Excellent
900—4-Cyl.—Equipment Schedule 3						
W.B. 102.4"; 2.3 Liter.						
S Hatchback 4D	DD55B	27505	**1675**	**2200**	**4150**	**6725**
S Convertible 2D	DD75B	36945	**4050**	**4825**	**7025**	**10050**
Auto Trans			**200**	**200**	**265**	**265**
900—4-Cyl. Turbo—Equipment Schedule 3						
W.B. 102.4"; 2.0 Liter.						
S Coupe 2D	DD35N	25050	**2075**	**2650**	**4625**	**7250**
SE Coupe 2D	DF35N	31545	**2950**	**3625**	**5700**	**8500**
SE Hatchback 4D	DF55N	32545	**2850**	**3525**	**5600**	**8400**
SE Convertible 2D	DF75N	42745	**5575**	**6500**	**8900**	**12150**
Auto Trans			**200**	**200**	**265**	**265**
9000—4-Cyl. Turbo—Equipment Schedule 3						
W.B. 105.2"; 2.3 Liter.						
CSE Hatchback 4D	CF68M	40175	**4175**	**4950**	**7250**	**10400**
Manual Trans	5		**(475)**	**(475)**	**(635)**	**(635)**

1999 SAAB — YS3(DD38N)-X-#

Body Type	VIN	List	Trade-In Fair	Good	Pvt-Party Good	Retail Excellent
9-3—4-Cyl. Turbo—Equipment Schedule 3						
W.B. 102.6"; 2.0 Liter.						
Hatchback 2D	DD38N	26225	**2825**	**3475**	**5275**	**7775**
Hatchback 4D	DD58N	26725	**3000**	**3650**	**5500**	**8000**
Convertible 2D	DD78N	38725	**6150**	**7150**	**9300**	**12300**
SE Hatchback 4D	DF58N	33275	**3900**	**4650**	**6600**	**9275**
SE Convertible 2D	DF78N	44570	**7100**	**8200**	**10500**	**13750**
Auto Trans			**200**	**200**	**265**	**265**
4-Cyl. 2.0L HO Turbo	P		**250**	**250**	**335**	**335**
9-3—4-Cyl. HO Turbo—Equipment Schedule 3						
W.B. 102.6"; 2.3 Liter.						
Viggen Coupe 2D	DP35G	38325	**7275**	**8375**	**10600**	**13800**
9-5—V6 Turbo—Equipment Schedule 2						
W.B. 106.4"; 3.0 Liter.						
Sedan 4D	ED48Z	35640	**5125**	**6025**	**8275**	**11400**
Wagon 4D	ED58Z	37475	**5550**	**6500**	**8775**	**12000**
SE Sedan 4D	EF48Z	37825	**5775**	**6725**	**9050**	**12250**
Manual Trans			**(500)**	**(500)**	**(665)**	**(665)**
4-Cyl. 2.3L Turbo	E		**(1025)**	**(1025)**	**(1365)**	**(1365)**

2000 SAAB — YS3(DD35H)-Y-#

Body Type	VIN	List	Trade-In Fair	Good	Pvt-Party Good	Retail Excellent
9-3—4-Cyl. Turbo—Equipment Schedule 3						
W.B. 102.6"; 2.0 Liter.						
Hatchback 2D	DD35H	27675	**3650**	**4375**	**6400**	**9200**
Hatchback 4D	DD55H	28175	**3850**	**4600**	**6675**	**9475**
Convertible 2D	DD75H	41225	**7475**	**8575**	**10950**	**14350**
Auto Trans	8		**225**	**225**	**300**	**300**
9-3—4-Cyl. HO Turbo—Equipment Schedule 3						
W.B. 102.6"; 2.0 Liter, 2.3 Liter.						
SE Hatchback 4D	DF55K	33670	**4950**	**5800**	**7925**	**10900**

2000 SAAB

Body	Type	VIN	List	Trade-In Fair	Good	Pvt-Party Good	Retail Excellent
SE Convertible 2D		DF75K	44770	8550	9800	12300	15950
Viggen Hatchback 2D		DP35G	38325	8725	10000	12450	16000
Viggen Hatchback 4D		DP55G	38325	7750	8900	11300	14750
Viggen Convertible 2D		DP75G	45570	11200	12700	15550	19700
Auto Trans			8	225	225	300	300

9-5—4-Cyl. Turbo—Equipment Schedule 2
W.B. 106.4", 106.6" (Wagon); 2.3 Liter.

Body	Type	VIN	List	Trade-In Fair	Good	Pvt-Party Good	Retail Excellent
Sedan 4D		ED48E	35300	6425	7425	9900	13350
Wagon 4D		ED58E	35300	6900	7975	10500	14000
Gary Fisher Edition				700	700	935	935
Manual Trans			5	(550)	(550)	(735)	(735)

9-5—4-Cyl. HO Turbo—Equipment Schedule 2
W.B. 106.4", 106.6" (Wagon); 2.3 Liter.

Body	Type	VIN	List	Trade-In Fair	Good	Pvt-Party Good	Retail Excellent
Aero Sedan 4D		EH48G	41550	8200	9375	12050	15750
Aero Wagon 4D		EH58G	44145	8950	10225	12900	16700
Manual Trans			5	(550)	(550)	(735)	(735)

9-5—V6 Turbo—Equipment Schedule 2
W.B. 106.4", 106.6" (Wagon); 3.0 Liter.

Body	Type	VIN	List	Trade-In Fair	Good	Pvt-Party Good	Retail Excellent
SE Sedan 4D		EF48Z	38325	7175	8275	10800	14350
SE Wagon 4D		EF58Z	38325	7650	8800	11400	15050

2001 SAAB — YS3(DD35H)-1-#

9-3—4-Cyl. Turbo—Equipment Schedule 3
W.B. 102.6"; 2.0 Liter.

Body	Type	VIN	List	Trade-In Fair	Good	Pvt-Party Good	Retail Excellent
Hatchback 2D		DD35H	27070	4675	5525	7825	10950
Hatchback 4D		DD55H	27570	4925	5775	8075	11250
Auto Trans				250	250	335	335

9-3—4-Cyl. HO Turbo—Equipment Schedule 3
W.B. 102.6"; 2.0 Liter, 2.3 Liter.

Body	Type	VIN	List	Trade-In Fair	Good	Pvt-Party Good	Retail Excellent
SE Hatchback 4D		DF55K	33170	6175	7175	9600	12950
SE Convertible 2D		DF75K	40570	10175	11600	14350	18400
Viggen Hatchback 2D		DP35G	38570	10425	11875	14600	18550
Viggen Hatchback 4D		DP55G	38570	9300	10625	13300	17050
Viggen Convertible 2D		DP75G	45570	13100	14850	17950	22500
Auto Trans				250	250	335	335

9-5—4-Cyl. Turbo—Equipment Schedule 2
W.B. 106.4"; 2.3 Liter.

Body	Type	VIN	List	Trade-In Fair	Good	Pvt-Party Good	Retail Excellent
Sedan 4D		ED48E	34570	7925	9125	11800	15500
Wagon 4D		ED58E	35270	8525	9750	12450	16300
Manual Trans				(600)	(600)	(800)	(800)

9-5—4-Cyl. HO Turbo—Equipment Schedule 2
W.B. 106.4"; 2.3 Liter.

Body	Type	VIN	List	Trade-In Fair	Good	Pvt-Party Good	Retail Excellent
Aero Sedan 4D		EH48G	40750	9950	11350	14150	18200
Aero Wagon 4D		EH58G	41450	10775	12275	15150	19300
Manual Trans				(600)	(600)	(800)	(800)

9-5—V6 Turbo—Equipment Schedule 2
W.B. 106.4"; 3.0 Liter.

Body	Type	VIN	List	Trade-In Fair	Good	Pvt-Party Good	Retail Excellent
SE Sedan 4D		EF48Z	39225	8825	10100	12800	16700
SE Wagon 4D		EF58Z	39925	9300	10625	13450	17350

2002 SAAB — YS3(DF55K)-2-#

9-3—4-Cyl. Turbo—Equipment Schedule 3
W.B. 102.6"; 2.0 Liter.

Body	Type	VIN	List	Trade-In Fair	Good	Pvt-Party Good	Retail Excellent
SE Hatchback 4D		DF55K	29820	7700	8850	11550	15350
SE Convertible 2D		DF75K	41820	12125	13725	16800	21200
Auto Trans				275	275	365	365

9-3—4-Cyl. HO Turbo—Equipment Schedule 3
W.B. 102.6"; 2.3 Liter.

Body	Type	VIN	List	Trade-In Fair	Good	Pvt-Party Good	Retail Excellent
Viggen Hatchback 2D		DP35G	38720	12375	14025	17000	21400
Viggen Hatchback 4D		DP55G	38720	11150	12650	15550	19800
Viggen Convertible 2D		DP75G	45620	15325	17275	20700	25600

9-5—4-Cyl. Turbo—Equipment Schedule 2
W.B. 106.4"; 2.3 Liter.

Body	Type	VIN	List	Trade-In Fair	Good	Pvt-Party Good	Retail Excellent
Linear Sedan 4D		EB49E	35820	9750	11100	14000	18150
Linear Wagon 4D		EB59E	36520	10375	11775	14750	18950
Manual Trans			5	(650)	(650)	(865)	(865)

9-5—4-Cyl. HO Turbo—Equipment Schedule 2
W.B. 106.4"; 2.3 Liter.

Body	Type	VIN	List	Trade-In Fair	Good	Pvt-Party Good	Retail Excellent
Aero Sedan 4D		EH49G	40475	11925	13525	16600	21000
Aero Wagon 4D		EH59G	41175	12850	14550	17650	22200
Manual Trans			5	(650)	(650)	(865)	(865)

9-5—V6 Turbo—Equipment Schedule 2
W.B. 106.4"; 3.0 Liter.

Body Type	VIN	List	Trade-In Fair	Good	Pvt-Party Good	Retail Excellent
Arc Sedan 4D	ED49Z	39275	10675	12175	15150	19400
Arc Wagon 4D	ED59Z	39975	11300	12800	15800	20200

2003 SAAB — YS3(FB45S)-3-#

9-3—4-Cyl. Turbo—Equipment Schedule 3
W.B. 105.3"; 2.0 Liter.

Body Type	VIN	List	Trade-In Fair	Good	Pvt-Party Good	Retail Excellent
Linear Sedan 4D	FB45S	26525	10525	11975	14600	18500
Auto Trans			300	300	400	400

9-3—4-Cyl. HO Turbo—Equipment Schedule 3
W.B. 102.6", 105.3" (Sed); 2.0 Liter.

Arc Sedan 4D	FD46Y	30620	12550	14200	17000	21000
Vector Sedan 4D	FF46Y	33120	13525	15275	18100	22300
SE Convertible 2D	DF75K	40620	16450	18525	21600	26300
Auto Trans			300	300	400	400

9-5—4-Cyl. Turbo—Equipment Schedule 2
W.B. 106.4"; 2.3 Liter.

Linear Sedan 4D	EB49E	35920	11825	13375	16650	21200
Linear Wagon 4D	EB59E	36620	12525	14150	17400	22100
Manual Trans			(675)	(675)	(900)	(900)

9-5—4-Cyl. HO Turbo—Equipment Schedule 2
W.B. 106.4"; 2.3 Liter.

Aero Sedan 4D	EH49G	40575	14250	16050	19400	24300
Aero Wagon 4D	EH59G	41275	15225	17175	20700	25700
Manual Trans			(675)	(675)	(900)	(900)

9-5—V6 Turbo—Equipment Schedule 2
W.B. 106.4"; 3.0 Liter.

Arc Sedan 4D	ED49Z	39275	12850	14550	17850	22600
Arc Wagon 4D	ED59Z	39975	13475	15225	18600	23500

2004 SAAB — YS3(FB45S)-4-#

9-3—4-Cyl. Turbo—Equipment Schedule 3
W.B. 105.3"; 2.0 Liter.

Linear Sedan 4D	FB45S	26765	12850	14550	17500	21900
Auto Trans			300	300	400	400

9-3—4-Cyl. HO Turbo—Equipment Schedule 3
W.B. 105.3"; 2.0 Liter.

Arc Sedan 4D	FD46Y	30860	15075	16975	20100	24600
Arc Convertible 2D	FD75Y	40670	20850	23375	26700	31900
Aero Sedan 4D	FF45Y	34710	15775	17800	20900	25600
Aero Convertible 2D	FH76Y	43175	21625	24250	27500	32900
Auto Trans			300	300	400	400

9-5—4-Cyl. Turbo—Equipment Schedule 2
W.B. 106.4"; 2.3 Liter.

Linear Sedan 4D	EB59E	34225	15125	17025	20600	25800
Arc Sedan 4D	ED49G	36455	15475	17450	21000	26200
Arc Wagon 4D	ED59G	37165	16200	18225	21800	27200
Manual Trans			(700)	(700)	(935)	(935)

9-5—4-Cyl. HO Turbo—Equipment Schedule 2
W.B. 106.4"; 2.3 Liter.

Aero Sedan 4D	EH49G	41490	17025	19150	22800	28200
Aero Wagon 4D	EH59G	42195	18150	20375	24100	29600
Manual Trans			(700)	(700)	(935)	(935)

2005 SAAB — (YS3orJF4)(GG616)-5-#

9-2X AWD—4-Cyl.—Equipment Schedule 3
W.B. 99.4"; 2.5 Liter.

Linear Wagon 4D	GG616	24935	13475	15225	18650	23600

9-2X AWD—4-Cyl. Turbo—Equipment Schedule 3
W.B. 99.4"; 2.0 Liter.

Aero Sedan 4D	GG226	28895				

9-3—4-Cyl. Turbo—Equipment Schedule 3
W.B. 105.3"; 2.0 Liter.

Linear Sedan 4D	FB45S	28920	15275	17225	20600	25400
Linear Convertible 2D	FB75S	39170	21625	24250	27700	33200
Auto Trans			300	300	400	400

9-3—4-Cyl. HO Turbo—Equipment Schedule 3
W.B. 105.3"; 2.0 Liter.

Arc Sedan 4D	FD45Y	32320	17600	19800	23200	28200
Arc Convertible 2D	FD75Y	42170	23950	26775	30400	36100
Aero Sedan 4D	FF45Y	34920				
Aero Convertible 2D	FH75Y	44670				
Auto Trans			300	300	400	400

2005 SAAB

Body Type	VIN	List	Trade-In Fair	Good	Pvt-Party Good	Retail Excellent

9-5—4-Cyl. Turbo—Equipment Schedule 2
W.B. 106.4"; 2.3 Liter.

Body Type	VIN	List	Fair	Good	Good	Excellent
Linear Wagon 4D	EB59E	34620	**17800**	**19975**	**23900**	**29600**
Arc Sedan 4D	ED49A	36970	**18150**	**20375**	**24300**	**30000**
Arc Wagon 4D	ED59A	37770	**18975**	**21250**	**25200**	**31000**
Manual Trans			**(725)**	**(725)**	**(965)**	**(965)**

9-5—4-Cyl. HO Turbo—Equipment Schedule 2
W.B. 106.4"; 2.3 Liter.

Body Type	VIN	List	Fair	Good	Good	Excellent
Aero Sedan 4D	EH49G	42020				
Aero Wagon 4D	EH59G	42820				
Manual Trans						

SATURN

1991 SATURN — 1G8Z(F549)–M–#

SATURN—4-Cyl.—Equipment Schedule 6
W.B. 99.2", 102.4" (4D); 1.9 Liter.

Body Type	VIN	List	Fair	Good	Good	Excellent
SL Sedan 4D	F549	9045	350	475	1150	2150
SL1 Sedan 4D	G549	9645	450	625	1350	2450
SL2 Sedan 4D	J547	11345	550	800	1575	2800
SC Coupe 2D	J147	12825	600	850	1625	2875

1992 SATURN — 1G8Z(F549)–N–#

SATURN—4-Cyl.—Equipment Schedule 6
W.B. 99.2", 102.4" (4D); 1.9 Liter.

Body Type	VIN	List	Fair	Good	Good	Excellent
SL Sedan 4D	F549	9265	400	550	1225	2250
SL1 Sedan 4D	G549	10065	500	725	1450	2625
SL2 Sedan 4D	J547	11465	625	900	1725	3000
SC Coupe 2D	J147	12945	675	950	1800	3125

1993 SATURN — 1G8Z(F559)–P–#

SATURN—4-Cyl.—Equipment Schedule 6
W.B. 99.2", 102.4" (4D); 1.9 Liter.

Body Type	VIN	List	Fair	Good	Good	Excellent
SL Sedan 4D	F559	10325	400	600	1275	2325
SL1 Sedan 4D	G559	11125	550	800	1575	2800
SL2 Sedan 4D	J557	12625	700	1025	1900	3225
SC1 Coupe 2D	E159	12125	600	875	1675	2925
SC2 Coupe 2D	G157	13925	750	1075	2000	3400
SW1 Wagon 4D	G859	12025	650	925	1750	3050
SW2 Wagon 4D	J857	13325	775	1100	2025	3450

1994 SATURN — 1G8Z(F559)–R–#

SATURN—4-Cyl.—Equipment Schedule 6
W.B. 99.2", 102.4" (4D); 1.9 Liter.

Body Type	VIN	List	Fair	Good	Good	Excellent
SL Sedan 4D	F559	11210	450	625	1375	2550
SL1 Sedan 4D	G559	12010	625	900	1750	3100
SL2 Sedan 4D	J557	13010	775	1125	2100	3575
SC1 Coupe 2D	E159	12910	675	975	1900	3275
SC2 Coupe 2D	G157	14110	850	1200	2325	3950
SW1 Wagon 4D	G859	12910	725	1050	1975	3400
SW2 Wagon 4D	J857	13810	850	1225	2350	3975

1995 SATURN — 1G8Z(F528)–S–#

SATURN—4-Cyl.—Equipment Schedule 6
W.B. 99.2", 102.4" (4D); 1.9 Liter.

Body Type	VIN	List	Fair	Good	Good	Excellent
SL Sedan 4D	F528	11260	500	725	1550	2825
SL1 Sedan 4D	G528	12260	700	1025	2000	3475
SL2 Sedan 4D	J527	13260	900	1250	2425	4100
SC1 Coupe 2D	E128	13130	775	1125	2150	3675
SC2 Coupe 2D	G127	14260	975	1350	2575	4275
SW1 Wagon 4D	G828	12960	825	1175	2325	3975
SW2 Wagon 4D	J827	13960	975	1375	2600	4300

1996 SATURN — 1G8Z(F528)–T–#

SATURN—4-Cyl.—Equipment Schedule 6
W.B. 99.2", 102.4" (4D); 1.9 Liter.

Body Type	VIN	List	Fair	Good	Good	Excellent
SL Sedan 4D	F528	11805	600	850	1775	3175
SL1 Sedan 4D	G528	12705	825	1175	2350	4025
SL2 Sedan 4D	J527	13605	1025	1450	2700	4425
SC1 Coupe 2D	E128	13505	925	1300	2525	4225

1996 SATURN

Body	Type	VIN	List	Trade-In Fair	Good	Pvt-Party Good	Retail Excellent
SC2 Coupe 2D		G127	14605	**1125**	**1575**	**2850**	**4625**
SW1 Wagon 4D		G828	13305	**975**	**1350**	**2575**	**4300**
SW2 Wagon 4D		J827	14205	**1125**	**1575**	**2875**	**4650**

1997 SATURN — 1G8Z(F528)-V-#

SATURN—4-Cyl.—Equipment Schedule 6
W.B. 102.4"; 1.9 Liter.

SL Sedan 4D		F528	11925	**700**	**1000**	**2075**	**3675**
SL1 Sedan 4D		G528	12925	**975**	**1350**	**2650**	**4425**
SL2 Sedan 4D		J527	13825	**1200**	**1650**	**2975**	**4825**
SC1 Coupe 2D		E128	13825	**1075**	**1500**	**2825**	**4600**
SC2 Coupe 2D		G127	15025	**1325**	**1825**	**3175**	**5050**
SW1 Wagon 4D		G828	13525	**1125**	**1575**	**2875**	**4700**
SW2 Wagon 4D		J827	14425	**1350**	**1850**	**3200**	**5100**

1998 SATURN — 1G8Z(F528)-W-#

SATURN—4-Cyl.—Equipment Schedule 6
W.B. 102.4"; 1.9 Liter.

SL Sedan 4D		F528	11995	**850**	**1225**	**2500**	**4300**
SL1 Sedan 4D		G528	12695	**1150**	**1600**	**2950**	**4825**
SL2 Sedan 4D		J527	13195	**1450**	**1950**	**3350**	**5250**
SC1 Coupe 2D		E128	13995	**1275**	**1775**	**3150**	**5050**
SC2 Coupe 2D		G127	15295	**1625**	**2125**	**3575**	**5500**
SW1 Wagon 4D		G828	13695	**1350**	**1850**	**3225**	**5125**
SW2 Wagon 4D		J827	14695	**1650**	**2150**	**3600**	**5550**

1999 SATURN — 1G8Z(F528)-X-#

SATURN—4-Cyl.—Equipment Schedule 6
W.B. 102.4"; 1.9 Liter.

SL Sedan 4D		F528	11995	**1025**	**1450**	**2825**	**4700**
SL1 Sedan 4D		G528	12695	**1375**	**1900**	**3325**	**5250**
SL2 Sedan 4D		J527	13195	**1750**	**2275**	**3725**	**5750**
SC1 Coupe 2D		E128	13345	**1525**	**2025**	**3500**	**5475**
SC1 Coupe 3D		E128	13845	**1550**	**2050**	**3525**	**5500**
SC2 Coupe 2D		G127	14945	**1925**	**2450**	**3950**	**6000**
SC2 Coupe 3D		G127	15445	**1975**	**2525**	**4025**	**6075**
SW1 Wagon 4D		G828	13695	**1600**	**2100**	**3575**	**5550**
SW2 Wagon 4D		J827	14695	**1975**	**2500**	**4000**	**6050**

2000 SATURN — 1G8(JorZ)(F528)-Y-#

SATURN—4-Cyl.—Equipment Schedule 6
W.B. 102.4"; 1.9 Liter.

SL Sedan 4D		F528	12085	**1225**	**1725**	**3200**	**5225**
SL1 Sedan 4D		G528	12885	**1700**	**2225**	**3750**	**5850**
SL2 Sedan 4D		J527	13335	**2125**	**2700**	**4250**	**6400**
SC1 Coupe 3D		N128	12975	**1925**	**2450**	**4000**	**6100**
SC2 Coupe 3D		R127	15585	**2375**	**2950**	**4550**	**6750**
SW2 Wagon 4D		J827	14730	**2350**	**2925**	**4525**	**6725**

SATURN L-SERIES—4-Cyl.—Equipment Schedule 3
W.B. 106.5"; 2.2 Liter.

LS Sedan 4D		R52F	16700	**3225**	**3900**	**5250**	**7150**
LS1 Sedan 4D		T52F	18150	**3650**	**4375**	**5725**	**7700**
LW1 Wagon 4D		U82F	19375	**3925**	**4675**	**6075**	**8100**
Manual Trans				**(500)**	**(500)**	**(665)**	**(665)**

SATURN L-SERIES—V6—Equipment Schedule 3
W.B. 106.5"; 3.0 Liter.

LS2 Sedan 4D		W52R	20575	**4650**	**5475**	**6900**	**9050**
LW2 Wagon 4D		W82R	21800	**4975**	**5850**	**7300**	**9500**

2001 SATURN — 1G8(JorZ)(F528)-1-#

SATURN—4-Cyl.—Equipment Schedule 6
W.B. 102.4"; 1.9 Liter.

SL Sedan 4D		F528	11995	**1850**	**2375**	**3900**	**5975**
SL1 Sedan 4D		G528	12910	**2350**	**2925**	**4475**	**6625**
SL2 Sedan 4D		J527	13360	**2825**	**3450**	**5025**	**7225**
SC1 Coupe 3D		N128	13960	**2575**	**3200**	**4750**	**6925**
SC2 Coupe 3D		R127	16110	**3100**	**3750**	**5375**	**7625**
SW2 Wagon 4D		J827	14755	**3075**	**3725**	**5350**	**7600**

SATURN L-SERIES—4-Cyl.—Equipment Schedule 3
W.B. 106.5"; 2.2 Liter.

L100 Sedan 4D		R52F	16245	**3800**	**4550**	**5975**	**8025**

Body	Type	VIN	List	Trade-In Fair	Good	Pvt-Party Good	Retail Excellent
L200 Sedan 4D		T52F	18210	**4275**	**5075**	**6500**	**8625**
LW200 Wagon 4D		U82F	19335	**4600**	**5425**	**6875**	**9075**
Manual Trans				**(525)**	**(525)**	**(700)**	**(700)**

SATURN L-SERIES—V6—Equipment Schedule 3
W.B. 106.5"; 3.0 Liter.

| L300 Sedan 4D | | W52R | 19995 | **5400** | **6325** | **7850** | **10150** |
| LW300 Wagon 4D | | W82R | 21860 | **5825** | **6775** | **8325** | **10650** |

2002 SATURN — 1G8(JorZ)(F528)-2-#

SATURN—4-Cyl.—Equipment Schedule 6
W.B. 102.4"; 1.9 Liter.

SL Sedan 4D		F528	11995	**3100**	**3750**	**5100**	**7025**
SL1 Sedan 4D		G528	13275	**3650**	**4375**	**5725**	**7725**
SL2 Sedan 4D		J527	13800	**4150**	**4925**	**6325**	**8400**
SC1 Coupe 3D		N128	14325	**3900**	**4650**	**6050**	**8075**
SC2 Coupe 3D		R127	16545	**4475**	**5275**	**6725**	**8825**

SATURN L-SERIES—4-Cyl.—Equipment Schedule 3
W.B. 106.5"; 2.2 Liter.

L100 Sedan 4D		R52F	16870	**4500**	**5325**	**6875**	**9100**
L200 Sedan 4D		T52F	19070	**5025**	**5900**	**7450**	**9750**
LW200 Wagon 4D		U82F	20515	**5400**	**6300**	**7875**	**10250**
Manual Trans				**(550)**	**(550)**	**(735)**	**(735)**

SATURN L-SERIES—V6—Equipment Schedule 3
W.B. 106.5"; 3.0 Liter.

| L300 Sedan 4D | | W52R | 20920 | **6300** | **7325** | **8975** | **11450** |
| LW300 Wagon 4D | | W82R | 22850 | **6775** | **7825** | **9475** | **12050** |

2003 SATURN — 1G8(AF54F)-3-#

ION—4-Cyl.—Equipment Schedule 6
W.B. 103.2"; 2.2 Liter.

1 Sedan 4D		AF54F	12955	**4975**	**5850**	**7375**	**9625**
2 Sedan 4D		AZ52F	14075	**5425**	**6350**	**7875**	**10200**
3 Sedan 4D		AK52F	15575	**5850**	**6825**	**8375**	**10700**
2 Quad Coupe 2D		AM12F	14595	**6375**	**7400**	**8975**	**11400**
3 Quad Coupe 2D		AV12F	16095	**6800**	**7850**	**9450**	**11950**

SATURN L-SERIES—4-Cyl.—Equipment Schedule 3
W.B. 106.5"; 2.2 Liter.

L200 Sedan 4D		JT54F	19040	**5900**	**6875**	**8525**	**11000**
LW200 Wagon 4D		JU84F	20850	**6300**	**7325**	**9025**	**11550**
Manual Trans				**(575)**	**(575)**	**(765)**	**(765)**

SATURN L-SERIES—V6—Equipment Schedule 3
W.B. 106.5"; 3.0 Liter.

| L300 Sedan 4D | | JW54R | 21255 | **7350** | **8450** | **10200** | **12850** |
| LW300 Wagon 4D | | JW84R | 23185 | **7850** | **9025** | **10750** | **13550** |

2004 SATURN — 1G8(AF54F)-4-#

ION—4-Cyl.—Equipment Schedule 6
W.B. 103.2"; 2.2 Liter.

1 Sedan 4D		AF54F	10995	**5825**	**6775**	**8225**	**10500**
2 Sedan 4D		AZ52F	14750	**6300**	**7325**	**8800**	**11100**
3 Sedan 4D		AK52F	16275	**6775**	**7825**	**9325**	**11700**
2 Quad Coupe 2D		AM12F	14850	**7350**	**8450**	**10000**	**12400**
3 Quad Coupe 2D		AV12F	16800	**7775**	**8950**	**10500**	**13000**

ION—4-Cyl. Supercharged—Equipment Schedule 6
W.B. 103.3"; 2.0 Liter.

| Red Line Quad Cpe 2D | | AY12P | 20950 | | | | |

SATURN L-SERIES—4-Cyl.—Equipment Schedule 3
W.B. 106.5"; 2.2 Liter.

| L300 Sedan 4D | | JC54F | 16995 | **6925** | **8000** | **9700** | **12250** |
| L300 Wagon 4D | | JC84F | 19045 | **7400** | **8500** | **10250** | **12850** |

SATURN L-SERIES—V6—Equipment Schedule 3
W.B. 106.5"; 3.0 Liter.

| L300 Sedan 4D | | JD54R | 21410 | **8525** | **9750** | **11550** | **14300** |
| L300 Wagon 4D | | JD84R | 23560 | **9125** | **10425** | **12200** | **15050** |

2005 SATURN — 1G8(AF52F)-5-#

ION—4-Cyl.—Equipment Schedule 6
W.B. 103.2"; 2.2 Liter.

1 Sedan 4D		AF52F	12955	**6825**	**7875**	**9300**	**11600**
2 Sedan 4D		AZ52F	14945	**7350**	**8475**	**9950**	**12300**
3 Sedan 4D		AK52F	16470	**7850**	**9025**	**10550**	**12950**
2 Quad Coupe 2D		AM12F	15495	**8500**	**9700**	**11200**	**13700**

Body	Type	VIN	List	Trade-In Fair	Good	Pvt-Party Good	Retail Excellent
3 Quad Coupe 2D		AV12F	17245	**8975**	**10275**	**11850**	**14400**

ION—4-Cyl. Supercharged—Equipment Schedule 6
W.B. 103.2"; 2.0 Liter.

| Red Line Quad Cpe 2D | | AV12P | 21450 | | | | |

SATURN L-SERIES—V6—Equipment Schedule 3
W.B. 106.5"; 3.0 Liter.

| L300 Sedan 4D | | JD54R | 21995 | **9525** | **10875** | **12650** | **15450** |

SCION

2004 SCION — JT(KorL)(KT624)-4-#

xA—4-Cyl.—Equipment Schedule 6
W.B. 93.3"; 1.5 Liter.

| Hatchback 4D | | KT624 | 12965 | **7075** | **8175** | **9950** | **12550** |

xB—4-Cyl.—Equipment Schedule 6
W.B. 98.4"; 1.5 Liter.

| Sport Wagon 4D | | KT324 | 14165 | **8550** | **9800** | **11550** | **14300** |

2005 SCION — JT(KorL)(KT624)-5-#

xA—4-Cyl.—Equipment Schedule 6
W.B. 93.3"; 1.5 Liter.

| Hatchback 4D | | KT624 | 12995 | **7650** | **8775** | **10400** | **12900** |
| Release Series 1.0 | | | | **400** | **400** | **535** | **535** |

xB—4-Cyl.—Equipment Schedule 6
W.B. 98.4"; 1.5 Liter.

| Sport Wagon 4D | | KT324 | 14195 | **9250** | **10525** | **12150** | **14750** |

tC—4-Cyl.—Equipment Schedule 4
W.B. 106.3"; 2.4 Liter.

| Hatchback Coupe 2D | | DE177 | 17265 | **10950** | **12425** | **14350** | **17450** |

STERLING

1991 STERLING — SAXXS(43H)-M-#

827—V6—Equipment Schedule 1
W.B. 108.6"; 2.7 Liter.

Si Sedan 4D		43H,K	26960	**350**	**475**	**1150**	**2150**
SL Sedan 4D		83H,K	28960	**400**	**575**	**1275**	**2375**
SLi Hatchback 4D		56H,K	28960	**425**	**625**	**1325**	**2450**
Manual Trans				**(200)**	**(200)**	**(265)**	**(265)**

SUBARU

1991 SUBARU — JF(1or2)(KA722)-M-#

JUSTY—3-Cyl.—Equipment Schedule 6
W.B. 90.0"; 1.2 Liter.

Hatchback 2D		KA722	6390	**200**	**300**	**750**	**1425**
GL Hatchback 2D		KA732	7794	**250**	**350**	**800**	**1525**
GL 4WD H'Back 2D		KA83A	8594	**275**	**375**	**850**	**1600**
GL 4WD H'Back 4D		KD83A	8694	**275**	**375**	**850**	**1600**

LOYALE—4-Cyl.—Equipment Schedule 4
W.B. 97.0", 97.2" (Sed); 1.8 Liter.

Sedan 4D		AC422	9894	**600**	**850**	**1475**	**2500**
Wagon 4D		AN422	10694	**550**	**800**	**1425**	**2425**
4WD				**475**	**475**	**635**	**635**
Auto Trans				**150**	**150**	**200**	**200**

LEGACY—4-Cyl.—Equipment Schedule 4
W.B. 101.6"; 2.2 Liter.

L Sedan 4D		BC632	15259	**475**	**700**	**1525**	**2800**
L Wagon 4D		BJ632	15859	**625**	**900**	**1800**	**3175**
LS Sedan 4D		BC652	18164	**550**	**775**	**1625**	**2950**
LS Wagon 4D		BJ652	18764	**675**	**975**	**1925**	**3350**
LSi Sedan 4D		BC652	19094	**550**	**800**	**1675**	**3000**
4WD		C		**475**	**475**	**635**	**635**
Manual Trans				**(175)**	**(175)**	**(235)**	**(235)**

LEGACY 4WD—4-Cyl. Turbo—Equipment Schedule 4
W.B. 101.6"; 2.2 Liter.

| Sport Sedan 4D | | BC67C | 19294 | **825** | **1175** | **2300** | **3950** |
| Manual Trans | | | | **(175)** | **(175)** | **(235)** | **(235)** |

1991 SUBARU

Body Type	VIN	List	Trade-In Fair	Good	Pvt-Party Good	Retail Excellent
XT—4-Cyl.—Equipment Schedule 4						
W.B. 97.0"; 1.8 Liter.						
GL Coupe 2D	AX432	13833	**675**	**975**	**1650**	**2775**
Auto Trans			**150**	**150**	**200**	**200**
XT6—6-Cyl.—Equipment Schedule 4						
W.B. 97.0"; 2.7 Liter.						
Coupe 2D	AX842	17873	**900**	**1275**	**2100**	**3400**
4WD Coupe 2D	AX942	18713	**975**	**1350**	**2250**	**3625**
Auto Trans			**150**	**150**	**200**	**200**

1992 SUBARU — (JF1,JF2,4S3or4S4)(KA722)-N-#

Body Type	VIN	List	Trade-In Fair	Good	Pvt-Party Good	Retail Excellent
JUSTY—3-Cyl.—Equipment Schedule 6						
W.B. 90.0"; 1.2 Liter.						
Hatchback 2D	KA722	7090	**200**	**300**	**750**	**1475**
GL Hatchback 2D	KA732	8494	**250**	**350**	**825**	**1575**
GL AWD H'Back 2D	KA832	9294	**275**	**375**	**875**	**1650**
GL AWD H'Back 4D	KD83A	9394	**275**	**375**	**875**	**1650**
LOYALE—4-Cyl.—Equipment Schedule 4						
W.B. 97.0", 97.2" (Sed); 1.8 Liter.						
Sedan 4D	AC422	10244	**675**	**975**	**1650**	**2800**
Wagon 4D	AN422	11094	**650**	**925**	**1625**	**2775**
AWD		5*	**550**	**550**	**735**	**735**
Auto Trans			**150**	**150**	**200**	**200**
LEGACY—4-Cyl.—Equipment Schedule 4						
W.B. 101.6"; 2.2 Liter.						
L Sedan 4D	BC632	16229	**550**	**775**	**1725**	**3175**
L Wagon 4D	BJ632	16729	**675**	**975**	**2025**	**3625**
LS Sedan 4D	BC652	19744	**600**	**875**	**1900**	**3400**
LS Wagon 4D	BJ652	20244	**775**	**1100**	**2275**	**4000**
LSi Sedan 4D	BC652	21144	**625**	**900**	**1925**	**3450**
4WD		6	**550**	**550**	**735**	**735**
Manual Trans			**(175)**	**(175)**	**(235)**	**(235)**
LEGACY 4WD—4-Cyl. Turbo—Equipment Schedule 4						
W.B. 101.6"; 2.2 Liter.						
Sport Sedan 4D	BC672	21029	**925**	**1300**	**2550**	**4325**
LE Touring Wagon	BJ672	22090	**1075**	**1500**	**2825**	**4625**
Manual Trans			**(175)**	**(175)**	**(235)**	**(235)**
SVX AWD—6-Cyl.—Equipment Schedule 4						
W.B. 102.8"; 3.3 Liter.						
Sport Coupe 2D	CX343	25445	**1225**	**1675**	**3475**	**5825**
Touring Pkg			**275**	**275**	**365**	**365**

1993 SUBARU — (JF1,JF2,4S3or4S4)(KA722)-P-#

Body Type	VIN	List	Trade-In Fair	Good	Pvt-Party Good	Retail Excellent
JUSTY—3-Cyl.—Equipment Schedule 6						
W.B. 90.0"; 1.2 Liter.						
Hatchback 2D	KA722	7783	**200**	**300**	**775**	**1525**
GL Hatchback 2D	KA732	9558	**250**	**350**	**875**	**1650**
GL AWD H'Back 2D	KA832	10358	**275**	**400**	**925**	**1750**
GL AWD H'Back 4D	KD83A	9923	**275**	**400**	**925**	**1750**
LOYALE—4-Cyl.—Equipment Schedule 4						
W.B. 97.0", 97.2" (Sed); 1.8 Liter.						
Sedan 4D	AC422	10923	**775**	**1100**	**1900**	**3125**
Wagon 4D	AN422	11773	**775**	**1100**	**1925**	**3175**
AWD			**625**	**625**	**835**	**835**
Auto Trans			**175**	**175**	**235**	**235**
IMPREZA—4-Cyl.—Equipment Schedule 5						
W.B. 99.2"; 1.8 Liter.						
Sedan 4D	GC214	11444	**525**	**750**	**1550**	**2800**
L Sedan 4D	GC224	14244	**625**	**900**	**1750**	**3100**
L Wagon 4D	GF244	14644	**825**	**1175**	**2175**	**3675**
LS Sedan 4D	GC254	16144	**825**	**1175**	**2175**	**3675**
LS Wagon 4D	GF254	16544	**950**	**1325**	**2525**	**4175**
AWD			**625**	**625**	**835**	**835**
LEGACY—4-Cyl.—Equipment Schedule 4						
W.B. 101.6"; 2.2 Liter.						
L Sedan 4D	BC633	17495	**625**	**900**	**2000**	**3625**
L Wagon 4D	BJ633	18195	**775**	**1125**	**2400**	**4200**
LS Sedan 4D	BC653	19595	**700**	**1025**	**2250**	**4025**
LS Wagon 4D	BJ653	20295	**900**	**1275**	**2600**	**4450**
AWD			**625**	**625**	**835**	**835**
Manual Trans			**(225)**	**(225)**	**(300)**	**(300)**
LEGACY AWD—4-Cyl.—Equipment Schedule 4						
W.B. 101.6"; 2.2 Liter.						

Body	Type	VIN	List	Trade-In Fair	Trade-In Good	Pvt-Party Good	Retail Excellent
LSi Sedan 4D		BC653	22095	**1225**	**1700**	**3125**	**5075**
LSi Wagon 4D		BJ653	23095	**1525**	**2025**	**3525**	**5525**
LEGACY AWD—4-Cyl. Turbo—Equipment Schedule 4							
W.B. 101.6"; 2.2 Liter.							
Sport Sedan 4D		BC673	21295	**1075**	**1500**	**2875**	**4775**
Touring Wagon 4D		BJ673	23095	**1250**	**1750**	**3175**	**5125**
Manual Trans				**(225)**	**(225)**	**(300)**	**(300)**
SVX AWD—6-Cyl.—Equipment Schedule 4							
W.B. 102.8"; 3.3 Liter.							
Special Edition Cpe 2D		CX343	34445	**1675**	**2175**	**4050**	**6525**

1994 SUBARU — (JF1,JF2,4S3or4S4)(KA722)–R–#

Body	Type	VIN	List	Trade-In Fair	Trade-In Good	Pvt-Party Good	Retail Excellent
JUSTY—3-Cyl.—Equipment Schedule 6							
W.B. 90.0"; 1.2 Liter.							
DL Hatchback 2D		KA722	8194	**200**	**300**	**825**	**1600**
GL AWD Hatchback 5D		KD83A	10048	**300**	**400**	**1000**	**1875**
LOYALE AWD—4-Cyl.—Equipment Schedule 4							
W.B. 96.9"; 1.8 Liter.							
Wagon 4D		AN52B	13998	**1425**	**1925**	**3100**	**4775**
Auto Trans				**200**	**200**	**265**	**265**
IMPREZA—4-Cyl.—Equipment Schedule 5							
W.B. 99.2"; 1.8 Liter.							
Sedan 4D		GC214	11645	**575**	**825**	**1725**	**3125**
L Sedan 4D		GC224	15195	**700**	**1000**	**2000**	**3475**
L Wagon 4D		GF224	15595	**900**	**1275**	**2500**	**4200**
AWD				**700**	**700**	**935**	**935**
IMPREZA—4-Cyl.—Equipment Schedule 5							
W.B. 99.2"; 1.8 Liter.							
LS Sedan 4D		GC255	18995	**1975**	**2500**	**3825**	**5700**
LS Wagon 4D		GF255	19395	**2200**	**2800**	**4150**	**6075**
LEGACY—4-Cyl.—Equipment Schedule 4							
W.B. 101.6"; 2.2 Liter.							
L Sedan 4D		BC633	17395	**700**	**1025**	**2300**	**4150**
L Wagon 4D		BJ633	18695	**900**	**1275**	**2675**	**4575**
LS Sedan 4D		BC653	20145	**825**	**1175**	**2550**	**4450**
LS Wagon 4D		BJ653	20845	**1050**	**1450**	**2900**	**4875**
AWD				**700**	**700**	**935**	**935**
Manual Trans				**(275)**	**(275)**	**(365)**	**(365)**
LEGACY AWD—4-Cyl.—Equipment Schedule 4							
W.B. 101.6"; 2.2 Liter.							
LSi Sedan 4D		BC653	22295	**1475**	**1975**	**3525**	**5575**
LSi Wagon 4D		BJ653	23295	**1825**	**2350**	**3925**	**6075**
LEGACY AWD—4-Cyl. Turbo—Equipment Schedule 4							
W.B. 101.6"; 2.2 Liter.							
Sport Sedan 4D		BC673	22645	**1250**	**1750**	**3250**	**5250**
Touring Wagon 4D		BJ673	23645	**1525**	**2025**	**3575**	**5625**
Manual Trans				**(275)**	**(275)**	**(365)**	**(365)**
SVX—6-Cyl.—Equipment Schedule 4							
W.B. 102.8"; 3.3 Liter.							
L Coupe 2D		CX323	24345	**1075**	**1525**	**3325**	**5675**
LS Coupe 2D		CX345	28995	**1450**	**1950**	**3800**	**6250**
LSi AWD Coupe 2D		CX355	34295	**2150**	**2750**	**4700**	**7325**

1995 SUBARU — 4S3orJF1(GC215)–S–#

Body	Type	VIN	List	Trade-In Fair	Trade-In Good	Pvt-Party Good	Retail Excellent
IMPREZA—4-Cyl.—Equipment Schedule 5							
W.B. 99.2"; 1.8 Liter, 2.2 Liter.							
Sedan 4D		GC215	13420	**675**	**950**	**2025**	**3625**
Coupe 2D		GM215	13715	**550**	**800**	**1800**	**3300**
L Sedan 4D		GC235	15025	**800**	**1150**	**2350**	**4100**
L Coupe 2D		GM235	15025	**725**	**1050**	**2225**	**3925**
AWD				**775**	**775**	**1035**	**1035**
IMPREZA AWD—4-Cyl.—Equipment Schedule 5							
W.B. 99.2"; 1.8 Liter, 2.2 Liter.							
L Wagon 4D		GF235	16425	**2325**	**2900**	**4325**	**6275**
LX Sedan 4D		GC655	17470	**2325**	**2900**	**4325**	**6275**
LX Coupe 2D		GM655	17770	**2150**	**2750**	**4100**	**6050**
LX Wagon 4D		GF655	17870	**2600**	**3225**	**4650**	**6700**
Outback Wagon 4D		GF235	17225	**2800**	**3425**	**4900**	**6950**
LEGACY—4-Cyl.—Equipment Schedule 4							
W.B. 103.5"; 2.2 Liter.							
Sedan 4D		BD625	16517	**975**	**1375**	**2850**	**4900**
L Sedan 4D		BD635	18264	**950**	**1325**	**2825**	**4850**
L Wagon 4D		BK635	18964	**1200**	**1650**	**3225**	**5325**

1995 SUBARU

Body	Type	VIN	List	Trade-In Fair	Trade-In Good	Pvt-Party Good	Retail Excellent
AWD				**775**	**775**	**1035**	**1035**
	Manual Trans (Sedan)			**(325)**	**(325)**	**(435)**	**(435)**

LEGACY AWD—4-Cyl.—Equipment Schedule 4
W.B. 103.5"; 2.2 Liter.

Body	Type	VIN	List	Fair	Good	Good	Excellent
	Brighton Wagon 4D	BK625	17643	**1575**	**2075**	**3725**	**5925**
	Outback Wagon 4D	BK635	21095	**2725**	**3325**	**5125**	**7575**
	LS Sedan 4D	BD655	21595	**1775**	**2300**	**3950**	**6175**
	LS Wagon 4D	BK655	22295	**2025**	**2600**	**4300**	**6600**
	LSi Sedan 4D	BD655	24095	**1950**	**2475**	**4175**	**6425**
	LSi Wagon 4D	BK655	24795	**2300**	**2875**	**4625**	**6950**

SVX—6-Cyl.—Equipment Schedule 4
W.B. 102.8"; 3.3 Liter.

Body	Type	VIN	List	Fair	Good	Good	Excellent
	L Coupe 2D	CX335	27275	**1500**	**2000**	**3900**	**6400**
	L AWD Coupe 2D	CX335	28775	**2050**	**2625**	**4575**	**7200**
	LSi Coupe 2D	CX355	34825	**2725**	**3350**	**5425**	**8200**

1996 SUBARU — JF1or4S3(GM225)—T-#

IMPREZA AWD—4-Cyl.—Equipment Schedule 5
W.B. 99.2"; 1.8 Liter, 2.2 Liter.

Body	Type	VIN	List	Fair	Good	Good	Excellent
	Brighton Coupe 2D	GM225	13990	**1975**	**2500**	**3875**	**5800**
	L Sedan 4D	GC435	16890	**2375**	**2950**	**4400**	**6375**
	L Coupe 2D	GM435	16890	**2175**	**2775**	**4150**	**6100**
	L Wagon 4D	GF435	16490	**2700**	**3300**	**4775**	**6850**
	LX Sedan 4D	GC455	18290	**2725**	**3325**	**4800**	**6875**
	LX Coupe 2D	GM455	18590	**2525**	**3125**	**4550**	**6600**
	LX Wagon 4D	GF455	18690	**3000**	**3650**	**5175**	**7300**
	Outback Wagon 4D	GF485	18890	**3175**	**3850**	**5400**	**7575**
	2WD			**(825)**	**(825)**	**(1100)**	**(1100)**

LEGACY—4-Cyl.—Equipment Schedule 4
W.B. 103.5"; 2.2 Liter.

Body	Type	VIN	List	Fair	Good	Good	Excellent
	L Sedan 4D	BD335	18775	**1125**	**1575**	**3225**	**5400**
	L Wagon 4D	BK335	19475	**1450**	**1950**	**3650**	**5925**
	AWD	4		**825**	**825**	**1100**	**1100**
	Manual Trans (Sedan)			**(375)**	**(375)**	**(500)**	**(500)**

LEGACY AWD—4-Cyl.—Equipment Schedule 4
W.B. 103.5"; 2.2 Liter, 2.5 Liter.

Body	Type	VIN	List	Fair	Good	Good	Excellent
	Brighton Wagon 4D	BK425	18075	**1900**	**2425**	**4200**	**6575**
	Outback Wagon 4D	BG685	22490	**3150**	**3800**	**5750**	**8400**
	LS Sedan 4D	BD455	22590	**2125**	**2700**	**4475**	**6875**
	LS Wagon 4D	BK455	23290	**2425**	**3025**	**4875**	**7375**
	GT Sedan 4D	BD675	22790	**2325**	**2900**	**4725**	**7175**
	GT Wagon 4D	BK675	23490	**2725**	**3325**	**5225**	**7750**
	LSi Sedan 4D	BD665	25290	**2275**	**2850**	**4675**	**7125**
	LSi Wagon 4D	BK665	25990	**2700**	**3300**	**5175**	**7675**
	4-Cyl. 2.5L (Outback)	6		**225**	**225**	**300**	**300**

SVX AWD—6-Cyl.—Equipment Schedule 4
W.B. 102.8"; 3.3 Liter.

Body	Type	VIN	List	Fair	Good	Good	Excellent
	L Coupe 2D	CX835	30490	**2600**	**3225**	**5300**	**8075**
	LSi Coupe 2D	CX865	35990	**3325**	**4025**	**6200**	**9150**

1997 SUBARU — JF1or4S3(GM425)—V-#

IMPREZA AWD—4-Cyl.—Equipment Schedule 5
W.B. 99.2"; 1.8 Liter, 2.2 Liter.

Body	Type	VIN	List	Fair	Good	Good	Excellent
	Brighton Coupe 2D	GM425	15290	**2275**	**2825**	**4325**	**6350**
	L Sedan 4D	GC435	17190	**2725**	**3350**	**4875**	**6975**
	L Coupe 2D	GM435	17190	**2525**	**3125**	**4600**	**6700**
	L Sport Wagon 4D	GF435	17590	**3050**	**3725**	**5275**	**7475**
	Outback Sport Wagon	GF485	19290	**3625**	**4325**	**5950**	**8225**

LEGACY AWD—4-Cyl.—Equipment Schedule 4
W.B. 103.5"; 2.2 Liter, 2.5 Liter.

Body	Type	VIN	List	Fair	Good	Good	Excellent
	Brighton Wagon 4D	BK425	18490	**2600**	**3225**	**5100**	**7625**
	L Sedan 4D	BD435	20490	**2375**	**2950**	**4800**	**7275**
	L Wagon 4D	BK435	21190	**2800**	**3425**	**5300**	**7850**
	Outback Wagon 4D	BG685	23790	**3900**	**4650**	**6675**	**9450**
	Outback Ltd Wag 4D	BG685	25490	**4150**	**4925**	**7000**	**9850**
	GT Sedan 4D	BD675	24090	**3225**	**3900**	**5875**	**8500**
	GT Wagon 4D	BK675	24790	**3625**	**4325**	**6325**	**9050**
	LSi Sedan 4D	BD665	25490	**3150**	**3800**	**5750**	**8400**
	LSi Wagon 4D	BK665	26190	**3525**	**4225**	**6200**	**8825**
	Manual Trans (Sedan)			**(400)**	**(400)**	**(535)**	**(535)**

SVX AWD—6-Cyl.—Equipment Schedule 4
W.B. 102.8"; 3.3 Liter.

Body	Type	VIN	List	Fair	Good	Good	Excellent
	L Coupe 2D	CX835	31120	**3200**	**3875**	**6100**	**9075**

Body Type	VIN	List	Trade-In Fair	Good	Pvt-Party Good	Retail Excellent
LSi Coupe 2D	CX865	36740	**4000**	**4750**	**7100**	**10250**

1998 SUBARU — JF1or4S3(GC435)–W–#

IMPREZA AWD—4-Cyl.—Equipment Schedule 5
W.B. 99.2"; 2.2 Liter, 2.5 Liter.

L Sedan 4D	GC435	17190	**3150**	**3800**	**5400**	**7650**
L Coupe 2D	GM435	17190	**2900**	**3575**	**5150**	**7325**
L Sport Wagon 4D	GF435	17590	**3500**	**4200**	**5825**	**8125**
Outback Sport Wag 4D	GF485	19290	**4050**	**4825**	**6500**	**8900**
2.5RS Coupe 2D	GM675	20490	**4300**	**5100**	**6800**	**9250**

LEGACY AWD—4-Cyl.—Equipment Schedule 4
W.B. 103.5"; 2.2 Liter, 2.5 Liter.

Brighton Wagon 4D	BK425	18524	**3100**	**3750**	**5800**	**8525**
L Sedan 4D	BD435	20490	**2850**	**3500**	**5475**	**8175**
L Wagon 4D	BK435	21190	**3300**	**3975**	**6025**	**8775**
Outback Wagon 4D	BG685	23790	**4500**	**5300**	**7500**	**10500**
Outback Ltd Wag 4D	BG685	25890	**4800**	**5625**	**7850**	**10900**
GT Sedan 4D	BD675	24090	**3775**	**4525**	**6650**	**9500**
GT Limited Sedan 4D	BE656	25390	**3950**	**4700**	**6850**	**9750**
GT Wagon 4D	BK675	24790	**4200**	**4975**	**7100**	**10050**
Manual Trans (Sedan)			**(425)**	**(425)**	**(565)**	**(565)**
Dual Power Moon Roofs			**175**	**175**	**235**	**235**

1999 SUBARU — JF1or4S3(GC435)–X–#

IMPREZA AWD—4-Cyl.—Equipment Schedule 5
W.B. 99.2"; 2.2 Liter, 2.5 Liter.

L Sedan 4D	GC435	17190	**3625**	**4350**	**6025**	**8375**
L Coupe 2D	GM435	17190	**3350**	**4050**	**5700**	**8000**
L Sport Wagon 4D	GF435	17590	**4000**	**4750**	**6475**	**8900**
Outback Sport Wag 4D	GF485	19290	**4600**	**5425**	**7175**	**9700**
2.5RS Coupe 2D	GM675	20490	**4850**	**5700**	**7500**	**10050**

LEGACY AWD—4-Cyl.—Equipment Schedule 4
W.B. 103.5"; 2.2 Liter, 2.5 Liter.

Brighton Wagon 4D	BK425	18524	**3650**	**4375**	**6500**	**9350**
L Sedan 4D	BD435	20490	**3400**	**4100**	**6175**	**9025**
L Wagon 4D	BK435	21190	**3875**	**4625**	**6775**	**9675**
Outback Wagon 4D	BG686	23790	**5175**	**6050**	**8325**	**11450**
Outback Ltd Wag 4D	BG686	25890	**5550**	**6475**	**8775**	**12000**
GT Sedan 4D	BD675	24090	**4425**	**5225**	**7425**	**10450**
GT Limited Sedan 4D	BE656	25390	**4575**	**5400**	**7650**	**10650**
GT Wagon 4D	BK675	24790	**4850**	**5700**	**7925**	**11000**
Sport Util Sedan 4D	BD685	23890	**4900**	**5750**	**7975**	**11050**
Ltd Sport Util Sed 4D	BD685	26090	**5400**	**6300**	**8600**	**11800**
Dual Moon Roofs			**225**	**225**	**300**	**300**
Manual Trans (Sedan)			**(450)**	**(450)**	**(600)**	**(600)**

2000 SUBARU — JF1or4S3{GC435)–Y–#

IMPREZA AWD—4-Cyl.—Equipment Schedule 5
W.B. 99.2"; 2.2 Liter, 2.5 Liter.

L Sedan 4D	GC435	17190	**4300**	**5100**	**6875**	**9350**
L Coupe 2D	GM435	17190	**3975**	**4725**	**6475**	**8950**
L Sport Wagon 4D	GF435	17590	**4700**	**5550**	**7350**	**9950**
Outback Sport Wag 4D	GF485	19390	**5400**	**6300**	**8175**	**10850**
2.5RS Sedan 4D	GC675	20590	**5925**	**6875**	**8775**	**11550**
2.5RS Coupe 2D	GM675	20590	**5700**	**6625**	**8500**	**11250**

LEGACY AWD—4-Cyl.—Equipment Schedule 4
W.B. 104.3"; 2.5 Liter.

Brighton Wagon 4D	BH625	19690	**5550**	**6500**	**8375**	**11050**
L Sedan 4D	BE635	20490	**5250**	**6150**	**8025**	**10650**
L Wagon 4D	BH635	21190	**5850**	**6800**	**8675**	**11400**
GT Sedan 4D	BE645	24090	**6450**	**7450**	**9375**	**12200**
GT Limited Sedan 4D	BE656	25590	**6625**	**7675**	**9600**	**12450**
GT Wagon 4D	BH645	24990	**6925**	**8000**	**10000**	**12900**
Dual Moon Roofs			**300**	**300**	**400**	**400**
Manual Trans (Sedan)			**(500)**	**(500)**	**(665)**	**(665)**

OUTBACK AWD—4-Cyl.—Equipment Schedule 4
W.B. 104.3"; 2.5 Liter.

Wagon 4D	BH666	23990	**7325**	**8425**	**10450**	**13400**
Limited Sedan 4D	BE686	26390	**7575**	**8700**	**10700**	**13750**
Limited Sedan 4D	BH686	27390	**7725**	**8875**	**10950**	**13950**
Dual Moon Roofs			**300**	**300**	**400**	**400**

2001 SUBARU

Body	Type	VIN	List	Trade-In Fair	Trade-In Good	Pvt-Party Good	Retail Excellent

2001 SUBARU — JF1or4S3(GC435)-1-#

IMPREZA AWD—4-Cyl.—Equipment Schedule 5
W.B. 99.2"; 2.2 Liter, 2.5 Liter.

Body Type	VIN	List	Fair	Good	Good	Excellent
L Sedan 4D	GC435	17290	**5000**	**5875**	**7725**	**10400**
L Coupe 2D	GM435	17290	**4650**	**5500**	**7350**	**9950**
L Sport Wagon 4D	GF435	17690	**5475**	**6400**	**8300**	**11000**
Outback Sport Wag 4D	GF485	19490	**6250**	**7250**	**9200**	**12050**
2.5RS Sedan 4D	GC675	20790	**6850**	**7875**	**9900**	**12850**
2.5RS Coupe 2D	GM675	20790	**6600**	**7625**	**9600**	**12500**

LEGACY AWD—4-Cyl.—Equipment Schedule 4
W.B. 104.3"; 2.5 Liter.

Body Type	VIN	List	Fair	Good	Good	Excellent
L Sedan 4D	BE635	20590	**6075**	**7050**	**9025**	**11850**
L Wagon 4D	BH635	21290	**6725**	**7750**	**9750**	**12650**
GT Sedan 4D	BE645	24190	**7400**	**8500**	**10550**	**13600**
GT Limited Sedan 4D	BE656	25690	**7625**	**8750**	**10800**	**13800**
GT Wagon 4D	BH645	25090	**7975**	**9175**	**11250**	**14350**
Dual Moon Roofs			**375**	**375**	**500**	**500**
Manual Trans (Sedan)			**(525)**	**(525)**	**(700)**	**(700)**

OUTBACK AWD—4-Cyl.—Equipment Schedule 4
W.B. 104.3"; 2.5 Liter.

Body Type	VIN	List	Fair	Good	Good	Excellent
Wagon 4D	BH665	24190	**8400**	**9625**	**11750**	**14900**
Limited Sedan 4D	BE686	26490	**8675**	**9950**	**12100**	**15300**
Limited Wagon 4D	BH686	27590	**8850**	**10125**	**12250**	**15450**
Dual Moon Roofs			**375**	**375**	**500**	**500**

OUTBACK AWD—H6—Equipment Schedule 4
W.B. 104.3"; 3.0 Liter.

Body Type	VIN	List	Fair	Good	Good	Excellent
L.L. Bean Wagon 4D	BH806	29990	**9300**	**10625**	**12800**	**16100**
VDC Wagon 4D	BH896	32390	**10475**	**11925**	**14200**	**17650**
Dual Moon Roofs			**375**	**375**	**500**	**500**

2002 SUBARU — JF1or4S3(GG655)-2-#

IMPREZA AWD—4-Cyl.—Equipment Schedule 5
W.B. 99.4"; 2.5 Liter.

Body Type	VIN	List	Fair	Good	Good	Excellent
2.5 TS Sport Wagon 4D	GG655	18820	**6300**	**7325**	**9325**	**12250**
Outback Sport Wag 4D	GF485	20020	**7175**	**8275**	**10350**	**13400**
2.5RS Sedan 4D	GC675	20320	**7800**	**8975**	**11100**	**14200**

IMPREZA AWD—4-Cyl. Turbo—Equipment Schedule 4
W.B. 99.4"; 2.0 Liter.

Body Type	VIN	List	Fair	Good	Good	Excellent
WRX Sedan 4D	GD295	25520	**9950**	**11350**	**13900**	**17650**
WRX Sport Wagon 4D	GG295	25020	**9600**	**10950**	**13550**	**17200**

LEGACY AWD—4-Cyl.—Equipment Schedule 4
W.B. 104.3"; 2.5 Liter.

Body Type	VIN	List	Fair	Good	Good	Excellent
L Sedan 4D	BE635	20620	**7000**	**8075**	**10200**	**13200**
L Wagon 4D	BH635	21320	**7675**	**8825**	**11000**	**14150**
GT Sedan 4D	BE645	24220	**8500**	**9700**	**11900**	**15150**
GT Limited Sedan 4D	BE656	26020	**8675**	**9950**	**12150**	**15450**
GT Wagon 4D	BH645	25120	**9125**	**10425**	**12650**	**15950**
Dual Moon Roofs			**475**	**475**	**635**	**635**
Manual Trans (Sedan)			**(550)**	**(550)**	**(735)**	**(735)**

OUTBACK AWD—4-Cyl.—Equipment Schedule 4
W.B. 104.3"; 2.5 Liter.

Body Type	VIN	List	Fair	Good	Good	Excellent
Wagon 4D	BH665	24220	**9575**	**10925**	**13200**	**16550**
Limited Sedan 4D	BE686	26520	**9900**	**11300**	**13600**	**17000**
Limited Wagon 4D	BH686	27620	**10100**	**11450**	**13750**	**17150**
Dual Moon Roofs			**475**	**475**	**635**	**635**

OUTBACK AWD—H6—Equipment Schedule 4
W.B. 104.3"; 3.0 Liter.

Body Type	VIN	List	Fair	Good	Good	Excellent
Sedan 4D	BE896	28520	**9950**	**11350**	**13650**	**17000**
L.L. Bean Wagon 4D	BH806	30020	**10625**	**12075**	**14400**	**17900**
VDC Sedan 4D	BH806	30920	**11150**	**12650**	**15050**	**18600**
VDC Wagon 4D	BH896	32420	**11875**	**13425**	**15850**	**19600**
Dual Moon Roofs			**475**	**475**	**635**	**635**

2003 SUBARU — JF1or4S3(GG655)-3-#

IMPREZA AWD—4-Cyl.—Equipment Schedule 5
W.B. 99.4"; 2.5 Liter.

Body Type	VIN	List	Fair	Good	Good	Excellent
2.5 TS Sport Wagon 4D	GG655	18920	**7200**	**8325**	**10500**	**13600**
Outback Sport Wag	GG685	20120	**8150**	**9325**	**11550**	**14800**
2.5RS Sedan 4D	GD675	20420	**8850**	**10125**	**12350**	**15650**

IMPREZA AWD—4-Cyl. Turbo—Equipment Schedule 4
W.B. 99.4"; 2.0 Liter.

Body Type	VIN	List	Trade-In Fair	Good	Pvt-Party Good	Retail Excellent
WRX Sedan 4D	GD296	25720	11200	12700	15400	19400
WRX Sport Wag 4D	GG296	25220	10875	12325	15050	19000
LEGACY AWD—4-Cyl.—Equipment Schedule 4						
W.B. 104.3"; 2.5 Liter.						
L Sedan 4D	BE635	20820	8075	9275	11500	14800
L Wagon 4D	BH635	21520	8825	10100	12350	15700
L Special Ed Sed 4D	BE635	21320	8225	9425	11700	15000
L Special Ed Wag 4D	BH635	22420	8975	10275	12550	15950
GT Sedan 4D	BE646	26320	9700	11050	13400	16850
GT Wagon 4D	BH646	27220	10375	11775	14150	17700
Dual Moon Roofs		------	575	575	765	765
Manual Trans (Sedan)		------	(575)	(575)	(765)	(765)
OUTBACK AWD—4-Cyl.—Equipment Schedule 4						
W.B. 104.3"; 2.5 Liter.						
Wagon 4D	BH675	24370	10875	12325	14750	18350
Limited Sedan 4D	BE686	26820	11250	12750	15200	18800
Limited Wagon 4D	BH686	27920	11400	12950	15350	19000
Dual Moon Roofs		------	575	575	765	765
OUTBACK AWD—H6—Equipment Schedule 4						
W.B. 104.3"; 3.0 Liter.						
Sedan 4D	BE896	29020	11300	12800	15250	18850
Wagon 4D	BH896	29520	10775	12275	14650	18250
L.L. Bean Wagon 4D	BH806	30520	12025	13625	16050	19800
VDC Sedan 4D	BE896	31420	12600	14250	16800	20600
VDC Wagon 4D	BH896	32920	13375	15125	17650	21500

2004 SUBARU — JF1or4S3(GG655)-4-#

IMPREZA AWD—4-Cyl.—Equipment Schedule 5
W.B. 99.4"; 2.5 Liter.

2.5 TS Sport Wagon 4D	GG655	19245	8225	9425	11650	14850
Outback Sport Wag	GG685	20445	9275	10575	12850	16200
2.5RS Sedan 4D	GD675	20745	10050	11400	13700	17100
IMPREZA AWD—4-Cyl. Turbo—Equipment Schedule 4						
W.B. 99.4"; 2.0 Liter.						
WRX Sedan 4D	GD296	26045	12600	14250	17000	21100
WRX Sport Wagon 4D	GG296	25545	12225	13875	16600	20700
IMPREZA AWD—4-Cyl. HO Turbo—Equipment Schedule 4						
W.B. 99.4"; 2.5 Liter.						
WRX STi Sedan 4D	GD706	31545	17125	19250	22200	26800
LEGACY AWD—4-Cyl.—Equipment Schedule 4						
W.B. 104.3"; 2.5 Liter.						
L Sedan 4D	BE635	21245	9250	10525	12900	16350
L Wagon 4D	BH635	21945	10100	11450	13850	17400
GT Sedan 4D	BE646	26645	11000	12475	14950	18600
GT Wagon 4D	BH646	27545	11725	13300	15750	19500
Dual Moon Roofs		------	675	675	900	900
Manual Trans (Sedan)		------	(600)	(600)	(800)	(800)
OUTBACK AWD—4-Cyl.—Equipment Schedule 4						
W.B. 104.3"; 2.5 Liter.						
Wagon 4D	BH675	24695	12275	13925	16400	20200
Limited Sedan 4D	BE686	27145	12650	14300	16850	20700
Limited Wagon 4D	BH686	28245	12850	14550	17050	21000
Dual Moon Roofs		------	675	675	900	900
OUTBACK AWD—H6—Equipment Schedule 4						
W.B. 104.3"; 3.0 Liter.						
Sedan 4D	BE896	29345	12750	14400	17000	20900
35th Anniv Wagon 4D	BH815	27645	12175	13775	16300	20100
L.L. Bean Wagon 4D	BH806	30845	13525	15275	17850	21800
VDC Sedan 4D	BE896	31545	14200	16000	18600	22600
VDC Wagon 4D	BH896	33045	15075	16975	19600	23800

2005 SUBARU — (JFor4S)(1,3or4)(GG675)-5-#

IMPREZA AWD—4-Cyl.—Equipment Schedule 4
W.B. 99.4"; 2.5 Liter.

2.5RS Sport Wagon 4D	GG675	19470	9425	10775	13100	16550
Outback Sport Wag	GG685	20370	10525	11975	14350	17950
2.5RS Sedan 4D	GD675	19470	11400	12950	15350	19100
IMPREZA AWD—4-Cyl. Turbo—Equipment Schedule 4						
W.B. 99.4"; 2.0 Liter.						
WRX Sedan 4D	GD296	26470	13625	15375	18150	22300
WRX Sport Wagon 4D	GG296	25970	13200	14950	17650	21800
IMPREZA AWD—4-Cyl. HO Turbo—Equipment Schedule 4						
W.B. 99.4"; 2.5 Liter.						

2005 SUBARU

Body	Type	VIN	List	Trade-In Fair	Trade-In Good	Pvt-Party Good	Retail Excellent
WRX STi Sedan 4D		GD706	32770	**18425**	**20750**	**23800**	**28600**

LEGACY AWD—4-Cyl.—Equipment Schedule 4
W.B. 105.1"; 2.5 Liter.

2.5i Sedan 4D		BL616	22870	**11450**	**13000**	**14800**	**17750**
2.5i Wagon 4D		BP616	23870	**12325**	**13975**	**15800**	**18900**
2.5i Limited Sedan 4D		BL626	26120	**13050**	**14750**	**16650**	**19800**
2.5i Limited Wagon 4D		BP626	27320	**13975**	**15800**	**17750**	**21000**
Dual Moon Roofs				775	775	1035	1035
Manual Trans (Sedan)				(625)	(625)	(835)	(835)

LEGACY AWD—4-Cyl. Turbo—Equipment Schedule 4
W.B. 105.1"; 2.5 Liter.

2.5 GT Sedan 4D		BL686	27870	**13375**	**15075**	**17000**	**20300**
2.5 GT Wagon 4D		BP686	28870	**14150**	**15950**	**17950**	**21200**
2.5 GT Limited Sed 4D		BL696	30370	**16150**	**18200**	**20300**	**23800**
2.5 GT Limited Wag 4D		BP676	31570	**16925**	**19050**	**21000**	**24600**
Dual Moon Roofs				775	775	1035	1035
Manual Trans (Sedan)				(625)	(625)	(835)	(835)

OUTBACK AWD—4-Cyl.—Equipment Schedule 4
W.B. 105.1"; 2.5 Liter.

2.5i Wagon 4D		BP61C	25870	**14750**	**16625**	**18600**	**21900**
2.5i Limited Wagon		BP62C	28670	**15375**	**17325**	**19300**	**22700**
Dual Moon Roofs				775	775	1035	1035

OUTBACK AWD—4-Cyl. Turbo—Equipment Schedule 4
W.B. 105.1"; 2.5 Liter.

2.5 XT Wagon 4D		BP68C	29870	**15775**	**17800**	**19800**	**23300**
2.5 XT Limited Wag		BP67C	32570	**16150**	**18200**	**20300**	**23800**
Dual Moon Roofs				775	775	1035	1035

OUTBACK AWD—H6—Equipment Schedule 4
W.B. 105.1"; 3.0 Liter.

3.0 R Sedan 4D		BL84C	31670	**18525**	**20850**	**22900**	**26600**
3.0 R L.L. Bean Wagon		BP86C	32870	**19300**	**21625**	**23800**	**27500**
3.0 R VDC Ltd Wagon		BP85C	34070	**20475**	**22900**	**25100**	**29000**
Dual Moon Roofs				775	775	1035	1035

SUZUKI

1991 SUZUKI — JS2(AE35S)–M–#

SWIFT—4-Cyl.—Equipment Schedule 6
W.B. 89.2", 93.1" (Sed); 1.3 Liter.

GA Sedan 4D		AE35S	7769	**200**	**275**	**725**	**1400**
GA Hatchback 2D		AE35S	6669	**150**	**225**	**625**	**1250**
GS Sedan 4D		AE35S	8869	**275**	**400**	**900**	**1650**
GT Hatchback 2D		AC34S	9669	**350**	**475**	**1025**	**1875**

1992 SUZUKI — JS2(AE34S)–N–#

SWIFT—4-Cyl.—Equipment Schedule 6
W.B. 89.2", 93.1" (Sed); 1.3 Liter.

GA Sedan 4D		AE34S	7984	**200**	**300**	**750**	**1475**
GA Hatchback 2D		AC34S	7184	**175**	**225**	**675**	**1350**
GA Limited Ed H'Back		AC34S	8484	**175**	**250**	**700**	**1400**
GS Sedan 4D		AE34S	9384	**300**	**400**	**950**	**1750**
GT Hatchback 2D		AC34S	9884	**400**	**525**	**1125**	**2025**

1993 SUZUKI — (JSor2S)2(AE34S)–P–#

SWIFT—4-Cyl.—Equipment Schedule 6
W.B. 89.2", 93.1" (Sed); 1.3 Liter.

GA Sedan 4D		AE34S	8299	**250**	**350**	**875**	**1650**
GA Hatchback 2D		AC34S	7599	**200**	**275**	**750**	**1475**
GS Sedan 4D		AE34S	9699	**350**	**475**	**1050**	**1925**
GT Hatchback 2D		AC34S	10299	**425**	**625**	**1250**	**2250**

1994 SUZUKI — (JSor2S)2(AE34S)–R–#

SWIFT—4-Cyl.—Equipment Schedule 6
W.B. 89.2", 93.1" (Sed); 1.3 Liter.

GA Sedan 4D		AE34S	8844	**275**	**400**	**975**	**1875**
GA Hatchback 2D		AC34S	7864	**225**	**325**	**875**	**1700**
GS Sedan 4D		AE34S	10344	**400**	**525**	**1175**	**2150**
GT Hatchback 2D		AC34S	10974	**475**	**700**	**1400**	**2550**

1995 SUZUKI

Body	Type	VIN	List	Trade-In Fair	Good	Pvt-Party Good	Retail Excellent

1995 SUZUKI — (JSor2S)2(AB21H)-S-#

SWIFT—4-Cyl.—Equipment Schedule 6
W.B. 93.1"; 1.3 Liter.
Hatchback 2D	AB21H	9029	275	375	925	1775

ESTEEM—4-Cyl.—Equipment Schedule 6
W.B. 97.6"; 1.6 Liter.
| GL Sedan 4D | GB31S | 11789 | 575 | 825 | 1500 | 2600 |
| GLX Sedan 4D | GB31S | 14789 | 625 | 900 | 1625 | 2775 |

1996 SUZUKI — (JSor2S)2(AB21H)-T-#

SWIFT—4-Cyl.—Equipment Schedule 6
W.B. 93.1"; 1.3 Liter.
| Hatchback 2D | AB21H | 9359 | 325 | 450 | 1100 | 2025 |

ESTEEM—4-Cyl.—Equipment Schedule 6
W.B. 97.6"; 1.6 Liter.
| GL Sedan 4D | GB31S | 11989 | 675 | 975 | 1725 | 2925 |
| GLX Sedan 4D | GB31S | 13289 | 750 | 1075 | 1875 | 3125 |

1997 SUZUKI — (JSor2S)2(AB21H)-V-#

SWIFT—4-Cyl.—Equipment Schedule 6
W.B. 93.1"; 1.3 Liter.
| Hatchback 2D | AB21H | 9359 | 400 | 550 | 1275 | 2425 |

ESTEEM—4-Cyl.—Equipment Schedule 6
W.B. 97.6"; 1.6 Liter.
| GL Sedan 4D | GB31S | 13319 | 775 | 1125 | 2025 | 3400 |
| GLX Sedan 4D | GB31S | 14419 | 875 | 1225 | 2200 | 3650 |

1998 SUZUKI — (JSor2S)2(AB21H)-W-#

SWIFT—4-Cyl.—Equipment Schedule 6
W.B. 93.1"; 1.3 Liter.
| Hatchback 2D | AB21H | 9479 | 625 | 900 | 1900 | 3350 |

ESTEEM—4-Cyl.—Equipment Schedule 6
W.B. 97.6", 97.7" (Wag); 1.6 Liter.
GL Sedan 4D	GB31S	12429	925	1300	2450	4050
GL Wagon 4D	GB31W	12929	1050	1475	2650	4300
GLX Sedan 4D	GB31S	13529	1050	1450	2625	4250
GLX Wagon 4D	GB31W	14029	1175	1625	2825	4475

1999 SUZUKI — (JSor2S)3(AB21H)-X-#

SWIFT—4-Cyl.—Equipment Schedule 6
W.B. 93.1"; 1.3 Liter.
| Hatchback 2D | AB21H | 9479 | 800 | 1150 | 2300 | 3975 |

ESTEEM—4-Cyl.—Equipment Schedule 6
W.B. 97.6"; 1.6 Liter, 1.8 Liter.
GL Sedan 4D	GB31S	12629	1125	1575	2825	4525
GL Wagon 4D	GB31W	13129	1275	1775	3000	4750
GLX Sedan 4D	GB31S	13729	1275	1775	3000	4750
GLX Wagon 4D	GB31W	14229	1475	1975	3250	5025

2000 SUZUKI — (JSor2S)3(AB21H)-Y-#

SWIFT—4-Cyl.—Equipment Schedule 6
W.B. 93.1"; 1.3 Liter.
| GA Hatchback 2D | AB21H | 9499 | 925 | 1300 | 2575 | 4375 |
| GL Hatchback 2D | AB21H | 10499 | 1050 | 1450 | 2775 | 4575 |

ESTEEM—4-Cyl.—Equipment Schedule 6
W.B. 97.6"; 1.6 Liter, 1.8 Liter.
GL Sedan 4D	GB31S	13349	1525	2025	3350	5200
GL Wagon 4D	GB31W	13849	1725	2250	3625	5475
GLX Sedan 4D	GB31S	14449	1725	2250	3625	5475
GLX Wagon 4D	GB31W	14849	1950	2475	3850	5750

2001 SUZUKI — (JSor2S)2(AB21H)-1-#

SWIFT—4-Cyl.—Equipment Schedule 6
W.B. 93.1"; 1.3 Liter.
| GA Hatchback 2D | AB21H | 9729 | 1075 | 1525 | 2925 | 4875 |
| GL Hatchback 2D | AB21H | 10729 | 1250 | 1750 | 3175 | 5150 |

ESTEEM—4-Cyl.—Equipment Schedule 6
W.B. 97.6"; 1.8 Liter.
| GL Sedan 4D | GB41S | 13679 | 1975 | 2525 | 3975 | 5975 |
| GL Wagon 4D | GB41W | 14179 | 2200 | 2800 | 4250 | 6275 |

2001 SUZUKI

Body Type	VIN	List	Trade-In Fair	Good	Pvt-Party Good	Retail Excellent
GLX Sedan 4D	GB41S	14479	**2200**	**2800**	**4250**	**6275**
GLX Sedan 4D	GB41W	14979	**2425**	**3025**	**4500**	**6575**

2002 SUZUKI — JS2(RA41S)-2-#

AERIO—4-Cyl.—Equipment Schedule 6
W.B. 97.6"; 2.0 Liter.

S Sedan 4D	RA41S	13999	**3625**	**4350**	**5900**	**8100**
GS Sedan 4D	RA41S	14999	**3950**	**4700**	**6275**	**8525**
SX Wagon 4D	RC41H	14999	**4250**	**5050**	**6625**	**8900**

ESTEEM—4-Cyl.—Equipment Schedule 6
W.B. 97.6"; 1.8 Liter.

GL Sedan 4D	GB41S	13799	**2525**	**3125**	**4700**	**6875**
GL Wagon 4D	GB41W	14299	**2775**	**3400**	**5000**	**7200**
GLX Sedan 4D	GB41S	14799	**2775**	**3400**	**5000**	**7200**
GLX Wagon 4D	GB41W	15299	**3000**	**3675**	**5275**	**7525**

2003 SUZUKI — JS2(RA41S)-3-#

AERIO—4-Cyl.—Equipment Schedule 6
W.B. 97.6"; 2.0 Liter.

S Sedan 4D	RA41S	14094	**4200**	**4975**	**6625**	**8975**
GS Sedan 4D	RA41S	15294	**4525**	**5350**	**7025**	**9425**
SX Wagon 4D	RC41H	15594	**4875**	**5725**	**7425**	**9850**
AWD			**500**	**500**	**665**	**665**

2004 SUZUKI — JS2orKL5(RA61S)-4-#

AERIO—4-Cyl.—Equipment Schedule 6
W.B. 97.6"; 2.3 Liter.

S Sedan 4D	RA61S	13499	**5050**	**5925**	**7550**	**9950**
LX Sedan 4D	RA61S	15199	**5400**	**6325**	**7975**	**10450**
SX Wagon 4D	RC61H	15499	**5800**	**6750**	**8425**	**10900**
AWD			**550**	**550**	**735**	**735**

FORENZA—4-Cyl.—Equipment Schedule 3
W.B. 102.4"; 2.0 Liter.

S Sedan 4D	JD52Z	13799	**5250**	**6150**	**7875**	**10400**
LX Sedan 4D	JJ52Z	15699	**5650**	**6575**	**8325**	**10850**
EX Sedan 4D	JJ52Z	16499	**5850**	**6825**	**8550**	**11150**
Manual Trans			**(600)**	**(600)**	**(800)**	**(800)**

VERONA—6-Cyl.—Equipment Schedule 3
W.B. 106.3"; 2.5 Liter.

S Sedan 4D	VJ52L	16999	**7975**	**9175**	**11150**	**14150**
LX Sedan 4D	VJ52L	18299	**8375**	**9575**	**11600**	**14650**
EX Sedan 4D	VM52L	19999	**8725**	**10000**	**12050**	**15150**

2005 SUZUKI — JS2orKL5(RA62S)-5-#

AERIO—4-Cyl.—Equipment Schedule 6
W.B. 97.6"; 2.3 Liter.

S Sedan 4D	RA62S	13994	**6025**	**6975**	**8675**	**11200**
LX Sedan 4D	RA61S	15994	**6425**	**7425**	**9175**	**11750**
SX Wagon 4D	RC61H	15994	**6825**	**7875**	**9625**	**12250**
AWD	B,D		**575**	**575**	**765**	**765**

FORENZA—4-Cyl.—Equipment Schedule 3
W.B. 102.4"; 2.0 Liter.

S Sedan 4D	JD52Z	14794	**6275**	**7275**	**9075**	**11750**
S Wagon 4D	JD86Z	15294	**6675**	**7700**	**9550**	**12250**
LX Sedan 4D	JJ52Z	16694	**6675**	**7700**	**9550**	**12250**
LX Wagon 4D	JJ86Z	17194	**7050**	**8150**	**10050**	**12800**
EX Sedan 4D	JJ52Z	17494	**6875**	**7950**	**9800**	**12550**
EX Wagon 4D	JJ86Z	17994	**7325**	**8425**	**10300**	**13100**
Manual Trans			**(625)**	**(625)**	**(835)**	**(835)**

RENO—4-Cyl.—Equipment Schedule 4
W.B. 102.4"; 2.0 Liter.

S Hatchback 4D	JD66Z	14794	**5400**	**6325**	**8275**	**11050**
LX Hatchback 4D	JJ66Z	16694	**6600**	**7650**	**9675**	**12600**
EX Hatchback 4D	JJ66Z	17494	**7000**	**8075**	**10150**	**13100**
Manual Trans			**(625)**	**(625)**	**(835)**	**(835)**

VERONA—6-Cyl.—Equipment Schedule 3
W.B. 106.3"; 2.5 Liter.

S Sedan 4D	VJ56L	17994	**9150**	**10425**	**12550**	**15750**
LX Sedan 4D	VJ56L	19794	**9575**	**10925**	**13100**	**16350**
EX Sedan 4D	VM56L	20994	**9950**	**11350**	**13550**	**16850**

Body	Type	VIN	List	Trade-In Fair	Good	Pvt-Party Good	Retail Excellent

TOYOTA

1991 TOYOTA — (1,4orJ)T(1,2orX)(EL46B)–M–#

TERCEL—4-Cyl.—Equipment Schedule 6
W.B. 93.7"; 1.5 Liter.

Body	Type	VIN	List	Fair	Good	Good	Excellent
Sedan 2D		EL46B	7728	400	525	1200	2200
DX Sedan 2D		EL43B	9288	500	725	1450	2600
DX Sedan 4D		EL43A	9388	550	800	1550	2775
LE Sedan 4D		EL44A	10878	550	800	1550	2775

COROLLA—4-Cyl.—Equipment Schedule 6
W.B. 95.7"; 1.6 Liter.

Sedan 4D		AE91A	10508	500	725	1550	2825
Deluxe Sedan 4D		AE94A	11508	500	725	1550	2825
Deluxe Wagon 4D		AE94K	12178	675	950	1900	3300
Dlx All-Trac Wag 4D		AE94V	13878	725	1050	2025	3475
LE Sedan 4D		AE97A	12477	550	775	1625	2950
SR5 Sport Coupe 2D		AE96J	13048	625	900	1825	3225
GT-S Sport Coupe 2D		AE98J	14638	675	975	1925	3350

CAMRY—4-Cyl.—Equipment Schedule 4
W.B. 102.4"; 2.0 Liter.

Sedan 4D		SV24E	14513	925	1300	2525	4200
Deluxe Sedan 4D		SV21E	15127	975	1375	2600	4300
Deluxe Wagon 4D		SV21W	15837	1050	1475	2750	4450
Dlx All-Trac Sed 4D		SV21J	17107	1175	1625	2900	4675
LE Sedan 4D		SV22E	16242	1100	1550	2825	4550
LE All-Trac Sed 4D		SV22J	18232	1225	1700	2975	4775
Manual Trans				(175)	(175)	(235)	(235)
V6 2.5 Liter		V		100	100	135	135

CAMRY—V6—Equipment Schedule 4
W.B. 102.4"; 2.5 Liter.

LE Wagon 4D		VV22W	18483	1350	1850	3175	5000

MR2—4-Cyl.—Equipment Schedule 6
W.B. 94.5"; 2.2 Liter.

Coupe 2D		SW21M	16848	1050	1475	2750	4450

MR2—4-Cyl. Turbo—Equipment Schedule 6
W.B. 94.5"; 2.0 Liter.

Coupe 2D		SW22M	20178	1475	1975	3325	5200

CELICA—4-Cyl.—Equipment Schedule 4
W.B. 99.4"; 1.6 Liter, 2.2 Liter.

ST Sport Coupe 2D		AT86F	14323	1000	1425	2650	4375
GT Sport Coupe 2D		ST87F	16328	1075	1500	2750	4475
GT Liftback 2D		ST87N	16713	1125	1575	2850	4600
GT Convertible 2D		ST87K	21188	1900	2425	3850	5825
GT-S Liftback 2D		ST85N	18553	1450	1950	3300	5150
Auto Trans				100	100	135	135

CELICA AWD—4-Cyl. Turbo—Equipment Schedule 4
W.B. 99.4"; 2.0 Liter.

All-Trac Liftback 2D		ST88P	22673	1900	2425	3850	5825

SUPRA—6-Cyl.—Equipment Schedule 4
W.B. 102.2"; 3.0 Liter.

Liftback 2D		MA70M	24845	1200	1650	3350	5600
Auto Trans				100	100	135	135

SUPRA—6-Cyl. Turbo—Equipment Schedule 4
W.B. 102.2"; 3.0 Liter.

Liftback 2D		MA71M	28315	1775	2300	4125	6525
Sport Roof		N		200	200	265	265
Auto Trans				100	100	135	135

CRESSIDA—6-Cyl.—Equipment Schedule 4
W.B. 105.5"; 3.0 Liter.

Luxury Sedan 4D		MX83E	22473	1200	1650	3150	5200

1992 TOYOTA — (1,4orJ)(NorT)(1,2orX)(EL46B)–N

TERCEL—4-Cyl.—Equipment Schedule 6
W.B. 93.7"; 1.5 Liter.

Sedan 2D		EL46B	8303	400	600	1300	2425
DX Sedan 2D		EL43B	9983	550	800	1600	2875
DX Sedan 4D		EL43A	10083	625	900	1775	3100
LE Sedan 4D		EL44A	11253	625	900	1775	3100

PASEO—4-Cyl.—Equipment Schedule 6
W.B. 93.7"; 1.5 Liter.

Body	Type	VIN	List	Trade-In Fair	Trade-In Good	Pvt-Party Good	Retail Excellent
Coupe 2D		EL45F	11433	**700**	**1025**	**1950**	**3350**
COROLLA—4-Cyl.—Equipment Schedule 6							
W.B. 95.7"; 1.6 Liter.							
Sedan 4D		AE91A	11123	**600**	**850**	**1825**	**3300**
Deluxe Sedan 4D		AE94A	12113	**600**	**875**	**1900**	**3400**
Deluxe Wagon 4D		AE94K	12653	**800**	**1150**	**2350**	**4100**
Dlx All-Trac Wag 4D		AE94V	14393	**850**	**1225**	**2475**	**4225**
LE Sedan 4D		AE97A	13713	**650**	**925**	**2000**	**3575**
CAMRY—4-Cyl.—Equipment Schedule 4							
W.B. 103.1"; 2.2 Liter.							
Deluxe Sedan 4D		SK11E	16713	**1125**	**1575**	**2925**	**4775**
Deluxe Wagon 4D		SK11V	18443	**1275**	**1775**	**3150**	**5050**
LE Sedan 4D		SK12E	17293	**1200**	**1650**	**3000**	**4875**
LE Wagon 4D		SK12V	19093	**1350**	**1850**	**3225**	**5150**
XLE Sedan 4D		SK13E	19143	**1225**	**1725**	**3075**	**4950**
Manual Trans				**(175)**	**(175)**	**(235)**	**(235)**
V6 3.0 Liter		V		**150**	**150**	**200**	**200**
CAMRY—V6—Equipment Schedule 4							
W.B. 103.1"; 3.0 Liter.							
SE Sedan 4D		VK14E	20538	**1550**	**2050**	**3500**	**5450**
Manual Trans				**(175)**	**(175)**	**(235)**	**(235)**
MR2—4-Cyl.—Equipment Schedule 6							
W.B. 94.5"; 2.2 Liter.							
Coupe 2D		SW21M	17813	**1275**	**1775**	**3125**	**5000**
MR2—4-Cyl. Turbo—Equipment Schedule 6							
W.B. 94.5"; 2.0 Liter.							
Coupe 2D		SW22M	21143	**1825**	**2350**	**3800**	**5825**
CELICA—4-Cyl.—Equipment Schedule 4							
W.B. 99.4"; 1.6 Liter, 2.2 Liter.							
ST Sport Coupe 2D		AT86F	15063	**1225**	**1675**	**3025**	**4875**
GT Sport Coupe 2D		ST87F	17733	**1275**	**1775**	**3150**	**5025**
GT Liftback 2D		ST87N	17818	**1375**	**1875**	**3250**	**5150**
GT Convertible 2D		ST87K	22313	**2250**	**2825**	**4375**	**6500**
GT-S Liftback 2D		ST85N	19353	**1750**	**2275**	**3700**	**5675**
Auto Trans				**100**	**100**	**135**	**135**
CELICA AWD—4-Cyl. Turbo—Equipment Schedule 4							
W.B. 99.4"; 2.0 Liter.							
All-Trac Liftback 2D		ST88P	23393	**2250**	**2825**	**4375**	**6500**
SUPRA—6-Cyl.—Equipment Schedule 4							
W.B. 102.2"; 3.0 Liter.							
Liftback 2D		MA70M	25575	**1475**	**1975**	**3775**	**6175**
Auto Trans				**100**	**100**	**135**	**135**
SUPRA—6-Cyl. Turbo—Equipment Schedule 4							
W.B. 102.2"; 3.0 Liter.							
Liftback 2D		MA71M	29045	**2125**	**2700**	**4650**	**7250**
Sport Roof				**225**	**225**	**300**	**300**
Auto Trans				**100**	**100**	**135**	**135**
CRESSIDA—6-Cyl.—Equipment Schedule 4							
W.B. 105.5"; 3.0 Liter.							
Luxury Sedan 4D		MX83E	23783	**1400**	**1900**	**3500**	**5600**

1993 TOYOTA — (1,4orJ)(NorT)(1,2orX)(EL46S)-P-#

Body	Type	VIN	List	Trade-In Fair	Trade-In Good	Pvt-Party Good	Retail Excellent
TERCEL—4-Cyl.—Equipment Schedule 6							
W.B. 93.7"; 1.5 Liter.							
Sedan 2D		EL46S	9223	**475**	**675**	**1450**	**2675**
DX Sedan 2D		EL43S	11313	**650**	**925**	**1850**	**3225**
DX Sedan 4D		EL43T	11413	**750**	**1050**	**2025**	**3475**
LE Sedan 4D		EL44T	12473	**750**	**1075**	**2050**	**3525**
PASEO—4-Cyl.—Equipment Schedule 6							
W.B. 93.7"; 1.5 Liter.							
Coupe 2D		EL45U	12663	**825**	**1175**	**2300**	**3900**
COROLLA—4-Cyl.—Equipment Schedule 6							
W.B. 97.0"; 1.6 Liter, 1.8 Liter.							
Sedan 4D		AE04E	12983	**750**	**1075**	**2275**	**3975**
Deluxe Sedan 4D		AE09E	13823	**825**	**1175**	**2425**	**4175**
Deluxe Wagon 4D		AE09W	14503	**1075**	**1500**	**2825**	**4675**
LE Sedan 4D		AE00E	15543	**900**	**1275**	**2550**	**4350**
CAMRY—4-Cyl.—Equipment Schedule 4							
W.B. 103.2"; 2.2 Liter.							
Deluxe Sedan 4D		SK11E	17578	**1325**	**1825**	**3250**	**5225**
Deluxe Wagon 4D		SK11W	18908	**1550**	**2050**	**3575**	**5600**
LE Sedan 4D		SK12E	18233	**1400**	**1900**	**3350**	**5325**
LE Wagon 4D		SK12W	19553	**1625**	**2125**	**3650**	**5700**

1993 TOYOTA

Body Type	VIN	List	Trade-In Fair	Good	Pvt-Party Good	Retail Excellent
XLE Sedan 4D	SK13E	20203	**1500**	**2000**	**3475**	**5475**
Manual Trans		......	**(225)**	**(225)**	**(300)**	**(300)**
V6 3.0 Liter	V	......	**225**	**225**	**300**	**300**
CAMRY—V6—Equipment Schedule 4						
W.B. 103.2"; 3.0 Liter.						
SE Sedan 4D	VK14E	21188	**1850**	**2375**	**3925**	**6050**
Manual Trans		......	**(225)**	**(225)**	**(300)**	**(300)**
MR2—4-Cyl.—Equipment Schedule 4						
W.B. 94.5"; 2.2 Liter.						
Coupe 2D	SW21M	20208	**1600**	**2100**	**3575**	**5525**
MR2—4-Cyl. Turbo—Equipment Schedule 6						
W.B. 94.5"; 2.0 Liter.						
Coupe 2D	SW22M	24923	**2225**	**2825**	**4375**	**6500**
CELICA—4-Cyl.—Equipment Schedule 4						
W.B. 99.4"; 1.6 Liter, 2.2 Liter.						
ST Sport Coupe 2D	AT86F	15983	**1450**	**1950**	**3425**	**5400**
GT Sport Coupe 2D	ST87F	18108	**1575**	**2075**	**3575**	**5600**
GT Liftback 2D	ST87N	18383	**1675**	**2175**	**3675**	**5725**
GT Convertible 2D	ST87K	23903	**2700**	**3300**	**4975**	**7275**
GT-S Liftback 2D	ST85N	20863	**2000**	**2550**	**4100**	**6225**
Auto Trans		......	**125**	**125**	**165**	**165**
CELICA AWD—4-Cyl. Turbo—Equipment Schedule 4						
W.B. 100.4"; 2.0 Liter.						
All-Trac Liftback 2D	ST88P	28623	**2875**	**3550**	**5250**	**7600**
SUPRA—6-Cyl.—Equipment Schedule 4						
W.B. 100.4"; 3.0 Liter.						
Liftback 2D	JA81L	34225	**5475**	**6400**	**9000**	**12500**
Sport Roof	J	......	**250**	**250**	**335**	**335**
Auto Trans		......	**125**	**125**	**165**	**165**
SUPRA—6-Cyl. Turbo—Equipment Schedule 4						
W.B. 100.4"; 3.0 Liter.						
Liftback 2D	JA82L	40225	**8650**	**9900**	**13050**	**17350**
Sport Roof	J	......	**250**	**250**	**335**	**335**
6-Spd Manual Trans		......	**325**	**325**	**435**	**435**

1994 TOYOTA — (1,4orJ)(NorT)(1,2orX)(EL46S)-R-#

Body Type	VIN	List	Trade-In Fair	Good	Pvt-Party Good	Retail Excellent
TERCEL—4-Cyl.—Equipment Schedule 6						
W.B. 93.7"; 1.5 Liter.						
Sedan 2D	EL46S	10223	**525**	**750**	**1650**	**3000**
DX Sedan 2D	EL43S	12028	**750**	**1050**	**2100**	**3650**
DX Sedan 4D	EL43T	12028	**850**	**1200**	**2375**	**4075**
PASEO—4-Cyl.—Equipment Schedule 6						
W.B. 93.7"; 1.5 Liter.						
Coupe 2D	EL45U	13753	**950**	**1325**	**2550**	**4250**
COROLLA—4-Cyl.—Equipment Schedule 6						
W.B. 97.0"; 1.6 Liter, 1.8 Liter.						
Sedan 4D	AE04B	13308	**825**	**1175**	**2425**	**4225**
DX Sedan 4D	AE09B	14998	**950**	**1325**	**2700**	**4525**
DX Wagon 4D	AE09V	15553	**1225**	**1725**	**3150**	**5125**
LE Sedan 4D	AE00B	18113	**1050**	**1475**	**2875**	**4775**
CAMRY—4-Cyl.—Equipment Schedule 4						
W.B. 103.1"; 2.2 Liter.						
DX Sedan 4D	SK11E	19293	**1550**	**2050**	**3625**	**5700**
DX Coupe 2D	SK11C	18963	**1225**	**1725**	**3200**	**5225**
DX Wagon 4D	SK11W	20703	**1850**	**2375**	**4000**	**6150**
LE Sedan 4D	SK12E	19613	**1675**	**2175**	**3725**	**5850**
LE Coupe 2D	SK12C	19323	**1400**	**1900**	**3425**	**5450**
LE Wagon 4D	SK12W	21003	**1925**	**2450**	**4075**	**6250**
XLE Sedan 4D	SK13E	21643	**1775**	**2300**	**3850**	**6000**
Manual Trans		......	**(275)**	**(275)**	**(365)**	**(365)**
V6 3.0 Liter	G	......	**275**	**275**	**365**	**365**
CAMRY—V6—Equipment Schedule 4						
W.B. 103.1"; 3.0 Liter.						
SE Sedan 4D	GK14E	22913	**2150**	**2750**	**4400**	**6625**
SE Coupe 2D	GK14C	22623	**1975**	**2525**	**4150**	**6325**
MR2—4-Cyl.—Equipment Schedule 6						
W.B. 94.5"; 2.2 Liter.						
Coupe 2D	SW21M	23613	**2425**	**3025**	**4650**	**6875**
MR2—4-Cyl. Turbo—Equipment Schedule 6						
W.B. 94.5"; 2.0 Liter.						
Coupe 2D	SW22M	28663	**3175**	**3825**	**5575**	**8000**
CELICA—4-Cyl.—Equipment Schedule 4						
W.B. 99.9"; 1.8 Liter, 2.2 Liter.						

1994 TOYOTA

Body Type	VIN	List	Trade-In Fair	Good	Pvt-Party Good	Retail Excellent
ST Sport Coupe 2D	AT00F	18628	**1800**	**2325**	**3875**	**6000**
ST Liftback 2D	AT00N	18968	**1925**	**2450**	**4050**	**6200**
GT Sport Coupe 2D	ST07F	20053	**1975**	**2500**	**4100**	**6275**
GT Liftback 2D	ST07N	20523	**2025**	**2600**	**4225**	**6400**
Auto Trans			**150**	**150**	**200**	**200**
SUPRA—6-Cyl.—Equipment Schedule 4						
W.B. 100.4"; 3.0 Liter.						
Liftback 2D	JA81L	36185	**6425**	**7425**	**10250**	**14000**
Sport Roof	J		**275**	**275**	**365**	**365**
Auto Trans			**150**	**150**	**200**	**200**
SUPRA—6-Cyl. Turbo—Equipment Schedule 4						
W.B. 100.4"; 3.0 Liter.						
Liftback 2D	JA82L	43185	**10050**	**11400**	**14750**	**19400**
Sport Roof	J		**275**	**275**	**365**	**365**
6-Spd Manual Trans			**375**	**375**	**500**	**500**

1995 TOYOTA — (1,4orJ)(NorT)(1,2,5orX)(EL55D)–S

Body Type	VIN	List	Trade-In Fair	Good	Pvt-Party Good	Retail Excellent
TERCEL—4-Cyl.—Equipment Schedule 6						
W.B. 93.7"; 1.5 Liter.						
Sedan 2D	EL55D	11535	**825**	**1175**	**2825**	**4150**
DX Sedan 2D	EL56D	12685	**1075**	**1500**	**2825**	**4650**
DX Sedan 4D	EL56E	13125	**1225**	**1675**	**3025**	**4900**
PASEO—4-Cyl.—Equipment Schedule 6						
W.B. 93.7"; 1.5 Liter.						
Coupe 2D	EL45U	14725	**1100**	**1550**	**2825**	**4625**
COROLLA—4-Cyl.—Equipment Schedule 6						
W.B. 97.0"; 1.6 Liter, 1.8 Liter.						
Sedan 4D	AE04B	13782	**925**	**1300**	**2675**	**4525**
DX Sedan 4D	AE09B	14525	**1125**	**1575**	**3000**	**4975**
DX Wagon 4D	AE09V	16527	**1525**	**2025**	**3550**	**5600**
LE Sedan 4D	AE00B	17075	**1275**	**1775**	**3250**	**5250**
CAMRY—4-Cyl.—Equipment Schedule 4						
W.B. 103.1"; 2.2 Liter.						
DX Sedan 4D	SK11E	19815	**1850**	**2375**	**4050**	**6300**
DX Coupe 2D	SK11C	19430	**1525**	**2025**	**3650**	**5800**
LE Sedan 4D	SK12E	19955	**1975**	**2525**	**4200**	**6475**
LE Coupe 2D	SK12C	19665	**1675**	**2200**	**3825**	**6050**
LE Wagon 4D	SK12W	21365	**2275**	**2825**	**4575**	**6925**
XLE Sedan 4D	SK13E	22015	**2100**	**2675**	**4375**	**6675**
Manual Trans			**(325)**	**(325)**	**(435)**	**(435)**
V6 3.0 Liter	G		**325**	**325**	**435**	**435**
CAMRY—V6—Equipment Schedule 4						
W.B. 103.1"; 3.0 Liter.						
SE Sedan 4D	GK14E	23895	**2550**	**3150**	**4925**	**7325**
SE Coupe 2D	GK14C	23605	**2325**	**2900**	**4650**	**7025**
MR2—4-Cyl.—Equipment Schedule 6						
W.B. 94.5"; 2.2 Liter.						
Coupe 2D	SW21M	24655	**2900**	**3575**	**5300**	**7675**
MR2—4-Cyl. Turbo—Equipment Schedule 6						
W.B. 94.5"; 2.0 Liter.						
Coupe 2D	SW22N	29755	**3750**	**4475**	**6350**	**8925**
CELICA—4-Cyl.—Equipment Schedule 4						
W.B. 99.9"; 1.8 Liter, 2.2 Liter.						
ST Sport Coupe 2D	AT00F	19410	**2125**	**2700**	**4400**	**6675**
ST Liftback 2D	AT00N	19760	**2275**	**2825**	**4575**	**6900**
GT Sport Coupe 2D	ST07F	20925	**2325**	**2900**	**4650**	**7000**
GT Liftback 2D	ST07N	21415	**2425**	**3000**	**4750**	**7125**
GT Convertible 2D	ST07K	25635	**3725**	**4450**	**6400**	**9050**
Auto Trans			**175**	**175**	**235**	**235**
AVALON—V6—Equipment Schedule 4						
W.B. 107.1"; 3.0 Liter.						
XL Sedan 4D	GB10E	23155	**1950**	**2475**	**4100**	**6300**
XLS Sedan 4D	GB11E	27085	**2875**	**3550**	**5325**	**7800**
SUPRA—6-Cyl.—Equipment Schedule 4						
W.B. 100.4"; 3.0 Liter.						
SE Liftback 2D	JA81L	31497	**6875**	**7900**	**10750**	**14650**
Liftback 2D	JA81L	37297	**7425**	**8525**	**11500**	**15500**
Sport Roof	J		**300**	**300**	**400**	**400**
Auto Trans			**175**	**175**	**235**	**235**
SUPRA—6-Cyl. Turbo—Equipment Schedule 4						
W.B. 100.4"; 3.0 Liter.						
Liftback 2D	JA82L	46997	**11450**	**13000**	**16500**	**21400**
Sport Roof	J		**300**	**300**	**400**	**400**

1995 TOYOTA

Body	Type	VIN	List	Trade-In Fair	Good	Pvt-Party Good	Retail Excellent
6-Spd Manual Trans				400	400	535	535

1996 TOYOTA — (4T,JTor1N)(1,2,5orX)(AC52L)-T-#

TERCEL—4-Cyl.—Equipment Schedule 6
W.B. 93.7"; 1.5 Liter.
Sedan 2D		AC52L	11981	950	1325	2675	4500
DX Sedan 2D		AC52L	13458	1225	1725	3150	5075
DX Sedan 4D		BC52L	13768	1425	1925	3375	5325

PASEO—4-Cyl.—Equipment Schedule 6
W.B. 93.7"; 1.5 Liter.
Coupe 2D		CC52H	14383	1300	1800	3150	5050

COROLLA—4-Cyl.—Equipment Schedule 6
W.B. 97.0"; 1.6 Liter, 1.8 Liter.
Sedan 4D		BA02E	14538	1050	1450	2925	4925
DX Sedan 4D		BB02E	15448	1350	1850	3375	5450
DX Wagon 4D		EB02E	16598	1825	2350	3950	6125

CAMRY—4-Cyl.—Equipment Schedule 6
W.B. 103.1"; 2.2 Liter.
DX Sedan 4D		BG12K	19848	2200	2800	4575	7000
DX Coupe 2D		CG12K	19458	1825	2350	4125	6450
LE Sedan 4D		BG12K	20588	2325	2900	4725	7175
LE Coupe 2D		CG12K	20298	2000	2550	4350	6725
LE Wagon 4D		EG12K	22028	2675	3275	5175	7675
XLE Sedan 4D		BG12K	22698	2475	3075	4925	7400
Manual Trans				(375)	(375)	(500)	(500)
V6 3.0 Liter		F		375	375	500	500

CAMRY—V6—Equipment Schedule 4
W.B. 103.1"; 3.0 Liter.
SE Sedan 4D		BF12K	24538	2950	3625	5500	8100
SE Coupe 2D		CF12K	24248	2725	3350	5250	7750

CELICA—4-Cyl.—Equipment Schedule 4
W.B. 99.9"; 1.8 Liter, 2.2 Liter.
ST Sport Coupe 2D		CB02T	19638	2500	3100	4950	7425
ST Liftback 2D		DB02T	19998	2675	3275	5175	7675
GT Sport Coupe 2D		CG02T	21183	2750	3375	5250	7800
GT Liftback 2D		DG02T	21693	2825	3475	5350	7925
GT Convertible 2D		FG02T	25893	4275	5075	7150	10050
Auto Trans				200	200	265	265

AVALON—V6—Equipment Schedule 4
W.B. 107.1"; 3.0 Liter.
XL Sedan 4D		BF12B	23838	2400	2975	4675	7000
XLS Sedan 4D		BF12B	27868	3450	4150	6050	8650

SUPRA—6-Cyl.—Equipment Schedule 4
W.B. 100.4"; 3.0 Liter.
Liftback 2D		DD82A	39020	8525	9750	12850	17100
Sport Roof				325	325	435	435
Auto Trans				200	200	265	265

SUPRA—6-Cyl. Turbo—Equipment Schedule 4
W.B. 100.4"; 3.0 Liter.
Liftback 2D		DE82A	50820	12950	14650	18300	23500

1997 TOYOTA—(4T,JTor1N)(1,2,5orX)(AC52L)-V-#

TERCEL—4-Cyl.—Equipment Schedule 6
W.B. 93.7"; 1.5 Liter.
CE Sedan 2D		AC52L	12508	1600	2100	3600	5600
CE Sedan 4D		BC52L	13968	1900	2425	3950	6025
Limited Edition				25	25	35	35

PASEO—4-Cyl.—Equipment Schedule 6
W.B. 93.7"; 1.5 Liter.
Coupe 2D		CC52H	14553	1550	2050	3550	5525
Convertible 2D		FC52H	18073	2500	3100	4675	6875

COROLLA—4-Cyl.—Equipment Schedule 6
W.B. 97.0"; 1.6 Liter, 1.8 Liter.
Sedan 4D		BA02E	15028	1225	1675	3300	5425
CE Sedan 4D		BA02E	15063	1375	1900	3525	5725
DX Sedan 4D		BB02E	16445	1650	2150	3825	6075

CAMRY—4-Cyl.—Equipment Schedule 4
W.B. 105.1"; 2.2 Liter.
CE Sedan 4D		BG22K	19918	2775	3400	4850	6900
LE Sedan 4D		BG22K	20288	2875	3550	5000	7075
XLE Sedan 4D		BG22K	22228	3050	3725	5200	7300
Manual Trans				(400)	(400)	(535)	(535)
V6 3.0 Liter		F		425	425	565	565

Body	Type	VIN	List	Trade-In Fair	Good	Pvt-Party Good	Retail Excellent
CELICA—4-Cyl.—Equipment Schedule 4							
W.B. 99.9"; 1.8 Liter, 2.2 Liter.							
ST Sport Coupe 2D	CB02T	19703	**2900**	**3575**	**5575**	**8275**
ST Liftback 2D	DB02T	20063	**3125**	**3775**	**5850**	**8600**
GT Liftback 2D	DG02T	21893	**3300**	**3975**	**6050**	**8825**
GT Convertible 2D	FG02T	26093	**4850**	**5700**	**7950**	**11050**
Auto Trans			**200**	**200**	**265**	**265**
AVALON—V6—Equipment Schedule 4							
W.B. 107.1"; 3.0 Liter.							
XL Sedan 4D	BF12B	23958	**2900**	**3575**	**5400**	**7900**
XLS Sedan 4D	BF12B	27468	**4050**	**4800**	**6850**	**9650**
SUPRA—6-Cyl.—Equipment Schedule 4							
W.B. 100.4"; 3.0 Liter.							
Ltd Edition L'Back 2D	DD82A	30340	**9600**	**10950**	**14200**	**18750**
Sport Roof	P		**350**	**350**	**465**	**465**
Auto Trans			**200**	**200**	**265**	**265**
SUPRA—6-Cyl. Turbo—Equipment Schedule 4							
W.B. 100.4"; 3.0 Liter.							
Ltd Edition L'Back 2D	DE82A	39040	**15625**	**17600**	**21600**	**27400**
6-Spd Manual Trans			**450**	**450**	**600**	**600**

1998 TOYOTA—(4T,JTor1N)(1,2,5orX)(AC52L)-W-#

Body	Type	VIN	List	Trade-In Fair	Good	Pvt-Party Good	Retail Excellent
TERCEL—4-Cyl.—Equipment Schedule 6							
W.B. 93.7"; 1.5 Liter.							
CE Sedan 4D	AC52L	13110	**1900**	**2425**	**4000**	**6125**
COROLLA—4-Cyl.—Equipment Schedule 6							
W.B. 97.0"; 1.8 Liter.							
VE Sedan 4D	BR12E	13443	**2050**	**2625**	**4050**	**6025**
CE Sedan 4D	BR12E	14208	**2275**	**2850**	**4325**	**6350**
LE Sedan 4D	BR12E	15218	**2575**	**3175**	**4650**	**6750**
CAMRY—4-Cyl.—Equipment Schedule 4							
W.B. 105.2"; 2.2 Liter.							
CE Sedan 4D	BG22K	20464	**3325**	**4025**	**5575**	**7775**
LE Sedan 4D	BG22K	20858	**3475**	**4175**	**5725**	**7950**
XLE Sedan 4D	BG22K	23279	**3625**	**4350**	**5925**	**8175**
Manual Trans			**(425)**	**(425)**	**(565)**	**(565)**
V6 3.0 Liter	F		**475**	**475**	**635**	**635**
CELICA—4-Cyl.—Equipment Schedule 4							
W.B. 99.9"; 2.2 Liter.							
GT Sport Coupe 2D	CG02T	20531	**3700**	**4450**	**6475**	**9275**
GT Liftback 2D	DG02T	21701	**4025**	**4775**	**6875**	**9700**
GT Convertible 2D	FG02T	24970	**5700**	**6650**	**8925**	**12100**
Auto Trans			**200**	**200**	**265**	**265**
AVALON—V6—Equipment Schedule 4							
W.B. 107.1"; 3.0 Liter.							
XL Sedan 4D	BF18B	24698	**3575**	**4275**	**6250**	**8950**
XLS Sedan 4D	BF18B	28548	**4775**	**5600**	**7800**	**10800**
SUPRA—6-Cyl.—Equipment Schedule 4							
W.B. 100.4"; 3.0 Liter.							
Liftback 2D	DD82A	31338	**10825**	**12275**	**15750**	**20600**
Sport Roof	P		**375**	**375**	**500**	**500**
SUPRA—6-Cyl. Turbo—Equipment Schedule 4							
W.B. 100.4"; 3.0 Liter.							
Liftback 2D	DE82A	40728	**17225**	**19400**	**23600**	**29600**
6-Spd Manual Trans			**475**	**475**	**635**	**635**

1999 TOYOTA—(J,1,2or4)(NorT)(X,1,2or5)(BR12E)-X

Body	Type	VIN	List	Trade-In Fair	Good	Pvt-Party Good	Retail Excellent
COROLLA—4-Cyl.—Equipment Schedule 6							
W.B. 97.0"; 1.8 Liter.							
VE Sedan 4D	BR12E	13588	**2475**	**3075**	**4550**	**6625**
CE Sedan 4D	BR12E	14278	**2750**	**3375**	**4875**	**6975**
LE Sedan 4D	BR12E	15288	**3025**	**3700**	**5225**	**7375**
CAMRY—4-Cyl.—Equipment Schedule 4							
W.B. 105.2"; 2.2 Liter.							
CE Sedan 4D	BG22K	19444	**3950**	**4700**	**6325**	**8625**
LE Sedan 4D	BG22K	20218	**4075**	**4850**	**6475**	**8800**
XLE Sedan 4D	BG22K	23178	**4275**	**5075**	**6725**	**9075**
Manual Trans			**(450)**	**(450)**	**(600)**	**(600)**
V6 3.0 Liter	F		**525**	**525**	**700**	**700**
SOLARA—4-Cyl.—Equipment Schedule 4							
W.B. 105.1"; 2.2 Liter.							
SE Coupe 2D	CG22P	19858	**4175**	**4950**	**6625**	**9025**
Manual Trans			**(450)**	**(450)**	**(600)**	**(600)**

Body	Type	VIN	List	Trade-In Fair	Trade-In Good	Pvt-Party Good	Retail Excellent
V6 3.0 Liter		F		525	525	700	700
SOLARA—V6—Equipment Schedule 4							
W.B. 105.1"; 3.0 Liter.							
SLE Coupe 2D		CF22P	25408	5300	6200	8000	10550
CELICA—4-Cyl.—Equipment Schedule 4							
W.B. 99.9"; 2.2 Liter.							
GT Liftback 2D		DG02T	22240	4650	5500	7700	10750
GT Convertible 2D		FG02T	25319	6500	7525	9950	13300
Auto Trans				200	200	265	265
AVALON—V6—Equipment Schedule 4							
W.B. 107.1"; 3.0 Liter.							
XL Sedan 4D		BF18B	24988	4250	5050	7125	10000
XLS Sedan 4D		BF18B	28998	5550	6475	8775	12000

2000 TOYOTA—(J,1,2or4)(NorT)(X,1,2or5)(BT123)—Y

Body	Type	VIN	List	Trade-In Fair	Trade-In Good	Pvt-Party Good	Retail Excellent
ECHO—4-Cyl.—Equipment Schedule 6							
W.B. 93.3"; 1.5 Liter.							
Sedan 4D		BT123	11945	3575	4275	5525	7400
Coupe 2D		AT123	11645	3350	4050	5275	7125
COROLLA—4-Cyl.—Equipment Schedule 6							
W.B. 97.0"; 1.8 Liter.							
VE Sedan 4D		BR12E	13603	2850	3500	5050	7225
CE Sedan 4D		BR12E	14653	3175	3825	5425	7675
LE Sedan 4D		BR12E	15523	3500	4200	5825	8100
CAMRY—4-Cyl.—Equipment Schedule 4							
W.B. 105.2"; 2.2 Liter.							
CE Sedan 4D		BG22K	19820	4600	5425	7100	9525
LE Sedan 4D		BG22K	20743	4750	5575	7300	9750
XLE Sedan 4D		BG22K	24423	5000	5875	7575	10050
Manual Trans				(500)	(500)	(665)	(665)
V6 3.0 Liter		F		600	600	800	800
SOLARA—4-Cyl.—Equipment Schedule 4							
W.B. 105.1"; 2.2 Liter.							
SE Coupe 2D		CG22P	20193	4825	5675	7450	10000
SE Convertible 2D		FG22P	25523	6450	7450	9350	12150
Manual Trans				(500)	(500)	(665)	(665)
V6 3.0 Liter		F		600	600	800	800
SOLARA—V6—Equipment Schedule 4							
W.B. 105.1"; 3.0 Liter.							
SLE Coupe 2D		CF22P	26293	6125	7125	9000	11750
SLE Convertible 2D		FF22P	30943	7775	8950	10950	13950
MR2 SPYDER—4-Cyl.—Equipment Schedule 4							
W.B. 96.5"; 1.8 Liter.							
Convertible 2D		FG320	23553	6300	7300	9525	12700
CELICA—4-Cyl.—Equipment Schedule 4							
W.B. 102.3"; 1.8 Liter.							
GT Liftback 2D		DR32T	17970	5725	6675	8425	10950
GT-S Liftback 2D		DY32T	21620	6750	7800	9625	12300
Auto Trans				225	225	300	300
AVALON—V6—Equipment Schedule 4							
W.B. 107.1"; 3.0 Liter.							
XL Sedan 4D		BF28B	25650	7050	8150	10300	13400
XLS Sedan 4D		BF28B	30210	8550	9800	12150	15800

2001 TOYOTA—(J,1,2or4)(NorT)(D,X,1or2)(BT123)—1

Body	Type	VIN	List	Trade-In Fair	Trade-In Good	Pvt-Party Good	Retail Excellent
ECHO—4-Cyl.—Equipment Schedule 6							
W.B. 93.3"; 1.5 Liter.							
Sedan 4D		BT123	11930	4225	5000	6300	8275
Coupe 2D		AT123	11400	3975	4725	6050	7975
COROLLA—4-Cyl.—Equipment Schedule 6							
W.B. 97.0"; 1.8 Liter.							
CE Sedan 4D		BR12E	13753	4075	4850	6375	8575
S Sedan 4D		BR12E	14343	4375	5175	6725	8975
LE Sedan 4D		BR12E	14863	4450	5250	6825	9075
PRIUS—4-Cyl. HYBRID—Equipment Schedule 3							
W.B. 100.4"; 1.5 Liter.							
Hatchback 4D		BK12U	20450	9300	10625	12750	16000
CAMRY—4-Cyl.—Equipment Schedule 4							
W.B. 105.1"; 2.2 Liter.							
CE Sedan 4D		BG22K	19733	5325	6225	8025	10600
LE Sedan 4D		BG22K	20895	5500	6425	8225	10800
XLE Sedan 4D		BG22K	24575	5800	6750	8550	11200
Manual Trans				(525)	(525)	(700)	(700)

Body	Type	VIN	List	Trade-In Fair	Trade-In Good	Pvt-Party Good	Retail Excellent
V6 3.0 Liter		F		675	675	900	900
SOLARA—4-Cyl.—Equipment Schedule 4							
W.B. 105.1"; 2.2 Liter.							
SE Coupe 2D		CG22P	20245	5575	6500	8400	11100
SE Convertible 2D		FG22P	25575	7400	8500	10500	13550
Manual Trans				(525)	(525)	(700)	(700)
V6 3.0 Liter		F		675	675	900	900
SOLARA—V6—Equipment Schedule 4							
W.B. 105.1"; 3.0 Liter.							
SLE Coupe 2D		CF22P	25645	7050	8150	10150	13050
SLE Convertible 2D		FF22P	30995	8950	10225	12300	15450
MR2 SPYDER—4-Cyl.—Equipment Schedule 4							
W.B. 96.5"; 1.8 Liter.							
Convertible 2D		FG320	24065	7300	8400	10800	14200
CELICA—4-Cyl.—Equipment Schedule 4							
W.B. 102.3"; 1.8 Liter.							
GT Liftback 2D		DR32T	18285	6675	7700	9550	12250
GT-S Liftback 2D		DY32T	21935	7850	9025	10950	13800
Auto Trans				250	250	335	335
AVALON—V6—Equipment Schedule 4							
W.B. 107.1"; 3.0 Liter.							
XL Sedan 4D		BF28B	26325	8075	9275	11550	14850
XLS Sedan 4D		BF28B	30885	9750	11100	13500	17300

2002 TOYOTA—(J,1,2or4)(NorT)(D,X,1or2)(BT123)—2

Body	Type	VIN	List	Trade-In Fair	Trade-In Good	Pvt-Party Good	Retail Excellent
ECHO—4-Cyl.—Equipment Schedule 6							
W.B. 93.3"; 1.5 Liter.							
Sedan 4D		BT123	12265	4925	5775	7175	9300
Coupe 2D		AT123	11675	4650	5500	6875	8975
COROLLA—4-Cyl.—Equipment Schedule 6							
W.B. 97.0"; 1.8 Liter.							
CE Sedan 4D		BR12E	13533	4725	5575	7200	9550
S Sedan 4D		BR12E	14073	5075	5950	7600	10000
LE Sedan 4D		BR12E	14443	5150	6050	7675	10100
PRIUS—4-Cyl. HYBRID—Equipment Schedule 3							
W.B. 100.4"; 1.5 Liter.							
Hatchback 4D		BK12U	20480	10475	11925	14150	17600
CAMRY—4-Cyl.—Equipment Schedule 4							
W.B. 107.1"; 2.4 Liter.							
LE Sedan 4D		BE32K	20285	8075	9275	10800	13300
SE Sedan 4D		BE32K	21625	8225	9425	11000	13500
XLE Sedan 4D		BF32K	22780	8550	9800	11400	13900
Manual Trans				(550)	(550)	(735)	(735)
V6 3.0 Liter		F		750	750	1000	1000
SOLARA—4-Cyl.—Equipment Schedule 4							
W.B. 105.1"; 2.4 Liter.							
SE Coupe 2D		CE22P	20650	6450	7475	9475	12350
SE Convertible 2D		FE22P	25980	8500	9700	11850	15000
Manual Trans				(550)	(550)	(735)	(735)
V6 3.0 Liter		F		750	750	1000	1000
SOLARA—V6—Equipment Schedule 4							
W.B. 105.1"; 3.0 Liter.							
SLE Coupe 2D		CF22P	25160	8100	9300	11400	14550
SLE Convertible 2D		FF22P	31010	10125	11550	13750	17150
MR2 SPYDER—4-Cyl.—Equipment Schedule 4							
W.B. 96.5"; 1.8 Liter.							
Convertible 2D		FR320	25000	8450	9675	12200	15850
CELICA—4-Cyl.—Equipment Schedule 4							
W.B. 102.4"; 1.8 Liter.							
GT Liftback 2D		DR32T	18390	7725	8875	10850	13750
GT-S Liftback 2D		DY32T	22040	9125	10425	12450	15550
Auto Trans				275	275	365	365
AVALON—V6—Equipment Schedule 4							
W.B. 107.1"; 3.0 Liter.							
XL Sedan 4D		BF28B	26330	9250	10525	13000	16600
XLS Sedan 4D		BF28B	30890	11100	12600	15350	19300

2003 TOYOTA—J,1,2or4(NorT)D,X,1or2(BT123)—3

Body	Type	VIN	List	Trade-In Fair	Trade-In Good	Pvt-Party Good	Retail Excellent
ECHO—4-Cyl.—Equipment Schedule 6							
W.B. 93.3"; 1.5 Liter.							
Sedan 4D		BT123	12375	5700	6625	8125	10400
Coupe 2D		AT123	11785	5400	6325	7800	10050

2003 TOYOTA

Body	Type	VIN	List	Trade-In Fair	Trade-In Good	Pvt-Party Good	Retail Excellent
COROLLA—4-Cyl.—Equipment Schedule 6							
W.B. 102.4"; 1.8 Liter.							
CE Sedan 4D		BR32E	14055	7100	8200	9850	12350
S Sedan 4D		BR32E	15000	7475	8575	10250	12800
LE Sedan 4D		BR32E	15165	7550	8675	10350	12900
Sport Pkg				100	100	135	135
TRD Pkg				200	200	265	265
PRIUS—4-Cyl. Hybrid—Equipment Schedule 3							
W.B. 100.4"; 1.5 Liter.							
Hatchback 4D		BK12U	20730	11725	13300	15700	19400
MATRIX—4-Cyl.—Equipment Schedule 6							
W.B. 102.4"; 1.8 Liter.							
Sport Wagon 4D		KR32E	15155	7475	8575	10300	12850
XR Sport Wagon 4D		KR32E	16665	7725	8875	10600	13250
XRS Sport Wagon 4D		KY32E	19235	8400	9625	11350	14050
4WD Sport Wagon 4D		LR32E	17600	8100	9300	11000	13700
4WD XR Sport Wag 4D		LR32E	18930	8225	9425	11150	13800
TRD Pkg				400	400	535	535
CAMRY—4-Cyl.—Equipment Schedule 4							
W.B. 107.1"; 2.4 Liter.							
LE Sedan 4D		BE30K	20285	9275	10575	12200	14850
SE Sedan 4D		BE30K	21625	9475	10825	12450	15100
XLE Sedan 4D		BF30K	22780	9850	11250	12900	15550
Manual Trans				(575)	(575)	(765)	(765)
V6 3.0 Liter		F		825	825	1100	1100
SOLARA—4-Cyl.—Equipment Schedule 4							
W.B. 105.1"; 2.4 Liter.							
SE Coupe 2D		CE22P	20650	7475	8575	10700	13850
SE Convertible 2D		FE22P	25980	9650	11000	13300	16700
Manual Trans				(575)	(575)	(765)	(765)
V6 3.0 Liter		F		825	825	1100	1100
SOLARA—V6—Equipment Schedule 4							
W.B. 105.1"; 3.0 Liter.							
SLE Coupe 2D		CF22P	25160	9275	10575	12850	16200
SLE Convertible 2D		FF22P	31010	11550	13100	15400	19000
MR2 SPYDER—4-Cyl.—Equipment Schedule 4							
W.B. 96.5"; 1.8 Liter.							
Convertible 2D		FR320	25055	9700	11050	13800	17750
CELICA—4-Cyl.—Equipment Schedule 4							
W.B. 102.4"; 1.8 Liter.							
GT Liftback 2D		DR32T	18610	8950	10225	12300	15500
GT-S Liftback 2D		DY32T	22455	10425	11875	14050	17400
Auto Trans				300	300	400	400
AVALON—V6—Equipment Schedule 4							
W.B. 107.1"; 3.0 Liter.							
XL Sedan 4D		BF28B	26330	10625	12075	14700	18600
XLS Sedan 4D		BF28B	27150	12650	14300	17200	21500

2004 TOYOTA—(J,1,2or4)(NorT)D,Xor1(BT123)—4—#

Body	Type	VIN	List	Trade-In Fair	Trade-In Good	Pvt-Party Good	Retail Excellent
ECHO—4-Cyl.—Equipment Schedule 6							
W.B. 93.3"; 1.5 Liter.							
Sedan 4D		BT123	12215	6600	7625	9075	11350
Coupe 2D		AT123	11685	6300	7300	8725	10950
COROLLA—4-Cyl.—Equipment Schedule 6							
W.B. 102.4"; 1.8 Liter.							
CE Sedan 4D		BR32E	14085	8200	9375	11000	13550
S Sedan 4D		BR32E	15030	8550	9800	11450	14000
LE Sedan 4D		BR32E	15295	8650	9900	11550	14100
PRIUS—4-Cyl. Hybrid—Equipment Schedule 3							
W.B. 106.3"; 1.5 Liter.							
Hatchback 4D		KB20U	20510	15800	17800	19600	22800
MATRIX—4-Cyl.—Equipment Schedule 6							
W.B. 102.4"; 1.8 Liter.							
Sport Wagon 4D		KR32E	15185	8725	10000	11600	14200
XR Sport Wagon 4D		KR32E	16695	9025	10325	12000	14600
XRS Sport Wagon 4D		KY32E	19265	9800	11150	12800	15500
4WD Sport Wagon 4D		LR32E	17630	9400	10725	12400	15100
4WD XR Sport Wag 4D		LR32E	18960	9575	10925	12550	15300
Sport Pkg				400	400	535	535
CAMRY—4-Cyl.—Equipment Schedule 4							
W.B. 107.1"; 2.4 Liter.							
Sedan 4D		BE32K	19390	10325	11725	13300	15850
LE Sedan 4D		BE32K	20390	10675	12175	13750	16350

Body Type	VIN	List	Trade-In Fair	Good	Pvt-Party Good	Retail Excellent
SE Sedan 4D	BE32K	21220	10925	12375	13900	16600
XLE Sedan 4D	BE32K	22810	11300	12850	14400	17100
Manual Trans			(600)	(600)	(800)	(800)
V6 3.0/3.3 Liter	F,A		900	900	1200	1200

SOLARA—4-Cyl.—Equipment Schedule 4
W.B. 107.2"; 2.4 Liter.

Body Type	VIN	List	Trade-In Fair	Good	Pvt-Party Good	Retail Excellent
SE Coupe 2D	CE38P	20465	10675	12125	13600	16150
SE Sport Coupe 2D	CE38P	21960	11775	13350	14900	17600
SLE Coupe 2D	CE38P	23510	12650	14300	15900	18700
Manual Trans			(600)	(600)	(800)	(800)
V6 3.3 Liter	A		900	900	1200	1200

SOLARA—V6—Equipment Schedule 4
W.B. 107.2"; 3.3 Liter.

Body Type	VIN	List	Trade-In Fair	Good	Pvt-Party Good	Retail Excellent
SE Convertible 2D	FA22P	26465	13050	14750	16350	19200
SLE Convertible 2D	FA22P	29965	15075	16975	18700	21800

MR2 SPYDER—4-Cyl.—Equipment Schedule 4
W.B. 96.5"; 1.8 Liter.

Body Type	VIN	List	Trade-In Fair	Good	Pvt-Party Good	Retail Excellent
Convertible 2D	FR320	25410	11100	12600	15500	19700

CELICA—4-Cyl.—Equipment Schedule 4
W.B. 102.4"; 1.8 Liter.

Body Type	VIN	List	Trade-In Fair	Good	Pvt-Party Good	Retail Excellent
GT Liftback 2D	DR32T	17905	10275	11700	13850	17200
GT-S Liftback 2D	DY32T	22570	11925	13525	15800	19350
Auto Trans			300	300	400	400

AVALON—V6—Equipment Schedule 4
W.B. 107.1"; 3.0 Liter.

Body Type	VIN	List	Trade-In Fair	Good	Pvt-Party Good	Retail Excellent
XL Sedan 4D	BF28B	26560	12175	13825	16650	20800
XLS Sedan 4D	BF28B	31020	14400	16250	19300	23900

2005 TOYOTA—(J,1,2or4)(NorT)D,Xor1(BT123)-5

ECHO—4-Cyl.—Equipment Schedule 6
W.B. 93.3"; 1.5 Liter.

Body Type	VIN	List	Trade-In Fair	Good	Pvt-Party Good	Retail Excellent
Sedan 4D	BT123	12620	7675	8800	10350	12700
Coupe 2D	AT123	12090	7350	8475	9950	12250

COROLLA—4-Cyl.—Equipment Schedule 6
W.B. 102.4"; 1.8 Liter.

Body Type	VIN	List	Trade-In Fair	Good	Pvt-Party Good	Retail Excellent
CE Sedan 4D	BR32E	14220	8900	10175	11650	14500
S Sedan 4D	BR32E	15265	9275	10575	12100	14500
LE Sedan 4D	BR32E	15430	9350	10675	12150	14600
XRS Sedan 4D	BY32E	17995	9900	11300	12750	15300

PRIUS—4-Cyl. Hybrid—Equipment Schedule 3
W.B. 106.3"; 1.5 Liter.

Body Type	VIN	List	Trade-In Fair	Good	Pvt-Party Good	Retail Excellent
Hatchback 4D	KB22U	21515	17135	19250	21300	24100

MATRIX—4-Cyl.—Equipment Schedule 6
W.B. 102.4"; 1.8 Liter.

Body Type	VIN	List	Trade-In Fair	Good	Pvt-Party Good	Retail Excellent
Sport Wagon 4D	KR32E	15300	10225	11650	13250	15850
XR Sport Wagon 4D	KR32E	16780	10575	12025	13600	16250
XRS Sport Wagon 4D	KY32E	19290	11350	12900	14500	17250
4WD Sport Wagon 4D	LR32E	17835	10950	12425	14000	16750
4WD XR Sport Wag 4D	LR32E	19175	11100	12600	14250	17000

CAMRY—4-Cyl.—Equipment Schedule 4
W.B. 107.1"; 2.4 Liter.

Body Type	VIN	List	Trade-In Fair	Good	Pvt-Party Good	Retail Excellent
Sedan 4D	BE32K	19415	11450	13000	14400	17000
LE Sedan 4D	BE32K	20515	11825	13375	14900	17450
SE Sedan 4D	BE32K	21345	12075	13675	15150	17750
XLE Sedan 4D	BE32K	22935	12525	14150	15650	18350
Manual Trans			(625)	(625)	(835)	(835)
V6 3.0/3.3 Liter	F,A		950	950	1265	1265

SOLARA—4-Cyl.—Equipment Schedule 4
W.B. 107.1"; 2.4 Liter.

Body Type	VIN	List	Trade-In Fair	Good	Pvt-Party Good	Retail Excellent
SE Coupe 2D	CE38P	20590	11725	13300	14750	17250
SE Sport Coupe 2D	CE38P	22085	12950	14650	16150	18800
SLE Coupe 2D	CE38P	23635	13875	15675	17150	20000
Manual Trans			(625)	(625)	(835)	(835)
V6 3.3 Liter	A		950	950	1265	1265

SOLARA—V6—Equipment Schedule 4
W.B. 107.1"; 3.3 Liter.

Body Type	VIN	List	Trade-In Fair	Good	Pvt-Party Good	Retail Excellent
SE Convertible 2D	FA38P	26920	14300	16150	17700	20600
SLE Convertible 2D	FA38P	30190	16550	18625	20300	23500

MR2 SPYDER—4-Cyl.—Equipment Schedule 4
W.B. 96.5"; 1.8 Liter.

Body Type	VIN	List	Trade-In Fair	Good	Pvt-Party Good	Retail Excellent
Convertible 2D	FR320	26685	12175	13825	16750	21000

CELICA—4-Cyl.—Equipment Schedule 4
W.B. 102.4"; 1.8 Liter.

Body Type	VIN	List	Trade-In Fair	Good	Pvt-Party Good	Retail Excellent
GT Liftback 2D	DR32T	19830	11300	12850	15050	18450
GT-S Liftback 2D	DY32T	23575	13100	14850	17100	20800
Auto Trans			300	300	400	400
AVALON—V6—Equipment Schedule 4						
W.B. 111.0"; 3.5 Liter.						
XL Sedan 4D	BK36B	26890	13675	15425	18350	22700
Touring Sedan 4D	BK36B	29140	15225	17175	20200	24700
XLS Sedan 4D	BK36B	31340	16050	18050	21200	26100
Limited Sedan 4D	BK36B	34080	17125	19250	22300	27100

VOLKSWAGEN

1991 VOLKSWAGEN — (9orW)(BorV)W(BA230)–M

Body Type	VIN	List	Fair	Good	Good	Excellent
FOX—4-Cyl.—Equipment Schedule 6						
W.B. 92.8"; 1.8 Liter.						
Sedan 2D	BA230	8405	375	500	925	1575
GL Sedan 4D	GA230	9595	400	600	1050	1750
Wolfsburg Edition			25	25	35	35
GOLF—4-Cyl.—Equipment Schedule 6						
W.B. 97.3"; 1.8 Liter.						
GL Hatchback 2D	BA21G	10340	350	475	1225	2375
GL Hatchback 4D	FA21G	10640	375	500	1250	2425
Wolfsburg Edition			25	25	35	35
GTI—4-Cyl.—Equipment Schedule 6						
W.B. 97.3"; 1.8 Liter, 2.0 Liter.						
Hatchback 2D	DB21G	11355	400	600	1375	2600
16V Hatchback 2D	HE21G	14060	600	850	1725	3100
Wolfsburg Edition			25	25	35	35
JETTA—4-Cyl.—Equipment Schedule 6						
W.B. 97.3"; 1.8 Liter, 2.0 Liter.						
GL Sedan 2D	MA21G	11355	550	800	1700	3050
GL Sedan 4D	RA21G	11655	600	850	1750	3125
Carat Sedan 4D	RB21G	12370	650	925	1875	3300
GLI 16V Sedan 4D	TE21G	15155	825	1175	2325	3975
Wolfsburg Edition			25	25	35	35
4-Cyl. 1.6L Diesel	G		(200)	(200)	(265)	(265)
CABRIOLET—4-Cyl.—Equipment Schedule 6						
W.B. 94.5"; 1.8 Liter.						
Convertible 2D	CA515	17740	850	1225	2400	4075
Carat Convertible 2D	CA515	19300	925	1300	2500	4200
Etienne Aigner Conv 2D	EA515	19600	975	1375	2600	4325
Power Top			50	50	65	65
PASSAT—4-Cyl.—Equipment Schedule 4						
W.B. 103.3"; 2.0 Liter.						
GL Sedan 4D	FB431	17355	500	725	1600	2925
GL Wagon 4D	GB431	17760	625	900	1850	3275
Manual Trans			(175)	(175)	(235)	(235)
CORRADO—4-Cyl. Supercharged—Equipment Schedule 3						
W.B. 97.3"; 1.8 Liter.						
Coupe 2D	DB450	19440	1000	1425	2650	4375

1992 VOLKSWAGEN–(9,3orW)(BorV)W(BA230)–N

Body Type	VIN	List	Fair	Good	Good	Excellent
FOX—4-Cyl.—Equipment Schedule 6						
W.B. 92.8"; 1.8 Liter.						
Sedan 2D	BA230	8770	400	550	1000	1700
GL Sedan 4D	GA230	9990	450	625	1125	1875
GOLF—4-Cyl.—Equipment Schedule 6						
W.B. 97.3"; 1.8 Liter.						
GL Hatchback 2D	BA21G	11135	425	625	1525	2875
GL Hatchback 4D	FA21G	11445	450	625	1550	2925
GTI—4-Cyl.—Equipment Schedule 6						
W.B. 97.3"; 1.8 Liter, 2.0 Liter.						
Hatchback 2D	DB21G	12320	500	725	1675	3100
16V Hatchback 2D	HE21G	15120	700	1025	2200	3900
JETTA—4-Cyl.—Equipment Schedule 6						
W.B. 97.3"; 1.8 Liter, 2.0 Liter.						
GL Sedan 4D	RA21G	12580	700	1000	2025	3575
Carat Sedan 4D	SB21G	13600	750	1075	2225	3900
GLI 16V Sedan 4D	TE21G	16690	975	1350	2625	4400
4-Cyl. 1.6L Diesel	F		(200)	(200)	(265)	(265)

1992 VOLKSWAGEN

Body	Type	VIN	List	Trade-In Fair	Good	Pvt-Party Good	Retail Excellent
CABRIOLET—4-Cyl.—Equipment Schedule 6							
W.B. 94.5"; 1.8 Liter.							
Convertible 2D		CB515	18585	**1000**	**1425**	**2725**	**4475**
Carat Convertible 2D		DB515	20215	**1075**	**1500**	**2825**	**4625**
Wolfsburg Edition				25	25	35	35
Power Top				50	50	65	65
PASSAT—4-Cyl.—Equipment Schedule 4							
W.B. 103.3"; 2.0 Liter.							
CL Sedan 4D		EB431	16955	**550**	**775**	**1750**	**3225**
GL Sedan 4D		FB431	18715	**575**	**825**	**1850**	**3350**
GL Wagon 4D		GB431	19135	**700**	**1000**	**2075**	**3675**
Manual Trans				(175)	(175)	(235)	(235)
CORRADO—4-Cyl. Supercharged—Equipment Schedule 3							
W.B. 97.3"; 1.8 Liter.							
G60 Coupe 2D		DB450	20230	**1225**	**1700**	**3050**	**4925**
CORRADO—V6—Equipment Schedule 3							
W.B. 97.3"; 2.8 Liter.							
SLC Coupe 2D		ED450	22210	**1925**	**2450**	**3950**	**6025**

1993 VOLKSWAGEN — (9orW)(BorV)W(BA230)–P

Body	Type	VIN	List	Trade-In Fair	Good	Pvt-Party Good	Retail Excellent
FOX—4-Cyl.—Equipment Schedule 6							
W.B. 92.8"; 1.8 Liter.							
Wolfsburg Sedan 2D		BA230	9065	**450**	**625**	**1125**	**1875**
Polo Sedan 2D		BA230	9285	**450**	**625**	**1125**	**1875**
Wolfsburg GL Sedan 4D		GA230	9895	**525**	**750**	**1225**	**2075**
GOLF III—4-Cyl.—Equipment Schedule 6							
W.B. 103.3"; 2.0 Liter.							
GL Hatchback 4D		FL21H	12830	**850**	**1200**	**2450**	**4225**
JETTA III—4-Cyl.—Equipment Schedule 6							
W.B. 97.4"; 2.0 Liter.							
GL Sedan 4D		RL21H	14030	**850**	**1225**	**2475**	**4250**
CABRIOLET—4-Cyl.—Equipment Schedule 6							
W.B. 94.5"; 1.8 Liter.							
Convertible 2D		AB515	19665	**1125**	**1575**	**2950**	**4850**
Classic Conv 2D		BB515	20320	**1225**	**1725**	**3125**	**5050**
PASSAT—4-Cyl.—Equipment Schedule 4							
W.B. 103.3"; 2.0 Liter.							
GL Sedan 4D		FB431	19125	**600**	**850**	**1950**	**3575**
Manual Trans				(225)	(225)	(300)	(300)
PASSAT—V6—Equipment Schedule 4							
W.B. 103.3"; 2.8 Liter.							
GLX Sedan 4D		JD431	22395	**1225**	**1700**	**3150**	**5125**
GLX Wagon 4D		ND431	22825	**1300**	**1800**	**3275**	**5250**
Manual Trans				(225)	(225)	(300)	(300)
CORRADO—V6—Equipment Schedule 3							
W.B. 97.3"; 2.8 Liter.							
SLC Coupe 2D		ED450	23260	**2350**	**2925**	**4550**	**6800**

1994 VOLKSWAGEN — (9orW)(BorV)W(BA81H)–R

Body	Type	VIN	List	Trade-In Fair	Good	Pvt-Party Good	Retail Excellent
GOLF III—4-Cyl.—Equipment Schedule 6							
W.B. 97.3"; 2.0 Liter.							
GL Hatchback 2D		BA81H	13565	**900**	**1250**	**2600**	**4450**
GL Hatchback 4D		FB21H	13140	**925**	**1300**	**2675**	**4525**
JETTA III—4-Cyl.—Equipment Schedule 6							
W.B. 97.3"; 2.0 Liter.							
GL Sedan 4D		RB21H	14365	**975**	**1350**	**2725**	**4600**
GLS Sedan 4D		SB81H	16090	**1125**	**1575**	**3000**	**4950**
JETTA III—V6—Equipment Schedule 6							
W.B. 97.3"; 2.8 Liter.							
GLX Sedan 4D		TS81H	20365	**2125**	**2725**	**4325**	**6525**
PASSAT—V6—Equipment Schedule 4							
W.B. 103.3"; 2.8 Liter.							
GLX Sedan 4D		JF431	24340	**1525**	**2025**	**3600**	**5725**
GLX Wagon 4D		NF431	24765	**1625**	**2125**	**3725**	**5875**
Manual Trans				(275)	(275)	(365)	(365)
CORRADO—V6—Equipment Schedule 3							
W.B. 97.2"; 2.8 Liter.							
SLC Coupe 2D		EF450	25540	**2825**	**3475**	**5250**	**7650**

1995 VOLKSWAGEN — (3VWorWVW)(JB81H)–S–#

GOLF III—4-Cyl.—Equipment Schedule 6
W.B. 97.3"; 2.0 Liter.

1995 VOLKSWAGEN

Body	Type	VIN	List	Trade-In Fair	Good	Pvt-Party Good	Retail Excellent
City Hatchback 4D		JB81H	11915	**825**	**1175**	**2550**	**4450**
Hatchback 4D		KA81H	12890	**925**	**1300**	**2725**	**4650**
GL Hatchback 2D		BA81H	14265	**1025**	**1450**	**2875**	**4875**
GL Hatchback 4D		FA81H	14590	**1050**	**1475**	**2950**	**4950**
Sport Hatchback 2D		BA81H	15640	**1750**	**2275**	**3875**	**6050**
GTI—V6—Equipment Schedule 6							
W.B. 97.3"; 2.8 Liter.							
Coupe 2D		HD81H	19265	**2575**	**3200**	**4925**	**7275**
JETTA III—4-Cyl.—Equipment Schedule 6							
W.B. 97.3"; 2.0 Liter.							
City Sedan 4D		VB81H	12915	**1050**	**1450**	**2900**	**4900**
Sedan 4D		PB81H	13865	**1075**	**1525**	**3000**	**5000**
GL Sedan 4D		RA81H	16065	**1350**	**1850**	**3375**	**5450**
GLS Sedan 4D		SB81H	17415	**1550**	**2050**	**3650**	**5750**
JETTA III—V6—Equipment Schedule 6							
W.B. 97.3"; 2.8 Liter.							
GLX Sedan 4D		TD81H	20365	**2550**	**3150**	**4875**	**7200**
CABRIO—4-Cyl.—Equipment Schedule 3							
W.B. 97.4"; 2.0 Liter.							
Convertible 2D		BC81E	21215	**2400**	**2975**	**4650**	**6950**
Manual Trans				**(175)**	**(175)**	**(235)**	**(235)**
PASSAT—4-Cyl.—Equipment Schedule 4							
W.B. 103.3"; 2.0 Liter.							
GLS Sedan 4D		CC83A	19215	**800**	**1150**	**2625**	**4650**
Manual Trans				**(325)**	**(325)**	**(435)**	**(435)**
PASSAT—V6—Equipment Schedule 4							
W.B. 103.3"; 2.8 Liter.							
GLX Sedan 4D		EE83A	22080	**1850**	**2375**	**4125**	**6450**
GLX Wagon 4D		FE83A	22510	**1975**	**2525**	**4300**	**6650**
Manual Trans				**(325)**	**(325)**	**(435)**	**(435)**

1996 VOLKSWAGEN — (3VWorWVW)(FA81H)–T–#

Body	Type	VIN	List	Trade-In Fair	Good	Pvt-Party Good	Retail Excellent
GOLF—4-Cyl.—Equipment Schedule 6							
W.B. 97.4"; 2.0 Liter.							
GL Hatchback 4D		FA81H	14435	**1650**	**2150**	**3500**	**5325**
GTI Hatchback 2D		DA81H	16425	**2175**	**2775**	**4175**	**6125**
GOLF—4-Cyl. Turbo Diesel—Equipment Schedule 6							
W.B. 97.4"; 1.9 Liter.							
TDI Hatchback 4D		FF81H	15660	**2025**	**2575**	**3975**	**5925**
GOLF GTI VR6—V6—Equipment Schedule 6							
W.B. 97.4"; 2.8 Liter.							
Hatchback 2D		HD81H	20110	**3500**	**4200**	**5800**	**8050**
JETTA—4-Cyl.—Equipment Schedule 6							
W.B. 97.4"; 2.0 Liter.							
GL Sedan 4D		RA81H	15535	**1675**	**2175**	**3575**	**5475**
GLS Sedan 4D		SA81H	16725	**1925**	**2450**	**3875**	**5850**
Trek Edition		W		**50**	**50**	**65**	**65**
Wolfsburg Edition		P		**50**	**50**	**65**	**65**
JETTA—4-Cyl. Turbo Diesel—Equipment Schedule 6							
W.B. 97.4"; 1.9 Liter.							
TDI Sedan 4D		RF81H	16760	**2200**	**2800**	**4275**	**6300**
JETTA—V6—Equipment Schedule 6							
W.B. 97.4"; 2.8 Liter.							
GLX Sedan 4D		TD81H	21035	**3175**	**3850**	**5450**	**7700**
CABRIO—4-Cyl.—Equipment Schedule 3							
W.B. 97.2"; 2.0 Liter.							
Convertible 2D		BB81E	21260	**2775**	**3400**	**5175**	**7575**
Manual Trans				**(200)**	**(200)**	**(265)**	**(265)**
PASSAT—4-Cyl.—Equipment Schedule 4							
W.B. 103.3"; 2.0 Liter.							
GLS Sedan 4D		GC83A	19715	**950**	**1325**	**3025**	**5250**
Manual Trans				**(375)**	**(375)**	**(500)**	**(500)**
PASSAT—4-Cyl. Turbo Diesel—Equipment Schedule 4							
W.B. 103.3"; 1.9 Liter.							
TDI Sedan 4D		GG83A	19905	**2400**	**2975**	**4900**	**7450**
TDI Wagon 4D		HG83A	20335	**2600**	**3225**	**5125**	**7675**
PASSAT—V6—Equipment Schedule 4							
W.B. 103.3"; 2.8 Liter.							
GLX Sedan 4D		EE83A	23115	**2225**	**2825**	**4700**	**7250**
GLX Wagon 4D		FE83A	23545	**2375**	**2950**	**4875**	**7450**
Manual Trans				**(375)**	**(375)**	**(500)**	**(500)**

1997 VOLKSWAGEN

Body	Type	VIN	List	Trade-In Fair	Good	Pvt-Party Good	Retail Excellent

1997 VOLKSWAGEN — (3VWorWVW)(FA81H)-V-#

GOLF—4-Cyl.—Equipment Schedule 6
W.B. 97.4"; 2.0 Liter.

GL Hatchback 4D		FA81H	14830	**2025**	**2575**	**4000**	**5975**
GTI Hatchback 2D		DA81H	16820	**2600**	**3225**	**4725**	**6825**
Jazz Edition		M		**50**	**50**	**65**	**65**
Trek Edition		L		**50**	**50**	**65**	**65**
K2 Edition		K		**50**	**50**	**65**	**65**

GOLF GTI VR6—V6—Equipment Schedule 6
W.B. 97.4"; 2.8 Liter.

Hatchback 2D		HD81H	20210	**4050**	**4800**	**6500**	**8875**

JETTA—4-Cyl.—Equipment Schedule 6
W.B. 97.4"; 2.0 Liter.

GL Sedan 4D		RA81H	15930	**2050**	**2625**	**4100**	**6125**
GT Sedan 4D		VA81H	16325	**2300**	**2875**	**4425**	**6500**
GLS Sedan 4D		SA81H	17420	**2575**	**3175**	**4700**	**6875**
Trek Edition		W		**50**	**50**	**65**	**65**

JETTA—4-Cyl. Turbo Diesel—Equipment Schedule 6
W.B. 97.4"; 1.9 Liter.

TDI Sedan 4D		RF81H	17105	**2650**	**3275**	**4800**	**6950**

JETTA—V6—Equipment Schedule 6
W.B. 97.4"; 2.8 Liter.

GLX Sedan 4D		TD81H	21055	**3750**	**4475**	**6175**	**8550**

CABRIO—4-Cyl.—Equipment Schedule 3
W.B. 97.4"; 2.0 Liter.

Convertible 2D		AA81E	20785	**3175**	**3850**	**5725**	**8275**
Highline Conv 2D		BA81E	23050	**3550**	**4250**	**6075**	**8625**
Manual Trans				**(200)**	**(200)**	**(265)**	**(265)**

PASSAT—4-Cyl. Turbo Diesel—Equipment Schedule 4
W.B. 103.3"; 1.9 Liter.

TDI Sedan 4D		GG83A	19930	**2825**	**3450**	**5525**	**8325**
TDI Wagon 4D		HG83A	20360	**3025**	**3700**	**5750**	**8500**

PASSAT—V6—Equipment Schedule 4
W.B. 103.3"; 2.8 Liter.

GLX Sedan 4D		EE83A	23190	**2675**	**3275**	**5350**	**8125**
GLX Wagon 4D		FE83A	23620	**2825**	**3475**	**5575**	**8375**
Manual Trans				**(400)**	**(400)**	**(535)**	**(535)**

1998 VOLKSWAGEN–(3VWorWVW)(FA81H)-W-#

GOLF—4-Cyl.—Equipment Schedule 6
W.B. 97.4"; 2.0 Liter.

GL Hatchback 4D		FA81H	14855	**2425**	**3025**	**4525**	**6650**
GTI Hatchback 2D		DA81H	17170	**3050**	**3725**	**5300**	**7550**
K2 Edition		K		**50**	**50**	**65**	**65**

GOLF GTI VR6—V6—Equipment Schedule 6
W.B. 97.4"; 2.8 Liter.

Hatchback 2D		HD81H	20735	**4625**	**5450**	**7225**	**9750**

NEW BEETLE—4-Cyl.—Equipment Schedule 6
W.B. 98.9"; 2.0 Liter.

Hatchback 2D		BB61C	15700	**3650**	**4375**	**5700**	**7675**

NEW BEETLE—4-Cyl. Turbo Diesel—Equipment Schedule 6
W.B. 98.9"; 1.9 Liter.

TDI Hatchback 2D		BF61C	16975	**4575**	**5400**	**6850**	**9000**

JETTA—4-Cyl.—Equipment Schedule 6
W.B. 97.4"; 2.0 Liter.

GL Sedan 4D		RA81H	15955	**2500**	**3100**	**4675**	**6875**
GT Sedan 4D		VA81H	16350	**2750**	**3375**	**4975**	**7200**
GLS Sedan 4D		SA81H	17445	**3025**	**3700**	**5350**	**7650**
K2 Edition		Y		**50**	**50**	**65**	**65**
Wolfsburg		P		**50**	**50**	**65**	**65**

JETTA—4-Cyl. Turbo Diesel—Equipment Schedule 6
W.B. 97.4"; 1.9 Liter.

TDI Sedan 4D		RF81H	17130	**3100**	**3750**	**5400**	**7675**

JETTA—V6—Equipment Schedule 6
W.B. 97.4"; 2.8 Liter.

GLX Sedan 4D		TD81H	21455	**4375**	**5150**	**6925**	**9475**

CABRIO—4-Cyl.—Equipment Schedule 3
W.B. 97.4"; 2.0 Liter.

GL Convertible 2D		AA81E	20835	**3650**	**4375**	**6350**	**9050**
GLS Convertible 2D		BA81E	23665	**4050**	**4800**	**6750**	**9400**
Manual Trans				**(200)**	**(200)**	**(265)**	**(265)**

1998 VOLKSWAGEN

Body Type	VIN	List	Trade-In Fair	Good	Pvt-Party Good	Retail Excellent
PASSAT—4-Cyl. Turbo—Equipment Schedule 4						
W.B. 106.4"; 1.8 Liter.						
GLS Sedan 4D	MA63B	22325	**4300**	**5100**	**6875**	**9375**
GLS Wagon 4D	NA63B	22875	**4450**	**5250**	**7050**	**9600**
Manual Trans			(425)	(425)	(565)	(565)
V6 2.8 Liter	D		375	375	500	500
PASSAT—4-Cyl. Turbo Diesel—Equipment Schedule 4						
W.B. 106.4"; 1.9 Liter.						
GLS TDI Sedan 4D	MG63B	22575	**4675**	**5525**	**7350**	**9950**
Manual Trans			(425)	(425)	(565)	(565)
PASSAT—V6—Equipment Schedule 4						
W.B. 106.4"; 2.8 Liter.						
GLX Sedan 4D	PD63B	27825	**6300**	**7325**	**9325**	**12200**
Manual Trans			(425)	(425)	(565)	(565)

1999 VOLKSWAGEN — (3orW)VW(FB81H)-X-#

Body Type	VIN	List	Trade-In Fair	Good	Pvt-Party Good	Retail Excellent
GOLF—4-Cyl.—Equipment Schedule 6						
W.B. 97.4"; 2.0 Liter.						
GL Hatchback 4D	FB81H	14855	**2875**	**3550**	**5125**	**7325**
Wolfsburg	J		50	50	65	65
GOLF GTI VR6—V6—Equipment Schedule 6						
W.B. 97.4"; 2.8 Liter.						
Hatchback 2D	HD81H	20735	**5275**	**6175**	**7975**	**10550**
NEW GOLF—4-Cyl.—Equipment Schedule 6						
W.B. 98.9"; 2.0 Liter.						
GL Hatchback 2D	BC31J	15425	**4175**	**4950**	**6375**	**8475**
GLS Hatchback 4D	GC31J	16875	**4375**	**5150**	**6600**	**8700**
NEW GOLF—4-Cyl. Turbo Diesel—Equipment Schedule 6						
W.B. 98.9"; 1.9 Liter.						
GL TDI H'Back 2D	BF31J	16720	**5275**	**6175**	**7700**	**10000**
GLS TDI H'Back 4D	GF31J	17925	**5450**	**6375**	**7925**	**10250**
NEW GTI—4-Cyl.—Equipment Schedule 6						
W.B. 98.9"; 2.0 Liter.						
GLS Hatchback 2D	DC31J	18025	**4900**	**5750**	**7250**	**9450**
NEW GTI—V6—Equipment Schedule 6						
W.B. 98.9"; 2.8 Liter.						
GLX Hatchback 2D	DE21J	22675	**6500**	**7525**	**9175**	**11650**
NEW BEETLE—4-Cyl.—Equipment Schedule 6						
W.B. 98.9"; 2.0 Liter.						
GL Hatchback 2D	BC21C	16425	**4275**	**5075**	**6400**	**8450**
GLS Hatchback 2D	CC21C	17375	**4475**	**5275**	**6650**	**8700**
NEW BEETLE—4-Cyl. Turbo—Equipment Schedule 6						
W.B. 98.9"; 1.8 Liter.						
GLS Hatchback 2D	CD21C	19525	**4700**	**5550**	**6925**	**9025**
GLS Hatchback 2D	DD21C	21425	**4875**	**5725**	**7125**	**9275**
NEW BEETLE—4-Cyl. Turbo Diesel—Equipment Schedule 6						
W.B. 98.9"; 1.9 Liter.						
GLS TDI H'Back 2D	CF21C	18425	**5250**	**6150**	**7625**	**9800**
JETTA—4-Cyl.—Equipment Schedule 6						
W.B. 97.4"; 2.0 Liter.						
GL Sedan 4D	RB81H	16205	**2975**	**3650**	**5250**	**7525**
Wolfsburg	P		50	50	65	65
JETTA—4-Cyl. Turbo Diesel—Equipment Schedule 6						
W.B. 97.4"; 1.9 Liter.						
TDI Sedan 4D	RF81H	17130	**3625**	**4350**	**6050**	**8425**
JETTA—V6—Equipment Schedule 6						
W.B. 97.4"; 2.8 Liter.						
GLX Sedan 4D	TD81H	21455	**5050**	**5925**	**7725**	**10350**
NEW JETTA—4-Cyl.—Equipment Schedule 6						
W.B. 98.9"; 2.0 Liter.						
GL Sedan 4D	RC29M	16400	**4425**	**5225**	**6725**	**8925**
GLS Sedan 4D	SC29M	16875	**4700**	**5550**	**6925**	**9025**
NEW JETTA—4-Cyl. Turbo Diesel—Equipment Schedule 6						
W.B. 98.9"; 1.9 Liter.						
GL TDI Sedan 4D	RF29M	17695	**5850**	**6825**	**8275**	**10500**
GLS TDI Sedan 4D	SF29M	17925	**6050**	**7000**	**8475**	**10700**
NEW JETTA VR6—V6—Equipment Schedule 6						
W.B. 98.9"; 2.8 Liter.						
GLS Sedan 4D	SE29M	20475	**6075**	**7025**	**8550**	**10850**
GLX Sedan 4D	TE29M	24025	**6150**	**7150**	**8950**	**11600**
CABRIO—4-Cyl.—Equipment Schedule 3						
W.B. 97.4"; 2.0 Liter.						
GL Convertible 2D	AB81E	20835	**4200**	**4975**	**6975**	**9750**

1999 VOLKSWAGEN

Body	Type	VIN	List	Trade-In Fair	Trade-In Good	Pvt-Party Good	Retail Excellent
GLS Convertible 2D		BB81E	23665	**4625**	**5450**	**7400**	**10150**
Manual Trans				**(200)**	**(200)**	**(265)**	**(265)**
NEW CABRIO—4-Cyl.—Equipment Schedule 3							
W.B. 97.4"; 2.0 Liter.							
GL Convertible 2D		CB81E	22015	**5025**	**5900**	**7700**	**10350**
GLS Convertible 2D		DB81E	24700	**5300**	**6200**	**8050**	**10700**
Manual Trans				**(200)**	**(200)**	**(265)**	**(265)**
PASSAT—4-Cyl. Turbo—Equipment Schedule 4							
W.B. 106.4"; 1.8 Liter.							
GLS Sedan 4D		MA63B	22775	**5000**	**5875**	**7675**	**10300**
GLS Wagon 4D		NA63B	23325	**5175**	**6050**	**7875**	**10500**
Manual Trans				**(450)**	**(450)**	**(600)**	**(600)**
V6 2.8 Liter		D		**425**	**425**	**565**	**565**
PASSAT—V6—Equipment Schedule 4							
W.B. 106.4"; 2.8 Liter.							
GLX Sedan 4D		UD63B	30300	**7200**	**8325**	**10350**	**13350**

2000 VOLKSWAGEN — (3orW)VW(BC21J)-Y-#

Body	Type	VIN	List	Trade-In Fair	Trade-In Good	Pvt-Party Good	Retail Excellent
GOLF—4-Cyl.—Equipment Schedule 6							
W.B. 98.9"; 2.0 Liter.							
GL Hatchback 2D		BC21J	15425	**4800**	**5625**	**7100**	**9300**
GLS Hatchback 4D		GC21J	16875	**5025**	**5900**	**7375**	**9575**
GOLF—4-Cyl. Turbo—Equipment Schedule 6							
W.B. 98.9"; 1.8 Liter.							
GLS Hatchback 4D		GH21J	18425	**5400**	**6325**	**7850**	**10150**
GOLF—4-Cyl. Turbo Diesel—Equipment Schedule 6							
W.B. 98.9"; 1.9 Liter.							
GL TDI H'Back 2D		BF21J	16720	**6075**	**7050**	**8625**	**11000**
GLS TDI H'Back 4D		GF21J	17295	**6300**	**7300**	**8875**	**11300**
GTI—4-Cyl.—Equipment Schedule 6							
W.B. 98.9"; 2.0 Liter.							
GLS Hatchback 2D		DC21J	18200	**5625**	**6550**	**8075**	**10400**
GTI—4-Cyl. Turbo—Equipment Schedule 6							
W.B. 98.9"; 1.8 Liter.							
GLS Hatchback 2D		DH21J	19750	**6750**	**7775**	**9400**	**11900**
GTI—V6—Equipment Schedule 6							
W.B. 98.9"; 2.8 Liter.							
GLX Hatchback 2D		DE21J	23145	**7475**	**8575**	**10300**	**12900**
NEW BEETLE—4-Cyl.—Equipment Schedule 6							
W.B. 98.9"; 2.0 Liter.							
GL Hatchback 2D		BC21C	16425	**5050**	**5925**	**7300**	**9375**
GLS Hatchback 2D		CC21C	17375	**5275**	**6175**	**7600**	**9750**
NEW BEETLE—4-Cyl. Turbo—Equipment Schedule 6							
W.B. 98.9"; 1.8 Liter.							
GLS Hatchback 2D		CD21C	19525	**5550**	**6475**	**7875**	**10050**
GLS Hatchback 2D		DD21C	21600	**5750**	**6700**	**8125**	**10350**
NEW BEETLE—4-Cyl. Turbo Diesel—Equipment Schedule 6							
W.B. 98.9"; 1.9 Liter.							
GLS TDI H'Back 2D		CF21C	18425	**6200**	**7200**	**8675**	**10950**
JETTA—4-Cyl.—Equipment Schedule 6							
W.B. 98.9"; 2.0 Liter.							
GL Sedan 4D		RC29M	17225	**5150**	**6050**	**7550**	**9800**
GLS Sedan 4D		SC29M	18175	**5500**	**6425**	**7800**	**9950**
JETTA—4-Cyl. Turbo—Equipment Schedule 6							
W.B. 98.9"; 1.8 Liter.							
GLS Sedan 4D		SD29M	19725	**5900**	**6875**	**8275**	**10500**
JETTA—4-Cyl. Turbo Diesel—Equipment Schedule 6							
W.B. 98.9"; 1.9 Liter.							
GL TDI Sedan 4D		RF29M	18520	**6875**	**7900**	**9375**	**11700**
GLS TDI Sedan 4D		SF29M	19225	**7025**	**8125**	**9600**	**11950**
JETTA—V6—Equipment Schedule 6							
W.B. 98.9"; 2.8 Liter.							
GLS Sedan 4D		SE29M	20475	**7025**	**8125**	**9650**	**12050**
GLX Sedan 4D		TE29M	24695	**7175**	**8275**	**10100**	**12850**
CABRIO—4-Cyl.—Equipment Schedule 3							
W.B. 97.4"; 2.0 Liter.							
GL Convertible 2D		CC21V	22015	**5775**	**6725**	**8650**	**11450**
GLS Convertible 2D		DC21V	24700	**6100**	**7075**	**9050**	**11900**
Manual Trans				**(250)**	**(250)**	**(335)**	**(335)**
PASSAT—4-Cyl. Turbo—Equipment Schedule 4							
W.B. 106.4"; 1.8 Liter.							
GLS Sedan 4D		MA23B	22800	**5875**	**6850**	**8700**	**11400**
GLS Wagon 4D		NA23B	23600	**6075**	**7025**	**8925**	**11650**

DEDUCT FOR RECONDITIONING   0106

2000 VOLKSWAGEN

Body Type	VIN	List	Trade-In Fair	Good	Pvt-Party Good	Retail Excellent
Manual Trans			**(500)**	**(500)**	**(665)**	**(665)**
V6 2.8 Liter	D		500	500	665	665
PASSAT—V6—Equipment Schedule 4						
W.B. 106.4"; 2.8 Liter.						
GLX Sedan 4D	PD23B	29255	8400	9625	11700	14800
GLX Wagon 4D	VD23B	30055	8600	9850	11950	15100
Manual Trans			**(500)**	**(500)**	**(665)**	**(665)**
PASSAT 4MOTION AWD—V6—Equipment Schedule 4						
W.B. 106.4"; 2.8 Liter.						
GLS Sedan 4D	TH23B	27050	8725	10000	12100	15250
GLS Wagon 4D	RH23B	27850	8900	10175	12300	15450
GLX Sedan 4D	UH23B	30905	9400	10725	12900	16150
GLX Wagon 4D	WH23B	31705	9750	11100	13300	16600

2001 VOLKSWAGEN — (3orW)VW(BK21J)-1-#

Body Type	VIN	List	Trade-In Fair	Good	Pvt-Party Good	Retail Excellent
GOLF—4-Cyl.—Equipment Schedule 6						
W.B. 98.9"; 2.0 Liter.						
GL Hatchback 2D	BK21J	15425	5500	6425	7925	10250
GLS Hatchback 4D	GK21J	16875	5775	6725	8250	10550
GOLF—4-Cyl. Turbo—Equipment Schedule 6						
W.B. 98.9"; 1.8 Liter.						
GLS Hatchback 4D	GC21J	18425	6200	7200	8775	11150
GOLF—4-Cyl. Turbo Diesel—Equipment Schedule 6						
W.B. 98.9"; 1.9 Liter.						
GL TDI H'Back 4D	BP21J	16720	6950	8025	9675	12150
GLS TDI H'Back 4D	GP21J	17925	7200	8325	9950	12500
GTI—4-Cyl. Turbo—Equipment Schedule 6						
W.B. 98.9"; 1.8 Liter.						
GLS Hatchback 2D	DC21J	19800	7675	8825	10500	13150
GTI—V6—Equipment Schedule 6						
W.B. 98.9"; 2.8 Liter.						
GLX Hatchback 2D	PG21J	23425	8525	9750	11500	14200
NEW BEETLE—4-Cyl.—Equipment Schedule 6						
W.B. 98.7"; 2.0 Liter.						
GL Hatchback 2D	BK21C	16425	5900	6875	8275	10500
GLS Hatchback 2D	CK21C	17375	6175	7175	8625	10850
NEW BEETLE—4-Cyl. Turbo—Equipment Schedule 6						
W.B. 98.7"; 1.8 Liter.						
GLS Hatchback 2D	CD21C	19525	6450	7475	8925	11200
Sport Hatchback 2D	ED21C	21175	6525	7550	9025	11300
GLX Hatchback 2D	DD21C	21700	6725	7750	9250	11550
NEW BEETLE—4-Cyl. Turbo Diesel—Equipment Schedule 6						
W.B. 98.7"; 1.9 Liter.						
GLS TDI H'Back 2D	CP21C	18425	7225	8350	9850	12200
JETTA—4-Cyl.—Equipment Schedule 6						
W.B. 98.9", 99.0" (Wag); 2.0 Liter.						
GL Sedan 4D	RK29M	17225	5950	6900	8475	10800
GLS Sedan 4D	SK29M	18175	6350	7375	8775	11000
GLS Wagon 4D	SK21J	19150	6625	7675	9100	11350
JETTA—4-Cyl. Turbo—Equipment Schedule 6						
W.B. 98.9"; 1.8 Liter.						
GLS Sedan 4D	SD29M	19725	6800	7850	9300	11600
Wolfsburg Edition			100	100	135	135
JETTA—4-Cyl. Turbo Diesel—Equipment Schedule 6						
W.B. 98.9"; 1.9 Liter.						
GL TDI Sedan 4D	RP29M	18520	7925	9125	10550	12950
GLS TDI Sedan 4D	SP29M	19225	8100	9300	10750	13200
JETTA—V6—Equipment Schedule 6						
W.B. 98.9", 99.0" (Wag); 2.8 Liter.						
GLS Sedan 4D	SG29M	20475	8100	9300	10800	13300
GLS Wagon 4D	SG21J	21450	8275	9475	11050	13600
GLX Sedan 4D	TG29M	24825	8225	9425	11300	14150
GLX Wagon 4D	TG21J	25950	8450	9675	11600	14500
CABRIO—4-Cyl. Equipment Schedule 3						
W.B. 97.4"; 2.0 Liter.						
GL Convertible 2D	BC21V	21625	6600	7650	9675	12600
GLS Convertible 2D	CC21V	22000	6975	8050	10150	13150
GLX Convertible 2D	DC21V	23700	7300	8400	10500	13600
Manual Trans			**(275)**	**(275)**	**(365)**	**(365)**
PASSAT—4-Cyl. Turbo—Equipment Schedule 4						
W.B. 106.4"; 1.8 Liter.						
GLS Sedan 4D	AD23B	23050	6825	7875	9800	12650
GLS Wagon 4D	HD23B	23850	7025	8100	10050	12950

Body	Type	VIN	List	Trade-In Fair	Good	Pvt-Party Good	Retail Excellent
Manual Trans		H		(525)	(525)	(700)	(700)
V6 2.8 Liter		H		550	550	735	735

NEW PASSAT—4-Cyl. Turbo—Equipment Schedule 4
W.B. 106.4"; 1.8 Liter.

Body	Type	VIN	List	Fair	Good	Good	Excellent
GLS Sedan 4D		PD23B	23375	7025	8100	10050	12950
GLS Wagon 4D		VD23B	24175	7225	8350	10350	13250
Manual Trans				(525)	(525)	(700)	(700)
V6 2.8 Liter		H		550	550	735	735

PASSAT—V6—Equipment Schedule 4
W.B. 106.4"; 2.8 Liter.

GLX Sedan 4D		BH23B	29810	9650	11000	13200	16450
GLX Wagon 4D		JH23B	30610	9850	11250	13400	16700
Manual Trans				(525)	(525)	(700)	(700)

NEW PASSAT—V6—Equipment Schedule 4
W.B. 106.4"; 2.8 Liter.

GLX Sedan 4D		RD23B	30375	9750	11100	13250	16550
GLX Wagon 4D		WD23B	31175	10000	11350	13600	16900
Manual Trans				(525)	(525)	(700)	(700)

PASSAT 4MOTION AWD—V6—Equipment Schedule 4
W.B. 106.4"; 2.8 Liter.

GLS Sedan 4D		DH23B	27400	10000	11350	13600	16900
GLS Wagon 4D		KH23B	28200	10175	11600	13750	17100
GLX Sedan 4D		EH23B	31560	10725	12225	14450	17850
GLX Wagon 4D		LH23B	32360	11150	12650	14950	18400

NEW PASSAT 4MOTION AWD—V6—Equipment Schedule 4
W.B. 106.4"; 2.8 Liter.

GLS Sedan 4D		SH23B	27625	10000	11350	13600	16900
GLS Wagon 4D		XH23B	28425	10175	11600	13750	17100
GLX Sedan 4D		TH23B	32125	10875	12325	14600	18050
GLX Wagon 4D		YH23B	32925	11200	12700	15000	18500

2002 VOLKSWAGEN—(3,9orW)(BorV)W(BK21J)—2

GOLF—4-Cyl.—Equipment Schedule 6
W.B. 98.9"; 2.0 Liter.

GL Hatchback 2D		BK21J	15600	6300	7300	8900	11350
GL Hatchback 4D		FK21J	15800	6450	7450	9075	11550
GLS Hatchback 4D		GK21J	17150	6600	7625	9275	11750

GOLF—4-Cyl. Turbo Diesel—Equipment Schedule 6
W.B. 98.9"; 1.9 Liter.

GL TDI H'Back 2D		BP21J	16895	7925	9125	10800	13450
GL TDI H'Back 4D		FP21J	17095	8025	9225	10950	13650
GLS TDI H'Back 4D		GP21J	18200	8225	9425	11150	13800

GTI—4-Cyl. Turbo—Equipment Schedule 6
W.B. 98.9"; 1.8 Liter.

Hatchback 2D		DE61J	19460	8725	10000	11750	14500
337 Edition H'Back 2D		DE61J	22775	9350	10675	12450	15300

GTI VR6—V6—Equipment Schedule 6
W.B. 98.9"; 2.8 Liter.

Hatchback 2D		DH61J	20845	9650	11000	12800	15650

NEW BEETLE—4-Cyl.—Equipment Schedule 6
W.B. 98.7"; 2.0 Liter.

GL Hatchback 2D		BK21C	16450	6850	7875	9350	11700
GLS Hatchback 2D		CK21C	17400	7175	8275	9750	12150

NEW BEETLE—4-Cyl. Turbo—Equipment Schedule 6
W.B. 98.7"; 1.8 Liter.

GLS Hatchback 2D		CD21C	19750	7475	8575	10100	12550
Sport Hatchback 2D		ED21C	20800	7525	8650	10200	12550
GLX Hatchback 2D		DD21C	22050	7750	8900	10500	12900
S Hatchback 2D		FE21C	23905	8775	10050	11650	14200

NEW BEETLE—4-Cyl. Turbo Diesel—Equipment Schedule 6
W.B. 98.7"; 1.8 Liter.

GLS TDI H'Back 2D		CP21C	18450	8375	9575	11150	13700

JETTA—4-Cyl.—Equipment Schedule 6
W.B. 98.9", 99.0" (Wag); 2.0 Liter.

GL Sedan 4D		RK69M	17400	6825	7875	9500	12050
GL Wagon 4D		RK61J	18200	7050	8150	9800	12300
GLS Sedan 4D		SK69M	18450	7300	8400	9900	12200
GLS Wagon 4D		SK21J	19250	7575	8700	10200	12550

JETTA—4-Cyl. Turbo—Equipment Schedule 6
W.B. 98.9", 99.0" (Wag); 1.8 Liter.

GLS Sedan 4D		SE69M	20100	7775	8925	10450	12850
GLS Wagon 4D		SE61J	20900	8150	9325	10850	13350

2002 VOLKSWAGEN

Body	Type	VIN	List	Trade-In Fair	Good	Pvt-Party Good	Retail Excellent
JETTA—4-Cyl. Turbo Diesel—Equipment Schedule 6							
W.B. 98.9", 99.0" (Wag); 1.9 Liter.							
GL TDI Sedan 4D		RP69M	18695	9075	10375	11900	14350
GL TDI Wagon 4D		RP69M	19495	9275	10575	12100	14600
GLS TDI Sedan 4D		SP69M	19500	9275	10575	12100	14600
GLS TDI Wagon 4D		SP69M	20300	9400	10725	12200	14750
JETTA—V6—Equipment Schedule 6							
W.B. 98.9", 99.0" (Wag); 2.8 Liter.							
GLS Sedan 4D		SH69M	20750	9250	10525	12150	14700
GLS Wagon 4D		SH61J	21550	9425	10775	12350	15000
GLI Sedan 4D		VH69M	23500	9600	10950	12550	15250
GLX Sedan 4D		TH69M	25250	9350	10675	12650	15650
GLX Wagon 4D		TH61J	26050	9600	10950	12950	16000
CABRIO—4-Cyl.—Equipment Schedule 3							
W.B. 97.4"; 2.0 Liter.							
GL Convertible 2D		BC21V	21025	7525	8650	10800	13900
GLS Convertible 2D		CC21V	22025	7925	9125	11300	14500
GLX Convertible 2D		DC21V	23725	8325	9525	11750	15000
Manual Trans				(300)	(300)	(400)	(400)
PASSAT—4-Cyl. Turbo—Equipment Schedule 4							
W.B. 106.4"; 1.8 Liter.							
GLS Sedan 4D		PD63B	23375	8100	9300	11350	14400
GLS Wagon 4D		VD63B	24175	8375	9575	11650	14750
Manual Trans				(550)	(550)	(735)	(735)
V6 2.8 Liter		H		600	600	800	800
PASSAT—V6—Equipment Schedule 4							
W.B. 106.4"; 2.8 Liter.							
GLX Sedan 4D		RH63B	30375	11100	12600	14900	18350
GLX Wagon 4D		WH63B	31175	11350	12900	15150	18600
Manual Trans				(550)	(550)	(735)	(735)
PASSAT 4MOTION AWD—V6—Equipment Schedule 4							
W.B. 106.4"; 2.8 Liter.							
GLS Sedan 4D		SH63B	27625	11300	12850	15100	18600
GLS Wagon 4D		XH63B	28425	11600	13200	15450	18950
GLX Sedan 4D		TH63B	32125	12375	14025	16350	20000
GLX Wagon 4D		YH63B	32925	12750	14400	16800	20500
PASSAT 4MOTION AWD—W8—Equipment Schedule 4							
W.B. 106.4"; 4.0 Liter.							
Sedan 4D		UH63B	38450	15375	17325	20600	25400
Wagon 4D		ZH63B	39250	15475	17450	20800	25600

2003 VOLKSWAGEN — (3,9orW)(BorV)W(BK21J)-3

Body	Type	VIN	List	Trade-In Fair	Good	Pvt-Party Good	Retail Excellent
GOLF—4-Cyl.—Equipment Schedule 6							
W.B. 98.9"; 2.0 Liter.							
GL Hatchback 2D		BK21J	15870	7175	8275	10000	12650
GL Hatchback 4D		FK21J	16070	7350	8450	10200	12850
GLS Hatchback 4D		GK21J	18095	7500	8600	10400	13050
GOLF—4-Cyl. Turbo Diesel—Equipment Schedule 6							
W.B. 98.9"; 1.9 Liter.							
GL TDI H'Back 2D		BP21J	17295	8975	10275	12100	14950
GL TDI H'Back 4D		FP21J	17495	9125	10425	12250	15150
GLS TDI H'Back 4D		GP21J	19285	9300	10625	12450	15350
GTI—4-Cyl. Turbo—Equipment Schedule 6							
W.B. 98.9"; 1.8 Liter.							
Hatchback 2D		DE61J	19640	9800	11200	13100	16050
20th Anniv H'Back 2D		D61J	23800	11975	13575	14800	17100
GTI VR6—V6—Equipment Schedule 6							
W.B. 98.9"; 2.8 Liter.							
Hatchback 2D		DH61J	22570	10875	12325	14250	17300
NEW BEETLE—4-Cyl.—Equipment Schedule 6							
W.B. 98.7", 98.8" (Conv); 2.0 Liter.							
GL Hatchback 2D		BK21C	16525	7900	9075	10600	13050
GL Convertible 2D		BK21Y	21025	11825	13375	15150	18050
GLS Hatchback 2D		CK21C	18390	8275	9475	11050	13550
GLS Convertible 2D		CK21Y	22425	13050	14750	16550	19600
NEW BEETLE—4-Cyl. Turbo—Equipment Schedule 6							
W.B. 98.7", 98.8" (Conv); 1.8 Liter.							
GL Hatchback 2D		BD21C	19025	8325	9525	11100	13600
GLS Hatchback 2D		CD21C	20430	8600	9850	11450	13950
GLS Convertible 2D		CD21Y	24675	13250	14975	16800	19900
GLX Hatchback 2D		DE21C	22215	8950	10225	11850	14400
GLX Convertible 2D		DD21Y	26125	15025	16925	18850	22100
S Hatchback 2D		FE21C	24115	10050	11400	13050	15750

2003 VOLKSWAGEN

Body	Type	VIN	List	Trade-In Fair	Good	Pvt-Party Good	Retail Excellent
NEW BEETLE—4-Cyl. Turbo Diesel—Equipment Schedule 6							
W.B. 98.7"; 1.9 Liter.							
GL TDI H'Back 2D		BP21C	17770	**9400**	**10725**	**12350**	**15000**
GLS TDI H'Back 2D		CP21C	19570	**9575**	**10925**	**12500**	**15200**
JETTA—4-Cyl.—Equipment Schedule 6							
W.B. 98.9", 99.0" (Wag); 2.0 Liter.							
GL Sedan 4D		RK69M	17675	**7825**	**9000**	**10700**	**13400**
GL Wagon 4D		RK61J	18475	**8100**	**9300**	**11050**	**13750**
GLS Sedan 4D		SK69M	19365	**8375**	**9575**	**11100**	**13600**
GLS Wagon 4D		SK61J	20165	**8650**	**9900**	**11450**	**13950**
JETTA—4-Cyl. Turbo—Equipment Schedule 6							
W.B. 98.9", 99.0" (Wag); 1.8 Liter.							
GL Sedan 4D		RE69M	19325	**8200**	**9375**	**11150**	**13850**
GL Wagon 4D		RE61J	20125	**8550**	**9800**	**11550**	**14300**
Wolfsburg Sedan 4D		PE69M	20075	**8725**	**10000**	**11550**	**14050**
GLS Sedan 4D		SE29M	21015	**8900**	**10175**	**11750**	**14300**
GLS Wagon 4D		SE61J	21815	**9300**	**10625**	**12200**	**14850**
JETTA—4-Cyl. Turbo Diesel—Equipment Schedule 6							
W.B. 98.9", 99.0" (Wag); 1.9 Liter.							
GL TDI Sedan 4D		RP69M	19065	**10325**	**11725**	**13350**	**16000**
GL TDI Wagon 4D		RP61J	19865	**10525**	**11975**	**13550**	**16200**
GLS TDI Sedan 4D		SP69M	20545	**10525**	**11975**	**13550**	**16200**
GLS TDI Wagon 4D		SP61J	21345	**10675**	**12125**	**13700**	**16350**
JETTA—V6—Equipment Schedule 6							
W.B. 98.9"; 2.8 Liter.							
GLI Sedan 4D		VH69M	23525	**10925**	**12375**	**14050**	**16850**
GLX Sedan 4D		TH69M	27515	**10625**	**12075**	**14100**	**17300**
PASSAT—4-Cyl. Turbo—Equipment Schedule 4							
W.B. 106.4"; 1.8 Liter.							
GL Sedan 4D		MD63B	23400	**8400**	**9625**	**11800**	**14950**
GL Wagon 4D		ND63B	24200	**8675**	**9950**	**12100**	**15300**
GLS Sedan 4D		PD63B	24535	**9300**	**10625**	**12800**	**16100**
GLS Wagon 4D		VD63B	27835	**9575**	**10925**	**13100**	**16400**
Manual Trans				**(575)**	**(575)**	**(765)**	**(765)**
V6 2.8 Liter		H		**650**	**650**	**865**	**865**
PASSAT—V6—Equipment Schedule 4							
W.B. 106.4"; 2.8 Liter.							
GLX Sedan 4D		RH63B	30400	**12600**	**14250**	**16650**	**20300**
GLX Wagon 4D		WH63B	31200	**12900**	**14600**	**17000**	**20700**
Manual Trans				**(575)**	**(575)**	**(765)**	**(765)**
PASSAT 4MOTION AWD—V6—Equipment Schedule 4							
W.B. 106.4"; 2.8 Liter.							
GLS Sedan 4D		TH63B	32150	**13975**	**15800**	**18200**	**22000**
GLX Sedan 4D		YH63B	32950	**14400**	**16250**	**18700**	**22600**
PASSAT 4MOTION AWD—W8—Equipment Schedule 4							
W.B. 106.4"; 4.0 Liter.							
Sedan 4D		UK63B	38475	**17275**	**19400**	**22900**	**28000**
Wagon 4D		ZK63B	39275	**17375**	**19500**	**23000**	**28100**

2004 VOLKSWAGEN—(W,3or9)(VorB)W(BK21J)—4—#

Body	Type	VIN	List	Trade-In Fair	Good	Pvt-Party Good	Retail Excellent
GOLF—4-Cyl.—Equipment Schedule 6							
W.B. 98.9"; 2.0 Liter.							
GL Hatchback 2D		BK21J	16155	**8200**	**9375**	**11100**	**13750**
GL Hatchback 4D		FK21J	16355	**8375**	**9575**	**11300**	**13950**
GLS Hatchback 4D		GK21J	18715	**8525**	**9750**	**11500**	**14150**
GOLF—4-Cyl. Turbo Diesel—Equipment Schedule 6							
W.B. 98.9"; 1.9 Liter.							
GL TDI H'Back 4D		FP21J	17775	**10375**	**11775**	**13600**	**16500**
GLS TDI H'Back 4D		GP21J	19895	**10525**	**11975**	**13750**	**16700**
GTI—4-Cyl. Turbo—Equipment Schedule 6							
W.B. 98.9"; 1.8 Liter.							
Hatchback 2D		DE61J	19825	**11050**	**12550**	**14400**	**17400**
GTI VR6—V6—Equipment Schedule 6							
W.B. 98.9"; 2.8 Liter.							
Hatchback 2D		DH61J	22645	**12175**	**13825**	**15700**	**18800**
R32 AWD—V6—Equipment Schedule 3							
W.B. 99.1"; 3.2 Liter.							
Hatchback 2D		KG61J	29675	**21250**	**23850**	**27100**	**32200**
NEW BEETLE—4-Cyl.—Equipment Schedule 6							
W.B. 98.7", 98.8" (Conv); 2.0 Liter.							
GL Hatchback 2D		BK21C	16905	**9075**	**10375**	**11850**	**14800**
GL Convertible 2D		BK21Y	21475	**13350**	**15025**	**16750**	**19700**
GLS Hatchback 2D		CK21C	19095	**9425**	**10775**	**12250**	**14800**

2004 VOLKSWAGEN

Body	Type	VIN	List	Trade-In Fair	Good	Pvt-Party Good	Retail Excellent
GLS Convertible 2D		CK21Y	23215	14650	16550	18300	21300
NEW BEETLE—4-Cyl. Turbo—Equipment Schedule 6							
W.B. 98.7", 98.8 (Conv); 1.8 Liter.							
GLS Hatchback 2D		CD21C	21055	9800	11200	12700	15300
GLS Convertible 2D		CD21Y	25395	14900	16825	18550	21600
S Hatchback 2D		FE21C	24425	11350	12900	14500	17200
NEW BEETLE—4-Cyl. Turbo—Equipment Schedule 6							
W.B. 98.7"; 1.9 Liter.							
GL TDI H'Back 2D		BP21C	18205	10675	12175	13750	16350
GLS TDI H'Back 2D		CP21C	20335	10925	12375	13900	16600
JETTA—4-Cyl.—Equipment Schedule 6							
W.B. 98.9", 99.0" (Wag); 2.0 Liter.							
GL Sedan 4D		RK29M	18005	8975	10275	11950	14600
GL Wagon 4D		RK61J	19005	9275	10575	12250	14950
GLS Sedan 4D		SK29M	20035	9525	10875	12300	14800
GLS Wagon 4D		SK21J	21035	9800	11200	12650	15200
JETTA—4-Cyl. Turbo—Equipment Schedule 6							
W.B. 98.9", 99.0" (Wag); 1.8 Liter.							
GL Sedan 4D		RE29M	19485	9350	10675	12350	15100
GLS Sedan 4D		SE29M	21515	10100	11500	13000	15500
GLS Wagon 4D		SE61J	22515	10575	12025	13550	16100
GLI Sedan 4D		VH69M	24375	12275	13925	15500	18300
JETTA—4-Cyl. Turbo Diesel—Equipment Schedule 6							
W.B. 98.9", 99.0" (Wag); 1.9 Liter.							
GL TDI Sedan 4D		RP29M	19245	11700	13250	14800	17450
GL TDI Wagon 4D		RP21J	20245	11925	13525	15050	17650
GLS TDI Sedan 4D		SP69M	21055	11925	13525	15050	17650
GLS TDI Wagon 4D		SP61J	22055	12075	13675	15200	17850
JETTA—V6—Equipment Schedule 6							
W.B. 98.9"; 2.8 Liter.							
GLI Sedan 4D		VH29M	23785	12275	13925	15500	18300
PASSAT—4-Cyl. Turbo—Equipment Schedule 4							
W.B. 106.4"; 1.8 Liter.							
GL Sedan 4D		MD63B	23430	9700	11050	13200	16450
GL Wagon 4D		ND63B	24430	10050	11400	13600	16900
GLS Sedan 4D		PD63B	25030	10675	12175	14350	17700
GLS Wagon 4D		VD63B	26030	11000	12475	14700	18100
Manual Trans				(600)	(600)	(800)	(800)
PASSAT 4MOTION AWD—4-Cyl. Turbo—Equipment Schedule 4							
W.B. 106.4"; 1.8 Liter.							
GLS Sedan 4D		PD63B	26780	14400	16250	18600	22400
GLS Wagon 4D		VD63B	27780	14850	16775	19150	23000
Manual Trans				(600)	(600)	(800)	(800)
PASSAT—4-Cyl. Turbo Diesel—Equipment Schedule 4							
W.B. 106.4"; 2.0 Liter.							
GL TDI Sedan 4D		ME63B	23635	12900	14600	16900	20500
GL TDI Wagon 4D		NE63B	24635	13625	15375	17750	21400
GLS TDI Sedan 4D		PE63B	25235	14300	16150	18550	22300
GLS TDI Wagon 4D		VE63B	26235	15075	16975	19350	23200
Manual Trans				(600)	(600)	(800)	(800)
PASSAT—V6—Equipment Schedule 4							
W.B. 106.4"; 2.8 Liter.							
GLX Sedan 4D		RH63B	31430	14250	16100	18500	22200
GLX Wagon 4D		WH63B	32430	14550	16450	18850	22700
Manual Trans				(600)	(600)	(800)	(800)
PASSAT 4MOTION AWD—V6—Equipment Schedule 4							
W.B. 106.4"; 2.8 Liter.							
GLX Sedan 4D		TH63B	33180	15775	17800	20200	24200
GLX Wagon 4D		YH63B	34180	16300	18325	20900	24800
PASSAT 4MOTION AWD—W8—Equipment Schedule 4							
W.B. 106.4"; 4.0 Liter.							
Sedan 4D		UK63B	39235	19350	21725	25200	30700
Wagon 4D		ZK63B	40235	19500	21825	25300	30700
Sport Pkg				350	350	465	465
PHAETON AWD—V8—Equipment Schedule 1							
W.B. 118.1"; 4.2 Liter.							
Sedan 4D		AF63D	65215	31925	35600	40600	48500
4-Seater Pkg				900	900	1200	1200
PHAETON AWD—W12—Equipment Schedule 1							
W.B. 118.1"; 6.0 Liter.							
Sedan 4D		AH63D	80515	40650	45200	50600	59500
4-Seater Pkg				900	900	1200	1200

Body	Type	VIN	List	Trade-In Fair	Trade-In Good	Pvt-Party Good	Retail Excellent

2005 VOLKSWAGEN–(W,3or9)(VorB)W(BL61J)–5–#

GOLF—4-Cyl.—Equipment Schedule 6
W.B. 98.9"; 2.0 Liter.

GL Hatchback 2D	BL61J	15830	**9400**	**10725**	**12150**	**14650**
GL Hatchback 4D	FL61J	16030	**9575**	**10925**	**12400**	**14900**
GLS Hatchback 4D	GL61J	18390	**9800**	**11150**	**12600**	**15150**

GOLF—4-Cyl. Turbo Diesel—Equipment Schedule 6
W.B. 98.9"; 1.9 Liter.

GL TDI H'Back 4D	FR61Y	17450	**11775**	**13350**	**14950**	**17700**
GLS TDI H'Back 4D	GR61Y	19580	**11925**	**13525**	**15200**	**17950**

GTI—4-Cyl. Turbo—Equipment Schedule 6
W.B. 98.9"; 1.8 Liter.

Hatchback 2D	DE61Y	19510	**12525**	**14150**	**15800**	**18650**

GTI VR6—V6—Equipment Schedule 6
W.B. 98.9"; 2.8 Liter.

Hatchback 2D	DH61Y	22330	**13675**	**15475**	**17150**	**20200**

NEW BEETLE—4-Cyl.—Equipment Schedule 6
W.B. 98.7", 98.8" (Conv); 2.0 Liter.

GL Hatchback 2D	BK31C	17145	**9850**	**11250**	**12550**	**14900**
GL Convertible 2D	BM31Y	21865	**14450**	**16300**	**17850**	**20700**
GLS Hatchback 2D	CK31C	19345	**10275**	**11700**	**13050**	**15400**
GLS Convertible 2D	CM31Y	23615	**15900**	**17900**	**19600**	**22600**
Bi-Color H'Back 2D	CK31C	21360				
Dark Flint Ed Conv	CM31Y	26405				

NEW BEETLE—4-Cyl. Turbo—Equipment Schedule 6
W.B. 98.7", 98.8" (Conv); 1.8 Liter.

GLS Hatchback 2D	CD31Y	21515	**10675**	**12125**	**13500**	**15900**
GLS Convertible 2D	CD31Y	26025	**16150**	**18200**	**19900**	**22900**

NEW BEETLE—4-Cyl. Turbo Diesel—Equipment Schedule 6
W.B. 98.7"; 1.9 Liter.

GLS TDI H'Back 2D	CR31C	20585	**11875**	**13425**	**14850**	**17300**

JETTA—4-Cyl.—Equipment Schedule 6
W.B. 98.9", 99.0" (Wag); 2.0 Liter.

GL Sedan 4D	RK69M	18255	**9750**	**11100**	**12450**	**15100**
GL Wagon 4D	RL61J	19255	**10050**	**11400**	**12950**	**15500**
GLS Sedan 4D	SK69M	20295	**10275**	**11700**	**13000**	**15300**
GLS Wagon 4D	SL61J	21295	**10625**	**12075**	**13400**	**15700**

JETTA—4-Cyl. Turbo—Equipment Schedule 6
W.B. 98.9", 99.0" (Wag); 1.8 Liter.

GLS Wagon 4D	SE61J	22775	**11400**	**12950**	**14300**	**16750**
GLI Sedan 4D	SE69M	24645	**13300**	**15025**	**16500**	**19150**

JETTA—4-Cyl. Turbo Diesel—Equipment Schedule 6
W.B. 98.9", 99.0" (Wag); 1.9 Liter.

GL TDI Wagon 4D	RR61J	20505	**12900**	**14600**	**15950**	**18500**
GLS TDI Sedan 4D	SR69M	21315	**12900**	**14600**	**15950**	**18500**
GLS TDI Wagon 4D	SR61J	22315	**13050**	**14750**	**16100**	**18650**

NEW JETTA—5-Cyl.—Equipment Schedule 6
W.B. 101.5"; 2.5 Liter.

Value Edition Sed 4D	PF71K	18515				
2.5 Sedan 4D	SF71K	21005				

NEW JETTA—4-Cyl. Turbo Diesel—Equipment Schedule 6
W.B. 101.5"; 1.9 Liter.

TDI Sedan 4D	RT71K	22000				

PASSAT—4-Cyl. Turbo—Equipment Schedule 4
W.B. 106.4"; 1.8 Liter.

GLS Sedan 4D	AD63B	26030	**11825**	**13375**	**15550**	**18950**
GLS Wagon 4D	CD63B	27030	**12125**	**13725**	**15900**	**19300**
Manual Trans			**(625)**	**(625)**	**(835)**	**(835)**

PASSAT 4MOTION AWD—4-Cyl. Turbo—Equipment Schedule 4
W.B. 106.4"; 1.8 Liter.

GLS Sedan 4D	BD63B	27780	**15775**	**17800**	**20100**	**24000**
GLS Wagon 4D	DD63B	28780	**16350**	**18425**	**20900**	**24700**
Manual Trans			**(625)**	**(625)**	**(835)**	**(835)**

PASSAT—4-Cyl. Turbo Diesel—Equipment Schedule 4
W.B. 106.4"; 2.0 Liter.

GL TDI Sedan 4D	ME63B	23935	**14200**	**16000**	**18350**	**22000**
GL TDI Wagon 4D	NE63B	24935	**14975**	**16875**	**19200**	**23000**
GLS TDI Sedan 4D	AE63B	26235	**15775**	**17750**	**20100**	**24000**
GLS TDI Wagon 4D	CE63B	27235	**16550**	**18625**	**21000**	**25000**

PASSAT—V6—Equipment Schedule 4
W.B. 106.4"; 2.8 Liter.

GLX Sedan 4D	RU63B	31440	**15725**	**17700**	**20100**	**24000**

2005 VOLKSWAGEN

Body	Type	VIN	List	Trade-In Fair	Good	Pvt-Party Good	Retail Excellent
GLX Wagon 4D		WU63B	32440	**16050**	**18050**	**20500**	**24300**
Manual Trans				(625)	(625)	(835)	(835)

PASSAT 4MOTION AWD—V6—Equipment Schedule 4
W.B. 106.4"; 2.8 Liter.

GLX Sedan 4D		TU63B	33190	**17375**	**19500**	**21900**	**26000**
GLX Wagon 4D		YU63B	34190	**17800**	**19975**	**22500**	**26700**

PHAETON—V8—Equipment Schedule 1
W.B. 118.1"; 4.2 Liter.

Sedan 4D		AF93D	68865				
4-Seater Pkg							

PHAETON—W12—Equipment Schedule 1
W.B. 118.1"; 6.0 Liter.

Sedan 4D		AH93D	99715				
4-Seater Pkg							

VOLVO

1991 VOLVO — YV1(AA884)–M–#

240—4-Cyl.—Equipment Schedule 3
W.B. 104.3"; 2.3 Liter.

Sedan 4D		AA884	19680	**1375**	**1875**	**3200**	**5050**
Wagon 4D		AA885	20175	**1550**	**2050**	**3475**	**5375**
SE Wagon 4D		AA885	22915	**1600**	**2100**	**3525**	**5425**
Manual Trans				(100)	(100)	(135)	(135)

740—4-Cyl.—Equipment Schedule 3
W.B. 109.1"; 2.3 Liter.

Sedan 4D		FA884	23135	**1225**	**1700**	**3000**	**4800**
Wagon 4D		FA885	23815	**1475**	**1975**	**3350**	**5250**
Manual Trans				(100)	(100)	(135)	(135)

740—4-Cyl. Turbo—Equipment Schedule 3
W.B. 109.1"; 2.3 Liter.

Sedan 4D		FA874	25190	**1425**	**1925**	**3275**	**5150**
Wagon 4D		FA875	25870	**1675**	**2200**	**3625**	**5525**
SE Sedan 4D		FA874	28335	**1525**	**2025**	**3400**	**5275**
SE Wagon 4D		FA875	29015	**1975**	**2525**	**3975**	**5975**
Coupe 2D		HA872	42325	**1225**	**1725**	**3025**	**4825**
Manual Trans				(100)	(100)	(135)	(135)

940—4-Cyl.—Equipment Schedule 1
W.B. 109.1"; 2.3 Liter.

GLE Sedan 4D		JA894	28265	**1375**	**1875**	**3200**	**5050**
GLE Wagon 4D		JA895	28945	**1450**	**1950**	**3325**	**5225**

940—4-Cyl. Turbo—Equipment Schedule 1
W.B. 109.1"; 2.3 Liter.

Sedan 4D		JA874	29675	**1675**	**2200**	**3625**	**5525**
Wagon 4D		JA875	30355	**2100**	**2675**	**4150**	**6200**
SE Sedan 4D		KA874	33330	**2025**	**2600**	**4075**	**6100**
SE Wagon 4D		KA875	34010	**2275**	**2825**	**4375**	**6475**

1992 VOLVO — YV1(AS881)–N–#

240—4-Cyl.—Equipment Schedule 3
W.B. 104.3"; 2.3 Liter.

Sedan 4D		AS881	21215	**1675**	**2175**	**3650**	**5650**
Wagon 4D		AW881	21715	**1900**	**2425**	**3950**	**6050**
GL Sedan 4D		AS881	21890	**1700**	**2225**	**3700**	**5725**
Manual Trans				(100)	(100)	(135)	(135)

740—4-Cyl.—Equipment Schedule 3
W.B. 109.1"; 2.3 Liter.

Sedan 4D		FS881	24680	**1500**	**2000**	**3425**	**5350**
Wagon 4D		FW881	25360	**1800**	**2325**	**3800**	**5875**
GL Wagon 4D		FW881	26070	**1800**	**2325**	**3800**	**5875**

740—4-Cyl. Turbo—Equipment Schedule 3
W.B. 109.1"; 2.3 Liter.

Wagon 4D		FW871	28190	**2025**	**2575**	**4125**	**6225**

940—4-Cyl.—Equipment Schedule 3
W.B. 109.1"; 2.3 Liter.

GL Sedan 4D		JS881	25390	**1675**	**2175**	**3650**	**5650**

940—4-Cyl. Turbo—Equipment Schedule 1
W.B. 109.1"; 2.3 Liter.

Sedan 4D		JS871	31190	**2025**	**2575**	**4125**	**6225**
Wagon 4D		JW871	31870	**2525**	**3125**	**4750**	**6975**

Body	Type	VIN	List	Trade-In Fair	Trade-In Good	Pvt-Party Good	Retail Excellent
960—6-Cyl.—Equipment Schedule 1							
W.B. 109.1"; 3.0 Liter.							
Sedan 4D		KS951	34370	**1350**	**1850**	**3250**	**5200**
Wagon 4D		KW951	35050	**1625**	**2125**	**3625**	**5625**

1993 VOLVO — YV1(AS881)-P-#

240—4-Cyl.—Equipment Schedule 3							
W.B. 104.3"; 2.3 Liter.							
Sedan 4D		AS881	22215	**2050**	**2625**	**4200**	**6350**
Wagon 4D		AW881	23215	**2350**	**2925**	**4575**	**6825**
Manual Trans				**(125)**	**(125)**	**(165)**	**(165)**
850—5-Cyl.—Equipment Schedule 3							
W.B. 104.9"; 2.4 Liter.							
GLT Sedan 4D		LS551	24495	**1350**	**1850**	**3300**	**5250**
Manual Trans				**(125)**	**(125)**	**(165)**	**(165)**
940—4-Cyl.—Equipment Schedule 3							
W.B. 109.1"; 2.3 Liter.							
Sedan 4D		JS881	25390	**1700**	**2225**	**3725**	**5800**
Wagon 4D		JW881	26390	**1900**	**2425**	**3975**	**6075**
940—4-Cyl. Turbo—Equipment Schedule 1							
W.B. 109.1"; 2.3 Liter.							
Sedan 4D		JS871	28890	**2125**	**2725**	**4300**	**6475**
Wagon 4D		JW871	29890	**2725**	**3325**	**5025**	**7325**
960—6-Cyl.—Equipment Schedule 1							
W.B. 109.1"; 2.9 Liter.							
Sedan 4D		KS951	36070	**1700**	**2225**	**3725**	**5800**
Wagon 4D		KW951	37070	**2050**	**2625**	**4200**	**6350**

1994 VOLVO — YV1(LS551)-R-#

850—5-Cyl.—Equipment Schedule 3							
W.B. 104.9"; 2.4 Liter.							
Sedan 4D		LS551	24725	**1675**	**2175**	**3750**	**5925**
Wagon 4D		LW551	28120	**1975**	**2500**	**4125**	**6325**
Manual Trans				**(150)**	**(150)**	**(200)**	**(200)**
850—5-Cyl. Turbo—Equipment Schedule 1							
W.B. 104.9"; 2.3 Liter.							
Sedan 4D		LS571	31900	**2425**	**3025**	**4750**	**7075**
Wagon 4D		LW571	32900	**2775**	**3400**	**5175**	**7575**
940—4-Cyl.—Equipment Schedule 3							
W.B. 109.1"; 2.3 Liter.							
Sedan 4D		JS881	23325	**2025**	**2600**	**4225**	**6450**
Wagon 4D		JW881	24425	**2300**	**2875**	**4575**	**6875**
940—4-Cyl. Turbo—Equipment Schedule 1							
W.B. 109.1"; 2.3 Liter.							
Sedan 4D		JS871	27220	**2575**	**3175**	**4900**	**7250**
Wagon 4D		JW871	28220	**3175**	**3850**	**5675**	**8175**
960—6-Cyl.—Equipment Schedule 1							
W.B. 109.1"; 2.9 Liter.							
Sedan 4D		KS951	33875	**2075**	**2650**	**4300**	**6525**
Wagon 4D		KW951	34875	**2525**	**3125**	**4850**	**7200**

1995 VOLVO — YV1(LS551)-S-#

850—5-Cyl.—Equipment Schedule 3							
W.B. 104.9"; 2.4 Liter.							
Sedan 4D		LS551	25540	**1375**	**1875**	**3500**	**5675**
Wagon 4D		LW551	26840	**1925**	**2450**	**4175**	**6475**
GLT Sedan 4D		LS551	27570	**1850**	**2375**	**4075**	**6350**
GLT Wagon 4D		LW551	28870	**2125**	**2700**	**4450**	**6800**
Manual Trans				**(175)**	**(175)**	**(235)**	**(235)**
850—5-Cyl. Turbo—Equipment Schedule 1							
W.B. 104.9"; 2.3 Liter.							
Sedan 4D		LS571	32000	**2950**	**3625**	**5475**	**8025**
Wagon 4D		LW571	33300	**3325**	**4025**	**5950**	**8550**
T-5 R Sedan 4D		LS581	36005	**3650**	**4375**	**6325**	**9025**
T-5 R Wagon 4D		LW581	37555	**4000**	**4750**	**6800**	**9575**
940—4-Cyl.—Equipment Schedule 3							
W.B. 109.1"; 2.3 Liter.							
Sedan 4D		JS831	24315	**2425**	**3025**	**4825**	**7250**
Wagon 4D		JW831	25615	**2800**	**3425**	**5250**	**7775**
GL Sedan 4D		JS831	25295	**2425**	**3025**	**4825**	**7250**
940—4-Cyl. Turbo—Equipment Schedule 1							
W.B. 109.1"; 2.3 Liter.							

1995 VOLVO

Body Type	VIN	List	Trade-In Fair	Trade-In Good	Pvt-Party Good	Retail Excellent
Sedan 4D	JS861	24820	3025	3700	5575	8150
Wagon 4D	JS861	26120	3725	4450	6425	9150
960—6-Cyl.—Equipment Schedule 1						
W.B. 109.1"; 2.9 Liter.						
Sedan 4D	KS961	30360	2525	3125	4925	7375
Wagon 4D	KW961	31660	3025	3700	5575	8150

1996 VOLVO — YV1(LS554)–T–#

Body Type	VIN	List	Trade-In Fair	Trade-In Good	Pvt-Party Good	Retail Excellent
850—5-Cyl.—Equipment Schedule 3						
W.B. 104.9"; 2.4 Liter.						
Sedan 4D	LS554	26620	1800	2325	4125	6500
Wagon 4D	LW554	27920	2375	2950	4850	7375
GLT Sedan 4D	LS554	29695	2275	2850	4725	7225
GLT Wagon 4D	LW554	30995	2650	3275	5200	7750
Manual Trans			(200)	(200)	(265)	(265)
850—5-Cyl. Turbo—Equipment Schedule 1						
W.B. 104.9"; 2.3 Liter.						
Sedan 4D	LS572	33145	3600	4300	6350	9125
Wagon 4D	LW572	34445	4000	4750	6850	9700
TLA Sedan 4D	LS572	37380	4350	5125	7250	10200
TLA Wagon 4D	LW572	38830	4700	5550	7725	10750
R Sedan 4D	LS572	38420	4775	5600	7825	10850
R Wagon 4D	LW572	39870	5250	6125	8425	11550
960—6-Cyl.—Equipment Schedule 1						
W.B. 109.1"; 2.9 Liter.						
Sedan 4D	KS960	34455	3050	3725	5675	8350
Wagon 4D	KW960	35755	3650	4400	6450	9250

1997 VOLVO — YV1(LS555)–V–#

Body Type	VIN	List	Trade-In Fair	Trade-In Good	Pvt-Party Good	Retail Excellent
850—5-Cyl.—Equipment Schedule 3						
W.B. 104.9"; 2.4 Liter.						
Sedan 4D	LS555	28180	2300	2875	4875	7500
Wagon 4D	LW555	29480	2925	3600	5650	8400
Manual Trans			(200)	(200)	(265)	(265)
850—5-Cyl. Turbo—Equipment Schedule 1						
W.B. 104.9"; 2.3 Liter, 2.4 Liter.						
GLT Sedan 4D	LS564	33525	3875	4625	6775	9700
GLT Wagon 4D	LW564	34825	4125	4900	7100	10100
T-5 Sedan 4D	LS572	36190	4325	5125	7350	10400
T-5 Wagon 4D	LW572	37490	4775	5600	7875	11000
R Sedan 4D	LS582	39180	5100	6000	8300	11500
R Wagon 4D	LW582	40630	5525	6450	8800	12100
960—6-Cyl.—Equipment Schedule 1						
W.B. 109.1"; 2.9 Liter.						
Sedan 4D	KS960	34795	3700	4450	6575	9475
Wagon 4D	KW960	36345	4400	5200	7425	10500
90 SERIES—6-Cyl.—Equipment Schedule 1						
W.B. 109.1"; 2.9 Liter.						
S90 Sedan 4D	KS960	34875	3950	4700	6875	9850
V90 Wagon 4D	KW960	36425	4725	5575	7850	10950

1998 VOLVO — YV1(LS553)–W–#

Body Type	VIN	List	Trade-In Fair	Trade-In Good	Pvt-Party Good	Retail Excellent
70 SERIES—5-Cyl.—Equipment Schedule 3						
W.B. 104.9"; 2.4 Liter.						
S70 Sedan 4D	LS553	28535	2975	3650	5425	7875
V70 Wagon 4D	LW553	29835	3650	4375	6250	8850
Manual Trans	4		(200)	(200)	(265)	(265)
70 SERIES—5-Cyl. Turbo—Equipment Schedule 1						
W.B. 104.9", 104.5" (AWD); 2.3 Liter, 2.4 Liter.						
C70 Coupe 2D	NK537	40545	6825	7875	10100	13300
C70 Convertible 2D	NC567	43570	7900	9075	11400	14800
S70 GLT Sedan 4D	LS564	33015	4550	5375	7350	10100
V70 GLT Wagon 4D	LW564	34315	5075	5950	7950	10800
S70 T-5 Sedan 4D	LS534	35560	5175	6050	8100	10950
V70 T-5 Wagon 4D	LW534	36860	5700	6625	8725	11700
V70 AWD Wagon 4D	LW564	36195	6275	7275	9425	12500
V70 XC AWD Wagon 4D	LZ564	38195	6525	7550	9750	12850
V70 R AWD Wagon 4D	LW524	41570	7600	8725	11050	14400
90 SERIES—6-Cyl.—Equipment Schedule 1						
W.B. 109.1"; 2.9 Liter.						
S90 Sedan 4D	KS960	34875	4750	5575	8000	11250
V90 Wagon 4D	KW960	36425	5575	6500	9000	12400

Body	Type	VIN	List	Trade-In Fair	Good	Pvt-Party Good	Retail Excellent

1999 VOLVO — YV1(LS55A)-X-#

70 SERIES—5-Cyl.—Equipment Schedule 3
W.B. 104.9"; 2.4 Liter.

S70 Sedan 4D		LS55A	28935	3700	4450	6325	8925
V70 Wagon 4D		LW55A	30235	4450	5250	7175	9900
Manual Trans		4		(200)	(200)	(265)	(265)

70 SERIES—5-Cyl. Turbo—Equipment Schedule 1
W.B. 104.5", 104.8" (XC), 104.9" (C70, S70/V70 GLT & T-5); 2.3 Liter, 2.4 Liter.

C70 LT Coupe 2D		NK56D	37570	6200	7200	9300	12300
C70 HT Coupe 2D		NK56D	40945	7900	9075	11350	14650
C70 Convertible 2D		NC56D	43970	9125	10425	12800	16300
S70 GLT Sedan 4D		LS56A	35105	5400	6325	8375	11250
V70 GLT Wagon 4D		LW56A	36405	6075	7025	9150	12150
S70 T-5 Sedan 4D		LS53A	37155	6100	7075	9200	12150
V70 T-5 Wagon 4D		LW53A	38455	6725	7750	9950	13050
S70 AWD Sedan 4D		LT56A	36985	6700	7725	9900	13000
V70 AWD Wagon 4D		LV56A	38285	7300	8400	10600	13800
V70 XC AWD Wag 4D		LZ56A	39460	7550	8675	10900	14150
V70 R AWD Wagon 4D		LV52A	41970	8725	10000	12300	15750

80 SERIES—6-Cyl.—Equipment Schedule 1
W.B. 109.9"; 2.9 Liter.

S80 2.9 Sedan 4D		TS97D	38790	6200	7200	9300	12300

80 SERIES—6-Cyl. Turbo—Equipment Schedule 1
W.B. 109.9"; 2.8 Liter.

S80 T-6 Sedan 4D		TS90D	43755	8075	9275	11550	14850

2000 VOLVO — YV1(VS252)-Y-#

40 SERIES—4-Cyl. Turbo—Equipment Schedule 3
W.B. 100.3"; 1.9 Liter.

S40 Sedan 4D		VS252	23475	5225	6075	7600	9850
V40 Wagon 4D		VW252	24475	6125	7125	8700	11100

70 SERIES—5-Cyl.—Equipment Schedule 3
W.B. 104.9"; 2.4 Liter.

S70 Sedan 4D		LS61J	29075	4550	5375	7475	10400
S70 SE Sedan 4D		LS61J	30075	4700	5550	7675	10550
V70 Wagon 4D		LW61J	30375	5400	6300	8475	11500
V70 SE Wagon 4D		LW61J	31575	5550	6475	8625	11700
Manual Trans		4		(225)	(225)	(300)	(300)

70 SERIES—5-Cyl. Turbo—Equipment Schedule 1
W.B. 104.5", 104.9" (C70, S70 & V70 ex. AWD); 2.3 Liter, 2.4 Liter.

C70 LT Coupe 2D		NK56D	36475	7575	8700	11050	14400
C70 LT Convertible 2D		NC56D	45675	10825	12275	14900	18750
C70 HT Coupe 2D		NK53D	40575	9350	10675	13200	16850
C70 HT Conv 2D		NC53D	47075	11650	13200	15900	19900
S70 GLT Sedan 4D		LS56D	34675	6575	7600	9850	13050
S70 GLT SE Sedan 4D		LS56D	33075	6825	7875	10150	13400
V70 GLT Wagon 4D		LW56D	35975	7300	8400	10700	14050
S70 T-5 Sedan 4D		LS53D	37275	7325	8425	10750	14050
S70 AWD Sedan 4D		LT56D	36575	7975	9175	11550	14950
V70 XC AWD Wag 4D		LZ56D	39575	8950	10225	12650	16250
V70 XC AWD SE Wag		LZ56D	37575	9250	10525	13050	16650
V70 R AWD Wagon 4D		LV60D	42075	10275	11700	14250	18050

80 SERIES—6-Cyl.—Equipment Schedule 1
W.B. 109.9"; 2.9 Liter.

S80 2.9 Sedan 4D		TS94D	37775	7575	8700	11000	14350

80 SERIES—6-Cyl. Turbo—Equipment Schedule 1
W.B. 109.9"; 2.8 Liter.

S80 T-6 Sedan 4D		TS90D	42275	9700	11050	13550	17200

2001 VOLVO — YV1(VS295)-1-#

40 SERIES—4-Cyl. Turbo—Equipment Schedule 3
W.B. 100.9"; 1.9 Liter.

S40 Sedan 4D		VS295	24075	6150	7150	8800	11300
S40 SE Sedan 4D		VS295	28025	7275	8375	10150	12750
V40 Wagon 4D		VW295	25075	7225	8350	10050	12650
V40 SE Wagon 4D		VW295	29025	8100	9300	11050	13800

60 SERIES—5-Cyl.—Equipment Schedule 3
W.B. 106.9"; 2.4 Liter.

S60 2.4 Sedan 4D		RS61N	27075	7725	8875	10800	13700

60 SERIES—5-Cyl. Turbo—Equipment Schedule 3
W.B. 106.9"; 2.3 Liter, 2.4 Liter.

2001 VOLVO

Body	Type	VIN	List	Trade-In Fair	Good	Pvt-Party Good	Retail Excellent
S60 2.4T Sedan 4D		RS58D	30375	9025	10325	12300	15350
S60 T5 Sedan 4D		RS53D	32375	10175	11600	13700	16950

70 SERIES—5-Cyl.—Equipment Schedule 3
W.B. 108.5"; 2.4 Liter.

| V70 Wagon 4D | | SW61N | 30075 | 8225 | 9425 | 12000 | 15600 |

70 SERIES—5-Cyl. Turbo—Equipment Schedule 1
W.B. 104.9", 108.5" (V70 ex XC), 108.8" (XC); 2.3 Liter, 2.4 Liter.

C70 LT Convertible 2D		NC56D	44075	12750	14400	17200	21400
C70 HT Coupe 2D		NK53D	38475	11000	12525	15250	19200
C70 HT Conv 2D		NC53D	47075	13675	15425	18350	22700
V70 2.4T Wagon 4D		SW58D	35375	9600	10950	13600	17400
V70 T5 Wagon 4D		SW53D	36675	10225	11650	14300	18200
V70 XC AWD Wag 4D		SZ58D	37975	11725	13300	16100	20200

80 SERIES—6-Cyl.—Equipment Schedule 1
W.B. 109.9"; 2.9 Liter.

| S80 2.9 Sedan 4D | | TS94D | 38675 | 9150 | 10425 | 13000 | 16650 |

80 SERIES—6-Cyl. Turbo—Equipment Schedule 1
W.B. 109.9"; 2.8 Liter.

| S80 T-6A Sedan 4D | | TS90D | 42675 | 11550 | 13100 | 15750 | 19800 |
| S80 T-6 Executive 4D | | TS90D | 48075 | 12550 | 14200 | 17000 | 21100 |

2002 VOLVO — YV1(VS295)-2-#

40 SERIES—4-Cyl. Turbo—Equipment Schedule 3
W.B. 100.9"; 1.9 Liter.

| S40 Sedan 4D | | VS295 | 24525 | 7400 | 8500 | 10400 | 13150 |
| V40 Wagon 4D | | VW295 | 25525 | 8600 | 9850 | 11800 | 14700 |

60 SERIES—5-Cyl.—Equipment Schedule 3
W.B. 106.9"; 2.4 Liter.

| S60 2.4 Sedan 4D | | RS61N | 27750 | 9350 | 10675 | 12750 | 15950 |

60 SERIES—5-Cyl. Turbo—Equipment Schedule 1
W.B. 106.9"; 2.3 Liter, 2.4 Liter.

S60 2.4T Sedan 4D		RS58D	32250	10875	12325	14550	17900
S60 T5 Sedan 4D		RS53D	34650	12075	13675	15950	19500
S60 2.4T AWD Sed 4D		RH58D	34000	11500	13050	15250	18650

70 SERIES—5-Cyl.—Equipment Schedule 3
W.B. 108.5"; 2.4 Liter.

| V70 Wagon 4D | | SW61N | 30650 | 9900 | 11300 | 14050 | 18100 |

70 SERIES—5-Cyl. Turbo—Equipment Schedule 1
W.B. 104.9", 108.5" (V70 ex XC), 108.8" (XC); 2.3 Liter, 2.4 Liter.

C70 LT Convertible 2D		NC56D	44750	14900	16825	20000	24600
C70 HT Coupe 2D		NK53D	38150	12950	14650	17650	22100
C70 HT Conv 2D		NC53D	46750	15900	17900	21000	25900
V70 2.4T Wagon 4D		SW58D	36150	11400	12950	15850	20100
V70 2.4T AWD Wag 4D		SJ58D	37900	12750	14450	17450	21900
V70 T5 Wagon 4D		SW53D	38350	12175	13775	16750	21000
V70 XC AWD Wag 4D		SZ58D	38425	13675	15475	18500	23000

80 SERIES—6-Cyl.—Equipment Schedule 1
W.B. 109.9"; 2.9 Liter.

| S80 2.9 Sedan 4D | | TS94D | 38775 | 11000 | 12525 | 15300 | 19350 |

80 SERIES—6-Cyl. Turbo—Equipment Schedule 1
W.B. 109.9"; 2.9 Liter.

| S80 T-6 Sedan 4D | | TS90D | 42775 | 13675 | 15425 | 18400 | 22800 |
| S80 T-6 Executive 4D | | TS90D | 50575 | 14850 | 16725 | 19700 | 24300 |

2003 VOLVO — YV1(VS275)-3-#

40 SERIES—4-Cyl. Turbo—Equipment Schedule 3
W.B. 100.9"; 1.9 Liter.

| S40 Sedan 4D | | VS275 | 24560 | 8950 | 10225 | 12300 | 15450 |
| V40 Wagon 4D | | VW275 | 25560 | 10225 | 11650 | 13800 | 17100 |

60 SERIES—5-Cyl.—Equipment Schedule 3
W.B. 107.0"; 2.4 Liter.

| S60 2.4 Sedan 4D | | RS61T | 28030 | 11250 | 12750 | 15100 | 18600 |

60 SERIES—5-Cyl. Turbo—Equipment Schedule 3
W.B. 107.0"; 2.3 Liter, 2.4 Liter, 2.5 Liter.

S60 2.4T Sedan 4D		RS58D	31085	12950	14650	17050	20900
S60 2.5T AWD Sed 4D		RH59H	32835	13675	15425	17900	21700
S60 T5 Sedan 4D		RS53D	34685	14250	16050	18600	22500

70 SERIES—5-Cyl.—Equipment Schedule 1
W.B. 108.5"; 2.4 Liter.

| V70 Wagon 4D | | SW61T | 29530 | 11875 | 13425 | 16550 | 21000 |

70 SERIES—5-Cyl. Turbo—Equipment Schedule 1
W.B. 104.9", 108.5" (V70), 108.8" (XC70); 2.3 Liter, 2.4 Liter, 2.5 Liter.

Body Type	VIN	List	Trade-In Fair	Trade-In Good	Pvt-Party Good	Retail Excellent
C70 LT Convertible 2D	NC63D	44785	17450	19600	23000	28100
C70 HT Conv 2D	NC62D	47785	18525	20850	24300	29500
V70 2.4T Wagon 4D	SW58D	31530	13525	15275	18450	23100
V70 2.5T AWD Wag 4D	SJ58H	33280	15025	16925	20300	25100
V70 T5 Wagon 4D	SW53D	35730	14400	16250	19500	24300
XC70 AWD Wagon 4D	SZ59H	34530	16000	18000	21300	26300
80 SERIES—6-Cyl.—Equipment Schedule 1						
W.B. 109.9"; 2.9 Liter.						
S80 2.9 Sedan 4D	TS92D	39110	13150	14900	17950	22500
80 SERIES—6-Cyl. Turbo—Equipment Schedule 1						
W.B. 109.9"; 2.9 Liter.						
S80 T6 Sedan 4D	TS91D	44595	16050	18050	21300	26200
S80 T6 Elite Sedan 4D	TS91Z	48880	17225	19400	22700	27700

2004 VOLVO — YV1(VS275)-4-#

Body Type	VIN	List	Trade-In Fair	Trade-In Good	Pvt-Party Good	Retail Excellent
40 SERIES—4-Cyl. Turbo—Equipment Schedule 3						
W.B. 101.0"; 1.9 Liter.						
S40 Sedan 4D	VS275	25385	10950	12425	14750	18300
S40 LSE Sedan 4D	VS275	29530	12175	13825	16200	19900
V40 Wagon 4D	VW275	26385	12375	14025	16400	20100
V40 LSE Wagon 4D	VW275	30530	13575	15325	17800	21600
40 SERIES—5-Cyl.—Equipment Schedule 3						
W.B. 103.9"; 2.4 Liter.						
S40 2.4i Sedan 4D	MS382	27170	12475	14125	16500	20200
40 SERIES—5-Cyl. Turbo—Equipment Schedule 3						
W.B. 103.9"; 2.5 Liter.						
S40 T5 Sedan 4D	MS682	29970	13875	15675	18150	22000
60 SERIES—5-Cyl.—Equipment Schedule 3						
W.B. 106.9" 2.4 Liter.						
S60 2.4 Sedan 4D	RS61T	28645	13575	15325	17950	21900
60 SERIES—5-Cyl. Turbo—Equipment Schedule 3						
W.B. 106.9", 107.6" (R); 2.3 Liter, 2.5 Liter.						
S60 2.5T Sedan 4D	RS59V	30295	15475	17450	20200	24300
S60 2.5T AWD Sed 4D	RH59H	32070	16300	18325	21000	25400
S60 T5 Sedan 4D	RS53D	35170	16775	18875	21600	26000
S60 R AWD Sedan 4D	RH52Y	39185	19200	21525	24400	29000
70 SERIES—5-Cyl.—Equipment Schedule 3						
W.B. 108.5"; 2.4 Liter.						
V70 Wagon 4D	SW61T	30145	14250	16050	19500	24500
70 SERIES—5-Cyl. Turbo—Equipment Schedule 1						
W.B. 104.9" (V70), 108.8" (XC70); 2.3 Liter, 2.4 Liter, 2.5 Liter.						
C70 LT Convertible 2D	NC63D	40565	20375	22900	26600	32200
C70 HT Conv 2D	NC62D	43565	21525	24150	27900	33800
V70 2.5T Wagon 4D	SW59V	35070	16050	18100	21600	26900
V70 2.5T AWD Wag 4D	SJ59H	36895	17700	19875	23500	28900
V70 T5 Wagon 4D	SW53D	38145	17125	19250	22800	28100
V70 R AWD Wagon 4D	SJ52Y	40635	19350	21725	25400	30900
XC70 AWD Wagon 4D	SZ59H	38145	18725	21050	24600	30100
80 SERIES—6-Cyl.—Equipment Schedule 1						
W.B. 109.9"; 2.9 Liter.						
S80 2.9 Sedan 4D	TS92D	39725	15775	17800	21100	26200
80 SERIES—5-Cyl. Turbo—Equipment Schedule 1						
W.B. 109.9"; 2.5 Liter.						
S80 2.5T Sedan 4D	TR59V	38630	16350	18425	21800	27000
S80 2.5T AWD Sed 4D	TH59H	40380	17225	19350	22800	27900
80 SERIES—6-Cyl. Twin Turbo—Equipment Schedule 1						
W.B. 109.9"; 2.9 Liter.						
S80 T6 Sedan 4D	TS91Z	45210	18975	21250	24800	30200
S80 T6 Premier Sed 4D	TS91Z	49200	21250	23775	27400	33000

2005 VOLVO — YV1(MS382)-5-#

Body Type	VIN	List	Trade-In Fair	Trade-In Good	Pvt-Party Good	Retail Excellent
40 SERIES—5-Cyl.—Equipment Schedule 3						
W.B. 103.9"; 2.4 Liter.						
S40 2.4i Sedan 4D	MS382	25145	14550	16450	19200	23500
40 SERIES—5-Cyl. Turbo—Equipment Schedule 3						
W.B. 103.9"; 2.5 Liter.						
S40 T5 Sedan 4D	MS682	27945	16150	18200	21100	25400
S40 T5 AWD Sedan 4D	MH682	29595	16925	19050	21800	26300
50 SERIES—5-Cyl.—Equipment Schedule 3						
W.B. 103.9"; 2.4 Liter.						
2.4i Sport Wagon 4D	MW382	28640	15075	16975	19600	23800
50 SERIES—5-Cyl. Turbo—Equipment Schedule 3						
W.B. 103.9"; 2.5 Liter.						

0106

Body Type	VIN	List	Trade-In Fair	Good	Pvt-Party Good	Retail Excellent
T5 Sport Wagon 4D	MW682	30159	17375	19500	22200	26500
T5 AWD Sport Wag 4D	MJ682	31809	18200	20475	23200	27600
60 SERIES—5-Cyl.—Equipment Schedule 3						
W.B. 106.9"; 2.4 Liter.						
S60 2.4 Sedan 4D	RS612	28920	15950	17950	20900	25300
60 SERIES—5-Cyl. Turbo—Equipment Schedule 3						
W.B. 106.9"; 2.5 Liter.						
S60 2.5T Sedan 4D	RS592	30420	18150	20375	23300	27900
S60 2.5T AWD Sed 4D	RH592	32070	18975	21250	24300	29000
S60 T5 Sedan 4D	RS547	35170	19500	21825	24800	29600
S60 R AWD Sedan 4D	RH527	37935	22025	24725	27700	32800
70 SERIES—5-Cyl.—Equipment Schedule 3						
W.B. 108.5"; 2.4 Liter.						
V70 Wagon 4D	SW612	30445	16675	18775	22500	28000
70 SERIES—5-Cyl. Turbo—Equipment Schedule 1						
W.B. 108.5"; 2.5 Liter.						
V70 2.5T Wagon 4D	SW592	36895	18725	21050	24800	30600
V70 T5 Wagon 4D	SW547	39345	19875	22300	26100	31900
V70 R AWD Wagon 4D	SJ527	40635	22225	24825	28800	34800
XC70 AWD Wagon 4D	SZ592	38145	21425	24050	27900	33900
80 SERIES—5-Cyl.—Equipment Schedule 1						
W.B. 109.9"; 2.5 Liter.						
S80 2.5T Sedan 4D	TS592	39185	19100	21425	25100	30700
S80 2.5T AWD Sed 4D	TH592	40835	19975	22400	26100	31700
80 SERIES—6-Cyl. Twin Turbo—Equipment Schedule 1						
W.B. 109.9"; 2.9 Liter.						
S80 T6 Sedan 4D	TS911	45210	21825	24550	28300	34100
S80 T6 Premier Sed 4D	TR911	49200	24250	27150	31000	37100

Body	Type	VIN	List	Trade-In Fair	Good	Pvt-Party Good	Retail Excellent

TRUCKS & VANS

Truck & Van Section

ACURA

1996 ACURA — JAE(DJ58V)-T-#

SLX 4WD—V6—Truck Equipment Schedule T3
| Sport Utility 4D | DJ58V | 38420 | 3225 | 3900 | 5450 | 7650 |

1997 ACURA — JAE(DJ58V)-V-#

SLX 4WD—V6—Truck Equipment Schedule T3
| Sport Utility 4D | DJ58V | 38735 | 3750 | 4475 | 6125 | 8475 |

1998 ACURA — JAE(DJ58X)-W-#

SLX 4WD—V6—Truck Equipment Schedule T3
| Sport Utility 4D | DJ58X | 36735 | 4400 | 5200 | 6925 | 9400 |

1999 ACURA — JAE(DJ58X)-X-#

SLX 4WD—V6—Truck Equipment Schedule T3
| Sport Utility 4D | DJ58X | 36755 | 5250 | 6100 | 7725 | 10150 |

2000 ACURA — No Production

2001 ACURA — 2HN(YD182)-1-#

MDX 4WD—V6—Truck Equipment Schedule T3
| Sport Utility 4D | YD182 | 34850 | 14650 | 16550 | 19200 | 23400 |
| Touring Spt Util 4D | YD186 | 37450 | 15900 | 17900 | 20700 | 25000 |

2002 ACURA — 2HN(YD182)-2-#

MDX 4WD—V6—Truck Equipment Schedule T3
| Sport Utility 4D | YD182 | 35180 | 16625 | 18725 | 21400 | 25800 |
| Touring Spt Util 4D | YD186 | 37780 | 17950 | 20175 | 23000 | 27500 |

2003 ACURA — 2HN(YD182)-3-#

MDX 4WD—V6—Truck Equipment Schedule T3
| Sport Utility 4D | YD182 | 36200 | 18875 | 21150 | 24100 | 28700 |
| Touring Spt Util 4D | YD186 | 38800 | 20375 | 22900 | 25800 | 30700 |

2004 ACURA — 2NH(YD182)-4-#

MDX 4WD—V6—Truck Equipment Schedule T3
| Sport Utility 4D | YD182 | 36945 | 21525 | 24150 | 27100 | 31900 |
| Touring Spt Util 4D | YD186 | 39545 | 23075 | 25900 | 28900 | 33900 |

2005 ACURA — 2HN(YD182)-5-#

MDX 4WD—V6—Truck Equipment Schedule T3
| Sport Utility 4D | YD182 | 37270 | 24250 | 27150 | 30200 | 35300 |
| Touring Spt Util 4D | YD186 | 40095 | 26000 | 29100 | 32200 | 37400 |

BMW

2000 BMW — WBA(FB335)-Y-#

X5 AWD—V8—Truck Equipment Schedule T3
| 4.4i Sport Utility 4D | FB335 | 49970 | 18375 | 20650 | 23700 | 28500 |
| Sport Pkg | | | 250 | 250 | 335 | 335 |

2001 BMW — WBA(FA535)-1-#

X5 AWD—6-Cyl.—Truck Equipment Schedule T3
| 3.0i Sport Utility 4D | FA535 | 42195 | 18150 | 20375 | 23300 | 27900 |
| Sport Pkg | | | 275 | 275 | 365 | 365 |

X5 AWD—V8—Truck Equipment Schedule T3
| 4.4i Sport Utility 4D | FB335 | 49970 | 21150 | 23675 | 26900 | 31900 |
| Sport Pkg | | | 275 | 275 | 365 | 365 |

Body	Type	VIN	List	Trade-In Fair	Good	Pvt-Party Good	Retail Excellent

2002 BMW — 5UX(FA535)-2-#

X5 AWD—6-Cyl.—Truck Equipment Schedule T3
| 3.0i Sport Utility 4D | FA535 | 42270 | 20650 | 23175 | 26300 | 31300 |
| Sport Pkg | | | 300 | 300 | 400 | 400 |

X5 AWD—V8—Truck Equipment Schedule T3
4.4i Sport Utility 4D	FB335	50045	24050	26875	30300	35700
4.6is Sport Utility 4D	FB935	66845	32000	35700	39500	46000
Sport Pkg			300	300	400	400

2003 BMW — 5UX(FA535)-3-#

X5 AWD—6-Cyl.—Truck Equipment Schedule T3
| 3.0i Sport Utility 4D | FA535 | 42920 | 23675 | 26475 | 29700 | 35000 |
| Sport Pkg | | | 325 | 325 | 435 | 435 |

X5 AWD—V8—Truck Equipment Schedule T3
4.4i Sport Utility 4D	FB335	50645	27250	30450	34000	39700
4.6is Sport Utility 4D	FB935	67495	35975	40050	43900	50700
Sport Pkg			325	325	435	435

2004 BMW — WBXor5UX(PA734)-4-#

X3 AWD—6-Cyl.—Truck Equipment Schedule T3
2.5i Sport Utility 4D	PA734	33740	18875	21150	24500	29800
3.0i Sport Utility 4D	PA934	38270	22400	25025	28600	34200
Sport Pkg			350	350	465	465
Premium Pkg			1000	1000	1335	1335

X5 AWD—6-Cyl.—Truck Equipment Schedule T3
| 3.0i Sport Utility 4D | FA135 | 40995 | 26875 | 30075 | 33400 | 38900 |
| Sport Pkg | | | 350 | 350 | 465 | 465 |

X5 AWD—V8—Truck Equipment Schedule T3
4.4i Sport Utility 4D	FB535	52195	30850	34425	37900	43900
4.8is Sport Utility 4D	FA935	70495	41800	46550	50400	57600
Sport Pkg			350	350	465	465

2005 BMW — WBXor5UX(PA734)-5-#

X3 AWD—6-Cyl.—Truck Equipment Schedule T3
2.5i Sport Utility 4D	PA734	34715	21625	24250	27800	33400
3.0i Sport Utility 4D	PA934	38445	25425	28425	32100	38000
Sport Pkg			375	375	500	500
Premium Pkg			1000	1000	1335	1335

X5 AWD—6-Cyl.—Truck Equipment Schedule T3
| 3.0i Sport Utility 4D | FA135 | 45120 | 30275 | 33850 | 37200 | 43200 |
| Sport Pkg | | | 375 | 375 | 500 | 500 |

X5 AWD—V8—Truck Equipment Schedule T3
4.4i Sport Utility 4D	FB535	53495				
4.8is Sport Utility 4D	FA935	70795				
Sport Pkg						

BUICK

2002 BUICK — 3G5-(A03E)-2-#

RENDEZVOUS—V6—Truck Equipment Schedule T3
| CX Sport Utility 4D | A03E | 26279 | 7325 | 8425 | 10250 | 13000 |
| AWD | B | | 825 | 825 | 1100 | 1100 |

RENDEZVOUS AWD—V6—Truck Equipment Schedule T3
| CXL Sport Utility 4D | B03E | 31502 | 8325 | 9525 | 11450 | 14300 |

2003 BUICK — 3G5-(A03E)-3-#

RENDEZVOUS—V6—Truck Equipment Schedule T3
CX Sport Utility 4D	A03E	26975	8825	10100	12050	15000
CXL Sport Utility 4D	B03E	30200	9900	11300	13300	16350
AWD	B		900	900	1200	1200

2004 BUICK — (3G5or5GA)-(A03E)-4-#

RENDEZVOUS—V6—Truck Equipment Schedule T3
CX Sport Utility 4D	A03E	26545	10675	12125	14050	17100
CXL Sport Utility 4D	A03E	26545	11875	13425	15450	18650
AWD	B		975	975	1300	1300
V6 3.6 Liter	7		400	400	535	535

TRUCKS & VANS

Body Type	VIN	List	Trade-In Fair	Good	Pvt-Party Good	Retail Excellent
RENDEZVOUS AWD—V6—Truck Equipment Schedule T3						
Ultra Sport Utility 4D	B037	39695	**13300**	**15025**	**17050**	**20500**
RAINIER AWD—6-Cyl.—Truck Equipment Schedule T1						
CXL Sport Utility 4D	T13S	37895	**13625**	**15375**	**17500**	**21000**
2WD	S		**(1500)**	**(1500)**	**(2000)**	**(2000)**
V8 5.3 Liter	P		**400**	**400**	**535**	**535**

2005 BUICK — (3G5or5GA)-(V23L)-5-#

TERRAZA—V6—Truck Equipment Schedule T3						
CX Minivan 4D	V23L	28825	**13825**	**15625**	**17950**	**21600**
CXL Minivan 4D	V33L	31885	**15175**	**17075**	**19500**	**23400**
AWD	X		**1050**	**1050**	**1400**	**1400**
RENDEZVOUS—V6—Truck Equipment Schedule T3						
CX Sport Utility 4D	A03E	27270	**12700**	**14350**	**16450**	**19800**
CXL Sport Utility 4D	A03E	31600	**13975**	**15800**	**17950**	**21400**
Ultra Sport Utility 4D	A03E	36840	**14800**	**16675**	**18750**	**22300**
AWD	B		**1050**	**1050**	**1400**	**1400**
V6 3.6 Liter	7		**400**	**400**	**535**	**535**
RAINIER AWD—6-Cyl.—Truck Equipment Schedule T1						
CXL Sport Utility 4D	T13S	37590	**15850**	**17850**	**20100**	**23700**
2WD	S		**(1550)**	**(1550)**	**(2065)**	**(2065)**
V8 5.3 Liter	M		**400**	**400**	**535**	**535**

CADILLAC

1999 CADILLAC — 1GY-(K13R)-X-#

ESCALADE 4WD—V8—Truck Equipment Schedule T3						
Sport Utility 4D	K13R	46525	**9850**	**11250**	**13800**	**17600**

2000 CADILLAC — 1GY-(K13R)-Y-#

ESCALADE 4WD—V8—Truck Equipment Schedule T3						
Sport Utility 4D	K13R	46875	**11650**	**13200**	**16000**	**20100**

2001 CADILLAC — No Production

2002 CADILLAC — (1or3)GY-(K63N)-2-#

ESCALADE AWD—V8—Truck Equipment Schedule T3						
Sport Utility 4D	K63N	51980	**22300**	**24925**	**28500**	**34000**
2WD	C		**(1400)**	**(1400)**	**(1865)**	**(1865)**
V8 5.3 Liter	T		**(400)**	**(400)**	**(535)**	**(535)**
ESCALADE EXT AWD—V8—Truck Equipment Schedule T3						
Sport Util Pickup 4D	K13N	49990	**23275**	**26100**	**28500**	**32900**

2003 CADILLAC — (1or3)GY-(K63N)-3-#

ESCALADE AWD—V8—Truck Equipment Schedule T3						
Sport Utility 4D	K63N	53975	**25325**	**28325**	**32000**	**38000**
2WD	C		**(1450)**	**(1450)**	**(1935)**	**(1935)**
V8 5.3 Liter	T		**(425)**	**(425)**	**(565)**	**(565)**
ESCALADE EXT AWD—V8—Truck Equipment Schedule T3						
Sport Util Pickup 4D	K63N	51215	**26275**	**29400**	**31800**	**36300**
ESCALADE ESV AWD—V8—Truck Equipment Schedule T3						
Sport Utility 4D	K66N	56160	**28225**	**31525**	**35200**	**41300**

2004 CADILLAC — (1or3)GY-(E63A)-4-#

SRX—V8—Truck Equipment Schedule T3						
Sport Utility 4D	E63A	46995	**26000**	**29000**	**31900**	**37000**
Luxury Performance			**325**	**325**	**435**	**435**
Power Third Seat			**0**	**0**	**0**	**0**
AWD			**975**	**975**	**1300**	**1300**
V6 3.6 Liter	7		**(550)**	**(550)**	**(735)**	**(735)**
ESCALADE AWD—V8—Truck Equipment Schedule T3						
Sport Utility 4D	K63N	55695	**28700**	**32100**	**35900**	**42200**
2WD	C		**(1500)**	**(1500)**	**(2000)**	**(2000)**
V8 5.3 Liter	T		**(450)**	**(450)**	**(600)**	**(600)**
ESCALADE EXT AWD—V8—Truck Equipment Schedule T3						
Sport Util Pickup 4D	K63N	52975	**29575**	**33075**	**35400**	**40000**
ESCALADE ESV AWD—V8—Truck Equipment Schedule T3						
Sport Utility 4D	K66N	58095	**31925**	**35600**	**39300**	**45700**
Platinum Utility 4D	K66N	69730	**35500**	**39475**	**43500**	**50200**

Body	Type	VIN	List	Trade-In Fair	Good	Pvt-Party Good	Retail Excellent

2005 CADILLAC — (1or3)GY–(E63A)–5–#

SRX—V8—Truck Equipment Schedule T3
Sport Utility 4D	E63A	50830	29400	32775	35600	40800
Luxury Performance			1950	1950	2600	2600
AWD			1050	1050	1400	1400
V6 3.6 Liter	7		(575)	(575)	(765)	(765)

ESCALADE AWD—V8—Truck Equipment Schedule T3
Sport Utility 4D	K63N	56615	32300	35975	39900	46500
2WD			(1550)	(1550)	(2065)	(2065)
V8 5.3 Liter	T		(475)	(475)	(635)	(635)

ESCALADE EXT AWD—V8—Truck Equipment Schedule T3
| Sport Util Pickup 4D | K62N | 53895 | 32975 | 36775 | 39000 | 43700 |

ESCALADE ESV AWD—V8—Truck Equipment Schedule T3
| Sport Utility 4D | K66N | 59015 | 35800 | 39875 | 43700 | 50200 |
| Platinum Sport Util | K66N | 70385 | 39775 | 44225 | 48100 | 55100 |

CHEVROLET/GMC

1991 CHEVY/GMC — 1G(C,T,BorD)–(T18Z)–M–#

S10 BLAZER/S15 JIMMY 4WD—V6—Truck Equipment Sch T1
Sport Utility 2D	T18Z	17786	875	1225	2025	3225
Sport Utility 4D	T13Z	19426	1150	1600	2675	4175
2WD	S		(350)	(350)	(465)	(465)

BLAZER/JIMMY 4WD—V8—Truck Equipment Schedule T1
| Sport Utility 2D | V18K | 19986 | 1100 | 1550 | 2600 | 4075 |
| V8 6.2 Liter Diesel | C,J | | (100) | (100) | (135) | (135) |

SUBURBAN—V8—Truck Equipment Schedule T1
R1500 Sport Utility	R16K	19244	1350	1850	3125	4900
R2500 Sport Utility	R26K	20661	1475	1975	3275	5100
w/o Third Seat			(200)	(200)	(265)	(265)
4WD	V		500	500	665	665
V8 454/7.4 Liter	N		150	150	200	200
V8 6.2 Liter Diesel	C,J		(100)	(100)	(135)	(135)

APV—V6—Truck Equipment Schedule T2
| Cargo Minivan | U06D | 14102 | 100 | 150 | 425 | 900 |

LUMINA APV—V6—Truck Equipment Schedule T1
| Minivan | U06D | 16045 | 250 | 350 | 700 | 1300 |
| 5 Passenger | | | (200) | (200) | (265) | (265) |

ASTRO/SAFARI—V6—Truck Equipment Schedule T2
Cargo Minivan	M15Z	14081	400	575	1050	1775
Extended Cargo	M19Z	14751	425	625	1125	1925
AWD	L		250	250	335	335
V6 4.3L High Output	B		100	100	135	135

ASTRO/SAFARI—V6—Truck Equipment Schedule T1
Minivan	M15Z	17145	575	825	1400	2375
Extended Minivan	M19Z	17835	675	950	1575	2625
5 Passenger			(200)	(200)	(265)	(265)
AWD	L		250	250	335	335
V6 4.3L High Output	B		100	100	135	135

SPORTVAN/RALLY WAGON—V8—Truck Equipment Sch T1
G10 Passenger Van	G15H	18518	750	1075	1825	3000
G20 Passenger Van	G25H	18983	775	1125	1900	3100
G30 Passenger Van	G35K	20252	825	1175	1950	3175
5 Passenger			(200)	(200)	(265)	(265)
110" W.B.			0	0	0	0
146" W.B.	9		50	50	65	65
V6 4.3 Liter	Z		(200)	(200)	(265)	(265)
V8 454/7.4 Liter	N		100	100	135	135
V8 6.2 Liter Diesel	C,J		(100)	(100)	(135)	(135)

G-SERIES/VANDURA—V6—Truck Equipment Schedule T1
G10 Cargo Van	G15Z	15496	725	1050	1675	2775
G20 Cargo Van	G25Z	15686	775	1125	1800	2925
G30 Cargo Van	G35Z	15456	825	1175	1875	3000
110" W.B.			0	0	0	0
146" W.B.	9		50	50	65	65
V8 5.0, 5.7 Liter	H,K		100	100	135	135
V8 454/7.4 Liter	N		200	200	265	265
V6 6.2 Liter Diesel	C,J		(75)	(75)	(100)	(100)

S10/SONOMA PICKUP—4-Cyl.—Truck Equipment Schedule T2
| EL/Spcl Short Bed | S14E | 8832 | 325 | 425 | 850 | 1475 |

Body	Type	VIN	List	Trade-In Fair	Good	Pvt-Party Good	Retail Excellent
Short Bed		S14E	10150	**400**	**550**	**1025**	**1750**
Long Bed		S14E	10320	**325**	**450**	**900**	**1575**
Extended Cab		S19E	11420	**600**	**850**	**1425**	**2375**
4WD		T		**500**	**500**	**665**	**665**
V6 2.8 Liter		R		**125**	**125**	**165**	**165**
V6 4.3 Liter		Z		**150**	**150**	**200**	**200**

SONOMA PICKUP 4WD—V6 Turbo—Truck Equipment Sch T3

Body	Type	VIN	List	Trade-In Fair	Good	Pvt-Party Good	Retail Excellent
Syclone Short Bed		T14Z	25970	**7125**	**8225**	**9950**	**12550**

REGULAR CAB PICKUP—V8—Truck Equipment Schedule T1

Body	Type	VIN	List	Trade-In Fair	Good	Pvt-Party Good	Retail Excellent
C1500 Short Bed		C14H	13125	**1200**	**1650**	**2700**	**4175**
C1500 Long Bed		C14H	15425	**1125**	**1575**	**2600**	**4050**
C2500 Long Bed		C24H	16065	**1000**	**1400**	**2250**	**3575**
C3500 Long Bed		C34K	18795	**1050**	**1450**	**2350**	**3675**
Work Truck/Special				**(250)**	**(250)**	**(335)**	**(335)**
4WD		K		**500**	**500**	**665**	**665**
V6 4.3 Liter		Z		**(350)**	**(350)**	**(465)**	**(465)**
V8 5.7 Liter		K		**75**	**75**	**100**	**100**
V8 454/7.4 Liter		N		**150**	**150**	**200**	**200**
V8 6.2 Liter Diesel		C,J		**(100)**	**(100)**	**(135)**	**(135)**

REGULAR CAB PICKUP—V8—Truck Equipment Schedule T3

Body	Type	VIN	List	Trade-In Fair	Good	Pvt-Party Good	Retail Excellent
454SS Short Bed		C14N	20185	**3000**	**3650**	**5000**	**6925**

EXTENDED CAB PICKUP—V8—Truck Equipment Schedule T1

Body	Type	VIN	List	Trade-In Fair	Good	Pvt-Party Good	Retail Excellent
C1500 Short Bed		C19H	16075	**1450**	**1950**	**3025**	**4575**
C1500 Long Bed		C19H	16365	**1375**	**1900**	**2950**	**4475**
C2500 Short Bed		C29H	17185	**1575**	**2075**	**3200**	**4800**
C2500 Long Bed		C29H	17465	**1425**	**1925**	**3000**	**4550**
C3500 Long Bed		C39K	19290	**1425**	**1925**	**3000**	**4550**
4WD		K		**500**	**500**	**665**	**665**
V6 4.3 Liter		Z		**(350)**	**(350)**	**(465)**	**(465)**
V8 5.7 Liter		K		**75**	**75**	**100**	**100**
V8 454/7.4 Liter		N		**150**	**150**	**200**	**200**
V8 6.2 Liter Diesel		C,J		**(100)**	**(100)**	**(135)**	**(135)**

BONUS CAB PICKUP—V8—Truck Equipment Schedule T1

Body	Type	VIN	List	Trade-In Fair	Good	Pvt-Party Good	Retail Excellent
R3500 Long Bed		R34K	18592	**1425**	**1925**	**3000**	**4550**
4WD		V		**500**	**500**	**665**	**665**
V8 454/7.4 Liter		N		**150**	**150**	**200**	**200**
V8 6.2 Liter Diesel		C,J		**(100)**	**(100)**	**(135)**	**(135)**

CREW CAB PICKUP—V8—Truck Equipment Schedule T1

Body	Type	VIN	List	Trade-In Fair	Good	Pvt-Party Good	Retail Excellent
R3500 Long Bed		R33K	19132	**1975**	**2500**	**3675**	**5375**
4WD		V		**500**	**500**	**665**	**665**
V8 454/7.4 Liter		N		**150**	**150**	**200**	**200**
V8 6.2 Liter Diesel		C,J		**(100)**	**(100)**	**(135)**	**(135)**

1992 CHEVY/GMC — 1G(C,T,N,BorD)-(T18Z)-N-#

S10 BLAZER/JIMMY 4WD—V6—Truck Equipment Schedule Sch T1

Body	Type	VIN	List	Trade-In Fair	Good	Pvt-Party Good	Retail Excellent
Sport Utility 2D		T18Z	18859	**975**	**1350**	**2200**	**3475**
Sport Utility 4D		T13Z	20229	**1300**	**1800**	**2850**	**4400**
2WD		S		**(375)**	**(375)**	**(500)**	**(500)**
V6 4.3L High Output		W		**100**	**100**	**135**	**135**

JIMMY 4WD—V6 Turbo—Truck Equipment Schedule T3

Body	Type	VIN	List	Trade-In Fair	Good	Pvt-Party Good	Retail Excellent
Typhoon Spt Util 2D		T18Z	33006	**9025**	**10325**	**12750**	**16300**

BLAZER/YUKON 4WD—V8—Truck Equipment Schedule T1

Body	Type	VIN	List	Trade-In Fair	Good	Pvt-Party Good	Retail Excellent
Sport Utility 2D		K18K	21780	**1975**	**2525**	**3750**	**5525**

SUBURBAN—V8—Truck Equipment Schedule T1

Body	Type	VIN	List	Trade-In Fair	Good	Pvt-Party Good	Retail Excellent
C1500 Sport Utility		C16K	20905	**1775**	**2300**	**3675**	**5600**
C2500 Sport Utility		C26K	22109	**1900**	**2425**	**3825**	**5775**
w/o Third Seat				**(225)**	**(225)**	**(300)**	**(300)**
4WD		K		**550**	**550**	**735**	**735**
V8 454/7.4 Liter		N		**150**	**150**	**200**	**200**

APV—V6—Truck Equipment Schedule T2

Body	Type	VIN	List	Trade-In Fair	Good	Pvt-Party Good	Retail Excellent
Cargo Minivan		U06D	14905	**125**	**175**	**475**	**975**

LUMINA APV—V6—Truck Equipment Schedule T1

Body	Type	VIN	List	Trade-In Fair	Good	Pvt-Party Good	Retail Excellent
Minivan		U06D	16930	**275**	**400**	**800**	**1425**
5 Passenger				**(225)**	**(225)**	**(300)**	**(300)**
V6 3.8 Liter		L		**50**	**50**	**65**	**65**

ASTRO/SAFARI—V6—Truck Equipment Schedule T2

Body	Type	VIN	List	Trade-In Fair	Good	Pvt-Party Good	Retail Excellent
Cargo Minivan		M15Z	14636	**450**	**650**	**1175**	**2000**
Extended Cargo		M19Z	15306	**500**	**725**	**1225**	**2100**
AWD		L		**275**	**275**	**365**	**365**
V6 4.3L High Output		W		**100**	**100**	**135**	**135**

ASTRO/SAFARI—V6—Truck Equipment Schedule T1

Body	Type	VIN	List	Trade-In Fair	Good	Pvt-Party Good	Retail Excellent
Minivan		M15Z	16726	**675**	**950**	**1575**	**2625**
Extended Minivan		M19Z	17416	**775**	**1100**	**1800**	**2925**

0106

1992 CHEVROLET/GMC

Body	Type	VIN	List	Trade-In Fair	Good	Pvt-Party Good	Retail Excellent
5 Passenger		L	------	(225)	(225)	(300)	(300)
AWD		L	------	275	275	365	365
V6 4.3L High Output		W	------	100	100	135	135
SPORTVAN/RALLY WAGON—V8—Truck Equipment Sch T1							
G10 Passenger Van		G15H	19266	875	1225	2075	3400
G20 Passenger Van		G25H	19456	900	1275	2150	3475
G30 Passenger Van		G35K	20631	925	1300	2225	3625
5 Passenger			------	(225)	(225)	(300)	(300)
110" W.B.			------	0	0	0	0
146" W.B.		9	------	50	50	65	65
V6 4.3 Liter		Z	------	(225)	(225)	(300)	(300)
V8 454/7.4 Liter		N	------	100	100	135	135
V8 6.2 Liter Diesel		C,J	------	(100)	(100)	(135)	(135)
G-SERIES/VANDURA—V6—Truck Equipment Schedule T1							
G10 Cargo Van		G15Z	16246	850	1200	1950	3100
G20 Cargo Van		G25Z	16486	900	1275	2050	3275
G30 Cargo Van		G35Z	16206	925	1300	2100	3350
110" W.B.			------	0	0	0	0
146" W.B.		9	------	50	50	65	65
V8 5.0, 5.7 Liter		H,K	------	100	100	135	135
V8 454/7.4 Liter		N	------	225	225	300	300
V8 6.2 Liter Diesel		C,J	------	(75)	(75)	(100)	(100)
S10/SONOMA PICKUP—4-Cyl.—Truck Equipment Schedule T2							
EL/Spcl Short Bed		S14A	9524	350	475	925	1650
Short Bed		S14A	10459	425	625	1125	1950
Long Bed		S19A	10759	375	500	1000	1750
Extended Cab		S19A	11959	675	950	1600	2675
4WD		T	------	550	550	735	735
V6 2.8 Liter		R	------	125	125	165	165
V6 4.3 Liter		Z	------	175	175	235	235
V6 4.3L High Output		W	------	225	225	300	300
SONOMA PICKUP—V6—Truck Equipment Schedule T1							
GT Short Bed		S14W	16770	1050	1450	2450	3900
SONOMA PICKUP 4WD—V6 Turbo—Truck Equipment Sch T3							
Syclone Short Bed		T14Z	27465	7975	9175	11200	14200
REGULAR CAB PICKUP—V8—Truck Equipment Schedule T1							
C1500 Short Bed		C14H	16130	2175	2775	3925	5650
C1500 Long Bed		C14H	16430	2075	2650	3800	5500
C2500 Short Bed		C24H	17070	1925	2450	3625	5250
C3500 Long Bed		C34K	17895	1975	2525	3675	5350
Work Truck/Special			------	(275)	(275)	(365)	(365)
4WD		K	------	550	550	735	735
V6 4.3 Liter		Z	------	(350)	(350)	(465)	(465)
V8 5.7 Liter		K	------	100	100	135	135
V8 454/7.4 Liter		N	------	150	150	200	200
V8 6.2 Liter Diesel		C,J	------	(150)	(150)	(200)	(200)
V8 6.5L Turbo Diesel		F	------	275	275	365	365
REGULAR CAB PICKUP—V8—Truck Equipment Schedule T3							
454SS Short Bed		C14N	21180	4075	4850	6400	8650
EXTENDED CAB PICKUP—V8—Truck Equipment Schedule T1							
C1500 Short Bed		C19H	17080	2500	3100	4375	6150
C1500 Long Bed		C19H	17370	2425	3000	4250	6050
C2500 Short Bed		C29H	18190	2675	3275	4575	6475
C2500 Long Bed		C29H	18470	2475	3075	4350	6150
C3500 Long Bed		C39K	18965	2475	3075	4350	6150
4WD		K	------	550	550	735	735
V6 4.3 Liter		Z	------	(350)	(350)	(465)	(465)
V8 5.7 Liter		K	------	100	100	135	135
V8 454/7.4 Liter		N	------	150	150	200	200
V8 6.2 Liter Diesel		C,J	------	(150)	(150)	(200)	(200)
CREW CAB PICKUP—V8—Truck Equipment Schedule T1							
C3500 Long Bed		C33K	19867	3075	3725	5125	7100
4WD		K	------	550	550	735	735
V8 454/7.4 Liter		N	------	150	150	200	200

1993 CHEVY/GMC — 1G(C,T,NorB)–(T18Z)–P–#

Body	Type	VIN	List	Trade-In Fair	Good	Pvt-Party Good	Retail Excellent
S10 BLAZER/JIMMY 4WD—V6—Truck Equipment Sch T1							
Sport Utility 2D		T18Z	19129	900	1275	2125	3450
Sport Utility 4D		T13Z	20499	1300	1800	2875	4450
2WD		S	------	(400)	(400)	(535)	(535)
V6 4.3L High Output		W	------	125	125	165	165
JIMMY 4WD—V6 Turbo—Truck Equipment Schedule T3							
Typhoon Spt Util 2D		T18Z	29795	9600	10950	13450	17050

TRUCKS & VANS

1993 CHEVROLET/GMC

Body	Type	VIN	List	Trade-In Fair	Trade-In Good	Pvt-Party Good	Retail Excellent
BLAZER/YUKON 4WD—V8—Truck Equipment Schedule T1							
Sport Utility 2D		K18K	22505	2325	2900	4250	6125
SUBURBAN—V8—Truck Equipment Schedule T1							
C1500 Sport Utility		C16K	21830	2050	2625	4100	6125
C2500 Sport Utility		C26K	23035	2200	2800	4275	6350
w/o Third Seat				(250)	(250)	(335)	(335)
4WD		K		650	650	865	865
V8 454/7.4 Liter		N		175	175	235	235
APV—V6—Truck Equipment Schedule T2							
Cargo Minivan		U06D	15225	75	100	450	975
LUMINA APV—V6—Truck Equipment Schedule T1							
Minivan		U06D	17255	275	375	825	1525
5 Passenger				(250)	(250)	(335)	(335)
V6 3.8 Liter		L		75	75	100	100
ASTRO/SAFARI—V6—Truck Equipment Schedule T2							
Cargo Minivan		M15Z	15336	475	675	1225	2150
Extended Cargo		M19Z	16006	550	775	1375	2375
Dutch Doors				25	25	35	35
AWD				325	325	435	435
V6 4.3L High Output		W		125	125	165	165
ASTRO/SAFARI—V6—Truck Equipment Schedule T1							
Minivan		M15Z	17146	725	1050	1775	2925
Extended Minivan		M19Z	17836	850	1200	2025	3275
5 Passenger				(250)	(250)	(335)	(335)
Dutch Doors				25	25	35	35
AWD		L		325	325	435	435
V6 4.3L High Output		W		125	125	165	165
SPORTVAN/RALLY WAGON—V8—Truck Equipment Sch T1							
G10 Passenger Van		G15H	18756	950	1325	2275	3675
G20 Passenger Van		G25H	18946	1000	1400	2450	3975
G30 Passenger Van		G35K	20696	1050	1450	2550	4100
5 Passenger				(250)	(250)	(335)	(335)
110" W.B.		9		0	0	0	0
146" W.B.		9		75	75	100	100
V6 4.3 Liter		Z		(250)	(250)	(335)	(335)
V8 454/7.4 Liter		N		125	125	165	165
V8 6.2 Liter Diesel		C,J		(125)	(125)	(165)	(165)
G-SERIES/VANDURA—V6—Truck Equipment Schedule T1							
G10 Cargo Van		G15Z	16431	900	1275	2100	3400
G20 Cargo Van		G25Z	16571	975	1375	2275	3625
G30 Cargo Van		G35Z	16691	1000	1425	2325	3675
110" W.B.				0	0	0	0
146" W.B.		9		75	75	100	100
V8 5.0, 5.7 Liter		H,K		125	125	165	165
V8 454/7.4 Liter		N		250	250	335	335
V8 6.2 Liter Diesel		C,J		(100)	(100)	(135)	(135)
S10/SONOMA PICKUP—4-Cyl.—Truck Equipment Schedule T2							
EL/Special Short Bed		S14A	9547	375	500	1000	1775
Short Bed		S14A	10731	475	675	1225	2100
Long Bed		S14A	11031	400	550	1075	1875
Extended Cab		S19A	12231	750	1050	1775	2925
4WD		T		675	675	900	900
V6 2.8 Liter		R		150	150	200	200
V6 4.3 Liter		Z		200	200	265	265
V6 4.3L High Output		W		250	250	335	335
REGULAR CAB PICKUP—V8—Truck Equipment Schedule T1							
1500 Short Bed		C14H	16120	2275	2825	4075	5825
1500 Long Bed		C14H	16420	2125	2725	3900	5625
2500 Long Bed		C24H	16885	2075	2650	3850	5575
3500 Long Bed		C34K	18624	2150	2750	3950	5700
Work Truck/Special				(325)	(325)	(435)	(435)
4WD		K		650	650	865	865
V6 4.3 Liter		Z		(375)	(375)	(500)	(500)
V8 5.7 Liter		K		150	150	200	200
V8 454/7.4 Liter		N		175	175	235	235
V8 6.2 Liter Diesel		C,J		(225)	(225)	(300)	(300)
V8 6.5L Turbo Diesel		F		325	325	435	435
REGULAR CAB PICKUP—V8—Truck Equipment Schedule T3							
454SS Short Bed		C14N	21835	4500	5325	6950	9300
EXTENDED CAB PICKUP—V8—Truck Equipment Schedule T1							
1500 Short Bed		C19H	17590	2725	3325	4625	6525
1500 Long Bed		C19H	17850	2600	3225	4500	6350
2500 Short Bed		C29H	18700	2950	3625	4975	6925

Body	Type	VIN	List	Trade-In Fair	Trade-In Good	Pvt-Party Good	Retail Excellent
2500 Long Bed		C29H	18980	2725	3350	4675	6575
3500 Long Bed		C39K	20284	2750	3375	4700	6600
4WD		K		650	650	865	865
V6 4.3 Liter		Z		(375)	(375)	(500)	(500)
V8 5.7 Liter		K		150	150	200	200
V8 454/7.4 Liter		N		175	175	235	235
V8 6.2 Liter Diesel		C,J		(225)	(225)	(300)	(300)
V8 6.5L Turbo Diesel		F		325	325	435	435
CREW CAB PICKUP—V8—Truck Equipment Schedule T1							
3500 Long Bed		C33K	20604	3450	4150	5575	7675
4WD		K		650	650	865	865
V8 454/7.4 Liter		N		175	175	235	235
V8 6.5L Turbo Diesel		F		325	325	435	435

1994 CHEVY/GMC — 1G(C,T,NorB)–(T18Z)–R–#

Body	Type	VIN	List	Trade-In Fair	Trade-In Good	Pvt-Party Good	Retail Excellent
S10 BLAZER/JIMMY 4WD—V6—Truck Equipment Sch T1							
Sport Utility 2D		T18Z	19649	875	1225	2150	3525
Sport Utility 4D		T13Z	21377	1350	1850	3000	4650
2WD		S		(425)	(425)	(565)	(565)
V6 4.3L High Output		W		150	150	200	200
BLAZER/YUKON 4WD—V8—Truck Equipment Schedule T1							
Sport Utility 2D		K18K	23460	2725	3350	4775	6800
V8 6.5L Turbo Diesel		S		375	375	500	500
SUBURBAN—V8—Truck Equipment Schedule T1							
C1500 Sport Utility		C16K	21651	2425	3000	4600	6800
C2500 Sport Utility		C26K	22883	2575	3200	4825	7050
w/o Third Seat				(275)	(275)	(365)	(365)
4WD		K		750	750	1000	1000
V8 454/7.4 Liter		N		200	200	265	265
V8 6.5L Turbo Diesel		F		375	375	500	500
LUMINA—V6—Truck Equipment Schedule T2							
Cargo		U06D	16015	275	375	875	1650
LUMINA—V6—Truck Equipment Schedule T1							
Passenger		U06D	18175	475	675	1275	2275
5 Passenger				(275)	(275)	(365)	(365)
V6 3.8 Liter		L		100	100	135	135
ASTRO/SAFARI—V6—Truck Equipment Schedule T2							
Cargo Minivan		M15Z	15985	500	725	1350	2375
Extended Cargo		M19Z	16458	600	875	1550	2675
Dutch Doors				50	50	65	65
AWD		L		375	375	500	500
V6 4.3L High Output		W		150	150	200	200
ASTRO/SAFARI—V6—Truck Equipment Schedule T1							
Minivan		M15Z	17819	800	1150	1975	3275
Extended Minivan		M19Z	18121	925	1300	2250	3650
5 Passenger				(275)	(275)	(365)	(365)
Dutch Doors				50	50	65	65
AWD		L		375	375	500	500
V6 4.3L High Output		W		150	150	200	200
SPORTVAN/RALLY WAGON—V8—Truck Equipment Sch T1							
G20 Passenger Van		G25H	20344	1125	1575	2725	4325
G30 Passenger Van		G35K	21696	1200	1650	2825	4450
5 Passenger				(275)	(275)	(365)	(365)
146" W.B.		9		100	100	135	135
V6 4.3 Liter		Z		(275)	(275)	(365)	(365)
V8 454/7.4 Liter		N		150	150	200	200
V8 6.5 Liter Diesel		P		(150)	(150)	(200)	(200)
G-SERIES/VANDURA—V6—Truck Equipment Schedule T1							
G10 Cargo Van		G15Z	17544	1000	1425	2450	3950
G20 Cargo Van		G25Z	17534	1075	1525	2600	4100
G30 Cargo Van		G35Z	17661	1125	1575	2675	4200
110" W.B.				0	0	0	0
146" W.B.		9		100	100	135	135
V8 5.0, 5.7 Liter		H,K		150	150	200	200
V8 454/7.4 Liter		P		275	275	365	365
V8 6.5 Liter Diesel		P		(125)	(125)	(165)	(165)
S10/SONOMA PICKUP—4-Cyl.—Truck Equipment Schedule T2							
Short Bed		S144	10201	650	925	1575	2675
Long Bed		S144	10501	550	775	1375	2375
Extended Cab		S194	12260	950	1325	2225	3575
4WD				800	800	1065	1065
V6 4.3 Liter		Z		225	225	300	300
V6 4.3L High Output		W		275	275	365	365

TRUCKS & VANS

1994 CHEVROLET/GMC

Body Type	VIN	List	Trade-In Fair	Good	Pvt-Party Good	Retail Excellent
REGULAR CAB PICKUP—V8—Truck Equipment Schedule T1						
1500 Short Bed	C14H	16322	2425	3000	4275	6075
1500 Long Bed	C14H	16602	2275	2850	4100	5850
2500 Long Bed	C24H	17579	2300	2875	4150	5925
3500 Long Bed	C34K	19313	2425	3000	4275	6075
Work Truck/Special			(375)	(375)	(500)	(500)
4WD	K		750	750	1000	1000
V6 4.3 Liter	Z		(400)	(400)	(535)	(535)
V8 5.7 Liter	K		175	175	235	235
V8 454/7.4 Liter	N		200	200	265	265
V8 6.5 Liter Diesel	P,Y		(275)	(275)	(365)	(365)
V8 6.5L Turbo Diesel	F,S		375	375	500	500
EXTENDED CAB PICKUP—V8—Truck Equipment Schedule T1						
1500 Short Bed	C19H	18319	3000	3650	5025	6950
1500 Long Bed	C19H	19162	2850	3500	4800	6725
2500 Short Bed	C29H	20107	3325	4000	5400	7450
2500 Long Bed	C29K	20995	3025	3700	5050	7000
3500 Long Bed	C39K	22547	3075	3725	5125	7075
4WD	K		750	750	1000	1000
V6 4.3 Liter	Z		(400)	(400)	(535)	(535)
V8 5.7 Liter	K		175	175	235	235
V8 454/7.4 Liter	N		200	200	265	265
V8 6.5 Liter Diesel	P,Y		(275)	(275)	(365)	(365)
V8 6.5L Turbo Diesel	F,S		375	375	500	500
CREW CAB PICKUP—V8—Truck Equipment Schedule T1						
3500 Long Bed	C33K	21652	3850	4600	6075	8250
4WD	K		750	750	1000	1000
V8 454/7.4 Liter	N		200	200	265	265
V8 6.5L Turbo Diesel	F,S		375	375	500	500

1995 CHEVY/GMC — 1G(C,T,NorB)-(T18W)-S-#

Body Type	VIN	List	Trade-In Fair	Good	Pvt-Party Good	Retail Excellent
BLAZER/JIMMY 4WD—V6—Truck Equipment Schedule T1						
Sport Utility 2D	T18W	20390	1125	1575	2750	4400
Sport Utility 4D	T13W	22438	1775	2300	3600	5375
2WD	S		(450)	(450)	(600)	(600)
TAHOE/YUKON 4WD—V8—Truck Equipment Schedule T1						
Sport Utility 2D	K18K	24215	1925	2450	4025	6175
Sport Utility 4D	K13K	29195	3000	3675	5400	7800
2WD	C		(450)	(450)	(600)	(600)
V8 6.5L Turbo Diesel	S		400	400	535	535
SUBURBAN—V8—Truck Equipment Schedule T1						
C1500 Sport Utility	C16K	24264	2850	3525	5225	7575
C2500 Sport Utility	C26K	25497	3050	3725	5450	7850
w/o Third Seat			(300)	(300)	(400)	(400)
4WD	K		850	850	1135	1135
V8 454/7.4 Liter	N		225	225	300	300
V8 6.5L Turbo Diesel	F		400	400	535	535
LUMINA—V6—Truck Equipment Schedule T2						
Cargo	U06D	16775	325	450	1025	1925
LUMINA—V6—Truck Equipment Schedule T1						
Passenger	U06D	19625	550	800	1500	2625
5 Passenger			(300)	(300)	(400)	(400)
V6 3.8 Liter	L		100	100	135	135
ASTRO/SAFARI—V6—Truck Equipment Schedule T2						
Cargo Minivan	M19W	18340	1025	1450	2550	4100
Dutch Doors			75	75	100	100
AWD	L		425	425	565	565
ASTRO/SAFARI—V6—Truck Equipment Schedule T1						
Minivan	M19W	19886	1475	1975	3175	4850
5 Passenger			(300)	(300)	(400)	(400)
Dutch Doors			75	75	100	100
AWD	L		425	425	565	565
SPORTVAN/RALLY WAGON—V8—Truck Equipment Sch T1						
G20 Passenger Van	G25H	21776	1300	1800	3000	4725
G30 Passenger Van	G35K	22595	1400	1900	3150	4875
5 Passenger			(300)	(300)	(400)	(400)
146" W.B.	9		100	100	135	135
V6 4.3 Liter	Z		(300)	(300)	(400)	(400)
V8 454/7.4 Liter	N		175	175	235	235
V8 6.5 Liter Diesel	Y		(175)	(175)	(235)	(235)
G-SERIES/VANDURA—V6—Truck Equipment Schedule T1						
G10 Cargo Van	G15Z	18588	1150	1600	2725	4275
G20 Cargo Van	G25Z	18578	1225	1725	2825	4425

Body Type	VIN	List	Trade-In Fair	Trade-In Good	Pvt-Party Good	Retail Excellent
G30 Cargo Van	G35Z	18732	1300	1800	2900	4500
110" W.B.			0	0	0	0
146" W.B.			100	100	135	135
V8 5.0, 5.7 Liter	H,K		175	175	235	235
V8 454/7.4 Liter	N		300	300	400	400
V8 6.5 Liter Diesel	Y		(125)	(125)	(165)	(165)

S10/SONOMA PICKUP—4-Cyl.—Truck Equipment Schedule T2

Body Type	VIN	List	Fair	Good	Good	Excellent
Short Bed	S144	10820	775	1100	1850	3050
Long Bed	S144	11130	650	925	1600	2725
Extended Cab	S194	12990	1100	1550	2600	4125
4WD	T		900	900	1200	1200
V6 4.3 Liter	Z		250	250	335	335
V6 4.3L High Output			300	300	400	400

REGULAR CAB PICKUP—V8—Truck Equipment Schedule T1

Body Type	VIN	List	Fair	Good	Good	Excellent
1500 Short Bed	C14H	17217	2650	3275	4550	6450
1500 Long Bed	C14H	17497	2500	3100	4375	6200
2500 Short Bed	C24H	18679	2625	3250	4550	6425
3500 HD Long Bed	C34K	19803	2725	3350	4675	6575
Work Truck/Special			(400)	(400)	(535)	(535)
4WD	K		850	850	1135	1135
V6 4.3 Liter	Z		(425)	(425)	(565)	(565)
V8 5.7 Liter	K		200	200	265	265
V8 454/7.4 Liter	N		225	225	300	300
V8 6.5 Liter Diesel	P		(325)	(325)	(435)	(435)
V8 6.5L Turbo Diesel	S		400	400	535	535

EXTENDED CAB PICKUP—V8—Truck Equipment Schedule T1

Body Type	VIN	List	Fair	Good	Good	Excellent
1500 Short Bed	C19H	19177	3350	4050	5450	7525
1500 Long Bed	C19H	19545	3175	3850	5250	7250
2500 Short Bed	C29H	21115	3725	4450	5950	8075
2500 Long Bed	C29H	21172	3625	4350	5800	7900
3500 HD Long Bed	C39K	23129	3475	4200	5625	7675
4WD	K		850	850	1135	1135
V6 4.3 Liter	Z		(425)	(425)	(565)	(565)
V8 5.7 Liter	K		200	200	265	265
V8 454/7.4 Liter	N		225	225	300	300
V8 6.5 Liter Diesel	P		(325)	(325)	(435)	(435)
V8 6.5L Turbo Diesel	S		400	400	535	535

CREW CAB PICKUP—V8—Truck Equipment Schedule T1

Body Type	VIN	List	Fair	Good	Good	Excellent
3500 Long Bed	C33K	22389	4350	5125	6700	8975
4WD	K		850	850	1135	1135
V8 454/7.4 Liter	N		225	225	300	300
V8 6.5L Turbo Diesel	F,S		400	400	535	535

BLAZER/JIMMY 4WD—V6—Truck Equipment Schedule T1

Body Type	VIN	List	Fair	Good	Good	Excellent
Sport Utility 2D	T18W	21694	1275	1775	3025	4775
Sport Utility 4D	T13W	23742	2025	2575	3925	5850
2WD	S		(475)	(475)	(635)	(635)

TAHOE/YUKON 4WD—V8—Truck Equipment Schedule T1

Body Type	VIN	List	Fair	Good	Good	Excellent
Sport Utility 2D	K18R	26596	2425	3000	4725	7050
Sport Utility 4D	K13R	31079	3625	4350	6225	8825
2WD	C		(475)	(475)	(635)	(635)
V8 6.5L Turbo Diesel	S		425	425	565	565

SUBURBAN—V8—Truck Equipment Schedule T1

Body Type	VIN	List	Fair	Good	Good	Excellent
C1500 Sport Utility	C16R	26709	3425	4125	5975	8500
C2500 Sport Utility	C26R	27942	3625	4350	6200	8800
w/o Third Seat			(325)	(325)	(435)	(435)
4WD	K		950	950	1265	1265
V8 454/7.4 Liter	J		250	250	335	335
V8 6.5L Turbo Diesel	F		425	425	565	565

LUMINA—V6—Truck Equipment Schedule T2

Body Type	VIN	List	Fair	Good	Good	Excellent
Cargo	U06E	18415	400	550	1225	2275

LUMINA—V6—Truck Equipment Schedule T1

Body Type	VIN	List	Fair	Good	Good	Excellent
Passenger	U06E	20435	675	950	1800	3100
5 Passenger			(325)	(325)	(435)	(435)

ASTRO/SAFARI—V6—Truck Equipment Schedule T2

Body Type	VIN	List	Fair	Good	Good	Excellent
Cargo/SL Cargo	M19W	19152	1225	1675	2850	4525
Dutch Doors			100	100	135	135
AWD	L		475	475	635	635

ASTRO/SAFARI—V6—Truck Equipment Schedule T1

Body Type	VIN	List	Fair	Good	Good	Excellent
Minivan/SL Minivan	M19W	19736	1750	2275	3550	5325
5 Passenger			(325)	(325)	(435)	(435)
Dutch Doors			100	100	135	135

TRUCKS & VANS

Body Type	VIN	List	Trade-In Fair	Good	Pvt-Party Good	Retail Excellent
AWD	L		475	475	635	635
EXPRESS/SAVANA—V8—Truck Equipment Schedule T1						
1500 Passenger Van	G15M	23342	1825	2350	3675	5575
2500 Passenger Van	G25R	25767	1925	2450	3825	5725
3500 Passenger Van	G35R	25927	2025	2600	3975	5925
5 Passenger	9		(325)	(325)	(435)	(435)
155" W.B.	9		100	100	135	135
V6 4.3 Liter	W		(325)	(325)	(435)	(435)
V8 454/7.4 Liter	J		200	200	265	265
V8 6.5L Turbo Diesel	F		150	150	200	200
SPORTVAN/RALLY WAGON—V8—Truck Equipment Sch T1						
G30 Passenger Van	G35K	23451	1650	2150	3500	5325
146" W.B.			100	100	135	135
V8 454/7.4 Liter	N		(200)	(200)	(265)	(265)
G-SERIES/SAVANA—V6—Truck Equip Schedule T1						
1500 Cargo Van	G15W	20314	1825	2350	3625	5350
2500 Cargo Van	G25W	20639	1950	2475	3725	5525
3500 Cargo Van	G35R	22019	2000	2550	3800	5600
155" W.B.	9		100	100	135	135
V8 5.0, 5.7 Liter	M,R		200	200	265	265
V8 454/7.4 Liter	J		325	325	435	435
V8 6.5L Turbo Diesel	F		225	225	300	300
G-SERIES/VANDURA—V8—Truck Equipment Schedule T1						
G30 Classic	G39K	20469	1825	2350	3625	5350
146" W.B.			100	100	135	135
V6 4.3 Liter	Z		(325)	(325)	(435)	(435)
V8 454/7.4 Liter	N		200	200	265	265
V8 6.5 Liter Diesel	Y		(125)	(125)	(165)	(165)
S10/SONOMA PICKUP—4-Cyl.—Truck Equipment Schedule T2						
Short Bed	S144	11755	900	1250	2150	3525
Long Bed	S144	12065	750	1075	1875	3125
Extended Cab	S194	14470	1275	1775	2900	4500
Third Door			200	200	265	265
4WD	T		1000	1000	1335	1335
V6 4.3 Liter	X		275	275	365	365
V6 4.3L High Output	W		325	325	435	435
REGULAR CAB PICKUP—V8—Truck Equipment Schedule T1						
1500 Short Bed	C14M	18311	2950	3625	5000	6950
1500 Long Bed	C14M	18591	2800	3425	4750	6675
2500 Long Bed	C24M	19273	3000	3675	5050	7025
3500 Long Bed	C34R	20477	3125	3775	5200	7175
Work Truck/Special			(425)	(425)	(565)	(565)
4WD	K		950	950	1265	1265
V6 4.3 Liter	W		(450)	(450)	(600)	(600)
V8 5.7 Liter	R		225	225	300	300
V8 454/7.4 Liter	J		250	250	335	335
V8 6.5L Turbo Diesel	F,S		425	425	565	565
EXTENDED CAB PICKUP—V8—Truck Equipment Schedule T1						
1500 Short Bed	C19M	20371	3775	4525	6025	8175
1500 Long Bed	C19M	20819	3625	4325	5775	7875
2500 Short Bed	C29M	21889	4225	5025	6575	8825
2500 HD Long Bed	C29M	21946	4100	4875	6400	8600
3500 Long Bed	C39R	23903	3950	4700	6225	8425
Third Door			200	200	265	265
4WD	K		950	950	1265	1265
V6 4.3 Liter	W		(450)	(450)	(600)	(600)
V8 5.7 Liter	R		225	225	300	300
V8 454/7.4 Liter	J		250	250	335	335
V8 6.5L Turbo Diesel	F,S		425	425	565	565
CREW CAB PICKUP—V8—Truck Equipment Schedule T1						
3500 Long Bed	C33R	23611	4900	5750	7400	9800
4WD	K		950	950	1265	1265
V8 454/7.4 Liter	J		250	250	335	335
V8 6.5L Turbo Diesel	F		425	425	565	565

1997 CHEVY/GMC — 1G(C,K,NorT)-T18W-V-#

Body Type	VIN	List	Trade-In Fair	Good	Pvt-Party Good	Retail Excellent
BLAZER/JIMMY 4WD—V6—Truck Equipment Schedule T1						
Sport Utility 2D	T18W	22631	1525	2025	3400	5250
Sport Utility 4D	T13W	24631	2325	2900	4375	6400
2WD	S		(500)	(500)	(665)	(665)
TAHOE/YUKON 4WD—V8—Truck Equipment Schedule T1						
Sport Utility 2D	K18R	27642	3000	3675	5550	8100

Body Type	VIN	List	Trade-In Fair	Good	Pvt-Party Good	Retail Excellent
Sport Utility 4D	K13R	32125	4350	5125	7175	10000
2WD	C		(1100)	(1100)	(1465)	(1465)
V8 6.5L Turbo Diesel	S		450	450	600	600
SUBURBAN—V8—Truck Equipment Schedule T1						
C1500 Sport Utility	C16R	27350	4050	4825	6825	9575
C2500 Sport Utility	C26R	28583	4300	5100	7100	9900
w/o Third Seat			(350)	(350)	(465)	(465)
4WD	K		1050	1050	1400	1400
V8 454/7.4 Liter			275	275	365	365
V8 6.5L Turbo Diesel	F		450	450	600	600
VENTURE—V6—Truck Equipment Schedule T1						
Minivan	U03E	20495	1175	1625	3000	4875
Extended Minivan	X06E	21660	1525	2025	3475	5400
w/o 2nd Sliding Door			(450)	(450)	(600)	(600)
ASTRO/SAFARI—V6—Truck Equipment Schedule T2						
Cargo/SL Cargo	M19W	19583	1500	2000	3300	5100
Dutch Doors			100	100	135	135
AWD	L		500	500	665	665
ASTRO/SAFARI—V6—Truck Equipment Schedule T1						
Base/SLX Minivan	M19W	20167	2075	2650	4000	5900
5 Passenger			(350)	(350)	(465)	(465)
Dutch Doors			100	100	135	135
AWD	L		500	500	665	665
EXPRESS/SAVANA—V8—Truck Equipment Schedule T1						
1500 Passenger Van	G15M	23380	2275	2825	4325	6350
2500 Passenger Van	G25R	25411	2425	2950	4450	6500
3500 Passenger Van	G35R	25571	2525	3125	4600	6700
5 Passenger			(350)	(350)	(465)	(465)
155" W.B.			100	100	135	135
V6 4.3 Liter	W		(350)	(350)	(465)	(465)
V8 454/7.4 Liter	J		200	200	265	265
V8 6.5L Turbo Diesel	F		150	150	200	200
G-SERIES/SAVANA—V6—Truck Equipment Schedule T1						
1500 Cargo Van	G15W	20662	2275	2825	4200	6075
2500 Cargo Van	G25W	21087	2375	2950	4325	6225
3500 Cargo Van	G35R	22467	2425	3025	4400	6300
155" W.B.			100	100	135	135
V8 5.0, 5.7 Liter	M,R		200	200	265	265
V8 454/7.4 Liter	J		350	350	465	465
V8 6.5L Turbo	J		250	250	335	335
S10/SONOMA PICKUP—4-Cyl.—Truck Equipment Schedule T2						
Short Bed	S144	12008	1050	1475	2575	4150
Long Bed	S144	12308	900	1275	2225	3650
Extended Cab	S194	14863	1550	2050	3250	4950
Third Door			200	200	265	265
4WD	T		1100	1100	1465	1465
V6 4.3 Liter	X		300	300	400	400
V6 4.3L High Output	W		350	350	465	465
REGULAR CAB PICKUP—V8—Truck Equipment Schedule T1						
1500 Short Bed	C14M	18837	3350	4050	5450	7525
1500 Long Bed	C14M	19137	3175	3825	5250	7225
2500 Long Bed	C24M	19819	3500	4200	5650	7700
3500 Long Bed	C34R	20807	3625	4325	5775	7850
Work Truck/Special			(450)	(450)	(600)	(600)
4WD	K		1050	1050	1400	1400
V6 4.3 Liter	W		(450)	(450)	(600)	(600)
V8 5.7 Liter	R		250	250	335	335
V8 454/7.4 Liter	J		275	275	365	365
V8 6.5L Turbo Diesel	F,S		450	450	600	600
EXTENDED CAB PICKUP—V8—Truck Equipment Schedule T1						
1500 Short Bed	C19M	20917	4325	5125	6650	8900
1500 Long Bed	C19M	21417	4100	4875	6375	8550
2500 Short Bed	C29M	22435	4800	5650	7275	9625
2500 HD Long Bed	C29M	22272	4650	5475	7050	9350
3500 Long Bed	C39R	24229	4500	5325	6900	9200
Third Door			225	225	300	300
4WD	K		1050	1050	1400	1400
V6 4.3 Liter	W		(450)	(450)	(600)	(600)
V8 5.7 Liter	R		250	250	335	335
V8 454/7.4 Liter	J		275	275	365	365
V8 6.5L Turbo Diesel	F,S		450	450	600	600
CREW CAB PICKUP—V8—Truck Equipment Schedule T1						
3500 Long Bed	C33R	23937	5550	6475	8175	10650

TRUCKS & VANS

1997 CHEVROLET/GMC

Body	Type	VIN	List	Trade-In Fair	Good	Pvt-Party Good	Retail Excellent
4WD		K		1050	1050	1400	1400
V8 454/7.4 Liter		J		275	275	365	365
V8 6.5L Turbo Diesel		F		450	450	600	600

1998 CHEVY/GMC–1G(C,K,NorT)–J186–W–#

TRACKER 4WD—4-Cyl.—Truck Equipment Schedule T2
Sport Util Conv 2D		J186	15301	1000	1400	2750	4575
Sport Utility 4D		J136	16251	1550	2050	3500	5450
2WD		E		(475)	(475)	(635)	(635)

BLAZER/JIMMY 4WD—V6—Truck Equipment Schedule T1
Sport Utility 2D		T18W	24166	1950	2475	3925	5925
Sport Utility 4D		T13W	25691	2775	3400	4950	7100
2WD		S		(525)	(525)	(700)	(700)

ENVOY 4WD—V6—Truck Equipment Schedule T3
Sport Utility 4D		K13W	34650	5500	6425	8275	10950

TAHOE/YUKON 4WD—V8—Truck Equipment Schedule T1
Sport Utility 2D		K18R	27670	3750	4475	6550	9325
Sport Utility 4D		K13R	32625	5175	6050	8250	11300
2WD		C		(1175)	(1175)	(1565)	(1565)
V8 6.5L Turbo Diesel		S		475	475	635	635

SUBURBAN—V8—Truck Equipment Schedule T1
C1500 Sport Utility		C16R	27767	4825	5675	7825	10800
C2500 Sport Utility		C26R	29351	5100	5975	8125	11150
w/o Third Seat				(375)	(375)	(500)	(500)
4WD		K		1150	1150	1535	1535
V8 454/7.4 Liter		J		300	300	400	400
V8 6.5L Turbo Diesel		F		475	475	635	635

VENTURE—V6—Truck Equipment Schedule T2
Cargo Minivan		G05E	21329	1225	1675	3125	5075
w/o 2nd Sliding Door				(475)	(475)	(635)	(635)

VENTURE—V6—Truck Equipment Schedule T1
Minivan		U05E	21999	1525	2025	3525	5525
Extended Minivan		X09E	22829	1925	2450	3975	6075
w/o 2nd Sliding Door				(475)	(475)	(635)	(635)

ASTRO/SAFARI—V6—Truck Equipment Schedule T2
Cargo/SL Cargo		M19W	19925	1875	2400	3800	5725
Dutch Doors				100	100	135	135
AWD		L		525	525	700	700

ASTRO/SAFARI—V6—Truck Equipment Schedule T1
Base/SLX Minivan		M19W	21628	2475	3075	4525	6575
5 Passenger				(375)	(375)	(500)	(500)
Dutch Doors				100	100	135	135
AWD		L		525	525	700	700

EXPRESS/SAVANA—V8—Truck Equipment Schedule T1
1500 Passenger Van		G15M	23871	2825	3475	5050	7250
2500 Passenger Van		G25R	25876	2925	3600	5175	7400
3500 Passenger Van		G35M	26165	3100	3750	5375	7650
5 Passenger				(375)	(375)	(500)	(500)
155" W.B.		9		100	100	135	135
V6 4.3 Liter		W		(375)	(375)	(500)	(500)
V8 454/7.4 Liter		J		200	200	265	265
V8 6.5L Turbo Diesel		F		150	150	200	200

G-SERIES/SAVANA—V6—Truck Equipment Schedule T1
1500 Cargo Van		G15M	21102	2825	3450	4875	6900
2500 Cargo Van		G25W	21527	2900	3575	5000	7050
3500 Cargo Van		G35M	23061	2975	3650	5075	7125
155" W.B.				100	100	135	135
V8 5.0, 5.7 Liter		M,R		200	200	265	265
V8 454/7.4 Liter		J		375	375	500	500
V8 6.5L Turbo Diesel		F		275	275	365	365

S10/SONOMA PICKUP—4-Cyl.—Truck Equipment Schedule T2
Short Bed		S144	12508	1525	2025	3250	4975
Long Bed		S144	13172	1325	1825	3000	4675
Extended Cab		S194	15740	2125	2700	3975	5825
Third Door				200	200	265	265
4WD		T		1200	1200	1600	1600
V6 4.3 Liter		X		325	325	435	435
V6 4.3L High Output		W		375	375	500	500

REGULAR CAB PICKUP—V8—Truck Equipment Schedule T1
1500 Short Bed		C14M	19250	3825	4575	6075	8200
1500 Long Bed		C14M	19550	3625	4350	5800	7875
2500 Long Bed		C24M	20232	4050	4825	6325	8525
3500 Long Bed		C34R	21419	4200	4975	6500	8700

1998 CHEVROLET/GMC

Body Type	VIN	List	Fair	Good	Good	Excellent
			Trade-In		Pvt-Party	Retail
Work Truck/Special			(475)	(475)	(635)	(635)
4WD	K		1150	1150	1535	1535
V6 4.3 Liter	W		(450)	(450)	(600)	(600)
V8 5.7 Liter	R		275	275	365	365
V8 454/7.4 Liter	J		300	300	400	400
V8 6.5L Turbo Diesel	F,S		475	475	635	635
EXTENDED CAB PICKUP—V8—Truck Equipment Schedule T1						
1500 Short Bed	C19M	21250	4925	5775	7400	9750
1500 Long Bed	C19M	22045	4675	5525	7075	9375
2500 Short Bed	C29M	22848	5475	6400	8075	10500
2500 HD Long Bed	C29M	22884	5250	6150	7800	10250
3500 Long Bed	C39R	24842	5175	6050	7675	10100
Third Door			250	250	335	335
4WD	K		1150	1150	1535	1535
V6 4.3 Liter	W		(450)	(450)	(600)	(600)
V8 5.7 Liter	R		275	275	365	365
V8 454/7.4 Liter	J		300	300	400	400
V8 6.5L Turbo Diesel	F,S		475	475	635	635
CREW CAB PICKUP—V8—Truck Equipment Schedule T1						
3500 Long Bed	C33R	24549	6275	7275	9025	11650
4WD	K		1150	1150	1535	1535
V8 454/7.4 Liter	J		300	300	400	400
V8 6.5L Turbo Diesel	F		475	475	635	635

1999 CHEVY/GMC—(1,2or3)(CorG)(A,CorN)–J186–X

Body Type	VIN	List	Fair	Good	Good	Excellent
TRACKER 4WD—4-Cyl.—Truck Equipment Schedule T2						
Sport Util Conv 2D	J186	15095	1200	1650	3000	4875
Sport Utility 4D	J136	16295	1875	2400	3825	5825
2WD	E		(525)	(525)	(700)	(700)
BLAZER/JIMMY 4WD—V6—Truck Equipment Schedule T1						
Sport Utility 2D	T18W	22995	2475	3075	4450	6375
Sport Utility 4D	T13W	25945	3375	4075	5525	7625
2WD	S		(575)	(575)	(765)	(765)
ENVOY 4WD—V6—Truck Equipment Schedule T3						
Sport Utility 4D	K13W	34125	6500	7525	9275	11900
TAHOE/YUKON 4WD—V8—Truck Equipment Schedule T1						
Sport Utility 2D	K18R	27995	4575	5400	7500	10400
Sport Utility 4D	K13R	32950	6125	7125	9350	12500
2WD	C		(1225)	(1225)	(1635)	(1635)
V8 6.5L Turbo Diesel	S		525	525	700	700
YUKON DENALI 4WD—V8—Truck Equipment Schedule T3						
Sport Utility 4D	K13R	43505	9600	10950	13550	17250
SUBURBAN—V8—Truck Equipment Schedule T1						
C1500 Sport Utility	C16R	28267	5725	6675	8875	12000
C2500 Sport Utility	C26R	29851	6000	6950	9200	12300
w/o Third Seat			(425)	(425)	(565)	(565)
4WD	K		1225	1225	1635	1635
V8 454/7.4 Liter	J		300	300	400	400
V8 6.5L Turbo Diesel	F		525	525	700	700
VENTURE—V6—Truck Equipment Schedule T2						
Cargo Minivan 4D	G05E	22025	1625	2125	3575	5525
VENTURE—V6—Truck Equipment Schedule T1						
Minivan 4D	U05E	22625	1975	2500	3975	6000
Extended Minivan	X09E	23625	2400	2975	4475	6575
w/o 2nd Sliding Door			(500)	(500)	(665)	(665)
ASTRO/SAFARI—V6—Truck Equipment Schedule T2						
Cargo/SL Cargo	M19W	20268	2300	2875	4275	6175
Dutch Doors			100	100	135	135
AWD	L		575	575	765	765
ASTRO/SAFARI—V6—Truck Equipment Schedule T1						
Minivan/SL Minivan	M19W	21547	2975	3650	5075	7100
Dutch Doors			100	100	135	135
AWD	L		575	575	765	765
EXPRESS/SAVANA—V8—Truck Equipment Schedule T1						
1500 Passenger Van	G15M	24100	3550	4250	5925	8250
2500 Passenger Van	G25R	26105	3650	4375	6050	8375
3500 Passenger Van	G35R	26394	3825	4575	6250	8625
5 Passenger			(425)	(425)	(565)	(565)
155" W.B.	9		100	100	135	135
V6 4.3 Liter	W		(425)	(425)	(565)	(565)
V8 454/7.4 Liter	J		200	200	265	265
V8 6.5L Turbo Diesel	F,S		150	150	200	200

TRUCKS & VANS

1999 CHEVROLET/GMC

Body	Type	VIN	List	Trade-In Fair	Good	Pvt-Party Good	Retail Excellent
EXPRESS/SAVANA—V6—Truck Equipment Schedule T1							
1500 Cargo Van	G15W	21505	**3475**	**4200**	**5625**	**7700**
2500 Cargo Van	G25W	21955	**3600**	**4300**	**5750**	**7850**
3500 Cargo Van	G35R	23489	**3650**	**4400**	**5875**	**7975**
155" W.B.	9		100	100	135	135
V8 5.0, 5.7 Liter	M,R		200	200	265	265
V8 454/7.4 Liter			425	425	565	565
V8 6.5L Turbo Diesel	F,S		300	300	400	400
S10/SONOMA PICKUP—4-Cyl.—Truck Equipment Schedule T2							
Short Bed	S144	12658	**1925**	**2450**	**3700**	**5475**
Long Bed	S144	13322	**1700**	**2225**	**3450**	**5200**
Extended Cab	S194	15890	**2575**	**3175**	**4475**	**6350**
Third Door			200	200	265	265
4WD	T		1275	1275	1700	1700
V6 4.3 Liter	X		375	375	500	500
V6 4.3L High Output	W		425	425	565	565
SILVERADO/SIERRA REGULAR CAB—V8 (New)—Truck Sch T1							
1500 Short Bed	C14V	18390	**4800**	**5625**	**7000**	**9100**
1500 Long Bed	C14V	18690	**4525**	**5350**	**6725**	**8750**
2500 Long Bed	C24T	21601	**5250**	**6100**	**7525**	**9675**
2500 HD Long Bed	C24T	22445	**5400**	**6300**	**7725**	**9900**
4WD	K		1225	1225	1635	1635
V6 4.3 Liter	W		(475)	(475)	(635)	(635)
V8 5.3 Liter	T		300	300	400	400
V8 6.0 Liter	U		300	300	400	400
V8 6.5L Turbo Diesel	F,S		525	525	700	700
SILVERADO/SIERRA EXTENDED CAB—V8 (New)—Truck Sch T1							
1500 Short Bed	C19V	22635	**6250**	**7250**	**8750**	**11050**
1500 Long Bed	C19V	22935	**6000**	**6950**	**8450**	**10700**
2500 Short Bed	C29T	24051	**6875**	**7950**	**9525**	**12000**
2500 HD Short Bed	K29T	27995	**7050**	**8150**	**9750**	**12150**
2500 HD Long Bed	C29T	25195	**6875**	**7900**	**9475**	**11900**
4WD	K		1225	1225	1635	1635
V6 4.3 Liter	W		(475)	(475)	(635)	(635)
V8 5.3 Liter	T		300	300	400	400
V8 6.0 Liter	U		300	300	400	400
V8 6.5L Turbo Diesel	F,S		525	525	700	700
REGULAR CAB PICKUP—V8—Truck Equipment Schedule T1							
2500 HD Long Bed	C24R	21558	**5000**	**5875**	**7400**	**9650**
3500 Long Bed	C34R	21856	**4875**	**5725**	**7250**	**9475**
4WD	K		1225	1225	1635	1635
V8 454/7.4 Liter	J		300	300	400	400
V8 6.5L Turbo Diesel	F,S		525	525	700	700
EXTENDED CAB PICKUP—V8—Truck Equipment Schedule T1							
1500 Short Bed	C19M	23366	**5650**	**6575**	**8150**	**10500**
2500 HD Short Bed	K29M	26268	**6450**	**7475**	**9150**	**11650**
2500 HD Long Bed	C29M	23162	**6050**	**7000**	**8625**	**11050**
3500 Long Bed	C39R	25282	**5950**	**6900**	**8500**	**10900**
4WD	K		1225	1225	1635	1635
V8 5.7 Liter	R		300	300	400	400
V8 454/7.4 Liter	J		300	300	400	400
V8 6.5L Turbo Diesel	F,S		525	525	700	700
CREW CAB PICKUP—V8—Truck Equipment Schedule T1							
2500 Short Bed	C23R	24547	**6475**	**7500**	**9175**	**11700**
3500 Short Bed	C33J	26466	**7350**	**8475**	**10200**	**12850**
3500 Long Bed	C33R	24986	**7150**	**8250**	**10000**	**12600**
4WD	K		1225	1225	1635	1635
V8 454/7.4 Liter	J		300	300	400	400
V8 6.5L Turbo Diesel	F,S		525	525	700	700

2000 CHEVY/GMC—(1,2or3)(CorG)(1,CorN)—J186–Y

Body	Type	VIN	List	Trade-In Fair	Good	Pvt-Party Good	Retail Excellent
TRACKER 4WD—4-Cyl.—Truck Equipment Schedule T2							
Sport Util Conv 2D	J186	15425	**1525**	**2025**	**3525**	**5500**
Sport Utility 4D	J13C	16650	**2350**	**2925**	**4475**	**6600**
2WD	E		(600)	(600)	(800)	(800)
BLAZER/JIMMY 4WD—V6—Truck Equipment Schedule T1							
Sport Utility 2D	T18W	23495	**3050**	**3725**	**5200**	**7275**
Sport Utility 4D	T13W	26995	**4100**	**4875**	**6425**	**8650**
2WD	S		(650)	(650)	(865)	(865)
ENVOY 4WD—V6—Truck Equipment Schedule T3							
Sport Utility 4D	T13W	34695	**7675**	**8825**	**10650**	**13500**
TAHOE 4WD—V8 4.8L Engine (New)—Truck Equipment Sch T1							
Sport Utility 4D	K13V	29441	**9125**	**10425**	**13000**	**16700**

TRUCKS & VANS

Body Type	VIN	List	Trade-In Fair	Trade-In Good	Pvt-Party Good	Retail Excellent
w/o Third Seat	C		(500)	(500)	(665)	(665)
2WD			(1300)	(1300)	(1735)	(1735)
V8 5.3 Liter	T		325	325	435	435
TAHOE 4WD—V8 5.7L Engine—Truck Equipment Schedule T1						
LT Sport Utility 4D	K13R	39544	7700	8850	11350	14850
w/o Third Seat	C		(1300)	(1300)	(1735)	(1735)
YUKON 4WD—V8 (New)—Truck Equipment Schedule T1						
SLE Sport Utility 4D	K13V	35835	9125	10425	13000	16700
w/o Third Seat	C		(500)	(500)	(665)	(665)
2WD			(1300)	(1300)	(1735)	(1735)
V8 5.3 Liter	T		325	325	435	435
YUKON DENALI 4WD—V8—Truck Equipment Schedule T3						
Sport Utility 4D	K13R	44185	11875	13425	16250	20400
SUBURBAN—V8—Truck Equipment Schedule T1						
C1500 Sport Utility	C16T	27651	8025	9225	11500	14850
C2500 Sport Utility	C26U	29535	8325	9525	11850	15250
w/o Third Seat			(500)	(500)	(665)	(665)
4WD	K		1400	1400	1865	1865
YUKON XL—V8—Truck Equipment Schedule T1						
1500 Sport Utility	C13T	35178	8025	9225	11500	14850
2500 Sport Utility	C23U	36696	8325	9525	11850	15250
w/o Third Seat			(500)	(500)	(665)	(665)
4WD	K		1400	1400	1865	1865
VENTURE—V6—Truck Equipment Schedule T2						
Cargo Minivan 4D	U05E	22330	2050	2625	4150	6250
VENTURE—V6—Truck Equipment Schedule T1						
Minivan 4D	U05E	21230	2475	3075	4650	6825
Extended Minivan	X09E	24930	2975	3650	5250	7500
ASTRO/SAFARI—V6—Truck Equipment Schedule T2						
Cargo/SL Cargo	M19W	20635	2725	3350	4775	6825
Dutch Doors			150	150	200	200
AWD	L		675	675	900	900
ASTRO/SAFARI—V6—Truck Equipment Schedule T1						
Minivan/SL Minivan	M19W	21982	3650	4400	5900	8075
Dutch Doors			150	150	200	200
AWD	L		675	675	900	900
EXPRESS/SAVANA—V8—Truck Equipment Schedule T1						
1500 Passenger Van	G15M	24240	4500	5300	7125	9700
2500 Passenger Van	G25R	26245	4625	5450	7275	9850
3500 Passenger Van	G35R	26534	4825	5675	7525	10150
5 Passenger	9		(500)	(500)	(665)	(665)
155" W.B.			150	150	200	200
V6 4.3 Liter	W		(500)	(500)	(665)	(665)
V8 454/7.4 Liter	J		250	250	335	335
V8 6.5L Turbo Diesel	F		175	175	235	235
EXPRESS/SAVANA—V6—Truck Equipment Schedule T1						
1500 Cargo Van	G15W	21910	4350	5125	6700	8975
2500 Cargo Van	G25W	22360	4450	5250	6850	9150
3500 Cargo Van	G35R	23894	4575	5400	6975	9300
155" W.B.			150	150	200	200
V8 5.0, 5.7 Liter	M,R		250	250	335	335
V8 454/7.4 Liter	J		500	500	665	665
V8 6.5L Turbo Diesel	F		350	350	465	465
S10/SONOMA PICKUP—4-Cyl.—Truck Equipment Schedule T2						
Short Bed	S144	12610	2400	2975	4325	6225
Long Bed	S144	12661	2150	2750	4050	5925
Extended Cab	S194	15309	3150	3800	5225	7225
Third Door			225	225	300	300
4WD	T		1450	1450	1935	1935
V6 4.3 Liter	W		500	500	665	665
SILVERADO/SIERRA REGULAR CAB—V8 (New)—Truck Sch T1						
1500 Short Bed	C14V	18510	5550	6475	7850	10000
1500 Long Bed	C14V	18810	5250	6125	7525	9625
2500 Long Bed	C24T	21950	6050	7000	8450	10650
2500 HD Long Bed	C24T	23074	6225	7225	8650	10900
4WD	K		1400	1400	1865	1865
V6 4.3 Liter	W		(550)	(550)	(735)	(735)
V8 5.3 Liter	T		325	325	435	435
V8 6.0 Liter	U		350	350	465	465
SILVERADO/SIERRA EXTENDED CAB—V8 (New)—Truck Sch T1						
1500 Short Bed	C19V	22884	7200	8325	9850	12200
1500 Short Bed	C19V	23184	6900	7975	9475	11850
2500 Short Bed	C29T	24400	7975	9175	10750	13300

TRUCKS & VANS

Body Type	VIN	List	Trade-In Fair	Good	Pvt-Party Good	Retail Excellent
2500 HD Short Bed	C29T	28324	8150	9325	10950	13500
2500 HD Long Bed	C29T	25524	7925	9125	10700	13250
4WD	K		1400	1400	1865	1865
Fourth Door			250	250	335	335
V6 4.3 Liter	W		(550)	(550)	(735)	(735)
V8 5.3 Liter	T		325	325	435	435
V8 6.0 Liter	U		350	350	465	465
REGULAR CAB PICKUP—V8—Truck Equipment Schedule T1						
2500 HD Long Bed	C24R	21837	5700	6625	8175	10500
3500 Long Bed	C34R	22435	5600	6525	8100	10450
4WD	K		1400	1400	1865	1865
V8 454/7.4 Liter	J		350	350	465	465
V8 6.5L Turbo Diesel	F		600	600	800	800
EXTENDED CAB PICKUP—V8—Truck Equipment Schedule T1						
2500 HD Short Bed	K29R	26547	7450	8550	10300	12900
2500 HD Long Bed	C29R	23441	7025	8100	9750	12300
3500 Long Bed	C39R	25861	6950	8025	9700	12200
4WD	K		1400	1400	1865	1865
V8 454/7.4 Liter	J		350	350	465	465
V8 6.5L Turbo Diesel	F		600	600	800	800
CREW CAB PICKUP—V8—Truck Equipment Schedule T1						
2500 Short Bed	C23R	24826	7600	8725	10450	13100
3500 Short Bed	C33R	27045	8500	9700	11500	14300
3500 Long Bed	C33R	25565	8225	9425	11200	13950
4WD	K		1400	1400	1865	1865
V8 454/7.4 Liter	J		350	350	465	465
V8 6.5L Turbo Diesel	F		600	600	800	800

2001 CHEVY/GMC—(1,2or3)(CorG)(A,CorN)–J186–1

Body Type	VIN	List	Trade-In Fair	Good	Pvt-Party Good	Retail Excellent
TRACKER 4WD—4-Cyl.—Truck Equipment Schedule T2						
Sport Util Conv 2D	J1B6	16760	2025	2575	4150	6300
Sport Utility 4D	J13C	17380	2925	3600	5250	7525
ZR2 Spt Util Conv 2D	J78C	18835	2575	3200	4800	7025
ZR2 Sport Utility 4D	J734	21200	3675	4425	6100	8500
LT Sport Utility 4D	J634	21880	4225	5025	6750	9225
2WD			(675)	(675)	(900)	(900)
V6 2.5 Liter	4		550	550	735	735
BLAZER/JIMMY 4WD—V6—Truck Equipment Schedule T1						
Sport Utility 2D	T18W	23745	3900	4650	6200	8450
Sport Utility 4D	T13W	27345	5075	5950	7600	10000
2WD	S		(725)	(725)	(965)	(965)
TAHOE 4WD—V8—Truck Equipment Schedule T1						
Sport Utility 4D	K13V	31021	10775	12275	15000	19000
w/o Third Seat			(550)	(550)	(735)	(735)
2WD	C		(1350)	(1350)	(1800)	(1800)
V8 5.3 Liter	T		350	350	465	465
YUKON 4WD—V8—Truck Equipment Schedule T1						
SLE Sport Utility 4D	K13T	36128	10775	12275	15000	19000
w/o Third Seat			(550)	(550)	(735)	(735)
2WD	C		(1350)	(1350)	(1800)	(1800)
V8 5.3 Liter	T,Z		350	350	465	465
YUKON DENALI 4WD—V8—Truck Equipment Schedule T3						
Sport Utility 4D	K13U	46680	15475	17400	20600	25200
SUBURBAN—V8—Truck Equipment Schedule T1						
C1500 Sport Utility	C16T	29428	9475	10825	13300	16950
C2500 Sport Utility	C26U	31287	9800	11200	13700	17350
w/o Third Seat			(550)	(550)	(735)	(735)
4WD	K		1575	1575	2100	2100
V8 8.1 Liter	G		400	400	535	535
YUKON XL—V8—Truck Equipment Schedule T1						
1500 Sport Utility	C13T	36287	9475	10825	13300	16950
2500 Sport Utility	C23U	37659	9800	11200	13700	17350
4WD	K		1575	1575	2100	2100
V8 8.1 Liter	G		400	400	535	535
YUKON XL DENALI AWD—V8—Truck Equipment Schedule T3						
1500 Sport Utility	K16U	48185	16875	18975	22000	26700
VENTURE—V6—Truck Equipment Schedule T1						
Minivan 4D	U05E	21605	3150	3800	5525	7900
Extended Minivan	X09E	26085	3700	4450	6175	8625
ASTRO/SAFARI—V6—Truck Equipment Schedule T2						
Cargo/SL Cargo	M19W	21238	3300	3975	5525	7700
Dutch Doors			200	200	265	265
AWD	L		750	750	1000	1000

Body Type	VIN	List	Trade-In Fair	Trade-In Good	Pvt-Party Good	Retail Excellent
ASTRO/SAFARI—V6—Truck Equipment Schedule T1						
Minivan 3D	M19W	23886	4500	5300	6925	9300
Dutch Doors			200	200	265	265
AWD	L		750	750	1000	1000
EXPRESS/SAVANA VAN—V8—Truck Equipment Schedule T1						
1500 Passenger Van	G15M	24730	5700	6625	8625	11500
2500 Passenger Van	G25R	26735	5850	6800	8800	11700
3500 Passenger Van	G35R	27024	6075	7025	9075	12000
155" W.B.			175	175	235	235
V6 8.3 Liter	W		(550)	(550)	(735)	(735)
V8 8.1 Liter	G		275	275	365	365
V8 6.5L Turbo Diesel	F		200	200	265	265
EXPRESS/SAVANA VAN—V6—Truck Equipment Schedule T1						
1500 Cargo Van	G15W	22520	5400	6300	8000	10500
2500 Cargo Van	G25W	22650	5550	6475	8175	10650
3500 Cargo Van	G35R	24929	5700	6650	8350	10850
155" W.B.			175	175	235	235
V8 5.0, 5.7 Liter	M,R		275	275	365	365
V8 8.1 Liter	G		550	550	735	735
V8 6.5L Turbo Diesel	F		400	400	535	535
S10/SONOMA PICKUP—4-Cyl. Flex Fuel—Truck Equip Sch T2						
Short Bed	S145	12859	2975	3650	5075	7125
Long Bed	S145	13210	2725	3350	4775	6800
Extended Cab	S195	16203	3825	4575	6075	8250
Third Door			250	250	335	335
4WD	T		1625	1625	2165	2165
V6 4.3 Liter	W		550	550	735	735
S10/SONOMA CREW CAB 4WD—V6—Truck Equip Sch T1						
LS/SLS Short Bed	T13W	25369	6675	7700	9400	12000
SILVERADO/SIERRA REGULAR CAB—V8—Truck Equip Sch T1						
1500 Short Bed	C14V	19185	6475	7500	8925	11150
1500 Long Bed	C14V	19485	6125	7125	8525	10700
2500 Long Bed	C24U	23689	7025	8125	9575	11900
2500 HD Long Bed	C24U	24109	7250	8350	9850	12150
3500 Long Bed	C34U	25361	7300	8400	9900	12200
4WD	K		1575	1575	2100	2100
V6 4.3 Liter	W		(625)	(625)	(835)	(835)
V8 5.3 Liter	T		350	350	465	465
V8 8.1 Liter	G		400	400	535	535
V8 6.6L Turbo Diesel	1		5050	5050	6730	6730
SILVERADO/SIERRA EXTENDED CAB—V8—Truck Equip Sch T1						
1500 Short Bed	C19V	23889	8375	9575	11150	13650
1500 Long Bed	C19V	23889	8025	9225	10700	13200
2500 HD Short Bed	K29U	29039	9250	10525	12150	14800
2500 HD Short Bed	K29U	26614	9425	10775	12400	15050
2500 HD Long Bed	C29U	26859	9200	10475	12100	14700
3500 Long Bed	C39U	28141	9250	10525	12150	14800
4WD	K		1575	1575	2100	2100
V6 4.3 Liter	W		(625)	(625)	(835)	(835)
V8 5.3 Liter	T		350	350	465	465
V8 8.1 Liter	G		400	400	535	535
V8 6.6L Turbo Diesel	1		5050	5050	6730	6730
SIERRA EXTENDED CAB PICKUP—V8—Truck Equip Sch T1						
1500 C3 Short Bed	C19V	38995	13425	15175	17100	20400
SILVERADO/SIERRA CREW CAB—V8—Truck Equipment Sch T1						
1500 HD Short Bed	C13U	28912	9475	10825	12450	15100
2500 HD Short Bed	C23U	27984	10375	11825	13550	16300
2500 HD Long Bed	C23U	28284	10225	11650	13350	16100
3500 Long Bed	C33U	30766	10275	11700	13400	16150
4WD	K		1575	1575	2100	2100
V8 8.1 Liter	G		400	400	535	535
V8 6.6L Turbo Diesel	1		5050	5050	6730	6730
2002 CHEVY/GMC—1,2or3(CorG)A,CorN—(J18C)—2						
TRACKER 4WD—4-Cyl.—Truck Equipment Schedule T2						
Sport Util Conv 2D	J18C	17415	2650	3275	4950	7275
Sport Utility 4D	J13C	18105	3650	4400	6150	8600
ZR2 Spt Utl Conv 2D	J78C	19395	3275	3950	5700	8100
ZR2 Sport Utility 4D	J734	21845	4500	5300	7125	9700
LT Sport Utility 4D	J634	22270	5100	6000	7825	10500
2WD	E		(750)	(750)	(1000)	(1000)
V6 2.5 Liter	4		600	600	800	800

TRUCKS & VANS

2002 CHEVROLET/GMC

Body	Type	VIN	List	Trade-In Fair	Good	Pvt-Party Good	Retail Excellent
BLAZER 4WD—V6—Truck Equipment Schedule T1							
Sport Utility 2D	T18W	23895	**4950**	**5800**	**7475**	**9900**
Sport Utility 4D	T13W	26130	**6225**	**7225**	**9000**	**11600**
2WD	S		**(800)**	**(800)**	**(1065)**	**(1065)**
TRAILBLAZER 4WD—6-Cyl.—Truck Equipment Schedule T1							
Sport Utility 4D	T1S3	28130	**8950**	**10225**	**12150**	**15150**
Extended Spt Util 4D	T16S	33610	**9200**	**10475**	**12400**	**15350**
2WD	S		**(1400)**	**(1400)**	**(1865)**	**(1865)**
ENVOY 4WD—6-Cyl.—Truck Equipment Schedule T1							
Sport Utility 4D	T13S	31770	**8950**	**10225**	**12150**	**15150**
2WD	S		**(1400)**	**(1400)**	**(1865)**	**(1865)**
ENVOY XL 4WD—6-Cyl.—Truck Equipment Schedule T1							
Sport Utility 4D	T16S	33820	**9200**	**10475**	**12400**	**15350**
2WD	S		**(1400)**	**(1400)**	**(1865)**	**(1865)**
TAHOE 4WD—V8—Truck Equipment Schedule T1							
Sport Utility 4D	K13V	36345	**12600**	**14250**	**17200**	**21500**
w/o Third Seat			**(600)**	**(600)**	**(800)**	**(800)**
2WD	C		**(1400)**	**(1400)**	**(1865)**	**(1865)**
V8 5.3 Liter	T,Z		**375**	**375**	**500**	**500**
YUKON 4WD—V8—Truck Equipment Schedule T1							
Sport Utility 4D	K13V	37000	**12600**	**14250**	**17200**	**21500**
w/o Third Seat			**(600)**	**(600)**	**(800)**	**(800)**
2WD	C		**(1400)**	**(1400)**	**(1865)**	**(1865)**
V8 5.3 Liter	T,Z		**375**	**375**	**500**	**500**
YUKON DENALI 4WD—V8—Truck Equipment Schedule T3							
Sport Utility 4D	K13U	47355	**17800**	**19975**	**23300**	**28200**
SUBURBAN—V8—Truck Equipment Schedule T1							
C1500 Sport Utility	C16T	35988	**11200**	**12700**	**15350**	**19300**
C2500 Sport Utility	C26U	37601	**11600**	**13150**	**15800**	**19800**
4WD	K		**1750**	**1750**	**2335**	**2335**
V8 8.1 Liter	G		**450**	**450**	**600**	**600**
YUKON XL—V8—Truck Equipment Schedule T1							
1500 Sport Utility	C13T	37047	**11200**	**12700**	**15350**	**19300**
2500 Sport Utility	C23U	38419	**11600**	**13150**	**15800**	**19800**
4WD	K		**1750**	**1750**	**2335**	**2335**
V8 8.1 Liter	G		**450**	**450**	**600**	**600**
YUKON XL DENALI AWD—V8—Truck Equipment Schedule T3							
1500 Sport Utility 4D	K16U	48890	**19350**	**21725**	**24900**	**29900**
VENTURE—V6—Truck Equipment Schedule T2							
Cargo Minivan 4D	U05E	24697	**3450**	**4150**	**5975**	**8500**
VENTURE—V6—Truck Equipment Schedule T1							
Minivan 4D	U03E	22035	**4025**	**4775**	**6650**	**9250**
Extended Minivan 4D	X03E	26255	**4650**	**5475**	**7375**	**10050**
5 Passenger			**(600)**	**(600)**	**(800)**	**(800)**
AWD			**825**	**825**	**1100**	**1100**
ASTRO/SAFARI—V6—Truck Equipment Schedule T2							
Cargo/SL Cargo	M19W	21768	**4050**	**4825**	**6500**	**8850**
Dutch Doors			**250**	**250**	**335**	**335**
AWD	L		**825**	**825**	**1100**	**1100**
ASTRO/SAFARI—V6—Truck Equipment Schedule T1							
Minivan 3D	M19W	24416	**5550**	**6475**	**8225**	**10750**
Dutch Doors			**250**	**250**	**335**	**335**
AWD	L		**825**	**825**	**1100**	**1100**
EXPRESS/SAVANA VAN—V8—Truck Equipment Schedule T1							
1500 Passenger Van	G15M	25287	**7175**	**8275**	**10500**	**13700**
2500 Passenger Van	G25R	27292	**7350**	**8450**	**10650**	**13850**
3500 Passenger Van	G35R	27581	**7600**	**8725**	**10950**	**14200**
155" W.B.			**200**	**200**	**265**	**265**
V6 4.3 Liter	W		**(600)**	**(600)**	**(800)**	**(800)**
V8 8.1 Liter	G		**225**	**225**	**300**	**300**
V8 6.5L Turbo Diesel	F		**300**	**300**	**400**	**400**
EXPRESS/SAVANA VAN—V6—Truck Equipment Schedule T1							
1500 Cargo Van	G15W	22948	**6750**	**7800**	**9625**	**12300**
2500 Cargo Van	G25W	23078	**6900**	**7975**	**9800**	**12500**
3500 Cargo Van	G35R	25357	**7125**	**8225**	**10050**	**12800**
155" W.B.			**200**	**200**	**265**	**265**
V8 5.0, 5.7 Liter	M,R		**300**	**300**	**400**	**400**
V8 8.1 Liter	G		**600**	**600**	**800**	**800**
V8 6.5L Turbo Diesel	F		**450**	**450**	**600**	**600**
S10/SONOMA PICKUP—4-Cyl. Flex Fuel—Truck Equip Sch T2							
Short Bed	S145	14327	**3675**	**4425**	**5975**	**8175**
Long Bed	S145	15772	**3425**	**4125**	**5650**	**7825**
Extended Cab	S195	16309	**4625**	**5450**	**7050**	**9375**

DEDUCT FOR RECONDITIONING 0106

2002 CHEVROLET/GMC

Body	Type	VIN	List	Trade-In Fair	Good	Pvt-Party Good	Retail Excellent
4WD		T		1800	1800	2400	2400
V6 4.3 Liter		W		600	600	800	800

S10/SONOMA CREW CAB PICKUP 4WD—V6—Truck Sch T1

| LS/SLS Short Bed | | T13W | 24584 | 8025 | 9225 | 11050 | 13800 |

AVALANCHE 4WD—V8—Truck Equipment Schedule T1

1500 Spt Util Pickup		C13T	33965	12600	14250	16050	19000
2500 Spt Util Pickup		C23G	35865	13375	15125	17000	20100
2WD				(800)	(800)	(1065)	(1065)
NorthFace Edition				800	800	1065	1065

SILVERADO/SIERRA REGULAR CAB—V8—Truck Equip Sch T1

1500 Short Bed		C14V	20028	7625	8750	10200	12500
1500 Long Bed		C14V	20328	7225	8350	9750	12050
2500 Long Bed		C24U	24182	8225	9425	10900	13350
2500 HD Long Bed		C24U	24672	8500	9700	11200	13700
3500 Long Bed		C34U	29017	8525	9750	11250	13750
4WD		K		1750	1750	2335	2335
V6 4.3 Liter		W,X		(700)	(700)	(935)	(935)
V8 5.3 Liter		T		375	375	500	500
V8 8.1 Liter		G		450	450	600	600
V8 6.6L Turbo Diesel		1		5300	5300	7065	7065

SILVERADO/SIERRA EXTENDED CAB—V8—Truck Equip Sch T1

1500 Short Bed		C19V	23952	9700	11050	12600	15250
1500 Long Bed		C19V	25052	9300	10625	12150	14750
2500 Short Bed		K29U	29407	10675	12125	13750	16500
2500 HD Short Bed		K29U	27177	10925	12375	14000	16800
2500 HD Long Bed		C29U	27452	10625	12075	13750	16450
3500 Long Bed		C39U	28734	10675	12125	13750	16500
Quadrasteer				775	775	1035	1035
4WD		K		1750	1750	2335	2335
V6 4.3 Liter		W,X		(700)	(700)	(935)	(935)
V8 5.3 Liter		T		375	375	500	500
V8 8.1 Liter		G		450	450	600	600
V8 6.6L Turbo Diesel		1		5300	5300	7065	7065

SIERRA DENALI EXT CAB PICKUP AWD—V8—Truck Sch T3

| 1500 Short Bed | | K69U | 44105 | 15675 | 17650 | 19600 | 23000 |

SILVERADO/SIERRA CREW CAB PICKUP—V8—Truck Sch T1

1500 HD Short Bed		C13U	29425	10950	12425	14100	16900
2500 HD Short Bed		C23U	28577	11975	13575	15300	18200
2500 HD Long Bed		C23U	28877	11775	13350	15100	17950
3500 Long Bed		C33U	30159	11375	13425	15200	18300
4WD		K		1750	1750	2335	2335
V8 8.1 Liter		G		450	450	600	600
V8 6.6L Turbo Diesel		1		5300	5300	7065	7065

2003 CHEVY/GMC—1,2or3(CorG)A,CorN—(J18C)—3

TRACKER 4WD—4-Cyl.—Truck Equipment Schedule T2

Sport Util Conv 2D		J18C	17815	3475	4175	5975	8475
Sport Utility 4D		J13C	18505	4575	5400	7275	9900
ZR2 Spt Util Conv 2D		J78C	19675	4150	4925	6775	9350
ZR2 Sport Utility 4D		J734	22125	5475	6400	8325	11050
LT Sport Utility 4D		J634	22550	6125	7125	9075	11900
2WD		E		(825)	(825)	(1100)	(1100)
V6 2.5 Liter		4		650	650	865	865

BLAZER 4WD—V6—Truck Equipment Schedule T1

Sport Utility 2D		T18X	24705	6225	7225	9025	11700
Sport Utility 4D		T13X	26585	7650	8800	10650	13500
2WD		S		(875)	(875)	(1165)	(1165)

TRAILBLAZER 4WD—6-Cyl.—Truck Equipment Schedule T1

Sport Utility 4D		T13S	28800	10625	12075	14050	17200
Extended Spt Util 4D		T16S	33510	11300	12800	14850	18050
2WD		S		(1450)	(1450)	(1935)	(1935)
V8 5.3 Liter		P		400	400	535	535

ENVOY 4WD—6-Cyl.—Truck Equipment Schedule T1

| Sport Utility 4D | | T13S | 30820 | 10625 | 12075 | 14050 | 17200 |
| 2WD | | S | | (1450) | (1450) | (1935) | (1935) |

ENVOY XL 4WD—6-Cyl.—Truck Equipment Schedule T1

Sport Utility 4D		T16S	33220	11300	12800	14850	18050
2WD		S		(1450)	(1450)	(1935)	(1935)
V8 5.3 Liter		P		400	400	535	535

TAHOE 4WD—V8—Truck Equipment Schedule T1

Sport Utility 4D		K13V	37387	14750	16625	19800	24400
w/o Third Seat				(650)	(650)	(865)	(865)
2WD		C		(1450)	(1450)	(1935)	(1935)

TRUCKS & VANS

TRUCKS & VANS

Body	Type	VIN	List	Trade-In Fair	Good	Pvt-Party Good	Retail Excellent
V8 5.3 Liter		T,Z		400	400	535	535
YUKON 4WD—V8—Truck Equipment Schedule T1							
Sport Utility 4D		K13V	37920	14750	16625	19800	24400
w/o Third Seat				(650)	(650)	(865)	(865)
2WD		C		(1450)	(1450)	(1935)	(1935)
V8 5.3 Liter		T,Z		400	400	535	535
YUKON DENALI 4WD—V8—Truck Equipment Schedule T3							
Sport Utility 4D		K13U	49195	20375	22900	26300	31600
SUBURBAN—V8—Truck Equipment Schedule T1							
C1500 Sport Utility		C16T	37030	13150	14900	17750	22000
C2500 Sport Utility		C26U	38643	13575	15325	18250	22600
Quadrasteer				850	850	1135	1135
4WD		K		1925	1925	2565	2565
V8 8.1 Liter		G		500	500	665	665
YUKON XL—V8—Truck Equipment Schedule T1							
1500 Sport Utility		C13T	37967	13150	14900	17750	22000
2500 Sport Utility		C23U	39435	13575	15325	18250	22600
Quadrasteer				850	850	1135	1135
4WD		K		1925	1925	2565	2565
V8 8.1 Liter		G		500	500	665	665
YUKON XL DENALI AWD—V8—Truck Equipment Schedule T3							
1500 Sport Utility 4D		K16U	50859	22125	24725	28000	33400
VENTURE—V6—Truck Equipment Schedule T2							
Cargo Minivan 4D		U03E	22925	4500	5300	7300	10100
VENTURE—V6—Truck Equipment Schedule T1							
Minivan 4D		U03E	23139	5175	6050	8075	10900
Extended Minivan 4D		X03E	24509	5850	6825	8875	11800
5 Passenger				(650)	(650)	(865)	(865)
AWD		V		900	900	1200	1200
ASTRO/SAFARI—V6—Truck Equipment Schedule T2							
Cargo/SL Cargo 3D		M19X	21952	5100	5975	7775	10400
Dutch Doors				300	300	400	400
AWD		L		900	900	1200	1200
ASTRO/SAFARI—V6—Truck Equipment Schedule T1							
Minivan 3D		M19X	23801	6850	7875	9800	12600
Dutch Doors				300	300	400	400
AWD		L		900	900	1200	1200
EXPRESS/SAVANA VAN—V8—Truck Equipment Schedule T1							
1500 Passenger Van		G15X	27005	9075	10375	12800	16350
2500 Passenger Van		G25U	28000	9275	10575	13050	16650
3500 Passenger Van		G35U	28504	9525	10875	13350	16950
155" W.B.				225	225	300	300
AWD		H		(650)	(650)	(865)	(865)
V6 4.3 Liter		X		900	900	1200	1200
EXPRESS/SAVANA VAN—V6—Truck Equipment Schedule T1							
1500 Cargo Van		G15X	23265	8500	9700	11650	14600
2500 Cargo Van		G25X	23415	8675	9950	11900	14900
3500 Cargo Van		G35U	25969	8950	10225	12150	15200
155" W.B.				225	225	300	300
V8 4.8, 5.3 Liter		T,V		325	325	435	435
V8 6.0 Liter		U		650	650	865	865
S10/SONOMA PICKUP—4-Cyl.—Truck Equipment Schedule T2							
Short Bed		S14H	14771	4500	5325	7000	9425
Long Bed		S14H	16216	4225	5025	6700	9075
Extended Cab		S19H	16593	5550	6475	8200	10700
4WD		T		1975	1975	2635	2635
V6 4.3 Liter		X		650	650	865	865
S10/SONOMA CREW CAB PICKUP 4WD—V6—Truck Equip Sch T1							
LS/SLS Short Bed		T13X	24404	9525	10875	12800	15750
SSR REGULAR CAB PICKUP—V8—Truck Equipment Schedule T3							
LS Convertible 2D		S14P	41995	23275	26100	28300	32500
AVALANCHE—V8—Truck Equipment Schedule T1							
1500 Spt Util Pickup		K13T	35139	14550	16450	18250	21300
2500 Spt Util Pickup		K23G	37039	15375	17325	19150	22400
North Face Edition				850	850	1135	1135
2WD		C		(875)	(875)	(1165)	(1165)
SILVERADO/SIERRA REGULAR CAB PICKUP—V8—Truck Sch T1							
1500 Short Bed		C14V	20726	8975	10275	11800	14250
1500 Long Bed		C14V	21026	8600	9850	11350	13750
2500 Long Bed		C24U	23627	9700	11050	12550	15150
2500 HD Long Bed		C24U	23877	9950	11350	12900	15450
3500 Long Bed		K34U	29317	10000	11350	12950	15500
Work Truck				(1125)	(1125)	(1500)	(1500)

Body / Type	VIN	List	Trade-In Fair	Trade-In Good	Pvt-Party Good	Retail Excellent
4WD	K		1925	1925	2565	2565
V6 4.3 Liter	X		(750)	(750)	(1000)	(1000)
V8 5.3 Liter	T		400	400	535	535
V8 8.1 Liter	G		500	500	665	665
V8 6.6L Turbo Diesel	1		5550	5550	7400	7400
SILVERADO/SIERRA EXTENDED CAB PICKUP—V8—Truck Sch T1						
1500 Short Bed	C19V	24465	11300	12800	14400	17150
1500 Long Bed	C19V	25565	10875	12325	13900	16650
2500 Short Bed	K29U	29822	12325	13975	15600	18500
2500 HD Short Bed	K29U	26257	12550	14200	15900	18800
2500 HD Long Bed	C29U	26532	12275	13925	15625	18450
3500 Long Bed	C39U	28909	12325	13975	15600	18500
Quadrasteer			850	850	1135	1135
Work Truck			(1125)	(1125)	(1500)	(1500)
4WD	K		1925	1925	2565	2565
V6 4.3 Liter	X		(750)	(750)	(1000)	(1000)
V8 5.3 Liter	T		400	400	535	535
V8 8.1 Liter	G		500	500	665	665
V8 6.6L Turbo Diesel	1		5550	5550	7400	7400
SILVERADO SS EXTENDED CAB PICKUP AWD—V8—Truck Sch T3						
1500 Short Bed	K19V	39995	17125	19250	21100	24600
SIERRA DENALI EXT CAB PICKUP AWD—V8—Truck Sch T3						
1500 Short Bed	K19W	44995	17800	19975	21900	25400
SILVERADO/SIERRA CREW CAB PICKUP—V8—Truck Equip Sch T1						
1500 Short Bed	C13U	30442	12650	14300	16000	18900
2500 HD Short Bed	C23U	29277	13825	15625	17350	20400
2500 HD Long Bed	C23U	29577	13575	15325	17050	20100
3500 Long Bed	C33U	30714	13675	15425	17150	20200
Quadrasteer			850	850	1135	1135
4WD	K		1925	1925	2565	2565
V8 8.1 Liter	G		500	500	665	665
V8 6.6L Turbo Diesel	1		5550	5550	7400	7400

2004 CHEVY/GMC—(1,2or3)(CorG)(A,CorN)–J134–4

Body / Type	VIN	List	Trade-In Fair	Trade-In Good	Pvt-Party Good	Retail Excellent
TRACKER 4WD—V6—Truck Equipment Schedule T2						
Sport Utility 4D	J134	21355	5725	6675	8500	11200
ZB2 Sport Utility 4D	J734	22705	6700	7725	9650	12450
LT Sport Utility 4D	J634	23105	7425	8525	10500	13350
2WD	E		(900)	(900)	(1200)	(1200)
BLAZER 4WD—V6—Truck Equipment Schedule T1						
Sport Utility 2D	T18X	25395	7825	9000	10800	13600
Sport Utility 4D	T13X	27345	9400	10725	12600	15500
2WD	S		(950)	(950)	(1265)	(1265)
TRAILBLAZER 4WD—6-Cyl.—Truck Equipment Schedule T1						
Sport Utility 4D	T13S	30045	12550	14200	16300	19600
Extended Spt Util 4D	T16S	32595	13675	15425	17500	21000
2WD	S		(1500)	(1500)	(2000)	(2000)
V8 5.3 Liter	P		400	400	535	535
ENVOY 4WD—6-Cyl.—Truck Equipment Schedule T1						
Sport Utility 4D	T13S	31745	12550	14200	16300	19600
2WD	S		(1500)	(1500)	(2000)	(2000)
ENVOY XL 4WD—6-Cyl.—Truck Equipment Schedule T1						
Sport Utility 4D	T16S	33845	13675	15425	17500	21000
2WD	S		(1500)	(1500)	(2000)	(2000)
V8 5.3 Liter	P		400	400	535	535
ENVOY XUV 4WD—6-Cyl.—Truck Equipment Schedule T1						
Sport Utility 4D	T12S	34115	14800	16675	18800	22400
2WD	S		(1500)	(1500)	(2000)	(2000)
V8 5.3 Liter	P		400	400	535	535
TAHOE 4WD—V8—Truck Equipment Schedule T1						
Sport Utility 4D	K13V	38425	17225	19350	22700	27700
w/o Third Seat			(700)	(700)	(935)	(935)
2WD	C		(1500)	(1500)	(2000)	(2000)
V8 5.3 Liter	T,Z		400	400	535	535
YUKON 4WD—V8—Truck Equipment Schedule T1						
Sport Utility 4D	K13V	38785	17225	19350	22700	27700
w/o Third Seat			(700)	(700)	(935)	(935)
2WD	C		(1500)	(1500)	(2000)	(2000)
V8 5.3 Liter	T		400	400	535	535
YUKON DENALI AWD—V8—Truck Equipment Schedule T3						
Sport Utility 4D	K13U	50125	23275	26100	29700	35400
SUBURBAN—V8—Truck Equipment Schedule T1						
C1500 Sport Utility	C16T	37865	15475	17400	20500	25100

2004 CHEVROLET/GMC

Body	Type	VIN	List	Trade-In Fair	Trade-In Good	Pvt-Party Good	Retail Excellent
C2500 Sport Utility		C26U	39465	15900	17900	21000	25700
	Quadrasteer			925	925	1235	1235
	4WD	K		2100	2100	2800	2800
	V8 8.1 Liter	G		550	550	735	735
YUKON XL—V8—Truck Equipment Schedule T1							
1500 Sport Utility		C13T	38775	15475	17400	20500	25100
2500 Sport Utility		C23U	40275	15900	17900	21000	25700
	Quadrasteer			925	925	1235	1235
	4WD	K		2100	2100	2800	2800
	V8 8.1 Liter	G		550	550	735	735
YUKON XL DENALI AWD—V8—Truck Equipment Schedule T3							
1500 Sport Utility 4D		K16U	51775	25225	28225	31600	37300
VENTURE—V6—Truck Equipment Schedule T2							
Cargo Minivan 4D		U03E	23120	6000	6950	9000	11950
VENTURE—V6—Truck Equipment Schedule T1							
Minivan 4D		U03E	21995	6725	7750	9850	12850
Extended Minivan 4D		X09E	23570	7475	8575	10700	13800
	5 Passenger			(700)	(700)	(935)	(935)
	AWD	V		975	975	1300	1300
ASTRO/SAFARI—V6—Truck Equipment Schedule T2							
Cargo 3D		M19X	22965	6500	7525	9400	12150
	Dutch Doors			350	350	465	465
	AWD	L		975	975	1300	1300
ASTRO/SAFARI—V6—Truck Equipment Schedule T1							
Minivan 3D		M19X	24395	8525	9750	11750	14750
	Dutch Doors			350	350	465	465
	AWD	L		975	975	1300	1300
EXPRESS/SAVANA VAN—V8—Truck Equipment Schedule T1							
1500 Passenger Van		G15T	27280	11450	13000	15650	19600
2500 Passenger Van		G25U	28685	11650	13200	15900	19900
3500 Passenger Van		G35U	29089	11925	13525	16200	20200
	155" W.B.			250	250	335	335
	AWD	H		900	900	1200	1200
	V6 4.3 Liter	X		(700)	(700)	(935)	(935)
EXPRESS/SAVANA VAN—V6—Truck Equipment Schedule T1							
1500 Cargo Van		G15X	23185	10675	12175	14200	17400
2500 Cargo Van		G25X	23965	10925	12375	14450	17650
3500 Cargo Van		G35U	27194	11200	12700	14800	18050
3500 Van Cab-Ch		G35U		10575	12025	14050	17200
	155" W.B.			250	250	335	335
	AWD			900	900	1200	1200
	V8 4.8, 5.3 Liter	V,T		350	350	465	465
	V8 6.0 Liter	U		700	700	935	935
S10/SONOMA CREW CAB PICKUP 4WD—V6—Truck Sch T1							
LS/SLS Short Bed		T13X	25095	11200	12700	14700	17850
COLORADO/CANYON PICKUP—4-Cyl.—Truck Equip Sch T1							
Short Bed		S148	16200	5700	6625	8325	10800
Extended Cab		S198	18545	6800	7850	9600	12200
Crew Cab		S138	20670	7900	9075	10850	13650
	4WD	T		2150	2150	2865	2865
	5-Cyl. 3.5 Liter	6		200	200	265	265
SSR REGULAR CAB PICKUP—V8—Truck Equipment Schedule T1							
Convertible 2D		S14P	41995	26475	29575	31800	36100
AVALANCHE 4WD—V8—Truck Equipment Schedule T1							
1500 Spt Util Pickup		K12T	36100	16775	18875	20700	24000
2500 Spt Util Pickup		K22G	37935	17600	19800	21500	24800
	2WD			(950)	(950)	(1265)	(1265)
SILVERADO/SIERRA REGULAR CAB PICKUP—V8—Truck Sch T1							
1500 Short Bed		C14V	23400	10675	12125	13550	16050
1500 Long Bed		C14V	23700	10225	11650	13050	15500
2500 Short Bed		C24U	26660	11400	12950	14400	17000
2500 HD Long Bed		C24U	26910	11700	13250	14800	17400
3500 Long Bed		K34U	30940	11775	13350	14850	17500
	Work Truck			(1275)	(1275)	(1700)	(1700)
	4WD	K		2100	2100	2800	2800
	V6 4.3 Liter	X		(800)	(800)	(1065)	(1065)
	V8 5.3 Liter	T		400	400	535	535
	V8 8.1 Liter	G		550	550	735	735
	V8 6.6L Turbo Diesel	1,2		5800	5800	7730	7730
SILVERADO/SIERRA EXTENDED CAB PICKUP—V8—Truck Sch T1							
1500 Short Bed		C19V	26260	13150	14900	16450	19250
1500 Long Bed		C19V	27360	12700	14350	15900	18650
2500 Short Bed		K29U	31615	14250	16100	17750	20700

TRUCKS & VANS

Body	Type	VIN	List	Trade-In Fair	Trade-In Good	Pvt-Party Good	Retail Excellent
2500 HD Short Bed		C29U	29160	14550	16450	18100	21000
2500 HD Long Bed		C29U	29460	14250	16050	17700	20700
3500 Long Bed		C39U	30400	14250	16100	17750	20700
Work Truck				(1275)	(1275)	(1700)	(1700)
Quadrasteer				925	925	1235	1235
4WD		K		2100	2100	2800	2800
V6 4.3 Liter		X		(800)	(800)	(1065)	(1065)
V8 5.3 Liter		T		400	400	535	535
V8 6.0 Liter (1500)		U		550	550	735	735
V8 8.1 Liter		G		550	550	735	735
V8 6.6L Turbo Diesel		1,2		5800	5800	7730	7730
SILVERADO SS EXTENDED CAB PICKUP AWD—V8—Truck Sch T3							
1500 Short Bed		K19N	40195	19500	21925	23900	27500
SIERRA DENALI EXTENDED CAB PICKUP AWD—V8—Truck Sch T3							
1500 Short Bed		K19U	41995	20275	22800	24600	28200
SILVERADO/SIERRA CREW CAB PICKUP—V8—Truck Sch T1							
1500 Short Bed		C13T	31020	14650	16550	18200	21100
2500 Short Bed		C23U	31540	15375	17325	18950	22000
2500 HD Short Bed		C23U	31460	15900	17950	19700	22900
2500 HD Long Bed		C23U	31160	15675	17650	19350	22400
3500 Long Bed		C33U	32400	15775	17800	19400	22500
Work Truck				(1275)	(1275)	(1700)	(1700)
Quadrasteer				925	925	1235	1235
4WD		K		2100	2100	2800	2800
V8 8.1 Liter		G		550	550	735	735
V8 6.6L Turbo Diesel		1,2		5800	5800	7730	7730

2005 CHEVY/GMC–(1,2or3)(CorG)(A,CorN)–T18X–5

Body	Type	VIN	List	Trade-In Fair	Trade-In Good	Pvt-Party Good	Retail Excellent
BLAZER 4WD—V6—Truck Equipment Schedule T1							
Sport Utility 2D		T18X	25850	9700	11050	12900	15850
Sport Utility 4D		T13X	28025	11350	12900	14900	18050
2WD		S		(1000)	(1000)	(1335)	(1335)
EQUINOX—V6—Truck Equipment Schedule T1							
LS Sport Utility 4D		L13F	21660	11600	13200	15350	18800
AWD		2		1050	1050	1400	1400
TRAILBLAZER 4WD—6-Cyl.—Truck Equipment Schedule T1							
Sport Utility 4D		T13S	30655	14750	16625	18750	22300
Extended Spt Util 4D		T16S	32775	16300	18325	20600	24300
2WD		S		(1550)	(1550)	(2065)	(2065)
V8 5.3 Liter		M		400	400	535	535
ENVOY 4WD—6-Cyl.—Truck Equipment Schedule T1							
Sport Utility 4D		T13S	32685	14750	16625	18750	22300
2WD		S		(1550)	(1550)	(2065)	(2065)
ENVOY DENALI 4WD—V8—Truck Equipment Schedule T3							
Sport Utility 4D		T13M	39640	18725	21050	23300	27200
2WD		S		(1550)	(1550)	(2065)	(2065)
ENVOY XL 4WD—6-Cyl.—Truck Equipment Schedule T1							
Sport Utility 4D		T16S	34355	16300	18325	20600	24300
2WD		S		(1550)	(1550)	(2065)	(2065)
V8 5.3 Liter		M		400	400	535	535
ENVOY XL DENALI 4WD—V8—Truck Equipment Schedule T3							
Sport Utility 4D		T16M	40920	20175	22700	25000	29100
2WD		S		(1550)	(1550)	(2065)	(2065)
ENVOY XUV 4WD—6-Cyl.—Truck Equipment Schedule T1							
Sport Utility 4D		T12S	34440	17125	19250	21400	25200
2WD		S		(1550)	(1550)	(2065)	(2065)
V8 5.3 Liter		M		400	400	535	535
TAHOE 4WD—V8—Truck Equipment Schedule T1							
Sport Utility 4D		K13V	39185	19875	22300	25800	31200
w/o Third Seat				(750)	(750)	(1000)	(1000)
2WD		C		(1550)	(1550)	(2065)	(2065)
V8 5.3 Liter		T		400	400	535	535
YUKON 4WD—V8—Truck Equipment Schedule T1							
Sport Utility 4D		K13V	39545	19875	22300	25800	31200
w/o Third Seat				(750)	(750)	(1000)	(1000)
2WD		C		(1550)	(1550)	(2065)	(2065)
V8 5.3 Liter		T		400	400	535	535
YUKON DENALI AWD—V8—Truck Equipment Schedule T3							
Sport Utility 4D		K63U	50855	26375	29500	33200	39200
SUBURBAN—V8—Truck Equipment Schedule T1							
C1500 Sport Utility		C16Z	38875	17950	20175	23400	28300
C2500 Sport Utility		C26U	40475	18425	20750	24000	29000
Quadrasteer				1000	1000	1335	1335

Body	Type	VIN	List	Trade-In Fair	Good	Pvt-Party Good	Retail Excellent
4WD		K		2275	2275	3035	3035
V8 8.1 Liter		G		575	575	765	765
YUKON XL—V8—Truck Equipment Schedule T1							
1500 Sport Utility		C16Z	39535	17950	20175	23400	28300
2500 Sport Utility		C26U	41035	18425	20750	24000	29000
Quadrasteer				1000	1000	1335	1335
4WD		K		2275	2275	3035	3035
V8 8.1 Liter		G		575	575	765	765
YUKON XL DENALI AWD—V8—Truck Equipment Schedule T3							
1500 Sport Utility 4D		K66U	52535	28425	31825	35300	41300
VENTURE—V6—Truck Equipment Schedule T2							
Cargo Minivan 4D		V03E	23880	7900	9075	11300	14550
VENTURE—V6—Truck Equipment Schedule T2							
Extended Minivan 4D		V09E	24080	9475	10825	13150	16600
5 Passenger				(750)	(750)	(1000)	(1000)
ASTRO/SAFARI—V6—Truck Equipment Schedule T2							
Cargo 3D		M19X	23540	8375	9575	11600	14600
Dutch Doors				375	375	500	500
AWD		L		1050	1050	1400	1400
ASTRO/SAFARI—V6—Truck Equipment Schedule T2							
Minivan 3D		M19X	25040	10675	12125	14250	17600
Dutch Doors				375	375	500	500
AWD		L		1050	1050	1400	1400
UPLANDER—V6—Truck Equipment Schedule T2							
Cargo Minivan 4D		V13L	21415	10375	11775	13900	17200
UPLANDER—V6—Truck Equipment Schedule T2							
Extended Minivan 4D		V03L	24350	10825	12275	14450	17800
LS Extended Minivan		V23L	26955	11250	12750	14950	18350
LT Extended Minivan		V38L	29385	11600	13200	15350	18800
LT AWD Ext Minivan		X33L	32100	12425	14075	16350	19900
EXPRESS/SAVANA VAN—V8—Truck Equipment Schedule T1							
1500 Passenger Van		G15T	26305	13100	14800	17600	21800
2500 Passenger Van		G25V	29405	13350	15025	17900	22100
3500 Passenger Van		G35U	30009	13625	15375	18200	22400
155" W.B.				275	275	365	365
AWD		H		950	950	1265	1265
V6 4.3 Liter		X		(750)	(750)	(1000)	(1000)
EXPRESS/SAVANA VAN—V6—Truck Equipment Schedule T1							
1500 Cargo Van		G15T	23575	12800	14500	16750	20300
2500 Cargo Van		G25V	24275	13100	14800	17000	20600
3500 Cargo Van		G35U	26809	13375	15075	17350	21000
155" W.B.				275	275	365	365
AWD		H		950	950	1265	1265
V8 4.8, 5.3 Liter		V,T		375	375	500	500
V8 6.0 Liter		U		750	750	1000	1000
COLORADO/CANYON PICKUP—4-Cyl.—Truck Equip Sch T2							
Short Bed		S198	16430	7050	8150	9950	12650
Extended Cab		S198	18775	8275	9475	11400	14250
Crew Cab		S138	21920	9425	10775	12750	15800
4WD		T		2325	2325	3100	3100
5-Cyl, 3.5 Liter		6		200	200	265	265
SSR REGULAR CAB PICKUP—V8—Truck Equipment Schedule T3							
Convertible 2D		S14H	43055				
AVALANCHE 4WD—V8—Truck Equipment Schedule T1							
1500 Spt Util Pickup		K12T	37170	19100	21425	23200	26600
2500 Spt Util Pickup		K22G	39005	19975	22400	24200	27600
2WD		C		(1000)	(1000)	(1335)	(1335)
SILVERADO/SIERRA REGULAR CAB PICKUP—V8—Truck Sch T1							
1500 Short Bed		C14V	23635	12475	14125	15500	18150
1500 Long Bed		C14V	23935	11975	13575	15000	17550
2500 HD Long Bed		C24U	27700	13525	15275	16800	19500
3500 Long Bed		K34U	31730	13625	15375	16950	19700
Work Truck				(1400)	(1400)	(1865)	(1865)
4WD		K		2275	2275	3035	3035
V6 4.3 Liter		X		(850)	(850)	(1135)	(1135)
V8 5.3 Liter		T,Z		400	400	535	535
V8 8.1 Liter		G		575	575	765	765
V8 6.6L Turbo Diesel		2		6025	6025	8030	8030
SILVERADO/SIERRA EXTENDED CAB PICKUP—V8—Truck Sch T1							
1500 Short Bed		C19V	27295	15125	17025	18650	21600
1500 Long Bed		C19V	28295	14650	16550	18150	21000
2500 HD Short Bed		C29U	30000	16625	18725	20400	23600
2500 HD Long Bed		C29U	30300	16300	18325	20000	23100

0106

Body	Type	VIN	List	Trade-In Fair	Good	Pvt-Party Good	Retail Excellent
3500 Long Bed		C39U	31240	16300	18325	20000	23100
Work Truck				(1400)	(1400)	(1865)	(1865)
Quadrasteer				1000	1000	1335	1335
4WD		K		2275	2275	3035	3035
V6 4.3 Liter		X		(850)	(850)	(1135)	(1135)
V8 5.3 Liter		B,T,Z		400	400	535	535
V8 6.0 Liter (1500)		U		550	550	735	735
V8 8.1 Liter		G		575	575	765	765
V8 6.6L Turbo Diesel		2		6025	6025	8030	8030
SILVERADO SS EXTENDED CAB PICKUP—V8—Truck Sch T3							
1500 Short Bed		K19N	36440	20075	22600	24300	27800
AWD				2275	2275	3035	3035
SILVERADO/SIERRA CREW CAB PICKUP—V8—Truck Sch T1							
1500 Short Bed		C13T,V	30875	16675	18775	20500	23700
1500 HD Short Bed		C13U	32480	17450	19600	21300	24500
2500 HD Short Bed		C23U	32100	18200	20475	22200	25500
2500 HD Long Bed		C23U	32400	17800	19975	21700	25000
3500 Long Bed		C33U	33340	17950	20175	21900	25200
Work Truck				(1400)	(1400)	(1865)	(1865)
Quadrasteer				1000	1000	1335	1335
4WD		K		2275	2275	3035	3035
V8 8.1 Liter		G		575	575	765	765
V8 6.6L Turbo Diesel		2		6025	6025	8030	8030
SIERRA DENALI CREW CAB PICKUP AWD—V8—Truck Sch T3							
1500 Short Bed		K63N	42585	24550	27450	29400	33300

CHRYSLER

1991 CHRYSLER — (1,3orZ)C4(BY54R)—M—#

TOWN & COUNTRY—V6—Truck Equipment Schedule T3							
Minivan		BY54R	24425	1150	1600	2725	4300
5 Passenger				(200)	(200)	(265)	(265)
w/o Rear Air Conditioning				(100)	(100)	(135)	(135)

1992 CHRYSLER — (1or3)C4—(H54R)—N—#

TOWN & COUNTRY—V6—Truck Equipment Schedule T3							
Minivan		H54R	25161	1400	1900	2975	4525
5 Passenger				(225)	(225)	(300)	(300)
AWD		K		275	275	365	365
w/o Rear Air Conditioning				(100)	(100)	(135)	(135)

1993 CHRYSLER — (1or3)C4—(H54R)—P—#

TOWN & COUNTRY—V6—Truck Equipment Schedule T3							
Minivan		H54R	26078	1600	2100	3250	4900
5 Passenger				(250)	(250)	(335)	(335)
AWD		K		325	325	435	435
w/o Rear Air Conditioning				(125)	(125)	(165)	(165)

1994 CHRYSLER — (1or3)C4—(H54L)—R—#

TOWN & COUNTRY—V6—Truck Equipment Schedule T3							
Minivan		H54L	27844	1825	2350	3600	5325
5 Passenger				(275)	(275)	(365)	(365)
w/o Rear Air Conditioning				(150)	(150)	(200)	(200)
AWD		K		375	375	500	500

1995 CHRYSLER — (1or3)C4—(H54L)—S—#

TOWN & COUNTRY—V6—Truck Equipment Schedule T3							
Minivan		H54L	28240	2125	2700	3975	5800
5 Passenger				(300)	(300)	(400)	(400)
w/o Rear Air Conditioning				(175)	(175)	(235)	(235)
AWD		K		425	425	565	565

1996 CHRYSLER — 1C4—(P55R)—T—#

TOWN & COUNTRY—V6—Truck Equipment Schedule T3							
LX Minivan		P55R	25850	3150	3800	5275	7375
Minivan		P54R	25865	3325	4025	5500	7650
LXi Minivan		P64L	30605	3625	4325	5850	8025
5 Passenger				(325)	(325)	(435)	(435)
w/o Quad Seating				(150)	(150)	(200)	(200)
w/o 2nd Sliding Door				(425)	(425)	(565)	(565)

TRUCKS & VANS

1996 CHRYSLER

Body	Type	VIN	List	Trade-In Fair	Trade-In Good	Pvt-Party Good	Retail Excellent
w/o Rear Air Conditioning				(200)	(200)	(265)	(265)

1997 CHRYSLER — 1C4-(P55R)-V-#

TOWN & COUNTRY—V6—Truck Equipment Schedule T3

Body	Type	VIN	List	Fair	Good	Good	Excellent
SX Minivan		P55R	28070	3600	4300	5850	8050
LX Minivan		P54R	28285	3775	4525	6075	8350
LXi Minivan		P64L	32045	4075	4850	6450	8750
5 Passenger				(350)	(350)	(465)	(465)
w/o Quad Seating				(150)	(150)	(200)	(200)
w/o Rear Air Conditioning				(225)	(225)	(300)	(300)
AWD		T		500	500	665	665

1998 CHRYSLER — 1C4-(P55B)-W-#

TOWN & COUNTRY—V6—Truck Equipment Schedule T3

Body	Type	VIN	List	Fair	Good	Good	Excellent
SX Minivan		P55R	28150	4075	4850	6475	8800
LX Minivan		P54R	28605	4325	5125	6775	9150
LXi Minivan		P64L	32300	4625	5450	7125	9550
w/o Quad Seating				(150)	(150)	(200)	(200)
w/o Rear Air Conditioning				(250)	(250)	(335)	(335)
AWD		T		525	525	700	700

1999 CHRYSLER — 1C4-(P55R)-X-#

TOWN & COUNTRY—V6—Truck Equipment Schedule T3

Body	Type	VIN	List	Fair	Good	Good	Excellent
SX Minivan		P55R	28855	4700	5550	7125	9450
LX Minivan		P54R	29130	4950	5825	7450	9800
LXi Minivan		P64L	31955	5300	6200	7850	10300
Limited Minivan		P64L	34345	6150	7150	8875	11450
w/o Rear Air Conditioning				(250)	(250)	(335)	(335)
AWD		T		575	575	765	765

2000 CHRYSLER — 1C4-(J253)-Y-#

VOYAGER—V6—Truck Equipment Schedule T1

Body	Type	VIN	List	Fair	Good	Good	Excellent
Minivan 4D		J253	20895	2725	3325	4750	6800
SE Minivan 4D		J453	23840	3175	3825	5300	7400
Grand Minivan 4D		J243	22545	3400	4100	5575	7700
SE Grand Minivan 4D		J443	24835	3725	4450	6000	8175
5 Passenger				(500)	(500)	(665)	(665)
w/o 2nd Sliding Door				(550)	(550)	(735)	(735)
4-Cyl. 2.4 Liter		B		(900)	(900)	(1200)	(1200)

TOWN & COUNTRY—V6—Truck Equipment Schedule T3

Body	Type	VIN	List	Fair	Good	Good	Excellent
LX Minivan		P44R	26950	5875	6850	8525	11050
LXi Minivan		P54L	31530	6375	7400	9150	11750
Limited Minivan		P64L	34855	7300	8400	10250	12950
w/o Rear Air Conditioning				(300)	(300)	(400)	(400)
AWD		T		675	675	900	900

2001 CHRYSLER—1C(4or8)-(J24G)-1-#

VOYAGER—V6—Truck Equipment Schedule T1

Body	Type	VIN	List	Fair	Good	Good	Excellent
Minivan		J24G	20770	3675	4425	6000	8225
LX Minivan		J54G	24165	4200	4975	6575	8875
5 Passenger				(550)	(550)	(735)	(735)
4-Cyl. 2.4 Liter		B		(1025)	(1025)	(1365)	(1365)

TOWN & COUNTRY—V6—Truck Equipment Schedule T3

Body	Type	VIN	List	Fair	Good	Good	Excellent
LX Minivan		P44G	26155	7100	8200	10050	12750
EX Minivan		P54L	26830	7425	8525	10400	13200
LXi Minivan		P64G	30705	7650	8800	10600	13450
Limited Minivan		P64L	35490	8725	10000	11950	14900
w/o Quad Seating				(250)	(250)	(335)	(335)
w/o Rear Air Conditioning				(350)	(350)	(465)	(465)
AWD		T		750	750	1000	1000

2002 CHRYSLER—1C(4or8)-(J15B)-2-#

VOYAGER—V6—Truck Equipment Schedule T1

Body	Type	VIN	List	Fair	Good	Good	Excellent
eC Minivan		J15B	16995	3375	4075	5675	7950
Minivan		J253	19995	4600	5425	7125	9550
LX Minivan		J453	24060	5150	6050	7750	10300
5 Passenger				(600)	(600)	(800)	(800)
4-Cyl. 2.4 Liter		B		(1125)	(1125)	(1500)	(1500)

TOWN & COUNTRY—V6—Truck Equipment Schedule T3

Body	Type	VIN	List	Fair	Good	Good	Excellent
eL Minivan		P343	24330	7300	8400	10300	13100
LX Minivan		P443	27065	8325	9525	11450	14350

Body	Type	VIN	List	Trade-In Fair	Good	Pvt-Party Good	Retail Excellent
EX Minivan		P74L	26830	8775	10050	12000	15000
LXi Minivan		P543	30970	9025	10325	12250	15300
Limited Minivan		P64L	35990	10175	11600	13650	16800
w/o Quad Seating		------		(300)	(300)	(400)	(400)
w/o Rear Air Conditioning		------		(400)	(400)	(535)	(535)
AWD		T		825	825	1100	1100

2003 CHRYSLER—1C(4or8)–(J453)–3–#

VOYAGER—V6—Truck Equipment Schedule T1

Body	Type	VIN	List	Trade-In Fair	Good	Pvt-Party Good	Retail Excellent
LX Minivan		J453	24025	6375	7400	9275	12050
5 Passenger				(650)	(650)	(865)	(865)
4-Cyl. 2.4 Liter		B		(1225)	(1225)	(1635)	(1635)

TOWN & COUNTRY—V6—Truck Equipment Schedule T3

Body	Type	VIN	List	Trade-In Fair	Good	Pvt-Party Good	Retail Excellent
Minivan		P24R	25975	9150	10425	12450	15500
eL Minivan		P343	24830	8775	10050	12050	15050
LX Minivan		P443	27010	9800	11200	13250	16350
EX Minivan		P74L	27235	10375	11775	13850	17050
LXi Minivan		P54L	34080	10625	12075	14150	17400
Limited Minivan		P64L		11875	13425	15600	19000
w/o Quad Seating		------		(325)	(325)	(435)	(435)
w/o Rear Air Conditioning		------		(425)	(425)	(565)	(565)
AWD		T		900	900	1200	1200

2004 CHRYSLER–(1or2)C(4or8)–(P45R)–4–#

TOWN & COUNTRY—V6—Truck Equipment Schedule T3

Body	Type	VIN	List	Trade-In Fair	Good	Pvt-Party Good	Retail Excellent
Minivan		P45R	23520	9800	11150	13200	16350
LX Minivan		P44R	27490	11700	13250	15350	18700
eX Minivan		P74L	30110	12325	13975	16150	19600
Touring Minivan		P54L	33245	12600	14250	16500	20000
Limited Minivan		P64L	38380	13975	15775	18000	21600
w/o Quad Seating		------		(350)	(350)	(465)	(465)
w/o Rear Air Conditioning		------		(450)	(450)	(600)	(600)
AWD		T		975	975	1300	1300

PACIFICA—V6—Truck Equipment Schedule T3

Body	Type	VIN	List	Trade-In Fair	Good	Pvt-Party Good	Retail Excellent
Minivan		M684	30410	14025	15850	17450	20400
AWD		F		975	975	1300	1300

2005 CHRYSLER–(1or2)C(4or8)–(P45R)–5

TOWN & COUNTRY—V6—Truck Equipment Schedule T3

Body	Type	VIN	List	Trade-In Fair	Good	Pvt-Party Good	Retail Excellent
Minivan		P45R	21185	11975	13575	15850	19350
LX Minivan		P44R	25640	13975	15800	18150	21800
Touring Minivan		P54L	27940	15075	16975	19350	23200
Limited Minivan		P64L	35940	16450	18525	21000	24900
w/o Quad Seating		------		(375)	(375)	(500)	(500)
w/o Rear Air Conditioning		------		(475)	(475)	(635)	(635)
Signature Series				500	500	665	665

PACIFICA—V6—Truck Equipment Schedule T3

Body	Type	VIN	List	Trade-In Fair	Good	Pvt-Party Good	Retail Excellent
Minivan		M48L	24995	14700	16575	18200	21100
Touring Minivan		M684	28525	16300	18325	20100	23200
AWD		F		1050	1050	1400	1400

PACIFICA AWD—V6—Truck Equipment Schedule T3

Body	Type	VIN	List	Trade-In Fair	Good	Pvt-Party Good	Retail Excellent
Limited Minivan		F784	36995	18275	20575	22300	25600

DAIHATSU

1991 DAIHATSU — JD2(FF310)–M–#

ROCKY 4WD—4-Cyl.—Truck Equipment Schedule T2

Body	Type	VIN	List	Trade-In Fair	Good	Pvt-Party Good	Retail Excellent
SE Spt Utility Conv		FF310	11586	475	700	1225	2100
SX Spt Utility HT		FF320	13286	600	875	1450	2450
Hard Top		B		50	50	65	65

1992 DAIHATSU — JD2(FF310)–N–#

ROCKY 4WD—4-Cyl.—Truck Equipment Schedule T2

Body	Type	VIN	List	Trade-In Fair	Good	Pvt-Party Good	Retail Excellent
SE Spt Utility Conv		FF310	11994	550	775	1375	2375
SX Spt Utility HT		FF320	13794	675	950	1600	2675
Hard Top		B		50	50	65	65

Body	Type	VIN	List	Trade-In Fair	Good	Pvt-Party Good	Retail Excellent

TRUCKS & VANS

DODGE/PLYMOUTH

1991 DODGE/PLYM — (1orJ)BorP(4or7)-(M07Y)-M

Body	Type	VIN	List	Fair	Good	Good	Excellent
RAMCHARGER 4WD—V8—Truck Equipment Schedule T1							
AW150 S Sport Util 2D	M07Y	19022	975	1375	2250	3575
AW150 Sport Util 2D	M17Y	20373	1025	1450	2350	3675
2WD	E		(350)	(350)	(465)	(465)
V8 5.9 Liter	Z		75	75	100	100
CARAVAN C/V—4-Cyl.—Truck Equipment Schedule T2							
Cargo Minivan	-11L	12806	175	225	575	1100
AWD	D		250	250	335	335
V6 3.0 Liter	3		200	200	265	265
CARAVAN C/V—V6—Truck Equipment Schedule T2							
Extended Minivan	-14R	14546	375	500	1000	1750
AWD	D		250	250	335	335
CARAVAN/VOYAGER—4-Cyl.—Truck Equipment Schedule T1							
Minivan	-25K	14989	350	475	925	1650
SE Minivan	-45K	15722	350	475	975	1700
LE Minivan	-55K	18165	400	550	1050	1825
5 Passenger	D		(200)	(200)	(265)	(265)
AWD	D		250	250	335	335
V6 3.0 Liter	3		200	200	265	265
V6 3.3 Liter	R		200	200	265	265
CARAVAN/VOYAGER—V6—Truck Equipment Schedule T1							
ES/LX Minivan	-25R	19660	600	850	1475	2500
SE Grand Minivan	-44R	17472	675	975	1650	2775
LE Grand Minivan	-54R	19775	750	1050	1775	2925
5 Passenger			(200)	(200)	(265)	(265)
AWD	D		250	250	335	335
RAM WAGON—V8—Truck Equipment Schedule T1							
B150 Passenger Van	B15Y	17511	750	1075	1825	3000
B250 Passenger Van	B25Y	18139	800	1150	1925	3125
B350 Passenger Van	B35Y	18808	900	1275	2150	3475
5 Passenger			(200)	(200)	(265)	(265)
110" W.B.			0	0	0	0
Maxi-Wagon	4		50	50	65	65
V6 3.9 Liter	X		(200)	(200)	(265)	(265)
V8 5.9 Liter	Z		25	25	35	35
VAN—V6—Truck Equipment Schedule T1							
B150 Cargo Van	B11X	14881	725	1050	1675	2775
B250 Cargo Van	B21X	15122	775	1125	1800	2925
110" W.B.			0	0	0	0
Maxi-Van	4		50	50	65	65
V8 5.2, 5.9 Liter	Y,Z		100	100	135	135
VAN—V8—Truck Equipment Schedule T1							
B350 Cargo Van	B31Y	16622	875	1225	2000	3175
Maxi-Van	4		50	50	65	65
V8 5.9 Liter	z,5		25	25	35	35
RAM 50 PICKUP—4-Cyl.—Truck Equipment Schedule T2							
Short Bed	L24W	8356	275	400	775	1400
Long Bed	L24W	8889	300	400	800	1425
Sport Cab	L25W	9395	475	700	1225	2075
SE Short Bed	L44W	9067	375	500	950	1650
LE Sport Cab	L55W	11296	575	825	1350	2275
4WD			500	500	665	665
V6 3.0 Liter	S		200	200	265	265
RAM 50 PICKUP 4WD—V6—Truck Equipment Schedule T2							
SE Sport Cab	M45S	13454	975	1350	2125	3350
DAKOTA PICKUP—4-Cyl.—Truck Equipment Schedule T2							
S Short Bed	L16G	9177	450	650	1150	1950
Short Bed	L26G	10622	500	725	1225	2075
Long Bed	L26G	10773	450	625	1125	1925
Club Cab	L23G	11691	700	1025	1650	2725
4WD			500	500	665	665
V6 3.9 Liter	X		125	125	165	165
V8 5.2 Liter	Y		150	150	200	200
DAKOTA PICKUP—V6—Truck Equipment Schedule T2							
Sport Short Bed	L66X	13324	600	875	1450	2425
Sport Club Cab	L63X	14443	925	1300	2050	3275
4WD	G		500	500	665	665
V8 5.2 Liter	Y		125	125	165	165

TRUCKS & VANS

Body	Type	VIN	List	Trade-In Fair	Trade-In Good	Pvt-Party Good	Retail Excellent
REGULAR CAB PICKUP—V8—Truck Equipment Schedule T1							
D150 S Short Bed		E06Y	13317	825	1175	1900	3050
D150 S Long Bed		E06Y	13526	825	1175	1900	3050
D150 Short Bed		E16Y	14770	850	1200	1950	3125
D150 Long Bed		E16Y	14978	825	1175	1900	3050
D250 Long Bed		E26Y	15581	900	1250	2025	3275
D350 Long Bed		E36Z	17308	900	1250	2025	3275
4WD		M		500	500	665	665
6-Cyl. 3.9 Liter		X		(350)	(350)	(465)	(465)
6-Cyl. 5.9L Turbo Dsl		8		2100	2100	2800	2800
V8 5.9 Liter				75	75	100	100
CLUB CAB PICKUP—V8—Truck Equipment Schedule T1							
D150 Short Bed		E13Y	16463	900	1250	2025	3275
D150 Long Bed		E13Y	16672	825	1175	1925	3100
D250 Long Bed		E23Y	18059	1050	1475	2500	3950
4WD		M		500	500	665	665
V8 5.9 Liter				75	75	100	100

1992 DODGE/PLYM — (1orJ)BorP(4or7)—(M07Y)—N

Body	Type	VIN	List	Trade-In Fair	Trade-In Good	Pvt-Party Good	Retail Excellent
RAMCHARGER 4WD—V8—Truck Equipment Schedule T1							
AW150 S Sport Util 2D		M07Y	20451	1100	1550	2575	4050
AW150 Sport Util 2D		M17Y	21913	1150	1600	2650	4125
2WD		E		(375)	(375)	(500)	(500)
V8 5.9 Liter		Z		100	100	135	135
CARAVAN C/V—4-Cyl.—Truck Equipment Schedule T2							
Minivan		H11G	13360	175	250	575	1100
AWD		K		275	275	365	365
V6 3.0 Liter		3		225	225	300	300
V6 3.3 Liter		R		225	225	300	300
CARAVAN C/V—V6—Truck Equipment Schedule T2							
Extended Minivan		H14R	15749	400	600	1100	1875
AWD		K		275	275	365	365
V6 3.0 Liter		3		(100)	(100)	(135)	(135)
CARAVAN/VOYAGER—4-Cyl.—Truck Equipment Schedule T1							
Minivan		H25G	15379	400	550	1025	1775
SE Minivan		H45G	16926	400	575	1050	1825
5 Passenger				(225)	(225)	(300)	(300)
AWD		K		275	275	365	365
V6 3.0 Liter		3		225	225	300	300
V6 3.3 Liter		R		225	225	300	300
CARAVAN/VOYAGER—V6—Truck Equipment Schedule T1							
LE Minivan		H553	20785	675	950	1575	2625
ES/LX Minivan		H553	21328	700	1000	1625	2725
Grand Minivan		H443	18723	725	1050	1700	2800
SE Grand Minivan		H44R	18908	775	1125	1825	2950
LE Grand Minivan		H54R	21505	850	1200	1950	3175
ES Grand Minivan		H54R	22016	850	1200	1950	3125
5 Passenger				(225)	(225)	(300)	(300)
AWD		K		275	275	365	365
RAM WAGON—V8—Truck Equipment Schedule T1							
B150 Passenger Van		B15Y	18152	875	1225	2075	3400
B250 Passenger Van		B25Y	18796	925	1300	2175	3525
B350 Passenger Van		B35Z	19497	1050	1450	2525	4050
5 Passenger				(225)	(225)	(300)	(300)
110" W.B.				0	0	0	0
Maxi-Wagon		4		50	50	65	65
V6 3.9 Liter		X		(225)	(225)	(300)	(300)
V8 5.9 Liter		Z		25	25	35	35
VAN—V6—Truck Equipment Schedule T1							
B150 Cargo Van		B11X	16148	850	1200	1925	3050
B250 Cargo Van		B21X	16561	900	1275	2025	3225
110" W.B.				0	0	0	0
Maxi-Van		4		50	50	65	65
V8 5.2, 5.9 Liter		Y,Z		100	100	135	135
VAN—V8—Truck Equipment Schedule T1							
B350 Cargo Van		B31Y	18428	1025	1450	2300	3625
Maxi-Van		4		50	50	65	65
V6 3.9 Liter		X		(225)	(225)	(300)	(300)
V8 5.9 Liter		Z		25	25	35	35
RAM 50 PICKUP—4-Cyl.—Truck Equipment Schedule T2							
Short Bed		L24W	8787	300	400	825	1475
Long Bed		L29W	9332	325	425	850	1525
SE Short Bed		L44W	9907	400	525	1000	1750

TRUCKS & VANS

Body	Type	VIN	List	Trade-In Fair	Good	Pvt-Party Good	Retail Excellent
4WD		M		550	550	735	735
DAKOTA PICKUP—4-Cyl.—Truck Equipment Schedule T2							
S Short Bed		L16G	9659	475	675	1225	2075
Sport Short Bed		L66G	9934	525	750	1300	2200
Short Bed		L26G	11175	550	800	1375	2325
Long Bed		L26G	11458	475	700	1225	2100
Club Cab		L23G	12342	800	1150	1875	3050
4WD		G		550	550	735	735
V6 3.9 Liter		X		125	125	165	165
V8 5.2 Liter		Y		175	175	235	235
REGULAR CAB PICKUP—V8—Truck Equipment Schedule T1							
D150 Short Bed		E16Y	15949	975	1350	2150	3400
D150 Long Bed		E16Y	16166	925	1300	2075	3300
D250 Long Bed		E26Y	17107	1025	1450	2275	3575
D350 Long Bed		E36Z	17386	1025	1450	2275	3575
4WD		M		550	550	735	735
V6 3.9 Liter		X		(350)	(350)	(465)	(465)
6-Cyl. 5.9L Turbo Dsl		C		2200	2200	2935	2935
V8 5.9 Liter		Z		100	100	135	135
CLUB CAB PICKUP—V8—Truck Equipment Schedule T1							
D150 Short Bed		E13Y	17444	1000	1425	2250	3525
D150 Long Bed		E13Y	17663	950	1325	2125	3350
D250 Long Bed		E23Y	18404	1225	1700	2725	4175
D350 Long Bed		E33C	23289	1225	1675	2700	4175
4WD		M		550	550	735	735
6-Cyl. 5.9L Turbo Dsl		C		2200	2200	2935	2935
V8 5.9 Liter		Z		100	100	135	135

1993 DODGE/PLYM — (1orJ)BorP(4or7)—(M07Y)—P

Body	Type	VIN	List	Trade-In Fair	Good	Pvt-Party Good	Retail Excellent
RAMCHARGER 4WD—V8—Truck Equipment Schedule T1							
AW150 S Sport Util 2D		M07Y	21610	1075	1500	2575	4075
AW150 Sport Util 2D		M17Y	23127	1125	1575	2675	4200
2WD				(400)	(400)	(535)	(535)
V8 5.9 Liter		Z		150	150	200	200
CARAVAN C/V—4-Cyl.—Truck Equipment Schedule T2							
Minivan		H11K	14106	125	175	525	1075
V6 3.0 Liter		3		250	250	335	335
CARAVAN C/V—V6—Truck Equipment Schedule T2							
Extended Minivan		H14R	16560	400	575	1100	1950
CARAVAN/VOYAGER—4-Cyl.—Truck Equipment Schedule T1							
Minivan		H25K	16071	375	500	1025	1825
SE Minivan		H45K	17498	400	525	1050	1875
5 Passenger				(250)	(250)	(335)	(335)
AWD		K		325	325	435	435
V6 3.0 Liter		3		250	250	335	335
V6 3.3 Liter		R		275	275	365	365
CARAVAN/VOYAGER—V6—Truck Equipment Schedule T1							
LE Minivan		H553	21381	725	1050	1775	2925
ES/LX Minivan		H553	21863	750	1075	1825	3000
Grand Minivan		H443	18140	775	1125	1900	3100
SE Grand Minivan		H54R	18688	850	1225	2025	3300
LE Grand Minivan		H54R	22324	925	1300	2200	3525
ES Grand Minivan		H54R	22785	925	1300	2150	3475
5 Passenger				(250)	(250)	(335)	(335)
AWD		K		325	325	435	435
RAM WAGON—V8—Truck Equipment Schedule T1							
B150 Passenger Van		B15Y	19145	925	1300	2250	3650
B250 Passenger Van		B25Y	19789	1000	1400	2450	3975
B350 Passenger Van		B35Y	20490	1125	1575	2725	4300
5 Passenger				(250)	(250)	(335)	(335)
110" W.B.				0	0	0	0
Maxi-Wagon		4		75	75	100	100
V6 3.9 Liter		X		(250)	(250)	(335)	(335)
V8 5.9 Liter		Z		50	50	65	65
VAN—V6—Truck Equipment Schedule T1							
B150 Cargo Van		B11X	16933	875	1225	2025	3275
B250 Cargo Van		B21X	17346	950	1325	2175	3475
110" W.B.				0	0	0	0
Maxi-Van		4		75	75	100	100
V8 5.2, 5.9 Liter		Y,Z		125	125	165	165
VAN—V8—Truck Equipment Schedule T1							
B350 Cargo Van		B31Y	18626	1075	1525	2550	4025
Maxi-Van		4		75	75	100	100

1993 DODGE/PLYMOUTH

Body Type	VIN	List	Trade-In Fair	Good	Pvt-Party Good	Retail Excellent
V6 3.9 Liter	X		(250)	(250)	(335)	(335)
V8 5.9 Liter			50	50	65	65
RAM 50 PICKUP—4-Cyl.—Truck Equipment Schedule T2						
Short Bed	S21G	9506	325	425	875	1575
Long Bed	S22G	10073	350	475	925	1650
SE Short Bed	S41G	10676	400	575	1075	1875
4WD	T		675	675	900	900
DAKOTA PICKUP—4-Cyl.—Truck Equipment Schedule T2						
S Short Bed	L16G	9818	500	725	1275	2200
Sport Short Bed	L16G	10413	550	775	1350	2325
Short Bed	L26G	11844	600	875	1475	2500
Long Bed	L26G	12027	525	750	1300	2250
Club Cab	L23G	13096	875	1225	2025	3300
4WD	G		675	675	900	900
V6 3.9 Liter	X		150	150	200	200
V8 5.2 Liter	Y		225	225	300	300
REGULAR CAB PICKUP—V8—Truck Equipment Schedule T1						
D150 Short Bed	E16Y	16360	925	1300	2100	3350
D150 Long Bed	E16Y	16577	900	1250	2025	3275
D250 Long Bed	E26Y	17637	1000	1425	2300	3625
D350 Long Bed	E36Z	18155	1000	1425	2300	3625
4WD	M		650	650	865	865
V6 3.9 Liter	X		(375)	(375)	(500)	(500)
6-Cyl. 5.9L Turbo Dsl	C		2500	2500	3335	3335
V8 5.9 Liter	Z		150	150	200	200
CLUB CAB PICKUP—V8—Truck Equipment Schedule T1						
D150 Short Bed	E13Y	18294	1000	1400	2250	3575
D150 Long Bed	E13Y	18513	925	1300	2125	3400
D250 Long Bed	E23Y	19454	1225	1700	2750	4225
D350 Long Bed	E33C	24339	1275	1775	2825	4350
4WD	M		650	650	865	865
6-Cyl. 5.9L Turbo Dsl	C		2500	2500	3335	3335
V8 5.9 Liter	Z		150	150	200	200

1994 DODGE/PLYM — (1orJ)BorP(4or7)-(H11K)-R

Body Type	VIN	List	Trade-In Fair	Good	Pvt-Party Good	Retail Excellent
CARAVAN C/V—4-Cyl.—Truck Equipment Schedule T2						
Cargo Minivan	H11K	14972	100	125	500	1100
V6 3.0 Liter	3		275	275	365	365
CARAVAN C/V—V6—Truck Equipment Schedule T2						
Extended Minivan	H14R	17426	400	600	1200	2100
CARAVAN/VOYAGER—4-Cyl.—Truck Equipment Schedule T1						
Minivan	H25K	17135	375	500	1075	1950
5 Passenger			(275)	(275)	(365)	(365)
V6 3.0 Liter	3		275	275	365	365
CARAVAN/VOYAGER—V6—Truck Equipment Schedule T1						
SE Minivan	H453	19113	525	750	1425	2500
LE Minivan	H553	22523	825	1175	2000	3300
ES/LX Minivan	H553	23230	850	1200	2050	3400
Grand Minivan	H243	19595	875	1225	2125	3475
SE Grand Minivan	H44R	20278	950	1325	2275	3675
LE Grand Minivan	H54R	23443	1050	1450	2550	4075
ES Grand Minivan	H54R	23952	1025	1450	2500	4025
5 Passenger			(275)	(275)	(365)	(365)
AWD	K		375	375	500	500
V6 3.8 Liter	L		100	100	135	135
RAM WAGON—V8—Truck Equipment Schedule T1						
B150 Passenger Van	B15Y	16643	1025	1450	2550	4125
B250 Passenger Van	B25Y	20412	1100	1550	2675	4275
B350 Passenger Van	B35Y	21113	1275	1775	2950	4600
5 Passenger			(275)	(275)	(365)	(365)
Maxi-Wagon	4		100	100	135	135
V6 3.9 Liter	X		(275)	(275)	(365)	(365)
V8 5.9 Liter	Z		50	50	65	65
VAN—V6—Truck Equipment Schedule T1						
B150 Cargo Van	B11X	17431	775	1125	1900	3125
B250 Cargo Van	B21X	17844	875	1225	2075	3400
110" W.B.			0	0	0	0
Maxi-Van	4		100	100	135	135
V8 5.2 Liter	Y		150	150	200	200
V8 5.9 Liter	Z		275	275	365	365
VAN—V8—Truck Equipment Schedule T1						
B350 Cargo Van	B31Y	19124	1025	1450	2500	4000
Maxi-Van	4		100	100	135	135

1994 DODGE/PLYMOUTH

Body Type	VIN	List	Trade-In Fair	Good	Pvt-Party Good	Retail Excellent
V8 5.9 Liter	Z		50	50	65	65
DAKOTA PICKUP—4-Cyl.—Truck Equipment Schedule T2						
WS Short Bed	L26G	10249	550	775	1375	2375
WS Long Bed	L26G	11774	600	850	1475	2500
Sport Short Bed	L26G	11237	600	850	1475	2500
Short Bed	L26G	11927	675	950	1625	2725
Long Bed	L26G	12777	575	825	1425	2450
4WD	G		800	800	1065	1065
V6 3.9 Liter	X		175	175	235	235
V8 5.2 Liter	Y		275	275	365	365
DAKOTA PICKUP—V6—Truck Equipment Schedule T2						
Sport Club Cab	L23X	14537	1225	1725	2825	4350
Club Cab	L23X	14794	1350	1850	2925	4475
4WD	G		800	800	1065	1065
V8 5.2 Liter	Y		150	150	200	200
REGULAR CAB PICKUP—V8—Truck Equipment Schedule T1						
1500 Short Bed	C16Y	17265	1625	2125	3275	4875
1500 Long Bed	C16Y	17537	1425	1925	3025	4575
2500 Long Bed	C26Y	18205	1875	2400	3575	5250
3500 Long Bed	C36Z	20706	2050	2625	3800	5500
Work Special	F,M		(375)	(375)	(500)	(500)
4WD			750	750	1000	1000
V6 3.9 Liter	X		(400)	(400)	(535)	(535)
6-Cyl. 5.9L Turbo Dsl	C		2800	2800	3730	3730
V8 5.9 Liter	Z		175	175	235	235
V10 8.0 Liter	W		150	150	200	200

1995 DODGE/PLYM — (1orJ)BorP(4or7)-(H11K)-S

Body Type	VIN	List	Trade-In Fair	Good	Pvt-Party Good	Retail Excellent
CARAVAN C/V—4-Cyl.—Truck Equipment Schedule T2						
Cargo Minivan	H11K	16705	100	150	575	1225
V6 3.0 Liter	3		300	300	400	400
CARAVAN C/V—V6—Truck Equipment Schedule T2						
Extended Minivan	H14R	18245	475	675	1325	2375
CARAVAN/VOYAGER—4-Cyl.—Truck Equipment Schedule T1						
Minivan	H25K	17930	400	600	1225	2200
5 Passenger			(300)	(300)	(400)	(400)
V6 3.0 Liter	3		300	300	400	400
CARAVAN/VOYAGER—V6—Truck Equipment Schedule T1						
SE Minivan	H453	20275	625	900	1625	2825
LE Minivan	H553	23940	925	1300	2375	3900
ES Minivan	H553	24895	975	1375	2450	4000
Grand Minivan	H243	20025	1000	1425	2500	4050
SE Grand Minivan	H44R	20375	1075	1525	2650	4225
LE Grand Minivan	H54R	24240	1200	1650	2800	4400
ES Grand Minivan	H54R	25095	1200	1650	2800	4400
5 Passenger			(300)	(300)	(400)	(400)
AWD	K		425	425	565	565
V6 3.8 Liter	L		100	100	135	135
RAM WAGON—V8—Truck Equipment Schedule T1						
1500 Passenger Van	B15Y	17951	1150	1600	2825	4475
2500 Passenger Van	B25Y	21627	1250	1750	2950	4650
3500 Passenger Van	B35Y	22627	1500	2000	3250	5025
5 Passenger			(300)	(300)	(400)	(400)
Maxi-Wagon	4		100	100	135	135
V6 3.9 Liter	X		(300)	(300)	(400)	(400)
V8 5.9 Liter	Z		50	50	65	65
VAN—V6—Truck Equipment Schedule T1						
1500 Cargo Van	B11X	18605	925	1300	2250	3650
2500 Cargo Van	B21X	18743	1025	1450	2500	4025
110" W.B.			0	0	0	0
Maxi-Van	4		100	100	135	135
V8 5.2 Liter	Y		175	175	235	235
V8 5.9 Liter	Z		300	300	400	400
VAN—V8—Truck Equipment Schedule T1						
3500 Cargo Van	B31Y	20673	1225	1700	2825	4425
Maxi-Van	4		100	100	135	135
V8 5.9 Liter	Z		50	50	65	65
DAKOTA PICKUP—4-Cyl.—Truck Equipment Schedule T2						
WS Short Bed	L26G	10975	625	900	1550	2625
WS Long Bed	L26G	12291	675	950	1625	2775
Sport Short Bed	L26G	11489	675	950	1625	2775
Short Bed	L26G	12710	750	1075	1825	3000
Long Bed	L26G	13921	675	950	1625	2775

1995 DODGE/PLYMOUTH

Body Type	VIN	List	Trade-In Fair	Good	Pvt-Party Good	Retail Excellent
4WD	G	......	900	900	1200	1200
V6 3.9 Liter	X	......	200	200	265	265
V8 5.2 Liter	Y	......	300	300	400	400
DAKOTA PICKUP—V6—Truck Equipment Schedule T2						
Sport Club Cab	L23X	14722	1450	1950	3050	4650
Club Cab	L23X	16006	1575	2075	3225	4850
V6 3.9 Liter	G	......	900	900	1200	1200
V8 5.2 Liter	Y	......	175	175	235	235
REGULAR CAB PICKUP—V8—Truck Equipment Schedule T1						
1500 Short Bed	C16Y	17594	1825	2350	3575	5250
1500 Long Bed	C16Y	17878	1625	2125	3300	4975
2500 Long Bed	C26Y	18851	2100	2675	3900	5675
3500 Long Bed	C36Z	21468	2300	2875	4150	5975
Work Special			(400)	(400)	(535)	(535)
4WD	F	......	850	850	1135	1135
V6 3.9 Liter	X	......	(425)	(425)	(565)	(565)
6-Cyl. 5.9L Turbo Dsl.	C	......	3100	3100	4130	4130
V8 5.9 Liter	Z	......	200	200	265	265
V10 8.0 Liter	W	......	175	175	235	235
CLUB CAB PICKUP—V8—Truck Equipment Schedule T1						
1500 Short Bed	C13Y	20040	2725	3350	4675	6600
1500 Long Bed	C13Y	20321	2500	3100	4425	6275
2500 Short Bed	C23Z	21840	3175	3850	5250	7300
2500 Long Bed	C23Z	22046	3050	3725	5100	7075
3500 Long Bed	C33Z	23667	3175	3850	5250	7300
4WD	F	......	850	850	1135	1135
6-Cyl. 5.9L Turbo Dsl.	C	......	3100	3100	4130	4130
V8 5.9 Liter	Z	......	200	200	265	265
V10 8.0 Liter	W	......	175	175	235	235

1996 DODGE/PLYM—(1,2or3)BorP(4or7)–(P253)–T

Body Type	VIN	List	Trade-In Fair	Good	Pvt-Party Good	Retail Excellent
CARAVAN/VOYAGER—V6—Truck Equipment Schedule T1						
Minivan	P253	18510	1175	1625	2825	4475
SE Minivan	P453	21070	1450	1950	3200	4925
LE Minivan	P55R	24180	1975	2525	3825	5675
ES Minivan	P55R	25665	2050	2625	3925	5800
Grand Minivan	P243	19410	1625	2125	3400	5175
SE Grand Minivan	P443	21810	1875	2400	3700	5525
LE Grand Minivan	P54R	24670	2275	2850	4225	6100
ES Grand Minivan	P54R	26595	2575	3175	4525	6500
5 Passenger			(325)	(325)	(435)	(435)
w/o 2nd Sliding Door			(425)	(425)	(565)	(565)
4-Cyl. 2.4 Liter	B	......	(625)	(625)	(835)	(835)
V6 3.8 Liter	L	......	100	100	135	135
RAM WAGON—V8—Truck Equipment Schedule T1						
1500 Passenger Van	B15Y	19965	1400	1900	3200	4975
2500 Passenger Van	B24Y	21374	1550	2050	3375	5200
3500 Passenger Van	B34Y	22575	1825	2350	3675	5575
Maxi-Wagon			100	100	135	135
V6 3.9 Liter	X	......	(325)	(325)	(435)	(435)
V8 5.9 Liter	Z	......	50	50	65	65
RAM VAN—V6—Truck Equipment Schedule T1						
1500 Cargo Van	B11X	18460	1150	1600	2775	4375
2500 Cargo Van	B21X	18563	1250	1750	2900	4525
110" W.B.			0	0	0	0
Maxi-Van			100	100	135	135
V8 5.2 Liter	Y	......	200	200	265	265
V8 5.9 Liter	Z	......	325	325	435	435
RAM VAN—V8—Truck Equipment Schedule T1						
3500 Cargo Van	B31Y	21075	1550	2050	3275	4975
Maxi-Van			100	100	135	135
V8 5.9 Liter	Z	......	50	50	65	65
DAKOTA PICKUP—4-Cyl.—Truck Equipment Schedule T2						
WS Short Bed	L26G	11764	700	1000	1750	2950
WS Long Bed	L26G	12380	750	1075	1875	3125
Sport Short Bed	L26G	12440	750	1075	1875	3125
Short Bed	L26G	13665	850	1200	2050	3400
Long Bed	L26X	14176	750	1075	1875	3125
4WD	G	......	1000	1000	1335	1335
V6 3.9 Liter	X	......	225	225	300	300
V8 5.2 Liter	Y	......	325	325	435	435
DAKOTA PICKUP—V6—Truck Equipment Schedule T2						
Sport Club Cab	L23X	15616	1675	2175	3375	5050

Body Type	VIN	List	Trade-In Fair	Trade-In Good	Pvt-Party Good	Retail Excellent
Club Cab	L23X	16746	1825	2350	3550	5250
4WD	G	----	1000	1000	1335	1335
V8 5.2 Liter	Y	----	200	200	265	265
REGULAR CAB PICKUP—V8—Truck Equipment Schedule T1						
1500 Short Bed	C16Y	18032	2125	2725	3975	5800
1500 Long Bed	C16Y	18316	1925	2450	3675	5450
2500 Long Bed	C26Y	19569	2425	3025	4350	6200
3500 Long Bed	C365	22286	2675	3275	4600	6525
Work Special			(425)	(425)	(565)	(565)
4WD	F	----	950	950	1265	1265
V6 3.9 Liter	X	----	(450)	(450)	(600)	(600)
6-Cyl. 5.9L Turbo Diesel	C	----	3400	3400	4530	4530
V8 5.9 Liter		----	225	225	300	300
V10 8.0 Liter	W	----	200	200	265	265
CLUB CAB PICKUP—V8—Truck Equipment Schedule T1						
1500 Short Bed	C13Y	20190	3125	3775	5225	7225
1500 Long Bed	C13Y	20471	2850	3525	4900	6875
2500 Short Bed	C23Z	22958	3625	4350	5825	7950
2500 Long Bed	C23Z	23164	3475	4200	5625	7700
3500 Long Bed	C33Z	24685	3625	4350	5825	7950
4WD	F	----	950	950	1265	1265
6-Cyl. 5.9L Turbo Diesel	C	----	3400	3400	4530	4530
V8 5.9 Liter	Z,5	----	225	225	300	300
V10 8.0 Liter	W	----	200	200	265	265

Body Type	VIN	List	Trade-In Fair	Trade-In Good	Pvt-Party Good	Retail Excellent
CARAVAN/VOYAGER—V6—Truck Equipment Schedule T1						
Minivan	P253	19570	1400	1900	3175	4950
SE Minivan	P453	22495	1750	2275	3600	5425
LE Minivan	P55R	25715	2300	2875	4300	6225
ES Minivan	P55R	27055	2400	2975	4400	6350
Grand Minivan	P243	20565	1925	2450	3800	5675
SE Grand Minivan	P443	23325	2175	2775	4125	6050
LE Grand Minivan	P54R	26405	2650	3275	4675	6700
ES Grand Minivan	P54R	26995	2925	3600	5050	7100
5 Passenger			(350)	(350)	(465)	(465)
w/o 2nd Sliding Door			(450)	(450)	(600)	(600)
AWD	T	----	500	500	665	665
4-Cyl. 2.4 Liter	B	----	(675)	(675)	(900)	(900)
V6 3.8 Liter	L	----	100	100	135	135
RAM WAGON—V8—Truck Equipment Schedule T1						
1500 Passenger Van	B15Y	21192	1800	2325	3700	5650
2500 Passenger Van	B25Y	22555	1975	2500	3900	5875
3500 Passenger Van	B35Y	23755	2225	2825	4250	6250
Maxi-Wagon			100	100	135	135
V6 3.9 Liter	X	----	(350)	(350)	(465)	(465)
V8 5.9 Liter	Z	----	50	50	65	65
RAM VAN—V6—Truck Equipment Schedule T1						
1500 Cargo Van	B11X	19090	1500	2000	3225	4975
2500 Cargo Van	B21X	19295	1625	2125	3400	5150
110" W.B.			0	0	0	0
Maxi-Van			100	100	135	135
V8 5.2 Liter	Y	----	200	200	265	265
V8 5.9 Liter	Z	----	350	350	465	465
RAM VAN—V8—Truck Equipment Schedule T1						
3500 Cargo Van	B31Y	21885	1975	2500	3800	5650
Maxi-Van			100	100	135	135
V8 5.9 Liter	Z	----	50	50	65	65
DAKOTA PICKUP—4-Cyl.—Truck Equipment Schedule T1						
Short Bed	L26P	14959	1950	2475	3850	5800
Long Bed	L26P	15419	1825	2350	3700	5600
4WD	G	----	1100	1100	1465	1465
V6 3.9 Liter	X	----	250	250	335	335
V8 5.2 Liter	Y	----	350	350	465	465
DAKOTA PICKUP—V6—Truck Equipment Schedule T1						
Club Cab	L23X	18654	3125	3775	5325	7500
4WD	G	----	1100	1100	1465	1465
V8 5.2 Liter	Y	----	200	200	265	265
REGULAR CAB PICKUP—V8—Truck Equipment Schedule T1						
1500 Short Bed	C16Y	18831	2550	3150	4475	6375
1500 Long Bed	C16Y	19116	2275	2850	4175	6025
2500 Long Bed	C26Z	21134	2850	3500	4850	6825
3500 Long Bed	C36Z	22619	3100	3750	5175	7150

TRUCKS & VANS

Body Type	VIN	List	Trade-In Fair	Trade-In Good	Pvt-Party Good	Retail Excellent
Work Special			**(450)**	**(450)**	**(600)**	**(600)**
4WD	F		1050	1050	1400	1400
V6 3.9 Liter	X		(450)	(450)	(600)	(600)
6-Cyl. 5.9L Turbo Diesel	D		3700	3700	4930	4930
V8 5.9 Liter	5,Z		250	250	335	335
V10 8.0 Liter	W		225	225	300	300
CLUB CAB PICKUP—V8—Truck Equipment Schedule T1						
1500 Short Bed	C13Y	20914	3625	4325	5800	7900
1500 Long Bed	C13Y	21194	3350	4050	5475	7550
2500 Short Bed	C23Z	23139	4150	4925	6450	8675
2500 Long Bed	C23Z	23344	3975	4725	6225	8425
3500 Long Bed	C33Z	24964	4150	4925	6450	8675
4WD	F		1050	1050	1400	1400
6-Cyl. 5.9L Turbo Diesel	D		3700	3700	4930	4930
V8 5.9 Liter	5,Z		250	250	335	335
V10 8.0 Liter	W		225	225	300	300

1998 DODGE/PLYM–1(BorP)4–(S28Y)–W–#

Body Type	VIN	List	Trade-In Fair	Trade-In Good	Pvt-Party Good	Retail Excellent
DURANGO 4WD—V8—Truck Equipment Schedule T1						
SLT Sport Utility 4D	S28Y	28575	4375	5175	6900	9375
w/o Third Seat			(475)	(475)	(635)	(635)
V6 3.9 Liter	X		(525)	(525)	(700)	(700)
V6 5.9 Liter	Z		250	250	335	335
CARAVAN/VOYAGER—V6—Truck Equipment Schedule T1						
Minivan	P253	20535	1725	2250	3625	5500
SE Minivan	P453	22065	2100	2650	4075	6050
LE Minivan	P55R	25610	2725	3325	4800	6875
Grand Minivan	P243	20730	2275	2825	4300	6275
SE Grand Minivan	P443	23060	2575	3175	4625	6675
LE Grand Minivan	P54R	26605	3050	3725	5250	7375
ES Grand Minivan	P54R	27760	3375	4075	5625	7800
5 Passenger			(375)	(375)	(500)	(500)
w/o 2nd Sliding Door			(475)	(475)	(635)	(635)
AWD	T		525	525	700	700
4-Cyl. 2.4 Liter	B		(725)	(725)	(965)	(965)
V6 3.8 Liter	L		100	100	135	135
RAM WAGON—V8—Truck Equipment Schedule T1						
1500 Passenger Van	B15Y	21655	2275	2825	4375	6450
2500 Passenger Van	B25Y	23480	2425	3025	4550	6675
3500 Maxi Passenger	B35Y	26185	2725	3350	4925	7075
V6 3.9 Liter	X		(375)	(375)	(500)	(500)
V8 5.9 Liter			50	50	65	65
RAM VAN—V6—Truck Equipment Schedule T1						
1500 Cargo Van	B11X	19440	1975	2500	3825	5700
110" W.B.			0	0	0	0
Maxi-Van			100	100	135	135
V8 5.2 Liter	Y		200	200	265	265
V8 5.9 Liter	Z		375	375	500	500
RAM VAN—V8—Truck Equipment Schedule T1						
2500 Cargo Van	B21Y	21375	2400	2975	4375	6300
3500 Cargo Van	B31Y	22545	2450	3050	4450	6425
Maxi-Van			100	100	135	135
V8 5.9 Liter	Z		50	50	65	65
DAKOTA PICKUP—4-Cyl.—Truck Equipment Schedule T1						
Short Bed	L26P	15235	2225	2825	4275	6325
R/T Short Bed	L26Z	19205	2825	3450	5000	7175
Long Bed	L26P	15695	2100	2675	4125	6150
4WD	G		1200	1200	1600	1600
V6 3.9 Liter	X		250	250	335	335
V8 5.2 Liter	Y		375	375	500	500
V8 5.9 Liter (ex. R/T)	Z		575	575	765	765
DAKOTA PICKUP—V6—Truck Equipment Schedule T1						
Club Cab	L22X	18430	3525	4225	5850	8150
R/T Club Cab	L22Z	21360	4000	4750	6425	8800
4WD	G		1200	1200	1600	1600
4-Cyl. 2.5 Liter	P		(275)	(275)	(365)	(365)
V8 5.2 Liter	Y		200	200	265	265
V8 5.9 Liter (ex. R/T)	Z		375	375	500	500
REGULAR CAB PICKUP—V8—Truck Equipment Schedule T1						
1500 Short Bed	C16Y	19240	3025	3700	5100	7100
1500 Long Bed	C16Y	19525	2775	3400	4775	6750
2500 Long Bed	C26Z	21900	3375	4075	5500	7575
3500 Long Bed	C36Z	23190	3625	4350	5825	7925

TRUCKS & VANS

Body Type	VIN	List	Trade-In Fair	Trade-In Good	Pvt-Party Good	Retail Excellent
Work Special			(475)	(475)	(635)	(635)
4WD	F		1150	1150	1535	1535
V6 3.9 Liter	F		(450)	(450)	(600)	(600)
6-Cyl. 5.9L Turbo Dsl	6,D		4000	4000	5330	5330
V8 5.9 Liter	5,Z		275	275	365	365
V10 8.0 Liter	W		225	225	300	300
CLUB CAB PICKUP—V8—Truck Equipment Schedule T1						
1500 Short Bed	C12Y	21365	4175	4950	6475	8700
1500 Long Bed	C12Y	21645	3900	4650	6150	8350
2500 Short Bed	C22Z	23680	4750	5575	7200	9525
2500 Long Bed	C22Z	23870	4550	5375	6950	9250
4WD	F		1150	1150	1535	1535
6-Cyl. 5.9L Turbo Dsl	6,D		4000	4000	5330	5330
V8 5.9 Liter	Z		275	275	365	365
V10 8.0 Liter	W		225	225	300	300
QUAD CAB PICKUP—V8—Truck Equipment Schedule T1						
1500 Short Bed	C13Y	22115	4475	5275	6875	9150
1500 Long Bed	C13Y	22395	4250	5050	6575	8800
2500 Short Bed	C23Z	24430	5100	5975	7600	10000
2500 Long Bed	C23Z	24620	4875	5725	7350	9700
3500 Long Bed	C33Z	26325	5100	5975	7600	10000
4WD	F		1150	1150	1535	1535
6-Cyl. 5.9L Turbo Dsl	6,D		4000	4000	5330	5330
V8 5.9 Liter	5,Z		275	275	365	365
V10 8.0 Liter	W		225	225	300	300

1999 DODGE/PLYM—(1,2,3or4)B4—(S28Y)—X—#

Body Type	VIN	List	Trade-In Fair	Trade-In Good	Pvt-Party Good	Retail Excellent
DURANGO 4WD—V8—Truck Equipment Schedule T1						
SLT Sport Utility 4D	S28Y	29030	5200	6075	7675	10100
w/o Third Seat	R		(525)	(525)	(700)	(700)
2WD	X		(575)	(575)	(765)	(765)
V6 3.9 Liter	X		(575)	(575)	(765)	(765)
V8 5.9 Liter	Z		250	250	335	335
CARAVAN/VOYAGER—V6—Truck Equipment Schedule T1						
Minivan 4D	P253	21185	2125	2725	4075	5975
SE Minivan 4D	P453	22460	2575	3175	4550	6525
LE Minivan 4D	P55R	26280	3200	3875	5325	7400
Grand Minivan 4D	P243	22580	2750	3375	4775	6800
SE Grand Minivan 4D	P443	23455	3025	3700	5150	7175
LE Grand Minivan 4D	P54R	27275	3625	4325	5825	7950
ES Grand Minivan 4D	P54L	29485	3925	4675	6200	8425
5 Passenger			(425)	(425)	(565)	(565)
w/o 2nd Sliding Door			(500)	(500)	(665)	(665)
AWD	T		575	575	765	765
4-Cyl. 2.4 Liter	B		(775)	(775)	(1035)	(1035)
V6 3.8 Liter	L		100	100	135	135
RAM WAGON—V8—Truck Equipment Schedule T1						
1500 Passenger Van	B15Y	22000	2875	3550	5150	7350
2500 Passenger Van	B25Y	23725	3050	3725	5325	7600
3500 Maxi Passenger	B35Y	26430	3375	4075	5700	8000
V6 3.9 Liter	X		(425)	(425)	(565)	(565)
V8 5.9 Liter	Z		50	50	65	65
RAM VAN—V6—Truck Equipment Schedule T1						
1500 Cargo Van	B11X	19685	2550	3150	4500	6450
110" W.B.			0	0	0	0
Maxi-Van			100	100	135	135
V8 5.2 Liter	Y		200	200	265	265
V8 5.9 Liter	Z		425	425	565	565
RAM VAN—V8—Truck Equipment Schedule T1						
2500 Cargo Van	B21Y	21620	3000	3675	5100	7100
3500 Cargo Van	B31Y	22790	3100	3750	5200	7200
Maxi-Van			100	100	135	135
V8 5.9 Liter	Z		50	50	65	65
DAKOTA PICKUP—4-Cyl.—Truck Equipment Schedule T1						
Short Bed	L26P	15545	2675	3275	4775	6875
Long Bed	L26P	16005	2550	3150	4625	6725
R/T Short Bed	L26Z	19745	3325	4000	5575	7775
4WD	G		1275	1275	1700	1700
V6 3.9 Liter	X		250	250	335	335
V8 5.2 Liter	Y		425	425	565	565
V8 5.9 Liter (ex. R/T)	Z		625	625	835	835
DAKOTA PICKUP—V6—Truck Equipment Schedule T1						
Club Cab	L22X	18740	4050	4825	6475	8800

0106

Body Type	VIN	List	Trade-In Fair	Trade-In Good	Pvt-Party Good	Retail Excellent
R/T Club Cab	L22Z	20215	4575	5400	7075	9500
4WD	G		1275	1275	1700	1700
4-Cyl. 2.5 Liter	P		(300)	(300)	(400)	(400)
V8 5.2 Liter	Y		200	200	265	265
V8 5.9 Liter (ex. R/T)	Z		425	425	565	565
REGULAR CAB PICKUP—V8—Truck Equipment Schedule T1						
1500 Short Bed	C16Y	19485	3600	4300	5700	7700
1500 Long Bed	C16Y	19770	3300	3975	5325	7325
2500 Long Bed	C26Z	22145	3925	4675	6100	8200
3500 Long Bed	C36Z	23935	4200	4975	6400	8525
Work Special			(525)	(525)	(700)	(700)
4WD	F		1225	1225	1635	1635
V6 3.9 Liter	X		(475)	(475)	(635)	(635)
6-Cyl. 5.9L Turbo Diesel	6		4225	4225	5630	5630
V8 5.9 Liter	5,Z		300	300	400	400
V10 8.0 Liter	W		225	225	300	300
CLUB CAB PICKUP—V8—Truck Equipment Schedule T1						
1500 Short Bed	C12Y	21515	4800	5625	7125	9350
1500 Long Bed	C12Y	21795	4525	5350	6850	9025
2500 Short Bed	C22Y	23330	5425	6350	7900	10250
2500 Long Bed	C22Z	23520	5225	6075	7650	9950
4WD	F		1225	1225	1635	1635
6-Cyl. 5.9L Turbo Diesel	6		4225	4225	5630	5630
V8 5.9 Liter	Z		300	300	400	400
V10 8.0 Liter	W		225	225	300	300
QUAD CAB PICKUP—V8—Truck Equipment Schedule T1						
1500 Short Bed	C13Y	22310	5150	6050	7575	9850
1500 Long Bed	C13Y	22590	4875	5725	7250	9475
2500 Short Bed	C23Z	24125	5775	6725	8325	10700
2500 Long Bed	C23Z	24315	5550	6500	8075	10450
3500 Long Bed	C33Z	26915	5775	6725	8325	10700
4WD	F		1225	1225	1635	1635
6-Cyl. 5.9L Turbo Dsl	6		4225	4225	5630	5630
V8 5.9 Liter	5,Z		300	300	400	400
V10 8.0 Liter	W		225	225	300	300

2000 DODGE/PLYM—(1,2,3or4)B4—(S28N)—Y—#

Body Type	VIN	List	Trade-In Fair	Trade-In Good	Pvt-Party Good	Retail Excellent
DURANGO 4WD—V8—Truck Equipment Schedule T1						
SLT Sport Utility 4D	S28N	29060	6150	7150	8875	11450
R/T Sport Utility 4D	S28Z	33810	6675	7700	9475	12150
w/o Third Seat			(600)	(600)	(800)	(800)
2WD	R		(650)	(650)	(865)	(865)
V8 5.2 Liter	Y		0	0	0	0
V8 5.9 Liter (ex. R/T)	Z		300	300	400	400
CARAVAN/VOYAGER—V6—Truck Equipment Schedule T1						
Minivan 4D	P243	21905	2725	3325	4750	6800
SE Minivan 4D	P443	23675	3175	3825	5300	7400
Grand Minivan 4D	P243	22380	3400	4100	5575	7700
SE Grand Minivan 4D	P443	24670	3725	4450	6000	8175
LE Grand Minivan 4D	P54R	27785	4375	5175	6750	9025
ES Grand Minivan 4D	P54L	29995	4750	5575	7200	9525
5 Passenger			(500)	(500)	(665)	(665)
w/o 2nd Sliding Door			(550)	(550)	(735)	(735)
AWD	T		675	675	900	900
4-Cyl. 2.4 Liter	B		(900)	(900)	(1200)	(1200)
V6 3.8 Liter	L		150	150	200	200
GRAND CARAVAN AWD—V6—Truck Equipment Schedule T1						
Sport Minivan 4D	T44L	28670	5400	6300	7950	10400
5 Passenger			(500)	(500)	(665)	(665)
RAM WAGON—V8—Truck Equipment Schedule T1						
1500 Passenger Van	B15Y	22245	3650	4375	6100	8550
2500 Passenger Van	B25Y	23670	3850	4600	6350	8825
3500 Maxi Passenger	B35Y	26675	4175	4950	6750	9275
V6 3.9 Liter	X		(500)	(500)	(665)	(665)
V8 5.9 Liter			100	100	135	135
RAM VAN—V8—Truck Equipment Schedule T1						
1500 Cargo Van	B11X	19575	3200	3875	5350	7475
110" W.B.			0	0	0	0
Maxi-Van			150	150	200	200
V8 5.2 Liter	T,Y		250	250	335	335
V8 5.9 Liter	Z		500	500	665	665
RAM VAN—V8—Truck Equipment Schedule T1						
2500 Cargo Van	B21Y	21075	3750	4475	6025	8200

TRUCKS & VANS

Body	Type	VIN	List	Trade-In Fair	Good	Pvt-Party Good	Retail Excellent
3500 Cargo Van		B31Y	23260	3850	4600	6100	8325
Maxi-Van				150	150	200	200
V8 5.9 Liter		Z		100	100	135	135
DAKOTA PICKUP—4-Cyl.—Truck Equipment Schedule T1							
Short Bed		L26P	15850	3275	3950	5575	7875
R/T Short Bed		L26Z	20090	4025	4775	6475	8900
4WD		G		1450	1450	1935	1935
V6 3.9 Liter		Y		300	300	400	400
V8 4.7 Liter		Y		500	500	665	665
V8 5.9 Liter (ex. R/T)		Z		725	725	965	965
DAKOTA PICKUP—V6—Truck Equipment Schedule T1							
Club Cab		L22X	19045	4800	5650	7425	9950
R/T Club Cab		L22Z	22340	5450	6375	8200	10800
Quad Cab		L2AX	20290	5250	6100	7925	10500
4WD		G		1450	1450	1935	1935
4-Cyl. 2.5 Liter		P		(350)	(350)	(465)	(465)
V8 4.7 Liter		N		250	250	335	335
V8 5.9 Liter (ex. R/T)		Z		500	500	665	665
REGULAR CAB PICKUP—V8—Truck Equipment Schedule T1							
1500 Short Bed		C16Y	19695	4075	4850	6275	8400
1500 Long Bed		C16Y	19980	3750	4500	5925	7950
2500 Long Bed		C26Z	22570	4500	5325	6825	8975
3500 Long Bed		C36Z	24330	4800	5625	7125	9325
Work Special				(675)	(675)	(900)	(900)
4WD		F		1400	1400	1865	1865
V6 3.9 Liter		X		(550)	(550)	(735)	(735)
6-Cyl. 5.9L Turbo Diesel		6		4425	4425	5900	5900
V8 5.9 Liter		Z,5		325	325	435	435
V10 8.0 Liter		W		250	250	335	335
CLUB CAB PICKUP—V8—Truck Equipment Schedule T1							
1500 Short Bed		C12Y	21890	5550	6475	8000	10350
4WD		F		1400	1400	1865	1865
V8 5.9 Liter		Z		325	325	435	435
QUAD CAB PICKUP—V8—Truck Equipment Schedule T1							
1500 Short Bed		C13Y	22750	5975	6925	8500	10900
1500 Long Bed		C13Y	23030	5650	6575	8150	10500
2500 Short Bed		C23Z	24335	6675	7700	9325	11850
2500 Long Bed		C23Z	24525	6450	7450	9075	11550
3500 Long Bed		C32Z	27125	6675	7700	9325	11850
4WD		F		1400	1400	1865	1865
6-Cyl. 5.9L Turbo Dsl		6		4425	4425	5900	5900
V8 5.9 Liter		Z,5		325	325	435	435
V10 8.0 Liter		W		250	250	335	335

2001 DODGE—(1or2)B(4,7or8)—(S28N)–1

Body	Type	VIN	List	Trade-In Fair	Good	Pvt-Party Good	Retail Excellent
DURANGO 4WD—V8—Truck Equipment Schedule T1							
SLT Sport Utility 4D		S28N	30740	7350	8475	10300	13000
R/T Sport Utility 4D		S28Z	30990	7925	9125	10950	13750
w/o Third Seat				(675)	(675)	(900)	(900)
2WD		R		(725)	(725)	(965)	(965)
V8 5.9 Liter (ex. R/T)		Z		350	350	465	465
CARAVAN—V6—Truck Equipment Schedule T1							
SE Minivan 4D		P44B	19800	3675	4425	6000	8225
Sport Minivan 4D		P64G	24165	4200	4975	6575	8875
SE Grand Minivan 4D		P44G	22440	4575	5400	7025	9400
Sport Grand 4D		P64G	24915	4825	5675	7350	9750
EX Grand Minivan 4D		P44L	26725	5850	6825	8525	11100
ES Grand Minivan 4D		P54L	29750	6000	6950	8675	11250
5 Passenger				750	750	1000	1000
AWD		T		(550)	(550)	(735)	(735)
4-Cyl. 2.4 Liter		B		(1025)	(1025)	(1365)	(1365)
V6 3.8 Liter		L		675	675	900	900
RAM WAGON—V8—Truck Equipment Schedule T1							
1500 Passenger Van		B15Y	22615	4650	5475	7400	10100
2500 Passenger Van		B25Y	24040	4875	5725	7675	10400
3500 Maxi Passenger		B35Y	27055	5225	6075	8050	10800
V6 3.9 Liter		X		(550)	(550)	(735)	(735)
V8 5.9 Liter		Z		150	150	200	200
RAM VAN—V6—Truck Equipment Schedule T1							
1500 Cargo Van		B11X	19890	4100	4875	6475	8750
2500 Cargo Van		B21X	21390	4275	5075	6675	8975
110" W.B.				0	0	0	0
Maxi-Van				175	175	235	235

0106

2001 DODGE/PLYMOUTH

Body Type	VIN	List	Trade-In Fair	Trade-In Good	Pvt-Party Good	Retail Excellent
V8 5.2 Liter	Y		275	275	365	365
V8 5.9 Liter	Z		550	550	735	735
RAM VAN—V8—Truck Equipment Schedule T1						
3500 Cargo Van	B31Y	23575	4825	5675	7325	9700
Maxi-Van			175	175	235	235
V8 5.9 Liter	Z		150	150	200	200
DAKOTA PICKUP—4-Cyl.—Truck Equipment Schedule T1						
Short Bed	L26P	16255	3975	4725	6500	8975
R/T Short Bed	L26Z	20505	4825	5675	7500	10100
4WD	G		1625	1625	2165	2165
V6 3.9 Liter	X		350	350	465	465
V8 4.7 Liter	N		575	575	765	765
V8 5.9 Liter (ex. R/T)	Z		825	825	1100	1100
DAKOTA PICKUP—V6—Truck Equipment Schedule T1						
Club Cab	L22X	19580	5675	6600	8500	11200
R/T Club Cab	L22Z	22885	6450	7450	9375	12200
Quad Cab	L23X	21950	6175	7175	9100	11900
4WD	G		1625	1625	2165	2165
4-Cyl. 2.5 Liter	P		(400)	(400)	(535)	(535)
V8 4.7 Liter	N		300	300	400	400
V8 5.9 Liter (ex. R/T)	Z		550	550	735	735
REGULAR CAB PICKUP—V8—Truck Equipment Schedule T1						
1500 Short Bed	C16Y	20145	4750	5575	7050	9275
1500 Long Bed	C16Y	20430	4425	5225	6675	8825
2500 Long Bed	C26Z	23475	5250	6150	7675	9950
3500 Long Bed	C36Z	25360	5550	6500	8025	10350
Work Special			(825)	(825)	(1100)	(1100)
4WD	F		1575	1575	2100	2100
V6 3.9 Liter	X		(625)	(625)	(835)	(835)
6-Cyl. 5.9L Turbo Diesel	6		4625	4625	6165	6165
6-Cyl. 5.9L HO Turbo Dsl	7		5625	5625	7500	7500
V8 5.9 Liter	Z		350	350	465	465
V10 8.0 Liter	W		275	275	365	365
CLUB CAB PICKUP—V8—Truck Equipment Schedule T1						
1500 Short Bed	C12Y	21465	6450	7475	9100	11550
4WD	F		1575	1575	2100	2100
V8 5.9 Liter	Z		350	350	465	465
QUAD CAB PICKUP—V8—Truck Equipment Schedule T1						
1500 Short Bed	C13Y	23375	6900	7975	9625	12150
1500 Long Bed	C13Y	23655	6600	7625	9250	11700
2500 Short Bed	C23Z	25440	7725	8875	10600	13250
2500 Long Bed	C23Z	25630	7475	8875	10300	12850
3500 Long Bed	C33Z	28155	7725	8875	10600	13250
4WD	F		1575	1575	2100	2100
6-Cyl. 5.9L Turbo Dsl	6		4625	4625	6165	6165
6-Cyl. 5.9L HO Turbo Dsl	7		5625	5625	7500	7500
V8 5.9 Liter	Z		350	350	465	465
V10 8.0 Liter	W		275	275	365	365

2002 DODGE — 1B(4,7or8)-(S38N)-2-#

Body Type	VIN	List	Trade-In Fair	Trade-In Good	Pvt-Party Good	Retail Excellent
DURANGO 4WD—V8—Truck Equipment Schedule T1						
Sport Utility 4D	S38N	27595	8775	10050	11950	14850
R/T Sport Utility 4D	S78Z	37070	9475	10825	12750	15750
w/o Third Seat			(750)	(750)	(1000)	(1000)
2WD	R		(800)	(800)	(1065)	(1065)
V8 5.9 Liter (ex. R/T)	Z		400	400	535	535
CARAVAN—Truck Equipment Schedule T1						
eC Minivan 4D	P15B	16995	3375	4075	5675	7950
SE Minivan 4D	P44B	19795	4600	5425	7125	9550
Sport Minivan 4D	P64G	24060	5150	6050	7750	10300
SE Grand Minivan 4D	P44G	22440	5600	6525	8300	10850
eL Grand Minivan 4D	P343	24175	5850	6800	8550	11150
Sport Grand 4D	P64G	24930	5875	6850	8600	11200
EX Grand Minivan 4D	P44L	26725	7000	8075	9950	12700
ES Grand Minivan 4D	P54L	30135	7150	8250	10100	12850
5 Passenger			(600)	(600)	(800)	(800)
AWD	T		825	825	1100	1100
4-Cyl. 2.4 Liter	B		(1125)	(1125)	(1500)	(1500)
V6 3.8 Liter	L		750	750	1000	1000
RAM WAGON—V8—Truck Equipment Schedule T1						
1500 Passenger Van	B15Y	22035	5950	6900	9025	12050
2500 Passenger Van	B25Y	24050	6175	7175	9300	12350
3500 Maxi Passenger	B35Y	27055	6550	7575	9750	12850

TRUCKS & VANS

2002 DODGE/PLYMOUTH

Body Type	VIN	List	Trade-In Fair	Trade-In Good	Pvt-Party Good	Retail Excellent
V6 3.9 Liter	X		(600)	(600)	(800)	(800)
V8 5.9 Liter	Z		200	200	265	265
RAM VAN—V6—Truck Equipment Schedule T1						
1500 Cargo Van	B11X	20050	5275	6175	7900	10450
2500 Cargo Van	B21X	21595	5475	6400	8125	10650
110" W.B.			0	0	0	0
Maxi-Van			200	200	265	265
V8 5.2 Liter	Y		300	300	400	400
V8 5.9 Liter	Z		600	600	800	800
RAM VAN—V8—Truck Equipment Schedule T1						
3500 Cargo Van	B31Y	23780	6100	7075	8875	11500
Maxi-Van			200	200	265	265
V8 5.9 Liter	Z		200	200	265	265
DAKOTA PICKUP—4-Cyl.—Truck Equipment Schedule T1						
Short Bed	L26P	16370	4800	5650	7550	10200
R/T Short Bed	L26Z	21290	5750	6700	8650	11450
4WD	G		1800	1800	2400	2400
V6 3.9 Liter	X		400	400	535	535
V8 4.7 Liter	N		650	650	865	865
V8 5.9 Liter (ex. R/T)	Z		925	925	1235	1235
DAKOTA PICKUP—V6—Truck Equipment Schedule T1						
Club Cab	L22X	19695	6650	7675	9675	12550
R/T Club Cab	L22Z	23585	7550	8675	10700	13750
Quad Cab	L23X	21985	7275	8375	10450	13400
4WD	G		1800	1800	2400	2400
4-Cyl. 2.5 Liter	P		(450)	(450)	(600)	(600)
V8 4.7 Liter	N		350	350	465	465
V8 5.9 Liter (ex. R/T)	Z		600	600	800	800
REGULAR CAB PICKUP—V8—Truck Equipment Schedule T1						
1500 Short Bed	C16Y	19620	6875	7925	9550	12050
1500 Long Bed	C16Y	19905	6500	7525	9125	11550
2500 HD Long Bed	C26Z	23490	6225	7225	8800	11200
3500 Long Bed	C36Z	25375	6550	7575	9175	11600
4WD	F		1750	1750	2335	2335
V6 3.7 Liter	K		(700)	(700)	(935)	(935)
6-Cyl. 5.9L Turbo Diesel	6		4825	4825	6430	6430
6-Cyl. 5.9L HO Turbo Dsl	7		5850	5850	7800	7800
V8 5.9 Liter	Z		375	375	500	500
V10 8.0 Liter	W		300	300	400	400
QUAD CAB PICKUP—V8—Truck Equipment Schedule T1						
1500 Short Bed	C13Y	23840	9275	10575	12350	15150
1500 Long Bed	C13Y	24120	8900	10175	11950	14650
2500 Short Bed	C23Z	25455	9025	10325	12050	14800
2500 Long Bed	C23Z	25645	8675	9950	11700	14400
3500 Long Bed	C33Z	28170	9025	10325	12050	14800
4WD	F		1750	1750	2335	2335
6-Cyl. 5.9L Turbo Dsl	6		4825	4825	6430	6430
6-Cyl. 5.9L HO Turbo Dsl	7		5850	5850	7800	7800
V8 5.9 Liter	Z		375	375	500	500
V10 8.0 Liter	W		300	300	400	400

2003 DODGE — (1,2or3)D(3,4,7or8)-(S38N)-3

Body Type	VIN	List	Trade-In Fair	Trade-In Good	Pvt-Party Good	Retail Excellent
DURANGO 4WD—V8—Truck Equipment Schedule T1						
Sport Utility 4D	S38N	28875	10375	11825	13800	16950
R/T Sport Utility 4D	S78Z	38670	11200	12700	14750	17950
w/o Third Seat			(650)	(650)	(865)	(865)
2WD	R		(875)	(875)	(1165)	(1165)
V8 5.9 Liter (ex. R/T)	Z		425	425	565	565
CARAVAN—V6—Truck Equipment Schedule T1						
Cargo Minivan	P253	21965	4900	5750	7575	10150
Grand Cargo Minivan	P253	22850	5250	6125	7950	10550
CARAVAN—V6—Truck Equipment Schedule T2						
SE Minivan 4D	P25B	21440	6375	7400	9275	12050
Sport Minivan 4D	P453	25110	7475	8575	10500	13400
SE Grand Minivan 4D	P24R	22890	6875	7950	9900	12700
eL Grand Minivan 4D	P343	24425	7150	8250	10150	13000
Sport Grand 4D	P44R	28040	7175	8300	10200	13050
EX Grand Minivan 4D	P74L	30450	8450	9675	11650	14600
ES Grand Minivan 4D	P54L	33335	8600	9850	11850	14850
5 Passenger			(650)	(650)	(865)	(865)
AWD	T		900	900	1200	1200
4-Cyl. 2.4 Liter	B		(1225)	(1225)	(1635)	(1635)
V6 3.8 Liter	L		825	825	1100	1100

DEDUCT FOR RECONDITIONING 0106

Body Type	VIN	List	Trade-In Fair	Trade-In Good	Pvt-Party Good	Retail Excellent
RAM VAN—V6—Truck Equipment Schedule T1						
1500 Cargo Van	B11X	20685	7425	8525	10450	13300
2500 Cargo Van	B21X	21640	7650	8775	10650	13550
110" W.B.			0	0	0	0
Maxi-Van			225	225	300	300
V8 5.2 Liter	Y		325	325	435	435
V8 5.9 Liter	Z		650	650	865	865
RAM VAN—V8—Truck Equipment Schedule T1						
3500 Cargo Van	B31Y	24415	8325	9525	11500	14450
Maxi-Van			225	225	300	300
V8 5.9 Liter	Z		250	250	335	335
DAKOTA PICKUP—V6—Truck Equipment Schedule T1						
Short Bed	L16X	17680	5775	6725	8750	11650
R/T Short Bed	L76Z	22800	6800	7850	9950	12950
Club Cab	L22X	19375	7750	8900	11050	14150
R/T Club Cab	L22Z	25100	8775	10050	12200	15450
Quad Cab	L23X	22550	8500	9700	11900	15100
4WD	G		1975	1975	2635	2635
V8 4.7 Liter	N		375	375	500	500
V8 5.9 Liter (ex. R/T)	Z		650	650	865	865
REGULAR CAB PICKUP—V8—Truck Equipment Schedule T1						
1500 Short Bed	A16N	20225	8450	9675	11350	14000
1500 Long Bed	A16N	20510	8025	9225	10850	13500
4WD	U		1925	1925	2565	2565
V6 3.7 Liter	K		(750)	(750)	(1000)	(1000)
V8 5.7 Liter HEMI	D		1125	1125	1500	1500
V8 5.9 Liter	Z,5		325	325	435	435
REGULAR CAB PICKUP—V8 HEMI—Truck Equipment Schedule T1						
2500 Long Bed	A26D	24255	9125	10425	12150	14900
3500 Long Bed	A36D	26140	9425	10775	12500	15300
4WD	U		1925	1925	2565	2565
6-Cyl. 5.9L Turbo Diesel	6		5025	5025	6700	6700
6-Cyl. 5.9L HO Turbo Dsl	C		6075	6075	8100	8100
V10 8.0 Liter	W		300	300	400	400
QUAD CAB PICKUP—V8—Truck Equipment Schedule T1						
1500 Short Bed	A18N	24960	10625	12075	13850	16800
1500 Long Bed	A18N	25240	10175	11600	13400	16250
4WD	U		1925	1925	2565	2565
V6 3.7 Liter	K		(750)	(750)	(1000)	(1000)
V8 5.7 Liter HEMI	D		1125	1125	1500	1500
V8 5.9 Liter	Z,5		325	325	435	435
QUAD CAB PICKUP—V8 HEMI—Truck Equipment Schedule T1						
2500 Short Bed	A28D	26600	11650	13200	15100	18150
2500 Long Bed	A28D	26790	11300	12850	14700	17700
3500 Short Bed	A386	32455	11975	13575	15450	18550
3500 Long Bed	A38D	29315	11650	13200	15100	18150
4WD	U		1925	1925	2565	2565
6-Cyl. 5.9L Turbo Dsl	6		5025	5025	6700	6700
6-Cyl. 5.9L HO Turbo Dsl	C		6075	6075	8100	8100
V10 8.0 Liter	W		300	300	400	400
2004 DODGE—(1,3orW)D(2,3,4,5,7or8)—(S38N)-4						
DURANGO 4WD—V8—Truck Equipment Schedule T1						
Sport Utility 4D	S38N	29350	12025	13625	16100	19900
w/o Third Seat			(700)	(700)	(935)	(935)
2WD	R		(950)	(950)	(1265)	(1265)
V6 3.7 Liter	K		(1125)	(1125)	(1500)	(1500)
V8 5.7 Liter	D		1075	1075	1435	1435
CARAVAN—V6—Truck Equipment Schedule T2						
Cargo Minivan	P21R	22585	6400	7425	9300	12050
Grand Cargo Minivan	P23R	23455	6800	7850	9750	12500
CARAVAN—V6—Truck Equipment Schedule T1						
SE Minivan 4D	P25B	21795	8025	9225	11150	14050
SXT Minivan 4D	P45R	24850	9200	10475	12500	15550
SE Grand Minivan 4D	P24R	24975	8550	9800	11800	14800
EX Grand Minivan 4D	P74L	27225	10225	11650	13750	16950
SXT Grand Minivan	P44L	30335	11200	12700	14800	18100
5 Passenger			(700)	(700)	(935)	(935)
AWD	T		975	975	1300	1300
4-Cyl. 2.4 Liter	B		(1325)	(1325)	(1765)	(1765)
V6 3.8 Liter	L		900	900	1200	1200
DAKOTA PICKUP—V6—Truck Equipment Schedule T1						
Short Bed	L16X	18725	6925	8000	10100	13100

TRUCKS & VANS

Body Type	VIN	List	Trade-In Fair	Trade-In Good	Pvt-Party Good	Retail Excellent
Club Cab	L22X	21395	9075	10375	12550	15800
Quad Cab	L23X	23595	9850	11250	13500	16850
4WD	G		2150	2150	2865	2865
V8 4.7 Liter	N		750	750	1000	1000

REGULAR CAB PICKUP—V8—Truck Equipment Schedule T1

Body Type	VIN	List	Fair	Good	Good	Excellent
1500 Short Bed	A16N	21900	10100	11450	13100	15800
1500 Long Bed	A16N	22185	9650	11000	12600	15300
4WD	U		2100	2100	2800	2800
V6 3.7 Liter	K		(800)	(800)	(1065)	(1065)
V8 5.7 Liter HEMI	D		1200	1200	1600	1600

REGULAR CAB PICKUP—V8 HEMI—Truck Equipment Schedule T1

Body Type	VIN	List	Fair	Good	Good	Excellent
2500 Long Bed	A26D	25695	10825	12275	13950	16800
3500 Long Bed	A36D	27715	11150	12650	14350	17150
4WD	U		2100	2100	2800	2800
6-Cyl. 5.9L Turbo Diesel	6		5225	5225	6965	6965
6-Cyl. 5.9L HO Turbo Dsl	C		6300	6300	8400	8400

REGULAR CAB PICKUP—V10—Truck Equipment Schedule T1

Body Type	VIN	List	Fair	Good	Good	Excellent
SRT-10 1500 Short	A16H	45795	28525	31925	34100	38700
6-Spd Manual Trans			0	0	0	0

QUAD CAB PICKUP—V8—Truck Equipment Schedule T1

Body Type	VIN	List	Fair	Good	Good	Excellent
1500 Short Bed	A18N	26060	12475	14125	15900	18850
1500 Long Bed	A18N	26415	12025	13625	15350	18300
4WD	U		2100	2100	2800	2800
V6 3.7 Liter	K		(800)	(800)	(1065)	(1065)
V8 5.7 Liter HEMI	D		1200	1200	1600	1600

QUAD CAB PICKUP—V8 HEMI—Truck Equipment Schedule T1

Body Type	VIN	List	Fair	Good	Good	Excellent
2500 Short Bed	A28D	28150	13625	15375	17150	20300
2500 Long Bed	A28D	28340	13250	14975	16750	19800
3500 Short Bed	A386	34530	13975	15800	17600	20800
3500 Long Bed	A38D	30790	13625	15375	17150	20300
4WD	U		2100	2100	2800	2800
6-Cyl. 5.9L Turbo Dsl	6		5225	5225	6965	6965
6-Cyl. 5.9L HO Turbo Dsl	C		6300	6300	8400	8400

2005 DODGE — (1,3orW)D(2,3,4,5,7or8)—(B38N)—5

DURANGO 4WD—V8—Truck Equipment Schedule T1

Body Type	VIN	List	Fair	Good	Good	Excellent
Sport Utility 4D	B38N	30360	14200	16000	18600	22600
w/o Third Seat			(750)	(750)	(1000)	(1000)
2WD	D		(1000)	(1000)	(1335)	(1335)
V6 3.7 Liter	D		(1225)	(1225)	(1635)	(1635)
V8 5.7 Liter HEMI	D		1150	1150	1535	1535

CARAVAN—V6—Truck Equipment Schedule T2

Body Type	VIN	List	Fair	Good	Good	Excellent
Cargo Minivan	P21R	20185	8375	9575	11600	14600
Grand Cargo Minivan	P23R	20885	8775	10050	12100	15150

CARAVAN—V6—Truck Equipment Schedule T1

Body Type	VIN	List	Fair	Good	Good	Excellent
Minivan 4D	P25B	18995	10100	11450	13600	16850
SXT Minivan 4D	P45R	22485	11350	12900	15100	18550
Grand Minivan 4D	P24R	22185	10675	12175	14300	17650
SXT Grand Minivan	P44L	27185	13475	15225	17550	21200
5 Passenger			(750)	(750)	(1000)	(1000)
4-Cyl. 2.4 Liter	B		(1425)	(1425)	(1900)	(1900)
V6 3.3L Flex Fuel	E		0	0	0	0

DAKOTA PICKUP—V6—Truck Equipment Schedule T1

Body Type	VIN	List	Fair	Good	Good	Excellent
Club Cab	E22K	20305	10575	12025	14750	18650
Quad Cab	E28K	22514	11500	13050	15750	19800
4WD	W		2325	2325	3100	3100
V8 4.7 Liter/V8 4.7L HO	N,J		800	800	1065	1065

REGULAR CAB PICKUP—V8—Truck Equipment Schedule T1

Body Type	VIN	List	Fair	Good	Good	Excellent
1500 Short Bed	A16N	22910	11825	13375	15050	17850
1500 Long Bed	A16N	23195	11300	12850	14450	17200
4WD	U		2275	2275	3035	3035
V6 3.7 Liter	K		(850)	(850)	(1135)	(1135)
V8 5.7 Liter HEMI	D		1250	1250	1665	1665

REGULAR CAB PICKUP—V8 HEMI—Truck Equipment Schedule T1

Body Type	VIN	List	Fair	Good	Good	Excellent
2500 Long Bed	R26D	26510	12600	14250	16000	18900
3500 Long Bed	R36D	28395	13000	14700	16450	19400
4WD	S		2275	2275	3035	3035
6-Cyl. 5.9L HO Turbo Dsl	C		6525	6525	8700	8700

REGULAR CAB 4WD—V8 HEMI—Truck Equipment Schedule T1

Body Type	VIN	List	Fair	Good	Good	Excellent
2500 Power Wagon	S26D	36660				

REGULAR CAB PICKUP—V10—Truck Equipment Schedule T1

Body Type	VIN	List	Fair	Good	Good	Excellent
SRT-10 1500 Short	A16H	45850				
6-Spd Manual Trans						

2005 DODGE/PLYMOUTH

Body	Type	VIN	List	Trade-In Fair	Good	Pvt-Party Good	Retail Excellent
QUAD CAB PICKUP—V8—Truck Equipment Schedule T1							
1500 Short Bed	A18N	26920	14450	16300	18100	21200
1500 Long Bed	A18N	27275	13975	15800	17550	20700
4WD	S		2275	2275	3035	3035
V6 3.7 Liter	K		(850)	(850)	(1135)	(1135)
V8 5.7 Liter HEMI	D		1250	1250	1665	1665
QUAD CAB PICKUP 4WD—V8 HEMI—Truck Equipment Sch T1							
2500 Power Wagon	R28D	41040				
QUAD CAB PICKUP—V10—Truck Equipment Schedule T1							
SRT-10 1500 Short	A18H	50850				
QUAD CAB PICKUP—V8 HEMI—Truck Equipment Schedule T1							
2500 Short Bed	R28D	28890	15675	17650	19500	22800
2500 Long Bed	R28D	29080	15225	17175	19050	22300
3500 Short Bed	R48D	35480	16050	18050	20000	23400
3500 Long Bed	R48D	31605	15675	17650	19500	22800
4WD	S		2275	2275	3035	3035
6-Cyl. 5.9L HO Turbo Dsl	C		6525	6525	8700	8700

FORD

1991 FORD — 1F(MorT)-(U24X)-M-#

Body	Type	VIN	List	Trade-In Fair	Good	Pvt-Party Good	Retail Excellent
EXPLORER 4WD—V6—Truck Equipment Schedule T1							
Sport Utility 2D	U24X	18340	950	1325	2175	3475
Sport Utility 4D	U34X	19319	1325	1825	2900	4450
2WD	2		(350)	(350)	(465)	(465)
BRONCO 4WD—V8—Truck Equipment Schedule T1							
Sport Utility 2D	U15N	20599	1450	1950	3050	4625
6-Cyl. 4.9 Liter	Y		(350)	(350)	(465)	(465)
V8 5.8 Liter	H		75	75	100	100
AEROSTAR—V6—Truck Equipment Schedule T2							
Cargo Minivan	A14U	13310	475	675	1175	2000
Extended Cargo	A34U	14057	475	675	1200	2025
Window Minivan	A15U	13693	475	675	1200	2025
Extended Window	A35U	14440	475	675	1225	2075
4WD	2,4		250	250	335	335
V6 4.0 Liter	X		50	50	65	65
AEROSTAR—V6—Truck Equipment Schedule T1							
Minivan	A11U	15466	525	750	1325	2250
Extended Minivan	A31U	16363	600	875	1475	2500
5 Passenger			(200)	(200)	(265)	(265)
4WD	2,4		250	250	335	335
V6 4.0 Liter	X		50	50	65	65
CLUB WAGON—V8—Truck Equipment Schedule T1							
E150 Passenger Van	E11N,H	19461	750	1075	1825	3000
E250 Passenger Van	E21H	20408	775	1125	1900	3100
E350 Passenger Van	E31H	22390	825	1175	2000	3225
5 Passenger			(200)	(200)	(265)	(265)
6-Cyl. 4.9 Liter	Y		(200)	(200)	(265)	(265)
V8 460/7.5 Liter	G		100	100	135	135
V8 7.3 Liter Diesel	M		200	200	265	265
ECONOLINE—6-Cyl.—Truck Equipment Schedule T1							
E150 Cargo Van	E14Y	15366	725	1050	1675	2775
E250 Cargo Van	E24Y	15716	775	1100	1775	2875
E350 Cargo Van	E34Y	16767	850	1200	1950	3100
Super Van	S		50	50	65	65
V8 5.0, 5.8 Liter	N,H		100	100	135	135
V8 460/7.5 Liter	G		200	200	265	265
V8 7.3 Liter Diesel	M		200	200	265	265
RANGER PICKUP—4-Cyl.—Truck Equipment Schedule T1							
S Short Bed	R10A	8729	275	375	750	1350
Sport Short Bed	R10A	8834	300	400	800	1425
Sport Long Bed	R10A	8990	225	325	675	1250
Custom Short Bed	R10A	10213	300	400	800	1425
Custom Long Bed	R10A	10376	225	325	675	1250
Custom Super Cab	R14A	11741	500	725	1225	2025
4WD	1,5		500	500	665	665
V6 2.9, 3.0 Liter	T,U		125	125	165	165
V6 4.0 Liter	X		150	150	200	200
REGULAR CAB PICKUP—V8—Truck Equipment Schedule T1							
F150 Short Bed	F15N	14977	1100	1550	2575	4050
F150 Long Bed	F15N	15221	1075	1500	2525	3975
F250 Long Bed	F25H	16650	1125	1575	2625	4100

Body	Type	VIN	List	Trade-In Fair	Good	Pvt-Party Good	Retail Excellent
TRUCKS & VANS	F350 Long Bed	F35H	17636	1150	1600	2650	4125
	Special			(250)	(250)	(335)	(335)
	4WD	4,6		500	500	665	665
	6-Cyl. 4.9 Liter	Y		(350)	(350)	(465)	(465)
	V8 5.8 Liter	H		75	75	100	100
	V8 460/7.5 Liter	G		150	150	200	200
	V8 7.3 Liter Diesel	M		200	200	265	265
	SUPER CAB PICKUP—V8—Truck Equipment Schedule T1						
	F150 Short Bed	X15N	16361	1400	1900	3000	4550
	F150 Long Bed	X15N	16595	1375	1875	2925	4475
	F250 Long Bed	X25H	19059	1675	2175	3325	4975
	F350 Long Bed	X35G	19756	1525	2025	3175	4775
	Special			(250)	(250)	(335)	(335)
	4WD	4,6		500	500	665	665
	6-Cyl. 4.9 Liter	Y		(350)	(350)	(465)	(465)
	V8 5.8 Liter	H		75	75	100	100
	V8 460/7.5 Liter	G		150	150	200	200
	V8 7.3 Liter Diesel	M		200	200	265	265
	CREW CAB PICKUP—V8—Truck Equipment Schedule T1						
	F350 Long Bed	W35H	19588	1775	2300	3475	5125
	4WD	6		500	500	665	665
	V8 460/7.5 Liter	G		150	150	200	200
	V8 7.3 Liter Diesel	M		200	200	265	265

1992 FORD — 1F(MorT)–(U24X)–N–#

Body	Type	VIN	List	Trade-In Fair	Good	Pvt-Party Good	Retail Excellent
EXPLORER 4WD—V6—Truck Equipment Schedule T1							
Sport Utility 2D	U24X	19799	1075	1500	2525	3975
Sport Utility 4D	U34X	20660	1550	2050	3200	4800
2WD	2		(375)	(375)	(500)	(500)
BRONCO 4WD—V8—Truck Equipment Schedule T1							
Sport Utility 2D	U15N	21879	2400	2975	4275	6075
6-Cyl. 4.9 Liter	Y		(350)	(350)	(465)	(465)
V8 5.8 Liter	H		100	100	135	135
AEROSTAR—V6—Truck Equipment Schedule T2							
Cargo Minivan	A14U	14478	525	750	1275	2150
Extended Cargo	A34U	15275	550	775	1300	2200
Window Minivan	A15U	14855	550	775	1300	2200
Extended Window	A35U	15602	550	775	1325	2250
4WD	4		275	275	365	365
V6 4.0 Liter	X		50	50	65	65
AEROSTAR—V6—Truck Equipment Schedule T1							
Minivan	A11U	15881	600	875	1450	2425
Extended Minivan	A31U	17673	700	1000	1625	2675
5 Passenger			(225)	(225)	(300)	(300)
4WD	4		275	275	365	365
V6 4.0 Liter	X		50	50	65	65
CLUB WAGON—V8—Truck Equipment Schedule T1							
Passenger Van	E11N,H	19154	875	1225	2075	3400
Heavy Duty Van	E31H	20363	925	1300	2200	3575
Super Passenger Van	S31H	22413	975	1375	2300	3675
5 Passenger			(225)	(225)	(300)	(300)
6-Cyl. 4.9 Liter	Y		100	100	135	135
V8 460/7.5 Liter	G		100	100	135	135
V8 7.3 Liter Diesel	M		200	200	265	265
ECONOLINE—6-Cyl.—Truck Equipment Schedule T1							
E150 Cargo Van	E14Y	16636	850	1200	1950	3100
E250 Cargo Van	E24Y	17050	900	1250	2025	3225
E350 Cargo Van	E34Y	18150	975	1350	2200	3475
Super Van	S		50	50	65	65
V8 5.0, 5.8 Liter	N,H		100	100	135	135
V8 460/7.5 Liter	G		225	225	300	300
V8 7.3 Liter Diesel	M		200	200	265	265
RANGER PICKUP—4-Cyl.—Truck Equipment Schedule T2							
S Short Bed	R10A	9190	300	400	875	1575
Sport Short Bed	R10A	9306	325	450	925	1650
Sport Long Bed	R10A	9463	250	350	775	1425
Custom Short Bed	R10A	10723	325	450	925	1650
Custom Long Bed	R10A	11048	250	350	775	1425
Custom Super Cab	R14A	12144	550	775	1375	2375
4WD	1,5		550	550	735	735
V6 2.9, 3.0 Liter	T,U		125	125	165	165
V6 4.0 Liter	X		175	175	235	235

DEDUCT FOR RECONDITIONING 0106

Body	Type	VIN	List	Trade-In Fair	Trade-In Good	Pvt-Party Good	Retail Excellent
REGULAR CAB PICKUP—V8—Truck Equipment Schedule T1							
F150 Short Bed		F15N	15853	**1400**	**1900**	**2950**	**4475**
F150 Long Bed		F15N	16097	**1375**	**1875**	**2900**	**4425**
F250 Long Bed		F25H	17699	**1475**	**1975**	**3050**	**4575**
F350 Long Bed		F35H	18963	**1500**	**2000**	**3050**	**4600**
Special				(275)	(275)	(365)	(365)
4WD		4,6		550	550	735	735
6-Cyl. 4.9 Liter		Y		(350)	(350)	(465)	(465)
V8 5.8 Liter		H		100	100	135	135
V8 460/7.5 Liter		G		150	150	200	200
V8 7.3 Liter Diesel		M		200	200	265	265
SUPER CAB PICKUP—V8—Truck Equipment Schedule T1							
F150 Short Bed		X15N	17219	**1775**	**2300**	**3425**	**5025**
F150 Long Bed		X15N	17453	**1725**	**2250**	**3350**	**4950**
F250 Long Bed		X25H	19237	**2075**	**2650**	**3825**	**5525**
F350 Long Bed		X35G	20829	**1975**	**2500**	**3650**	**5300**
Special				(275)	(275)	(365)	(365)
4WD		4,6		550	550	735	735
6-Cyl. 4.9 Liter		Y		(350)	(350)	(465)	(465)
V8 5.8 Liter		H		100	100	135	135
V8 460/7.5 Liter		G		150	150	200	200
V8 7.3 Liter Diesel		M		200	200	265	265
CREW CAB PICKUP—V8—Truck Equipment Schedule T1							
F350 Long Bed		W35H	20322	**2225**	**2825**	**4025**	**5775**
4WD		6		550	550	735	735
V8 460/7.5 Liter		G		150	150	200	200
V8 7.3 Liter Diesel		M		200	200	265	265

1993 FORD — 1F(MorT)–(U24X)–P–#

Body	Type	VIN	List	Trade-In Fair	Trade-In Good	Pvt-Party Good	Retail Excellent
EXPLORER 4WD—V6—Truck Equipment Schedule T1							
Sport Utility 2D		U24X	20613	**1075**	**1525**	**2600**	**4100**
Sport Utility 4D		U34X	21401	**1675**	**2175**	**3375**	**5050**
Limited				200	200	265	265
2WD		2		(400)	(400)	(535)	(535)
BRONCO 4WD—V8—Truck Equipment Schedule T1							
Sport Utility 2D		U15N	22589	**2525**	**3125**	**4450**	**6350**
V8 5.8 Liter		H		150	150	200	200
AEROSTAR—V6—Truck Equipment Schedule T2							
Cargo Minivan		A14U	14977	**450**	**650**	**1225**	**2075**
Extended Cargo		A34U	15724	**475**	**700**	**1250**	**2150**
Window Minivan		A15U	15272	**475**	**700**	**1275**	**2200**
Extended Window		A35U	16020	**500**	**725**	**1300**	**2250**
4WD		2,4		325	325	435	435
V6 4.0 Liter		X		75	75	100	100
AEROSTAR—V6—Truck Equipment Schedule T1							
Minivan		A11U	15682	**575**	**825**	**1425**	**2450**
Extended Minivan		A31U	17081	**675**	**975**	**1650**	**2775**
5 Passenger				(250)	(250)	(335)	(335)
4WD		2,4		325	325	435	435
V6 4.0 Liter		X		75	75	100	100
CLUB WAGON—V8—Truck Equipment Schedule T1							
Passenger Van		E11N	18925	**975**	**1350**	**2400**	**3900**
Heavy Duty Van		E31H	20850	**1050**	**1450**	**2550**	**4075**
Super Passenger Van		S31N	21652	**1075**	**1525**	**2625**	**4175**
Chateau				200	200	265	265
5 Passenger				(250)	(250)	(335)	(335)
6-Cyl. 4.9 Liter		Y		(250)	(250)	(335)	(335)
V8 460/7.5 Liter		G		125	125	165	165
V8 7.3 Liter Diesel		M		225	225	300	300
ECONOLINE—6-Cyl.—Truck Equipment Schedule T1							
E150 Cargo Van		E14Y	17022	**925**	**1300**	**2175**	**3475**
E250 Cargo Van		E24Y	17437	**1000**	**1400**	**2300**	**3650**
E350 Cargo Van		E34Y	18536	**1075**	**1525**	**2550**	**4025**
Super Van		S		75	75	100	100
V8 5.0, 5.8 Liter		N,H		125	125	165	165
V8 460/7.5 Liter		G		250	250	335	335
V8 7.3 Liter Diesel		M		225	225	300	300
RANGER PICKUP—4-Cyl.—Truck Equipment Schedule T2							
XL Short Bed		R10A	9190	**475**	**675**	**1225**	**2100**
XL Long Bed		R10A	9903	**400**	**550**	**1075**	**1875**
XL Super Cab		R14A	12346	**750**	**1050**	**1775**	**2925**
Splash Short Bed		R10A	12635	**675**	**950**	**1625**	**2725**
4WD		1,5		675	675	900	900

TRUCKS & VANS

1993 FORD

Body	Type	VIN	List	Trade-In Fair	Trade-In Good	Pvt-Party Good	Retail Excellent
V6 3.0 Liter	U		150	150	200	200
V6 4.0 Liter	X		200	200	265	265
REGULAR CAB PICKUP—V8—Truck Equipment Schedule T1							
F150 Short Bed	F15N	15407	1475	1975	3075	4650
F150 Lightning	F15R	21669	2350	2925	4225	6050
F150 Long Bed	F15N	15651	1400	1900	3000	4550
F250 Long Bed	F25H	17160	1550	2050	3175	4775
F350 Long Bed	F35H	19390	1525	2025	3150	4750
Special			(325)	(325)	(435)	(435)
4WD	4,6		650	650	865	865
6-Cyl. 4.9 Liter	Y		(375)	(375)	(500)	(500)
V8 5.8 Liter	H,R		150	150	200	200
V8 460/7.5 Liter	G		175	175	235	235
V8 7.3 Liter Diesel	M		225	225	300	300
V8 7.3L Turbo Diesel	K		750	750	1000	1000
SUPER CAB PICKUP—V8—Truck Equipment Schedule T1							
F150 Short Bed	X15N	17483	1800	2425	3625	5275
F150 Long Bed	X15N	17717	1825	2350	3525	5200
F250 Long Bed	X25H	19616	2275	2850	4125	5925
F350 Long Bed	X35G	21572	2400	2975	4275	6075
4WD	4,6		650	650	865	865
6-Cyl. 4.9 Liter	Y		(375)	(375)	(500)	(500)
V8 5.8 Liter	H		150	150	200	200
V8 460/7.5 Liter	G		175	175	235	235
V8 7.3 Liter Diesel	M		225	225	300	300
V8 7.3L Turbo Diesel	K		750	750	1000	1000
CREW CAB PICKUP—V8—Truck Equipment Schedule T1							
F350 Long Bed	W35H	20641	2475	3075	4375	6225
4WD	6		650	650	865	865
V8 460/7.5 Liter	G		175	175	235	235
V8 7.3 Liter Diesel	M		225	225	300	300
V8 7.3L Turbo Diesel	K		750	750	1000	1000

1994 FORD — 1F(MorT)-(U24X)-R-#

Body	Type	VIN	List	Trade-In Fair	Trade-In Good	Pvt-Party Good	Retail Excellent
EXPLORER 4WD—V6—Truck Equipment Schedule T1							
Sport Utility 2D	U24X	21145	1125	1575	2725	4325
Sport Utility 4D	U34X	22055	1825	2350	3600	5350
2WD	2		(425)	(425)	(565)	(565)
BRONCO 4WD—V8—Truck Equipment Schedule T1							
Sport Utility 2D	U15N	24036	2700	3300	4700	6675
V8 5.8 Liter	H		175	175	235	235
AEROSTAR—V6—Truck Equipment Schedule T2							
Cargo Minivan	A14U	15796	400	575	1150	2025
Extended Cargo	A34U	16346	450	625	1225	2150
Window Minivan	A15U	16091	450	650	1275	2250
Extended Window	A35U	16641	475	675	1275	2275
4WD	2,4		375	375	500	500
V6 4.0 Liter	X		100	100	135	135
AEROSTAR—V6—Truck Equipment Schedule T1							
Minivan	A11U	16302	550	800	1475	2550
Extended Minivan	A31U	17747	675	975	1700	2875
5 Passenger			(275)	(275)	(365)	(365)
4WD	2,4		375	375	500	500
V6 4.0 Liter	X		100	100	135	135
CLUB WAGON—V8—Truck Equipment Schedule T1							
Passenger Van	E11N	19790	1075	1525	2650	4250
Heavy Duty Van	E31H	21739	200	1650	2825	4450
Super Passenger Van	S31H	22925	1225	1725	2875	4525
5 Passenger			(275)	(275)	(365)	(365)
6-Cyl. 4.9 Liter	Y		(275)	(275)	(365)	(365)
V8 460/7.5 Liter	G		150	150	200	200
V8 7.3 Liter Diesel	M		(150)	(150)	(200)	(200)
ECONOLINE—6-Cyl.—Truck Equipment Schedule T1							
E150 Cargo Van	E14Y	17806	1075	1500	2575	4075
E250 Cargo Van	E24Y	18201	1125	1575	2675	4200
E350 Cargo Van	E34Y	19299	1250	1750	2825	4425
Super Van			100	100	135	135
V8 5.0, 5.8 Liter	N,H		150	150	200	200
V8 460/7.5 Liter	G		275	275	365	365
V8 7.3 Liter Diesel	M		250	250	335	335
RANGER PICKUP—4-Cyl.—Truck Equipment Schedule T2							
XL Short Bed	R10A	9826	550	800	1425	2425
XL Long Bed	R10A	10200	450	650	1225	2100

302   **DEDUCT FOR RECONDITIONING**

0106

Body Type	VIN	List	Trade-In Fair	Trade-In Good	Pvt-Party Good	Retail Excellent
XL Super Cab	R14A	12469	850	1225	2025	3300
Splash Short Bed	R10A	13305	825	1175	1950	3175
Splash Super Cab	R14A	14774	1100	1550	2600	4100
4WD	1,5		800	800	1065	1065
V6 3.0 Liter	U		175	175	235	235
V6 4.0 Liter	X		225	225	300	300
REGULAR CAB PICKUP—V8—Truck Equipment Schedule T1						
F150 Short Bed	F15N	16434	1625	2125	3275	4900
F150 Lightning	F15R	23127	2675	3275	4600	6500
F150 Long Bed	F15N	16658	1525	2025	3175	4775
F250 Long Bed	F25H	17480	1725	2250	3400	5050
F350 Long Bed	F35H	20088	1750	2275	3425	5075
Special			(375)	(375)	(500)	(500)
4WD	4,6		750	750	1000	1000
6-Cyl. 4.9 Liter	Y		(400)	(400)	(535)	(535)
V8 5.8 Liter	H,R		175	175	235	235
V8 460/7.5 Liter	G		200	200	265	265
V8 7.3 Liter Diesel	M		250	250	335	335
V8 7.3L Turbo Diesel	K		850	850	1135	1135
V8 7.3L Power Stroke	F		2500	2500	3335	3335
SUPER CAB PICKUP—V8—Truck Equipment Schedule T1						
F150 Short Bed	X15N	18040	2100	2675	3875	5600
F150 Long Bed	X15N	18283	2025	2575	3750	5475
F250 Long Bed	X25H	20578	2575	3200	4475	6325
F350 Long Bed	X35G	22410	2725	3325	4650	6550
Special			(375)	(375)	(500)	(500)
4WD	4,6		750	750	1000	1000
6-Cyl. 4.9 Liter	Y		(400)	(400)	(535)	(535)
V8 5.8 Liter	H		175	175	235	235
V8 460/7.5 Liter	G		200	200	265	265
V8 7.3 Liter Diesel	M		250	250	335	335
V8 7.3L Turbo Diesel	K		850	850	1135	1135
V8 7.3L Power Stroke	F		2500	2500	3335	3335
CREW CAB PICKUP—V8—Truck Equipment Schedule T1						
F350 Long Bed	W35H	21591	2825	3450	4775	6725
4WD	6		750	750	1000	1000
V8 460/7.5 Liter	G		200	200	265	265
V8 7.3 Liter Diesel	M		250	250	335	335
V8 7.3L Turbo Diesel	K		850	850	1135	1135
V8 7.3L Power Stroke	F		2500	2500	3335	3335

1995 FORD—(1or2)F(B,MorT)—(U24X)—S—#

Body Type	VIN	List	Trade-In Fair	Trade-In Good	Pvt-Party Good	Retail Excellent
EXPLORER 4WD—V6—Truck Equipment Schedule T1						
Sport Utility 2D	U24X	22380	1225	1700	2900	4600
Sport Utility 4D	U34X	23735	2000	2550	3875	5750
2WD	2		(450)	(450)	(600)	(600)
BRONCO 4WD—V8—Truck Equipment Schedule T1						
Sport Utility 2D	U15N	24305	2925	3600	5050	7125
V8 5.8 Liter	H		200	200	265	265
AEROSTAR—V6—Truck Equipment Schedule T2						
Cargo Minivan	A14U	17486	400	550	1175	2075
AEROSTAR—V6—Truck Equipment Schedule T1						
Minivan	A11U	17895	725	1050	1850	3100
Extended Minivan	A31U	22261	850	1225	2125	3525
5 Passenger			(300)	(300)	(400)	(400)
V6 4.0 Liter	X		425	425	565	565
WINDSTAR—V6—Truck Equipment Schedule T2						
Cargo Minivan	A544	18655	625	900	1625	2800
WINDSTAR—V6—Truck Equipment Schedule T1						
GL Minivan	A514	19995	1225	1675	2825	4425
LX Minivan	A514	24080	1450	1950	3125	4775
CLUB WAGON—V8—Truck Equipment Schedule T1						
Passenger Van	E11N	21286	1250	1750	2950	4650
Heavy Duty Van	E31H	22967	1400	1900	3150	4875
Super Passenger Van	S31H	24780	1475	1975	3225	4975
6-Cyl. 4.9 Liter	Y		(300)	(300)	(400)	(400)
V8 460/7.5 Liter	G		175	175	235	235
V8 7.3L Turbo Diesel	F		1500	1500	2000	2000
ECONOLINE—6-Cyl.—Truck Equipment Schedule T1						
E150 Cargo Van	E14Y	18676	1250	1750	2850	4450
E250 Cargo Van	E24Y	19098	1350	1850	2975	4575
E350 Cargo Van	E34Y	20624	1525	2025	3175	4825

TRUCKS & VANS

Body Type	VIN	List	Trade-In Fair	Trade-In Good	Pvt-Party Good	Retail Excellent
Super Van..................S		....	100	100	135	135
V8 5.0, 5.8 Liter..........N,H		....	175	175	235	235
V8 460/7.5 Liter..........G		....	300	300	400	400
V8 7.3L Turbo Diesel		....	1675	1675	2235	2235
RANGER PICKUP—4-Cyl.—Truck Equipment Schedule T2						
XL Short Bed..............R10A	10746	....	675	950	1625	2775
XL Long Bed...............R10A	11130	....	550	775	1400	2425
XL Super Cab.............R14A	13298	....	1000	1400	2425	3900
Splash Short Bed........R10A	13825	....	975	1375	2300	3675
Splash Super Cab.......R14A	15400	....	1325	1825	2900	4475
4WD........................1,5		....	900	900	1200	1200
V6 3.0 Liter................U		....	200	200	265	265
V6 4.0 Liter................X		....	250	250	335	335
REGULAR CAB PICKUP—V8—Truck Equipment Schedule T1						
F150 Short Bed...........F15N	17418	....	1825	2350	3550	5250
F150 Lightning............F15R		....	3000	3675	5075	7050
F150 Long Bed............F15N	17642	....	1700	2175	3425	5100
F250 Long Bed............F25H	18264	....	1950	2475	3675	5425
F350 Long Bed............F35H	20236	....	2000	2550	3750	5500
Special		....	(400)	(400)	(535)	(535)
4WD........................4,6		....	850	850	1135	1135
6-Cyl. 4.9 Liter...........Y,Z		....	(425)	(425)	(565)	(565)
V8 5.8 Liter................H,R		....	200	200	265	265
V8 460/7.5 Liter..........G		....	225	225	300	300
V8 7.3L Turbo Diesel....F		....	2800	2800	3730	3730
SUPER CAB PICKUP—V8—Truck Equipment Schedule T1						
F150 Short Bed...........X15N	19297	....	2350	2925	4225	6050
F150 Long Bed............X15N	19540	....	2250	2825	4075	5875
F250 Long Bed............X25H	20670	....	2900	3575	4925	6875
F350 Long Bed............X35G	22730	....	3050	3725	5125	7125
Special		....	(400)	(400)	(535)	(535)
4WD........................4,6		....	850	850	1135	1135
6-Cyl. 4.9 Liter...........Y		....	(425)	(425)	(565)	(565)
V8 5.8 Liter................H		....	200	200	265	265
V8 460/7.5 Liter..........G		....	225	225	300	300
V8 7.3L Turbo Diesel....F		....	2800	2800	3730	3730
CREW CAB PICKUP—V8—Truck Equipment Schedule T1						
F350 Long Bed............W35H	21938	....	3175	3850	5250	7300
4WD........................6		....	850	850	1135	1135
V8 460/7.5 Liter..........G		....	225	225	300	300
V8 7.3L Turbo Diesel....F		....	2800	2800	3730	3730

1996 FORD—(1or2)F(B,MorT)—(U24X)—T—#

Body Type	VIN	List	Trade-In Fair	Trade-In Good	Pvt-Party Good	Retail Excellent
EXPLORER 4WD—V6—Truck Equipment Schedule T1						
Sport Utility 2D..........U24X	22980	....	1575	2075	3400	5225
XL Sport Utility 4D.......U34X	24335	....	2425	3000	4450	6450
2WD........................2		....	(475)	(475)	(635)	(635)
AWD........................5		....	0	0	0	0
V8 5.0 Liter................P		....	200	200	265	265
BRONCO 4WD—V8—Truck Equipment Schedule T1						
XL Sport Utility 2D.......U15N	25375	....	3275	3950	5475	7675
V8 5.8 Liter................H		....	225	225	300	300
AEROSTAR—V6—Truck Equipment Schedule T2						
Cargo Minivan............A14U	17966	....	400	575	1225	2275
AEROSTAR—V6—Truck Equipment Schedule T2						
XLT Minivan...............A11U	18375	....	775	1125	2025	3450
XLT Extended.............A31U	22840	....	925	1300	2425	4025
5 Passenger		....	(325)	(325)	(435)	(435)
4WD........................4		....	475	475	635	635
V6 4.0 Liter................X		....	100	100	135	135
WINDSTAR—V6—Truck Equipment Schedule T2						
Cargo Minivan............A544	18825	....	725	1050	1925	3275
V6 3.0 Liter................U		....	(200)	(200)	(265)	(265)
WINDSTAR—V6—Truck Equipment Schedule T1						
GL Minivan.................A514	20785	....	1425	1925	3150	4875
LX Minivan.................A514	25340	....	1700	2225	3500	5250
V6 3.0 Liter................U		....	(200)	(200)	(265)	(265)
CLUB WAGON—V8—Truck Equipment Schedule T1						
XL Passenger Van........E11N	22224	....	1550	2050	3375	5200
XL Heavy Duty Van.......E31H	23925	....	1725	2250	3600	5425
XL Super Pass Van.......S31H	25764	....	1800	2325	3650	5525
6-Cyl. 4.9 Liter...........Y		....	(325)	(325)	(435)	(435)
V8 460/7.5 Liter..........G		....	200	200	265	265

1996 FORD

Body Type	VIN	List	Trade-In Fair	Trade-In Good	Pvt-Party Good	Retail Excellent
V8 7.3L Turbo Diesel	F		1650	1650	2200	2200
ECONOLINE—6-Cyl.—Truck Equipment Schedule T1						
E150 Cargo Van	E14Y	19346	1575	2075	3275	4975
E250 Cargo Van	E24Y	19771	1675	2175	3400	5100
E350 Cargo Van	E34Y	21396	1850	2375	3625	5350
Super Van			100	100	135	135
V8 5.0, 5.8 Liter	N,H		200	200	265	265
V8 460/7.5 Liter	G		325	325	435	435
V8 7.3L Turbo Diesel	F		1825	1825	2435	2435
RANGER PICKUP—4-Cyl.—Truck Equipment Schedule T2						
XL Short Bed	R10A	11087	775	1100	1925	3175
XL Long Bed	R10A	11472	625	900	1625	2800
XL Super Cab	R14A	14311	1125	1575	2700	4275
Splash Short Bed	R10A	14645	1150	1600	2725	4300
Splash Super Cab	R14U	16305	1575	2075	3250	4925
4WD	1,5		1000	1000	1335	1335
V6 3.0 Liter	U		225	225	300	300
V6 4.0 Liter	X		275	275	365	365
REGULAR CAB PICKUP—V8—Truck Equipment Schedule T1						
F150 Short Bed	F15N	18327	2075	2650	3900	5700
F150 Long Bed	F15N	18552	1975	2500	3750	5525
F250 Long Bed	F25H	19017	2225	2825	4100	5925
F350 Long Bed	F35H	20157	2325	2900	4225	6075
Special			(425)	(425)	(565)	(565)
4WD	4,6		950	950	1265	1265
6-Cyl. 4.9 Liter	Y		(450)	(450)	(600)	(600)
V8 5.8 Liter	H		225	225	300	300
V8 460/7.5 Liter	G		250	250	335	335
V8 7.3L Turbo Diesel	F		3100	3100	4130	4130
SUPER CAB PICKUP—V8—Truck Equipment Schedule T1						
F150 Short Bed	X15N	20352	2725	3325	4675	6600
F150 Long Bed	X15N	20597	2575	3200	4500	6400
F250 Short Bed	X25H	21667	3500	4200	5675	7775
F250 Long Bed	X25H	21487	3325	4025	5450	7525
F350 Long Bed	X35G	23485	3500	4200	5675	7775
Special			(425)	(425)	(565)	(565)
4WD	4,6		950	950	1265	1265
6-Cyl. 4.9 Liter	Y		(450)	(450)	(600)	(600)
V8 5.8 Liter	H		225	225	300	300
V8 460/7.5 Liter	G		250	250	335	335
V8 7.3L Turbo Diesel	F		3100	3100	4130	4130
CREW CAB PICKUP—V8—Truck Equipment Schedule T1						
F250 Short Bed	W25G	23422	3950	4700	6225	8450
F350 Long Bed	W35H	23482	3625	4350	5825	7950
4WD	6		950	950	1265	1265
V8 460/7.5 Liter	G		250	250	335	335
V8 7.3L Turbo Diesel	F		3100	3100	4130	4130

1997 FORD—(1or2)F(B,M,orT)—(U24X)—V—#

Body Type	VIN	List	Trade-In Fair	Trade-In Good	Pvt-Party Good	Retail Excellent
EXPLORER 4WD—V6—Truck Equipment Schedule T1						
Sport Utility 2D	U24X	24065	2000	2550	3975	5950
XL Sport Utility 4D	U34X	25420	2875	3550	5075	7225
2WD			(500)	(500)	(665)	(665)
AWD	5		0	0	0	0
V6 4.0 Liter SOHC	E		150	150	200	200
V8 5.0 Liter	P		200	200	265	265
EXPEDITION 4WD—V8—Truck Equipment Schedule T1						
XLT Sport Utility 4D	U18W	30510	4150	4925	6925	9700
w/o Third Seat			(525)	(525)	(700)	(700)
2WD	7		(1100)	(1100)	(1465)	(1465)
V8 5.4 Liter	L		250	250	335	335
AEROSTAR—V6—Truck Equipment Schedule T2						
Cargo Minivan	A14U	17995	475	675	1450	2675
AEROSTAR—V6—Truck Equipment Schedule T1						
XLT Minivan	A11U	18405	900	1275	2425	4050
XLT Extended	A31U	21170	1075	1500	2725	4425
5 Passenger			(350)	(350)	(465)	(465)
2WD	4		500	500	665	665
V6 4.0 Liter	X		100	100	135	135
WINDSTAR—V6—Truck Equipment Schedule T2						
Cargo Minivan	A544	19600	900	1250	2400	4025
V6 3.0 Liter	U		(225)	(225)	(300)	(300)

SEE BACK PAGES FOR TRUCK EQUIPMENT

Body	Type	VIN	List	Trade-In Fair	Trade-In Good	Pvt-Party Good	Retail Excellent
WINDSTAR—V6—Truck Equipment Schedule T1							
Minivan		A514	19995	1300	1800	3025	4775
GL Minivan		A514	23070	1725	2250	3575	5375
LX Minivan		A514	26195	2025	2575	3900	5800
V6 3.0 Liter		U		(225)	(225)	(300)	(300)
CLUB WAGON—V8—Truck Equipment Schedule T1							
XL Passenger Van		E11N	23210	1975	2500	3900	5875
XL Heavy Duty Van		E31L	25255	2125	2700	4125	6100
XL Super Pass Van		S31L	27135	2200	2800	4225	6225
V6 4.2 Liter		2		(350)	(350)	(465)	(465)
V8 7.3L Turbo Diesel		F		1800	1800	2400	2400
V10 6.8 Liter		S		525	525	700	700
ECONOLINE—V6—Truck Equipment Schedule T1							
E150 Cargo Van		E142	20505	1975	2500	3775	5600
E250 Cargo Van		E242	20930	2025	2600	3875	5725
E350 Cargo Van		E34L	23565	2250	2825	4150	6025
Super Van		S		100	100	135	135
V8 4.6, 5.4 Liter		6,L		200	200	265	265
V8 7.3L Turbo Diesel		F		1950	1950	2600	2600
V10 6.8 Liter		S		1050	1050	1400	1400
RANGER PICKUP—4-Cyl.—Truck Equipment Schedule T2							
XL Short Bed		R10A	11060	925	1300	2375	3900
XL Long Bed		R10A	11445	775	1125	1975	3300
XL Super Cab		R14A	14905	1375	1900	3050	4700
Splash Short Bed		R10A	15385	1450	1950	3125	4775
Splash Super Cab		R14U	17010	1925	2450	3675	5425
4WD		1,5		1100	1100	1465	1465
V6 3.0 Liter		U		250	250	335	335
V6 4.0 Liter		X		300	300	400	400
REGULAR CAB PICKUP—V8—Truck Equipment Schedule T1							
F150 Short Bed		F176,W	17480	2725	3350	4700	6650
F150 Long Bed		F176,W	17750	2500	3100	4425	6300
F250 Long Bed		F276,W	18770	3075	3725	5150	7125
F250 H.D. Long Bed		F25H	20265	3625	4335	5775	7850
F350 Long Bed		F35H	20775	3925	4675	6175	8375
Standard (Work Truck)		6,8		(450)	(450)	(600)	(600)
4WD				1050	1050	1400	1400
V6 4.2 Liter		2		(450)	(450)	(600)	(600)
V8 5.4 Liter		L		250	250	335	335
V8 460/7.5 Liter		G		275	275	365	365
V8 7.3L Turbo Diesel		F		3400	3400	4530	4530
SUPER CAB PICKUP—V8—Truck Equipment Schedule T1							
F150 Short Bed		X176,W	19635	3975	4725	6225	8425
F150 Long Bed		X176,W	19920	3750	4500	6000	8125
F250 Short Bed		X276,W	20620	4500	5325	6900	9225
F250 H.D. Short Bed		X25H	22285	3925	4675	6175	8375
F250 H.D. Long Bed		X25H	22105	3750	4500	6000	8125
F350 Long Bed		X35G	23875	4275	5075	6600	8825
Standard (Work Truck)		6,8		(450)	(450)	(600)	(600)
4WD				1050	1050	1400	1400
V6 4.2 Liter		2		(450)	(450)	(600)	(600)
V8 5.4 Liter		L		250	250	335	335
V8 460/7.5 Liter		G		275	275	365	365
V8 7.3L Turbo Diesel		F		3400	3400	4530	4530
CREW CAB PICKUP—V8—Truck Equipment Schedule T1							
F250 Short Bed		W25G	24160	4475	5275	6875	9175
F350 Long Bed		W35H	24220	4675	5525	7125	9450
4WD		6		1050	1050	1400	1400
V8 460/7.5 Liter		G		275	275	365	365
V8 7.3L Turbo Diesel		F		3400	3400	4530	4530

1998 FORD –(1or2)F(B,MorT)–(U24X)–W–#

Body	Type	VIN	List	Trade-In Fair	Trade-In Good	Pvt-Party Good	Retail Excellent
EXPLORER 4WD—V6—Truck Equipment Schedule T1							
Sport Utility 2D		U24X	24315	2550	3150	4675	6800
XL Sport Utility 4D		U34X	24995	3500	4200	5850	8150
2WD		2		(525)	(525)	(700)	(700)
AWD		5		0	0	0	0
V6 4.0 Liter SOHC		E		150	150	200	200
V8 5.0 Liter		P		200	200	265	265
EXPEDITION 4WD—V8—Truck Equipment Schedule T1							
XLT Sport Utility 4D		U18W	31225	4950	5825	8025	11050
w/o Third Seat				(575)	(575)	(765)	(765)
2WD		7		(1175)	(1175)	(1565)	(1565)

Body Type	VIN	List	Trade-In Fair	Good	Pvt-Party Good	Retail Excellent
V8 5.4 Liter	L		275	275	365	365
WINDSTAR—V6—Truck Equipment Schedule T2						
Cargo Minivan	A544	18590	1100	1550	2825	4575
V6 3.0 Liter	U		(250)	(250)	(335)	(335)
WINDSTAR—V6—Truck Equipment Schedule T1						
Minivan	A514	20970	1650	2150	3525	5375
GL Minivan	A514	24025	2075	2650	4050	6000
LX Minivan	A514	28365	2400	2975	4425	6425
Limited Minivan	A514	30085	3050	3725	5250	7375
V6 3.0 Liter	U		(250)	(250)	(335)	(335)
CLUB WAGON—V8—Truck Equipment Schedule T1						
XL Passenger Van	E11N	23090	2450	3050	4575	6725
XL Heavy Duty Van	E31L	25255	2625	3250	4775	6925
XL Super Pass Van	S31L	26970	2725	3350	4925	7075
V6 4.2 Liter	2		(375)	(375)	(500)	(500)
V8 7.3L Turbo Diesel	F		1925	1925	2565	2565
V10 6.8 Liter	S		575	575	765	765
ECONOLINE—V6—Truck Equipment Schedule T1						
E150 Cargo Van	E142	19795	2425	3025	4425	6350
E250 Cargo Van	E242	20105	2525	3125	4500	6475
E350 Cargo Van	E34L	22705	2750	3375	4775	6800
Super Van	S		100	100	135	135
V8 4.6, 5.4 Liter	6,L		200	200	265	265
V8 7.3L Turbo Diesel	F		2075	2075	2765	2765
V10 6.8 Liter	S		1150	1150	1535	1535
RANGER PICKUP—4-Cyl.—Truck Equipment Schedule T2						
XL Short Bed	R10C	11575	1150	1600	2800	4450
XL Long Bed	R10C	12045	1000	1400	2550	4150
Splash Short Bed	R10C	15195	1825	2350	3625	5375
XL Super Cab 2D	R14C	14625	1725	2250	3500	5250
XLT Super Cab 4D	R14C	15625	2650	3275	4600	6525
Splash Super Cab 2D	R14U	16825	2300	2875	4200	6075
Splash Super Cab 4D	R14C	17420	2725	3325	4675	6625
4WD	1,5		1200	1200	1600	1600
V6 3.0 Liter	U		250	250	335	335
V6 4.0 Liter	X		325	325	435	435
REGULAR CAB PICKUP—V8—Truck Equipment Schedule T1						
F150 Short Bed	F176,W	18815	3225	3900	5325	7375
F150 Long Bed	F176,W	19115	3000	3650	5050	7050
F250 Long Bed	F276,W	20225	3625	4350	5825	7925
Standard (Work Truck)			(475)	(475)	(635)	(635)
4WD	6,8		1150	1150	1535	1535
V6 4.2 Liter	2		(450)	(450)	(600)	(600)
V8 5.4 Liter	L		275	275	365	365
SUPER CAB PICKUP—V8—Truck Equipment Schedule T1						
F150 Short Bed	X176,W	21255	4575	5400	6975	9275
F150 Long Bed	X176,W	21555	4375	5150	6700	8950
F250 Short Bed	X276,W	22300	5175	6050	7675	10100
Standard (Work Truck)			(475)	(475)	(635)	(635)
4WD	6,8		1150	1150	1535	1535
V6 4.2 Liter	2		(450)	(450)	(600)	(600)
V8 5.4 Liter	L		275	275	365	365

1999 FORD—(1,2or3)F(B,MorT)—(U24X)–X–

Body Type	VIN	List	Trade-In Fair	Good	Pvt-Party Good	Retail Excellent
EXPLORER 4WD—V6—Truck Equipment Schedule T1						
Sport Utility 2D	U24X	24545	3200	3875	5300	7375
XL Sport Utility 4D	U34X	25310	4225	5025	6550	8775
2WD	2		(575)	(575)	(765)	(765)
AWD	5		0	0	0	0
V6 4.0 Liter SOHC	E		150	150	200	200
V8 5.0 Liter	P		200	200	265	265
EXPEDITION 4WD—V8—Truck Equipment Schedule T1						
XLT Sport Utility 4D	U18W	32610	6075	7025	8950	11750
w/o Third Seat			(625)	(625)	(835)	(835)
2WD	7		(1225)	(1225)	(1635)	(1635)
V8 5.4 Liter	L		300	300	400	400
WINDSTAR—V6—Truck Equipment Schedule T2						
Cargo Minivan	A544	18955	1525	2025	3300	5100
V6 3.0 Liter	U		(250)	(250)	(335)	(335)
WINDSTAR—V6—Truck Equipment Schedule T1						
Minivan	A51U	21300	2125	2700	4025	5925
LX Minivan	A514	24590	2600	3225	4600	6575
SE Minivan	A524	28075	2950	3625	5025	7050

TRUCKS & VANS

1999 FORD

Body Type	VIN	List	Trade-In Fair	Good	Pvt-Party Good	Retail Excellent
SEL Minivan	A534	30995	3650	4375	5875	8000
w/o 2nd Sliding Door			(500)	(500)	(665)	(665)
ECONOLINE WAGON—V8—Truck Equipment Schedule T1						
E150 XL Passenger	E112	22710	3125	3775	5400	7675
E350 XL Super Duty	S31L	25595	3300	3975	5600	7875
E350 XL S.D. Ext	S31L	27285	3450	4150	5800	8100
V6 4.2 Liter	2		(425)	(425)	(565)	(565)
V8 7.3L Turbo Diesel	F		2050	2050	2735	2735
V10 6.8 Liter	S		600	600	800	800
ECONOLINE VAN—V6—Truck Equipment Schedule T1						
E150 Cargo Van	E142	20025	3050	3725	5150	7150
E250 Cargo Van	E24L	21325	3150	3800	5250	7275
E350 Super Cargo	E34L	24085	3425	4125	5500	7650
Super Van (E250)	S		100	100	135	135
V8 4.6, 5.4 Liter	W,L		200	200	265	265
V8 7.3L Turbo Diesel	F		2200	2200	2935	2935
V10 6.8 Liter	S		1225	1225	1635	1635
RANGER PICKUP—4-Cyl.—Truck Equipment Schedule T2						
XL Short Bed	R10C	11795	1500	2000	3200	4900
XL Long Bed	R10C	12265	1275	1775	2950	4625
XL Super Cab 2D	R14C	15250	2125	2725	3975	5800
XLT Super Cab 4D	R14X	15910	3125	3775	5175	7125
4WD	1,5		1275	1275	1700	1700
V6 3.0L Flex Fuel	V		250	250	335	335
V6 4.0 Liter	X		375	375	500	500
REGULAR CAB PICKUP—V8—Truck Equipment Schedule T1						
F150 Short Bed	F17W	19205	3800	4550	5975	8025
F150 Long Bed	F17W	19505	3575	4275	5675	7675
F250 Long Bed	F276,W	20575	4250	5050	6500	8625
Work Truck			(525)	(525)	(700)	(700)
4WD	6,8		1225	1225	1635	1635
V6 4.2 Liter	2		(475)	(475)	(635)	(635)
V8 5.4 Liter	L		300	300	400	400
REGULAR CAB PICKUP—V8 Supercharged—Truck Sch T1						
F150 Lightning	F073	29355	8600	9850	11650	14400
SUPER CAB PICKUP—V8—Truck Equipment Schedule T1						
F150 Short Bed	X17W	21985	5250	6150	7700	10050
F150 Long Bed	X17W	22285	5025	5900	7425	9675
F250 Long Bed	X276,W	23355	5925	6875	8500	10900
Work Truck			(525)	(525)	(700)	(700)
4WD	6,8		1225	1225	1635	1635
V6 4.2 Liter	2		(475)	(475)	(635)	(635)
V8 5.4 Liter	L		300	300	400	400
SUPER DUTY REGULAR CAB—V8—Truck Equipment Sch T1						
F250 Long Bed	F20L	21505	5150	6050	7575	9850
F350 Long Bed	F30L	22150	5350	6250	7800	10150
4WD	1		1225	1225	1635	1635
V10 6.8 Liter	S		500	500	665	665
V8 7.3L Turbo Diesel	F		3950	3950	5265	5265
SUPER DUTY SUPER CAB—V8—Truck Equipment Sch T1						
F250 Short Bed	X20L	23560	6825	7875	9550	12150
F250 Long Bed	X20L	23460	6600	7650	9300	11850
F350 Short Bed	X30L	24245	7025	8100	9800	12400
F350 Long Bed	X30L	24445	6825	7875	9550	12150
4WD	1		1225	1225	1635	1635
V8 7.3L Turbo Diesel	F		3950	3950	5265	5265
V10 6.8 Liter	S		500	500	665	665
SUPER DUTY CREW CAB—V8—Truck Equipment Sch T1						
F250 Short Bed	W20L	24985	7675	8800	10600	13350
F250 Long Bed	W20L	25185	7475	8575	10400	13050
F350 Short Bed	W30L	25835	7900	9075	10850	13650
F350 Long Bed	W30L	26035	7675	8800	10600	13350
4WD	1		1225	1225	1635	1635
V8 7.3L Turbo Diesel	F		3950	3950	5265	5265
V10 6.8 Liter	S		500	500	665	665

2000 FORD–(1,2or3)F(B,MorT)–(U70X)–Y–

Body Type	VIN	List	Trade-In Fair	Good	Pvt-Party Good	Retail Excellent
EXPLORER SPORT 4WD—V6—Truck Equipment Schedule T1						
Utility 2D	U70X	24690	3900	4650	6175	8400
2WD	6		(650)	(650)	(865)	(865)
V6 4.0 Liter SOHC	E		175	175	235	235
EXPLORER 4WD—V6—Truck Equipment Schedule T1						
XL Sport Utility 4D	U72X	26790	5075	5950	7575	9950

Body Type	VIN	List	Trade-In Fair	Trade-In Good	Pvt-Party Good	Retail Excellent
2WD	6	......	(650)	(650)	(865)	(865)
AWD	5	......	0	0	0	0
V6 4.0 Liter SOHC	E	......	175	175	235	235
V8 5.0 Liter	P	......	250	250	335	335
EXPEDITION 4WD—V8—Truck Equipment Schedule T1						
XLT Sport Utility 4D	U166	33165	7150	8250	10350	13400
w/o Third Seat			(725)	(725)	(965)	(965)
2WD			(1300)	(1300)	(1735)	(1735)
V8 5.4 Liter	L		325	325	435	435
EXCURSION 4WD—V10—Truck Equipment Schedule T1						
XLT Sport Utility 4D	U41S	38090	8550	9800	12000	15250
w/o Third Seat			(725)	(725)	(965)	(965)
2WD			(1300)	(1300)	(1735)	(1735)
V8 5.4 Liter	L		(500)	(500)	(665)	(665)
V8 7.3L Turbo Diesel	F		4200	4200	5600	5600
WINDSTAR—V6—Truck Equipment Schedule T2						
Cargo Minivan	A544	20395	1900	2425	3800	5700
WINDSTAR—V6—Truck Equipment Schedule T1						
Minivan	A504	23080	2600	3225	4625	6650
LX Minivan	A514	25045	3175	3825	5300	7400
SE Minivan	A524	28195	3600	4300	5800	7950
SEL Minivan	A534	31095	4375	5175	6750	9025
Limited Minivan	A534	33990	5675	6600	8300	10750
w/o 2nd Sliding Door	0		(550)	(550)	(735)	(735)
V6 3.0 Liter	U		(275)	(275)	(365)	(365)
ECONOLINE WAGON—V8—Truck Equipment Schedule T1						
E150 Passenger Van	E112	23810	4000	4750	6525	9025
E350 Super Duty Van	E31L	25900	4225	5000	6800	9300
E350 Super Duty Ext.	S31L	27570	4400	5200	7000	9550
V6 4.2 Liter	2		(500)	(500)	(665)	(665)
V8 7.3L Turbo Diesel	F		2275	2275	3035	3035
V10 6.8 Liter	S		650	650	865	865
ECONOLINE VAN—V6—Truck Equipment Schedule T1						
E150 Cargo Van	E142	20805	3825	4575	6075	8300
E250 Cargo Van	E24L	21835	3925	4675	6225	8450
E350 Super Cargo	E34L	24355	4250	5050	6600	8850
Super Van	S		150	150	200	200
V8 4.6, 5.4 Liter	W,L		250	250	335	335
V8 7.3L Turbo Diesel	F		2525	2525	3365	3365
V10 6.8 Liter	S		1300	1300	1735	1735
RANGER PICKUP—4-Cyl.—Truck Equipment Schedule T2						
XL Short Bed	R10C	11995	1950	2475	3775	5625
XL Long Bed	R10C	12445	1675	2200	3500	5275
XL Super Cab 2D	R14C	15655	2700	3300	4675	6625
XL Super Cab 4D	R14C	16230	3425	4125	5525	7600
4WD	1,5		1450	1450	1935	1935
V6 3.0L Flex Fuel	V		300	300	400	400
V6 4.0 Liter	X		450	450	600	600
REGULAR CAB PICKUP—V8—Truck Equipment Schedule T1						
F150 Short Bed	F17W	19510	4450	5250	6750	8900
F150 Long Bed	F17W	19810	4175	4950	6375	8500
4WD	6,8		1400	1400	1865	1865
Work Truck			(675)	(675)	(900)	(900)
V6 4.2 Liter	2		(550)	(550)	(735)	(735)
V8 5.4 Liter	L		325	325	435	435
REGULAR CAB—V8 Supercharged—Truck Equip Sch T1						
F150 Lightning	F073	30895	10050	11400	13250	16150
SUPER CAB PICKUP—V8—Truck Equipment Schedule T1						
F150 Short Bed	X17W	22195	6125	7100	8700	11100
F150 Harley Davidson	X17L	33800	9200	10475	12350	15250
F150 Long Bed	X17W	22495	5850	6800	8375	10700
4WD	6,8		1400	1400	1865	1865
Work Truck			(675)	(675)	(900)	(900)
V6 4.2 Liter	2		(550)	(550)	(735)	(735)
V8 5.4 Liter	L		325	325	435	435
SUPER DUTY REGULAR CAB PICKUP—V8—Truck Equip Sch T1						
F250 Long Bed	F20L	22450	5925	6875	8475	10850
F350 Long Bed	F30L	23175	6150	7150	8775	11200
4WD	1		1400	1400	1865	1865
V8 7.3L Turbo Diesel	F		4200	4200	5600	5600
V10 6.8 Liter	S		550	550	735	735
SUPER DUTY SUPER CAB PICKUP—V8—Truck Equip Sch T1						
F250 Short Bed	X20L	24620	7825	9000	10750	13450

TRUCKS & VANS

Body Type	VIN	List	Trade-In Fair	Trade-In Good	Pvt-Party Good	Retail Excellent
F250 Long Bed	X20L	24820	7600	8725	10450	13100
F350 Short Bed	X30L	25410	8100	9300	11050	13750
F350 Long Bed	X30L	25610	7825	9000	10750	13450
4WD	1		1400	1400	1865	1865
V8 7.3L Turbo Diesel	F		4200	4200	5600	5600
V10 6.8 Liter	S		550	550	735	735
SUPER DUTY CREW CAB PICKUP—V8—Truck Equipment Sch T1						
F250 Short Bed	W20L	25930	8825	10100	11950	14800
F350 Short Bed	W20L	26130	8600	9850	11650	14450
F350 Short Bed	W30L	26590	9075	10375	12200	15150
F350 Short Bed	W30L	26790	8825	10100	11950	14800
4WD	1		1400	1400	1865	1865
V8 7.3L Turbo Diesel	F		4200	4200	5600	5600
V10 6.8 Liter	S		550	550	735	735

2001 FORD — (1or2)F(B,MorT)–(U021)–1–#

Body Type	VIN	List	Trade-In Fair	Trade-In Good	Pvt-Party Good	Retail Excellent
ESCAPE 4WD—V6—Truck Equipment Schedule T1						
XLS Sport Utility 4D	U021	21185	6325	7350	8925	11350
XLT Sport Utility 4D	U041	22815	6875	7925	9575	12100
2WD	B		(725)	(725)	(965)	(965)
4-Cyl. 2.0 Liter	B		(725)	(725)	(965)	(965)
EXPLORER SPORT 4WD—V6—Truck Equipment Schedule T1						
Sport Utility 2D	U70E	24435	4800	5650	7275	9650
2WD	6		(720)	(720)	(965)	(965)
EXPLORER 4WD—V6—Truck Equipment Schedule T1						
XLS Sport Utility 4D	U71E	27570	6125	7100	8825	11400
2WD	6		(725)	(725)	(965)	(965)
AWD	8		0	0	0	0
V8 5.0 Liter	P		300	300	400	400
EXPLORER SPORT TRAC 4WD—V6—Truck Equipment Sch T1						
Utility Pickup 4D	U77E	25010	6875	7950	9750	12400
2WD	6		(725)	(725)	(965)	(965)
EXPEDITION 4WD—V8—Truck Equipment Schedule T1						
XLT Sport Utility 4D	U16W	33405	8450	9675	11950	15300
w/o Third Seat			(825)	(825)	(1100)	(1100)
2WD	5		(1350)	(1350)	(1800)	(1800)
V8 5.4 Liter	L		350	350	465	465
EXCURSION 4WD—V10—Truck Equipment Schedule T1						
XLT Sport Utility 4D	U41S	38925	10050	11400	13800	17350
w/o Third Seat			(825)	(825)	(1100)	(1100)
2WD	0		(1350)	(1350)	(1800)	(1800)
V8 5.4 Liter	L		(500)	(500)	(665)	(665)
V8 7.3L Turbo Diesel	F		4450	4450	5930	5930
WINDSTAR—V6—Truck Equipment Schedule T2						
Cargo Minivan	A544	20540	2425	3025	4500	6575
WINDSTAR—V6—Truck Equipment Schedule T1						
LX Minivan	A514	25320	3875	4625	6200	8475
SE Sport Minivan	A574	27755	4225	5000	6600	8925
SE Minivan	A524	28915	4350	5125	6750	9075
SEL Minivan	A534	31435	5250	6125	7825	10300
Limited Minivan	A584	34085	6725	7750	9550	12200
w/o 2nd Sliding Door	0		(600)	(600)	(800)	(800)
ECONOLINE WAGON—V8—Truck Equipment Schedule T1						
E150 Passenger Van	E11W	24060	5125	6025	7950	10700
E350 Super Duty	E31L	26350	5350	6250	8225	11000
E350 Super Duty Ext.	S31L	27970	5575	6500	8500	11350
V6 4.2 Liter	2		(550)	(550)	(735)	(735)
V8 7.3L Turbo Diesel	F		2500	2500	3335	3335
V10 6.8 Liter	S		675	675	900	900
ECONOLINE VAN—V6—Truck Equipment Schedule T1						
E150 Cargo Van	E142	21175	4825	5675	7325	9700
E250 Cargo Van	E24L	22445	4950	5825	7475	9900
E350 Super Cargo	E34L	24875	5275	6175	7875	10350
Super Van	S		175	175	235	235
Crew Van Pkg.			275	275	365	365
V8 4.6, 5.4 Liter	W,L		275	275	365	365
V8 7.3L Turbo Diesel	F		2850	2850	3800	3800
V10 6.8 Liter	S		1350	1350	1800	1800
RANGER PICKUP—4-Cyl.—Truck Equipment Schedule T2						
XL Short Bed	R10C	12400	2475	3075	4475	6475
XL Long Bed	R10C	13515	2175	2775	4150	6075
XL Super Cab 2D	R14C	16465	3325	4025	5475	7600
XL Super Cab 4D	R14C	20960	4150	4925	6450	8650

Body Type	VIN	List	Trade-In Fair	Good	Pvt-Party Good	Retail Excellent
4WD	1,5		1625	1625	2165	2165
V6 3.0 Liter	U		350	350	465	465
V6 4.0 Liter	E		500	500	665	665
REGULAR CAB PICKUP—V8—Truck Equipment Schedule T1						
F150 Short Bed	F17W	20170	5250	6150	7675	9950
F150 Long Bed	F17W	20470	4950	5800	7300	9525
4WD	6,8		1575	1575	2100	2100
Work Truck			(825)	(825)	(1100)	(1100)
V6 4.2 Liter	2		(625)	(625)	(835)	(835)
V8 5.4 Liter	L,Z		350	350	465	465
REGULAR CAB PICKUP—V8 Supercharged—Truck Sch T1						
F150 Lightning	F073	32460	11600	13150	15050	18100
SUPER CAB PICKUP—V8—Truck Equipment Schedule T1						
F150 Short Bed	X17W	22855	7150	8250	9900	12400
F150 Long Bed	X17W	23155	6825	7875	9500	12000
4WD	6,8		1575	1575	2100	2100
Work Truck			(825)	(825)	(1100)	(1100)
V6 4.2 Liter	2		(625)	(625)	(835)	(835)
V8 5.4 Liter	L,Z		350	350	465	465
SUPERCREW PICKUP—V8—Truck Equipment Schedule T1						
F150 Short Bed 4D	W07W	26940	8275	9475	11200	13850
F150 King Ranch	W07W	31455	9700	11050	12900	15750
F150 HarleyDavidson	W07L	34495	12950	14650	16750	20100
4WD	8		1575	1575	2100	2100
V8 5.4 Liter	L		350	350	465	465
SUPER DUTY REGULAR CAB—V8—Truck Equipment Sch T1						
F250 Long Bed	F20L	23155	6875	7925	9550	12050
F350 Long Bed	F30L	23580	7150	8250	9900	12400
4WD	1		1575	1575	2100	2100
V8 7.3L Turbo Diesel	F		4450	4450	5930	5930
V10 6.8 Liter	S		575	575	765	765
SUPER DUTY SUPER CAB—V8—Truck Equipment Schedule T1						
F250 Short Bed	X20L	25295	9025	10325	12100	14900
F250 Long Bed	X20L	25495	8725	10000	11750	14500
F350 Short Bed	X30L	26085	9300	10625	12400	15300
F350 Long Bed	X30L	26285	9025	10325	12100	14900
4WD	1		1575	1575	2100	2100
V8 7.3L Turbo Diesel	F		4450	4450	5930	5930
V10 6.8 Liter	S		575	575	765	765
SUPER DUTY CREW CAB—V8—Truck Equipment Schedule T1						
F250 Short Bed	W20L	25295	10125	11550	13400	16350
F250 Long Bed	W20L	26805	9900	11300	13150	16050
F350 Short Bed	W30L	27265	10375	11825	13750	16700
F350 Long Bed	W30L	27465	10125	11550	13400	16350
Platinum Edition	1		125	125	165	165
4WD			1575	1575	2100	2100
V8 7.3L Turbo Diesel	F		4450	4450	5930	5930
V10 6.8 Liter	S		575	575	765	765

2002 FORD — (1or2)F(B,MorT)–(U021)–2–#

Body Type	VIN	List	Trade-In Fair	Good	Pvt-Party Good	Retail Excellent
ESCAPE 4WD—V6—Truck Equipment Schedule T1						
XLS Sport Utility 4D	U021	21910	7625	8750	10500	13100
XLT Sport Utility 4D	U041	23935	8200	9375	11100	13800
2WD			(800)	(800)	(1065)	(1065)
4-Cyl. 2.0 Liter	B		(825)	(825)	(1100)	(1100)
EXPLORER SPORT 4WD—V6—Truck Equipment Schedule T1						
Sport Utility 2D	U70E	24785	6475	7500	9450	12300
2WD	6		(800)	(800)	(1065)	(1065)
EXPLORER 4WD—V6—Truck Equipment Schedule T1						
XLS Sport Utility 4D	U71E	27775	7925	9125	11150	14200
Third Seat			600	600	800	800
2WD	6		(800)	(800)	(1065)	(1065)
V8 4.6 Liter	W		350	350	465	465
EXPLORER SPORT TRAC 4WD—V6—Truck Equipment Sch T1						
Utility Pickup 4D	U77E	25410	8525	9750	11850	15000
2WD			(800)	(800)	(1065)	(1065)
EXPEDITION 4WD—V8—Truck Equipment Schedule T1						
XLT Sport Utility 4D	U16W	33810	10000	11350	13850	17500
w/o Third Seat			(925)	(925)	(1235)	(1235)
2WD	5		(1400)	(1400)	(1865)	(1865)
V8 5.4 Liter	L		375	375	500	500
EXCURSION 4WD—V10—Truck Equipment Schedule T1						
XLT Sport Utility 4D	U41S	38985	11725	13300	15900	19800

Body Type	VIN	List	Trade-In Fair	Good	Pvt-Party Good	Retail Excellent
w/o Third Seat			(925)	(925)	(1235)	(1235)
2WD			(1400)	(1400)	(1865)	(1865)
V8 5.4 Liter	L		(500)	(500)	(665)	(665)
V8 7.3L Turbo Diesel	F		4700	4700	6265	6265
WINDSTAR—V6—Truck Equipment Schedule T2						
Cargo Minivan	A544	20905	3175	3850	5450	7700
WINDSTAR—V6—Truck Equipment Schedule T1						
LX Minivan	A514	22995	4800	5625	7350	9800
SE Minivan	A524	29280	5275	6175	7900	10450
SEL Minivan	A534	31950	6325	7350	9150	11800
Limited Minivan	A584	34360	7975	9175	11050	13900
w/o 2nd Sliding Door	0		(650)	(650)	(865)	(865)
ECONOLINE WAGON—V8—Truck Equipment Schedule T1						
E150 Passenger Van	E11W	24660	6550	7575	9750	12850
E350 Super Duty	E31L	26950	6800	7850	10050	13200
E350 Super Duty Ext	S31L	28370	7050	8150	10400	13600
V6 4.2 Liter	2		(600)	(600)	(800)	(800)
V8 7.3L Turbo Diesel	F		2725	2725	3630	3630
V10 6.8 Liter	S		700	700	935	935
ECONOLINE VAN—V6—Truck Equipment Schedule T1						
E150 Cargo Van	E142	21880	6125	7100	8875	11500
E250 Cargo Van	E242	22750	6250	7250	9050	11700
E350 Super Cargo	E34L	25230	6625	7675	9475	12150
Super Van	S		200	200	265	265
Crew Van Pkg			300	300	400	400
V8 4.6, 5.4 Liter	W,L		300	300	400	400
V8 7.3L Turbo Diesel	F		3150	3150	4200	4200
V10 6.8 Liter	S		1400	1400	1865	1865
RANGER PICKUP—4-Cyl.—Truck Equipment Schedule T2						
XL Short Bed	R10C	12725	3150	3800	5325	7475
XL Long Bed	R10C	13655	2825	3450	4950	7025
XL Super Cab 2D	R14C	16400	4075	4850	6425	8675
XL Super Cab 4D	R14C	18075	5000	5875	7500	9900
4WD	1,5		1800	1800	2400	2400
V6 3.0 Liter	U		400	400	535	535
V6 4.0 Liter	E		550	550	735	735
REGULAR CAB PICKUP—V8—Truck Equipment Schedule T1						
F150 Short Bed	F17W	20640	6300	7325	8900	11300
F150 Long Bed	F17W	20940	5950	6900	8475	10800
4WD	6,8		1750	1750	2335	2335
Work Truck			(975)	(975)	(1300)	(1300)
V6 4.2 Liter	2		(700)	(700)	(935)	(935)
V8 5.4 Liter	L,Z		375	375	500	500
REGULAR CAB PICKUP—V8 Supercharged—Truck Sch T1						
F150 Lightning	F073	32490	13375	15075	17000	20200
SUPER CAB PICKUP—V8—Truck Equipment Schedule T1						
F150 Short Bed	X17W	23290	8400	9625	11300	13950
F150 Long Bed	X17W	22840	8025	9225	10850	13500
F150 King Ranch	X17W	29735	9400	10725	12450	15300
4WD	6,8		1750	1750	2335	2335
Work Truck			(975)	(975)	(1300)	(1300)
V6 4.2 Liter	2		(700)	(700)	(935)	(935)
V8 5.4 Liter	L,Z		375	375	500	500
SUPERCREW PICKUP—V8—Truck Equipment Schedule T1						
F150 Short Bed 4D	W07W	27660	9650	11000	12800	15600
F150 King Ranch 4D	W07W	32135	11200	12700	14600	17600
4WD	8		1750	1750	2335	2335
V8 5.4 Liter	L		375	375	500	500
SUPERCREW PICKUP—V8 Supercharged—Truck Equip Sch T1						
F150 HarleyDavidson	W073	36520	14950	16875	18950	22500
SUPER DUTY REGULAR CAB PICKUP—V8—Truck Equip Sch T1						
F250 Long Bed	F20L	22725	8025	9225	10850	13500
F350 Long Bed	F30L	23985	8325	9525	11200	13850
4WD	1		1750	1750	2335	2335
V8 7.3L Turbo Diesel	F		4700	4700	6265	6265
V10 6.8 Liter	S		600	600	800	800
SUPER DUTY SUPER CAB PICKUP—V8—Truck Equip Sch T1						
F250 Short Bed	X20L	25715	10375	11825	13700	16600
F250 Long Bed	X20L	25915	10100	11450	13300	16150
F350 Short Bed	X30L	26505	10725	12225	14050	17000
F350 Long Bed	X30L	26705	10375	11825	13700	16600
4WD	1		1750	1750	2335	2335
V8 7.3L Turbo Diesel	F		4700	4700	6265	6265

Body	Type	VIN	List	Trade-In Fair	Trade-In Good	Pvt-Party Good	Retail Excellent
	V10 6.8 Liter	S		600	600	800	800
SUPER DUTY CREW CAB PICKUP—V8—Truck Equipment Sch T1							
	F250 Short Bed	W20L	27025	11650	13200	15150	18200
	F250 Long Bed	W20L	27225	11350	12900	14800	17850
	F350 Short Bed	W30L	27685	11925	13525	15450	18600
	F350 Long Bed	W30L	27885	11650	13200	15150	18200
	4WD	1		1750	1750	2335	2335
	V8 7.3L Turbo Diesel	F		4700	4700	6265	6265
	V10 6.8 Liter	S		600	600	800	800

2003 FORD — (1or2)F(B,MorT)–(U921)-3-#

Body	Type	VIN	List	Trade-In Fair	Trade-In Good	Pvt-Party Good	Retail Excellent
ESCAPE 4WD—V6 Flex Fuel—Truck Equipment Schedule T1							
	XLS Sport Utility 4D	U921	23565	9150	10425	12200	15050
	XLT Sport Utility 4D	U931	25475	9800	11150	12950	15800
	Limited Sport Util 4D	U941	27475	10525	11975	13800	16800
	2WD	0		(875)	(875)	(1165)	(1165)
	4-Cyl. 2.0 Liter	B		(925)	(925)	(1235)	(1235)
EXPLORER SPORT 4WD—V6—Truck Equipment Schedule T1							
	Sport Utility 2D	U70E	25825	7900	9075	11150	14250
	2WD	6		(875)	(875)	(1165)	(1165)
EXPLORER 4WD—V6 Flex Fuel—Truck Equipment Schedule T1							
	XLS Sport Utility 4D	U72K	28470	9475	10825	13000	16250
	Third Seat			650	650	865	865
	2WD	6		(875)	(875)	(1165)	(1165)
	AWD	8		0	0	0	0
	V8 4.6 Liter	W		400	400	535	535
EXPLORER SPORT TRAC 4WD—V6—Truck Equipment Sch T1							
	XLS Util Pickup 4D	U77E	26185	10125	11550	13750	17100
	2WD	6		(875)	(875)	(1165)	(1165)
EXPEDITION 4WD—V8—Truck Equipment Schedule T1							
	XLT Sport Utility 4D	U16W	34165	12125	13725	16750	21100
	w/o Third Seat			(1000)	(1000)	(1335)	(1335)
	2WD	5,7		(1450)	(1450)	(1935)	(1935)
	V8 5.4 Liter	L		400	400	535	535
EXCURSION 4WD—V10—Truck Equipment Schedule T1							
	XLT Sport Utility 4D	U41S	39635	13675	15475	18350	22600
	w/o Third Seat			(650)	(650)	(865)	(865)
	2WD	0,2,4		(1450)	(1450)	(1935)	(1935)
	V8 5.4 Liter	L		(500)	(500)	(665)	(665)
	V8 6.0L Turbo Diesel	P		5225	5225	6965	6965
	V8 7.3L Turbo Diesel	F		4950	4950	6600	6600
WINDSTAR—V6—Truck Equipment Schedule T2							
	Cargo Minivan	A544	21360	4225	5000	6750	9250
WINDSTAR—V6—Truck Equipment Schedule T1							
	LX Minivan	A514	23365	6000	6950	8800	11500
	SE Minivan	A524	29675	6525	7550	9400	12150
	SEL Minivan	A534	32405	7675	8825	10800	13750
	Limited Minivan	A584	35110	9475	10825	12850	16000
	w/o 2nd Sliding Door			(700)	(700)	(935)	(935)
ECONOLINE WAGON—V8—Truck Equipment Schedule T1							
	E150 Passenger Van	E11W	25250	8375	9575	12000	15450
	E350 Super Duty	E31L	24790	8650	9900	12300	15800
	E350 Super Duty Ext	S31L	28910	8950	10225	12650	16200
	V6 4.2 Liter	2		(650)	(650)	(865)	(865)
	V8 7.3L Turbo Diesel	F		2925	2925	3900	3900
	V10 6.8 Liter	S		725	725	965	965
ECONOLINE VAN—V6—Truck Equipment Schedule T1							
	E150 Super Cargo	E142	22420	7775	8925	10850	13750
	E250 Super Cargo	E242	23290	7900	9075	11000	13900
	E350 Super Cargo	E34L	25770	8325	9525	11500	14450
	Super Van	S		225	225	300	300
	Crew Van Pkg			325	325	435	435
	V8 4.6, 5.4 Liter	W,L		325	325	435	435
	V8 7.3L Turbo Diesel	F		3450	3450	4600	4600
	V10 6.8 Liter	S		1450	1450	1935	1935
RANGER PICKUP—4-Cyl.—Truck Equipment Schedule T2							
	XL Short Bed	R10D	13620	3925	4675	6325	8675
	XL Long Bed	R10D	14370	3600	4300	5950	8250
	XL Super Cab 2D	R14U	17320	4950	5825	7525	10000
	XL Super Cab 4D	R44E	18605	5975	6925	8675	11250
	4WD	1,5		1975	1975	2635	2635
	V6 3.0 Liter	U		450	450	600	600
	V6 4.0 Liter	E		600	600	800	800

TRUCKS & VANS

Body	Type	VIN	List	Trade-In Fair	Trade-In Good	Pvt-Party Good	Retail Excellent
REGULAR CAB PICKUP—V8—Truck Equipment Schedule T1							
F150 Short Bed		F17W	21300	7575	8700	10400	12950
F150 Long Bed		F17W	21600	7175	8275	9950	12450
4WD		6,8		1925	1925	2565	2565
Work Truck				(1125)	(1125)	(1500)	(1500)
V6 4.2 Liter		2		(750)	(750)	(1000)	(1000)
V8 5.4 Liter		L,Z		400	400	535	535
REGULAR CAB PICKUP—V8 Supercharged—Truck Sch T1							
F150 Lightning		F073	33255	15375	17325	19250	22600
SUPER CAB PICKUP—V8—Truck Equipment Schedule T1							
F150 Short Bed		X17W	23495	9850	11250	13050	15900
F150 Long Bed		X17W	24250	9425	10775	12550	15350
F150 King Ranch 4D		X17W	31680	11000	12475	14300	17300
4WD		6,8		1925	1925	2565	2565
Work Truck				(1125)	(1125)	(1500)	(1500)
V6 4.2 Liter		2		(750)	(750)	(1000)	(1000)
V8 5.4 Liter		L,Z		400	400	535	535
SUPERCREW PICKUP—V8—Truck Equipment Schedule T1							
F150 Short Bed 4D		W07W	28320	11250	12750	14650	17650
F150 King Ranch 4D		W07W	33115	12950	14650	16600	19800
4WD		8		1925	1925	2565	2565
V8 5.4 Liter		L		400	400	535	535
SUPERCREW PICKUP—V8 Supercharged—Truck Equip Sch T1							
F150 Harley-Davidson		W073	37295	17125	19250	21400	25100
SUPER DUTY REGULAR CAB PICKUP—V8—Truck Sch T1							
F250 Long Bed		F20L	23760	9425	10775	12500	15300
F350 Long Bed		F30L	24215	9750	11100	12850	15650
4WD		1		1925	1925	2565	2565
V8 6.0L Turbo Diesel		P		5225	5225	6965	6965
V8 7.3L Turbo Diesel		F		4950	4950	6600	6600
V10 6.8 Liter		S		625	625	835	835
SUPER DUTY SUPER CAB PICKUP—V8—Truck Sch T1							
F250 Short Bed		X20L	25945	12025	13625	15500	18600
F250 Long Bed		X20L	26145	11700	13250	15150	18200
F350 Short Bed		X30L	26735	12425	14075	15950	19050
F350 Long Bed		X30L	26935	12025	13625	15500	18600
4WD		1		1925	1925	2565	2565
V8 6.0L Turbo Diesel		P		5225	5225	6965	6965
V8 7.3L Turbo Diesel		F		4950	4950	6600	6600
V10 6.8 Liter		S		625	625	835	835
SUPER DUTY CREW CAB PICKUP—V8—Truck Equipment Schedule T1							
F250 Short Bed		W20L	27355	13375	15125	17100	20400
F250 King Ranch 6'		W20L	36460	14450	16300	18300	21600
F250 Long Bed		W20L	27555	13100	14800	16700	19900
F250 King Ranch 8'		W20L	36660	14125	15950	17900	21200
F350 Short Bed		W30L	28015	13675	15475	17450	20800
F350 King Ranch 6'		W30L	37325	14800	16675	18700	22100
F350 Long Bed		W30L	28215	13375	15125	17100	20400
F350 King Ranch 8'		W30L	37525	14450	16300	18300	21600
4WD		1		1925	1925	2565	2565
V8 6.0L Turbo Diesel		P		5225	5225	6965	6965
V8 7.3L Turbo Diesel		F		4950	4950	6600	6600
V10 6.8 Liter		S		625	625	835	835

2004 FORD—(1or2)F(B,MorT)–(U921)–4–#

Body	Type	VIN	List	Trade-In Fair	Trade-In Good	Pvt-Party Good	Retail Excellent
ESCAPE 4WD—V6—Truck Equipment Schedule T1							
XLS Sport Utility 4D		U921	22515	11000	12475	14250	17150
XLT Sport Utility 4D		U931	24770	11600	13200	15000	18000
Limited Sport Util 4D		U941	26830	12475	14125	16000	19100
2WD		0		(950)	(950)	(1265)	(1265)
4-Cyl. 2.0 Liter		B		(1025)	(1025)	(1365)	(1365)
EXPLORER 4WD—V6 Flex Fuel—Truck Equipment Schedule T1							
XLS Sport Utility 4D		U72K	29155	11350	12900	15100	18550
Third Seat				700	700	935	935
2WD		6		(950)	(950)	(1265)	(1265)
AWD		8		0	0	0	0
V8 4.6 Liter		W		450	450	600	600
EXPLORER SPORT TRAC 4WD—V6 Flex Fuel—Truck Sch T1							
XLS Utility Pickup		U77K	26460	12125	13725	15950	19500
2WD		6		(950)	(950)	(1265)	(1265)
EXPEDITION 4WD—V8—Truck Equipment Schedule T1							
XLS Sport Utility 4D		U16W	35305	14350	16200	19500	24300
w/o Third Seat				(1075)	(1075)	(1435)	(1435)

Body	Type	VIN	List	Trade-In Fair	Trade-In Good	Pvt-Party Good	Retail Excellent
2WD		3,5,7		(1500)	(1500)	(2000)	(2000)
V8 5.4 Liter		L		400	400	535	535

EXCURSION 4WD—V10—Truck Equipment Schedule T1
XLS Sport Utility 4D	U41S	40485	16000	18000	21000	25700
w/o Third Seat			(1075)	(1075)	(1435)	(1435)
2WD	0,2,4		(1500)	(1500)	(2000)	(2000)
V8 5.4 Liter	L		(500)	(500)	(665)	(665)
V8 6.0L Turbo Diesel	P		5500	5500	7330	7330

FREESTAR—V6—Truck Equipment Schedule T2
Cargo Minivan	A546	22070	6450	7475	9325	12100

FREESTAR—V6—Truck Equipment Schedule T1
S Minivan	A546	24460	7925	9125	11000	13900
SE Minivan	A526	26930	8325	9525	11450	14400
SES Minivan	A576	28750	8675	9950	11900	14900
SEL Minivan	A532	29995	9075	10375	12350	15350
Limited Minivan	A582	33630	9425	10775	12800	15850

ECONOLINE WAGON—V8—Truck Equipment Schedule T1
E150 Passenger Van	E11W	25255	10675	12175	14800	18600
E350 Super Duty	E31L	27995	11000	12475	15150	19000
E350 Super Duty Ext.	S31L	29415	11350	12900	15550	19500
V8 6.0L Turbo Diesel	P		3125	3125	4165	4165
V10 6.8 Liter	S		750	750	1000	1000

ECONOLINE VAN—V8—Truck Equipment Schedule T1
E150 Super Cargo	E14W	23060	9950	11350	13350	16450
E250 Super Cargo	E24W	24105	10100	11450	13500	16600
E350 Super Cargo	E34L	26110	10525	11975	14000	17150
Super Van	S		250	250	335	335
Crew Van Pkg			350	350	465	465
V8 5.4 Liter	L		350	350	465	465
V8 6.0L Turbo Diesel	P		5500	5500	7330	7330
V10 6.8 Liter	S		1500	1500	2000	2000

RANGER PICKUP—4-Cyl.—Truck Equipment Schedule T2
XL Short Bed	R10D	14385	4950	5800	7450	9850
XL Long Bed	R10D	15135	4550	5375	7000	9350
XL Super Cab 2D	R14U	18120	6050	7000	8725	11250
XL Super Cab 4D	R44E	19405	7125	8225	10000	12650
4WD	1,5		2150	2150	2865	2865
V6 3.0 Liter	U		500	500	665	665
V6 4.0 Liter	E		650	650	865	865

HERITAGE REGULAR CAB PICKUP—V8—Truck Equipment Sch T1
F150 Short Bed	F17W	21765	9025	10325	12150	15000
F150 Long Bed	F17W	22065	8500	9700	11500	14300
Work Truck			(1275)	(1275)	(1700)	(1700)
4WD	6,8		2100	2100	2800	2800
V6 4.2 Liter			(800)	(800)	(1065)	(1065)
V8 5.4L Bi-Fuel	Z		400	400	535	535

REGULAR CAB PICKUP—V8 Supercharged—Truck Equip Sch T1
F150 Lightning	F073	33560	18775	21050	23400	27300

HERITAGE SUPER CAB PICKUP—V8—Truck Equipment Schedule T1
F150 Short Bed	X17W	24415	11400	12950	14900	18050
F150 Long Bed	X17W	24715	10950	12425	14350	17450
Work Truck			(1275)	(1275)	(1700)	(1700)
4WD	8		2100	2100	2800	2800
V6 4.2 Liter			(800)	(800)	(1065)	(1065)
V8 5.4L Bi-Fuel	Z		400	400	535	535

REGULAR CAB PICKUP—V8—Truck Equipment Schedule T1
F150 Short Bed	F12W	22010	10225	11650	13550	16550
F150 Long Bed	F12W	22310	9800	11200	13050	16000
4WD	4		2100	2100	2800	2800
V8 5.4 Liter	5		400	400	535	535

SUPER CAB PICKUP—V8—Truck Equipment Schedule T1
F150 5 1/2'	X12W	25010	12750	14400	16450	19700
F150 6 1/2'	X12W	24660	12750	14400	16450	19700
F150 8'	X12W	24960	12275	13925	15900	19150
4WD	4		2100	2100	2800	2800
V8 5.4 Liter	5		400	400	535	535

SUPERCREW PICKUP—V8—Truck Equipment Schedule T1
F150 Monster Bed 4D	W12W	29815	14250	16050	18200	21600
4WD	4		2100	2100	2800	2800
V8 5.4 Liter	5		400	400	535	535

SUPER DUTY REGULAR CAB PICKUP—V8—Truck Equip Sch T1
F250 Long Bed	F20L	24430	11100	12600	14300	17100
F350 Long Bed	F30L	24885	11450	13000	14700	17550

Body	Type	VIN	List	Trade-In Fair	Trade-In Good	Pvt-Party Good	Retail Excellent
4WD		1		2100	2100	2800	2800
V8 6.0L Turbo Diesel		P		5500	5500	7330	7330
V10 6.8 Liter		S		650	650	865	865
SUPER DUTY SUPER CAB PICKUP—V8—Truck Equipment Sch T1							
F250 Short Bed		X20L	26615	13975	15775	17600	20800
F250 Harley 6'		X20S	39890	21250	23775	26000	30000
F250 Long Bed		X20L	26815	13575	15325	17150	20300
F250 Harley 8'		X20S	40090	20750	23275	25500	29500
F350 Short Bed		X30L	27405	14300	16150	18050	21200
F350 Harley 6'		X31S	40895	21525	24150	26400	30400
F350 Long Bed		X30L	27605	13975	15775	17600	20800
F350 Harley 8'		X31S	41095	21250	23775	26000	30000
4WD		1		2100	2100	2800	2800
V8 6.0L Turbo Diesel		P		5500	5500	7330	7330
V10 6.8 Liter		S		650	650	865	865
SUPER DUTY CREW CAB PICKUP—V8—Truck Equipment Sch T1							
F250 Short Bed		W20L	28025	15475	17400	19300	22600
F250 King Ranch 6'		W20L	37350	16625	18725	20700	24100
F250 Harley 6'		W21S	42385	22700	25425	27600	31800
F250 Long Bed		W20L	28225	15075	16975	18850	22100
F250 King Ranch 8'		W20L	37550	16200	18225	20200	23700
F250 Harley 8'		W21S	42585	22300	24925	27300	31300
F350 Short Bed		W30L	28685	15775	17800	19700	23000
F350 King Ranch 6'		W30L	38215	16925	19050	21000	24500
F350 Harley 6'		W35S	43000	23075	25800	28100	32300
F350 Long Bed		W30L	28885	15475	17400	19300	22600
F350 King Ranch 8'		W30L	38415	16625	18725	20700	24100
F350 Harley 8'		W35S	43200	22700	25425	27600	31800
4WD		1		2100	2100	2800	2800
V8 6.0L Turbo Diesel		P		5500	5500	7330	7330
V10 6.8 Liter		S		650	650	865	865

2005 FORD—(1or2)F(B,MorT)—(U96H)—5—#

Body	Type	VIN	List	Trade-In Fair	Trade-In Good	Pvt-Party Good	Retail Excellent
ESCAPE 4WD—4-Cyl. Hybrid—Truck Equipment Schedule T1							
Sport Utility 4D		U96H	28595	19000	21350	23500	27300
2WD		0		(1000)	(1000)	(1335)	(1335)
ESCAPE 4WD—V6—Truck Equipment Schedule T1							
XLS Sport Utility 4D		U92Z	22045	13050	14750	16650	19800
XLT Utility 4D		U931	25545	13675	15475	17400	20700
Limited Sport Util 4D		U941	27145	14600	16450	18500	21800
2WD		0		(1000)	(1000)	(1335)	(1335)
4-Cyl. 2.3 Liter		Z		(950)	(950)	(1265)	(1265)
FREESTYLE AWD—V6—Truck Equipment Schedule T1							
SE Sport Utility 4D		K041	27295	14400	16250	18400	21900
SEL Sport Utility 4D		K051	28695	14850	16725	18850	22400
Limited Sport Utility		K061	30895	15175	17125	19300	22900
2WD				(1000)	(1000)	(1335)	(1335)
EXPLORER 4WD—V6 Flex Fuel—Truck Equipment Schedule T1							
XLS Sport Utility 4D		U72K	29880	13475	15225	17600	21300
Third Seat				750	750	1000	1000
2WD		6		(1000)	(1000)	(1335)	(1335)
V8 4.6 Liter		W		475	475	635	635
EXPLORER SPORT TRAC 4WD—V6 Flex Fuel—Truck Equip Sch T1							
XLS Utility Pickup		U77K	27125	14250	16100	18550	22300
2WD		6		(1000)	(1000)	(1335)	(1335)
EXPEDITION 4WD—V8—Truck Equipment Schedule T1							
XLS Sport Utility 4D		U145	35935	16775	18875	22300	27500
King Ranch Sport Util		U185	46560				
w/o Third Seat				(1150)	(1150)	(1535)	(1535)
2WD				(1150)	(1150)	(1535)	(1535)
EXCURSION 4WD—V10—Truck Equipment Schedule T1							
XLS Sport Utility 4D		U41S	41065	18525	20850	24100	29000
w/o Third Seat				(1150)	(1150)	(1535)	(1535)
2WD				(1550)	(1550)	(2065)	(2065)
V8 5.4 Liter		L		(500)	(500)	(665)	(665)
V8 6.0L Turbo Diesel		P		5775	5775	7700	7700
FREESTAR—V6—Truck Equipment Schedule T2							
Cargo Minivan		A546	22295	8400	9625	11650	14700
FREESTAR—V6—Truck Equipment Schedule T1							
S Minivan		A506	24595	10000	11350	13550	16800
SE Minivan		A516	27195	10375	11825	14000	17300
SES Minivan		A576	28695	10775	12275	14450	17800
SEL Minivan		A522	29695	11200	12700	14950	18350

Body Type	VIN	List	Trade-In Fair	Trade-In Good	Pvt-Party Good	Retail Excellent
Limited Minivan	A582	33395	11600	13150	15350	18800
ECONOLINE WAGON—V8—Truck Equipment Schedule T1						
E150 Super Duty	E11W	25525	12275	13925	16700	20900
E350 Super Duty	E31L	28265	12600	14250	17050	21200
E350 Super Duty Ext.	S31L	30865	13000	14700	17500	21700
V8 6.0L Turbo Diesel	P		3325	3325	4430	4430
V10 6.8 Liter	S		775	775	1035	1035
ECONOLINE VAN—V8—Truck Equipment Schedule T1						
E150 Super Cargo	E14W	23330	12025	13625	15800	19200
E250 Super Cargo	E24W	24375	12175	13775	15950	19400
E350 Super Cargo	E34L	27160	12650	14300	16550	20100
Super Van	S		275	275	365	365
Crew Van Pkg.			375	375	500	500
V8 5.4 Liter	L		375	375	500	500
V8 6.0L Turbo Diesel	P		5775	5775	7700	7700
V10 6.8 Liter	S		1550	1550	2065	2065
RANGER PICKUP—4-Cyl.—Truck Equipment Schedule T2						
XL Short Bed	R10D	14985	6275	7275	9000	11600
XLT Long Bed	R10D	17865	5875	6850	8525	11050
XL Super Cab 2D	R14U	17685	7475	8575	10450	13200
Edge Super Cab 4D	R44U	20250	8650	9900	11850	14750
4WD	1,5		2325	2325	3100	3100
V6 3.0 Liter	U		525	525	700	700
V6 4.0 Liter	E		700	700	935	935
REGULAR CAB PICKUP—V8—Truck Equipment Schedule T1						
F150 Short Bed	F12W	21436	12025	13625	15500	18600
F150 Long Bed	F12W	21736	11600	13150	15000	18000
4WD	4		2275	2275	3035	3035
V6 4.2 Liter	2		(850)	(850)	(1135)	(1135)
V8 5.4 Liter	5		400	400	535	535
SUPER CAB PICKUP—V8—Truck Equipment Schedule T1						
F150 5 1/2'	X12W	25430	14700	16575	18600	22000
F150 6 1/2'	X12W	25080	14700	16575	18600	22000
F150 8'	X125	26580	14250	16050	18100	21400
4WD	4		2275	2275	3035	3035
V8 5.4 Liter	5		400	400	535	535
SUPERCREW PICKUP—V8—Truck Equipment Schedule T1						
F150 Short Bed 4D	W12W	30185	16300	18325	20500	24100
F150 King Ranch	W125	36325				
4WD	4		2275	2275	3035	3035
V8 5.4 Liter	5		400	400	535	535
SUPER DUTY REGULAR CAB PICKUP—V8—Truck Equip Sch T1						
F250 Long Bed	F205	25525	12950	14650	16250	19100
F350 Long Bed	F305	26270	13350	15025	16700	19600
4WD	1		2275	2275	3035	3035
V8 6.0L Turbo Diesel	P		5775	5775	7700	7700
V10 6.8 Liter	Y		675	675	900	900
SUPER DUTY SUPER CAB PICKUP—V8—Truck Equipment Sch T1						
F250 Short Bed	X205	27110	16000	18000	19800	23000
F250 Long Bed	X205	27910	15625	17600	19350	22500
F350 Short Bed	X305	28790	16350	18425	20300	23600
F350 Long Bed	X305	28990	16000	18000	19800	23000
4WD	1		2275	2275	3035	3035
V8 6.0L Turbo Diesel	P		5775	5775	7700	7700
V10 6.8 Liter	Y		675	675	900	900
SUPER DUTY CREW CAB PICKUP—V8—Truck Equipment Sch T1						
F250 Short Bed	W205	29120	17600	19800	21600	25000
F250 King Ranch 6'	W205	37105	18875	21150	23100	26700
F250 Long Bed	W205	29320	17225	19350	21100	24500
F250 King Ranch 8'	W205	37305	18425	20750	22600	26100
F250 Harley 8'	W215	42035	25025	28025	30200	34300
F350 Short Bed	W305	30070	17950	20175	22100	25600
F350 King Ranch 6'	W305	38450	19200	21525	23600	27200
F350 Harley 6'	W315	42610	25800	28800	31000	35300
F350 Long Bed	W305	30305	17600	19800	21600	25000
F350 King Ranch 8'	W305	38650	18875	21150	23100	26700
F350 Harley 8'	W315	42810	25425	28425	30700	34800
4WD	1		2275	2275	3035	3035
V8 6.0L Turbo Diesel	P		5775	5775	7700	7700
V10 6.8 Liter	Y		675	675	900	900

Body	Type	VIN	List	Trade-In Fair	Trade-In Good	Pvt-Party Good	Retail Excellent

TRUCKS & VANS

GMC — See CHEVROLET TRUCKS

GEO

1991 GEO — JGC–(J18U)–M–#

TRACKER 4WD—4-Cyl.—Truck Equipment Schedule T2

Body Type	VIN	List	Fair	Good	Good	Excellent
Sport Utility 2D	J18U	11867	450	625	1175	2000
Spt Utility Conv 2D	J18U	11467	450	625	1175	2000
LSi Sport Utility 2D	J18U	12865	550	800	1375	2325
LSi Spt Util Conv 2D	J18U	12275	525	750	1325	2250
2WD	E		(300)	(300)	(400)	(400)

1992 GEO — JGC–(J18U)–N–#

TRACKER 4WD—4-Cyl.—Truck Equipment Schedule T2

Body Type	VIN	List	Fair	Good	Good	Excellent
Sport Utility 2D	J18U	12502	500	725	1275	2200
Spt Utility Conv 2D	J18U	12102	475	700	1250	2150
LSi Sport Utility 2D	J18U	13500	625	900	1500	2550
LSi Spt Util Conv 2D	J18U	12900	600	850	1450	2450
2WD	E		(325)	(325)	(435)	(435)

1993 GEO — 2CC–(J18U)–P–#

TRACKER 4WD—4-Cyl.—Truck Equipment Schedule T2

Body Type	VIN	List	Fair	Good	Good	Excellent
Sport Utility 2D	J18U	12351	475	675	1275	2250
Spt Utility Conv 2D	J18U	12186	450	650	1250	2200
LSi Sport Utility 2D	J18U	13250	625	900	1550	2675
LSi Spt Util Conv 2D	J18U	12985	600	850	1500	2600
2WD	E		(350)	(350)	(465)	(465)

1994 GEO — 2CC–(J18U)–R–#

TRACKER 4WD—4-Cyl.—Truck Equipment Schedule T2

Body Type	VIN	List	Fair	Good	Good	Excellent
Sport Utility 2D	J18U	12901	475	675	1325	2375
Spt Utility Conv 2D	J18U	12741	450	650	1300	2325
LSi Sport Utility 2D	J18U	14065	650	925	1675	2875
LSi Spt Util Conv 2D	J18U	13800	625	900	1625	2800
2WD	E		(375)	(375)	(500)	(500)

1995 GEO — 2C(CorN)–(J186)–S–#

TRACKER 4WD—4-Cyl.—Truck Equipment Schedule T2

Body Type	VIN	List	Fair	Good	Good	Excellent
Sport Utility 2D	J186	13631	500	725	1475	2675
Spt Utility Conv 2D	J186	13551	475	700	1450	2625
LSi Sport Utility 2D	J186	14795	700	1025	1925	3275
LSi Spt Util Conv 2D	J186	14615	675	950	1800	3125
2WD	E		(400)	(400)	(535)	(535)

1996 GEO — 2C(CorN)–(J186)–T–#

TRACKER 4WD—4-Cyl.—Truck Equipment Schedule T2

Body Type	VIN	List	Fair	Good	Good	Excellent
Spt Utility Conv 2D	J186	15071	550	800	1675	3000
Sport Utility 4D	J136	15941	925	1300	2475	4125
LSi Spt Util Conv 2D	J136	15501	750	1075	2075	3575
LSi Sport Utility 4D	J136	16331	1150	1600	2850	4575
2WD	E		(425)	(425)	(565)	(565)

1997 GEO — 2C(CorN)–(J186)–V–#

TRACKER 4WD—4-Cyl.—Truck Equipment Schedule T2

Body Type	VIN	List	Fair	Good	Good	Excellent
Spt Utility Conv 2D	J186	15096	675	950	2025	3575
Sport Utility 4D	J136	15966	1050	1475	2775	4550
LSi Sport Utility 4D	J186	16356	1350	1850	3175	5050
2WD	E		(450)	(450)	(600)	(600)

HONDA

1994 HONDA — 4S6(CG58E)–R–#

PASSPORT—4-Cyl.—Truck Equipment Schedule T1

Body Type	VIN	List	Fair	Good	Good	Excellent
DX Sport Utility 4D	CG58E	16035	1125	1575	2750	4350
Manual Trans			(150)	(150)	(200)	(200)

1994 HONDA

Body Type	VIN	List	Trade-In Fair	Good	Pvt-Party Good	Retail Excellent
PASSPORT 4WD—V6—Truck Equipment Schedule T1						
LX Sport Utility 4D	CY58V	22825	**2050**	**2625**	**3900**	**5750**
EX Sport Utility 4D	CY58V	25375	**2425**	**3025**	**4400**	**6325**
2WD	G		(375)	(375)	(500)	(500)

1995 HONDA — (JHMor4S6)(CG58E)-S-#

Body Type	VIN	List	Trade-In Fair	Good	Pvt-Party Good	Retail Excellent
PASSPORT—4-Cyl.—Truck Equipment Schedule T1						
DX Sport Utility 4D	CG58E	16610	**1275**	**1775**	**2975**	**4700**
Dual Air Bags			0	0	0	0
Manual Trans			(175)	(175)	(235)	(235)
PASSPORT 4WD—V6—Truck Equipment Schedule T1						
LX Sport Utility 4D	CY58V	23830	**2325**	**2900**	**4300**	**6225**
EX Sport Utility 4D	CY58V	26930	**2750**	**3375**	**4825**	**6875**
2WD	G		(400)	(400)	(535)	(535)
Dual Air Bags			0	0	0	0
ODYSSEY—4-Cyl.—Truck Equipment Schedule T1						
LX Minivan 4D	RA184	23380	**2925**	**3600**	**5000**	**7000**
EX Minivan 4D	RA187	25390	**3100**	**3750**	**5225**	**7250**

1996 HONDA — (JHMor4S6)(CK58E)-T-#

Body Type	VIN	List	Trade-In Fair	Good	Pvt-Party Good	Retail Excellent
PASSPORT—4-Cyl.—Truck Equipment Schedule T1						
DX Sport Utility 4D	CK58E	18385	**1525**	**2025**	**3350**	**5175**
Manual Trans			(200)	(200)	(265)	(265)
PASSPORT 4WD—V6—Truck Equipment Schedule T1						
LX Sport Utility 4D	CM58V	25895	**2700**	**3300**	**4775**	**6850**
EX Sport Utility 4D	CM58V	29425	**3150**	**3800**	**5350**	**7525**
2WD	G		(425)	(425)	(565)	(565)
ODYSSEY—4-Cyl.—Truck Equipment Schedule T1						
LX Minivan 4D	RA184	23955	**3300**	**3975**	**5450**	**7575**
EX Minivan 4D	RA187	25945	**3475**	**4200**	**5675**	**7825**

1997 HONDA — (JHL,JHMor4S6)(RD184)-V

Body Type	VIN	List	Trade-In Fair	Good	Pvt-Party Good	Retail Excellent
CR-V 4WD—4-Cyl.—Truck Equipment Schedule T2						
Sport Utility 4D	RD184	19695	**3900**	**4650**	**6225**	**8475**
PASSPORT 4WD—V6—Truck Equipment Schedule T1						
LX Sport Utility 4D	CM58V	25895	**3100**	**3750**	**5325**	**7525**
EX Sport Utility 4D	CM58V	29425	**3625**	**4325**	**5950**	**8250**
2WD	G		(450)	(450)	(600)	(600)
ODYSSEY—4-Cyl.—Truck Equipment Schedule T1						
LX Minivan 4D	RA184	23955	**3700**	**4450**	**6000**	**8225**
EX Minivan 4D	RA187	25945	**3900**	**4650**	**6250**	**8500**

1998 HONDA — (JHL,JHMor4S6)(RD174)-W

Body Type	VIN	List	Trade-In Fair	Good	Pvt-Party Good	Retail Excellent
CR-V 4WD—4-Cyl.—Truck Equipment Schedule T2						
LX Sport Utility 4D	RD174	19145	**4075**	**4850**	**6425**	**8700**
EX Sport Utility 4D	RD176	20645	**4400**	**5200**	**6825**	**9150**
2WD	2		(475)	(475)	(635)	(635)
PASSPORT 4WD—V6—Truck Equipment Schedule T1						
LX Sport Utility 4D	CM58W	26995	**3750**	**4500**	**6175**	**8550**
EX Sport Utility 4D	CM58W	29345	**4325**	**5125**	**6875**	**9325**
2WD	K		(475)	(475)	(635)	(635)
ODYSSEY—4-Cyl.—Truck Equipment Schedule T1						
LX Minivan 4D	RA386	24205	**4200**	**4975**	**6600**	**8950**
EX Minivan 4D	RA387	26195	**4400**	**5200**	**6875**	**9250**

1999 HONDA — (JHL,2HKor4S6)(RD174)-X

Body Type	VIN	List	Trade-In Fair	Good	Pvt-Party Good	Retail Excellent
CR-V 4WD—4-Cyl.—Truck Equipment Schedule T2						
LX Sport Utility 4D	RD174	19365	**4750**	**5575**	**7150**	**9425**
EX Sport Utility 4D	RD176	20865	**5100**	**6000**	**7575**	**9900**
2WD	2		(525)	(525)	(700)	(700)
PASSPORT 4WD—V6—Truck Equipment Schedule T1						
LX Sport Utility 4D	CM58V	27015	**4550**	**5375**	**6950**	**9250**
EX Sport Utility 4D	CM58V	29365	**5175**	**6050**	**7675**	**10050**
2WD	K		(525)	(525)	(700)	(700)
ODYSSEY—V6—Truck Equipment Schedule T1						
LX Minivan 4D	RL184	23615	**5950**	**6900**	**8600**	**11150**
EX Minivan 4D	RL186	26215	**6550**	**7575**	**9325**	**12000**

2000 HONDA — (JHL,2HKor4S6)(RD174)-Y-

Body Type	VIN	List	Trade-In Fair	Good	Pvt-Party Good	Retail Excellent
CR-V 4WD—4-Cyl.—Truck Equipment Schedule T2						
LX Sport Utility 4D	RD174	19465	**5600**	**6525**	**8175**	**10600**

TRUCKS & VANS

Body Type	VIN	List	Trade-In Fair	Trade-In Good	Pvt-Party Good	Retail Excellent
EX Sport Utility 4D	RD176	20965	6025	6975	8675	11200
SE Sport Utility 4D	RD187	23015	6275	7275	8975	11500
2WD	2		(600)	(600)	(800)	(800)
PASSPORT 4WD—V6—Truck Equipment Schedule T1						
LX Sport Utility 4D	CM58V	27515	5550	6475	8125	10550
EX Sport Utility 4D	CM58V	29465	6250	7250	8975	11550
2WD	K		(600)	(600)	(800)	(800)
ODYSSEY—V6—Truck Equipment Schedule T1						
LX Minivan 4D	RL185	23815	7025	8100	9900	12550
EX Minivan 4D	RL186	26415	7700	8850	10700	13500

2001 HONDA—(JHL,2HKor4S6)(RD174)—1—

Body Type	VIN	List	Trade-In Fair	Trade-In Good	Pvt-Party Good	Retail Excellent
CR-V 4WD—4-Cyl.—Truck Equipment Schedule T2						
LX Sport Utility 4D	RD174	19590	6600	7625	9325	11950
EX Sport Utility 4D	RD176	21190	7025	8125	9900	12550
SE Sport Utility 4D	RD187	23240	7400	8500	10300	13000
2WD	2		(675)	(675)	(900)	(900)
PASSPORT 4WD—V6—Truck Equipment Schedule T1						
LX Sport Utility 4D	CM58W	27670	6725	7750	9525	12150
EX Sport Utility 4D	CM58W	29690	7525	8650	10500	13250
2WD	K		(675)	(675)	(900)	(900)
ODYSSEY—V6—Truck Equipment Schedule T1						
LX Minivan 4D	RL185	24340	8275	9475	11400	14250
EX Minivan 4D	RL186	26840	9075	10375	12300	15350

2002 HONDA—(JHL,2HKor4S6)(RD784)—2—

Body Type	VIN	List	Trade-In Fair	Trade-In Good	Pvt-Party Good	Retail Excellent
CR-V 4WD—4-Cyl.—Truck Equipment Schedule T2						
LX Sport Utility 4D	RD784	19640	7700	8850	10650	13450
EX Sport Utility 4D	RD788	21940	8225	9425	11300	14100
2WD	2		(750)	(750)	(1000)	(1000)
PASSPORT 4WD—V6—Truck Equipment Schedule T1						
LX Sport Utility 4D	CM58W	28040	8100	9300	11150	13950
EX Sport Utility 4D	CM58W	29990	9025	10325	12200	15200
2WD	K		(750)	(750)	(1000)	(1000)
ODYSSEY—V6—Truck Equipment Schedule T1						
LX Minivan 4D	RL185	24690	9700	11050	13050	16150
EX Minivan 4D	RL186	27190	10575	12025	14050	17250

2003 HONDA—(Jor5)HorJ(L,Kor6)(YH282)—3—

Body Type	VIN	List	Trade-In Fair	Trade-In Good	Pvt-Party Good	Retail Excellent
ELEMENT 4WD—4-Cyl.—Truck Equipment Schedule T2						
DX Sport Utility 4D	YH282	18760	7625	8750	10550	13350
EX Sport Utility 4D	YH285	21310	8650	9900	11800	14650
2WD	1		(825)	(825)	(1100)	(1100)
CR-V 4WD—4-Cyl.—Truck Equipment Schedule T2						
LX Sport Utility 4D	RD774	19760	9025	10325	12150	15100
EX Sport Utility 4D	RD778	22060	9575	10925	12800	15750
2WD	2		(825)	(825)	(1100)	(1100)
PILOT 4WD—V6—Truck Equipment Schedule T1						
LX Sport Utility 4D	YF181	27360	14200	16000	18250	21800
EX Sport Utility 4D	YF184	29730	15325	17275	19500	23200
ODYSSEY—V6—Truck Equipment Schedule T1						
LX Minivan 4D	RL185	24860	11400	12950	15100	18450
EX Minivan 4D	RL186	27360	12375	14025	16200	19700

2004 HONDA—(J,2or5)F,HorJ(K,L,Nor6)(YH282)—4

Body Type	VIN	List	Trade-In Fair	Trade-In Good	Pvt-Party Good	Retail Excellent
ELEMENT 4WD—4-Cyl.—Truck Equipment Schedule T2						
DX Sport Utility 4D	YH282	17990	9025	10325	12050	14800
LX Sport Utility 4D	YH273	18990	9800	11150	12900	15750
EX Sport Utility 4D	YH285	20790	10125	11550	13350	16250
2WD	1		(900)	(900)	(1200)	(1200)
CR-V 4WD—4-Cyl.—Truck Equipment Schedule T2						
LX Sport Utility 4D	RD774	19890	10525	11975	13750	16700
EX Sport Utility 4D	RD778	22240	11100	12600	14450	17450
2WD	2		(900)	(900)	(1200)	(1200)
PILOT 4WD—V6—Truck Equipment Schedule T1						
LX Sport Utility 4D	YF181	27590	16350	18425	20600	24300
EX Sport Utility 4D	YF184	29960	17750	19700	21900	25700
ODYSSEY—V6—Truck Equipment Schedule T1						
LX Minivan 4D	RL185	24980	13525	15275	17450	21000
EX Minivan 4D	RL186	27480	14550	16450	18600	22200

Body	Type	VIN	List	Trade-In Fair	Good	Pvt-Party Good	Retail Excellent

TRUCKS & VANS

2005 HONDA—(J,2or5)F,HorJ(K,L,Nor6)(YH273)-5

ELEMENT 4WD—4-Cyl.—Truck Equipment Schedule T2

LX Sport Utility 4D	YH273	18990	**11450**	**13000**	**14750**	**17650**
EX Sport Utility 4D	YH276	20790	**11875**	**13425**	**15250**	**18200**
2WD		1	**(950)**	**(950)**	**(1265)**	**(1265)**

CR-V 4WD—4-Cyl.—Truck Equipment Schedule T2

LX Sport Utility 4D	RD774	21710	**12225**	**13875**	**15650**	**18700**
EX Sport Utility 4D	RD778	22965	**12850**	**14550**	**16400**	**19500**
SE Sport Utility 4D	RD779	25565	**13675**	**15425**	**17350**	**20600**
2WD		6	**(950)**	**(950)**	**(1265)**	**(1265)**

PILOT 4WD—V6—Truck Equipment Schedule T1

| LX Sport Utility 4D | YF181 | 27865 | **18725** | **21050** | **23300** | **27200** |
| EX Sport Utility 4D | YF184 | 30435 | **19975** | **22400** | **24700** | **28800** |

ODYSSEY—V6—Truck Equipment Schedule T1

LX Minivan 4D	RL185	25510	**16050**	**18050**	**20400**	**24200**
EX Minivan 4D	RL186	28510	**17125**	**19250**	**21600**	**25600**
Touring Minivan 4D	RL188	35010	**19200**	**21525**	**24100**	**28200**

HUMMER

1993 HUMMER—137(XE82)--P-#

H1 4WD—V8 DIESEL—Truck Equipment Schedule T3

Hard Top 2D	XE82	48620	**18150**	**20375**	**24300**	**30100**
Open Top 4D	XE85	50570	**19100**	**21425**	**25600**	**31600**
Hard Top 4D	XE83	52020	**19600**	**22025**	**26200**	**32300**
Wagon 4D	XE84	55020	**20075**	**22600**	**26800**	**33100**
GA Pkg			**1200**	**1200**	**1600**	**1600**
GC Pkg			**1850**	**1850**	**2465**	**2465**
Winch			**525**	**525**	**700**	**700**

1994 HUMMER—137(YA82)--R-#

H1 4WD—V8 DIESEL—Truck Equipment Schedule T3

Hard Top 2D	YA82	42706	**18875**	**21150**	**25100**	**31000**
Open Top 4D	YA85	47440	**19975**	**22400**	**26600**	**32700**
Hard Top 4D	YA83	53960	**20575**	**23000**	**27300**	**33500**
Wagon 4D	YA84	57019	**21150**	**23675**	**27900**	**34300**
GA Pkg			**1350**	**1350**	**1800**	**1800**
GC Pkg			**2075**	**2075**	**2765**	**2765**
Winch			**575**	**575**	**765**	**765**

1995 HUMMER—137(YA82)--S-#

H1 4WD—V8 DIESEL—Truck Equipment Schedule T3

Hard Top 2D	YA82	43265	**19800**	**22225**	**26000**	**31800**
HardTop Enlarged 2D	YA82	46970	**20275**	**22800**	**26800**	**32700**
OpenTop Recruit 4D	YA85	50317	**20950**	**23475**	**27500**	**33700**
Open Top 4D	YA85	53239	**20950**	**23475**	**27500**	**33700**
Hard Top 4D	YA83	57652	**21725**	**24350**	**28400**	**34600**
Wagon 4D	YA84	60858	**22300**	**24925**	**29200**	**35600**
GA Pkg			**1500**	**1500**	**2000**	**2000**
GC Pkg			**2300**	**2300**	**3065**	**3065**
Winch			**625**	**625**	**835**	**835**
V8 5.7 Liter	D		**(1275)**	**(1275)**	**(1700)**	**(1700)**

1996 HUMMER — 137(YA82)--T-#

H1 4WD—V8 DIESEL—Truck Equipment Schedule T3

Hard Top 2D	YA82	46765	**20650**	**23175**	**27100**	**33000**
HardTop Enlarged 2D	YA82	50649	**21250**	**23850**	**27700**	**33800**
OpenTop Recruit 4D	YA85	54230	**22025**	**24725**	**28700**	**34800**
Open Top 4D	YA85	57346	**22025**	**24725**	**28700**	**34800**
Hard Top 4D	YA83	62037	**22800**	**25500**	**29700**	**36100**
Wagon 4D	YA84	65421	**23475**	**26275**	**30600**	**37100**
GA Pkg			**1650**	**1650**	**2200**	**2200**
GC Pkg			**2525**	**2525**	**3365**	**3365**
Winch			**675**	**675**	**900**	**900**
V8 5.7 Liter	D		**(1350)**	**(1350)**	**(1800)**	**(1800)**
V8 6.5L Turbo Diesel	Z		**1250**	**1250**	**1665**	**1665**

Body	Type	VIN	List	Trade-In Fair	Good	Pvt-Party Good	Retail Excellent
1997 HUMMER — 137(YA82)--V-#							
H1 4WD—V8 DIESEL—Truck Equipment Schedule T3							
Hard Top 2D		YA82	55749	22400	25025	29000	35100
Open Top 4D		YA85	61954	23175	26000	30100	36300
Hard Top 4D		YA83	67330	24050	26875	31000	37400
Wagon 4D		YA84	70614	24825	27750	32000	38500
GA Pkg				1800	1800	2400	2400
GC Pkg				2750	2750	3665	3665
Winch				725	725	965	965
V8 6.5L Turbo Diesel		Z		1350	1350	1800	1800
1998 HUMMER — 137(YA82)--W-#							
H1 4WD—V8 DIESEL—Truck Equipment Schedule T3							
Hard Top 2D		YA82	57859	23675	26475	30500	36600
Open Top 4D		YA85	64451	24450	27350	31400	37800
Hard Top 4D		YA83	70174	25425	28425	32600	39100
Wagon 4D		YA84	73605	26200	29300	33600	40300
GA Pkg				1925	1925	2565	2565
GC Pkg				2975	2975	3965	3965
Winch				775	775	1035	1035
V8 6.5L Turbo Diesel		Z		1450	1450	1935	1935
1999 HUMMER — 137(YA82)--X-#							
H1 4WD—V8 DIESEL—Truck Equipment Schedule T3							
Hard Top 2D		YA82	66522	25225	28225	32200	38600
Open Top 4D		YA85	73580	26275	29400	33600	40100
Hard Top 4D		YA83	79677	27350	30550	34800	41500
Wagon 4D		YA84	83211	28225	31525	35800	42700
GA Pkg				2050	2050	2735	2735
GC Pkg				3175	3175	4230	4230
Winch				825	825	1100	1100
2000 HUMMER — 137(ZA89)--Y-#							
H1 4WD—V8 Turbo Diesel—Truck Equipment Sch T3							
Hard Top 2D		ZA89	70819	28525	31925	36000	42700
Open Top 4D		ZA90	80499	30175	33650	37900	44800
Hard Top 4D		ZA83	87058	31425	35125	39500	46700
Wagon 4D		ZA84	90844	32600	36375	40900	48200
Slantback 4D		ZA91	93197	33075	36850	41400	48800
GA Pkg				2350	2350	3135	3135
GC Pkg				3625	3625	4830	4830
Winch				950	950	1265	1265
2001 HUMMER — 137(ZA82)--1-#							
H1 4WD—V8 Turbo Diesel—Truck Equipment Sch T3							
Hard Top 2D		ZA82	76862	32700	36475	40800	47900
Open Top 4D		ZA85	84608	35025	39000	43500	50800
Hard Top 4D		ZA83	91553	36575	40750	45300	53000
Wagon 4D		ZA84	95404	37925	42300	46900	54800
GA Pkg				2650	2650	3530	3530
GC Pkg				4075	4075	5430	5430
Winch				1075	1075	1435	1435
2002 HUMMER — 137(ZA85)--2-#							
H1 4WD—V8 Turbo Diesel—Truck Equipment Sch T3							
Open Top 4D		ZA85	98681	39775	44225	48800	56600
Enclosed Wagon 4D		ZA84	109234	43250	48100	53000	61200
Winch				1200	1200	1600	1600
2003 HUMMER — 5GR-(A903)-3-#							
H1 4WD—V8 Turbo Diesel—Truck Equipment Sch T3							
Open Top 4D		A903	106185	44725	49750	54500	62800
Wagon 4D		A843	117508	48700	54225	59100	67800
Winch				1325	1325	1765	1765
H2 4WD—V8—Truck Equipment Schedule T3							
Sport Utility 4D		N23U	50200	24725	27650	31300	37200
Third Seat				650	650	865	865
Adventure Pkg				425	425	565	565
Lux Pkg				425	425	565	565
Air Suspension				400	400	535	535

Body	Type	VIN	List	Trade-In Fair	Trade-In Good	Pvt-Party Good	Retail Excellent
2004 HUMMER — 5GR–(A903)–4–#							
H1 4WD—V8 Turbo Diesel—Truck Equipment Sch T3							
Open Top 4D		A903	106185	50150	55775	60400	69000
Wagon 4D		ZA84	117508	54600	60725	65600	74600
Winch				1425	1425	1900	1900
Adventure Pkg				450	450	600	600
H2 4WD—V8—Truck Equipment Schedule T3							
Sport Utility 4D		N23U	51395	28125	31425	35200	41400
Limited Ed Spt Util		N23U	59840	28525	31925	35700	42000
Third Seat				700	700	935	935
Adventure Pkg				450	450	600	600
Lux Pkg				450	450	600	600
Air Suspension				400	400	535	535
2005 HUMMER — 5GR–(N23U)–5–#							
H2 4WD—V8—Truck Equipment Schedule T3							
Sport Utility 4D		N23U	52000	31825	35500	39400	45900
Third Seat				750	750	1000	1000
Adventure Pkg				475	475	635	635
Lux Pkg				475	475	635	635
Air Suspension				400	400	535	535
H2 SUT 4WD—V8—Truck Equipment Schedule T3							
Sport Utility Pickup		N22U	53055				
Adventure Pkg							
Lux Pkg							
Air Suspension							

HYUNDAI

Body	Type	VIN	List	Trade-In Fair	Trade-In Good	Pvt-Party Good	Retail Excellent
2001 HYUNDAI — KM8S(B72D)–1–#							
SANTA FE 4WD—V6—Truck Equipment Schedule T2							
GL Sport Utility 4D		B72D	20234	4650	5500	6950	9150
GLS Sport Utility 4D		C72D	21234	5475	6400	7900	10200
LX Sport Utility 4D		C72D	22434	5925	6875	8550	11050
2WD		8		(675)	(675)	(900)	(900)
4-Cyl. 2.4 Liter		B		(550)	(550)	(735)	(735)
2002 HYUNDAI — KM8S(B82B)–2–#							
SANTA FE—4-Cyl.—Equipment Schedule T2							
Sport Utility 4D		B82B	17694	5575	6500	8050	10400
SANTA FE 4WD—V6—Truck Equipment Schedule T2							
GLS Sport Utility 4D		C72D	21594	6525	7550	9150	11600
LX Sport Utility 4D		C72D	23794	7025	8100	9850	12500
2WD		8		(750)	(750)	(1000)	(1000)
2003 HYUNDAI — KM8S(B82B)–3–#							
SANTA FE—4-Cyl.—Truck Equipment Schedule T2							
Sport Utility 4D		B82B	17894	6675	7700	9300	11800
SANTA FE 4WD—V6—Truck Equipment Schedule T2							
GLS Sport Utility 4D		C72D	21894	7700	8850	10500	13150
LX Sport Utility 4D		C72D	24394	8275	9475	11350	14150
2WD		8		(825)	(825)	(1100)	(1100)
V6 3.5 Liter		8		500	500	665	665
2004 HYUNDAI — KM8S(B82B)–4–#							
SANTA FE—4-Cyl.—Truck Equipment Schedule T2							
Sport Utility 4D		B82B	18589	7975	9175	10700	13250
SANTA FE 4WD—V6—Truck Equipment Schedule T2							
GLS Sport Utility 4D		C72D	23089	9150	10425	12100	14750
LX Sport Utility 4D		C72E	26089	9800	11150	13000	15900
2WD		8		(900)	(900)	(1200)	(1200)
V6 3.5 Liter		E		500	500	665	665
2005 HYUNDAI — KM8(SC73D)–5–#							
SANTA FE 4WD—V6—Truck Equipment Schedule T2							
GLS Sport Util 4D		SC73D	23594	10775	12275	13950	16800
LX Sport Utility 4D		SC73E	26594	11500	13050	15000	18150
2WD		1		(950)	(950)	(1265)	(1265)

TRUCKS & VANS

Body	Type	VIN	List	Trade-In Fair	Good	Pvt-Party Good	Retail Excellent
	V6 3.5 Liter	E		500	500	665	665

TUCSON 4WD—4-Cyl.—Truck Equipment Schedule T1

GL Sport Utility 4D		JM72B	19594	10725	12225	13600	16050
2WD		1		(950)	(950)	(1265)	(1265)

TUCSON 4WD—V6—Truck Equipment Schedule T1

GLS Sport Util 4D		JN72D	22094	12325	13975	15450	18150
LX Sport Utility 4D		JN72D	23344	13375	15075	16700	19500
2WD		1		(950)	(950)	(1265)	(1265)

INFINITI

1997 INFINITI — JN6(AR05Y)-V-#

QX4 4WD—V6—Truck Equipment Schedule T3

Sport Utility 4D		AR05Y	36045	5600	6525	8425	11100

1998 INFINITI — JN6(AR05Y)-W-#

QX4 4WD—V6—Truck Equipment Schedule T3

Sport Utility 4D		AR05Y	36045	6425	7425	9375	12200

1999 INFINITI — JN6(AR05Y)-X-#

QX4 4WD—V6—Truck Equipment Schedule T3

Sport Utility 4D		AR05Y	36075	7375	8500	10350	13100

2000 INFINITI — JNR(AR05Y)-Y-#

QX4 4WD—V6—Truck Equipment Schedule T3

Sport Utility 4D		AR05Y	36075	8725	10000	12050	15100

2001 INFINITI — JNR(DR07Y)-1-#

QX4 4WD—V6—Truck Equipment Schedule T3

Sport Utility 4D		DR07Y	36075	11775	13350	15550	19050
2WD		X		(725)	(725)	(965)	(965)

2002 INFINITI — JNR(DR07Y)-2-#

QX4 4WD—V6—Truck Equipment Schedule T3

Sport Utility 4D		DR07Y	36095	13675	15425	17750	21400
2WD		X		(800)	(800)	(1065)	(1065)

2003 INFINITI — JNR(AS08W)-3-#

FX35 AWD—V6—Truck Equipment Schedule T3

Sport Utility 4D		AS08W	36245	19975	22400	24900	29300
Intelligent Cruise Cntrl				450	450	600	600
Sport Pkg				1000	1000	1335	1335
2WD		U		(875)	(875)	(1165)	(1165)

FX45 AWD—V8—Truck Equipment Schedule T3

Sport Utility 4D		BS08W	44770	24050	26875	29700	34400
Intelligent Cruise Cntrl				450	450	600	600

QX4 4WD—V6—Truck Equipment Schedule T3

Sport Utility 4D		DR09Y	36695	15775	17800	20200	24200
2WD		X		(875)	(875)	(1165)	(1165)

2004 INFINITI — JNR(AS08W)-4-#

FX35 AWD—V6—Truck Equipment Schedule T3

Sport Utility 4D		AS08W	36395	22900	25600	28200	32800
Intelligent Cruise Cntrl				475	475	635	635
Sport Pkg				1000	1000	1335	1335
2WD		U		(950)	(950)	(1265)	(1265)

FX45 AWD—V8—Truck Equipment Schedule T3

Sport Utility 4D		BS08W	44920	27250	30450	33400	38400
Intelligent Cruise Cntrl				475	475	635	635

QX56 AWD—V8—Truck Equipment Schedule T3

Sport Utility 4D		AA08C	51080	29000	32400	36200	42500
2WD				(950)	(950)	(1265)	(1265)

2005 INFINITI — JNR(AS08W)-5-#

FX35 AWD—V6—Truck Equipment Schedule T3

Sport Utility 4D		AS08W	37060	26000	29000	31700	36600
Adaptive Cruise Control				500	500	665	665
Sport Pkg				1000	1000	1335	1335
2WD		U		(1000)	(1000)	(1335)	(1335)

TRUCKS & VANS

Body	Type	VIN	List	Trade-In Fair	Good	Pvt-Party Good	Retail Excellent
FX45 AWD—V8—Truck Equipment Schedule T3							
Sport Utility 4D		BS08W	46060	30850	34350	37200	42500
Adaptive Cruise Control				500	500	665	665
QX56 4WD—V8—Truck Equipment Schedule T3							
Sport Utility 4D		AA08C	51700	32600	36375	40300	46900
Adaptive Cruise Control				500	500	665	665
2WD				(1000)	(1000)	(1335)	(1335)

ISUZU

1991 ISUZU — (JAA,JACor4S2)–(Y01E)–M

Body	Type	VIN	List	Trade-In Fair	Good	Pvt-Party Good	Retail Excellent
AMIGO 4WD—4-Cyl.—Truck Equipment Schedule T2							
S Sport Utility 2D		Y01E	12988	450	650	1200	2025
XS Sport Utility 2D		Y01E	14268	525	725	1250	2150
Rear Seat				100	100	135	135
2WD		G		(300)	(300)	(400)	(400)
4-Cyl. 2.3 Liter		L		(100)	(100)	(135)	(135)
RODEO 4WD—V6—Truck Equipment Schedule T1							
S Sport Utility 4D		Y58Z	15498	1275	1775	2825	4400
XS Sport Utility 4D		Y58Z	18098	1475	1975	3100	4700
LS Sport Utility 4D		Y58Z	18998	1600	2100	3250	4900
2WD		G		(350)	(350)	(465)	(465)
4-Cyl. 2.6 Liter		E		(300)	(300)	(400)	(400)
TROOPER 4WD—4-Cyl.—Truck Equipment Schedule T1							
S Sport Utility 4D		H58E	16068	650	925	1550	2625
V6 2.8 Liter		R		150	150	200	200
TROOPER 4WD—V6—Truck Equipment Schedule T1							
XS Sport Utility 4D		H58R	18688	875	1225	2025	3300
SE Sport Utility 4D		H58R	18838	875	1225	2025	3300
LS Sport Utility 4D		H58R	20838	900	1250	2075	3350
PICKUP—4-Cyl.—Truck Equipment Schedule T2							
S Short Bed		L11E	8818	350	475	900	1575
S Long Bed		L14E	10258	350	475	925	1600
S 1 Ton Long Bed		L34E	10218	425	625	1100	1875
S Spacecab		L16E	10068	550	775	1300	2200
LS Spacecab		L16E	12548	750	1050	1700	2775
4WD		R		500	500	665	665
4-Cyl. 2.3 Liter		L		(100)	(100)	(135)	(135)
V6 3.1 Liter		Z		100	100	135	135
PICKUP 4WD—V6—Truck Equipment Schedule T2							
LS Spacecab		L16E	11988	900	1275	2025	3225

1992 ISUZU — (JAA,4S1or4S2)–(Y01E)–N

Body	Type	VIN	List	Trade-In Fair	Good	Pvt-Party Good	Retail Excellent
AMIGO 4WD—4-Cyl.—Truck Equipment Schedule T2							
S Sport Utility 2D		Y01E	14318	525	750	1350	2325
XS Sport Utility 2D		Y01E	15668	575	825	1425	2450
2WD		G		(325)	(325)	(435)	(435)
4-Cyl. 2.3 Liter		L		(100)	(100)	(135)	(135)
RODEO 4WD—V6—Truck Equipment Schedule T1							
S Sport Utility 4D		Y58Z	16668	1500	2000	3100	4700
XS Sport Utility 4D		Y58Z	19748	1700	2225	3400	5050
LS Sport Utility 4D		Y58Z	20068	1850	2375	3575	5250
2WD		G		(375)	(375)	(500)	(500)
4-Cyl. 2.6 Liter		E		(325)	(325)	(435)	(435)
TROOPER 4WD—V6—Truck Equipment Schedule T1							
S Sport Utility 4D		H58V	21169	1750	2275	3450	5100
LS Sport Utility 4D		H58W	25769	2225	2825	4050	5850
PICKUP—4-Cyl.—Truck Equipment Schedule T2							
S Short Bed		L11E	9438	375	500	975	1700
S Long Bed		L14E	9718	400	525	1000	1750
S 1 Ton Long Bed		L34E	10958	475	675	1200	2025
S Spacecab		L16E	10758	600	850	1425	2425
LS Spacecab		L16E	13438	800	1150	1850	3000
4WD		R		550	550	735	735
4-Cyl. 2.3 Liter		L		(100)	(100)	(135)	(135)
V6 3.1 Liter		Z		150	150	200	200

1993 ISUZU — (JAA,4S1or4S2)–(Y01E)–P

Body	Type	VIN	List	Trade-In Fair	Good	Pvt-Party Good	Retail Excellent
AMIGO 4WD—4-Cyl.—Truck Equipment Schedule T2							
S Sport Utility 2D		Y01E	14988	600	850	1500	2600
XS Sport Utility 2D		Y01E	16338	650	925	1625	2775

1993 ISUZU

Body	Type	VIN	List	Trade-In Fair	Good	Pvt-Party Good	Retail Excellent
2WD		G		(350)	(350)	(465)	(465)
4-Cyl. 2.3 Liter		L		(125)	(125)	(165)	(165)
RODEO 4WD—V6—Truck Equipment Schedule T1							
S Sport Utility 4D		Y58V	20158	1450	1950	3075	4675
LS Sport Utility 4D		Y58V	23258	1875	2400	3625	5325
2WD		G		(400)	(400)	(535)	(535)
4-Cyl. 2.6 Liter		E		(350)	(350)	(465)	(465)
TROOPER 4WD—V6—Truck Equipment Schedule T1							
S Sport Utility 4D		H58V	22119	1775	2300	3500	5200
RS Sport Utility 2D		H57W	23869	1850	2375	3600	5300
LS Sport Utility 4D		H58W	26519	2325	2900	4225	6075
PICKUP—4-Cyl.—Truck Equipment Schedule T2							
S Short Bed		L11E	9338	375	500	1000	1750
S Long Bed		L14E	10438	400	550	1050	1825
S Spacecab		L16E	11888	650	925	1550	2625
4WD		R		675	675	900	900
4-Cyl. 2.3 Liter		L		(125)	(125)	(165)	(165)
V6 3.1 Liter		Z		225	225	300	300

1994 ISUZU — (JAA,4S1or4S2)-(Y07E)-R

Body	Type	VIN	List	Trade-In Fair	Good	Pvt-Party Good	Retail Excellent
AMIGO 4WD—4-Cyl.—Truck Equipment Schedule T1							
S Sport Utility 2D		Y07E	17149	675	975	1700	2875
XS Sport Utility 2D		Y07E	17549	750	1075	1875	3100
2WD		G		(375)	(375)	(500)	(500)
RODEO 4WD—V6—Truck Equipment Schedule T1							
S Sport Utility 4D		Y58V	21574	1475	1975	3175	4875
LS Sport Utility 4D		Y58V	25274	1975	2500	3775	5600
2WD		G		(425)	(425)	(565)	(565)
4-Cyl. 2.6 Liter		E		(375)	(375)	(500)	(500)
TROOPER 4WD—V6—Truck Equipment Schedule T1							
S Sport Utility 4D		H58V	23700	1850	2375	3650	5400
RS Sport Utility 2D		H57W	25550	1975	2500	3775	5575
LS Sport Utility 4D		H58W	28400	2475	3075	4450	6375
SE Sport Utility 4D		H58W	33200	2950	3625	5050	7075
PICKUP—4-Cyl.—Truck Equipment Schedule T2							
S Short Bed		L11E	12349	400	550	1075	1875
S Long Bed		L14E	11159	400	600	1125	1950
S Spacecab		L16E	13059	725	1050	1750	2875
4WD		R		800	800	1065	1065
4-Cyl. 2.3 Liter		L		(150)	(150)	(200)	(200)
V6 3.1 Liter		Z		300	300	400	400

1995 ISUZU — (JAA,JACor4S2)-(Y58V)-S

Body	Type	VIN	List	Trade-In Fair	Good	Pvt-Party Good	Retail Excellent
RODEO 4WD—V6—Truck Equipment Schedule T1							
S Sport Utility 4D		Y58V	22750	1575	2075	3350	5125
LS Sport Utility 4D		Y58V	26670	2125	2700	4050	5950
2WD		G,K		(450)	(450)	(600)	(600)
4-Cyl. 2.6 Liter		E		(400)	(400)	(535)	(535)
TROOPER 4WD—V6—Truck Equipment Schedule T1							
S Sport Utility 4D		J58V	26270	2000	2550	3875	5725
RS Sport Utility 2D		J57V	29220	2125	2700	4025	5925
LS Sport Utility 4D		J58V	30400	2700	3300	4750	6775
SE Sport Utility 4D		J58V	34445	3225	3900	5400	7550
Ltd Sport Utility 4D		J58W	37220	3525	4225	5775	7950
PICKUP—4-Cyl.—Truck Equipment Schedule T2							
S Short Bed		L11L	10399	450	625	1200	2075
S Long Bed		L14L	11809	475	675	1225	2150
PICKUP 4WD—4-Cyl.—Truck Equipment Schedule T2							
S Short Bed		R11E	14519	1350	1850	2925	4475

1996 ISUZU-(JR2,1GG,4S2orJAC)-(M58V)-T

Body	Type	VIN	List	Trade-In Fair	Good	Pvt-Party Good	Retail Excellent
RODEO 4WD—V6—Truck Equipment Schedule T1							
S Sport Utility 4D		M58V	25085	1775	2300	3650	5475
LS Sport Utility 4D		M58V	28705	2375	2950	4400	6375
2WD		K		(475)	(475)	(635)	(635)
4-Cyl. 2.6 Liter		E		(425)	(425)	(565)	(565)
OASIS—4-Cyl.—Truck Equipment Schedule T1							
S Minivan 4D		J184	23940	2675	3275	4675	6650
LS Minivan 4D		J187	26435	2925	3600	5025	7050
TROOPER 4WD—V6—Truck Equipment Schedule T1							
S Sport Utility 4D		J58V	28585	2225	2825	4200	6125
LS Sport Utility 4D		J58V	32015	2975	3650	5150	7250

Body	Type	VIN	List	Trade-In Fair	Trade-In Good	Pvt-Party Good	Retail Excellent
	Ltd Sport Utility 4D	J58V	38435	3900	4650	6250	8550
	SE Sport Utility 4D	J58V	38945	3600	4300	5875	8100
HOMBRE—4-Cyl.—Truck Equipment Schedule T2							
	S Short Bed	S144	11719	750	1050	1850	3100
	XS Short Bed	S144	12548	775	1100	1925	3175

1997 ISUZU—(JR2,1GG,4S2orJAC)—(M58V)-V

Body	Type	VIN	List	Trade-In Fair	Trade-In Good	Pvt-Party Good	Retail Excellent
RODEO 4WD—V6—Truck Equipment Schedule T1							
	S Sport Utility 4D	M58V	25235	2025	2575	4000	5975
	LS Sport Utility 4D	M58V	28855	2700	3300	4825	6925
	2WD	K		(500)	(500)	(665)	(665)
	4-Cyl. 2.6 Liter	E		(450)	(450)	(600)	(600)
OASIS—4-Cyl.—Truck Equipment Schedule T1							
	S Minivan 4D	J184	24175	3025	3700	5175	7250
	LS Minivan 4D	J187	26435	3325	4025	5525	7675
TROOPER 4WD—V6—Truck Equipment Schedule T1							
	S Sport Utility 4D	J58V	28245	2525	3125	4600	6675
	LS Sport Utility 4D	J58V	32715	3325	4025	5600	7825
	Ltd Sport Utility 4D	J58V	38435	4350	5125	6825	9250
HOMBRE—4-Cyl.—Truck Equipment Schedule T2							
	S Short Bed	S144	11992	900	1275	2225	3650
	XS Short Bed	S144	12419	925	1300	2375	3900
	XS Spacecab	S194	14774	1550	2050	3250	4950
	V6 4.3 Liter	X		250	250	335	335

1998 ISUZU—(JR2,1GG,4S2orJAC)—(M57D)-W

Body	Type	VIN	List	Trade-In Fair	Trade-In Good	Pvt-Party Good	Retail Excellent
AMIGO 4WD—4-Cyl.—Truck Equipment Schedule T2							
	S Sport Utility 2D	M57D	17945	2425	3000	4400	6350
	2WD	K		(475)	(475)	(635)	(635)
	V6 3.2 Liter	W		575	575	765	765
RODEO 4WD—V6—Truck Equipment Schedule T1							
	S Sport Utility 4D	M58W	25635	2475	3075	4600	6725
	LS Sport Utility 4D	M58W	29355	3175	3850	5450	7700
	2WD	K		(525)	(525)	(700)	(700)
	4-Cyl. 2.2 Liter	D		(475)	(475)	(635)	(635)
OASIS—4-Cyl.—Truck Equipment Schedule T1							
	S Minivan 4D	J286	23977	3475	4200	5750	7950
	LS Minivan 4D	J287	26247	3775	4525	6125	8425
TROOPER 4WD—V6—Truck Equipment Schedule T1							
	S Sport Utility 4D	J58X	28245	2825	3450	5025	7200
HOMBRE—4-Cyl.—Truck Equipment Schedule T2							
	S Short Bed	S144	12169	1075	1525	2700	4325
	XS Short Bed	S144	12704	1125	1575	2750	4375
	XS Spacecab	S194	15650	1850	2375	3650	5425
	4WD	T		1200	1200	1600	1600
	V6 4.3 Liter	X		250	250	335	335

1999 ISUZU—(JAC,JR2,4S2or1GG)—(M57D)-X-

Body	Type	VIN	List	Trade-In Fair	Trade-In Good	Pvt-Party Good	Retail Excellent
AMIGO 4WD—4-Cyl.—Truck Equipment Schedule T2							
	S Sport Utility 2D	M57D	18825	2925	3600	4975	6950
	2WD	K		(525)	(525)	(700)	(700)
	Hard Top			100	100	135	135
	V6 3.2 Liter	W		625	625	835	835
RODEO 4WD—V6—Truck Equipment Schedule T1							
	S Sport Utility 4D	M58W	26135	3000	3650	5075	7100
	LS Sport Utility 4D	M58W	27985	3750	4500	6000	8150
	LSE Sport Utility 4D	M58W	31145	4325	5125	6650	8900
	2WD	K		(575)	(575)	(765)	(765)
	4-Cyl. 2.2 Liter	D		(525)	(525)	(700)	(700)
VEHICROSS 4WD—V6—Truck Equipment Schedule T1							
	Sport Utility 2D	N57X	29595	4700	5550	7125	9425
OASIS—4-Cyl.—Truck Equipment Schedule T1							
	S Minivan 4D	J286	24175	4025	4775	6300	8500
TROOPER 4WD—V6—Truck Equipment Schedule T1							
	S Sport Utility 4D	J58X	27595	3500	4200	5675	7775
	Performance Pkg			200	200	265	265
HOMBRE—4-Cyl.—Truck Equipment Schedule T2							
	S Short Bed	S144	12040	1400	1900	3100	4800
	XS Short Bed	S144	12575	1475	1975	3175	4875
	XS Spacecab	S194	15695	2275	2825	4125	5975
	Third Door			200	200	265	265
	4WD	T		1275	1275	1700	1700

TRUCKS & VANS

Body	Type	VIN	List	Trade-In Fair	Good	Pvt-Party Good	Retail Excellent
V6 4.3 Liter		X	......	250	250	335	335

2000 ISUZU–(JAC,4S2or1GG)–(M57D)–Y–#

AMIGO 4WD—4-Cyl.—Truck Equipment Schedule T2

Body	Type	VIN	List	Fair	Good	Good	Excellent
S Sport Utility 2D		M57D	20190	3550	4250	5725	7850
2WD				(600)	(600)	(800)	(800)
Hard Top				125	125	165	165
V6 3.2 Liter		W		700	700	935	935

RODEO 4WD—V6—Truck Equipment Schedule T1

S Sport Utility 4D		M58N	24935	3675	4425	5925	8100
LS Sport Utility 4D		M58N	27615	4550	5375	6975	9300
LSE Sport Utility 4D		M58N	31760	5200	6075	7700	10150
2WD		K		(650)	(650)	(865)	(865)
4-Cyl. 2.2 Liter		D		(600)	(600)	(800)	(800)

VEHICROSS 4WD—V6—Truck Equipment Schedule T1

Sport Utility 2D		N57X	31045	5650	6575	8250	10700

TROOPER 4WD—V6—Truck Equipment Schedule T1

S Sport Utility 4D		J58X	29445	4225	5025	6575	8825
LS Sport Utility 4D		J58X	31145	5300	6200	7850	10300
Limited Sport Util 4D		J58X	35193	6600	7650	9400	12050
2WD				(950)	(950)	(1265)	(1265)

HOMBRE—4-Cyl.—Truck Equipment Schedule T2

S Short Bed		S144	11855	1825	2350	3650	5450
XS Short Bed		S144	13355	1950	2475	3775	5625
S Spacecab		S194	14180	2575	3175	4525	6450
XS Spacecab		S194	16005	2800	3425	4800	6775
Third Door				225	225	300	300
4WD		T		1450	1450	1935	1935
V6 4.3 Liter		W		300	300	400	400

2001 ISUZU–(JACor4S2)–(M57W)–1–#

RODEO SPORT 4WD—V6—Truck Equipment Schedule T2

Soft Top 2D		M57W	20270	4350	5125	6700	8975
Hard Top 2D		M57W	20880	4475	5275	6875	9175
2WD		K		(725)	(725)	(965)	(965)
4-Cyl. 2.2 Liter		D		(675)	(675)	(900)	(900)

RODEO 4WD—V6—Truck Equipment Schedule T1

S Sport Utility 4D		M58N	26025	4575	5400	7000	9350
LS Sport Utility 4D		M58N	27480	5550	6500	8175	10650
LSE Sport Utility 4D		M58N	31950	6275	7275	9000	11600
2WD		K		(725)	(725)	(965)	(965)
4-Cyl. 2.2 Liter		D		(675)	(675)	(900)	(900)

VEHICROSS 4WD—V6—Truck Equipment Schedule T1

Sport Utility 2D		N57X	31045	6800	7850	9625	12250

TROOPER 4WD—V6—Truck Equipment Schedule T1

S Sport Utility 4D		J58X	29690	5175	6050	7700	10150
LS Sport Utility 4D		J58X	31285	6400	7425	9150	11750
Limited Sport Util 4D		J58X	35333	7775	8950	10800	13650
2WD				(1075)	(1075)	(1435)	(1435)

2002 ISUZU–(JACor4S2)–(M57W)–2–#

RODEO SPORT 4WD—V6—Truck Equipment Schedule T2

Soft Top 2D		M57W	22655	5250	6100	7750	10200
Hard Top 2D		M57W	22380	5400	6300	7975	10450
2WD		K		(800)	(800)	(1065)	(1065)
4-Cyl. 2.2 Liter		D		(750)	(750)	(1000)	(1000)

RODEO 4WD—V6—Truck Equipment Schedule T1

S Sport Utility 4D		M58W	25305	5700	6650	8375	10900
LS Sport Utility 4D		M58W	28355	6800	7850	9650	12300
LSE Sport Utility 4D		M58W	32340	7600	8725	10550	13350
2WD		K		(800)	(800)	(1065)	(1065)
4-Cyl. 2.2 Liter		D		(750)	(750)	(1000)	(1000)

AXIOM 4WD—V6—Truck Equipment Schedule T1

Sport Utility 4D		F58X	29625	6400	7425	9175	11800
XS Sport Utility 4D		F58X	31945	6650	7675	9450	12150
2WD				(800)	(800)	(1065)	(1065)

TROOPER 4WD—V6—Truck Equipment Schedule T1

S Sport Utility 4D		J58X	30015	6300	7325	9075	11700
LS Sport Utility 4D		J58X	33300	7675	8800	10650	13450
Limited Sport Util 4D		J58X	37270	9200	10475	12450	15450
2WD				(1200)	(1200)	(1600)	(1600)

(Side tab: TRUCKS & VANS)

TRUCKS & VANS

Body	Type	VIN	List	Trade-In Fair	Trade-In Good	Pvt-Party Good	Retail Excellent

2003 ISUZU — (4NUor4S2)–(K57D)–3–#

RODEO SPORT—4-Cyl.—Truck Equipment Schedule T2
S Soft Top 2D	K57D	14624	5100	5975	7650	10100

RODEO SPORT 4WD—V6—Truck Equipment Schedule T2
S Hard Top 2D	M57W	20040	6475	7500	9275	11900
2WD	K		(875)	(875)	(1165)	(1165)
4-Cyl. 2.2 Liter	D		(825)	(825)	(1100)	(1100)

RODEO 4WD—V6—Truck Equipment Schedule T1
S Sport Utility 4D	M58W	22004	7075	8175	10000	12750
2WD	K		(875)	(875)	(1165)	(1165)
4-Cyl. 2.2 Liter	D		(825)	(825)	(1100)	(1100)

AXIOM 4WD—V6—Truck Equipment Schedule T1
S Sport Utility 4D	F58X	27620	7800	8975	10850	13750
XS Sport Utility 4D	F58X	30620	8100	9300	11200	14050
2WD	E		(875)	(875)	(1165)	(1165)

ASCENDER 4WD—6-Cyl.—Truck Equipment Schedule T1
S Sport Utility 4D	T16S	31974	10925	12375	14450	17650
LS			500	500	665	665
Limited			900	900	1200	1200
2WD	S		(1450)	(1450)	(1935)	(1935)
V8 5.3 Liter	T		500	500	665	665

2004 ISUZU — (4NUor4S2)–(M58W)–4–#

RODEO 4WD—V6—Truck Equipment Schedule T1
S Sport Utility 4D	M58W	23479	8775	10050	11900	14750
2WD	K		(950)	(950)	(1265)	(1265)
V6 3.5 Liter	Y		500	500	665	665

AXIOM 4WD—V6—Truck Equipment Schedule T1
S Sport Utility 4D	F58X	28149	9575	10925	12800	15750
XS Sport Utility 4D	F58X	31149	9850	11250	13150	16100
2WD	E		(950)	(950)	(1265)	(1265)

ASCENDER 4WD—6-Cyl.—Truck Equipment Schedule T1
S Sport Utility 4D	T16S	31849	13300	15025	17050	20500
w/o Third Seat			(900)	(900)	(1200)	(1200)
LS			500	500	665	665
Limited			900	900	1200	1200
2WD	S		(1500)	(1500)	(2000)	(2000)
V8 5.3 Liter	T		550	550	735	735

2005 ISUZU — 4NU–(T16S)–5–#

ASCENDER 4WD—6-Cyl.—Truck Equipment Schedule T1
S Sport Utility 4D	T16S	32083	15900	17900	20100	23800
w/o Third Seat	3		(900)	(900)	(1200)	(1200)
LS			500	500	665	665
Limited			900	900	1200	1200
2WD	S		(1550)	(1550)	(2065)	(2065)
V8 5.3 Liter	M		575	575	765	765

JEEP

1991 JEEP — 1J(4or7)–(Y19P)–M–#

WRANGLER 4WD—4-Cyl.—Truck Equipment Schedule T2
S Sport Utility 2D	Y19P	10645	1525	2025	3150	4725
Sport Utility 2D	Y29P	12673	1675	2200	3350	5000
Islander Spt Util 2D	Y39P	13681	1800	2325	3475	5150
Sahara Spt Util 2D	Y49P	14829	1825	2350	3525	5225
Hard Top			250	250	335	335
6-Cyl. 4.0 Liter	S		500	500	665	665

WRANGLER 4WD—6-Cyl.—Truck Equipment Schedule T2
| Renegade Spt Util 2D | Y59S | 17209 | 2350 | 2925 | 4225 | 6050 |
| Hard Top | | | 250 | 250 | 335 | 335 |

CHEROKEE 4WD—4-Cyl.—Truck Equipment Schedule T1
Sport Utility 2D	J27P	16632	1025	1450	2450	3900
Sport Utility 4D	J28P	17615	1125	1575	2600	4100
2WD	T		(350)	(350)	(465)	(465)
6-Cyl. 4.0 Liter	S		150	150	200	200

CHEROKEE 4WD—6-Cyl.—Truck Equipment Schedule T3
| Briarwood Spt Util 4D | J78S | 24643 | 1950 | 2475 | 3700 | 5475 |
| Limited Sport Util 4D | J78S | 25164 | 1975 | 2525 | 3750 | 5525 |

Body	Type	VIN	List	Trade-In Fair	Trade-In Good	Pvt-Party Good	Retail Excellent

GRAND WAGONEER 4WD—V8—Truck Equipment Schedule T3
| Sport Utility 4D | | S587 | 29819 | 1375 | 1875 | 2950 | 4500 |

COMANCHE PICKUP 4WD—4-Cyl.—Truck Equipment Sch T2
Short Bed		J26P	12588	400	575	1050	1775
Long Bed		J26P	13000	400	525	975	1700
2WD		T		(300)	(300)	(400)	(400)
6-Cyl. 4.0 Liter		S		300	300	400	400

1992 JEEP — 1J(4or7)-(Y19P)-N-#

WRANGLER 4WD—4-Cyl.—Truck Equipment Schedule T2
S Sport Utility 2D		Y19P	11250	1725	2250	3400	5050
Sport Utility 2D		Y29P	13324	1900	2425	3650	5325
Hard Top				250	250	335	335
6-Cyl. 4.0 Liter		S		550	550	735	735

WRANGLER 4WD—6-Cyl.—Truck Equipment Schedule T2
Islander Spt Util 2D		Y39S	14674	2425	3000	4325	6150
Sahara Spt Util 2D		Y49S	15823	2550	3150	4450	6350
Renegade Spt Util 2D		Y69S	17590	2625	3250	4550	6475
Hard Top				250	250	335	335

CHEROKEE 4WD—4-Cyl.—Truck Equipment Schedule T1
Sport Utility 2D		J27P	18030	1150	1600	2650	4125
Sport Utility 4D		J28P	19040	1275	1775	2825	4375
Laredo				75	75	100	100
Sport				75	75	100	100
2WD		T		(375)	(375)	(500)	(500)
6-Cyl. 4.0 Liter		S		175	175	235	235

CHEROKEE 4WD—6-Cyl.—Truck Equipment Schedule T3
| Briarwood Spt Util 4D | | N78S | 25284 | 2225 | 2825 | 4050 | 5850 |
| Limited Sport Util 4D | | J78S | 25819 | 2275 | 2825 | 4125 | 5925 |

COMANCHE PICKUP 4WD—4-Cyl.—Truck Equipment Sch T2
Short Bed		J26P	13108	450	625	1175	2000
Long Bed		J26P	13839	400	600	1100	1925
Eliminator or Sport				75	75	100	100
Pioneer				75	75	100	100
2WD		T		(325)	(325)	(435)	(435)
6-Cyl. 4.0 Liter		S		325	325	435	435

1993 JEEP — 1J4-(Y19P)-P-#

WRANGLER 4WD—4-Cyl.—Truck Equipment Schedule T2
S Sport Utility 2D		Y19P	11680	1900	2425	3650	5375
Sport Utility 2D		Y29P	13828	2100	2675	3900	5700
Hard Top				275	275	365	365
6-Cyl. 4.0 Liter		S		625	625	835	835

WRANGLER 4WD—6-Cyl.—Truck Equipment Schedule T2
Sahara Spt Util 2D		Y49S	16327	2850	3500	4875	6850
Renegade Spt Util 2D		Y69S	18094	2925	3600	4975	6950
Hard Top				275	275	365	365

CHEROKEE 4WD—6-Cyl.—Truck Equipment Schedule T1
Sport Utility 2D		J27S	16432	1300	1800	2875	4450
Sport Utility 4D		J28S	17442	1500	2000	3150	4775
Sport 2D		J67S	18033	1275	1775	2850	4450
Sport 4D		J68S	19043	1525	2025	3175	4825
Country Sport Util 2D		J77S	19721	1300	1800	2875	4450
Country Sport Util 4D		J78S	20731	1500	2000	3150	4775
2WD		T		(400)	(400)	(535)	(535)
4-Cyl. 2.5 Liter		P		(350)	(350)	(465)	(465)

GRAND CHEROKEE 4WD—6-Cyl.—Truck Equipment Sch T1
Sport Utility 4D		Z68S	21898	2250	2825	4075	5875
Sport Utility 4D		Z88S	21898	2250	2825	4075	5875
Laredo Sport Util 4D		Z58S	23082	2550	3150	4450	6350
2WD		X		(400)	(400)	(535)	(535)
V8 5.2 Liter		Y		275	275	365	365

GRAND CHEROKEE 4WD—V8—Truck Equipment Schedule T3
Wagoneer Spt Util 4D		Z88Y	29826	3700	4450	5950	8125
Limited Sport Util 4D		Z78Y	28925	3800	4550	6075	8325
6-Cyl. 4.0L (Limited)				(275)	(275)	(365)	(365)

1994 JEEP — 1J4-(Y19P)-R-#

WRANGLER 4WD—4-Cyl.—Truck Equipment Schedule T2
S Sport Utility 2D		Y19P	12610	2125	2700	3925	5725
w/o Rear Seat				(100)	(100)	(135)	(135)
Hard Top				300	300	400	400

0106

Body Type	VIN	List	Trade-In Fair	Good	Pvt-Party Good	Retail Excellent
WRANGLER 4WD—6-Cyl.—Truck Equipment Schedule T2						
SE Sport Utility 2D	Y29S	14949	3075	3725	5175	7175
Sahara Spt Util 2D	Y49S	17372	3200	3875	5300	7350
Renegade Spt Util 2D	Y69S	19201	3300	3975	5400	7475
w/o Rear Seat		......	(100)	(100)	(135)	(135)
Hard Top		......	300	300	400	400
CHEROKEE 4WD—6-Cyl.—Truck Equipment Schedule T1						
SE Sport Utility 2D	J27S	17402	1325	1825	2975	4600
SE Sport Utility 4D	J28S	18412	1525	2025	3250	4950
Sport 2D	J67S	18947	1300	1800	2950	4575
Sport 4D	J68S	19957	1575	2075	3300	5025
Country Sport Util 2D	J77S	20584	1325	1825	2975	4600
Country Sport Util 4D	J78S	21594	1525	2025	3250	4950
2WD	T	......	(425)	(425)	(565)	(565)
4-Cyl. 2.5 Liter	P	......	(375)	(375)	(500)	(500)
GRAND CHEROKEE 4WD—6-Cyl.—Truck Equipment Sch T1						
SE Sport Utility 4D	Z68S	23488	2325	2900	4225	6075
Laredo Sport Util 4D	Z58S	23627	2675	3275	4650	6625
2WD	X	......	(425)	(425)	(565)	(565)
V8 5.2 Liter	Y	......	325	325	435	435
GRAND CHEROKEE 4WD—V8—Truck Equipment Schedule T3						
Limited Sport Util 4D	Z78Y	30113	4175	4950	6600	8975
6-Cyl. 4.0 Liter	S	......	(325)	(325)	(435)	(435)

1995 JEEP — 1J4-(Y19P)-S-#

Body Type	VIN	List	Trade-In Fair	Good	Pvt-Party Good	Retail Excellent
WRANGLER 4WD—4-Cyl.—Truck Equipment Schedule T2						
S Sport Utility 2D	Y19P	13038	2400	2975	4325	6175
w/o Rear Seat		......	(100)	(100)	(135)	(135)
Rio Grande Pkg		......	400	400	535	535
Hard Top		......	325	325	435	435
WRANGLER 4WD—6-Cyl.—Truck Equipment Schedule T2						
SE Sport Utility 2D	Y29S	15932	3475	4175	5650	7750
Sahara Spt Util 2D	Y49S	17957	3600	4300	5800	7925
w/o Rear Seat		......	(100)	(100)	(135)	(135)
Hard Top		......	325	325	435	435
CHEROKEE 4WD—6-Cyl.—Truck Equipment Schedule T1						
SE Sport Utility 2D	J27S	18194	1425	1925	3175	4900
SE Sport Utility 4D	J28S	19228	1675	2200	3475	5250
Sport 2D	J67S	19800	1400	1900	3125	4850
Sport 4D	J68S	20834	1725	2250	3550	5325
Country Sport Util 4D	J78S	22398	1675	2200	3475	5250
2WD	T	......	(450)	(450)	(600)	(600)
4-Cyl. 2.5 Liter	P	......	(400)	(400)	(535)	(535)
GRAND CHEROKEE 4WD—6-Cyl.—Truck Equipment Sch T1						
SE Sport Utility 4D	Z68S	25075	2475	3075	4450	6400
Laredo Sport Util 4D	Z58S	25706	2850	3500	4925	6950
2WD	X	......	(450)	(450)	(600)	(600)
V8 5.2 Liter	Y	......	375	375	500	500
GRAND CHEROKEE 4WD—V8—Truck Equipment Schedule T3						
Limited/Orvis 4D	Z78Y	31182	4500	5300	7050	9525
2WD	X	......	(450)	(450)	(600)	(600)
6-Cyl. 4.0 Liter	S	......	(375)	(375)	(500)	(500)

1996 JEEP — 1J4-(J27S)-T-#

Body Type	VIN	List	Trade-In Fair	Good	Pvt-Party Good	Retail Excellent
CHEROKEE 4WD—6-Cyl.—Truck Equipment Schedule T1						
SE Sport Utility 2D	J27S	18369	1650	2150	3475	5300
SE Sport Utility 4D	J28S	19403	1925	2450	3800	5700
Sport 2D	J67S	19908	1600	2100	3425	5225
Sport 4D	J68S	20942	1975	2500	3850	5750
Country Sport Util 4D	J78S	22476	1925	2450	3800	5700
2WD	T	......	(475)	(475)	(635)	(635)
4-Cyl. 2.5 Liter	P	......	(425)	(425)	(565)	(565)
GRAND CHEROKEE 4WD—6-Cyl.—Truck Equipment Sch T1						
Laredo Sport Util 4D	Z68S	27071	2400	2975	4450	6450
2WD	X	......	(475)	(475)	(635)	(635)
V8 5.2 Liter	Y	......	425	425	565	565
GRAND CHEROKEE 4WD—V8—Truck Equipment Schedule T3						
Limited/Orvis 4D	Z78Y	33406	4200	4975	6725	9225
2WD	X	......	(475)	(475)	(635)	(635)
6-Cyl. 4.0 Liter	S	......	(425)	(425)	(565)	(565)

TRUCKS & VANS

TRUCKS & VANS

Body Type	VIN	List	Trade-In Fair	Good	Pvt-Party Good	Retail Excellent

1997 JEEP — 1J4–(Y29P)–V–#

WRANGLER 4WD—4-Cyl.—Truck Equipment Schedule T2
SE Sport Utility 2D	Y29P	14857	3475	4200	5675	7800
w/o Rear Seat			(100)	(100)	(135)	(135)
Hard Top			375	375	500	500

WRANGLER 4WD—6-Cyl.—Truck Equipment Schedule T2
Sport Utility 2D	Y19S	17665	4375	5175	6775	9100
Sahara Spt Util 2D	Y49S	19363	4425	5225	6850	9175
w/o Rear Seat			(100)	(100)	(135)	(135)
Hard Top			375	375	500	500

CHEROKEE 4WD—6-Cyl.—Truck Equipment Schedule T1
SE Sport Utility 2D	J27S	19280	1925	2450	3850	5825
SE Sport Utility 4D	J28S	20315	2200	2800	4225	6225
Sport 2D	J67S	20895	1850	2375	3775	5725
Sport 4D	J68S	21930	2250	2825	4275	6275
Country Sport Util 4D	J78S	23945	2200	2800	4225	6225
2WD	T		(500)	(500)	(665)	(665)
4-Cyl. 2.5 Liter	P		(450)	(450)	(600)	(600)

GRAND CHEROKEE 4WD—6-Cyl.—Truck Equipment Sch T1
Laredo Sport Util 4D	Z58S	28040	2875	3550	5100	7250
TSi Sport Util 4D	Z58Y	30190	3125	3775	5350	7575
2WD	X		(500)	(500)	(665)	(665)
V8 5.2 Liter	Y		475	475	635	635

GRAND CHEROKEE 4WD—V8—Truck Equipment Schedule T3
Limited/Orvis 4D	Z78Y	34315	4825	5675	7575	10250
2WD	X		(500)	(500)	(665)	(665)
6-Cyl. 4.0 Liter	S		(475)	(475)	(635)	(635)

1998 JEEP — 1J4–(Y29P)–W–#

WRANGLER 4WD—4-Cyl.—Truck Equipment Schedule T2
SE Sport Utility 2D	Y29P	15480	3950	4700	6250	8500
w/o Rear Seat			(100)	(100)	(135)	(135)
Hard Top			400	400	535	535

WRANGLER 4WD—6-Cyl.—Truck Equipment Schedule T2
Sport Utility 2D	Y19S	18030	4925	5775	7425	9850
Sahara Spt Util 2D	Y49S	20140	4950	5825	7475	9900
w/o Rear Seat			(100)	(100)	(135)	(135)
Hard Top			400	400	535	535

CHEROKEE 4WD—6-Cyl.—Truck Equipment Schedule T1
SE Sport Utility 2D	J27S	20270	2300	2875	4400	6475
SE Sport Utility 4D	J28S	21305	2625	3250	4775	6900
Sport 2D	J67S	21885	2250	2825	4325	6375
Sport 4D	J68S	22920	2675	3275	4825	6950
Classic Sport Util 4D	J68S	23370	2625	3250	4775	6900
Limited Sport Util 4D	J78S	24885	3625	4350	6100	8575
2WD	T		(525)	(525)	(700)	(700)
4-Cyl. 2.5 Liter	P		(475)	(475)	(635)	(635)

GRAND CHEROKEE 4WD—6-Cyl.—Truck Equipment Sch T1
Laredo Sport Util 4D	Z58S	28340	3525	4225	5875	8200
Special Ed Sport Util	Z48S	30040	3650	4375	6050	8400
TSi Sport Utility 4D	Z58S	30490	3750	4475	6150	8525
2WD	X		(525)	(525)	(700)	(700)
V8 5.2 Liter	Y		525	525	700	700

GRAND CHEROKEE 4WD—V8—Truck Equipment Schedule T3
Limited Sport Util 4D	Z78Y	35195	5575	6500	8500	11350
5.9 Limited Sport Util	Z88Z	38700	5750	6700	8850	11900
2WD	X		(525)	(525)	(700)	(700)
6-Cyl. 4.0 Liter	S		(525)	(525)	(700)	(700)

1999 JEEP — 1J4–(Y29P)–X–#

WRANGLER 4WD—4-Cyl.—Truck Equipment Schedule T2
SE Sport Utility 2D	Y29P	15670	4500	5325	6875	9125
w/o Rear Seat			(100)	(100)	(135)	(135)
Hard Top			425	425	565	565

WRANGLER 4WD—6-Cyl.—Truck Equipment Schedule T2
Sport Utility 2D	Y19S	18335	5550	6475	8100	10500
Sahara Spt Util 2D	Y49S	20495	5600	6525	8150	10550
w/o Rear Seat			(100)	(100)	(135)	(135)
Hard Top			425	425	565	565

CHEROKEE 4WD—6-Cyl.—Truck Equipment Schedule T1
| SE Sport Utility 2D | F27P | 20815 | 2850 | 3500 | 4900 | 6875 |

Body	Type	VIN	List	Trade-In Fair	Good	Pvt-Party Good	Retail Excellent
SE Sport Utility 4D	F28P	21850	3200	3875	5300	7375
Sport 2D	F67S	22540	2825	3475	4875	6875
Sport 4D	F68S	23575	3275	3950	5400	7475
Classic Sport Util 4D	F68S	23945	3225	3900	5325	7400
Limited Sport Util 4D	F78S	25505	4275	5075	6725	9125
2WD	T	......	(575)	(575)	(765)	(765)
4-Cyl. 2.5 Liter	P	......	(525)	(525)	(700)	(700)

GRAND CHEROKEE 4WD—6-Cyl.—Truck Equipment Sch T1

Laredo Sport Util 4D	W58S	28225	4975	5850	7450	9800
2WD	2	......	(575)	(575)	(765)	(765)
V8 4.7 Liter	N	......	575	575	765	765

GRAND CHEROKEE 4WD—V8—Truck Equipment Schedule T3

Limited Sport Util	W68N	35480	7200	8325	10300	13150
2WD	2	......	(575)	(575)	(765)	(765)
6-Cyl. 4.0 Liter	S	......	(575)	(575)	(765)	(765)

2000 JEEP — 1J4-(A29P)-Y-#

WRANGLER 4WD—4-Cyl.—Truck Equipment Schedule T2

SE Sport Utility 2D	A29P	16305	5025	5900	7525	9900
w/o Rear Seat		......	(150)	(150)	(200)	(200)
Hard Top		......	500	500	665	665

WRANGLER 4WD—6-Cyl.—Truck Equipment Schedule T2

Sport Utility 2D	A49S	18995	6175	7175	8900	11450
Sahara Spt Util 2D	A59S	20925	6300	7325	9050	11650
w/o Rear Seat		......	(150)	(150)	(200)	(200)
Hard Top		......	500	500	665	665

CHEROKEE 4WD—6-Cyl.—Truck Equipment Schedule T1

SE Sport Utility 2D	F27P	21285	3575	4275	5775	7925
SE Sport Utility 4D	F28P	22320	3950	4700	6250	8475
Sport 2D	F47S	21860	3650	4400	5900	8075
Sport 4D	F48S	22895	4175	4950	6500	8750
Classic Sport Util 4D	F58S	23420	4175	4950	6500	8750
Limited Sport Util 4D	F68S	25745	5200	6075	7850	10450
2WD	T	......	(650)	(650)	(865)	(865)
4-Cyl. 2.5 Liter	P	......	(600)	(600)	(800)	(800)

GRAND CHEROKEE 4WD—6-Cyl.—Truck Equipment Sch T1

Laredo Sport Util 4D	W48S	29075	5925	6875	8575	11100
2WD	X	......	(650)	(650)	(865)	(865)
V8 4.7 Liter	N	......	675	675	900	900

GRAND CHEROKEE 4WD—V8—Truck Equipment Schedule T3

Limited Spt Util 4D	258N	35950	8500	9700	11800	14850
2WD	X	......	(650)	(650)	(865)	(865)
6-Cyl. 4.0 Liter	S	......	(700)	(700)	(935)	(935)

2001 JEEP — 1J4-(A29P)-1-#

WRANGLER 4WD—4-Cyl.—Truck Equipment Schedule T2

SE Sport Utility 2D	A29P	16095	5650	6575	8300	10800
w/o Rear Seat		......	(175)	(175)	(235)	(235)
Hard Top		......	550	550	735	735

WRANGLER 4WD—6-Cyl.—Truck Equipment Schedule T2

Sport Utility 2D	A49S	19615	6950	8025	9850	12550
Sahara Spt Util 2D	A59S	22895	7150	8250	10100	12800
Hard Top		......	550	550	735	735

CHEROKEE 4WD—6-Cyl.—Truck Equipment Schedule T1

SE Sport Utility 2D	F27S	21780	4475	5275	6875	9225
SE Sport Utility 4D	F28S	22815	4925	5775	7425	9800
Sport Utility 2D	F47S	22410	4700	5550	7175	9575
Sport Utility 4D	F48S	23445	5250	6150	7825	10300
Classic Sport Util 4D	F58S	23835	5275	6175	7850	10300
Limited Sport Util 4D	F68S	23970	6300	7325	9225	12000
2WD	T	......	(725)	(725)	(965)	(965)

GRAND CHEROKEE 4WD—6-Cyl.—Truck Equipment Sch T1

Laredo Sport Util 4D	W48S	29855	7050	8150	9950	12600
2WD	X	......	(725)	(725)	(965)	(965)
V8 4.7 Liter	N	......	750	750	1000	1000

GRAND CHEROKEE 4WD—V8—Truck Equipment Schedule T3

Limited Spt Util 4D	W58N	35870	9950	11350	13550	16850
2WD	X	......	(725)	(725)	(965)	(965)
6-Cyl. 4.0 Liter	S	......	(825)	(825)	(1100)	(1100)

TRUCKS & VANS

Body	Type	VIN	List	Trade-In Fair	Good	Pvt-Party Good	Retail Excellent

2002 JEEP — 1J(4or8)-(A29P)-2-#

WRANGLER 4WD—4-Cyl.—Truck Equipment Schedule T2
SE Sport Utility 2D	A29P	16410	6425	7425	9250	11950
w/o Rear Seat			(200)	(200)	(265)	(265)
Hard Top			600	600	800	800

WRANGLER 4WD—6-Cyl.—Truck Equipment Schedule T2
X Sport Utility 2D	A49S	18995	7450	8550	10450	13250
Sport Utility 2D	A49S	20665	7900	9075	10950	13800
Sahara Spt Util 2D	A59S	24035	8150	9325	11250	14150
Hard Top			600	600	800	800

LIBERTY 4WD—V6—Truck Equipment Schedule T1
Sport Utility 4D	L48K	21070	6875	7900	9700	12400
Limited Utility 4D	L58K	23305	7850	9025	10900	13750
Renegade Utility 4D	L38K	23855	8325	9525	11450	14300
2WD			(800)	(800)	(1065)	(1065)
4-Cyl. 2.4 Liter		1	(825)	(825)	(1100)	(1100)

GRAND CHEROKEE 4WD—6-Cyl.—Truck Equipment Schedule T1
Laredo Sport Util 4D	W48S	27995	8450	9675	11550	14400
Sport Utility 4D	W38S	29140	8675	9950	11850	14750
2WD		X	(800)	(800)	(1065)	(1065)
V8 4.7 Liter		N	825	825	1100	1100

GRAND CHEROKEE 4WD—V8—Truck Equipment Schedule T3
Limited Spt Util 4D	W58N	33300	11600	13200	15450	18950
Overland Spt Utl 4D	W68N	37430	12850	14550	16750	20200
2WD		X	(800)	(800)	(1065)	(1065)
6-Cyl. 4.0 Liter		S	(925)	(925)	(1235)	(1235)

2003 JEEP — 1J(4or8)-(A291)-3-#

WRANGLER 4WD—4-Cyl.—Truck Equipment Schedule T2
SE Sport Utility 2D	A291	16910	7350	8475	10400	13250
w/o Rear Seat			(225)	(225)	(300)	(300)
Hard Top			650	650	865	865

WRANGLER 4WD—6-Cyl.—Truck Equipment Schedule T2
X Sport Utility 2D	A39S	19295	8550	9800	11800	14800
Sport Utility 2D	A49S	21105	8975	10275	12250	15300
Sahara Spt Util 2D	A59S	24695	9275	10575	12600	15650
Rubicon Spt Util 2D	A59S	24995	10100	11450	13550	16700
Hard Top			650	650	865	865

LIBERTY 4WD—V6—Truck Equipment Schedule T1
Sport Utility 4D	L48K	21880	8375	9575	11500	14350
Limited Utility 4D	L58K	24045	9475	10825	12750	15750
Renegade Utility 4D	L38K	24630	10000	11350	13350	16400
2WD		K	(875)	(875)	(1165)	(1165)
4-Cyl. 2.4 Liter		1	(925)	(925)	(1235)	(1235)

GRAND CHEROKEE 4WD—6-Cyl.—Truck Equipment Schedule T1
Laredo Sport Util 4D	W48S	28640	10050	11400	13450	16550
2WD		X	(875)	(875)	(1165)	(1165)
V8 4.7 Liter		N	900	900	1200	1200

GRAND CHEROKEE 4WD—V8—Truck Equipment Schedule T3
Limited Spt Util 4D	W58N	34920	13525	15275	17700	21400
Overland Spt Utl 4D	W68J	37975	14850	16775	19000	22700
2WD		X	(875)	(875)	(1165)	(1165)
6-Cyl. 4.0 Liter		S	(1025)	(1025)	(1365)	(1365)

2004 JEEP — 1J(4or8)-(A291)-4-#

WRANGLER 4WD—4-Cyl.—Truck Equipment Schedule T2
SE Sport Utility 2D	A291	17515	8525	9750	11700	14600
w/o Rear Seat			(250)	(250)	(335)	(335)
Hard Top			700	700	935	935

WRANGLER 4WD—6-Cyl.—Truck Equipment Schedule T2
X Sport Utility 2D	A49S	19945	9900	11300	13300	16350
Sport Utility 2D	A49S	21930	10275	11700	13750	16850
Unlimited Spt Utl 2D	A49S	24995	10375	11775	13750	16950
Sahara Spt Util 2D	A59S	25520	10675	12125	14100	17250
Rubicon Spt Utl 2D	A59S	25695	11450	13000	15050	18300
Hard Top			700	700	935	935

LIBERTY 4WD—V6—Truck Equipment Schedule T2
Sport Utility 4D	L48K	21855	10125	11550	13500	16500
Limited Utility 4D	L58K	24045	11350	12900	14900	18050
Renegade Utility 4D	L38K	25455	11875	13475	15500	18700
2WD		K	(950)	(950)	(1265)	(1265)

Body Type	VIN	List	Trade-In Fair	Trade-In Good	Pvt-Party Good	Retail Excellent
4-Cyl. 2.4 Liter	1		(1025)	(1025)	(1365)	(1365)
GRAND CHEROKEE 4WD—6-Cyl.—Truck Equipment Schedule T1						
Laredo Sport Util 4D	W48S	29875	11925	13525	15550	18750
2WD	X		(950)	(950)	(1265)	(1265)
V8 4.7 Liter	N,J		975	975	1300	1300
GRAND CHEROKEE 4WD—V8—Truck Equipment Schedule T3						
Limited Spt Util 4D	W58N	35655	15775	17750	20200	24200
Overland Spt Util 4D	W68J	39920	17225	19350	21600	25500
2WD	X		(950)	(950)	(1265)	(1265)
6-Cyl. 4.0 Liter	S		(1125)	(1125)	(1500)	(1500)

Body Type	VIN	List	Trade-In Fair	Trade-In Good	Pvt-Party Good	Retail Excellent
WRANGLER 4WD—4-Cyl.—Truck Equipment Schedule T2						
SE Sport Utility 2D	A291	18510	9950	11350	13300	16300
w/o Rear Seat			(275)	(275)	(365)	(365)
6-Cyl. 4.0 Liter	S		1000	1000	1335	1335
WRANGLER 4WD—6-Cyl.—Truck Equipment Schedule T2						
X Sport Utility 2D	A39S	20820	11500	13050	15100	18300
Sport Utility 2D	A49S	23600	11875	13425	15550	18750
Unlimited Spt Util 2D	A44S	24355	11875	13475	15550	18800
Rubicon Spt Util 2D	A69S	27825	13100	14850	16950	20400
Rubicon LWB Util 2D	A69S	28825	13200	14950	17050	20600
Hard Top			750	750	1000	1000
LIBERTY 4WD—V6—Truck Equipment Schedule T1						
Sport Utility 4D	L48K	22985	12175	13775	15800	19100
Limited Utility 4D	L58K	25645	13425	15175	17300	20800
Renegade Utility 4D	L38K	24920	14075	15900	18050	21500
2WD	K		(1000)	(1000)	(1335)	(1335)
4-Cyl. 2.4 Liter	1		(1125)	(1125)	(1500)	(1500)
4-Cyl. Turbo Diesel	5		2000	2000	2665	2665
GRAND CHEROKEE 4WD—V6—Truck Equipment Schedule T1						
Laredo Sport Util 4D	R48K	28745	13875	15675	18250	22200
2WD	S		(1000)	(1000)	(1335)	(1335)
V8 4.7 Liter	N		1050	1050	1400	1400
GRAND CHEROKEE 4WD—V8—Truck Equipment Schedule T3						
Limited Spt Util 4D	R58N	34690	17950	20175	23100	27700
2WD	S		(1000)	(1000)	(1335)	(1335)
V8 5.7 Liter HEMI	2		1050	1050	1400	1400

KIA

Body Type	VIN	List	Trade-In Fair	Trade-In Good	Pvt-Party Good	Retail Excellent
SPORTAGE 4WD—4-Cyl.—Truck Equipment Schedule T2						
Sport Utility 4D	JA721	14895	825	1175	2025	3400
EX Sport Utility 4D	JA721	15895	975	1350	2425	3975
2WD			(400)	(400)	(535)	(535)
4-Cyl. 2.0L DOHC	3		100	100	135	135

Body Type	VIN	List	Trade-In Fair	Trade-In Good	Pvt-Party Good	Retail Excellent
SPORTAGE 4WD—4-Cyl.—Truck Equipment Schedule T2						
Sport Utility 4D	JA723	15720	975	1375	2475	4050
EX Sport Utility 4D	JA723	16420	1150	1600	2775	4400
2WD	B		(425)	(425)	(565)	(565)

Body Type	VIN	List	Trade-In Fair	Trade-In Good	Pvt-Party Good	Retail Excellent
SPORTAGE 4WD—4-Cyl.—Truck Equipment Schedule T2						
Sport Utility 4D	JA723	16420	1200	1650	2850	4550
EX Sport Utility 4D	JA723	17040	1425	1925	3175	4900
2WD	B		(450)	(450)	(600)	(600)

Body Type	VIN	List	Trade-In Fair	Trade-In Good	Pvt-Party Good	Retail Excellent
SPORTAGE 4WD—4-Cyl.—Truck Equipment Schedule T2						
Sport Utility 4D	JA723	17845	1525	2025	3325	5125
EX Sport Utility 4D	JA723	18945	1825	2350	3650	5500
2WD	B		(475)	(475)	(635)	(635)

Body Type	VIN	List	Trade-In Fair	Trade-In Good	Pvt-Party Good	Retail Excellent
SPORTAGE 4WD—4-Cyl.—Truck Equipment Schedule T2						
Sport Util Conv 2D	JA623	14945	1650	2150	3425	5200
Sport Utility 4D	JA723	16745	2000	2550	3850	5675

TRUCKS & VANS

Body	Type	VIN	List	Trade-In Fair	Good	Pvt-Party Good	Retail Excellent
	EX Sport Utility 4D	JA723	19045	**2275**	**2850**	**4200**	**6075**
	2WD	B		**(525)**	**(525)**	**(700)**	**(700)**

2000 KIA — KNM(JA623)-Y-#

SPORTAGE 4WD—4-Cyl.—Truck Equipment Schedule T2

Sport Util Conv 2D		JA623	14945	**2025**	**2600**	**3950**	**5850**
Sport Utility 4D		JA723	16745	**2450**	**3050**	**4450**	**6400**
EX Sport Utility 4D		JA723	19045	**2800**	**3425**	**4825**	**6850**
2WD		B		**(600)**	**(600)**	**(800)**	**(800)**

2001 KIA — KND(JB623)-1-#

SPORTAGE 4WD—4-Cyl.—Truck Equipment Schedule T2

Sport Util Conv 2D		JB623	15345	**2575**	**3200**	**4625**	**6675**
Sport Utility 4D		JB723	17245	**3025**	**3700**	**5200**	**7275**
EX Sport Utility 4D		JB723	19545	**3425**	**4125**	**5625**	**7750**
Limited Spt Util 4D		JB723	20090	**3925**	**4675**	**6225**	**8450**
2WD		B		**(675)**	**(675)**	**(900)**	**(900)**

2002 KIA — KND(JA623)-2-#

SPORTAGE 4WD—4-Cyl.—Truck Equipment Schedule T2

Sport Util Conv 2D		JA623	15640	**3275**	**3950**	**5475**	**7675**
Sport Utility 4D		JA723	18715	**3750**	**4500**	**6075**	**8325**
2WD		B		**(750)**	**(750)**	**(1000)**	**(1000)**

SEDONA—V6—Truck Equipment Schedule T1

LX Minivan		UP131	19590	**4000**	**4750**	**6925**	**9900**
EX Minivan		UP131	21590	**4625**	**5450**	**7675**	**10650**

2003 KIA — KND(UP131)-3-#

SEDONA—V6—Truck Equipment Schedule T1

LX Minivan		UP131	19965	**5125**	**6025**	**8375**	**11600**
EX Minivan		UP131	22180	**5825**	**6775**	**9175**	**12450**

SORENTO 4WD—V6—Truck Equipment Schedule T1

LX Sport Utility 4D		JC733	21795	**7800**	**8975**	**10600**	**13250**
EX Sport Utility 4D		JC733	24595	**8525**	**9750**	**11450**	**14100**
2WD				**(875)**	**(875)**	**(1165)**	**(1165)**

2004 KIA — KND(UP131)-4-#

SEDONA—V6—Truck Equipment Schedule T1

LX Minivan		UP131	20615	**6650**	**7675**	**10200**	**13650**
EX Minivan		UP131	22725	**7400**	**8500**	**11050**	**14600**

SORENTO 4WD—V6—Truck Equipment Schedule T1

LX Sport Utility 4D		JC733	23290	**9575**	**10925**	**12550**	**15250**
EX Sport Utility 4D		JC733	25490	**10325**	**11725**	**13450**	**16200**
2WD		D		**(950)**	**(950)**	**(1265)**	**(1265)**

2005 KIA — KND(JE723)-5-#

SPORTAGE 4WD—V6—Truck Equipment Schedule T2

LX Sport Utility 4D		JE723	20290				
EX Sport Utility 4D		JE723	21990				
2WD		F					
4-Cyl. 2.0 Liter		4					

SEDONA—V6—Truck Equipment Schedule T1

LX Minivan		UP131	20840	**8600**	**9850**	**12550**	**16400**
EX Minivan		UP131	23240	**9400**	**10725**	**13500**	**17400**

SORENTO 4WD—V6—Truck Equipment Schedule T1

LX Sport Utility 4D		JC733	23840	**11550**	**13100**	**14800**	**17700**
EX Sport Utility 4D		JC733	26140	**12325**	**13975**	**15700**	**18700**
2WD		D		**(1000)**	**(1000)**	**(1335)**	**(1335)**

LAND ROVER

1991 LAND ROVER — SAL(HV124)-M-#

RANGE ROVER 4WD—V8—Truck Equipment Schedule T3

Hunter Sport Util 4D		HV124	36525	**750**	**1075**	**1950**	**3275**
Sport Utility 4D		HV124	44475	**1225**	**1700**	**2875**	**4550**
Great Divide Util 4D		HV124	45075	**1325**	**1825**	**3000**	**4700**
County SE Util 4D		HV124	46975	**1600**	**2100**	**3375**	**5150**

Body	Type	VIN	List	Trade-In Fair	Good	Pvt-Party Good	Retail Excellent

1992 LAND ROVER — SAL(HV124)-N-#

RANGE ROVER 4WD—V8—Truck Equipment Schedule T3
| Sport Utility 4D | | HV124 | 39475 | 1500 | 2000 | 3250 | 5025 |
| County Sport Util 4D | | HV124 | 45075 | 1950 | 2475 | 3825 | 5725 |

1993 LAND ROVER — SAL(DH128)-P-#

DEFENDER 110 4WD—V8—Truck Equipment Schedule T2
| Sport Utility 4D | | DH128 | 40575 | **** | **** | **** | 24100 |

RANGE ROVER 4WD—V8—Truck Equipment Schedule T3
| County Sport Util 4D | | HC124 | 45125 | 1650 | 2150 | 3525 | 5375 |
| County LWB Util 4D | | HC134 | 49825 | 2225 | 2825 | 4250 | 6150 |

1994 LAND ROVER — SAL(DV228)-R-#

DEFENDER 90 4WD—V8—Truck Equipment Schedule T2
| Sport Utility 2D | | DV228 | 28495 | **** | **** | **** | 25800 |

DISCOVERY 4WD—V8—Truck Equipment Schedule T3
Sport Utility 4D		JY124	30725	1750	2275	3575	5350
Dual Moon Roofs		------		575	575	765	765
Rear Jump Seats		------		275	275	365	365
Manual Trans		------		(275)	(275)	(365)	(365)
Rear Air Conditioning		------		150	150	200	200

RANGE ROVER 4WD—V8—Truck Equipment Schedule T3
| County Sport Utl 4D | | HV124 | 47525 | 1800 | 2325 | 3750 | 5750 |
| County LWB 4D | | HC134 | 50825 | 2450 | 3050 | 4600 | 6750 |

1995 LAND ROVER — SAL(DV228)-S-#

DEFENDER 90 4WD—V8—Truck Equipment Schedule T2
| Soft Top Spt Utl 2D | | DV228 | 29275 | **** | **** | **** | 27300 |
| Hard Top Spt Utl 2D | | DV228 | | **** | **** | **** | 28200 |

DISCOVERY 4WD—V8—Truck Equipment Schedule T3
Sport Utility 4D		JY124	32375	2225	2825	4200	6150
Dual Moon Roofs		------		600	600	800	800
Rear Jump Seats		------		300	300	400	400
Rear Air Conditioning		------		175	175	235	235
Manual Trans		------		(300)	(300)	(400)	(400)

RANGE ROVER 4WD—V8—Truck Equipment Schedule T3
County Classic 4D		HV124	45625	2075	2650	4200	6300
County LWB 4D		HC134	53125	2675	3275	4900	7150
4.0 SE Sport Util 4D		PV124	54625	4750	5575	7525	10250

1996 LAND ROVER — SAL(JY124)-T-#

DISCOVERY 4WD—V8—Truck Equipment Schedule T3
SD Sport Utility 4D		JY124	32975	2775	3400	4900	7000
SE Sport Utility 4D		JY124	35975	3675	4425	6050	8350
SE7 Sport Utility 4D		JY124	38550	3900	4650	6300	8650
Rear Jump Seats (Ex SE7)		------		325	325	435	435
Dual Moon Roofs		------		625	625	835	835
Manual Trans		8		(325)	(325)	(435)	(435)

RANGE ROVER 4WD—V8—Truck Equipment Schedule T3
| 4.0 SE Spt Util 4D | | PV124 | 55625 | 5250 | 6150 | 8200 | 11050 |
| 4.6 HSE Spt Util 4D | | PV144 | 62625 | 7775 | 8950 | 11350 | 14750 |

1997 LAND ROVER — SAL(DV224)-V-#

DEFENDER 90 4WD—V8—Truck Equipment Schedule T2
| Soft Top Spt Util 2D | | DV224 | 32625 | **** | **** | **** | 30400 |
| Hard Top Spt Util 2D | | DV324 | 34625 | **** | **** | **** | 31800 |

DISCOVERY 4WD—V8—Truck Equipment Schedule T3
SD Sport Utility 4D		JY124	34625	3375	4075	5675	7950
XD Sport Utility 4D		JY124	36325	4300	5100	6825	9275
SE Sport Utility 4D		JY124	36625	4375	5175	6900	9375
SE7 Sport Utility 4D		JY124	39125	4600	5425	7175	9700
Rear Jump Seats (Ex SE7)		------		350	350	465	465
Dual Moon Roofs		------		650	650	865	865
Manual Trans		8		(350)	(350)	(465)	(465)

RANGE ROVER 4WD—V8—Truck Equipment Schedule T3
| 4.0 SE Spt Util 4D | | PV124 | 56125 | 5900 | 6875 | 9000 | 12050 |
| 4.6 HSE Spt Util 4D | | PV144 | 63625 | 8650 | 9900 | 12350 | 15950 |

1998 LAND ROVER

Body	Type	VIN	List	Trade-In Fair	Trade-In Good	Pvt-Party Good	Retail Excellent

1998 LAND ROVER — SAL(JY124)-W-#

DISCOVERY 4WD—V8—Truck Equipment Schedule T3

Body Type	VIN	List	Fair	Good	Good	Excellent
LE Sport Utility 4D	JY124	35125	5200	6075	7925	10550
LSE Sport Utility 4D	JY124	38625	5425	6350	8225	10900
Rear Jump Seats			375	375	500	500
Rear Air Conditioning			250	250	335	335
Dual Moon Roofs			675	675	900	900

RANGE ROVER 4WD—V8—Truck Equipment Schedule T3

Body Type	VIN	List	Fair	Good	Good	Excellent
4.0 SE Spt Util 4D	PV124	56625	6650	7675	10000	13250
4.6 HSE Spt Util 4D	PV144	64125	9650	11000	13600	17350

1999 LAND ROVER — SAL(JY124)-X-#

DISCOVERY 4WD—V8—Truck Equipment Schedule T3

Body Type	VIN	List	Fair	Good	Good	Excellent
SD Sport Utility 4D	JY124	33625	4975	5850	7700	10400
Rear Jump Seats			425	425	565	565
Dual Moon Roofs			700	700	935	935

DISCOVERY SERIES II 4WD—V8—Truck Equipment Schedule T3

Body Type	VIN	List	Fair	Good	Good	Excellent
Sport Utility 4D	TY124	36725	6050	7000	9000	11850
Rear Jump Seats			425	425	565	565
Rear Air Conditioning			250	250	335	335
Dual Moon Roofs			700	700	935	935
Performance Pkg			625	625	835	835

RANGE ROVER 4WD—V8—Truck Equipment Schedule T3

Body Type	VIN	List	Fair	Good	Good	Excellent
4.0 Sport Utility 4D	PA124	57625	6175	7175	10000	13750
4.0 S Sport Utility 4D	PA124	57625	6175	7175	10000	13750
4.0 SE Sport Util 4D	PV124	58625	6750	7775	10600	14500
4.6 HSE Sport Utl 4D	PV144	66625	10000	11350	14550	18950

2000 LAND ROVER — SAL(TY124)-Y-#

DISCOVERY SERIES II 4WD—V8—Truck Equipment Schedule T3

Body Type	VIN	List	Fair	Good	Good	Excellent
SD Sport Utility 4D	TY124	33975	6725	7750	9800	12700
SD7 Sport Utility 4D	TY124	35725	7425	8525	10600	13700
Sport Utility 4D	TY124	36725	7925	9125	11230	14350
Rear Jump Seats			500	500	665	665
Rear Air Conditioning			300	300	400	400
Dual Moon Roofs			750	750	1000	1000
Performance Pkg			725	725	965	965

RANGE ROVER 4WD—V8—Truck Equipment Schedule T3

Body Type	VIN	List	Fair	Good	Good	Excellent
County Sport Utl 4D	PA124	58925	7475	8575	11650	15800
4.0 Sport Util 4D	PA124	59625	7975	9175	12250	16500
4.0 SE Sport Util 4D	PV124	59625	8650	9800	12950	17250
4.6 HSK Spt Utl 4D	PF164	67625	11875	13425	16850	21600
4.6 HSE Spt Util 4D	PV144	67925	12275	13925	17300	22200
4.6 Vitesse Util 4D	PF164	68625	12325	13975	17400	22300
4.6 Holland Holland	PV164	79625	14975	16875	20600	25800

2001 LAND ROVER — SAL(TY124)-1-#

DISCOVERY SERIES II 4WD—V8—Truck Equipment Schedule T3

Body Type	VIN	List	Fair	Good	Good	Excellent
SD Sport Utility 4D	TY124	33975	8600	9850	12050	15250
SD7 Sport Utility 4D	TY124	35725	9400	10725	12950	16250
LE Sport Utility 4D	TY124	34975	10100	11450	13750	17100
LE7 Sport Utility 4D	TY124	36725	10325	11725	14000	17450
SE Sport Utility 4D	TY124	36975	10525	11975	14250	17750
SE7 Sport Utility 4D	TY124	38725	10825	12275	14600	18150
Rear Jump Seats			550	550	735	735
Rear Air Conditioning			350	350	465	465
Dual Moon Roofs			775	775	1035	1035
Performance Pkg			825	825	1100	1100

RANGE ROVER 4WD—V8—Truck Equipment Schedule T3

Body Type	VIN	List	Fair	Good	Good	Excellent
4.6 SE Sport Util 4D	PV164	62625	10625	12075	15450	20300
4.6 HSE Sport Util	PV164	68625	14800	16675	20400	25800

2002 LAND ROVER — SAL(NM222)-2-#

FREELANDER AWD—V6—Truck Equipment Schedule T3

Body Type	VIN	List	Fair	Good	Good	Excellent
S Sport Utility 4D	NM222	25600	7850	9025	10850	13700
SE Sport Utility 4D	NY222	28400	9125	10425	12300	15300
HSE Sport Util 4D	NE222	32200	10325	11725	13750	16900

DISCOVERY SERIES II 4WD—V8—Truck Equipment Schedule T3

Body Type	VIN	List	Fair	Good	Good	Excellent
SD Sport Utility 4D	TL144	33995	10725	12225	14500	17950
SD7 Sport Utility 4D	TK144	34995	11600	13200	15450	19050

2002 LAND ROVER

Body Type	VIN	List	Trade-In Fair	Good	Pvt-Party Good	Retail Excellent
SE Sport Utility 4D	TY144	37795	12900	14600	17000	20800
SET Sport Utility 4D	TW124	38875	13200	14950	17350	21100
Rear Jump Seats			600	600	800	800
Rear Air Conditioning			400	400	535	535
Dual Moon Roofs			800	800	1065	1065
Performance Pkg			925	925	1235	1235
RANGE ROVER 4WD—V8—Truck Equipment Schedule T3						
4.6 HSE Sport Util	PL162	68665	17550	19700	23700	29500

2003 LAND ROVER — SAL(NM222)-3-#

Body Type	VIN	List	Trade-In Fair	Good	Pvt-Party Good	Retail Excellent
FREELANDER AWD—V6—Truck Equipment Schedule T3						
S Sport Utility 4D	NM222	25600	9525	10875	12850	15950
SE3 Sport Utility 2D	NY222	26995	10575	12025	14050	17250
SE Sport Utility 4D	NY222	28400	10925	12375	14450	17700
HSE Sport Utility 4D	NE222	32200	12225	13875	16000	19400
DISCOVERY 4WD—V8—Truck Equipment Schedule T3						
S Sport Utility 4D	TL144	34995	13100	14800	17200	21000
SE Sport Utility 4D	TY144	38895	15525	17500	20000	24100
SET Sport Utility 4D	TW124	39995	15775	17800	20300	24300
HSE Sport Utility 4D	TP144	40995	17225	19350	21900	26200
HSET Sport Util 4D	TR144	41995	17375	19500	22100	26400
Rear Jump Seats			650	650	865	865
Rear Air Conditioning			425	425	565	565
Dual Moon Roofs			825	825	1100	1100
Suspension Pkg			1000	1000	1335	1335
RANGE ROVER 4WD—V8—Truck Equipment Schedule T3						
HSE Sport Util 4D	MB114	71865	40250	44825	49100	56600

2004 LAND ROVER — SAL(NY222)-4-#

Body Type	VIN	List	Trade-In Fair	Good	Pvt-Party Good	Retail Excellent
FREELANDER AWD—V6—Truck Equipment Schedule T3						
SE Sport Utility 4D	NY222	25995	13050	14750	16950	20500
SE3 Sport Utility 2D	NY222	28195	12650	14300	16500	20000
HSE Sport Utility 4D	NE222	28995	14450	16300	18600	22200
DISCOVERY 4WD—V8—Truck Equipment Schedule T3						
S Sport Utility 4D	TL194	34995	15775	17750	20200	24200
SE Sport Utility 4D	TY194	39250	18425	20750	23300	27500
SET Sport Utility 4D	TW194	40350	18725	21050	23600	27800
HSE Sport Utility 4D	TP194	41250	20275	22800	25400	29900
HSET Sport Util 4D	TR194	42250	20475	22900	25600	30100
G4 Sport Utility 4D	TL194	39995	19200	21525	24200	28500
Rear Jump Seats			700	700	935	935
Rear Air Conditioning			450	450	600	600
Dual Moon Roofs			850	850	1135	1135
Suspension Pkg			1075	1075	1435	1435
RANGE ROVER 4WD—V8—Truck Equipment Schedule T3						
HSE Sport Util 4D	ME114	72250	45000	50050	54300	62100
Westminister Util	MH114	84700	53050	58975	63600	72300

2005 LAND ROVER — SAL(NY222)-5-#

Body Type	VIN	List	Trade-In Fair	Good	Pvt-Party Good	Retail Excellent
FREELANDER AWD—V6—Truck Equipment Schedule T3						
SE Sport Utility 4D	NY222	27495	15275	17225	19600	23500
SE3 Sport Utility 2D	NM222	27495	14900	16825	19100	22900
LR3 4WD—V8—Truck Equipment Schedule T3						
SE Sport Utility 4D	AD254	44995	30450	33950	36600	41400
HSE Sport Utility 4D	AF254	49995	33650	37550	40200	45300
Third Row Seat			750	750	1000	1000
RANGE ROVER 4WD—V8—Truck Equipment Schedule T3						
HSE Sport Util 4D	ME114	73750				
Westminister Util	MH114	86000				

LEXUS

1996 LEXUS — JT6(HJ88J)-T-#

Body Type	VIN	List	Trade-In Fair	Good	Pvt-Party Good	Retail Excellent
LX 450 4WD—6-Cyl.—Truck Equipment Schedule T3						
Sport Utility 4D	HJ88J	47995	8500	9700	12250	15900

1997 LEXUS — JT6(HJ88J)-V-#

Body Type	VIN	List	Trade-In Fair	Good	Pvt-Party Good	Retail Excellent
LX 450 4WD—6-Cyl.—Truck Equipment Schedule T3						
Sport Utility 4D	HJ88J	48945	9650	11000	13700	17550

Body Type	VIN	List	Trade-In Fair	Trade-In Good	Pvt-Party Good	Retail Excellent

1998 LEXUS — JT6(HT00W)–W–#

LX 470 4WD—V8—Truck Equipment Schedule T3
Sport Utility 4D HT00W 55445 **13975 15800 19000 23800**

1999 LEXUS — JT6(HF10U)–X–#

RX 300 4WD—V6—Truck Equipment Schedule T3
Sport Utility 4D HF10U 34980 **10375 11825 14100 17600**
2WD .... G .... (825) (825) (1100) (1100)
LX 470 4WD—V8—Truck Equipment Schedule T3
Sport Utility 4D HT00W 56400 **15950 17950 21000 25800**

2000 LEXUS — JT6(HF10U)–Y–#

RX 300 4WD—V6—Truck Equipment Schedule T3
Sport Utility 4D HF10U 35680 **12475 14125 16600 20400**
2WD .... G .... (950) (950) (1265) (1265)
LX 470 4WD—V8—Truck Equipment Schedule T3
Sport Utility 4D HT00W 59500 **19600 22025 25500 30800**

2001 LEXUS — JTJ(HF10U)–1–#

RX 300 4WD—V6—Truck Equipment Schedule T3
Sport Utility 4D HF10U 37430 **14800 16675 19300 23400**
Silversport Edition 275 275 365 365
2WD .... G .... (1075) (1075) (1435) (1435)
LX 470 4WD—V8—Truck Equipment Schedule T3
Sport Utility 4D HT00W 61950 **23575 26375 30100 35900**

2002 LEXUS — JTJ(HF10U)–2–#

RX 300 4WD—V6—Truck Equipment Schedule T3
Sport Utility 4D HF10U 37580 **17275 19400 22200 26700**
Coach Edition 400 400 535 535
2WD .... G .... (1200) (1200) (1600) (1600)
LX 470 4WD—V8—Truck Equipment Schedule T3
Sport Utility 4D HT00W 63051 **27750 30950 34900 41200**

2003 LEXUS — JTJ(HF10U)–3–#

RX 300 4WD—V6—Truck Equipment Schedule T3
Sport Utility 4D HF10U 38800 **20075 22600 25500 30400**
2WD .... G .... (1325) (1325) (1765) (1765)
GX 470 4WD—V8—Truck Equipment Schedule T3
Sport Utility 4D BT20X 45500 **26775 29975 33700 39800**
Third Row Seat 800 800 1065 1065
LX 470 4WD—V8—Truck Equipment Schedule T3
Sport Utility 4D HT00W 63700 **32100 35800 39900 46700**

2004 LEXUS — JTJ(HA31U)–4–#

RX 330 AWD—V6—Truck Equipment Schedule T3
Sport Utility 4D HA31U 39195 **23275 26100 29100 34200**
Dynamic Cruise Control 475 475 635 635
Performance Pkg 2500 2500 3335 3335
2WD .... G .... (1425) (1425) (1900) (1900)
GX 470 4WD—V8—Truck Equipment Schedule T3
Sport Utility 4D BT20X 45700 **30275 33850 37700 44100**
Third Row Seat 800 800 1065 1065
LX 470 4WD—V8—Truck Equipment Schedule T3
Sport Utility 4D HT00W 64800 **36850 41125 45200 52400**

2005 LEXUS — JTJ(HA31U)–5–#

RX 330 AWD—V6—Truck Equipment Schedule T3
Sport Utility 4D HA31U 37800
Dynamic Cruise Control
Performance Pkg
2WD .... G ....
GX 470 4WD—V8—Truck Equipment Schedule T3
Sport Utility 4D BT20X 46425
Third Row Seat
LX 470 4WD—V8—Truck Equipment Schedule T3
Sport Utility 4D HT00W 65400

Body	Type	VIN	List	Trade-In Fair	Trade-In Good	Pvt-Party Good	Retail Excellent

TRUCKS & VANS

LINCOLN

1999 LINCOLN — 5LM-(U28L)-X-#

NAVIGATOR 4WD—V8—Truck Equipment Schedule T3

Body	Type	VIN	List	Fair	Good	Good	Excellent
Sport Utility 4D		U28L	43800	10475	11925	14250	17750
w/o Rear Air Conditioning				(250)	(250)	(335)	(335)
2WD		7		(1225)	(1225)	(1635)	(1635)

2000 LINCOLN — 5LM-(U28A)-Y-#

NAVIGATOR 4WD—V8—Truck Equipment Schedule T3

Body	Type	VIN	List	Fair	Good	Good	Excellent
Sport Utility 4D		U28A	46500	12225	13875	16350	20200
w/o Rear Air Conditioning				(300)	(300)	(400)	(400)
2WD		7		(1300)	(1300)	(1735)	(1735)

2001 LINCOLN — 5LM-(U28A,R)-1-#

NAVIGATOR 4WD—V8—Truck Equipment Schedule T3

Body	Type	VIN	List	Fair	Good	Good	Excellent
Sport Utility 4D		U28A,R	48085	14200	16000	18700	22900
2WD		7		(1350)	(1350)	(1800)	(1800)

2002 LINCOLN — 5LM-(U28R)-2-#

NAVIGATOR 4WD—V8—Truck Equipment Schedule T3

Body	Type	VIN	List	Fair	Good	Good	Excellent
Sport Utility 4D		U28R	48680	16350	18425	21300	25800
2WD		7		(1400)	(1400)	(1865)	(1865)

BLACKWOOD—V8—Truck Equipment Schedule T3

Body	Type	VIN	List	Fair	Good	Good	Excellent
Sport Util Pickup 4D		W05A	52500	17275	19400	21700	25500

2003 LINCOLN — 5LM-(U88H)-3-#

AVIATOR AWD—V8—Truck Equipment Schedule T3

Body	Type	VIN	List	Fair	Good	Good	Excellent
Sport Utility 4D		U88H	42945	18375	20650	23300	27500
2WD		6		(1450)	(1450)	(1935)	(1935)

NAVIGATOR 4WD—V8—Truck Equipment Schedule T3

Body	Type	VIN	List	Fair	Good	Good	Excellent
Sport Utility 4D		U28R	52425	21050	23575	27100	32500
2WD				(1450)	(1450)	(1935)	(1935)

2004 LINCOLN — 5LM-(U88H)-4-#

AVIATOR AWD—V8—Truck Equipment Schedule T3

Body	Type	VIN	List	Fair	Good	Good	Excellent
Sport Utility 4D		U88H	43400	21350	23950	26600	31100
2WD		6		(1500)	(1500)	(2000)	(2000)

NAVIGATOR 4WD—V8—Truck Equipment Schedule T3

Body	Type	VIN	List	Fair	Good	Good	Excellent
Sport Utility 4D		U28R	52775	24250	27150	30800	36700
2WD				(1500)	(1500)	(2000)	(2000)

2005 LINCOLN — 5LM-(U88H)-5-#

AVIATOR AWD—V8—Truck Equipment Schedule T3

Body	Type	VIN	List	Fair	Good	Good	Excellent
Sport Utility 4D		U88H	44150	24650	27550	30200	34900
2WD		6		(1550)	(1550)	(2065)	(2065)

NAVIGATOR 4WD—V8—Truck Equipment Schedule T3

Body	Type	VIN	List	Fair	Good	Good	Excellent
Sport Utility 4D		U285	53985	27750	30950	34700	40800
2WD		7		(1550)	(1550)	(2065)	(2065)

MAZDA

1991 MAZDA — JM(2or3)(LV521)-M-#

MPV—4-Cyl.—Truck Equipment Schedule T1

Body	Type	VIN	List	Fair	Good	Good	Excellent
Minivan		LV521	18073	600	850	1425	2425
V6 3.0 Liter		2		200	200	265	265

MPV 4WD—V6—Truck Equipment Schedule T1

Body	Type	VIN	List	Fair	Good	Good	Excellent
Minivan		LV523	20743	900	1250	2050	3300

NAVAJO 4WD—V6—Truck Equipment Schedule T1

Body	Type	VIN	List	Fair	Good	Good	Excellent
Sport Utility 2D		CU44X	20000	950	1325	2175	3475

B2200 PICKUP—4-Cyl.—Truck Equipment Schedule T2

Body	Type	VIN	List	Fair	Good	Good	Excellent
Short Bed		UF113	8748	400	525	975	1700
Long Bed		UF213	9408	425	625	1100	1875
Cab Plus		UF313	10268	725	1050	1650	2725
SE-5 Sport Pkg				100	100	135	135
LE-5 Luxury Pkg				100	100	135	135

1991 MAZDA

Body	Type	VIN	List	Trade-In Fair	Good	Pvt-Party Good	Retail Excellent
B2600i PICKUP—4-Cyl.—Truck Equipment Schedule T2							
Short Bed		UF414	9108	450	650	1150	1950
Cab Plus		UF314	10358	825	1175	1850	2950
SE-5 Sport Pkg				100	100	135	135
LE-5 Luxury Pkg				100	100	135	135
4WD		4,6		500	500	665	665

1992 MAZDA — (4ForJM)(2or3)(LV521)-N-#

Body	Type	VIN	List	Trade-In Fair	Good	Pvt-Party Good	Retail Excellent
MPV—4-Cyl.—Truck Equipment Schedule T1							
Minivan		LV521	17844	675	975	1600	2675
V6 3.0 Liter		2		225	225	300	300
MPV 4WD—V6—Truck Equipment Schedule T1							
Minivan		LV523	21394	1025	1450	2350	3675
NAVAJO 4WD—V6—Truck Equipment Schedule T1							
DX Sport Utility 2D		CU44X	18680	1075	1500	2525	3975
LX Sport Utility 2D		CU44X	19785	1225	1675	2725	4225
2WD		2		(375)	(375)	(500)	(500)
B2200 PICKUP—4-Cyl.—Truck Equipment Schedule T2							
Short Bed		UF113	8845	400	600	1100	1875
Long Bed		UF213	9560	475	675	1225	2075
Cab Plus		UF313	10345	800	1150	1875	3050
SE-5 Pkg				100	100	135	135
LE-5 Pkg				100	100	135	135
B2600i PICKUP—4-Cyl.—Truck Equipment Schedule T2							
Short Bed		UF114	9470	500	725	1250	2150
Cab Plus		UF314	10695	900	1275	2075	3350
SE-5 Pkg				100	100	135	135
LE-5 Pkg				100	100	135	135
4WD		4,6		550	550	735	735

1993 MAZDA — (JMor4F)(2or3)(LV521)-P

Body	Type	VIN	List	Trade-In Fair	Good	Pvt-Party Good	Retail Excellent
MPV—4-Cyl.—Truck Equipment Schedule T1							
Minivan		LV521	19255	750	1050	1800	2950
Air Bag				0	0	0	0
V6 3.0 Liter		2		275	275	365	365
MPV 4WD—V6—Truck Equipment Schedule T1							
Minivan		LV523	22960	1200	1650	2750	4300
Air Bag				0	0	0	0
NAVAJO 4WD—V6—Truck Equipment Schedule T1							
DX Sport Utility 2D		CU44X	20700	1075	1525	2600	4100
LX Sport Utility 2D		CU44X	22470	1225	1725	2825	4400
2WD		2		(400)	(400)	(535)	(535)
B2200 PICKUP—4-Cyl.—Truck Equipment Schedule T2							
Short Bed		UF113	9275	425	625	1150	2000
Long Bed		UF213	9990	525	750	1300	2250
Cab Plus		UF313	10935	875	1225	2025	3300
SE-5 Sport Pkg				125	125	165	165
LE-5 Luxury Pkg				125	125	165	165
B2600i PICKUP—4-Cyl.—Truck Equipment Schedule T2							
Cab Plus		UF314	11785	1000	1400	2300	3650
SE-5 Pkg				125	125	165	165
LE-5 Pkg				125	125	165	165
4WD		4,6		675	675	900	900
B2600i PICKUP 4WD—4-Cyl.—Truck Equipment Schedule T2							
Short Bed		UF114	12235	950	1325	2200	3525
SE-5 Sport Pkg				125	125	165	165
LE-5 Luxury Pkg				125	125	165	165

1994 MAZDA — (JMor4F)(2or3)-(V521)-R

Body	Type	VIN	List	Trade-In Fair	Good	Pvt-Party Good	Retail Excellent
MPV—4-Cyl.—Truck Equipment Schedule T1							
Minivan		V521	20900	825	1175	2000	3300
V6 3.0 Liter		U		325	325	435	435
MPV 4WD—V6—Truck Equipment Schedule T1							
Minivan		V523	24700	1400	1900	3050	4700
NAVAJO 4WD—V6—Truck Equipment Schedule T1							
DX Sport Utility 2D		U44X	20350	1125	1575	2725	4325
LX Sport Utility 2D		U44X	23260	1350	1850	3000	4650
2WD		2		(425)	(425)	(565)	(565)
B2300 PICKUP—4-Cyl.—Truck Equipment Schedule T2							
Short Bed		R12A	10025	625	900	1550	2625
Cab Plus		R16A	12480	1000	1425	2425	3900
SE Short Bed		R12A	11670	725	1050	1750	2875

1994 MAZDA

Body	Type	VIN	List	Trade-In Fair	Good	Pvt-Party Good	Retail Excellent
B3000 PICKUP—V6—Truck Equipment Schedule T2							
SE Short Bed		R12U	12140	850	1200	2025	3275
SE Long Bed		R21U	12785	875	1225	2050	3350
Cab Plus		R16U	12950	1175	1625	2700	4225
SE Cab Plus		R16U	13630	1275	1775	2850	4425
B3000 PICKUP 4WD—V6—Truck Equipment Schedule T2							
Short Bed		R13U	14895	1100	1550	2600	4100
Cab Plus		R17U	15955	1575	2075	3225	4825
B4000 PICKUP—V6—Truck Equipment Schedule T2							
SE Long Bed		R21X	12960	875	1225	2050	3350
LE Cab Plus		R16X	15815	1100	1550	2600	4100
B4000 PICKUP 4WD—V6—Truck Equipment Schedule T2							
SE Short Bed		R13X	16885	1125	1575	2650	4150
SE Cab Plus		R17X	17755	1575	2075	3225	4825
LE Cab Plus		R17X	19960	1800	2325	3500	5175

1995 MAZDA — (JM3or4F4)—(V522)–S–#

Body	Type	VIN	List	Trade-In Fair	Good	Pvt-Party Good	Retail Excellent
MPV—V6—Truck Equipment Schedule T1							
L Minivan		V522	22505	925	1300	2375	3900
LX Minivan		V522	23155	1050	1450	2575	4125
LXE Minivan		V522	24845	1225	1700	2850	4475
4WD		3		425	425	565	565
B2300 PICKUP—4-Cyl.—Truck Equipment Schedule T2							
Short Bed		R12A	10765	750	1050	1800	2950
Long Bed		R12A	11155	775	1100	1850	3050
Cab Plus		R16A	13485	1150	1600	2700	4225
SE Short Bed		R12A	12485	850	1200	2025	3275
SE Cab Plus		R16A	14185	1375	1900	3000	4575
4WD		3		900	900	1200	1200
B3000 PICKUP—V6—Truck Equipment Schedule T2							
SE Short Bed		R12U	13155	975	1375	2300	3675
SE Cab Plus		R16U	14855	1525	2025	3175	4775
B3000 PICKUP 4WD—V6—Truck Equipment Schedule T2							
Cab Plus		R17U	17715	1875	2400	3600	5250
B4000 PICKUP—V6—Truck Equipment Schedule T2							
SE Cab Plus		R16X	15400	1225	1725	2825	4375
LE Cab Plus		R16X	16925	1300	1800	2875	4450
B4000 PICKUP 4WD—V6—Truck Equipment Schedule T2							
SE Short Bed		R13X	18360	1350	1850	2925	4500
SE Cab Plus		R17X	19485	1850	2375	3575	5250
LE Cab Plus		R17X	20975	2100	2675	3875	5625

1996 MAZDA — (JM3or4F4)(LV522)–T–#

Body	Type	VIN	List	Trade-In Fair	Good	Pvt-Party Good	Retail Excellent
MPV—V6—Truck Equipment Schedule T1							
DX Minivan		LV522	22845	1550	2050	3300	5050
LX Minivan		LV522	22735	1725	2250	3525	5275
ES Minivan		LV522	25135	1975	2525	3825	5675
4WD		3		475	475	635	635
B2300 PICKUP—4-Cyl.—Truck Equipment Schedule T2							
Short Bed		R12A	10600	850	1200	2050	3400
Long Bed		R12A	10985	875	1225	2125	3475
Cab Plus		R16A	13720	1325	1825	2950	4550
SE Short Bed		R12A	12545	975	1350	2400	3900
SE Cab Plus		R16A	14840	1625	2125	3300	4975
4WD		3,7		1000	1000	1335	1335
B3000 PICKUP—V6—Truck Equipment Schedule T2							
SE Cab Plus		R16U	15675	1800	2325	3525	5225
B3000 PICKUP 4WD—V6—Truck Equipment Schedule T2							
Cab Plus		R17U	18170	2150	2750	3975	5750
B4000 PICKUP—V6—Truck Equipment Schedule T2							
LE Cab Plus		R16X	17845	1525	2025	3175	4825
B4000 PICKUP 4WD—V6—Truck Equipment Schedule T2							
SE Short Bed		R13X	18810	1575	2075	3250	4925
SE Cab Plus		R17X	20065	2125	2700	3925	5700
LE Cab Plus		R17X	22140	2425	3000	4300	6125

1997 MAZDA — (JM3or4F4)(LV522)–V–#

Body	Type	VIN	List	Trade-In Fair	Good	Pvt-Party Good	Retail Excellent
MPV—V6—Truck Equipment Schedule T1							
LX Minivan		LV522	24370	2025	2575	3925	5825
ES Minivan		LV522	28270	2300	2875	4300	6225
4WD		3		500	500	665	665

TRUCKS & VANS

TRUCKS & VANS

Body	Type	VIN	List	Trade-In Fair	Good	Pvt-Party Good	Retail Excellent
B2300 PICKUP—4-Cyl.—Truck Equipment Schedule T2							
Short Bed		R12A	11060	1000	1425	2500	4050
SE Short Bed		R12A	13225	1125	1575	2725	4300
SE Cab Plus		R16A	15480	1950	2475	3700	5450
B4000 PICKUP—V6—Truck Equipment Schedule T2							
SE Cab Plus		R16X	16225	2250	2825	4100	5900
B4000 PICKUP 4WD—V6—Truck Equipment Schedule T2							
Short Bed		R13X	16775	1900	2425	3650	5400
Cab Plus		R17X	18660	2425	3025	4325	6150
SE Cab Plus		R17X	20275	2475	3075	4375	6225

1998 MAZDA — (JM3or4F4)(LV522)-W-#

Body	Type	VIN	List	Trade-In Fair	Good	Pvt-Party Good	Retail Excellent
MPV—V6—Truck Equipment Schedule T1							
LX Minivan		LV522	24370	2400	2975	4450	6450
ES Minivan		LV522	28270	2725	3325	4800	6875
4WD		3		525	525	700	700
B2500 PICKUP—4-Cyl.—Truck Equipment Schedule T2							
SX Short Bed		R12C	11575	1300	1800	2975	4650
SE Short Bed		R12C	13215	1475	1975	3200	4900
SE Cab Plus		R16C	15355	2000	2550	3825	5650
SE Cab Plus 4D		R16C	15950	2575	3175	4500	6425
B3000 PICKUP—V6—Truck Equipment Schedule T2							
SE Cab Plus 2D		R16U	16305	2375	2950	4300	6150
SE Cab Plus 4D		R14U	16900	2625	3250	4575	6500
B3000 PICKUP 4WD—V6—Truck Equipment Schedule T2							
SX Short Bed		R13U	15925	1975	2550	3800	5600
SE Short Bed		R13U	17455	2225	2825	4100	5975
SE Cab Plus 2D		R17U	18940	3000	3675	5075	7050
SE Cab Plus 4D		R15U	19535	3325	4025	5450	7500
B4000 PICKUP—V6—Truck Equipment Schedule T2							
SE Cab Plus 2D		R16X	17155	2725	3325	4675	6625
SE Cab Plus 4D		R14X	17750	2925	3600	4975	6925
B4000 PICKUP 4WD—V6—Truck Equipment Schedule T2							
SE Cab Plus 2D		R17X	19840	2950	3625	5000	6950
SE Cab Plus 4D		R15X	20435	3425	4125	5550	7650

1999 MAZDA — (JM3or4F4)—(R12C)-X-#

Body	Type	VIN	List	Trade-In Fair	Good	Pvt-Party Good	Retail Excellent
B2500 PICKUP—4-Cyl.—Truck Equipment Schedule T2							
SX Short Bed		R12C	11795	1675	2175	3425	5150
SE Short Bed		R12C	14170	1850	2375	3650	5375
Troy Lee Short Bed		R12C	15130	2050	2625	3875	5675
SE Cab Plus 2D		R16C	16225	2425	3025	4350	6175
SE Cab Plus 4D		R16C	16885	3000	3675	5025	6975
B3000 PICKUP—V6—Truck Equipment Schedule T2							
SE Cab Plus 2D		R16U	16800	2825	3450	4775	6700
SE Cab Plus 4D		R16U	17460	3075	3725	5100	7050
Troy Lee Cab Plus 4D		R16U	18955	3375	4075	5450	7475
B3000 PICKUP 4WD—V6—Truck Equipment Schedule T2							
SE Short Bed		R13U	18060	2650	3275	4575	6475
SE Cab Plus 2D		R17U	19715	3525	4225	5625	7675
SE Cab Plus 4D		R17U	20375	3875	4625	6075	8150
B4000 PICKUP—V6—Truck Equipment Schedule T2							
SE Short Bed		R12X	18090	2275	2825	4125	5975
SE Cab Plus 2D		R16X	20145	3175	3850	5250	7200
SE Cab Plus 4D		R16X	20805	3450	4150	5525	7550
B4000 PICKUP 4WD—V6—Truck Equipment Schedule T2							
SE Cab Plus 2D		R17X	22140	3475	4200	5575	7625
SE Cab Plus 4D		R17X	22800	3975	4725	6175	8300
Troy Lee Cab Plus 4D		R17X	23995	4325	5125	6575	8750

2000 MAZDA-(JM3,4F2or4F4)-(LW28)-Y-

Body	Type	VIN	List	Trade-In Fair	Good	Pvt-Party Good	Retail Excellent
MPV—V6—Truck Equipment Schedule T1							
DX Minivan 4D		LW28	20475	4075	4850	6500	8850
LX Minivan 4D		LW28	22530	4300	5100	6750	9150
ES Minivan 4D		LW28	26030	4675	5525	7225	9675
B2500 PICKUP—4-Cyl.—Truck Equipment Schedule T2							
SX Short Bed		R12C	12005	2125	2725	4025	5900
SE Short Bed		R12C	14315	2400	2975	4325	6225
SE Cab Plus 2D		R16C	16505	3075	3725	5150	7150
B3000 PICKUP—V6—Truck Equipment Schedule T2							
SX Short Bed		R12V	12400	2575	3175	4525	6450
SE Short Bed		R12V	14710	2725	3325	4700	6650

2000 MAZDA

Body	Type	VIN	List	Trade-In Fair	Good	Pvt-Party Good	Retail Excellent
SE Cab Plus 2D		R16V	16975	3475	4175	5600	7675
SE Cab Plus 4D		R16V	17715	3800	4550	6025	8125
Troy Lee Cab Plus 4D		R16V	19120	4100	4875	6350	8525
B3000 PICKUP 4WD—V6—Truck Equipment Schedule T2							
SE Short Bed		R13V	18235	3275	3950	5350	7400
SE Cab Plus 4D		R17V	20720	4675	5525	7050	9300
B4000 PICKUP—V6—Truck Equipment Schedule T2							
SE Cab Plus 4D		R16X	21140	4200	4975	6450	8625
B4000 PICKUP 4WD—V6—Truck Equipment Schedule T2							
SE Cab Plus 4D		R17X	23050	4800	5650	7200	9475
Troy Lee Cab Plus 4D		R17X	26000	5175	6050	7625	9950

2001 MAZDA—(JM3,4F2or4F4)—(U06B)-1-

Body	Type	VIN	List	Trade-In Fair	Good	Pvt-Party Good	Retail Excellent
TRIBUTE 4WD—V6—Truck Equipment Schedule T1							
DX Sport Utility 4D		U06B	21055	5775	6725	8275	10600
LX Sport Utility 4D		U08B	22535	6050	7000	8575	10950
ES Sport Utility 4D		U081	23540	6325	7350	8925	11350
2WD				(725)	(725)	(965)	(965)
4-Cyl. 2.0 Liter		B		(725)	(725)	(965)	(965)
MPV—V6—Truck Equipment Schedule T1							
DX Minivan 4D		LW28	21155	4800	5625	7475	10100
LX Minivan 4D		LW28	23280	5025	5900	7725	10400
ES Minivan 4D		LW28	26760	5475	6400	8300	11000
B2300 PICKUP—4-Cyl.—Truck Equipment Schedule T2							
SX Short Bed		R12D	12930	2825	3450	4875	6900
SE Short Bed		R12D	15130	3100	3750	5225	7300
B2500 PICKUP—4-Cyl.—Truck Equipment Schedule T2							
SX Short Bed		R12C	12785	2725	3375	4775	6800
SE Short Bed		R12C	14985	3000	3675	5125	7175
B3000 PICKUP—V6—Truck Equipment Schedule T2							
SE Short Bed		R12V	15280	3350	4050	5500	7625
Dual Sport Short Bed		R12V	15315	3425	4125	5600	7700
SE Cab Plus 2D		R16V	17515	4225	5000	6525	8750
SE Cab Plus 4D		R16V	18180	4650	5475	7025	9325
Dual Sport Cab + 2D		R16V	17735	4675	5525	7075	9375
B3000 PICKUP 4WD—V6—Truck Equipment Schedule T2							
SE Short Bed		R13V	18810	4000	4750	6275	8475
SE Cab Plus 2D		R13V	20480	5100	5975	7550	9900
B4000 PICKUP—V6—Truck Equipment Schedule T2							
Dual Sport Cab + 4D		R17X	19935	5025	5900	7500	9850
B4000 PICKUP 4WD—V6—Truck Equipment Schedule T2							
Dual Sport Cab + 4D		R17X	22780	5750	6700	8350	10750

2002 MAZDA—(JM3,4F2or4F4)—(U06B)-2

Body	Type	VIN	List	Trade-In Fair	Good	Pvt-Party Good	Retail Excellent
TRIBUTE 4WD—V6—Truck Equipment Schedule T1							
DX Sport Utility 4D		U06B	22575	6975	8050	9700	12250
LX Sport Utility 4D		U08B	23225	7275	8375	10100	12650
ES Sport Utility 4D		U081	24455	7625	8750	10500	13100
2WD				(800)	(800)	(1065)	(1065)
4-Cyl. 2.0 Liter		B		(825)	(825)	(1100)	(1100)
MPV—V6—Truck Equipment Schedule T1							
LX Minivan 4D		LW28	22770	6000	6950	9000	11950
ES Minivan 4D		LW28	27712	6500	7525	9575	12550
B2300 PICKUP—4-Cyl.—Truck Equipment Schedule T2							
Short Bed		R12D	13240	3525	4225	5775	7950
SE Cab Plus		R16D		4475	5275	6875	9225
B3000 PICKUP—V6—Truck Equipment Schedule T2							
Dual Sport Short Bed		R12V	15870	4225	5000	6575	8850
Dual Sport Cab + 2D		R16V	18290	5600	6525	8200	10650
B3000 PICKUP 4WD—V6—Truck Equipment Schedule T2							
Cab Plus 2D		R13V	20775	6050	7000	8725	11250
B4000 PICKUP—V6—Truck Equipment Schedule T2							
Dual Sport Cab + 4D		R17X	20085	6000	6950	8625	11150
B4000 PICKUP 4WD—V6—Truck Equipment Schedule T2							
Cab Plus 4D		R17X	22830	6825	7875	9600	12200

2003 MAZDA—(JM3,4F2or4F4)—(Z92B)-3

Body	Type	VIN	List	Trade-In Fair	Good	Pvt-Party Good	Retail Excellent
TRIBUTE 4WD—4-Cyl.—Truck Equipment Schedule T1							
DX Sport Utility 4D		Z92B	20440	7225	8350	10050	12600
2WD		0		(875)	(875)	(1165)	(1165)
Manual Trans		0		0	0	0	0

TRUCKS & VANS

Body Type	VIN	List	Trade-In Fair	Trade-In Good	Pvt-Party Good	Retail Excellent

TRUBUTE 4WD—V6—Truck Equipment Schedule T1

Body Type	VIN	List	Fair	Good	Good	Excellent
LX Sport Utility 4D	Z941	22125	**8825**	**10100**	**11850**	**14600**
ES Sport Utility 4D	Z961	24885	**9150**	**10425**	**12200**	**15050**
2WD	0		**(875)**	**(875)**	**(1165)**	**(1165)**

MPV—V6—Truck Equipment Schedule T1

LX S-V Minivan 4D	LW28A	21895	**6600**	**7625**	**9850**	**13000**
LX Minivan 4D	LW28A	23120	**7200**	**8325**	**10550**	**13800**
ES Minivan 4D	LW28A	26520	**7775**	**8925**	**11200**	**14500**

B2300 PICKUP—4-Cyl.—Truck Equipment Schedule T2

Short Bed	R12D	13740	**4375**	**5150**	**6825**	**9225**
SE Cab Plus	R16D	17960	**5400**	**6325**	**8050**	**10550**

B3000 PICKUP—V6—Truck Equipment Schedule T2

Dual Sport Short Bed	R12U	16590	**5100**	**6000**	**7675**	**10200**
Dual Sport Cab + 2D	R16V	18700	**6650**	**7675**	**9450**	**12150**
SE Cab Plus 4D	R46V	18935	**6600**	**7650**	**9425**	**12100**

B4000 PICKUP—V6—Truck Equipment Schedule T2

Dual Sport Cab + 4D	R17E	20495	**7050**	**8150**	**10000**	**12700**

B4000 PICKUP 4WD—V6—Truck Equipment Schedule T2

Cab Plus 2D	R17X	20260	**6950**	**8025**	**9850**	**12550**
SE Cab Plus 2D	R17X	21705	**7625**	**8750**	**10550**	**13400**
SE Cab Plus 4D	R17X	23240	**8025**	**9225**	**11050**	**13850**

TRIBUTE 4WD—4-Cyl.—Truck Equipment Schedule T1

DX Sport Utility 4D	Z92B	21087	**8900**	**10175**	**11850**	**14500**
2WD	0		**(950)**	**(950)**	**(1265)**	**(1265)**
Manual Trans			**0**	**0**	**0**	**0**

TRIBUTE 4WD—V6—Truck Equipment Schedule T1

LX Sport Utility 4D	Z941	23972	**10625**	**12075**	**13800**	**16700**
ES Sport Utility 4D	Z961	25562	**11000**	**12475**	**14250**	**17150**
2WD	0		**(950)**	**(950)**	**(1265)**	**(1265)**

MPV—V6—Truck Equipment Schedule T1

LX Minivan 4D	W28A	23780	**8850**	**10125**	**12500**	**15950**
ES Minivan 4D	W28A	28750	**9475**	**10825**	**13250**	**16800**

B2300 PICKUP—4-Cyl.—Truck Equipment Schedule T2

Short Bed	R12D	14840	**5400**	**6300**	**7975**	**10450**
SE Cab Plus	R16D	18980	**6575**	**7600**	**9325**	**11950**

B3000 PICKUP—V6—Truck Equipment Schedule T2

Dual Sport Short Bed	R12U	17915	**6200**	**7200**	**8925**	**11500**
Dual Sport Cab + 2D	R16V	19871	**7900**	**9075**	**10900**	**13700**
SE Cab Plus 4D	R46V	20140	**7850**	**9025**	**10850**	**13650**

B4000 PICKUP—V6—Truck Equipment Schedule T2

Dual Sport Cab + 4D	R17E	21865	**8375**	**9575**	**11450**	**14250**

B4000 PICKUP 4WD—V6—Truck Equipment Schedule T2

Cab Plus 2D	R17X	20850	**8225**	**9425**	**11300**	**14100**
SE Cab Plus 2D	R17X	22350	**8950**	**10225**	**12150**	**15050**
SE Cab Plus 4D	R17X	24090	**9400**	**10725**	**12650**	**15600**

TRIBUTE 4WD—4-Cyl.—Truck Equipment Schedule T1

i Sport Utility 4D	Z92Z	22325	**10775**	**12275**	**14000**	**16900**
2WD	0		**(1000)**	**(1000)**	**(1335)**	**(1335)**

TRIBUTE 4WD—V6—Truck Equipment Schedule T1

s Sport Utility 4D	Z941	24980	**12650**	**14300**	**16200**	**19350**
2WD	0		**(1000)**	**(1000)**	**(1335)**	**(1335)**

MPV—V6—Truck Equipment Schedule T1

LX-SV Minivan 4D	W28A	22665	**10175**	**11600**	**14200**	**18050**
LX Minivan 4D	W28A	23485	**10925**	**12375**	**15050**	**18950**
ES Minivan 4D	W28J	29050	**11550**	**13100**	**15750**	**19800**

B2300 PICKUP—4-Cyl.—Truck Equipment Schedule T2

Short Bed	R12D	15935	**6750**	**7800**	**9600**	**12250**

B3000 PICKUP—V6—Truck Equipment Schedule T2

Extended Cab 4D	R46U	19480	**9425**	**10775**	**12750**	**15800**
Dual Sport Short Bed	R12U	20120	**7650**	**8775**	**10600**	**13450**
Dual Sport Ext 4D	R46U	21870	**9475**	**10825**	**12800**	**15850**

B4000 PICKUP 4WD—V6—Truck Equipment Schedule T2

Extended Cab 4D	R47E	22220	**9800**	**11200**	**13250**	**16350**
SE Extended Cab 4D	R47E	26765	**11100**	**12600**	**14750**	**18050**

Body	Type	VIN	List	Trade-In Fair	Trade-In Good	Pvt-Party Good	Retail Excellent

MERCEDES-BENZ

1998 MERCEDES-BENZ — 4JG(AB54E)-W-#

ML-CLASS 4WD—V6—Truck Equipment Schedule T3

Body	Type	VIN	List	Fair	Good	Good	Excellent
ML320 Sport Util 4D		AB54E	38590	7725	8875	11050	14250
Third Seat				300	300	400	400

1999 MERCEDES-BENZ — 4JG(AB54E)-X-#

ML-CLASS 4WD—V6—Truck Equipment Schedule T3

Body	Type	VIN	List	Fair	Good	Good	Excellent
ML320 Sport Util 4D		AB54E	39590	9200	10475	12600	15800
Third Seat				300	300	400	400

ML-CLASS 4WD—V8—Truck Equipment Schedule T3

| ML430 Sport Util 4D | | AB72E | 44345 | 10625 | 12075 | 14300 | 17750 |
| Third Seat | | | | 300 | 300 | 400 | 400 |

2000 MERCEDES-BENZ — 4JG(AB54E)-Y-#

ML-CLASS 4WD—V6—Truck Equipment Schedule T3

Body	Type	VIN	List	Fair	Good	Good	Excellent
ML320 Sport Util 4D		AB54E	36895	11050	12550	14900	18400
Third Seat				350	350	465	465

ML-CLASS 4WD—V8—Truck Equipment Schedule T3

ML430 Sport Util 4D		AB72E	44345	12700	14350	16800	20600
ML55 Sport Util 4D		AB74E	65495	20850	23375	26500	31500
Third Seat				350	350	465	465

2001 MERCEDES-BENZ — 4JG(AB54E)-1-#

ML-CLASS 4WD—V6—Truck Equipment Schedule T3

Body	Type	VIN	List	Fair	Good	Good	Excellent
ML320 Sport Util 4D		AB54E	38045	13150	14900	17300	21100
Sport Pkg				275	275	365	365
Third Seat				400	400	535	535
designo Edition				475	475	635	635

ML-CLASS 4WD—V8—Truck Equipment Schedule T3

ML430 Sport Util 4D		AB72E	44845	14975	16875	19500	23500
ML55 Sport Util 4D		AB74E	66545	24150	26975	30300	35600
Sport Pkg				275	275	365	365
Third Seat				400	400	535	535
designo Edition				475	475	635	635

2002 MERCEDES-BENZ — WDCor4JG(AB54E)-2-#

ML-CLASS 4WD—V6—Truck Equipment Schedule T3

Body	Type	VIN	List	Fair	Good	Good	Excellent
ML320 Sport Util 4D		AB54E	36945	15475	17400	20000	24100
designo Edition				600	600	800	800
Third Seat				450	450	600	600
Sport Pkg				300	300	400	400

ML-CLASS 4WD—V8—Truck Equipment Schedule T3

ML500 Sport Util 4D		AB75E	45595	18725	21050	23800	28300
ML55 Sport Util 4D		AB74E	66545	27650	30850	34200	39900
Sport Pkg				300	300	400	400
Third Seat				450	450	600	600
designo Edition				600	600	800	800

G-CLASS AWD—V8—Truck Equipment Schedule T3

| G500 Sport Util 4D | | YR49E | 73145 | 34050 | 37925 | 42300 | 49400 |
| designo Edition | | | | 600 | 600 | 800 | 800 |

2003 MERCEDES-BENZ — WDCor4JG(AB54E)-3-#

ML-CLASS 4WD—V6—Truck Equipment Schedule T3

Body	Type	VIN	List	Fair	Good	Good	Excellent
ML320 Sport Util 4D		AB54E	40315	18050	20275	23000	27500
ML350 Sport Util 4D		AB57E	40665	18725	21050	23800	28300
Sport Pkg				325	325	435	435
Inspiration Edition				725	725	965	965
designo Edition				725	725	965	965
Third Seat				500	500	665	665

ML-CLASS 4WD—V8—Truck Equipment Schedule T3

ML500 Sport Util 4D		AB75E	46015	21625	24250	27200	32000
ML55 Sport Util 4D		AB74E	66565	31425	35025	38400	44400
Sport Pkg				325	325	435	435
Inspiration Edition				725	725	965	965
designo Edition				725	725	965	965
Third Seat				500	500	665	665

TRUCKS & VANS

Body	Type	VIN	List	Trade-In Fair	Good	Pvt-Party Good	Retail Excellent
G-CLASS AWD—V8—Truck Equipment Schedule T3							
G500 Sport Utility 4D		YR49	74265	38325	42675	46900	54400
G55 Sport Utility 4D		YR46	90565	45675	50725	55500	63800
designo Edition				725	725	965	965

2004 MERCEDES-BENZ — WDCor4JG(AB57E)-4-#

ML-CLASS 4WD—V6—Truck Equipment Schedule T3							
ML350 Sport Utl 4D		AB57E	39720	21725	24350	27300	32200
Inspiration Edition				750	750	1000	1000
designo Edition				825	825	1100	1100
Third Seat				550	550	735	735
ML-CLASS 4WD—V8—Truck Equipment Schedule T3							
ML500 Sport Utl 4D		AB75E	46470	24825	27750	30800	36000
Inspiration Edition				750	750	1000	1000
designo Edition				825	825	1100	1100
Third Seat				550	550	735	735
G-CLASS AWD—V8—Truck Equipment Schedule T3							
G500 Sport Utility 4D		YR49	76870	42875	47725	52200	59900
G55 Sport Utility 4D		YR46	93420	50925	56550	61300	69900
designo Edition				825	825	1100	1100

2005 MERCEDES-BENZ — WDCor4JG(AB57E)-5-#

ML-CLASS 4WD—V6—Truck Equipment Schedule T3							
ML350 Sport Utl 4D		AB57E	40370	24825	27850	30800	36100
Special Edition				775	775	1035	1035
designo Edition				925	925	1235	1235
Third Seat				575	575	765	765
ML-CLASS 4WD—V8—Truck Equipment Schedule T3							
ML500 Sport Utl 4D		AB75E	47120	28225	31525	34600	40200
Special Edition				775	775	1035	1035
designo Edition				925	925	1235	1235
Third Seat				575	575	765	765
G-CLASS AWD—V8—Truck Equipment Schedule T3							
G500 Sport Util 4D		YR49E	78420				
G500 Grand Ed Util		YR49C					
designo Edition							
G-CLASS AWD—V8 Supercharged—Truck Equipment Sch T3							
G55 Sport Utility 4D		YR46E	100620				
G55 Grand Ed Util		YR46C					

MERCURY

1993 MERCURY — 4M2-(V11W)-P-#

VILLAGER—V6—Truck Equipment Schedule T1							
GS Minivan		V11W	18851	1075	1525	2600	4100
LS Minivan		V11W	22683	1425	1925	3050	4675
5 Passenger				(250)	(250)	(335)	(335)

1994 MERCURY — 4M2-(V11W)-R-#

VILLAGER—V6—Truck Equipment Schedule T1							
GS Minivan		V11W	19292	1225	1700	2825	4450
LS Minivan		V11W	22975	1650	2150	3375	5075
Nautica Minivan		V11W	26218	1900	2425	3675	5450
5 Passenger				(275)	(275)	(365)	(365)

1995 MERCURY — 4M2-(V11W)-S-#

VILLAGER—V6—Truck Equipment Schedule T1							
GS Minivan		V11W	21090	1450	1950	3150	4825
LS Minivan		V11W	24650	1925	2450	3700	5500
Nautica Minivan		V11W	27535	2175	2775	4075	5925
5 Passenger				(300)	(300)	(400)	(400)

1996 MERCURY — 4M2-(V11W)-T-#

VILLAGER—V6—Truck Equipment Schedule T1							
GS Minivan		V11W	21745	1700	2225	3500	5275
LS Minivan		V11W	25595	2200	2800	4125	6025
Nautica Minivan		V11W	28375	2500	3100	4475	6450
5 Passenger				(325)	(325)	(435)	(435)

Body	Type	VIN	List	Trade-In Fair	Good	Pvt-Party Good	Retail Excellent

1997 MERCURY — 4M(2or4)–(U55P)–V–#

MOUNTAINEER AWD—V8—Truck Equipment Schedule T1

Sport Utility 4D		U55P	29995	3175	3850	5425	7650
2WD		2		(500)	(500)	(665)	(665)

VILLAGER—V6—Truck Equipment Schedule T1

GS Minivan		V111	22395	2025	2575	3925	5825
LS Minivan		V111	27595	2575	3175	4575	6600
Nautica Minivan		V111	28995	2850	3525	4975	7050
5 Passenger				(350)	(350)	(465)	(465)

1998 MERCURY — 4M(2or4)–(U55P)–W–#

MOUNTAINEER AWD—V8—Truck Equipment Schedule T1

Sport Utility 4D		U55P	29785	3800	4550	6225	8575
2WD		2		(525)	(525)	(700)	(700)
4WD		4		0	0	0	0
V6 4.0 Liter		E		(275)	(275)	(365)	(365)

VILLAGER—V6—Truck Equipment Schedule T1

GS Minivan		V111	22885	2400	2975	4450	6450
LS Minivan		V111	27485	2975	3650	5150	7275
Nautica Minivan		V111	28885	3325	4000	5550	7725
5 Passenger				(375)	(375)	(500)	(500)

1999 MERCURY — 4M2–(U55P)–X–#

MOUNTAINEER AWD—V8—Truck Equipment Schedule T1

Sport Utility 4D		U55P	30015	4575	5400	6975	9275
2WD		2		(575)	(575)	(765)	(765)
4WD		4		0	0	0	0
V6 4.0 Liter		E		(300)	(300)	(400)	(400)

VILLAGER—V6—Truck Equipment Schedule T1

Minivan 4D		V11T	22995	3250	3925	5250	7125
Sport Minivan 4D		V11T	25595	4225	5025	6400	8475
Estate Minivan 4D		V11T	25595	4275	5075	6450	8500

2000 MERCURY — 4M2–(U86P)–Y–#

MOUNTAINEER AWD—V8—Truck Equipment Schedule T1

Sport Utility 4D		U86P	30360	5500	6425	8075	10500
Premier				825	825	1100	1100
2WD		6		(650)	(650)	(865)	(865)
4WD		7		0	0	0	0
V6 4.0 Liter		E		(350)	(350)	(465)	(465)

VILLAGER—V6—Truck Equipment Schedule T1

Minivan 4D		V11T	22995	3950	4700	6075	8075
Sport Minivan 4D		V12T	25995	5100	5975	7400	9575
Estate Minivan 4D		V14T	27695	5200	6075	7550	9750

2001 MERCURY — 4M2–(U86P)–1–#

MOUNTAINEER AWD—V8—Truck Equipment Schedule T1

Sport Utility 4D		U86P	30695	6650	7675	9450	12100
Premier				925	925	1235	1235
2WD		6		(725)	(725)	(965)	(965)
4WD		7		0	0	0	0
V6 4.0 Liter		E		(400)	(400)	(535)	(535)

VILLAGER—V6—Truck Equipment Schedule T1

Minivan 4D		V11T	23140	4800	5650	7100	9275
Sport Minivan 4D		V12T	26365	6075	7050	8600	10950
Estate Minivan 4D		V14T	27840	6175	7175	8725	11100

2002 MERCURY — 4M2–(U86W)–2–#

MOUNTAINEER AWD—V8—Truck Equipment Schedule T1

Sport Utility 4D		U86W	31310	9025	10325	12400	15600
Premier				1025	1025	1365	1365
w/o Third Seat				(800)	(800)	(1065)	(1065)
2WD		6		(800)	(800)	(1065)	(1065)
V6 4.0 Liter		E		(450)	(450)	(600)	(600)

VILLAGER—V6—Truck Equipment Schedule T1

Minivan 4D		V11T	19995	5850	6825	8375	10700
Sport Minivan 4D		V12T	24995	7275	8375	10050	12550
Estate Minivan 4D		V14T	26995	7375	8500	10150	12700

TRUCKS & VANS

Body Type	VIN	List	Trade-In Fair	Good	Pvt-Party Good	Retail Excellent

2003 MERCURY — 4M2–(U86W)-3-#

MOUNTAINEER AWD—V8—Truck Equipment Schedule T1
Sport Utility 4D	U86W	32605	10675	12125	14350	17750
Premier			1125	1125	1500	1500
w/o Third Seat			(800)	(800)	(1065)	(1065)
2WD	6		(875)	(875)	(1165)	(1165)
V6 4.0L Flex Fuel	K		(500)	(500)	(665)	(665)

2004 MERCURY — (2MRor4M2)–(A202)-4-#

MONTEREY—V6—Truck Equipment Schedule T1
Minivan	A202	29995	7925	9125	11000	13900
Premier			725	725	965	965

MOUNTAINEER AWD—V8—Truck Equipment Schedule T1
Sport Utility 4D	U86W	32855	12650	14300	16600	20200
Premier			1225	1225	1635	1635
w/o Third Seat			(800)	(800)	(1065)	(1065)
2WD	6		(950)	(950)	(1265)	(1265)
V6 4.0L Flex Fuel	6		(550)	(550)	(735)	(735)

2005 MERCURY — (2MRor4M2)–(A222)-5

MONTEREY—V6—Truck Equipment Schedule T1
Minivan	A222	29695	10000	11350	13550	16800
Premier			775	775	1035	1035

MARINER 4WD—V6—Truck Equipment Schedule T1
Sport Utility 4D	U571	25245	13825	15625	17550	20900
2WD	6		(1000)	(1000)	(1335)	(1335)
4-Cyl. 2.3 Liter	Z		(950)	(950)	(1265)	(1265)

MOUNTAINEER AWD—V8—Truck Equipment Schedule T1
Sport Utility 4D	U86W	33505	14850	16775	19200	23100
Premier			1325	1325	1765	1765
w/o Third Seat			(800)	(800)	(1065)	(1065)
2WD	6		(1000)	(1000)	(1335)	(1335)
V6 4.0 Liter	E,K		(575)	(575)	(765)	(765)

MITSUBISHI

1991 MITSUBISHI–JA(4or7)–(J31S)-M-#

MONTERO 4WD—V6—Truck Equipment Schedule T1
Sport Utility 4D	J31S	17342	1500	2000	3100	4700
RS Sport Utility 4D	J31S	17822	1500	2000	3125	4725
LS Sport Utility 4D	J51S	20652	1525	2025	3175	4800

MIGHTY MAX PICKUP—4-Cyl.—Truck Equipment Schedule T2
Short Bed	L24W	8329	350	475	900	1575
1 Ton Long Bed	L29W	9322	400	575	1050	1775
Macro Cab Short Bed	L25W	9559	725	1050	1650	2725

MIGHTY MAX PICKUP 4WD—V6—Truck Equipment Sch T2
Short Bed	M24S	12339	550	800	1350	2275

1992 MITSUBISHI–JA(4or7)–(K31S)-N-#

MONTERO 4WD—V6—Truck Equipment Schedule T1
Sport Utility 4D	K31S	19967	2150	2750	3950	5725
RS Sport Utility 4D	K41S	21627	2150	2750	3975	5750
LS Sport Utility 4D	K41S	24247	2225	2825	4050	5850
SR Sport Utility 4D	K51S	23657	2250	2825	4075	5875

MIGHTY MAX PICKUP—4-Cyl.—Truck Equipment Schedule T2
Short Bed	L24W	8744	400	525	1000	1750
1 Ton Long Bed	L29W	10094	450	650	1175	2000
Macro Cab Short Bed	L25W	10044	825	1175	1900	3050

MIGHTY MAX PICKUP 4WD—V6—Truck Equipment Sch T2
Short Bed	M24S	12954	625	900	1525	2550

1993 MITSUBISHI–JA(4or7)–(R31H)-P-#

MONTERO 4WD—V6—Truck Equipment Schedule T1
Sport Utility 4D	R31H	21037	2225	2825	4075	5875
RS Sport Utility 4D	R41H	22887	2275	2825	4125	5975
LS Sport Utility 4D	R41H	25928	2350	2925	4250	6075
SR Sport Utility 4D	R51H	26528	2400	2975	4300	6150

MIGHTY MAX PICKUP—4-Cyl.—Truck Equipment Schedule T2
Short Bed	S21G	9253	400	575	1075	1875

Body Type	VIN	List	Trade-In Fair	Trade-In Good	Pvt-Party Good	Retail Excellent
Macro Cab Short Bed	S23G	10623	875	1225	2025	3225
MIGHTY MAX PICKUP 4WD—V6—Truck Equipment Sch T2						
Short Bed	T21H	13693	700	1000	1650	2775

1994 MITSUBISHI–JA(4or7)–(R41H)–R–#

Body Type	VIN	List	Trade-In Fair	Trade-In Good	Pvt-Party Good	Retail Excellent
MONTERO 4WD—V6—Truck Equipment Schedule T1						
LS Sport Utility 4D	R41H	26024	2525	3125	4475	6425
SR Sport Utility 4D	R51M	31920	3425	4125	5625	7775
MIGHTY MAX PICKUP—4-Cyl.—Truck Equipment Schedule T2						
Short Bed	S21G	10170	450	625	1175	2025
Macro Cab Short Bed	S23G	11640	925	1300	2150	3450
MIGHTY MAX PICKUP 4WD—V6—Truck Equipment Sch T2						
Short Bed	T21H	14639	775	1100	1825	3000

1995 MITSUBISHI–JA(4or7)–(R41H)–S–#

Body Type	VIN	List	Trade-In Fair	Trade-In Good	Pvt-Party Good	Retail Excellent
MONTERO 4WD—V6—Truck Equipment Schedule T1						
LS Sport Utility 4D	R41H	28920	2750	3375	4800	6850
SR Sport Utility 4D	R51M	35070	3750	4475	6075	8325
MIGHTY MAX PICKUP—4-Cyl.—Truck Equipment Schedule T2						
Short Bed	S21G	10779	525	750	1325	2275

1996 MITSUBISHI — JA4–(R41H)–T–#

Body Type	VIN	List	Trade-In Fair	Trade-In Good	Pvt-Party Good	Retail Excellent
MONTERO 4WD—V6—Truck Equipment Schedule T1						
LS Sport Utility 4D	R41H	31458	3075	3725	5250	7400
SR Sport Utility 4D	R51M	38200	4200	4975	6625	9000
MIGHTY MAX PICKUP—4-Cyl.—Truck Equipment Schedule T2						
Short Bed	S21G	11590	600	850	1525	2625

1997 MITSUBISHI — JA4–(S21G)–V–#

Body Type	VIN	List	Trade-In Fair	Trade-In Good	Pvt-Party Good	Retail Excellent
MONTERO SPORT 2WD—4-Cyl.—Truck Equipment Schedule T1						
ES Utility 4D	S21G	18980	1250	1750	3100	4950
MONTERO SPORT 4WD—Truck Equipment Schedule T1						
LS Utility 4D	T31P	25452	2875	3550	5100	7250
XLS Utility 4D	T41P	31555	3050	3725	5275	7500
2WD	S		(500)	(500)	(665)	(665)
MONTERO 4WD—V6—Truck Equipment Schedule T1						
LS Sport Util 4D	R41R	31040	3475	4200	5800	8050
SR Sport Util 4D	R51R	38827	4650	5500	7250	9750

1998 MITSUBISHI — JA4–(S21G)–W–#

Body Type	VIN	List	Trade-In Fair	Trade-In Good	Pvt-Party Good	Retail Excellent
MONTERO SPORT 2WD—4-Cyl.—Truck Equipment Schedule T1						
ES Utility 4D	S21G	19390	1750	2275	3725	5725
MONTERO SPORT 4WD—V6—Truck Equipment Schedule T1						
LS Utility 4D	T31P	26140	3525	4225	5875	8200
XLS Utility 4D	T41P	32695	3675	4425	6075	8450
2WD	S		(525)	(525)	(700)	(700)
MONTERO 4WD—V6—Truck Equipment Schedule T1						
Sport Utility 4D	R51R	33975	4650	5475	7225	9750

1999 MITSUBISHI — JA4–(S21G)–X–#

Body Type	VIN	List	Trade-In Fair	Trade-In Good	Pvt-Party Good	Retail Excellent
MONTERO SPORT 2WD—4-Cyl.—Truck Equipment Schedule T1						
ES Utility 4D	S21G	19680	2350	2925	4300	6200
MONTERO SPORT 4WD—V6—Truck Equipment Schedule T1						
LS Utility 4D	T31N	27445	4275	5075	6600	8825
XLS Utility 4D	T31N	29355	4450	5250	6800	9075
Limited Utility 4D	T41N	33085	5225	6075	7700	10100
2WD	S		(575)	(575)	(765)	(765)
MONTERO 4WD—V6—Truck Equipment Schedule T1						
Sport Utility 4D	R51R	31825	5475	6400	8050	10500

2000 MITSUBISHI — JA4–(S21H)–Y–#

Body Type	VIN	List	Trade-In Fair	Trade-In Good	Pvt-Party Good	Retail Excellent
MONTERO SPORT 2WD—V6—Truck Equipment Schedule T1						
ES Utility 4D	S21H	22982	2800	3425	4875	6900
MONTERO SPORT 4WD—V6—Truck Equipment Schedule T1						
LS Utility 4D	T31N	27262	4975	5850	7475	9850
XLS Utility 4D	T31N	29782	5200	6075	7700	10150
Limited Utility 4D	T41N	31812	6075	7025	8750	11300
2WD	S		(650)	(650)	(865)	(865)
MONTERO 4WD—V6—Truck Equipment Schedule T1						
Sport Utility 4D	R51R	32262	6550	7575	9300	11950
Endeavor Pkg			250	250	335	335

TRUCKS & VANS

TRUCKS & VANS

Body	Type	VIN	List	Trade-In Fair	Trade-In Good	Pvt-Party Good	Retail Excellent

2001 MITSUBISHI — JA4–(T21H)–1–#

MONTERO SPORT 4WD—V6—Truck Equipment Schedule T1

Body	Type	VIN	List	Fair	Good	Good	Excellent
ES Utility 4D		T21H	25467	5075	5950	7600	10000
LS Utility 4D		T31H	28177	5925	6875	8575	11100
XS Sport Utility 4D		T31R	29187	6050	7000	8750	11300
XLS Utility 4D		T31H	29827	6125	7125	8850	11400
Limited Utility 4D		T41R	33297	7150	8250	10050	12750
2WD		S		(725)	(725)	(965)	(965)

MONTERO 4WD—V6—Truck Equipment Schedule T1

XLS Sport Utility 4D		W31R	31817	7975	9175	11000	13800
Limited Spt Util 4D		W51R	35817	8675	9950	11900	14800

2002 MITSUBISHI — JA4–(T21H)–2–#

MONTERO SPORT 4WD—V6—Truck Equipment Schedule T1

ES Utility 4D		T21H	25647	6125	7100	8875	11500
LS Utility 4D		T31H	28337	7050	8150	10000	12700
XLS Utility 4D		T31H	30187	7325	8425	10250	13000
Limited Utility 4D		T41R	33447	8450	9675	11600	14500
2WD		S		(800)	(800)	(1065)	(1065)

MONTERO 4WD—V6—Truck Equipment Schedule T1

XLS Sport Utility 4D		W31R	32247	9475	10825	12800	15800
Limited Spt Util 4D		W51R	36357	10275	11700	13750	16900

2003 MITSUBISHI — JA4–(Z31G)–3–#

OUTLANDER AWD—4-Cyl.—Truck Equipment Schedule T1

LS Utility 4D		Z31G	19877	6600	7650	9500	12250
XLS Sport Utility 4D		Z41G	21370	7300	8400	10350	13200
2WD				(825)	(825)	(1100)	(1100)

MONTERO SPORT 4WD—V6—Truck Equipment Schedule T1

ES Utility 4D		T21H	25802	7475	8575	10500	13300
LS Utility 4D		T21H	28362	8500	9700	11650	14550
XLS Utility 4D		T31H	30212	8775	10050	12000	14950
Limited Utility 4D		T41R	33472	10000	11350	13400	16500
2WD		S		(875)	(875)	(1165)	(1165)

MONTERO 4WD—V6—Truck Equipment Schedule T1

XLS Sport Utility 4D		W31S	33072	11250	12750	14800	18050
Limited Spt Util 4D		W51S	37182	12075	13675	15750	19100

2004 MITSUBISHI — (Jor4)A4–(Z31G)–4–#

OUTLANDER AWD—4-Cyl.—Truck Equipment Schedule T1

LS Sport Utility 4D		Z31G	20692	7925	9125	10950	13750
XLS Sport Utility 4D		Z41G	22792	8675	9950	11850	14750
2WD		X		(900)	(900)	(1200)	(1200)

MONTERO SPORT 4WD—V6—Truck Equipment Schedule T1

LS Utility 4D		T31R	26392	10225	11650	13600	16600
XLS Utility 4D		T31R	28592	10525	11975	13900	17000
2WD		S		(950)	(950)	(1265)	(1265)

ENDEAVOR AWD—V6—Truck Equipment Schedule T1

LS Sport Utility 4D		N21S	28192	11150	12650	14650	17750
XLS Sport Utility 4D		N31S	30492	12475	14125	16100	19400
Limited Sport Util 4D		N41S	33792	13675	15425	17500	21000
2WD		M		(950)	(950)	(1265)	(1265)

MONTERO 4WD—V6—Truck Equipment Schedule T1

Limited Spt Util 4D		W51R	35624	14250	16050	18250	21700

2005 MITSUBISHI — (Jor4)A4(LZ31F)–5

OUTLANDER AWD—4-Cyl.—Truck Equipment Schedule T1

LS Sport Utility 4D		LZ31F	21244	9475	10825	12750	15700
XLS Sport Utility 4D		LZ41F	23724	10275	11700	13700	16800
Limited Sport Util		LZ81F	25774	11250	12750	14800	18050
2WD		X		(950)	(950)	(1265)	(1265)

ENDEAVOR AWD—V6—Truck Equipment Schedule T1

LS Sport Utility 4D		MN21S	28294	13250	14975	17100	20600
XLS Sport Util 4D		MN31S	30894	14600	16500	18650	22200
Limited Sport Util		MN41S	33794	15950	17950	20200	23900
2WD		M		(1000)	(1000)	(1335)	(1335)

MONTERO 4WD—V6—Truck Equipment Schedule T1

Limited Spt Util 4D		NW51S	36424	16625	18725	21000	24600

Body	Type	VIN	List	Trade-In Fair	Trade-In Good	Pvt-Party Good	Retail Excellent

TRUCKS & VANS

NISSAN

1991 NISSAN — (JN8or1N6)(HD17Y)-M-#

PATHFINDER 4WD—V6—Truck Equipment Schedule T1

Type	VIN	List	Fair	Good	Good	Excellent
XE Sport Utility 4D	HD17Y	19950	1725	2250	3400	5050
SE Sport Utility 4D	HD17Y	22579	2050	2625	3850	5600
2WD	S		(350)	(350)	(465)	(465)

PICKUP—4-Cyl.—Truck Equipment Schedule T2

Type	VIN	List	Fair	Good	Good	Excellent
Short Bed	SD11S	8554	450	650	1150	1950
King Cab	SD16S	10124	900	1250	2025	3175
4WD	Y		500	500	665	665

PICKUP—V6—Truck Equipment Schedule T2

Type	VIN	List	Fair	Good	Good	Excellent
Long Bed	HD12H	9899	600	850	1400	2325
SE King Cab	HD16S	12974	925	1300	2050	3275
4WD	Y		500	500	665	665

1992 NISSAN — (JN8or1N6)(HD17Y)-N-#

PATHFINDER 4WD—V6—Truck Equipment Schedule T1

Type	VIN	List	Fair	Good	Good	Excellent
XE Sport Utility 4D	HD17Y	21275	2025	2575	3775	5500
SE Sport Utility 4D	HD17Y	23225	2400	2975	4275	6075
2WD	S		(375)	(375)	(500)	(500)

PICKUP—4-Cyl.—Truck Equipment Schedule T2

Type	VIN	List	Fair	Good	Good	Excellent
Short Bed	SD11S	9165	500	725	1225	2100
King Cab	SD16S	10825	975	1350	2200	3475
4WD	Y		550	550	735	735

PICKUP—V6—Truck Equipment Schedule T2

Type	VIN	List	Fair	Good	Good	Excellent
Long Bed	HD12S	10580	625	900	1525	2550
SE King Cab	HD16S	13805	1000	1400	2275	3625
4WD	Y		550	550	735	735

1993 NISSAN — (JN8or1N6)(HD17Y)-P-#

PATHFINDER 4WD—V6—Truck Equipment Schedule T1

Type	VIN	List	Fair	Good	Good	Excellent
XE Sport Utility 4D	HD17Y	22380	2125	2700	3925	5725
SE Sport Utility 4D	HD17Y	24680	2575	3175	4500	6400
2WD	S		(400)	(400)	(535)	(535)

QUEST—V6—Truck Equipment Schedule T2

Type	VIN	List	Fair	Good	Good	Excellent
XE Minivan	DN11W	17895	1350	1850	2950	4550
GXE Minivan	DN11W	21800	1700	2225	3425	5100
5 Passenger			(250)	(250)	(335)	(335)

PICKUP—4-Cyl.—Truck Equipment Schedule T2

Type	VIN	List	Fair	Good	Good	Excellent
Short Bed	SD11S	9545	525	750	1325	2275
King Cab	SD16S	11845	1050	1450	2450	3900
4WD	Y		675	675	900	900

PICKUP—V6—Truck Equipment Schedule T2

Type	VIN	List	Fair	Good	Good	Excellent
Long Bed	HD12S	11015	700	1025	1675	2800
SE King Cab	HD16S	14405	1125	1575	2600	4100
4WD	Y		675	675	900	900

1994 NISSAN — (JN8or1N6)(HD17Y)-R-#

PATHFINDER 4WD—V6—Truck Equipment Schedule T1

Type	VIN	List	Fair	Good	Good	Excellent
XE Sport Utility 4D	HD17Y	23844	2275	2825	4175	6050
SE Sport Utility 4D	HD17Y	27484	2775	3400	4800	6800
LE Sport Utility 4D	HD17Y	29379	3275	3950	5425	7575
2WD	S		(425)	(425)	(565)	(565)

QUEST—V6—Truck Equipment Schedule T1

Type	VIN	List	Fair	Good	Good	Excellent
XE Minivan	DN11W	18909	1550	2050	3250	4950
GXE Minivan	DN11W	23419	1975	2500	3750	5525

PICKUP—4-Cyl.—Truck Equipment Schedule T2

Type	VIN	List	Fair	Good	Good	Excellent
Short Bed	SD11S	9739	650	925	1575	2675
XE Short Bed	SD11S	10509	725	1050	1750	2875
XE King Cab	SD16S	12059	1175	1625	2725	4250
4WD	Y		800	800	1065	1065
V6 3.0 Liter	H		175	175	235	235

PICKUP—V6—Truck Equipment Schedule T2

Type	VIN	List	Fair	Good	Good	Excellent
Long Bed	HD12S	11569	925	1300	2150	3475
SE King Cab	HD16S	14659	1450	1950	3075	4675
4WD	Y		800	800	1065	1065

1995 NISSAN

Body	Type	VIN	List	Trade-In Fair	Trade-In Good	Pvt-Party Good	Retail Excellent
1995 NISSAN — (JN8or4N2)(HD17Y)–S–#							
PATHFINDER 4WD—V6—Truck Equipment Schedule T1							
XE Sport Utility 4D	HD17Y	24988	**2500**	3100	4475	6450
SE Sport Utility 4D	HD17Y	29028	**3025**	3700	5200	7275
LE Sport Utility 4D	HD17Y	30749	**3600**	4300	5850	8075
2WD	S		**(450)**	(450)	(600)	(600)
QUEST—V6—Truck Equipment Schedule T1							
XE Minivan	DN11W	20229	**1825**	2350	3625	5375
GXE Minivan	DN11W	24999	**2275**	2825	4175	6050
PICKUP—4-Cyl.—Truck Equipment Schedule T2							
Short Bed	SD11S	10319	**750**	1075	1825	3000
XE Short Bed	SD11S	11399	**825**	1175	2000	3225
XE King Cab	SD16S	13079	**1425**	1925	3050	4650
4WD	Y		**900**	900	1200	1200
V6 3.0 Liter	H		**200**	200	265	265
PICKUP—V6—Truck Equipment Schedule T2							
Long Bed	HD11S	12479	**1075**	1525	2600	4100
4WD	Y		**900**	900	1200	1200
PICKUP 4WD—V6—Truck Equipment Schedule T2							
SE King Cab	HD16Y	20989	**2500**	3100	4375	6450
1996 NISSAN — (JN8or4N2)(AR05Y)–T–#							
PATHFINDER 4WD—V6—Truck Equipment Schedule T1							
XE Sport Utility 4D	AR05Y	26803	**2725**	3350	4825	6875
SE Sport Utility 4D	AR05Y	29748	**3325**	4000	5550	7750
LE Sport Utility 4D	AR05Y	32129	**3900**	4650	6275	8600
2WD	S		**(475)**	(475)	(635)	(635)
QUEST—V6—Truck Equipment Schedule T1							
XE Minivan	DN11W	21304	**2125**	2700	4025	5925
GXE Minivan	DN11W	26104	**2600**	3225	4600	6600
PICKUP—4-Cyl.—Truck Equipment Schedule T2							
Short Bed	SD11S	11404	**850**	1225	2100	3450
XE Short Bed	SD11S	12904	**925**	1300	2250	3650
XE King Cab	SD16S	14554	**1700**	2225	3450	5150
SE King Cab	SD16S	17004	**2125**	2725	3950	5750
4WD	Y		**1000**	1000	1335	1335
1997 NISSAN — (JN8,1N6or4N2)(AR05Y)–V–#							
PATHFINDER 4WD—V6—Truck Equipment Schedule T1							
XE Sport Utility 4D	AR05Y	27318	**3225**	3900	5475	7675
SE Sport Utility 4D	AR05Y	30568	**3850**	4600	6250	8600
LE Sport Utility 4D	AR05Y	32719	**4475**	5275	7025	9500
2WD	S		**(500)**	(500)	(665)	(665)
QUEST—V6—Truck Equipment Schedule T1							
XE Minivan	DN111	21669	**2475**	3075	4475	6450
GXE Minivan	DN111	26469	**3000**	3650	5150	7225
PICKUP—4-Cyl.—Truck Equipment Schedule T2							
Short Bed	SD11S	11469	**1025**	1450	2525	4075
XE Short Bed	SD11S	13469	**1100**	1550	2675	4250
XE King Cab	SD16S	15119	**2050**	2625	3875	5675
SE King Cab	SD16S	17519	**2575**	3200	4500	6400
4WD	Y		**1100**	1100	1465	1465
1998 NISSAN — (JN8,4N2or1N6)(AR05Y)–W–#							
PATHFINDER 4WD—V6—Truck Equipment Schedule T1							
XE Sport Utility 4D	AR05Y	27489	**3850**	4600	6250	8625
SE Sport Utility 4D	AR05Y	30589	**4500**	5325	7100	9600
LE Sport Utility 4D	AR05Y	33339	**5200**	6075	7900	10500
2WD	S		**(525)**	(525)	(700)	(700)
QUEST—V6—Truck Equipment Schedule T1							
XE Minivan	DN111	23589	**2850**	3525	5000	7100
GXE Minivan	DN111	26539	**3450**	4150	5700	7925
GLE Minivan	DN111	27868	**3650**	4400	6000	8250
FRONTIER PICKUP—4-Cyl.—Truck Equipment Schedule T2							
Short Bed	DD21S	12480	**1625**	2125	3350	5050
XE Short Bed	DD21S	13680	**1725**	2250	3475	5200
XE King Cab	DD26S	15130	**2825**	3475	4825	6775
SE King Cab	DD26S	18480	**3450**	4150	5550	7600
4WD	Y		**1200**	1200	1600	1600

Body	Type	VIN	List	Trade-In Fair	Trade-In Good	Pvt-Party Good	Retail Excellent

1999 NISSAN — (1N6,4N2orJN8)(AR05Y)-X

PATHFINDER 4WD—V6—Truck Equipment Schedule T1
XE Sport Utility 4D		AR05Y	27669	4600	5425	7000	9300
SE Sport Utility 4D		AR05Y	30769	5325	6225	7875	10300
LE Sport Utility 4D		AR05Y	33469	6075	7025	8750	11300
2WD		S		(575)	(575)	(765)	(765)

PATHFINDER 4WD (1999.5)—V6—Truck Equip Schedule T1
XE Sport Utility 4D		AR07Y	28819	5050	5925	7525	9900
SE Sport Utility 4D		AR07Y	30769	5775	6725	8400	10850
LE Sport Utility 4D		AR07Y	31719	6500	7525	9275	11900
2WD		S		(575)	(575)	(765)	(765)

QUEST—V6—Truck Equipment Schedule T1
GXE Minivan		XN11T	22679	3750	4500	5850	7825
SE Minivan		XN11T	24419	4375	5150	6550	8625
GLE Minivan		XN11T	26819	4625	5450	6875	9000

FRONTIER—4-Cyl.—Truck Equipment Schedule T2
XE Short Bed		DD21S	12010	2125	2700	3925	5700
XE King Cab		DD26S	14010	3325	4025	5375	7350
SE King Cab		DD26S	15510	4000	4750	6175	8275
4WD		Y		1275	1275	1700	1700
V6 3.3 Liter		E		250	250	335	335

2000 NISSAN–(1N6,4N2,5N1orJN8)(ED28Y)-Y-#

XTERRA 4WD—V6—Truck Equipment Schedule T1
XE Sport Utility 4D		ED28Y	22019	5400	6325	7950	10400
SE Sport Utility 4D		ED28Y	26069	6425	7425	9175	11750
2WD		T		(600)	(600)	(800)	(800)
4-Cyl. 2.4 Liter		D		(500)	(500)	(665)	(665)

PATHFINDER 4WD—V6—Truck Equipment Schedule T1
XE Sport Utility 4D		AR05Y	28919	5550	6500	8250	10800
SE Sport Utility 4D		AR05Y	30869	6350	7375	9200	11900
LE Sport Utility 4D		AR05Y	31819	7300	8400	10350	13200
2WD		S		(650)	(650)	(865)	(865)

QUEST—V6—Truck Equipment Schedule T1
GXE Minivan		XN11T	22779	4550	5375	6800	8900
SE Minivan		XN11T	24919	5250	6100	7600	9800
GLE Minivan		XN11T	26919	5550	6475	7950	10200

FRONTIER—4-Cyl.—Truck Equipment Schedule T2
XE Short Bed		DD21S	12110	2800	3425	4775	6725
XE King Cab		DD26S	14060	4050	4800	6250	8400
4WD		Y		1450	1450	1935	1935
V6 3.3 Liter		E		300	300	400	400

FRONTIER—V6—Truck Equipment Schedule T2
Desrt Rnr XE King		ED26S	16260	4450	5250	6750	8925
Desrt Rnr SE King		ED26S	18410	4675	5525	7025	9275
SE King Cab		DD26Y	21010	4650	5500	7000	9225
XE Crew Cab 4D		ED27S	17810	5050	5925	7475	9750
SE Crew Cab 4D		ED27S	19110	5350	6250	7800	10150
4WD		Y		1450	1450	1935	1935

2001 NISSAN–(1N6,4N2,5N1orJN8)(ED28Y)-1-#

XTERRA 4WD—V6—Truck Equipment Schedule T1
XE Sport Utility 4D		ED28Y	22569	6375	7400	9125	11700
SE Sport Utility 4D		ED28Y	26619	7525	8650	10500	13200
2WD		T		(675)	(675)	(900)	(900)
4-Cyl. 2.4 Liter		D		(550)	(550)	(735)	(735)

PATHFINDER 4WD—V6—Truck Equipment Schedule T1
XE Sport Utility 4D		DR07Y	30169	6675	7700	9575	12300
SE Sport Utility 4D		DR07Y	30869	7550	8675	10600	13550
LE Sport Utility 4D		DR07Y	31819	8675	9950	11950	15000
2WD		X		(725)	(725)	(965)	(965)
AWD				0	0	0	0

QUEST—V6—Truck Equipment Schedule T1
GXE Minivan		ZN15T	22959	5500	6425	7925	10200
SE Minivan		ZN16T	24919	6250	7250	8800	11150
GLE Minivan		ZN17T	27569	6600	7250	9225	11650

FRONTIER—4-Cyl.—Truck Equipment Schedule T2
XE Short Bed		DD21S	12219	3550	4250	5700	7775
XE King Cab		DD26S	14169	4850	5700	7250	9525
4WD		Y		1625	1625	2165	2165
V6 3.3 Liter		E		350	350	465	465

Body Type	VIN	List	Trade-In Fair	Trade-In Good	Pvt-Party Good	Retail Excellent
FRONTIER—V6—Truck Equipment Schedule T2						
Desrt Rnr XE King	ED26T	16469	5250	6150	7725	10100
Desrt Rnr SE King	ED26T	18619	5600	6525	8150	10500
SE King Cab	ED26Y	21219	5625	6550	8150	10500
XE Crew Cab 4D	ED27T	18569	6000	6950	8575	11000
SE Crew Cab 4D	ED27T	20719	6400	7425	9050	11550
4WD	Y		1625	1625	2165	2165
FRONTIER—V6 Supercharged—Truck Equipment Schedule T2						
King Cab	MD26T	20519	5550	6500	8100	10500
Crew Cab 4D	MD27T	21969	6425	7425	9100	11600
4WD	Y		1625	1625	2165	2165

Body Type	VIN	List	Trade-In Fair	Trade-In Good	Pvt-Party Good	Retail Excellent
XTERRA 4WD—V6—Truck Equipment Sch T1						
XE Sport Utility 4D	ED28Y	22739	7500	8600	10450	13150
SE Sport Utility 4D	ED28Y	26739	8775	10050	11950	14800
2WD	T		(750)	(750)	(1000)	(1000)
4-Cyl. 2.4 Liter	D		(600)	(600)	(800)	(800)
XTERRA 4WD—V6 Supercharged—Truck Equipment Sch T1						
XE S/C Spt Util 4D	MD28T	26239	8100	9300	11100	13900
SE S/C Spt Util 4D	MD28T	28039	9400	10725	12650	15600
2WD	T		(750)	(750)	(1000)	(1000)
PATHFINDER 4WD—V6—Truck Equipment Schedule T1						
SE Sport Utility 4D	DR07Y	29189	8950	10225	12250	15350
LE Sport Utility 4D	DR07Y	32039	10275	11700	13800	17050
2WD	X		(800)	(800)	(1065)	(1065)
QUEST—V6—Truck Equipment Schedule T1						
GXE Minivan	ZN15T	23279	6625	7675	9300	11750
SE Minivan	ZN16T	25039	7425	8575	10250	12800
GLE Minivan	ZN17T	27689	7850	9025	10700	13350
FRONTIER KING CAB—4-Cyl.—Truck Equipment Sch T2						
Short Bed	ED27S	13339	5475	6400	8000	10400
XE Short Bed	DD26S	14339	5775	6725	8350	10750
4WD	Y		1800	1800	2400	2400
V6 3.3 Liter	E		400	400	535	535
FRONTIER KING CAB—V6—Truck Equipment Schedule T2						
Desert Runner XE	ED26T	16539	6225	7225	8875	11350
Desert Runner SE	ED26T	19739	6650	7675	9375	11950
SE Short Bed	ED26Y	22339	6725	7750	9425	12000
4WD	Y		1800	1800	2400	2400
FRONTIER CREW CAB—V6—Truck Equipment Schedule T2						
XE Short Bed	ED27T	18739	7025	8125	9850	12400
XE Long Bed	ED27T	19299	7000	8075	9800	12350
SE Short Bed	ED27T	22239	7575	8700	10500	13150
SE Long Bed	ED27T	22799	7550	8675	10450	13100
4WD	Y		1800	1800	2400	2400
FRONTIER KING CAB—V6 Supercharged—Truck Equip Sch T2						
Short Bed	MD26T	20889	6750	7775	9475	12050
4WD	Y		1800	1800	2400	2400
FRONTIER CREW CAB—V6 Supercharged—Truck Equip Sch T2						
Short Bed	MD27T	23739	7675	8825	10600	13300
Long Bed	MD27T	24299	7675	8800	10550	13250
4WD	Y		1800	1800	2400	2400

Body Type	VIN	List	Trade-In Fair	Trade-In Good	Pvt-Party Good	Retail Excellent
XTERRA 4WD—V6—Truck Equipment Schedule T1						
XE Sport Utility 4D	ED28Y	23939	8725	10000	11900	14800
SE Sport Utility 4D	ED28Y	27239	10175	11600	13600	16650
2WD	T		(825)	(825)	(1100)	(1100)
4-Cyl. 2.4 Liter	D		(650)	(650)	(865)	(865)
XTERRA 4WD—V6 Supercharged—Truck Equipment Schedule T1						
SE S/C Spt Util 4D	MD28T	28539	10875	12325	14300	17450
2WD	T		(825)	(825)	(1100)	(1100)
MURANO AWD—V6—Equipment Schedule T1						
SL Sport Utility 4D	AZ08W	30339	14200	16000	17950	21100
SE Sport Utility 4D	AZ08W	31139	14550	16450	18400	21600
2WD	X		(875)	(875)	(1165)	(1165)
PATHFINDER 4WD—V6—Truck Equipment Schedule T1						
SE Sport Utility 4D	DR09Y	29339	10625	12075	14200	17500
LE Sport Utility 4D	DR09Y	34339	12125	13725	15950	19400
2WD	X		(875)	(875)	(1165)	(1165)
FRONTIER KING CAB—4-Cyl.—Truck Equipment Schedule T2						
Short Bed	ED27S	13529	6450	7450	9200	11800

Body Type	VIN	List	Trade-In Fair	Trade-In Good	Pvt-Party Good	Retail Excellent
XE Short Bed	DD26S	14579	6800	7850	9600	12200
4WD	Y		1975	1975	2635	2635
V6 3.3 Liter	E		450	450	600	600
FRONTIER KING CAB—V6—Truck Equipment Schedule T2						
Desert Runner XE	ED26T	16709	7300	8400	10200	12850
Desert Runner SE	ED26T	21109	7775	8950	10750	13500
FRONTIER KING CAB 4WD—V6—Truck Equipment Schedule T2						
SE Short Bed	ED26Y	23709	7900	9075	10900	13700
FRONTIER CREW CAB—V6—Truck Equipment Schedule T2						
XE Short Bed	ED27T	18979	8225	9425	11250	14000
XE Long Bed	ED27T	19529	8225	9425	11250	14050
SE Short Bed	ED27T	22829	8825	10100	11950	14850
SE Long Bed	ED27T	23379	8900	10175	12050	14900
4WD	Y		1975	1975	2635	2635
FRONTIER KING CAB—V6 Supercharged—Truck Equip Sch T2						
Short Bed	MD26T	21359	7975	9175	11000	13750
4WD	Y		1975	1975	2635	2635
FRONTIER CREW CAB—V6 Supercharged—Truck Equip Sch T2						
Short Bed	MD27T	24329	9075	10375	12200	15150
Long Bed	MD27T	24879	9125	10425	12250	15150
4WD	Y		1975	1975	2635	2635

Body Type	VIN	List	Trade-In Fair	Trade-In Good	Pvt-Party Good	Retail Excellent
XTERRA 4WD—V6—Truck Equipment Schedule T1						
XE Sport Utility 4D	ED28Y	22940	10225	11650	13500	16450
SE Sport Utility 4D	ED28Y	27240	11825	13375	15350	18500
2WD	T		(900)	(900)	(1200)	(1200)
4-Cyl. 2.4 Liter	D		(700)	(700)	(935)	(935)
XTERRA 4WD—V6 Supercharged—Truck Equipment Schedule T1						
SE S/C Spt Util 4D	MD28T	28540	12550	14200	16200	19400
2WD	T		(900)	(900)	(1200)	(1200)
MURANO AWD—V6—Truck Equipment Schedule T1						
SL Sport Utility 4D	AZ08N	30340	16550	18625	20500	23900
SE Sport Utility 4D	AZ08N	31290	16925	19050	21000	24400
2WD	T		(950)	(950)	(1265)	(1265)
QUEST—V6—Truck Equipment Schedule T1						
S Minivan	BV28U	24780	12650	14300	16500	20000
SL Minivan	BV28U	27280	13375	15125	17350	21000
SE Minivan	BV28U	32780	14400	16250	18550	22200
PATHFINDER 4WD—V6—Truck Equipment Schedule T1						
SE Sport Utility 4D	DR09Y	29440	12550	14200	16450	19900
LE Sport Utility 4D	DR09Y	34590	14250	16100	18400	22000
2WD	X		(950)	(950)	(1265)	(1265)
PATHFINDER ARMADA 4WD—V8—Truck Equipment Schedule T1						
SE Sport Utility 4D	AA08B	36750	16550	18625	21900	27000
SE Off-Road Spt Utl	AA08B	39900	17275	19400	22800	27800
LE Sport Utility 4D	AA08B	41250	18050	20275	23700	28800
2WD	A		(950)	(950)	(1265)	(1265)
FRONTIER KING CAB—4-Cyl.—Truck Equipment Schedule T2						
Short Bed	ED27S	13830	7600	8725	10450	13100
XE Short Bed	DD26S	14880	8025	9225	10950	13700
4WD	Y		2150	2150	2865	2865
V6 3.3 Liter	E		500	500	665	665
FRONTIER KING CAB—V6—Truck Equipment Schedule T2						
Desert Runner XE	ED26T	17030	8550	9800	11600	14350
FRONTIER KING CAB 4WD—V6 Supercharged—Truck Sch T2						
Short Bed	MD26T	25430	9425	10775	12600	15450
FRONTIER CREW CAB—V6—Truck Equipment Schedule T2						
XE Short Bed	ED27T	19360	9600	10950	12800	15650
XE Long Bed	ED27T	19910	9700	11050	12900	15750
LE Short Bed	ED27T	24900	10275	11700	13600	16550
LE Long Bed	ED27T	25450	10375	11825	13750	16700
4WD	Y		2150	2150	2865	2865
FRONTIER CREW CAB—V6 Supercharged—Truck Equip T2						
Short Bed	MD27T	24810	10675	12125	14000	17000
Long Bed	MD27T	25360	10725	12225	14050	17050
4WD	Y		2150	2150	2865	2865
TITAN KING CAB—V8—Truck Equipment Schedule T1						
XE Short Bed	AA06A	23050	11875	13475	15300	18250
SE Short Bed	AA06A	25050	12425	14075	15850	18900
LE Short Bed	AA06A	29450	13100	14800	16650	19800
4WD	B		2100	2100	2800	2800

Body Type	VIN	List	Trade-In Fair	Good	Pvt-Party Good	Retail Excellent
TITAN CREW CAB—V8—Truck Equipment Schedule T1						
XE Short Bed	AA07A	25750	13375	15125	17000	20200
SE Short Bed	AA07A	27350	13975	15775	17650	20900
LE Short Bed	AA07A	31750	14500	16350	18300	21500
4WD	B		2100	2100	2800	2800

2005 NISSAN–(1N6,5N1orJN8)(AN08W)-5-#

Body Type	VIN	List	Trade-In Fair	Good	Pvt-Party Good	Retail Excellent
XTERRA 4WD—V6—Truck Equipment Schedule T1						
S Sport Utility 4D	AN08W	24280	12175	13775	15700	18900
Off-Road Sport Util	AN08W	27280	12950	14650	16650	19900
SE Sport Utility 4D	AN08W	27880	13925	15725	17750	21100
2WD			(950)	(950)	(1265)	(1265)
MURANO AWD—V6—Truck Equipment Schedule T1						
S Sport Utiltiy 4D	AZ08W	29180	18625	20950	22900	26400
SL Sport Utility 4D	AZ08W	30680	19000	21350	23400	27000
SE Sport Utility 4D	AZ08W	31630	19500	21825	23900	27500
2WD			(1000)	(1000)	(1335)	(1335)
QUEST—V6—Truck Equipment Schedule T1						
Minivan	BV28U	23910	14025	15850	18200	21900
S Minivan	BV28U	25110	15125	17025	19400	23300
SL Minivan	BV28U	26810	15900	17900	20400	24300
SE Minivan	BV28U	32810	19350	21800	23800	25800
PATHFINDER 4WD—V6—Truck Equipment Schedule T1						
XE Sport Utility 4D	AR18W	23700	13675	15425	17700	21300
SE Sport Utility 4D	AR18W	28500	14800	16675	18900	22600
LE Sport Utility 4D	AR18W	35400	16625	18725	21000	25000
2WD	U		(1000)	(1000)	(1335)	(1335)
ARMADA 4WD—V8—Truck Equipment Schedule T1						
SE Sport Utility 4D	AA08B	37050	19100	21425	24900	30300
SE Off-Road Spt Utl	AA08B	40420	19975	22400	25900	31300
LE Sport Utility 4D	AA08B	42150	20650	23175	26800	32300
2WD	A		(1000)	(1000)	(1335)	(1335)
FRONTIER KING CAB—4-Cyl.—Truck Equipment Schedule T2						
XE Short Bed	BD06T	16080	9075	10375	12150	15050
FRONTIER KING CAB—V6—Truck Equipment Schedule T2						
SE Short Bed	AD06T	18980	9600	10950	12800	15700
LE Short Bed	AD06T	22780	11150	12650	14650	17750
Nismo Short Bed	AD06U	22580	11400	12900	14950	18100
4WD	Y		2325	2325	3100	3100
FRONTIER CREW CAB—V6—Truck Equipment Schedule T2						
SE Short Bed	AD07T	21130	11300	12850	14800	17950
LE Short Bed	AD07T	24480	12075	13675	15700	18950
Nismo Short Bed	AD07U	24630	12750	14400	16500	19800
4WD	Y		2325	2325	3100	3100
TITAN KING CAB—V8—Truck Equipment Schedule T1						
XE Short Bed	AA06A	23300	13975	15800	17600	20800
SE Short Bed	AA06A	25450	14450	16300	18150	21300
LE Short Bed	AA06A	29900	15225	17175	19050	22300
4WD	B		2275	2275	3035	3035
TITAN CREW CAB—V8—Truck Equipment Schedule T1						
XE Short Bed	AA07A	26150	15575	17550	19400	22700
SE Short Bed	AA07A	27950	16050	18100	20900	23400
LE Short Bed	AA07A	32700	16775	18875	20900	24300
4WD	B		2275	2275	3035	3035

OLDSMOBILE

1991 OLDSMOBILE — 1GH–(U06D)-M-#

Body Type	VIN	List	Trade-In Fair	Good	Pvt-Party Good	Retail Excellent
SILHOUETTE—V6—Truck Equipment Schedule T1						
Minivan	U06D	18705	425	625	1125	1950
BRAVADA AWD—V6—Truck Equipment Schedule T3						
Sport Utility 4D	T13Z	24250	1475	1975	3100	4700

1992 OLDSMOBILE — 1GH–(U06D)-N-#

Body Type	VIN	List	Trade-In Fair	Good	Pvt-Party Good	Retail Excellent
SILHOUETTE—V6—Truck Equipment Schedule T1						
Minivan	U06D	19625	500	725	1250	2150
V6 3.8 Liter	L		50	50	65	65
BRAVADA AWD—V6—Truck Equipment Schedule T3						
Sport Utility 4D	T13Z	25070	1675	2200	3350	5000
V6 4.3L High Output	W		100	100	135	135

TRUCKS & VANS

Body	Type	VIN	List	Trade-In Fair	Trade-In Good	Pvt-Party Good	Retail Excellent

1993 OLDSMOBILE — 1GH–(U06D)–P–#

SILHOUETTE—V6—Truck Equipment Schedule T1

Minivan		U06D	20029	**525**	750	1375	2375
V6 3.8 Liter		L		**75**	75	100	100

BRAVADA AWD—V6—Truck Equipment Schedule T3

| Sport Utility 4D | | T13W | 26474 | **1750** | 2275 | 3475 | 5175 |

1994 OLDSMOBILE — 1GH–(U06D)–R–#

SILHOUETTE—V6—Truck Equipment Schedule T1

Minivan		U06D	20625	**800**	1150	1975	3275
V6 3.8 Liter		L		**100**	100	135	135

BRAVADA AWD—V6—Truck Equipment Schedule T3

| Sport Utility 4D | | T13W | 27120 | **1850** | 2375 | 3650 | 5400 |

1995 OLDSMOBILE — 1GH–(U06L)–S–#

SILHOUETTE—V6—Truck Equipment Schedule T1

Minivan		U06L	20795	**925**	1300	2250	3675

1996 OLDSMOBILE — 1GH–(U06E)–T–#

SILHOUETTE—V6—Truck Equipment Schedule T1

Minivan		U06E	21900	**1050**	1475	2650	4275

BRAVADA AWD—V6—Truck Equipment Schedule T3

| Sport Utility 4D | | T13W | 29995 | **2600** | 3225 | 4675 | 6725 |

1997 OLDSMOBILE — 1GH–(U06E)–V–#

SILHOUETTE—V6—Truck Equipment Schedule T1

Minivan		U06E	22245	**1400**	1900	3325	5250
Extended Minivan		X06E	23075	**1800**	2325	3750	5750
GL Extended		X06E	25145	**1975**	2500	3975	6000
GLS Extended		X06E	26805	**2025**	2575	4050	6100
w/o 2nd Sliding Door				**(450)**	(450)	(600)	(600)

BRAVADA AWD—V6—Truck Equipment Schedule T3

| Sport Utility 4D | | T13W | 30800 | **2950** | 3625 | 5150 | 7300 |

1998 OLDSMOBILE — 1GH–(U03E)–W–#

SILHOUETTE—V6—Truck Equipment Schedule T1

GS Minivan		U03E	25000	**1800**	2325	3825	5900
GL Extended		X03E	24535	**2350**	2925	4500	6675
GLS Extended		X03E	27735	**2425**	3025	4600	6800

BRAVADA AWD—V6—Truck Equipment Schedule T3

| Sport Utility 4D | | T13W | 31160 | **3450** | 4150 | 5775 | 8050 |

1999 OLDSMOBILE — 1GH–(U03E)–X–#

SILHOUETTE—V6—Truck Equipment Schedule T1

GS Minivan		U03E	25370	**2275**	2825	4350	6400
GL Extended		X03E	24990	**2850**	3525	5075	7225
GLS Extended		X03E	28665	**2950**	3625	5175	7350
Premiere Extended		X03E	31580	**3650**	4375	6000	8300

BRAVADA AWD—V6—Truck Equipment Schedule T3

| Sport Utility 4D | | T13W | 31568 | **4125** | 4900 | 6425 | 8625 |

2000 OLDSMOBILE — 1GH–(X03E)–Y–#

SILHOUETTE—V6—Truck Equipment Schedule T1

GL Extended		X03E	25530	**3550**	4250	5925	8250
GLS Extended		X03E	29220	**3625**	4350	6025	8375
Premiere Extended		X03E	32130	**4425**	5225	6925	9400

BRAVADA AWD—V6—Truck Equipment Schedule T3

| Sport Utility 4D | | T13W | 31923 | **4950** | 5800 | 7425 | 9800 |

2001 OLDSMOBILE — 1GH–(X03E)–1–#

SILHOUETTE—V6—Truck Equipment Schedule T1

GL Extended		X03E	26920	**4350**	5125	6900	9450
GLS Extended		X03E	31055	**4450**	5250	7050	9600
Premiere Extended		X03E	33855	**5300**	6200	8075	10750

BRAVADA AWD—V6—Truck Equipment Schedule T3

| Sport Utility 4D | | T13W | 32335 | **6000** | 6950 | 8675 | 11200 |

2002 OLDSMOBILE

Body	Type	VIN	List	Trade-In Fair	Trade-In Good	Pvt-Party Good	Retail Excellent

2002 OLDSMOBILE — 1GH-(X23E)-2-#

SILHOUETTE—V6—Truck Equipment Schedule T1
GL Extended	X23E	27560	5325	6225	8175	10900
GLS Extended	X03E	31635	5450	6375	8325	11100
Premiere Extended	X13E	33535	6425	7425	9425	12300
AWD	V		825	825	1100	1100

BRAVADA AWD—6-Cyl.—Truck Equipment Schedule T3
| Sport Utility 4D | T13W | 34967 | 8950 | 10225 | 12150 | 15150 |
| 2WD | S | | (800) | (800) | (1065) | (1065) |

2003 OLDSMOBILE — 1GH-(X23E)-3-#

SILHOUETTE—V6—Truck Equipment Schedule T1
GL Extended	X23E	28510	6600	7650	9750	12750
GLS Extended	X03E	32175	6750	7800	9900	12950
Premiere Extended	X13E	34225	7775	8950	11100	14300
AWD	V		900	900	1200	1200

BRAVADA AWD—6-Cyl.—Truck Equipment Schedule T3
| Sport Utility 4D | T13S | 35145 | 10625 | 12075 | 14050 | 17200 |
| 2WD | S | | (875) | (875) | (1165) | (1165) |

2004 OLDSMOBILE — 1GH-(X23E)-4-#

SILHOUETTE—V6—Truck Equipment Schedule T1
GL Extended	X23E	28790	8275	9475	11700	14900
GLS Extended	X03E	32450	8450	9675	11900	15150
Premiere Extended	X13E	34510	9575	10925	13200	16550
AWD	V		975	975	1300	1300

BRAVADA AWD—6-Cyl.—Truck Equipment Schedule T3
| Sport Utility 4D | T13S | 36245 | 12550 | 14200 | 16300 | 19600 |
| 2WD | S | | (950) | (950) | (1265) | (1265) |

2005 OLDSMOBILE — No Longer Produced

PLYMOUTH — See DODGE TRUCKS

PONTIAC

1991 PONTIAC — 1GM-(U06D)-M-#

TRANS SPORT—V6—Truck Equipment Schedule T1
Minivan	U06D	17609	400	575	1075	1875
SE Minivan	U06D	19509	450	625	1175	2000
5 Passenger			(200)	(200)	(265)	(265)

1992 PONTIAC — 1GM-(U06D)-N-#

TRANS SPORT—V6—Truck Equipment Schedule T1
SE Minivan	U06D	17585	375	500	975	1700
GT Minivan	U06L	21465	850	1200	1975	3175
5 Passenger			(225)	(225)	(300)	(300)
V6 3.8 Liter			50	50	65	65

1993 PONTIAC — 1G(YorM)-(U06D)-P-#

TRANS SPORT—V6—Truck Equipment Schedule T1
SE Minivan	U06D	18049	350	475	1025	1825
5 Passenger			(250)	(250)	(335)	(335)
V6 3.8 Liter	L		75	75	100	100

1994 PONTIAC — 1G(YorM)-(U06D)-R-#

TRANS SPORT—V6—Truck Equipment Schedule T1
SE Minivan	U06D	18279	575	825	1500	2625
5 Passenger			(275)	(275)	(365)	(365)
V6 3.8 Liter	L		100	100	135	135

1995 PONTIAC — 1G(YorM)-(U06D)-S-#

TRANS SPORT—V6—Truck Equipment Schedule T1
SE Minivan	U06D	19964	675	975	1750	3000
5 Passenger			(300)	(300)	(400)	(400)
V6 3.8 Liter	L		100	100	135	135

Body	Type	VIN	List	Trade-In Fair	Trade-In Good	Pvt-Party Good	Retail Excellent

1996 PONTIAC — 1GM–(U06E)–T–#

TRANS SPORT—V6—Truck Equipment Schedule T1

SE Minivan	U06E	21595		800	1150	2075	3525
5 Passenger				(325)	(325)	(435)	(435)

1997 PONTIAC — 1GM–(U06E)–V–#

TRANS SPORT—V6—Truck Equipment Schedule T1

SE Minivan	U06E	21049		1525	2025	3475	5400
SE Extended Minivan	X09E	23939		2200	2800	4300	6375
Montana				325	325	435	435
w/o 2nd Sliding Door				(450)	(450)	(600)	(600)

1998 PONTIAC — 1GM–(U03E)–W–#

TRANS SPORT—V6—Truck Equipment Schedule T1

Minivan	U03E	22950		1925	2450	3975	6075
Extended Minivan	X03E	23660		2625	3250	4850	7075
Montana				100	100	135	135
w/o 2nd Sliding Door				(475)	(475)	(635)	(635)

1999 PONTIAC — 1GM–(U03E)–X–#

MONTANA—V6—Truck Equipment Schedule T1

Minivan	U03E	23455		2400	2975	4475	6575
Extended Minivan	X03E	24455		3175	3825	5400	7650
w/o 2nd Sliding Door				(500)	(500)	(665)	(665)

2000 PONTIAC — 1GM–(U03E)–Y–#

MONTANA—V6—Truck Equipment Schedule T1

Minivan	U03E	24255		2975	3650	5250	7500
Extended Minivan	X03E	25365		3875	4625	6300	8675

2001 PONTIAC — (1GMor3G7)–(A03E)–1–#

AZTEK—V6—Truck Equipment Schedule T1

Sport Utility 4D	A03E	21995		3400	4100	5625	7775
GT Sport Utility 4D	A03E	24995		4075	4850	6425	8700
AWD	B			750	750	1000	1000

MONTANA—V6—Truck Equipment Schedule T1

Minivan 4D	U03E	24810		3700	4450	6175	8625
Extended Minivan 4D	X03E	27150		4700	5550	7350	9950

2002 PONTIAC — (1GMor3G7)–(A03E)–2–#

AZTEK—V6—Truck Equipment Schedule T1

Sport Utility 4D	A03E	20545		4375	5175	6825	9200
AWD	B			825	825	1100	1100

MONTANA—V6—Truck Equipment Schedule T1

Minivan 4D	U03E	24990		4650	5475	7375	10050
Extended Minivan 4D	X03E	27390		5750	6700	8675	11500

2003 PONTIAC — (1GMor3G7)–(A03E)–3–#

AZTEK—V6—Truck Equipment Schedule T1

Sport Utility 4D	A03E	20870		5600	6525	8300	10850
AWD	B			900	900	1200	1200

MONTANA—V6—Truck Equipment Schedule T1

Minivan 4D	U03E	24845		5850	6825	8875	11800
Extended Minivan 4D	X03E	26645		7050	8150	10300	13350
AWD	V			1000	1000	1335	1335

2004 PONTIAC — (1GMor3G7)–(A03E)–4–#

AZTEK—V6—Truck Equipment Schedule T1

Sport Utility 4D	A03E	21595		7150	8250	10000	12650
AWD	B			975	975	1300	1300

MONTANA—V6—Truck Equipment Schedule T1

Minivan 4D	U03E	23845		7475	8575	10700	13800
Extended Minivan 4D	X03E	26220		8775	10050	12250	15500
AWD	V			1000	1000	1335	1335

2005 PONTIAC — (1GMor3G7)–(A03E)–5–#

AZTEK—V6—Truck Equipment Schedule T1

Sport Utility 4D	A03E	22060		8950	10225	12050	14900
AWD	B			1050	1050	1400	1400

TRUCKS & VANS

Body	Type	VIN	List	Trade-In Fair	Good	Pvt-Party Good	Retail Excellent

MONTANA—V6—Truck Equipment Schedule T1
Extended Minivan 4D V23E 26755 **10925 12375 14850 18500**
MONTANA SV6—V6—Truck Equipment Schedule T1
Minivan 4D V03L 25235 **10100 11450 13600 16850**
AWD .... X **1000 1000 1335 1335**
5 Passenger .... **(750) (750) (1000) (1000)**

PORSCHE

2003 PORSCHE — WP1-(AB29P)-3-#

CAYENNE AWD—V8—Truck Equipment Schedule T3
S Sport Utility 4D 56665 **34425 38400 41600 47400**
CAYENNE AWD—V8 Twin Turbo—Truck Equipment Schedule T3
Sport Utility 4D AC29P 89665 **54125 60150 64300 72500**

2004 PORSCHE — WP1-(AB29P)-4-#

CAYENNE AWD—V6—Truck Equipment Schedule T3
Sport Utility 4D AB29P 43665 **28425 31825 34500 39600**
CAYENNE AWD—V8—Truck Equipment Schedule T3
S Sport Utility 4D AB29P 56665 **37725 42000 45100 51100**
CAYENNE AWD—V8 Twin Turbo—Truck Equipment Schedule T3
Sport Utility 4D AC29P 89665 **59175 65675 69700 78000**

2005 PORSCHE — WP1-(AB29P)-5-#

CAYENNE AWD—V6—Truck Equipment Schedule T3
Sport Utility 4D AB29P 44995 **31225 34825 37400 42600**
CAYENNE AWD—V8—Truck Equipment Schedule T3
S Sport Utility 4D AB29P 57195 **41225 45875 48900 54900**
CAYENNE AWD—V8 Twin Turbo—Truck Equipment Schedule T3
Sport Utility 4D AC29P 90195

SAAB

2005 SAAB — 5S3E(T13S)-5-#

9-7X AWD—6-Cyl.—Truck Equipment Schedule T3
Linear Sport Util 4D T13S 38990
9-7X AWD—V8—Truck Equipment Schedule T3
Arc Sport Utility 4D T13M 40990

SATURN

2002 SATURN — 5GZ-(Z23D)-2-#

VUE—4-Cyl.—Truck Equipment Schedule T1
Sport Utility 4D Z23D 17775 **6300 7325 9275 12100**
AWD **825 825 1100 1100**
V6 3.0 Liter .... B **600 600 800 800**

2003 SATURN — 5GZ-(Z23D)-3-#

VUE—4-Cyl.—Truck Equipment Schedule T1
Sport Utility 4D Z23D 18295 **7475 8575 10650 13700**
AWD .... 4,6 .... **900 900 1200 1200**
V6 3.0 Liter .... B **650 650 865 865**

2004 SATURN — 5GZ-(Z23D)-4-#

VUE—4-Cyl.—Truck Equipment Schedule T1
Sport Utility 4D Z23D 19135 **8850 10125 12150 15300**
AWD .... 4,6 .... **975 975 1300 1300**
V6 3.5 Liter .... B **700 700 935 935**

2005 SATURN — 5GZ-(Z23D)-5-#

VUE—4-Cyl.—Truck Equipment Schedule T1
Sport Utility 4D Z23D 21190 **10425 11875 14000 17300**
AWD .... 4,6 .... **1050 1050 1400 1400**
V6 3.5 Liter .... 4 .... **750 750 1000 1000**
RELAY—V6—Truck Equipment Schedule T1
Minivan 4D V03L 24485
AWD X

Body	Type	VIN	List	Trade-In Fair	Good	Pvt-Party Good	Retail Excellent

SUBARU

1998 SUBARU — JF1(SF615)-W-#

FORESTER AWD—4-Cyl.—Truck Equipment Schedule T1
Sport Utility 4D	SF615	19190	4125	4900	6475	8750
L Sport Utility 4D	SF635	21290	4500	5325	6950	9300
S Sport Utility 4D	SF655	23490	4925	5775	7450	9900

1999 SUBARU — JF1(SF615)-X-#

FORESTER AWD—4-Cyl.—Truck Equipment Schedule T1
Sport Utility 4D	SF615	19190	4800	5625	7200	9475
L Sport Utility 4D	SF635	21290	5250	6100	7700	10100
S Sport Utility 4D	SF655	23790	5650	6575	8225	10650

2000 SUBARU — JF1(SF635)-Y-#

FORESTER AWD—4-Cyl.—Truck Equipment Schedule T1
| L Sport Utility 4D | SF635 | 21390 | 6175 | 7175 | 8875 | 11400 |
| S Sport Utility 4D | SF655 | 23890 | 6675 | 7700 | 9425 | 12050 |

2001 SUBARU — JF1(SF635)-1-#

FORESTER AWD—4-Cyl.—Truck Equipment Schedule T1
| L Sport Utility 4D | SF635 | 21590 | 7275 | 8375 | 10150 | 12850 |
| S Sport Utility 4D | SF655 | 24190 | 7800 | 8975 | 10800 | 13600 |

2002 SUBARU — JF1(SF635)-2-#

FORESTER AWD—4-Cyl.—Truck Equipment Schedule T1
| L Sport Utility 4D | SF635 | 21625 | 8500 | 9700 | 11550 | 14400 |
| S Sport Utility 4D | SF655 | 24220 | 9125 | 10425 | 12300 | 15250 |

2003 SUBARU—(JF1or4S4)(BorS)(G636)-3

FORESTER AWD—4-Cyl.—Truck Equipment Schedule T1
| X Sport Utility 4D | G636 | 21870 | 9900 | 11300 | 13200 | 16200 |
| XS Sport Utility 4D | G656 | 24220 | 10575 | 12025 | 13950 | 17050 |
BAJA AWD—4-Cyl.—Truck Equipment Schedule T1
| Sport Util Pickup 4D | T61C | 24520 | 8400 | 9625 | 11650 | 14700 |

2004 SUBARU—(JF1or4S4)(BorS)(G636)-4

FORESTER AWD—4-Cyl.—Truck Equipment Schedule T1
| X Sport Utility 4D | G636 | 22245 | 11500 | 13050 | 14950 | 18050 |
| XS Sport Utility 4D | G656 | 24495 | 12225 | 13875 | 15800 | 19000 |
FORESTER AWD—4-Cyl. Turbo—Truck Equipment Schedule T1
| XT Sport Utility 4D | G696 | 26320 | 13100 | 14800 | 16800 | 20100 |
BAJA AWD—4-Cyl.—Truck Equipment Schedule T1
| Sport Util Pickup 4D | T61C | 22545 | 10100 | 11450 | 13600 | 16800 |
BAJA AWD—4-Cyl. Turbo—Truck Equipment Schedule T1
| Sport Util Pickup 4D | T63C | 24545 | 11600 | 13150 | 15300 | 18650 |

2005 SUBARU—(JF1or4S4)(BorS)(G636)-5

FORESTER AWD—4-Cyl.—Truck Equipment Schedule T1
X Sport Utility 4D	G636	22670	13300	15025	17050	20500
XS Sport Utility 4D	G656	25070	14075	15900	18000	21400
XS LL Bean Spt Util	G676	26970	14850	16775	18800	22300
FORESTER AWD—4-Cyl. Turbo—Truck Equipment Schedule T1
| XT Sport Utility 4D | G696 | 27070 | 15025 | 16925 | 19000 | 22500 |
BAJA AWD—4-Cyl.—Truck Equipment Schedule T1
| Sport Util Pickup 4D | T62C | 22770 | 12125 | 13725 | 16000 | 19600 |
BAJA AWD—4-Cyl. Turbo—Truck Equipment Schedule T1
| Sport Util Pickup 4D | T63C | 24770 | 13675 | 15475 | 17800 | 21500 |

SUZUKI

1991 SUZUKI — JS(3or4)(JD31C)-M-#

SAMURAI—4-Cyl.—Truck Equipment Schedule T2
| JA Convertible | JD31C | 6279 | 400 | 550 | 1050 | 1825 |
| JS Convertible | JD31C | 7279 | 400 | 550 | 1050 | 1825 |

TRUCKS & VANS

1991 SUZUKI

Body	Type	VIN	List	Trade-In Fair	Good	Pvt-Party Good	Retail Excellent
SAMURAI 4WD—4-Cyl.—Truck Equipment Schedule T2							
JL	Convertible	JC31C	8579	475	675	1225	2075
	Fiberglass Hard Top			50	50	65	65
SIDEKICK—4-Cyl.—Truck Equipment Schedule T2							
JS	Convertible 2D	TC01C	10579	300	400	825	1475
SIDEKICK 4WD—4-Cyl.—Truck Equipment Schedule T2							
JL	Convertible 2D	TA01C	11279	450	625	1175	2000
JX	Convertible 2D	TA01C	12079	475	675	1225	2075
JX	Sport Utility 4D	TD01V	12294	625	900	1550	2600
JLX	Sport Util 4D	TD01V	13294	750	1075	1800	2925

1992 SUZUKI — JS(3or4)(JD31C)–N–#

Body	Type	VIN	List	Fair	Good	Good	Excellent
SAMURAI—4-Cyl.—Truck Equipment Schedule T2							
JA	Convertible	JD31C	6599	400	600	1100	1925
SAMURAI 4WD—4-Cyl.—Truck Equipment Schedule T2							
JL	Convertible	JC31C	8499	500	725	1250	2150
	Fiberglass Hard Top			50	50	65	65
SIDEKICK—4-Cyl.—Truck Equipment Schedule T2							
JS-Plus	Conv 2D	TC01C	10999	325	450	900	1600
JS	Sport Utility 4D	TE01C	11959	550	800	1400	2375
SIDEKICK 4WD—4-Cyl.—Truck Equipment Schedule T2							
JX	Convertible 2D	TA01C	12299	500	725	1275	2200
JX	Limited Conv 2D	TA01C	13599	525	750	1300	2250
JX	Sport Utility 4D	TD01V	12809	700	1025	1700	2825
JLX	Sport Util 4D	TD01V	14009	850	1200	2000	3225
JLX	Ltd Spt Util 4D	TD01V	15509	875	1225	2025	3300

1993 SUZUKI — (JSor2S)(3or4)(JD31C)–P

Body	Type	VIN	List	Fair	Good	Good	Excellent
SAMURAI—4-Cyl.—Truck Equipment Schedule T2							
JA	Convertible	JD31C	7019	325	425	900	1650
SAMURAI 4WD—4-Cyl.—Truck Equipment Schedule T2							
JL	Convertible	JC31C	8919	400	575	1100	1950
	Fiberglass Hard Top			75	75	100	100
SIDEKICK—4-Cyl.—Truck Equipment Schedule T2							
JS	Convertible 2D	TC01C	11319	275	375	850	1575
JS	Sport Utility 4D	TE01C	12229	550	775	1425	2450
SIDEKICK 4WD—4-Cyl.—Truck Equipment Schedule T2							
JX	Convertible 2D	TA01C	12719	475	675	1275	2250
JX	Sport Utility 4D	TD01V	13329	725	1050	1800	3000
JLX	Sport Util 4D	TD01V	14529	875	1225	2100	3450

1994 SUZUKI — (JSor2S)(3or4)(JC31C)–R

Body	Type	VIN	List	Fair	Good	Good	Excellent
SAMURAI 4WD—4-Cyl.—Truck Equipment Schedule T2							
JL	Convertible	JC31C	9799	350	475	1025	1825
	Fiberglass Hard Top			100	100	135	135
SIDEKICK—4-Cyl.—Truck Equipment Schedule T2							
JS	Convertible 2D	TC01C	11779	250	350	875	1650
JS	Sport Utility 4D	TE01C	13199	550	800	1500	2625
SIDEKICK 4WD—4-Cyl.—Truck Equipment Schedule T2							
JX	Convertible 2D	TA01C	13179	475	675	1325	2375
JX	Sport Utility 4D	TD01V	14429	775	1100	1975	3275
JLX	Sport Util 4D	TD01V	15509	925	1300	2375	3900

1995 SUZUKI — (JS3,JS4or2S3)(JC31C)–S

Body	Type	VIN	List	Fair	Good	Good	Excellent
SAMURAI 4WD—4-Cyl.—Truck Equipment Schedule T2							
JL	Convertible	JC31C	10234	325	450	1025	1875
	Fiberglass Hard Top			100	100	135	135
SIDEKICK—4-Cyl.—Truck Equipment Schedule T2							
JS	Convertible 2D	TC01C	12344	275	375	1000	1925
JS	Sport Utility 4D	TE02V	13869	600	875	1675	2950
	Limited			100	100	135	135
SIDEKICK 4WD—4-Cyl.—Truck Equipment Schedule T2							
JX	Convertible 2D	TA02C	13844	500	725	1475	2675
JX	Sport Utility 4D	TD03V	15179	850	1200	2175	3650
JLX	Sport Util 4D	TD03V	16689	1025	1450	2600	4250
	Limited			100	100	135	135

1996 SUZUKI — (2SorJS)3(TC02C)–T–#

Body	Type	VIN	List	Fair	Good	Good	Excellent
SIDEKICK—4-Cyl.—Truck Equipment Schedule T2							
JS	Convertible 2D	TC02C	13274	325	450	1175	2250
JS	Utility 4D	TE02V	14789	700	1000	1950	3400

Body Type	VIN	List	Trade-In Fair	Trade-In Good	Pvt-Party Good	Retail Excellent
SIDEKICK 4WD—4-Cyl.—Truck Equipment Schedule T2						
JX Convertible 2D	TA02C	15044	575	825	1700	3050
JX Utility 4D	TD03V	16389	950	1325	2525	4175
Sport JX Utility 4D	TD21V	18389	1625	2125	3450	5275
Sport JLX Util 4D	TD21V	19389	1675	2175	3500	5325
X-90 4WD—4-Cyl.—Truck Equipment Schedule T2						
Sport Utility 2D	LB11S	15389	550	800	1550	2775
2WD	A		(425)	(425)	(565)	(565)

1997 SUZUKI — (2SorJS)3(TC02C)-V-#

Body Type	VIN	List	Trade-In Fair	Trade-In Good	Pvt-Party Good	Retail Excellent
SIDEKICK—4-Cyl.—Truck Equipment Schedule T2						
JS Convertible 2D	TC02C	13299	400	575	1450	2775
JS Utility 4D	TE02V	14819	825	1175	2350	4075
Sport JS Utility 4D	TE21V	17119	875	1225	2475	4200
SIDEKICK 4WD—4-Cyl.—Truck Equipment Schedule T2						
JX Convertible 2D	TA02C	15069	700	1000	2050	3650
JX Utility 4D	TD03V	16419	1075	1525	2825	4600
Sport JX Utility 4D	TD21V	18119	1875	2400	3825	5800
Sport JLX Util 4D	TD21V	19619	1950	2475	3900	5875
X-90 4WD—4-Cyl.—Truck Equipment Schedule T2						
Sport Utility 2D	LB11S	15019	750	1050	2025	3450
2WD	A		(450)	(450)	(600)	(600)

1998 SUZUKI — (2SorJS)3(TC02C)-W-#

Body Type	VIN	List	Trade-In Fair	Trade-In Good	Pvt-Party Good	Retail Excellent
SIDEKICK—4-Cyl.—Truck Equipment Schedule T2						
JS Convertible 2D	TC02C	13519	550	775	1850	3400
JS Utility 4D	TE02V	14829	1000	1400	2750	4575
Sport JS Utility 4D	TE02V	17329	1050	1475	2825	4675
SIDEKICK 4WD—4-Cyl.—Truck Equipment Schedule T2						
JX Convertible 2D	TA02C	15289	875	1225	2525	4350
JX Utility 4D	TD03V	16429	1325	1825	3200	5125
Sport JX Utility 4D	TD21V	18329	2200	2800	4275	6350
Sport JLX Util 4D	TD21V	19829	2275	2850	4400	6475
X-90 4WD—4-Cyl.—Truck Equipment Schedule T2						
Sport Utility 2D	LB11S	15229	975	1375	2575	4250
2WD	A		(475)	(475)	(635)	(635)

1999 SUZUKI — (Jor2)S3(TC52C)-X-#

Body Type	VIN	List	Trade-In Fair	Trade-In Good	Pvt-Party Good	Retail Excellent
VITARA—4-Cyl.—Truck Equipment Schedule T2						
JS Convertible 2D	TC52C	14719	675	975	2175	3925
JS Hard Top 4D	TE52V	15829	1200	1650	3000	4875
4-Cyl. 1.6 Liter			(200)	(200)	(265)	(265)
VITARA 4WD—4-Cyl.—Truck Equipment Schedule T2						
JX Convertible 2D	TA52C	16519	925	1300	2600	4400
JX Hard Top 4D	TD52V	17429	1475	1975	3375	5250
4-Cyl. 1.6 Liter			(200)	(200)	(265)	(265)
GRAND VITARA—V6—Truck Equipment Schedule T1						
JS Utility 4D	TE62V	18429	2225	2825	4275	6300
GRAND VITARA 4WD—V6—Truck Equipment Schedule T1						
JLX Utility 4D	TD62V	19429	2650	3275	4750	6875

2000 SUZUKI — (Jor2)S3(TC03C)-Y-#

Body Type	VIN	List	Trade-In Fair	Trade-In Good	Pvt-Party Good	Retail Excellent
VITARA—4-Cyl.—Truck Equipment Schedule T2						
JS Convertible 2D	TC03C	13939	875	1225	2600	4450
JS Hard Top 4D	TE52V	15949	1525	2025	3525	5500
JLS Convertible 2D	TC52C	15439	1275	1775	3200	5175
JLS Hard Top 4D	TE52V	16749	1800	2325	3800	5850
VITARA 4WD—4-Cyl.—Truck Equipment Schedule T2						
JX Convertible 2D	TA03C	15739	1125	1575	3000	4950
JX Hard Top 4D	TD52V	17549	1875	2400	3900	5950
JLX Convertible 2D	TA52C	17239	2525	3125	4675	6825
JLX Hard Top 4D	TD52V	18349	2775	3400	4975	7150
GRAND VITARA—V6—Truck Equipment Schedule T1						
JLS Hard Top 4D	TE62V	19749	2775	3400	4975	7150
Ltd Hard Top 4D	TE62V	22149	2975	3650	5225	7450
GRAND VITARA 4WD—V6—Truck Equipment Schedule T1						
JLX Hard Top 4D	TD62V	20749	3250	3925	5550	7800
Ltd Hard Top 4D	TD62V	23149	3325	4025	5625	7900

Body Type	VIN	List	Trade-In Fair	Trade-In Good	Pvt-Party Good	Retail Excellent

2001 SUZUKI — (Jor2)S3(TC03C)-1-#

VITARA—4-Cyl.—Truck Equipment Schedule T2

Body Type	VIN	List	Fair	Good	Good	Excellent
JS Convertible 2D	TC03C	14369	1175	1625	3125	5175
JS Hard Top 4D	TE52C	16079	2025	2575	4150	6300
JLS Convertible 2D	TC52C	15869	1725	2250	3800	5925
JLS Hard Top 2D	TE52C	16869	2175	2775	4350	6525
JLS Hard Top 4D	TE52C	17079	2300	2875	4475	6700

VITARA 4WD—4-Cyl.—Truck Equipment Schedule T2

JX Convertible 2D	TA03C	15969	1550	2050	3625	5700
JX Hard Top 4D	TD52D	17579	2400	2975	4575	6800
JLX Convertible 2D	TA52C	17469	3125	3775	5450	7750
JLX Hard Top 2D	TD52D	18469	3250	3950	5950	8325
JLX Hard Top 4D	TD52V	18579	3400	4100	5775	8125

GRAND VITARA—V6—Truck Equipment Schedule T1

JLS Hard Top 4D	TE62V	19879	3450	4150	5825	8175
Ltd Hard Top 4D	TE62V	22279	3625	4350	6050	8425

GRAND VITARA 4WD—V6—Truck Equipment Schedule T1

JLX Hard Top 4D	TD62V	21079	3975	4725	6450	8875
Ltd Hard Top 4D	TD62V	23479	4050	4825	6550	9000

XL-7 4WD—V6—Truck Equipment Schedule T1

Sport Utility 4D	TX92V	21499	4375	5175	6775	9075
Plus Sport Util 4D	TX92V	23999	4600	5425	7025	9375
Touring Spt Util 4D	TX92V	24999	4650	5500	7100	9450
Limited Spt Util 4D	TX92V	26499	4700	5550	7175	9525
2WD			(725)	(725)	(965)	(965)

2002 SUZUKI — (Jor2)S3(TC52C)-2-#

VITARA—4-Cyl.—Truck Equipment Schedule T2

JLS Convertible 2D	TC52C	16089	2300	2875	4575	6875
JLS Hard Top 4D	TE52C	17299	2975	3650	5325	7700

VITARA 4WD—4-Cyl.—Truck Equipment Schedule T2

JLX Convertible 2D	TA52C	17489	3875	4625	6400	8875
JLX Hard Top 4D	TD52D	18699	4175	4950	6750	9275

GRAND VITARA—V6—Truck Equipment Schedule T1

JLS Hard Top 4D	TE62V	19099	4250	5050	6850	9350
Ltd Hard Top 4D	TE62V	22299	4425	5225	7025	9575

GRAND VITARA 4WD—V6—Truck Equipment Schedule T1

JLX Hard Top 4D	TD62V	20299	4850	5700	7550	10150
Ltd Hard Top 4D	TD62V	23490	4950	5800	7650	10300

XL-7 4WD—V6—Truck Equipment Schedule T1

Sport Utility 4D	TX92V	22319	5500	6425	8125	10600
Plus Spt Util 4D	TX92V	23899	5750	6700	8425	10950
Touring Spt Util 4D	TX92V	25319	5850	6800	8500	11050
Limited Spt Util 4D	TX92V	26519	5875	6850	8550	11100
2WD	Y		(800)	(800)	(1065)	(1065)

2003 SUZUKI — (Jor2)S3(TC52C)-3-#

VITARA—4-Cyl.—Truck Equipment Schedule T2

Convertible 2D	TC52C	16109	3100	3750	5550	8025
Hard Top 4D	TE52V	17319	3800	4550	6375	8925

VITARA 4WD—4-Cyl.—Truck Equipment Schedule T2

Convertible 2D	TA52C	17509	4800	5650	7550	10200
Hard Top 4D	TD52V	18719	5125	6025	7900	10600

GRAND VITARA—V6—Truck Equipment Schedule T1

Hard Top 4D	TE62V	20119	5250	6100	8025	10700

GRAND VITARA 4WD—V6—Truck Equipment Schedule T1

Hard Top 4D	TD62V	20319	5900	6875	8800	11600

XL-7 4WD—V6—Truck Equipment Schedule T1

Touring Spt Util 4D	TX92V	22339	7225	8350	10200	12950
Limited Spt Util 4D	TX92V	25399	7300	8400	10250	13000
w/o Third Seat			(500)	(500)	(665)	(665)
2WD	Y		(875)	(875)	(1165)	(1165)

2004 SUZUKI — (Jor2)S3(TE52V)-4-#

VITARA—V6—Truck Equipment Schedule T2

LX Hard Top 4D	TE52V	16799	4875	5725	7525	10100

VITARA 4WD—V6—Truck Equipment Schedule T2

LX Hard Top 4D	TD52V	17999	6300	7325	9200	11950

GRAND VITARA—V6—Truck Equipment Schedule T1

LX Hard Top 4D	TE62V	18999	6450	7450	9350	12150
EX Hard Top 4D	TE62V	20799	7025	8125	10050	12850

Body	Type	VIN	List	Trade-In Fair	Good	Pvt-Party Good	Retail Excellent
GRAND VITARA 4WD—V6—Truck Equipment Schedule T1							
LX Hard Top 4D	TD62V	19499	**7175**	**8275**	**10200**	**13050**
EX Hard Top 4D	TD62V	22499	**7775**	**8925**	**10900**	**13800**
XL-7 4WD—V6—Truck Equipment Schedule T1							
LX Sport Utility 4D	TX92V	22899	**8950**	**10225**	**12100**	**14950**
EX Sport Utility 4D	TX92V	25399	**9025**	**10325**	**12150**	**15050**
w/o Third Seat			**(700)**	**(700)**	**(935)**	**(935)**
2WD	Y		**(950)**	**(950)**	**(1265)**	**(1265)**

2005 SUZUKI — JS3(TE62V)-5-#

Body	Type	VIN	List	Trade-In Fair	Good	Pvt-Party Good	Retail Excellent
GRAND VITARA—V6—Truck Equipment Schedule T1							
LX Hard Top 4D	TE62V	19994	**7900**	**9075**	**11000**	**13850**
EX Hard Top 4D	TE62V	21474	**8525**	**9750**	**11750**	**14700**
GRAND VITARA 4WD—V6—Truck Equipment Schedule T1							
LX Hard Top 4D	TD62V	21694	**8675**	**9950**	**11900**	**14900**
EX Hard Top 4D	TD62V	23194	**9300**	**10625**	**12650**	**15700**
XL-7 4WD—V6—Truck Equipment Schedule T1							
LX Sport Utility 4D	TX92V	25394	**10950**	**12425**	**14350**	**17450**
EX Sport Utility 4D	TX92V	28394	**11000**	**12525**	**14500**	**17600**
w/o Third Seat			**(750)**	**(750)**	**(1000)**	**(1000)**
2WD	Y		**(1000)**	**(1000)**	**(1335)**	**(1335)**

TOYOTA

1991 TOYOTA — JT(3or4)(RN37J)-M-#

Body	Type	VIN	List	Trade-In Fair	Good	Pvt-Party Good	Retail Excellent
4RUNNER 4WD—4-Cyl.—Truck Equipment Schedule T1							
SR5 Sport Util 2D	RN37J	18918	**2075**	**2650**	**3850**	**5600**
SR5 Sport Util 4D	RN37W	18908	**2275**	**2850**	**4125**	**5925**
2WD	2		**(350)**	**(350)**	**(465)**	**(465)**
V6 3.0 Liter	V		**150**	**150**	**200**	**200**
LAND CRUISER 4WD—6-Cyl.—Truck Equipment Schedule T1							
Sport Utility 4D	FJ80W	23553	**3100**	**3750**	**5375**	**7650**
PREVIA—4-Cyl.—Truck Equipment Schedule T1							
Deluxe Minivan	AC11R	17173	**1275**	**1775**	**2875**	**4450**
LE Minivan	AC12R	19573	**1550**	**2050**	**3250**	**4900**
4WD	2		**250**	**250**	**335**	**335**
PICKUP—4-Cyl.—Truck Equipment Schedule T2							
Short Bed	RN81A	8683	**1075**	**1525**	**2500**	**3900**
Deluxe Short Bed	RN81P	9503	**1125**	**1575**	**2600**	**4050**
Deluxe Long Bed	RN82P	10033	**1175**	**1625**	**2650**	**4100**
Deluxe Xtra Cab	RN93P	10743	**1675**	**2175**	**3300**	**4900**
4WD	0,1		**500**	**500**	**665**	**665**
V6 3.0 Liter	V		**100**	**100**	**135**	**135**
PICKUP—V6—Truck Equipment Schedule T2							
1 Ton Long Bed	VN82N	11803	**1250**	**1750**	**2800**	**4300**
SR5 Xtra Cab	VN93G	13533	**1925**	**2450**	**3625**	**5275**
4WD	0,1		**500**	**500**	**665**	**665**

1992 TOYOTA — (JT3or1N4)(RN37J)-N-#

Body	Type	VIN	List	Trade-In Fair	Good	Pvt-Party Good	Retail Excellent
4RUNNER 4WD—4-Cyl.—Truck Equipment Schedule T1							
SR5 Sport Util 2D	RN37J	20723	**2400**	**2975**	**4250**	**6075**
SR5 Sport Util 4D	RN37W	20593	**2625**	**3250**	**4550**	**6425**
2WD	2		**(375)**	**(375)**	**(500)**	**(500)**
V6 3.0 Liter	V		**175**	**175**	**235**	**235**
LAND CRUISER 4WD—6-Cyl.—Truck Equipment Schedule T1							
Sport Utility 4D	FJ80W	25923	**3650**	**4400**	**6125**	**8550**
PREVIA—4-Cyl.—Truck Equipment Schedule T1							
Deluxe Minivan	AC11R	19453	**1550**	**2050**	**3250**	**4925**
LE Minivan	AC12R	21743	**1875**	**2400**	**3650**	**5425**
All-Trac AWD	2		**275**	**275**	**365**	**365**
PICKUP—4-Cyl.—Truck Equipment Schedule T2							
Short Bed	RN81A	9503	**1200**	**1650**	**2675**	**4125**
Deluxe Short Bed	RN81P	10373	**1225**	**1725**	**2775**	**4275**
Deluxe Long Bed	RN82P	10903	**1275**	**1775**	**2825**	**4325**
Deluxe Xtra Cab	RN93P	11613	**1825**	**2350**	**3525**	**5200**
4WD	0		**550**	**550**	**735**	**735**
V6 3.0 Liter	V		**150**	**150**	**200**	**200**
PICKUP—V6—Truck Equipment Schedule T2							
1 Ton Long Bed	VN82N	12593	**1400**	**1900**	**2975**	**4525**
SR5 Xtra Cab	VN93G	14353	**2100**	**2675**	**3875**	**5600**
4WD	0		**550**	**550**	**735**	**735**

TRUCKS & VANS

Body	Type	VIN	List	Trade-In Fair	Good	Pvt-Party Good	Retail Excellent

TRUCKS & VANS

1993 TOYOTA — (JT3or1N4)(RN37W)-P-#

4RUNNER 4WD—4-Cyl.—Truck Equipment Schedule T1
SR5 Spt Utility 4D		RN37W	20143	2825	3450	4825	6800
2WD		2		(400)	(400)	(535)	(535)
V6 3.0 Liter		V		225	225	300	300

LAND CRUISER 4WD—6-Cyl.—Truck Equipment Schedule T1
| Sport Utility 4D | | DJ81W | 31503 | 4300 | 5100 | 6925 | 9550 |
| Third Seat Pkg | | | | 250 | 250 | 335 | 335 |

PREVIA—4-Cyl.—Truck Equipment Schedule T1
Deluxe Minivan		AC11R	21198	1750	2275	3550	5300
LE Minivan		AC12R	23583	2125	2700	4025	5925
All-Trac AWD		2		325	325	435	435

PICKUP—4-Cyl.—Truck Equipment Schedule T2
Short Bed		RN81A	9723	1225	1675	2725	4200
Deluxe Short Bed		RN81P	10743	1325	1825	2875	4425
Deluxe Long Bed		RN82P	11283	1400	1900	2975	4525
Deluxe Xtra Cab		RN93P	12203	2000	2550	3725	5425
4WD		0,1		675	675	900	900
V6 3.0 Liter		V		225	225	300	300

PICKUP—V6—Truck Equipment Schedule T2
| SR5 Xtra Cab | | VN93G | 14963 | 2300 | 2875 | 4150 | 5925 |
| 4WD | | 1 | | 675 | 675 | 900 | 900 |

T100 PICKUP—V6—Truck Equipment Schedule T2
Long Bed		VD10A	14533	1375	1875	2950	4500
1 Ton Long Bed		VD10B	15253	1625	2125	3275	4900
SR5 Long Bed		VD10C	16043	1625	2125	3275	4900
4WD		2		675	675	900	900

1994 TOYOTA — (JT3or1N4)(RN37W)-R-#

4RUNNER 4WD—4-Cyl.—Truck Equipment Schedule T1
SR5 Spt Utility 4D		RN37W	21338	3050	3725	5175	7225
2WD		2		(425)	(425)	(565)	(565)
V6 3.0 Liter		V		275	275	365	365

LAND CRUISER 4WD—6-Cyl.—Truck Equipment Schedule T1
| Sport Utility 4D | | DJ81W | 34653 | 5900 | 6875 | 9025 | 12100 |
| Third Seat Pkg | | | | 275 | 275 | 365 | 365 |

PREVIA—4-Cyl.—Truck Equipment Schedule T1
DX Minivan		AC11R	24218	1975	2525	3850	5750
LE Minivan		AC12R	26183	2400	2975	4425	6400
All-Trac AWD		2		375	375	500	500

PREVIA—4-Cyl. Supercharged—Truck Equipment Schedule T1
| LE S/C Minivan | | AC14R | 28543 | 2900 | 3575 | 5075 | 7175 |
| All-Trac AWD | | 2 | | 375 | 375 | 500 | 500 |

PICKUP—4-Cyl.—Truck Equipment Schedule T2
Short Bed		RN81A	10443	1250	1750	2825	4325
DX Short Bed		RN81P	11533	1450	1950	3050	4600
DX Xtra Cab		RN93P	13083	2175	2775	3975	5725
4WD		0,1		800	800	1065	1065
V6 3.0 Liter		V		300	300	400	400

PICKUP—V6—Truck Equipment Schedule T2
| SR5 Xtra Cab | | VN93G | 15943 | 2550 | 3150 | 4425 | 6250 |
| 4WD | | 1 | | 800 | 800 | 1065 | 1065 |

T100 PICKUP—4-Cyl.—Truck Equipment Schedule T2
| Long Bed | | UD10D | 13623 | 1375 | 1900 | 2975 | 4550 |

T100 PICKUP—6-Cyl.—Truck Equipment Schedule T2
DX Long Bed		VD10A	15323	1625	2125	3275	4900
DX 1 Ton Long Bed		VD10B	16063	1925	2450	3650	5350
SR5 Long Bed		VD10C	17153	1925	2450	3650	5350
4WD		2		750	750	1000	1000

1995 TOYOTA—(JT3,JT4or4TA)(RN37W)-S-#

4RUNNER 4WD—4-Cyl.—Truck Equipment Schedule T1
SR5 Spt Utility 4D		RN37W	22450	3375	4075	5600	7750
Limited				425	425	565	565
2WD		2		(450)	(450)	(600)	(600)
V6 3.0 Liter		V		325	325	435	435

LAND CRUISER 4WD—6-Cyl.—Truck Equipment Schedule T1
| Sport Utility 4D | | DJ81W | 39085 | 6775 | 7825 | 10100 | 13350 |
| Third Seat Pkg | | | | 300 | 300 | 400 | 400 |

PREVIA—4-Cyl.—Truck Equipment Schedule T1
| DX Minivan | | AC11R | 24400 | 2275 | 2825 | 4250 | 6200 |

Body Type	VIN	List	Trade-In Fair	Trade-In Good	Pvt-Party Good	Retail Excellent
LE Minivan	AC12R	26975	2725	3350	4825	6900
All-Trac AWD	2		425	425	565	565
PREVIA—4-Cyl. Supercharged—Truck Equipment Schedule T1						
DX S/C Minivan	AC13R	24900	2850	3525	5025	7125
LE Minivan	AC14R	27475	3325	4025	5575	7775
All-Trac AWD	2		425	425	565	565
PICKUP—4-Cyl.—Truck Equipment Schedule T2						
Short Bed	RN81A	10985	1375	1875	2925	4475
DX Short Bed	RN81P	11885	1625	2125	3275	4875
DX Xtra Cab	RN93P	13495	2425	3000	4275	6075
4WD	0,1		900	900	1200	1200
V6 3.0 Liter	V		375	375	500	500
PICKUP—V6—Truck Equipment Schedule T2						
SR5 Xtra Cab	VN93G	16455	2825	3450	4750	6650
4WD	1		900	900	1200	1200
TACOMA—4-Cyl.—Truck Equipment Sch T2						
Short Bed	UN41B	12435	1825	2350	3525	5200
Xtra Cab	UN53B	14545	2325	2900	4175	5975
4WD	6,7		900	900	1200	1200
V6 3.4 Liter	V		375	375	500	500
TACOMA 4WD—V6—Truck Equipment Sch T2						
SR5 Xtra Cab	VN73K	21715	4025	4775	6300	8500
T100 PICKUP—V6—Truck Equipment Schedule T2						
Long Bed	VD10D	15135	1675	2175	3325	4975
DX Long Bed	VD11E	16155	1925	2450	3650	5325
DX 1 Ton Long Bed	VD11G	16935	2250	2825	4050	5825
DX Xtra Cab	VD12E	18000	2850	3500	4800	6725
SR5 Xtra Cab	VD12F	19275	3375	4075	5475	7525
4WD	2		900	900	1200	1200
4-Cyl. 2.7 Liter	U		(200)	(200)	(265)	(265)

1996 TOYOTA—(JT3,JT4or4TA)(YP10V)—T–#

Body Type	VIN	List	Trade-In Fair	Trade-In Good	Pvt-Party Good	Retail Excellent
RAV4 4WD—4-Cyl.—Truck Equipment Schedule T2						
Sport Utility 2D	YP10V	17058	2600	3225	4450	6225
Sport Utility 4D	HP10V	17758	3000	3675	4975	6875
2WD	G,X		(425)	(425)	(565)	(565)
Dual Sun Roofs			50	50	65	65
4RUNNER 4WD—4-Cyl.—Truck Equipment Schedule T1						
Sport Utility 4D	HM84R	23853	3425	4125	5700	7925
2WD	G		(475)	(475)	(635)	(635)
4RUNNER 4WD—V6—Truck Equipment Schedule T1						
SR5 Spt Utility 4D	HN86R	27453	4800	5650	7425	9950
Limited Spt Util 4D	HN87R	33408	5775	6725	8600	11350
2WD	G		(475)	(475)	(635)	(635)
LAND CRUISER 4WD—6-Cyl.—Truck Equipment Schedule T3						
Sport Utility 4D	HJ85J	45483	7700	8850	11300	14800
Third Seat Pkg			325	325	435	435
PREVIA—4-Cyl. Supercharged—Truck Equipment Schedule T1						
DX S/C Minivan	GK12M	26473	3275	3950	5525	7750
LE S/C Minivan	GK13M	29278	3750	4500	6125	8475
AWD			475	475	635	635
TACOMA—4-Cyl.—Truck Equipment Schedule T2						
Short Bed	NL42M	12643	2100	2675	3900	5675
Xtra Cab	VL52M	14793	2700	3300	4625	6525
4WD	6,7		1000	1000	1335	1335
V6 3.4 Liter	N		450	450	600	600
TACOMA 4WD—V6—Truck Equipment Schedule T2						
SR5 Xtra Cab	WN74N	22648	4650	5500	7100	9425
T100 PICKUP—4-Cyl.—Truck Equipment Schedule T2						
Long Bed	JM11D	15113	1925	2450	3675	5400
T100 PICKUP—V6—Truck Equipment Schedule T2						
Xtra Cab	TN12D	18683	3200	3875	5250	7275
SR5 Xtra Cab	UN14D	20158	3800	4550	6025	8150
4WD			950	950	1265	1265

1997 TOYOTA—(JT3,JT4or4TA)(YP10V)—V

Body Type	VIN	List	Trade-In Fair	Trade-In Good	Pvt-Party Good	Retail Excellent
RAV4 4WD—4-Cyl.—Truck Equipment Schedule T2						
Sport Utility 2D	YP10V	17128	3050	3725	5025	6925
Sport Utility 4D	HP10V	17828	3525	4225	5575	7575
2WD	G,X		(450)	(450)	(600)	(600)
Dual Sun Roofs			50	50	65	65
4RUNNER 4WD—4-Cyl.—Truck Equipment Schedule T1						
Sport Utility 4D	HM84R	24293	4000	4750	6450	8825

Body	Type	VIN	List	Trade-In Fair	Good	Pvt-Party Good	Retail Excellent
2WD		G		(500)	(500)	(665)	(665)
4RUNNER 4WD—V6—Truck Equipment Schedule T1							
SR5 Sport Util 4D		HN86R	27983	5525	6450	8325	11000
Limited Spt Util 4D		HN87R	34158	6575	7600	9600	12500
2WD		G		(500)	(500)	(665)	(665)
LAND CRUISER 4WD—6-Cyl.—Truck Equipment Schedule T3							
Sport Utility 4D		HJ85J	46293	8775	10050	12600	16300
Third Seat Pkg				450	450	600	600
PREVIA—4-Cyl. Supercharged—Truck Equipment Schedule T1							
DX S/C Minivan		GK12M	26963	3725	4450	6100	8475
LE S/C Minivan		GK13M	29858	4275	5075	6775	9225
All-Trac AWD		2		500	500	665	665
TACOMA—4-Cyl.—Truck Equipment Schedule T2							
Short Bed		NL42N	12813	2450	3050	4350	6200
Xtra Cab		VL52N	14983	3100	3750	5150	7125
4WD				1100	1100	1465	1465
V6 3.4 Liter		N		525	525	700	700
TACOMA 4WD—V6—Truck Equipment Schedule T2							
SR5 Xtra Cab		WN74N	22868	5375	6275	7925	10400
T100—4-Cyl.—Truck Equipment Schedule T2							
Long Bed		JM11D	15303	2250	2825	4100	5900
T100—V6—Truck Equipment Schedule T2							
DX Xtra Cab		TN12D	19213	3650	4375	5825	7900
SR5 Xtra Cab		UN14D	20428	4325	5125	6625	8825
4WD				1050	1050	1400	1400

1998 TOYOTA–(JT3,JT4or4TA)(YP10V)–W

Body	Type	VIN	List	Trade-In Fair	Good	Pvt-Party Good	Retail Excellent
RAV4 4WD—4-Cyl.—Truck Equipment Schedule T2							
Sport Util Conv 2D		YP10V	17218	3700	4450	5800	7800
Sport Utility 2D		YP10V	17218	3625	4350	5700	7675
Sport Utility 4D		HP10V	18078	4100	4875	6275	8350
2WD		G,X		(475)	(475)	(635)	(635)
4RUNNER 4WD—4-Cyl.—Truck Equipment Schedule T1							
Sport Utility 4D		HM84R	25013	4700	5550	7350	9900
2WD				(525)	(525)	(700)	(700)
4RUNNER 4WD—V6—Truck Equipment Schedule T1							
SR5 Sport Util 4D		HN86R	28573	6350	7375	9325	12150
Limited Spt Util 4D		HN87R	35038	7475	8575	10650	13750
2WD		G		(525)	(525)	(700)	(700)
LAND CRUISER 4WD—V8—Truck Equipment Schedule T3							
Sport Utility 4D		HT05J	46413	11825	13375	16350	20700
Third Seat Pkg				475	475	635	635
SIENNA—V6—Truck Equipment Schedule T1							
CE Minivan		GF19C	21560	4050	4825	6450	8775
LE Minivan		ZF13C	24395	4600	5425	7125	9550
XLE Minivan		ZF13C	27520	5275	6175	7950	10500
w/o 2nd Sliding Door				(475)	(475)	(635)	(635)
TACOMA—4-Cyl.—Truck Equipment Schedule T2							
Short Bed		NL42N	13228	2825	3475	4825	6800
Xtra Cab		VL52N	15128	3500	4250	5700	7800
PreRunner Xtra		SM92N	17658	4400	5200	6750	9000
4WD		6,7		1200	1200	1600	1600
V6 3.4 Liter		N		575	575	765	765
TACOMA 4WD—V6—Truck Equipment Schedule T2							
Limited Xtra Cab		WN74N	24448	5825	6775	8500	11000
T100—4-Cyl.—Truck Equipment Schedule T2							
Long Bed		JM11D	15248	2600	3225	4550	6475
T100—V6—Truck Equipment Schedule T2							
DX Xtra Cab		TN12D	19218	4100	4875	6375	8575
SR5 Xtra Cab		TN14D	20848	4825	5675	7275	9600
4WD		2		1150	1150	1535	1535

1999 TOYOTA–(4,5orJ)T(3,AorB)(YP10V)–X

Body	Type	VIN	List	Trade-In Fair	Good	Pvt-Party Good	Retail Excellent
RAV4 4WD—4-Cyl.—Truck Equipment Schedule T2							
Sport Util Conv 2D		YP10V	17508	4900	5750	7100	9175
Sport Utility 4D		HP10V	18198	4800	5650	7000	9075
2WD		G,X		(525)	(525)	(700)	(700)
4RUNNER 4WD—4-Cyl.—Truck Equipment Schedule T1							
Sport Utility 4D		HM84R	25443	5550	6475	8125	10550
2WD		G		(575)	(575)	(765)	(765)
4RUNNER 4WD—V6—Truck Equipment Schedule T1							
SR5 Sport Util 4D		HN86R	28773	7350	8450	10300	13050
Limited Spt Util 4D		HN87R	36088	8550	9800	11750	14700

TRUCKS & VANS

Body	Type	VIN	List	Trade-In Fair	Trade-In Good	Pvt-Party Good	Retail Excellent
2WD		G		(575)	(575)	(765)	(765)
LAND CRUISER 4WD—V8—Truck Equipment Schedule T3							
Sport Utility 4D		HT05J	48718	13575	15325	18300	22700
Third Seat Pkg				525	525	700	700
SIENNA—V6—Truck Equipment Schedule T1							
CE Minivan		GF19C	22738	4650	5500	7075	9400
LE Minivan		ZF13C	24778	5250	6150	7800	10250
XLE Minivan		ZF13C	28099	6000	6950	8675	11200
w/o 2nd Sliding Door				(500)	(500)	(665)	(665)
TACOMA—4-Cyl.—Truck Equipment Schedule T2							
Short Bed		NL42N	13388	3325	4000	5375	7375
Xtra Cab		VL52N	15288	4075	4850	6300	8450
PreRunner Short		NM92N	16348	4050	4800	6250	8375
PreRunner Xtra		SM92N	18028	5025	5900	7425	9700
4WD		6,7		1275	1275	1700	1700
V6 3.4 Liter		N		625	625	835	835
TACOMA 4WD—V6—Truck Equipment Schedule T2							
Limited Xtra Cab		WN74N	25108	6650	7675	9375	11950

Body	Type	VIN	List	Trade-In Fair	Trade-In Good	Pvt-Party Good	Retail Excellent
RAV4 4WD—4-Cyl.—Truck Equipment Schedule T2							
Sport Utility 4D		HP10V	18558	5700	6650	8050	10250
2WD		G,X		(600)	(600)	(800)	(800)
4RUNNER 4WD—4-Cyl.—Truck Equipment Schedule T1							
Sport Utility 4D		HM84R	26046	6475	7500	9250	11850
2WD		G		(650)	(650)	(865)	(865)
4RUNNER 4WD—V6—Truck Equipment Schedule T1							
SR5 Sport Util 4D		HN86R	29786	8525	9750	11650	14550
Limited Spt Util 4D		HN87R	36948	9950	11350	13350	16500
2WD		G		(650)	(650)	(865)	(865)
LAND CRUISER 4WD—V8—Truck Equipment Schedule T3							
Sport Utility 4D		HT05J	51308	16675	18775	22000	27000
Third Seat Pkg				600	600	800	800
SIENNA—V6—Truck Equipment Schedule T1							
CE Minivan		ZF19C	23338	5575	6500	8200	10650
LE Minivan		ZF13C	25378	6300	7300	9025	11600
XLE Minivan		ZF13C	27414	7100	8200	10000	12700
w/o 2nd Sliding Door				(550)	(550)	(735)	(735)
TACOMA—4-Cyl.—Truck Equipment Schedule T2							
Short Bed		NL42N	12208	3850	4600	6075	8200
Xtra Cab		VL52N	14458	4700	5550	7075	9325
PreRunner Short		NM92N	14298	4675	5525	7050	9300
PreRunner Xtra		SM92N	17418	5775	6725	8350	10750
4WD				1450	1450	1935	1935
V6 3.4 Liter		N		725	725	965	965
TACOMA 4WD—V6—Truck Equipment Schedule T2							
Limited Xtra Cab		WN74N	24758	7775	8925	10700	13450
TUNDRA—V6—Truck Equipment Schedule T2							
Long Bed		JN321	15475	5275	6175	7475	9450
TUNDRA 4WD—V8—Truck Equipment Schedule T2							
SR5 Long Bed		KT441	23190	6925	8000	9400	11650
V6 3.4 Liter		N		(600)	(600)	(800)	(800)
TUNDRA—V8—Truck Equipment Schedule T2							
SR5 Access Cab 4D		RT341	22730	7650	8800	10300	12600
Ltd Access Cab 4D		RT381	24975	7925	9125	10600	13000
4WD		4		1400	1400	1865	1865
V6 3.4 Liter		N		(600)	(600)	(800)	(800)

Body	Type	VIN	List	Trade-In Fair	Trade-In Good	Pvt-Party Good	Retail Excellent
RAV4 4WD—4-Cyl.—Truck Equipment Schedule T2							
Sport Utility 4D		HH20V	18095	7025	8125	9625	12000
2WD		G,Z		(675)	(675)	(900)	(900)
HIGHLANDER 4WD—V6—Truck Equipment Schedule T1							
Sport Utility 4D		HF21A	26950	8975	10275	12350	15500
Limited Spt Utl 4D		HF21A	30445	9850	11250	13400	16700
2WD				(725)	(725)	(965)	(965)
4-Cyl. 2.4 Liter				(725)	(725)	(965)	(965)
4RUNNER 4WD—V6—Truck Equipment Schedule T1							
SR5 Sport Util 4D		HN86R	29375	9900	11300	13300	16350
Limited Spt Util 4D		HN87R	38085	11500	13050	15150	18500
2WD				(725)	(725)	(965)	(965)
SEQUOIA 4WD—V8—Truck Equipment Schedule T1							
SR5 Spt Util 4D		BT44A	34825	12850	14550	16800	20300

Body Type	VIN	List	Trade-In Fair	Trade-In Good	Pvt-Party Good	Retail Excellent
Limited Spt Util 4D	BT48A	42755	13775	15575	18000	21800
2WD			(725)	(725)	(965)	(965)
LAND CRUISER 4WD—V8—Truck Equipment Schedule T3						
Sport Utility 4D	HT05J	53375	20075	22600	26000	31400
Third Seat Pkg			675	675	900	900
SIENNA—V6—Truck Equipment Schedule T1						
CE Minivan	ZF19C	24385	6650	7675	9450	12150
LE Minivan	ZF13C	26235	7475	8575	10450	13250
XLE Minivan	ZF13C	28916	8375	9575	11500	14440
TACOMA—4-Cyl.—Truck Equipment Schedule T2						
Short Bed	NL42N	12325	4500	5300	6875	9150
Xtra Cab	VL52N	14965	5425	6350	7975	10400
PreRunner Short	NM92N	14215	5425	6350	7975	10400
PreRunner Xtra	SM92N	16815	6625	7675	9350	11950
PreRunner 4D	GM92N	18335	7650	8800	10550	13300
PreRunner Ltd 4D	GM92N	22690	8325	9525	11350	14150
4WD			1625	1625	2165	2165
V6 3.4 Liter	N		825	825	1100	1100
TACOMA—V6—Truck Equipment Schedule T2						
S-Runner Xtra Cab	VN52N	18385	6475	7500	9200	11750
TACOMA 4WD—V6—Truck Equipment Schedule T2						
Limited Xtra Cab	WN74N	24895	9025	10325	12150	15100
Double Cab 4D	HN72N	22345	8675	9950	11800	14650
Ltd Double Cab 4D	HN72N	25840	9075	10375	12250	15200
4-Cyl. 2.7 Liter	M		(725)	(725)	(965)	(965)
TUNDRA—V6—Truck Equipment Schedule T2						
Long Bed	JN321	16085	6275	7275	8600	10700
TUNDRA 4WD—V8—Truck Equipment Schedule T2						
SR5 Long Bed	RT441	23885	8075	9275	10700	13150
TUNDRA—V8—Truck Equipment Schedule T2						
SR5 Access Cab 4D	RT341	23455	8900	10175	11700	14200
Ltd Access Cab 4D	RT381	26205	9275	10575	12150	14650
4WD	4		1575	1575	2100	2100
V6 3.4 Liter	N		(675)	(675)	(900)	(900)

2002 TOYOTA—(4,5orJ)T(3,B,DorE)(HH20V)–2

Body Type	VIN	List	Trade-In Fair	Trade-In Good	Pvt-Party Good	Retail Excellent
RAV4 4WD—4-Cyl.—Truck Equipment Schedule T2						
Sport Utility 4D	HH20V	18435	8275	9475	11050	13600
2WD	G		(750)	(750)	(1000)	(1000)
HIGHLANDER 4WD—V6—Truck Equipment Schedule T1						
Sport Utility 4D	HF21A	27370	10575	12025	14200	17600
Limited Spt Utl 4D	HF21A	31305	11550	13100	15350	18850
2WD	G		(800)	(800)	(1065)	(1065)
4-Cyl. 2.4 Liter	D		(825)	(825)	(1100)	(1100)
4RUNNER 4WD—V6—Truck Equipment Schedule T1						
SR5 Sport Util 4D	HN86R	29385	11500	13050	15100	18400
Limited Spt Util 4D	HN87R	36615	13250	14975	17150	20700
2WD	G		(800)	(800)	(1065)	(1065)
SEQUOIA 4WD—V8—Truck Equipment Schedule T1						
SR5 Spt Util 4D	BT44A	35305	15025	16925	19250	23000
Limited Spt Util 4D	BT48A	42235	16050	18100	20600	24600
2WD	G		(800)	(800)	(1065)	(1065)
LAND CRUISER 4WD—V8—Truck Equipment Schedule T3						
Sport Utility 4D	HT05J	53105	23675	26575	30200	36000
SIENNA—V6—Truck Equipment Schedule T1						
CE Minivan	ZF19C	24415	7925	9125	11000	13850
LE Minivan	ZF13C	26265	8850	10125	12100	15100
XLE Minivan	ZF13C	28522	9850	11250	13250	16400
TACOMA—4-Cyl.—Truck Equipment Schedule T2						
Short Bed	NL42N	12410	5250	6150	7800	10250
Xtra Cab	VL52N	15050	6300	7300	9000	11550
PreRunner Short	NM92N	14400	6300	7325	9025	11600
PreRunner Xtra	SM92N	17000	7625	8750	10550	13300
PreRunner 4D	GM92N	18620	8775	10050	11900	14750
4WD			1800	1800	2400	2400
V6 3.4 Liter	N		925	925	1235	1235
TACOMA—V6—Truck Equipment Schedule T2						
S-Runner Xtra Cab	VN52N	18570	7650	8775	10550	13300
PreRunner Ltd 4D	GM92N	23000	9475	10825	12750	15700
TACOMA 4WD—V6—Truck Equipment Schedule T2						
Limited Xtra Cab	WN72N	23655	10375	11775	13750	16900
Double Cab 4D	HN72N	22630	9950	11350	13250	16250
Ltd Double Cab 4D	HN72N	26150	10425	11875	13850	17000

Body	Type	VIN	List	Trade-In Fair	Trade-In Good	Pvt-Party Good	Retail Excellent
TUNDRA—V6—Truck Equipment Schedule T2							
Long Bed		JN321	16115	7375	8500	9900	12150
TUNDRA 4WD—V8—Truck Equipment Schedule T2							
SR5 Long Bed		KT441	23915	9300	10625	12150	14700
TUNDRA—V8—Truck Equipment Schedule T2							
SR5 Access Cab 4D		RT341	23485	10275	11700	13300	15950
Ltd Access Cab 4D		RT381	27230	10675	12175	13750	16500
4WD		4		1750	1750	2335	2335
V6 3.4 Liter		N		(750)	(750)	(1000)	(1000)

2003 TOYOTA–(4,5orJ)T(B,DorE)(HH20V)–3

Body	Type	VIN	List	Trade-In Fair	Trade-In Good	Pvt-Party Good	Retail Excellent
RAV4 4WD—4-Cyl.—Truck Equipment Schedule T2							
Sport Utility 4D		HH20V	18435	9700	11050	12650	15300
2WD		G,Z		(825)	(825)	(1100)	(1100)
HIGHLANDER 4WD—V6—Truck Equipment Schedule T1							
Sport Utility 4D		HF21A	25790	12475	14125	16400	20000
Limited Spt Util 4D		HF21A	31305	13475	15225	17600	21300
2WD		G		(925)	(875)	(1165)	(1165)
4-Cyl. 2.4 Liter		D		(925)	(925)	(1235)	(1235)
4RUNNER 4WD—V6—Truck Equipment Schedule T1							
SR5 Sport Util 4D		BU14R	29990	13525	15275	17450	21000
Sport Utility 4D		BU14R	31785	13675	15425	17600	21100
Limited Spt Util 4D		BU17R	36190	15475	17400	19700	23500
2WD		Z		(875)	(875)	(1165)	(1165)
V8 4.7 Liter		T		425	425	565	565
SEQUOIA 4WD—V8—Truck Equipment Schedule T1							
SR5 Spt Util 4D		BT44A	35565	17450	19600	21900	25900
Limited Spt Util 4D		BT48A	44030	18625	20950	23500	27600
2WD		Z		(875)	(875)	(1165)	(1165)
LAND CRUISER 4WD—V8—Truck Equipment Schedule T3							
Sport Utility 4D		HT05J	53915	27650	30850	34700	40900
SIENNA—V6—Truck Equipment Schedule T1							
CE Minivan		ZF19C	24415	9475	10825	12850	15950
LE Minivan		ZF19C	26265	10475	11925	14000	17200
XLE Minivan		ZF13C	28522	11600	13150	15250	18600
TACOMA—4-Cyl.—Truck Equipment Schedule T2							
Short Bed		NL42N	12610	6025	6975	8750	11350
Xtra Cab		VL52N	15250	7100	8200	10050	12750
PreRunner Short		NM92N	14525	7175	8275	10100	12800
PreRunner Xtra		SM92N	17200	8550	9800	11700	14600
PreRunner 4D		GM92N	18820	9850	11250	13200	16200
4WD		N		1975	1975	2635	2635
V6 3.4 Liter		N		1025	1025	1365	1365
TACOMA—V6—Truck Equipment Schedule T2							
PreRunner Ltd 4D		GN92N	23430	10675	12125	14100	17250
TACOMA 4WD—V6—Truck Equipment Schedule T2							
Limited Xtra Cab		WN72N	22830	11700	13250	15350	18600
Double Cab 4D		HN72N	22830	11150	12650	14650	17850
Ltd Double Cab 4D		HN72N	26580	11825	13375	15450	18750
TUNDRA—V6—Truck Equipment Schedule T2							
Long Bed		JN321	16465	8600	9850	11350	13750
TUNDRA 4WD—V8—Truck Equipment Schedule T2							
SR5 Long Bed		KT441	24265	10675	12175	13750	16400
TUNDRA—V8—Truck Equipment Schedule T2							
SR5 Access Cab 4D		RT341	23835	11775	13350	15000	17800
Ltd Access Cab 4D		RT381	27465	12225	13875	15500	18400
4WD		4		1925	1925	2565	2565
V6 3.4 Liter		N		(825)	(825)	(1100)	(1100)

2004 TOYOTA–(5orJ)T(B,DorE)(HD20V)–4–#

Body	Type	VIN	List	Trade-In Fair	Trade-In Good	Pvt-Party Good	Retail Excellent
RAV4 4WD—4-Cyl.—Truck Equipment Schedule T2							
Sport Utility 4D		HD20V	20290	11300	12850	14400	17000
2WD		G		(900)	(900)	(1200)	(1200)
HIGHLANDER 4WD—V6—Truck Equipment Schedule T1							
Sport Utility 4D		HD21A	27930	14600	16500	18750	22500
Limited Spt Utl 4D		HF21A	31920	15775	17750	20100	23900
Third Seat				700	700	935	935
2WD		G		(950)	(950)	(1265)	(1265)
4-Cyl. 2.4 Liter		D		(1025)	(1025)	(1365)	(1365)
4RUNNER 4WD—V6—Truck Equipment Schedule T1							
SR5 Sport Util 4D		BU14R	29985	15725	17700	19800	23400
Sport Util 4D		BU14R	31225	15800	17800	20000	23700
Limited Spt Util 4D		BU17R	36260	17800	19975	22200	26100

Body Type	VIN	List	Trade-In Fair	Good	Pvt-Party Good	Retail Excellent
2WD	Z	.....	(950)	(950)	(1265)	(1265)
V8 4.7 Liter	T	.....	450	450	600	600
SEQUOIA 4WD—V8—Truck Equipment Schedule T1						
SR5 Spt Util 4D	BT44A	35695	20075	22600	24900	29000
Limited Spt Util 4D	BT48A	44760	21350	23950	26600	31000
2WD	Z	.....	(950)	(950)	(1265)	(1265)
SIENNA—V6—Truck Equipment Schedule T3						
Sport Utility 4D	HT05J	54765	31825	35500	39500	46100
SIENNA—V6—Truck Equipment Schedule T1						
CE Minivan	ZA23C	23495	11600	13200	15050	18050
LE Minivan	ZA23C	24800	12700	14350	16250	19400
XLE Minivan	ZA22C	28800	13925	15725	17650	21000
XLE Limited	ZA22C	35020	14450	16300	18300	21600
4WD	B	.....	975	975	1300	1300
TACOMA PICKUP—4-Cyl.—Truck Equipment Schedule T2						
Short Bed	NL42N	12800	7075	8175	9900	12450
Xtra Cab	VL52N	15460	8225	9425	11200	13950
PreRunner Short	NM92N	14715	8375	9575	11350	14050
PreRunner Xtra	SM92N	17410	9850	11250	13050	15950
PreRunner 4D	GM92N	19030	11250	12750	14700	17750
4WD	W,H	.....	2150	2150	2865	2865
V6 3.4 Liter	N	.....	1125	1125	1500	1500
TACOMA PICKUP—V6—Truck Equipment Schedule T2						
S-Runner Xtra Cab	VN52N	20700	10175	11600	13450	16400
PreRunner Ltd 4D	GN92N	23640	12175	13775	15700	18850
TACOMA PICKUP 4WD—V6—Truck Equipment Schedule T2						
Limited Xtra Cab	WN72N	24295	13350	15025	17050	20400
Double Cab 4D	HN72N	23040	12650	14300	16350	19600
Ltd Double Cab 4D	HN72N	26790	13525	15275	17300	20700
TUNDRA—V6—Truck Equipment Schedule T2						
Long Bed	RN32I	16495	10100	11450	12900	15350
TUNDRA 4WD—V8—Truck Equipment Schedule T2						
SR5 Long Bed	RT441	24415	12325	13975	15450	18150
TUNDRA—V8—Truck Equipment Schedule T2						
SR5 Access Cab 4D	RN341	23985	13475	15225	16800	19600
Ltd Access Cab 4D	RT381	27615	14025	15850	17400	20300
SR5 Double Cab 4D	ET341	26185	15325	17275	18900	21900
Ltd Double Cab 4D	ET381	29810	15800	17800	19500	22600
4WD	4	.....	2100	2100	2800	2800
V6 3.4 Liter	N	.....	(900)	(900)	(1200)	(1200)

2005 TOYOTA—(5orJ)T(B,DorE)(HD20V)-5-#

Body Type	VIN	List	Trade-In Fair	Good	Pvt-Party Good	Retail Excellent
RAV4 4WD—4-Cyl.—Truck Equipment Schedule T1						
Sport Utility 4D	HD20V	20515	13150	14900	16400	19100
2WD	G	.....	(950)	(950)	(1265)	(1265)
HIGHLANDER 4WD—V6—Truck Equipment Schedule T1						
Sport Utility 4D	HD21A	27955	17025	19150	21500	25500
Limited Spt Util 4D	EP21A	31945	18200	20475	22900	27000
Third Seat		.....	750	750	1000	1000
2WD	E,G	.....	(1000)	(1000)	(1335)	(1335)
4-Cyl. 2.4 Liter	D	.....	(1125)	(1125)	(1500)	(1500)
4RUNNER 4WD—V6—Truck Equipment Schedule T1						
SR5 Sport Util 4D	BU14R	30335	18200	20475	22700	26600
Sport Utility 4D	BU14R	31605	18275	20575	22800	26700
Limited Spt Util 4D	BU17R	36610	20375	22900	25200	29300
2WD	Z	.....	(1000)	(1000)	(1335)	(1335)
V8 4.7 Liter	T	.....	475	475	635	635
SEQUOIA 4WD—V8—Truck Equipment Schedule T1						
SR5 Spt Util 4D	BT44A	36520	23075	25800	28200	32600
Limited Spt Util 4D	BT48A	45525	24350	27250	30000	34700
2WD	Z	.....	(1000)	(1000)	(1335)	(1335)
LAND CRUISER 4WD—V8—Truck Equipment Schedule T3						
Sport Utility 4D	HT05J	55590				
SIENNA—V6—Truck Equipment Schedule T1						
CE Minivan	ZA23C	23790	13975	15775	17750	21000
LE Minivan	ZA23C	25295	15125	17025	19050	22500
XLE Minivan	ZA22C	29590	16350	18425	20600	24200
XLE Limited	ZA22C	35860	17025	19150	21200	24900
4WD	B	.....	1050	1050	1400	1400
TACOMA PICKUP—4-Cyl.—Truck Equipment Schedule T1						
Short Bed	NX22N	13980	8950	10225	11400	13500
Access Cab	TX22N	17395	10925	12375	13700	16000
PreRunner Short	NX62N	14850	9850	11250	12450	14650

Body	Type	VIN	List	Trade-In Fair	Trade-In Good	Pvt-Party Good	Retail Excellent
	PreRunner Access	TX62N	18155	**11975**	**13575**	**14950**	**17400**
	4WD	4,5		2325	2325	3100	3100
	V6 4.0 Liter	U		1225	1225	1635	1635
TACOMA PICKUP—V6—Truck Equipment Schedule T2							
	X-Runner Access	TU62N	23650				
	PreRunner Access	TU62N	19610	**13425**	**15175**	**16650**	**19250**
	PreRunner Dbl 5'	JU62N	22240	**15025**	**16925**	**18500**	**21300**
	PreRunner Dbl 6'	KU72N	22740	**15375**	**17325**	**18850**	**21700**
TACOMA PICKUP 4WD—V6—Truck Equipment Schedule T2							
	Double Cab Short	LU42N	24435	**16625**	**18725**	**20400**	**23400**
	Double Cab Long	MU52N	25815	**16350**	**18425**	**20000**	**23000**
TUNDRA—V6—Truck Equipment Schedule T2							
	Long Bed	JU321	16520	**10950**	**12425**	**13750**	**16200**
TUNDRA—V8—Truck Equipment Schedule T2							
	Work Truck Long	JT321	18995	**12225**	**13875**	**15350**	**17900**
	SR5 Access Cab 4D	RT341	24700	**15475**	**17450**	**19050**	**22000**
	Ltd Access Cab 4D	RT381	27640	**16050**	**18100**	**19800**	**22800**
	SR5 Double Cab 4D	ET341	26685	**17450**	**19600**	**21300**	**24600**
	Ltd Double Cab 4D	ET381	30310	**18050**	**20275**	**22100**	**25400**
	4WD	4		2275	2275	3035	3035
	V6 4.0 Liter	U		(950)	(950)	(1265)	(1265)

VOLKSWAGEN

1991 VOLKSWAGEN — WV2(YB025)-M-#

Body	Type	VIN	List	Fair	Good	Good	Excellent
VANAGON—4-Cyl.—Truck Equipment Schedule T2							
	Minivan	YB025	14680	**1475**	**1975**	**3100**	**4725**
	GL Minivan	YB025	17140	**1500**	**2000**	**3150**	**4775**
	Carat Minivan	YB025	18780	**1725**	**2250**	**3450**	**5150**
	Multi-Van	TB025	21160	**4800**	**5625**	**7400**	**9900**
	GL Camper	ZB025	21730	**5250**	**6100**	**7975**	**10600**
	4WD Syncro			2000	2000	2665	2665

1992 VOLKSWAGEN — Not Imported

1993 VOLKSWAGEN — WV2(HD070)-P-#

Body	Type	VIN	List	Fair	Good	Good	Excellent
EUROVAN—5-Cyl.—Truck Equipment Schedule T2							
	CL Minivan	HD070	17130	**1275**	**1775**	**2925**	**4550**
	GL Minivan	KD070	20910	**1525**	**2025**	**3250**	**4975**
	MV Minivan	MD070	22340	**1975**	**2525**	**3800**	**5625**
	Weekender Pkg			2625	2625	3500	3500

1994 - 1998 VOLKSWAGEN — Not Imported

1999 VOLKSWAGEN — WV2(KH270)-X-#

Body	Type	VIN	List	Fair	Good	Good	Excellent
EUROVAN—V6—Truck Equipment Schedule T1							
	GLS Minivan	KH270	30465	**6300**	**7300**	**9125**	**11800**
	MV Minivan	MH270	31965	**6775**	**7825**	**9700**	**12450**
	Weekender Pkg			7000	7000	9330	9330

2000 VOLKSWAGEN — WV2(KH270)-Y-#

Body	Type	VIN	List	Fair	Good	Good	Excellent
EUROVAN—V6—Truck Equipment Schedule T1							
	GLS Minivan	KH270	31890	**7650**	**8775**	**10750**	**13700**
	MV Minivan	MH270	33390	**8200**	**9375**	**11400**	**14450**
	Weekender Pkg			7000	7000	9330	9330

2001 VOLKSWAGEN — WV2(KH470)-1-#

Body	Type	VIN	List	Fair	Good	Good	Excellent
EUROVAN—V6—Truck Equipment Schedule T1							
	Minivan	KH470	26815	**9250**	**10525**	**12650**	**15850**
	MV Minivan	MH470	28315	**9900**	**11300**	**13450**	**16750**
	Weekender Pkg			7000	7000	9330	9330

2002 VOLKSWAGEN — WV2(KB470)-2-#

Body	Type	VIN	List	Fair	Good	Good	Excellent
EUROVAN—V6—Truck Equipment Schedule T1							
	GLS Minivan	KB470	26815	**11100**	**12600**	**14950**	**18500**
	MV Minivan	MB470	28315	**11875**	**13425**	**15850**	**19500**
	Weekender Pkg			7000	7000	9330	9330

TRUCKS & VANS

TRUCKS & VANS

Body	Type	VIN	List	Trade-In Fair	Trade-In Good	Pvt-Party Good	Retail Excellent
2003 VOLKSWAGEN — WV2(KB470)-3-#							
EUROVAN—V6—Truck Equipment Schedule T1							
GLS Minivan		KB470	26815	**13375**	**15075**	**17650**	**21500**
MV Minivan		MB470	28315	**14200**	**16000**	**18600**	**22600**
Weekender Pkg				**7000**	**7000**	**9330**	**9330**
2004 VOLKSWAGEN — WVG(BC67L)-4-#							
TOUAREG—V6—Truck Equipment Schedule T3							
Sport Utility 4D		BC67L	35515	**21825**	**24450**	**27100**	**31600**
V8 4.2 Liter		M		**1325**	**1325**	**1765**	**1765**
TOUAREG—V8—Truck Equipment Schedule T3							
x Sport Utility 4D		GM67L	46165	**26575**	**29675**	**32600**	**37700**
TOUAREG—V10 Turbo Diesel—Truck Equipment Schedule T3							
TDI Sport Util 4D		GH67L	58415	**36275**	**40450**	**43700**	**49900**
2005 VOLKSWAGEN — WVG(BG77L)-5-#							
TOUAREG—V6—Truck Equipment Schedule T3							
Sport Utility 4D		BG77L	37755	**24825**	**27750**	**30500**	**35200**
V8 4.2 Liter		M		**1425**	**1425**	**1900**	**1900**

VOLVO

Body	Type	VIN	List	Trade-In Fair	Trade-In Good	Pvt-Party Good	Retail Excellent
2003 VOLVO — YV1(CN59H)-3-#							
XC90—5-Cyl. Turbo—Truck Equipment Schedule T3							
Sport Utility 4D		CN59H	36610	**21250**	**23850**	**26600**	**31100**
Third Row Seat				**500**	**500**	**665**	**665**
AWD				**1200**	**1200**	**1600**	**1600**
XC90 AWD—6-Cyl. Twin Turbo—Truck Equipment Schedule T3							
T6 Sport Utility 4D		CM91L	40640	**23675**	**26475**	**29300**	**34100**
Third Row Seat				**500**	**500**	**665**	**665**
2004 VOLVO — YV1(CN59V)-4-#							
XC90—5-Cyl. Turbo—Truck Equipment Schedule T3							
Sport Utility 4D		CN59V	35475	**24150**	**26975**	**29800**	**34600**
Third Row Seat				**550**	**550**	**735**	**735**
AWD				**1200**	**1200**	**1600**	**1600**
XC90 AWD—6-Cyl. Twin Turbo—Truck Equipment Schedule T3							
T6 Sport Utility 4D		CM91H	41650	**26675**	**29775**	**32700**	**37800**
Third Row Seat				**550**	**550**	**735**	**735**
2005 VOLVO — YV1(CN592)-5-#							
XC90—5-Cyl. Turbo—Truck Equipment Schedule T3							
Sport Utility 4D		CN592	35525				
Third Row Seat		Y					
AWD							
XC90 AWD—6-Cyl. Twin Turbo—Truck Equipment Schedule T3							
T6 Sport Utility 4D		CM911	41700				
Third Row Seat		Y					
XC90 AWD—V8—Truck Equipment Schedule T3							
Sport Utility 4D		CM852	46080				
Third Row Seat		Z					

1991-1998 TRUCK FACTORY EQUIPMENT

Equipment	91-92	93	94	95	96	97	98

MODEL PACKAGES (Truck Schedules T1 & T2)
(Add Only If Not Listed on Individual Vehicle Listing)

CHEVROLET/GMC:

LT (Astro)/SLT (Safari)							
	100	100	100	100	125	150	175

FORD:

Limited, Chateau	125	200	275	350	425	500	575
Eddie Bauer, Silver Anniversary							
	125	150	175	225	275	325	375

ALL MAKES: (All Other Model Packages Not Listed)

	75	75	75	75	75	75	100

TRUCK SCHEDULE T1 (Deduct For)

	91-92	93	94	95	96	97	98
Manual Trans	(225)	(250)	(275)	(300)	(325)	(350)	(375)
w/o Pwr Steering	(100)	(125)	(150)	(150)	(150)	(150)	(150)
w/o Air Cond	(150)	(175)	(200)	(225)	(250)	(250)	(250)

TRUCK SCHEDULE T2 (Add For)

	91-92	93	94	95	96	97	98
Auto Trans	175	200	225	250	275	300	325
Power Steering	50	75	75	75	75	75	75
Air Cond	150	175	200	200	200	200	200
TOTAL	375	450	500	525	550	575	600

TRUCK SCHEDULE T3 (See Page 378)

OTHER OPTIONS (Truck Schedules T1 & T2)

	91-92	93	94	95	96	97	98
Cassette	25	25	25	25	25	50	75
Power Windows	50	75	100	100	100	100	100
Pwr Door Locks	25	50	50	50	50	50	50
Tilt Wheel	25	50	75	75	75	75	75
Cruise Control	25	25	25	25	25	25	25
TOTAL	150	225	275	275	275	300	325

	91-92	93	94	95	96	97	98
w/o AM/FM	(25)	(50)	(50)	(50)	(50)	(50)	(50)
CD (Single Disc)	50	50	100	100	100	100	100
CD (Multi Disc)	100	100	150	175	200	200	200
Premium Sound	25	50	50	50	50	50	50
Air Cond, Rear	100	125	150	175	200	225	250
Leather	25	50	75	100	125	150	175
Quad Seating (4 Buckets)	100	125	150	150	150	150	150

SEE PAGE 13 FOR PVT PARTY & RETAIL EQUIPMENT

TRUCKS & VANS

Equipment	91-92	93	94	95	96	97	98
Van Seating Pkgs							
(11/12 Pass)	250	275	300	325	350	375	400
(15 Passenger)	400	425	450	475	500	525	550
Privacy Glass (Vans/Wagons/Sport Utilities)							
	25	50	50	50	50	50	50
Sliding Rear Window (Pickups)							
	25	25	25	25	25	25	25
Roof Rack	25	25	25	25	25	25	25
Sun Roof or Moon Roof							
(Flip-Up)	50	50	50	50	50	50	50
(Sliding)	125	150	175	200	225	250	275
Pickup Shell/Cap	50	75	100	100	100	100	100
Bed Liner	50	50	50	50	50	50	75
Grille Guard	25	50	50	50	50	50	50
Winch	50	50	50	50	75	100	125
Custom Bumper	25	50	50	50	50	50	50
Stepside							
(Short Bed PU)	25	50	75	100	125	150	150
(Long Bed PU)	(250)	(250)	(250)	(250)	(250)	(250)	(250)
Running Boards	200	200	200	200	200	200	200
Alloy Wheels	50	75	100	125	150	150	150
Premium Wheels	125	150	175	200	225	250	275
Wide Tires or Oversize Off-Road Tires							
	50	50	50	50	50	50	75
ABS (4-Wheel)	50	75	100	125	150	150	150
Opt Fuel Tank	25	50	50	50	50	50	50
Towing Pkg	100	125	150	175	200	200	200
Dual Rear Wheels (Add Only on Models Not Listed as DR)							
	575	625	675	700	725	750	775

TRUCK SCHEDULE T3 (This Equipment Only)

Equipment	91-92	93	94	95	96	97	98
CD (Single Disc)	50	50	100	125	150	150	150
CD (Multi Disc)	100	100	150	175	200	225	250
Premium Sound	50	75	100	125	150	150	150
Sun/Moon Roof	125	150	175	200	225	250	275
Grille Guard	25	50	50	50	50	50	50
Running Boards	200	200	200	200	200	200	200
Premium Wheels	125	150	175	200	225	250	275
Towing Pkg	100	125	150	175	200	200	200
w/o Leather	—	(25)	(50)	(75)	(100)	(125)	(175)

FOR MILEAGE ADJUSTMENT — SEE PAGE 13

Equipment	99	00	01	02	03	04	05

TRUCKS & VANS

MODEL & TRIM PACKAGES (Truck Schedules T1 & T2)
(Add Only If Not Listed on Individual Vehicle Listing)

CHEVROLET/GMC:

Silverado, LS, LT, LTZ, TrailBlazer, Xtreme, SLE (Full-Size), SLT, Diamond, Warner Bros Ed

	99	00	01	02	03	04	05
	400	450	500	550	600	675	750

SLE (Sonoma/Jimmy/Safari), Sport, LS (S10/Colorado), ZR2 Suspension

	250	275	300	325	375	425	475

SLS

	200	225	250	275	300	—	—

SL, Z71 Off-Road, Cheyenne

	125	125	125	125	150	175	200

DODGE/PLYMOUTH:

SLT, SXT, Laramie, Limited

	300	325	375	425	475	525	575

Expresso

	250	—	—	—	—	—	—

ST, Sport, Off-Road

	125	125	125	125	150	175	200

FORD:

Eddie Bauer (Explorer/Expedition), Limited, Chateau

	825	950	1075	1225	1375	1525	1675

Lariat, Lariat LE	600	675	750	825	900	975	1050

XLT, XLT Sport, XLT NBX, Edge Plus, Adrenaline

	400	450	500	550	600	675	750

STX, XLS, Edge	250	275	300	325	375	425	475

XL, Sport, Off-Road, Tremor, LE, FX4, Heritage, NBX

	125	125	125	125	150	175	200

ALL MAKES: (All Other Model Pkgs Not Listed)

	125	125	125	125	150	175	200

TRUCK SCHEDULE T1 (Deduct For)

	99	00	01	02	03	04	05
5-Spd Manual	(425)	(500)	(550)	(600)	(650)	(700)	(750)
6-Spd Manual	(250)	(300)	(350)	(400)	(425)	(450)	(475)
w/o Pwr Steering	(150)	(175)	(200)	(225)	(250)	(275)	(300)
w/o Air Cond	(250)	(300)	(350)	(400)	(450)	(500)	(550)

TRUCK SCHEDULE T2 (Add For)

	99	00	01	02	03	04	05
Auto Trans	350	400	450	500	550	600	650
Power Steering	75	100	125	150	150	150	150
Air Cond	200	250	300	350	400	450	475
TOTAL	625	750	875	1000	1100	1200	1275

TRUCK SCHEDULE T3 (See Page 381)

SEE PAGE 13 FOR PVT PARTY & RETAIL EQUIPMENT 379

1999-2005 TRUCK FACTORY EQUIPMENT

Equipment	99	00	01	02	03	04	05
OTHER OPTIONS (Truck Schedules T1 & T2)							
Cassette	100	100	100	100	100	125	150
Power Windows	100	125	150	175	200	225	250
Pwr Door Locks	50	75	100	125	150	175	175
Tilt Wheel	75	100	125	150	175	200	200
Cruise Control	25	50	75	100	125	150	150
TOTAL	350	450	550	650	750	875	925
w/o AM/FM	(50)	(75)	(100)	(100)	(100)	(100)	(100)
CD (Single Disc)	100	125	150	175	200	225	250
CD (Multi Disc)	200	250	275	300	325	350	375
Premium Sound	50	100	125	150	175	200	225
Integrated Phone	50	75	100	125	150	175	200
Video/DVD	200	250	275	300	325	350	375
NavigationSystm	400	450	475	500	525	550	575
Air Cond, Rear	250	300	350	400	425	450	475
Leather	200	250	275	300	325	350	375
Power Seat	25	25	25	50	75	100	125
Dual Pwr Seats	75	100	125	150	175	200	225
Quad Seating							
(4 Buckets)	150	200	250	300	325	350	375
Van Seating Packages							
(11/12 Pass)	400	450	500	550	600	650	700
(14/15 Pass)	550	600	650	700	750	800	850
Power Sliding Doors (Minivans)							
Single	25	25	25	25	25	50	75
Dual	50	50	75	100	125	150	175
Privacy Glass (Vans/Wagons/Sport Utilities)							
	50	75	100	100	100	100	100
Sliding Rear Window (Pickups)							
	25	50	75	75	75	75	75
Roof Rack	25	50	75	100	100	100	100
Sun Roof or Moon Roof							
(Flip-Up)	50	75	100	125	150	175	200
(Sliding)	300	350	400	450	500	550	575
Pickup Shell/Cap	100	150	175	200	225	250	275
Hard Tonneau	50	100	125	150	175	200	225
Bed Liner	100	100	100	100	125	150	175
Grille Guard	50	75	75	75	75	75	75
Winch	150	150	175	200	225	250	275
Custom Bumper	50	75	100	100	100	100	100
Parking Sensors	50	50	75	100	125	150	175
Custom Paint	25	25	25	50	75	100	125
Two-Tone Paint	25	25	25	50	75	100	125
Stepside Bed	150	200	250	300	325	350	375
Running Boards	200	200	200	200	200	200	200
Alloy Wheels	150	175	200	225	250	275	300

TRUCKS & VANS

Equipment	99	00	01	02	03	04	05
Premium Wheels	300	350	375	400	425	450	475
Oversize Premium Wheels (20" Plus)							
	475	550	625	700	750	800	850
Wide Tires or Oversize Off-Road Tires							
	100	100	100	100	125	150	175
ABS (4 Wheel)	150	175	200	200	200	200	200
Towing Pkg	200	225	250	275	300	300	300
Dual Rear Wheels (Add Only on Models Not Listed as DR)							
	825	950	1075	1200	1325	1450	1575

TRUCK SCHEDULE T3 (This Equipment Only)

Equipment	99	00	01	02	03	04	05
CD (Single Disc)	150	175	200	225	250	275	300
CD (Multi Disc)	250	300	350	400	425	450	475
Premium Sound	150	200	250	300	325	350	375
Integrated Phone	50	75	100	125	150	175	200
Video/DVD	200	250	275	300	325	350	375
NavigationSystm	400	450	475	500	525	550	575
Sun/Moon Roof	300	350	400	450	500	550	575
Premium Wheels	300	350	375	400	425	450	475
Oversize Premium Wheels (20" Plus)							
	475	550	625	700	750	800	850
Grille Guard	50	75	75	75	75	75	75
Parking Sensors	50	50	75	100	125	150	175
Running Boards	200	200	200	200	200	200	200
Power Sliding Doors (Minivans)							
Single	25	25	25	25	25	50	75
Dual	50	50	75	100	125	150	175
Towing Pkg	200	225	250	275	300	300	300
w/o Leather	(200)	(250)	(300)	(350)	(400)	(475)	(550)

FOR MILEAGE ADJUSTMENT — SEE PAGE 13